# EDUCATIONAL PSYCHOLOGY
## DEVELOPING LEARNERS

### JEANNE ELLIS ORMROD

Professor Emerita, University of Northern Colorado

**EIGHTH EDITION**

**PEARSON**

Boston  Columbus  Indianapolis  New York  San Francisco  Upper Saddle River
Amsterdam  Cape Town  Dubai  London  Madrid  Milan  Munich  Paris  Montreal  Toronto
Delhi  Mexico City  São Paulo  Sydney  Hong Kong  Seoul  Singapore  Taipei  Tokyo

**Vice President and Editorial Director:** *Jeffery W. Johnston*
**Vice President and Publisher:** *Kevin Davis*
**Editorial Assistant:** *Lauren Carlson*
**Development Editor:** *Christina Robb*
**Vice President, Director of Marketing:** *Margaret Waples*
**Marketing Manager:** *Joanna Sabella*
**Senior Managing Editor:** *Pamela D. Bennett*
**Project Manager:** *Kerry Rubadue*
**Senior Operations Supervisor:** *Matthew Ottenweller*

**Senior Art Director:** *Diane Lorenzo*
**Text Designer:** *Candace Rowley*
**Cover Designer:** *Candace Rowley*
**Media Project Manager:** *Noelle Chun*
**Cover Image:** *© Purestock / Alamy*
**Full-Service Project Management:** *Jouve North America*
**Composition:** *Jouve North America*
**Printer/Binder:** *Courier / Kendallvile*
**Cover Printer:** *Lehigh-Phoenix Color / Hagerstown*
**Text Font:** *Adobe Garamond Pro*

Credits and acknowledgments for materials borrowed from other sources and reproduced, with permission, in this textbook appear on appropriate page within text.

**Photo Credits:** Moodboard Premium / Glow Images, p. 2; Losevsky Photo and Video / Shutterstock.com, p. 18; © Monkey Business / Fotolia, pp. 54, 422; © Infoto / Fotolia, p. 90; Jim Carter / Photo Researches, Inc., p. 96; Fotosearch / Glow Images, p. 118; michaeljung / Fotolia, p. 154; © Jacek Chabraszewski / Fotolia, p. 194; © Ian Shaw / Alamy, p. 226; Monashee Frantz / Glow Images, p. 264; © Jamie Wilson / Fotolia, p. 289; © Jim Cummins / CORBIS / Glow Images, p. 298; David Mager / Pearson Learning Group, p. 300; © Greatstock Photographic Library / Alamy, p. 332; © Will Hart / PhotoEdit, p. 357; © Gabe Palmer / Alamy, p. 374; © Alexander Raths / Fotolia, p. 380; Jeffrey Ormrod, p. 425; © Blend Images / Alamy, pp. 439, 460, 504; Gabe Palmer / CORBIS, p. 489; © Jeff Greenberg / Alamy; Rex Interstock / Stock Connection, p. 531. All video stills are from Pearson Education videos.

Every effort has been made to provide accurate and current Internet information in this book. However, the Internet and information posted on it are constantly changing, so it is inevitable that some of the Internet addresses listed in this textbook will change.

**Library of Congress Cataloging-in-Publication Data**

Ormrod, Jeanne Ellis.
  Educational psychology : developing learners / Jeanne Ellis Ormrod. — Eighth edition.
    pages cm
  Includes bibliographical references and index.
  ISBN-13: 978-0-13-297442-4
  ISBN-10: 0-13-297442-8
 1. Educational psychology.   2. Teaching.   3. Learning.   4. Classroom management.   I. Title.
  LB1051.O66 2014
  370.15—dc23
                                                        2012040629

10 9 8 7 6 5 4 3 2 1

ISBN 10: 0-13-297442-8
ISBN 13: 978-0-13-297442-4

# To Olivia

whose curiosity and good humor are daily reminders
of the importance of education and the joy of life

# About the Author

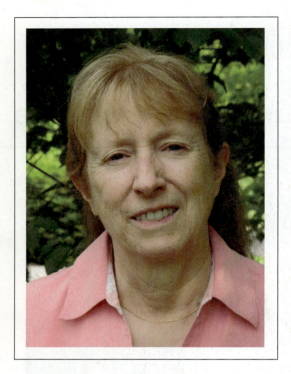

**JEANNE ELLIS ORMROD** received her A.B. in psychology from Brown University and her M.S. and Ph.D. in educational psychology from The Pennsylvania State University. She earned licensure in school psychology through postdoctoral work at Temple University and the University of Colorado at Boulder and has worked as a middle school geography teacher and school psychologist. She was Professor of Educational Psychology at the University of Northern Colorado until 1998, when she moved east to return to her native New England. She has published numerous research articles on cognition and memory, cognitive development, and giftedness but is probably best known for this book and four others: *Human Learning* (currently in its sixth edition); *Essentials of Educational Psychology* (currently in its third edition); *Child Development and Education* (co-authored with Teresa McDevitt, currently in its fifth edition); and *Practical Research* (co-authored with Paul Leedy, currently in its tenth edition). She has also recently published a non-textbook for a broad audience: *Our Minds, Our Memories: Enhancing Thinking and Learning at All Ages*. With her three children now grown and out on their own, she lives in New Hampshire with her husband, Richard.

# Preface

## New to This Edition

This eighth edition of *Educational Psychology: Developing Learners* retains features that have made it so popular with both instructors and students—for example, its engaging writing style and emphasis on classroom applications—but has significantly increased coverage in three areas:

- **Social, cultural, and academic contexts of learning:** Users of previous editions will notice a new Chapter 8, "Learning and Cognition in Context," which draws heavily from contemporary contextual theories as it describes the multiple contexts (e.g., immediate physical and social environment, culture and society) that directly and/or indirectly affect classroom learning and achievement. This new chapter also includes a section on academic content domains as specific contexts in which thinking and learning may be uniquely situated.

- **Neuropsychology and brain development and its relevance to classroom practice:** Findings from research are updated in numerous places throughout the book, but this increased emphasis is most obvious in the addition of five new "Applying Brain Research" boxes in Chapters 2, 3, 6, 10, and 11.

- **Technological innovations and their classroom applications:** Recent innovations in technology are included in many chapters but are especially apparent in the sections "Technology and Peer Relationships" (Chapter 3); "Technological Innovations," including a subsection on fostering students' technological literacy (Chapter 8); "Creating a Class Website to Share Goals and Facilitate Communication throughout the School Year," "Using Instructional Websites," "Using Technology to Individualize Instruction," "Using Computer Simulations and Games,"

"Conducting Technology-Based Collaborative Learning Activities" (all in Chapter 12); and "Using Digital Technologies in Classroom Assessments" (Chapter 14).

- The online resource that accompanies this book, MyEducationLab™, has also been updated and expanded, with many new illustrative videos plus several Simulation exercises related to classroom management. I'm probably most excited about the fact that the book itself is now available not only in paper but also in an electronic form that can be read on various electronic devices. Electronic versions of the book will enable readers to connect directly to illustrative videos and other supportive pedagogical aids in MyEducationLab™.

- In order to keep the book at 15 chapters in length, I've incorporated much of the "old" Chapter 7 into Chapter 6, now called "Learning, Cognition, and Memory" but also moved some of it into the new Chapter 8. Meanwhile, the "old" Chapter 8, "Complex Cognitive Processes," is now Chapter 7.

Throughout the book, I have, as always, updated the content to reflect advances in theory, research, and classroom practices. Especially noteworthy additions and changes to this edition include the following:

- **Every chapter:** All chapters are now written to stand alone and so can be read in whatever order an instructor prefers; cross-references to other chapters appear in margin notes rather than within the running text. Each chapter now begins with four to six Learning Outcomes that are revisited in a final "What Have You Learned?" summary section. Also, the "Developmental Trends" tables that appear in most chapters now have an "Example" column to illustrate characteristics listed for the K–2, 3–5, 6–8, and 9–12 grade levels.

- **Chapter 1:** New opening case study illustrating action research; revisions to the OOPS test items to reflect common misconceptions about the brain and technology; new discussions of quasi-experimental and mixed-methods research; an additional study-strategy recommendation that I'm hoping will encourage occasional conceptual change in my readers.

- **Chapter 2:** Expansion of section on Bronfenbrenner's theory to include the idea of the environment as a dynamic system; new "Applying Brain Research" feature "Taking Developmental Changes in the Brain into Account"; expansion of the section on Vygotsky's theory to include the concept of *appropriation;* new section contrasting Piaget's and Vygotsky's theories.

- **Chapter 3:** New discussions of effortful control, mirror neurons, and cheating; new "Applying Brain Research" feature "Understanding and Addressing Adolescent Risk Taking"; new "Experiencing Firsthand" exercise on bullying.

- **Chapter 4:** New discussion of verbal assertiveness in the section on cultural and ethnic differences; new "Experience with Technology" subsection in the section on gender differences; additional recommendations for creating a culturally inclusive classroom and addressing students' stereotypes and prejudices.

- **Chapter 5:** New sections on "Developmental Views of Intelligence" and "Intelligence and the Brain"; increased focus on assistive technologies for students with disabilities; new recommendation regarding addressing gifted students' emotional needs.

- **Chapter 6:** Inclusion of the section on misconceptions and conceptual change that was in the "old" Chapter 7; addition of contextual theories to Table 6.1; new discussion of *cognitive load* as a key term.

- **Chapter 7** (Chapter 8 in the seventh edition): Section on problem solving reorganized around a general model of problem solving; new discussion of metacognitive processes in creativity.

- **Chapter 8** (new chapter): Explicit focus on the various broad contexts that both shape and situate learning and cognition; new section on assumptions of contextual theories (including *situated learning, distributed cognition, social construction,* and *sociocultural theory* as key terms), with a new "Principles/Assumptions" table; sections on the important roles of social interactions with both more experienced individuals and equal-ability peers, as well as a section on communities of learners (all adapted from the "old" Chapter 7); new section on cultures as contexts, including discussions of worldviews and communities of practice; new section on society and technology as contexts, including authentic activities (moved from the "old" Chapter 7) and technological innovations; new section on content domains (literacy, math, science, social studies) as contexts, with a new "Developmental Trends" table on reading development.

- **Chapter 9:** Inclusion of *operant conditioning* as a key term (it was replaced with the broader term *instrumental conditioning* in the seventh edition), with a discussion of how operant conditioning is essentially the "reinforcement" half of instrumental conditioning; new discussion of schoolwide positive behavior support.

- **Chapter 10:** Broadened definition of *modeling* to include verbal instructions (in keeping with Bandura's use of the term); addition of *outcome expectations* and *coping model* as key terms; addition of a learner's current emotional state as a factor influencing self-efficacy; broadened view of co-regulated learning to include collaboration with peers; new "Applying Brain Research" feature "Understanding and Accommodating Individual Differences in Self-Regulation"; new recommendations and examples added to both "Into the Classroom" features.

- **Chapter 11:** Revamped introductory section to include three general principles of motivation; new "Contextual Theories" row in Table 11.1 to replace and subsume the "Sociocultural Theories" row of the seventh edition; additions of doing-just-enough goals, long-term life goals, and boredom as important factors in motivation and/or affect; revision of "TARGET" mnemonic to seven "TARGETS" principles (including "social support").

- **Chapter 12:** Reorganization of the chapter, now with a "General Principles" section at the beginning and later discussions of instructional strategies divided into "Teacher-Directed" and "Learner-Directed" sections; new figure illustrating the general nature of backward design (Figure 12.2); new discussions of the Common Core standards, Wiggins and McTighe's (2005) six facets of understanding, and recent technological innovations in instruction (e.g., class discussion boards and chat rooms, educational video games).

- **Chapter 13:** Discussion of arranging a classroom to monitor and support students' use of individual laptops or computer tablets; discussion of schoolwide positive behavior support (which needs to be in this chapter as well as in Chapter 9); a class website as a possible additional mechanism for communicating with parents (appropriate only when parents have knowledge of and access to the Internet, of course).

- **Chapter 14:** Reorganization of the chapter to give more prominence and visibility to formative assessment and use of rubrics (the terms *formative evaluation* and *summative evaluation* now changed to *formative assessment* and *summative assessment* to be in keeping with current usage); addition of *response to intervention* and *curriculum-based measurement* as key terms; new "Comments" column added to Table 14.2 to address considerations regarding formative versus summative assessments (contemporary literature on formative assessment hasn't focused much on RSVP characteristics, so much of this column is my own perspective on the topic); new section on "Using Digital Technologies in Classroom Assessments."

- **Chapter 15:** New discussions of normal curve equivalent (NCE) scores and the issue of addressing late and missing assignments in determination of final grades; updated discussions of standardized achievement test results (including a new Figure 15.12) and No Child Left Behind; new Figure 15.13 that can help parents understand stanines and NCE scores.

## My Rationale for the Book

As teachers, we play critical roles in the lives of children and adolescents. Some of us help them learn to read and write. Some of us help them understand their physical and social worlds through explorations of science, mathematics, geography, history, or literature. Some of us help them express themselves through physical movement, the visual arts, or music. But regardless of the subject matter we teach, we help the generation that follows us to become knowledgeable, self-confident, and productive citizens.

In my mind, teaching is the most rewarding profession we could possibly choose. Yet it's often a challenging profession as well. Students don't always come to us ready or eager to learn classroom subject matter. How can we help them develop the knowledge and skills they need to become productive adults? What strategies can we use to motivate them? What tasks and instructional materials are appropriate for children at different developmental levels? Over the years, researchers and practitioners have worked together to answer such questions. We're in the fortunate position of being able to benefit from the many insights that such experts offer.

I've been teaching educational psychology since 1974, and I've loved every minute of it. How children and adolescents learn and think, how they change as they grow and develop, why they do the things they do, how they're often very different from one another—our understanding of all these things has innumerable implications for classroom practice and, ultimately, for the lives of young people.

I've written this textbook in much the same way that I've taught my college classes. Because I want the field of educational psychology to captivate you the way it has captivated me, I've tried to make the book interesting, meaningful, and thought-provoking as well as informative. I have a definite philosophy about how future teachers can best learn and apply educational psychology, and this philosophy has guided me as I've written all eight editions of the book. In particular, I believe that human learners of all ages actively *construct* their own understandings of what they read in textbooks—an idea reflected in the puzzle-piece motif you'll see throughout the book.

## Helping My Readers Learn and Apply Educational Psychology

You can gain much more from your study of educational psychology when you:

- Focus on core concepts and principles of the discipline
- See these principles in action in your own learning and behavior
- Use the principles to understand the learning and behavior of children and adolescents
- Consistently apply the principles to classroom practice

**FIGURE 6.7** This drawing by 9-year-old Trisha effectively illustrates the water cycle.

I've incorporated numerous features into the book to help you do all these things. I hope that you'll learn a great deal from what educational psychology has to offer, not only about the students you may be teaching but also about yourself—a human being who continues to learn and develop even as an adult.

## FOCUSING ON CORE CONCEPTS AND PRINCIPLES

Rather than superficially explore every aspect of educational psychology, this book zeroes in on fundamental concepts and principles that have broad applicability to classroom practice. Throughout the book, core concepts appear in boldfaced blue font. Core principles are clearly identified in sections labeled "Basic Principles" or "Basic Assumptions" and then often summarized in "Principles/Assumptions" tables. Each table includes educational implications and concrete examples.

## SEEING CONCEPTS AND PRINCIPLES IN ACTION IN YOUR OWN LEARNING

A central goal of this book has always been to help my readers discover more about themselves as thinkers and learners. Thus I include "Experiencing Firsthand" exercises throughout the book—exercises that illustrate such diverse concepts as constructive processes, working memory, sense of self, social cognition, ethnic stereotyping, and confidentiality in assessment. All of these exercises are designed to do exactly what their name implies: help my readers observe principles of educational psychology *in themselves.*

## UNDERSTANDING CHILDREN'S AND ADOLESCENTS' LEARNING AND BEHAVIOR

Throughout the book I continually urge my readers to look closely at and try to make sense of what children and adolescents do and say. Each chapter begins with a "Case Study" that situates chapter content in a real-life scenario. I also make frequent use of *real artifacts* from children's journals and school assignments to illustrate concepts and principles in action.

**Examining Developmental Trends**   Unique to this book is a focus on children's development in almost every chapter. For example, Chapters 2 through 4 and 6 through 15 all have one or more "Developmental Trends" tables that summarize age-typical characteristics at four grade levels (K–2, 3–5, 6–8, and 9–12), present concrete examples, and offer suggested classroom strategies for each level.

## APPLYING CORE IDEAS OF EDUCATIONAL PSYCHOLOGY TO CLASSROOM PRACTICE

Throughout this text, psychological concepts and principles are consistently applied to classroom practice. I also provide "Into the Classroom" and "Creating a Productive Classroom Environment" boxes that suggest and illustrate strategies related to particular areas of concern for teachers.

This book is consistently praised for its emphasis on application, application, application. Throughout the book I identify suggested strategies—within the text, in tables, and in the margins—with apple icons that look like this: 🍏

**Helping You Prepare for Licensure**   All chapters end with "Practice for Your Licensure Exam" exercises designed to resemble the kinds of case-study questions that appear on many teacher licensure tests. Students can complete these exercises on MyEducationLab™.

**Building Your Teaching Skills**   At the end of each chapter, readers can apply chapter content and build their teaching skills by going to the new MyEducationLab™ to complete scaffolded exercises.

> **Practice for Your Licensure Exam**
>
> **Cooperative Learning Project**
>
> One Monday morning Ms. Mihara begins the unit "Customs in Other Lands" in her fourth-grade class. She asks students to choose two or three students with whom they would like to study a particular country. After the students have assembled into six small groups, she assigns each group a country: Australia, Colombia, Ireland, Greece, Japan, or South Africa. She tells the students, "Today we'll go to the school library, where your group can find information on the customs of your country and check out materials you think will be useful. Every day over the next two weeks you'll have time to work with your group. A week from Friday, each group will give an oral report to the class.
>
> During the next few class sessions, Ms. Mihara runs into many more problems than she anticipated. She realizes that the high achievers have gotten together to form two of the groups, and many socially oriented, "popular" students have flocked to two others. The remaining two groups are comprised of whichever students were left over. Some groups get to work immediately on their task, others spend their group time joking and sharing gossip, and still others are neither academically nor socially productive.
>
> As the unit progresses, Ms. Mihara hears more and more complaints from students about their task: "Janet and I are doing all the work; Karen and Mary Kay aren't helping at all." "Eugene thinks he can boss the rest of us around because we're studying Ireland and he's Irish." "We're spending all this time but just can't seem to get anywhere!" And the group reports at the end of the unit differ markedly in quality: Some are carefully planned and informative, whereas others are disorganized and have little substance.
>
> "So much for this cooperative learning stuff," Ms. Mihara mumbles to herself. "If I want students to learn something, I'll just have to teach it to them myself."

# MyEducationLab™

Classroom applications are by no means limited to the book itself! MyEducationLab™, a valuable online resource that includes media and other materials to help instructors bring educational psychology to life and to help students come to a deep and applied understanding of this content, can be found at www.myeducationlab.com. I alert you to many of its resources in margin notes, as follows:

- Videos that illustrate key concepts and principles
- Simulations that provide opportunities to explore strategies related to typical classroom management issues
- Supplementary readings that provide more information on certain topics

In addition, at the end of each chapter, readers are directed to MyEducationLab™, where they can self-assess their knowledge of chapter concepts by taking a pretest, extend their knowledge by completing one or more scaffolded exercises, and apply what they've learned in a new case study by completing the "Practice for Your Licensure Exam" exercise.

In *Preparing Teachers for a Changing World,* Linda Darling-Hammond and her colleagues point out that grounding teacher education in real classrooms—among real teachers and students and among actual examples of students' and teachers' work—is an important, and perhaps even an essential, part of training teachers for the complexities of teaching in today's classrooms. MyEducationLab™ is an online learning solution that provides contextualized interactive exercises, simulations, and other resources designed to help readers develop the knowledge and skills that teachers need. All of the activities and exercises in MyEducationLab™ are built around essential learning outcomes for teachers and are mapped to professional teaching standards. Utilizing classroom video, authentic student and teacher artifacts, case studies, and other resources and assessments, the scaffolded learning experiences in MyEducationLab™ offer readers a unique and valuable education tool.

For each topic covered in the course, readers will find most or all of the following features and resources.

### Advanced Data and Performance Reporting Aligned to National Standards
Advanced data and performance reporting helps educators quickly identify gaps in student learning and gauge and address individual and classroom performance. Educators easily see the connection between coursework, concept mastery, and national teaching standards with highly visual views of performance reports. Data and assessments align directly to national teaching standards, including InTASC Model Core Teaching Standards, National Council for Accreditation of Teacher Education Standards, and National Board for Professional Teaching Standards, and support reporting for state and accreditation requirements.

### Assignments and Activities
Designed to enhance understanding of concepts covered in class, these assignable exercises show concepts in action (through videos, cases, and/or student and teacher artifacts). They help readers deepen content knowledge and synthesize and apply concepts and strategies read about in the book. For example, "Understanding Research" exercises (just one possible type of "Assignments and Activities" exercise) provide summaries of real research articles and present questions for readers to respond to that help them apply research-based information to educational psychology and classroom practice. (Correct answers for these assignments are available to the instructor only.)

Knowledge about fishing enhances children's ability to separate and control variables in a fishing problem. Contrast 10-year-old Kent (an experienced fisherman) with 14-year-old Alicia (who has never fished) in "Cognitive Development: Middle Childhood" and "Cognitive Development: Late Adolescence."

Classroom rules are more likely to be effective when students are involved in creating and evaluating them. Explore effective strategies in the simulation "Creating Classroom Behavioral Expectations."

Track changes in psychological perspectives of learning in a supplementary reading "How Learning Theories Have Evolved Over Time."

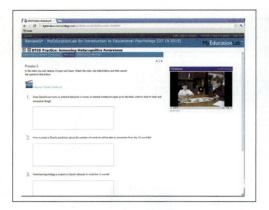

**Building Teaching Skills and Dispositions**  These learning units help readers practice and strengthen skills that are essential to effective teaching. After presenting the steps involved in a core teaching process, readers are given an opportunity to practice applying this skill via videos, student and teacher artifacts, and/or case studies of authentic classrooms. Providing multiple opportunities to practice a single teaching concept, each activity encourages a deeper understanding and application of concepts, as well as the use of critical thinking skills. After practice, students take a quiz that is reported to the instructor gradebook and performance reporting features of MyEducationLab™.

**IRIS Center Resources**  The IRIS Center at Vanderbilt University (http://iris.peabody .vanderbilt.edu), funded by the U.S. Department of Education's Office of Special Education Programs (OSEP), develops training-enhancement materials for preservice and practicing teachers. The Center works with experts from across the country to create challenge-based interactive modules, case study units, and podcasts that provide research-validated information about working with students in inclusive settings. In your MyEducationLab™ course we have integrated this content where appropriate.

**Simulations in Classroom Management**  One of the most difficult challenges facing teachers today is how to balance classroom instruction with classroom management. These interactive cases focus on the classroom management issues teachers most frequently encounter on a daily basis. Each simulation presents a challenge scenario at the beginning and then offers a series of choices to solve each challenge. Along the way, readers receive mentor feedback on their choices and have the opportunity to make better choices if necessary. After completing each simulation, readers will have a clear understanding of how to address these common classroom management issues and will be better equipped to handle them in the classroom.

MyEducationLab™ is easy to use and integrate into both assignments and courses. Download the correlation guide (see the "Ancillary Materials" section of this preface) which connects chapter sections with appropriate assignable exercises on MyEducationLab™.

## Additional Course Resources

- The **Lesson Plan Builder** is an effective and easy-to-use tool that readers can use to create, update, and share quality lesson plans. The software also makes it easy to integrate state content standards into any lesson plan.
- The "Certification and Licensure" section is designed to help readers pass their licensure exam by giving them access to state test requirements, overviews of what tests cover, and sample test items. The Certification and Licensure section includes the following:

  - **State Certification Test Requirements:** Here, you can click on a state and will then be taken to a list of state certification tests.
  - You can click on the **Licensure Exams** you need to take in order to find:

    - Basic information about each test
    - Descriptions of what is covered on each test
    - Sample test questions with explanations of correct answers

  - **National Evaluation Series**™ by Pearson: Here, readers can see the tests in the NES, learn what is covered on each exam, and access sample test items with descriptions and rationales of correct answers. Readers can also purchase interactive online tutorials developed by Pearson Evaluation Systems and the Pearson Teacher Education and Development group.
  - **ETS Online Praxis Tutorials:** Here, readers can purchase interactive online tutorials developed by ETS and by the Pearson Teacher Education and Development group. Tutorials are available for the Praxis I exams and for select Praxis II exams.

**Book-Specific Resources**  The "Book-Specific Resources" section of MyEducationLab™ contains useful materials organized by book chapter rather than by topic. The "Book-Specific Resources" section offers the following resources:

*Study Plan* A MyEducationLab™ Study Plan offers readers a chance to assess their current level of content mastery, receive individualized study material to help bolster it, and take another assessment to confirm improvement. It consists of the following components:

- **Chapter Learning Outcomes** give readers targets to shoot for as they read and study.
- **Pretests** allow readers to assess mastery of the content. These assessments are mapped to chapter "Learning Outcomes." Not only do these pretests provide overall scores for each Learning Outcome but they also explain why responses to particular items are correct or incorrect. After readers have completed this pretest, they are given a report showing which Learning Outcomes they appear to have troubles with.
- **Review, Practice, and Enrichment** provides an individualized set of study materials to work with to develop mastery of certain "Learning Outcomes." This consists of excerpts of chapter material to reread and activities to complete based on media assets (video, simulations, cases, etc.) or vignettes that help scaffold and develop content knowledge. If readers wish, they may access the Review, Practice, and Enrichment material relevant to a Learning Outcome, even if they have mastered that outcome as demonstrated in the pretest report.
- **Posttests** present unique questions to assess the *same* important concepts as the items in the pretest. Readers receive results on this assessment as well and can see if their level of mastery has changed.

**Other book-specific resources include:**

- **Flashcards** help readers review the core concepts and principles within each chapter.
- **Focus Questions** help guide the reading of chapter content.
- **Common Beliefs and Misconceptions About Educational Psychology** help alert readers to typical misunderstandings in educational psychology classes.
- **Video Examples,** referenced by margin notes in every chapter, provide concrete illustrations of various concepts and principles illustrated in each chapter.
- **Supplementary Readings** related to chapter concepts give readers an opportunity to explore certain topics in more depth—for example, the ecological systems perspective of child development (Chapter 2), the evolution of learning theories (Chapter 6), and programmed instruction and computer-assisted instruction (Chapter 12).
- **"Practice for Your Licensure Exam"** exercise resembles the kinds of questions that appear on many teacher licensure tests. The same chapter-ending exercise is also located on MyEducationLab™. Once on MyEducationLab™, readers can complete the exercise while receiving hints that scaffold their efforts to make correct responses. Readers can also compare their responses to the expert feedback provided.

**Visit www.myeducationlab.com for a demonstration of this exciting new online teaching resource.**

## CUSTOMIZING YOUR TEXTBOOK

It is now possible for instructors to customize textbooks by selecting portions of this book and perhaps combining them with portions of other Pearson Education books. Instructors should contact their local Pearson sales representative for information on how to customize their textbook.

# Ancillary Materials

## SUPPORT MATERIALS FOR INSTRUCTORS

The following resources are available for instructors to download on www.pearsonhighered.com/educators. Instructors can enter the author or title of this book, select this particular edition of the book, and then click on the "Resources" tab to log in and download textbook supplements.

**Instructor's Resource Manual (0-13-297783-4)** An Instructor's Resource Manual includes suggestions for learning activities, additional "Experiencing Firsthand" exercises, supplementary lectures, case study analyses, discussion topics, group activities, and additional media resources.

**PowerPoint™ Slides (0-13-297784-2**   The PowerPoint™ slides include key concept summarizations, diagrams, and other graphic aids to enhance learning. They are designed to help students understand, organize, and remember core concepts and theories.

**Test Bank (0-13-297793-1)**   I've personally written many of the test questions in the Test Bank that accompanies the book; Test Bank co-author Karen Zabrucky added new ones to reflect the many updates to this eighth edition. Some items (lower-level questions) simply ask students to identify or explain concepts and principles they have learned. But many others (higher-level questions) ask students to apply those same concepts and principles to specific classroom situations—that is, to actual student behaviors and teaching strategies. Ultimately, it is these higher-level questions that assess students' ability to use principles of educational psychology in their own teaching practice.

**TestGen (0-13-297792-3)**   TestGen is a powerful test generator available exclusively from Pearson Education publishers. You install TestGen on your personal computer (Windows or Macintosh) and create your own tests for classroom testing and for other specialized delivery options, such as over a local area network or on the web. A test bank, which is also called a Test Item File (TIF), typically contains a large set of test items, organized by chapter and ready for your use in creating a test, based on the associated textbook material. Assessments—including equations, graphs, and scientific notation—may be created for both print or testing online.

The tests can be downloaded in the following formats:

TestGen Testbank file—PC
TestGen Testbank file—MAC
TestGen Testbank—Blackboard 9 TIF
TestGen Testbank—Blackboard CE/Vista (WebCT) TIF
Angel Test Bank (zip)
D2L Test Bank (zip)
Moodle Test Bank
Sakai Test Bank (zip)

**MyEducationLab™ Correlation Guide (0-13-296512-7)**   This guide connects chapter sections with appropriate assignable exercises on MyEducationLab™.

## SUPPLEMENTARY MATERIALS FOR STUDENTS

**Case Studies: Applying Educational Psychology (*2nd ed.*)**   Many instructors use Ormrod and McGuire's *Case Studies* book (0-13-198046-7) as a supplement to this book. It includes 48 real cases involving students and classrooms ranging from preschool to high school. It illustrates concepts and principles in many areas of educational psychology, including child and adolescent development, learning and cognition, motivation, classroom management, instructional practices, and assessment.

**Artifact Case Studies: Interpreting Children's Work and Teachers' Classroom Strategies**   Another possible supplement to the book is my *Artifact Case Studies* book (0-13-114671-8). The artifact cases in this supplement offer work samples and instructional materials that cover a broad range of topics, including literacy, mathematics, science, social studies, and art. Every artifact case includes background information and questions to consider as readers examine the artifact. Instructors should contact their local Pearson sales representative to order a copy of this book.

**Simulations in Educational Psychology and Research (version 2.1)**   This CD-ROM (0-13-113717-4) features five interactive psychological/educational experiments, along with exercises and readings that can help students explore the research components and procedures connected to the experiments. Qualitative and quantitative designs are included. Instructors should contact their local Pearson sales representative to order a copy of these simulations.

# Acknowledgments

Although I'm listed as the sole author of this textbook, I've been fortunate to have had a great deal of help in writing it. First and foremost, this book wouldn't be what it is today without a long-term partnership with my editor, Kevin Davis. Kevin first came on board as developmental editor for the book in 1989 and, except for a two-year "leave of absence" while he filled other roles at Pearson, has continued to stand by my side through several promotions. Kevin hasn't penned the words, but his influence permeates every page, and with each new edition he has insisted that I stretch my knowledge and skills in ways I never imagined and didn't think were possible. I thank Kevin for his inspiration, guidance, friendship, and undying dedication to the quality of teacher education.

Paul Smith took over Kevin's role as editor for the seventh edition to help make this book the very best that it could be. I'm deeply appreciative of Paul's professional advice, emotional support, and indefatigable sense of humor.

I continue to be indebted to Christie Robb, developmental editor, for the seventh and eighth editions. Christie has always "been there" for me, generously dropping what she's doing at a moment's notice to provide counsel or assistance. She's kept me on course—no doubt about it—whenever I've gone astray from my mission, and her guidance about both the big picture and many, many nitty-gritty details have been invariably on target.

Four previous developmental editors have left footprints on the book as well. Linda Peterson helped shape many of the book's pedagogical features in the first and second editions. Linda Bishop and Julie Peters brought fresh perspectives and creative ideas to the third and fourth editions, respectively, as did Autumn Benson for the fifth and sixth editions. All of these women kept me upbeat and on-task throughout my arduous, year-long writing efforts. Fortunately, I can continue to work with Autumn in her role as Senior Media Producer.

For this eighth edition of the book, people at the production end of things have gone far beyond the call of duty. Turning a lengthy textbook manuscript into an actual book is a complex endeavor under any circumstances, but the task of creating an e-book as well as a paper book has presented challenges beyond any that we all could have imagined. Kerry Rubadue ably and patiently coordinated the production effort at Pearson's end. Kay Banning was, as always, delightfully compulsive in creating the indexes. But most importantly, I must thank Lynda Griffiths, who painstakingly copyedited my words, double-checked every reference (possibly the world's most thankless job), and then steered the manuscript through several rounds of page proofs until the layout was logically and pedagogically sound. Amazingly, Lynda kept her good humor throughout the whole process—even during eleventh-hour crises—and yet also found time to "oooh" and "aaah" in response to the many pictures of Olivia I sent her way.

And, of course, I must thank Joanna Sabella and her colleagues in Pearson's marketing department, who have always been skillful in getting out the word about a new edition. Without their help, my books wouldn't have much of an impact on the field of educational psychology—a field about which I'm deeply passionate.

In addition to the folks at Pearson Education and Jouve, several colleagues across the country have provided assistance with various ancillary materials. Karen Zabrucky at Georgia State has graciously taken on the task of updating the test bank to be in line with this new edition. Audrey Ambrosino, also at George State, is updating the instructor's resource manual, PowerPoint™ slides, and correlation guide for the book. Joanne Rojas at the University of Kentucky has lended her expertise to the Book-Specific Resources and Study Plans sections of MyEducationLab™. Gail Gottfried and several people at the University of Nebraska's Center for Instructional Innovation—especially Roger Bruning, Christy A. Horn, Katherine Smith, and Jeremy J. Sydik—have created many of the interactive features now on MyEducationLab™. Vern Jones of Lewis and Clark College wrote the engaging new interactive simulations related to classroom management. To all these individuals, I must say, "Thank you, thank you, thank you." In this multimedia age, writing any textbook and its accompanying materials must truly be a team effort.

Many other colleagues have strengthened the book itself by reviewing one or more of its previous versions. Reviewers for the first seven editions were Jane Abraham, Virginia Tech University; Joyce Alexander, Indiana University; Eric Anderman, University of Kentucky; Linda M. Anderson, Michigan State University; Margaret D. Anderson, SUNY–Cortland; J. C. Barton, Tennessee Technical University; Timothy A. Bender, Southwest Missouri State University; Stephen L. Benton, Kansas State University; Kathryn J. Biacindo, California State University–Fresno; Barbara Bishop, Eastern New Mexico University; Karen L. Block, University of Pittsburgh; Phyllis Blumenfeld, University of Michigan; Robert Braswell, Winthrop College; Kathy Brown, University of Central Oklahoma; Randy L. Brown, University of Central Oklahoma; Kay S. Bull, Oklahoma State University; Margaret W. Cohen, University of Missouri–St. Louis; Theodore Coladarci, University of Maine; Sharon Cordell, Roane State Community College; Roberta Corrigan, University of Wisconsin–Milwaukee; Richard D. Craig, Towson State University; José Cruz, Jr., The Ohio State University; Peggy Dettmer, Kansas State University; Joan Dixon, Gonzaga University; Leland K. Doebler, University of Montevallo; Catherine Emilhovich, SUNY–Buffalo; Joanne B. Engel, Oregon State University; Kathy Farber, Bowling Green State University; William R. Fisk, Clemson University; Victoria Fleming, Miami University of Ohio; M. Arthur Garmon, Western Michigan University; Roberta J. Garza, Pan American University–Brownsville; Mary Gauvain, University of California–Riverside; Cheryl Greenberg, University of North Carolina–Greensboro; Richard Hamilton, University of Houston; Jennifer Mistretta Hampston, Youngstown State University; Arthur Hernandez, University of Texas–San Antonio; Heather Higgins, University of North Carolina–Greensboro; Frederick C. Howe, Buffalo State College; Peggy Hsieh, University of Texas–San Antonio; Dinah Jackson, University of Northern Colorado; Janina M. Jolley, Clarion University of Pennsylvania; Caroline Kaczala, Cleveland State University; CarolAnne M. Kardash, University of Missouri–Columbia; Pamela Kidder-Ashley, Appalachian State University; Kenneth Kiewra, University of Nebraska–Lincoln; Nancy F. Knapp, University of Georgia; Mary Lou Koran, University of Florida; Randy Lennon, University of Northern Colorado; Susan C. Losh, Florida State University; Pamela Manners, Troy State University; Hermine H. Marshall, San Francisco State University; Teresa McDevitt, University of Northern Colorado; Sharon McNeely, Northeastern Illinois University; Michael Meloth, University of Colorado–Boulder; Kelly S. Mix, Michigan State University; Bruce P. Mortenson, Louisiana State University; Janet Moursund, University of Oregon; P. Karen Murphy, The Pennsylvania State University; Gary A. Negin, California State University; Joe Olmi, The University of Southern Mississippi; Helena Osana, Concordia University; James Persinger, Emporia State University; Judy Pierce, Western Kentucky University; James R. Pullen, Central Missouri State University; Gary F. Render, University of Wyoming; Robert S. Ristow, Western Illinois University; Jeff Sandoz, University of Louisiana—Lafayette; Rolando Santos, California State University–Los Angeles; Gregg Schraw, University of Nebraska–Lincoln; Dale H. Schunk, University of North Carolina–Greensboro; Mark Seng, University of Texas; Glenn E. Snelbecker, Temple University; Johnna Shapiro, University of California–Davis; Kenneth Springer, Southern Methodist University; Harry L. Steger, Boise State University; Bruce Torff, Hofstra University; Ann Turnbull, University of Kansas; Julianne C. Turner, University of Notre Dame; Enedina Vazquez, New Mexico State University; Alice A. Walker, SUNY–Cortland; Mary Wellman, Rhode Island College; Jane A. Wolfle, Bowling Green State University; and Karen Zabrucky, Georgia State University.

Coming on board for the eighth edition were these reviewers, who offered many helpful suggestions now reflected in the book: Cindy Ballantyne, Northern Arizona University; Angela Bloomquist, California University of Pennsylvania; Gregory Braswell, Illinois State University; David Yun Dai, SUNY–University at Albany; Kellah Edens, University of South Carolina; Sister Nancy Gilchriest, St. Joseph's College; Nathan Gonyea, SUNY–Oneonta; Ken Hay, Indiana University; Howard Lloyd, University of Kentucky; Traci Van Prooyen, Heartland Community College; Courtney Vorell, Minnesota School of Business; and Ya-Shu Yang, University of Nebraska–Lincoln.

Some of my own students and teacher interns—especially Jenny Bressler, Kathryn Broadhead, Ryan Francoeur, Gerry Holly, Shelly Lamb, Michele Minichiello, Kim Sandman, Melissa Tillman, Nick Valente, and Brian Zottoli—have agreed to let me use their interviews, essays, and experiences as examples. Teachers and administrators at schools both home and abroad (including two of my own children, now teachers themselves) have allowed me to share their strategies with my readers; I thank Liz Birnam, Berneen Bratt, Don Burger, Tom Carroll, Barbara Dee, Jackie Filion, Tina Ormrod Fox, Sarah Gagnon, Dinah Jackson, Sheila Johnson, Don Lafferty, Carol Lincoln, Gary MacDonald, Sharon McManus, Linda Mengers, Mark Nichols, Susan O'Byrne, Jeff Ormrod, Ann Reilly, and Gwen Ross.

Many young people, too, deserve thanks for letting me use their work. In particular, I acknowledge the contributions of the following present and former students: Andrew and Katie Belcher; Noah and Shea Davis; Zachary Derr; Amaryth, Andrew, and Anthony Gass; Ben and Darcy Geraud; Dana Gogolin; Colin Hedges; Erin Islo; Charlotte Jeppsen; Laura Linton; Michael McShane; Frederik Meissner; Meghan Milligan; Alex, Jeff, and Tina Ormrod; Patrick Paddock; Isabelle Peters; Ian Rhoads; David and Laura Riordan; Corey and Trisha Ross; Ashton and Haley Russo; Alex and Connor Sheehan; Matt and Melinda Shump; Andrew Teplitz; Emma Thompson; Grace Tober; Grant Valentine; and Geoff Wuehrmann.

Last but certainly not least, I must thank my husband and children, who have for many years forgiven my countless hours spent either buried in my books and journals or else glued to my computer. Without their continuing support and understanding of what has, for me, become an enduring passion, this book would never have seen the light of day.

J. E. O.

# Brief Contents

# Contents

# PART II LEARNING AND MOTIVATION

# 7 Complex Cognitive Processes 194

# 8 Learning and Cognition in Context 226

# 9 Behaviorist Views of Learning 264

# PART III
# CLASSROOM STRATEGIES

## 13 Creating a Productive Learning Environment 422

## 14 Classroom Assessment Strategies 460

## 15 Summarizing Students' Achievement and Abilities 504

# Special Topics

## THE BRAIN IN LEARNING AND DEVELOPMENT

## CULTURAL AND ETHNIC DIFFERENCES

## STUDENTS AT RISK

## TECHNOLOGICAL INNOVATIONS AND THEIR IMPLICATIONS

# 1

# Teaching and Educational Psychology

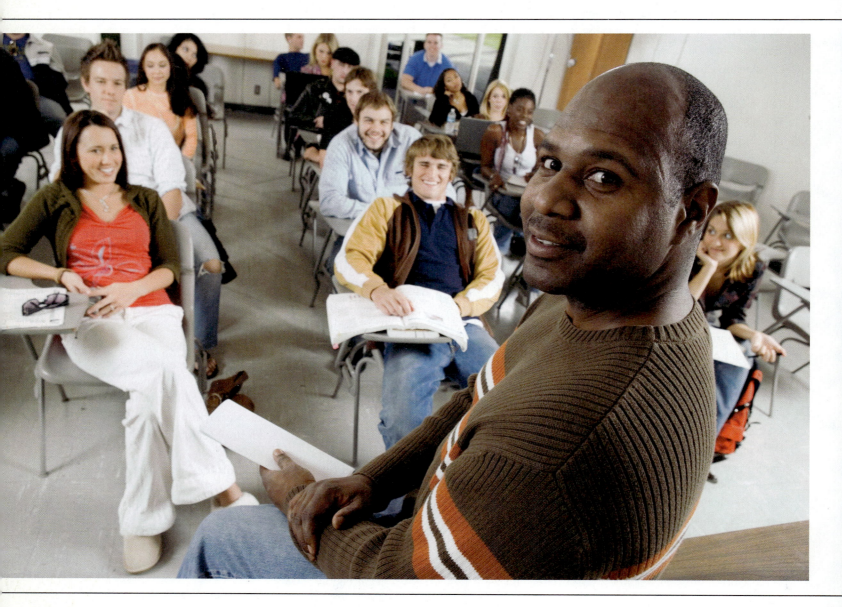

## LEARNING OUTCOMES

**1.1:** Explain the importance of research in classroom decision making.

**1.2:** Draw appropriate conclusions from different types of research studies.

**1.3:** Describe several strategies for collecting information about your own students.

**1.4:** Plan long-term strategies for gaining expertise as a teacher.

**1.5:** Use effective strategies when you read and study.

## CASE STUDY: THE "NO D" POLICY

Anne Smith is a ninth-grade English teacher with 10 years of teaching experience, and by all accounts she is an excellent teacher. Even so, in previous years many of her students haven't invested much time or energy in their writing assignments and seemingly haven't been bothered by the Cs and Ds they've eventually earned in her classes. In an effort to more fully engage this year's students in their schoolwork, Ms. Smith begins fall semester by initiating two new policies. First, to pass her course, students must earn at least a C; she won't give anyone a final grade of D. Second, students will have multiple opportunities to revise and resubmit assignments; she'll give whatever feedback students need—and, if necessary, one-on-one instruction—to help them improve their work. She solicits students' questions and concerns about the new policies, gains their agreement to "try something new," and engages them in a discussion of specific, concrete characteristics of A-quality, B-quality, and C-quality work. Then, as the semester progresses, she regularly administers brief surveys to get students' feedback about her innovations, asking such questions as "How is the 'no D' working for you?" "Do you think your grade is an accurate reflection of your learning?" and "Any suggestions?"

Students' responses on the surveys are overwhelmingly positive. Students mention noticeable improvements in the quality of their writing and increasingly report that they believe themselves to be in control of both their learning and their grades. Furthermore, they begin to see their teacher in a new light—"as one who will help them achieve their best work, not as one who just gives out grades . . . as a coach encouraging them along the long race of learning." Final course grades also confirm the value of the new policies: A much higher percentage of students earn grades of C or better than has been true in past years. (Action research project described in A. K. Smith, 2009.)

- Effective teachers don't simply transmit new information and skills to students; they also work hard to help students *master* the information and skills. In the case study just presented, what various strategies does Ms. Smith use to foster her students' writing development?

---

Teaching other people—especially teaching the generation that will follow you into the adult world—can be one of the most rewarding professions on the planet. It can also be a very challenging profession. Certainly effective teaching involves presenting a topic or skill in such a way that students can understand and master it. Yet it involves many other things as well. For instance, teachers must motivate students to *want* to learn the subject matter, must help students recognize what true mastery involves, and—in order to appropriately individualize instruction—must assess where each student currently is in his or her learning and development. And, in general, effective teachers create an environment in which students believe that if they work hard and have reasonable support, they can achieve at high levels. In the opening case study, Anne Smith does all of these things.

Mastering the multifaceted nature of teaching takes time and practice, of course. But it also takes knowledge about human learning and motivation, developmental trends, individual and group differences, and effective classroom practices. Such topics are the domain of educational psychology. This book will help you understand children and adolescents—how they learn and develop, how they're likely to be similar to but also different from one another, what topics and activities are apt to engage them in the classroom, and so on. It will also give you a toolbox of strategies for planning and carrying out instruction, creating an environment that keeps students motivated and on task, and assessing students' progress and achievement.

**educational psychology**
Academic discipline that (1) systematically studies the nature of learning, child development, motivation, and related topics and (2) applies its research findings to the identification and development of effective classroom practices.

# Teaching as Evidence-Based Practice

You yourself have been a student for many years now, and in the process you've undoubtedly learned a great deal about how children change over time and about how teachers can foster their learning and development. But exactly how much *do* you know? To help you find out, I've developed a short pretest, Ormrod's Own Psychological Survey (OOPS).

### ■ EXPERIENCING FIRSTHAND

### ORMROD'S OWN PSYCHOLOGICAL SURVEY

Decide whether each of the following statements is *true* or *false.*

**True/False**

_____ **1.** Children most effectively acquire new knowledge and skills in the first three years of life.

_____ **2.** Some children are predominantly left-brain thinkers, whereas others are predominantly right-brain thinkers.

_____ **3.** Children's personalities are largely the result of their home environments.

_____ **4.** The best way to learn and remember a new fact is to repeat it over and over.

_____ **5.** Students often misjudge how much they know about a topic.

_____ **6.** Anxiety sometimes helps students learn and perform more successfully in the classroom.

_____ **7.** Playing video games interferes with children's cognitive development.

_____ **8.** The ways in which teachers assess students' learning influence what and how students actually learn.

Now let's see how well you did on the OOPS. Following are the answers, along with an explanation for each one.

**1.** *Children most effectively acquire new knowledge and skills in the first three years of life.* FALSE. As brain researchers have discovered, neurons in the human brain spontaneously generate many new interconnections *(synapses)* in the first two or three years of life. Then, beginning in the preschool years, synapses that aren't used gradually begin to disintegrate—a process known as *synaptic pruning.* Some educators have interpreted these developmental processes as an indication that the first three years of life are the most important ones for learning new skills, but nothing could be further from the truth! Synaptic pruning plays a beneficial role in children's cognitive development, in part by eliminating unproductive and counterproductive responses and thereby making thinking and behavior more efficient. Furthermore, the human brain continues to develop in important ways throughout childhood, adolescence, and early adulthood, enabling the acquisition of increasingly sophisticated thought processes—and therefore it enables increasingly effective *learning*—with age (Haier, 2001; Luna & Sweeney, 2004; Steinberg, 2009).

**2.** *Some children are predominantly left-brain thinkers, whereas others are predominantly right-brain thinkers.* FALSE. With the development of new medical technologies in recent years, researchers have learned a great deal about how the human brain works and which parts of it specialize in which aspects of human thinking. The two halves, or *hemispheres,* of the brain do seem to have somewhat different specialties, but they continually communicate and collaborate in tackling even the simplest of daily tasks. Practically speaking, there is no such thing as left-brain or right-brain thinking (Bressler, 2002; M. I. Posner & Rothbart, 2007).

**3.** *Children's personalities are largely the result of their home environments.* FALSE. Certainly children's home environments mold their behaviors to some extent. But heredity also has a significant impact. From Day 1, infants are noticeably different in the extent to which they're calm or fussy, shy or outgoing, fearful or adventurous, and so on. Such differences in *temperament* appear to have their roots in biology and genetics, and they persist throughout the childhood years and into adulthood (Kagan & Snidman, 2007; Keogh, 2003; Rothbart, 2011).

**4.** *The best way to learn and remember a new fact is to repeat it over and over.* FALSE. Although repeating information numerous times is better than doing nothing at all, repetition of specific facts is a relatively *in*effective way to learn. Students learn information more easily and remember it longer when they relate it to things they already know. One especially effective strategy is **elaboration**: using prior knowledge to expand or embellish on a new idea in some way, perhaps by drawing inferences from a historical fact, identifying new examples of a scientific concept, or thinking of situations in which a mathematical procedure might be helpful (J. R. Anderson, 2005; Graesser & Bower, 1990).

**5.** *Students often misjudge how much they know about a topic.* TRUE. Contrary to popular opinion, students are usually *not* the best judges of what they do and don't know. For example, many students think that if they've spent a long time studying a textbook chapter, they must know its contents very well. Yet if they've spent most of their study time inefficiently—perhaps by "reading" while thinking about something else altogether or by mindlessly copying definitions—they may know far less than they think they do (N. J. Stone, 2000; Thiede, Griffin, Wiley, & Redford, 2009).

**6.** *Anxiety sometimes helps students learn and perform more successfully in the classroom.* TRUE. Many people think that anxiety is always a bad thing. In fact, a little bit of anxiety can actually *improve* learning and performance, especially when students perceive a task to be something they can accomplish with reasonable effort. For instance, a small, manageable amount of anxiety can spur students to complete their work carefully and to study for tests (Cassady, 2010b; N. E. Perry, Turner, & Meyer, 2006; Shipman & Shipman, 1985).

**7.** *Playing video games interferes with children's cognitive development.* FALSE—or more accurately, NOT NECESSARILY. A great deal of time spent playing video games *instead of* reading, doing homework, and engaging in other school-related activities can definitely interfere with children's long-term academic success. But some video games can be powerful tools for promoting important cognitive abilities and life skills. For example, practice in using a joystick to quickly move people or animals on a computer screen can significantly enhance young children's ability to focus and maintain their attention—an ability that then transfers to many other situations and tasks (M. I. Posner & Rothbart, 2007). And increasingly, educational technologists have been designing highly motivating video games that simulate real-world problems and foster complex problem-solving skills (e.g., Barab, Gresalfi, & Ingram-Goble, 2010; Gee, 2010).

**8.** *The ways in which teachers assess students' learning influence what and how students actually learn.* TRUE. What and how students learn depend, in part, on how they expect their learning to be assessed. For example, students typically spend more time studying the things they think will be on a test than the things they think the test won't cover, and they're more likely to pull class material into an integrated, meaningful whole if they expect assessment activities to require such integration (N. Frederiksen, 1984b; Lundeberg & Fox, 1991). We see this principle in action in the opening case study: Anne Smith's "No D" and multiple-submission policies encourage students to seek feedback about their work, benefit from their mistakes, and enhance their writing skills.

How many of the OOPS items did you answer correctly? Did some of the false items seem convincing enough that you marked them true? Did one or more of the true items contradict certain beliefs you had? If either of these was the case, you're hardly alone. College students often agree with statements that seem obvious but are, in fact, completely wrong (Gage, 1991; Lennon, Ormrod, Burger, & Warren, 1990).

---

The brain's structure, functioning, and development are discussed in Chapter 2 and in *Applying Brain Research* features throughout the book.

Chapter 3 discusses temperament and personality development.

Chapter 6 discusses elaboration and its implications for instructional practice.

Chapter 7 describes this *illusion of knowing* in more detail.

Chapter 11 explores anxiety's effects in different situations.

Chapter 3 describes potential adverse effects of violent video games on children's aggression. Chapter 12 explores potential benefits of appropriately designed video games.

Chapter 14 and Chapter 15 explore numerous ways in which assessment practices affect students' learning.

**elaboration** Cognitive process in which learners embellish on new information based on what they already know.

Effective teachers are passionate about what they do. Watch the many "Why I Teach" videos in MyEducationLab™.

It's easy to be persuaded by common sense and assume that what seems logical must be true. Yet common sense and logic don't always give us the real scoop about how people actually learn and develop, nor do they always give us accurate information about how best to help students succeed in the classroom. Instead, our knowledge about learning and instruction must come from a more objective source of information—that is, from systematic research.

As professionals, teachers are *decision makers* who must choose among many, many possible strategies for helping students learn and develop. Certainly teaching is an art to some degree: Effective teachers are creative and innovative, and they add many imaginative touches to enhance the things they do in the classroom. But that art must be based on a firm foundation of research findings both about how human beings learn and about how teachers can help them learn effectively; in other words, it must be based on the *science of learning* and the *science of instruction*. Ultimately, good teaching involves evidence-based practices—the use of instructional methods and other classroom strategies that research has consistently shown to bring about significant gains in students' development and academic achievement.

# Understanding and Interpreting Research Findings

Historically, most research related to learning, development, and educational practice has been quantitative research; that is, it has involved collecting data that either take the form of numbers or can easily be converted into numbers. These numbers are tabulated and usually statistically analyzed to determine underlying trends and other patterns in the data. For example, we're apt to get quantitative information from students' performance on achievement tests, students' responses to rating-scale questionnaires, and school district records of students' attendance and dropout rates.

In recent years, educational researchers have also made considerable use of qualitative research, in which they examine complex phenomena that can't easily be reduced to numerical values. For example, a qualitative research study might involve lengthy interviews in which students describe their hopes for the future, a detailed case study of interpersonal relationships within a tight-knit clique of teenage girls, or in-depth observations of particular teachers who create distinctly different psychological "climates" in their classrooms.

To a considerable degree, the research study described at the beginning of the chapter is a quantitative one: Anne Smith tabulates students' responses to various survey questions and computes the percentages of various final class grades. But when she collects the completed surveys, she also looks closely at students' specific comments and suggestions—qualitative information.

Not all research on learning and instruction is *good* research, of course. Furthermore, people sometimes draw inappropriate conclusions from even the best of research studies. It's important, therefore, that teachers understand what various kinds of research studies can and cannot tell us about learning and instruction.

## QUANTITATIVE RESEARCH

Quantitative research studies vary widely in nature, but you might think of them as falling into four general categories: descriptive, correlational, experimental, and quasi-experimental. These categories yield different kinds of information and warrant different kinds of conclusions.

### DESCRIPTIVE STUDIES

A descriptive study does exactly what its name implies: It *describes* a situation. Descriptive studies might give us information about the characteristics of students, teachers, or schools. They might also provide information about how often certain events or behaviors occur. In general, descriptive studies enable us to draw conclusions about the way things are—the current state of affairs.

### CORRELATIONAL STUDIES

A correlational study explores possible associations among two or more variables. For instance, it might tell us how closely various human characteristics are associated with one another, or it might give us information about the consistency with which certain human behaviors occur in conjunction with certain environmental conditions. In general, correlational studies enable us to draw conclusions about correlation: the extent to which two characteristics or phenomena

**evidence-based practice** Instructional method or other classroom strategy that research has consistently shown to bring about significant gains in students' development and/or academic achievement.

**quantitative research** Research yielding information that is inherently numerical in nature or can easily be reduced to numbers.

**qualitative research** Research yielding information that cannot easily be reduced to numbers; typically involves an in-depth examination of a complex phenomenon.

**descriptive study** Research study that enables researchers to draw conclusions about the current state of affairs regarding an issue but not about correlation or cause–and–effect relationships.

**correlational study** Research study that explores possible associations among two or more variables.

**correlation** Extent to which two variables are associated, such that when one variable increases, the other either increases or decreases somewhat predictably.

tend to be found together or to change together. Two variables are correlated when one tends to *increase* as the other increases (a *positive correlation*) or when one tends to *decrease* as the other increases (a *negative correlation*). Correlations are often described numerically with a statistic known as a *correlation coefficient*.

Correlation coefficients are described in Appendix A.

Sometimes correlational studies involve comparing two or more groups that differ with respect to a particular characteristic, such as age, gender, or background.[1] For example, a correlational study might compare the average achievement test scores of boys and girls, or it might investigate whether young children who have had considerable exposure to reading materials at home learn to read more quickly at school than children without such exposure.

Any correlation between two variables allows us to make *predictions* about one variable if we know the status of the other. For example, if we find that 15-year-olds are more capable of abstract thought than 10-year-olds—in other words, if age and abstract thinking ability are correlated—we can predict that high school students will benefit more from an abstract discussion of democratic government than fourth graders will. And if we find that children learn to read more easily if they've had many previous experiences with books at home, we might take proactive steps to enhance the early literacy skills of children without such experiences.

In general, although correlational studies demonstrate that an association exists, they can never tell us for certain *why* it exists. They don't tell us what specific factors—previous experiences, personality, motivation, or perhaps other things we haven't thought of—are the cause of the association we see. In other words, *correlation does not necessarily indicate causation.*

## EXPERIMENTAL AND QUASI-EXPERIMENTAL STUDIES

Descriptive and correlational studies describe things as they exist or have previously existed naturally in the environment. In contrast, an experimental study is a study in which the researcher intentionally changes, or *manipulates,* one or more aspects of the environment (called *independent variables*) and then measures the effects of such changes on something else. In educational research the "something else" being affected (called the *dependent variable*) is often some aspect of student behavior—perhaps end-of-semester grades, persistence in trying to solve difficult math problems, or ability to interact appropriately with peers. In a good experiment a researcher *separates and controls variables,* testing the possible effects of one independent variable while holding all other potentially influential variables constant.

Some experimental studies involve giving a single group of individuals two or more distinct treatments and comparing the specific effects of each treatment. Other experimental studies involve two or more groups that are treated differently. The following are examples.

- A researcher uses two different instructional methods to teach reading comprehension skills to two different groups of students. (Instructional method is the independent variable.) The researcher then assesses the students' reading ability (the dependent variable) and compares the average performances of the two groups.

- A researcher gives three different groups of students varying amounts of practice with woodworking skills. (Amount of practice is the independent variable.) The researcher subsequently scores the quality of each student's woodworking project (the dependent variable) and compares the average quality scores of the three groups.

- A researcher gives one group of students an intensive instructional program designed to improve their study skills. The researcher gives another group either no instruction or, better still, instruction in subject matter unrelated to study skills. (Presence or absence of instruction in study skills is the independent variable.) The researcher later assesses the students' study skills and obtains their grade point averages (two dependent variables) to see whether the program had an effect.

Each of these examples includes one or more treatment groups, which are recipients of a planned intervention. The third example also includes a control group, which receives either no intervention or a *placebo* intervention that is unlikely to affect the dependent variable(s) in question.

**experimental study** Research study that involves both (1) the manipulation of one variable to determine its possible effect on another variable and (2) control of additional variables that might potentially have an impact on the outcome; allows conclusions about cause-and-effect relationships.

**treatment group** Group of people in a research study who are given a particular experimental intervention (e.g., a particular method of instruction).

**control group** Group of people in a research study who are given either no intervention or a *placebo* treatment that is unlikely to have an effect on the dependent variable.

---

[1]Such group-comparison studies are sometimes called *causal-comparative studies*. However, as B. Johnson (2001) has pointed out, this label may mislead us to believe that such studies reveal cause-and-effect relationships, when in fact they do not.

**quasi-experimental study** Research study that involves the manipulation of one variable to determine its possible effect on another variable, but without total control of additional variables that might have an impact on the outcome.

In many experimental studies, participants are assigned to groups *randomly*—for instance, by drawing names out of a hat. Such random assignment is apt to yield groups that are, on average, roughly equivalent on other variables (e.g., ability levels, personality characteristics, motivation) that might affect the dependent variable.

Random assignment to groups isn't always possible or practical, however, especially in research studies conducted in actual schools and classrooms. For example, when studying the potential benefits of a new teaching technique or therapeutic intervention, a researcher may not be able to completely control which students receive the experimental treatment and which do not, *or* a particular treatment or intervention may have important benefits for *all* students. In such situations, researchers often conduct a quasi-experimental study, in which they take into account but do not complete control other influential factors. The following are examples.

- A researcher implements a new after-school homework program at one high school and identifies a comparable high school without such a program to serve as a control group. The researcher obtains achievement test data for students at both schools both before and after the program's implementation. Ideally, the average test scores for the two high schools will be the same *before* the program begins but different *after* its implementation. (Such an approach is known as a *pretest–posttest study*.)
- Three researchers want to study the effects of safety instructions on children's behaviors on the playground. The researchers present the instructional intervention to first graders one week, second graders the following week, and kindergartners and third graders the week after that. The researchers monitor students' playground behavior before, during, and after the intervention to determine whether each grade-level group's risky playground behavior decreases immediately after its intervention. (Such an approach is known as a *multiple-base-lines study;* study described is by Heck, Collins, & Peterson, 2001.)

When researchers conduct such quasi-experimental studies, they don't control for all potentially influential variables and so can't completely rule out alternative explanations for the results they obtain. For instance, in the after-school homework program example, possibly the school getting the new homework program—but *only* that school—has simultaneously begun to use more effective instructional methods, and those methods are the reason for any increase in achievement scores. And in the playground safety example, perhaps certain other things coincidentally happened in the four classrooms during their respective safety-instructions weeks, and those things were the true cause of children's behavior improvement.

When carefully designed and conducted, experimental studies and, to a lesser degree, quasi-experimental studies enable us to draw conclusions about *causation*—about *why* behaviors occur. Yet for practical or ethical reasons, many important questions in education don't easily lend themselves to experimental manipulation and tight control of other potentially influential variables. For instance, although we might reasonably hypothesize that children can better master difficult math concepts if they receive individual tutoring, most public school systems can't afford such a luxury, and it would be unfair to provide tutoring for some students and deny it to a control group of other, equally needy students. And, of course, it would be highly unethical to study the effects of aggression by intentionally placing some children in a violent environment. Some important educational questions, then, can be addressed only with descriptive or correlational studies, even though such studies can't help us pin down precise cause–and–effect relationships.

Columns 2, 3, and 4 of Table 1.1 contrast descriptive, correlational, and experimental and quasi-experimental studies and give examples of the kinds of questions each type of study might address.

## QUALITATIVE RESEARCH

Rather than address questions related to quantity—questions regarding *how much, how many,* or *how frequently*—researchers sometimes want to look in depth at the nature of certain characteristics or behaviors. Imagine, for example, that a researcher wants to find out what kinds of study strategies high-achieving students tend to use. One approach would be simply to ask the students questions such as "What things do you do to help you remember what you read in your textbooks?" and "How do you prepare for tests in your classes?" Students' responses to such open-ended questions are apt to go in many different directions, sometimes focusing on various

# COMPARE/CONTRAST

| TABLE 1.1 • Contrasting Various Types of Research | | | | |
|---|---|---|---|---|
| | **QUANTITATIVE RESEARCH STUDIES** | | | **QUALITATIVE RESEARCH STUDIES** |
| | **Descriptive Studies** | **Correlational Studies** | **Experimental and Quasi-Experimental Studies** | |
| **General Nature and Purposes** | • Capture the current state of affairs regarding a real-world issue or problem. | • Identify associations among characteristics, behaviors, and/or environmental conditions.<br>• Enable predictions about one variable, given knowledge of the degree or quantity of another variable.<br>• Provide an alternative when experimental manipulations are unethical or impossible. | • Systematically manipulate one (independent) variable in order to observe its possible effect on another (dependent) variable.<br>• Eliminate other plausible explanations for observed outcomes (especially in carefully controlled experimental studies).<br>• Enable conclusions about cause-and-effect relationships. | • Portray the complex, multifaceted nature of human behavior, especially in real-world social settings. |
| **Limitations** | • Don't enable either (1) predictions about one variable based on another variable or (2) conclusions about cause-and-effect relationships. | • Don't enable conclusions about cause-and-effect relationships. | • May not completely eliminate alternative explanations for observed outcomes (especially true for quasi-experimental studies).<br>• In some cases, involve artificial laboratory conditions that don't resemble real-life learning environments (true for many tightly controlled experimental studies). | • Don't enable either predictions or conclusions about cause-and-effect relationships. |
| **Examples of Questions That Might Be Addressed** | • How pervasive are gender stereotypes in popular children's literature?<br><br>• What kinds of aggressive behaviors occur in schools, and with what frequencies?<br><br>• How well have students performed on a recent national achievement test? | • Are better readers also better spellers?<br><br>• Are students more likely to be aggressive at school if they often see violence at home or in their neighborhoods?<br><br>• To what extent are students' class grades correlated with their scores on achievement tests? | • Which of two reading programs produces greater gains in reading comprehension?<br><br>• Which method is most effective in reducing aggressive behavior—reinforcing appropriate behavior, punishing aggressive behavior, or a combination of both?<br><br>• Do different kinds of tests (e.g., multiple choice vs. essay tests) encourage students to study in different ways? | • What things do high-achieving students say they do "in their heads" when they read and study their textbooks?<br>• What distinct qualities characterize high schools in which members of various adolescent gangs interact congenially and respectfully?<br>• In what ways do teachers' instructional practices change when their jobs and salaries depend on their students' scores on statewide or national achievement tests? |

behaviors (e.g., taking notes, working on practice problems) and at other times focusing on various mental processes (e.g., trying to make sense of a passage, generating new examples of concepts). Although it might be possible to categorize students' responses and count those falling into each category (thereby obtaining some quantitative data), the researcher may also want to preserve the multifaceted qualities of students' responses by reporting lengthy excerpts from the interviews.

Qualitative research is often used to explore the complex nature of human behavior in social settings—perhaps in particular social groups, classrooms, schools, or cultures. For instance, in-depth qualitative studies have contributed in important ways to our knowledge of school characteristics that affect the academic and social success of students from diverse backgrounds (e.g., Hemmings, 2004; Ladson-Billings, 1995b; Ogbu, 2003). The right-most column of Table 1.1 presents examples of questions that might best be answered by qualitative research.

Ultimately, you shouldn't think of quantitative and qualitative research as an either-or situation. Like Anne Smith in the opening case study, many educational researchers effectively combine elements of both quantitative and qualitative research in what is known as a

**mixed-methods study** Research study that includes elements of both quantitative and qualitative research.

mixed-methods study. For example, in a study described in the *American Educational Research Journal* in 1999, researchers Melissa Roderick and Eric Camburn tracked more than 27,000 students' academic progress as they made the transition from small elementary or middle schools to much larger high schools in the Chicago public school system. Many students showed a sharp decline in academic achievement in ninth grade, their first year of high school. More than 40% of first-semester ninth graders (males especially) failed at least one course, and students who achieved at low levels early in their high school career were more likely to drop out before graduation.

Such troubling findings are examples of quantitative data, but the researchers also obtained qualitative information that can help us understand the data. For instance, they described a student named Anna, who had done well in her neighborhood K–8 school and seemingly had the basic skills she needed to successfully tackle a high school curriculum. Unfortunately, Anna was overwhelmed by the new demands that her ninth-grade classes placed on her, and her first-semester final grades included several Ds and an F. In an interview with one of the researchers, she gave the following explanation:

> [In geography, the teacher] said the reason why I got a lower grade is 'cause I missed one assignment and I had to do a report, and I forgot that one. [In English,] I got a C . . . 'cause we were supposed to keep a journal, and I keep on forgetting it 'cause I don't have a locker. Well I do, but my locker partner she lets her cousins use it, and I lost my two books there. . . . I would forget to buy a notebook, and then I would have them on separate pieces of paper, and I would lose them. [And, in biology,] the reason I failed was because I lost my folder . . . it had everything I needed, and I had to do it again, and, by the time I had to turn in the new folder, I did, but he said it was too late . . . . (Roderick & Camburn, 1999, p. 305)

Additionally, the interview revealed Anna's perception of most school faculty members as being uncaring, inattentive to students' difficulties, and inflexible in evaluating students' achievement.

If Anna's behaviors, experiences, and perceptions are common ones—and apparently they are—they point to the need for greater faculty support as students make the transition from a close-knit elementary or K–8 school to a more impersonal high school environment. This support might not only be emotional but also *academic*—for instance, including instruction and guidance in organizational skills and effective study habits. We must be careful in drawing such inferences, however. Qualitative data are essentially *descriptive* in nature. Just as is true for a descriptive quantitative study, a qualitative study tells us *how things are* rather than *what causes what*. Any hypotheses about cause–and–effect relationships are only that—hypotheses—that ideally should be tested with experimental, quantitative studies.

## INTERPRETING RESEARCH RESULTS: A CAUTIONARY NOTE

Whenever we look at the results of a research study, we can determine that a particular condition or intervention has led to a particular outcome—that is, there is a cause–and–effect relationship between the two—only if we've eliminated all other possible explanations for the results we've observed. As an example, imagine that Hometown School District wants to find out which of two reading programs, *Reading Is Great* (RIG) or *Reading and You* (RAY), leads to better reading in third grade. The district asks each of its third-grade teachers to choose one of these two reading programs and use it throughout the school year. The district then compares the end-of-year achievement test scores of students in the RIG and RAY classrooms and finds that RIG students have substantially higher reading comprehension scores than RAY students. We might quickly jump to the conclusion that RIG promotes better reading comprehension than RAY—in other words, that a cause–and–effect relationship exists between the instructional method and reading comprehension. But is this really so?

Not necessarily. The fact is, the school district hasn't eliminated all other possible explanations for the difference in students' reading comprehension scores. Remember, the third-grade teachers personally *selected* the instructional program they used. Were the teachers who chose RIG different in some way from those who chose RAY? For instance, were RIG teachers more open-minded and enthusiastic about using innovative methods, did they have higher expectations for their students, or did they devote more class time to reading? Or, perhaps, did the RIG teachers have students who were, on average, better readers to begin with? If the RIG and RAY classrooms were different from each other in any of these ways—or perhaps different in some other way we haven't thought of—then the district hasn't eliminated alternative explanations for why the RIG students have acquired better reading skills than the RAY students. A better way to study the causal influence of a reading program on reading comprehension would be to *randomly assign* third-grade classes to the RIG and RAY programs, thereby making the two groups similar (on average) in terms of student abilities and teacher characteristics.

Be careful that you don't jump too quickly to conclusions about what factors are affecting students' learning, development, and behavior in particular research studies. Scrutinize research reports carefully, always with these questions in mind: *Have the researchers separated and controlled variables that might have an influence on the outcome? Have they ruled out other possible explanations for their results?* Only when the answers to these questions are undeniably *yes* and *yes* should you draw a conclusion about a cause–and–effect relationship.

> Draw conclusions about cause–and–effect relationships only when other possible explanations for an outcome have been eliminated.

## FROM RESEARCH TO PRACTICE: THE IMPORTANCE OF THEORIES

Some research studies have obvious, direct implications for educational practice. Other studies contribute to educational practice indirectly through the **theories** that researchers develop to integrate and explain their findings. In these theories, researchers typically speculate about the underlying (and often unobservable) mechanisms involved in thinking, learning, development, motivation, or some other aspect of human functioning. By giving us ideas about such underlying mechanisms, theories can ultimately help us create learning environments that facilitate students' learning and achievement to the greatest extent possible.

Let's take an example. One prominent theory of how people learn—information processing theory—proposes that attention is an essential ingredient in the learning process. More specifically, if a learner pays attention to new information, the information moves from the first component of the human memory system (the sensory register) to the second component (working memory). If the learner *doesn't* pay attention, the information disappears from the memory system; in the words of a common expression, the information "goes in one ear and out the other." The importance of attention in information processing theory suggests that strategies that capture and maintain students' attention—perhaps presenting interesting reading materials or intriguing real-world problems—are apt to enhance students' learning and achievement.

> Chapter 6 describes information processing theory in depth.

Psychological theories are rarely, if ever, set in stone. Instead, they're continually expanded and modified as additional data come to light, and in some cases one theory may be abandoned in favor of another that better explains a particular phenomenon. Furthermore, different theories focus on different aspects of human functioning, and psychologists haven't yet pulled them together into a single mega-theory that adequately accounts for all the diverse phenomena and experiences that comprise human existence.

Although current theories related to thinking, learning, development, motivation, and behavior will inevitably change in the future, they can be quite useful even in their unfinished forms. They help us integrate thousands of research studies into concise understandings of how children typically learn and develop, and they enable us to draw inferences and make predictions about how students are apt to perform and achieve in particular classroom situations. In general, theories help us to both *explain* and *predict* human behavior, thereby giving us numerous ideas about how best to promote students' academic and social success at school.

## Collecting Data and Drawing Conclusions about Your Own Students

Certainly the collection and interpretation of data aren't restricted only to highly trained researchers who work in universities and research laboratories. In fact, practicing teachers continually collect and interpret data about their own students through formal and informal assessments of students' written work and classroom behaviors. Furthermore, many teachers plan and conduct their own research to help them better understand their students and schools—a process known as *action research*.

> **theory** Integrated set of concepts and principles developed to explain a particular phenomenon.

**FIGURE 1.1**  Seven-year-old Justin's story "The Pet Who Came to Dinner"

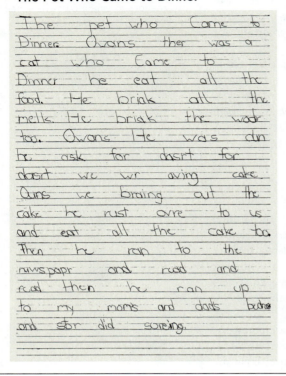

🍏 Use assessment results to form hypotheses—but *not* to draw hard-and-fast conclusions— about students' current characteristics and abilities and about effective instructional strategies.

## ASSESSING STUDENTS' ACHIEVEMENTS AND BEHAVIORS

Most teachers regularly assess what their students know and can do, perhaps through assignments, projects, oral presentations, and quizzes. But effective teachers don't limit themselves only to such formal, planned evaluations. They continually observe their students in a variety of contexts—not only in the classroom but also in the hallways and cafeteria, on the playground, during parent–teacher conferences, and so on—for clues about what students might be thinking, believing, feeling, and learning. Students' comments, questions, body language, work habits, and interactions with friends and classmates can provide valuable insights into their learning, development, and motivation.

To get your feet wet in the process of assessment, read 7-year-old Justin's short story "The Pet Who Came to Dinner," presented in Figure 1.1. As you read it, consider what you might conclude about Justin's progress in writing. Consider, too, what inferences you might make about Justin's family and home life.

As you can see, Justin has learned how to spell some words (e.g., *dinner, came*) but not others (e.g., he spells *once* as "owans" and *started* as "stor did"). Overall, he knows which alphabet letters represent which sounds in speech, but he sometimes reverses the letter *d* so that it looks like a *b,* and he occasionally leaves out sounds in his word spellings (e.g., his spelling of *drink* begins with *b* and omits the *n* sound). Justin has made some progress in common spelling patterns (e.g., the -*ing* suffix for verbs) and in the use of periods and apostrophes. He has learned to tell a simple story, but he does so merely by listing a series of seemingly unrelated events, and he hasn't yet learned that the title of a story should appear in a line by itself, centered at the top of the page.

Justin's story offers a few hints about home life as well. For instance, it appears that Justin lives with two parents, and he talks about the pet reading the newspaper ("nuwspapr"), suggesting that reading is a familiar activity in the home. Are such inferences about Justin accurate? Not necessarily. The conclusions we reach about our students are— like the theories that researchers formulate about learning and development—only reasonable guesses based on the evidence at hand. We must think of such conclusions as tentative *hypotheses* to be tested further, rather than as indisputable *facts.*

## CONDUCTING ACTION RESEARCH

Like Anne Smith in the opening case study, teachers sometimes have questions that existing research findings don't fully answer. In action research, teachers conduct systematic studies of issues and problems in their own schools, with the goal of seeking more effective strategies in working with students. For instance, an action research project might involve examining the effectiveness of a new teaching technique, seeking students' opinions on a controversial school policy, or ascertaining reasons why many students rarely complete homework assignments.

Any action research study typically involves the following steps (Mills, 2011):

**1.** *Identify an area of focus.* The teacher–researcher begins with a problem and gathers preliminary information that might shed light on the problem, perhaps by reading relevant books or journal articles, surfing the Internet, or discussing the issue with colleagues or students. The teacher–researcher then identifies one or more specific questions to address and develops a research plan (data collection techniques, necessary resources, schedule, etc.) for answering those questions. At this point, the teacher also seeks permission from school administrators and any other appropriate authorities to conduct the study. Depending on the nature of the study, parents' permission may be necessary as well.

**2.** *Collect data.* The teacher–researcher collects data relevant to the research questions. Such data might, for example, be obtained from questionnaires, interviews, achievement tests, students' journals or portfolios, existing school records (e.g., attendance patterns, school suspension rates), observations, or any combination of these.

**3.** *Analyze and interpret the data.* The teacher–researcher looks for patterns in the data. Sometimes the analysis involves computing particular statistics (e.g., percentages, averages,

**action research** Research conducted by teachers and other school personnel to address issues and problems in their own schools or classrooms.

correlation coefficients)—this would be a quantitative study. At other times, the analysis involves an in-depth, nonnumerical inspection of the data—this would be a qualitative study. In either case, the teacher–researcher relates the findings to the original research questions.

    **4.** *Develop an action plan.* The final step distinguishes action research from the more traditional research studies described earlier in the chapter. In particular, the teacher–researcher uses the information collected to *take action*—for instance, to change instructional strategies, school policies, or the classroom environment.

    Many colleges and universities now offer courses in action research. You can also find inexpensive paperback books on the topic (e.g., Cochran-Smith & Lytle, 1993; Craig, 2009; Mills, 2011; A. P. Johnson, 2012).

## Developing as a Teacher

As a beginning teacher, you may initially find your role a bit overwhelming. Virtually any classroom will be one of nonstop action requiring you to be constantly attentive and on your toes, and there will always be a great deal to think about.

    If you are currently enrolled in a teacher education program, you should think of your program as a very good start on the road to becoming a skillful teacher (Bransford, Darling-Hammond, & LePage, 2005; Brouwer & Korthagen, 2005). However, it is *only* a start. Developing true expertise in any profession, including teaching, takes many years of experience to acquire, but even a single year of teaching experience can make a significant difference (Berliner, 2001; Clotfelter, Ladd, & Vigdor, 2007; Henry, Bastian, & Fortner, 2011). So be patient with yourself, and recognize that occasionally feeling a bit unsure and making mistakes is par for the course. As you gain experience, you'll gradually become able to make decisions about routine situations and problems quickly and efficiently, giving you the time and energy to think creatively and flexibly about how best to teach classroom subject matter (Borko & Putnam, 1996; Bransford, Derry, Berliner, & Hammerness, 2005; Feldon, 2007).

    Conducting action research is, of course, one effective way of developing your knowledge and skills as a teacher. But in addition, I offer the following strategies—all of them based on research on teacher effectiveness.

    🍏 *Keep up to date on research findings and innovations in education.* Additional university coursework and in-service training sessions at your school are two good ways to increase your teaching effectiveness (Desimone, 2009; Hattie, 2009; McDonald, Robles-Piña, & Polnick, 2011). In addition, effective teachers typically subscribe to one or more professional journals, and as time allows, they occasionally attend professional conferences in their area.

    🍏 *Learn as much as you can about the subject matter you teach.* When we look at effective teachers—for example, those who are flexible in their approaches to instruction, help students develop a thorough understanding of classroom topics, and convey obvious enthusiasm for whatever they're teaching—we typically find teachers who know their subject matter extremely well (Borko & Putnam, 1996; Cochran & Jones, 1998; H. C. Hill et al., 2008).

    🍏 *Learn as much as you can about specific strategies for teaching your particular subject matter.* In addition to knowing general teaching strategies, it's helpful to acquire strategies specific to the topic you're teaching—strategies that are collectively known as pedagogical content knowledge. Effective teachers typically have a large number of strategies for teaching particular topics and skills. Furthermore, they can usually anticipate—and so can also address—the difficulties students will have and the kinds of errors students will make in the process of mastering a skill or body of knowledge (Baumert et al., 2010; Borko & Putnam, 1996; Krauss et al., 2008; L. S. Shulman, 1986).

    🍏 *Learn as much as you can about the culture(s) of the community in which you are working.* Students are more likely to do well in school when the school curriculum and classroom environment take the students' cultural backgrounds into account (Brayboy & Searle, 2007; Moje & Hinchman, 2004; Tyler et al., 2008). Reading about various cultures can be helpful, of course. But ideally, you can best inform yourself about students' cultural beliefs and practices if you participate in local community activities and converse regularly with community members (Castagno & Brayboy, 2008; McIntyre, 2010).

**pedagogical content knowledge**
Knowledge about effective methods of teaching a specific topic or content area.

You can find discussions of cultural differences in many chapters of this book, and especially in Chapter 4.

**reflective teaching** Regular, ongoing examination and critique of one's assumptions and instructional strategies, and revision of them as necessary to enhance students' learning and development.

**self-efficacy** Belief that one is capable of executing certain behaviors or reaching certain goals.

🍎 *Continually reflect on and critically examine your assumptions, inferences, and teaching practices.* In the opening case study, Anne Smith reflects on her students' performance in previous years and then institutes new assessment policies that she thinks might be more motivating and productive. Like Ms. Smith, effective teachers engage in **reflective teaching**: They continually examine and critique their assumptions, inferences, and instructional practices, and they regularly adjust their beliefs and strategies in the face of new evidence (Hammerness, Darling-Hammond, & Bransford, 2005; T. Hogan, Rabinowitz, & Craven, 2003; Larrivee, 2006).

🍎 *Communicate and collaborate with colleagues.* Effective teachers rarely work in isolation. Instead, they frequently communicate with colleagues in their own school district, across the nation, and, often, in other countries. Furthermore, they regularly coordinate their efforts to enhance students' learning and personal well-being at a schoolwide level (Bransford, Darling-Hammond, et al., 2005; Raudenbush, 2009). Teacher lounges, e-mail, Internet websites, and blogs—all of these can potentially offer ideas for lesson plans and instructional activities on a wide range of topics. One helpful resource is www.tappedin.org, an online community of educators from around the world. You should also look at the websites of professional organizations related to your field; websites for the National Council of Teachers of Mathematics (www.nctm.org) and the National Council for the Social Studies (www.socialstudies.org) are just two of the many possibilities.

Keep in mind, too, that even the most masterful of teachers had to begin their teaching careers as novices, and they probably entered their first classroom with the same concerns and uncertainties that you may initially have. Most experienced teachers are happy to offer you advice and support during challenging times. In fact, they're apt to be flattered that you're asking them!

Chapter 10 discusses the nature and effects of self-efficacy.

🍎 *Believe that you can make a difference in students' lives.* In general, human beings achieve at higher levels in their endeavors when they have high **self-efficacy**—that is, when they believe they are capable of executing certain behaviors or reaching certain goals. Students are more likely to try to learn something if they believe they *can* learn it—in other words, if they have high self-efficacy. But as a teacher, you, too, must have high self-efficacy. Believing that you can be a good teacher will give you confidence to try new strategies and help you persist in the face of occasional setbacks. Students who achieve at high levels are apt to be those whose teachers have confidence that, *as teachers,* they can make a genuine difference as they work both individually in their classrooms and collectively with their colleagues (J. A. Langer, 2000; Skaalvik & Skaalvik, 2008; Tschannen-Moran, Woolfolk Hoy, & Hoy, 1998). Ultimately, what teachers do in the classroom *matters* for students, not only in the short term but for years to come (Hattie, 2009; Konstantopoulos & Chung, 2011).

## Strategies for Studying and Learning Effectively

As you learn more about educational psychology—and especially as you learn about the nature of human thinking and learning—you'll gain many insights into how you can help students more effectively master classroom subject matter. I hope you'll also gain insights into how *you yourself* can better learn and remember course material. For now, I suggest five general strategies.

You'll learn much more about effective learning and study strategies in upcoming chapters, especially in Chapter 6 and Chapter 7.

🍎 *Relate what you read to your existing knowledge and prior experiences.* For example, connect new concepts and principles with memorable childhood events, previous coursework, or your general knowledge about human beings and their behavior. In general, people learn and remember things more easily and effectively when they engage in *meaningful learning*—that is, when they connect new information and ideas to things they've previously learned.

🍎 *Actively consider how some new information might contradict your existing beliefs.* As the earlier OOPS test may have shown you, some of what you currently "know" and believe may be sort-of-but-not-quite accurate or even out-and-out *in*accurate. People's existing beliefs can occasionally wreak havoc with new learning. For example, many students in teacher education classes reject research findings that appear to be inconsistent with their personal beliefs and experiences (Darling-Hammond, 2006; Gregoire, 2003; Richardson, 2003).

As you read about and study educational psychology, then, think about how some ideas and research findings might actually contradict and discredit your prior "knowledge." When you encounter puzzling or seemingly "wrong" ideas and findings, I hope you'll keep an open mind and, in particular, consider how and why they might have some validity and worth. Ideally, effective learners undergo *conceptual change*: They revise their existing notions to accommodate new and discrepant information.

🍎 *Tie abstract concepts and principles to concrete examples.* Children become increasingly able to think about abstract ideas as they get older, but people of *all* ages can more readily understand and remember abstract information when they tie it to concrete objects and events. Short examples and lengthier case studies that involve real children and teachers, videos that depict classrooms in action, Experiencing Firsthand exercises such as my OOPS test—all of these can enhance your understanding and memory of new concepts and help you recognize them when you see them in your own work with children and adolescents.

🍎 *Elaborate on what you read, going beyond it and adding to it.* Earlier in the chapter I mentioned that the process of *elaboration*—using prior knowledge to embellish on new information—enhances learning and memory of the information. So try to think *beyond* the information you read. Draw inferences from the ideas presented. Generate new examples of concepts. Identify your own educational applications of various principles of learning, development, and motivation.

🍎 *Periodically check yourself to make sure you remember and understand what you have read.* There are times when even the most diligent students don't concentrate on what they're reading—when they're actually thinking about something else as their eyes go down the page. So stop once in a while (perhaps once every two or three pages) to make sure you have really learned and understood the things you've been reading. Try to summarize the material. Ask yourself questions about it. Make sure everything makes sense to you. Tackle the "Practice for Your Licensure Exam" exercises that appear at the end of each chapter. Check your mastery of various concepts by doing activities and taking quizzes in MyEducationLab™.

When all is said and done, your goal in studying educational psychology isn't to memorize enough facts that you can get good grades on tests and quizzes. Instead, your goal is to become the best teacher—and also the best *learner*—you can possibly be. As you look forward to your entry into the teaching profession, I urge you to be confident that with time, practice, a solid understanding of how children and adolescents learn and develop, a large toolkit of instructional strategies, and every student's best interests at heart, you can truly make a significant difference in young people's lives.

Chapter 6 explores meaningful learning and conceptual change in greater depth.

Chapter 2 discusses the development of abstract thinking and other significant cognitive advancements during the school years.

For additional strategies, read "Study Tips."

# 1 What Have You Learned?

The beginning of the chapter lists five *learning outcomes*—five general things you should accomplish—while reading and studying this chapter. Let's return now to these outcomes and identify key points related to each one.

■ **1.1: Explain the importance of research in classroom decision making.** As teachers, we must make countless daily decisions about how to interact with, instruct, and guide students in our classrooms. Although we can sometimes use simple common sense in making these decisions, such "sense" may occasionally lead us to draw unwarranted, even inaccurate, conclusions. We are most likely to make good decisions—those that maximize students' learning and development over the long run—when we base them on contemporary research findings and on theoretical syntheses of those findings.

Evaluate your knowledge related to this learning outcome in MyEducationLab™.

■ **1.2: Draw appropriate conclusions from different types of research studies.** Knowledge of findings from both quantitative and qualitative research can greatly enhance our teaching effectiveness, but different kinds of studies are appropriate for different kinds of issues and conclusions. Qualitative studies and descriptive quantitative studies can yield a great deal of information about *how things are* at the present time. Correlational quantitative studies enable conclusions about *what variables are associated with what other variables*. But only carefully controlled experimental studies—and, to a lesser extent, quasi-experimental studies—yield dependable conclusions about *what causes what*.

Evaluate and apply your knowledge related to this learning outcome in MyEducationLab™.

■ **1.3: Describe several strategies for collecting information about your own students.** To be effective teachers, we must regularly collect data about our students, sometimes by giving them preplanned assignments or quizzes and sometimes by observing them "on the fly" as they act and interact in class, on the playground, and elsewhere. In addition, we may often find it helpful to conduct action research in order to address questions about our own particular students or about local issues and concerns.

Evaluate and apply your knowledge related to this learning outcome in MyEducationLab™.

■ **1.4: Plan long-term strategies for gaining expertise as a teacher.** Truly effective teachers are also life-long learners. To maximize our development as teachers, we must think critically and reflectively about our assumptions, beliefs, and classroom strategies. We must also continue to modify what we think and do as we acquire new information related to our profession. Such information can come from a variety of sources, including formal coursework, in-service training sessions, professional journals and conferences, Internet websites, consultation with

colleagues and community members, and, of course, our own action research.

Evaluate and apply your knowledge related to this learning outcome in MyEducationLab™.

■ **1.5: Use effective strategies when you read and study.** Successful learning is *active, strategic learning.* A few simple strategies can greatly enhance your learning and memory of what you read and study. In particular, I urge you to (1) connect new concepts and principles to things you already know; (2) reconsider your existing beliefs when new information potentially discredits them; (3) tie abstract ideas to concrete examples; (4) embellish (elaborate) on the concepts and principles you learn, perhaps by drawing inferences or thinking of potential applications; and (5) regularly check yourself to make sure you understand and can remember what you've read—for instance, by summarizing it or asking yourself questions about it.

Evaluate your knowledge related to this learning outcome in MyEducationLab™.

## Practice for Your Licensure Exam

### New Software

High school math teacher Mr. Gualtieri begins his class one Monday with an important announcement: "Our school has just purchased a new instructional software program for the school's computer lab. This program, called Problem-Excel, will give you practice in applying the mathematical concepts and procedures we'll be studying this year. I strongly encourage you to stay after school once or twice a week to get extra practice with the software whenever you're having trouble with the assignments I give you."

Mr. Gualtieri is firmly convinced that the new instructional software will help his students better understand and apply mathematics. To test his hypothesis, he keeps a record of which students report to the computer lab after school and which students do not. He then looks at how well the two groups of students perform on his next classroom test. Much to his surprise, he discovers that, on average, the students who have stayed after school to use the computer software have earned *lower* scores than those who have not used the software. "How can this be?" he puzzles. "Is the computer software actually doing more harm than good?"

1. **Constructed-response question:**

Mr. Gualtieri wonders whether the computer software is actually hurting, rather than helping, his students. Assume that the software has been carefully designed by an experienced educator. Assume, too, that Mr. Gualtieri's classroom test is a good measure of how well his students have learned the material they've been studying.

A. Explain why Mr. Gualtieri cannot draw a conclusion about a cause–and–effect relationship from the evidence he has. Base your response on principles of educational research.

B. Identify another plausible explanation for the results Mr. Gualtieri has obtained.

2. **Multiple-choice question:**

Which one of the following results would provide the most convincing evidence that the Problem-Excel software enhances students' mathematics achievement?

a. Ten high schools in New York City purchase Problem-Excel and make it available to their students. Students at these high schools get higher mathematics achievement test scores than students at ten other high schools that have *not* purchased the software.

b. A high school purchases Problem-Excel, but only four of the eight math teachers at the school decide to have their students use it. The students of these four teachers score at higher levels on a mathematics achievement test than the students of the other four teachers.

c. All tenth graders at a large high school take a mathematics achievement test in September. At some point during the next two months, each student spends 20 hours working with Problem-Excel. The students all take the same math achievement test again in December and, on average, get substantially higher scores than they did in September.

d. Students at a high school are randomly assigned to two groups. One group works with Problem-Excel, and the other group works with a software program called Write-Away, designed to teach better writing skills. The Problem-Excel group scores higher than the Write-Away group on a subsequent mathematics achievement test.

---

**PRAXIS** Go to Appendix C, "Matching Book and MyEducationLab™ to the Praxis Principles of Learning and Teaching Tests," to discover sections of this chapter that may be especially applicable to the Praxis tests.

# 2 Cognitive and Linguistic Development

## LEARNING OUTCOMES

**2.1:** Describe four principles portraying the general nature of child development and the roles of both heredity and environment in guiding it.

**2.2:** Explain how the brain and its development influence children's learning and thinking.

**2.3:** Apply Piaget's theory of cognitive development to classroom practice.

**2.4:** Apply Vygotsky's theory of cognitive development to classroom practice.

**2.5:** Describe developmental changes in language during the school years, and explain how you might adapt instruction to children with diverse language abilities and needs.

# CASE STUDY: APPLE TARTS

Ms. Lombard's fourth-grade class has learned how to add and subtract fractions but has not yet studied how to divide by fractions. Nevertheless, students are working in small groups to tackle the following problem, which requires dividing 20 by $\frac{3}{4}$:

> Mom makes small apple tarts, using three-quarters of an apple for each small tart. She has 20 apples. How many small apple tarts can she make? (J. Hiebert et al., 1997, p. 118)

One group has already agreed that Mom can use three-fourths of each apple to make 20 tarts, with one-fourth of each apple being left to make additional tarts.

> **Liz:** So you've got twenty quarters *left*.
>
> **Jeanette:** Yes, . . . and twenty quarters is equal to five apples, . . . so five apples divided by—
>
> **Liz:** Six, seven, eight.
>
> **Jeanette:** But three-quarters equals three.
>
> **Kerri:** But she can't make only three apple tarts!
>
> **Jeanette:** No, you've still got twenty.
>
> **Liz:** But you've got twenty quarters, if you've got twenty quarters you might be right.
>
> **Jeanette:** I'll show you.
>
> **Liz:** No, I've drawn them all here.
>
> **Kerri:** How many quarters have you got? Twenty?
>
> **Liz:** Yes, one quarter makes five apples and out of five apples she can make five tarts which will make that twenty-five tarts and then she will have, wait, one, two, three, four, five quarters, she'll have one, two, three, four, five quarters. . . . (J. Hiebert et al., 1997, p. 121)

Eventually the group arrives at the correct answer: Mom can make 26 tarts and will have half an apple left over.

- Is the apple-tarts problem developmentally appropriate for Ms. Lombard's students? Why or why not?
- What advantages might there be for making this task a group activity?

---

As you undoubtedly know from your own experiences as a student, fractions are more difficult to understand and work with than are whole numbers. But Liz, Jeanette, and Kerri rise to the challenge of the apple-tarts problem and, in the process, possibly acquire new mathematical understandings and problem-solving skills. In other words, the task is *developmentally appropriate* for them.

Classroom instruction must take into account the physical, cognitive, personal, and social characteristics and abilities that students at a particular age are likely to have. In this chapter we'll look at general principles of development and then zero in on children's cognitive development—that is, developmental changes in thinking, reasoning, and language. As we look at these topics in the pages ahead, we'll be better able to answer the preceding questions about Ms. Lombard's apple-tarts activity.

**cognitive development**
Development of increasingly sophisticated thinking, reasoning, and language with age.

Keep in mind that students of any single age show considerable diversity in what they can and cannot do.

Chapter 3 examines temperamental differences in greater depth.

# General Principles of Human Development

Four general principles characterize children's physical, cognitive, personal, and social development:

- *The sequence of development is somewhat predictable.* Researchers have observed many universals in development; that is, they've seen similar patterns in how children change over time despite considerable differences in the environments in which the children grow up. Some of this universality is marked by the acquisition of developmental milestones—new, developmentally more advanced behaviors—in predictable sequences. For example, children typically become capable of using fractions in mathematical problem solving only after they have mastered counting and the use of whole numbers.

- *Children develop at different rates.* Not all children reach particular milestones at the same age: Some reach them earlier, some later. Accordingly, we are apt to see considerable *diversity* in students' developmental accomplishments at any single grade level. As teachers, we should never jump to conclusions about what individual students can and cannot do based on age alone. For example, although Ms. Lombard's apple-tarts problem appears to be developmentally appropriate for some of her students, it might be too advanced for others.

- *Development is often marked by periods of relatively rapid growth (spurts) between periods of slower growth (plateaus).* Development doesn't necessarily proceed at a constant rate. For example, toddlers may speak with a limited vocabulary and one-word "sentences" for several months, yet sometime around their second birthday their vocabulary expands rapidly and their sentences become longer and longer within just a few weeks. And, of course, after seemingly stalling out height-wise, many young adolescents undergo an adolescent growth spurt, shooting up several inches within a year or so. Occasionally children even take a temporary step *backward,* apparently because they're in the process of overhauling a particular physical or cognitive skill and are about to make a major leap forward (Gershkoff-Stowe & Thelen, 2004; Morra, Gobbo, Marini, & Sheese, 2008). Some developmental theorists use such patterns of uneven growth and change as evidence of qualitatively distinct periods, or *stages,* in development.

- *Heredity and environment interact in their effects on development.* Virtually all aspects of development are influenced either directly or indirectly by a child's genetic makeup. For example, soon after birth children begin to show genetic inclinations, or *temperaments,* that predispose them to respond to physical and social events in certain ways—perhaps to be calm or irritable, outgoing or shy, cheerful or fearful. Not all inherited characteristics appear so early, however. Heredity continues to guide a child's growth through the process of maturation, a gradual, genetically controlled progression of physical advancements as the child develops. For example, motor skills such as walking, running, and jumping develop primarily as a result of neurological development, increased strength, and increased muscular control— changes that are largely determined by inherited biological "instructions."

Yet environmental factors also make substantial contributions to development. For example, although height and body build are primarily inherited characteristics, good nutrition and regular physical exercise also make a difference. And although children's behaviors are partly the result of inherited temperaments, the ways in which their environment encourages them to behave are just as influential, sometimes even more so.

Historically, many researchers have sought to determine the degree to which various human characteristics are the result of heredity versus environment—a question often referred to as *nature versus nurture.* But increasingly psychologists have come to realize that heredity and environment interact in ways we can probably never disentangle (e.g., Belsky, Bakermans-Kranenburg, & van IJzendoorn, 2007; Scarr & McCartney, 1983; J. P. Spencer et al., 2009). First and foremost, genes need environmental support in order to do their work. For instance, a child with "tall" genes can grow tall only if good nutrition supports such growth. Furthermore, some genetically driven maturational processes seem to be characterized by sensitive periods, limited time periods during which certain environmental conditions are especially important for normal development (we'll see examples in the upcoming sections on the brain and language development). In addition, children's inherited characteristics may lead other people to treat them in particular ways. For instance, a physically attractive child will be accepted more readily by peers than a less attractive one, and a temperamentally hyperactive child may be disciplined more harshly than a quieter one. Finally, children can *choose* their environments to some extent, especially as they get older, and they're apt to seek out situations that match their inherited temperaments and abilities.

The last point in the preceding paragraph is important enough to repeat: *Children can choose their environments to some extent.* Children are hardly passive recipients of their environmental legacies. Instead, they actively and intentionally *think about* and *act on* their environments, and in doing so they alter their environments—and the effects of those environments—in significant ways (Mareschal et al., 2007; Nettles, Caughy, & O'Campo, 2008; Nuemi, 2008).

**universals** Similar patterns in how children change and progress over time regardless of their specific environment.

**developmental milestone** Appearance of a new, more advanced behavior that indicates significant progress in a child's development.

**maturation** Occurrence of genetically controlled physical advancements as a child develops.

**sensitive period** Age range during which a certain aspect of a child's development is especially susceptible to environmental conditions (you may sometimes see the term *critical period*).

**culture** Behaviors and belief systems of a long-standing social group.

## THE MULTIPLE LAYERS OF ENVIRONMENTAL INFLUENCE: BRONFENBRENNER'S THEORY

As we consider the various ways in which the environment might influence children's development, we must be careful that we don't limit our thinking only to children's immediate surroundings. In fact, as the developmental theorist Urie Bronfenbrenner pointed out, any large society encompasses various "layers" of environment that all have significant impacts on children's development (Bronfenbrenner, 1989, 2005; Bronfenbrenner & Morris, 1998). The most basic level for most children is the *family*, which can potentially support development in a number of ways—for instance, by providing good nutrition, encouraging physical exercise, helping with homework, and giving guidance during challenging tasks. Surrounding the family is another layer, the *neighborhood and community*, which can offer additional support, definitely through its schools (in industrialized societies, at least) and perhaps also through preschools, after-school homework assistance programs, libraries, museums, zoos, and internships in local businesses. At a still broader level, the *state (or province) and country* in which children reside influence development through legislation that governs school policy, tax dollars that flow back to local schools, agencies and professional groups that offer information and training in new teaching strategies, and so on. Figure 2.1 illustrates the kinds of environmental influences that the different layers might involve.

Learn more about children's physical development in "Physical Development Across Childhood and Adolescence."

Permeating and impacting all of these layers is a child's culture—the behaviors and belief systems that characterize one or more long-standing social groups of which the child is a member. Culture is pervasive in many aspects of a child's home environment—for instance, in the behaviors family members encourage, the disciplinary practices parents use, the books children have access to, the television shows they watch, and so on. Culture influences the broader environmental levels as well—for instance, by offering certain outlets for leisure time (e.g., basketball courts, Cinco de Mayo festivals) and by advocating or discouraging certain activities (e.g., seeking a college degree, playing video games). Ultimately, culture is an inside-the-head thing as well as an out-there-in-the-world thing: It provides an overall framework by which a child comes to determine what things are normal and abnormal, true and not true, rational and irrational, good and bad (M. Cole, 2006; Shweder et al., 1998).

The various environmental layers interact with one another and with children's existing characteristics in their influences on children's development; in the process, they also *change* one another. For example, a temperamentally hyperactive child might initially elicit stringent disciplinary actions at school (the neighborhood/community layer), but concerned parents (the family layer) might seek out teachers and suggest alternative strategies that effectively channel the child's behavior into productive activities. And government agencies (the state/province/country layer) might provide websites that help both parents and teachers better

Learn more about Bronfenbrenner's *ecological systems perspectives* in "Ecological Systems Perspectives of Child Development."

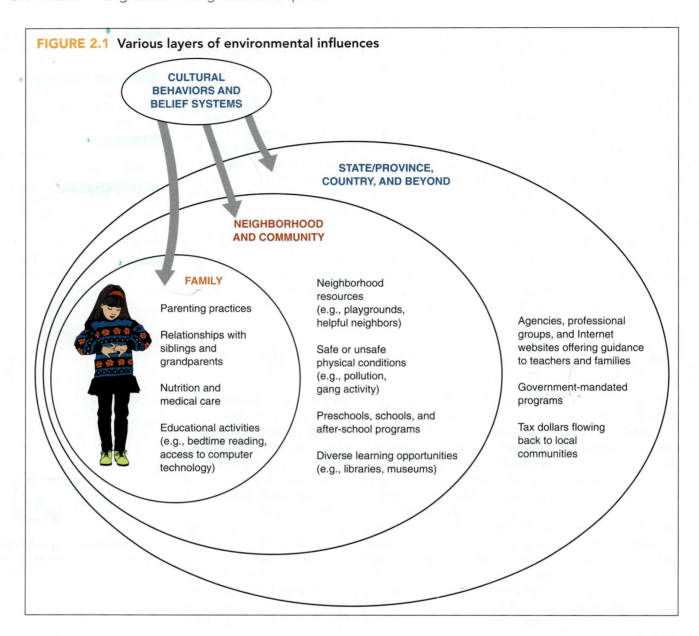

**FIGURE 2.1** Various layers of environmental influences

foster children's cognitive development. In general, children's environments are *dynamic systems* encompassing mutually influencing variables that are in constant flux (C. D. Lee, 2010; Thelen & Smith, 1998).

## Role of the Brain in Learning and Development

One key player in children's development is, of course, the brain. The human brain is an incredibly complicated organ that includes several *trillion* cells. About one hundred billion of them are nerve cells, or neurons, that are microscopic in size and interconnected in innumerable ways. Some neurons receive information from the rest of the body, others synthesize and interpret that information, and still others send messages that tell the body how to respond to its present circumstances. Accompanying neurons are perhaps one to five trillion glial cells, which serve a variety of specialized functions that enhance the functioning of neurons or in other ways keep the brain going.

Like all cells in living creatures, every neuron has a *cell body,* which contains its nucleus and is responsible for its general well-being (see Figure 2.2). But in addition, a neuron has numerous branchlike structures, called *dendrites,* that receive messages from other neurons. A neuron also

**neuron** Cell in the brain or another part of the nervous system that transmits information to other cells.

**glial cell** Cell in the brain that supports neurons or general brain functioning.

**FIGURE 2.2  Neurons and their interconnections**

has an *axon,* a long, armlike structure that transmits information on to still other neurons. The axon may branch out many times, and the ends of its branches have *terminal buttons* that contain certain chemical substances (more about these substances in a moment). For some (but not all) neurons, much of the axon has a white, fatty coating called a *myelin sheath.*

When a neuron's dendrites are stimulated by other neurons (either those in the brain or those extending from other parts of the body), the dendrites become electrically charged. If the total charge reaches a certain level, the neuron fires, sending an electrical impulse along its axon to the terminal buttons. If the axon has a myelin sheath, the impulse travels quite rapidly because it leaps from one gap in the myelin to the next, almost as if it were playing leap frog. If the axon doesn't have a myelin sheath, the impulse travels more slowly.

Curiously, neurons don't actually touch one another. Instead, they send chemical messages to their neighbors across tiny spaces known as **synapses**. When an electrical impulse moves along a neuron's axon, it signals the terminal buttons to release chemicals known as **neurotransmitters** that travel across the synapses and stimulate neighboring neurons. Any single neuron may have synaptic connections with hundreds or even thousands of other neurons (Goodman & Tessier-Lavigne, 1997; Lichtman, 2001).

With these basics in mind, let's consider four key points about the brain and its role in cognitive development:

• *Different parts of the brain have different specialties, but they all work closely with one another.* Brain structures in the lower and middle parts of the brain specialize in essential physiological processes (e.g., breathing), habitual body movements (e.g., riding a bicycle), and basic perceptual skills (e.g., diverting attention to potentially life-threatening stimuli). Complex, conscious thinking takes place primarily in the **cortex**, which rests on the top and sides of the brain like a thick, lumpy toupee (see Figure 2.3). The portion of the cortex located near the forehead, known as the *prefrontal cortex,* is largely responsible for a wide variety of very human activities, including sustained attention, planning, reasoning, decision making, coordination of complex activities, and inhibition of nonproductive thoughts and behaviors. Other areas of the cortex are actively involved in interpreting visual and auditory information, identifying the spatial characteristics of objects and events, and retaining general knowledge about the world.

To some degree, the left and right halves of the cortex—its two *hemispheres*—also have somewhat distinct specialties. For most people, the left hemisphere takes primary responsibility for language and logical thinking, whereas the right hemisphere is more dominant in visual and spatial tasks (Byrnes, 2001; Ornstein, 1997; Siegel, 2012). Yet contrary to a popular belief, people rarely, if ever, think exclusively in one hemisphere. There's no such thing as "left-brain" or "right-brain" thinking: The two hemispheres constantly collaborate in day-to-day tasks. In fact, learning

**synapse** Junction between two neurons that allows transmission of messages from one to the other.

**neurotransmitter** Chemical substance through which one neuron sends a message to another.

**cortex** Upper part of the brain; site of complex, conscious thinking processes.

**FIGURE 2.3** Cortex of the human brain

Prefrontal cortex

or thinking about virtually anything, even a fairly simple idea, tends to be *distributed* across many parts of the brain (Bressler, 2002; Gonsalves & Cohen, 2010; Haxby et al., 2001).

• *Most learning probably involves changes in neurons and synapses.* In many instances, learning involves strengthening existing synapses or forming new ones. Sometimes, however, making progress actually involves *eliminating* synapses. Effective learning requires not only that people think and do certain things but also that they *not* think and do other things—in other words, that they inhibit tendencies to think or behave in particular ways (Bruer & Greenough, 2001; Lichtman, 2001; Merzenich, 2001).

• *Developmental changes in the brain enable increasingly complex and efficient thought.* Neurons begin to form synapses long before a child is born. But shortly after birth the rate of synapse formation increases dramatically. Neurons sprout new dendrites in many directions, and so they come into contact with many of their neighbors, especially in the first two or three years of life. Much of this early synaptogenesis appears to be driven primarily by genetic programming rather than by learning experiences. Thanks to synaptogenesis, children in the elementary grades have many more synapses than adults do (Bruer, 1999; C. A. Nelson, Thomas, & de Haan, 2006).

As children encounter different stimuli and experiences in their daily lives, some synapses come in quite handy and are used repeatedly. Others are largely useless, and these gradually fade away through a process known as synaptic pruning, a process that continues throughout the elementary and secondary school years and into adulthood. Synaptic pruning is a *good* thing—not a bad one—because it eliminates "nuisance" synapses that are inconsistent with typical environmental events and appropriate responses. Synaptic pruning, then, may be Mother Nature's way of making the brain more efficient (Bruer & Greenough, 2001; Huttenlocher & Dabholkar, 1997; Spear, 2007). Meanwhile, children and adults alike continue to form new synapses in response to their experiences (R. D. Brown & Bjorklund, 1998; Bruer, 1999; O'Boyle & Gill, 1998; Silveri et al., 2006).

Another important developmental process in the brain is myelination. When neurons first develop, their axons have no myelin sheath. As they acquire this myelin over time, they fire much more quickly, greatly enhancing the brain's overall efficiency. Myelination continues throughout childhood, adolescence, and early adulthood, especially in the cortex (Lenroot & Giedd, 2007; Merzenich, 2001; Paus et al., 1999).

In addition, the onset of puberty is marked by significant changes in hormone levels, which affect the continuing maturation of brain structures and possibly also affect the production and effectiveness of neurotransmitters (Kolb, Gibb, & Robinson, 2003; Shen et al., 2010; E. F. Walker, 2002). Such changes can have an impact on adolescents' functioning in a variety of areas, including attention, planning, and impulse control. To some degree, adolescents' abilities to learn and respond appropriately may temporarily *decrease* until brain functioning restabilizes (McGivern, Andersen, Byrd, Mutter, & Reilly, 2002; Shen et al., 2010; Steinberg, 2009).

• *The brain remains adaptable throughout life.* Some aspects of cognitive development appear to have sensitive periods in which certain kinds of environmental stimulation are crucial. For example, if infants don't have normal exposure to patterns of light (e.g., if congenital cataracts make them functionally blind), they may soon lose the ability to see normally, and if children don't hear spoken language until age 5, they may never acquire the language's subtle grammatical complexities (Bruer, 1999; M. S. C. Thomas & Johnson, 2008). But seeing patterned light and hearing spoken language are *normal* experiences, not exceptional ones. There is *no* evidence to indicate that sensitive periods exist for traditional academic subjects such as reading and mathematics.

From a physiological standpoint, the brain's ability to reorganize itself in order to adapt to changing circumstances—that is, its plasticity—persists throughout the life span (Kolb et al., 2003; C. A. Nelson et al., 2006). The early years are important for development, to be sure, but so are the later years. For most topics and skills, there isn't a single "best" or "only" time to learn (Bruer, 1999; Byrnes & Fox, 1998; Geary, 1998, 2008). The human brain never goes into lockdown mode.

**synaptogenesis** Universal process in early brain development in which many new synapses form spontaneously.

**synaptic pruning** Universal process in brain development in which many previously formed synapses wither away.

**myelination** Growth of a fatty sheath (myelin) around the axons of neurons, enabling faster transmission of electrical impulses.

**plasticity** Ability to reorganize in order to adapt to changing circumstances; term often used in describing the human brain.

## Applying Brain Research

### Taking Developmental Changes in the Brain into Account

Be careful—many recently published books and articles about "using brain research" and "brain-based learning" either misrepresent or misapply researchers' findings about brain development. The following three recommendations are consistent with current knowledge about the brain and how it changes with age.

🍎 **Provide reasonable stimulation for young children; don't overload them with new information and activities for fear of their "losing synapses."** Some well-meaning educators have proposed that the proliferation of new synapses in the preschool and early elementary years points to a sensitive period in brain development. Accordingly, they urge us to maximize children's educational experiences—providing reading instruction, violin lessons, art classes, and so on—during this time period. Before you, too, jump to such a conclusion, consider this point: Although adequate nutrition and everyday forms of stimulation are critical for normal brain development, there is *no* evidence that jam-packed, information- and skills-intensive experiences in the early years enhance brain power over the long run (Bruer, 1999; R. A. Thompson & Nelson, 2001).

🍎 **Keep in mind that adolescents' brains have not yet fully matured.** Synaptic pruning and myelination—two developmental processes that enhance the brain's efficiency—continue throughout adolescence and beyond. Adolescents' brains are *not* adult brains, especially in the prefrontal cortex—that part of the brain that controls sustained attention, planning, reasoning, impulse control, and other abilities so important for independent learning and responsible behavior (Steinberg, 2009). Thus, many middle school and high school students need considerable structure and guidance in order to get and keep them on the road to academic success.

🍎 **Be optimistic that students of all ages can acquire a wide variety of new topics and skills.** For some content areas—for instance, in music and foreign languages—instruction in the preschool or early elementary years appears to mold the brain somewhat differently than does instruction in the later school years (K. L. Hyde et al., 2009; P. K. Kuhl et al., 2005). Furthermore, children of differing ages have differing levels of prior knowledge and experience on which to draw as they work to acquire new information and skills. Ultimately, we must keep in mind the *plasticity* of the human brain: With reasonable effort, practice, and support, human learners of any age can master a great many things.

---

As researchers gradually pin down how the brain works and develops, they're also beginning to get clues about how we can best foster children's and adolescents' cognitive development; three research-based recommendations are presented in the Applying Brain Research feature "Taking Developmental Changes in the Brain into Account." Even so, current knowledge of brain physiology doesn't yield many specifics about how best to foster students' learning and cognitive development (Byrnes, 2007; G. A. Miller, 2010; Varma, McCandliss, & Schwartz, 2008). By and large, if we want to understand the nature of human learning and cognitive development, we must look primarily at what psychologists, rather than neurologists, have discovered. Two early theories—those of Jean Piaget and Lev Vygotsky—have been especially influential in molding contemporary views of how children learn and develop.

# Piaget's Theory of Cognitive Development

Do you think of yourself as a logical person? Just how logical *are* you? Try your logical reasoning abilities in the following exercise.

### EXPERIENCING FIRSTHAND
#### BEADS, BEINGS, AND BASKETBALLS

Take a moment to solve the following three problems:

1. In the margin are 12 wooden beads, 10 brown ones and 2 white ones. Are there more brown beads or more wooden beads?

2. If all children are human beings,
   And if all human beings are living creatures,
   Then must all children be living creatures?

3. If all children are basketballs,
   And if all basketballs are jellybeans,
   Then must all children be jellybeans?

**clinical method** Procedure in which an adult presents a task or problem and asks a child a series of questions about it, tailoring later questions to the child's responses to previous ones.

**class inclusion** Recognition that an object simultaneously belongs to a particular category and to one of its subcategories.

You undoubtedly found the first problem quite easy; there are, of course, more wooden beads than brown beads. You may have found the second problem more difficult but probably concluded fairly quickly that, yes, all children must be living creatures. The third problem is a bit tricky: It follows the same line of reasoning as the second, but the logical conclusion—all children must be jellybeans—contradicts what is true in reality.

In the early 1920s Swiss biologist Jean Piaget began studying children's responses to problems of this nature. He used an approach he called the clinical method, in which an adult presents a task or problem and asks a child a series of questions about it, tailoring later questions to the child's responses to previous ones. For example, let's look at what happened when a researcher in Piaget's laboratory presented the wooden beads problem to a 6-year-old, whom we'll call Brian:[1]

> *Adult:* Are there more wooden beads or more brown beads?
>
> *Brian:* More brown ones, because there are two white ones.
>
> *Adult:* Are the white ones made of wood?
>
> *Brian:* Yes.
>
> *Adult:* And the brown ones?
>
> *Brian:* Yes.
>
> *Adult:* Then are there more brown ones or more wooden ones?
>
> *Brian:* More brown ones. (Piaget, 1952a, pp. 163–164)

During further questioning, Brian continues to assert that the brown beads outnumber the wooden beads. In an effort to help him see otherwise, the adult asks him to draw two necklaces, one made of the brown beads and another made of the wooden beads. Brian draws a series of black rings for the brown-beads necklace; he draws a series of black rings plus two white rings for the wooden-beads necklace.

> *Adult:* Good. Now which will be longer, the one with the brown beads or the one with the wooden beads?
>
> *Brian:* The one with the brown beads. (Piaget, 1952a, p. 164)

Piaget suggested that young children such as Brian have trouble with class inclusion tasks in which they must think of an object as simultaneously belonging to a category and to one of its subcategories—in this case, thinking of a bead as being both *wooden* and *brown* at the same time. Piaget found that many 4- and 5-year-olds have difficulty with class inclusion tasks such as the beads problem but that 7- and 8-year-olds almost always respond to such tasks correctly. He found, too, that 10-year-olds have an easier time with logic problems that involve real-world phenomena (such as categories and subcategories of living creatures) than with problems involving hypothetical and contrary-to-fact ideas (such as jellybean children), whereas adolescents can effectively deal with both kinds of problems.

Through a wide variety of thought-provoking questions and tasks, Piaget and his research colleagues discovered a great deal about what and how children think about the world around them (e.g., Inhelder & Piaget, 1958; Piaget, 1929, 1952b, 1959, 1970, 1980). Piaget integrated his findings into a theory of cognitive development that has made major contributions to contemporary understandings of children's learning and development.

## PIAGET'S BASIC ASSUMPTIONS

Piaget introduced a number of ideas and concepts to describe and explain the changes in logical thinking he observed in children and adolescents:

> • *Children are active and motivated learners.* Piaget believed that children are naturally curious about their world and actively seek out information to help them make sense of it. They continually experiment with the objects they encounter, manipulating them and observing the effects of their actions.

Young children are naturally curious about objects in their environment. For example, watch 2-year-old Maddie in "Cognitive Development: Early Childhood."

---

[1]Piaget used abbreviations to identify specific children in his studies. In this case he used the letters *BRI*, but I've given the child a name to allow for easier discussion.

- *Children construct rather than absorb knowledge.* In their day-to-day experiences, children don't just passively soak up a collection of isolated facts. Instead, they pull their experiences together into an integrated view of how the world operates. For example, by observing that objects always fall down (never up) when released, children begin to construct a basic understanding of gravity. As they interact with family pets, visit farms and zoos, and look at picture books, they develop more complex understandings of animals. Because Piaget proposed that children construct their own beliefs and understandings from their experiences, his theory is sometimes called a *constructivist* theory or, more generally, constructivism.

In Piaget's terminology, the things children do and know are organized as schemes—groups of similar actions or thoughts that are used repeatedly in response to the environment. Initially, children's schemes are largely behavioral in nature, but over time they become increasingly mental and, eventually, abstract. For example, an infant may have a putting-things-in-mouth scheme that she applies to a variety of objects, including her thumb, cookies, and toys. A 7-year-old may have a scheme for identifying snakes that includes their long, thin bodies, lack of legs, and slithery nature. A 13-year-old may have a scheme for what constitutes *fashion,* allowing him to classify his peers as being either very cool or "total losers."

Over time, children's schemes are modified with experience, and many become integrated with one another. For instance, children begin to take hierarchical interrelationships into account: They learn that poodles and cocker spaniels are both dogs, that dogs and cats are both animals, and so on. A progressively more organized body of knowledge and thought processes allows children to think in increasingly complex and logical ways.

- *Children continually learn new things through two complementary processes: assimilation and accommodation.* Assimilation entails dealing with an object or event in a way that's consistent with an existing scheme. For example, an infant may assimilate a new teddy bear into her putting-things-in-mouth scheme. A 7-year-old may quickly identify a new slithery creature in the garden as a snake. A 13-year-old may readily label a classmate's clothing as being either quite fashionable or "soooo yesterday."

But sometimes children can't easily interpret and respond to a new object or event using existing schemes. In these situations one of two forms of accommodation occurs: Children either (1) modify an existing scheme to account for the new object or event or (2) form a new scheme to deal with it. For example, an infant may have to open her mouth wider than usual to accommodate a teddy bear's fat paw. A 13-year-old may have to revise his existing scheme of fashion according to changes in what's hot and what's not. A 7-year-old who encounters a long, slithery creature with four legs can't apply the *snake* scheme (snakes don't have legs) and thus, after some research, may acquire a new scheme—*salamander.*

Assimilation and accommodation typically work hand in hand as children develop their knowledge and understanding of the world. Children interpret each new event within the context of their existing knowledge (assimilation) but at the same time may modify their knowledge as a result of the new event (accommodation). Accommodation rarely happens without assimilation: Children can benefit from, or accommodate to, new experiences only when they can relate those experiences to their current knowledge and beliefs.

- *Interactions with one's physical and social environments are essential for cognitive development.* According to Piaget, active experimentation with the physical world is critical for cognitive growth. By exploring and manipulating physical objects—fiddling with sand and water, playing games with balls and bats, and the like—children learn the nature of such characteristics as volume and weight, discover principles related to force and gravity, and so on.

In Piaget's view, interaction with other people is equally important. Frequent social interactions—both pleasant (e.g., conversations) and unpleasant (e.g., conflicts about sharing and fair play)—help young children come to realize that different people see things differently and that their own view of the world isn't necessarily completely accurate or logical. As children get older, discussions and disagreements about complex issues and problems—for instance, the apple-tarts problem in the opening case study—help them recognize and reexamine inconsistencies in their reasoning.

- *The process of equilibration promotes progression toward increasingly complex thought.* Piaget suggested that children are often in a state of equilibrium: They can comfortably interpret and

---

**constructivism** Theoretical perspective proposing that learners actively construct (rather than passively absorb) knowledge from their experiences.

**scheme** Organized group of similar actions or thoughts that are used repeatedly in response to the environment.

**assimilation** Process of dealing with an object or event in a way that is consistent with an existing scheme.

**accommodation** Process of dealing with a new object or event by either modifying an existing scheme or forming a new one.

**equilibrium** State of being able to address new events with existing schemes.

When introducing a new concept or procedure, show students how it relates to something they already know.

An event that contradicts what we currently know and believe about the world creates *disequilibrium*—a feeling of discomfort that motivates us to try to resolve the contradiction in some way.

Present puzzling phenomena that students cannot easily explain using their existing understandings.

respond to new events using existing schemes. But as children grow older and expand their horizons, they sometimes encounter situations for which their current knowledge and skills are inadequate. Such situations create disequilibrium, a sort of mental discomfort that spurs them to try to make sense of what they're observing. By replacing, reorganizing, or better integrating certain schemes (i.e., through accommodation), children can better understand and address previously puzzling events. The process of moving from equilibrium to disequilibrium and back to equilibrium again is known as equilibration. In Piaget's view, equilibration and children's intrinsic desire to achieve equilibrium promote the development of more complex levels of thought and knowledge.

As an example, let's return to Brian's responses to the beads problem. Recall that the adult asks Brian to draw two necklaces, one made with the brown beads and one made with the wooden beads. The adult hopes that after Brian draws a brown-and-white necklace that is longer than an all-brown necklace, he will notice that his drawings are inconsistent with his statement that there are more brown beads. The inconsistency might lead Brian to experience disequilibrium, perhaps to the point where he would revise his conclusion. In this case, however, Brian is apparently oblivious to the inconsistency, remains in equilibrium, and thus has no need to revise his thinking.

•  *In part as a result of maturational changes in the brain, children think in qualitatively different ways at different ages.*  Long before researchers knew much about how the brain changes with age, Piaget speculated that it *does* change in significant ways and that such changes enable more complex thought processes. He suggested that major neurological changes take place when children are about 2 years old, again when they're 6 or 7, and yet again around puberty. Changes at each of these times allow new abilities to emerge, such that children progress through a sequence of stages that reflect increasingly sophisticated thought. As we've seen, the brain does, in fact, continue to develop throughout childhood and adolescence, but whether such changes are specifically related to the cognitive changes Piaget described is still an open question.

**disequilibrium**  State of being unable to address new events with existing schemes; typically accompanied by some mental discomfort.

**equilibration**  Movement from equilibrium to disequilibrium and back to equilibrium, a process that promotes development of more complex thought and understandings.

## PIAGET'S STAGES OF COGNITIVE DEVELOPMENT

Piaget proposed that as a result of brain maturation, innumerable experiences, and children's natural desire to make sense of and adapt to their world, cognitive development proceeds through four distinct stages (e.g., Piaget, 1971). Abilities at any one stage are constructed out of the accomplishments of any preceding stages. Thus, the four stages are *hierarchical*—each one provides a foundation for any subsequent stages—and so children progress through them in a particular order.

Table 2.1 summarizes these stages and presents examples of abilities acquired during each one. As you look at the table, keep in mind that many children are apt to be in *transition* from one stage to the next, displaying characteristics of two adjacent stages at the same time. Furthermore, as children gain abilities associated with more advanced stages, they don't necessarily leave behind the characteristics they acquired in previous stages.

The preoperational, concrete operations, and formal operations stages all occur during the school years, and so we'll look at these three stages more closely.

**sensorimotor stage** Piaget's first stage of cognitive development, in which schemes are based largely on behaviors and perceptions.

## COMPARE/CONTRAST

### TABLE 2.1 • Piaget's Four Stages of Cognitive Development

| STAGE | AGE OF ONSET | GENERAL DESCRIPTION | EXAMPLES OF ABILITIES ACQUIRED |
|---|---|---|---|
| Sensorimotor | Begins at birth | Schemes are based largely on behaviors and perceptions. Especially in the early part of this stage, children cannot think about things that are not immediately in front of them, and so they focus on what they are doing and seeing at the moment. | • **Trial-and-error experimentation with physical objects:** Exploration and manipulation of objects to determine their properties<br>• **Object permanence:** Realization that objects continue to exist even when removed from view<br>• **Symbolic thought:** Representation of physical objects and events as mental entities (*symbols*) |
| Preoperational | Emerges at about age 2 | Thanks in part to their rapidly developing symbolic thinking abilities, children can now think and talk about things beyond their immediate experience. However, they do not yet reason in logical, adultlike ways. | • **Language:** Rapid expansion of vocabulary and grammatical structures<br>• **Extensive pretend play:** Enactment of imaginary scenarios with plots and assigned roles (e.g., mommy, doctor, Superman)<br>• **Intuitive thought:** Some logical thinking (especially after age 4), but based primarily on hunches and intuition rather than on conscious awareness of logical principles |
| Concrete Operations | Emerges at about age 6 or 7 | Adultlike logic appears but is limited to reasoning about concrete, real-life situations. | • **Distinction between one's own and others' perspectives:** Recognition that one's own thoughts and feelings may be different from those of others and do not necessarily reflect reality<br>• **Class inclusion:** Ability to classify objects as belonging to two or more categories simultaneously<br>• **Conservation:** Realization that amount stays the same if nothing is added or taken away, regardless of alterations in shape or arrangement |
| Formal Operations | Emerges at about age 11 or 12 | Logical reasoning processes are applied to abstract ideas as well as to concrete objects and situations. Many capabilities essential for advanced reasoning in science and mathematics appear. | • **Logical reasoning about abstract, hypothetical, and contrary-to-fact ideas:** Ability to draw logical deductions about situations that have no basis in physical reality<br>• **Proportional reasoning:** Conceptual understanding of fractions, percentages, decimals, and ratios<br>• **Formulation of multiple hypotheses:** Ability to identify two or more competing hypotheses about possible cause–and–effect relationships<br>• **Separation and control of variables:** Ability to test hypotheses by manipulating one variable while holding other relevant variables constant<br>• **Idealism:** Ability to envision alternatives to current social and political practices, sometimes with little regard for what is realistically possible under existing circumstances |

## PREOPERATIONAL STAGE (AGE 2 UNTIL AGE 6 OR 7)

In the early part of the preoperational stage, children's language skills virtually explode, and the many words in their rapidly increasing vocabularies serve as *symbols* that enable them to mentally represent and think about a wide variety of objects and events. However, preoperational thought has some definite limitations, especially when compared to the concrete operational thinking that emerges later. For example, Piaget described young children as exhibiting preoperational egocentrism, an inability to view situations from another person's perspective. Thus, preschoolers may play games together without checking to be sure they're all playing by the same rules, and they may tell stories in which they leave out details that are critical for listeners' understanding.

Young children's thinking also tends to be somewhat illogical at times, at least from an adult's point of view. We've already seen how young children have difficulty with class inclusion problems (recall Brian's insistence that the brown beads outnumber the wooden ones). In addition, they're apt to have trouble with conservation: They fail to realize that if nothing is added or taken away, the amount of one or more substances or objects must stay the same regardless of changes in shape or arrangement. As illustrations, consider what happens when we present two conservation tasks to 5-year-old Nathan:

*Conservation of liquid:* We show Nathan the three glasses in Figure 2.4. We ask him whether Glasses A and B contain the same amount of water, and he replies confidently that they do. We then pour the water from Glass B into Glass C and ask him whether A and C have the same amount. Nathan replies, "No, that glass [pointing to Glass A] has more because it's taller."

*Conservation of number:* We next show Nathan two rows of seven pennies each, like so:

Nathan counts the pennies in each row and agrees that the two rows have the same amount. We spread the second row out, and the pennies now look like this:

When we ask Nathan whether the two rows still have the same number, he replies, "No, this one [pointing to the bottom row] has more because it's longer."

As children approach the later part of the preoperational stage, perhaps at around age 4 or 5, they show early signs of adultlike logic. For example, they sometimes draw correct conclusions about class inclusion and conservation problems. But they base their reasoning on hunches and intuition rather than on any conscious awareness of underlying logical principles, and thus they can't yet explain *why* their conclusions are correct.

## CONCRETE OPERATIONS STAGE (AGE 6 OR 7 UNTIL AGE 11 OR 12)

Piaget proposed that as children enter the concrete operations stage, their thought processes become organized into larger systems of mental processes—*operations*—that allow them to think more logically than they have previously. They now realize that their own perspectives and feelings aren't necessarily shared by others and may reflect personal opinions rather than reality. They also exhibit such logical reasoning abilities as class inclusion and conservation. For example, they should readily conclude, as you presumably did in an earlier Experiencing Firsthand exercise, that in a group of brown and white wooden beads, there obviously must be more wooden beads than brown ones.

Children continue to refine their newly acquired logical thinking capabilities for several years. For instance, some forms of conservation, such as conservation of liquid and conservation of number, appear at age 6 or 7, whereas other forms emerge later. Consider the problem in Figure 2.5. Using a balance scale, an adult shows a child that two balls of clay have the same weight. One ball is removed from the scale and smashed into a pancake shape. Does the pancake weigh the same as the unsmashed ball, or are the weights different? Children typically don't achieve conservation of weight—they don't realize that the flattened pancake weighs the same as the round ball it was earlier—until about age 9 (Morra et al., 2008).

**FIGURE 2.4  Do Glasses A and C contain the same amount of water?**

A    B    C
Before

A    B    C
After

**preoperational stage**  Piaget's second stage of cognitive development, in which children can think about objects and events beyond their immediate view but do not yet reason in logical, adultlike ways.

**preoperational egocentrism**  Inability of children in Piaget's preoperational stage to view situations from another person's perspective.

**conservation**  Recognition that if nothing is added or taken away, amount stays the same regardless of alterations in shape or arrangement.

**concrete operations stage**  Piaget's third stage of cognitive development, in which adultlike logic appears but is limited to concrete reality.

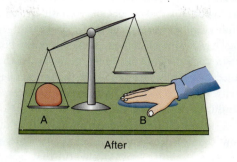

**FIGURE 2.5** Conservation of weight: Ball A and Ball B initially weigh the same. When Ball B is flattened into a pancake shape, how does its weight now compare with that of Ball A?

Before

After

**formal operations stage**
Piaget's fourth and final stage of cognitive development, in which logical reasoning processes are applied to abstract ideas as well as to concrete objects.

Although students displaying concrete operational thought show many signs of logical thinking, their cognitive development isn't yet complete. For example, they have trouble understanding abstract ideas, and they may struggle with problems involving fractions and other proportions, as Liz, Jeanette, and Kerri do in the opening case study.

## FORMAL OPERATIONS STAGE (AGE 11 OR 12 THROUGH ADULTHOOD)

Once children acquire abilities characterizing the formal operations stage, they can think about concepts that have little or no basis in concrete reality. Furthermore, they recognize that what is logically valid is different from what is true in the real world. For example, recall the earlier children-basketballs-jellybeans problem: *If* all children are basketballs and *if* all basketballs are jellybeans, then formal operational thinkers can logically conclude that all children must be jellybeans, even though in the real world children *aren't* jellybeans.

From Piaget's perspective, students' capabilities in mathematics are likely to improve when formal operational thinking develops. Abstract problems, such as mathematical word problems, should become easier to solve. And students should become capable of understanding such concepts as *negative number, pi* ($\pi$), and *infinity*. For instance, they should now comprehend how temperature can be below zero and how two parallel lines will never touch even if they go on forever. In addition, because students can now understand proportions (see Table 2.1), they can more easily use fractions, decimals, and ratios when solving problems.

Scientific reasoning is also likely to improve when students are capable of formal operational thought. Three of the formal operational abilities listed in Table 2.1—reasoning logically about hypothetical ideas, formulating multiple hypotheses, and separating and controlling variables—together allow many adolescents to use the *scientific method*, in which they test several possible explanations for an observed phenomenon in a systematic manner. As an example, consider the pendulum problem in the following exercise.

Children in Piaget's concrete operations stage exhibit conservation in their reasoning. For example, listen to 10-year-old Kent in "Cognitive Development: Middle Childhood."

## EXPERIENCING FIRSTHAND
## PENDULUM PROBLEM

In the absence of other forces, an object suspended by a rope or string—a pendulum—swings at a constant rate. (A yo-yo and a playground swing are two everyday examples.) Some pendulums swing back and forth rather slowly; others move more quickly. What characteristics of a pendulum determine how quickly it swings? Write down at least three hypotheses about the variable(s) that might affect a pendulum's oscillation rate.

Now gather several small objects of varying weights (e.g., a paperclip, a house key, a heavy bolt) and a piece of string. Tie one of the objects to one end of the string, and set your pendulum in motion. Conduct one or more experiments to test each of your hypotheses.

What can you conclude? What variable or variables affect the rate with which a pendulum swings?

According to Piaget, students gradually acquire formal reasoning abilities as they progress through adolescence. Observe seventh graders' difficulty in separating and controlling variables in "Designing Experiments."

Encourage adolescents to discuss their visions for a better world, but point out instances when their ideals are unrealistic.

What hypotheses did you generate? Four common ones involve weight of the object, length of the string, force with which the object is pushed, and height from which the object is released. Did you test each of your hypotheses in a systematic fashion? That is, did you *separate and control variables,* testing one at a time while holding all others constant? For example, if you were testing the hypothesis that weight makes a difference, you might have tried objects of different weights while keeping constant the length of the string, the force with which you pushed each object, and the height from which you released or pushed each one. Similarly, if you hypothesized that length was a critical factor, you might have varied the string length while continuing to use the same object and setting the pendulum in motion in a consistent manner. If you carefully separated and controlled each variable, you should have come to the correct conclusion: Only *length* affects a pendulum's oscillation rate.

An additional outcome of abstract and hypothetical thinking is the ability to envision how the world might be different from the way it actually is (e.g., see Figure 2.6). In some cases adolescents envision a world that is *better* than the one they live in, and they exhibit considerable concern and idealism about social and political issues. Some secondary school students devote a great deal of energy to local or global problems, such as water pollution and animal rights. However, they may offer recommendations for change that seem logical but aren't practical in today's world. For example, a teenager might argue that racism could disappear overnight if people would just begin to "love one another" or that a nation should eliminate its armed forces and weaponry as a way of moving toward world peace. Piaget proposed that adolescent idealism reflects **formal operational egocentrism**, an inability to separate one's own logical abstractions from the perspectives of others and from practical considerations. Only through experience do adolescents eventually begin to temper their optimism with some realism about what is possible in a given time frame and with limited resources.

**formal operational egocentrism**
Inability of adolescents in Piaget's formal operations stage to separate their own abstract logic from the perspectives of others and from practical considerations.

**FIGURE 2.6** In this excerpt from a comic book he has created, 12-year-old Zach shows an ability to think about contrary-to-fact ideas, such as an army of noses (led by Napoleon Nose), a time-warp trap, and villain Dark Fang's evil new weapon.

## CRITIQUING PIAGET'S THEORY

Perhaps Piaget's greatest contribution to our understanding of cognitive development was the nature of the *questions* he asked and tried to answer about how children think and reason. In addition, some of his key ideas—for instance, that children construct their own knowledge about the world, that they must relate new experiences to what they already know, and that encountering puzzling phenomena can sometimes spur them to revise their understandings—have stood the test of time.

Piaget's descriptions of processes that *propel* development—especially assimilation, accommodation, and equilibration—can be frustratingly vague, however (M. Chapman, 1988; diSessa, 2006; Klahr, 2001). And interaction with one's physical environment, although certainly valuable, may be less critical than Piaget believed. For instance, children with significant physical disabilities, who cannot actively experiment with physical objects, learn a great deal about the world simply by observing what happens around them (Bebko, Burke, Craven, & Sarlo, 1992; Brainerd, 2003).

### A SECOND LOOK AT PIAGET'S STAGES

Piaget's proposal that cognitive development progresses in stages has sparked a great deal of follow-up research. In general, this research supports Piaget's proposed *sequence* in which different abilities emerge but not necessarily the *ages* at which they emerge. Piaget probably underestimated the thinking capabilities of preschoolers and elementary school students. For example, under some circumstances preschoolers are capable of class inclusion and conservation, and they have some ability to comprehend abstract and contrary-to-fact ideas (S. R. Beck, Robinson, Carroll, & Apperly, 2006; Goswami & Pauen, 2005; McNeil & Uttal, 2009; Rosser, 1994). Many first and second graders can understand and use simple proportions (e.g., $\frac{1}{2}$, $\frac{1}{3}$, $\frac{1}{4}$) if they can relate the proportions to everyday objects and situations (Empson, 1999; Van Dooren, De Bock, Hessels, Janssens, & Verschaffel, 2005). And some older elementary school children can separate and control variables if a task is simplified in some way (Lorch et al., 2010; Metz, 1995; Ruffman, Perner, Olson, & Doherty, 1993).

Yet Piaget seems to have *over*estimated what adolescents can do. Formal operational thinking processes emerge more gradually than he suggested, and even high school students and adults don't necessarily use them regularly (Flieller, 1999; Kuhn & Franklin, 2006; Morra et al., 2008; Tourniaire & Pulos, 1985). Furthermore, students may demonstrate formal operational thought in one content domain while thinking concretely in another (Lovell, 1979; Tamburrini, 1982).

Explicit training and other structured experiences can sometimes help children acquire reasoning abilities sooner than Piaget thought was possible (Brainerd, 2003; Kuhn, 2006). For instance, children as young as age 4 or 5 begin to show conservation after having experience with conservation tasks, especially if they can actively manipulate the task materials and discuss their reasoning with someone who already exhibits conservation (Halford & Andrews, 2006; Siegler & Chen, 2008; Siegler & Lin, 2010). Similarly, instruction with concrete manipulatives can help children grasp the nature of proportions (Fujimura, 2001; Sarama & Clements, 2009). Children ages 10 and 11 can more easily solve logical problems involving hypothetical ideas if they're taught relevant problem-solving strategies, and they become increasingly able to separate and control variables when they have numerous experiences that require them to do so (Kuhn & Pease, 2008; S. Lee, 1985; Lorch et al., 2010; Schauble, 1990).

In light of all the evidence, does it still make sense to talk about discrete stages of cognitive development? As we'll see shortly, a few theorists have offered stage-based theories that may more adequately account for current findings about children's logical thinking in specific skill areas or content domains. But most theorists now believe that cognitive development can more accurately be described in terms of gradual *trends* rather than discrete stages. They also suggest—and Piaget himself acknowledged—that the four stages better describe how children and adolescents *can* think, rather than how they always *do* think, at any particular age (Flavell, 1994; Halford & Andrews, 2006; Klaczynski, 2001; Tanner & Inhelder, 1960).

## CONSIDERING DIVERSITY FROM THE PERSPECTIVE OF PIAGET'S THEORY

As a researcher working in Switzerland, Piaget conducted his studies with a particular population: Swiss children. However, the course of cognitive development appears to vary somewhat from one cultural group to another, probably because different cultures provide somewhat

Expect that even high school students will sometimes have difficulty with abstract subject matter.

Providing manipulatives often helps fourth graders understand fractions. Observe a fourth-grade teacher use this approach in "Manipulative Strategies.

**FIGURE 2.7**  **What are some possible reasons that Herb is catching more fish than the others?**

*Source:* Based on image created by Steven Pulos. Adapted with permission.

different experiences (Maynard & Greenfield, 2003; Morra et al., 2008). For example, Mexican children whose families make pottery for a living acquire conservation skills earlier than their peers in other Mexican families—presumably because making pottery requires children to make frequent judgments about needed quantities of clay regardless of its shape (Price-Williams, Gordon, & Ramirez, 1969). In other cultures, especially in some in which children don't attend school, conservation and other concrete operational abilities may appear several years later than they do in Western societies (Artman & Cahan, 1993; Fahrmeier, 1978).

Formal operational reasoning skills—for example, reasoning about hypothetical ideas and separating and controlling variables—also vary from culture to culture (Flieller, 1999; Norenzayan, Choi, & Peng, 2007; Rogoff, 2003). Mainstream Western culture actively nurtures these skills through formal instruction in such academic content domains as science, mathematics, literature, and social studies. In some other cultures, however, such skills may have little relevance to people's daily lives (M. Cole, 1990; J. G. Miller, 1997; Norenzayan et al., 2007).

Even within a single cultural group, logical reasoning abilities vary considerably from one individual to another, in part as a result of differences in background knowledge about particular topics. For instance, adolescents (adults, too) often apply formal operational thought to topics about which they know a great deal yet think concretely about topics with which they're unfamiliar (Girotto & Light, 1993; M. C. Linn, Clement, Pulos, & Sullivan, 1989; Schliemann & Carraher, 1993). For example, in a study by Pulos and Linn (1981), 13-year-olds were shown a picture similar to the one in Figure 2.7 and told, "These four children go fishing every week, and one child, Herb, always catches the most fish. The other children wonder why." If you look at the picture, you can see that Herb differs from the other children in several ways, including his location, the bait he uses, and the length of his fishing rod. Students who had fished a great deal more effectively separated and controlled variables for this situation than they did for the pendulum problem presented earlier, whereas the reverse was true for students with little or no experience fishing.

Knowledge about fishing enhances children's ability to separate and control variables in a fishing problem. Contrast 10-year-old Kent (an experienced fisherman) with 14-year-old Alicia (who has never fished) in "Cognitive Development: Middle Childhood" and "Cognitive Development: Late Adolescence."

## CONTEMPORARY EXTENSIONS AND APPLICATIONS OF PIAGET'S THEORY

Despite its shortcomings, Piaget's theory has had considerable influence on present-day thinking about cognitive development and classroom practice. A few contemporary *neo-Piagetian* theories integrate elements of Piaget's theory with current theories of thinking and learning. Furthermore, educators have found many of Piaget's ideas quite useful in instructional settings. We'll examine three of his ideas—his clinical method, his emphasis on the importance of hands-on experiences, and his concept of disequilibrium—in upcoming sections. The Into the Classroom feature "Applying Piaget's Theory" offers additional suggestions for translating Piaget's ideas into classroom practice.

### NEO-PIAGETIAN THEORIES

**Neo-Piagetian theories** echo Piaget's belief that cognitive development depends somewhat on brain maturation. For instance, some neo-Piagetian theorists suggest that a component of the human memory system known as *working memory* is especially important for cognitive development. In particular, working memory is a brain-based mechanism that enables people to temporarily hold and think about a small amount of new information. Children's working memory capacity increases with age, and thus their ability to think about several things simultaneously increases as well (Case & Mueller, 2001; Fischer & Bidell, 2006; Lautrey, 1993).

Chapter 6 looks more closely at the nature of working memory.

## Applying Piaget's Theory

🍎 **Use Piaget's stages as a rough guide to what students at different grade levels can do, but don't take them too literally.**

Knowing from both research and her own experience that 6- and 7-year-olds can understand simple proportions in familiar situations, a first-grade teacher asks her students to tackle this problem: "Two children want to share five cupcakes so that each child gets the same amount. Show how much each child can have." When some of the students decide that each child can have two cupcakes, she points to the fifth cupcake and says, "They want to share this one too. How can they do that?"

🍎 **When young children show signs of egocentric thinking, express confusion or explain that others think differently.**

A kindergartner asks, "What's this?" about an object that is out of the teacher's view. The teacher responds, "What's *what*? I can't see the object you're looking at."

🍎 **Relate abstract and hypothetical ideas to concrete objects and observable events.**

To help students understand that even seemingly weightless substances such as air have mass and weight, an eighth-grade teacher blows up a balloon and places it on one side of a balance scale. She then places an uninflated balloon on the other side of the scale. The inflated balloon tips the scale downward, showing that it weighs more than the uninflated one.

🍎 **Ask students to explain their reasoning about physical phenomena, and challenge illogical explanations.**

When learning about pendulums, cooperative groups in a middle school science class conduct experiments with three variables (weight, length, and height from which the pendulum is dropped) to see which variable or variables determine the rate at which a pendulum swings. After a student in one group asserts that weight affects the oscillation rate, her teacher asks a series of questions that eventually lead the student's group to realize it has simultaneously varied both weight and length in its experiments. (Observe this example in "Designing Experiments.")

🍎 **Draw on adolescents' idealism to engage them in public service projects and other charitable endeavors.**

In a unit on Africa, several students in a ninth-grade social studies class express their horror about the extreme poverty in which some Africans live. The teacher mentions that a friend is traveling to Rwanda the following month and wants to take several large suitcases full of used children's clothing to give to an especially poor Rwandan village. Over the next few days the students ask their parents and neighbors for donations and gather many usable items for the teacher's friend to take.

*Sources:* Empson, 1999, p. 295 (cupcake example); C. L. Smith, 2007 (balloon example).

Neo-Piagetian theorists reject Piaget's notion that a single series of stages characterizes children's overall cognitive development. However, they speculate that cognitive development in specific content domains—for instance, in understanding numbers or spatial relationships—often has a stagelike nature (e.g., Case, 1985; Case & Okamoto, 1996; Fischer & Immordino-Yang, 2002). Children's entry into a particular stage is marked by the acquisition of new abilities, which children practice and gradually master over time. Eventually, they integrate these abilities into more complex structures that mark their transition into a subsequent stage. Thus, as is true in Piaget's theory, the stages are *hierarchical,* with each one being constructed out of abilities acquired in the preceding stage.

Even in a particular subject area, however, cognitive development isn't necessarily a single series of stages through which children progress as if they were climbing rungs on a ladder. In some cases development might be better characterized as progression along "multiple strands" of skills that occasionally interconnect, consolidate, or separate in a weblike fashion (Fischer & Daley, 2007; Fischer & Immordino-Yang, 2002). From this perspective, children may acquire more advanced levels of competence in a particular area through any one of several pathways. For instance, as they become increasingly proficient in reading, children may gradually develop their word decoding skills, their comprehension skills, and so on, and they draw on all of these skills when reading a book. However, the rate at which each of the skills is mastered varies from one child to the next.

### PIAGET'S CLINICAL METHOD AS AN ASSESSMENT TOOL

Earlier in the chapter I described Piaget's clinical method, in which an adult probes children's thoughts about a particular task or problem through a sequence of individually tailored questions

**neo-Piagetian theory** Theoretical perspective that combines elements of Piaget's theory with more contemporary research and theories and suggests that development in specific content domains is often stagelike in nature.

**sociocognitive conflict** Situation in which one encounters and has to wrestle with ideas and viewpoints inconsistent with one's own.

![apple icon] Probe students' reasoning about various logical thinking tasks and problems.

![apple icon] Combine hands-on experiences with age-appropriate instruction that enables students to draw appropriate conclusions from their observations.

Hands-on experiences can be quite valuable in helping students understand the nature of the physical world. Watch an effective second-grade lesson in "Investigating Particles: Part 1."

![apple icon] Have students wrestle with complex issues and problems in small groups, where they can hear opinions and arguments that might conflict with their own ways of thinking. Monitor such interactions to be sure that they are mutually respectful and socially appropriate.

(recall the dialogue with Brian about the wooden beads). By presenting a variety of Piagetian tasks involving either concrete or formal operational thinking skills (e.g., conservation or separation and control of variables) and asking students to explain what they're thinking, we can gain valuable insights into their logical reasoning abilities (e.g., diSessa, 2007). We need not stick to traditional Piagetian reasoning tasks, however. To illustrate, a teacher might present various kinds of maps (e.g., a road map of Pennsylvania, an aerial map of Chicago, a three-dimensional relief map of a mountainous area) and ask students to interpret what they see. Children in the early elementary grades are apt to interpret maps very concretely, perhaps thinking that lines separating states and countries are actually painted on the earth or that an airport symbolized by a small airplane has only one plane. They might also have difficulty with the scale of a map, perhaps thinking that a line can't be a road because "it's not fat enough for two cars to go on" or that a mountain depicted by a bump on a relief map isn't really a mountain because "it's not high enough" (Liben & Downs, 1989; Liben & Myers, 2007, p. 202). Understanding the concept of *scale* in a map requires proportional reasoning—an ability that doesn't fully emerge until after puberty—and thus it's hardly surprising that young children will be confused by it.

### HANDS-ON EXPERIENCES

Piaget suggested that exploration of the physical environment should be largely a child-initiated and child-directed effort. Young children can certainly learn a great deal from their informal interactions with sand, water, and other natural substances (Hutt, Tyler, Hutt, & Christopherson, 1989). And in the elementary and secondary school grades, opportunities to manipulate physical objects—or their virtual equivalents on a computer screen—can enhance students' understanding of basic mathematical and scientific concepts (M. C. Brown, McNeil, & Glenberg, 2009; Lorch et al., 2010; Sarama & Clements, 2009; Sherman & Bisanz, 2009).

Researchers are finding, however, that hands-on experiences are typically more effective *when combined with instruction* that helps students draw appropriate conclusions from what they observe (Fujimura, 2001; Hardy, Jonen, Möller, & Stern, 2006; R. E. Mayer, 2004). In the absence of teacher guidance and directive questions, students may draw inferences based solely on what they see and feel—for instance, erroneously concluding that a very small piece of Styrofoam must have no weight whatsoever (M. C. Brown et al., 2009; C. L. Smith, 2007). And, of course, they may fail to separate and control variables in their experimentation (Lorch et al., 2010).

### CREATING DISEQUILIBRIUM: THE VALUE OF SOCIOCOGNITIVE CONFLICT

In the opening case study, the girls argue about various ways to solve a problem involving the use of a fraction ($^3/_4$) in making apple tarts. When Jeanette offers a seemingly nonproductive idea ("But three-quarters equals three"), Kerri points out her illogical thinking ("But she can't make only three apple tarts!"). As noted earlier, interaction with peers helps children realize that others often view the world differently than they do and that their own ideas aren't always completely logical or accurate. Furthermore, interactions with age-mates that involve wrestling with contradictory viewpoints—interactions that involve sociocognitive conflict—create disequilibrium that may spur children to reevaluate and possibly revise their current understandings. Whereas children may accept an adult's ideas without argument, some may be quite willing to disagree with and challenge the ideas of their peers (D. W. Johnson & Johnson, 2009b; Lampert, Rittenhouse, & Crumbaugh, 1996; M. C. Linn, 2008).

Ultimately, social interaction—not only with peers but also with adults—is probably even more important for children's cognitive development than Piaget realized. Lev Vygotsky's theory, which we turn to now, describes additional ways in which interactions with fellow human beings promote cognitive growth.

## Vygotsky's Theory of Cognitive Development

In Piaget's view, children are largely in control of their own cognitive development; for example, they initiate interactions with objects in their environment and develop self-constructed understandings of what they observe. In contrast, an early Russian developmentalist, Lev Vygotsky, believed that the adults in any society foster children's cognitive development in an intentional and somewhat systematic manner. Because Vygotsky emphasized the importance of adult instruction and guidance for promoting cognitive development—and more generally because he emphasized the influence of social and cultural factors on children's cognitive growth—his perspective is known as a sociocultural theory.

Vygotsky and his students conducted numerous studies of children's thinking from the 1920s until Vygotsky's early death from tuberculosis in 1934. Rather than determine the kinds of tasks children could successfully perform *on their own* (as Piaget did), Vygotsky often examined the kinds of tasks children could complete *only with adult assistance.* For example, he described two hypothetical children who could, without help, do things that a typical 8-year-old might be able to do. He would give each of the children progressively more difficult tasks and offer some help, perhaps asking a leading question or suggesting a reasonable first step. With such assistance, both children could almost invariably tackle more difficult tasks than they could handle on their own. However, the *range* of tasks that the two children could complete with assistance might be quite different, with one child stretching his or her abilities to succeed at typical 12-year-old-level tasks and the other succeeding only with typical 9-year-old-level tasks (Vygotsky, 1934/1986, p. 187).

Western psychologists were largely unfamiliar with Vygotsky's work until the last few decades of the twentieth century, when his major writings were translated from Russian into English (e.g., Vygotsky, 1978, 1934/1986, 1997). Although Vygotsky never had the chance to develop his theory fully, his views are clearly evident in many contemporary theorists' discussions of learning and development. In fact, Piaget's influence has been on the wane in recent years (Bjorklund, 1997), whereas Vygotsky's influence has become increasingly prominent.

## VYGOTSKY'S BASIC ASSUMPTIONS

Vygotsky acknowledged that biological factors (e.g., brain maturation) play a role in cognitive development. Children bring certain characteristics and dispositions to the situations they encounter, and their responses vary accordingly. Furthermore, children's behaviors, which are influenced in part by inherited traits, affect the particular experiences children have (Vygotsky, 1997). However, Vygotsky's primary focus was on the role of children's social and cultural environments in fostering cognitive growth—and especially in fostering those complex mental abilities that are unique to human beings as a species. Following are central ideas and concepts in Vygotsky's theory.

• *Through both informal conversations and formal schooling, adults convey to children the ways in which their culture interprets and responds to the world.* Vygotsky proposed that as adults interact with children, they share the *meanings* they attach to objects, events, and, more generally, human experience. In the process they transform, or *mediate,* the situations children encounter. Meanings are conveyed through a variety of mechanisms, including language (spoken words, writing, etc.), mathematical symbols, art, music, and so on.

Informal conversations are one common mechanism through which adults pass along culturally relevant ways of interpreting situations. But even more important is formal education, through which teachers systematically impart the ideas, concepts, and terminology used in various academic disciplines (Vygotsky, 1934/1986). Although Vygotsky, like Piaget, saw value in allowing children to make some discoveries themselves, he also saw value in having adults pass along the discoveries of previous generations (Vygotsky, 1934/1986).

• *Every culture passes along physical and cognitive tools that make daily living more productive and efficient.* Not only do adults teach children specific ways of interpreting experience but they also pass along specific tools that can help children tackle the various tasks and problems they're apt to face. Some tools, such as scissors, sewing machines, and computers, are physical objects. Others, such as writing systems, maps, and spreadsheets, are partly physical and partly symbolic. Still others, such as the concept of *fraction* and the process of division (recall the opening case study involving fractions of apples), may have little physical basis at all. In Vygotsky's view, acquiring tools that are at least partly symbolic or mental in nature—cognitive tools—greatly enhances growing children's thinking and functioning.

• *Thought and language become increasingly interdependent in the first few years of life.* One very important cognitive tool is language. For us as adults, thought and language are closely interconnected. We often think by using specific words that our language provides. For example, when

**sociocultural theory** Theoretical perspective emphasizing the importance of society and culture in promoting learning and development.

**cognitive tool** Concept, symbol, strategy, procedure, or other culturally constructed mechanism that helps people think about and respond to situations more effectively.

Show students how various academic disciplines conceptualize the world.

we think about household pets, our thoughts contain such words as *dog* and *cat.* In addition, we usually express our thoughts when we converse with others. In other words, we "speak our minds."

Vygotsky proposed that thought and language are separate functions for infants and young toddlers. In these early years, thinking occurs independently of language, and when language appears, it's first used primarily as a means of communication rather than as a mechanism of thought. But sometime around age 2, thought and language become intertwined: Children begin to express their thoughts when they speak, and they begin to think in words.

When thought and language first merge, children often talk to themselves, a phenomenon known as self-talk (you may also see the term *private speech*). Vygotsky suggested that self-talk serves an important function in cognitive development. By talking to themselves, children learn to guide and direct their own behaviors through difficult tasks and complex maneuvers in much the same way that adults have previously guided them. Self-talk eventually evolves into inner speech, in which children talk to themselves mentally rather than aloud. They continue to direct themselves verbally through tasks and activities, but others can no longer see and hear them do it (Vygotsky, 1934/1986). In other words, both self-talk and inner speech help children engage in *self-regulation.*

Chapter 10 more fully describes the nature and development of self-regulation.

• *Complex mental processes begin as social activities and gradually evolve into internal mental activities that children can use independently.* Vygotsky proposed that many complex thought processes have their roots in social interactions. As children discuss objects, events, tasks, and problems with adults and other knowledgeable individuals, they gradually incorporate into their own thinking the ways in which the people around them talk about and interpret the world, and they begin to use the words, concepts, symbols, and strategies—in essence, the cognitive tools—that are commonly used in their culture.

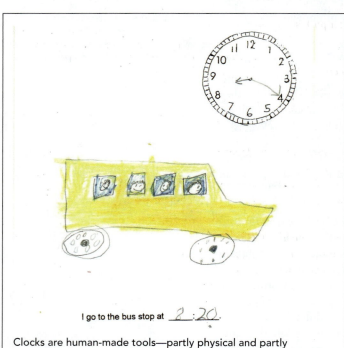

I go to the bus stop at ___8___:___20___.

Clocks are human-made tools—partly physical and partly symbolic—that enhance our daily functioning both as individuals and as a society. In this excerpt from his "My Day" book, 6-year-old David practices using and interpreting analog clocks.

The process through which social activities evolve into internal mental activities is called internalization. The progression from self-talk to inner speech just described illustrates this process: Over time, children gradually internalize adults' directions so that they are eventually giving *themselves* the directions.

Not all mental processes emerge as children interact with adults; some instead develop as children interact with peers. For example, children frequently argue with one another about a variety of matters—how best to carry out an activity, what games to play, who did what to whom, and so on. According to Vygotsky, having arguments helps children discover that there are often several ways to view the same situation. Eventually, he suggested, children internalize the arguing process, developing the ability to look at a situation from a variety of angles *on their own.*

• *Children appropriate their culture's tools in their own idiosyncratic manner.* Children don't necessarily internalize *exactly* what they see and hear in a social context. Rather, they often transform ideas, strategies, and other cognitive tools to suit their own needs and purposes—thus, Vygotsky's theory has a constructivist element to it. The term appropriation is often used to refer to this process of internalizing but also adapting the ideas and strategies of one's culture for one's own use.

• *Children can accomplish more difficult tasks when assisted by more advanced and competent individuals.* Vygotsky distinguished between two kinds of abilities that characterize children's skills at any particular point in development. A child's actual developmental level is the upper limit of tasks that he or she can perform independently, without help from anyone else. A child's level of potential development is the upper limit of tasks that he or she can perform with the assistance of a more competent individual. To get a true sense of children's cognitive development, Vygotsky suggested, we should assess their capabilities not only when performing alone but also when performing with assistance—a strategy that contemporary educators call *dynamic assessment.*

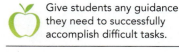 Give students any guidance they need to successfully accomplish difficult tasks.

Chapter 14 provides more details about dynamic assessment.

As mentioned earlier, Vygotsky found that children can typically do more difficult things in collaboration with adults than they can do on their own. For example, they can play more difficult piano pieces when an adult helps them locate some of the notes on the keyboard or provides suggestions about which fingers to use where. They can solve more difficult math problems when their teacher helps them identify critical problem components and potentially fruitful problem-solving strategies. And they can often read more complex prose in a reading group at school than they're likely to read independently at home.

• *Challenging tasks promote maximum cognitive growth.* The range of tasks that children cannot yet perform independently but *can* perform with the help and guidance of others is, in Vygotsky's terminology, the zone of proximal development (ZPD) (see Figure 2.8). A child's zone of proximal development includes learning and problem-solving abilities that are just beginning to emerge and develop.

Vygotsky proposed that children learn very little from performing tasks they can already do independently. Instead, they develop primarily by attempting tasks they can accomplish only with assistance and support—that is, when they attempt tasks within their zone of proximal development. In a nutshell, it's the challenges in life, not the easy successes, that promote cognitive development. But whereas challenging tasks are beneficial, impossible tasks, which children can't do even with considerable structure and guidance, are of no benefit whatsoever (Vygotsky, 1987). A child's ZPD therefore sets an upper limit on what he or she is cognitively capable of learning.

As teachers, then, we should assign some tasks that students can accomplish successfully *only* with other people's support. In some instances this support must come from more skilled individuals, such as adults or older students. In other situations, students of equal ability can work together to jointly accomplish difficult assignments—such as the apple-tarts problem in the opening case study—with each student bringing unique strengths to contribute to the overall effort.

Regardless of the nature of the support we provide, we must remember that every student's ZPD will change over time. As some tasks are mastered, other, more complex ones will appear on the horizon to take their place. In addition, students' ZPDs may vary considerably in "width." Some students may, with assistance, be able to stretch several years above their actual (independent) developmental level, whereas others may be able to handle tasks that are only slightly more difficult than what they can currently do on their own. In some instances, students with different zones of proximal development will need individualized tasks and assignments so that they all have challenges that optimally promote their personal cognitive growth.

• *Play allows children to stretch themselves cognitively.* As a young child, my son Jeff often played restaurant with his friend Scott. In a corner of our basement, the boys created a restaurant "kitchen" with a toy sink and stove and stocked it with plastic dishes, cooking utensils, and "food" items. They created a separate dining area with child-sized tables and chairs and made menus for their customers. On one occasion they invited both sets of parents to "dine" at the restaurant,

**self-talk** Process of talking to oneself as a way of guiding oneself through a task.

**inner speech** Process of talking to and guiding oneself mentally rather than aloud.

**internalization** Process through which a learner gradually incorporates socially based activities into his or her internal cognitive processes.

**appropriation** Process of internalizing but also adapting the cognitive tools of one's culture for one's own use.

**actual developmental level** Upper limit of tasks that a learner can successfully perform independently.

**level of potential development** Upper limit of tasks that a learner can successfully perform with the assistance of a more competent individual.

**zone of proximal development (ZPD)** Range of tasks that a learner can perform with the help and guidance of others but cannot yet perform independently.

**FIGURE 2.8** In Vygotsky's view, tasks in a child's zone of proximal development promote maximal learning and cognitive growth.

Give students time to explore new activities and roles through play.

In Vygotsky's view, children are more likely to make cognitive advancements when they work on tasks for which they need some support and assistance— that is, when they work within their zone of proximal development. See an example in "Zone of Proximal Development: Cognitive."

taking our orders, serving us our food, and eventually giving us our bills. (Fortunately, they seemed content with the few pennies we paid them for our meals.)

In their restaurant play, the two boys took on several adult roles (restaurant manager, waiter, cook) and practiced a variety of adultlike behaviors. In real life such a scenario would, of course, be impossible: Very few young children have the many skills necessary to run a restaurant. Yet the element of make-believe brought restaurant management within the boys' reach. In Vygotsky's words, "In play a child always behaves beyond his average age, above his daily behavior; in play it is as though he were a head taller than himself" (Vygotsky, 1978, p. 102).

Furthermore, as children play, their behaviors must conform to certain standards or expectations. In the early elementary school years, children often act in accordance with how a father, teacher, or waiter would behave. In the organized group games and sports that come later, children must follow specific sets of rules. By adhering to such restrictions on their behavior, children learn to plan ahead, to think before they act, and to engage in self-restraint—skills critical for successful participation in the adult world (also see Coplan & Arbeau, 2009; A. Diamond, Barnett, Thomas, & Munro, 2007; Pellegrini, 2009).

## CRITIQUING VYGOTSKY'S THEORY

Vygotsky focused more on the processes through which children develop than on the characteristics that children of particular ages are likely to exhibit. He described stages of development but portrayed them in only the most general terms (e.g., see Vygotsky, 1997, pp. 214–216). In addition, Vygotsky's descriptions of developmental processes were often vague and speculative (Gauvain, 2001; Haenan, 1996; Moran & John-Steiner, 2003). For such reasons, Vygotsky's theory has been more difficult for researchers to test and either verify or disprove than has the case for Piaget's theory.

Nevertheless, contemporary theorists and educators have found Vygotsky's ideas insightful and helpful. Most significantly, his theory points out the many ways in which *culture* influences cognitive development. A society's culture ensures that each new generation benefits from the accumulating wisdom of preceding generations. Any culture guides children in certain directions by encouraging them to pay attention to particular stimuli (and not to others) and to engage in particular activities (and not in others). In addition, it provides a lens through which children come to view and interpret their experiences in culturally appropriate ways. We see obvious effects of culture in many of children's everyday activities—in the books they read, the roles they enact in pretend play, the extracurricular activities they pursue—but we must remember that culture permeates their unobservable thinking processes as well.

Furthermore, some research has supported Vygotsky's views regarding the progression and role of self-talk and inner speech. The frequency of children's audible self-talk decreases during the preschool and early elementary years, but this decrease is at first accompanied by an increase in whispered mumbling and silent lip movements, presumably reflecting a transition to inner speech (Bivens & Berk, 1990; Winsler & Naglieri, 2003). Self-talk increases when children are performing more challenging tasks, at which they must exert considerable effort to be successful (Berk, 1994; Schimmoeller, 1998). As you undoubtedly know from your own experience, even adults occasionally talk to themselves when they face new challenges!

## CONSIDERING DIVERSITY FROM THE PERSPECTIVE OF VYGOTSKY'S THEORY

Vygotsky's theory leads us to expect greater diversity among children, at least in cognitive development, than Piaget's theory does. As we've seen, children in any single age-group are likely to have different zones of proximal development: Tasks that are easy for some children may be quite challenging or virtually impossible for others. In addition, to the extent that specific cultural groups pass along unique concepts, ideas, and beliefs, children from different cultural backgrounds will acquire somewhat different knowledge, skills, and ways of thinking. For instance, children are more likely to acquire map-reading skills if they regularly encounter maps (e.g., of roads, subway systems, and shopping malls) in their community and family life (Liben & Myers, 2007). And children are more apt to have a keen sense of time if cultural activities are tightly regulated by clocks and calendars (K. Nelson, 1996).

# CONTEMPORARY EXTENSIONS AND APPLICATIONS OF VYGOTSKY'S THEORY

The Into the Classroom feature "Applying Vygotsky's Theory" presents concrete examples of how teachers might make use of Vygotsky's ideas. In the upcoming sections, we'll consider several ways in which contemporary theorists and educators have built on the foundation that Vygotsky laid.

## SOCIAL CONSTRUCTION OF MEANING

Contemporary psychologists have elaborated on Vygotsky's proposal that adults help children attach meaning to the objects and events around them. Often an adult will help a child make sense of the world through a joint discussion of a phenomenon or event they are both experiencing (Feuerstein, Feuerstein, & Falik, 2010; P. K. Murphy, Wilkinson, & Soter, 2011). Such an interaction, sometimes called a mediated learning experience, encourages the child to think about the phenomenon or event in particular ways—to attach labels to it, recognize principles that underlie it, draw certain conclusions from it, and so on. As an example, consider the following exchange, in which a 5-year-old boy and his mother are talking about a prehistoric animal exhibit at a natural history museum.

> *Boy:* Cool. Wow, look. Look giant teeth. Mom, look at his giant teeth.
>
> *Mom:* He looks like a saber tooth. Do you think he eats meat or plants?
>
> *Boy:* Mom, look at his giant little tooth, look at his teeth in his mouth, so big.
>
> *Mom:* He looks like a saber tooth, doesn't he. Do you think he eats plants or meat?

**mediated learning experience** Discussion between an adult and a child in which the adult helps the child make sense of an event they are mutually experiencing.

---

## Into the Classroom

### Applying Vygotsky's Theory

🍏 **Provide cognitive tools that students can use in thinking about and tackling new tasks.**
A high school chemistry teacher places two equal-size inflated balloons into two beakers of water, one heated to 25°C and the other heated to 50°C. The students all agree that the balloon placed in the warmer water expands more. "How much more did the 50-degree balloon expand?" the teacher asks. "Let's use Charles's law to figure it out."

🍏 **Encourage students to talk themselves through difficult tasks.**
As his students work on complex mathematical equations such as this one,

$$x = \frac{2(4 \times 9)^2}{6} + 3$$

a junior high school mathematics teacher gives students a mnemonic (**P**lease **e**xcuse **m**y **d**ear **A**unt **S**ally) they might repeat to themselves to help them remember the order in which they should perform various operations (**p**arentheses, **e**xponents, **m**ultiplication and **d**ivision, **a**ddition and **s**ubtraction).

🍏 **Present some tasks that students can perform successfully only with assistance.**
When a fifth-grade teacher assigns students their first research paper, he breaks the process into several discrete steps and provides a great deal of structure and guidance.

🍏 **Provide sufficient support, or scaffolding, to enable students to perform challenging tasks successfully;** gradually withdraw the support as they become more proficient.
An elementary physical education teacher begins a lesson on tumbling by demonstrating forward and backward rolls in slow motion and physically guiding her students through the correct movements. As the students become more skillful, the teacher stands back from the mat and gives verbal feedback about how to improve.

🍏 **Have students work in small groups to accomplish complex, multifaceted tasks.**
A middle school art teacher asks his students to work in groups of four or five to design large murals that depict various ecosystems—rainforest, desert, grassland, tundra, and so on—and the kinds of plant and animal species that live in each one. The groups then paint their murals on the walls of the school corridors.

🍏 **Engage students in adult activities that are common in their culture.**
A high school publishes a monthly school newspaper with news articles, editorials, cartoons, announcements of upcoming events, advertisements for local businesses, and classified ads. Students assume various roles, including reporters, cartoonists, editors, proofreaders, photocopiers, marketers, and distributors.

🍏 **Give young children time to practice adult roles and behaviors through play.**
A kindergarten teacher equips his classroom with many household items (dress-up clothes, cooking utensils, a toy telephone, etc.) so that students can play house during free-play time.

**scaffolding** Support mechanism that helps a learner successfully perform a challenging task (i.e., a task within the learner's zone of proximal development).

*Boy:* Ouch, ouch, ouch, ouch. (referring to sharp tooth)

*Mom:* Do you think he eats plants or meat?

*Boy:* Meat.

*Mom:* How come?

*Boy:* Because he has sharp teeth. (growling noises) (Ash, 2002, p. 378)

Even without Mom's assistance, the boy would learn something about saber tooth tigers from his museum visit. Yet Mom helps him make better sense of what he's seeing than he might do on his own—for instance by using the label *saber tooth* and connecting tooth characteristics to eating preferences. Notice Mom's persistence regarding the tooth–food connection: She continues to ask questions about meat versus plants until the boy finally infers, correctly, that the tigers must have been meat eaters.

In addition to co-constructing meanings with adults, children and adolescents often talk among themselves to make sense of their experiences. School provides an ideal setting in which young people can toss around ideas and perhaps reach consensus about how best to interpret and understand a complex issue or problem—perhaps about a challenging math problem involving apple tarts, perhaps about troubling interpersonal dynamics with peers, or perhaps about moral dilemmas with no easy right and wrong answers.

Interacting with adults and interacting with peers possibly play somewhat different roles in children's development. Adults usually have more experience and expertise than age-mates do, and they tend to be more skillful teachers. Accordingly, adults are often the partners of choice when children are trying to master complex new tasks and procedures (Gauvain, 2001; Radziszewska & Rogoff, 1988). Working with peers has a different set of advantages. First, as mentioned in the earlier discussion of Piaget's theory, children who hear age-mates express perspectives quite different from their own may experience sociocognitive conflict that motivates them to overhaul their own understandings. Second, as Vygotsky suggested, peer interactions provide a social context in which children practice and eventually internalize complex cognitive processes, such as effective reading comprehension and argumentation skills (Andriessen, 2006; Chinn, Anderson, & Waggoner, 2001; P. K. Murphy et al., 2011). A third benefit is that children learn valuable social behaviors—including how to plan a joint enterprise and how to coordinate differing roles—when they work on cognitive tasks with their peers (Gauvain, 2001).

## SCAFFOLDING

Recall Vygotsky's suggestion that children are most likely to benefit from tasks and activities they can successfully accomplish only with the assistance and support of more competent individuals—that is, tasks within their zone of proximal development. Contemporary theorists have identified a variety of techniques—collectively known as **scaffolding**—that can help students accomplish challenging tasks in instructional contexts. The following are examples.

- Help students develop a plan for dealing with a complex new task.
- Demonstrate proper performance in a manner that students can easily imitate.
- Divide a multifaceted task into several smaller, simpler tasks.
- Give specific guidelines for accomplishing the task (e.g., see Figure 2.9).
- Ask questions that encourage students to think about the task in productive ways.
- Provide a calculator, computer software (word processing program, spreadsheet, etc.), or other technology that makes some aspects of the task easier.
- Remind students of what their goals are in performing the task (e.g., what a problem solution should look like).
- Give frequent feedback about how students are progressing. (A. Collins, 2006; Hmelo-Silver, 2006; Lajoie & Derry, 1993; Lodewyk & Winne, 2005; P. F. Merrill et al., 1996; Rogoff, 1990; Rosenshine & Meister, 1992; D. Wood, Bruner, & Ross, 1976)

Depending on their particular knowledge and ability levels, different students in any single grade may need different kinds of scaffolding to support their success in a task. As students become more adept at performing a task, scaffolding is ideally modified to nurture newly emerging skills. And over time the scaffolding is gradually phased out—a process known as *fading*—until students can complete the task entirely on their own.

Teacher scaffolding can take a variety of forms. For example, watch "Salamander Investigation."

---

**FIGURE 2.9** High school language arts teacher Jeff Ormrod uses this checklist to scaffold ninth graders' efforts to write a five-paragraph essay.

### Essay Checklist

Use the following checklist each time you write an essay to make sure that you have completed the steps and have every part you need.

**Introduction**

- My first sentence is a Hook sentence.
- I have a clear Thesis sentence that answers the question of the assignment.
- I have a List sentence that introduces my three main body paragraphs.
- I have a Transition sentence at the end.

**Main Body Paragraphs**

- Each of my main body paragraphs talks about one main idea or point.
- Each of my main body paragraphs gives information that supports this point.

**Conclusion**

- My conclusion paragraph restates my List sentence in a different way.
- My conclusion paragraph restates my Thesis sentence.
- My conclusion paragraph connects my essay to me or to the world.

*Source:* Excerpt by Jeffrey Ormrod. Copyright © by Jeffrey Ormrod. Reprinted with permission of the author.

---

**guided participation** A child's performance of a real-world adult activity, facilitated by developmentally appropriate adult support.

**apprenticeship** Mentorship in which a novice works intensively with an expert to learn how to perform complex new skills.

**cognitive apprenticeship** Mentorship in which a teacher and a student work together on a challenging task and the teacher provides guidance in how to think about the task.

## GUIDED PARTICIPATION IN ADULT ACTIVITIES

When you were a young child, did you sometimes help a parent or older sibling bake pastries in the kitchen? Did the cook let you pour, measure, and mix ingredients when you were old enough to do so? Did the cook also give you directions or suggestions as you performed these tasks?

Virtually all cultures allow children—and in fact usually require them—to be involved in adult activities to some degree. Children's early experiences often occur at the fringe of an activity, and their involvement is mediated, scaffolded, and supervised through what is sometimes called guided participation (Rogoff, 2003). From a Vygotskian perspective, gradual entry into adult activities enables children to engage in behaviors and thinking skills within their zone of proximal development. It also helps children tie newly acquired skills and thinking abilities to the specific contexts in which they're likely to be useful later on. As children acquire greater competence, they gradually take a more central role in a particular activity until, eventually, they're full-fledged participants (Lave & Wenger, 1991; Rogoff et al., 2007).

Adultlike activities can take many forms in the classroom. For instance, we might ask students to conduct laboratory experiments, write letters to government officials, or search the Internet for specific information, while always providing the support students need to accomplish such tasks successfully. As we engage students in these activities, we might also use some of the language that adults frequently use in such contexts. For example, when students conduct scientific experiments, we should use such words as *hypothesis, evidence,* and *theory* as we help them evaluate their procedures and results (Perkins, 1992).

## APPRENTICESHIPS

An especially intensive form of guided participation is an apprenticeship, in which a novice works with an expert mentor for a lengthy period to learn how to perform complex tasks within a particular domain. The expert provides considerable structure and guidance throughout the process, gradually removing scaffolding and giving the novice more independence and responsibility as competence increases (A. Collins, 2006; Rogoff, 1990, 1991). Many cultures use apprenticeships as a means of gradually introducing children to particular skills and trades in the adult community—perhaps weaving, tailoring, or playing a musical instrument (D. J. Elliott, 1995; Lave & Wenger, 1991; Rogoff, 1990).

In an apprenticeship a student often learns not only how to perform a task but also how to *think about* the task—a situation known as a cognitive apprenticeship (J. S. Brown, Collins, & Duguid, 1989; A. Collins, 2006; Dennen & Burner, 2008). For instance, a student and a teacher

 Have students apply new skills in adultlike activities.

In classroom settings, adultlike, real-world activities are often called *authentic activities,* discussed in Chapter 8.

might work together to accomplish a challenging task or solve a difficult problem—perhaps collecting data samples in biology fieldwork, solving a mathematical brainteaser, or translating a difficult passage from German to English. In the process of talking about various aspects of the task or problem, the teacher and the student together analyze the situation and develop the best approach to take, and the teacher models effective ways of thinking about and mentally processing the situation.

Apprenticeships differ widely from one context to another, but they typically have some or all of these features (A. Collins, 2006; A. Collins, Brown, & Newman, 1989):

- *Modeling:* The mentor carries out the task, simultaneously thinking aloud about the process, while the learner observes and listens.
- *Coaching:* As the learner performs the task, the mentor gives frequent suggestions, hints, and feedback.
- *Scaffolding:* The mentor provides various forms of support for the learner, perhaps by simplifying the task, breaking it into smaller and more manageable components, or providing less complicated equipment.
- *Articulation:* The learner explains what he or she is doing and why, allowing the mentor to examine the student's knowledge, reasoning, and problem-solving strategies.
- *Reflection:* The mentor asks the learner to compare his or her performance with that of experts, or perhaps with an ideal model of how the task should be done.
- *Increasing complexity and diversity of tasks:* As the learner gains greater proficiency, the mentor presents more complex, challenging, and varied tasks to complete.
- *Exploration:* The mentor encourages the learner to frame questions and problems on his or her own, and in doing so to expand and refine acquired skills.

Because apprenticeships are clearly labor intensive, their use in the classroom isn't always practical or logistically feasible (De Corte, Greer, & Verschaffel, 1996). Even so, we can certainly use elements of an apprenticeship to help students develop more complex skills. For example, we might help students think about writing tasks in the same ways that expert writers do by giving them such prompts as "To liven this up, I'll . . ." and "I can tie this together by . . . ." Such prompts provide the same sort of scaffolding that an expert writer might provide, and they help students develop more sophisticated writing strategies (S. L. Benton, 1997; Scardamalia & Bereiter, 1985; Wong, Hoskyn, Jai, Ellis, & Watson, 2008).

Give prompts that get students thinking about a complex task as an expert might.

## CONTRASTING PIAGET'S AND VYGOTSKY'S THEORIES

Both Piaget and Vygotsky have had a profound influence on contemporary views of learning, thinking, and cognitive development. If we look beyond their differing terminologies, we can see some common themes in the two perspectives. First, both theorists suggested that children acquire increasingly complex thinking processes with age and experience. Second, both argued for the importance of challenge, perhaps in the form of puzzling new information (Piaget's *disequilibrium*) or perhaps in the form of tasks that can be completed only with assistance (Vygotsky's *zone of proximal development*). And third, at any given point in development children are cognitively ready for some experiences but not for others. In Piaget's view, a child can accommodate to new objects and events only when the child can, to some degree, also assimilate them into existing schemes—that is, there must be some overlap between the "new" and the "old." From Vygotsky's perspective, some challenging new tasks may fall within a child's ZPD—and thus be accomplishable with guidance and support—but other tasks are likely to be out of reach for the time being.

Nevertheless, Piaget's and Vygotsky's theories differ in significant ways. For one thing, Piaget maintained that children's cognitive development is largely the result of their own efforts—their informal experiments with physical objects, their attempts to restore equilibrium in the face of puzzling events, and so on. In contrast, Vygotsky placed considerable emphasis on the role of adults and other more advanced individuals, who can mediate new experiences and provide needed support during challenging activities. The difference, then, is one of self-exploration and discovery (Piaget) versus guided exploration and instruction (Vygotsky).

A second key difference lies in the potential influence of the culture in which children grow up. Piaget recognized that cultural differences might have an impact, but he didn't systematically explore them in children's thinking processes. In Vygotsky's theory, however, culture is of paramount importance in molding the specific thinking skills children acquire—a perspective that Bronfenbrenner echoed in describing the multiple layers of environmental influence on children's development. Increasingly, contemporary researchers have come to the same conclusion: Children's cultural environments can have a *huge* influence on what children learn and how they develop.

Finally, the two theorists offer differing perspectives on how language enters into the picture. For Piaget, language certainly enhances cognitive development: It provides many labels *(symbols)* that help children mentally represent their world, and it's the primary means through which children gain knowledge of other people's diverse perspectives on various situations and topics. For Vygotsky, on the other hand, language is absolutely essential for cognitive growth. Children's thought processes are internalized versions of social interactions that are largely verbal in nature. Furthermore, in their conversations with adults, children learn the meanings their culture ascribes to particular events and gradually begin to interpret the world in culture-specific ways. In addition, through two language-based phenomena—self-talk and inner speech—children begin to guide their own behaviors in ways that others have previously guided them.

With such benefits in mind, many contemporary theorists share Piaget's and Vygotsky's belief that acquiring language is an important—perhaps the *most* important—factor in cognitive development (e.g., Pinker, 2007; Premack, 2004; Spelke, 2003). We can better understand cognitive development, then, when we also know something about language development.

# Language Development

Acquiring the language of one's culture is an extremely complex and challenging undertaking. To understand and use a language effectively, children must master four basic components of the language. First, they must master their language's *phonology:* They must know how words sound and be able to produce the sequence of sounds that make up any given word. Second, they must master *semantics,* the meanings of many thousands of words. Third, they must have a good command of *syntax,* knowing how words can legitimately be combined to form understandable phrases and sentences. And finally, children must master the *pragmatics* of their language—the social conventions and speaking strategies that enable effective communication with others.

Mastering these four components of language is a remarkable achievement for any child, yet before they reach kindergarten, most children have acquired sufficient proficiency in language to carry on productive conversations with the people around them. Their language development continues throughout childhood and adolescence, in part as a result of informal social interactions and in part as a result of formal instruction (see Table 2.2).

Some aspects of language development during the school years reflect an increasing ability to think abstractly about the world. For example, abstract thought enables children to reflect, deliberately and consciously, on the general nature and functions of language—an acquisition known as metalinguistic awareness (Owens, 2008; Yaden & Templeton, 1986). With such awareness comes an ability to recognize the figurative nature of words—the nonliteral meanings of proverbs, the symbolism in poems and literature, and so on. At the same time, children's ever-expanding language capabilities probably also *help* them think abstractly (K. Nelson, 1996; Pinker, 2007).

## THEORETICAL ISSUES REGARDING LANGUAGE DEVELOPMENT

Without a doubt children's immediate environments play a significant role in their language development. The richer the language that children hear—that is, the greater the variety of words and the greater the complexity of syntactic structures to which other people expose them—the faster their vocabulary develops (Hoff, 2003; Raikes et al., 2006; Risley & Hart, 2006). Yet children don't simply absorb the language spoken around them. Instead, they appear to use what they hear to construct their own understanding of the language, including knowledge about what words mean, rules governing how words can be combined into meaningful sentences, and so on (Cairns, 1996; Cromer, 1987; Karmiloff-Smith, 1993). Thus, we see in language development some of the knowledge *construction* of which Piaget spoke.

Chapter 4 describes a variety of cultural and ethnic differences that can shape children's behaviors and development.

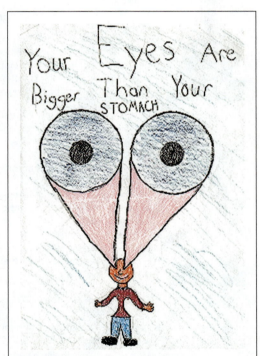

Children in the early and middle elementary grades have only limited ability to make sense of figurative language. Here, 8-year-old Jeff takes a common expression at face value, rather than recognizing its underlying meaning: that someone has ordered more food than can possibly be eaten.

**metalinguistic awareness** Ability to think consciously about the nature and functions of language.

# DEVELOPMENTAL TRENDS

| GRADE LEVEL | AGE-TYPICAL CHARACTERISTICS | EXAMPLE | SUGGESTED STRATEGIES |
|---|---|---|---|
| **TABLE 2.2** • Examples of Linguistic Characteristics and Abilities at Different Grade Levels | | | |
| K–2 | • Knowledge of 8,000–14,000 words by age 6; understandings of some words only partially correct (e.g., use of the word *animal* may be restricted largely to 4-legged mammals)<br>• Difficulty understanding lengthy, complex sentences (e.g., those with multiple clauses)<br>• Superficial understanding of being a "good listener" (e.g., just sitting quietly)<br>• Literal interpretations of messages and requests (e.g., not realizing that "Goodness, this class is noisy" means "Be quiet")<br>• Increasing ability to tell a story, both orally and in writing<br>• Mastery of most sounds; some difficulty pronouncing r, th, dr, sl, and str<br>• Occasional use of regular word endings (-s, -ed, -er) with irregular words (sheeps, goed, gooder)<br>• Basic etiquette in conversations (e.g., taking turns, answering questions)<br>• Reluctance to initiate conversations with adults (for many students from Asian and Mexican American backgrounds) | When two police officers visit a first-grade class to talk about how to go to and from school safely each day, the students listen quietly and respectfully. After the visit, however, the students can recall very little about what the officers have told them. | • Read age-appropriate storybooks as a way of enhancing vocabulary.<br>• Give corrective feedback when students' use of words indicates inaccurate understanding.<br>• Work on listening skills (e.g., sitting quietly, paying attention, trying to understand and remember).<br>• Ask follow-up questions to make sure students accurately understand important messages.<br>• Ask students to construct narratives about recent events (e.g., "Tell me about your camping trip last weekend"). |
| 3-5 | • Incomplete knowledge of irregular word forms<br>• Correct pronunciation of all sounds in one's language (by age 9)<br>• Sustained conversations about concrete topics<br>• Increasing ability to take listeners' prior knowledge into account during explanations<br>• Construction of stories with plots and cause–and–effect relationships<br>• Linguistic creativity and word play (e.g., rhymes, word games) | Students in a third-grade class love corny jokes and riddles that involve a play on words. For example, many are amused by "Why did the cookie go to the doctor?" ("He felt crumby") and "Why couldn't the sailors play cards?" ("Because the captain was standing on the deck"). | • Teach irregular word forms (e.g., the past tense of *ring* is *rang*, the past tense of *bring* is *brought*).<br>• Consult with a speech-language specialist if articulation problems persist in the upper elementary grades.<br>• Use group discussions as a way to explore academic subject matter.<br>• Have students create short stories that they present orally or in writing.<br>• Encourage jokes and rhymes that capitalize on double meanings and homonyms (i.e., sound-alike words). |
| 6-8 | • Knowledge of about 50,000 words at age 12<br>• Increasing awareness of terminologies used in various academic disciplines<br>• Emerging ability to carry on lengthy conversations about abstract topics<br>• Emerging ability to look beyond literal interpretations; comprehension of simple proverbs and increasing ability to detect sarcasm<br>• Increasing metalinguistic awareness; that is, increasing ability to reflect on the underlying nature of language<br>• Increasing proficiency in expository (nonfiction) writing, especially with teacher scaffolding | Students in a sixth-grade class write better persuasive essays when their teacher gives them explicit guidance about elements to include, including (1) an introductory statement expressing one's opinion, (2) supporting evidence for that opinion, (3) reasons why other people might disagree, and (4) explanations of why those reasons are invalid. | • Assign reading materials that introduce new vocabulary.<br>• Introduce some of the terminology used by experts in various content areas (e.g., *simile* in language arts, *molecule* in science).<br>• Conduct structured debates to explore controversial issues.<br>• Ask students to consider the underlying meanings of common proverbs.<br>• Explore the nature of words and language as entities in and of themselves.<br>• Frequently ask students to write about topics; provide guidance about effective writing and frequent feedback about what students have written. |

*(continued)*

**TABLE 2.2 • (Continued)**

9-12

| | | |
|---|---|---|
| • Knowledge of about 80,000 words<br>• Acquisition of many vocabulary words related to particular academic disciplines<br>• Subtle refinements in syntax, mostly as a result of formal instruction<br>• General ability to understand figurative language (e.g., metaphors, proverbs, hyperbole)<br>• Significant improvements in expository writing, especially with experience and constructive feedback | When a ninth-grade class reads Robert Frost's poem "The Road Not Taken," most students realize that the poem is only superficially about choosing one of two paths through the woods—that at a deeper level it's about choosing among various paths in life. | 🍏 Consistently use the terminology associated with various academic disciplines.<br>🍏 Distinguish between similar abstract words (e.g., *weather* vs. *climate*, *velocity* vs. *acceleration*).<br>🍏 Explore complex syntactic structures (e.g., multiple embedded clauses).<br>🍏 Consider the underlying meanings and messages in poetry and fiction.<br>🍏 When students have a native dialect other than Standard English, encourage them to use it in informal conversations and creative writing; encourage Standard English for more formal situations. |

*Sources:* Adger, Wolfram, & Christian, 2007; Byrnes, 1996; Capelli, Nakagawa, & Madden, 1990; S. Carey, 1978, 1985; Ferretti, MacArthur, & Dowdy, 2000; C. A. Grant & Gomez, 2001; K. R. Harris, Graham, & Mason, 2006; K. R. Harris, Santangelo, & Graham, 2010; Karmiloff-Smith, 1979; Maratsos, 1998; T. M McDevitt & Ford, 1987; T. M. McDevitt, Spivey, Sheehan, Lennon, & Story, 1990; Nippold, 1988; O'Grady, 1997; Owens, 2008; Reich, 1986; Stanovich, 2000; Thelen & Smith, 1998.

Most developmental theorists agree that heredity is also involved in language development to some degree. Human beings have the capacity to acquire a far more complex language than any other species on the planet. Exactly *what* human beings inherit that enables them to learn language is a matter of considerable controversy, however. At a minimum, infants inherit a few key predispositions—for instance, a preference for human voices over other sounds and an ability to hear very subtle differences among speech sounds—that make language learning possible (DeCasper & Fifer, 1980; Jusczyk, 1995; P. K. Kuhl, 2004; J. L. Locke, 1993). In addition, some theorists believe that part of our genetic heritage is a *language acquisition device,* a language-specific learning mechanism that enables infants and toddlers to acquire many intricacies of language in an amazingly short amount of time (Chomsky, 1972, 2006; M. Gopnik, 1997; Karmiloff-Smith, 1993). Other theorists believe instead that children learn language in much the same way they learn other things about their environment and culture: through detecting and making use of regular patterns of input from their social environment (Gentner & Namy, 2006; Pelucchi, Hay, & Saffran, 2009; Saffran, 2003).

Research evidence does point to a language-specific developmental mechanism for at least *some* aspects of language learning (Flavell, Miller, & Miller, 2002; Maratsos, 1998; Siegler & Alibali, 2005; Trout, 2003). Children of all cultures learn language very quickly and acquire complex syntactic structures even when those structures aren't necessary for effective communication. In addition, brain research reveals that certain parts of the left hemisphere seem to be biologically predisposed to specialize in either understanding or producing speech (Aitchison, 1996; J. L. Locke, 1993).

Additional evidence for heredity's influence comes from research findings suggesting that there may be *sensitive periods* in some aspects of language development (Bortfeld & Whitehurst, 2001; Bruer, 1999; J. L. Locke, 1993). Children who have little or no exposure to *any* language in the early years often have trouble acquiring language later on, even with intensive language instruction (Curtiss, 1977; Newport, 1990). Furthermore, when learning a *second* language, people have an easier time mastering pronunciation and various verb tenses if they're immersed in the language during childhood or early adolescence (Bialystok, 1994; Bortfeld & Whitehurst, 2001; Bruer, 1999; M. S. C. Thomas & Johnson, 2008). Such sensitive periods may reflect biologically built-in time frames for learning language. Alternatively, perhaps what appear to be predetermined "best" times for learning particular aspects of language are simply the result of the brain's tendency to adapt fairly quickly to whatever form its early auditory environment takes (P. K. Kuhl, 2004; P. K. Kuhl, Conboy, Padden, Nelson, & Pruitt, 2005).

## DIVERSITY IN LANGUAGE DEVELOPMENT

Some diversity in language development seems to be the result of biology. For instance, children with a specific language impairment develop normally in all respects except for language. These children have difficulty perceiving and mentally processing particular aspects of spoken

**specific language impairment**
Disability characterized by abnormalities in the production or comprehension of spoken language, to the point that special educational services are required.

**phonological awareness** Ability to hear the distinct sounds that comprise spoken words.

Chapter 4 looks more closely at the nature and implications of children's dialects.

language—perhaps the quality, pitch, duration, or intensity of specific sounds in speech. Often, although not always, the source of the impairment can be traced to heredity or a specific brain abnormality (Bishop, 2006; Bishop, McDonald, Bird, & Hayiou-Thomas, 2009; Corriveau, Pasquini, & Goswami, 2007; Spinath, Price, Dale, & Plomin, 2004).

Cultural factors play a role in linguistic diversity as well. For example, different cultural groups may nurture different dialects—distinct forms of English that characterize particular ethnicities or geographic regions—and different social conventions for human conversation (i.e., different pragmatic skills) (Adger, Wolfram, & Christian, 2007; Kitayama & Cohen, 2007; Tyler et al., 2008). Occasionally a cultural or ethnic group specifically nurtures certain aspects of language development. For example, many inner-city African American communities make heavy use of figurative language—such as similes, metaphors, and hyperbole (intentional exaggeration)—in their day-to-day conversations, jokes, and stories (C. D. Lee, 2005; H. L. Smith, 1998; Smitherman, 2007). The following anecdote illustrates this point:

> I once asked my mother, upon her arrival from church, "Mom, was it a good sermon?" To which she replied, "Son, by the time the minister finished preaching, the men were crying and the women had passed out on the floor." (H. L. Smith, 1998, p. 202)

With such a rich oral tradition, it isn't surprising that many inner-city African American youth are especially advanced in their use and understanding of figurative language (Ortony, Turner, & Larson-Shapiro, 1985; H. L. Smith, 1998; Smitherman, 2007).

## SECOND-LANGUAGE LEARNING AND ENGLISH LANGUAGE LEARNERS

As mentioned earlier, exposure to a second language in childhood or early adolescence may be especially important for acquiring flawless pronunciation and certain aspects of syntax. Early exposure to a second language seems to be most advantageous if the second language is very different from the first. For example, a native English speaker benefits more from an early start in Japanese or Arabic than from an early start in, say, Spanish or German (Bialystok, 1994; Strozer, 1994). Aside from such caveats, there appears to be no definitive "best" time to begin studying a second language (e.g., P. K. Kuhl et al., 2005; G. Stevens, 2004).

Although there may be no hard-and-fast sensitive period for learning a second language, beginning second-language instruction in the early years has definite advantages. For one thing, it appears that learning a second language facilitates achievement in such other academic areas as reading, vocabulary, and grammar (Diaz, 1983; Reich, 1986). Instruction in a foreign language also sensitizes young children to the international and multicultural nature of the world. Students who learn a second language during the elementary school years express more positive attitudes toward people who speak that language and are more likely to enroll in foreign language classes in high school (Reich, 1986).

 Encourage students of all ages to learn one or more foreign languages.

### BILINGUALISM

At least half of the world's children are *bilingual;* that is, they speak at least two languages fluently (Hoff-Ginsberg, 1997). Although children who grow up in bilingual environments may initially have more limited vocabularies in each language, research reveals clear long-term advantages of bilingualism. Bilingual children appear to have a head start in their development of metalinguistic awareness (Bialystok, 2001; Adesope, Lavin, Thompson, & Ungerleider, 2010). For instance, in the early elementary grades, bilingual children have greater phonological awareness—awareness of the individual sounds, or *phonemes,* that make up spoken words—and this awareness can get them off to an especially good start in learning to read (X. Chen et al., 2004; Rayner, Foorman, Perfetti, Pesetsky, & Seidenberg, 2001). Furthermore, when children are truly fluent in both languages, they tend to perform better on tasks requiring focused attention and on tasks requiring flexible, creative thinking (Adesope et al., 2010; Bialystok, Craik, Green, & Gollan, 2009). Their superior performance on such tasks may be partly the result of enhanced development in certain areas of the brain (Espinosa, 2008; Mechelli et al., 2004).

Being bilingual can have cultural and social advantages as well. In any English-speaking country, mastery of spoken and written English is, of course, essential for long-term educational and professional success. But when a resident of that country belongs to a cultural group that speaks a different language, maintaining social relationships within the culture requires knowledge of its language (McBrien, 2005b). For instance, in many Native American groups, the ancestral language is important for communicating oral history and cultural heritage and for conducting local business (McCarty & Watahomigie, 1998). And Puerto Rican children in the United States often speak Spanish at home as a way of showing respect to their elders (Torres-Guzmán, 1998). Finally, at school, when different students in a single classroom each speak only one of two different languages (perhaps some speaking only English and others speaking only Spanish), teaching students both languages increases student interaction and cross-cultural understanding (A. Doyle, 1982; Padilla, 2006).

## TEACHING A SECOND LANGUAGE

Most children in Western, English-speaking countries are exposed to only one language before they reach school age. That single language may or may not be English. School-age children who are fluent in their native language but not in English are often referred to as **English language learners (ELLs)**. To the extent that elementary and secondary school students have limited knowledge of English, they're apt to have trouble with schoolwork in an English-based classroom (Kieffer, 2008; Padilla, 2006; Slavin & Cheung, 2005; Valdés, Bunch, Snow, & Lee, 2005).

Just as very young children typically learn their native language through informal daily exposure, so, too, can they learn two languages simultaneously if they have frequent, ongoing exposure to both languages. However, when children begin to learn a second language at an older age, perhaps in the elementary grades or even later, they often learn it more quickly if their language-learning experiences are fairly structured (Strozer, 1994).

Yet teaching a second language for one 45-minute period a day—as is typically done in high schools—hardly promotes mastery. Two more intensive approaches, immersion and bilingual education, can be quite effective, with each being useful in somewhat different situations. To keep our discussion simple, let's assume that students are living in an English-speaking country. If these students are native English speakers, total **immersion** in the second language—hearing and speaking it almost exclusively in the classroom during the school day—appears to be the more effective approach. A variation of this approach is a *dual-immersion* program, in which some topics are taught exclusively in English and others are taught exclusively in the second language. For native English speakers living in an English-speaking country, immersion in the second language for part or all of the school day helps students acquire proficiency in the language fairly quickly, and any adverse effects on achievement in other academic areas appear to be short lived (Bialystok et al., 2009; Collier, 1992; Genesee, 1985; Padilla, 2006).

In contrast, English language learners living in an English-speaking country typically fare better in **bilingual education**, in which they receive intensive instruction in English while studying other academic subject areas in their native language. Not only is their academic achievement at least as good or better in bilingual education but they also have greater self-esteem and better attitudes toward school (Garcia & Jensen, 2009; Marsh, Hau, & Kong, 2002; Tong, Lara-Alecio, Irby, Mathes, & Kwok, 2008; Wright, Taylor, & Macarthur, 2000). The optimal bilingual education program proceeds through a gradual phase-in of English in instruction, perhaps in a sequence such as the following:

1. Students join native English-speakers for classes in subject areas that don't depend too heavily on language skills (e.g., art, music, physical education). They study other subject areas in their native language and also begin classes in English as a second language (ESL).

2. After students have acquired some English proficiency, instruction in English begins for one or two additional subject areas (perhaps math and science).

3. When it's clear that students can learn successfully in English in the subject areas identified in Step 2, they join their English-speaking classmates in regular classes in these subjects.

4. Eventually students are sufficiently proficient in English to join the mainstream in all subject areas, and they may no longer require their ESL classes (Krashen, 1996; Padilla, 2006; Valdés et al., 2005).

Ideally, the transition from instruction in a student's native language to instruction in English occurs very gradually over a period of several years. Simple knowledge of basic conversational

---

**English language learner (ELL)** School-age child who is not fully fluent in English because of limited exposure to English prior to enrollment in an English-speaking school.

**immersion** Second-language instruction in which students hear and speak that language almost exclusively in the classroom.

**bilingual education** Second-language instruction in which students are instructed in academic subject areas in their native language while simultaneously being taught to speak and write in the second language.

To maximize second-language learning for native English speakers who live in an English-speaking country, completely immerse them in the second language for part or all of the school day.

**basic interpersonal communication skills (BICS)** Proficiency in English sufficient for day-to-day conversation with English speakers but *not* sufficient for academic success in an English-only curriculum.

**cognitive academic language proficiency (CALP)** Mastery of English vocabulary and syntax sufficient for English language learners to achieve academic success in an English-only curriculum.

English—knowledge collectively known as basic interpersonal communication skills (BICS)—isn't enough for academic success in an English-only curriculum. Ultimately, students must have sufficient mastery of English vocabulary and syntax that they can easily understand and learn from English-based textbooks and lectures; in other words, they must have cognitive academic language proficiency (CALP). Such mastery of English takes considerable time to achieve—often five to seven years (Carhill, Suárez-Orozco, & Páez, 2008; Cummins, 1981, 1984, 2000, 2008; Padilla, 2006).

Why is immersion better for some students whereas bilingual education is better for others? As we've learned, language is an important foundation for cognitive development: It provides symbols for mentally representing the world, enables children to exchange ideas with others, helps them internalize sophisticated cognitive strategies, and so on. Students in an English-speaking country who are immersed in a different language at school still have many opportunities—at home, with their friends, and in the local community—to continue using and developing their English. In contrast, nonnative English speakers may have few opportunities outside their homes to use their native language. If they're taught exclusively in English, they may very well

## Into the Classroom

### Working with English Language Learners

🍏 **Teach early reading skills in students' native languages.**
When working with students whose families recently immigrated from Mexico, a first-grade teacher teaches basic letter–sound relationships and word decoding skills in Spanish (e.g., showing how the printed word *dos*, meaning "two," can be broken up into the sounds "duh," "oh," and "sss").

🍏 **If you don't speak a student's native language yourself, recruit and train parents, community volunteers, or other students to assist in providing instruction in that language.**
A boy in a kindergarten class has grown up speaking a language spoken in some Asian immigrant communities in the United States. His teacher recruits a fourth grader who can read an English picture book to the boy and translate it. At one point the teacher points to a lily pad on a page of the book and asks the fourth grader to describe a lily pad in the boy's language, as he has never seen lily pads in his own neighborhood.

🍏 **Use bilingual software.**
Conducting a quick Google search using the key terms *bilingual, educational,* and *software*, a teacher finds many educational software programs with both English and Spanish options, including some free programs he can easily download to his classroom's computers.

🍏 **When using English to communicate, speak more slowly than you might otherwise, and clearly enunciate each word.**
A third-grade teacher is careful that he always says "going to" rather than "gonna" and "want to" rather than "wanna."

🍏 **Use visual aids to supplement verbal explanations.**
A high school history teacher uses photographs she has downloaded from the Internet to illustrate her verbal description of ancient Egypt. She also gives students a one-page outline that identifies the main ideas in her lesson.

🍏 **During small-group learning activities, encourage same-language students to communicate with one another in their native language.**
When a high school science teacher breaks students into cooperative groups to study the effects of weight, length, and amount of push on a pendulum's oscillation rate, she puts three native Chinese speakers in a single group. She suggests that they can talk in either English or Chinese as they do their experiments.

🍏 **Encourage—but don't force—students to contribute to class discussions in English; be understanding of students who are initially reluctant to participate.**
A high school social studies teacher often breaks his class into small groups to discuss controversial social and political issues. He intentionally places two recent immigrants with peers who are likely to be supportive as these English language learners struggle in their efforts to communicate.

🍏 **Have students work in pairs to make sense of textbook material.**
As two middle school students read a section of their geography textbook, one reads aloud while the other listens and takes notes. They frequently stop to talk about what they've just read or to switch roles.

🍏 **Have students read, write, and report about their native countries; also have them create art that depicts aspects of their countries and cultures.**
A middle school social studies teacher has students conduct research on a country from which they or their ancestors emigrated. The students create posters to display what they've learned, and they proudly talk about their posters at a class-sponsored International Day that students from other classes attend.

*Sources:* Strategies are based on research and recommendations by Carhill et al., 2008; Comeau, Cormier, Grandmaison, & Lacroix, 1999; Duff, 2001; Egbert, 2009; Espinosa, 2007; García, 1995; Herrell & Jordan, 2004; Igoa, 1995, 2007; Janzen, 2008; Krashen, 1996; McClelland, 2001; McClelland, Fiez, & McCandliss, 2002; Padilla, 2006; Slavin & Cheung, 2005; Solórzano, 2008; Tong et al., 2008; Valdés et al., 2005; Walshaw & Anthony, 2008.

lose proficiency in their native language before developing adequate proficiency in English—a phenomenon known as subtractive bilingualism—and their cognitive development suffers as a result. Because bilingual education is designed to foster growth in *both* English and a child's native language, it's apt to promote cognitive development as well as English proficiency (Pérez, 1998; Tse, 2001; Winsler, Díaz, Espinosa, & Rodriguez, 1999).

We must remember that students' native languages are very much a part of their sense of identity—their sense of who they are as people (Nieto, 1995; Tatum, 1997). A high school student named Marisol made the point this way:

> I'm proud of [being Puerto Rican]. I guess I speak Spanish whenever I can. . . . I used to have a lot of problems with one of my teachers 'cause she didn't want us to talk Spanish in class and I thought that was like an insult to us, you know?  (Nieto, 1995, p. 127)

Incorporating children's cultural backgrounds as well as their native language into the classroom curriculum can further promote their academic success (Igoa, 1995, 2007; U.S. Department of Education, 1993). The strategies in the Into the Classroom feature "Working with English Language Learners" take language, sense of identity, and culture into account.

**subtractive bilingualism**
Phenomenon in which immersion in a new-language environment leads to deficits in a child's native language.

Remember that English language learners fare better when they study other school subjects in their native language.

## 2  What Have You Learned?

As a way of summing up our discussion of development in this chapter, we now return to the learning outcomes identified at the beginning of the chapter.

■ **2.1: Describe four principles portraying the general nature of child development and the roles of both heredity and environment in guiding it.** Children develop skills and abilities in a somewhat predictable sequence, but they don't all develop at the same rate, and their development in any particular domain is apt to show occasional spurts within periods of slower growth. To some degree, children's developing physical, cognitive, personal, and social characteristics depend on maturation—that is, on a genetically driven unfolding of physiological advancements. But equally critical is an environment that nurtures and supports the acquisition of new knowledge and skills. As developmental theorist Urie Bronfenbrenner has pointed out, children grow up within several layers of environmental influence, including their immediate families, their neighborhoods and communities, and the larger state (or province) and country in which they reside; each of these layers reflects the particular practices and beliefs of one or more cultural groups. At the same time, children also *change* their environment—and thus also change how their environment affects them—in part by eliciting certain kinds of behaviors from others and in part by choosing among the various opportunities and activities that come their way.

Evaluate and apply your knowledge related to this learning outcome in MyEducationLab™.

■ **2.2: Explain how the brain and its development influence children's learning and thinking.** The human brain changes in significant ways throughout childhood, adolescence, and early adulthood, in part as a result of environmental experiences and in part as a result of such genetically driven processes as synaptogenesis, synaptic pruning, and myelination. Although different parts of the brain have different specialties, they are closely interconnected and all work together to support complex

human activities. The brain has considerable *plasticity*—that is, it can learn a great many new things at virtually any age. As teachers, we should be optimistic that students can acquire a wide variety of knowledge and skills in both the elementary and secondary grades. Yet we must keep in mind that even at the high school level, many students' brains haven't sufficiently matured to support planning, reasoning, impulse control, and other abilities important for independent learning and responsible behavior.

Evaluate and apply your knowledge related to this learning outcome in MyEducationLab™.

■ **2.3: Apply Piaget's theory of cognitive development to classroom practice.** Swiss psychologist Jean Piaget proposed that children are intrinsically motivated to make sense of their world and self-construct increasingly complex understandings of it through the two complementary processes of assimilation and accommodation. His four stages of cognitive development give us a rough idea of when various logical thinking capabilities are likely to emerge; however, most contemporary developmental theorists believe that children's developmental progress can probably be better characterized as gradual trends that depend at least partly on experience.

Piaget's theory has numerous implications for classroom practice. For example, his clinical method offers a way of exploring children's reasoning processes in depth. His proposal that abstract thinking doesn't appear until adolescence encourages us to make heavy use of concrete, hands-on experiences in the elementary and middle school grades. And his concept of disequilibrium suggests that by challenging students' illogical reasoning, we can sometimes spur them to revise incomplete understandings and think in more sophisticated ways.

Evaluate and apply your knowledge related to this learning outcome in MyEducationLab™.

**■ 2.4: Apply Vygotsky's theory of cognitive development to classroom practice.**

In contrast to Piaget, who portrayed children as being largely in control of their own cognitive development, Russian psychologist Lev Vygotsky proposed that children's cognitive development is a very social enterprise. In particular, adults and other more advanced individuals communicate the meanings their culture assigns to objects and events, pass along physical and cognitive tools that make everyday tasks and problems easier, and assist children with tasks in their zone of proximal development. In Vygotsky's view, social activities are often precursors to and form the basis for complex mental processes: Children initially use new skills in the course of interacting with adults or peers and slowly internalize and adapt these skills for their own, independent use.

Vygotsky's theory suggests that, as teachers, we should help students make sense of their experiences (e.g., by tying their observations to particular scientific concepts and principles), assign activities that require them to stretch their existing abilities, scaffold their efforts on challenging new tasks, have them work in small groups to tackle multifaceted issues and problems, and meaningfully engage them in adult-like activities.

Evaluate and apply your knowledge related to this learning outcome in MyEducationLab™.

**■ 2.5: Describe developmental changes in language during the school years, and explain how you might adapt instruction to children with diverse language abilities and needs.**
Although most children have considerable proficiency in their native language by the time they reach kindergarten, their language development continues throughout the school years. For example, in addition to acquiring an ever-expanding vocabulary, children become increasingly able to listen effectively, conduct sustained conversations about particular topics, and comprehend the underlying meanings of figurative speech.

Both hereditary and environmental factors contribute to language development. One important environmental variable is, of course, the particular language—or languages—that children speak at home and in their communities. Researchers have identified many advantages to knowing two more languages, including more advanced metalinguistic awareness, more creative thinking, and greater cross-cultural understanding. Different approaches to promoting bilingualism are recommended in different situations. In an English-speaking community, native English speakers can gain fluency in a second language through complete or partial immersion in that language at school, but students who speak a language other than English at home typically achieve at higher levels in bilingual education programs.

Evaluate and apply your knowledge related to this learning outcome in MyEducationLab™.

## Practice for Your Licensure Exam

### Stones Lesson

Ms. Hennessey is conducting a demonstration in her first-grade class. She shows the children a large glass tank filled with water. She also shows them two stones. One stone, a piece of granite, is fairly small (about 2 cm in diameter). The other stone, a piece of pumice (i.e., cooled volcanic lava), is much larger (about 10 cm in diameter). Because Ms. Hennessey does not allow the children to touch or hold the stones, they have no way of knowing that the piece of pumice, which has many small air pockets in it, is much lighter than the piece of granite. The demonstration proceeds as follows:

*Ms. H.:* Would anyone like to predict what he or she thinks will happen to these stones? Yes, Brianna.

*Brianna:* I think the . . . both stones will sink because I know stones sink. I've seen lots of stones sink and every time I throw a rock into the water, like it always sinks, yeah, it always does.

*Ms. H.:* You look like you want to say something else.

*Brianna:* Yeah the water can't hold up rocks like it holds up boats and I know they'll sink.

*Ms. H.:* You sound so sure, let me try another object.

*Brianna:* No you gotta throw it in, you gotta test my idea first. [Ms. H. places the smaller stone in the tank; it sinks.] See, I told you I knew it would sink. [Ms. H. puts the larger, pumice stone down and picks up another object.] No you've gotta test the big one too because if the little one sunk the big one's gotta sunk. [Ms. H. places the pumice stone in the tank; it floats.] No! No! That's not right! That doesn't go with my mind [Brianna grabs hold of her head]; it just doesn't go with my mind.*

**1. Constructed-response question:**

Brianna is noticeably surprised, maybe even a little upset, when she sees the pumice stone float.

A. Use one or more concepts from Jean Piaget's theory of cognitive development to explain why Brianna reacts as strongly as she does to the floating pumice.

B. Again drawing on Piaget's theory, explain why Ms. Hennessey intentionally presents a phenomenon that will surprise the children.

*Excerpt from "Students' Reflective Thoughts About Science Content: A Relationship to Conceptual Change Learning" by M. Gertrude Hennessey and M.E. Beeth, April 1993, paper presented at the meeting of the American Educational Research Association, Atlanta, GA. Copyright © 1993 by Gertrude Hennessey and M. E. Beeth. Reprinted with permission.

2. **Multiple-choice question:**

   Imagine that you perform the same demonstration with high school students rather than first graders. If you were to follow Vygotsky's theory of cognitive development, which one of the following approaches would you take in helping the students understand the floating pumice?

   a. Before performing the demonstration, ask students to draw a picture of the tank and two stones.

   b. Drop several light objects (e.g., a feather, a piece of paper, a small sponge) into the tank before dropping either stone into it.

   c. Teach the concept of *density,* and explain that an object's average density relative to water determines whether it floats or sinks.

   d. Praise students who correctly predict that the larger stone will float, even if they initially give an incorrect explanation about why it will float.

---

**PRAXIS** Go to Appendix C, "Matching Book and MyEducationLab™ to the Praxis Principles of Learning and Teaching Tests," to discover sections of this chapter that may be especially applicable to the Praxis tests.

---

# 3 Personal and Social Development

## LEARNING OUTCOMES

**3.1:** Describe the nature and origins of children's temperaments and personality characteristics, and explain how you might adapt your classroom practices to students' diverse personalities.

**3.2:** Explain how students' sense of self is apt to influence their behavior and how you can help students develop healthy self-perceptions.

**3.3:** Apply your knowledge of peer relationships and social cognition in promoting productive social skills and addressing student aggression.

**3.4:** Describe typical advancements in moral and prosocial development over the course of childhood and adolescence, and identify strategies for promoting moral and prosocial development in the classroom.

## CASE STUDY: HIDDEN TREASURE

Six-year-old Lupita has spent most of her life in Mexico with her grandmother, but she has recently joined her migrant-worker parents in the United States and is now a quiet, well-behaved student in Ms. Padilla's kindergarten class. Ms. Padilla rarely calls on her because of her apparent lack of academic skills and is thinking about holding her back for a second year of kindergarten. Yet a researcher's video camera captures a side of Lupita that her teacher hasn't noticed. On one occasion Lupita is quick to finish her Spanish assignment and starts to work on a puzzle during her free time. A classmate approaches, and he and Lupita begin playing with a box of toys. A teacher aide asks the boy whether he has finished his Spanish assignment, implying that he should return to complete it, but the boy doesn't understand the aide's subtle message. Lupita gently persuades the boy to go finish his schoolwork and then returns to her puzzle. Two classmates having trouble with their own puzzles request Lupita's assistance, and she competently and patiently shows them how to work cooperatively to assemble the pieces.

Ms. Padilla is amazed when she views the videotape. She readily admits, "I had written her off—her and three others. They had met my expectations, and I just wasn't looking for anything else." Ms. Padilla and her aides begin working closely with Lupita on academic skills and often allow her to take a leadership role in group activities. At the end of the school year, Lupita earns achievement test scores indicating exceptional competence in language skills and mathematics, and she is promoted to first grade. (Based on case described by Carrasco, 1981)

- What distinctive personality characteristics and social skills does Lupita exhibit? Which of them are likely to enhance her classroom success? Which of them might potentially interfere with her classroom success?
- What might have happened to Lupita if her many strengths had gone unnoticed?

---

Lupita's behaviors during free time reveal a conscientious, socially astute child with strong teaching and leadership skills. However, perhaps because of Lupita's quiet, restrained nature—or perhaps because of her family background—Ms. Padilla initially concludes that Lupita hasn't mastered the knowledge and skills she'll need in first grade. If the researcher's videotape hadn't captured Lupita's social skills and proficiency and persistence with puzzles, Lupita might very well have remained on the sidelines throughout much of the school year, getting little assistance on academic skills and few opportunities to capitalize on her many positive personal qualities. Thus, Ms. Padilla's low expectations for Lupita may have ensured that Lupita *wouldn't* gain the knowledge and skills she would need in first grade—a self-fulfilling prophecy.

School isn't just a place for acquiring cognitive and linguistic skills. It's also a place for personal development, whereby children and adolescents build on and possibly modify their distinctive patterns of behavior (i.e., their *personalities*) and gain an increasing understanding of who they are as individuals. Furthermore, the very social nature of school makes it an ideal context for social development, in which young people come to better understand their fellow human beings, develop productive social skills and interpersonal relationships, and gradually internalize their society's standards for behavior.

# Personality Development

Long before children begin school, they show noticeable differences in personality. That is, they show some consistency in their behaviors and thought patterns in a wide variety of situations. For instance, whereas Lupita tends to be quiet and well behaved in class, some of her peers are probably noisy and rambunctious. And whereas Lupita is conscientious about completing her work,

**personal development** Development, with age, of distinctive behavioral styles and increasingly complex self-understandings.

**social development** Development, with age, of increasingly sophisticated understandings of other people and of society as a whole, as well as increasingly effective interpersonal skills and more internalized standards for behavior.

**personality** Characteristic ways in which an individual behaves and thinks in a wide range of circumstances.

at least one of her classmates—and probably several others—are easily distracted and must be prodded to stay on task.

Children's personalities are the result of both heredity—especially in the form of inherited temperaments—and environmental factors. As you will see, heredity and environment often interact in their influences.

## TEMPERAMENT

A child's temperament is his or her general tendency to respond to and deal with environmental stimuli and events in particular ways. Children seem to have distinct temperaments almost from birth. Researchers have identified many temperamental styles that emerge early in life and are relatively enduring, including general activity level, adaptability, self-control, persistence, adventurousness, outgoingness, shyness, fearfulness, irritability, and distractibility. Most psychologists agree that such temperamental differences are biologically based and have genetic origins, and to some degree the differences persist into adolescence and adulthood (Caspi & Silva, 1995; Keogh, 2003; Rothbart, 2011; A. Thomas & Chess, 1977).

By influencing children's behaviors, inherited temperaments also influence the specific environmental circumstances they experience and so indirectly affect other aspects of personal and social development (N. A. Fox, Henderson, Rubin, Calkins, & Schmidt, 2001; Rothbart, 2011; Strelau, 2008). For example, children who are energetic and adventuresome seek out a wider variety of experiences than those who are quiet and restrained. And children who are naturally vivacious and outgoing typically have more opportunities to learn social skills and establish rewarding interpersonal relationships than do children who are subdued and shy.

Furthermore, many temperamental characteristics affect how students engage in and respond to classroom activities and thus indirectly affect their academic achievement (Keogh, 2003; Rothbart, 2011; Saudino & Plomin, 2007). For instance, students are more likely to achieve at high levels if they are persistent, reasonably (but not overly) energetic, and able to ignore minor distractions. They can also achieve greater academic success if their behaviors lead to friendly, productive relationships with teachers and peers—people who can bolster their self-confidence and support their efforts to learn. Underlying some of their academic and social success is an aspect of temperament known as effortful control—their general ability to inhibit immediate impulses in order to think and act productively (Rothbart, 2011; Valiente, Lemery-Chalfant, & Swanson, 2010).

## ENVIRONMENTAL INFLUENCES ON PERSONALITY DEVELOPMENT

Genetic differences in temperament are only *predispositions* to behave in certain ways, and environmental conditions and experiences point different children with the same predispositions in somewhat different directions. Two key environmental factors influencing personality development are family dynamics and cultural expectations for behavior.

### FAMILY DYNAMICS

Many parents and other family caregivers (e.g., grandparents, older siblings) lovingly interact with a new infant and consistently and dependably provide for the infant's physical and psychological needs. When they do such things, a strong, affectionate caregiver–child bond known as attachment typically forms (Ainsworth, Blehar, Waters, & Wall, 1978). Infants who become closely attached to parents or other caregivers early in life are apt to develop into amiable, independent, self-confident children and adolescents who adjust easily to new classroom environments, establish productive relationships with teachers and peers, and have an inner conscience that guides their behavior. In contrast, children who don't become closely attached to a parent or some other individual early in life can be immature, dependent, unpopular, and prone to disruptive and aggressive behaviors later on (J. P. Allen, Porter, McFarland, McElhaney, & Marsh, 2007; Kochanska, Aksan, Knaack, & Rhines, 2004; Mikulincer & Shaver, 2005; S. Shulman, Elicker, & Sroufe, 1994; Sroufe, Carlson, & Shulman, 1993).

In addition to forming emotional attachments with children, parents and other family caregivers adopt fairly consistent *parenting styles* they use in raising the children. In mainstream Western culture, the ideal situation seems to be authoritative parenting, which combines affection and respect for children with reasonable restrictions on behavior. Authoritative parents provide a loving and supportive home, hold high expectations and standards for performance, explain why behaviors are or are not acceptable, enforce household rules consistently, include children in decision making, and provide age-appropriate opportunities for autonomy. Children from authoritative homes tend to be happy, energetic, self-confident, and likeable. They make friends easily and show self-control and concern for the rights and needs of others. Children of authoritative parents appear well adjusted, in part, because their behavior fits well with the values espoused by mainstream Western culture. They listen respectfully to others, follow reasonable rules for behavior, work well independently, and strive for academic achievement (Barber, Stolz, & Olsen, 2005; Baumrind, 1989, 1991; Bradley, 2010; M. R. Gray & Steinberg, 1999; J. M. T. Walker & Hoover-Dempsey, 2006). Given such benefits, authoritative parenting provides a good model for how we, as teachers, should generally conduct our classrooms.

Authoritative parenting isn't universally "best," however. Certain other parenting styles may be better suited to particular cultures and environments. For instance, in authoritarian parenting, parents expect complete and immediate compliance; they neither negotiate expectations nor provide reasons for their requests. In many Asian American and Hispanic families, high demands for obedience are made within the context of close, supportive parent–child relationships. Underlying the message of control is a more important message: "I love you and want you to do well, but it's equally important that you act for the good of the family and community" (X. Chen & Wang, 2010; Halgunseth, Ispa, & Rudy, 2006; Rothbaum & Trommsdorff, 2007). Authoritarian parenting is also more common in impoverished economic environments. When families live in low-income, inner-city neighborhoods where danger potentially lurks around every corner, parents may better serve their children by being strict and directive about activities (Hale-Benson, 1986; McLoyd, 1998).

Some degree of parental guidance and discipline seems to be important for optimal personal and social development. Parents who are overly permissive—for instance, those who let their children come and go as they please and impose few consequences for inappropriate actions—tend to have children who are immature and impulsive, do poorly in school, and act aggressively with peers (Aunola & Nurmi, 2005; Joussemet et al., 2008; Lamborn, Mounts, Steinberg, & Dornbusch, 1991). Yet we must take care not to point accusatory fingers or in other ways be judgmental about how parents are bringing up their children. Some parents may have learned ineffective parenting strategies from their own parents. Others may have challenges in their lives—perhaps mental illness, marital conflict, or serious financial problems—that hamper their ability to nurture and support their children.

It's important to note, too, that most research on parenting involves correlational studies that reveal associations between parents' behaviors and children's characteristics but don't necessarily demonstrate cause–and–effect relationships. A few experimental studies have documented that specific parenting styles probably *do* influence children's personalities to some degree (Bakermans-Kranenburg, van IJzendoorn, Pijlman, Mesman, & Juffer, 2008; W. A. Collins, Maccoby, Steinberg, Hetherington, & Bornstein, 2000). In other cases, however, parents' disciplinary strategies seem to be the *result*, rather than the cause, of how children behave. For instance, temperamentally lively or adventuresome children typically require more parental control than quieter, restrained ones (J. R. Harris, 1998; Rothbart, 2011; Stice & Barrera, 1995).

As teachers, we can certainly serve as sources of information about effective disciplinary strategies. But we should keep in mind that parenting styles have, at most, only a *moderate* influence on children's personalities. Many children and adolescents thrive despite their caregivers' diverse parenting styles, provided that those caregivers aren't severely neglectful or abusive. Children with certain temperaments—for instance, those who tend to be adaptable, self-disciplined, and outgoing—seem to be especially resilient in the face of difficult family

**temperament** Genetic predisposition to respond in particular ways to one's physical and social environments.

**effortful control** One's general ability to inhibit immediate impulses in order to think and act productively; believed to be a distinct aspect of temperament that has a biological basis in the brain.

**attachment** Strong, affectionate bond formed between a child and a caregiver.

**authoritative parenting** Parenting style characterized by emotional warmth, high standards for behavior, explanation and consistent enforcement of rules, and inclusion of children in decision making.

**authoritarian parenting** Parenting style characterized by rigid rules and expectations for behavior that children are asked to obey without question.

 Adopt a generally authoritative style in the classroom.

 Serve as a resource regarding effective parenting strategies, perhaps through newsletters or parent discussion groups.

**child maltreatment** Consistent neglect or abuse of a child that jeopardizes the child's physical and psychological well-being.

**socialization** Process of molding a child's behavior and beliefs to be appropriate for his or her cultural group.

**culture shock** Sense of confusion when a student encounters a new environment with behavioral expectations very different from those previously learned.

Chapter 5 describes possible warning signs that a student is contemplating suicide.

 Report suspected cases of child maltreatment *immediately*.

Chapter 4 examines cultural differences such as these in greater depth.

Teach students behaviors they will need for long-term success in Western society, but be patient when such behaviors are very different from those learned at home.

circumstances (Bates & Pettit, 2007; Belsky & Pluess, 2009; D. Hart, Atkins, & Fegley, 2003; Rothbart, 2011).

**Child maltreatment**   In a few unfortunate instances, parents' behaviors toward their children constitute **child maltreatment**. In some cases, parents neglect children: They fail to provide nutritious meals, adequate clothing, and other basic necessities of life. In other cases, parents or other family members abuse children physically, sexually, or emotionally. Possible indicators of neglect or abuse are chronic hunger, lack of warm clothing in cold weather, untreated medical needs, frequent or serious physical injuries (e.g., bruises, burns, broken bones), and exceptional knowledge about sexual matters.

Parental neglect and abuse can have significant adverse effects on children's personal and social development. On average, children who have been routinely neglected or abused have low self-esteem, poorly developed social skills, and low school achievement. Many are angry, aggressive, and defiant. Others can be depressed, anxious, socially withdrawn, and possibly suicidal (Crosson-Tower, 2010; J. Kim & Cicchetti, 2006; Maughan & Cicchetti, 2002; R. A. Thompson & Wyatt, 1999).

Teachers are both morally and legally obligated to report any cases of suspected child abuse or neglect to the proper authorities (e.g., the school principal or child protective services). Two helpful resources are the National Child Abuse Hotline at 1-800-4-A-CHILD (1-800-422-4453) and the website for Childhelp at www.childhelp.org.

## CULTURAL EXPECTATIONS AND SOCIALIZATION

As we've seen, various cultural groups influence children's personalities indirectly through the parenting styles they encourage. Culture also has a more direct influence on children's personal and social development through a process known as **socialization**. That is, members of a cultural group work hard to help growing children adopt the behaviors and beliefs that the group holds dear. Children typically learn their earliest lessons about their culture's standards and expectations for behavior from parents and other family members, who teach them simple manners (e.g., saying please and thank you), encourage them to do well in school, and so on (W.-B. Chen & Gregory, 2008; Eccles, 2007). Once children reach school age, teachers become equally important socialization agents. For example, in mainstream Western society, teachers typically expect and encourage such behaviors as showing respect for authority figures, following rules and directions, controlling impulses, working independently, and asking for help when it's needed (Manning & Baruth, 2009; Wentzel & Looney, 2007). Cultures around the globe encourage many of these behaviors, but they don't necessarily endorse *all* of them. For instance, many children of Mexican heritage are more accustomed to observing events quietly and unobtrusively—as Lupita does in the opening case study—than to asking adults for explanations and help (Correa-Chávez, Rogoff, & Mejía Arauz, 2005; Gutiérrez & Rogoff, 2003).

Researchers have observed other cultural differences in socialization practices as well. For instance, European American families often encourage assertiveness and independence, but families from many other countries (e.g., Mexico, China, India) are more likely to encourage restraint, obedience, and deference to elders (Goodnow, 1992; Joshi & MacLean, 1994; Morelli & Rothbaum, 2007). And whereas many American children are encouraged to be outgoing and emotionally expressive, children in many Asian cultures are encouraged to be shy and emotionally reserved (X. Chen, Chung, & Hsiao, 2009; Huntsinger & Jose, 2006; Morelli & Rothbaum, 2007). However, considerable diversity exists *within* any culture, with different parents, teachers, and other adults encouraging somewhat different behaviors and beliefs.

When behaviors expected of students at school differ from those expected at home or when belief systems presented by teachers are inconsistent with those of children's parents, children may initially experience some **culture shock**. At a minimum, these children are apt to be confused and distracted, at least in the first few days or weeks of school. Some children with less adaptable or more irritable temperaments may even become angry or resistant (Rothbart, 2011; Ward, Bochner, & Furnham, 2001).

As teachers, we must certainly encourage behaviors essential for students' long-term success, such as obeying rules, following instructions, and working independently. At the same time, students will need our guidance, support, and patience when our expectations differ from those of their family or cultural group.

## THE "BIG FIVE" PERSONALITY TRAITS

As children grow older, the many interactions among their inherited temperaments and environmental circumstances lead to unique and somewhat stable personality profiles. Research with both children and adults has yielded five general personality traits that are relatively independent of one another and appear to involve somewhat different areas of the brain. You can remember them using the mnemonic *OCEAN*:

- *Openness:* The extent to which one is curious about the world and receptive to new experiences and ideas
- *Conscientiousness:* The extent to which one is careful, organized, self-disciplined, and likely to follow through on plans and commitments
- *Extraversion:* The extent to which one is socially outgoing and seeks excitement
- *Agreeableness:* The extent to which one is pleasant, kind, and cooperative in social situations
- *Neuroticism:* The extent to which one is prone to negative emotions (e.g., anxiety, anger, depression) (Caspi, 1998; DeYoung et al., 2010; G. Matthews, Zeidner, & Roberts, 2006; Saarni, Campos, Camras, & Witherington, 2006)

Such traits lead to some consistency—but not *total* consistency—in children's behaviors across situations (Hampson, 2008; Mendoza-Denton & Mischel, 2007). Variability is particularly common when circumstances change considerably. For instance, a student might be very outgoing and sociable with his close friends but shy and withdrawn with people he doesn't know very well. And a student is more likely to be conscientious about completing homework if she is given some guidance about how to organize her assignments in a "to-do" list (Belfiore & Hornyak, 1998).

> Remember that despite some consistency in students' personalities, their behaviors are likely to vary somewhat in different contexts.

## Creating a Productive Classroom Environment

### Accommodating Students' Diverse Temperaments and Personality Traits

**Minimize down time for students with high energy levels.**
As a way of letting a chronically restless third grader release pent-up energy throughout the school day, his teacher gives him small chores to do (e.g., erasing the board, sharpening pencils, cleaning art supplies) and shows him how to complete the chores quietly so as not to disturb his classmates.

**Provide numerous opportunities for highly sociable students to interact with classmates.**
In a unit on colonial America, a fifth-grade teacher assigns a project in which students must depict a typical colonial village in some way (e.g., by writing a research paper, drawing a map on poster board, or creating a miniature three-dimensional model). The students can choose to work on the project alone or with one or two classmates, with the stipulation that students who work with peers must undertake more complex projects than students who work alone.

**Be especially warm and attentive with very shy students.**
A ninth-grade teacher has a new student join one of his classes midway through the school year. The student comes to class alone each day and doesn't join in conversations with peers before or after class. When the teacher sees her eating lunch by herself in the cafeteria one day, he sits beside her and engages her in conversation about her previous school and community. The following day in class, he assigns a small-group, cooperative learning project that students will work on periodically over the next two weeks. He forms cooperative groups of three or four students each, making sure to place the new girl with two students whom he knows will be friendly and helpful to her.

**When students have trouble adapting to new circumstances, give them advance notice of unusual activities and provide extra structure and reassurance.**
A kindergarten teacher has discovered that two children in his class do well when the school day is orderly and predictable but often become anxious or upset when the class departs from its usual routine. To prepare the children for a field trip to the fire station on Friday, the teacher begins to talk about the trip at the beginning of the week, explaining what the class will do and see during the visit. He also recruits the father of one of the anxiety-prone children to serve as a parent assistant that day.

**If students seem overwhelmed by noisy or chaotic situations, find or create a more calm and peaceful environment for them.**
Several middle school students find the school cafeteria loud and unsettling. Their math teacher offers her classroom as a place where they can occasionally eat instead. On some days she eats with them. At other times she sits at her desk and grades papers, but the students know she will gladly stop to talk if they have a question or concern.

**Teach self-control strategies to students who act impulsively.**
A high school student often shouts out comments and opinions in her history class. One day the student's teacher takes her aside after school and gently explains that her lack of restraint is interfering with classmates' ability to participate in discussions. To sensitize the student to the extent of the problem, the teacher asks her to keep a daily tally of how many times she talks without first raising her hand. A week later the two meet again, and the teacher suggests a self-talk strategy that can help the student participate actively without dominating a discussion.

*Sources:* Some strategies based on suggestions by Keogh (2003).

Even when all students are productively engaged in a classroom activity, they show temperamental differences in such traits as general energy level and outgoingness. For example, observe the diverse student temperaments in "Water Wheels Activity."

## TEMPERAMENT, PERSONALITY, AND GOODNESS OF FIT

On average, students who are conscientious about their work and open to new experiences achieve at higher levels at school (Hattie, 2009; M. C. O'Connor & Paunonen, 2007). Yet there is no single best temperament or personality that maximizes students' adjustment and achievement in the classroom. Instead, children are more likely to succeed at school when there is a **goodness of fit**, rather than a mismatch, between their natural inclinations and typical behaviors, on the one hand, and classroom activities and expectations, on the other (A. Thomas & Chess, 1977). For example, when teachers want students to participate actively in whole-class discussions, highly energetic, outgoing children are apt to shine, but quieter students (like Lupita) might feel anxious or intimidated. When teachers require a lot of independent seatwork, quieter children often do well, but some energetic children may be viewed as disruptive (Keogh, 2003; Rothbart, 2011).

As teachers, we must keep in mind that students' distinctive ways of behaving in the classroom—their energy levels, sociability, impulsiveness, and so on—aren't entirely within their control. The Creating a Productive Classroom Environment feature "Accommodating Students' Diverse Temperaments and Personality Traits" offers several suggestions for adapting instruction and classroom management strategies to accommodate students' individual behavioral styles.

## Development of a Sense of Self

With their increasing capacity for symbolic thinking and (eventually) abstract reasoning, growing children begin to draw conclusions about who they are as people. As an example, try the following exercise.

### EXPERIENCING FIRSTHAND
### DESCRIBING YOURSELF

List at least 10 adjectives or phrases that describe you as a person.

How did you describe yourself? Are you smart? Friendly? Open-minded? Physically attractive? Moody? Your answers provide a window into a key component of your personality known as **sense of self**—your perceptions, beliefs, judgments, and feelings about who you are as a person. Many psychologists distinguish between two aspects of the sense of self: *self-concept*—assessments of one's own characteristics, strengths, and weaknesses—and *self-esteem*—judgments and feelings about one's own value and worth. These two aspects closely overlap, however, and thus the two terms are often used interchangeably (Bracken, 2009; Byrne, 2002; McInerney, Marsh, & Craven, 2008).

In overall self-assessments, young children tend to make distinctions between two general domains: how competent they are at day-to-day tasks (including schoolwork) and how well they are liked by family and friends. As they grow older, children make finer and finer distinctions—for instance, they realize that they may be more or less competent or "good" in various academic subjects, athletic activities, peer relationships, and physical attractiveness (Davis-Kean & Sandler, 2001; Harter, 1999; Yun, Farran, Lipsey, & Bilbrey, 2010). Each of these domains may have a greater or lesser influence on students' overall sense of self. For some, academic achievement may be the overriding factor, whereas for others, physical attractiveness or popularity with peers may be more important (Crocker & Knight, 2005; D. Hart, 1988; Harter, 1999).

Children and adolescents tend to behave in ways that mirror their beliefs about themselves (M. S. Caldwell, Rudolph, Troop-Gordon, & Kim, 2004; Marsh & O'Mara, 2008; Valentine, DuBois, & Cooper, 2004). For instance, if they see themselves as good students, they're more likely to pay attention, follow directions, persist at difficult problems, and enroll in challenging courses. If they see themselves as friendly and socially desirable, they're more likely to seek the company of their classmates and perhaps run for student council. If they see themselves as physically competent, they'll more eagerly pursue extracurricular athletics.

Students' beliefs about themselves are, like their beliefs about the world around them, largely self-constructed. Accordingly, their self-assessments may or may not be accurate. When students evaluate themselves fairly accurately, they're in a good position to choose age-appropriate tasks and activities (Baumeister, Campbell, Krueger, & Vohs, 2003; Harter, 1999). A slightly inflated self-assessment can be beneficial as well, because it encourages students to work toward challenging yet

**goodness of fit** Situation in which classroom conditions and expectations are compatible with students' temperaments and personality characteristics.

**sense of self** Perceptions, beliefs, judgments, and feelings about oneself as a person; includes *self-concept* and *self-esteem*.

potentially reachable goals (Bjorklund & Green, 1992; Pajares, 2009). However, a sense of self that is *too* inflated can give some students an unwarranted sense of superiority over classmates and lead them to bully or in other ways act aggressively toward peers (Baumeister et al., 2003; Baumeister, Smart, & Boden, 1996; Menon et al., 2007). And as you might guess, students who significantly *under*estimate their abilities are apt to avoid the many challenges that would enhance their cognitive and social growth (Schunk & Pajares, 2004; Zimmerman & Moylan, 2009).

## FACTORS INFLUENCING SENSE OF SELF

Students often gain initial insights about their general competence in a certain domain from their *own successes and failures* in that domain (Marsh, Gerlach, Trautwein, Lüdtke, & Brettschneider, 2007; Marsh & O'Mara, 2008). For instance, they may discover that they can easily solve—or consistently struggle with—simple math problems. Or they may find that they can run faster—or more slowly—than most of their peers. Through such experiences, students acquire a sense of self-efficacy about the degree to which they can succeed in certain activities and accomplish certain goals. Over time, students' specific self-efficacies for various tasks and activities contribute to their more general sense of self (Bong & Skaalvik, 2003; McInerney et al., 2008).

Unfortunately, an interplay between self-perceptions and behaviors can create a vicious cycle: A poor sense of self leads to less productive behaviors, which leads to fewer successes, which perpetuates the poor sense of self. However, simply telling students that they're good or smart or in some other way "special" is unlikely to break the cycle (Crocker & Knight, 2005; McMillan, Singh, & Simonetta, 1994; Pajares, 2009). Instead, we must make sure that students have many opportunities to improve and eventually succeed at academic, social, and physical tasks—not obviously easy tasks (which presumably anyone could do) but challenging ones that reflect a genuine sense of accomplishment. When we present such challenges, we must, of course, be sure that students have the prerequisite knowledge and age-appropriate scaffolding to facilitate their success (Bouchey & Harter, 2005; Dunning, Heath, & Suls, 2004; Leary, 1999).

Yet students' personal successes and failures aren't the only things affecting their sense of self. A second important factor is their social context—and more specifically, *other people's behaviors*—which influences students' self-perceptions in at least two ways. For one thing, how students evaluate themselves depends to some extent on how their own performance compares to that of their peers. For example, students who see themselves achieving at higher levels than classmates are apt to develop a more positive sense of self than those who consistently find themselves falling short (R. Butler, 2008; Dijkstra, Kuyper, van der Werf, Buunk, & van der Zee, 2008; Trautwein, Gerlach, & Lüdtke, 2008). Thus, peer comparisons can dampen high-ability students' sense of self when they attend classes made up largely of students with similarly high ability (Köller, Zeinz, & Trautwein, 2008; Seaton, Marsh, & Craven, 2010).

In addition, students' self-perceptions are affected by how others behave *toward* them. Peers often communicate information about children's social and athletic competence, perhaps by seeking out a child's companionship or ridiculing a child in front of others (M. S. Caldwell et al., 2004; Crosnoe, 2011; Rudolph, Caldwell, & Conley, 2005). Adults, too, influence children's sense of self, in part by the kinds of expectations they hold for children's performance and in part by drawing attention to various things children do well or poorly (M. J. Harris & Rosenthal, 1985; O'Mara, Marsh, Craven, & Debus, 2006; Pajares, 2009). As teachers, we should, of course, communicate realistically high expectations for achievement and give positive feedback about the specific things students do well. And when we find that we must give students negative feedback—and occasionally we must—we should do so while also communicating respect and affection for them as human beings. For instance, we might point out that mistakes are a natural part of the learning process, and we should offer concrete suggestions about how to improve.

A third general factor that can impact students' sense of self is *membership in a successful group* (Harter, 1999; Thorkildsen, Golant, & Cambray-Engstrom, 2008; Wigfield, Eccles, & Pintrich, 1996). If you think back to your own school years, perhaps you can recall taking pride in something your entire class accomplished or feeling good about a community service project completed through an extracurricular club. School groups aren't the only groups affecting students' sense of self. For instance, some cultures encourage children to take pride in the accomplishments of their families as well as—or perhaps instead of—their own accomplishments (Banks & Banks, 1995; P. M. Cole & Tan, 2007). And as we'll see a bit later in the chapter, students' membership in certain ethnic groups can also be a source of pride.

**self-efficacy**  Belief that one is capable of executing certain behaviors or achieving certain goals.

 Enhance students' sense of self by supporting their efforts to meet new challenges.

 Minimize competitive situations in which students might compare themselves unfavorably with peers.

Chapter 11 describes more specific effects of teacher expectations.

 Point out things that students do well, and present any negative feedback within the context of overall positive regard.

 Get students actively involved in successful group activities.

## DEVELOPMENTAL CHANGES IN SENSE OF SELF

We've already seen one way in which self-perceptions change with age: Children increasingly differentiate among the many aspects of who they are as people—academic aspects, physical aspects, social aspects, and so on. But children's and adolescents' beliefs and feelings about themselves change in other ways as well. Figure 3.1 presents Erik Erikson's early theory of how people's personalities and sense of self might continue to evolve throughout the life span. In the following sections, we'll look at what more contemporary researchers have learned about developmental changes in children's and adolescents' sense of self.

---

**FIGURE 3.1  Erikson's eight stages of psychosocial development**

**Overview of Erikson's Stages**

Erik Erikson (1963, 1972) proposed that people proceed through eight distinct stages over the course of their lives. Each stage presents a unique developmental task, and how a person addresses it influences her or his general mental health and progress through later stages.

**Trust versus mistrust (infancy).** According to Erikson, the major developmental task in infancy is to learn whether other people, especially primary caregivers, regularly satisfy basic needs. If caregivers are consistent sources of food and comfort, an infant learns *trust*—that others are dependable and reliable. If caregivers are neglectful or abusive, the infant learns *mistrust*—that the world is an undependable, unpredictable, and possibly dangerous place.

**Autonomy versus shame and doubt (toddler years).** As toddlers gain increasing muscular control, they begin to satisfy some of their own needs—for example, by feeding and dressing themselves. If caregivers encourage self-sufficient behavior, toddlers develop a sense of *autonomy*—a sense of being able to handle many problems on their own. But if caregivers demand too much too soon or, in contrast, restrict or ridicule early attempts at self-sufficiency, children may instead develop *shame and doubt* about their abilities.

**Initiative versus guilt (preschool years).** With their growing independence, preschoolers have many choices about the activities they pursue. If parents and preschool teachers encourage and support children's efforts while also helping them make realistic and appropriate choices, children develop *initiative*—independence in planning and undertaking activities. But if, instead, adults discourage the pursuit of independent activities or else dismiss them as silly and bothersome, children develop *guilt* about their needs and desires.

**Industry versus inferiority (elementary school years).** Elementary school provides many opportunities for children to achieve the recognition of teachers, parents, and peers by producing things—drawing pictures, writing short stories, and so on. If children are encouraged to make and do things and then praised for their accomplishments, they begin to demonstrate *industry* by being diligent, persevering at tasks until completed, and putting work before pleasure. If they are instead punished for their efforts or if they find they are incapable of meeting others' expectations, they develop a sense of *inferiority* about their capabilities.

**Identity versus role confusion (adolescence).** Adolescents begin to ponder the roles they might play in the adult world. Initially, they're apt to experience some *role confusion*—mixed ideas and feelings about the specific ways in which they will fit into society—and may experiment with a variety of behaviors and activities (e.g., tinkering with cars, babysitting for neighbors, affiliating with certain religious groups). Erikson proposed that eventually most adolescents achieve a sense of *identity* regarding who they are and where their lives are headed.

**Intimacy versus isolation (young adulthood).** Once young people have established their identities, they're ready to make long-term social commitments. Many become capable of *intimacy*, forming one or more reciprocal relationships that involve compromise and self-sacrifice. People who can't form intimate relationships—perhaps because they have trouble putting aside their own needs—develop a sense of *isolation*.

**Generativity versus stagnation (middle age).** During middle age the primary developmental task is one of contributing to society and helping to guide future generations. When a person makes a contribution during this period, he or she feels a sense of *generativity*—a sense of productivity and accomplishment. In contrast, a person who is self-centered and unable or unwilling to help society move forward develops a feeling of *stagnation*—a dissatisfaction with his or her relative lack of productivity.

**Integrity versus despair (retirement years).** As people reach retirement, they look back on their lives and accomplishments. They develop feelings of contentment and *integrity* if they believe that they have led a happy, productive life. Conversely, they may develop a sense of *despair* if they look back on a life of disappointments and unachieved goals.

**Critiquing Erikson's Theory**

Erikson's theory reminds us that development is a life-long process: Children and adults alike have new things to learn and new challenges to meet. At the same time, his theory has shortcomings. First, Erikson drew his ideas largely from personal anecdotes rather than systematic research (Crain, 2005). Second, he based his stages primarily on work with men; for many women, a focus on intimacy emerges either before or in conjunction with a focus on identity (Josselson, 1988). And third, Erikson didn't take into account the important role that culture plays in development. Many cultures intentionally discourage autonomy, initiative, and self-assertiveness in young children, sometimes as a way of protecting children from the very real dangers of their environments (X. Chen et al., 2009; Harwood, Miller, & Irizarry, 1995; G. J. Powell, 1983).

As teachers, we should keep in mind that the age ranges for accomplishing Erikson's eight developmental tasks are probably broader than Erikson proposed. For instance, most people probably don't achieve a sense of identity as early or as easily as Erikson suggested (see the discussion of older adolescents' sense of self). Nevertheless, the first five stages have implications for us as teachers, who must work hard to do the following:

- Help students overcome early difficulties with trust, autonomy, or initiative—in particular, by being reliable sources of affection and support (trust) and by giving students age-appropriate opportunities to work independently (autonomy) and undertake self-chosen activities (initiative).

- Promote a sense of industry by engaging students in meaningful tasks and completing worthwhile projects.

- Help adolescents in their search for identity by providing opportunities to explore various roles they might play in adult society.

**Childhood**   Elementary school children tend to think of themselves in terms of concrete, easily observable characteristics and behaviors—their age, sex, favorite activities, and so on (D. Hart, 1988; Harter, 1983). In racially and culturally diverse communities, where different skin colors, languages, and customs are obvious, children may also classify themselves as belonging to one or another racial or ethnic group (Phinney, 1990; Sheets, 1999). For instance, although my daughter Tina was raised in a European American family, her genetic heritage is Native American and Hispanic. In a self-portrait she drew in second grade (see Figure 3.2), she was clearly aware that her hair and skin tone were darker than those of most of her classmates.

Most young children have a generally positive sense of self. Sometimes they believe they're more capable than they really *are* and that they can easily overcome initial failures (R. Butler, 2008; Lockhart, Chang, & Story, 2002; Robins & Trzesniewski, 2005). As children have more opportunities to compare themselves with peers during the elementary grades and as they become cognitively more able to *make* such comparisons, their self-assessments become increasingly realistic (R. Butler, 2008; J. W. Chapman, Tunmer, & Prochnow, 2000; Davis-Kean et al., 2008). They also begin to pull together their many self-observations into generalizations about the kinds of people they are—perhaps friendly, good at sports, smart, or dumb—and such generalizations lead to the development of increasingly stable self-concepts (D. A. Cole et al., 2001; Harter, 1999).

**Early adolescence**   As students reach adolescence and gain greater capability for abstract thought, they increasingly think of themselves in terms of general, fairly stable traits. Consider my daughter Tina's self-description in sixth grade:

> I'm cool. I'm awesome. I'm way cool. I'm 12. I'm boy crazy. I go to Brentwood Middle School. I'm popular with my fans. I play viola. My best friend is Lindsay. I have a gerbil named Taj. I'm adopted. I'm beautiful.

Although Tina listed a few concrete features, she had clearly developed a fairly abstract self-perception. Her focus on coolness, popularity, and beauty, rather than on intelligence or academic achievement (or, I might add, modesty), is fairly typical: Social acceptance and physical appearance are far more important to many young adolescents than academic competence (D. Hart, 1988; Harter, 1999).

Students' self-concepts and self-esteem often drop as they make the transition from elementary school to middle school or junior high, with the drop being more pronounced for girls (D. A. Cole et al., 2001; Harter, 1999; Robins & Trzesniewski, 2005). The physiological changes accompanying puberty may be a factor: Many boys and girls think of themselves as being somewhat less attractive once they reach adolescence (S. Moore & Rosenthal, 2006; Stice, 2003). Changes in the school environment—including disrupted friendships, more superficial teacher–student relationships, and more rigorous academic standards—probably also have a negative impact.

Also with early adolescence come two new phenomena with implications for sense of self. First, students become more cognitively able to reflect on how others might see them (Harter, 1999). They may initially go to extremes, thinking that in any social situation everyone else's attention is focused squarely on them—a phenomenon known as the **imaginary audience** (Elkind, 1981; Lapsley, 1993; R. M. Ryan & Kuczkowski, 1994). Because they believe themselves to be the center of attention, young teenagers (especially girls) are often preoccupied with their physical appearance and can be quite self-critical.

A second noteworthy phenomenon in early adolescence is emergence of the **personal fable**: Young teenagers often believe they are completely unlike anyone else (Elkind, 1981; Lapsley, 1993). For instance, they may think that no one else—and certainly not parents and teachers—has ever experienced the intensity of emotions they feel about thwarted goals or unhappy love affairs. Furthermore, some have a sense of invulnerability and immortality, believing themselves immune to the normal dangers of life. Thus they may take foolish risks, such as experimenting with drugs and alcohol, having unprotected sexual intercourse, and driving at high speeds (DeRidder, 1993; Dodge et al., 2009; Jacobs & Klaczynski, 2002; Nell, 2002). It's important to note, however, that adolescents are apt to take risks even when they *don't* believe themselves to be invulnerable, for reasons you can discover in the Applying Brain Research feature "Understanding and Addressing Adolescent Risk Taking."

**FIGURE 3.2**   As early as the primary grades, students in racially diverse communities have some awareness of their membership in a particular racial group. Notice how 7-year-old Tina portrays herself as having darker hair and skin than the classmates behind her.

Remember that a student's sense of self becomes increasingly stable with age. In the upper elementary and secondary grades, then, enhancing a student's low self-esteem may take time and persistence.

**imaginary audience**   Belief that one is the center of attention in any social situation.

**personal fable**   Belief that one is completely unlike anyone else and so cannot be understood by others.

## Applying Brain Research

### Understanding and Addressing Adolescent Risk Taking

The human brain continues to mature in important ways throughout adolescence and early adulthood. With puberty come significant changes in brain regions that play a role in pleasure seeking, potentially heightening the desire for enjoyable activities and immediate rewards. Only later, perhaps in the late teens or early twenties, do regions of the prefrontal cortex that support rational decision making and self-restraint fully mature (Figner & Weber, 2011; Somerville, Jones, & Casey, 2010; Steinberg, 2009). Furthermore, young people show significant individual differences in brain activity levels in these important regions—differences that are correlated with their predisposition to seek out exciting but potentially dangerous activities, on the one hand, or to be cautious and prudent, on the other (Gianotti et al., 2009; Joseph, Liu, Jiang, Lynam, & Kelly, 2009).

For such reasons, many adolescents have trouble planning ahead and controlling their impulses (Spear, 2007; Steinberg, Cauffman, Woolard, Graham, & Banich, 2009). In addition, they tend to make choices based on emotions ("This will be fun") rather than on logic ("There's a high probability of a bad outcome") (Cleveland, Gibbons, Gerrard, Pomery, & Brody, 2005; V. F. Reyna & Farley, 2006; Steinberg, 2007). Thus, adolescent risk taking is most common in social contexts, where having fun is typically a high priority and it's easy to get swept away by what peers are doing or suggesting.

With such research findings in mind, I offer two recommendations.

🍏 **Channel adolescents' risk-taking tendencies into safe activities.** Many adolescents enjoy trying things that are new, different, and perhaps a bit risky; such activities are reasonable if appropriate safeguards are in place. Team sports provide one outlet for both risk taking and social camaraderie. Preplanned, organized activities during traditionally high-risk periods are also beneficial; for example, many high schools offer all-night after-prom parties to keep students sober and safe when they might otherwise be drinking and driving.

🍏 **Provide avenues through which students can safely and productively gain status with their peers.** Sometimes adolescents engage in risky behaviors—drinking, drug use, sexual intercourse, and the like—in an attempt to project an adultlike image, to be "cool" and "with it" (J. P. Allen & Antonishak, 2008; Blanton & Burkley, 2008; Crosnoe, 2011). There are much healthier ways to show one's coolness and withitness, some of which we can facilitate at school. Gaining competence and prominence in rock music, student government, and community service are just a few of the many possibilities.

---

**Late adolescence**  The majority of older adolescents recover sufficiently from the double whammy of puberty and a changing school social environment to enjoy positive self-concepts and overall mental health (Harter, 1999; S. I. Powers, Hauser, & Kilner, 1989). The imaginary audience and personal fable phenomena slowly decline, although remnants remain throughout the high school years.

Older teenagers increasingly reflect on their own characteristics and abilities and begin to struggle with seeming inconsistencies in their self-perceptions, as one ninth grader explained:

> I really don't understand how I can switch so fast from being cheerful with my friends, then coming home and feeling anxious, and then getting frustrated and sarcastic with my parents. Which one is the *real* me? (Harter, 1999, p. 67)

Eventually, perhaps around eleventh grade, most students integrate their various self-perceptions into a complex, multifaceted sense of self that reconciles apparent contradictions—for instance, recognizing that their inconsistent behaviors on different occasions mean they are "flexible" (Harter, 1999).

As older adolescents pull the numerous parts of themselves together, many of them begin to form a general sense of identity: a self-constructed definition of who they are, what things they find important, and what goals they want to accomplish in life. In their ongoing search for a long-term identity, adolescents may initially take on temporary identities, aligning themselves with a particular peer group, insisting on a certain mode of dress, or continually changing their photo and self-description on Facebook (Alemán & Vartman, 2009; Greenhow, Robelia, & Hughes, 2009; Seaton, Scottham, & Sellers, 2006). Adolescents may also have somewhat different identities in different contexts, depending on the traditional roles they have played in each context (Eccles, 2009; Greeno, 2006). For example, a student might be a "loser" at school but a "star" in an out-of-school activity or a "leader" in a neighborhood gang.

Erik Erikson proposed that most people achieve an overall sense of identity by the end of adolescence (see Figure 3.1). In contrast, many contemporary developmental theorists believe that identity formation continues to be a work-in-progress well into adulthood (e.g., Bandura, 2008;

**identity** Self-constructed definition of who one is and what things are important to accomplish in life.

Eccles, 2009; Kaplan & Flum, 2009). Marcia (1980, 1991) has described four distinct patterns of behavior that may characterize the status of a young person's search for identity:

- *Identity diffusion.* The individual has made no commitment to a particular career path or ideological belief system. Some haphazard experimentation with particular roles or beliefs may have taken place, but the individual hasn't yet embarked on a serious exploration of issues related to self-definition.
- *Foreclosure.* The individual has made a firm commitment to an occupation, a particular set of beliefs, or both. The choices have been based largely on what others (especially parents) have prescribed, without an earnest exploration of other possibilities.
- *Moratorium.* The individual has no strong commitment to a particular career or set of beliefs but is actively exploring and considering a variety of professions and ideologies. In essence, the individual is undergoing an identity crisis.
- *Identity achievement.* After going through a period of moratorium, the individual has emerged with a clear choice of occupation, a commitment to particular political or religious beliefs, or both.

For most young people, the ideal situation seems to be to proceed through a period of moratorium—an exploration that may continue into adulthood—and to eventually settle on a clear identity (Berzonsky & Kuk, 2000; Marcia, 1988; Seaton et al., 2006).

Table 3.1 presents developmental changes in children's and adolescents' sense of self and offers suggestions for how we, as teachers, can enhance their self-perceptions at different grade levels.

## DIVERSITY IN SENSE OF SELF

As you undoubtedly know from your own experiences, students differ considerably in their self-esteem and overall sense of self. Sometimes such differences are indirectly the result of biology. For instance, students who are physically attractive tend to have more positive self-concepts than students with less appealing physical features (Harter, Whitesell, & Junkin, 1998). And on average, students with cognitive, social, or physical disabilities have lower self-esteem than their classmates (T. Bryan, 1991; Marsh & Craven, 1997; Martinez & Huberty, 2010).

**Gender differences**   Some researchers find gender differences in overall self-esteem, with boys rating themselves more highly than girls, especially in adolescence. Many students' self-perceptions tend to be consistent with stereotypes about what males and females are supposedly "good at." For instance, even when actual ability levels are the same, boys tend to rate themselves more highly in math and sports, and girls tend to rate themselves more highly in language and literacy (Bracken, 2009; D. A. Cole et al., 2001; Herbert & Stipek, 2005; Joët, Usher, & Bressoux, 2011).

**Cultural and ethnic differences**   In many Native American communities and many Middle Eastern and Far Eastern countries, children and adolescents see their group membership and connections with other individuals as central parts of who they are as human beings (Kağitçibaşi, 2007; M. Ross & Wang, 2010; Whitesell, Mitchell, Kaufman, Spicer, & the Voices of Indian Teens Project Team, 2006). In addition, many young people have a strong **ethnic identity**: They're both aware and proud of their ethnic group and willingly adopt some of the group's behaviors. Occasionally, students' ethnic identities can lead them to reject mainstream Western values. In some ethnic minority groups, peers may accuse high-achieving students of "acting white," a label that essentially means "You're not one of us" (Bergin & Cooks, 2008; Cross, Strauss, & Fhagen-Smith, 1999; Ogbu, 2008a). For the most part, however, students with a strong and positive ethnic identity do *well* in school both academically and socially (Altschul, Oyserman, & Bybee, 2006; Smokowski, Buchanan, & Bacalleo, 2009; M. B. Spencer, Noll, Stoltzfus, & Harpalani, 2001). Furthermore, pride in one's ethnic heritage and high academic achievement can serve as an emotional buffer against other people's prejudicial insults and discrimination (L. Allen & Aber, 2006; P. J. Cook & Ludwig, 2008; DuBois, Burk-Braxton, Swenson, Tevendale, & Hardesty, 2002). Consider this statement by Eva, an African American high school student, as an example:

> I'm proud to be black and everything. But, um, I'm aware of, you know, racist acts and racist things that are happening in the world, but I use that as no excuse, you know. I feel as though I can succeed. . . . I just know that I'm not gonna let [racism] stop me. (Way, 1998, p. 257)

**ethnic identity**   Awareness of one's membership in a particular ethnic or cultural group, and willingness to adopt behaviors characteristic of the group.

Encourage students to take pride in their cultural heritage.

# DEVELOPMENTAL TRENDS

## TABLE 3.1 • Sense of Self at Different Grade Levels

| GRADE LEVEL | AGE-TYPICAL CHARACTERISTICS | EXAMPLE | SUGGESTED STRATEGIES |
|---|---|---|---|
| K–2 | • Self-descriptions largely limited to concrete, easily observable characteristics<br>• Some tendency to overestimate abilities and chances of future success, especially in domains in which one has little or no prior experience | When 6-year-old Jeff is asked to describe himself, he says, "I like animals. I like making things. I do good in school. I'm happy. Blue eyes, yellow hair, light skin." He mentions nothing about his shyness, sense of humor, and ability to work and play independently—characteristics that would require considerable self-reflection and abstract thought to identify. | • Encourage students to stretch their abilities by tackling the challenging tasks they think they can accomplish.<br>• Provide sufficient scaffolding to make success possible in various domains.<br>• Praise students for the things they do well; be specific about the behaviors you're praising. |
| 3–5 | • Increasing awareness of and differentiation among particular strengths and weaknesses<br>• Association of such emotions as pride and shame with various self-perceptions | When Kellen begins fifth grade at his neighborhood middle school, his class work rapidly deteriorates, despite individualized instruction in reading and spelling. At home one day, his mother finds him curled in a ball under his desk, crying and saying, "I can't do this anymore!" Alarmed, she takes him to a series of specialists, who diagnose severe dyslexia. Kellen's parents eventually find a school that provides considerable structure and scaffolding for students with learning disabilities. There Kellen shows dramatic improvement in virtually every area of the curriculum, and his self-esteem skyrockets. | • Focus students' attention on their improvement over time.<br>• Encourage pride in individual and group achievements, but be aware that students from some ethnic groups may prefer that recognition be given only for group achievements.<br>• Provide opportunities for students to look at one another's work only when *everyone* has something to be proud of. |
| 6–8 | • Increasingly abstract self-conceptions<br>• For many, a decline in self-esteem after the transition to middle or junior high school (especially for girls)<br>• Heightened concern about others' perceptions and judgments of oneself (imaginary audience)<br>• Excessive belief in one's own uniqueness, sometimes accompanied by risk taking and a sense of invulnerability to normal dangers (personal fable) | Meghan describes a recent event in her eighth-grade algebra class: "I had to cough but I knew if I did everyone would stare at me and think I was stupid, hacking away. So I held my breath until I turned red and tears ran down my face and finally I coughed anyway and everyone *really* noticed then. It was horrible." | • After students make the transition to middle school or junior high, be especially supportive and optimistic about their abilities and potential for success.<br>• Minimize opportunities for students to compare their own performance unfavorably with that of others.<br>• Be patient when students show exceptional self-consciousness; give them strategies for presenting themselves well to others. |
| 9–12 | • Search for the "real me" and an adult identity; experimentation with a variety of possible identities<br>• Increasing integration of diverse self-perceptions into an overall, multifaceted sense of self<br>• Gradual increase in self-esteem<br>• Continuing risk-taking behavior (especially for boys) | Sixteen-year-old Kayla often revises her profile on Facebook, editing her interests and favorites, the "About Me" section, and so on. And she regularly changes the photo that appears at the top of her profile. Sometimes she displays a happy Kayla, at other times a more sullen one; an early photo shows her in her basketball uniform, but a later one shows her in a skimpy party dress. | • Give students opportunities to examine and try out a variety of adultlike roles.<br>• Encourage students to explore and take pride in their cultural and ethnic heritages.<br>• When discussing the potential consequences of risky behaviors, present the facts but don't make students so anxious or upset that they can't effectively learn and remember the information (e.g., avoid scare tactics). |

*Sources:* Bracken, 2009; R. Butler, 2008; Davis-Kean et al., 2008; Dweck, 2000; Elkind, 1981; Figner & Weber, 2011; Greenhow, Robelia, & Hughes, 2009; Harter, 1999; Lockhart et al., 2002; Marcia, 1980, 1991; T. M. McDevitt & Ormrod, 2007 (Kellen example); Nell, 2002; Nuemi, 2008; O'Mara et al., 2006; Orenstein, 1994, p. 47 (Meghan example); Pajares, 2009; Robins & Trzesniewski, 2005; Seaton et al., 2006; Spear, 2007; Tatum, 1997; Whitesell et al., 2006.

Not all students from minority groups affiliate strongly with their cultural and ethnic groups. Some students—especially those with multiple racial or cultural heritages—fluctuate in the strength of their ethnic identity depending on the context and situation (Hitlin, Brown, & Elder, 2006; Y.-Y. Hong, Wan, No, & Chiu, 2007; Yip & Fuligni, 2002). In addition, older adolescents may experiment with varying forms of an ethnic identity. Some teens, for instance, may initially adopt a fairly intense, inflexible, and perhaps hostile ethnic identify before eventually retreating to a more relaxed, open-minded, and productive one (Cross et al., 1999; Nasir, McLaughlin, & Jones, 2009; Seaton et al., 2006).

# Development of Peer Relationships and Interpersonal Understandings

For many students, relationships with peers are a high priority. For example, listen to 15-year-old Greg in "Motivation: Late Adolescence."

For many students, interacting with and gaining the acceptance of peers—in some way *fitting in*—are more important than classroom learning and achievement (Crosnoe, 2011; Dowson & McInerney, 2001; LaFontana & Cillessen, 2010). Yet social success and academic success aren't an either-or situation. In fact, students who enjoy good relationships with their peers at school are *more* likely to achieve at high levels (Gest, Domitrovich, & Welsh, 2005; Patrick, Anderman, & Ryan, 2002; Pellegrini & Bohn, 2005).

## ROLES OF PEERS IN CHILDREN'S DEVELOPMENT

Peer relationships, especially friendships, serve at least three unique functions in children's and adolescents' personal and social development. For one thing, they provide an arena for learning and practicing a variety of social skills, including cooperation, negotiation, emotional control, and conflict resolution (J. P. Allen & Antonishak, 2008; Coplan & Arbeau, 2009; Larson & Brown, 2007). In addition, peers provide companionship, safety, and emotional support, as illustrated in Figure 3.3. They become a group with whom to eat lunch, a safe haven from playground bullies, and shoulders to cry on in times of trouble or confusion (Jordan, 2006; Laursen, Bukowski, Aunola, & Nurmi, 2007; Wentzel, 2009). Many adolescents (especially girls) reveal their innermost thoughts and feelings to their friends (Levitt, Guacci-Franco, & Levitt, 1993; Patrick et al., 2002; A. J. Rose, 2002). Friends often understand a teenager's perspectives—the preoccupation with physical appearance, concerns about the opposite sex, and so on—when others are seemingly clueless.

Peers play a third important role in personal and social development as well: They serve as socialization agents that help to mold children's behaviors and beliefs (B. B. Brown, Bakken, Ameringer, & Mahon, 2008; A. M. Ryan, 2000). For example, they define options for leisure time—perhaps getting together to study or, instead, to drink a few beers. They serve as role models and provide standards for acceptable behavior, showing what's possible, what's admirable, what's cool. And they sanction one another for stepping beyond acceptable bounds, perhaps through ridicule, gossip, or ostracism. Such **peer pressure** has its greatest effects during early adolescence, with teenagers who have weak emotional bonds to their families being especially susceptible (Berndt, Laychak, & Park, 1990; Erwin, 1993; Urdan & Maehr, 1995).

## THE REAL SCOOP ON PEER PRESSURE

A common misconception is that peer pressure is invariably a bad thing. In fact, it's a mixed bag. Many peers encourage such desirable qualities as working hard in school, treating people kindly, and engaging in community service. Others, however, encourage cutting class, engaging in aggression, consuming alcohol or drugs, or in other ways behaving unproductively (Mayeux, Houser, & Dyches, 2011; Prinstein & Dodge, 2008; Spinrad & Eisenberg, 2009; E. N. Walker, 2006; Wentzel & Looney, 2007).

Although peer pressure certainly is a factor affecting development, its overall influence on children's behaviors has probably been overrated. Most children acquire a strong set of values and behavioral standards from their families, and they don't necessarily abandon these values and standards in the company of peers (B. B. Brown, 1990; W. A. Collins et al., 2000; Galambos, Barker, & Almeida, 2003). Furthermore, they tend to choose friends who are similar to themselves in academic achievement, leisure-time activities, and long-term goals (Kindermann, 2007; Prinstein & Dodge, 2008; A. M. Ryan, 2001).

**FIGURE 3.3** In this writing sample, 7-year-old Andrew describes the many benefits of having friends.

> Friends our for you when you are lonley and sad. they play with you, they are nice, they are mean. they tell stores And the things they Do. they walk you to the nurse,

**peer pressure** Phenomenon whereby age-mates encourage some behaviors and discourage others.

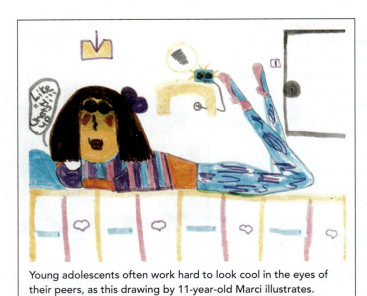

Young adolescents often work hard to look cool in the eyes of their peers, as this drawing by 11-year-old Marci illustrates.

Much of the pressure to conform to others' standards and expectations actually comes from within rather than from outside. In particular, most children and adolescents engage in self-socialization, putting pressure on *themselves* to adopt the behaviors they think others will find acceptable (B. B. Brown, 1990; Bukowski, Velasquez, & Brendgen, 2008; Crosnoe, 2011; Juvonen, 2006). For instance, many young adolescents are quite concerned about adhering to self-construed social norms, to the point of imitating peers' choices in dress, slang, and other behaviors. In some cases, they may lead double lives that enable them to attain academic success while maintaining peer acceptance (Grimes, 2002; Hemmings, 2004; Juvonen, 2006; Mac Iver, Reuman, & Main, 1995). For example, although they attend class and faithfully do homework, they may feign disinterest in scholarly activities, disrupt class with jokes or goofy behaviors, and express surprise at receiving high grades. In addition, they may act tough when they're in public, saving their softer sides for more private circumstances, as one sixth grader's reflection reveals:

You'd still have to have your bad attitude. You have to act—it's just like a movie. You have to act. And then at home you're a regular kind of guy, you don't act mean or nothing. But when you're around your friends you have to be sharp and stuff like that, like push everybody around. (Juvonen & Cadigan, 2002, p. 282)

Help students look good in the eyes of their peers.

As teachers, we can help students maintain a good public image in a variety of ways. For instance, we can help them acquire skills for presenting themselves in a favorable light—public-speaking techniques, personal hygiene strategies, and so on. We can assign small-group projects in which every student has a unique talent to contribute. And when valued classmates ridicule academic achievement, we can allow students to demonstrate their accomplishments privately (e.g., through written assignments or one-on-one conversations) instead of in front of classmates.

## CHARACTERISTICS OF PEER RELATIONSHIPS

Some peers are, of course, more influential than others. In this section we look at a variety of peer relationships and then consider the effects of popularity and social isolation.

### FRIENDSHIPS

Close friends find activities that are mutually meaningful and enjoyable, and over time they acquire a common set of experiences that enable them to share certain perspectives on life (Gottman, 1986; Suttles, 1970). Because friends typically have an emotional investment in their relationship, they work hard to look at situations from one another's point of view and to resolve disputes that threaten to separate them. As a result, they develop increased perspective-taking and conflict resolution skills. Close friendships also foster self-esteem and a general sense of well-being (Basinger, Gibbs, & Fuller, 1995; Berndt, 1992; Bukowski, Motzoi, & Meyer, 2009; Newcomb & Bagwell, 1995).

As children get older, their friendships increasingly involve emotional attachments as well as sources of recreation. Observe this developmental trend in "Friendships."

### LARGER SOCIAL GROUPS

With age and experience, many students form larger social groups that frequently get together. In early adolescence, cliques—moderately stable friendship groups of perhaps three to ten individuals—provide the setting for most voluntary social interactions. Clique boundaries tend to be fairly rigid and exclusive—some people are "in," others are "out"—and memberships in various cliques often affect students' social status (B. B. Brown, 2011; Crockett, Losoff, & Peterson, 1984; Goodwin, 2006; Kindermann, McCollam, & Gibson, 1996).

Crowds are considerably larger than cliques and don't have the tight-knit cohesiveness and carefully drawn boundaries of cliques. Their members tend to share certain characteristics and behaviors (e.g., "brains" study a lot, "jocks" are active in sports), attitudes about academic achievement, and (occasionally) ethnic background (B. B. Brown, 2011; Steinberg, 1996). Crowd membership may or may not be a voluntary thing; for instance, membership in a so-called "popular" crowd is apt to be based as much on a student's reputation as on his or her actual efforts to affiliate with certain peers (B. B. Brown et al., 2008; Juvonen & Galván, 2008).

Occasionally a crowd takes the form of a subculture, a group that resists a powerful dominant culture by adopting a significantly different lifestyle (J. S. Epstein, 1998). Some subcultures are relatively benign; for example, the baggy-pants skaters with whom my son Alex affiliated spent much of their free time riding skateboards and addressing everyone as "dude." Other subcultures are worrisome, such as those that endorse racist and anti-Semitic behaviors (e.g., skinheads) and those that practice Satanic worship and rituals. Adolescents are more likely to affiliate with troublesome subcultures when they feel alienated from the dominant culture—perhaps that of their school or that of society more generally—and want to distinguish themselves from it in some way (Crosnoe, 2011; J. R. Harris, 1998).

In the upper high school grades, a greater capacity for abstract thought allows many adolescents to think of other people more as unique individuals and less as members of stereotypical categories. They may also discover characteristics they have in common with peers from diverse backgrounds. Perhaps as a result of such changes, ties to specific social groups tend to dissipate, hostilities between groups soften, and students become more flexible in their friendship choices (B. B. Brown, Eicher, & Petrie, 1986; Gavin & Fuhrman, 1989; Shrum & Cheek, 1987).

### GANGS

A gang is a cohesive social group characterized by initiation rites, distinctive colors and symbols, "ownership" of a specific territory, and feuds with one or more rival groups. Typically, gangs are governed by strict rules for behavior and stiff penalties for violations. Adolescents (and sometimes younger children as well) affiliate with gangs for a variety of reasons. Some do so as a way of demonstrating loyalty to their family, friends, or neighborhood. Some seek the status and prestige that gang membership brings. Some have poor academic records and perceive gang activity as an alternative means of gaining recognition for accomplishments. Many members of gangs have troubled relationships with their families or have been consistently rejected by peers, and so they turn to gangs to get the emotional support they can find nowhere else (Dishion, Piehler, & Myers, 2008; Kodluboy, 2004; Petersen, 2004; Simons, Whitbeck, Conger, & Conger, 1991).

As teachers, we can definitely make a difference in the lives of any gang members in our classes (S. G. Freedman, 1990; Parks, 1995). We must, first and foremost, show these students that we truly care about them and their well-being. For instance, we can be willing listeners in times of trouble and can provide the support that gang members need to achieve both academic and social success. We must also have some knowledge of students' backgrounds—their cultural values, economic circumstances, and so on—so that we can better understand the issues with which they may be dealing. And we must certainly work cooperatively and proactively with our colleagues to minimize violent gang activity at school.

### ROMANTIC RELATIONSHIPS

As early as the primary grades, children talk of having boyfriends or girlfriends, and the opposite sex is a subject of interest throughout the elementary school years. With the onset of adolescence, the biological changes of puberty bring on new and sometimes unsettling feelings and sexual desires. Not surprisingly, then, romance is a frequent topic of conversation in the middle and high school grades. Middle school students' romances tend to exist more in their minds than in reality; for instance, two students might be identified as "going out" even if they never actually date. Young adolescents' romantic thoughts may also involve crushes on people who are out of reach—perhaps favorite teachers or movie stars (B. B. Brown, 1999; Eckert, 1989; B. C. Miller & Benson, 1999).

Eventually many adolescents begin to date, especially if their friends are dating. Early choices in dating partners are often based on physical attractiveness or social status, and dates may involve only limited and superficial interaction (B. B. Brown, 2011; Furman, Brown, & Feiring, 1999; Pellegrini, 2002). As adolescents move into the high school grades, some form more intense, affectionate, and long-term relationships with members of the opposite sex, and these relationships often (but by no means always) lead to sexual intimacy (J. Connolly & Goldberg, 1999; Furman & Collins, 2009). The age of first sexual intercourse has decreased steadily over the last few decades; in the United States in recent years, fewer than half of 18-year-olds have remained virgins (S. Moore & Rosenthal, 2006).

**self-socialization** Tendency to integrate personal observations and others' input into self-constructed standards for behavior and to choose actions consistent with those standards.

**clique** Moderately stable friendship group of perhaps three to ten members.

**crowd** Large, loose-knit social group that shares certain common interests and behaviors.

**subculture** Group that resists the ways of the dominant culture and adopts its own norms for behavior.

**gang** Cohesive social group characterized by initiation rites, distinctive colors and symbols, territorial orientation, and feuds with rival groups.

Provide the academic, social, and emotional support that gang members need to be successful at school.

Chapter 13 offers specific strategies for minimizing—and ideally eliminating—gang-related aggression and violence at school.

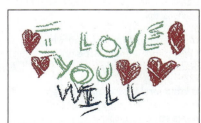

For many children, thoughts of romance emerge early, as 5-year-old Isabelle's artwork illustrates.

From a developmental standpoint, romantic relationships have definite benefits: They can address young people's needs for companionship, affection, and security, and they provide an opportunity to experiment with new social skills and interpersonal behaviors (Davila, 2008; Furman & Simon, 2008; B. C. Miller & Benson, 1999). At the same time, romance can wreak havoc with adolescents' emotions. Adolescents have more extreme mood swings than younger children or adults, and for many this instability may be partly due to the excitement and frustration of being romantically involved or *not* involved (Davila, 2008; Furman & Collins, 2009; Larson, Clore, & Wood, 1999).

As students reach high school (occasionally earlier), a significant minority of them find themselves attracted to their own sex either instead of or in addition to the opposite sex. Adolescence can be a particularly confusing time for gay, lesbian, and bisexual individuals. Some struggle to make sense of their sexual orientation and may experience considerable depression. Yet many others enjoy good mental health, especially if their home and school environments communicate acceptance of diverse sexual orientations (Espelage, Aragon, Birkett, & Koenig, 2008; J. P. Robinson & Espelage, 2011; Savin-Williams, 2008).

The extent to which we, as teachers, talk about sexuality with our students must be dictated, in part, by the policies of the school and the values of the community in which we work. At the same time, especially if we're teaching at the middle school or high school level, we must be aware that romantic and sexual relationships, whether real or imagined, are a considerable source of excitement, frustration, confusion, and distraction for students, and we must lend a sympathetic ear and an open mind to those students who seek our counsel and support.

 Offer emotional support when valued romantic relationships fizzle or don't materialize.

## POPULARITY AND SOCIAL ISOLATION

When my daughter Tina was in junior high school, she sometimes told me, "No one likes the popular kids." As self-contradictory as Tina's remark might seem, it's consistent with research findings. When students are asked to identify their most "popular" classmates, they identify peers who have dominant social status at school (perhaps those who belong to a prestigious social group) but in many cases are aggressive or snobby (Cillessen, Schwartz, & Mayeux, 2011; W. E. Ellis & Zarbatany, 2007). Truly popular students—those whom many classmates select as people they'd like to do things with—may or may not hold high-status positions, but they're kind and socially skillful, as Lupita is in the opening case study. They also tend to show genuine concern for others—for instance, by sharing, cooperating, and empathizing with peers (Asher & McDonald, 2009; Cillessen & Rose, 2005; Mayeux et al., 2011).

In contrast to popular students, rejected students are those whom classmates select as being the *least* preferred social companions. Students with few social skills—for example, those who are impulsive or aggressive—typically experience peer rejection (Bukowski, Brendgen, & Vitaro, 2007; S. Pedersen, Vitaro, Barker, & Borge, 2007; Pellegrini, Bartini, & Brooks, 1999). Students who are noticeably overweight and those who appear to be gay or lesbian are also frequent targets of ridicule, harassment, and rejection (Swearer, Espelage, Vaillancourt, & Hymel, 2010). When students experience consistent peer rejection over a lengthy period, they may withdraw either physically or mentally from classroom activities, or they may engage in inappropriate attention-getting behaviors; in either case, their academic achievement suffers as a result (Bellmore, 2011; Ladd, Herald-Brown, & Reiser, 2008; Snyder et al., 2008).

A third group, controversial students, are a mixed bag, in that some peers really like them and others really *dis*like them. These students can, like rejected students, be quite aggressive, but they also have good social skills that make them popular with at least some of their peers (Asher & McDonald, 2009; Mayeux et al., 2011; D. Schwartz & Gorman, 2011).

Researchers have described a fourth category as well. Neglected students are those whom peers rarely choose as someone they would either most like or least like to do something with (Asher & Renshaw, 1981). Some neglected students prefer to be alone, others are quite shy or don't know how to go about initiating interaction, and still others are content with having only one or two close friends (Gazelle & Ladd, 2003; Guay, Boivin, & Hodges, 1999; McElhaney, Antonishak, & Allen, 2008). For some students, neglected status is a relatively temporary situation. Others are totally friendless for extended periods—for instance, this is often the case for recent immigrants and for students with disabilities—and these students are at increased risk for depression (Gazelle & Ladd, 2003; Igoa, 2007; Yuker, 1988).

In this self-portrait, 10-year-old Sarah characterizes herself as a nerd ("neard")—that is, as someone who isn't as "cool" as she might be within her peer group.

**popular student**  Student whom many peers like and perceive to be kind and trustworthy.

**rejected student**  Student whom many peers identify as being an undesirable social partner.

**controversial student**  Student whom some peers strongly like and other peers strongly dislike.

**neglected student**  Student about whom most peers have no strong feelings, either positive or negative.

Especially in the middle school and high school grades, most students are well aware of which peers do and don't have high social status. Some students put considerable pressure on themselves to gain or maintain membership in an allegedly "popular" group, occasionally casting old friends aside and engaging in socially hurtful behaviors in an effort to gain the admiration of prestigious peers. Not all of these students successfully climb to the top of the social hierarchy, of course, and their failure to do so can leave them feeling isolated, depressed, and uninterested in school achievement (Cillessen et al., 2011; Crosnoe, 2011).

As teachers, we can help offset the hard feelings that peer rejection or neglect may engender by being particularly warm and attentive to socially isolated students (Crosnoe, 2011; Wentzel, 1999). In fact, when *we* show that we like particular students, their classmates are more likely to accept and act positively toward them as well (Chang, 2003; Chang et al., 2004). We can also assist with interpersonal skills. Because of their social isolation, rejected and neglected students have fewer opportunities to develop the social skills that many of them desperately need (Coie & Cillessen, 1993; McElhaney et al., 2008).

 Model positive feelings and behaviors toward rejected and neglected students, and help these students acquire good social skills.

## SOCIAL COGNITION

To be effective in interpersonal relationships, students must engage in social cognition: They must consider how people around them are likely to think about, behave in, and react to various situations. Those who think regularly about other people's thoughts and feelings tend to be socially skillful and make friends easily (Bosacki, 2000; P. L. Harris, 2006; Izard et al., 2001). Some psychologists propose that social cognition is a distinct human ability—which they call *emotional intelligence*—whereas others believe that it is simply an integral part of people's general intellectual and social functioning (J. D. Mayer, Salovey, & Caruso, 2008; Waterhouse, 2006; Zeidner, Roberts, & Matthews, 2002).

### PERSPECTIVE TAKING

One important element of social cognition is perspective taking, looking at the world from other people's viewpoints. The following situation provides an example.

### ■ ■ EXPERIENCING FIRSTHAND
### LAST PICKED

Consider this scenario:

> Kenny and Mark are co-captains of the soccer team. They have one person left to choose for the team. Without saying anything, Mark winks at Kenny and looks at Tom, who is one of the remaining children left to be chosen for the team. Mark looks back at Kenny and smiles. Kenny nods and chooses Tom to be on their team. Tom sees Mark and Kenny winking and smiling at each other. Tom, who is usually one of the last to be picked for team sports, wonders why Kenny wants him to be on his team. . . .

- Why did Mark smile at Kenny?
- Why did Kenny nod?
- Why did Kenny choose Tom to be on the team? How do you know this?
- Do you think that Tom has any idea of why Kenny chose him to be on the team? How do you know this? . . .
- How do you think Tom feels? (Bosacki, 2000, p. 711)

To answer these questions, you must look at the situation from the perspectives of the three children involved. For instance, if you put yourself in Tom's shoes, you might suspect that he has mixed feelings. If he enjoys soccer, he may be happy to have a chance to play, but he may also be wondering whether the other boys' nonverbal signals indicate a malicious intention to make him look foolish on the soccer field. And, of course, Tom may feel embarrassed or demoralized at consistently being one of the last children picked for a team. (Accordingly, asking some students to select classmates for team games is generally *not* recommended.)

Recent brain research indicates that, to some degree, human beings may be "prewired" to look at situations from other people's perspectives as well as their own. In particular, certain

**social cognition** Process of thinking about how other people are likely to think, act, and react.

**perspective taking** Ability to look at a situation from someone else's viewpoint.

**mirror neuron**  Neuron in the brain that fires either when a person is performing a particular behavior or when the person sees someone else perform the behavior.

**theory of mind**  Self-constructed understanding of one's own and other people's mental and psychological states (thoughts, feelings, etc.).

**recursive thinking**  Thinking about what other people may be thinking about oneself, possibly through multiple iterations.

neurons in the brain, known as mirror neurons, fire either when a person is performing a particular behavior *or* when the person watches *someone else* perform that behavior. Some of these mirror neurons are involved both in feeling certain emotions—perhaps disgust or anguish—and in observing such emotions in others' facial expressions (Gallese, Gernsbacher, Heyes, Hickok, & Iacoboni, 2011; Rizzolatti & Sinigaglia, 2008).

Yet truly effective perspective taking also involves active, conscious thinking and learning about human beings' general mental and psychological states. As children grow older, most develop and increasingly refine a theory of mind—a self-constructed understanding of their own and others' thoughts, beliefs, feelings, and motives. The development of a theory of mind appears to involve the prefrontal cortex of the brain—a part of the brain that continues to mature over the course of childhood and adolescence (Liu, Sabbagh, Gehring, & Wellman, 2009; Steinberg, 2009).

Probably as a result of both experience and brain maturation, children gain an increasingly complex understanding of human thought processes and feelings as they grow older, enabling them to become increasingly effective in interacting with others (Flavell, 2000; A. Gopnik & Meltzoff, 1997; Wellman & Gelman, 1998).

**Childhood**    Consistent with what we know about cognitive development, young children tend to focus on other people's concrete, observable characteristics and behaviors (e.g., look once again at Andrew's essay in Figure 3.3). However, they do have some awareness of other people's inner worlds. As early as age 4 or 5, they realize that what *they* know may be different from what *other people* know (Wellman, Cross, & Watson, 2001; Wimmer & Perner, 1983). They also have some ability to make inferences about other people's mental and emotional states—for instance, to deduce that people who behave in certain ways have certain intentions or feelings (P. L. Harris, 2006; Schult, 2002; Wellman, Phillips, & Rodriguez, 2000). As children progress through the elementary grades, they also begin to understand that people's actions don't always reflect their thoughts and feelings—for instance, that someone who appears to be happy may actually feel sad (Flavell, Miller, & Miller, 2002; Gnepp, 1989; Selman, 1980).

**Early adolescence**    Most young adolescents realize that people can have mixed feelings about events and other individuals (Donaldson & Westerman, 1986; Flavell & Miller, 1998; Harter & Whitesell, 1989). And courtesy of their expanding cognitive abilities, memory capacity, and social awareness, young adolescents become capable of recursive thinking (Oppenheimer, 1986; Perner & Wimmer, 1985). That is, they can think about what other people might be thinking about them and eventually can reflect on other people's thoughts about them through multiple iterations (e.g., "You think that I think that you think . . ."). This isn't to say that adolescents (or adults, for that matter) always use this capacity, however. Consistent with our earlier discussion of the *imaginary audience,* focusing primarily about one's *own* perspective is a common phenomenon in the early adolescent years (Tsethlikai & Greenhoot, 2006; Tsethlikai, Guthrie-Fulbright, & Loera, 2007).

When students seem focused only on their own points of view, encourage them to consider why others might reasonably think and behave as they do.

**Late adolescence**    In the high school years, teenagers can draw on a rich body of knowledge derived from numerous social experiences. Consequently, they become ever more skillful at drawing inferences about people's psychological characteristics, intentions, and needs (Eisenberg, Carlo, Murphy, & Van Court, 1995; Paget, Kritt, & Bergemann, 1984). In addition, they're more attuned to the complex dynamics that influence behavior—not only thoughts, feelings, and present circumstances but also past experiences (C. A. Flanagan & Tucker, 1999; Selman, 1980). What we see emerging in the high school years, then, is a budding psychologist: an individual who can be quite astute in deciphering and explaining the motives and actions of others.

Social cognition becomes increasingly sophisticated with age. For example, listen to children of various ages in "Emotions."

**Promoting perspective taking**    Virtually any classroom offers many opportunities for perspective taking. One strategy is to talk frequently about people's thoughts, feelings, and motives (Ruffman, Slade, & Crowe, 2002; Wittmer & Honig, 1994; Woolfe, Want, & Siegal, 2002). In the process, we must, of course, use age-appropriate language. With first graders we might use such words as *think, want,* and *sadness.* With fifth graders we might talk about *misunderstanding, frustration,* and *mixed feelings.* Most high school students have the cognitive and social reasoning capabilities to understand fairly abstract and complex psychological terms, such as *being passive-aggressive* and *having an inner moral compass.*

Another important strategy is to take advantage of situations in which people have diverse perspectives and beliefs about a situation. For example, in times of disagreement or conflict, students and teachers alike benefit from putting themselves in the other party's shoes (Adalbjarnardottir & Selman, 1997; Gehlbach, Brinkworth, & Harris, 2011). And when two or more students clash in the classroom or elsewhere on school grounds, an effective approach is *peer mediation,* in which specially trained peers elicit their differing points of view and help them reach an equitable solution (Deutsch, 1993; D. W. Johnson & Johnson, 1996, 2006).

Opportunities for perspective taking also arise in lessons about academic subject matter. For example, in discussions of current events, teachers might have different students—or, using the Internet, different classrooms—take different countries' perspectives as they explore significant world problems, such as climate change or arms control (Gehlbach et al., 2008).

## SOCIAL INFORMATION PROCESSING

Children and adolescents have a lot to think about when they consider what other people are thinking, feeling, and doing. The mental processes involved in understanding and responding to social events are collectively known as social information processing (e.g., Burgess, Wojslawowicz, Rubin, Rose-Krasnor, & Booth-LaForce, 2006; Fontaine, Yang, Dodge, Bates, & Pettit, 2008; E. R. Smith & Semin, 2007). Among other things, social information processing involves paying *attention* to certain behaviors in a social situation and trying to *interpret* and make sense of those behaviors. For example, when students interact with classmates, they might focus on certain remarks, facial expressions, and body language and try to figure out what a classmate really means by, say, a thoughtless comment or sheepish grin. Students also consider one or more *goals* they hope to achieve during an interaction—perhaps preserving a friendship, on the one hand, or teaching somebody a "lesson," on the other. Then, taking into account both their interpretations and their goals, students draw on their previous knowledge and experiences to identify a number of possible responses and choose what is, in their eyes, a productive course of action. As we'll see in the next section, an understanding of social information processing is especially helpful in explaining why some students are unusually aggressive toward their peers.

## AGGRESSION

Aggressive behavior is an action intentionally taken to hurt another person either physically or psychologically. It sometimes involves physical aggression, an action that can potentially cause bodily injury (e.g., hitting, shoving). In other cases it involves psychological aggression, an action intended to cause mental anguish or reduce self-esteem. One form of psychological aggression is relational aggression, an action that can adversely affect friendships and other interpersonal relationships (e.g., ostracizing a peer, spreading unkind rumors). As a general rule, aggression declines over the course of childhood and adolescence, but it increases for a short time after students make the transition from elementary school to middle school or junior high (Pellegrini, 2002).

Researchers have identified two distinct groups of aggressive students (Crick & Dodge, 1996; Poulin & Boivin, 1999; Vitaro, Gendreau, Tremblay, & Oligny, 1998). Those who engage in proactive aggression deliberately initiate aggressive behaviors as a means of obtaining desired goals. Those who engage in reactive aggression act aggressively primarily in response to frustration or provocation. Of the two groups, students who exhibit proactive aggression are more likely to have trouble maintaining productive friendships (Hanish, Kochenderfer-Ladd, Fabes, Martin, & Denning, 2004; Poulin & Boivin, 1999). Those who direct considerable aggression toward particular peers—whether it be physical or psychological aggression—are known as bullies. Students who are immature, anxious, and socially isolated are frequent victims of bullies, as are students with nontraditional sexual orientations and students with disabilities (Hamovitch, 2007; J. P. Robinson & Espelage, 2011; M. W. Watson, Andreas, Fischer, & Smith, 2005).

Some children and adolescents are genetically more predisposed to aggression than their peers, and others may exhibit heightened aggression as a result of neurological abnormalities (Brendgen et al., 2008; Raine, 2008; van Goozen, Fairchild, & Harold, 2008). But environmental factors can foster aggressive behavior as well. Many aggressive students live in dysfunctional conditions at home, perhaps including frequent conflicts and displays of anger, harsh punishment or child maltreatment, and a general lack of affection and appropriate social behavior (Christenson, 2004; Maikovich, Jaffee, Odgers, & Gallop, 2008; Pettit, 2004). In addition, regular exposure to violence

---

*Frequently ask students to reflect on other people's thoughts, feelings, and motives.*

*Chapter 10 describes peer mediation in more detail.*

*Chapter 6 discusses information processing theory, on which this concept of social information processing is based.*

**social information processing** Mental processes involved in making sense of and responding to social events.

**aggressive behavior** Action intentionally taken to hurt another either physically or psychologically.

**physical aggression** Action that can potentially cause bodily injury.

**psychological aggression** Action intended to cause mental anguish or reduce self-esteem.

**relational aggression** Action that can adversely affect interpersonal relationships; a form of psychological aggression.

**proactive aggression** Deliberate aggression against another as a means of obtaining a desired goal.

**reactive aggression** Aggressive response to frustration or provocation.

**bully** Person who frequently threatens, harasses, or causes injury to particular peers.

**hostile attributional bias** Tendency to interpret others' behaviors as reflecting hostile or aggressive intentions.

in the community or through various media (e.g., television, music, video games) seems to increase aggressive behavior in young people (C. A. Anderson et al., 2003; Greitemeyer, 2011; Guerra, Huesmann, & Spindler, 2003; Huesmann, Moise-Titus, Podolski, & Eron, 2003).

It's important to note that many children and adolescents who are routinely exposed to violence at home or elsewhere are *not* especially aggressive (Margolin & Gordis, 2004; M. J. Pearce, Jones, Schwab-Stone, & Ruchkin, 2003). Certain cognitive and motivational factors seem to underlie aggressive behavior, including the following:

- *Poor perspective-taking ability.* Students who are highly aggressive tend to have limited ability to look at situations from other people's perspectives or to empathize with their victims (Coie & Dodge, 1998; Damon & Hart, 1988; Marcus, 1980).
- *Misinterpretation of social cues.* Students who are aggressive toward peers tend to interpret others' behaviors as reflecting hostile intentions, especially when those behaviors have ambiguous meanings. This hostile attributional bias is especially prevalent in children who are prone to *reactive* aggression (Bukowski et al., 2007; Crick, Grotpeter, & Bigbee, 2002; Dodge et al., 2003).
- *Prevalence of self-serving goals.* For most students, establishing and maintaining interpersonal relationships is a high priority. For aggressive students, however, achieving more self-serving goals—perhaps maintaining an inflated self-image, seeking revenge, or gaining power and dominance—often takes precedence (Baumeister et al., 1996; Cillessen & Rose, 2005; Menon et al., 2007; Pellegrini, Roseth, Van Ryzin, & Solberg, 2011).
- *Ineffective social problem-solving strategies.* Aggressive students often have little knowledge of how to persuade, negotiate, or compromise. Instead, they're apt to resort to hitting, shoving, barging into play activities, and other ineffective strategies (Neel, Jenkins, & Meadows, 1990; D. Schwartz et al., 1998; Troop-Gordon & Asher, 2005).
- *Belief in the appropriateness and effectiveness of aggression.* Many aggressive students believe that violence and other forms of aggression are acceptable ways of resolving conflicts and retaliating against others' misdeeds (Paciello, Fida, Tramontano, Lupinetti, & Caprara, 2008; M. W. Watson et al., 2005; Zelli, Dodge, Lochman, & Laird, 1999). Those who display high rates of *proactive* aggression are also apt to believe that aggressive action will yield positive results—for instance, that it will enhance social status at school or restore "honor" to one's family or social group (R. P. Brown, Osterman, & Barnes, 2009; Mayeux et al., 2011; Pellegrini & Bartini, 2000). Not surprisingly, aggressive children tend to associate with one another, thereby confirming one another's beliefs that aggression is appropriate (Crick, Murray-Close, Marks, & Mohajeri-Nelson, 2009; Espelage & Swearer, 2004).

Both initiators and recipients of aggression often have problems later on. Unless adults actively intervene, many aggressive students (especially those who exhibit proactive aggression) show a continuing pattern of aggression and violence as they grow older, and such a pattern almost guarantees long-term maladjustment and difficulties with peers (Dodge et al., 2003; Ladd & Troop-Gordon, 2003; Swearer et al., 2010). Meanwhile, children who are frequent targets of bullying can become anxious and depressed—sometimes suicidal—and their classroom performance deteriorates as a result (Hoglund, 2007; Russell et al., 2011; D. Schwartz, Gorman, Nakamoto, & Toblin, 2005; Swearer et al., 2010). An entry in one high school student's journal illustrates just how devastating bullying can be:

> One day in junior high, I was getting off the school bus from a seat in the back. . . . I heard people shouting, "Hey, Fatso!" "You big buffalo!" . . . In order to leave the bus I had to walk through a long crowded aisle and face the obnoxious girls. As I stood up, the girls followed. They crowded together, and approached me as if they were ready to strike at me. . . . The girls began to kick and sock me repeatedly. . . . They continued to hurt me as if there was nothing more important to them than to see me in pain. The last few kicks were the hardest; all I wanted to do was get off the bus alive. . . . Finally, after what seemed like an eternity, I was able to release myself from their torture. I got off the bus alive. Imagining that the worst had already passed, I began to walk away from the bus and the girls stuck their heads out the window and spit on me. I could not believe it! They spit on my face! . . . While I was cleaning my face with a napkin, I could still hear the girls laughing. (Freedom Writers, 1999, pp. 37–38)

Often the psychological aggression involved in bullying—taunts, name-calling, blatant exclusion from social activities, and so on—is more harmful than any physical aggression that accompanies it (Doll, Song, & Siemers, 2004; Goodwin, 2006).

Even innocent bystanders tend to suffer from the aggression they witness at school. For example, when they observe one classmate bullying another, their own sense of safety at school diminishes (M. J. Mayer & Furlong, 2010; Rivers, Poteat, Noret, & Ashurst, 2009). Furthermore, if they see bullying and other aggressive behaviors going unpunished, they may come to believe that such actions are perfectly acceptable (E. J. Meyer, 2009; D. T. Miller & Prentice, 1994).

As teachers, we *must* intervene when some students victimize others, and we must keep a watchful eye for additional incidents of physical or psychological aggression down the road. Regular victims of aggression need social and emotional support from us and from their classmates. Some may also need one or more sessions with a school counselor, perhaps to address feelings of vulnerability and depression or perhaps to learn skills that will minimize future victimization incidents (Espelage & Swearer, 2004; R. S. Newman, 2008; Yeung & Leadbeater, 2007).

The perpetrators of aggression require intervention as well. They must be given appropriate consequences for their actions, of course, but they should also be helped to behave more appropriately. Specific strategies should be tailored to the thoughts and motives that underlie their aggression. Such strategies as encouraging perspective taking, helping students interpret social situations more accurately, and teaching effective social problem-solving skills are potentially useful in reducing aggression and other disruptive behaviors (Cunningham & Cunningham, 2006; Frey, Hirschstein, Edstrom, & Snell, 2009; Guerra & Slaby, 1990; Horne, Orpinas, Newman-Carlson, & Bartolomucci, 2004; Hudley & Graham, 1993). Putting students in situations where they must explicitly *help*, rather than harm, others—for instance, asking them to tutor younger children—can also be beneficial (J. R. Sullivan & Conoley, 2004). Ultimately, interventions with aggressive students are most likely to be effective if schools communicate the importance of acting kindly and respectfully toward all members of the school community, teachers and students alike (Espelage & Swearer, 2004; E. J. Meyer, 2009; Parada, Craven, & Marsh, 2008; S. W. Ross & Horner, 2009).

## TECHNOLOGY AND PEER RELATIONSHIPS

With the advent of cell telephone technology, text-messaging software, and easy access to the Internet, many students now communicate quite frequently—daily, sometimes almost hourly—with some of their peers (Crosnoe, 2011; Greenhow et al., 2009; Valkenburg & Peter, 2009). For instance, e-mail and instant messaging ("IM-ing") allow quick and easy ways of asking classmates about homework assignments, making plans for weekend social activities, and seeking friends' advice and emotional support. Networking sites (e.g., facebook.com, myspace.com) provide a means of sharing personal information (e.g., news, interests, photos) and potentially finding like-minded age-mates. Internet-based chat rooms allow group discussions about virtually any topic. Judicious use of such mechanisms can enhance students' self-esteem, connectedness with peers, social problem solving, and general psychological well-being (Ellison, Steinfield, & Lampe, 2007; Greenhow et al., 2009; Gross, Juvonen, & Gable, 2002; Valkenburg & Peter, 2009).

Unfortunately, wireless technologies and the Internet also provide vehicles for cyberbullying—electronically transmitting hostile messages, broadcasting personally embarrassing information, or in other ways causing an individual significant psychological distress. For example, a student might upload humiliating video footage on YouTube, post humiliating (and possibly false) gossip on Facebook, or set up a website on which classmates can "vote" for their class's "biggest loser" or "easiest slut" (Shariff, 2008; Valkenburg & Peter, 2009; Willard, 2007). Cyberbullying can be more harmful than face-to-face bullying, in part because the perpetrators often remain anonymous (and so can't be confronted) and in part because highly defamatory material can spread like wildfire among a large peer group (Kowalski & Limber, 2007; Rivers, Chesney, & Coyne, 2011).

To the extent that we have opportunities, then, we should talk with students about wise and socially appropriate uses of modern technology, and we must explain in no uncertain terms that cyberbullying in any form—whether it involves taunts, threats, unkind rumors, or any other material that can cause psychological harm to others—is totally unacceptable. And, of course, we must monitor students' in-class use of the Internet.

**cyberbullying** Engaging in psychological aggression via wireless technologies or the Internet.

Be on the lookout for bullying and other forms of aggression, and take appropriate actions with both the victims and the perpetrators.

Teachers must intervene when students are either the perpetrators or victims of aggression. Gain practice in the simulation "Dealing with Situations Where Students Are Being Bullied/Harassed."

Explain what cyberbullying is and why it is unacceptable.

## DIVERSITY IN PEER RELATIONSHIPS AND SOCIAL COGNITION

Some students with disabilities have delays in the development of social cognition and, as a result, often have trouble in interpersonal relationships. For example, students with significant delays in their overall cognitive development (i.e., children with intellectual disabilities) typically have limited understanding of appropriate behaviors in social situations (S. Greenspan & Granfield, 1992; Leffert, Siperstein, & Millikan, 2000). Also, some students with seemingly normal cognitive abilities have specific deficits in social cognition. In a mild form of autism known as *Asperger syndrome,* students may show average or above-average academic achievement but have great difficulty drawing accurate inferences from others' behaviors and body language, apparently as a result of a brain abnormality (G. Dawson & Bernier, 2007; Hobson, 2004; Tager-Flusberg, 2007). In addition, many students with chronic emotional and behavioral disabilities have poor perspective-taking and social problem-solving abilities and thus may have few, if any, friends (Harter et al., 1998; Lind, 1994).

**Gender differences**    Gender differences have been observed in interpersonal behaviors. Boys tend to hang out in large groups, whereas girls tend to favor smaller, more intimate gatherings with close friends (Maccoby, 2002). Also, girls seem to be more astute at reading other people's body language, and they work hard to maintain group harmony (Benenson et al., 2002; Bosacki, 2000; Rudolph et al., 2005). Furthermore, aggression tends to take different forms in boys (who are prone to physical aggression) and in girls (who are more apt to engage in relational aggression, disrupting friendships and tarnishing others' reputations) (Card, Stucky, Sawalani, & Little, 2008; Crick et al., 2002; Pellegrini, 2011; Pellegrini & Archer, 2005).

**Cultural and ethnic differences**    Interpersonal behaviors vary from culture to culture as well. For instance, some cultural groups (e.g., some groups in northern Canada and in the South Pacific) regularly use seemingly antisocial behaviors—especially teasing and ridicule—to teach children to remain calm and handle criticism (Rogoff, 2003). In contrast, many Native Americans, many people of Hispanic heritage, and certain African American communities place particular emphasis on group harmony, and many Asian groups strongly discourage aggression. Children from these backgrounds may be especially adept at negotiation and peace making (Gardiner & Kosmitzki, 2008; Guthrie, 2001; Halgunseth et al., 2006; Rubin, Cheah, & Menzer, 2010; Witmer, 1996).

## PROMOTING HEALTHY PEER RELATIONSHIPS

As teachers, we're in an excellent position to assess how students think about and behave in social situations and to help them interact more effectively with others. Following are several strategies that research has shown to be effective.

🍎 *Provide numerous opportunities for social interaction and cooperation.* For instance, students' play activities—whether the fantasy play of preschoolers and kindergartners or the rule-based games of older children and adolescents—can promote cooperation, sharing, perspective taking, and conflict resolution skills (Coplan & Arbeau, 2009; Creasey, Jarvis, & Berk, 1998; Gottman, 1986). Assignments and activities that require students to work cooperatively to achieve a common goal can foster leadership skills and a willingness to both help and get help from peers (Certo, 2011; Y. Li et al., 2007; N. M. Webb & Farivar, 1994). And activities in which students communicate with one another online—for example, by posting their ideas and questions about classroom topics on a class website—can be especially valuable for students who are shy or otherwise feel uncomfortable communicating with peers in a more public fashion (Hewitt & Scardamalia, 1998).

🍎 *Help students interpret social situations accurately and productively.* When students consistently have trouble getting along with others, explicit training in social cognition can make a difference. In one research study (Hudley & Graham, 1993), chronically aggressive boys attended a series of training sessions in which, through role-playing and similar activities, they practiced making inferences about other people's intentions and identifying appropriate courses of action. They also learned strategies for reminding themselves of how to behave in various situations—for example, "When I don't have the information to tell what he meant, I should act as if it were an accident" (p. 128). Following the training, the students were less

Extracurricular activities can promote productive peer relationships and a general "team spirit." They can also be a source of success for students who struggle with academic tasks. Here, 7-year-old Daniel, who has a learning disability, expresses his love of baseball.

likely to presume hostile intent or endorse aggressive retaliation in interpersonal situations than control-group students who didn't receive the training, and their teachers rated the trained students as less aggressive.

🍏 *Teach specific social skills, provide opportunities for students to practice them, and give feedback.* We can teach students appropriate ways of behaving both through explicit verbal instructions and through modeling desired behaviors. Such instruction is especially effective when we also ask students to practice their newly learned social skills (perhaps through role-playing) and give them concrete feedback about how they're doing (Bierman & Powers, 2009; Themann & Goldstein, 2001; S. Vaughn, 1991; Watkins & Wentzel, 2008).

🍏 *Promote understanding, communication, and interaction among diverse groups.* Even when students have good social skills, many of them interact almost exclusively within small, close-knit groups, and a few others remain socially isolated. For example, students often divide themselves along ethnic lines when they eat lunch and interact in the school yard. In fact, ethnic segregation *increases* once students reach the middle school grades. As young adolescents from ethnic minority groups begin to look closely and introspectively at issues of racism and ethnic identity, they often find it helpful to compare experiences and perspectives with other group members. Ethnic stereotypes and prejudices can also contribute to this self-imposed segregation (B. B. Brown et al., 2008; G. L. Cohen & Garcia, 2008; Ogbu, 2008b; Tatum, 1997).

Yet when students from diverse groups interact regularly—and especially when they come together as equals, work toward a common goal, and see themselves as members of the same team—they're more likely to accept and value one another's differences (Hodson, 2011; Oskamp, 2000; Pfeifer, Brown, & Juvonen, 2007). The Creating a Productive Classroom Environment box "Encouraging Positive Interactions among Diverse Individuals and Groups" offers several strategies for expanding students' friendship networks.

Some students need explicit instruction in social skills. As an example, watch "Social Skills Lesson."

## Creating a Productive Classroom Environment

### Encouraging Positive Interactions among Diverse Individuals and Groups

🍏 **Set up situations in which students can form cross-group friendships.**
To help her students get to know a greater number of their peers, a junior high school science teacher gives them assigned seats in her classroom and changes the seating chart once a month. She also decides how students will be paired for weekly lab activities.

🍏 **Minimize or eliminate barriers to social interaction.**
Students in a third-grade class learn basic words and phrases in American Sign Language so that they can work and play with a classmate who is deaf.

🍏 **Encourage and facilitate participation in extracurricular activities, and take steps to ensure that no single group dominates in membership or leadership in any particular activity.**
When recruiting members for the scenery committee for the eighth grade's annual class play, the committee's teacher-adviser encourages both "popular" and "unpopular" students to participate. Later he divides the workload in such a way that students who don't know one another well must work closely and cooperatively.

🍏 **As a class, discuss the undesirable consequences of intergroup hostilities.**
A high school English teacher in a low-income, inner-city school district uses a lesson on Shakespeare's *Romeo and Juliet* to initiate a discussion about an ongoing conflict between two rival ethnic-group gangs in the community. "Don't you think this family feud is stupid?" she asks her students, referring to Shakespeare's play. When they agree, she continues, "The Capulets are like the Latino gang, and the Montagues are like the Asian gang . . . Don't you think it's stupid that the Latino gang and the Asian gang are killing each other?" The students immediately protest, but when she presses them to justify their thinking, they gradually begin to acknowledge the pointlessness of a long-standing rivalry whose origins they can't even recall.

🍏 **Develop nondisabled students' understanding of students with disabilities, *provided that* the students and their parents give permission to share what might otherwise be confidential information.**
In a widely publicized case, Ryan White, a boy who had contracted AIDS from a blood transfusion, met considerable resistance against his return to his neighborhood school because parents and students thought he might infect others. After Ryan's family moved to a different school district, school personnel actively educated the community about the fact that AIDS doesn't spread through casual day-to-day contact. Ryan's reception at his new school was overwhelmingly positive. Later Ryan described his first day at school: "When I walked into classrooms or the cafeteria, several kids called out at once, 'Hey, Ryan! Sit with me!'"

*Sources:* Certo, Cauley, & Chafin, 2003; D. J. Connor & Baglieri, 2009; Dilg, 2010; Feddes, Noack, & Rutland, 2009; Feldman & Matjasko, 2005; Freedom Writers, 1999, p. 33 (Shakespeare example); Mahoney, Cairns, & Farmer, 2003; A. J. Martin & Dowson, 2009; Schofield, 1995; K. Schultz, Buck, & Niesz, 2000; Sleeter & Grant, 1999; Tatum, 1997; M. Thompson & Grace, 2001 (school play example); R. White & Cunningham, 1991, p. 149 (Ryan White example).

🍏 *Explain what bullying is and why it cannot be tolerated.* Students and teachers alike often have misconceptions about bullying. For instance, they may think it involves only physical aggression, even though psychological aggression—for instance, name calling, sexual harassment, deliberate social exclusion, and defamatory postings on the Internet—constitutes bullying as well. Another common misconception is that the victims of bullies somehow deserve what they get, perhaps because they display immature behaviors or need to "toughen up" and learn to defend themselves. Thus many students condone bullying and act as a supportive audience for the perpetrators (Salmivalli & Peets, 2009; Swearer et al., 2010). And teachers who refuse to intervene when they see or hear about bullying and harassment indirectly communicate the message that such behaviors are acceptable (Buston & Hart, 2001; Juvonen & Galván, 2008).

Earlier I urged you to be on the lookout for incidents of bullying. This is easier said than done, because many incidents of bullying occur beyond the watchful eyes of school faculty members (K. Carter & Doyle, 2006; Swearer et al., 2010). It's important, then, that students learn about the many forms bullying can take and the truly harmful effects it can have on its victims. One simple strategy is to use the mnemonic *PIC* to describe what bullying involves:

- **P**urposeful behavior—"He meant to do it."
- **I**mbalanced—"That's not fair, he's bigger."
- **C**ontinual—"I'm afraid to enter the classroom because she's always picking on me." (Horne et al., 2004, pp. 298–299)

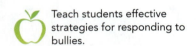

Teach students effective strategies for responding to bullies.

We can also teach students strategies to use when they're being bullied (e.g., they might walk away or respond with a humorous come-back) or when they observe others being victimized (e.g., they might say "Stop, you're being disrespectful" and escort the victim from the scene) (Juvonen & Galván, 2008; S. W. Ross & Horner, 2009).

🍏 *Help change the reputations of formerly antisocial students.* Unfortunately, students' bad reputations often live on long after their behavior has changed for the better, and thus their classmates may continue to dislike and reject them (Bierman, Miller, & Stabb, 1987; Caprara, Dodge, Pastorelli, & Zelli, 2007; Juvonen & Weiner, 1993). So when we work to improve the behaviors of aggressive and other antisocial students, we must work to improve their reputations as well. For example, we might encourage their active involvement in extracurricular activities or place them in structured cooperative learning groups where they can use their newly developed social skills. We should also demonstrate through our words and actions that *we* like and appreciate them, as our attitudes are apt to be contagious (Chang, 2003; Chang et al., 2004). In one way or another we must help students discover that formerly antisocial classmates have changed and are worth getting to know better.

🍏 *Create a general climate of respect for others.* Teachers who effectively cultivate friendships among diverse groups of students are often those who communicate a consistent message over and over: We must all respect one another as human beings. Fernando Arias, a high school vocational education teacher, has put it this way:

> In our school, our philosophy is that we treat everybody the way we'd like to be treated. . . . Our school is a unique situation where we have pregnant young ladies who go to our school. We have special education children. We have the regular kids, and we have the drop-out recovery program . . . we're all equal. We all have an equal chance. And we have members of every gang at our school, and we hardly have any fights, and there are close to about 300 gangs in our city. We all get along. It's one big family unit it seems like. (Turnbull, Pereira, & Blue-Banning, 2000, p. 67)

Truly productive interpersonal relationships depend on students' ability to respect one another's rights and needs and to support classmates who are going through hard times. Such capabilities are aspects of students' moral and prosocial development, a domain to which we turn now.

# Moral and Prosocial Development

In the opening case study, Lupita helps a classmate interpret a teacher aide's subtle message and assists two others with their puzzles. Such actions are examples of prosocial behavior, behavior aimed at benefiting others more than oneself. Prosocial behaviors—plus such traits as honesty, fairness, and concern about other people's rights and welfare—fall into the domain of morality. By and large, students who think and behave in moral and prosocial ways gain more support from their teachers and peers and, as a result, achieve greater academic and social success over the long run (Caprara, Barbaranelli, Pastorelli, Bandura, & Zimbardo, 2000; Spinrad & Eisenberg, 2009).

Morality and prosocial behavior are complex entities that appear to involve multiple parts of the brain. Certainly the mirror neurons mentioned earlier are involved, as they partially underlie people's ability to look at situations from someone else's perspective. But ultimately, moral and prosocial actions also have two components that involve distinctly different brain regions: *emotions* (e.g., affection and concern for others) and *complex reasoning abilities* (e.g., determining what actions are morally right and wrong) (Gallese et al., 2011; Greene, Sommerville, Nystrom, Darley, & Cohen, 2001; Moll et al., 2007; Young & Saxe, 2009).

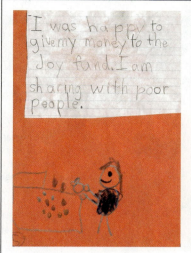

On a page in her "Happiness Book," 6-year-old Jaquita expresses her pleasure in behaving prosocially.

## DEVELOPMENTAL TRENDS IN MORALITY AND PROSOCIAL BEHAVIOR

Most children behave more morally and prosocially as they grow older. Table 3.2 describes the forms that morality and prosocial behavior are apt to take at various grade levels. Some entries in the table reflect the following developmental trends.

- *Even very young children use internal standards to evaluate behavior.* Well before their first birthday, children show that they value prosocial behavior over antisocial behavior, and by age 3 they have some understanding that behaviors causing physical or psychological harm are inappropriate (Hamlin & Wynn, 2011; Helwig, Zelazo, & Wilson, 2001). By age 4 most children understand that causing harm to another person is wrong regardless of what authority figures might tell them and regardless of what consequences certain behaviors may or may not bring (Laupa & Turiel, 1995; Smetana, 1981; Tisak, 1993).

- *Children increasingly distinguish between moral and conventional transgressions.* Virtually every culture discourages some behaviors—moral transgressions—because they cause damage or harm, violate human rights, or run counter to basic principles of equality, freedom, or justice. It discourages other behaviors—conventional transgressions—that, although not unethical, violate widely held understandings about how one should act (e.g., children shouldn't talk back to adults or burp at meals). Conventional transgressions are usually specific to a particular culture; in contrast, many moral transgressions are universal across cultures (Nucci, 2009; Smetana, 2006; Turiel, 2002).

Children's awareness of social conventions increases throughout the elementary school years (Helwig & Jasiobedzka, 2001; Laupa & Turiel, 1995; Nucci & Nucci, 1982). But especially as children reach adolescence, they don't always agree with adults about which behaviors constitute moral transgressions, which ones fall into the conventional domain, and which ones are simply a matter of personal choice. Hence, many adolescents resist rules they think are infringements on their personal freedoms—rules about clothing, hair style, talking in class, and so on (Nucci, 2009; Smetana, 2005).

- *Children's capacity to respond emotionally to others' harm and distress increases over the school years.* Within the first two or three years of life, two emotions important for moral development emerge (Kochanska, Gross, Lin, & Nichols, 2002; M. Lewis & Sullivan, 2005). First, children occasionally show guilt—a feeling of discomfort when they know they've inflicted damage or caused someone else pain or distress. They also feel shame: a feeling of embarrassment or humiliation when they fail to meet their own or other people's standards for moral behavior. Both guilt and shame, although unpleasant emotions, are good signs that children are developing a sense of right and wrong and will work hard to correct their misdeeds (Eisenberg, 1995; Harter, 1999; Narváez & Rest, 1995).

**prosocial behavior** Behavior directed toward promoting the well-being of people other than oneself.

**morality** One's general standards about right and wrong behavior.

**moral transgression** Action that causes harm or infringes on the needs or rights of others.

**conventional transgression** Action that violates a culture's general expectations regarding socially appropriate behavior.

**guilt** Feeling of discomfort about having caused someone else pain or distress.

**shame** Feeling of embarrassment or humiliation after failing to meet certain standards for moral behavior.

# DEVELOPMENTAL TRENDS

## TABLE 3.2 • Moral Reasoning and Prosocial Behavior at Different Grade Levels

| GRADE LEVEL | AGE-TYPICAL CHARACTERISTICS | EXAMPLE | SUGGESTED STRATEGIES |
|---|---|---|---|
|  K–2 | • Some awareness that behaviors causing physical or psychological harm are morally wrong<br>• Ability to distinguish between behaviors that violate human rights and dignity versus those that violate social conventions<br>• Guilt and shame about misbehaviors that cause obvious harm or damage<br>• Some empathy for, as well as attempts to comfort, people in distress<br>• Appreciation for the need to be fair; fairness seen as strict equality in how a desired commodity is divided | When Jake pushes Otis off the ladder of a playground slide, several classmates are horrified. One child shouts, "That's wrong!" and three others rush to Otis's side to make sure he's not hurt. | • Make standards for behavior very clear.<br>• When students misbehave, give reasons that such behaviors are unacceptable, focusing on the harm and distress they have caused others (i.e., use *induction*, a strategy described later in the chapter).<br>• Encourage students to comfort others in times of distress.<br>• Model sympathetic responses; explain what you're doing and why you're doing it.<br>• Keep in mind that some selfish behavior is typical for the age-group; when it occurs, encourage perspective taking and prosocial behavior. |
|   3-5 | • Knowledge of social conventions for appropriate behavior<br>• Increasing empathy for unknown individuals who are suffering or needy<br>• Recognition that one should strive to meet others' needs as well as one's own; growing appreciation for cooperation and compromise<br>• Growing realization that fairness doesn't necessarily mean equality—that some people (e.g., peers with disabilities) may need more of a desired commodity than others<br>• Increased desire to help others as an objective in and of itself | At the suggestion of his third-grade teacher, 8-year-old Jeff acts as a "special friend" to Evan, a boy with severe physical and cognitive disabilities who joins the class two or three days a week. Evan can't speak, but Jeff gives him things to feel and manipulate and talks to him whenever class activities allow conversation. And the two boys regularly sit together at lunch. Jeff comments, "Doing things that make Evan happy make me happy, too." | • Make prosocial behaviors (e.g., sharing, helping others) a high priority in the classroom.<br>• Explain how students can often meet their own needs while helping others (e.g., when asking students to be "reading buddies" for younger children, explain that doing so will help them become better readers themselves).<br>• Use prosocial adjectives (e.g., *kind, helpful*) when praising altruistic behaviors. |
|  6-8 | • Growing awareness that some rules and conventions are arbitrary; in some cases accompanied by resistance to these rules and conventions<br>• Interest in pleasing and helping others, but with a tendency to oversimplify what "helping" requires<br>• Tendency to believe that people in dire circumstances are entirely responsible for their own fate | After the midwinter break, 13-year-old Brooke returns to school with several large nose rings and her hair styled into long, vertical spikes above her head. The school principal tells her that her appearance is inappropriate and insists that she go home to make herself more presentable. Brooke resists, claiming, "I have a right to express myself however I want!" | • Talk about how rules for behavior enable classrooms and other groups to run more smoothly.<br>• Involve students in group projects that will benefit their school or community.<br>• When imposing discipline for moral transgressions, accompany it with explanations about the harm that has been caused (i.e., use *induction*). |
|  9-12 | • Understanding that rules and conventions help society run smoothly<br>• Increasing concern about doing one's duty and abiding by the rules of society as a whole rather than simply pleasing certain authority figures<br>• Genuine empathy for people in distress<br>• Belief that society has an obligation to help those in need | Several high school students propose and establish a school chapter of Amnesty International, an organization dedicated to the preservation of human rights around the world. The group invites knowledgeable guest speakers and conducts several fundraisers to help combat abusive practices against women. | • Explore moral issues in social studies, science, and literature.<br>• Encourage community service as a way of engendering feelings of commitment to helping others. Ask students to reflect on their experiences through group discussions or written essays.<br>• Have students read autobiographies and other literature that depict heroic figures who have actively worked to help people in need. |

*Sources:* Eisenberg, 1982; Eisenberg & Fabes, 1998; Eisenberg, Lennon, & Pasternack, 1986; Farver & Branstetter, 1994; C. A. Flanagan & Faison, 2001; Gibbs, 1995; Gummerum, Keller, Takezawa, & Mata, 2008; D. Hart & Fegley, 1995; Hastings et al., 2007; Helwig & Jasiobedzka, 2001; Helwig et al., 2001; Hoffman, 2000; Kohlberg, 1984; Krebs & Van Hesteren, 1994; Kurtines, Berman, Ittel, & Williamson, 1995; Laupa & Turiel, 1995; M. Lewis & Sullivan, 2005; Nucci, 2009; Nucci & Weber, 1995; Rothbart, 2011; Rushton, 1980; Smetana & Braeges, 1990; Spinrad & Eisenberg, 2009; Turiel, 1983, 1998; Wainryb, Brehl, & Matwin, 2005; Yates & Youniss, 1996; Yau & Smetana, 2003; Youniss & Yates, 1999; Zahn-Waxler, Radke-Yarrow, Wagner, & Chapman, 1992.

- Guilt and shame are the result of doing something wrong. In contrast, empathy—experiencing the same feelings as someone in unfortunate circumstances—appears in the absence of wrongdoing. Although those mirror neurons mentioned earlier may to some degree underlie human beings' ability to empathize, this ability continues to develop throughout childhood and adolescence (Eisenberg et al., 1995; Rizzolatti & Sinigaglia, 2008; Spinrad & Eisenberg, 2009). When empathy also evokes sympathy—whereby children not only assume another person's feelings but also have concerns for the individual's well-being—it tends to spur prosocial behavior (Batson, 1991; Eisenberg & Fabes, 1998; Malti, Gummerum, Keller, & Buchman, 2009).

- *With age, reasoning about moral issues becomes increasingly abstract and flexible.* To probe children's thinking about moral issues, researchers sometimes present moral dilemmas, situations in which two or more people's rights or needs may be at odds and for which there are no clear-cut right or wrong responses. The scenario in the following exercise is an example.

### EXPERIENCING FIRSTHAND
### MARTIN'S PLIGHT

Imagine that you're in the ninth grade. You're walking quickly down the school corridor on your way to your math class when you see three boys from the so-called "popular" crowd cornering a small, socially awkward boy named Martin. The boys first make fun of Martin's thick glasses and unfashionable clothing, then they start taunting him with names such as "fag" and "retard." What do you do?

    a. You look the other way, pretending you haven't heard anything, and hurry on to class. If you were to stop to help, the boys might taunt you as well, and that will only make the situation worse.

    b. You shoot Martin a sympathetic look and then head to class so that you won't be late. Afterward, you anonymously report the incident to the principal's office, because you know that the boys' behaviors have violated your school's antibullying policy.

    c. You stop and say, "Hey, you jerks, cut it out! Martin's a really nice guy and doesn't deserve your insulting labels. Come on, Martin, let's go. We might be late for math class, so we need to hurry."

I'm hoping that, given my earlier discussions of bullying, you've picked Alternative *c*. But if you were a ninth grader, is that *really* what you would do?

In his groundbreaking early research on moral development, Lawrence Kohlberg gave children and adults a variety of moral dilemmas and asked them both what they would do and why they would do it. Based on the hundreds of responses he obtained, Kohlberg proposed that as children grow older, they construct increasingly complex views of morality. In Kohlberg's view, development of moral reasoning is characterized by a sequence of six stages grouped into three general *levels* of morality: preconventional, conventional, and postconventional (see Table 3.3). Children with preconventional morality haven't yet adopted or internalized society's conventions regarding what things are right and wrong but instead focus largely on external consequences that certain actions might bring to themselves, as illustrated in Alternative *a* in the exercise. Kohlberg's second level, conventional morality, is characterized by general, often unquestioning obedience either to an authority figure's dictates or to established rules and norms, even when there are no consequences for disobedience. The exercise's Alternative *b* is an example: You report a violation of school rules to school authorities, but you don't want to be late to class—that would violate another school rule—and through your actions you don't jeopardize any good relationships you might have with the "popular" boys.

In contrast to the somewhat rigid nature of conventional morality, people at Kohlberg's third level, postconventional morality, view rules as useful but changeable mechanisms that ideally can maintain the general social order and protect human rights; rules aren't absolute dictates that must be obeyed without question. These people live by their own abstract principles about right and wrong and may disobey rules inconsistent with these principles. Alternative *c* shows some evidence of postconventional reasoning: You're more concerned about protecting Martin's physical and psychological safety than you are about getting to class on time.

---

hopes
goals
dreams
happiness
  broken
  destroyed
  eliminated
  exterminated
no steps forward
no evolution
no prosperity
no hope
But
maybe
perhaps
except
if we
help
together
we stand
a chance.

In this poem, Matt, a middle school student, shows empathy for victims of the Holocaust.

---

**empathy** Experience of sharing the same feelings as someone in unfortunate circumstances.

**sympathy** Feeling of sorrow for another person's distress, accompanied by concern for the person's well-being.

**moral dilemma** Situation in which two or more people's rights or needs may be at odds and the morally correct action is not clear-cut.

**preconventional morality** Lack of internalized standards about right and wrong; decision making based primarily on what seems best for oneself.

**conventional morality** Uncritical acceptance of society's conventions regarding right and wrong.

**postconventional morality** Thinking in accordance with self-constructed, abstract principles regarding right and wrong.

## COMPARE/CONTRAST

### TABLE 3.3 • Kohlberg's Three Levels and Six Stages of Moral Reasoning

| LEVEL | AGE RANGE | STAGE | NATURE OF MORAL REASONING |
|---|---|---|---|
| Level I: Preconventional morality | Seen in preschool children, most elementary school students, some junior high school students, and a few high school students | Stage 1: Punishment-avoidance and obedience | People make decisions based on what is best for themselves, without regard for others' needs or feelings. They obey rules only if established by more powerful individuals; they may disobey if they aren't likely to get caught. "Wrong" behaviors are those that will be punished. |
| | | Stage 2: Exchange of favors | People recognize that others also have needs. They may try to satisfy others' needs if their own needs are met simultaneously (e.g., "You scratch my back; I'll scratch yours"). They continue to define right and wrong primarily in terms of consequences to themselves. |
| Level II: Conventional morality | Seen in a few older elementary school students, some junior high school students, and many high school students (Stage 4 typically does not appear before high school) | Stage 3: Good boy/ good girl | People make decisions based on what actions will please others, especially authority figures (e.g., teachers, popular peers). They are concerned about maintaining relationships through sharing, trust, and loyalty, and they consider other people's perspectives and intentions when making decisions. |
| | | Stage 4: Law and order | People look to society as a whole for guidelines about right or wrong. They know that having rules is necessary for keeping society running smoothly and believe it is their duty to obey them. However, they perceive rules to be inflexible; they don't necessarily recognize that as society's needs change, rules should change as well. |
| Level III: Postconventional morality | Rarely seen before college | Stage 5: Social contract | People recognize that rules represent agreements among many individuals about what is appropriate behavior. Rules are seen as useful mechanisms that maintain the general social order and protect individual rights, rather than as absolute dictates that must be obeyed simply because they are the law. People also recognize the flexibility of rules; rules that no longer serve society's best interests can and should be changed. |
| | | Stage 6: Universal ethical principle | Stage 6 is a hypothetical, ideal stage that few people ever reach. People in this stage adhere to a few abstract, universal principles (e.g., equality of all people, respect for human dignity, commitment to justice) that transcend specific norms and rules. They answer to a strong inner conscience and willingly disobey laws that violate their own ethical principles. |

*Sources:* Colby & Kohlberg, 1984; Colby, Kohlberg, Gibbs, & Lieberman, 1983; Kohlberg, 1976, 1984, 1986; Reimer, Paolitto, & Hersh, 1983; Snarey, 1995.

A great deal of research on the development of moral reasoning has followed on the heels of Kohlberg's work. Some of it supports Kohlberg's proposed sequence: Generally speaking, people seem to make advancements in the order Kohlberg proposed (Boom, Brugman, & van der Heijden, 2001; Colby & Kohlberg, 1984; Snarey, 1995; Stewart & Pascual-Leone, 1992). Furthermore, as Kohlberg suggested, moral development emerges out of children's own, self-constructed beliefs—beliefs they often revisit, revise, and ultimately improve on over time. Nevertheless, contemporary psychologists have identified several weaknesses in Kohlberg's theory. For one thing, Kohlberg included both moral issues (e.g., causing harm) and social conventions (e.g., having rules to help society run smoothly) in his views of morality, but as we've seen, children distinguish between these two domains, and their views about each domain may change differently over time (Nucci, 2001, 2009). Furthermore, Kohlberg focused largely on *reasoning,* with little consideration of people's moral *behaviors* (Gilligan & Attanucci, 1988; P. L. Hill & Roberts, 2010). Kohlberg also underestimated young children, who, as we discovered earlier, acquire some internal standards of right and wrong long before they reach school age. Finally, Kohlberg largely overlooked situational factors that youngsters take into account when deciding what's morally right and wrong in specific contexts (more about these factors in a moment).

Many contemporary developmental psychologists believe that moral reasoning involves general *trends* rather than distinct stages. It appears that children and adolescents gradually construct several different standards that guide their moral reasoning, including their own personal interests, consideration of other people's needs and motives, a desire to abide by society's rules and conventions, and, eventually, an appreciation of abstract ideals regarding human rights and society's overall needs (Killen & Smetana, 2008; Krebs, 2008; Rest, Narvaez, Bebeau, & Thoma, 1999). With age, students increasingly apply more advanced standards, but even a fairly primitive one—satisfying one's own needs without regard for others—may occasionally take priority (Rest et al., 1999; Turiel, 1998).

• *As children get older, they increasingly behave in accordance with their self-constructed moral standards, but other factors come into play as well.* To some degree, students with more advanced moral reasoning behave in more moral and prosocial ways (e.g., Blasi, 1980; P. A. Miller, Eisenberg, Fabes, & Shell, 1996; Paciello et al., 2008). However, the correlation between moral reasoning and moral behavior isn't an especially strong one. Students' perspective-taking ability and emotions (shame, guilt, empathy, sympathy) also influence their decisions to behave morally or otherwise (Batson, 1991; Damon, 1988; Eisenberg, Zhou, & Koller, 2001). And although students may truly want to do the right thing, they may also be concerned about the consequences for themselves in specific situations—for instance, how much personal sacrifice will be involved and how much various actions will gain other people's approval or respect (Batson & Thompson, 2001; Cillessen et al., 2011; Narváez & Rest, 1995; Wentzel, Filisetti, & Looney, 2007).

Finally, students' sense of self seems to be an important factor affecting their inclinations to act morally and prosocially. For one thing, students must believe they're actually capable of helping other people—in other words, they must have high self-efficacy about their ability to "make a difference" (Narváez & Rest, 1995). Furthermore, in adolescence, some young people begin to integrate a commitment to moral values into their overall sense of identity: They think of themselves as moral, caring individuals who make other people's rights and well-being a high priority (Blasi, 1995; D. Hart & Fegley, 1995; Hastings, Utendale, & Sullivan, 2007; Thorkildsen et al., 2008).

## FACTORS INFLUENCING MORAL AND PROSOCIAL DEVELOPMENT

To some degree, advanced moral reasoning depends on *cognitive development.* In particular, it depends on the ability to think simultaneously about multiple issues (e.g., about various people's motives and intentions in a situation) and also on the ability to comprehend such abstract ideals as justice and basic human rights. However, cognitive development doesn't *guarantee* moral development. It's quite possible to think abstractly about academic subject matter and yet reason in a self-centered, preconventional manner (Kohlberg, 1976; Nucci, 2006, 2009; Turiel, 2002).

Children's social and cultural environments have a significant influence on their moral and prosocial development. For example, when children see adults or peers being generous and showing concern for others, they tend to do likewise (Hoffman, 2000; Rushton, 1980; Spinrad & Eisenberg, 2009). And when they watch television shows that emphasize perspective taking and prosocial actions, they're more inclined to exhibit such behaviors themselves (Dubow, Huesmann, & Greenwood, 2007; Hearold, 1986; Rushton, 1980; Singer & Singer, 1994). Prosocial video games, too, can have a positive impact (Gentile et al., 2009; Greitemeyer, 2011). Ideally, society's prosocial messages must be consistently conveyed through other people's behaviors. Children do *not* make advancements in moral reasoning and behavior simply by hearing adults advocate certain moral values—say, through a short "character education" program (Higgins, 1995; N. Park & Peterson, 2009; Turiel, 1998).

Children also tend to make gains in moral and prosocial development when adults consistently use induction, asking children to think about the harm and distress that some of their behaviors have caused others (Hoffman, 2000; Rothbart, 2011). Induction is victim centered: It helps students focus on others' distress and recognize that they themselves have been the cause. Consistent use of induction in disciplining children, especially when accompanied by *mild* punishment for misbehavior—for instance, insisting that children make amends for their wrongdoings—appears to promote compliance with rules and foster the development of empathy, compassion, and altruism (G. H. Brody & Shaffer, 1982; Hoffman, 1975; Nucci, 2001; Rushton, 1980).

Yet another factor that appears to promote moral and prosocial advancements is *disequilibrium*—in particular, encountering moral dilemmas and arguments that children can't adequately address with their current moral standards and viewpoints. For instance, classroom discussions of controversial topics and moral issues can promote increased perspective taking

induction Explanation of why a certain behavior is unacceptable, often with a focus on the pain or distress that someone has caused another.

and a gradual transition to more advanced reasoning (DeVries & Zan, 1996; Power, Higgins, & Kohlberg, 1989; Schlaefli, Rest, & Thoma, 1985). As Kohlberg suggested, children *construct* (rather than absorb) their moral beliefs; disequilibrium can spur them to revise their beliefs in ways that allow them to consider increasingly complex moral issues.

## DIVERSITY IN MORAL AND PROSOCIAL DEVELOPMENT

Some diversity in moral and prosocial development is, of course, the result of differences in children's environments. But biology seems to be involved as well. For example, other things being equal, children who have a somewhat fearful, anxious temperament in infancy tend to show more guilt and empathy in the early elementary grades than their less anxious classmates (Rothbart, 2011). And as children grow older, the degree to which they show effortful control—an ability to inhibit selfish and other unproductive impulses—appears to be a factor in their acquisition of a moral conscience (Eisenberg, Spinrad, & Sadovsky, 2006; Kochanska, Tjebkes, & Forman, 1998; Rothbart, 2011).

Genetically based disabilities, too, come into the picture. For example, certain human genes seem to give rise to the development of brain abnormalities that, in turn, predispose their owners to antisocial behavior (Raine, 2008).

**Gender differences**   Researchers have observed minor gender differences in moral and prosocial development. For instance, on average, girls are more likely than boys to feel guilt and shame—in part because they're more willing to take personal responsibility for their misdeeds. Girls are also more likely to feel empathy for people in distress (Alessandri & Lewis, 1993; Lippa, 2002; A. J. Rose, 2002; Zahn-Waxler & Robinson, 1995).

Yet historically, researchers have disagreed about the extent to which girls and boys *reason* differently about situations involving moral issues. In his work with college students, Kohlberg found that males reasoned at a slightly more advanced level than females (Kohlberg & Kramer, 1969). In response, psychologist Carol Gilligan argued that Kohlberg's stages don't adequately describe female moral development (Gilligan, 1982, 1987; Gilligan & Attanucci, 1988). She suggested that Kohlberg's stages reflect a *justice orientation*—an emphasis on fairness and equal rights—that characterizes males' moral reasoning. In contrast, females are socialized to take a *care orientation* toward moral issues—that is, to focus on interpersonal relationships and take responsibility for others' well-being. To see how these two orientations might play out differently, try the following exercise.

Chapter 4 describes many gender differences and their possible origins, including socialization practices.

### EXPERIENCING FIRSTHAND
### THE PORCUPINE DILEMMA

Consider the following scenario:

> A group of industrious, prudent moles have spent the summer digging a burrow where they will spend the winter. A lazy, improvident porcupine who has not prepared a winter shelter approaches the moles and pleads to share their burrow. The moles take pity on the porcupine and agree to let him in. Unfortunately, the moles did not anticipate the problem the porcupine's sharp quills would pose in close quarters. Once the porcupine has moved in, the moles are constantly being stabbed. (Meyers, 1987, p. 141, adapted from Gilligan, 1985)

What do you think the moles should do? Why?

According to Gilligan, males are apt to view the problem as involving a violation of someone's rights: The moles own the burrow and so can legitimately evict the porcupine. In contrast, females are more likely to show compassion, perhaps suggesting that the moles cover the porcupine with a blanket so that his quills won't annoy anyone (Meyers, 1987).

Gilligan raised a good point: Males and females are often socialized quite differently. Furthermore, by including compassion for other human beings as well as consideration for their rights, Gilligan broadened our conception of what morality *is* (L. J. Walker, 1995). But in fact, most research studies *don't* find major gender differences in moral reasoning (Eisenberg, Martin, & Fabes, 1996; Nunner-Winkler, 1984; L. J. Walker, 1991). And as Gilligan herself has acknowledged, males and females alike typically reveal concern for both justice and compassion in their reasoning (L. M. Brown, Tappan, & Gilligan, 1995; Gilligan & Attanucci, 1988; Turiel, 1998).

**Cultural and ethnic differences**   Virtually all cultures worldwide acknowledge the importance of both individual rights and fairness (reflecting a justice orientation) and compassion for others (reflecting a care orientation). However, different cultural groups tend to place greater emphasis on one than on the other (J. G. Miller, 2007; Snarey, 1995; Turiel, 2002). For instance, in much of North America, helping others (or not) is considered to be a voluntary choice, but in some societies (e.g., in many Asian and Arab countries) it is one's *duty* to help people in need. Such a sense of duty, which is often coupled with strong ties to family and the community, can lead to considerable prosocial behavior (X. Chen et al., 2009; Markus & Kitayama, 1991; Rubin, Cheah, & Menzer, 2010).

Some diversity is also seen in the behaviors that cultural groups view as moral transgressions versus those they see as conventional transgressions (Nucci, 2001, 2009). For example, in mainstream Western culture, how one dresses is largely a matter of convention and personal choice. In some deeply religious groups, however, certain forms of dress (e.g., head coverings) are seen as moral imperatives. As another example, in mainstream Western culture, telling lies to avoid punishment for inappropriate behavior is considered morally wrong, but it's a legitimate way of saving face in certain other cultures (Triandis, 1995). As teachers, then, we must remember that our students' notions of morally appropriate and inappropriate behaviors may sometimes be quite different from our own. At the same time, of course, we must never accept behaviors that violate such basic principles as equality and respect for other people's rights and well-being.

> Keep in mind that students from diverse cultures may have different ideas about behaviors that are morally desirable (and in some cases mandatory) versus behaviors that are morally wrong. If necessary, explain to a student in private that some behaviors considered appropriate in his or her culture are unacceptable in your classroom because they infringe on other people's rights and well-being.

## ENCOURAGING MORAL AND PROSOCIAL DEVELOPMENT IN THE CLASSROOM

As teachers, we play an important role in helping children and adolescents acquire the beliefs, values, and behaviors critical to their effective participation in a democratic and compassionate society—a society in which everyone's rights are respected and everyone's needs are taken into consideration. Following are several general suggestions based on research findings.

● *Encourage perspective taking, empathy, and prosocial behaviors.*  Systematic efforts to promote perspective taking, empathy, and such prosocial skills as cooperation and helping others do seem to enhance students' moral and prosocial development (Nucci, 2009; Spinrad & Eisenberg, 2009; N. M. Webb & Palincsar, 1996). Perspective taking and empathy can and should be encouraged in the study of academic subject matter as well (Brophy, Alleman, & Knighton, 2009; Davison, 2011). For example, Figure 3.4 shows two writing samples created during history lessons about slavery in the pre-Civil War United States. The reaction paper on the left was written by 10-year-old Charmaine, whose fifth-grade class had been watching *Roots,* a miniseries about a young African man (Kunta Kinte) who is captured and brought to America as a slave. Charmaine acknowledges that she can't fully grasp Kunta Kinte's physical pain. Even so, she talks about his "pain" and "fright" and about his parents' "hurt" at losing their firstborn son, and she is incensed by some colonists' view of African women as little more than "beeby [baby] warmers." The diary entries on the right were written by 14-year-old Craig, whose ninth-grade history teacher asked his class to write journal entries that might capture the life of a Southern plantation owner. Notice that Craig tries to imagine someone else (a plantation owner) taking *other people's* perspectives (those of slaves). Such two-tiered perspective taking is similar to recursive thinking but in this case involves thinking "I think that you think that someone else thinks . . . ."

● *Give reasons that some behaviors are unacceptable.*  Although it's important to impose consequences for immoral and antisocial behaviors, punishment by itself often focuses children's attention primarily on their own hurt and distress. To promote moral and prosocial development, we must accompany punishment with induction, focusing students' attention on the hurt and distress their behaviors have caused *others* (Hoffman, 2000; Nucci, 2009; M. Watson, 2008). For example, we might describe how a behavior harms someone else either physically ("Having your hair pulled the way you just pulled Mai's can really be painful") or emotionally ("You hurt John's feelings when you call him names like that"). We might also show students how they have caused someone else inconvenience ("Because you ruined Marie's jacket, her parents are making her work around the house to earn the money for a new one"). Still another approach is to explain someone else's perspective, intention, or motive ("This science project you've just ridiculed may not be as fancy as yours, but I know that Jacob spent many hours working on it and is quite proud of what he's done").

**FIGURE 3.4** Two examples of perspective taking related to slavery in the pre-Civil War United States

<u>Roots</u>    II ON THE BOAT
TO AMERICA

I could feel the pain Kunta-Kinte was having. Once I had a paper cut and when in the ocean it hurt more than a wasp sting, and that was just paper cut! I can't even imagine the pain or fright that Kunta-Kinte had being taken from his family and home. Or his parent's hurt finding out that their first son was being taken to be a slave, their son that had just become a man. I also am horrified about how they treated women. Belly-warmers! The makes angre!

**My Diary**

July 1, 1700
Dear Diary - Today was a scorcher. I could not stand it and I was not even working. The slaves looked so hot. I even felt for them. and it is affecting my tobacco. It's too hot too early in the season. The tobacco plants are not growing quickly enough. I can only hope that it rains. Also today Robert Smith invited me to a ball at his house in two days. In 5 days I am going to have my masked ball. We mailed out the invitations two days ago. My wife, Beth, and I thought of a great idea of a masked ball. We will hire our own band.

July 2, 1700
Dear Diary - It was another scorcher. I wish it would cool down. I don't think the salves can handle it. It looked like some of them would faint. I had them drink more water. Later in the day a nice breeze came up. Then I gave them the rest of the day off. Also today we planned a trip to Richmond. . . .

July 5, 1700
Dear Diary - Today we had to wake up before the sun had risen. After a breakfast of hot cakes, eggs, and sausage, we headed back home. We got there at the end of the morning. When I got back it was very, very hot. One of the slaves fainted so I gave him the rest of the day off, fearing revolt. I also gave them extra food and water. It makes me think that they are only people too. I know that this is unheard of but it really makes me think.

One behavior we must explicitly and consistently discourage is *cheating* in its various forms, whether it be submitting a research paper downloaded from the Internet (i.e., plagiarism), copying other students' responses to quizzes or homework, or giving friends unfair advance notice of test questions. Sadly, students don't always see cheating as being a violation of moral standards (L. H. Anderman, Freeman, & Mueller, 2007; Honz, Kiewra, & Yang, 2010). Perhaps they're trying to help a friend, they say, or perhaps they see an assignment as being a waste of time or hopelessly beyond their ability levels. Not only does cheating hinder students' classroom learning—students gain very little from copying other people's work—but it is also dishonest and therefore immoral. Several strategies can potentially discourage cheating:

- Explain in clear, concrete terms what cheating is—for example, that it includes not only representing another person's work as one's own but also giving certain classmates an unfair advantage over others.

- Contrast cheating with legitimate collaboration, in which everyone learns something and the submitted work is honestly represented as a joint effort.

- Provide enough guidance and support that students can reasonably accomplish assigned tasks on their own. (L. H. Anderman et al., 2007; Honz et al., 2010; Lenski, Husemann, Trautwein, & Lüdtke, 2010)

- *Expose students to numerous models of moral and prosocial behavior.* Children and adolescents are more likely to exhibit moral and prosocial behavior when they see others (including their teachers!) behaving in moral rather than immoral ways. Powerful models of moral behavior can be found in literature as well—for instance, in Harper Lee's *To Kill a Mockingbird* and in John Gunther's *Death Be Not Proud* (Ellenwood & Ryan, 1991; Nucci, 2001).

🍏 *Engage students in discussions of moral issues related to academic subject matter.* Social and moral dilemmas often arise within the school curriculum. Consider the following questions that might emerge in discussions about academic topics:

- Is military retaliation for acts of terrorism justified if it involves killing innocent people?

- Should laboratory rats be used to study the effects of cancer-producing agents?

- Was Hamlet justified in killing Claudius to avenge the murder of his father?

Such dilemmas don't always have clear-cut right or wrong answers. As teachers, we can encourage student discussions of such issues in several ways:

- 🍏 Create a trusting and nonthreatening classroom atmosphere in which students can express their beliefs without fear of censure or embarrassment.

- 🍏 Help students identify all aspects of a dilemma, including the needs and perspectives of the various individuals involved.

- 🍏 Encourage students to explore their reasons for thinking as they do—that is, to clarify and reflect on the moral principles on which they're basing their judgments. (Reimer, Paolitto, & Hersh, 1983)

🍏 *Get students actively involved in community service.* As we've seen, students are more likely to adhere to strong moral principles when they have high self-efficacy for helping others and when they have integrated a commitment to moral ideals into their overall sense of identity. Such self-perceptions don't appear out of the blue, of course. Children are more likely to have high self-efficacy for prosocial activities when they have the guidance and support they need to carry out the activities successfully. And they're more likely to integrate moral and prosocial values into their overall sense of self when they become actively involved in service to others, ideally even before they reach puberty (Hastings et al., 2007; Nucci, 2001; Youniss & Yates, 1999). Through ongoing community service activities—sometimes collectively referred to as service learning—elementary and secondary students alike learn that they have the skills and the responsibility for helping people in dire straits and in other ways making the world a better place in which to live. In the process they also begin to think of themselves as concerned, compassionate, and moral citizens who have an obligation to help those less fortunate than themselves (J. P. Allen & Antonishak, 2008; Kahne & Sporte, 2008; Thorkildsen et al., 2008).

**service learning** Activity that promotes learning and development through contributing to the betterment of other people and the outside community.

 **3**  What Have You Learned?

We now return to the learning outcomes listed at the beginning of the chapter and identify key ideas related to each one.

■ **3.1: Describe the nature and origins of children's temperaments and personality characteristics, and explain how you might adapt your classroom practices to students' diverse personalities.** Children exhibit distinct personalities—consistent ways of behaving across a wide range of situations—long before they begin school. To some degree their personalities reflect their temperaments—their genetic predispositions to be active or subdued, outgoing or shy, adventurous or fearful, and so on. Yet environmental factors affect personality as well: The quality of parent–child emotional bonds (reflecting attachment), the nature of caregivers' parenting styles, and cultural norms and expectations all play roles in molding children's characteristic ways of behaving.

Students are most likely to thrive and succeed when there is a *goodness of fit* between students' temperaments and personality traits, on the one hand, and classroom activities and assignments, on the other. For example, temperamentally quiet and self-controlled students may do well with independent seatwork; more energetic students may be more productive during hands-on activities; and students with poor impulse control may require greater-than-average guidance and supervision.

Evaluate and apply your knowledge related to this learning outcome in MyEducationLab™.

■ **3.2: Explain how students' sense of self is apt to influence their behavior and how you can help students develop healthy self-perceptions.** As young people progress through childhood and adolescence, they construct and continually revise their *sense of self*—their perceptions, beliefs, judgments, and feelings about themselves. Children derive such self-views not only from their own experiences (e.g., their successes and failures) but also from other people's behaviors and from the achievements of social and ethnic groups to which they belong. As children reach adolescence, their sense of self increasingly incorporates abstract qualities and, eventually, a general sense of identity regarding who they are as people, what things they find important, and what goals they hope to accomplish. With adolescence, too, come heightened concern about other people's opinions of oneself (the imaginary audience phenomenon) and an exaggerated belief in one's uniqueness relative to others (the personal fable phenomenon). Perhaps as a result of the personal fable—but also as a result of incomplete brain maturation— many adolescents take foolish risks and engage in dangerous activities.

As teachers, we must provide the support students need to be successful and give them feedback that engenders optimism about future accomplishments. And working either as individuals or as a team, we can offer and advocate for activities that channel teenagers' desires for risk and social status into safe, productive behaviors.

Evaluate and apply your knowledge related to this learning outcome in MyEducationLab™.

■ **3.3: Apply your knowledge of peer relationships and social cognition in promoting productive social skills and addressing student aggression.** Productive peer relationships (especially friendships) provide a testing ground for emerging social skills, offer emotional support in times of trouble or uncertainty, and, ideally, promote socially and culturally appropriate behaviors. In the middle school and high school years, many students become members of larger social groups (e.g., cliques, subcultures, or gangs) and form romantic relationships. Yet some students are consistently rejected or neglected by their classmates, and these students may especially need teachers' friendship and support.

Most children and adolescents actively try to make sense of their social world. With age, such social cognition becomes increasingly complex and insightful, allowing young people to interact effectively with adults and peers. But some students have trouble interpreting social cues correctly and may have few effective social skills. Furthermore, some students engage in either physical or psychological aggression toward certain peers, perhaps as a way of gaining prestige and status within their social group. As teachers, then, we may sometimes need to monitor and guide students' interpersonal interactions; for example, we must explain that psychological bullying (e.g., posting defamatory material on the Internet) is as harmful and inappropriate as physical aggression. We should also take active steps to promote communication and interaction across individuals and groups with diverse backgrounds and abilities.

Evaluate and apply your knowledge related to this learning outcome in MyEducationLab™.

■ **3.4: Describe typical advancements in moral and prosocial development over the course of childhood and adolescence, and identify strategies for promoting moral and prosocial development in the classroom.** As children move through the grade levels, most acquire an increasingly sophisticated sense of right and wrong. This developmental progression is the result of many things, including increasing capacities for abstract thought and empathy, an evolving appreciation for human rights and others' welfare, and ongoing encounters with moral dilemmas and problems. Even at the high school level, however, students don't always take the moral high road, as personal needs and self-interests almost invariably enter into their moral decision making to some degree. As teachers, we can help students develop more advanced moral reasoning and increasingly prosocial behavior by giving them reasons why certain behaviors are unacceptable, encouraging them to recognize how others feel in various situations, exposing them to models of moral behavior, challenging their thinking with moral dilemmas, and providing opportunities for community service and other prosocial behavior.

Evaluate and apply your knowledge related to this learning outcome in MyEducationLab™.

## Practice for Your Licensure Exam

Observe this lesson first-hand in the video "Scarlet Letter."

### The Scarlet Letter

Ms. Southam's eleventh-grade English class has been reading Nathaniel Hawthorne's *The Scarlet Letter.* Set in seventeenth-century Boston, the novel focuses largely on two characters who have been carrying on an illicit love affair: Hester Prynne, a young woman who has not seen or heard from her husband for the past two years, and the Reverend Arthur Dimmesdale, a pious and well-respected local preacher. When Hester becomes pregnant, she is imprisoned for adultery and soon bears a child. The class is currently discussing Chapter 3, in which the governor and town leaders, including Dimmesdale, are urging Hester to name the baby's father.

*Ms. Southam:* The father of the baby . . . How do you know it's Dimmesdale . . . the Reverend Arthur Dimmesdale? . . . What are the clues in the text in Chapter 3? . . . Nicole?

*Nicole:* He acts very withdrawn. He doesn't even want to be involved with the situation. He wants the other guy to question her, because he doesn't want to look her in the face and ask her to name *him.*

*Ms. Southam:* OK. Anything else? . . .

*Student:* The baby.

*Ms. Southam:* What about the baby?

*Student:* She starts to cry, and her eyes follow him.

*Ms. Southam:* That is one of my absolutely favorite little Hawthornisms.

Ms. Southam reads a paragraph about Dimmesdale and then asks students to jot down their thoughts about him. She walks around the room, monitoring what students are doing until they appear to have finished writing.

*Ms. Southam:* What pictures do you have in your minds of this man . . . if you were directing a film of *The Scarlet Letter?*

*Mike:* I don't have a person in mind, just characteristics. About five-foot-ten, short, well-groomed hair, well dressed. He looks really nervous and inexperienced. Guilty look on his face. Always nervous, shaking a lot.

*Ms. Southam:* He's got a guilty look on his face. His lips always trembling, always shaking.

*Mike:* He's very unsure about himself.

*Matt:* Sweating really bad. Always going like this. [He shows how Dimmesdale might be wiping his forehead.] He does . . . he has his hanky . . .

*Ms. Southam:* Actually, we don't see him mopping his brow, but we do see him doing what? What's the action? Do you remember? If you go to the text, he's holding his hand over his heart, as though he's somehow suffering some pain.

*Student:* Wire-framed glasses . . . I don't know why. He's like. . . .

*Mike:* He's kind of like a nerd-type guy . . . short pants.

*Ms. Southam:* But at the same time . . . I don't know if it was somebody in this class or somebody in another class . . . He said, "Well, she was sure *worth* it." Worth risking your immortal soul for, you know? . . . Obviously she's sinned, but so has he, right? And if she was worth it, don't we also have to see him as somehow having been worthy of her risking *her* soul for this?

*Student:* Maybe he's got a good personality . . .

*Ms. Southam:* He apparently is, you know, a spellbinding preacher. He really can grab the crowd.

*Student:* It's his eyes. Yeah, the eyes.

*Ms. Southam:* Those brown, melancholy eyes. Yeah, those brown, melancholy eyes. Absolutely.

1. **Constructed-response question:**

In this classroom dialogue Ms. Southam and her students speculate about what the characters in the novel, especially Arthur Dimmesdale, might be thinking and feeling. In other words, they are engaging in social cognition.

a. Identify two examples of student statements that show social cognition.

b. For each example you identify, explain what it reveals about the speaker's social cognition.

2. **Multiple-choice question:**

Ms. Southam does several things that are apt to enhance students' perspective-taking ability. Which one of the following is the best example?

a. She models enthusiasm for the novel ("That is one of my absolutely favorite little Hawthornisms").

b. She walks around the room as the students write down their thoughts about Dimmesdale.

c. She points out that Dimmesdale is "holding his hand over his heart, as though he's somehow suffering some pain."

d. She agrees with Mike's description of Dimmesdale as having a guilty look on his face.

---

**PRAXIS** Go to Appendix C, "Matching Book and MyEducationLab™ to the Praxis Principles of Learning and Teaching Tests," to discover sections of this chapter that may be especially applicable to the Praxis tests.

# 4 Group Differences

## LEARNING OUTCOMES

**4.1:** Describe frequently observed between-group differences and within-group variability for various cultural and ethnic groups; also describe the teacher attitudes and strategies that underlie culturally responsive teaching.

**4.2:** Describe the nature and origins of typical gender differences in school-age children and adolescents, and explain how you might best accommodate such differences in your classroom.

**4.3:** Identify challenges that students from low-income families often face; also identify several strategies through which you can foster their resilience and help them be successful at school.

**4.4:** Explain how you might recognize students who are at risk for academic failure and dropping out of school, and identify strategies for helping these students get on the path to academic and social success.

## CASE STUDY: WHY JACK WASN'T IN SCHOOL

Jack was a Native American seventh grader who lived in the Navajo Nation in the American Southwest. Although he enjoyed school, worked hard in his studies, and got along well with his classmates, he had been absent from school all week. In fact, he had been absent from home as well, and his family (which didn't have a telephone) wasn't sure exactly where he was.

Jack's English teacher described the situation to Donna Deyhle, an educator who had known Jack for many years:

> That seventh grader was away from home for 5 days, and his parents don't care! . . . Almost one-third of my Navajo students were absent this week. Their parents just don't support their education. How can I teach when they are not in my classes? (Deyhle & LeCompte, 1999, p. 127)

A few days later, Jack's sister explained why her parents had eventually begun to look for Jack:

> He went to see [the film] *Rambo II* with friends and never came home. If he was in trouble we would know. But now the family needs him to herd sheep tomorrow. (Deyhle & LeCompte, 1999, p. 127)

It was spring—time for the family to plant crops and shear the sheep—and all family members needed to help out. Jack's whereabouts were soon discovered, and the family stopped by Donna's house to share the news:

> Jack's dad said, "We found him." His mother turned in his direction and said teasingly, "Now maybe school will look easy!" Jack stayed at home for several days, helping with the irrigation of the corn field, before he decided to return to school. (Deyhle & LeCompte, 1999, p. 128)

- Did you interpret Jack's absence from school in the same way his English teacher did, concluding that "his parents don't care" about his education? If so, how might your own cultural background have influenced your conclusion?
- Like most parents, Jack's mother and father cared deeply about his school achievement and general well-being. What alternative explanations might account for their behaviors in this situation?

---

To fully understand what transpired in Jack's family, we need to know a couple of things about Navajo culture. First, Navajo people place high value on individual autonomy: Even children must be self-sufficient and make their own decisions (Deyhle & LeCompte, 1999). From this perspective, good parenting doesn't mean demanding that children do certain things or behave in certain ways; instead, Navajo parents offer suggestions and guidance, perhaps in the form of gentle teasing ("Now maybe school will look easy!"), that nudge children toward productive choices. But in addition to individual autonomy, Navajos value cooperation and interdependence, believing that community members should work together for the common good; hence Jack's highest priority was helping his family. Such respect for both individual decision making and cooperative interdependence is seen in many other Native American communities as well (Chisholm, 1996; Manning & Baruth, 2009; Rogoff, 2003; Tyler et al., 2008).

In this chapter we'll look in depth at group differences—differences we're apt to see on average among students of diverse cultural and ethnic groups, different genders, and different socioeconomic backgrounds. As we do so, we must keep in mind two very important points. First, *a great deal of individual variability exists within any group.* We'll be examining research regarding how students of different groups behave *on average*, even though many students in

**group differences**
Consistently observed differences (on average) among diverse groups of students (e.g., students of different genders or ethnic backgrounds).

Remember that despite average group differences, there is considerable variability within any group and considerable overlap between any two groups.

Chapter 11 describes and explains potential effects of teachers' expectations on students' achievement.

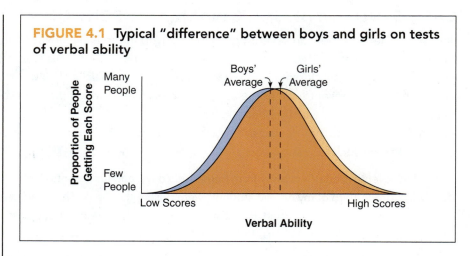

**FIGURE 4.1** Typical "difference" between boys and girls on tests of verbal ability

each group are not at all like those averages. Second, *a great deal of overlap typically exists between two groups.* Consider gender differences in verbal ability as an example. Many research studies have found girls to have slightly higher verbal ability than boys (Halpern & LaMay, 2000). The difference is often statistically significant—that is, it probably wasn't a one-time-in-a-hundred fluke that happened simply by chance. Yet the average difference between girls and boys in overall verbal ability is quite small, with a great deal of overlap between the sexes. Figure 4.1 shows the typical overlap between girls and boys on general measures of verbal ability. Notice that some boys (those whose scores fall in the rightmost part of their curve) have higher verbal ability than most of their female peers despite the average advantage for girls.

If we are to maximize the learning and development of all our students, we must be aware of group differences that may influence their classroom performance. Our challenge is to keep these differences in mind *without* either (1) imposing our own culturally based assumptions on what behaviors are "right" and "wrong" or (2) assuming that all members of a particular group fit typical group patterns. Our erroneous preconceptions about how various students will perform may actually *increase* differences among those students (de Boer, Bosker, & van der Werf, 2010; Rubie-Davies, Hattie, & Hamilton, 2006; Sirin & Ryce, 2010; van den Bergh, Denessen, Hornstra, Voeten, & Holland, 2010).

# Cultural and Ethnic Differences

The concept of **culture** encompasses the behaviors and belief systems that characterize a long-standing social group. The culture in which we live influences the perspectives and values we acquire, the skills we find important and master, and the adult roles to which we aspire. It also guides the development of our language and communication skills, our expression and regulation of emotions, and our formation of a sense of self.

Sometimes we use the word *culture* to refer to behaviors and beliefs that are widely shared over a large geographic area. For example, *mainstream Western culture* encompasses behaviors, beliefs, and values shared by many people in North America and western Europe. Members of this culture generally value self-reliance, academic achievement, democratic decision making, and respect for other individuals' rights and possessions, among other things. However, any single country in North America or western Europe—in fact, almost every country on the planet—encompasses considerable cultural diversity within its borders. Some of this within-country diversity is the result of growing up in particular geographic regions, religious groups, or socioeconomic circumstances (A. B. Cohen, 2009; Payne, 2005). In addition, most countries include citizens from a variety of ethnic groups. In general, an **ethnic group** is a group of individuals with a common culture and the following characteristics:

- Its roots either precede the creation of or are external to the country in which it resides. It may be comprised of people of the same race, national origin, or religious background.

- Its members share a sense of interdependence—a sense that their lives are intertwined. (NCSS Task Force on Ethnic Studies Curriculum Guidelines, 1992)

Cultures aren't static entities. Instead, they continue to change over time as they incorporate new ideas, innovations, and ways of thinking, particularly as they interact with other cultures (Kitayama, Duffy, & Uchida, 2007; O. Lee, 1999; Rogoff, 2003). Furthermore, there's considerable variation in attitudes and behaviors within a particular culture; individual members may adopt some cultural values and practices but reject others (Goodnow, 2010; Markus & Hamedani, 2007).

When people come into contact with a culture very different from their own (e.g., through immigration to a new country), many of them—especially children—gradually undergo acculturation, adopting some of the new culture's values and customs. Some acculturation is critical for success in the new cultural environment, but *rapid* acculturation can be detrimental to children's social and emotional well-being. In most instances, children's own cultural groups give them a support network and stable set of values that enable them to do well in school and maintain their self-esteem in the face of discrimination and other challenges (Deyhle, 2008; Matute-Bianchi, 2008; Sam & Berry, 2010).

In general, we can get the best sense of students' cultural backgrounds and ethnic-group memberships by learning the extent to which they have participated and continue to participate in various cultural and ethnic-group activities (Gutiérrez & Rogoff, 2003). For example, some Mexican American students live in small, close-knit communities where Spanish is spoken and traditional Mexican practices and beliefs permeate everyday life, but others live in more culturally heterogeneous communities in which Mexican traditions may be cast aside to make time for mainstream American activities. And in some instances students may participate actively in two or more cultures, perhaps because they have immigrated from one country to another or perhaps because their parents come from distinctly different ethnic or racial backgrounds (Herman, 2004; A. M. Lopez, 2003; Mohan, 2009). In general, *membership in a particular cultural or ethnic group is a more-or-less phenomenon rather than an either-or situation.* In this age of increasing cross-cultural interaction, many students cannot easily be pigeonholed.

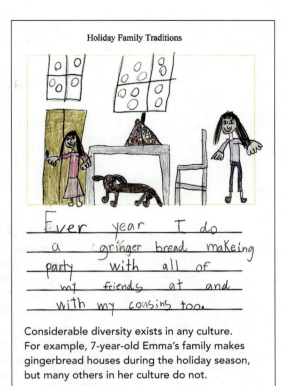

Holiday Family Traditions

Ever year I do a gringer bread makeing party with all of my friends at and with my cousins too.

Considerable diversity exists in any culture. For example, 7-year-old Emma's family makes gingerbread houses during the holiday season, but many others in her culture do not.

 Keep in mind that some students may have multiple cultural affiliations.

## NAVIGATING DIFFERENT CULTURES AT HOME AND AT SCHOOL

When they first begin school, many children experience some *culture shock*—some confusion about the behaviors expected of them in this new setting. Culture shock is more intense for some students than for others. Most schools in North America and western Europe embrace the norms and values of mainstream Western culture, and so students with this cultural background often adjust quickly to classroom practices. In contrast, students who come from cultural groups with radically different norms and values may experience a cultural mismatch between home and school. In particular, they may find school an unsettling place in which they don't know what to expect from others or what behaviors other people expect of *them*. Significant differences between home and school cultures can interfere with students' adjustment to the school setting and ultimately with their academic achievement as well (Phalet, Andriessen, & Lens, 2004; Phelan, Yu, & Davidson, 1994; Tyler et al., 2008; Ward, Bochner, & Furnham, 2001).

Cultural mismatch is compounded when teachers misinterpret the behaviors of students from cultural and ethnic minority groups. The following exercise provides an example.

### EXPERIENCING FIRSTHAND
#### ARGUMENT

Imagine that, as a new teacher, you're approaching the school building on the first day of school. You see seven or eight boys standing in a cluster just outside the front door. Two of them are

**culture** Behaviors and belief systems of a long-standing social group.

**ethnic group** People who have common historical roots, values, beliefs, and behaviors and who share a sense of interdependence.

**acculturation** Gradual process of adopting the values and customs of a new culture.

**cultural mismatch** Situation in which a child's home culture and the school culture hold conflicting expectations for behavior.

engaged in a heated argument, and the others are watching and listening with apparent delight. Here are just a few of the many insults you hear being hurled back and forth:

"Your momma so fat her driver's license says, 'Picture continued on other side'!"

"Yeah? Well, your momma so fat she got to iron her pants on the driveway!"

"That ain't nothin'. Your momma so fat her cereal bowl comes with a lifeguard!"

"Hey, man, your momma so fat she got smaller fat women orbitin' around her!"

The argument seems to be escalating, with the insults about the two boys' mothers becoming more and more outrageous. Should you intervene?

The incident you've just witnessed is probably an example of "sounding" or "playing the dozens," a friendly exchange of insults common among male youth in some African American communities. Some boys engage in such exchanges to achieve status among their peers—those who concoct the biggest, most creative insults are the winners—whereas others do it simply for amusement. But people unfamiliar with African American culture might misinterpret them as being potentially serious and worrisome (Adger, Wolfram, & Christian, 2007; R. E. Reynolds, Taylor, Steffensen, Shirey, & Anderson, 1982; Smitherman, 1998).

As students gain experience with the culture of their school, they become increasingly aware of their teachers' and peers' expectations for behavior and ways of thinking, and many eventually become adept at switching their cultural vantage point as they move from home to school and back again (Y. Hong, Morris, Chiu, & Benet-Martínez, 2000; LaFromboise, Coleman, & Gerton, 1993; Matute-Bianchi, 2008). One Mexican American student's recollection provides an example:

At home with my parents and grandparents the only acceptable language was Spanish; actually that's all they really understood. Everything was really Mexican, but at the same time they wanted me to speak good English. . . . But at school, I felt really different because everyone was American, including me. Then I would go home in the afternoon and be Mexican again. (Padilla, 1994, p. 30)

Not all students make an easy adjustment, however. Some students actively resist adapting to the school culture, perhaps because they view it as conflicting with their own cultural background and identity (Cross, Strauss, & Fhagen-Smith, 1999; Gay, 2010; Irving & Hudley, 2008; Phelan et al., 1994). Still others try desperately to fit in at school yet find the inconsistencies between home and school difficult to resolve, as illustrated by this report from a teacher whose students included immigrant Muslim children from Pakistan and Afghanistan:

During the days of preparation for Ramadan Feast, the children fasted with the adults. . . . They had breakfast [before dawn] and then went back to sleep until it was time to get themselves ready for school. In school they refrained from food or drink—even a drop of water—until sunset. By noon, especially on warm days, they were a bit listless. . . . They spoke about their obligation to pray five times daily. In their writing they expressed the conflict within:

*I always think about my country. I think about going there one day, seeing it and practicing my religion with no problems. . . . Before sunrise, I can pray with my family. But at school we can't say to my teacher, "Please, teacher, I need to pray."* (Igoa, 1995, p. 135)

As teachers, we must learn as much as we can about the ways in which students from various cultural and ethnic groups are apt to be different from one another and from ourselves. Equipped with such knowledge, we can make reasonable accommodations to help students from all backgrounds adjust to and thrive in our classrooms.

## EXAMPLES OF CULTURAL AND ETHNIC DIVERSITY

Tremendous cultural variation exists within African American, Hispanic, Asian American, Native American, and European American groups. Thus, we must be careful not to form stereotypes about *any* group. At the same time, knowledge of frequently observed cultural differences, such as those described in the following sections, can sometimes help us better understand why students behave as they do.

## LANGUAGE AND DIALECT

One obvious cultural difference is language. But even if children speak English at home, they may use a form of English different from the Standard English typically used at school. More specifically, they may speak in a different dialect, a form of a particular language that includes some unique pronunciations, idioms, and grammatical structures. Dialects tend to be associated either with particular geographical regions or with particular ethnic and cultural groups.

Perhaps the most widely studied ethnic dialect is African American English (you may also see the terms *Black English Vernacular* and *Ebonics*). This dialect—which is illustrated in the earlier "Argument" exercise and is actually a group of dialects that vary somewhat from place to place—is characterized by certain ways of speaking that are distinctly different from those of Standard English (e.g., "He got ten dollar," "Momma she mad," "He be talkin' ") (Hulit & Howard, 2006, p. 346; Owens, 1995, p. A-8). At one time, many researchers believed that an African American dialect represented a less complex form of speech than Standard English and thus urged educators to teach students to speak "properly" as quickly as possible. But most researchers now realize that African American dialects are, in fact, very complex languages with predictable sentence structures and that these dialects promote communication and sophisticated thinking processes as readily as Standard English (Alim & Baugh, 2007; Fairchild & Edwards-Evans, 1990; Hulit & Howard, 2006; Spears, 2007).

Many children and adolescents view their native dialect as an integral part of their ethnic identity. Furthermore, when a particular dialect is the language preferred by local community members, it's often the means through which people can most effectively connect with one another in face-to-face interactions and text messaging (Godley & Escher, 2011; Ogbu, 2003; D. Paris & Kirkland, 2011).

Nevertheless, lack of proficiency in Standard English can impede children's reading and writing development, and in later years, their use of a distinct regional or cultural dialect may lead other people to underestimate or discredit their abilities. For such reasons, many experts recommend that all students in English-speaking countries develop proficiency in Standard English. Ultimately, children and adolescents function most effectively when they can use both their local dialect and Standard English in appropriate settings. For example, although we may wish to encourage Standard English in most written work or in formal oral presentations, we might find other dialects quite appropriate in creative writing or informal classroom discussions (Adger et al., 2007; DeBose, 2007; Ogbu, 1999, 2003; Smitherman, 1994).

## TALKATIVENESS AND VERBAL ASSERTIVENESS

Relatively speaking, mainstream Western culture is a chatty one. People often say things to one another even when they have little to communicate, making small talk as a way of maintaining interpersonal relationships (Gay, 2010; Trawick-Smith, 2003). In some African American communities as well, people talk a lot, often with a great deal of energy and enthusiasm (Gay, 2006; Tyler et al., 2008). In certain other cultures, however, silence is golden (Norenzayan, Choi, & Peng, 2007; Trawick-Smith, 2003). For example, many people from Southeast Asian countries believe that effective learning is best accomplished through attentive listening rather than through speaking (J. Li, 2005; J. Li & Fischer, 2004; Volet, 1999).

Some talkative cultures are also assertive ones, in that people readily voice their opinions, perhaps interrupting those who are speaking; for example, this is the case for many African Americans, European Americans, and Hawaiians. People from quieter cultures, such as many Asian Americans, tend to be more subtle and tentative in expressing their opinions—for instance, they might begin a sentence by saying "I'm not sure, but perhaps . . . "—and they aren't as likely to reveal their emotions during conversations (Gay, 2010; Morelli & Rothbaum, 2007; Tyler et al., 2008; Ward et al., 2001).

In addition, different cultural and ethnic groups have diverse views about how assertive children should be with adults. In mainstream Western culture a common expectation is that children will speak up whenever they have comments or questions. Yet in many parts of the world, children are expected to learn primarily by close, quiet observation of adults, rather than by asking questions or otherwise interrupting what adults are doing (Correa-Chávez, Rogoff, & Mejía Arauz, 2005; Gutiérrez & Rogoff, 2003; Kağitçibaşi, 2007). And in some cultures—for instance, in many Mexican American and Southeast Asian communities and in some African

---

**Standard English** Form of English generally considered acceptable at school, as reflected in textbooks and grammar instruction.

**dialect** Form of a language that has certain unique pronunciations, idioms, and grammatical structures and is characteristic of a particular region or ethnic group.

**African American English** Dialect of some African American communities that includes some pronunciations, idioms, and grammatical constructions different from those of Standard English.

Encourage students to use both Standard English and their local dialect, each in appropriate settings.

Chapter 11 looks more closely at cultural differences in emotional expressiveness.

Keep in mind that some students have been taught that initiating a conversation with an adult is disrespectful.

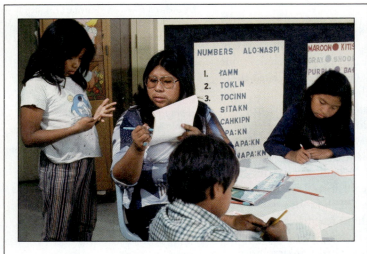

In some cultures, including many Native American communities, children are taught to look down as a sign of respect for an adult who speaks to them.

Don't rely on eye contact as the only indicator that students are paying attention.

American communities—children learn very early that they should engage in conversation with adults only when their participation has been directly solicited (Delgado-Gaitan, 1994; C. A. Grant & Gomez, 2001; Ochs, 1982).

## EYE CONTACT

For many of us, looking someone in the eye is a way to show that we're trying to communicate or are listening intently to what the person is saying. But in many Native American, African American, Mexican American, and Puerto Rican communities, a child who looks an adult in the eye is showing disrespect. In these communities children are taught to look down in the presence of adults (Jiang, 2010; McCarthy, Lee, Itakura, & Muir, 2006; Tyler et al., 2008). The following anecdote shows how a teacher's recognition of children's beliefs about eye contact can make a difference:

> A teacher [described a Native American] student who would never say a word, nor even answer when she greeted him. Then one day when he came in she looked in the other direction and said, "Hello, Jimmy." He answered enthusiastically, "Why hello Miss Jacobs." She found that he would always talk if she looked at a book or at the wall, but when she looked at him, he appeared frightened. (Gilliland, 1988, p. 26)

## PERSONAL SPACE

In some cultures, such as those of some African American and Hispanic communities, people stand close together when they talk, and they may touch one another frequently. In contrast, European Americans and East Asians tend to keep a fair distance from one another, maintaining some **personal space**, especially if they don't know each other very well (Slonim, 1991; Trawick-Smith, 2003; Ward et al., 2001). As teachers, we must be sensitive to the personal space that students from various cultural backgrounds need in order to feel comfortable in interactions with us and with classmates.

## RESPONDING TO QUESTIONS

A common interaction pattern in many Western classrooms is the **IRE cycle**: A teacher *initiates* an interaction by asking a question, a student *responds* to the question, and the teacher *evaluates* the response (Mehan, 1979). Similar interactions are often found in parent–child interactions in middle-income European American homes. For instance, when my own children were toddlers and preschoolers, I often asked them questions such as "How old are you?" and "What does a cow say?" and praised them when they answered correctly. But children reared in other cultural groups aren't necessarily familiar with such question-and-answer sessions when they first come to school. Furthermore, some children may be quite puzzled when a teacher asks questions to which he or she already knows the answer (Adger et al., 2007; Crago, Annahatak, & Ningiuruvik, 1993; Heath, 1989; Rogoff, 2003, 2007). And children in some communities are specifically taught *not* to answer questions from strangers about personal and home life—questions such as "What's your name?" and "Where do you live?" (Heath, 1982, 1989).

The issue, then, isn't that children are unaccustomed to questions; rather, it's that they have little experience with certain *kinds* of questions, as one child's mother explains:

> Miss Davis, she complain 'bout Ned not answerin' back. He says she asks dumb questions she already know about. (Heath, 1982, p. 107)

Meanwhile, teachers may misinterpret the children's silence, as this teacher does:

> The simplest questions are the ones they can't answer in the classroom; yet on the playground, they can explain a rule for a ballgame or describe a particular kind of bait with no problem. Therefore, I know they can't be as dumb as they seem in my class. (Heath, 1983, p. 269)

Cultural differences have also been observed in how long people wait before answering another person's question. People from some cultures use lengthy pauses before

**personal space** Personally or culturally preferred distance between people during social interaction.

**IRE cycle** Adult–child interaction marked by adult initiation (usually involving a question), child response, and adult evaluation.

responding as a way of indicating respect, as this statement by a Northern Cheyenne individual illustrates:

> Even if I had a quick answer to your question, I would never answer immediately. That would be saying that your question was not worth thinking about. (Gilliland, 1988, p. 27)

When teachers expect immediate answers to their questions—with a delay of, say, a second or less—students from these cultures may not have the time they need to show respect as they respond. Such students are more likely to participate in class and answer questions when their teacher provides a more extended wait time—that is, when several seconds of silence can elapse after the teacher's question or another student's comment (Castagno & Brayboy, 2008; Mohatt & Erickson, 1981; Tharp, 1989).

## PUBLIC VERSUS PRIVATE PERFORMANCE

In many classrooms learning is a very public enterprise. Individual students are often expected to answer questions or demonstrate skills in full view of their classmates, and they're encouraged to ask questions themselves when they don't understand. Such practices, which many teachers take for granted, may confuse or even alienate the students of some ethnic groups (Eriks-Brophy & Crago, 1994; García, 1994; Lomawaima, 1995). For example, many Native American children are accustomed to practicing a skill privately at first, performing in front of a group only after they've attained a reasonable level of mastery (Castagno & Brayboy, 2008; Suina & Smolkin, 1994). And children in some Native American and Hawaiian communities may feel more comfortable responding to questions as a group rather than interacting with adults one on one (K. H. Au, 1980; L. S. Miller, 1995).

## VIEWS ABOUT TEASING

Although people in some cultures think of teasing as mean spirited, it's a common form of social interaction in certain other cultures. For example, in the earlier "Argument" exercise, two African American boys engaged in playful one-upmanship, flinging increasingly outlandish insults at each other. And in the opening case study, Jack's mother teased him by suggesting that "Now maybe school will look easy!" When taken in the right spirit, teasing serves a variety of functions for particular cultural groups—perhaps providing a source of amusement and an outlet for verbal creativity, exerting gentle pressure to engage in more productive behavior, or helping children learn how to take criticism in stride (Adger et al., 2007; P. M. Cole, Tamang, & Shrestha, 2006; Rogoff, 2003).

## COOPERATION VERSUS COMPETITION

In a traditional Western classroom, students are rewarded when, as individuals, they achieve at high levels. In some cases—for example, when teachers grade on a curve or post "best" papers on a bulletin board—students must actually compete with one another in order to be successful.

Yet in some cultures—including many Native American, Mexican American, African, Southeast Asian, and Pacific Island communities—*group* achievement is valued over individual success. Students from these cultures are often more accustomed to working cooperatively and for the benefit of the community, rather than for themselves (X. Chen, Chung, & Hsiao, 2009; Lomawaima, 1995; Mejía-Arauz, Rogoff, Dexter, & Najafi, 2007; Tyler et al., 2008). Such a cooperative spirit is epitomized by the Zulu word *ubuntu,* which reflects the belief that people become fully human largely through caring relationships with others and regular contributions to the common good.

**wait time** Length of time a teacher pauses, either after asking a question or hearing a student's comment, before saying something.

Increase wait time as a means of encouraging students from diverse backgrounds to participate in discussions.

Increasing teacher wait time also enhances thinking and learning, as you'll discover in Chapter 6.

Remember that some students feel more comfortable practicing new skills in private.

Teachers often ask students questions for which they themselves already know the answers, but not all children are familiar with this strategy—known as an *IRE cycle*—for assessing students' knowledge.

Students from cooperative cultures may resist when asked to compete against their classmates, as 16-year-old Maria explains:

> I love sports, but not competitive sports. [My brother is] the same way. I think we learned that from our folks. They both try to set things up so that everyone wins in our family and no one is competing for anything. (Pipher, 1994, p. 280)

Students may also be confused when teachers scold them for helping one another on assignments or for sharing answers, and they may feel uncomfortable when their individual achievements are publicly acknowledged. Group work, with an emphasis on cooperation rather than competition, often facilitates the school achievement of these students (Deyhle & Margonis, 1995; Lipka, 1998; L. S. Miller, 1995; Rogoff, 2003).

Make frequent use of cooperative activities, especially when students' cultures place high value on cooperation.

### FAMILY RELATIONSHIPS AND EXPECTATIONS

In some groups—for example, in many Hispanic, Native American, Arab American, and Asian groups, as well as in some rural European American communities—family bonds and relationships are especially important, and extended family members often live nearby. Students growing up in these cultures are likely to feel responsibility for their family's well-being, to have a strong sense of loyalty to other family members, and to go to great lengths to please their elders. It isn't unusual for students in such communities to leave school when their help is needed at home, as Jack does in the opening case study (Banks & Banks, 1995; Fuligni, 1998; Kağitçibaşi, 2007; McIntyre, 2010).

In most cultures school achievement is highly valued, and parents encourage their children to do well in school (Monzó, 2010; R. R. Pearce, 2006; Spera, 2005). But some cultural groups place even higher priority on other accomplishments. For example, when preparing young children for school, many Hispanic families place particular emphasis on instilling appropriate social behaviors—for instance, showing respect for adults and cooperating with peers (Greenfield et al., 2006; Tyler et al., 2008). And in some cultural groups, an early pregnancy is a cause for joy even if the mother-to-be hasn't yet completed high school (Deyhle & Margonis, 1995; Stack & Burton, 1993).

We must certainly be sensitive to situations in which the achievements that *we* think are important are seemingly not valued by students' families. Whenever possible, we must show our students how the school curriculum and classroom activities relate to their cultural environment and their own life goals (Brayboy & Searle, 2007; Lipman, 1995; Moje & Hinchman, 2004). We must also maintain open lines of communication with students' parents. Because some parents of minority-group children feel intimidated by school personnel, teachers often need to take the first step in establishing productive parent–teacher relationships. When teachers and parents realize that both groups want students to succeed in the classroom, they're more apt to work cooperatively to promote student achievement (Banks & Banks, 1995; Edwards & Turner, 2010; Reschly & Christenson, 2009).

Relate the school curriculum to students' home environments and cultures. Establish and maintain open lines of communication with parents, and work with them to identify ways in which home and school can collaborate in helping students be successful at school.

Chapter 13 identifies many strategies for working effectively with parents.

### CONCEPTIONS OF TIME

Many people regulate their lives by the clock: Being on time to appointments, social engagements, and the dinner table is important. This emphasis on punctuality isn't characteristic of all cultures, however. For example, many Hispanic and Native American groups don't observe strict schedules and timelines (Tyler et al., 2008; Ward et al., 2001). Not surprisingly, children from these communities may sometimes be late for school and may have trouble understanding the need to complete school tasks within a certain time frame.

To succeed in mainstream Western society, students eventually need to learn punctuality. At the same time we must recognize that not all students will be especially concerned about clock time when they first enter our classrooms. Certainly we should expect students to come to class on time and to turn in assignments when they're due. But we must be patient and understanding when, for cultural reasons, students don't develop such habits immediately.

Encourage punctuality, but be patient if students' cultural backgrounds have placed little emphasis on clock time.

### WORLDVIEWS

The cultural and ethnic differences identified so far reveal themselves, in one way or another, in students' behaviors. Yet the definition of culture presented early in the chapter includes the behaviors *and belief systems* that characterize a social group. Our general beliefs and assumptions about the world—collectively known as our worldview—are often so integral to our everyday thinking that we take them for granted and aren't consciously aware of them (Koltko-Rivera, 2004; Losh, 2003). Some beliefs that permeate the curriculum in traditional Western schools aren't universally shared, however. Consider the following examples:

- After a major hurricane ripped through their community, many fourth and fifth graders attributed the hurricane to natural causes, but some children from minority-group backgrounds had heard explanations elsewhere that led them to believe that people's actions or supernatural forces also played a role in the hurricane's origins and destructiveness (O. Lee, 1999).

- Fourth graders from the Menominee culture (a Native American group) often show exceptionally high achievement scores in science, but by eighth grade their scores may decline considerably. Menominee culture encourages children to think about the many ways in which they are a *part* of nature, rather than taking care of or dominating it, and children increasingly find the school science curriculum at odds with this view (Atran, Medin, & Ross, 2005; Medin, 2005).

- When American high school students read newspaper articles about the appropriateness or inappropriateness of prayer in public schools, some view the trend away from prayer as a sign of progress toward greater religious freedom. But others—those from deeply religious Christian families, for instance—view the same trend as a decline that reflects abandonment of the country's religious heritage (Mosborg, 2002).

As you can see, then, students' worldviews are likely to influence their interpretations of current events and classroom subject matter (Kağitçibaşi, 2007; Keil & Newman, 2008).

## CREATING A CULTURALLY INCLUSIVE CLASSROOM ENVIRONMENT

Clearly, we must be aware of and responsive to the different ways in which students of various cultural and ethnic groups are likely to think and act. It's equally important that we help our *students* develop such awareness and responsiveness, enabling them to become productive members both of the school community and of our increasingly multicultural society. Following are several suggestions.

🍏 *Come to grips with your own cultural lens and biases.* In the opening case study Jack's English teacher complained that "his parents don't care" and that, in general, the parents of Navajo students "just don't support their [children's] education" (Deyhle & LeCompte, 1999, p. 127). This teacher was looking at parents' behaviors from the perspective of a non-Navajo. The assumptions and worldviews we've acquired in our own culture—for instance, the assumption that good parents actively direct and control their children's behaviors—are often so pervasive in our lives that we tend to treat them as common sense, or even as facts, rather than as the beliefs they really are. These beliefs become a *cultural lens* through which we view events—a lens that may lead us to perceive other cultures' practices as somehow irrational and inferior to our own.

Teachers who work effectively with students from diverse backgrounds are keenly aware that their own cultural beliefs are just that—beliefs. And they make a concerted effort *not* to pass judgment on cultural practices and beliefs very different from their own, but rather to try to understand *why* people of other cultural groups think and act as they do (Banks et al., 2005; Rogoff, 2003).

🍏 *Educate yourself about your students' cultural backgrounds.* One way to do this, of course, is to read as much as possible about various cultural groups. But in addition, effective teachers immerse themselves in students' daily lives and cultures—talking with students about their outside interests and activities, getting to know students' families, patronizing local businesses, and so on (Castagno & Brayboy, 2008; Ladson-Billings, 1995a; Moje & Hinchman, 2004). Only when we immerse ourselves in a very different cultural environment can we truly begin to understand how we, too, are products of our own cultures and to appreciate the potential benefits of growing up in a very different one (Banks et al., 2005; Rogoff, 2003).

🍏 *Be sensitive to the culture shock that recent immigrants may be experiencing.* In recent years, immigration has become a highly politicized topic in the United States and elsewhere. Whatever

worldview General, culturally based set of assumptions about reality that influence understandings of a wide variety of phenomena.

Consider how students' diverse worldviews might influence their interpretations of classroom subject matter.

**multicultural education** Instruction that integrates throughout the curriculum the perspectives and experiences of numerous cultural groups.

**culturally responsive teaching** Use of instructional strategies that build on students' existing knowledge and skills and are consistent with their culturally preferred ways of learning and behaving.

American history classes have traditionally presented only a European American view of historical events. Watch "Self-Concept Challenge" and "Genocide Impact."

Look for commonalities as well as differences among people from different cultural backgrounds.

Stress that people from diverse cultures can all benefit from considering one another's perspectives.

our own political views might be on the topic, we must realize that *all* children deserve our guidance and support in their efforts to acquire the knowledge and skills they will need to be successful in the adult world. For recent immigrants, such guidance and support might include not only extra academic assistance, but also explicit instruction in the typical practices and customs—"how things are done"—of their new culture (Vang, 2010; Ward et al., 2001). Also, some students may require accommodations for their religious beliefs; for instance, we might discreetly give devout Muslim students a private place for their early afternoon prayer, and we might excuse them from vigorous physical exercise when they're fasting during Ramadan (Sirin & Ryce, 2010).

🍎 *Incorporate the perspectives and traditions of many cultures into the curriculum.* True multicultural education isn't limited to cooking ethnic foods, celebrating Cinco de Mayo, or studying famous African Americans during Black History Month. Rather, it integrates throughout the curriculum the perspectives and experiences of numerous cultural groups and gives all students reason for pride in their own cultural heritage. Students from diverse backgrounds are more likely to be motivated to do well in school—and to *actually* do well there—when they perceive the school curriculum and classroom activities to be relevant to their own cultures (Brayboy & Searle, 2007; Gay, 2010; Moje & Hinchman, 2004; Tyler et al., 2008).

As teachers we can incorporate content from diverse cultures into many aspects of the school curriculum. Following are examples:

🍎 In language arts, study the work of authors and poets from a variety of ethnic groups (e.g., study the lyrics of popular hip-hop songs).

🍎 In math and science, draw on students' experiences with their community's building, hunting, farming, and cooking practices.

🍎 In social studies, look at different religious beliefs and their effects on people's behaviors (e.g., see Figure 4.2).

🍎 In history, look at wars and other major events from diverse perspectives (e.g., the Native American perspective on European settlers' westward migration, the Spanish perspective on the Spanish–American War, the Japanese perspective on World War II).

🍎 In both history and current events, consider such issues as discrimination and oppression. (J. M. Hughes, Bigler, & Levy, 2007; J. Kim, 2011; Lipka, Yanez, Andrew-Ihrke, & Adam, 2009; McIntyre, 2010; NCSS Task Force on Ethnic Studies Curriculum Guidelines, 1992; K. Schultz, Buck, & Niesz, 2000)

In our exploration of diverse cultures, we should look for commonalities as well as differences. For example, in the elementary grades we might study how people in various countries celebrate children's birthdays. In the secondary grades it can be beneficial to explore issues that adolescents of all cultures face: gaining the respect of elders, forming trusting relationships with peers, and finding a meaningful place in society. One important goal of multicultural education should be to communicate that, underneath it all, people are more alike than different (Brophy, Alleman, & Knighton, 2009; Ulichny, 1996).

Students should be encouraged to contribute to the multicultural curriculum—for example, by bringing in photographs and favorite foods from home and by expressing their varying experiences and perspectives without fear of ridicule or censure (Gollnick & Chinn, 2009; Jiang, 2010). Ultimately, we should help students realize that diverse cultural groups have much to learn from one another. As an example, students might be surprised to discover that several practices underlying many democratic governments—such as sending delegates to represent particular groups, allowing only one person in a governing council to speak at a time, and keeping government and military bodies separate—were adopted from Native American practices in the 1700s (Rogoff, 2003; Weatherford, 1988).

🍎 *Build on students' strengths, and adapt instructional methods to their preferred ways of learning and behaving.* Classroom strategies that build on students' existing knowledge, skills, and accustomed ways of learning and behaving are collectively known as culturally responsive teaching. For example, if students regularly collaborate with others at home and in the community, we should make frequent use of cooperative group activities (Castagno & Brayboy, 2008; Ladson-Billings, 1995a). If, in their informal interactions with peers, students are accustomed to talking simultaneously and elaborating on one another's ideas, we might ask them to answer questions in chorus rather than as individuals (K. H. Au, 1980). And if students' home environments are high-energy ones in which several activities often take place simultaneously—as is sometimes true in African American and Hispanic families—we might create a similarly high-energy, multiactivity classroom environment (Tyler et al., 2008).

🍎 *Work hard to break down students' stereotypes of particular ethnic groups.* Although we and our students should certainly be aware of real differences among various ethnic groups, it's counterproductive to hold a stereotype—a rigid, simplistic, and inevitably inaccurate caricature—of any particular group. Even the most open-minded of us are sometimes prone to holding ethnic stereotypes, as you might discover in the following exercise.

**stereotype** Rigid, simplistic, and erroneous view of a particular group of people.

### EXPERIENCING FIRSTHAND
### PICTURE THIS #1

Form a picture in your mind of someone from each of the following three places. Make note of the *first* image that comes to mind in each case:

> The Netherlands (Holland)
> Mexico
> Hawaii

Now answer yes or no to each of these questions:

- Was the person from the Netherlands wearing wooden shoes?
- Was the person from Mexico wearing a sombrero?
- Was the person from Hawaii wearing a hula skirt or flower lei?

If you answered *yes* to any of the three questions, then one or more of your images reflected an ethnic stereotype. Most people in the Netherlands, Mexico, and Hawaii *don't* routinely wear such stereotypical attire.

In the preceding exercise, your stereotypes involved only superficial qualities. Yet people's stereotypes can also include notions about typical personality characteristics and behaviors. Some stereotypes—for instance, perceptions of a certain group as being "stupid," "lazy," or "aggressive"—are derogatory and certainly *not* conducive to productive cross-group interactions.

Researchers have identified several possible origins of counterproductive stereotypes. In some instances family members, friends, or popular media communicate stereotypes through prejudicial remarks, practices, and caricatures (Branch, 1999; Nesdale, Maass, Durkin, & Griffiths, 2005; Theobald & Herley, 2009). In other cases a history of conflict and animosity between two groups may lead children to conclude that people in the opposing group have undesirable qualities (Pitner, Astor, Benbenishty, Haj-Yahia, & Zeira, 2003). Occasionally, stereotypes appear in curriculum materials and classroom instruction—as happens, for instance, when American children role-play the first Thanksgiving by dressing up in paper-bag "animal skins," painting their faces, and wearing feathers on their heads (Bigler & Liben, 2007; Brayboy & Searle, 2007). And sometimes students simply have little or no knowledge about a cultural group very different from their own. For example, when a Muslim girl wears a head scarf to school, a thoughtless classmate might ask, "Are you bald? Is something wrong with your hair?" (McBrien, 2005a, p. 86; Sirin & Ryce, 2010).

At a minimum, unflattering stereotypes lead to misunderstandings among members of diverse cultural groups. When left uncorrected, they can also lead to overtly

> Shinto gods are called Kami. It is believed that these spirits are found in the basic forces of fire, wind, and water. Most influence agriculture and this of course was how the earliest people survived. They relied on what they grew to live. So the gods had to help them grow their crops or they died. It seems natural for people to worship things that will help them survive, and worshiping forces that affect what you grow was the common practice in early history. These basic forces even affect the survival of modern people. We all still need agriculture to live and forces of nature really determine whether crops grow or not.
>
> Shintoists never developed strong doctrines, such as the belief in life after death that many other religions have. However they have developed some moral standards such as devotion, sincerity, and purity. . . .
>
> All Shintoists have a very good and simple set of rules or practice. They want to be honorable, have feelings for others, support the government, and keep their families safe and healthy. I think these are good principles for all people, whether they practice a religion or not. . . .

**FIGURE 4.2** In this paper for her language arts and social studies classes, 13-year-old Melinda explains what she has learned about Japan's Shinto religion and how in some ways it relates to her own life.

**stereotype threat** Awareness of a negative stereotype about one's own group and accompanying uneasiness that low performance will confirm the stereotype; leads (often unintentionally) to lower-quality performance.

Chapter 11 looks more closely at stereotype threat.

discriminatory and malicious behaviors—ethnic jokes, racial taunts, social exclusion, and so on (Killen, 2007; Pfeifer, Brown, & Juvonen, 2007). Students who are frequent victims of others' misunderstandings and prejudice are more likely than their peers to become chronically ill or depressed (Allison, 1998; G. H. Brody et al., 2006; Tatum, 1997). Negative stereotypes can also turn inward in a phenomenon known as **stereotype threat**: Students become overly anxious in domains in which their group stereotypically does poorly and, as a result, perform more poorly than they otherwise would (J. Aronson & Steele, 2005; Walton & Spencer, 2009).

As teachers, we must work hard to correct students' inaccurate and demeaning stereotypes of various cultural and ethnic groups, and we must vigorously address any acts of prejudice and discrimination we witness in the classroom and elsewhere. The Into the Classroom feature "Addressing Students' Stereotypes and Prejudices" offers several concrete strategies. By learning to appreciate multicultural differences within a single classroom, students take an important step toward appreciating the multicultural nature of the world at large.

🍏 *Bring cultural diversity to culturally homogeneous classrooms.* When students attend school only with peers who are culturally very similar to themselves, they may hold especially naive and potentially counterproductive stereotypes about other cultural and

## Into the Classroom

### Addressing Students' Stereotypes and Prejudices

🍏 **Use curriculum materials that represent all cultures and ethnic groups as competent, legitimate participants in mainstream society, rather than as exotic curiosities who live in a separate world.**

A history teacher peruses a history textbook to make sure it portrays members of all ethnic groups in a nonstereotypical manner. He supplements the text with readings that highlight the important roles that members of various ethnic groups have played in history.

🍏 **Assign literature depicting peers from diverse cultural backgrounds.**

As part of a research project in England, several elementary school teachers read to students a series of stories involving close friendships between English children and refugees from other countries. Following this experimental intervention, the students express more positive attitudes toward refugee children than do control-group students who have not heard the stories.

🍏 **Explore the nature and complexity of various dialects.**

A high school language arts class examines some unique features of a local African American dialect, including various forms of the verb *to be*. For example, African American members of the class explain that the word *is* is often dropped in simple descriptive sentences (e.g., "He a handsome man") and that the word *be* is sometimes used to indicate a constant or frequently occurring characteristic (e.g., "He be talking" describes someone who talks a lot).

🍏 **Conduct class discussions about prejudice and racism that exist in the school and local community.**

A middle school in a suburban community creates a number of mixed-race focus groups in which students regularly convene to share their views about interracial relations at the school. Although some students of European American ancestry initially feel uncomfortable talking about this topic with their minority-group peers, once the ice has been broken, greater cross-cultural understanding and communication result.

🍏 **Expose students to successful role models from various ethnic backgrounds.**

A teacher invites several successful professionals from minority groups to speak with her class about their careers. When some students seem especially interested in one or more of these careers, she arranges for the students to spend time with the professionals in their workplaces.

🍏 **Assign small-group cooperative projects in which students from diverse backgrounds must combine their unique talents to achieve a common goal.**

A fourth-grade teacher has small cooperative groups design and conduct schoolwide surveys soliciting other students' opinions on various topics (e.g., ideas for school fundraisers, preferences for cafeteria menu items, etc.). The teacher intentionally creates groups that are culturally heterogeneous, knowing that the group members will draw on diverse friendship networks in seeking volunteers to take the surveys. In addition, he makes sure that every member of a group has something unique to offer in survey design or data analysis—perhaps knowledge of word processing software, artistic talent, or math skills.

🍏 **Emphasize that some people affiliate with two or more cultural groups and that individual members of any single group are often very different from one another in behaviors, beliefs, and values.**

In a geography unit on major world religions, a middle school teacher regularly points out that members of any single religion often have very different customs. "For example," he says, "some Muslim women dress in much the same way that women in this country do; others also wear head scarves in addition to regular, modern clothes; and still others dress in a burqa that covers everything except their hands. Usually the women wear a scarf or burqa to show modesty about their bodies. In fact, some Jewish women, too, wear head scarves to show that they are modest, but many others don't."

*Sources:* Adger et al., 2007; Barbarin, Mercado, & Jigjidsuren, 2010; Boutte & McCormick, 1992; L. Cameron, Rutland, Brown, & Douch, 2006 (refugee stories example); Dovidio & Gaertner, 1999; Gutiérrez & Rogoff, 2003; Hulit & Howard, 2006, pp. 345–346 (dialect example); Mohan, 2009; Oskamp, 2000; Pfeifer et al., 2007; K. Schultz et al., 2000 (focus groups example); Tatum, 1997.

ethnic groups (McGlothlin & Killen, 2006; Pfeifer et al., 2007). In such situations we may have to take students beyond school boundaries, either physically or vicariously. For instance, we might engage students in community action projects that provide services to particular ethnic groups—perhaps in preschools, nursing homes, or city cultural centers (Sleeter & Grant, 1999). Alternatively, we might initiate a sister schools program in which students from two ethnically different communities regularly communicate, exchanging letters, photographs, stories, local news items, and the like (Koeppel & Mulrooney, 1992).

🍎 *Foster democratic ideals, and empower students to bring about meaningful change.* Any multicultural education program must include such democratic ideals as human dignity, equality, justice, and appreciation of diverse viewpoints (Gay, 2010; Gollnick & Chinn, 2009; NCSS Task Force on Ethnic Studies Curriculum Guidelines, 1992). We better prepare students to function effectively in a democratic society when we help them understand that virtually every nation includes numerous cultures and that such diversity provides a richness of ideas and perspectives that will inevitably yield a more creative, productive society overall. Such understanding is reflected in the writing sample in Figure 4.3, written by a student who was attending a rural, culturally homogenous high school in New Hampshire. The student's words were genuine; after earning his diploma, he spent two years in a very different cultural environment—a community in rural Brazil—before attending college.

Teaching respect for diverse perspectives doesn't necessarily mean that we treat all beliefs as equally acceptable. For instance, we should certainly not embrace a culture that blatantly violates some people's basic human rights. Respect does mean, however, that we and our students should try to understand another cultural group's behaviors within the context of its overall beliefs and assumptions.

Ideally, a democracy also provides a context in which students can bring about meaningful change. Students should be encouraged to challenge the status quo—perhaps substandard housing, poor voter turnout in certain neighborhoods, or misuse of natural resources (Ladson-Billings, 1995a; Lipman, 1995). For example, in some high schools in the Navajo Nation of the American Southwest, students have taken on controversial commercial practices (e.g., excessive tree cutting, landscape-scarring mining practices) that threaten their community's long-term well-being; they've conducted library research, interviewed community leaders, prepared written reports, and presented their findings at public meetings (Nelson-Barber & Estrin, 1995). Service learning projects such as these seem to instill a "can-do" spirit and optimism that all citizens can have a significant impact on the quality of their own and other people's lives (Eccles, 2007; Kahne & Sporte, 2008; Tate, 1995).

**FIGURE 4.3** In an essay for his American history class, 16-year-old Randy reveals his appreciation of cultural differences.

To me, diversity is not only a fact of life, but it is life. To be different and unique is what allows people to live a fulfilling life. To learn and admire other people's differences is perhaps one of the keys to life and without that key, there will be too many doors that will be locked, keeping you out and not allowing you to succeed. To learn that a majority of one kind in one place may be a minority of another kind in another place can help to initiate an outlook on life that promotes perspective and reason of any situation.

# Gender Differences

In their academic abilities, boys and girls are probably more similar than you think. But in other respects they may be more different than you realize.

## RESEARCH FINDINGS REGARDING GENDER DIFFERENCES

Researchers have identified a number of differences in the physical, cognitive, personal, and social domains.

### PHYSICAL ACTIVITY AND MOTOR SKILLS

Boys are temperamentally predisposed to be more active than girls. Thus, they have more trouble sitting still for long periods and are less likely to enjoy sedentary activities such as reading (W. O. Eaton & Enns, 1986; Newkirk, 2002). Before puberty, boys and girls seem to have similar *potential* for physical and psychomotor growth, although girls have a slight edge in fine motor skills (e.g., handwriting). But overall, boys develop their physical and motor skills more, perhaps

🍎 Make sure that students—especially boys—have frequent opportunities to release pent-up energy.

**visual–spatial ability** Ability to imagine and mentally manipulate two- and three-dimensional figures.

through participation in organized sports (Eccles, 2005; J. R. Thomas & French, 1985). After puberty, boys have a biological advantage in height and muscular strength: They're taller and, because of increased levels of the male sex hormone testosterone, they're stronger (Halpern, 2006; Hyde, 2005; J. R. Thomas & French, 1985).

Such differences are hardly justification for favoring either gender when enhancing students' physical fitness, of course. Physical education curricula and sports programs should provide equal opportunities for boys and girls to maximize their motor skills and physical well-being.

## COGNITIVE AND ACADEMIC ABILITIES

On average, boys and girls perform similarly on tests of general intelligence, in part because experts who construct the tests eliminate items that favor one group or the other (Halpern & LaMay, 2000). Researchers sometimes do find differences in more specific cognitive abilities, however. The most consistently observed gender difference is in visual–spatial ability, the ability to imagine and mentally manipulate two- and three-dimensional figures. As an example of what this ability involves, try the next exercise.

### EXPERIENCING FIRSTHAND
### MENTAL ROTATION

Are the three drawings shown here different rotations of the *same* object, or do they represent two or more *different* objects?

Object A          Object B          Object C

To correctly answer this question, you must "rotate" the objects in your head. If you mentally rotate Object B 180 degrees, you can see that it represents the same three-dimensional configuration as Object A. But if you rotate the right side of Object C down a bit and toward you, you can see that it's *not* the same as Object A; instead, it's a mirror image. Thus, Objects A and B are the same object; Object C is different. On average, males show greater proficiency in such visual–spatial thinking, even in infancy (Gallagher & Kaufman, 2005; Quinn & Liben, 2008). In contrast, females seem to have the advantage in certain verbal skills; for instance, girls have, on average, larger vocabularies and can more quickly think of the words they need to express their thoughts (Halpern, 2004, 2006; Halpern & LaMay, 2000; Lippa, 2002).

However, most gender differences in specific cognitive abilities tend to be *quite small*, with considerable overlap between the two groups (e.g., look once again at Figure 4.1). In addition, boys sometimes show greater *variability* in cognitive abilities than girls do, causing more boys than girls to demonstrate extremely high or low ability levels relative to their age-group (Halpern et al., 2007; Halpern & LaMay, 2000; Valla & Ceci, 2011).

Even though ability levels may be similar, girls consistently earn higher grades in school (Halpern et al., 2007; Halpern & LaMay, 2000). If achievement is measured by achievement tests rather than grades, research findings are inconsistent. When differences are found, girls typically have an advantage in reading and writing, and after puberty boys tend to have the upper hand in complex mathematical problem solving (Halpern, 2006; Halpern & LaMay, 2000; J. P. Robinson & Lubienski, 2011; Valla & Ceci, 2011).

Not only are gender differences in visual–spatial, verbal, and mathematical performance quite small, but some researchers have found them to be getting *smaller* in recent years. In other words, boys and girls are becoming increasingly similar in their academic performance (Hyde, Lindberg, Linn, Ellis, & Williams, 2008; Leaper & Friedman, 2007; Spelke, 2005). Thus, in general we should expect boys and girls to have similar academic aptitudes for different subject areas.

Expect boys and girls to have similar aptitudes for all academic subject areas.

## EXPERIENCE WITH TECHNOLOGY

As societies worldwide are gaining increasing access to computers and wireless technologies, boys and girls alike are becoming increasing proficient with technology—for example, they're apt to stay in frequent contact with peers by texting and sending photographs on cell phones and by posting messages on social networking websites such as Facebook (Greenhow, Robelia, & Hughes, 2009; Valkenburg & Peter, 2009). But overall, boys seem to spend more of their leisure time with technology than girls do. Boys are more likely to play video games, a pastime that may interfere with their reading and writing development but enhances their visual–spatial ability and probably also their comfort and expertise with computers (Feng, Spence, & Pratt, 2007; Ivory, 2006; Lucas & Sherry, 2004; Weis & Cerankosky, 2010).

## MOTIVATION IN ACADEMIC ACTIVITIES

On average, girls are more concerned about doing well in school: They're more engaged in classroom activities, more diligent in completing school assignments, and more likely to graduate from high school (H. M. Marks, 2000; Marsh, Martin, & Cheng, 2008; McCall, 1994; J. P. Robinson & Lubienski, 2011). Furthermore, girls are more interested in getting a college education than boys are, and in many countries more females than males earn college degrees (Halpern et al., 2007; National Science Foundation, 2007). However, this eagerness to achieve academically leads girls to prefer tasks at which they know they can succeed, and some find academic failure devastating. Boys are more willing to take on academic challenges and risks and more likely to take their failures in stride (Dweck, 2000; Yu, Elder, & Urdan, 1995).

> Make a special effort to motivate boys—for instance, by incorporating their personal interests into classroom activities.

> Help girls understand that taking risks and making mistakes reflect their willingness to take on challenges and stretch their abilities in new directions.

## SENSE OF SELF

Beginning in the upper elementary or middle school grades, boys appear to have a slightly more positive sense of self than girls do. This gender difference seems to be partly due to boys' tendency to *over*estimate their abilities and possibly also to girls' tendency to *under*estimate theirs (Hyde, 2007; Lundeberg & Mohan, 2009; Pajares, 2005). Boys' and girls' self-perceptions also tend to be consistent with stereotypes about what males and females are good at, especially in adolescence. Boys tend to rate themselves more highly in mathematics and sports, whereas girls tend to rate themselves more highly in reading and social studies. Such differences in self-perceptions persist even when boys' and girls' actual ability levels are *equal* (D. A. Cole, Martin, Peeke, Seroczynski, & Fier, 1999; Herbert & Stipek, 2005; Leaper & Friedman, 2007; Wigfield, Byrnes, & Eccles, 2006).

## INTERPERSONAL BEHAVIORS AND RELATIONSHIPS

One of the most consistently observed gender differences involves aggression. In early childhood and throughout the elementary and secondary school years, boys are more physically aggressive than girls, with the difference being especially large for *unprovoked* aggression (Card, Stucky, Sawalani, & Little, 2008; Hyde, 2007; Pellegrini, 2011). However, girls can be equally aggressive in a nonphysical way—for instance, by spreading rumors or snubbing peers (Crick, Grotpeter, & Bigbee, 2002; French, Jansen, & Pidada, 2002; Pellegrini & Archer, 2005). Some of their victims can be emotionally devastated by such treatment (Rudolph, Caldwell, & Conley, 2005).

Consistent differences are also seen in boys' and girls' interpersonal activities and relationships. Boys tend to congregate in large groups that engage in rough-and-tumble play, organized group games, and physical risk-taking activities (Maccoby, 2002; Pellegrini, Kato, Blatchford, & Baines, 2002; A. J. Rose & Smith, 2009). They enjoy competition and can be fairly assertive in their efforts to achieve their goals (Benenson et al., 2002; Eisenberg, Martin, & Fabes, 1996; Maccoby, 2002). They may often try to hide their true emotions in social situations, putting up a tough, "nothing-can-bother-me" front (Lippa, 2002; Pollack, 2006).

Whereas boys are apt to be competitive, girls are more likely to be affiliative and cooperative. Thus, they tend to form closer relationships with their teachers and to achieve at higher levels when classroom activities involve cooperation rather than competition (Inglehart, Brown, & Vida, 1994; Wentzel, Battle, Russell, & Looney, 2010). Girls also seem to be more attuned to others' mental states and more sensitive to the subtle, nonverbal messages—the body language—that others communicate (Bosacki, 2000; Deaux, 1984). Girls spend much of their leisure time with one or two close friends, with whom they may share their innermost thoughts and feelings (Leaper & Friedman, 2007; A. J. Rose & Smith, 2009). Although girls can be assertive in making their wishes known, they're also concerned about resolving conflicts and maintaining group

> Chapter 3 examines aggression in greater detail.

> Communicate that showing emotion is a natural human trait that is appropriate for males as well as females.

> Accommodate girls' affiliative nature by providing numerous opportunities for cooperative group work.

harmony, and so they may sometimes subordinate their own needs to those of others (Benenson et al., 2002; Leaper & Friedman, 2007; Rudolph et al., 2005).

### CLASSROOM BEHAVIORS

In part because boys tend to be physically more active than girls, they're more likely to misbehave in class (Altermatt, Jovanovic, & Perry, 1998; Gay, 2006; Sadker & Sadker, 1994). Boys talk more and ask more questions, sometimes without waiting to be called on. They also tend to dominate small-group discussions and work sessions. Girls are more reticent classroom participants. They're less likely to publicly volunteer ideas and ask questions, perhaps for fear of looking stupid or perhaps because they worry that looking too smart will reduce their popularity (Jovanovic & King, 1998; Sadker & Sadker, 1994; Théberge, 1994; Wentzel, 2009). Girls are more likely to express their opinions in small-group rather than large-group discussions, and they're more likely to assume the role of leader (thereby developing valuable leadership skills) in same-sex groups (Fennema, 1987; MacLean, Sasse, Keating, Stewart, & Miller, 1995; Théberge, 1994).

### CAREER ASPIRATIONS

Historically, boys have had more ambitious career aspirations than girls have. In recent years, however, many girls—especially those in Western countries—have also begun to set their sights on challenging professions. Often, boys and girls alike focus on careers that are stereotypically "appropriate" for their gender, in part because they have greater self-confidence about their ability to succeed in such careers (Bandura, Barbaranelli, Caprara, & Pastorelli, 2001; Leaper & Friedman, 2007; Weisgram, Bigler, & Liben, 2010). Students' general life goals come into the picture as well: Girls are more likely than boys to consider how their career choices might mesh with their desires to work with people (rather than objects) and to raise a family (Diekman, Brown, Johnston, & Clark, 2010; Eccles, 2009).

Some gender differences are especially prevalent for particular age-groups. Table 4.1 identifies differences you're apt to see at various grade levels and offers relevant classroom strategies for accommodating these differences.

## ORIGINS OF GENDER DIFFERENCES

Obviously, heredity determines basic physical differences between males and females; some are present at birth, some emerge at puberty. And because of inherited differences in sex-related hormones—especially estrogen for girls and testosterone for boys—girls reach puberty earlier and boys eventually become taller and stronger. Hormones may account for certain nonphysical gender differences as well. The gender difference in physical aggression appears to be related to testosterone levels (Lippa, 2002; S. Moore & Rosenthal, 2006). Hormones may also play a role in the small differences observed in visual–spatial and verbal abilities, possibly by affecting neurological development in different areas of the brain (Valla & Ceci, 2011; Vuoksimaa et al., 2010). Hormones even seem to influence children's preferences for male-stereotypical versus female-stereotypical behaviors (Auyeung et al., 2009; Hines et al., 2002).

Yet environmental factors clearly play a role as well, often by interacting with and amplifying existing biology-based gender differences (Lippa, 2002; Nuttall, Casey, & Pezaris, 2005). Virtually every culture teaches children that some behaviors are more appropriate for males and others more appropriate for females, as the following exercise may show you.

### EXPERIENCING FIRSTHAND
#### PICTURE THIS #2

Form a picture in your mind of each of the following individuals. Make note of the *first* image that comes to mind in each case:

| | |
|---|---|
| Secretary | Scientist |
| Bank president | Fashion model |
| Elementary school teacher | Building contractor |

Which individuals did you picture as male, and which did you picture as female?

Occasionally have students work in same-sex pairs or groups.

Compared to girls, boys are less likely to show their emotions or to actively work to resolve interpersonal conflicts. Watch "Emotions: Late Adolescence" and "Friendships: Late Adolescence."

# DEVELOPMENTAL TRENDS

**TABLE 4.1** • Gender-Related Characteristics at Different Grade Levels

| GRADE LEVEL | AGE-TYPICAL CHARACTERISTICS | EXAMPLE | SUGGESTED STRATEGIES |
|---|---|---|---|
| <br>**K–2** | • Physical abilities, general intelligence, and more specific cognitive abilities roughly equivalent for boys and girls<br>• More self-control in girls than in boys, leading to girls' easier adjustment to a classroom environment<br>• Rigid stereotypes about gender-appropriate behavior; eagerness to conform to these stereotypes<br>• Play groups largely segregated by gender<br>• Different themes in fantasy play (e.g., boys depict heroism, girls depict romance); play activities more active and forceful for boys than for girls | Most of the girls in a first-grade class can sit still during small-group reading instruction, but some of the boys quickly become fidgety and distracted. The boys are more likely to be attentive in their reading groups if they can physically act out a story they're reading. | • Expect and encourage equal achievement in all areas of the academic curriculum.<br>• Give students whatever structure they may need to stay on task in order to acquire basic skills, but also give them numerous opportunities to release pent-up energy.<br>• Provide materials for a wide range of play activities (e.g., household items, dress-up clothes, toy trucks, building blocks, balls).<br>• Monitor students' play activities for potentially dangerous behaviors; provide guidance about which actions are and are not safe. |
| <br>**3–5** | • Gender differences in self-evaluations of math ability, with boys rating themselves more highly than girls despite equal math achievement<br>• Play groups largely segregated by gender<br>• Organized large-group games more common for boys than for girls<br>• More competition, aggression, and risk taking in boys than in girls<br>• Onset of puberty earlier for girls (average age 10)<br>• Tendency for some early-maturing girls to feel out of sync with peers, putting them at greater risk for depression | During recess, many of the boys in a fourth-grade class organize a game of baseball or soccer. A few girls join in, but most of the girls stand on the sidelines and talk with one or two friends. | • Assure students that boys and girls have equal potential in all areas of the academic curriculum.<br>• Provide materials for group games (balls, bats, soccer goal nets, etc.).<br>• Set and enforce reasonable limits on play behaviors so that students' physical safety is ensured.<br>• Be especially sensitive and supportive as girls show signs of puberty (e.g., allow trips to the restroom as needed). |
| <br>**6–8** | • Onset of puberty later for boys (average age 11½)<br>• Greater physical ability for boys than for girls; participation in sports more widespread and prestigious for boys<br>• Emergence of gender differences in overall self-esteem and assessments of physical attractiveness and athletic competence, with self-ratings being higher for boys and preoccupation with physical appearance being greater for girls<br>• Increasing flexibility about which behaviors are gender-appropriate, especially for girls<br>• Tendency for boys' social groups to be larger and less intimate than girls'<br>• More emotional distress for girls than for boys when interpersonal relationships go badly; tendency for boys to try to hide feelings of sadness and distress | A student named Jason explains how he often hides his feelings at school: "If something happens to you, you have to say, 'Yeah, no big deal,' even when you're really hurting. . . . I've punched so many lockers in my life, it's not even funny. When I get home, I'll cry about it." | • Respect students' modesty and need for privacy when they must change clothes or take a shower in physical education or after-school sports.<br>• Encourage students to gain skills in domains stereotypically associated with the other gender (e.g., teach cooking and woodworking to boys and girls alike)<br>• Encourage both boys and girls to pursue extracurricular sports activities; encourage attendance at both boys' and girls' sports events.<br>• In appropriate contexts, teach good grooming habits and other skills for presenting oneself well to others.<br>• Communicate to boys that occasionally showing emotion and vulnerability is both manly and healthy. |
| <br>**9–12** | • Gradual improvement in girls' self-assessments of physical attractiveness<br>• Greater interest in a college education among girls than among boys<br>• Tendency for boys to aspire more to hands-on professions (e.g., working with tools and machines) and for girls to aspire more to social or artistic occupations (e.g., teaching, counseling, writing)<br>• Prosocial behavior seen more frequently in girls than in boys, despite equal ability to act prosocially<br>• Substance abuse and casual sexual intercourse more common in boys than in girls<br>• Depression and eating disorders more common in girls than in boys | Most members of a high school service club are girls. The club plans two community service projects for the year: making monthly after-school trips to a local nursing home and conducting a schoolwide fundraiser to buy holiday gifts for low-income children. | • Encourage students to cross stereotypical boundaries in course selection (e.g., girls taking advanced math, boys taking creative writing).<br>• Provide information about the benefits of a college education (e.g., invite recent high school graduates to come and share their college experiences).<br>• Expose students to diverse occupations and professions through guest lectures, trips to community businesses and agencies, and the like.<br>• Work with colleagues and parents to vigorously address unhealthful and risky out-of-school behaviors.<br>• Alert the school counselor when you suspect substance abuse, serious depression, an eating disorder, or some other potentially life-threatening condition. |

*Sources:* Benenson & Christakos, 2003; Binns, Steinberg, Amorosi, & Cuevas, 1997; Bussey & Bandura, 1992; Card, Stucky, Sawalani, & Little, 2008; D. A. Cole et al., 2001; Crouter, Whiteman, McHale, & Osgood, 2007; Davenport et al., 1998; Davila, 2008; Eisenberg et al., 1996; Evans-Winters & Ivie, 2009; Fabes, Martin, & Hanish, 2003; M. E. Ford, 1996; Grusec & Hastings, 2007; Halpern, 2004, 2006; Halpern et al., 2007; Hankin, Mermelstein, & Roesch, 2007; M. S. Hardy, 2002; J. R. Harris, 1995; Harter, 1999; Hayward, 2003; Herbert & Stipek, 2005; Hyde, 2005; Hyde & Durik, 2005; Leaper & Friedman, 2007; Liben & Bigler, 2002; Lippa, 2002; Maccoby, 2002; Matthews, Ponitz, & Morrison, 2009; T. M. McDevitt & Ormrod, 2013; S. Moore & Rosenthal, 2006; Pollack, 2006, p. 72 (Jason example); Ponitz, Rimm-Kaufman, Brock, & Nathanson, 2009; M. Rhodes & Gelman, 2008; Rogoff, 2003; A. J. Rose & Smith, 2009; Rudolph et al., 2005; R. M. Ryan & Kuczkowski, 1994; Sadker & Sadker, 1994; Seiffge-Krenke, Aunola, & Nurmi, 2009; J. R. Thomas & French, 1985; Wigfield, Byrnes, & Eccles, 2006; Wigfield, Eccles, & Pintrich, 1996; Zambo & Brozo, 2009 (reading group example).

**gender schema** Self-constructed, organized body of beliefs about characteristics and behaviors of males or females.

If you're like most people, your secretary, teacher, and fashion model were females, and your bank president, scientist, and building contractor were males. Gender stereotypes persist throughout our society, and even preschool children are aware of them (Bornholt, Goodnow, & Cooney, 1994; Eisenberg et al., 1996; Nosek & Smyth, 2011).

Numerous aspects of society conspire to socialize growing children to conform to gender stereotypes. For example, many adults believe—and communicate the message—that boys are "naturally" better in some domains (e.g., math) and that girls are "naturally" better in others (e.g., reading), even in cases where no gender differences in achievement exist (Bleeker & Jacobs, 2004; Eccles, 2009; Herbert & Stipek, 2005). Gender-stereotypical toys and games can also have impact: The dolls and board games that girls often get foster verbal and social skills, whereas the building blocks and soccer balls that boys get are more apt to foster visual–spatial skills (Feng et al., 2007; Frost, Shin, & Jacobs, 1998; Liss, 1983; Lytton & Romney, 1991).

Boys' and girls' personality characteristics, too, are socialized to some degree. Especially in cultural groups that espouse traditional gender roles, boys are often reinforced—by adults and peers alike—for being assertive and aggressive, whereas girls are encouraged to be restrained and nurturing (Leaper & Friedman, 2007; Manning & Baruth, 2009; Rothbart, 2011). And television and video games often portray males as aggressive leaders and successful problem solvers, whereas females are depicted as demure, obedient followers (Furnham & Mak, 1999; Leaper & Friedman, 2007; M. K. Miller & Summers, 2007; T. L. Thompson & Zerbinos, 1995).

As young children become increasingly aware of the typical characteristics and behaviors of boys, girls, men, and women, they gradually pull their knowledge together into self-constructed understandings, or gender schemas, of how males and females are different. These gender schemas, in turn, become part of their sense of self and guide them in their behaviors. By the time children reach school age, much of the pressure to act "appropriately" for their gender comes from within rather than from others (Bem, 1981; Eccles, 2009; Ruble, Martin, & Berenbaum, 2006).

Self-imposed adherence to gender stereotypes is an example of *self-socialization,* a concept described in Chapter 3.

Because gender schemas are self-constructed, their contents vary considerably from one individual to another (Liben & Bigler, 2002). For example, in adolescence some girls incorporate into their "female" schema unrealistic standards of beauty presented in popular media (films, fashion magazines, etc.). As girls compare themselves to these standards, they almost invariably come up short, and their self-assessments of physical attractiveness decline. In an effort to achieve the super-thin bodies they believe to be ideal, they may fall victim to eating disorders (Attie, Brooks-Gunn, & Petersen, 1990; Weichold, Silbereisen, & Schmitt-Rodermund, 2003). Likewise, some teenage boys go out of their way to meet self-constructed macho standards of male behavior by putting on a tough-guy act at school and bragging (perhaps accurately, but more often not) about their many sexual conquests (Pollack, 2006; K. M. Williams, 2001a).

Not all students have rigid or unrealistic stereotypes of what their gender should be like, of course. In fact, as students get older, many become increasingly flexible about what males and females can and should do. Those with more flexible gender schemas are more likely to pursue counterstereotypical interests and career paths (Liben & Bigler, 2002; C. L. Martin & Ruble, 2004).

## MAKING APPROPRIATE ACCOMMODATIONS FOR GENDER DIFFERENCES

Despite many teachers' best intentions to treat male and female students equitably, subtle inequities continue. For example, teachers tend to give more attention to boys, partly because boys ask more questions and present more discipline problems. Teachers also give boys more feedback—praise and criticism alike—than they give girls (Altermatt et al., 1998; Eisenberg et al., 1996; Gay, 2006; Halpern et al., 2007; S. M. Jones & Dindia, 2004).

The Into the Classroom feature "Promoting Gender Equity" offers several general suggestions for equitably fostering the learning and development of both sexes. At the same time, gender differences sometimes *do* warrant differential treatment of girls and boys. For example, girls are likely to improve their visual–spatial ability if we give them frequent opportunities to engage in activities requiring visual–spatial thinking (B. M. Casey et al., 2008; Gallagher & Kaufman, 2005). Meanwhile, boys are more likely to improve their literacy skills if we allow them to pursue typical "boy" interests (e.g., sports, adventure) while reading and writing (Newkirk, 2002).

Acknowledge that some differential treatment of girls and boys is appropriate, especially if it helps to *reduce* gender gaps in particular abilities and predispositions.

## Promoting Gender Equity

🍏 **Use your knowledge of typical gender differences to create greater equity for males and females, *not* to form expectations about how well males and females are likely to perform in various activities.**
An elementary physical education teacher realizes that most of the girls in her class probably haven't had as much experience as the boys in throwing a baseball or softball overhand, so she gives the girls extra instruction and practice in the overhand throw.

🍏 **When planning lessons and instructional strategies, consider typical interests and activity levels of both boys and girls.**
A sixth-grade math teacher teams up with her school's information technology teacher to create a month-long unit in which students learn how to use Game Maker, software that enables them to create simple video games using a variety of animated characters, graphics, and background music. The students then work in small groups to design games that will help them practice a particular mathematical concept or skill. At the end of the unit, each group demonstrates its game for the class, and the teachers copy the games onto compact discs so that students can play them at home.

🍏 **Use curriculum materials that represent both genders in a positive and competent light; include materials that portray both genders competently engaging in counterstereotypical behaviors.**
An English teacher assigns Harper Lee's *To Kill a Mockingbird*, in which an attorney named Atticus Finch is portrayed as a gentle, affectionate, and compassionate man, and his daughter Scout is portrayed as a courageous and adventuresome 8-year-old. The teacher also assigns Zora Neale Hurston's *Their Eyes Were Watching God*, in which an African American woman grows from a teenager who depends on others to meet her needs into a self-sufficient woman who can easily fend for herself.

🍏 **Monitor yourself to see whether you are unintentionally treating boys and girls in ways that limit the learning opportunities of one gender.**
A French teacher decides to count the number of times he calls on boys and girls during class. He finds that he calls on boys more than three times as frequently as girls, partly because the boys raise their hands more often. Therefore he institutes a new procedure: He alternates between boys and girls when he calls on students, and he sometimes calls on students who aren't raising their hands.

---

We must also help students recognize that gender stereotypes are just that—*stereotypes*—and don't necessarily limit what males and females can or should be. For example, we can:

🍏 Expose students to same-gender adults and peers who excel in domains commonly associated with the opposite gender.

🍏 Talk about the importance of all academic subject areas for students' future success.

🍏 Explain the historical roots of stereotypes. For instance, explain that differing expectations for males and females are a holdover from an era when many jobs outside the home required considerable strength (and thus were better suited for men) and jobs inside the home could easily be combined with breastfeeding (and thus were better suited for women).

🍏 Engage students in discussions about the adverse consequences of rigid gender roles—noting, for example, that adhering to such roles limits people's options and results in a lot of talent going to waste. (Bem, 1983, 1984; Evans-Winters & Ivie, 2009; Fennema, 1987; Huguet & Régner, 2007; A. Kelly & Smail, 1986; Pollack, 2006)

# Socioeconomic Differences

The concept of socioeconomic status (SES) encompasses a number of variables, including family income, parents' education levels, and parents' occupations. A family's socioeconomic status—whether high-SES, middle-SES, or low-SES—gives us a sense of family members' standing in the community: what type of neighborhood they live in, how much influence they have on political decision making, what educational opportunities are available to them, and so on.

Students' school performance is correlated with their socioeconomic status: Higher-SES students tend to have higher academic achievement, and lower-SES students tend to be at greater risk for dropping out of school (J.-S. Lee & Bowen, 2006; McLoyd, 1998; Sirin, 2005). As students from lower-SES families move through the grade levels, they tend to fall further and further behind their higher-SES peers (Farkas, 2008; Jimerson, Egeland, & Teo, 1999). When researchers find achievement differences among students from different ethnic groups, the differences in the students' socioeconomic status—*not* their cultural differences—seem to be mostly to blame (Byrnes, 2003; N. E. Hill, Bush, & Roosa, 2003; Murdock, 2000).

**socioeconomic status (SES)** One's general social and economic standing in society; encompasses family income, occupation, and educational level.

Life certainly isn't perfect for students from high-SES homes (Luthar, 2006; Luthar & Latendresse, 2005). Some high-income parents have such high expectations for their children's achievement that the children suffer from significant anxiety and depression. In addition, some high-income parents have demanding jobs that keep them both physically and emotionally distant from their children, thereby limiting the guidance and support they provide. But by and large it's children who live in poverty, especially *chronic* poverty, who face the most significant obstacles to academic success and personal well-being.

## CHALLENGES ASSOCIATED WITH POVERTY

Many, many children grow up in poverty, including more than *16 million* children (22%) in the United States (U.S. Census Bureau, 2010). Some of these children live in inner-city neighborhoods, but others live in rural areas or in modest apartments in wealthy suburbs. Some come from families that can meet life's basic necessities (e.g., food, warm clothing, adequate shelter) but have little money left over for luxuries. Many others live in extreme poverty; these students are the ones most at risk for academic failure and thus most in need of our attention and support.

Several factors tend to contribute to the generally lower school achievement of low-SES students. Students who face only one or two of these challenges often do quite well in school, but those who face many or all of them are at high risk for academic failure and other negative outcomes (Becker & Luthar, 2002; Gerard & Buehler, 2004; Grissmer, Williamson, Kirby, & Berends, 1998).

**Poor nutrition and health**    Lower-income families have fewer financial resources to ensure that their children have adequate nutrition and health care. Poor nutrition in the early years of life (including the nine months before birth) can lead to impairments in children's attention, memory, and learning ability (D'Amato, Chittooran, & Whitten, 1992; Noble, Tottenham, & Casey, 2005). Poor nutrition seems to influence school achievement both directly—for example, by hampering early brain development—and indirectly—for example, by leaving children listless and inattentive in class (Ashiabi & O'Neal, 2008; Sigman & Whaley, 1998). And inadequate health care means that some conditions that interfere with school attendance and performance, such as asthma and hearing problems, go unaddressed (Berliner, 2005).

*Help families apply for free and reduced-cost meal programs. Refer students with chronic health problems to the school nurse.*

**Inadequate housing and frequent moves**    Many poor children live in tight quarters, perhaps sharing one or two rooms with several other family members (Hawkins, 1997; Hernandez, Denton, & Macartney, 2008). Furthermore, children who move frequently from one rental apartment to another must often change schools as well. In the process they lose existing social support networks—both with teachers and with peers—and may miss lessons on fundamental academic skills (Croninger & Valli, 2009; Gruman, Harachi, Abbott, Catalano, & Fleming, 2008; Hattie, 2009).

**Exposure to toxic substances**    Especially when children live in poor, inner-city neighborhoods, their surroundings may expose them to excessive levels of environmental toxins that can seriously jeopardize their health and brain development (Hubbs-Tait, Nation, Krebs, & Bellinger, 2005; Koger, Schettler, & Weiss, 2005). For example, in old, badly maintained apartment buildings, children may be exposed to lead in the dust from deteriorating paint. In addition, the city water supply may contain pesticides or industrial waste, and the local air may be polluted by power plants and industrial incinerators.

**Unhealthy social environments**    On average, low-SES neighborhoods and communities have higher frequencies of violence and vandalism, greater prevalence of alcoholism and drug abuse, and greater numbers of antisocial peers. Furthermore, there are fewer productive outlets for leisure time—libraries, recreation centers, sports leagues, and so on—and fewer positive adult role models. Such factors appear to be partly responsible for the lower academic achievement of students who live in poverty (Aikens & Barbarin, 2008; T. D. Cook, Herman, Phillips, & Settersten, 2002; Duncan & Magnuson, 2005; Leventhal & Brooks-Gunn, 2000; Nettles, Caughy, & O'Campo, 2008).

**Emotional stress**   Students at all income levels experience stressful conditions at one time or another, but students from low-income families have more than their share. On average, low-SES homes are more chaotic and unpredictable than affluent ones. Children may wonder where their next meal is coming from or when the landlord might evict them for not paying rent. The preponderance of single-parent homes among low-SES families can come into play as well: A single parent may be too distracted by personal problems to offer much affection or consistent discipline. As a result of such factors, students from low-SES families show higher-than-average rates of depression and other emotional problems (Crosnoe & Cooper, 2010; G. W. Evans, Gonnella, Marcynyszyn, Gentile, & Salpekar, 2005; Morales & Guerra, 2006; Parke et al., 2004). Sometimes, too, chronic stress adversely affects students' physical development, which in turn can hamper their cognitive development (G. W. Evans & Schamberg, 2009).

Not all children from low-income homes live in chronically stressful conditions, of course, and those whose families provide consistent support, guidance, and discipline generally enjoy good mental health (N. E. Hill et al., 2003; M. O. Wright & Masten, 2006). Nevertheless, we should continually be on the lookout for signs that certain students are undergoing unusual stress at home and then provide whatever support we can. In some instances effective support may involve nothing more than being a willing listener. In other cases we may want to consult with a school counselor or social worker about possible support systems at school and resources in the local community.

Provide emotional support and appropriate referrals when students seem to be undergoing exceptional stress at home.

**Gaps in background knowledge**   Some students from low-SES families lack the basic knowledge and skills (e.g., knowledge of letters and numbers) on which successful school learning so often depends (Aikens & Barbarin, 2008; Brooks-Gunn, Linver, & Fauth, 2005; Siegler, 2009). Access to early educational opportunities that might foster such skills—books, computers, trips to zoos and museums, and so on—is always somewhat dependent on a family's financial resources. In addition, some parents have few basic academic skills that they might share with their children. However, as always, we must be careful not to overgeneralize. Some low-income parents have considerable education (perhaps a college degree) and may be well equipped to read to their children and provide other enriching educational experiences (Goldenberg, 2001; Raikes et al., 2006; Sidel, 1996).

Identify and address any missing basic skills.

**Lower-quality schools**   Unfortunately, the students who most need good schools are often least likely to have them. Schools in low-income neighborhoods and communities tend to receive less funding and, as a result, are often poorly equipped and maintained. Teacher turnover rates are high in these schools, and disciplinary tactics tend to be more harsh and less effective. Furthermore, some teachers at these schools have low expectations for students, offering a less-challenging curriculum, assigning less homework, and providing fewer opportunities to develop advanced thinking skills than do teachers in wealthier school districts (G. W. Evans, 2004; McLoyd, 1998; Pianta & Hamre, 2009; Raudenbush, 2009).

Of course, schools in low-income school districts don't have to be this way. In fact, we teachers can make a *huge* difference in the quality of children's educational experiences at even the poorest of schools. Consider a teacher whom researchers called Miss A (E. Pedersen, Faucher, & Eaton, 1978):

> Miss A taught at Ray School, an elementary school in a large, North American city. The school building—constructed like a fortress, with iron bars on its windows—was hardly appealing or welcoming. Its neighbors included old tenement buildings, a junkyard, and a brothel. Fewer than 10% of its students eventually completed high school.
>
> Nonetheless, Miss A worked wonders with the students in her first-grade classes. She showed obvious affection for them, insisted on appropriate behavior without ever losing her temper, and shared her lunch with those who hadn't brought one. She continually hammered home the importance of learning and education and had high expectations for achievement. She made sure her students learned to read, and she stayed after school with them whenever they needed extra help.
>
> Miss A's students got higher grades than students in other classes not only in their first-grade year but also for several years after that. On average, their IQ scores went *up*

Be optimistic that you *can* make a difference in students' lives.

between third and sixth grade (one girl's score changed from 93 to 126), whereas the IQs of most students at Ray School went down. When researchers tracked down some of Miss A's students many years later, they found that these students were far more financially and professionally successful than the typical Ray graduate. And every single one of them remembered her name.

## FOSTERING RESILIENCE

Remember that many bright, capable students come from low-income families.

Thanks in part to teachers like Miss A, many students of low-income families succeed in school despite exceptional hardships. Some are resilient students who acquire characteristics and coping skills that help them rise above their adverse circumstances. As a group, resilient students have likable personalities, a positive sense of self, and ambitious goals, and they believe that success comes with hard work and a good education (S. Goldstein & Brooks, 2006; Schoon, 2006; Werner & Smith, 2001).

Researchers have learned a great deal about factors that can foster resilience in students from challenging backgrounds. With their findings in mind, I offer the following suggestions.

*Be a dependable source of academic and emotional support.*  Resilient students usually have one or more individuals in their lives whom they trust and can turn to in difficult times (Masten, 2001; McLoyd, 1998; Werner, 1995, 2006). For example, resilient students often mention teachers who have taken a personal interest in them and been instrumental in their school success (R. M. Clark, 1983; McMillan & Reed, 1994; D. A. O'Donnell, Schwab-Stone, & Muyeed, 2002). As teachers, we're most likely to promote resilience in low-SES students when we show that we like and respect them, are available and willing to listen to their concerns, hold high expectations for their performance, and provide the encouragement and support they need to succeed both inside and outside the classroom (Kincheloe, 2009; Masten & Coatsworth, 1998; Milner, 2006; Schoon, 2006).

*Build on students' strengths.*  Although some students from lower-SES backgrounds may lag behind in basic academic skills, they're apt to bring many strengths to the classroom. For example, these students are often quite clever at improvising with everyday objects. If they work part-time to help their families make ends meet, they may have a good understanding of the working world. If they are children of single, working parents, they may know far more than their classmates about cooking, cleaning house, and taking care of younger siblings. Their own scarce resources are likely to have instilled genuine empathy and generosity for other people in need. And many of these students are quite knowledgeable about certain aspects of popular culture—characters and plot lines in television shows, lyrics from current rap songs, and so on (Freedom Writers, 1999; Kraus, Piff, & Keltner, 2011; Lareau, 2003; Torrance, 1995).

As teachers, then, we must remember that students who have grown up in poverty may, in some respects, have more knowledge and skills than their economically advantaged peers. Such knowledge and skills can often provide a basis for teaching classroom subject matter (Schoon, 2006; Varelas & Pappas, 2006). Furthermore, students who are willing to talk about challenges they have faced can sensitize their classmates to serious inequities in today's society.

*Identify and provide missing resources and experiences important for successful learning.*  Some students from very poor families lack basic essentials—such as nutritious meals, warm clothing, adequate health care, and school supplies—that will be important for their academic success. Many government programs and community agencies can help to provide such essentials. School districts offer free and reduced-cost meal programs for children from low-income families. Charitable organizations often distribute warm winter jackets gathered from annual clothing drives. Many communities have low-cost health clinics. And some office supply stores and large discount chains donate notebooks, pens, and other school supplies to children who need them.

Beyond connecting low-income students and families with community resources, we should identify any basic experiences that students may not have had. Field trips to zoos, farms, the mountains, or the ocean may be in order. And of course, we should identify and teach any basic skills that, for whatever reason, students haven't yet acquired. When we do so, we're likely to see significant improvements in students' classroom performance (S. A. Griffin, Case, &

Capodilupo, 1995; G. Phillips, McNaughton, & MacDonald, 2004; Siegler, 2009). However, we must be careful not to focus *exclusively* on basic skills, especially when doing so means a fair amount of drill and practice. Students' academic progress will suffer over the long run if they don't also have frequent opportunities to engage in complex academic tasks—reading for understanding, mastering new technologies, solving real-world problems, and so on (Cazden, 2001; Reis, McCoach, Little, Muller, & Kaniskan, 2011).

 Balance any needed instruction in basic skills with challenging and engaging real-world activities.

## WORKING WITH HOMELESS STUDENTS

Children of homeless families typically face far greater challenges than other students from low-income families. Many have chronic physical problems, limited social support networks, significant mental health issues, and inappropriate behaviors. Some may be reluctant to come to school because they lack bathing facilities and suitable clothing. And some may have moved so frequently from one school to another that they have large gaps in their academic skills (Coe, Salamon, & Molnar, 1991; McLoyd, 1998; P. M. Miller, 2011; Polakow, 2007).

As teachers we, too, face extra challenges when teaching students who live in homeless shelters. Following are several suggestions for giving these students the support they may need to achieve academic and social success at school (Pawlas, 1994):

- Pair new students with classmates who can provide guidance and assistance—for example, by explaining school procedures and making introductions to other students.
- Provide a notebook, clipboard, or other portable "desk" on which students can do their homework at the shelter.
- Find adult or teenage volunteers to serve as tutors at the shelter.
- Meet with students' parents at the shelter rather than at school.
- Share copies of homework assignments, school calendars, and newsletters with shelter officials.

When we use such strategies, however, we must keep in mind that students and their families are apt to feel embarrassed about their homeless status (Polakow, 2007). Accordingly, showing respect for their privacy and self-esteem must be a high priority.

# Students at Risk

**Students at risk** are those with a high probability of failing to acquire the minimum academic skills necessary for success in the adult world. Many students at risk drop out before high school graduation, and many others graduate without mastery of basic skills in reading or mathematics (e.g., Boling & Evans, 2008; Laird, Kienzl, DeBell, & Chapman, 2007). A common assumption is that the reasons for dropping out lie primarily in the students themselves (V. E. Lee & Burkam, 2003). But as we will see, school characteristics also play a significant role.

## CHARACTERISTICS OF STUDENTS AT RISK

Students at risk come from all socioeconomic levels, but children of poor, single-parent families are especially likely to leave school before high school graduation. Boys are more likely than girls to drop out, and African Americans, Hispanics, and Native Americans are more likely than European American and Asian American students to drop out. Also, students in large cities and rural areas are more likely to drop out than students in the suburbs are; graduation rates in some big cities are less than 40% (C. Chapman, Laird, & KewalRamani, 2010; Hardré & Reeve, 2003; L. S. Miller, 1995; National Research Council, 2004).

Students at risk, especially those who eventually drop out, typically have some or all of the following characteristics:

- *A history of academic failure.* On average, students who drop out have poorer reading and study skills, achieve at lower levels, and are more likely to have repeated a grade than their classmates who graduate. Consistent patterns of low achievement are sometimes seen as early as third grade (K. L. Alexander, Entwisle, & Dauber, 1995; Battin-Pearson et al., 2000; Belfiore & Hornyak, 1998; Hattie, 2009; Suh, Suh, & Houston, 2007).

**student at risk** Student with a high probability of failing to acquire minimal academic skills necessary for success in the adult world.

- *Emotional and behavioral problems.* Potential dropouts tend to have lower self-esteem than their more successful classmates. They're also more likely to exhibit serious behavioral problems (e.g., fighting, substance abuse) both in and out of school. Often their close friends are low achieving and, in some cases, antisocial peers (Battin-Pearson et al., 2000; Garnier, Stein, & Jacobs, 1997; Jozefowicz, Arbreton, Eccles, Barber, & Colarossi, 1994; Suh et al., 2007).

- *Lack of psychological attachment to school.* Students at risk for academic failure are less likely to identify with their school or to perceive themselves to be a vital part of the school community. For example, they engage in few extracurricular activities and are apt to express dissatisfaction with school in general (Christenson & Thurlow, 2004; Hymel, Comfort, Schonert-Reichl, & McDougall, 1996; Rumberger, 1995).

- *Increasing disinvolvement with school.* Dropping out isn't necessarily an all-or-nothing event. Many high school dropouts show lesser forms of dropping out many years before they officially leave school. Future dropouts are absent from school more frequently than their peers, even in the elementary grades. In addition, they're more likely to have been suspended from school and to show a long-term pattern of dropping out, returning to school, and dropping out again (Christenson & Thurlow, 2004; Suh et al., 2007).

The characteristics just described certainly aren't surefire indicators of which students will drop out, however. For example, some dropouts come from two-parent, middle-income homes, and some are actively involved in school activities almost until the time they drop out (Hymel et al., 1996; Janosz, Le Blanc, Boulerice, & Tremblay, 2000).

## WHY STUDENTS DROP OUT

Students drop out for a variety of reasons. Some have little family and peer encouragement and support for school success. Others have extenuating life circumstances; perhaps they have medical problems, take a job to help support the family, or get pregnant. Many simply become dissatisfied with school: They find the school environment unwelcoming or dangerous, perceive the curriculum to be boring and personally irrelevant, or doubt that they can pass high-stakes achievement tests on which graduation depends (Brayboy & Searle, 2007; Hardré & Reeve, 2003; Hursh, 2007; Portes, 1996; Rumberger, 1995; L. Steinberg, Blinde, & Chan, 1984).

*Chapter 15 looks more closely at the effects of high-stakes testing.*

Sadly, teacher behaviors can enter into the picture as well. For example, a teacher might communicate low expectations for students' achievement either explicitly (e.g., by telling them that their chances of earning passing grades are slim) or implicitly (e.g., by brushing off their requests for assistance on assigned tasks). Students are more likely to drop out when they perceive their teachers to be uninterested in helping them succeed (Becker & Luthar, 2002; Farrell, 1990; Suh et al., 2007).

## SUPPORTING STUDENTS AT RISK

Because students who are at risk for academic failure are a diverse group of individuals with a diverse set of needs, there is no single strategy that can keep all of them in school until high school graduation (Christenson & Thurlow, 2004; Janosz et al., 2000). Nevertheless, effective school and classroom practices will go a long way in helping these students stay on the road to academic success and high school graduation. Following are several suggestions based on research findings.

🍏 *Identify students at risk as early as possible.* We begin to see indicators of dropping out, such as low school achievement and high absenteeism, as early as elementary school. And other signs—such as disruptive behavior and lack of involvement in school activities—often appear years before students officially withdraw from school. Therefore it's quite possible to identify at-risk students early in their school careers and take steps to prevent or remediate academic difficulties before they become insurmountable. For students at risk, prevention, early intervention, and long-term support are more effective than later, short-term efforts (Brooks-Gunn, 2003; Christenson & Thurlow, 2004; McCall & Plemons, 2001; Ramey & Ramey, 1998).

*Chapter 13 offers many strategies for creating warm, emotionally supportive schools and classrooms.*

🍏 *Create a warm, supportive school and classroom atmosphere.* Teachers and schools that have high success rates with students at risk tend to be those that communicate a sense of caring, concern, and high regard for students (Christenson & Thurlow, 2004; Hamre & Pianta, 2005; Pianta, 1999).

## Into the Classroom

### Engaging Students at Risk in the Academic Curriculum

🍏 **Pique students' interest with stimulating activities.**
In a unit on the physics of sound, a junior high school science teacher shows students how basic principles of sound reveal themselves in rock music. On one occasion the teacher brings in a guitar and explains why holding down a string at different points along the neck of the guitar creates different frequencies and thus different notes.

🍏 **Make the curriculum relevant to students' lives and needs—for example, through service learning activities.**
A math teacher at an inner-city middle school consistently encourages her students to identify and work to solve problems in their community. One of her classes expresses concern about the many liquor stores located near the school and the questionable customers and drug dealers the stores attract. The students use yardsticks and maps to calculate the distance of each store from the school, gather information about zoning restrictions and other city government regulations, identify potential violations, meet with a local newspaper editor (who publishes an editorial describing the situation), and eventually meet with state legislators and the city council. As a result of the students' efforts, city police begin to monitor the liquor stores more closely, major violations are identified (leading to the closing of two stores), and the city council makes it illegal to consume alcohol within 600 feet of the school.

🍏 **Create a *community of learners*—a classroom in which students and teachers work collaboratively to increase everyone's understanding.**
In a high school science class's unit on weather, small groups of students specialize in different topics (e.g., humidity, wind, air pressure). Each group conducts research about its topic in the library and on the Internet and then prepares a lesson to teach students in other groups what it has learned.

🍏 **Use students' strengths to promote a positive sense of self.**
A low-income, inner-city elementary school forms a singing group (the Jazz Cats) for which students must try out. The group performs at a variety of community events, and the students enjoy considerable visibility for their talent. Group members exhibit increased self-esteem, improvement in other school subjects, and greater teamwork and leadership skills.

🍏 **Communicate high expectations for short-term and long-term academic success.**
A math teacher at a low-income, inner-city high school recruits students to participate in an intensive math program. The teacher and students work on evenings, Saturdays, and vacations, and all of them later pass the Advanced Placement calculus exam. (This real-life example is depicted in the 1988 film, *Stand and Deliver,* currently available on DVD.)

🍏 **Provide extra support for academic success.**
A middle school homework program meets every day after school in Room 103, where students find their homework assignments on a shelf. Students follow a particular sequence of steps to do each assignment (assembling materials, having someone check their work, etc.) and use a checklist to make sure they don't skip any steps. Initially, a supervising teacher closely monitors what they do, but with time and practice the students are able to complete their homework with only minimal help and guidance.

*Sources:* J. P. Allen & Antonishak, 2008; L. W. Anderson & Pellicer, 1998; Belfiore & Hornyak, 1998 (homework program example); Christenson & Thurlow, 2004; Cosden, Morrison, Albanese, & Macias, 2001; Evans-Winters & Ivie, 2009; L. S. Fuchs, D. Fuchs, et al., 2008; Jenlink, 1994 (Jazz Cats example); Kincheloe, 2009; Ladson-Billings, 1994a; Mathews, 1988 (inner-city math program example); Suh et al., 2007; Tate, 1995 (liquor store example).

🍏 *Make long-term, systematic efforts to engage students in the academic curriculum.* Students are more likely to stay in school and more likely to learn and achieve at high levels if they think their classes are worth their time and effort (e.g., L. W. Anderson & Pellicer, 1998; S. M. Miller, 2003; Ramey & Ramey, 1998; Suh et al., 2007). The Into the Classroom Environment feature "Engaging Students at Risk in the Academic Curriculum" offers several concrete examples of what we might do.

🍏 *Encourage and facilitate identification with school.* Students are far more likely to stay in school if they have an emotional attachment to their school and believe that they're important members of the school community (Christenson & Thurlow, 2004; Fredricks, Blumenfeld, & Paris, 2004). Following are several strategies that researchers have found to be effective:

🍏 Encourage participation in athletic programs, extracurricular activities, and student government. This strategy is especially important when students are having academic difficulties, because it provides an alternative way of experiencing school success.

🍏 Involve students in school policy and management decisions.

🍏 Give students positions of responsibility in managing school activities.

🍏 Provide rewards (e.g., a trip to a local amusement park) for good attendance records. (Eccles, 2007; Finn, 1989; Garibaldi, 1992; Newmann, 1981; M. G. Sanders, 1996)

In general, then, the most effective programs for students at risk are those that would be ideal for *any* student.

4  What Have You Learned?

We now return to the chapter's learning outcomes and identify key points associated with each one. As we do so, we must remember two critical principles regarding the group differences described in this chapter: There is *considerable individual variability within any group* and *a great deal of overlap between any two groups.*

■ **4.1: Describe frequently observed between-group differences and within-group variability for various cultural and ethnic groups; also describe the teacher attitudes and strategies that underlie culturally responsive teaching.** Cultural and ethnic group differences may be seen in language and dialect, talkativeness and verbal assertiveness, eye contact, personal space, responses to questions, comfort with public performance, views about teasing, attitudes toward cooperation and competition, family relationships and expectations, conceptions of time, and worldviews. For students from cultural and ethnic minority groups, there is often some degree of cultural mismatch between the home and school environments, and teachers' misinterpretations of students' behaviors can exacerbate this mismatch. All students benefit when we promote increased understanding of cultural and ethnic differences and foster social interaction among students from diverse groups.

Evaluate and apply your knowledge related to this learning outcome in MyEducationLab™.

■ **4.2: Describe the nature and origins of typical gender differences in school-age children and adolescents, and explain how you can best accommodate such differences in your classroom.** On average, males and females have similar academic abilities but differ somewhat in physical activity levels, experience with technology, motivation, sense of self, interpersonal relationships, classroom behavior, and career aspirations. Biological differences (e.g., gender-related hormone levels and subtle differences in brain development) account for a few gender differences, but socialization (which can amplify small biology-based differences) is probably at the root of many others. As teachers, we may occasionally need to tailor instructional strategies to the unique characteristics of boys versus girls; in general, however, we should hold equally high expectations for both sexes and make sure that both have equal opportunities to develop in all areas of the school curriculum.

Evaluate and apply your knowledge related to this learning outcome in MyEducationLab™.

■ **4.3: Identify challenges that students from low-income families often face; also identify several strategies through which you can foster their resilience and help them be successful at school.** Numerous factors can contribute to the generally lower achievement of students from low-income families, including poor nutrition and housing, unhealthy physical and social environments, emotional stress, lower-quality schools, gaps in basic knowledge and skills, and homelessness. Despite such challenges, many children from low-income backgrounds have a positive sense of self and do well in school; such *resilient students* often have one or more individuals in their lives whom they trust and can turn to in difficult times. As teachers, we can help students in lower socioeconomic groups succeed in the classroom by building on their many strengths and providing the academic and emotional support they may sometimes need to overcome their adverse circumstances.

Evaluate and apply your knowledge related to this learning outcome in MyEducationLab™.

■ **4.4: Explain how you might recognize students who are at risk for academic failure and dropping out of school, and identify strategies for helping these students get on the path to academic and social success.** *Students at risk* are those with a high probability of failing to acquire the minimum academic skills necessary for success in the adult world; they may graduate from high school without having learned to read or write, or they may drop out before graduation. To help such students succeed at school, we should identify them as early as possible, make the curriculum relevant to their needs and interests, communicate high expectations for academic success, provide sufficient support to make such success possible, and encourage involvement in school activities.

Evaluate and apply your knowledge related to this learning outcome in MyEducationLab™.

## Practice for Your Licensure Exam

### The Active and the Passive

Ms. Stewart has noticed that only a few students actively participate in her junior high school science classes. When she asks a question, especially one that requires students to draw inferences from information presented in class, the same hands always shoot up. She gives the matter some thought and realizes that all of the active participants are of European American descent and most of them are boys.

Ms. Stewart sees the same pattern in students' involvement in lab activities. When she forms small groups for particular lab assignments, the same students (notably the European American males) always take charge. The females and minority-group males take more passive roles, either providing assistance to the group leaders or else just sitting back and watching.

Ms. Stewart is a firm believer that students learn much more about science when they participate in class and when they engage in hands-on activities. Consequently, she is concerned about the lack of involvement of many of her students. She wonders whether they really even care about science.

1. **Constructed-response question:**

   Effective teachers place a high priority on *equity;* that is, they ensure that their classroom practices are not biased in ways that enhance some students' achievement more than others'. In this situation the European American boys appear to be benefiting more from instruction than their classmates are. Using what you know about group differences, identify at least three possible reasons that minority-group students are not actively participating in classroom lessons.

2. **Multiple-choice question:**

   Three of the following explanations are possible reasons that the boys in Ms. Stewart's class are participating more than the girls. Which alternative *contradicts* research findings on gender differences?

   a. On average, boys are more motivated to get good grades.

   b. On average, boys are more physically active in their classes.

   c. On average, boys tend to be more confident about their abilities.

   d. On average, boys are more likely to speak up without waiting to be called on.

3. **Constructed-response question:**

   Describe three different strategies you might use to increase the participation of both girls and minority-group students in Ms. Stewart's class.

---

**PRAXIS**   Go to Appendix C, "Matching Book and MyEducationLab™ to the Praxis Principles of Learning and Teaching Tests," to discover sections of this chapter that may be especially applicable to the Praxis tests.

---

# 5 Individual Differences and Special Educational Needs

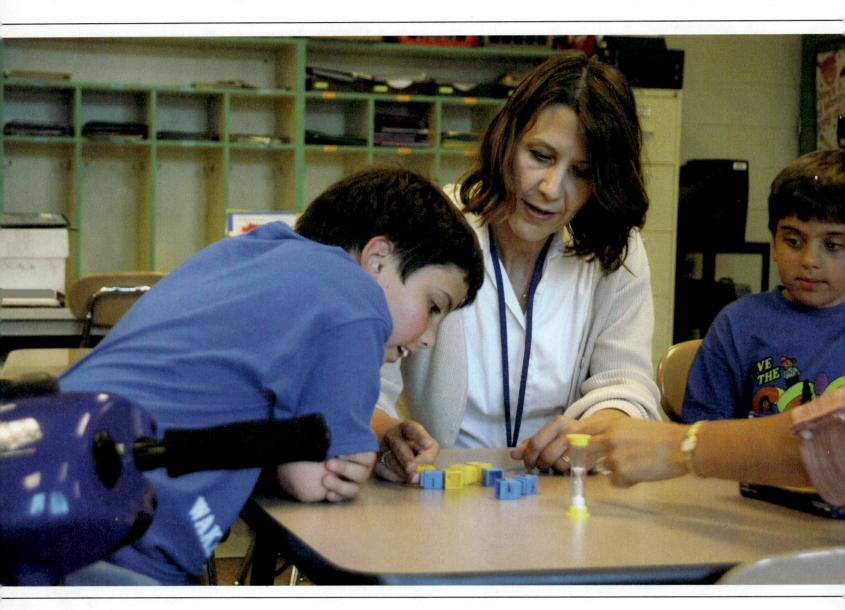

## LEARNING OUTCOMES

**5.1:** Describe various perspectives on the nature of intelligence, and identify several ways in which you can nurture intelligence in your own students.

**5.2:** Explain how students' cognitive styles and dispositions might influence their classroom performance.

**5.3:** Identify implications of the U.S. Individuals with Disabilities Education Act (IDEA) for your own work as a teacher.

**5.4:** Explain how you might adapt your instruction and classroom practices to the unique strengths and limitations of students with various disabilities.

**5.5:** Explain how you might nurture the development of students who show exceptional gifts and talents.

## CASE STUDY: TIM

In elementary school, Tim earned reasonable grades despite poor reading comprehension skills. And although he often appeared to be in a daze during classroom activities, he was generally well behaved. In middle school, his grades began to decline, and teachers complained of his spaciness and tendency to daydream. He had trouble staying on task in class and was so disorganized that he seldom completed homework. When Tim reached high school, he seemed unable to cope with the independence his teachers expected of students, and so he failed several ninth- and tenth-grade classes.

Now, as a 17-year-old eleventh grader, Tim undergoes an in-depth psychological evaluation at a university diagnostic clinic. An intelligence test yields a score of 96, reflecting average ability, and measures of social and emotional adjustment are also within an average range. However, measures of attention consistently show this to be an area of weakness. Tim explains that he has trouble ignoring distractions and must find a very quiet place to do his schoolwork. Even then, he says, he often has to reread something several times to grasp its meaning. (Based on Hathaway, Dooling-Litfin, & Edwards, 2006, pp. 410–412)

- Tim's attention problems have obviously been interfering with his academic achievement. But if you look closely at the facts presented in the case, you might realize that Tim also has strengths on which teachers can build. What particular characteristics might be working in Tim's favor?
- As a teacher, how might you adapt your instructional strategies and classroom environment to accommodate Tim's unique needs?

---

The clinic evaluation team eventually concludes that Tim has attention-deficit hyperactivity disorder, or ADHD. (Like Tim, some students identified as having ADHD exhibit attention problems *without* hyperactivity.) The team suspects that a learning disability might be at the root of the problem but doesn't have sufficiently precise diagnostic techniques to determine this with certainty. On the plus side, Tim is certainly motivated to do well in school: He's well behaved in class, seeks out quiet places to study, and may read something several times in an effort to make sense of it. With appropriately modified instruction and settings—for example, teaching Tim basic organizational skills, breaking a single complex task into several shorter and simpler ones, and giving him a quiet place to read and study—Tim can more readily stay on task and complete assignments (Barkley, 2006; Meltzer, 2007).

Some differences among students are related to their group membership—for instance, whether they're male or female or whether they have a particular ethnic heritage. Yet within any single group, students show significant individual differences in cognitive abilities, personalities, physical skills, and so on. In this chapter we'll look at individual differences in intelligence, cognitive styles, and dispositions. We'll then consider *students with special needs*—students who, like Tim, are different enough from their peers that they require specially adapted curriculum materials instructional practices, or both. As we go along, we'll find that the most effective instruction tends to be differentiated instruction—instruction that is tailored to align with each student's current knowledge, skills, and needs.

**individual differences**
Diversity in abilities and characteristics (intelligence, personality, etc.) among students at a particular age and within a particular gender or cultural group.

**differentiated instruction**
Practice of individualizing instructional methods—and possibly also individualizing specific content and instructional goals—to align with each student's existing knowledge, skills, and needs.

# Intelligence

Theorists define and conceptualize *intelligence* in a variety of ways, but most agree that it has several distinctive qualities:

- It is *adaptive:* It can be used flexibly to respond to a variety of situations and problems.

- It is related to *learning ability:* People who are intelligent in particular domains learn new information and skills in those domains more quickly and easily than people who are less intelligent in those domains.

- It involves the *use of prior knowledge* to analyze and understand new situations effectively.

- It involves the complex interaction and coordination of *many different mental processes.*

- It is *culture specific.* What is intelligent behavior in one culture isn't necessarily intelligent behavior in another culture. (Dai, 2010; Greenfield, 1998; Laboratory of Human Cognition, 1982; J. Li, 2004; Neisser et al., 1996; Sternberg, 1997, 2004, 2007; Sternberg & Detterman, 1986)

With these qualities in mind, I offer an intentionally broad definition of intelligence: the ability to apply prior knowledge and experiences flexibly to accomplish challenging new tasks.

For most theorists intelligence is somewhat different from what a person has actually learned (e.g., as reflected in school achievement). At the same time intelligent thinking and behavior *depend* on prior learning. The more students know about the world in general and about the specific tasks they need to perform, the more intelligently they can behave. Intelligence, then, isn't necessarily a permanent, unchanging characteristic; it can be modified through experience and learning.

## THEORETICAL PERSPECTIVES OF INTELLIGENCE

Some psychologists have suggested that intelligence is a single, general ability that people have to varying degrees and apply in a wide range of activities. Others have disagreed, citing evidence that people can be more or less intelligent on different kinds of tasks, at different points in development, and in different contexts. The theories of intelligence we examine in this section reflect these diverse perspectives on the nature of intelligence.

### SPEARMAN'S CONCEPT OF *g*

Imagine that you give a large group of students a wide variety of tests—some measuring verbal skills, others measuring visual–spatial thinking, still others measuring mathematical problem solving, and so on. Chances are that the test scores would all correlate with one another to some degree: Students who score high on one test would tend to score high on the other tests as well. The correlations would be strong among tests of very similar abilities; those among tests of distinctly different abilities would be weaker. For example, a student who scored very high on a vocabulary test would probably score high on other measures of verbal ability but might have only modest success in solving math problems (N. Brody, 1999; McGrew, Flanagan, Zeith, & Vanderwood, 1997; Neisser et al., 1996; Spearman, 1904).

In the early 1900s, Charles Spearman (1904, 1927) drew on such findings to propose that intelligence comprises both (1) a single, pervasive reasoning ability (a *general factor*) that is used across the board; and (2) a number of more narrow abilities, such as problem-solving ability and abstract reasoning (*specific factors*). The general factor and any relevant specific factors work together during the execution of particular tasks.

Many contemporary psychologists believe that sufficient evidence supports Spearman's concept of a general factor in intelligence—often known simply as Spearman's *g*. Underlying it, they suspect, may be a general ability to process information quickly and efficiently (Bornstein et al., 2006; Coyle, Pillow, Snyder, & Kochunov, 2011; Haier, 2003). A general ability to control and direct one's thinking may also be involved (Cornoldi, 2010; H. L. Swanson, 2008).

## CATTELL'S FLUID AND CRYSTALLIZED INTELLIGENCES

Several decades after Spearman's groundbreaking work, Raymond Cattell (1963, 1987) found evidence for two distinctly different components of general intelligence (*g*). First, people differ in fluid intelligence, their ability to acquire knowledge quickly and adapt to new situations effectively. Second, they differ in crystallized intelligence, the knowledge and skills they've accumulated from their experiences, schooling, and culture. Fluid intelligence is more important for new, unfamiliar tasks, especially those that require rapid decision making and involve nonverbal content. Crystallized intelligence is more important for familiar tasks, especially those that depend heavily on language and prior knowledge. Cattell suggested that fluid intelligence is largely the result of inherited biological factors, whereas crystallized intelligence depends on both fluid intelligence and experience and thus is influenced by both heredity and environment.

## CATTELL-HORN-CARROLL THEORY OF COGNITIVE ABILITIES

Some theorists have built on Cattell's distinction to suggest that intelligence may have three layers, or *strata* (Ackerman & Lohman, 2006; Carroll, 1993, 2003; D. P. Flanagan & Ortiz, 2001; Horn, 2008). In this *Cattell-Horn-Carroll theory of cognitive abilities,* the top stratum is general intelligence, or *g*. Underlying it in the middle stratum are 9 or 10 more specific abilities—processing speed, general reasoning ability, general world knowledge, ability to process visual input, and so on—that encompass fluid and/or crystallized intelligence to varying degrees. And underlying *these* abilities in the bottom stratum are more than 70 very specific abilities, such as reading speed, mechanical knowledge, and number and richness of associations in memory. With its large number of specific abilities, the Cattell–Horn–Carroll theory is too complex to describe in detail here, but you should be aware that psychologists are increasingly finding it useful in predicting and understanding students' achievement in various content domains (e.g., J. J. Evans, Floyd, McGrew, & Leforgee, 2001; Phelps, McGrew, Knopik, & Ford, 2005; B. E. Proctor, Floyd, & Shaver, 2005).

## GARDNER'S MULTIPLE INTELLIGENCES

Howard Gardner (1983, 1998, 1999; Gardner & Hatch, 1990) suggests that people have at least eight distinctly different abilities, or *multiple intelligences,* that are relatively independent of one another (see Table 5.1). In his view there may also be a ninth (existential) intelligence dedicated to philosophical and spiritual issues (e.g., Who are we? Why do we die?). However, because evidence for it is weaker than that for the other intelligences (Gardner, 1999, 2000a, 2003), I have omitted it from the table.

Gardner presents some evidence to support the existence of these distinctly different intelligences. For instance, he describes people who are quite skilled in one area, perhaps in composing music, yet have seemingly average abilities in other areas. He also points out that people who suffer brain damage sometimes lose abilities that are restricted primarily to one intelligence. One person might show deficits primarily in language, whereas another might have difficulty with tasks that require spatial reasoning.

Among psychologists, reviews of Gardner's theory are mixed. Some theorists don't believe that Gardner's evidence is sufficiently compelling to support the notion of eight or nine distinctly different abilities (N. Brody, 1992; Corno et al., 2002; Sternberg, 2003; Waterhouse, 2006). Others agree that people may have a variety of relatively independent abilities but argue for different distinctions than those Gardner makes (e.g., note the second-stratum abilities in the Cattell–Horn–Carroll theory just described). Still others reject the idea that abilities in certain domains, such as in music or bodily movement, are really "intelligences" per se (Bracken, McCallum, & Shaughnessy, 1999; Sattler, 2001).

Despite psychologists' lukewarm reception to Gardner's theory, many educators have wholeheartedly embraced it because of its optimistic view of human potential. Gardner's perspective encourages us to use many different teaching methods so that we can capitalize on students' diverse talents to help them learn and understand classroom subject matter (L. Campbell, Campbell, & Dickinson, 1998; Gardner,

**intelligence** Ability to apply prior knowledge and experiences flexibly to accomplish challenging new tasks.

***g*** Theoretical general factor in intelligence that influences one's ability to learn and perform in a wide variety of contexts.

**fluid intelligence** Ability to acquire knowledge quickly and adapt effectively to new situations.

**crystallized intelligence** Knowledge and skills accumulated from prior experience, schooling, and culture.

 Keep in mind that different students are likely to be intelligent in different ways.

Attention to detail in 10-year-old Luther's drawing of a plant suggests some talent in what Gardner calls *naturalist* intelligence.

## TABLE 5.1 • Gardner's Multiple Intelligences

| TYPE OF INTELLIGENCE | EXAMPLES OF RELEVANT BEHAVIORS |
|---|---|
| **Linguistic intelligence:**<br>Ability to use language effectively | • Making persuasive arguments<br>• Writing poetry<br>• Noticing subtle nuances in meanings of words |
| **Logical–mathematical intelligence:**<br>Ability to reason logically, especially in mathematics and science | • Solving mathematical problems quickly<br>• Generating mathematical proofs<br>• Formulating and testing hypotheses about observed phenomena[a] |
| **Spatial intelligence:**<br>Ability to notice details of what one sees and to imagine and manipulate visual objects in one's mind | • Conjuring up mental images<br>• Drawing a visual likeness of an object<br>• Seeing subtle differences among visually similar objects |
| **Musical intelligence:**<br>Ability to create, comprehend, and appreciate music | • Playing a musical instrument<br>• Composing a musical work<br>• Identifying the underlying structure of music |
| **Bodily–kinesthetic intelligence:**<br>Ability to use one's body skillfully | • Dancing<br>• Playing basketball<br>• Performing pantomime |
| **Interpersonal intelligence:**<br>Ability to notice subtle aspects of other people's behaviors | • Reading other people's moods<br>• Detecting other people's underlying intentions and desires<br>• Using knowledge of others to influence their thoughts and behaviors |
| **Intrapersonal intelligence:**<br>Awareness of one's own feelings, motives, and desires | • Discriminating among such similar emotions as sadness and regret<br>• Identifying the motives guiding one's own behavior<br>• Using self-knowledge to relate more effectively with others |
| **Naturalist intelligence:**<br>Ability to recognize patterns in nature and differences among various life-forms and natural objects | • Identifying members of particular plant or animal species<br>• Classifying natural forms (e.g., rocks, types of mountains)<br>• Applying one's knowledge of nature in such activities as farming, landscaping, or animal training |

[a]This example may remind you of Piaget's theory of cognitive development. Many of the stage-specific characteristics that Piaget described reflect logical–mathematical intelligence.
*Sources:* Gardner, 1983, 1999.

2000b; Kornhaber, Fierros, & Veenema, 2004). Consider how one eighth-grade teacher took advantage of two girls' musical talent to teach spelling, something with which both girls were having difficulty:

> [I] asked the girls to label the piano keys with the letters of the alphabet, so that the girls could "play" the words on their keyboards. Later, on spelling tests, the students were asked to recall the tones and sounds of each word and write its corresponding letters. Not only did spelling scores improve, but the two pianists began thinking of other "sound" texts to set to music. Soon, they performed each classmate's name and transcribed entire sentences. (L. Campbell et al., 1998, p. 142)

*Present classroom subject matter using a variety of approaches to capitalize on students' diverse abilities, but also give them tasks that require them to work on areas of weakness.*

Whether or not human beings have eight or more distinctly different intelligences, they certainly benefit when they're encouraged to think about a particular topic in two or more distinctly different ways—perhaps using both words and mental images (R. E. Mayer, 2011b; Moreno, 2006). We won't always want to teach to students' strengths, however. We must also give students tasks that encourage them to address and thereby strengthen their areas of weakness (Sternberg, 2002).

### STERNBERG'S TRIARCHIC THEORY

Robert Sternberg (e.g., 1998, 2004; Sternberg et al., 2000) has speculated that people may be more or less intelligent in three different domains—hence the name *triarchic* theory. *Analytical intelligence* involves making sense of, analyzing, contrasting, and evaluating the kinds of information and problems often seen in academic settings and on intelligence tests. *Creative intelligence* involves imagination, invention, and synthesis of ideas within the context of new situations. *Practical intelligence* involves applying knowledge and skills effectively to manage and respond to everyday problems and social situations.

In addition, Sternberg proposes that intelligent behavior involves an interplay of three factors, all of which vary from one occasion to the next (Sternberg, 1985, 1997, 2003):

- *The environmental context in which the behavior occurs.* Different behaviors may be more or less adaptive and effective in different cultures. For example, learning to read is an adaptive response in industrialized societies yet largely irrelevant to certain other cultures.

- *The relevance of prior experiences to a particular task.* Prior experiences can enhance intelligence in either of two ways. In some cases extensive practice with a particular kind of task enables students to perform that task with increasing speed and efficiency—that is, with greater *automaticity*. In other instances, students are able to draw on what they've learned in previous situations to help them with *new* tasks.

- *The cognitive processes required by the task.* Numerous cognitive processes are involved in intelligent behavior: separating important information from irrelevant details, identifying possible problem-solving strategies, seeing relationships among seemingly different ideas, and so on. Different cognitive processes may be more or less important in different contexts, and an individual may behave more or less intelligently depending on the specific cognitive processes needed at the time.

Chapter 6 looks more closely at automaticity.

To date, research neither supports nor refutes the notion that intelligence is structured in the specifically triarchic manner that Sternberg proposes. Certain aspects of Sternberg's theory (e.g., how various factors work together) are described in such general terms that they're difficult to either confirm or disconfirm through research (Sattler, 2001; Siegler & Alibali, 2005). And Sternberg himself acknowledges that most of the data supporting his theory have been collected by his own research team, rather than by outsiders who might be more objective or critical (Sternberg, 2003). Nevertheless, the theory reminds us that students' ability to behave intelligently may vary considerably depending on the cultural context, previously learned knowledge and skills, and cognitive processes that a task involves.

## DEVELOPMENTAL VIEWS OF INTELLIGENCE

Theories of cognitive development portray children as becoming increasingly intelligent over time; for example, with age and experience children gain greater proficiency in abstract thinking (Jean Piaget's theory) and effective use of complex cultural tools (Lev Vygotsky's theory). Yet with the possible exception of Sternberg's triarchic theory—which points out the importance of prior experiences—the perspectives of intelligence described so far don't really consider how intelligence might take different forms at different points in development (Dai, 2010).

Chapter 2 describes Piaget's and Vygotsky's theories of development.

Some psychologists working in the area of giftedness suggest that not only is intelligence somewhat specific to particular domains but also that its basic nature changes with age and experience. From this perspective, the developmental course of exceptional abilities and talents is as follows:

1. Initially (typically in childhood), people show exceptional *potential* in a certain domain, perhaps in reading, math, or music.

2. With appropriate instruction, guidance, and practice opportunities, people show exceptional *achievement* in the domain.

3. If people continue to pursue the domain and practice domain-specific tasks over a lengthy time period (typically into adulthood), they may eventually gain considerable *expertise and eminence,* to the point that their accomplishments are widely recognized (Dai, 2010; Subotnik, Olszewski-Kubilus, & Worrell, 2011).

Here, then, we see a very dynamic view of intelligence: Although its roots may be in certain natural endowments, over the long run intelligence requires both environmental nurturance and personal perseverance (Dai, 2010; Subotnik et al., 2011).

## DISTRIBUTED INTELLIGENCE

Many psychologists are beginning to realize that not only does a supportive environment context enhance people's intelligence over time, but in fact it can facilitate intelligent behavior in the here and now. People are far more likely to think and behave intelligently when they have assistance from their physical, cultural, and social environments—an idea that is sometimes called

Children can think and behave more intelligently when they acquire the cognitive tools of their culture, such as strategies for organizing and graphing data. For example, watch "Graphing in Second Grade Math."

 Identify physical, symbolic, and social supports that can help students think more intelligently.

As children get older, they become increasingly able to discern underlying meanings of proverbs such as "A rolling stone gathers no moss." Observe developmental differences in this ability in "Cognitive Development: Middle Childhood" and "Cognitive Development: Late Adolescence."

**distributed intelligence** (e.g., Hutchins, 1995; Pea, 1993; Perkins, 1992, 1995). People can "distribute" a challenging task—that is, they can pass some of the cognitive burden onto something or someone else—in at least three ways. First, they can use physical objects, especially technology (e.g., calculators, computers), to handle and manipulate large amounts of information. Second, they can represent and think about the situations they encounter by using their culture's various symbolic systems—words, charts, diagrams, mathematical equations, and so on—and other cognitive tools. And third, they can work with other people to explore ideas and solve problems—as we've often heard, two heads are (usually) better than one. In fact, when students work together on complex, challenging tasks and problems, they teach one another strategies and ways of thinking that can help each of them think even *more* intelligently on future occasions (Kuhn, 2001b; Palincsar & Herrenkohl, 1999; Slavin, 2011; Salomon, 1993).

From a distributed-intelligence perspective, then, intelligence is a highly variable, context-specific ability that increases when appropriate environmental supports are available. It certainly isn't an immutable trait that learners "carry around" with them, nor is it something that can be easily measured and then summarized with one or more test scores. However, psychologists coming from other theoretical perspectives often *do* try to measure intelligence, as we'll see now.

## MEASURING INTELLIGENCE

When a student consistently struggles with certain aspects of the school curriculum, as Tim does in the opening case study, psychologists sometimes find it helpful to get a measure of the student's general level of cognitive functioning. Such measures are commonly known as **intelligence tests**. To get a sense of what intelligence tests are like, try the following exercise.

### EXPERIENCING FIRSTHAND
### MOCK INTELLIGENCE TEST

Answer each of these questions:

1. What does the word *penitence* mean?
2. How are a goat and a beetle alike?
3. What should you do if you get separated from your family in a large department store?
4. What do people mean when they say, "A rolling stone gathers no moss"?
5. Complete the following analogy:  is to  as  is to:

   a. ●●     b. ●○     c. ○     d. ▷◀

These test items are modeled after items on many contemporary intelligence tests. Often the tests include a mixture of verbal tasks (such as Items 1 through 4) and less verbal, more visual tasks (such as Item 5).

Scores on intelligence tests were originally calculated using a formula that involves division. Hence, they were called intelligence quotient scores, or **IQ scores**. Although we still use the term IQ, intelligence test scores are no longer based on the old formula. Instead, they're determined by comparing a student's performance on a given test with the performance of others in the same age-group. A score of 100 indicates average performance on the test: Students with this score have performed better than half of their age-mates but not as well as the other half. Scores well below 100 indicate below-average performance on the test; scores well above 100 indicate above-average performance.

Figure 5.1 shows the percentages of students getting scores at different points along the scale (e.g., 12.9% get scores between 100 and 105). Notice that the curve is high in the middle and low at both ends, indicating that scores close to 100 are far more common than scores considerably higher or lower than 100. For example, if we add up the percentages in different parts of Figure 5.1, we find that approximately two-thirds (68%) of students score within 15 points of 100 (i.e., between 85 and 115). In contrast, only 2% of students score as low as 70, and only 2% score as high as 130. Such a many-in-the-middle-and-few-at-the-extremes distribution of scores seems to characterize a wide variety of human characteristics. Hence, psychologists have created a method of scoring intelligence test performance that intentionally yields this distribution.

In the opening case study, Tim's performance on an intelligence test yields an IQ score of 96, which we can now make some sense of. As you can see in Figure 5.1, a score of 96 is so close to 100 that we should consider it to be well within an average range.

## IQ SCORES AND SCHOOL ACHIEVEMENT

Studies repeatedly show that performance on intelligence tests is correlated with school achievement. On average, children with higher IQ scores earn higher course grades, do better on standardized achievement tests, and complete more years of education (N. Brody, 1997; Gustafsson & Undheim, 1996; Sattler, 2001).

It's important to keep three points in mind about this IQ–achievement relationship. First, intelligence doesn't necessarily *cause* achievement; it is simply correlated with it. Even though students with high IQs typically perform well in school, we cannot conclusively say that their high achievement is actually the result of their intelligence. Intelligence probably does play an important role in school achievement, but so, too, do many other factors—motivation, quality of instruction, family and neighborhood resources, peer-group expectations, and so on. Second, the relationship between IQ scores and achievement is an imperfect one, with many exceptions to the rule. For a variety of reasons, some students with high IQ scores don't perform well in the classroom, and others achieve at higher levels than we would predict from their IQ scores alone. Third and most important, we must remember that an IQ score simply reflects a child's performance on a particular test at a particular time—it's *not* a permanent characteristic etched in stone—and that some change is to be expected over time.

**FIGURE 5.1** **Percentages of IQ scores in different ranges**

If you have taken a course in descriptive statistics, you may realize that IQ scores are *standard scores* based on the *normal distribution*. Chapter 15 explains these concepts.

Don't use students' IQ scores to make long-term predictions about their school achievement.

## NATURE AND NURTURE IN THE DEVELOPMENT OF INTELLIGENCE

Research tells us that heredity probably plays some role in intelligence. For instance, identical twins (who have the same genetic makeup) tend to have more similar IQ scores than nonidentical (fraternal) twins do, even when the twins are adopted at birth by different parents and grow up in different homes. This is *not* to say, however, that children inherit a single IQ gene that determines their intellectual ability. Rather, they probably inherit a variety of characteristics that in one way or another affect particular cognitive abilities and talents (Bouchard, 1997; O. S. P. Davis, Haworth, & Plomin, 2009; Horn, 2008; Kovas & Plomin, 2007).

Environmental factors influence intelligence as well, sometimes for the better and sometimes for the worse. Poor nutrition in the early years of development (including the nine months before birth) leads to lower IQ scores, as does a mother's excessive use of alcohol during pregnancy (D'Amato, Chittooran, & Whitten, 1992; Neisser et al., 1996; Ricciuti, 1993). Moving a child from a neglectful, impoverished home environment to a more nurturing, stimulating one (e.g., through adoption) can result in IQ gains of 15 points or more (Beckett et al., 2006; Capron & Duyme, 1989; van IJzendoorn & Juffer, 2005). Effective, too, are long-term intervention programs designed to help children acquire basic cognitive and academic skills (e.g., F. A. Campbell & Burchinal, 2008; Kağitçibaşi, 2007). Even simply *going to school* has a positive effect on IQ scores (Ceci, 2003; Ramey, 1992). Furthermore, worldwide, there has been a slow but steady increase in people's performance on intelligence tests—a trend that is probably due to better nutrition, smaller family sizes, better schooling, increasing cognitive stimulation (through increased access to television, reading materials, etc.), and other improvements in people's environments (Flynn, 2007; E. Hunt, 2008; Neisser, 1998).

The question of how *much* nature and nurture each play a role in influencing intelligence has been a source of considerable controversy over the years. But in fact, genetic and environmental factors interact in their influences on cognitive development and intelligence in ways that can probably never be disentangled. First of all, genes require reasonable environmental support to do

**distributed intelligence**
Enhancement of thinking through the use of physical objects and technology, concepts and symbols of one's culture, and/or social collaboration and support.

**intelligence test** General measure of current level of cognitive functioning; often used to predict academic achievement in the short run.

**IQ score** Score on an intelligence test, determined by comparing a person's performance with that of others in the same age-group.

their work. In an extremely impoverished environment—one with a lack of adequate nutrition and stimulation—heredity may have little to say about children's intellectual growth, but under better circumstances it can have a significant influence (Ceci, 2003; D. C. Rowe, Jacobson, & Van den Oord, 1999; Turkheimer, Haley, Waldron, D'Onofrio, & Gottesman, 2003). Second, heredity seems to affect how susceptible or impervious a child is to particular environmental conditions (Rutter, 1997). For instance, some students—such as those with certain inherited disabilities, like Tim in the opening case study—may need a quiet, well-structured learning environment in which to acquire good reading comprehension skills, but other students might pick up good reading skills regardless of the quality of their environment. And third, children tend to seek out environmental conditions that match their inherited abilities (O. S. P. Davis et al., 2009; W. Johnson, 2010; Scarr & McCartney, 1983). For example, children who inherit exceptional quantitative reasoning ability may enroll in advanced math courses and in other ways nurture their inherited talent. Children with average quantitative ability are less likely to take on such challenges and thus have fewer opportunities to develop their mathematical skills.

### INTELLIGENCE AND THE BRAIN

Intelligence—at least that aspect of intelligence that can be measured by IQ tests—does seem to have some basis in the brain. For example, compared with their average-IQ peers, children with high IQ scores show a prolonged period of development in the cortex (P. Shaw et al., 2006). A high level of intelligence also seems to involve ongoing, efficient interactions among numerous brain regions (Jung & Haier, 2007). Although heredity appears to play some role in these differences, the extent to which they are the result of nature, nurture, or a nature–nurture interaction remains to be seen (Jung & Haier, 2007). And in any case, we must remember that the human brain has considerable ability to restructure itself—that is, it has *plasticity*—throughout childhood and adulthood.

See Chapter 2 for more information on the structure, development, and plasticity of the human brain.

## CULTURAL AND ETHNIC DIVERSITY IN INTELLIGENCE

Historically, some ethnic groups in the United States have, *on average,* performed better than other ethnic groups on intelligence tests. Most experts agree that such group differences in IQ are probably due to differences in environment and, more specifically, to economic circumstances that affect the quality of prenatal and postnatal nutrition, availability of stimulating books and toys, access to educational opportunities, and so on (Brooks-Gunn, Klebanov, & Duncan, 1996; Byrnes, 2003; McLoyd, 1998). Furthermore, various groups have become increasingly *similar* in average IQ score in recent years—a trend that can be attributed only to more equitable environmental conditions (Dickens & Flynn, 2006; Neisser et al., 1996).

Assume that when children from diverse ethnic groups all have reasonably stimulating environments, they have equal potential to develop their intellectual abilities.

   Yet it's important to note that different cultural groups have somewhat different views about what intelligence *is* and may therefore nurture somewhat different abilities in their children. Many people of European descent think of intelligence primarily as an ability that influences children's academic achievement and adults' professional success. In contrast, people in many African, Asian, Hispanic, and Native American cultures think of intelligence as involving social as well as academic skills—maintaining harmonious interpersonal relationships, working effectively together to accomplish challenging tasks, and so on (Greenfield et al., 2006; J. Li & Fischer, 2004; Sternberg, 2004, 2007). And in Buddhist and Confucian societies in the Far East (e.g., China, Taiwan), intelligence also involves acquiring strong moral values and making meaningful contributions to society (J. Li, 2004; Sternberg, 2003).

   Cultural groups differ, too, in the behaviors that they believe reflect intelligence. For example, many traditional measures of intelligence take speed into account on certain test items: Children score higher if they respond quickly as well as correctly. Yet people in some cultures tend to value thoroughness over speed and may be skeptical when tasks are completed very quickly (Sternberg, 2007). As another example, many people in mainstream Western culture interpret strong verbal skills as a sign of intelligence, but for many Japanese and many Inuit people of northern Quebec, talking a lot indicates immaturity or low intelligence (Crago, 1988; Minami & McCabe, 1996; Sternberg, 2003). One Inuit teacher had this concern about a boy whose language was quite advanced for his age-group:

> Do you think he might have a learning problem? Some of these children who don't have such high intelligence have trouble stopping themselves. They don't know when to stop talking. (Crago, 1988, p. 219)

As teachers, then, we must be careful not to assume that our own views of intelligence are shared by the students and families of cultures very different from our own.

## BEING SMART ABOUT INTELLIGENCE AND IQ SCORES

Whatever its nature and origins may be, intelligence appears to be an important factor in students' ability to learn and achieve in the classroom. Accordingly, we must have a good grasp of how we can best nurture students' intellectual growth and how we can reasonably interpret their performance on intelligence tests. Following are several recommendations.

🍏 *Place higher priority on developing—rather than on determining—intelligence.* As we've seen, intelligence is hardly a fixed, unchangeable characteristic: Environmental factors, including schooling, can lead to increases in children's measured intelligence. And the notion of distributed intelligence suggests that virtually all students can act more intelligently when they have tools, symbolic systems, and social groups to assist them in their efforts. As teachers, we should think more about *enhancing and supporting* students' intelligence than about measuring it (Dai, 2010; P. D. Nichols & Mittelholtz, 1997; Posner & Rothbart, 2007; B. Rhodes, 2008). Rather than ask, How intelligent are our students? we should instead ask, How can we help our students think as intelligently as possible? What tools and social networks can we give them? What useful concepts and procedures can we teach them?

🍏 *Think of intelligence tests as useful but imperfect measures.* Intelligence tests aren't magical instruments that mysteriously determine a learner's true intelligence—if, in fact, such a thing as "true" intelligence exists. Instead, these tests are simply collections of questions and tasks that psychologists have developed in order to get a handle on how well students can think, reason, and learn at a particular point in time. Used in conjunction with other information, they can often give us a general idea of a student's current cognitive functioning. To interpret IQ scores appropriately, however, we must be aware of their limitations:

- Different kinds of tests can yield somewhat different scores.
- A student's performance on any test will inevitably be affected by many temporary factors—general health, time of day, distracting circumstances, and so on. Such factors are especially influential for young children, who are apt to have high energy levels, short attention spans, and little interest in sitting still for more than a few minutes.
- Test items typically focus on certain skills that are important in mainstream Western culture—especially in school settings—and on tasks that can be accomplished within a single, short testing session. They don't necessarily tap into skills that are more highly valued and nurtured in other cultures, nor do they tap into skills that involve lengthy time periods (e.g., planning ahead, making wise decisions).
- Some students may be unfamiliar with the content or types of tasks involved in particular test items and may perform poorly on those items as a result.
- English language learners—students who have only limited proficiency in English as a result of growing up in a non-English-speaking environment—are at an obvious disadvantage when an intelligence test is administered in English. Thus, their IQ scores will typically be poor indicators of what they will be able to do once their English improves. (Dirks, 1982; Heath, 1989; Neisser et al., 1996; Perkins, 1995; Stanovich, 2009; Sternberg, 2007; Sternberg, Grigorenko, & Kidd, 2005; Zigler & Finn-Stevenson, 1992)

Obviously, then, we must be skeptical of IQ scores obtained for students who come from diverse cultural backgrounds, know little English, or were fairly young at the time of assessment.

🍏 *Use the results of more focused measures when you want to assess specific abilities.* Whenever we obtain and use IQ scores, we're buying into the idea that a general factor, or *g*, underlies students' school performance. But given the multifaceted nature of intelligence, no single test can possibly give us a complete picture of a student's current abilities. If we want to estimate a student's potential for success in a particular domain—say, in mathematics or mechanical reasoning—we're probably better off using measures of more specific abilities (Ackerman & Lohman, 2006; Horn, 2008; McGrew et al., 1997). However, I urge you to rely *only* on instruments available

Young children's distractibility during a testing session decreases the *reliability* of any test scores obtained (see Chapter 14 and Chapter 15).

Be skeptical of any IQ scores obtained for recent immigrants and other students who were not fluent in English when tested. And in general, never base expectations for students' achievement *solely* on IQ scores.

Don't use so-called "intelligence tests" you find posted on the Internet.

Chapter 14 provides more details about dynamic assessment.

from well-respected test publishers. Tests you might find on the Internet—for instance, tests that claim to be measures of Gardner's multiple intelligences—have typically undergone little or no research scrutiny, making their results questionable at best. Keep in mind, too, that intelligence tests should be administered only by school psychologists and other professionals who have been specifically trained in their use.

*Look for behaviors that reveal exceptional talents within the context of a student's culture.* For example, among students who have grown up in predominantly African American communities, intelligence might be reflected in oral language, such as colorful speech, creative storytelling, or humor. For students from Native American cultures, intelligence might be reflected in interpersonal skills, highly skilled craftsmanship, or an exceptional ability to notice and remember subtle landmarks in one's physical environment (Dai, 2010; Maker & Schiever, 1989; Sternberg, 2005; Torrance, 1989).

As teachers, then, we must be careful not to limit our conception of intelligence only to students' ability to succeed at traditional academic tasks and to perform well on traditional intelligence tests. One alternative is *dynamic assessment:* Rather than assess what students already know and can do, we might teach them something new and see how quickly and easily they master it (Feuerstein, Feuerstein, & Falik, 2010; Haywood & Lidz, 2007; Sternberg, 2007).

*Remember that many other factors also affect students' classroom achievement.* Most measures of intelligence focus on specific things that a student *can* do, with little consideration of what a student is *likely* to do. For instance, intelligence tests don't evaluate the extent to which students are willing to view a situation from multiple perspectives, examine data with a critical eye, or actively take charge of their own learning. Yet such traits are often just as important as intellectual ability in determining success on academic and real-world tasks (Duckworth & Seligman, 2005; Kuhn, 2001a; Perkins, Tishman, Ritchhart, Donis, & Andrade, 2000). In the next section we'll examine forms that these *cognitive styles* and *dispositions* might take.

## Cognitive Styles and Dispositions

Students with the same general level of intelligence often approach classroom tasks and think about classroom topics differently. Some of these individual differences reflect cognitive styles, over which students don't necessarily have much conscious control. Others reflect dispositions, which students voluntarily and intentionally bring to bear on their efforts to master school subject matter. Don't agonize over the distinction between the two concepts, because their meanings overlap considerably. Both involve not only specific cognitive tendencies but also personality characteristics (Messick, 1994b; Zhang & Sternberg, 2006). Dispositions also have a motivational component—an I-*want*-to-do-it-this-way quality (Kuhn, 2001a; Perkins & Ritchhart, 2004; Stanovich, 1999).

Over the past few decades, psychologists and educators have examined a wide variety of cognitive styles, sometimes instead using the *learning styles.* Many of the traits they've identified and assessment instruments they've developed don't hold up under the scrutiny of other researchers (J. Cassidy, 2004; Krätzig & Arbuthnott, 2006; Messick, 1994b). Furthermore, tailoring particular instructional strategies to students' self-reported styles—which in some cases are nothing more than students' *preferences*—doesn't necessarily enhance academic achievement (Curry, 1990; R. E. Mayer & Massa, 2003; Nieto & Bode, 2008; Snider, 1990). And neuroscientists have completely debunked the idea that we might teach to students' "left brains" or "right brains": Even the simplest of everyday thinking tasks requires the left and right hemispheres of the brain to work together (Bressler, 2002; Gonsalves & Cohen, 2010; Haxby et al., 2001).

One dimension of cognitive style worthy of our attention, however, is a distinction between analytic and holistic thinking.[1] In *analytic* thinking, learners tend to break new stimuli and tasks into their component parts and to see these parts somewhat independently

Don't plan instruction based on results you might get from easily available and aggressively marketed "learning style" inventories.

**cognitive style**   Characteristic way in which a learner tends to think about a task and process new information; typically comes into play automatically rather than by choice.

**disposition**   General inclination and desire to approach and think about learning and problem-solving tasks in a particular way; typically has a motivational component in addition to cognitive components.

---

[1]In the research literature you might see distinctions between *field independence* and *field dependence* or between *reflectivity* and *impulsivity.* Both of these distinctions overlap with the analytic-versus-holistic processing distinction.

of their context. In *holistic* thinking, learners tend to perceive situations as integrated, indivisible wholes that are closely tied to their context. Researchers have found cultural differences here: People from mainstream Western culture tend to be analytic thinkers, whereas people from East Asian cultures think more holistically (Norenzayan, Choi, & Peng, 2007; Park & Huang, 2010; Varnum, Grossmann, Kitayama, & Nisbett, 2010). In general, logical and scientific reasoning requires analytic thinking, but holistic thinking can help learners identify associations and relationships among seemingly very different phenomena. For example, holistically minded Chinese scientists identified the underlying cause of the ocean's tides—the moon's gravitational pull on any large body of water—many centuries before more narrowly focused, earth-centered European scientists did (Nisbett, 2009).

In contrast to the mixed research findings regarding cognitive styles and learning styles, research on dispositions has yielded more consistent and fruitful results. Some kinds of dispositions are clearly beneficial for classroom learning:

Children differ in their desires for intellectual stimulation and challenging cognitive tasks.

- *Stimulation seeking:* Eagerly interacting with one's physical and social environment in order to gain new experiences and information

- *Need for cognition:* Regularly seeking and engaging in challenging cognitive tasks

- *Critical thinking:* Consistently evaluating information or arguments in terms of their accuracy, credibility, and worth, rather than accepting them at face value

- *Open-mindedness:* Flexibly considering alternative perspectives and multiple sources of evidence, and suspending judgment for a time rather than leaping to immediate conclusions (Cacioppo, Petty, Feinstein, & Jarvis, 1996; DeBacker & Crowson, 2008, 2009; Halpern, 2008; Kang et al., 2009; Kardash & Scholes, 1996; Raine, Reynolds, & Venables, 2002; Southerland & Sinatra, 2003; Stanovich, 1999; West, Toplak, & Stanovich, 2008)

Chapter 7 describes critical thinking more thoroughly.

Such dispositions are often positively correlated with students' learning and achievement, and many theorists have suggested that they play a causal role in what and how much students learn. In fact, dispositions sometimes overrule intelligence in their influence on long-term achievement (Dai & Sternberg, 2004; Kuhn & Franklin, 2006; Perkins & Ritchhart, 2004). For instance, children who eagerly seek out physical and social stimulation as preschoolers later become better readers and earn better grades in school (Raine et al., 2002). Students with a high need for cognition learn more from what they read and are more likely to base conclusions on sound evidence and logical reasoning (Cacioppo et al., 1996; Dai, 2002; P. K. Murphy & Mason, 2006). And students who critically evaluate new evidence and open-mindedly listen to diverse perspectives show more advanced reasoning capabilities and are more likely to revise their beliefs in the face of contradictory information (DeBacker & Crowson, 2009; G. Matthews, Zeidner, & Roberts, 2006; Southerland & Sinatra, 2003).

Researchers haven't yet systematically addressed the origins of various dispositions. Perhaps inherited temperamental differences (e.g., in stimulation seeking) are involved (Raine et al., 2002). Beliefs about the underlying nature of knowledge—for instance, the belief that knowledge is fixed and unchanging, on the one hand, or dynamic and continually evolving, on the other— may also play a role (P. M. King & Kitchener, 2002; Kuhn, 2001b; Mason, 2003). And almost certainly teachers' actions and the general classroom atmosphere they create—for example, whether students are encouraged to pursue intriguing topics, take risks, and think critically— make a difference (Flum & Kaplan, 2006; Gresalfi, 2009; Kuhn, 2001b, 2006). In the following classroom interaction, a teacher actually seems to *discourage* any disposition to think analytically and critically about classroom material:

Beliefs about the underlying nature of knowledge are known as *epistemic beliefs* (see Chapter 7).

## Into the Classroom

### Promoting Productive Dispositions

🍎 **Communicate your own eagerness to learn about and master new topics.**

In a unit on poetry, a middle school English teacher says, "In our culture we're accustomed to poems that rhyme and have a steady beat. But many centuries ago the Japanese developed a very different form of poetry. This form, called *haiku,* is really cool. I'll give you some of my favorite examples, and then as a class we'll create some new haiku."

🍎 **Model open-mindedness about diverse viewpoints and a willingness to suspend judgment until all the facts are in.**

In a lesson about the properties of air—especially the fact that it takes up space—a first-grade teacher asks her students to predict whether the inside of a glass will get wet or stay dry when it is pushed upside down into a bowl of water. After the glass has been immersed, students come to different conclusions about the wetness or dryness of its inside. The teacher responds, "Uh-oh. Now we have two different opinions. We are going to have to figure out how to solve this problem." She devises a simple

strategy—stuffing a crumpled paper towel into the glass and then re-immersing it in the water—to get more conclusive evidence. (Observe this example in "Properties of Air.")

🍎 **Conduct learning activities in which students collaborate to address intriguing, multifaceted issues.**

A few weeks before a national presidential election, a high school social studies teacher says to his class, "Many of the campaign ads we see on television now are harshly criticizing opposing candidates, and some of them may be misrepresenting the facts. In your cooperative groups today, you'll be looking at transcripts of three political ads, one each from a different candidate's campaign. Each group has at least two laptops or tablets with wi-fi. Your job is to be fact checkers—to search the Internet for credible websites that can either confirm or disconfirm what the candidates are saying about their own records or those of their opponents. Tomorrow we'll compare the findings of various groups."

🍎 **Ask students to evaluate the quality of scientific evidence, and scaffold their efforts sufficiently that they can reach appropriate conclusions.**

Working in pairs, fifth graders conduct "experiments" in a computer program that simulates the effects of various factors (amount of rainfall, rate of snowmelt, type of soil, etc.) on local flooding. To guide students' inquiry, the program asks them to form and then test specific hypotheses, and it occasionally asks them if a particular series of tests has controlled for other potentially influential factors.

*Sources:* Strategies based on discussions by de Jong, 2011; Gresalfi, 2009; Halpern, 1998; Kuhn, 2001b; Perkins & Ritchhart, 2004; vanSledright & Limón, 2006.

---

*Teacher:*   Write this on your paper . . . it's simply memorizing this pattern. We have meters, centimeters, and millimeters. Let's say . . . write millimeters, centimeters, and meters. We want to make sure that our metric measurement is the same. If I gave you this decimal, let's say .234 m (yes, write that). In order to come up with .234 m in centimeters, the only thing that is necessary is that you move the decimal. How do we move the decimal? You move it to the right two places. . . . Simple stuff. (Turner, Meyer, et al., 1998, p. 741)

Undoubtedly this teacher means well, but notice the noncritical attitude she communicates: "Write this . . . it's simply memorizing this pattern." The Into the Classroom feature "Promoting Productive Dispositions" offers strategies that are more likely to be effective.

## Educating Students with Special Needs in General Education Classrooms

**students with special needs**
Students different enough from their peers that they require specially adapted instructional materials and practices to maximize their learning and achievement.

As teachers, we can typically accommodate many students' varying abilities and dispositions within the context of a single curriculum and everyday classroom lessons. But we're also likely to have students with special needs—students who are different enough from their peers that they require specially adapted instructional materials and practices to help them maximize their learning and achievement. Some of these students have cognitive, personal, social, or physical disabilities that adversely affect their performance in a typical classroom. Others, instead, are so advanced in a particular domain—that is, they are *gifted*—that they gain little from grade-level activities and assignments.

In the United States, most students with special educational needs are in general education classrooms for part or all of the school day—a practice known as inclusion (U.S. Department of Education, National Center for Education Statistics, 2010). In fact, federal legislation mandates that students with disabilities be educated in neighborhood schools and, ideally, in regular classrooms to the greatest extent possible.

## PUBLIC LAW 94-142: INDIVIDUALS WITH DISABILITIES EDUCATION ACT (IDEA)

In 1975 the U.S. Congress passed Public Law 94-142, which is now known as the Individuals with Disabilities Education Act (IDEA). This act has been amended and reauthorized several times since then, most recently in 2004 under the name *Individuals with Disabilities Education Improvement Act*. It currently grants educational rights from birth until age 21 for people with cognitive, emotional, or physical disabilities. It guarantees several rights for students with disabilities:

- *A free and appropriate education.* All students with disabilities are entitled to a free educational program designed specifically to meet their unique educational needs. For example, to acquire adequate reading skills, a student with a reading disability might require tailor-made reading materials and some one-on-one instruction.

- *Fair and nondiscriminatory evaluation.* A multidisciplinary team conducts an in-depth evaluation of any student who may be eligible for special services. The team's makeup depends on the student's needs but typically consists of two or more teachers, any appropriate specialists, and the student's parent(s) or guardian(s). Using a variety of tests and other evaluation tools, school personnel conduct a complete assessment of potential disabling conditions. Evaluation procedures must take a student's background and any suspected physical or communication difficulties into account. For example, tests must be administered in a student's primary language.

- *Education in the least restrictive environment.* To the greatest extent possible, students with disabilities should be included in the same academic environment, extracurricular activities, and social interactions as their nondisabled peers. That is, they must have the least restrictive environment, the most typical and standard educational environment that, with sufficient supplementary aids and support services, can reasonably meet their needs. Exclusion from general education is warranted only when others' safety would be jeopardized or when, even with proper support and assistance, a student can't make appreciable progress in a general education setting.

- *Individualized education program (IEP).* When an individual aged 3 to 21 is identified as having a disability, the multidisciplinary team collaboratively develops an instructional program, called an individualized education program (IEP), tailored to the individual's strengths and weaknesses (see Figure 5.2). The IEP is a written statement that the team

**inclusion** Practice of educating all students, including those with severe and multiple disabilities, in neighborhood schools and general education classrooms.

**Individuals with Disabilities Education Act (IDEA)** U.S. federal legislation granting educational rights from birth until age 21 for people with cognitive, emotional, or physical disabilities.

**least restrictive environment** Most typical and standard educational environment that can reasonably meet the needs of a student with a disability.

**individualized education program (IEP)** Written description of an appropriate instructional program for a student with special needs.

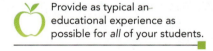
Provide as typical an educational experience as possible for *all* of your students.

---

## FIGURE 5.2 Components of an individualized education plan (IEP)

In the United States, any IEP written for a student with a disability must include the following information:

- *Current performance:* Information about the student's current school achievement levels, including classroom tests and assignments, teachers' and specialists' observations, and results of individually administered assessments.

- *Annual goals:* Objectives or benchmarks for the school year related to the student's academic, social, behavioral, and/or physical needs.

- *Special education and related services:* The special services, supplementary aids, and program modifications that will be provided in order to help the student meet the annual goals.

- *Participation with nondisabled children:* If applicable, explanation of the extent to which the student will *not* participate in regular classroom and extracurricular activities.

- *Measurement of progress:* Information regarding how the student's progress will be monitored and how parents will be informed of this progress.

- *Participation in state and district-wide tests:* Explanation of any modifications or exclusions with respect to regularly administered achievement tests and, if applicable, description of any alternative measures of achievement.

- *Dates and places:* Information regarding when and where services will begin and how long they will continue.

- *Transition services:* For any student aged 14 (or younger, if appropriate), any special services needed for reaching post-school goals and preparing to leave school.

*Source:* U.S. Department of Education, Office of Special Education and Rehabilitative Services, 2000.

continues to review and, if appropriate, revise at least once a year—more frequently if conditions warrant.

- *Due process.* IDEA mandates several practices that ensure that students' and parents' rights are preserved throughout the decision-making process. For instance, parents can give or withhold permission to have their child evaluated for special education services, and they must be notified in writing before the school takes any action that might change their child's educational program. Upon request, parents can see all school records about their child. And if the parents and school system disagree on the most appropriate placement for a child, mediation or a hearing before an impartial individual (i.e., someone who isn't employed by the school district) can be used to resolve the differences.

IDEA has now been in effect for four decades, and in that time it has had a significant impact on the nature of special education. More and more, teachers are realizing that truly inclusive practices require differentiated instruction for *all* students, not just those with formally identified needs. And rather than provide specialized instruction in a separate classroom, many special education teachers now partner with regular classroom teachers to jointly teach all students—both those with disabilities and those without—during part or all of the school day.

## POTENTIAL BENEFITS AND DRAWBACKS OF INCLUSION

Despite the mandates of IDEA, inclusive practices for students with disabilities have been controversial. Some experts argue that students are most likely to develop normal peer relationships and social skills when they participate fully in their school's overall social life. But others worry that when students with special needs are in a regular classroom for the entire school day, they can't get the intensive specialized instruction they may need to achieve essential skills in reading, math, and the like. Furthermore, nondisabled classmates may stigmatize, avoid, or bully students who appear to be odd or incompetent in some way (Hamovitch, 2007).

Numerous research studies have suggested that attending general education classes for part or all of the school day can have several positive outcomes for students with disabilities:

- Academic achievement equivalent to (and sometimes higher than) that in a self-contained classroom
- More appropriate classroom behavior
- Better social skills and more frequent interaction with nondisabled peers
- Better sense of self *if* the school environment is one in which all students accept and respect individual differences among their peers (C. M. Cole, Waldron, & Majd, 2004; Halvorsen & Sailor, 1990; Hamovitch, 2007; Hattie, 2009; P. Hunt & Goetz, 1997; MacMaster, Donovan, & MacIntyre, 2002; Scruggs & Mastropieri, 1994; Slavin, 1987; Soodak & McCarthy, 2006; Stainback & Stainback, 1992)

We're especially likely to see such outcomes when students understand the nature of their disabilities and when instruction and materials are tailored to students' specific needs, perhaps in their regular classrooms or perhaps in short resource-room sessions (e.g., H. L. Swanson, Hoskyn, & Lee, 1999). Appropriate assistive technology—electronic devices and other equipment that can enhance students' abilities and performance—is also extremely valuable in helping students successfully participate in the curriculum and social life of general education classrooms. In contrast, it's *not* helpful to pretend that students' difficulties don't exist—for instance, by saying that a student is simply "having a bad day."

Nondisabled students often benefit from inclusive practices as well. For example, they may be able to take advantage of special supports designed for students with disabilities—perhaps detailed study guides or supplementary explanations (C. M. Cole et al., 2004). Furthermore, they acquire an increasing awareness of the heterogeneous nature of the human race and discover that individuals with special needs are in many respects very much like themselves (P. Hunt & Goetz, 1997; D. Staub, 1998). I think of my son Jeff's friendship with Evan, a classmate with severe physical and cognitive disabilities, during their third-grade year. The boys' teacher had asked Jeff to be a special friend to Evan, interacting with him at lunch and whenever else the class schedule allowed. Although largely unable to speak, Evan always made it clear through gestures

**assistive technology** Any electronic or nonelectronic device that can enhance certain abilities or performance areas for students with disabilities.

and facial expressions that he was delighted to spend time with his friend, giving Jeff—who was quite shy—a considerable boost in social self-confidence. Several years later Jeff reflected on his friendship with Evan:

> It made me realize that Evan was a person too. It made me realize that I could have a friendship with a boy with disabilities. Doing things that made Evan happy made me happy as well. I knew that *Evan* knew that we were friends.

It's essential, of course, that nondisabled students treat classmates who have disabilities in respectful and supportive ways and, better still, forge friendships with these classmates. As teachers, we can do several things to nurture good relationships between students with and without disabilities:

- Explicitly point out the strengths of a student with a disability.
- Ask students with and without disabilities to assist others in their particular areas of strength.
- Plan academic and recreational activities that require cooperation.
- Encourage students with disabilities to participate in extracurricular activities and community events. (Bassett et al., 1996; DuPaul, Ervin, Hook, & McGoey, 1998; Hamovitch, 2007; Madden & Slavin, 1983; Turnbull, Pereira, & Blue-Banning, 2000)

## IDENTIFYING STUDENTS' SPECIAL NEEDS: RESPONSE TO INTERVENTION AND PEOPLE-FIRST LANGUAGE

Experts don't completely agree about how to define various categories of special needs—especially those not involving obvious physical conditions—or about how best to identify students who fit into each category. In the United States, IDEA provides specific identification criteria for various disabilities. Students with disabilities who don't meet IDEA's criteria are often eligible for special educational services under Section 504 of the Rehabilitation Act of 1973 (sometimes referred to simply as *Section 504*). This act stipulates that institutions that benefit from federal funding (including public schools) can't discriminate against individuals on the basis of a disability. Procedures for assessing and accommodating students' disabilities are less prescriptive in Section 504 than they are in IDEA—a situation that can be either advantageous or disadvantageous, depending on the circumstances. (For more details on the differences between IDEA and Section 504, see deBettencourt, 2002; alternatively, type "IDEA vs. 504" in an Internet search engine such as Google or Yahoo!)

One approach to identification that is gaining increasing support (and that is endorsed in the 2004 reauthorization of IDEA) involves determining response to intervention (RTI). In this approach, a teacher keeps an eye out for any student who has exceptional difficulty with basic skills in a certain domain (e.g., in reading or math) despite normal whole-class instruction *and* intensive follow-up small-group instruction that have both been shown *by research* to be effective for most children. Such a student is referred for in-depth assessments of various characteristics and abilities. If the assessment rules out obvious disabling conditions (e.g., significant genetic abnormalities, sensory impairments), the student is assumed to have a cognitive impairment—often, but not always, falling within the category of learning disabilities—and is therefore eligible for special services (e.g., Fletcher & Vaughn, 2009; L. S. Fuchs & Fuchs, 2009; Mellard & Johnson, 2008).

Whenever we identify a student as having a particular disability, however, we run the risk of focusing other people's attention on weaknesses rather than on the student's many strengths and age-typical characteristics. To minimize such an effect, special educators urge us all to use people-first language when referring to students with disabilities—in other words, to mention the person *before* the disability. For instance, we might say *student with a learning disability* rather than *learning disabled student* or *student who is blind* rather than *blind student*.

In upcoming sections of the chapter, I group students with special needs into five general categories. Table 5.2 lists the specific kinds of special needs that fall within each category. Disabilities covered by IDEA appear in a red color in the table.

**response to intervention** (RTI) Approach to diagnosing a cognitive impairment in which students are identified for in-depth assessment after failing to master certain basic skills despite both whole-class and remedial small-group instruction that research has shown to be effective for most students.

**people-first language** Language usage in which a student's disability is identified *after* the student is named.

Inclusive classrooms can promote genuine appreciation and respect for individual differences. Watch "Fifth Graders Discuss Different Abilities."

Use people-first language when talking about students with disabilities.

## STUDENTS IN INCLUSIVE SETTINGS

**TABLE 5.2 • General and Specific Categories of Students with Special Needs (Specific Categories Listed in Red Are Covered by IDEA)**

| GENERAL CATEGORY | SPECIFIC CATEGORIES | DESCRIPTION |
|---|---|---|
| **Students with specific cognitive or academic difficulties:** These students exhibit an uneven pattern of academic performance; they may have unusual difficulty with certain kinds of tasks yet perform quite successfully on other tasks. | Learning disabilities | Difficulties in specific cognitive processes (e.g., in perception, language, or memory) that cannot be attributed to other disabilities, such as mental retardation, emotional or behavioral disorders, or sensory impairments |
| | Attention-deficit hyperactivity disorder (ADHD) (not specifically covered by IDEA, but students are often eligible for special services under the IDEA category Other Health Impairments) | Disorder marked by either or both of these characteristics: (1) difficulty focusing and maintaining attention and (2) frequent hyperactive and impulsive behavior |
| | Speech and communication disorders | Impairments in spoken language (e.g., mispronunciations of certain sounds, stuttering, or abnormal syntactical patterns) or in language comprehension that significantly interfere with classroom performance |
| **Students with social or behavioral problems:** These students exhibit social, emotional, or behavioral difficulties serious enough to interfere significantly with their academic performance. | Emotional and behavioral disorders | Emotional states and behaviors that are present over a substantial period of time and significantly disrupt academic learning and performance |
| | Autism spectrum disorders | Disorders marked by impaired social cognition, social skills, and social interaction, as well as repetition of certain idiosyncratic behaviors; milder forms (e.g., Asperger syndrome) associated with normal development in other domains; extreme forms associated with delayed cognitive and linguistic development and highly unusual behaviors |
| **Students with general delays in cognitive and social functioning:** These students exhibit low achievement in virtually all academic areas and have social skills typical of much younger children. | Intellectual disabilities (mental retardation) | Significantly below-average general intelligence and deficits in adaptive behavior (i.e., in practical and social intelligence); deficits are evident in childhood and typically appear at an early age |
| **Students with physical or sensory challenges:** These students have disabilities caused by diagnosed physical or medical problems. | Physical and health impairments | Physical or medical conditions (usually long-term) that interfere with school performance as a result of limited energy and strength, reduced mental alertness, or little muscle control |
| | Visual impairments | Malfunctions of the eyes or optic nerves that prevent normal vision even with corrective lenses |
| | Hearing loss | Malfunctions of the ear or associated nerves that interfere with the perception of sounds within the frequency range of normal speech |
| **Students with advanced cognitive development:** These students have unusually high ability in one or more areas. | Giftedness (not covered by IDEA unless a disability is also present) | Unusually high ability or aptitude in one or more domains within the academic curriculum, requiring special educational services to help students meet their full potential |

# Students with Specific Cognitive or Academic Difficulties

Some students with special educational needs show no outward signs of physical disability yet have cognitive difficulties that interfere with their ability to learn certain kinds of academic material or perform certain kinds of classroom tasks. Such students include those with learning disabilities, attention-deficit hyperactivity disorder, and speech and communication disorders.

# LEARNING DISABILITIES

Students with **learning disabilities** have significant difficulties in one or more specific cognitive processes that can't be attributed to cultural or linguistic diversity, generally delayed cognitive development, emotional problems, sensory impairment, or environmental deprivation. Such difficulties often appear to result from specific and possibly inherited brain dysfunctions (N. Gregg, 2009; Price, Holloway, Räsänen, Vesterinen, & Ansari, 2007; K. Pugh & McCardle, 2009). Figure 5.3 lists several forms that a learning disability might take.

**learning disabilities** Deficiencies in one or more specific cognitive processes but not in overall cognitive functioning.

## COMMON CHARACTERISTICS

In general, students with learning disabilities are different from one another in many more ways than they are similar. They typically have many strengths but may face such challenges as these:

- Poor reading and writing skills
- Ineffective learning and memory strategies
- Trouble concentrating on and completing assigned tasks, especially in the face of distractions
- Poor sense of self and low motivation for academic tasks, especially in the absence of individualized assistance in areas of difficulty
- Poor motor skills
- Poor social skills (Bracken, 2009; Estell et al., 2008; Gathercole, Lamont, & Alloway, 2006; N. Gregg, 2009; K. Pugh & McCardle, 2009; Waber, 2010)

By no means do such characteristics describe *all* students with learning disabilities. For instance, some are attentive in class and work diligently on assignments, and some are socially skillful and popular with peers.

Sometimes learning disabilities reflect a mismatch between students' developing abilities, on the one hand, and grade-level expectations for performance, on the other (Waber, 2010). For instance, as students reach middle school, they're typically expected to work with little or no supervision, yet students with learning disabilities don't always have the time management skills they need to get things done (N. Gregg, 2009). And in high school, learning may require reading and studying relatively sophisticated textbooks, yet the average high school student with a learning disability reads at a fourth- to fifth-grade level and has few, if any, effective study strategies (Cutting, Eason, Young, & Alberstadt, 2009; Deshler et al., 2001; Meltzer & Krishnan, 2007). This exercise can give you a sense of how these students might feel under such circumstances.

## EXPERIENCING FIRSTHAND
## A READING ASSIGNMENT

Read the following passage carefully. I will test you on its contents later in the chapter.

> Personality research needs to refocus on global traits because such traits are an important part of everyday social discourse, because they embody a good deal of folk wisdom and common sense, because understanding and evaluating trait judgments can provide an important route toward the improvement of social judgment, and because global traits offer legitimate, if necessarily incomplete, explanations of behavior. A substantial body of evidence supporting the existence of global traits includes personality correlates of behavior, interjudge agreement in personality ratings, and the longitudinal stability of personality over time. Future research should clarify the origins of global traits, the dynamic mechanisms through which they influence behavior, and the behavioral cues through which they can most accurately be judged. (Funder, 1991, p. 31)

How well do you think you will perform on the upcoming test about this passage?

The passage you just read is a fairly typical one from *Psychological Science,* a professional journal written for people with advanced education (e.g., doctoral degrees) in psychology. Hence, it was written well above a typical college student's reading level. I won't *really* test you on the passage's contents, but I hope that the exercise gave you a feel for the frustration that high school students with learning disabilities might experience every day. For many students with learning

---

**FIGURE 5.3** Examples of cognitive processing deficiencies in students with learning disabilities

**Perceptual difficulty.** Students may have trouble understanding or remembering information they receive through a particular modality, such as vision or hearing.

**Memory difficulty.** Students may have less capacity for remembering information over either the short or long run (i.e., they may have problems with either *working memory* or *long-term memory*).

**Metacognitive difficulty.** Students may have difficulty using effective learning strategies, monitoring progress toward learning goals, and in other ways directing their own learning.

**Oral language processing difficulty.** Students may have trouble understanding spoken language or remembering what they have been told.

**Reading difficulty.** Students may have trouble recognizing printed words or comprehending what they read; extreme form is known as *dyslexia*.

**Written language difficulty.** Students may have problems in handwriting, spelling, or expressing themselves coherently on paper; an extreme form is known as *dysgraphia*.

**Mathematical difficulty.** Students may have trouble thinking about or remembering information involving numbers; an extreme form is known as *dyscalculia*.

**Social perception difficulty.** Students may have trouble interpreting others' social cues and signals and thus may respond inappropriately in social situations.

**Music processing difficulty.** Students may have little sensitivity to differences in pitch and be unable to recognize familiar tunes; an extreme form is known as *amusia*.

---

disabilities, completing school assignments may constantly seem like fighting an uphill battle. Perhaps for this reason, a higher-than-average percentage of students with learning disabilities drop out of school before graduation (N. Gregg, 2009).

## ADAPTING INSTRUCTION

Instructional strategies for students with learning disabilities must be tailored to students' specific strengths and weaknesses. Nevertheless, several strategies should benefit many of these students:

🍎 *Minimize distractions.* Because many students with learning disabilities are easily distracted, we should minimize the presence of other stimuli that might compete for their attention—for example, by pulling down window shades if other classes are playing outside and by asking students to clear away materials they don't immediately need (Buchoff, 1990).

🍎 *Present new information in an explicit and well-organized manner.* Most students with learning disabilities learn more successfully when instruction directly communicates what they need to learn, rather than requiring them to draw inferences and synthesize ideas on their own. Frequent and carefully structured practice of important skills is also critical (Fletcher, Lyon, Fuchs, & Barnes, 2007; Hallenbeck, 1996; J. A. Stein & Krishnan, 2007).

🍎 *Present information in multiple sensory modalities.* Because some students with learning disabilities have trouble learning through a particular sensory modality, we need to think broadly about the modalities we use to communicate information. For example, when teaching students to recognize alphabet letters, we might have them not only look at the letters but also trace large, textured letter shapes with their fingers (Florence, Gentaz, Pascale, & Sprenger-Charolles, 2004). And in lectures in the secondary grades, we might incorporate videos, graphics, and other visual materials, and we might encourage students to audiotape the lectures (J. A. Stein & Krishnan, 2007; J. W. Wood & Rosbe, 1985).

**FIGURE 5.4** Seven-year-old Daniel's attempt to write "I trust a policeman"

I trust a policeman.

🍎 *Analyze students' errors for clues about processing difficulties.* As an example of this strategy, look at 7-year-old Daniel's attempt to write "I trust a policeman" in Figure 5.4. Daniel captured several sounds correctly, including the "s" and final "t" sounds in *trust* and all of the consonant sounds in *policeman*. However, he misrepresented the first two consonant sounds in *trust,* replacing the *t* and *r* with an *N*. He also neglected to represent most of the vowel sounds, and two of the three vowels he did include (*I* for the article *a* and the *E* near the end of *policeman*) are incorrect. We might suspect that Daniel has difficulty hearing all the distinct sounds in spoken words and matching them with the letters he sees in written words. Such difficulties are quite common in students with significant reading disabilities (Goswami, 2007; N. Gregg, 2009; K. Pugh & McCardle, 2009).

🍏 *Teach study skills and learning strategies.* Many students with learning disabilities benefit from being taught specific strategies for completing assignments and remembering classroom subject matter (Fletcher et al., 2007; Meltzer, 2007; Wilder & Williams, 2001). For example, we might teach them concrete strategies for taking notes and organizing homework. We might also teach them specific *mnemonics,* or memory tricks, to help them remember particular facts (e.g., see Figure 5.5).

🍏 *Provide paper or electronic scaffolding that can support students as they study and work.* For example, we might develop study guides, outlines, or graphics that help students identify and interrelate important concepts and ideas. We could provide a copy of a high-achieving classmate's lecture notes. And we can teach students how to use the grammar and spell checkers in word processing software (N. Gregg, 2009; Mastropieri & Scruggs, 1992; Meltzer, 2007).

Chapter 6 and Chapter 7 provide many strategies for helping students study and learn.

**FIGURE 5.5 A mnemonic for remembering the letters *b* and *d***

Young children with learning disabilities often confuse lowercase b and d. By clenching their fists as shown here and "reading" their hands in the normal left-to-right direction, they can more easily remember the difference: b comes first in both the alphabet and the fists.

## ATTENTION-DEFICIT HYPERACTIVITY DISORDER (ADHD)

Virtually all students are apt to be inattentive, hyperactive, and impulsive at one time or another. But those with attention-deficit hyperactivity disorder (ADHD) typically have significant and chronic deficits in these areas, as reflected in the following identification criteria:

- *Inattention.* Students may have considerable difficulty focusing and maintaining attention on assigned tasks, especially when appealing alternatives are close at hand. They may have trouble listening to and following directions, and they may often make careless mistakes.
- *Hyperactivity.* Students may seem to have an excess amount of energy. They're apt to be fidgety and may move around the classroom at inappropriate times.
- *Impulsivity.* Students almost invariably have trouble inhibiting inappropriate behaviors. They may blurt out answers, begin assignments prematurely, or engage in risky or destructive behaviors without thinking about potential consequences. (American Psychiatric Association, 2000; Barkley, 2006; Gatzke-Kopp & Beauchaine, 2007; N. Gregg, 2009)

Students with ADHD don't necessarily show all three of these characteristics. For instance, some are inattentive without also being hyperactive, as is true for Tim in the opening case study. But all students with ADHD appear to have one characteristic in common: an *inability to inhibit inappropriate thoughts, inappropriate actions, or both* (Barkley, 2006, 2010; B. J. Casey, 2001; Nigg, 2010). Tim, for example, is easily distracted by his thoughts and daydreams when he should be focusing on a classroom lesson.

In many instances, ADHD appears to be the result of brain abnormalities that limit students' ability to focus their attention and control their behaviors. Sometimes these abnormalities are inherited, but sometimes, instead, they're the result of toxic substances in children's early environments—perhaps high lead content in the paint dust of old buildings (Accardo, 2008; Barkley, 2010; Faranoe et al., 2005; Gatzke-Kopp & Beauchaine, 2007; Nigg, 2010).

### COMMON CHARACTERISTICS

In addition to inattentiveness, hyperactivity, and impulsivity, students identified as having ADHD may have characteristics such as these:

- Exceptional imagination and creativity; exceptionally detailed memories
- Certain specific cognitive processing difficulties (e.g., see Figure 5.6) and low school achievement
- Problems with planning and time management
- Classroom behavior problems (e.g., disruptiveness, noncompliance)
- Poor social skills and interpersonal difficulties
- Increased probability of substance abuse in adolescence (Barkley, 2006; Gatzke-Kopp & Beauchaine, 2007; S. Goldstein & Rider, 2006; N. Gregg, 2009; Hallowell, 1996; Skowronek, Leichtman, & Pillemer, 2008)

Students' attention, hyperactivity, and impulsiveness problems may diminish somewhat in adolescence, but they don't entirely disappear, making it difficult for students to handle the increasing demands for independence and self-regulation that come in high school. Accordingly, students

**attention-deficit hyperactivity disorder (ADHD)** Disorder marked by inattention, hyperactivity, impulsive behavior, or some combination of these characteristics.

**FIGURE 5.6** Like many students with ADHD, 10-year-old Joshua has specific cognitive processing difficulties. Although he has the math skills of a typical fifth grader, he has delayed reading comprehension and writing skills, as reflected in the book report shown here. Josh can more easily express his thoughts orally.

> I am just doce with book. I really like ths book that I chose and it was a good chose. She dose not go back to Sac Frannsico and find her peo Pal She stay io the Arctc. , I would be saved too and cold. Mya X has survied there. About done.

with ADHD are at greater-than-average risk for dropping out of school (Barkley, 2006; S. Goldstein & Rider, 2006; N. Gregg, 2009; E. L. Hart, Lahey, Loeber, Applegate, & Frick, 1995).

## ADAPTING INSTRUCTION

Some students with ADHD take medication that helps them control their symptoms. But medication alone is rarely sufficient to enable classroom success; individually tailored educational interventions are also in order (Purdie, Hattie, & Carroll, 2002). The strategies previously listed for students with learning disabilities can often be helpful for students with ADHD. Researchers and practitioners have offered several additional suggestions:

🍎 *Modify students' work environments and schedules.* Students with ADHD do better in a work environment where there are minimal distractions, some degree of structure, and ongoing teacher monitoring. And ideally, students should have most academic subjects and challenging tasks in the morning rather than in the afternoon, as the symptoms of ADHD tend to get progressively worse as the day goes on (Barkley, 2006; N. Gregg, 2009).

🍎 *Explicitly facilitate attention and concentration.* Students may benefit from soundproof headphones or "white noise" machines that block out many potentially distracting sounds, or, for a low-tech alternative, we might encourage them to move to a new location if their current one presents too many distractions (Buchoff, 1990; N. Gregg, 2009). Also, some computer programs give students intense practice in focusing and keeping their attention on specific stimuli (e.g., see Klingberg, Keonig, & Bilbe, 2002; Rueda, Rothbart, McCandliss, Saccomanno, & Posner, 2005).

🍎 *Provide outlets for excess energy.* To help students control excess energy, we should intersperse quiet academic work with frequent opportunities for physical exercise (Pellegrini & Bohn, 2005; Pfiffner, Barkley, & DuPaul, 2006). We might also give students a settling-in time after recess or lunch—perhaps reading an excerpt from a high-interest storybook or magazine article—before asking them to engage in an activity that involves quiet concentration (Pellegrini & Horvat, 1995).

🍎 *Help students organize and use their time effectively.* For example, we can show them how to prioritize activities, create to-do lists, and establish a daily routine that they post on their desks. We can break large tasks into smaller ones and set a short time limit for each subtask. And we can provide a folder in which students transport homework assignments to and from school (Buchoff, 1990; N. Gregg, 2009; Pfiffner et al., 2006).

## SPEECH AND COMMUNICATION DISORDERS

Speech and communication disorders are impairments in spoken language or language comprehension that significantly interfere with students' classroom performance. Examples include persistent articulation problems (e.g., see Figure 5.7), stuttering, abnormal syntactical patterns, and difficulty understanding other people's speech. Sometimes, but not always, these children have difficulty perceiving and mentally processing particular aspects of spoken language—a subcategory of speech and communication disorders known as *specific language impairments*. And often—but again, not always—the source of the disorder can be traced to heredity or specific brain abnormalities (Bishop, 2006; J. L. Locke, 1993; Spinath, Price, Dale, & Plomin, 2004).

Specific language impairments are described in Chapter 2.

## COMMON CHARACTERISTICS

Although some students with speech and communication disorders have other disabilities as well, many of them are in most ways just typical students. Nevertheless, the following characteristics are fairly common:

- Reluctance to speak; embarrassment and self-consciousness when speaking
- Difficulties in reading and writing (Fey, Catts, & Larrivee, 1995; Heward, 2009; LaBlance, Steckol, & Smith, 1994; Rice, Hadley, & Alexander, 1993)

**speech and communication disorders** Impairments in spoken language or language comprehension that significantly interfere with classroom performance.

**FIGURE 5.7**  Seven-year-old Isaac receives speech therapy at school to address his consistent mispronunciation of certain sounds (such as pronouncing "th" as "v"). In his writing, he sometimes spells words as he says them rather than as he hears them (for instance, he writes *ven* for *then*).

## ADAPTING INSTRUCTION

Usually a trained specialist will work with students to help them improve or overcome their speech and communication difficulties. Nevertheless, general education teachers can assist in several ways:

🍏 *Encourage regular oral communication.*  Students with speech and communication disorders need as much practice in classroom-based public speaking as their classmates do. Thus, we should encourage them to talk in class, provided that doing so doesn't create exceptional stress (Hallahan, Kauffman, & Pullen, 2009; Patton, Blackbourn, & Fad, 1996).

🍏 *Listen patiently.*  When students have trouble expressing themselves, we might be tempted to assist them, perhaps by finishing their sentences for them. But we better help them when we allow them to complete their own thoughts, and we must encourage their classmates to be equally patient (Heward, 2009; Patton et al., 1996).

🍏 *Ask for clarification when a message is unclear.*  If we haven't entirely understood what students are saying, we should explain what we *did* understand and ask for clarification of the rest. Honest feedback helps students learn how well they're communicating (Patton et al., 1996).

🍏 *Use augmentative and alternative communication (AAC) when students have little or no oral language.*  Some forms of AAC involve computer technology; for example, a laptop or computer tablet might have a touch screen that "speaks" when a students puts a fingers on particular words or symbols. Others are nonelectronic; for example, we might give students a set of pictures or teach them some gestures they can use to represent their thoughts (Beukelman & Mirenda, 2005).

## GENERAL RECOMMENDATIONS

In addition to the strategies described in the preceding pages, several general ones apply to many students with specific cognitive or academic difficulties:

🍏 *Get an early start on appropriate interventions.*  When students lack basic concepts and skills on which their future learning will depend, intensive instruction to fill in the gaps—and the

**emotional and behavioral disorders** Emotional states and behavior patterns that consistently and significantly disrupt academic learning and performance.

**externalizing behavior** Symptom of an emotional or behavioral disorder that has a direct effect on other people (e.g., aggression, lack of self-control).

**internalizing behavior** Symptom of an emotional or behavioral disorder that adversely affects the student with the disorder but has little or no direct effect on other people (e.g., depression, social withdrawal).

earlier, the better—can often make a significant difference in their achievement over the long run (Fletcher et al., 2007; L. S. Fuchs et al., 2005; Waber, 2010; Wanzek & Vaughn, 2007).

🍎 *Take skill levels into account when assigning reading materials.* Even after intensive reading instruction, many students with specific cognitive or academic difficulties continue to have poor reading skills. Thus, we may sometimes need to identify alternatives to standard grade-level textbooks for presenting academic content. For example, we might reduce the amount of required reading, substitute materials written on a simpler (yet not babyish) level, or present information through some medium other than printed text—perhaps audiotapes or text-to-speech computer software (N. Gregg, 2009; Mastropieri & Scruggs, 2007). Students may also need extra guidance and support when assignments require them to find and read information on the Internet (Sampson, Szabo, Falk-Ross, Foote, & Linder, 2007).

🍎 *Clearly describe expectations for academic performance.* Students will have an easier time accomplishing classroom tasks if they're told, in concrete and precise terms, exactly what's expected of them (Meltzer & Krishnan, 2007). For example, before students begin a science lab activity, we might first remind them to carefully follow the steps described on the lab sheet, then review safety precautions, and finally provide a written list of components that should be included in lab reports.

🍎 *Take steps to enhance self-confidence and motivation.* Students with a long history of failure at academic tasks need to see that they're making progress and that they do some things quite well. For instance, we can give them daily or weekly goals we know they can attain. We can also have them keep journals in which they describe the successes they've achieved each day. And, of course, we should give them opportunities to do tasks at which they excel (Buchoff, 1990; J. A. Stein & Krishnan, 2007).

# Students with Social or Behavioral Problems

Many students have minor social, emotional, or behavioral difficulties at one time or another, particularly during times of unusual stress or major life changes. Often these problems are temporary ones that require only a little extra support from caring adults and peers. At other times problems are more enduring but *don't* reflect a disability. Perhaps a student's temperament is a poor fit with a teacher's instructional strategies—for instance, an especially fidgety child may perform poorly on lengthy seatwork assignments—or perhaps a teacher simply hasn't made clear the expectations and rules for classroom behavior (Keogh, 2003; Mehan, 1979). In such situations students' problems may decrease or disappear with a change in instructional practices or classroom management strategies.

For more information about matching instructional strategies to students' temperaments, see the section on *goodness of fit* in Chapter 3.

However, some students show a pattern of behaviors that consistently interfere with their learning and performance *regardless* of the teacher and the classroom environment. In this section we'll look at two groups of students who fit into this category: those with emotional and behavioral disorders and those with autism spectrum disorders.

## EMOTIONAL AND BEHAVIORAL DISORDERS

Students with **emotional and behavioral disorders** become identified as students with special needs—and therefore qualify for special educational services—when their problems have a substantial negative impact on classroom learning. Symptoms of emotional and behavioral disorders typically fall into one of two broad categories. **Externalizing behaviors** have direct or indirect effects on other people; examples include aggression, defiance, stealing, and general lack of self-control. **Internalizing behaviors** primarily affect the student with the disorder; examples include severe anxiety or depression, exaggerated mood swings, withdrawal from social interaction, and eating disorders. Students with externalizing behaviors—who are more likely to be boys than girls—are more likely to be referred for evaluation and possible special services. However, students with internalizing behaviors—who are more likely to be girls than boys—can be just as much at risk for school failure (Angold, Worthman, & Costello, 2003; Gay, 2006; Hayward, 2003).

Report suspicions about child maltreatment *immediately* to school administrators or child protective services.

Some emotional and behavioral disorders result from environmental factors, such as stressful living conditions, child maltreatment, or family alcohol or drug abuse (P. T. Davies & Woitach,

2008; D. Glaser, 2000; Maughan & Cicchetti, 2002). But biological causes (e.g., inherited predispositions, chemical imbalances, brain injuries) may also be involved, either by themselves or by interaction with adverse environmental conditions (Dodge, 2009; Raine, 2008; Yeo, Gangestad, & Thoma, 2007). Some students with a genetic predisposition for an emotional or behavioral disorder exhibit few if any signs of a problem until adolescence, as the following case illustrates:

> As a ninth grader, Kirk was a well-behaved, likeable student who earned As and Bs and showed particular promise in science and math. But in tenth grade, his grades began to decline, and he increasingly exhibited hostile and defiant behaviors. When Kirk failed three classes during the fall of his twelfth-grade year, the school principal convened a meeting with him, his parents, and his faculty advisor to discuss how to help Kirk get back on track. At the meeting the principal described several occasions on which Kirk had acted disoriented, belligerent, and seemingly "high" on drugs. Despite his strong desire to attend college the following year, Kirk sat at the meeting smirking (seemingly gleeful about his predicament) and focusing his attention on sorting pieces of trail mix in a bowl on the conference room table. By the end of the meeting, the principal was so infuriated that she expelled him from school.
>
> Over the next few weeks, Kirk's mental condition and behavior continued to deteriorate, to the point that he was soon arrested, placed in a juvenile detention facility, and eventually hospitalized in the state mental institution.

Kirk was ultimately diagnosed with *bipolar disorder,* a condition that is usually inherited and is characterized by excessive mood swings (hence, the disorder is sometimes called manic depression) and in some cases (like Kirk's) by distorted thought processes. Bipolar disorder often doesn't appear until adolescence, even though its biological underpinnings have been present since birth (Griswold & Pessar, 2000).

When students have emotional or behavioral disorders, their inappropriate behaviors interfere not only with academic achievement but also with peer relationships, leading to social as well as academic failure. Some of these students may seek the companionship of the few peers who will accept them—peers who typically behave in similarly inappropriate ways and may introduce one another to drugs, alcohol, or criminal activity (J. Snyder et al., 2008; Webber & Plotts, 2008).

## COMMON CHARACTERISTICS

Students with emotional and behavioral disorders differ considerably in their abilities and personalities. However, in addition to the difficulty in maintaining healthy peer relationships just mentioned, you may observe one or more of the following characteristics:

- Frequent absences from school
- Deteriorating academic performance with increasing age
- Low self-esteem
- Little or no empathy for others' distress
- Significant substance abuse (Espelage, Mebane, & Adams, 2004; Grinberg & McLean-Heywood, 1999; Harter, 1999; Leiter & Johnsen, 1997; McGlynn, 1998; C. M. Richards, Symons, Greene, & Szuszkiewicz, 1995; Turnbull, Turnbull, & Wehmeyer, 2010; Webber & Plotts, 2008)

Some students with emotional and behavioral disorders have other special needs as well, including learning disabilities, ADHD, or giftedness (Fessler, Rosenberg, & Rosenberg, 1991; Gatzke-Kopp & Beauchaine, 2007; Webber & Plotts, 2008).

## ADAPTING INSTRUCTION

Effective interventions must be tailored to each student's unique needs, but several strategies can benefit many of these students:

🍎 *Show an interest in students' well-being and personal growth.* A good first step in helping students with emotional and behavioral disorders is simply showing that we care about them (Chang & Davis, 2009; Clarke et al., 1995; S. C. Diamond, 1991; Heward, 2009). For example,

**autism spectrum disorders** Disorders marked by impaired social cognition, social skills, and social interaction, presumably due to a brain abnormality; extreme forms often associated with significant cognitive and linguistic delays and highly unusual behaviors.

**Asperger syndrome** Mild form of an autism spectrum disorder in which students have normal intelligence and language skills but show significant deficits in social cognition and social skills.

Students with emotional and behavioral disorders are more likely to succeed in inclusive settings if the general education teacher and special education teacher coordinate their efforts. For example, watch "Including Students with Emotional and Behavioral Disorders in General Education."

Mirror neurons are described in more detail in Chapter 3.

we can greet them warmly when we see them, express concern when they seem upset or overly stressed, and lend a supportive ear when they want to share their opinions or frustrations. And we can take students' personal interests into account when planning instruction and assignments.

🍎 *Give students a sense that they have some control over their circumstances.* Some students, especially those who are frequently defiant, often respond to efforts to control them by behaving even *less* appropriately. With such students it's important to avoid power struggles in which only one person wins and the other inevitably loses. Instead, we must create situations in which we ensure that students conform to classroom expectations yet feel that they have some control over what happens to them. For example, we can teach them techniques for observing and monitoring their own actions, with the goal of developing more productive classroom behavior. We can also give them choices, within reasonable limits, about what tasks to accomplish in particular situations (Chang & Davis, 2009; Kern, Dunlap, Childs, & Clark, 1994; Lane, Falk, & Wehby, 2006).

🍎 *Be alert for signs that a student may be contemplating suicide.* In the United States, suicide is the third-leading cause of death for adolescents; occasionally even younger students take their own lives (Goldston et al., 2008; Westefeld et al., 2010). Warning signs include the following:

- Sudden withdrawal from social relationships
- Increasing disregard for personal appearance
- Dramatic personality change (e.g., sudden elevation in mood)
- Preoccupation with death and morbid themes
- Overt or veiled threats (e.g., "I won't be around much longer")
- Actions that indicate putting one's affairs in order (e.g., giving away prized possessions) (Kerns & Lieberman, 1993; Wiles & Bondi, 2001)

As teachers, we must take any of these warning signs seriously and seek help *immediately* from trained professionals, such as school psychologists or counselors.

It's also essential, of course, that we help students with emotional and behavioral disorders acquire more appropriate behaviors. I describe strategies for doing so after the discussion of autism spectrum disorders in the next section.

## AUTISM SPECTRUM DISORDERS

The central, defining features of autism spectrum disorders are marked impairments in social cognition (e.g., perspective taking, interpreting other people's body language), social skills, and social interaction. Many students with these disorders prefer to be alone and form weak, if any, emotional attachments to other people. Common, too, are repetitive behaviors (often very odd ones rarely seen in age-mates) and inflexible adherence to certain routines or rituals (American Psychiatric Association, 2000; Lord, 2010; Pelphrey & Carter, 2007; Tager-Flusberg, 2007).

Aside from similarities in social impairments and repetitive behaviors, individuals with autism spectrum disorders differ considerably in the severity of their condition—hence the term *spectrum.* In Asperger syndrome, a fairly mild form, students have normal language skills and average or above-average intelligence. In severe cases, which are often referred to simply as *autism,* children have major delays in cognitive development and language and may exhibit certain bizarre behaviors—perhaps constantly rocking or waving fingers, continually repeating what someone else has said, or showing unusual fascination with a very narrow category of objects (American Psychiatric Association, 2000; Lord, 2010).

The vast majority of autism spectrum disorders are probably caused by abnormalities in the brain. Some researchers have observed abnormalities in *mirror neurons*—neurons that probably underlie people's perspective-taking abilities (Gallese, Gernsbacher, Heyes, Hickok, & Iacoboni, 2011). Other researchers have discovered abnormalities in interconnections among various parts of the brain—for example, in connections between parts that enable logical reasoning or inhibition of impulses, on the one hand, and parts that underlie emotions and emotional processing, on the other (Cherkassky, Kana, Keller, & Just, 2006; I. L. Cohen, 2007; Kana, Keller, Minshew, & Just, 2007). Also, students with autism spectrum disorders may be either undersensitive or oversensitive to environmental stimulation (Ratey, 2001; R. C. Sullivan, 1994; D. Williams, 1996). Temple Grandin, a woman who has gained international prominence as a designer of livestock facilities, recalls what it was like to be a child with autism:

> From as far back as I can remember, I always hated to be hugged. I wanted to experience the good feeling of being hugged, but it was just too overwhelming. It was like a great, all-engulfing tidal wave of stimulation, and I reacted like a wild animal. . . . When I was little, loud noises were also a problem, often feeling like a dentist's drill hitting a nerve. They actually caused pain. I was scared to death of balloons popping, because the sound was like an explosion in my ear. (Grandin, 1995, pp. 63, 67)

Children with autism sometimes need explicit instruction in social skills. For example, watch "Allyson Practices her Social Skills."

## COMMON CHARACTERISTICS

In addition to the traits already described, students with autism spectrum disorders may have characteristics such as these:

- Strong visual–spatial thinking skills and exceptional awareness of visual details
- Unusual ability to maintain attention and focus during distractions
- Good memory for a set of unrelated facts
- Difficulty planning and organizing a future course of action
- Strong need for a consistent, predictable environment (I. L. Cohen, 2007; M. Dawson, Soulières, Gernsbacher, & Mottron, 2007; Gernsbacher, Stevenson, Khandakar, & Goldsmith, 2008; Grandin & Johnson, 2005; Lord, 2010; Meltzer, 2007; Pelphrey & Carter, 2007; Tager-Flusberg, 2007)

Occasionally students with autism exhibit *savant syndrome,* possessing an extraordinary ability (e.g., exceptional mathematical, artistic, or musical talent) that is quite remarkable in contrast to other aspects of their mental functioning (I. L. Cohen, 2007; L. K. Miller, 2005; Treffert & Wallace, 2002).

## ADAPTING INSTRUCTION

Children with Asperger syndrome are typically in general education classes, and some students with more severe autism spectrum disorders also participate in general education classes for part or all of the school day. Many of the classroom strategies described in earlier sections are applicable for such students. Two additional strategies are helpful as well:

🍎 *Maximize consistency in the classroom layout and weekly schedule.* Many students with autism spectrum disorders feel more comfortable when their environments and schedules are predictable. At the beginning of the school year, then, we should arrange furniture and equipment in ways that will be serviceable throughout the school year, making adjustments later only if absolutely necessary. And to the greatest extent possible, we should schedule recurring activities at the same times each day or on particular days of the week. If the schedule must change for some reason, we should alert students well in advance (Dalrymple, 1995).

🍎 *Use visual approaches to instruction.* Because students with autism spectrum disorders often have strong visual–spatial skills but may have impaired language skills, a heavy emphasis on visual materials may be in order (Ozonoff & Schetter, 2007; C. C. Peterson, 2002; Quill, 1995). We might use objects, pictures, and photographs to convey ideas about academic topics, or we might use some sort of visual cue to signal the start of a new activity.

## GENERAL RECOMMENDATIONS

Although the causes of emotional and behavioral disorders and those of autism spectrum disorders are usually quite different, students with these disabilities can benefit from some of the same classroom interventions. Certainly we want to promote success on academic tasks, perhaps by using instructional strategies presented earlier for students with specific cognitive or academic difficulties. Following are additional suggestions:

A variety of simple technological devices are available to help students learn and practice appropriate classroom behaviors. For example, watch "Self-Management: Brandon's MotivAider."

🍎 *Insist on appropriate classroom behavior.* Although certain students with disabilities may be more prone to counterproductive classroom behaviors than most of their peers, teachers clearly *can* help them behave in productive ways—for instance, by putting reasonable limits on their behavior

## Creating a Productive Classroom Environment

### Encouraging Appropriate Behavior in Students with Social or Behavioral Problems

🍎 **Make expectations for behavior clear and specific.**
A teacher reminds a student, "You can't borrow Mary's bottle of glue without getting her permission. Check with Mary first to make sure it's all right for you to use her things. If Mary says no, ask someone else."

🍎 **Specify and follow through on consequences for appropriate and inappropriate behaviors.**
A teacher tells a student, "Sam, you know that certain four-letter words, such as the two you just used, are unacceptable in this classroom. You also know the consequence for such behavior, so please go to the time-out corner for 10 minutes."

🍎 **Give feedback about specific behaviors rather than general areas of performance.**
A teacher tells a student, "You did a good job in study hall today. You focused your attention on your homework, and you didn't retaliate when Jerome accidentally brushed past you on his way to my desk."

🍎 **Try to anticipate problems and nip them in the bud.**
A student has occasional temper tantrums that disrupt the entire class. Although the tantrums seemingly occur at random, his teacher eventually realizes that his ears always turn red just before an outburst. With this knowledge, she can divert the student's attention to a punching bag whenever a tantrum is imminent, thereby letting him unleash his feelings with only minimal distraction to others.

*Sources:* Hallahan et al., 2009; Heward, 2009; Myles & Simpson, 2001; Ormrod & McGuire, 2007 (temper tantrum example); Webber & Plotts, 2008

---

and imposing consequences when they go beyond those limits (Evertson & Weinstein, 2006; Webber & Plotts, 2008). The Creating a Productive Classroom Environment feature "Encouraging Appropriate Behavior in Students with Social or Behavioral Problems" offers several useful strategies.

🍎 *Foster social cognition and effective interpersonal skills.* Students with social or behavioral problems often benefit from training in social cognition and perspective taking. Explicit instruction in and reinforcement of social skills can also be quite powerful. And of course, students need numerous opportunities to *practice* their new skills (e.g., Chan & O'Reilly, 2008; Myles & Simpson, 2001; Nikopoulos & Keenan, 2004; Schrandt, Townsend, & Poulson, 2009; Theimann & Goldstein, 2004).

> You can find strategies for fostering social cognition and perspective taking in Chapter 3.

🍎 *Be persistent, and look for gradual improvement rather than overnight success.* Many students with social or behavioral problems will initially resist our efforts to help them. They may begin to recognize the value of our guidance and support only when they see the natural consequences of their changing behavior—for example, when they start to make new friends or get along better with their teachers. Their progress may be slow, but by focusing on small improvements, we and our students alike can be encouraged by the changes we *do* see, rather than being discouraged by problems that persist.

## Students with General Delays in Cognitive and Social Functioning

When I use the term *student with general delays in cognitive and social functioning,* I'm talking about any student who shows a consistent pattern of developmental delays, regardless of whether the student has specifically been identified as having a disability. Educators sometimes use the term *slow learner* to describe a student who obtains intelligence test scores in the 70s and has noticeable difficulties in most or all parts of the academic curriculum. A student with especially pronounced difficulties may be identified as having an intellectual disability.

### INTELLECTUAL DISABILITIES

You're undoubtedly familiar with the term *mental retardation*. In recent years, however, many special educators have instead advocated for the term intellectual disability in reference to students who show pronounced delays in most aspects of cognitive and social development. More specifically, students with intellectual disabilities exhibit *both* of the following characteristics (Luckasson et al., 2002):

**intellectual disability** Disability characterized by significantly below-average general intelligence and deficits in adaptive behavior, both of which first appear in infancy or childhood; also known as *mental retardation*.

- *Significantly below-average general intelligence.* These students have intelligence test scores that are quite low—usually no higher than 70, reflecting performance in the bottom 2% of their age-group. In addition, these students learn slowly and show consistently poor achievement in virtually all academic subject areas.

- *Deficits in adaptive behavior.* These students behave in ways that we would expect of much younger children. Their deficits in **adaptive behavior** include limitations in *practical intelligence*—that is, managing the ordinary activities of daily living—and *social intelligence*—that is, conducting themselves appropriately in social situations.

The preceding characteristics must be evident in childhood. Thus, a person who shows them beginning at age 18, perhaps as the result of a serious head injury, would *not* be classified as having an intellectual disability.

Intellectual disabilities are often caused by genetic conditions. For example, most children with Down syndrome have delayed cognitive and social development. Other cases of intellectual disabilities are due to biological but noninherited causes, such as severe malnutrition or excessive alcohol consumption during the mother's pregnancy or oxygen deprivation during a difficult birth. In still other situations, environmental factors, such as parental neglect or an extremely impoverished and unstimulating home environment, may be at fault (Beirne-Smith, Patton, & Kim, 2006).

## COMMON CHARACTERISTICS

Like students in any category of special needs, students with intellectual disabilities have differing personalities, strengths, and needs. Nevertheless, many of them are apt to exhibit characteristics such as the following:

- Sociability and a genuine desire to belong and fit in at school
- Less general knowledge about the world
- Poor reading and language skills
- Short attention span
- Poor memory; few or no effective learning and memory strategies
- Difficulty drawing inferences and understanding abstract ideas
- Difficulty generalizing something learned in one situation to a new situation
- Immature play behaviors and interpersonal skills
- Delayed motor skills; conditions that adversely affect performance in physical activities (e.g., heart defects, poor muscle tone) (Beirne-Smith et al., 2006; Bergeron & Floyd, 2006; Carlin et al., 2003; Heward, 2009; F. P. Hughes, 1998; Tager-Flusberg & Skwerer, 2007)

## ADAPTING INSTRUCTION

With proper support, many students with mild intellectual disabilities can learn basic skills in reading, writing, and math, perhaps even mastering components of a typical fifth- or sixth-grade curriculum (Hallahan et al., 2009; Heward, 2009). Most of the strategies previously described in this chapter can be useful for these students. Here are several additional strategies to keep in mind:

🍏 *Pace instruction slowly enough to ensure success.* When working with a student who has an intellectual disability, we should move through new topics and tasks slowly enough—and with enough support and repetition—that the student can eventually master them. Students with intellectual disabilities typically have a long history of failure at academic tasks. Thus, they need frequent success experiences to learn that, with hard work, they *can* succeed at many tasks (Feuerstein et al., 2010; Fidler, Hepburn, Mankin, & Rogers, 2005; Heward, 2009).

🍏 *Provide considerable scaffolding to promote effective cognitive processes and desired behaviors.* For example, we can develop simple study guides that tell students exactly what to focus on as they study. We can be explicit in our directions to perform various tasks—for instance, saying "John, go to the principal's office, give Mrs. Smith the absentee sheet, and come back here." And we can provide handheld, teacher-programmed prompters—which go by such labels as *visual assistant* and *digital memory aid*—to help students remember the specific things they need to do (Beirne-Smith et al., 2006; Mastropieri & Scruggs, 1992; Patton et al., 1996, p. 105; Turnbull et al., 2010).

🍏 *Include vocational and general life skills in the curriculum.* For most students with intellectual disabilities, training in general life and work skills is an important part of the high school curriculum. Such training is most likely to be effective when it takes place in realistic settings that closely resemble those in which students will find themselves once they leave school (Beirne-Smith et al., 2006; Turnbull et al., 2010).

**adaptive behavior** Behavior related to daily living skills or appropriate conduct in social situations; used as a criterion for identifying students with intellectual disabilities.

Learn more about adaptive behaviors in "Adaptive Behaviors and Intellectual Disabilities."

Many students with intellectual disabilities are sociable and eager to fit in at school. For example, watch a high school cheerleader with Down syndrome in "Trista."

**severe and multiple disabilities**
Combination of two or more disabilities that, taken together, require significant classroom adaptations and highly specialized educational services.

**physical and health impairment**
General physical or medical condition that interferes so significantly with school performance that special accommodations are required.

**visual impairment** Malfunction of the eyes or optic nerves that prevents normal vision even with corrective lenses.

# Students with Physical or Sensory Challenges

Some students with special needs have obvious physical disabilities caused by medically detectable physiological conditions. These include physical and health impairments, visual impairments, and hearing loss. A small subset of them have severe and multiple disabilities that require significant adaptations and highly specialized services; such students are typically accompanied by child-specific teacher aides or other specialists when attending general education classrooms.

## PHYSICAL AND HEALTH IMPAIRMENTS

Physical and health impairments are general physical or medical conditions (usually long term) that interfere with school performance to such a degree that special instruction, curricular materials, equipment, or facilities are necessary. Students in this category may have limited energy and strength, reduced mental alertness, or little muscle control. Examples of conditions that might qualify students for special services are traumatic brain injury, spinal cord injury, cerebral palsy, epilepsy, cancer, and acquired immune deficiency disorder (AIDS).

### COMMON CHARACTERISTICS

It's hard to generalize about students with physical and health impairments because their conditions are so very different from one another. Nevertheless, several common characteristics are noteworthy:

- Low stamina and a tendency to tire easily
- Varying degrees of intellectual functioning (many of these students have learning ability similar to that of nondisabled peers)
- Lower levels of academic achievement as a result of frequent school absences
- Fewer opportunities to experience and interact with the outside world in educationally important ways (e.g., less use of public transportation, fewer visits to museums and zoos)
- Possible low self-esteem, insecurity, or heavy dependence on adults, depending partly on how parents and others have responded to their impairments (Heward, 2009; Patton et al., 1996; J. W. Wood, 1998)

### ADAPTING INSTRUCTION

Although we won't necessarily need to modify the academic curriculum for students with physical and health impairments, we will definitely want to make certain accommodations:

🍏 *Be sensitive to specific limitations, and accommodate them flexibly.* One student may require extra time with a writing assignment and perhaps should not be held to the same standards of neatness and legibility. Another may need to respond to test questions orally rather than on paper. Still another might tire easily and need to take frequent breaks.

🍏 *Know what to do in emergencies.* A student with acute asthma may have trouble breathing. A student with diabetes may go into insulin shock. A student with epilepsy may have a grand mal seizure. We should consult with school medical personnel ahead of time so that we are prepared to respond appropriately in such life- and health-threatening situations.

🍏 *If students and parents give permission, educate classmates about the nature of students' disabilities.* Many children treat peers with physical disabilities kindly and respectfully, but some others do not. Sometimes peers are simply ignorant about the nature of a disability, and giving them accurate information can help them become more accepting and supportive (e.g., R. White & Cunningham, 1991).

## VISUAL IMPAIRMENTS

Students with visual impairments have malfunctions of their eyes or optic nerves that prevent normal vision even with corrective lenses. Some students are totally blind, others see only fuzzy patterns of light and dark, and still others have a restricted visual field *(tunnel vision)* that allows them to see just a very small area at a time. Visual impairments are caused by congenital abnormalities in or damage to either the eye or the visual pathway to the brain.

## COMMON CHARACTERISTICS

Students with visual impairments are apt to have many or all of these characteristics:

- Normal functioning of other senses (hearing, touch, etc.)
- General learning ability similar to that of nondisabled students
- More limited vocabulary and general world knowledge, in part because of fewer opportunities to experience the outside world in educationally important ways (e.g., less exposure to maps, films, and other visual material)
- Delayed motor development; reduced capability to imitate others' behaviors
- Inability to observe other people's body language and other nonverbal cues, leading to occasional misunderstanding of others' messages
- Uncertainty and anxiety (especially in chaotic environments, such as the lunchroom or playground) as a result of having no visual knowledge of ongoing events
- In the primary grades, less knowledge about the conventions of written language (direction of print, punctuation, etc.) (M. Harris, 1992; Heward, 2009; Hobson, 2004; Patton et al., 1996; Tompkins & McGee, 1986; Turnbull et al., 2010; Tuttle & Tuttle, 1996)

## ADAPTING INSTRUCTION

Specialists typically give students training in Braille, orientation and mobility, and specially adapted computer technology. But general education teachers play important roles as well, as reflected in the following strategies:

*Orient students ahead of time to the physical layout of the classroom.* Students should have a chance to explore the classroom before other students arrive—ideally, before the first day of class. At that time we can help students locate important objects (e.g., wastebasket and pencil sharpener) and point out special sounds (e.g., the buzzing of a wall clock) to help students get their bearings (J. W. Wood, 1998).

*Use visual materials with sharp contrast.* Some students with partial sight can use visual materials with clearly distinguishable features, such as enlarged documents on computer screens and large-print books available at most public libraries. Students' eyes may tire quickly, however, so we should limit use of visual materials to short time periods (Heward, 2009; Patton et al., 1996).

*Depend heavily on other modalities.* Print-reading computer software and portable print-reading devices easily translate most printed text into spoken language. Many novels, school textbooks, and published curriculum materials are available in Braille, many other books are available in audio form (e.g., see www.learningally.org), and volunteers can sometimes be enlisted to convert still other written materials into Braille or audiotape. We can also conduct hands-on activities involving objects that students can feel and manipulate. For example, we might use plastic relief maps that portray mountains, valleys, and coastlines in three dimensions, perhaps embellishing them with pin pricks to indicate country borders and small dabs of nail polish to indicate major cities.

*Allow extra time for learning and performance.* Learning by hearing often takes more time than learning by seeing. When students *look* at something, they perceive a great deal of information at once and thus learn many commonplace relationships (e.g., between the sight of a cat and the sound it makes). When they must *listen* to it, however, they receive it sequentially—only one piece at a time—and often without obvious interconnections (Ferrell, 1996; Heward, 2009; M. B. Rowe, 1978).

## HEARING LOSS

Students with **hearing loss** have a malfunction of the ears or associated nerves that interferes with the perception of sounds within the frequency range of normal human speech. Students who are completely *deaf* have insufficient sensation to understand any spoken language, even with the help of a hearing aid. Students who are *hard of hearing* understand some speech but experience exceptional difficulty in doing so.

**hearing loss** Malfunction of the ears or associated nerves that interferes with perception of sounds within the frequency range of normal human speech.

## COMMON CHARACTERISTICS

Most students with hearing loss have normal intellectual abilities (Braden, 1992; Schirmer, 1994). However, they may have characteristics such as these:

- Delayed language development because of reduced exposure to spoken language, especially if the impairment was present at birth or emerged early in life
- Proficiency in sign language, such as American Sign Language (ASL) or finger spelling
- Some ability to read lips (*speechreading*)
- Less oral language than that of hearing classmates; perhaps a monotonous, hollow quality to speech
- Less developed reading skills, especially if language development has been delayed
- Less general world knowledge because of reduced exposure to spoken language
- Some social isolation, more limited social skills, and reduced perspective-taking ability as a result of a reduced ability to communicate (Bassett et al, 1996; Chall, 1996; P. L. Harris, 2006; Heward, 2009; C. C. Peterson, 2002; M. B. Rowe, 1978; Schick, de Villiers, de Villiers, & Hoffmeister, 2007; Turnbull et al., 2010)

## ADAPTING INSTRUCTION

Specialists typically provide training in such communication skills as American Sign Language, finger spelling, and speechreading. With these additions (and possibly some remedial instruction in reading and vocabulary), a normal school curriculum is appropriate for most students with hearing loss. However, several accommodations can facilitate students' success in general education classrooms:

🍏 *Minimize irrelevant noise.* Even when students can benefit from hearing aids, what they hear is often diminished or distorted; consequently, it's helpful to minimize potentially distracting sounds. For example, carpeting and bulletin boards can absorb some extraneous noise, and fans and pencil sharpeners should be located as far away as possible.

🍏 *Supplement auditory presentations with visual information and hands-on experiences.* We can write important points on the chalkboard, illustrate key ideas with pictures, provide reading materials that duplicate lectures, and ask an aide or student volunteer to take notes on in-class discussions. We can also provide speech-to-text software, which enables students to translate spoken words into written language with reasonable accuracy. And we can use concrete activities (e.g., role-playing historical events) to make abstract ideas more understandable.

🍏 *Communicate in ways that help students hear and speechread.* Students who are hard of hearing are most likely to understand us when we speak in a normal tone of voice (not overly loud) and pronounce words distinctly but otherwise normally. To help students speechread, we should speak only while facing them and never while sitting in a dark corner or standing in front of a window or bright light (Gearheart, Weishahn, & Gearheart, 1992; J. W. Wood, 1998).

🍏 *Teach American Sign Language and finger spelling to classmates.* To facilitate communication with students who have hearing loss, other class members should gain some competence in American Sign Language and finger spelling. I once taught at a school where *every* student—those with hearing loss and those without—received instruction in signing. One girl in my class was totally deaf yet quite popular with her peers, thanks to everyone's ability to communicate easily.

## GENERAL RECOMMENDATIONS

In addition to the strategies just identified for specific physical disabilities, several more general strategies are useful with all students who have physical or sensory challenges:

🍏 *Ensure that all students have access to important educational resources and opportunities.* Such access may involve modifying instructional materials (e.g., obtaining large-print copies of textbooks), adjusting a classroom's physical arrangement (e.g., widening aisles and placing bulletin board displays at eye level to accommodate students in wheelchairs), or making special arrangements that enable students to participate in field trips or sports activities.

🍏 *Provide assistance only when students really need it.* Out of their eagerness to help students with physical and sensory challenges, many adults inadvertently perform tasks and solve problems that these students are perfectly capable of handling on their own. Yet one of our goals for these students should be to promote their independence, not their dependence on others (Wehmeyer et al., 2007).

🍏 *Use assistive technology to facilitate learning and performance.* I've already mentioned the value of print-reading software and speech-to-text software for students with sensory challenges. In addition, some computer printers can create Braille documents, enabling students with visual impairments to read their own class notes and compositions. Specially adapted joysticks and voice recognition systems can supplement or replace computer keyboards for students with limited muscle control. And machines known as augmentative communication devices provide synthesized speech for students incapable of producing normal speech.

# Students with Advanced Cognitive Development

Many students are apt to have advanced abilities, either in specific subject areas or across the curriculum, that warrant attention and encouragement. Some students—those who are *gifted*—are so far above the norm that special educational services are often appropriate.

## GIFTEDNESS

In general, giftedness is unusually high ability or aptitude in one or more areas (e.g., in math, science, creative writing, or music) to such a degree that special educational services are necessary to help the student meet his or her full potential. In most instances giftedness is probably the result of both a genetic predisposition and environmental nurturing (Dai, 2010; Simonton, 2001; Winner, 2000b). In some cases, however, special gifts and talents are largely the result of intensive practice and mentoring (Ericsson, 2003; Gladwell, 2006).

In the United States, the Jacob K. Javits Gifted and Talented Student Education Act of 1987 (reauthorized in 1994 and 2001) encourages but doesn't necessarily mandate special educational services for students who are gifted. Many state governments also either encourage or mandate such services. School districts often use multiple criteria—sometimes including intelligence test scores, sometimes not—to identify students who show exceptional promise in general academic ability, specific academic fields, creativity, or the arts.

### COMMON CHARACTERISTICS

Students who are gifted vary considerably in their unique strengths and talents, and those who show exceptional talent in one area may have only average ability in another (Winner, 2000b). Nevertheless, many students who are gifted have characteristics such as these:

- Advanced vocabulary, language, and reading skills
- Extensive general knowledge about the world
- Ability to learn more quickly, easily, and independently than peers
- Advanced and efficient cognitive processes and learning strategies
- Considerable flexibility in ideas and approaches to tasks
- High standards for performance (sometimes to the point of unhealthy perfectionism)
- High motivation to accomplish challenging tasks; boredom during easy tasks
- Positive self-concept, especially with regard to academic endeavors
- Average or above-average social development and emotional adjustment (although a few extremely gifted students may have difficulties because they are so *very* different from their peers) (Cornell et al., 1990; Dai, 2010; Mendaglio, 2010; Parker, 1997; Shavinina & Ferrari, 2004; Steiner & Carr, 2003; Winner, 2000a, 2000b)

To some degree, the nature of giftedness depends somewhat on where students are in their developmental journeys (Dai, 2010; D. J. Matthews, 2009). In the preschool and early elementary years, giftedness might take the form of precociousness in certain general domains; for example, a first grader might be reading sixth-grade-level books or exhibit exceptional facility with numbers. By the upper elementary and secondary school grades, some students are likely to show exceptional achievement in very specific areas—perhaps in creative writing, computer technology, or music. Yet we must keep in mind that students who are gifted may also have one or more disabilities; for instance, they may have dyslexia or Asperger syndrome. In planning instruction for such students, we must address their disabilities as well as their unique gifts.

giftedness Unusually high ability or aptitude in one or more areas, to such a degree that students require special educational services to help them meet their full potential.

## ADAPTING INSTRUCTION

From the perspective of Vygotsky's theory (Chapter 2), when gifted students are given the same assignments as their average-ability peers, they're unlikely to be working within their zone of proximal development and so unlikely to make significant cognitive advancements.

Exceptional talents and achievement levels typically require ongoing environmental nurturance and support, in the forms of both differentiated instruction and access to appropriate resources and practice opportunities. Furthermore, many high-achieving students become bored or frustrated when school assignments don't challenge them, and others become so accustomed to the "easy A" that they have trouble coping with the mistakes they're likely to make when they venture into new areas (Dai, 2010; Mendaglio, 2010; Parker, 1997). With such points in mind, I offer the following recommendations:

🍏 *Provide individualized tasks and assignments.* Different students are apt to need special services in very different areas—for example, in math, creative writing, or studio art. Some students who are gifted, especially those with only a limited background in English, may also need training in certain basic skills (C. R. Harris, 1991; Udall, 1989).

🍏 *Form study groups of students with similar interests and abilities.* In some cases a study group might explore a topic in greater depth and with more sophisticated analysis than other students (an *enrichment* approach). In other instances a study group might simply move through the standard school curriculum at a more rapid pace (an *acceleration* approach). Students benefit both academically and socially from increased contact with peers who have similar interests and talents (Hattie, 2009; J. A. Kulik & Kulik, 1997; McGinn, Viernstein, & Hogan, 1980).

🍏 *Teach complex cognitive skills within the context of specific subject areas.* Programs designed to enhance students' creativity, critical thinking, or other complex skills separately from specific content domains tend to have only limited impact. Teaching complex thinking skills within the context of specific topics—for example, creativity in writing or reasoning and problem-solving skills in science—is more likely to be effective (Dai, 2010; M. C. Linn, Clement, Pulos, & Sullivan, 1989; Moon, Feldhusen, & Dillon, 1994; Stanley, 1980).

🍏 *Provide opportunities for independent study and service-learning projects.* Independent study and community service projects in areas of interest are often beneficial and motivating for high-ability students, provided that they have the work habits, study strategies, and research skills they need to use their time and resources effectively (Candler-Lotven, Tallent-Runnels, Olivárez, & Hildreth, 1994; Lupart, 1995; Terry, 2008).

Working with a mentor often takes the form of a *cognitive apprenticeship* (see Chapter 2).

🍏 *Seek outside resources.* When students have high abilities in domains outside our own areas of expertise, it's often helpful to identify suitable mentors elsewhere in the school district or in the community at large—perhaps at a local university, government office, private business, or volunteer community group (Ambrose, Allen, & Huntley, 1994; Piirto, 1999; Seeley, 1989).

🍏 *Keep in mind that students with exceptional cognitive abilities aren't necessarily advanced in other aspects of their development.* Most students with special gifts and talents have the same personal and emotional concerns as their average-ability age-mates (D. J. Matthews, 2009). For example, gifted sixth graders making the transition to middle school are likely to have the typical thoughts and feelings of a young adolescent: whether they'll fit in with a new peer group, whom to sit with at lunch, and so on. They may worry that their peers will see their exceptional ability levels as odd or in some other way unacceptable (Mendaglio, 2010). And they're likely to be surprised or anxious when they discover that they must exert considerable effort to master challenging new skills and that they sometimes make errors in the process (Mendaglio, 2010). For such reasons, high-ability students are likely to need as much emotional support as their classmates, and they may occasionally need gentle reminders that only new challenges can truly help them grow.

# Considering Diversity When Identifying and Addressing Special Needs

Sadly, a disproportionately large number of minority-group students are identified as having disabilities, especially specific cognitive disabilities, general intellectual disabilities, and emotional and behavioral disorders (McLoyd, 1998; U.S. Department of Education, 2006; VanTassel-Baska, 2008). Most theorists attribute the differing identification rates to environmental conditions that often accompany low socioeconomic status: higher-than-normal exposure to environmental toxins, inadequate medical care, limited access to enriching educational resources, and so on (e.g., Dyson, 2008; Jacoby & Glauberman, 1995; McLoyd, 1998). Also, English language learners are identified as having learning disabilities or intellectual disabilities more often than native English speakers—a finding that probably reflects students' difficulty in understanding and responding to items on language-based diagnostic tests (A. L. Sullivan, 2008).

The higher-than-average identification rates for minority-group students pose a dilemma for educators. On the one hand, we don't want to assign a label such as *intellectual disability* or *emotional disorder* to students whose classroom performance and behavior may be due largely to their challenging living conditions. On the other hand, we don't want to deprive these students of special educational services that might help them learn and achieve more successfully over the long run. In such situations we must conduct fair and nondiscriminatory evaluations of students' needs, and if students qualify under a special-needs category, we must create IEPs to meet those needs. We should consider these categories of special needs as *temporary* classifications that may no longer be applicable as students' classroom performance improves. *All* students, with and without disability classifications, have changing needs that evolve over time.

In addition to being overrepresented in programs for students with disabilities, members of some minority groups are *under*represented in programs for gifted students (D. Y. Ford, Moore, & Whiting, 2006; Graham, 2009; VanTassel-Baska, 2008). On average, students from cultural and ethnic minority groups are at a disadvantage when traditional tests of ability are used to identify giftedness—in some cases because they've had little experience with the kinds of tasks that appear on those tests (Rogoff, 2003). It's critical, then, that we be on the lookout for other signs of giftedness, including the following:

- Exceptional talent in a specific area (e.g., in music or video game design)
- Ability to learn quickly from experiences
- Exceptional communication skills (e.g., articulateness, richness of language)
- Originality and resourcefulness in thinking and problem solving
- Ability to generalize concepts and ideas to new, seemingly unrelated situations (Dai, 2010; Haywood & Lidz, 2007; Maker & Schiever, 1989; Winner, 1996)

For the growth of our society over the long run, it's imperative that we nurture the many gifted students in *all* cultural and ethnic groups.

## General Recommendations for Working with Students Who Have Special Needs

Although students with special educational needs vary widely in their abilities and disabilities, several recommendations apply across the board:

🍏 *Be flexible in approaches to instruction and assessment.* Even when students clearly fall within a particular category of special needs, we can't always predict which instructional methods will be most effective for each of them. If we don't succeed with a particular approach, we should try again, but we might also want to try *differently.* Furthermore, we must keep open minds about how we assess students' achievement; depending on the nature of their disabilities, we may need to give them extra time, let them audiotape responses, tailor assessment tasks to an individualized curriculum, and so on.

🍏 *Seek new technologies that can facilitate students' learning and performance.* As we've seen, assistive technology takes a wide variety of forms—spell-checkers, hand-held prompters, speech-to-text software, and so on—and exciting new technologies emerge every year. Frequent searches of the Internet can alert us to recent innovations (e.g., search for "assistive technology devices" on Google or Yahoo!).

🍏 *Unless there is reason to do otherwise, hold the same expectations for students with disabilities as for other students.* Sometimes a disability makes it difficult or impossible for students to accomplish certain tasks, and we have to modify our expectations and assessment practices accordingly. Aside from such situations, however, we should generally have the same expectations for students with special needs that we have for other students. Rather than think of reasons that a student *can't* do something, we should think about how we can help the student *do* it.

🍏 *Identify and teach the prerequisite knowledge and skills students may not have acquired because of their disabilities.* As either a direct or indirect result of certain disabilities, some students lack the knowledge and skills essential for their school success. For instance, students with visual impairments haven't been able to observe many of the cause-and-effect relationships that

Especially when working with students identified as having cognitive, emotional, or behavioral difficulties, think of their disability labels as *temporary* classifications that may no longer be applicable as classroom performance improves.

Look beyond IQ scores in identifying students who may be gifted; for instance, look for specialized talents, richness of language, an ability to learn new things quickly, and exceptional resourcefulness in solving problems.

Chapter 14 and Chapter 15 offer numerous suggestions for accommodating disabilities in assessments.

form a foundation for learning science—such as the changes in the appearance of wood when it's burned (Ferrell, 1996; M. B. Rowe, 1978). And students whose medical conditions have limited their contact with peers may have had few opportunities to acquire effective interpersonal skills.

🍏 *Consult and collaborate with specialists.* School districts usually employ a variety of specialists, including special educators, counselors, school psychologists, nurses, speech pathologists, and physical and occupational therapists. Some students leave the classroom for part of the day to work with these individuals. However, in today's inclusive schools many special services are provided within a regular classroom context by teachers and specialists working in close collaboration.

🍏 *Communicate regularly with parents.* In accordance with IDEA, parents are part of the multidisciplinary team that determines the most appropriate program for a student with special needs. Parents can often tell us what works and what doesn't, and they can alert us to certain conditions or events at home that may trigger problem behaviors in class. Furthermore, we can bring about desired behavioral changes more effectively if the same expectations for behavior exist both at school and at home.

🍏 *Include students in planning and decision making.* Educational programs for most students with special needs—especially those with disabilities—are so highly structured that students have little say regarding what and how they learn. But increasingly, educators are recognizing the importance of letting *all* students make some choices about their academic goals and curriculum (Algozzine, Browder, Karvonen, Test, & Wood, 2001; Prout, 2009; Wehmeyer et al., 2007).

Such choice making can enhance both *self-regulation* and *self-determination*, discussed in Chapter 10 and Chapter 11, respectively.

🍏 *Keep your eyes open for students who may qualify for special services.* The more we work with students in a particular age-group, the more we learn about their age-typical abilities and behaviors. Hence, we teachers are in an excellent position to identify children who in one way or another are *not* typical. Although specialists usually conduct the in-depth assessments necessary to identify particular special needs, the job of referring students for such assessments—and thereby gaining them access to the specialized services they may need—is ultimately up to teachers in general education classrooms.

## 5    What Have You Learned?

Let's now review key points related to each of the chapter's learning outcomes.

**5.1: Describe various perspectives on the nature of intelligence, and identify several ways in which you can nurture intelligence in your own students.** Intelligence involves the ability to apply prior knowledge and experiences flexibly to accomplish challenging tasks; it's apt to manifest itself differently in different cultures. Some psychologists believe that intelligence is a single, biology-based entity that influences students' learning and performance across a wide variety of tasks and subject areas—a belief that's reflected in the use of IQ scores as general estimates of cognitive ability. Others disagree, proposing that intelligence consists of a number of somewhat independent abilities or, instead, that intelligent behavior varies considerably depending on a child's age and environmental support systems. As teachers, we must remember that human intelligence can and does change over time, especially with appropriate instruction and practice opportunities.

Evaluate and apply your knowledge related to this learning outcome in MyEducationLab™.

**5.2: Explain how students' cognitive styles and dispositions might influence their classroom performance.** *Cognitive styles* and *dispositions* are general inclinations to approach tasks in particular ways—for instance, to think analytically or holistically or to approach new ideas in an open-minded or close-minded manner. We can encourage productive styles and dispositions through

the messages we give about classroom subject matter (e.g., "Does the evidence support what scientists are saying about this topic?") and by modeling curiosity and enthusiasm for learning.

Evaluate and apply your knowledge related to this learning outcome in MyEducationLab™.

**5.3: Identify implications of the U.S. Individuals with Disabilities Education Act (IDEA) for your own work as a teacher.** Students with special needs are those students who are different enough from their classmates that they require specially adapted instructional materials and practices to help them maximize their cognitive and social development. Increasingly, students with special needs are being educated in general education classrooms for part or all of the school day; in the United States, such *inclusion* is in part the result of a mandate of the Individuals with Disabilities Education Act (IDEA). Students with special needs are most likely to flourish in general education settings when instruction and materials are individualized to address any missing basic skills but also present challenges that spur developmental advancements.

Evaluate and apply your knowledge related to this learning outcome in MyEducationLab™.

**5.4: Explain how you might adapt your instruction and classroom practices to the unique strengths and limitations of students with various disabilities.** Students with specific cognitive or academic difficulties include those with learning disabilities, those with attention-deficit hyperactivity disorder (ADHD), and those with speech and communication disorders. Many instructional strategies must be tailored to students' specific difficulty areas, but some strategies are widely applicable; for instance, virtually all of these students benefit from early interventions, clear expectations for performance, and feedback that documents ongoing progress.

Students with social or behavioral problems include those with emotional and behavioral disorders (which might involve either externalizing or internalizing behaviors) and those with autism spectrum disorders. Many students with these disabilities benefit from training in interpersonal skills. They may also perform more successfully in a structured environment in which appropriate behaviors are clearly identified and consequences for desired and undesired behaviors are consistently administered.

Some students have general delays in cognitive and social functioning, and a subset are formally diagnosed as having an intellectual disability. Effective instruction for these students usually involves a slow pace with considerable scaffolding and, eventually, explicit training in vocational and general life skills.

Students with physical and sensory challenges include those with physical and health impairments (conditions that result in reduced energy, alertness, or muscle control), visual impairments, or hearing loss. Although recommended instructional strategies vary considerably depending on students' specific disabilities, all of these students should have appropriate assistive technologies and access to the same educational resources and opportunities as their nondisabled peers.

**Evaluate** and **apply** your knowledge related to this learning outcome in MyEducationLab™.

■ **5.5: Explain how you might nurture the development of students who show exceptional gifts and talents.** Most students identified as gifted require individualized instruction that challenges them to stretch their existing abilities in new directions. We must be open-minded about how we identify such students, as giftedness may take different forms in different cultural and ethnic groups. Strategies for promoting the achievement of gifted students include forming small study groups on specific topics, teaching complex cognitive skills within the context of various academic subject areas, and providing opportunities for independent study and service learning either within or outside of school walls.

**Evaluate** and **apply** your knowledge related to this learning outcome in MyEducationLab™.

## Practice for Your Licensure Exam

### Quiet Amy

As a veteran kindergarten teacher, Mr. Mahoney knows that many kindergartners initially have difficulty adjusting to the school environment, especially if they haven't previously attended daycare or preschool. But Amy is giving him cause for concern. Amy never speaks, either to him or to the other children, even when she is directly spoken to. On the infrequent occasions when she wants to communicate, she does so primarily by looking and pointing at something or someone in the room. Amy also has trouble following simple directions, almost as if she hasn't heard what she's been asked to do. And she seems distracted during daily storybook readings and science lessons. The only activities that give her pleasure are arts and crafts. She may spend hours at a time working with construction paper, crayons, scissors, and glue, and her creations are often the most inventive and detailed in the class.

Mr. Mahoney suspects that Amy may have a disability that qualifies her for special services. To get permission for an in-depth evaluation of her abilities and needs, he and the school psychologist visit Amy's mother, a single woman raising five other children as well. "Amy doesn't talk at home either," the mother admits. "I work two jobs to make ends meet, and I haven't been able to spend as much time with her as I'd like. Her brothers and sisters take good care of her, though. They always seem to know what she wants, and they make sure she gets it."

1. **Multiple-choice question:**

   Mr. Mahoney suspects that Amy may qualify for special educational services. If she does, in which of the following categories of special needs is she *least* likely to fall?

   a. Hearing loss

   b. Autism spectrum disorders

   c. Speech and communication disorders

   d. Attention-deficit hyperactivity disorder

2. **Constructed-response question:**

   Amy's evaluation will undoubtedly take several weeks to complete. In the meantime, what strategies might Mr. Mahoney use to improve Amy's classroom behavior and performance? Describe at least three different things he might do. Be specific and concrete in your descriptions.

**PRAXIS** Go to Appendix C, "Matching Book and MyEducationLab™ to the Praxis Principles of Learning and Teaching Tests," to discover sections of this chapter that may be especially applicable to the Praxis tests.

# 6 Learning, Cognition, and Memory

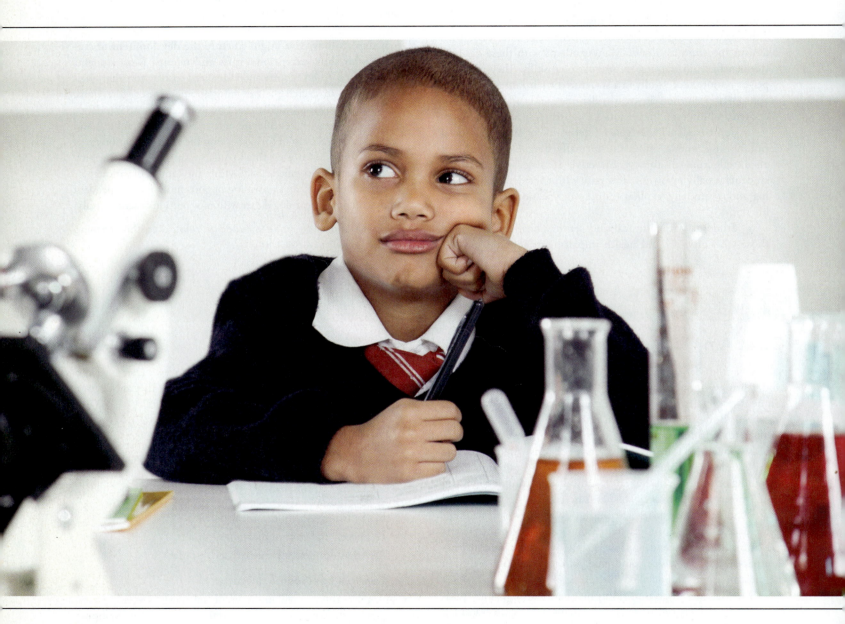

## LEARNING OUTCOMES

**6.1:** Distinguish among four distinct approaches to the study of human learning, and summarize one of these approaches—cognitive psychology—in terms of five basic assumptions.

**6.2:** Describe and illustrate the key components that many researchers believe may characterize the human memory system.

**6.3:** Apply your knowledge of long-term memory storage in identifying effective strategies for enhancing students' learning.

**6.4:** Explain how students' self-constructed beliefs can sometimes interfere with effective learning, and identify several ways of helping students productively revise such beliefs.

**6.5:** Describe six different factors that influence students' ability to recall what they have previously learned; also describe five possible reasons why students may either forget or incorrectly remember what they have learned.

**6.6:** Give examples of the diversity in cognitive processes you are likely to see in students, in some cases as a result of their cultural background or special educational needs.

## CASE STUDY: BONES

In biology class Kanesha has been struggling to learn the names of the bones in the human body, from head (cranium) to toe (metatarsus). She has learned a few bones quickly and easily. For example, she realizes that, logically, the *nasal bone* should form part of the nose, and she remembers the *humerus* (upper arm bone) by thinking of it as being just above one's funny ("humorous") bone. But she's still confused about some of the other bones. For example, the *tibia* and *fibula* have similar-sounding names and are both located in the lower leg. And she keeps thinking that the *sternum* (at the front of the chest) is actually in the back of the body, just as the stern of a boat is at its rear. She also has trouble remembering bones whose names don't provide any kind of clue for her—the coccyx, ulna, sacrum, clavicle, patella, and so on.

To prepare for an upcoming biology quiz, Kanesha looks at a diagram of the human skeleton and whispers the name of each bone to herself several times. She also writes each name on a sheet of paper. "These terms will certainly sink in if I repeat them enough times," she tells herself. But Kanesha scores only 70% on the biology quiz. As she looks over her incorrect answers, she sees that she confused the tibia and the fibula, labeled the ulna as "clavicle," put the sternum in the wrong place, and completely forgot about the coccyx, sacrum, and patella.

- Why are some bones easier for Kanesha to remember than others? Which ones would be easiest for *you* to remember? What do your answers to these questions suggest about the nature of human learning?

Kanesha seems to have an easier time learning bone names she can relate to things she already knows. In particular, she relates *nasal bone* to *nose* and *humerus* to *funny bone*. She applies her existing knowledge in trying to learn *sternum* as well, but her strategy backfires because a boat's *stern* is at its rear, whereas the sternum is in front of the chest cavity. Kanesha also has trouble with bone names she can't connect to anything in her previous experiences. Over the course of a lifetime, human beings learn many, many new pieces of information and many, many new behaviors. But as a general rule, people have an easier time learning and remembering things they can readily and appropriately connect to their existing knowledge and skills.

For our discussion in this book, we'll define **learning** as a long-term change in mental representations or associations as a result of experience. Let's divide this definition into its three parts. First, learning is a *long-term change* in that it isn't just a brief, transitory use of information—such as remembering a person's phone number only long enough to make a phone call—but it doesn't necessarily last forever. Second, learning involves *mental representations or associations;* at its core, it's a phenomenon that takes place in the brain. Third, learning is a change *due to experience,* rather than the result of physiological maturation, fatigue, use of alcohol or drugs, or onset of mental illness.

Psychologists have been studying the nature of learning for more than a century and in the process have taken a variety of theoretical perspectives. Table 6.1 summarizes four general ones, listed largely in the order in which they've gained influence in the field of psychology as a whole.

**learning** Long-term change in mental representations or associations as a result of experience.

Track changes in psychological perspectives of learning in a supplementary reading "How Learning Theories Have Evolved Over Time."

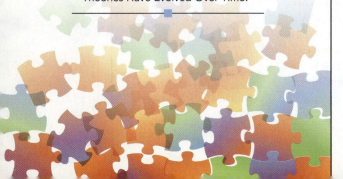

I urge you *not* to think of these perspectives as being mutually exclusive. In fact, they tend to complement one another, and together they give us a richer picture of human learning—and also give us many more strategies for facilitating learning in instructional settings—than any single perspective could give us alone.

In this chapter we'll look primarily at what goes on *inside* the learner. In doing so, we'll draw from cognitive psychology, a large body of research that addresses a variety of mental phenomena that underlie human behavior—perception, memory, reasoning, and so on.

# Basic Assumptions of Cognitive Psychology

At the core of cognitive psychology are several basic assumptions about how people learn:

- *Cognitive processes influence what is learned.* The specific things people mentally do as they try to interpret and remember what they see, hear, and study—that is, their cognitive processes—have a profound effect on what they specifically learn and remember. For example, in the opening case study, Kanesha thinks about the nasal bone and humerus in ways that should help her remember them. However, she thinks about the sternum in a way that *interferes* with her ability to remember it correctly, and she gives little or no thought to why certain other bones have particular names. The extent to which Kanesha thinks about the material she needs to learn—and also *how* she thinks about it—affects her performance on the quiz.

- *People's cognitive processes can sometimes be inferred from their behaviors.* Historically, some psychologists—especially behaviorists—have argued that we can't directly observe people's thinking and therefore can't study it objectively and scientifically. Cognitive psychologists disagree, suggesting that by observing people's responses to various objects and events, it's possible to draw reasonable *inferences*—to make educated guesses—about the cognitive processes that probably underlie the responses. As an example of how we might learn about people's cognitive processes by observing their behaviors, try the following exercise.

### EXPERIENCING FIRSTHAND
### REMEMBERING 12 WORDS

Read the 12 words below *one time only.* Then cover up the page, and write down the words in the order they come to mind.

| | | |
|---|---|---|
| shirt | table | hat |
| carrot | bed | squash |
| pants | potatoes | stool |
| chair | shoe | bean |

Did you write down the words in the order in which you read them? Probably not. If you're like most people, you recalled the words by category—perhaps clothing first, then vegetables, then furniture. From the order in which you wrote the words (i.e., from your *behavior*), we can draw an inference about an internal cognitive process that occurred as you learned the words: You mentally *organized* them into categories.

- *People are selective about what they mentally process and learn.* People are constantly bombarded with information. Consider the many stimuli you're encountering at this very moment—the many letters on this page, the many others objects you can see while you're reading, the many sounds reaching your ears,

## COMPARE/CONTRAST

| TABLE 6.1 • General Theoretical Approaches to the Study of Learning | |
|---|---|
| **THEORETICAL PERSPECTIVE** | **GENERAL DESCRIPTION** |
| **Behaviorism** | Early behaviorists argued that because thought processes cannot be directly observed and measured, it is difficult to study thinking objectively and scientifically. Thus, most behaviorists downplay the role of cognitive processes in learning and instead focus on two things that researchers *can* observe and measure: people's behaviors *(responses)* and the environmental events *(stimuli)* that precede and follow those responses. Learning is viewed as a process of acquiring and modifying associations among stimuli and responses, largely through a learner's direct interactions with the environment. Behaviorism has been especially helpful in identifying effective strategies for encouraging productive classroom behaviors. |
| **Social cognitive theory** | Historically, social cognitive theorists have focused largely on the ways in which people learn from observing one another. Environmental stimuli affect behavior, but cognitive processes (e.g., *awareness* of stimulus–response relationships, *expectations* about future events) also play a significant role. Often people learn through *modeling*—that is, they watch and imitate what others do. Whether people learn and perform effectively is also a function of their *self-efficacy,* the extent to which they believe they can successfully accomplish a particular task or activity. As social cognitive theory has evolved over time, it has increasingly incorporated the concept of *self-regulation,* in which people take charge of and direct their own actions. Social cognitive theory has had a significant impact on our understanding of motivation as well as learning. |
| **Cognitive psychology** | While not denying that the environment plays a critical role in learning, cognitive psychologists concern themselves with what goes on *inside* learners, focusing on the cognitive processes involved in learning, memory, and performance. From observations of how people execute various tasks and behave in various situations, these theorists make inferences about how people may perceive, interpret, and mentally manipulate the information they encounter. Many cognitive psychologists speculate about what internal mechanisms underlie human cognition (e.g., *working memory* and *long-term memory*) and about how people mentally process new information (e.g., through *elaboration* and *visual imagery*); this approach is called **information processing theory**. Other cognitive theorists (such as the developmental theorist Jean Piaget) focus on how individual learners create knowledge through their interactions with the environment; this approach is known as **individual constructivism**. |
| **Contextual theories** | Contextual theorists place considerable emphasis on the influence of learners' physical and social environments on cognition and learning. But rather than talk about specific stimuli (as behaviorists do), they focus on more general factors—physical, social, and cultural—that support "thoughtful" (i.e., cognition-based) learning. Some contextual theorists (such as the developmental psychologist Lev Vygotsky) suggest that young learners initially use sophisticated thinking strategies in social interactions and gradually *internalize* these strategies for their own, personal use; this approach is known as **sociocultural theory**. Other contextual theorists emphasize that by working together, two or more people can often gain better understandings than anyone could gain alone; this approach is sometimes called **social constructivism**. Still other theorists propose that various ways of thinking are inextricably tied to particular physical or social circumstances; this approach goes by a variety of labels, including **situated learning** and **distributed cognition**. |

the various articles of clothing touching your skin, and so on. I suspect that you've been ignoring most of these stimuli until just now, when I specifically asked you to think about them.

It's useful to distinguish between *sensation*—one's ability to detect stimuli in the environment—and *perception*—one's interpretation of stimuli. For reasons you'll discover a bit later, it's virtually impossible to perceive (interpret) everything the body senses. Because learners can handle only so much information at a given time, they must choose a few things to focus on and ignore the rest.

As an analogy, consider the hundreds of items a typical adult receives in the mail each year, not only in paper form from the post office but also in electronic form through e-mail. Do you open, examine, and respond to every piece of mail? Probably not. If you're like me, you process a few key items, inspect other items long enough to know that you don't need them, and discard still others without even opening them.

In much the same way, students encounter a great deal of new information every day—information delivered by way of teacher instruction, textbooks, bulletin boards, classmates' behaviors, and so on. They must inevitably make choices about which pieces of information are important for them. They select a few stimuli to examine and respond to in depth, give other stimuli only a cursory glance, and ignore other stimuli altogether.

**cognitive psychology** General theoretical perspective that focuses on the mental processes underlying learning and behavior.

**cognitive process** Particular way of thinking about and mentally responding to a certain event or piece of information.

• *Meanings and understandings are not derived directly from the environment; instead, they are constructed by the learner.* Like Kanesha, people often create their own unique understandings about a topic—understandings that may or may not be accurate. The process of construction lies at the core of many cognitive theories of learning: Learners take numerous, separate pieces of information and use them to create a general understanding, interpretation, or recollection of some aspect of their world (e.g., Brainerd & Reyna, 2005; Bransford & Franks, 1971; Neisser, 1967). Learning theories that focus primarily on the nature of this constructive process are collectively known as constructivism, and a subset of them that address how learners idiosyncratically construct knowledge on their own (rather than in collaboration with other people) are known as individual constructivism.

To experience the process of construction firsthand, try the following exercise.

### EXPERIENCING FIRSTHAND
### THREE FACES

Look at the three black-and-white figures shown here. What do you see in each one? Most people perceive the figure on the left to be that of a woman, even though many of her features are missing. Enough features are visible—an eye, parts of the nose, mouth, chin, and hair—that you can construct a meaningful perception from them. Is enough information available in the other two figures for you to construct two more faces? Construction of a face from the figure on the right may take a while, but it can be done.

*Source:* Figures from "Age in the Development of Closure Ability in Children" by C. M. Mooney, from *Canadian Journal of Psychology*, December 1957, Volume 11(4). Copyright © 1957 by Canadian Psychological Association. Reprinted with permission.

Objectively speaking, the three configurations of black splotches, and especially the two rightmost ones, leave a lot to the imagination. The woman in the middle is missing half of her face, and the man on the right is missing the top of his head. Yet knowing what human faces typically look like may have been enough to enable you to mentally add the missing features and perceive complete pictures. Curiously, once you've constructed faces from the figures, they then seem obvious. If you were to close this book now and not pick it up again for a week or more, you would probably see the faces almost immediately, even if you had had considerable difficulty perceiving them originally.

As teachers, we must remember that students won't necessarily learn information exactly as we present it to them. In fact, they'll each interpret classroom subject matter in their own, idiosyncratic ways. And occasionally they may construct *mis*information, as Kanesha does when she relates the *sternum* to the stern of a boat.

• *Maturational changes in the brain enable increasingly sophisticated cognitive processes with age.* With the advent of new technologies for studying the brain, cognitive psychologists are learning more and more about how the brain functions and how it changes with age and experience. This body of research, known as neuropsychology, has enabled cognitive psychologists to test various hypotheses about the precise nature of human learning and thinking. Furthermore, it has revealed that the human brain changes in many significant ways over the course of childhood

---

**construction** Mental process in which a learner takes many separate pieces of information and uses them to build an overall understanding or interpretation.

**constructivism** Theoretical perspective proposing that learners construct, rather than absorb, knowledge from their experiences.

**individual constructivism** Theoretical perspective that focuses on how people, as individuals, construct meaning from their experiences.

**neuropsychology** Study of how various brain structures and functions are related to human learning and behavior.

## PRINCIPLES/ASSUMPTIONS

### TABLE 6.2 • Basic Assumptions of Cognitive Psychology and Their Educational Implications

| ASSUMPTION | EDUCATIONAL IMPLICATION | EXAMPLE |
|---|---|---|
| **Influence of cognitive processes** | Encourage students to think about classroom subject matter in ways that will help them remember it. | When introducing the concept *mammal*, ask students to identify numerous examples. |
| **Behavior as a reflection of cognitive processes** | Ask students to explain their reasoning, and look closely at what they do and say to make educated guesses about how they are thinking about classroom topics. | When a student says that 16 + 19 = 25 and that 27 + 27 = 44, hypothesize that the student is forgetting to carry, and provide additional instruction about the carrying process. |
| **Selectivity about what is learned** | Help students identify the most important things for them to learn. Also help them understand why these things are important. | Give students questions they should try to answer as they read their textbooks. Include questions that ask them to apply what they read to their own lives. |
| **Construction of meanings and understandings** | Provide experiences that will help students make sense of the topics they are studying, and regularly monitor students' understandings. | When studying Nathaniel Hawthorne's *The Scarlet Letter*, have students convene in small groups to discuss possible reasons that the Reverend Dimmesdale refuses to acknowledge that he is the father of Hester Prynne's baby. |
| **Increasing capacity for sophisticated cognitive processes with age** | Take into account strengths and limitations in students' cognitive processing capabilities at different age levels. | When teaching kindergartners basic counting skills, accommodate their short attention spans by keeping verbal explanations short and conducting a variety of active, hands-on counting activities. |

and adolescence. Such changes are almost certainly a key reason why children become capable of increasingly effective cognitive processes—longer attention spans, enhanced ability to organize and integrate information, and so on (Kuhn, 2006; Luna, Garver, Urban, Lazar, & Sweeney, 2004; C. A. Nelson, Thomas, & de Haan, 2006). But rather than propose distinct stages of cognitive development (as Jean Piaget did), most cognitive psychologists believe that children's cognitive development can best be characterized as gradual *trends*. As we proceed through the chapter, we'll identify a number of developmental trends in children's cognitive processes.

Table 6.2 summarizes the assumptions just described and can help you apply them to your own teaching practice.

## A Model of Human Memory

Cognitive psychologists have offered numerous explanations of how people mentally process and remember new information and events—explanations that fall into the general category of **information processing theory**. Some early explanations portrayed human thinking and learning as being similar to the ways computers operate. It has since become clear, however, that the computer analogy is too simple: People often think about and interpret information in ways that are difficult to explain in the relatively simplistic, one-thing-always-leads-to-another ways that characterize computers (e.g., Hacker, Dunlosky, & Graesser, 2009a; G. Marcus, 2008; Minsky, 2006).

Central to information processing theory is the concept of **memory**. In some instances I'll use this term to refer to learners' ability to mentally save previously learned knowledge or skills over a period of time. In other instances I'll use it when talking about a particular location where learners put what they learn—perhaps *working memory* or *long-term memory*.

The process of putting what is being learned into memory is called **storage**. For example, each time you go to class, you undoubtedly *store* some of the ideas presented in a lecture or class discussion. You may store other information from class as well—perhaps the name of the person sitting next to you (George), the shape and size of the classroom (rectangular, about 15 by 30 meters), or the pattern of the instructor's shirt (a ghastly combination of orange and purple splotches). Yet learners rarely store information exactly as they receive it. Instead, they

Chapter 2 describes several ways in which the human brain matures over the course of childhood and adolescence; it also describes Jean Piaget's theory of cognitive development.

**information processing theory** Theoretical perspective that focuses on the specific ways in which learners mentally think about, or process, new information and events.

**memory** Ability to mentally save something that has been previously learned; also, the mental "location" where such information is saved.

**storage** Process of putting new information into memory.

**encoding** Changing the format of new information as it is being stored in memory.

**retrieval** Process of finding information previously stored in memory.

engage in encoding, modifying the information in some way. For instance, when listening to a story, you might imagine what certain characters look like—thus encoding some verbal input as visual images. And when you see your instructor's orange and purple shirt, you might think, "My instructor really needs a wardrobe makeover"—thus assigning a specific *meaning* and *interpretation* to what you've seen.

At some point after storing a piece of information, you may discover that you need to use it. The process of remembering previously stored information—that is, finding it in memory—is called retrieval. The following exercise illustrates this process.

### EXPERIENCING FIRSTHAND
### RETRIEVAL PRACTICE

See how quickly you can answer each of the following questions:

1. What is your name?
2. What is the capital of France?
3. In what year did Christopher Columbus first sail across the Atlantic Ocean to reach the New World?
4. When talking about appetizers at a party, we sometimes use a French term instead of the word *appetizer*. What is that French term, and how is it spelled?

As you probably noticed when you tried to answer these questions, retrieving some kinds of information from memory—your name, for instance—is quick and easy. Other things—perhaps the capital of France (Paris) and the year of Columbus's first voyage (1492)—can be retrieved only after some thought and effort. Still other pieces of information, even though you may have stored them in memory at one time, may be almost impossible to retrieve. Perhaps the correct spelling of *hors d'oeuvre* falls into this category.

Despite their common use of such terms as *storage, encoding,* and *retrieval,* information processing theorists don't all agree about the precise nature of human memory. However, many suggest that memory has three key components: a sensory register, a working (short-term) memory, and a long-term memory. A three-component model of human memory, based loosely on one proposed by Atkinson and Shiffrin in 1968 but modified to reflect more recent research findings, is presented in Figure 6.1. The model oversimplifies the nature of memory to some degree (more about this point later), but it provides a good way to organize much of what we know about how memory works.

**FIGURE 6.1 A model of the human memory system**

Please note that in referring to three components of memory, I'm *not* necessarily referring to three separate parts of the brain. The model of memory I describe here has been derived largely from studies of human behavior, rather than from studies of the brain.

## THE NATURE OF THE SENSORY REGISTER

If you have ever played with a lighted sparkler at night, then you've seen the tail of light that follows a sparkler as you wave it about. If you have ever daydreamed in class, you may have noticed that when you tune back in to a lecture, you can still hear the three or four words that were spoken just *before* you started paying attention to your instructor again. The sparkler's tail and the words that linger aren't actually out there in the environment. Instead, they're recorded in your sensory register.

The sensory register is the component of memory that holds the information you receive—the *input*—in more or less its original, *un*encoded form. Thus, visual input is stored in a visual form, auditory input in an auditory form, and so on (e.g., Coltheart, Lea, & Thompson, 1974; Cowan, 1995). The sensory register has a *large capacity:* It can hold a great deal of information at any one time.

That's the good news. The bad news is that information stored in the sensory register doesn't last very long (e.g., Cowan, 1995; Dahan, 2010; Wingfield & Byrnes, 1981). Visual information (i.e., what you see) probably lasts for less than a second. For example, as a child, I never could spell out my entire first name (Jeanne) with a sparkler: The *J* had always faded before I got to the first *n,* no matter how quickly I wrote. Auditory information (i.e., what you hear) probably lasts slightly longer, perhaps for two or three seconds. To keep information for any time at all, then, learners need to move it to *working memory.* Whatever information isn't moved is probably lost, or forgotten.

## MOVING INFORMATION TO WORKING MEMORY: THE ROLE OF ATTENTION

Sensory information, such as the light cast by a sparkler, doesn't last very long no matter what we do. But we can preserve a memory of it by encoding it in some minimal way—for instance, by perceiving the letters *Jea* written in a sparkler's curlicue tail. In the model of memory presented in Figure 6.1, the first step in this process is attention: *Whatever someone mentally pays attention to moves into working memory.* If information in the sensory register doesn't get a person's attention, it presumably disappears from the memory system.

Paying attention involves directing not only the appropriate sensory receptors (in the eyes, ears, etc.) but also the *mind* toward whatever needs to be learned and remembered. Imagine yourself reading a textbook for one of your classes. Your eyes are moving down each page, but you're thinking about something altogether different—a recent argument with a friend, a high-paying job advertised on the Internet, or your growling stomach. What will you remember from the textbook? Absolutely nothing. Even though your eyes have been focused on the words in the book, you haven't been *mentally* attending to the words.

Young children's attention often moves quickly from one thing to another and is easily drawn to objects and events unrelated to the task at hand. As children grow older, they become better able to focus their attention on a particular task and keep it there, and they're less distracted by irrelevant thoughts and events. Yet even adult learners can't keep their minds on a single task *all* the time (E. Barron, Riby, Greer, & Smallwood, 2011; S. M. Carlson & Moses, 2001; Dempster & Corkill, 1999).

Even when learners *are* paying attention, they can attend to only a very small amount of information at any one time. In other words, attention has a *limited capacity* (Cherry, 1953; Cowan, 2007). For example, if you're sitting in front of the television with your textbook open in your lap, you can attend to the *Simpsons* rerun playing on television *or* to your book, but not to both simultaneously. And if you're preoccupied in class with your instructor's desperate need for a fashion makeover, you're unlikely to be paying attention to the lecture itself.

Exactly *how* limited is the limited capacity of human attention? People can often perform two or three well-learned, automatic tasks at once. For example, you can walk and chew gum simultaneously, and you can probably drive a car and drink a cup of coffee at the same time. But when a stimulus or event is detailed and complex (as both textbooks and *Simpsons* reruns are)

**sensory register** Component of memory that holds incoming information in an unanalyzed form for a very brief period of time (two or three seconds at most, depending on the modality).

**attention** Focusing of mental processing on particular stimuli.

For learners of all ages, attention sometimes wanders; as 10-year-old David puts it, "My brain was turned off right now." Watch "Memory: Middle Childhood."

## Into the Classroom

### Getting and Keeping Students' Attention

🍎 **Create stimulating lessons in which students *want* to pay attention.**

In a unit on nutrition, a high school biology teacher has students determine the nutritional value of various menu items at a popular local fast-food restaurant.

🍎 **Get students physically involved with the subject matter.**

A middle school history teacher plans a day late in the school year when all of his classes "go back in time" to the American Civil War. In preparation for the event, the students spend several weeks learning about the Battle of Gettysburg, researching typical dress and meals of the era, gathering appropriate clothing and equipment, and preparing snacks and lunches. On the day of the "battle," students assume various roles: Union and Confederate soldiers, government officials, journalists, merchants, homemakers, doctors and nurses, and so on.

🍎 **Incorporate a variety of instructional methods into lessons.**

After explaining how to calculate the areas of squares and rectangles, a fourth-grade teacher has her students practice calculating areas in a series of increasingly challenging word problems. She then breaks the class into three- to four-member cooperative groups, gives each group a tape measure and calculator, and asks the students to calculate the area of their irregularly shaped classroom floor. To complete the task, the students must divide the room into several smaller rectangles, compute the area of each rectangle separately, and add the subareas together.

🍎 **Provide frequent breaks from sedentary activities, especially when working with students in the elementary grades.**

To provide practice with the alphabet, a kindergarten teacher occasionally has students make letters with their bodies: one child standing with arms extended up and out to make a Y, two children bending over and joining hands to form an M, and so on.

🍎 **In the middle school and high school grades, encourage students to take notes.**

In a middle school science class, different cooperative groups have been specializing in and researching various endangered species. As each group gives an oral report about its species to the rest of the class, the teacher asks students in the audience to jot down questions about things they would like to know about the animal. Upon the completion of their prepared report, members of the presenting group address their classmates' questions.

🍎 **Minimize distractions, especially when students must work quietly and independently.**

The windows of several classrooms look out onto an area where a new parking lot is being created. Teachers in those classrooms have noticed that many students are being distracted by the construction activity outside. The teachers ask the principal to request that the construction company work elsewhere on the day that an important statewide assessment is scheduled to be administered.

*Sources:* Some strategies based on Di Vesta & Gray, 1972; Kiewra, 1989; Ku, Chan, Wu, & Chen, 2008; Pellegrini & Bjorklund, 1997; M. I. Posner & Rothbart, 2007.

Teachers do many things that either capture or lose students' attention. Listen to 12-year-old Claudia in "Motivation: Early Adolescence."

When learners consciously and intentionally control their own thought processes, they are engaging in *metacognition*, discussed in depth in Chapter 7.

or when a task requires considerable thought (as understanding a lecture and driving a car on an icy mountain road would), then people can usually attend to only *one* thing at a time (J. R. Anderson, 2005; Lien, Ruthruff, & Johnston, 2006).

As teachers, we must remember that attention isn't just a behavior; it's also a mental process. The Into the Classroom feature "Getting and Keeping Students' Attention" presents several effective strategies for keeping students' minds on classroom topics.

## THE NATURE OF WORKING (SHORT-TERM) MEMORY

**Working memory** is the component of memory where we hold attended-to information for a short time while we try to make sense of it. Working memory is also where much of our active cognitive processing occurs. For instance, it's where we think about the content of a lecture, analyze a textbook passage, or solve a problem. Basically, this is the component that does most of the mental work of the memory system—hence its name, *working* memory.

Rather than being a single entity, working memory probably has several components for holding and working with different kinds of information—for example, visual information, auditory information, and the underlying meanings of events—as well as a component that integrates multiple kinds of information. As shown in Figure 6.1, working memory may also include a **central executive** that focuses attention, oversees the flow of information throughout the memory system, selects and controls complex voluntary behaviors, and inhibits counterproductive thoughts and actions (Aron, 2008; Baddeley, 2001; Banich, 2009; Logie, 2011).

Information stored in working memory doesn't last very long—perhaps 5 to 20 seconds at most—unless the learner consciously does something with it (e.g., Baddeley, 2001; L. R. Peterson & Peterson, 1959; W. Zhang & Luck, 2009). Accordingly, this component is sometimes called *short-term memory.* For example, imagine that you need to call a neighbor, so you look up the neighbor's number in the telephone book. But then you discover that you can't find your cell phone. You have no paper and pencil handy. What do you do to remember the number until you have access to a telephone? If you're like most people, you probably repeat it to yourself over and over again. This process, known as maintenance rehearsal, keeps information in working memory for as long as you're willing to continue talking to yourself. But once you stop, the number will disappear fairly quickly.

For reasons that aren't entirely clear, the amount of information children can hold in working memory increases somewhat with age (Ben-Yehudah & Fiez, 2007; Kail, 2007). Yet even adults have only so much room to simultaneously hold and think about information. To see what I mean, put your working memory to work for a moment in the following exercise.

### EXPERIENCING FIRSTHAND
### DIVISION PROBLEM

Try computing the answer to this division problem in your head:

$$59 \overline{)49{,}383}$$

Did you find yourself having trouble remembering some parts of the problem while you were dealing with other parts? Did you ever arrive at the correct answer of 837? Most people can't solve a division problem with this many digits unless they write it on paper. Working memory just doesn't have enough space both to hold all that information and to perform mathematical calculations with it. Like attention, working memory has a *limited capacity*—perhaps just enough for a telephone number or very short grocery list (Cowan, 2010; Logie, 2011; G. A. Miller, 1956).

Virtually any learning activity imposes a cognitive load—a certain amount of information that students must simultaneously think about, along with certain *ways* that they must think about it, in order to make sense of and remember what they're studying (R. E. Mayer, 2011b; Plass, Moreno, & Brünken, 2010; Sweller, 1988, 2008). When we design and conduct lessons, then, we must consider just how much of a load students' working memories can reasonably handle at any given time. For example, we should minimize information that's irrelevant to the topic at hand. We should pace the presentation of important information slowly enough that students have time to effectively process what they're seeing and hearing. And we might repeat the same idea several times (perhaps rewording it each time), stop to write important points on the board, and provide numerous examples and illustrations.

I sometimes hear students talking about putting class material in "short-term memory" so that they can do well on an upcoming exam. Such a statement reflects the common misconception that this component of memory lasts for several hours, days, or weeks. Now you know otherwise. Working memory is obviously *not* the place to leave information that you need for an exam later in the week or even information you need for a class later in the day. For such information, storage in long-term memory—the final component of the memory system—is in order.

## MOVING INFORMATION TO LONG-TERM MEMORY: CONNECTING NEW INFORMATION WITH PRIOR KNOWLEDGE

In the model of memory depicted in Figure 6.1, the arrow between working memory and long-term memory points in both directions. Effectively storing new information in long-term memory usually involves connecting it to relevant information that's *already* in long-term memory—a process that requires bringing the "old" information back into working memory. The following exercise can give you an idea of how this might happen.

### EXPERIENCING FIRSTHAND
### LETTERS AND A PICTURE

1  Study the two strings of letters below until you can remember each of them perfectly:

AIIRODFMLAWRS                    FAMILIARWORDS

2  Study the picture shown here until you can reproduce it accurately from memory.

**working memory**  Component of memory that holds and actively thinks about and processes a limited amount of information for a short time.

**central executive**  Component of the human memory system that oversees the flow of information throughout the system.

**maintenance rehearsal**  Rapid repetition of a small amount of information to keep it fresh in working memory.

**cognitive load**  Cognitive burden that a particular learning activity places on working memory at any one time; includes both the amount of information students must simultaneously think about and the specific cognitive processes students must engage in to understand what they're studying.

Keep the limited capacity of working memory in mind when designing and conducting lessons.

**long-term memory** Component of memory that holds knowledge and skills for a relatively long time.

**astrocyte** Star-shaped brain cell hypothesized to be involved in learning and memory; has chemically mediated connections with many other astrocytes and with neurons.

**activation** Degree to which something in memory is being actively attended to and mentally processed.

No doubt the second letter string was easier to learn because you could relate it to something you already knew: the words *familiar words*. How easily were you able to learn and remember the picture? Do you think you could draw it from memory a week from now? Do you think you could remember it more easily if it had the title "Bird's Eye View of a Cowboy Riding a Bicycle"? The answer to the last question is almost certainly *yes*, because the title would help you relate the picture to familiar shapes, such as those of a bicycle and a cowboy hat (Bower, Karlin, & Dueck, 1975).

## THE NATURE OF LONG-TERM MEMORY

**Long-term memory** is where learners store their general knowledge and beliefs about the world, the things they've learned in school (e.g., the capital of France, the correct spelling of *hors d'oeuvre*), and their recollections of events in their personal lives. It's also where learners store their knowledge about how to perform various actions, such as how to ride a bicycle, use a cell phone, and do long division.

Much of the information stored in long-term memory is interconnected. To see what I mean, try the next exercise.

### EXPERIENCING FIRSTHAND
### STARTING WITH A HORSE

What's the first word that comes to mind when you see the word *horse?* And what word does that second word remind you of? And what does the third word remind you of? Beginning with the word *horse,* follow your train of thought, letting each word remind you of a new word or short phrase, for a sequence of at least eight words or phrases. Write down the sequence of things that come to mind.

You probably found yourself easily following a train of thought from the word *horse,* perhaps something like the route I followed:

$$\text{horse} \rightarrow \text{cowboy} \rightarrow \text{lasso} \rightarrow \text{rope} \rightarrow \text{knot} \rightarrow \text{Girl Scouts} \rightarrow \text{cookies} \rightarrow \text{chocolate}$$

The last word in your sequence might be one with little or no obvious relationship to horses. Yet you can probably see a logical connection between each pair of items in the sequence. Related pieces of information tend to be associated with one another in long-term memory, perhaps in a network similar to the one depicted in Figure 6.2.

Information stored in long-term memory lasts much, much longer than information stored in working memory—perhaps a day, a week, a month, a year, or a lifetime, depending on a variety of factors that we'll examine in upcoming sections of the chapter. In addition to its indefinitely long duration, long-term memory seems to be capable of holding as much information as a learner needs to store there. There's probably no such thing as "running out of room." In fact, for reasons you'll discover shortly, the more information already stored in long-term memory, the easier it is to learn new things.

## LEARNING, MEMORY, AND THE BRAIN

Historically, theorists and researchers have believed that the physiological basis for most learning and memory lies in changes in the interconnections among neurons—in particular, in forming new synapses, strengthening existing ones, or eliminating counterproductive ones (e.g., Merzenich, 2001; M. I. Posner & Rothbart, 2007; Trachtenberg et al., 2002). In addition, some learning may involve the formation of new neurons, especially in a small, seahorse-shaped structure in the middle of each side of the brain—a structure called the *hippocampus*—and possibly also in certain areas of the cortex. New learning experiences appear to enhance the survival rate and maturation of the young neurons; without such experiences, these neurons slowly die away (Gould, Beylin, Tanapat, Reeves, & Shors, 1999; Leuner et al., 2004; C. A. Nelson et al., 2006; Sapolsky, 1999).

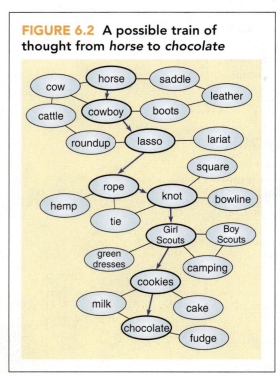

**FIGURE 6.2** **A possible train of thought from *horse* to *chocolate***

Within the last few years, some researchers have begun to speculate that certain star-shaped cells in the brain, known as **astrocytes**, are just as important as neurons—possibly even more important—in learning and memory. Figure 6.3 illustrates the general nature of an astrocyte and its connections with both neurons and the local blood supply. In human beings, astrocytes far outnumber neurons, have innumerable connections with one another and with neurons, and appear to have considerable control over what neurons do and don't do and how much neurons communicate with one another. A normal brain produces many new astrocytes throughout the lifespan (Koob, 2009; Oberheim et al., 2009; Verkhratsky & Butt, 2007).

As for *where* learning occurs, the answer is: many places. Key in the process is the *cortex,* the large, lumpy structure that covers the top and sides of the brain. The area of the brain immediately behind the forehead—the *prefrontal cortex*—seems to be the primary headquarters for working memory and its central executive, although all of the cortex may be active to a greater or lesser extent in interpreting new input in light of previously acquired knowledge (Byrnes, 2001; Gonsalves & Cohen, 2010; Huey, Krueger, & Grafman, 2006; Nee, Berman, Moore, & Jonides, 2008). The hippocampus is also actively involved in learning, in that it pulls together the information it simultaneously receives from various parts of the brain (Bauer, 2002; Squire & Alvarez, 1998).

As you might guess, a healthy brain is essential for effective learning. The Applying Brain Research feature "Enhancing Students' Brain Functioning" presents three general recommendations that are grounded in brain research.

## CRITIQUING THE THREE-COMPONENT MODEL

As mentioned earlier, the three-component model just described oversimplifies—and perhaps overcompartmentalizes—the nature of human memory. For example, attention may be a *part* of working memory, rather than the separate entity depicted in Figure 6.1 (Cowan, 2007; R. W. Engle, 2002; Wagner, 1996). Furthermore, studies conducted by neuropsychologists and other researchers yield mixed results about whether working memory and long-term memory are distinctly different entities (e.g., Baddeley, 2001; Nee et al., 2008; Öztekin, Davachi, & McElree, 2010; Talmi, Grady, Goshen-Gottstein, & Moscovitch, 2005).

Some psychologists have proposed that working memory and long-term memory simply reflect different **activation** states of a single memory (e.g., J. R. Anderson, 2005; Cowan, 1995; Ruchkin, Grafman, Cameron, & Berndt, 2003). According to this view, all information stored in memory is in either an active or inactive state. Active information, which may include both

Astrocytes are one variety of the brain's *glial cells,* described in Chapter 2.

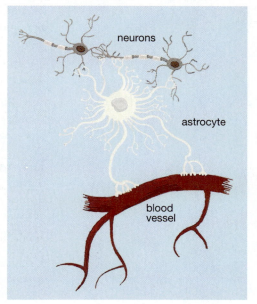

**FIGURE 6.3** Two neurons, an astrocyte, and their interconnections

## Applying Brain Research

### Enhancing Students' Brain Functioning

I urge you to be cautious when you read books, articles, and websites about "brain-based learning," because many of them are speculative at best. Following are three recommendations that have a solid foundation in neuropsychological research.

- **Provide ongoing intellectual stimulation.** New challenges and learning opportunities—age-appropriate ones, of course—seem to enhance brain functioning, in part by nourishing existing neurons, synapses, and astrocytes and in part by stimulating the growth of new ones (Koob, 2009; C. A. Nelson et al., 2006).

- **Encourage physical exercise.** Physical exercise appears to be good for brain health, especially if it includes aerobic activities that keep the cardiovascular system in good working order. A particular benefit is enhancement of the functioning of the central executive—that

component of working memory that controls attention, oversees the general flow of information throughout the memory system, and inhibits counterproductive thoughts (Castelli, Hillman, Buck, & Erwin, 2007; G. D. Cohen, 2005; Tomporowski, Davis, Miller, & Naglieri, 2008).

- **Encourage students to get plenty of sleep.** Unfortunately, typical school schedules, especially their early-morning starting times, are poor matches with the sleeping patterns of many high school students. As you well know, a good night's sleep improves mental alertness and can help people ward off germs that intend to do them harm. But in addition, sleep helps to firm up, or *consolidate,* new memories, rendering them more memorable over the long run (Dinges & Rogers, 2008; Kirby, Maggi, & D'Angiulli, 2011; J. D. Payne & Kensinger, 2010; Rasch & Born, 2008).

incoming information and information previously stored in memory, is what people are currently paying attention to and thinking about—information I've previously described as being in working memory. As attention shifts, other pieces of information in memory become activated, and the previously activated information gradually becomes inactive. The bulk of information stored in memory is in an inactive state, such that we aren't consciously aware of it; this is information I've previously described as being in long-term memory.

Despite its imperfections, the three-component model can help us remember aspects of learning and memory that we should take into account as we teach. For example, the model highlights the critical role of *attention* in learning, the *limited capacity* of attention and working memory, the *interconnectedness* of the knowledge learners acquire, and the importance of *relating* new information to things learned previously.

## Long-Term Memory Storage

Regardless of whether there are three truly distinct components of memory, some aspects of memory are definitely long term. Certainly human beings remember many things for a considerable length of time, and in this sense, at least, these things are in long-term memory.

It appears that information stored in long-term memory can be encoded in a variety of forms (e.g., Barsalou, Simmons, Barbey, & Wilson, 2003; Brainerd & Reyna, 2005; Sadoski & Paivio, 2001). Some information may be encoded in a *verbal* form, perhaps as actual words. Things you remember word for word (e.g., your name, your address, certain song lyrics) are all verbally encoded. Other information may be encoded as *imagery*—as it appears perceptually. For example, if, in your mind, you can see the face of a relative, hear that person's voice, or conjure up a mental whiff of the person's favorite perfume or aftershave lotion, you're retrieving images. Finally, a great deal of information in long-term memory is probably encoded *semantically*—as a set of underlying meanings.

All the preceding examples are instances of declarative knowledge—knowledge that relates to the nature of *how things are, were, or will be.* Declarative knowledge encompasses both general world knowledge (collectively known as *semantic memory*) and recollections of specific life experiences (collectively known as *episodic memory*). Not everything in long-term is declarative in nature, however. People also acquire procedural knowledge; that is, they learn *how to do things* (e.g., J. R. Anderson, 1983; Phye, 1997; Tulving, 1983). You probably know how to ride a bicycle, wrap a birthday present, and multiply a three-digit number by a two-digit number. To perform such actions successfully, you must adapt your behavior to changing conditions. For example, when you ride a bicycle, you must be able to turn left or right when an object blocks your path, and you must be able to come to a complete stop when you reach your destination. Accordingly, procedural knowledge must often include information about how to respond under different circumstances—it involves knowing *when to do certain things* (either physically or mentally). In such instances it's also known as conditional knowledge.

Most declarative knowledge is explicit knowledge: Once we recall it, we're quite conscious of what it is we know. But a good deal of procedural knowledge is implicit knowledge: We can't consciously recall or explain it, but it affects our thinking or behavior nonetheless (P. A. Alexander, Schallert, & Reynolds, 2009; J. R. Anderson, 2005; M. I. Posner & Rothbart, 2007). Another difference is that declarative knowledge can sometimes be learned very quickly, perhaps after a single presentation, whereas procedural knowledge is often acquired slowly and only with considerable practice.

## HOW KNOWLEDGE CAN BE ORGANIZED

As we consider the nature of long-term memory storage, it's helpful to remember that, to a considerable degree, learners *construct* their knowledge and understandings. In the process of constructing knowledge, learners often create well-integrated entities that encompass particular ideas or groups of ideas. For example, beginning in infancy, they form concepts that enable them to categorize objects and events (G. Mandler, 2011; J. M. Mandler, 2007; Quinn, 2002). Some concepts, such as *butterfly, chair,* and *backstroke,* refer to a fairly narrow range of objects or events. Other concepts are fairly general ones that encompass numerous more specific concepts.

**declarative knowledge**  Knowledge concerning the nature of how things are, were, or will be.

**procedural knowledge**  Knowledge concerning how to do something (e.g., a skill).

**conditional knowledge**  Knowledge concerning appropriate ways to respond (physically or mentally) under various circumstances.

**explicit knowledge**  Knowledge that a person is consciously aware of and can verbally describe.

**implicit knowledge**  Knowledge that a person cannot consciously recall or explain but that nevertheless affects the person's thinking or behavior.

**concept**  Mental grouping of objects or events that have something in common.

**schema**  Tightly organized set of facts about a specific topic.

For example, the concept *insect* includes ants, bees, and butterflies (e.g., see Figure 6.4). The concept *swimming* includes the backstroke, dog paddle, and butterfly. As you can see, some words (such as *butterfly*) can be associated with two very different, more general concepts (such as *insects* and *swimming*) and so might lead someone to follow a train of thought such as this one:

horse → cowboy → lasso → rope → knot → Girl Scouts → camping
→ outdoors → nature → insect → butterfly → swimming

By combining numerous objects or events into single entities, concepts take some of the strain off of working memory's limited capacity (G. Mandler, 2011; Oakes & Rakison, 2003). For instance, the concept *molecule* takes very little "space" in working memory despite the many things we know about molecules: their very tiny size, their essential role in the nature of matter, and so on. The Into the Classroom feature "Teaching Concepts" offers suggestions for fostering concept learning in a variety of academic disciplines.

Learners also pull some concepts together into general understandings of what things are typically like. Such understandings are sometimes called schemas (e.g., Rumelhart & Ortony, 1977; Schraw, 2006; Sweller, 2010). For example, let's return to the concept *horse,* which we've used in a couple of earlier examples. You know what horses look like, of course, and you can recognize one when you see one. Hence, you have a concept for *horse.* But now think about the many things you know *about* horses. What do they eat? How do they spend their time? Where are you most likely to see them? You probably have little difficulty retrieving many facts about horses, perhaps including their fondness for oats and carrots, their love of grazing and running, and their frequent appearance in pastures and at racetracks. The various things you know about horses are closely interrelated in your long-term memory in the form of a "horse" schema.

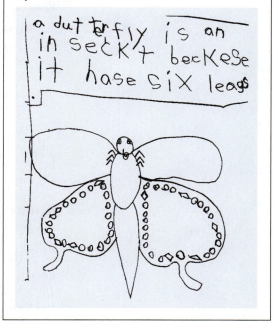

**FIGURE 6.4** In his classification of a butterfly as an *insect,* 8-year-old Noah identifies one characteristic that all insects have—six legs—but correctly doesn't mention the wings, which are optional.

a dutterfly is an inseckt beckese it hase six leags

## Into the Classroom

### Teaching Concepts

🍎 **Give a definition.**
A high school geometry teacher defines a *sphere* as "the set of points in three-dimensional space that are equidistant from a single point."

🍎 **Highlight the characteristics that all or most examples of a concept possess.**
A teacher illustrates the concept *insect* with a line drawing that emphasizes its three body parts, three pairs of legs, and two antennae in bold black lines. The drawing downplays other, irrelevant characteristics that might be visible, such as the insect's color and the presence of wings.

🍎 **Present a best example—a prototype that captures the key elements of the concept.**
To illustrate the concept *democracy,* a social studies teacher describes a hypothetical, ideal government.

🍎 **Present a wide range of examples in diverse contexts.**
On both a piano and a guitar, a music teacher plays a *primary chord* in several keys.

🍎 **Present nonexamples, especially near misses, to show what the concept is *not.***
When a teacher describes what a *mammal* is, he explains why frogs and lizards don't fall into this category.

🍎 **Ask students to identify examples and nonexamples from among numerous possibilities.**
A language arts teacher gives students a list of sentences and asks them to identify the sentences containing a *dangling participle.*

🍎 **Ask students to generate their own examples of the concept.**
A teacher asks students to think of examples of *adjectives* they frequently use in their own speech.

🍎 **Show students how various concepts are related to one another—their similarities and differences, their hierarchical relationships, and so on.**
A science teacher explains that the concepts *velocity* and *acceleration* have somewhat different meanings, even though they both involve speed.

*Sources:* Best, Dockrell, & Braisby, 2006; Brophy, Alleman, & Knighton, 2009; Carmichael & Hayes, 2001; R. G. Cook & Smith, 2006; R. M. Gagné, 1985; Ormrod, 2012; Rosch, 1977; B. H. Ross & Spalding, 1994; Tennyson & Cocchiarella, 1986.

**script** Schema that involves a predictable sequence of events related to a common activity.

**theory** Integrated set of concepts and principles developed to explain a particular phenomenon.

People have schemas not only about objects but also about events. When a schema involves a predictable sequence of events related to a particular activity, it's sometimes called a **script**. The next exercise provides an example.

## EXPERIENCING FIRSTHAND
### JOHN

Read the following passage *one time only.*

> John was feeling bad today so he decided to go see the family doctor. He checked in with the doctor's receptionist, and then looked through several medical magazines that were on the table by his chair. Finally the nurse came and asked him to take off his clothes. The doctor was very nice to him. He eventually prescribed some pills for John. Then John left the doctor's office and headed home. (Bower, Black, & Turner, 1979, p. 190)

You probably had no trouble making sense of the passage because you've been to a doctor's office yourself and have a schema for how those visits usually go. You can therefore fill in a number of details that the passage doesn't tell you. For example, you probably inferred that John actually *went* to the doctor's office, although the story omits this essential step. Likewise, you probably concluded that John took off his clothes in the examination room, *not* in the waiting room, even though the story never makes it clear where John did his striptease. When critical information is missing, as is true in the story about John, schemas and scripts often enable learners to fill in the gaps in a reasonable way.

On a much larger scale, human beings—young children included—construct general understandings and belief systems, or **theories**, about particular aspects of the world (Gelman, 2003; Keil & Newman, 2008; Wellman & Gelman, 1998.). Such theories include many concepts and the relationships among them (e.g., correlation, cause–and–effect). To see what some of your own theories are like, try the next exercise.

## EXPERIENCING FIRSTHAND
### COFFEEPOTS AND RACCOONS

Consider each of the following situations:

1  People took a coffeepot that looked like Drawing A. They removed the handle, sealed the top, took off the top knob, sealed the opening to the spout, and removed the spout. They also sliced off the base and attached a flat piece of metal. They attached a little stick, cut out a window, and filled the metal container with birdseed. When they were done, it looked like Drawing B. After these changes, was this a coffeepot or a bird feeder?

2  Doctors took the raccoon in Drawing C and shaved away some of its fur. They dyed what was left black and then bleached a single white stripe down the center of the animal's back. Then, with surgery, they put in its body a sac of super-smelly odor, just like the smell a skunk has. After they were all done, the animal looked like Drawing D. After the operation, was this a skunk or a raccoon?

*Source:* Both scenarios based on Keil, 1989, p. 184.

Chances are, you concluded that the coffeepot was transformed into a bird feeder but that the raccoon was still a raccoon despite its cosmetic makeover and stinky surgery. Now how is it possible that the coffeepot could be made into something entirely different, whereas the raccoon could not? Even young children seem to make a basic distinction between human-made objects (e.g., coffeepots, bird feeders) and biological entities (e.g., raccoons, skunks) (Gelman & Kalish, 2006; Inagaki & Hatano, 2006; Keil, 1986, 1989). For instance, human-made objects are defined largely by the *functions* they serve (e.g., brewing coffee, feeding birds), whereas biological entities are defined primarily by their origins (e.g., the parents who brought them into being, their DNA) (Greif, Kemler Nelson, Keil, & Gutierrez, 2006; Inagaki & Hatano, 2006; Keil, 1987, 1989). Thus, when a coffeepot begins to hold birdseed rather than coffee, it becomes a bird

## COMPARE/CONTRAST

| TABLE 6.3 • Long-Term Memory Storage Processes | | | |
|---|---|---|---|
| **PROCESS** | **DEFINITION** | **EXAMPLE** | **EFFECTIVENESS** |
| **Rote learning: Learning primarily through repetition and practice, with little or no attempt to make sense of what is being learned** | | | |
| Rehearsal | Repeating information verbatim, either mentally or aloud | Word-for-word repetition of a formula or definition | Relatively ineffective: Storage is slow, and later retrieval is difficult |
| **Meaningful learning: Making connections between new information and prior knowledge** | | | |
| Elaboration | Embellishing on new information based on what one already knows | Generating possible reasons that historical figures made the decisions they did | Effective if associations and additions made are appropriate and productive |
| Organization | Making connections among various pieces of new information | Thinking about how one's lines in a play relate to the play's overall story line | Effective if organizational structure is legitimate and consists of more than just a list of discrete facts |
| Visual imagery | Forming a mental picture of something, either by actually seeing it or by envisioning how it might look | Imagining how various characters and events in a novel might have looked | Individual differences in effectiveness; especially beneficial when used in combination with elaboration or organization |

feeder because its function has changed. But when a raccoon is cosmetically and surgically altered to look and smell like a skunk, it still has raccoon parents and raccoon DNA and so can't possibly *be* a skunk.

By the time children reach school age, they've already constructed basic theories about their physical, biological, social, and psychological worlds (Flavell, 2000; Geary, 2005; Torney-Purta, 1994; Wellman & Gelman, 1998). They've also constructed preliminary theories about the nature of their own and other people's thinking. In general, self-constructed theories help children make sense of and remember personal experiences, classroom subject matter, and other new information (Gelman, 2003; Reiner, Slotta, Chi, & Resnick, 2000; Wellman & Gelman, 1998). Yet because children's theories often evolve with little or no guidance from more knowledgeable individuals, they sometimes include erroneous beliefs about the world that can wreak havoc with new learning (more about this point later in the chapter).

## HOW DECLARATIVE KNOWLEDGE IS LEARNED

Especially when talking about the kinds of declarative knowledge learned in school, learning theorists distinguish between two general forms of long-term memory storage processes—rote learning and meaningful learning—and among more specific storage processes that differ considerably in their effectiveness (see Table 6.3).

### ROTE LEARNING

Learners engage in rote learning when they try to learn and remember something without attaching much meaning to it. For example, in the "Letters and a Picture" exercise presented earlier, you would be engaging in rote learning if you tried to remember the letter string FAMILIARWORDS simply as a list of isolated letters or if you tried to remember the cowboy/bicycle drawing as a collection of random, unrelated lines and curves.

One common form of rote learning is rehearsal, repeating something over and over within a short timeframe (typically a few minutes or less), either by saying it aloud or by continuously thinking about it in an unaltered, verbatim fashion. Earlier I described how maintenance rehearsal—verbally repeating something over and over—helps us keep information in working memory indefinitely. Contrary to what many students think, however, rehearsal is *not* a very effective way of storing information in *long-term* memory. If a learner repeats something often enough, it might eventually "sink in," but the process is slow, laborious, and not much fun. Furthermore, for reasons I'll identify later, people who use rehearsal and other forms of rote learning often have trouble remembering what they've learned (J. R. Anderson, 2005; Ausubel, Novak, & Hanesian, 1978; Craik & Watkins, 1973).

Verbally rehearsing information is probably better than not actively processing it at all, and rehearsal may be one of the few strategies students can use when they have little prior knowledge

A child's *theory of mind* is an example of a self-constructed theory (see Chapter 3).

Build on children's early theories about the world, but be on the lookout for beliefs that may get in the way of more advanced understandings.

**rote learning** Learning information in a relatively uninterpreted form, without making sense of it or attaching much meaning to it.

**rehearsal** Cognitive process in which information is repeated over and over within a short timeframe (typically a few minutes or less) as a possible way of learning and remembering it.

**meaningful learning** Cognitive process in which learners relate new information to things they already know.

**elaboration** Cognitive process in which learners embellish on new information based on what they already know.

The process of meaningful learning is similar to Piaget's concept of *assimilation* (see Chapter 2).

Meaningful learning takes many forms. Hear 16-year-old Hilary describe two of her strategies in "Memory: Late Adolescence."

Encourage students to go beyond the specific information they have learned—to draw inferences, speculate about possible implications, defend a position about a controversial topic, and so on. For example, have students work in pairs or small groups to formulate and ask one another elaborative questions.

to draw on to help them understand new material (E. Wood, Willoughby, Bolger, & Younger, 1993). For example, in the opening case study Kanesha resorts to rehearsal in her efforts to remember such seemingly nonsensical bone names as the coccyx, clavicle, and patella. Ideally, however, we should encourage students to engage in meaningful learning whenever possible.

## MEANINGFUL LEARNING

In contrast to rote learning, **meaningful learning** involves recognizing a relationship between new information and something already stored in long-term memory. When we use such words as *comprehension* and *understanding,* we're talking about meaningful learning. Here are examples that 16-year-old Hilary describes:

> When I'm trying to study for a test, I try to associate the things that I'm trying to learn with familiar things. Like, if I have a Spanish vocabulary test, I'll try to . . . with the Spanish words, I'll try to think of the English word that it sounds like, because sometimes it does sound like the English word. And then our government teacher is teaching us the amendments and we're trying to memorize them. He taught us one trick for memorizing Amendment 2, which is the right to bear arms. He said, "Bears have two arms, so that's Amendment 2."

In the vast majority of cases, meaningful learning is more effective than rote learning for storing information in long-term memory (R. E. Mayer, 1996; Sweller, 2010; Wittrock, 1974). It's especially effective when learners relate new ideas not only to what they already know about the world but also to what they know or believe about *themselves*—for instance, to self-descriptions or personal life experiences (Heatherton, Macrae, & Kelley, 2004; Kesebir & Oishi, 2010; Rogers, Kuiper, & Kirker, 1977).

Meaningful learning takes a variety of forms. Three forms that researchers have studied in depth are elaboration, organization, and visual imagery. All three are *constructive* in nature: They involve combining several pieces of information into a meaningful whole.

**Elaboration**   In **elaboration**, learners use their prior knowledge to embellish on a new idea, thereby storing *more* information than was actually presented. For example, when I took a course in Mandarin Chinese in high school, I learned that the Chinese word *wŏmen* means "we." "Aha!" I thought to myself, "the sign on the restroom that *we* girls use says *wŏmen*" (albeit without the tone mark over the *o*). Similarly, a student who reads that a certain species of dinosaurs had powerful jaws and sharp, pointed teeth might correctly deduce that those dinosaurs were meat eaters. And when a student learns that the crew on Columbus's first trip across the Atlantic threatened to revolt, the student might speculate, "I'll bet the men were really frightened when they continued to travel west day after day without ever seeing signs of land."

On average, the more students elaborate on new material—that is, the more they use what they already know to help them understand and interpret the new material—the more effectively they will store and remember it. Thus, students who regularly elaborate on what they learn in school usually show higher achievement than those who simply take information at face value (J. R. Anderson, 2005; McDaniel & Einstein, 1989; Paxton, 1999; Waters, 1982).

One effective way to encourage elaboration in the classroom is to have students write about a topic—for instance, to summarize what they've learned, relate new concepts to their personal experiences, or express and defend certain positions on controversial topics (Bangert-Drowns, Hurley, & Wilkinson, 2004; Shanahan, 2004). Another good strategy is to ask questions that require students to expand on something they've just learned—questions such as "How would you use . . . to . . . ?" and "What do you think would happen if . . . ?" (A. King, 1992, p. 309; McCrudden & Schraw, 2007). Still another approach is to have students work in pairs or small groups to formulate and answer their *own* elaborative questions. Different researchers call such group questioning either *elaborative interrogation* or *guided peer questioning* (Kahl & Woloshyn, 1994; A. King, 1994, 1999; Rosenshine, Meister, & Chapman, 1996; E. Wood et al., 1999). In the following dialogue, fifth graders Katie and Janelle are working together to study class material about tide pools. Katie's job is to ask Janelle questions that encourage elaboration:

> *Katie:* How are the upper tide zone and the lower tide zone different?
>
> *Janelle:* They have different animals in them. Animals in the upper tide zone and splash zone can handle being exposed—have to be able to use the rain and sand and wind and sun—and they don't need that much water and the lower tide animals do.

*Katie:* And they can be softer 'cause they don't have to get hit on the rocks.

*Janelle:* Also predators. In the spray zone it's because there's predators like us people and all different kinds of stuff that can kill the animals and they won't survive, but the lower tide zone has not as many predators.

*Katie:* But wait! Why do the animals in the splash zone have to survive? (A. King, 1999, p. 97)

Notice that the two girls are continually relating the animals' characteristics to survival in different tide zones, and eventually Katie asks why animals in the splash zone even *need* to survive. Such analyses are quite sophisticated for fifth graders. Imagine what high school students, with their increasing capacity for abstract and hypothetical thinking, might be able to do!

**Organization**    On average, we learn and remember a body of new information more easily when we pull it together in some reasonable way (e.g., Nesbit & Adesope, 2006; Novak, 1998; D. H. Robinson & Kiewra, 1995). Such organization involves making connections among various pieces of new information and forming an overall cohesive structure. For example, a learner might group information into categories, as you probably did in the "Remembering 12 Words" exercise near the beginning of the chapter.

Another way of organizing information is to identify interrelationships among its various parts. For instance, when learning about *velocity, acceleration, force,* and *mass* in a physics class, a student might better understand these concepts by seeing how they're interconnected—perhaps by learning that velocity is the product of acceleration and time $(v = a \times t)$ and that an object's force is determined by both its mass and its acceleration $(f = m \times a)$. The trick is not simply to memorize the formulas (that would be rote learning) but rather to make sense of the relationships that the formulas represent.

It's often helpful to give students specific structures they can use to organize information. For example, the weblike note-taking form shown in Figure 6.5 can help elementary students organize what they learn about tarantulas. Another effective structure is a two-dimensional matrix or table that enables students to compare several items with respect to various characteristics—for instance, how various geographical regions differ in topography, climate, economic activities, and cultural practices (R. K. Atkinson et al., 1999; Kiewra, DuBois, Christian, & McShane, 1988; D. H. Robinson & Kiewra, 1995). A third approach is to teach students how to create concept maps—diagrams that depict the concepts of a unit and their interrelationships (Hattie, 2009; Nesbit & Adesope, 2006; Novak, 1998). Figure 6.6 shows concept maps that two different students might construct after a lesson about gorillas. The concepts themselves are circled, and their interrelationships are indicated by lines with words or short phrases. Several concept-mapping software programs (e.g., Kidspiration, MindMapper Jr. for Kids) are available for creating and modifying concept maps quickly and easily.

Not only can self-constructed organizational structures help students learn more effectively, but they can also help teachers *assess* students' learning. For example, the concept map on the left side of Figure 6.6 reveals only spotty, fragmented knowledge about gorillas. Furthermore, the student has two ideas that need correction. First, contrary to a common stereotype, gorillas don't regularly swing from trees, although young ones may occasionally climb a tree to escape danger. Second, gorillas aren't especially "fierce" creatures. For the most part, they live a peaceful existence within their family group; they get nasty (e.g., by beating their chests) only when a human being, non-family-member gorilla, or other potential encroacher threatens their territory.

**Visual Imagery**    Earlier I mentioned imagery as one possible way in which information might be encoded in long-term memory. Numerous research studies indicate that visual imagery—forming mental pictures of objects or ideas—can be a highly effective method of storing information (Sadoski & Paivio, 2001; D. L. Schwartz & Heiser, 2006). To show you how effective visual imagery can be, I'll teach you a few of the Mandarin Chinese words I learned in high school.

**organization** Cognitive process in which learners make connections among various pieces of information they need to learn (e.g., by forming categories, identifying hierarchies, determining cause–and–effect relationships).

**concept map** Diagram of concepts and their interrelationships; used to enhance the learning and memory of a topic.

**visual imagery** Process of forming a mental picture of an object or idea.

 Explicitly show how various ideas are interrelated.

 Give students specific tools to help them organize what they're learning.

**FIGURE 6.5** **Using a form his second-grade teacher has provided, 7-year-old Tony organizes what he has learned about tarantulas.**

**FIGURE 6.6** Two concept maps about gorillas

### EXPERIENCING FIRSTHAND
## FIVE CHINESE WORDS

Try learning these five Chinese words by forming the visual images I describe (don't worry about learning the marks over the words):

| Chinese Word | English Meaning | Image |
|---|---|---|
| fáng | House | Picture a *house* with *fangs* growing on its roof and walls. |
| mén | door | Picture a restroom *door* with the word *MEN* painted on it. |
| ké | guest | Picture someone giving someone else (the *guest*) a *key* to the house. |
| fàn | food | Picture a plate of *food* being cooled by a *fan*. |
| shū | book | Picture a *shoe* with a book sticking out of it. |

Now find something else to do for a couple of minutes. Stand up and stretch, get a glass of water, or use the restroom. But be sure to come back to your reading in just a minute or two.

Now that you're back, cover the list of Chinese words, English meanings, and visual images. Then try to remember what each word means:

ké    fàn    mén    fáng    shū

Did the Chinese words remind you of the visual images you stored? Did the images, in turn, help you remember the English meanings? You may have remembered all five words easily, or you may have remembered only one or two. People differ in their ability to use visual imagery: Some form images quickly and easily, whereas others form them only slowly and with difficulty (Behrmann, 2000; J. M. Clark & Paivio, 1991; Kosslyn, 1985).

In the classroom we can promote the use of visual imagery in several ways. We can ask students to imagine how certain events in literature or history might have looked (Johnson-Glenberg, 2000; Sadoski & Paivio, 2001). We can provide visual materials (pictures, charts, graphs, etc.) that illustrate important but possibly abstract ideas (R. K. Atkinson et al., 1999; R. Carlson, Chandler, & Sweller, 2003; Verdi, Kulhavy, Stock, Rittschof, & Johnson, 1996). We can also ask students to draw their *own* illustrations or diagrams of the things they're studying, such as 9-year-old Trisha does in Figure 6.7 (Edens & Potter, 2001; Schwamborn, Mayer, Thillmann, Leopold, & Leutner, 2010; Van Meter & Garner, 2005).

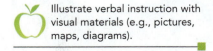
Illustrate verbal instruction with visual materials (e.g., pictures, maps, diagrams).

Visual imagery can be especially powerful when used in combination with other forms of encoding. For example, students more readily learn and remember information they receive in both a verbal form (e.g., a lecture or textbook passage) and a graphic form (e.g., a picture, map, or diagram) (R. E. Mayer, 2011b; Moreno, 2006; Winn, 1991). They're also likely to benefit from being explicitly asked to represent information both verbally and visually.

## DEVELOPMENTAL TRENDS IN STORAGE PROCESSES FOR DECLARATIVE INFORMATION

The tendency to relate new information to prior knowledge—meaningful learning—probably occurs in one form or another at virtually all age levels (Flavell, Miller, & Miller, 2002; Siegler & Alibali, 2005). More specific strategies—such as rehearsal, organization, and visual imagery—are fairly limited in the early elementary years but increase in both frequency and effectiveness over the course of childhood and adolescence. The frequency of elaboration—especially as a process that learners *intentionally* use—picks up a bit later, often not until adolescence, and is more common in high-achieving students. Table 6.4 provides more detailed information on the nature of long-term memory storage processes at different grade levels.

**FIGURE 6.7** **This drawing by 9-year-old Trisha effectively illustrates the water cycle.**

## HOW PROCEDURAL KNOWLEDGE IS LEARNED

Some of the procedures people learn—for example, baking a cake, serving a volleyball, driving a car with a stick shift—consist primarily of overt behaviors. Many others—for examples, writing a persuasive essay, solving for *x* in an algebraic equation, surfing the Internet—have a significant mental component as well. Many procedures involve a combination of physical behaviors and mental activities.

Procedural knowledge ranges from relatively simple actions (e.g., holding a pencil correctly or using scissors) to far more complex skills. Complex procedures usually aren't learned in one fell swoop. Instead, they're acquired slowly over a period of time, often only with a great deal of practice (Charness, Tuffiash, & Jastrzembski, 2004; Ericsson, 2003; Proctor & Dutta, 1995).

People appear to learn simple physical procedures primarily as actual behaviors—in other words, as specific actions that, with practice, are strengthened and gradually refined (Ennis & Chen, 2011; Féry & Morizot, 2000; Willingham, 1999). Yet many complex skills, especially those that have a mental component, may also be learned as declarative knowledge—in other words, as *information* about how to do something (J. R. Anderson, 1983; Beilock & Carr, 2004). Learners may initially use their declarative knowledge to guide them as they perform a new skill, but to the extent that they must do so, their performance is apt to be slow and laborious and to require a lot of concentration—that is, it consumes considerable working memory capacity. As learners continue to practice the skill, however, their declarative knowledge gradually evolves into procedural knowledge, perhaps eventually to the point that they can perform the activity quickly, efficiently, and effortlessly (we'll look at such *automaticity* more closely a bit later). People who show exceptional talent in a particular skill domain—say, in figure skating or playing the piano—typically practice a great deal, often a minimum of three to four hours a day over a period of 10 years or more (Ericsson, 1996; Horn, 2008).

Some of the storage processes we've already discussed play a role in acquiring procedural knowledge as well as declarative knowledge. For instance, verbally rehearsing a sequence of steps in a motor skill enhances people's ability to perform the skill (Weiss & Klint, 1987). Illustrations or live demonstrations of a procedure, which presumably foster visual imagery, are also beneficial (Kitsantas, Zimmerman, & Cleary, 2000; SooHoo, Takemoto, & McCullagh, 2004; Zimmerman & Kitsantas, 1999). In fact, imagining *oneself* performing a new skill (e.g., executing a gymnastics move or a basketball shot) can enhance acquisition of the skill, although this strategy obviously isn't as effective as actual practice (Feltz, Landers, & Becker, 1988; Kosslyn, 1985; SooHoo et al., 2004).

Perhaps the most effective way to teach new procedures is to model them for students, including both the overt behaviors and the internal thought processes involved (e.g., Rittle-Johnson, 2006; Schunk, 1998). The Into the Classroom feature "Helping Students Acquire New Procedures" illustrates several additional strategies for facilitating procedural learning.

With age and experience, children become increasingly strategic in their efforts to remember information. Watch "Remembering a List."

Chapter 8 explains how some procedural knowledge is an integral part of a culture's *communities of practice*. Chapter 10 offers suggestions for effectively modeling new behaviors for students.

# DEVELOPMENTAL TRENDS

## TABLE 6.4 • Typical Long-Term Memory Storage Processes at Different Grade Levels

| GRADE LEVEL | AGE-TYPICAL CHARACTERISTICS | EXAMPLE | SUGGESTED STRATEGIES |
|---|---|---|---|
| K–2 | • Organization of physical objects as a way to remember them<br>• Emergence of rehearsal to remember verbal material; used infrequently and relatively ineffectively<br>• Emerging ability to use visual imagery to enhance memory, especially if an adult suggests this strategy<br>• Few intentional efforts to learn | At the end of the school day, a first-grade teacher reminds students that they need to bring three things to school tomorrow: an object that begins with the letter W (for a phonics lesson), a signed permission slip for a field trip to a local historic site, and a warm jacket to wear on the field trip. Six-year-old Cassie briefly mumbles "jacket" to herself a couple of times and naively assumes she'll remember all three items without any further mental effort. | • Get students actively involved in topics, perhaps through hands-on activities, engaging reading materials, or fantasy play.<br>• Relate new topics to students' prior experiences.<br>• Model rehearsal as a strategy for remembering things over the short run.<br>• Provide pictures that illustrate verbal material.<br>• Give students short notes they can take home to help them and their parents remember items that need to be brought to school. |
| 3-5 | • Spontaneous, intentional, and increasingly effective use of rehearsal to remember things for a short time period<br>• Increasing use of organization as an intentional learning strategy for verbal information<br>• Increasing effectiveness in the use of visual imagery as a learning strategy | As 10-year-old Jonathan studies for an upcoming quiz on clouds, he looks at the photos of four different kinds of clouds in his science book and says each one's name aloud. Then he repeats the four cloud types several times: "Cumulus, cumulonimbus, cirrus, stratus. Cumulus, cumulonimbus, cirrus, stratus. Cumulus, cumulonimbus, cirrus, stratus." | • Emphasize the importance of making sense of, rather than memorizing, information.<br>• Encourage students to organize what they're studying; suggest possible organizational structures for topics.<br>• Provide a variety of visual aids to facilitate visual imagery, and suggest that students create their own drawings or visual images of things they need to remember. |
| 6-8 | • Predominance of rehearsal as a learning strategy<br>• Greater abstractness and flexibility in categories used to organize information<br>• Emergence of elaboration as an intentional learning strategy | Two middle school students, Raj and Owen, are studying for a quiz on various kinds of rocks. "Let's group them somehow," Raj says. Owen suggests grouping them by color (gray, white, reddish, etc.). But after further discussion, the boys agree that sorting them into *sedimentary, igneous,* and *metamorphic* would be a more strategic approach. | • Suggest questions that students might ask themselves as they study; emphasize questions that promote elaboration (e.g., "Why would ___ do that?" "How is ____ different from ____?").<br>• Assess true understanding rather than rote memorization in assignments and quizzes. |
| 9-12 | • Continuing reliance on rehearsal as an intentional learning strategy, especially by low-achieving students<br>• Increasing use of elaboration and organization to learn, especially by high-achieving students | In her high school world history class, Kate focuses her studying efforts on memorizing names, dates, and places. Meanwhile, Kate's classmate Janika likes to speculate about the personalities and motives of such historical characters as Alexander the Great, Napoleon Bonaparte, and Adolf Hitler. | • Ask thought-provoking questions that engage students' interest and help students see the relevance of topics to their own lives.<br>• Have students work in mixed-ability cooperative groups, in which high-achieving students can model effective learning strategies for low-achieving students. |

*Sources:* Bjorklund & Coyle, 1995; Bjorklund & Jacobs, 1985; Bjorklund, Schneider, Cassel, & Ashley, 1994; Cowan, Saults, & Morey, 2006; DeLoache & Todd, 1988; Gaskins & Pressley, 2007; Gathercole & Hitch, 1993; Kosslyn, Margolis, Barrett, Goldknopf, & Daly, 1990; Kunzinger, 1985; Lehmann & Hasselhorn, 2007; Lucariello, Kyratzis, & Nelson, 1992; Marley, Szabo, Levin, & Glenberg, 2008; L. S. Newman, 1990; P. A. Ornstein, Grammer, & Coffman, 2010; Plumert, 1994; Pressley, 1982; Pressley & Hilden, 2006; Schneider & Pressley, 1989.

## Into the Classroom

### Helping Students Acquire New Procedures

🍏 **Help students understand the logic behind the procedures they are learning.**
As a teacher demonstrates the correct way to swing a tennis racket, she asks her students, "Why is it important to have your feet apart rather than together? Why is it important to hold your arm straight as you swing?"

🍏 **When skills are especially complex, break them into simpler tasks that students can practice one at a time.**
Knowing how overwhelming the task of driving a car can initially be, a driver education teacher begins behind-the-wheel instruction by having students practice steering and braking in an empty school parking lot. Only later, after students have mastered these skills, does she have them drive in traffic on city streets.

🍏 **Provide mnemonics that can help students remember a sequence of steps.**
A math teacher shows students how to multiply in the expression $(3x + 4)(2x + 5)$ by working out the steps on the board. As she goes along, she explains what she's doing: "The word *FOIL* can help you remember what you need to do. You begin by multiplying the two *first* terms inside the parentheses—that would be $3x \times 2x$, or $6x^2$. Then you multiply the two *outer* terms—$3x \times 5$—which gives you $15x$. After that, you multiply the two *inner* terms—$4 \times 2x$—which gives you $8x$. Finally you multiply the two *last* terms—$4 \times 5$, which equals 20. Add them all together, and you get $6x^2 + 23x + 20$."

🍏 **Give students many opportunities to practice new skills, and provide the feedback they need to help them improve.**
A science teacher asks his students to write lab reports after each week's lab activity. Because many of his students have had little or no previous experience in scientific writing, he writes numerous comments when he grades the reports. Some comments describe the strengths he sees, and others provide suggestions for making the reports more objective, precise, or clear.

*Sources:* P. A. Alexander & Judy, 1988; J. R. Anderson, Reder, & Simon, 1996; Beilock & Carr, 2004; Ennis & Chen, 2011; Hattie & Timperley, 2007; Hecht, Close, & Santisi, 2003; Proctor & Dutta, 1995; Shute, 2008; van Merriënboer & Kester, 2008.

## ROLES OF PRIOR KNOWLEDGE AND WORKING MEMORY IN LONG-TERM MEMORY STORAGE

Students are more likely to engage in meaningful learning when they have a relevant knowledge base—that is, when they have existing knowledge to which they can connect whatever new information and skills they're trying to master. When, in contrast, they have little relevant knowledge on which to build, they're apt to struggle in their efforts to make sense of new information, as Kanesha sometimes does while studying bone names for her biology quiz.

Occasionally students' prior knowledge interferes with something they need to learn; this is the case when Kanesha tries to remember where the sternum is located. In general, however, a relevant knowledge base helps students learn and remember new material more effectively than they would otherwise (P. A. Alexander, Kulikowich, & Schulze, 1994; Kintsch, 2009; Schneider, 1993). For example, students will better understand scientific principles if they've already seen those principles in action either in their personal lives or in the classroom, and they'll better understand how large some dinosaurs were if they have previously seen life-sized dinosaur skeletons at a museum of natural history.

🍏 Provide concrete experiences (lab experiments, museum visits, etc.) to which students can relate more abstract ideas.

Students' prior knowledge contributes to their learning in several ways:

- It helps them determine what is most important to learn and therefore helps them direct their *attention* appropriately.

- It enhances their ability to *elaborate* on information—for example, to fill in missing details, clarify ambiguities, and draw inferences.

- It provides a framework for *organizing* new information. (Bjorklund, Muir-Broaddus, & Schneider, 1990; Haskell, 2001; Rumelhart & Ortony, 1977; P. T. Wilson & Anderson, 1986)

Children's knowledge about the world grows by leaps and bounds every year; on average, then, older students have more knowledge to help them understand and elaborate on new ideas and events than younger ones do (Flavell et al., 2002; Halford, 1989; Kail, 1990). When young children have more knowledge than their elders, however, they often have the upper hand

**knowledge base** One's existing knowledge about specific topics and the world in general.

**prior knowledge activation** Process of reminding learners of what they already know relative to a new topic.

(Chi, 1978; Rabinowitz & Glaser, 1985). For instance, when my son Alex and I used to read books about lizards together, Alex always remembered more than I did because, even as a 6-year-old, he knew much more about reptiles than I did.

Children don't all acquire the *same* knowledge bases, of course, and their differing knowledge can lead them to construct different meanings from the same situation. The next exercise illustrates this point.

### EXPERIENCING FIRSTHAND
### ROCKY

Read the following passage *one time only:*

> Rocky slowly got up from the mat, planning his escape. He hesitated a moment and thought. Things were not going well. What bothered him most was being held, especially since the charge against him had been weak. He considered his present situation. The lock that held him was strong but he thought he could break it. He knew, however, that his timing would have to be perfect. Rocky was aware that it was because of his early roughness that he had been penalized so severely—much too severely from his point of view. The situation was becoming frustrating; the pressure had been grinding on him for too long. He was being ridden unmercifully. Rocky was getting angry now. He felt he was ready to make his move. He knew that his success or failure would depend on what he did in the next few seconds. (R. C. Anderson, Reynolds, Schallert, & Goetz, 1977, p. 372)

Now summarize what you've just read in two or three sentences.

What did you think the passage was about? A prison escape? A wrestling match? Or perhaps something else altogether? When the Rocky passage was used in an experiment with college students, many physical education majors interpreted it as a wrestling match, but music education majors—most of whom had little or no knowledge of wrestling—were more likely to think it was about a prison break (R. C. Anderson et al., 1977).

Yet it isn't enough that students have the knowledge they need to make sense of new material. They must also be *aware* that some of their existing knowledge is relevant. They must retrieve that knowledge from long-term memory while thinking about the new material, so that *they have both the old and the new in working memory simultaneously and can make the appropriate connections* (Bellezza, 1986; Glanzer & Nolan, 1986; Kalyuga, 2010).

As teachers, we should use students' existing knowledge as a starting point whenever we introduce a new topic. Furthermore, we should explicitly remind students of things they know that bear directly on a topic of classroom study—an instructional strategy known as **prior knowledge activation** (Machiels-Bongaerts, Schmidt, & Boshuizen, 1993; Resnick, 1989; Spires & Donley, 1998). For instance, we might begin a first-grade unit about plants by asking students to describe what their parents do to keep flowers or vegetable gardens growing. In a secondary English literature class, we might introduce Sir Walter Scott's *Ivanhoe* (in which Robin Hood is a major character) by asking students to tell the tale of Robin Hood as they know it. We should also remember that students from diverse cultural backgrounds may have somewhat different knowledge bases and adjust our starting point accordingly (E. Fox, 2009; Nelson-Barber & Estrin, 1995; Pritchard, 1990).

Furthermore, we should encourage students to retrieve relevant knowledge *on their own* as they study. One approach is to model this strategy for students. For example, we might read aloud a portion of a textbook, stopping occasionally to tie an idea in the text to something previously studied in class or to something in our own personal experience. We can then encourage students to do likewise, giving suggestions and guiding their efforts as they proceed. Especially when working with students in the elementary grades, we might also want to provide specific questions that encourage students to reflect on their existing knowledge and beliefs as they read and study—for instance, asking themselves, "What do I already know about this topic?" and "Might I discover that something I think about this topic isn't correct?" (Baer & Garrett, 2010; Spires & Donley, 1998; H. Thompson & Carr, 1995).

Begin instruction with what students already know, and help them make connections between the "new" and the "old."

As students begin a reading assignment, encourage them to think about what they already know and believe about a topic.

## ENCOURAGING A MEANINGFUL LEARNING SET AND CONCEPTUAL UNDERSTANDING

We can't always blame students when they take a relatively meaning*less* approach to their studies. Inadvertently, some teachers tend to encourage students to learn school subjects by rote. Think back to your own experiences in school. How many times were you allowed to define a word by repeating its dictionary definition, rather than being expected to explain it in your own words? In fact, how many times were you *required* to learn something word for word? And how many times did an exam assess your knowledge of facts or principles without ever assessing your ability to relate those facts and principles to everyday life or to things learned in previous lessons or courses? When assignments and assessments require memory of isolated facts—and perhaps even require word-for-word recall—students are apt to engage in rote rather than meaningful learning, believing that a rote-learning approach will yield them better grades (Crooks, 1988; N. Frederiksen, 1984b; M. C. Linn & Eylon, 2011; L. Shepard, Hammerness, Darling-Hammond, & Rust, 2005).

As teachers, we should not only encourage meaningful learning through the strategies previously described—asking students to logically organize related ideas, think of new examples, speculate about implications, and so on—but we should also communicate that school topics are to be *understood* rather than memorized. In other words, we should encourage students to adopt a meaningful learning set. For example, we might frequently ask students to explain their reasoning, and our assignments and assessment tasks should require true understanding rather than rote memorization (Ausubel et al., 1978; Middleton & Midgley, 2002; L. Shepard et al., 2005).

Ideally, students should gain a conceptual understanding of classroom topics; that is, they should form many logical connections among related concepts and principles. For example, rather than simply memorize basic mathematical computation procedures, students should learn how those procedures reflect underlying principles of mathematics. And rather than learn historical facts as a list of unrelated people, places, and dates, students should place those facts within the context of major social and religious trends, migration patterns, economic conditions, human personality characteristics, and so on. The more interrelationships students form within the subject matter they're learning— in other words, the better they *organize* it—the more easily they'll be able to remember and apply it later on (e.g., Hecht & Vagi, 2010; M. C. Linn & Eylon, 2011; J. J. White & Rumsey, 1994).

Constructing an integrated understanding of any complex topic inevitably takes time. Accordingly, many educators advocate the principle *Less is more: Less* material studied thoroughly (rather than superficially) is learned *more* completely and with greater understanding (e.g., Sizer, 1992, 2004). Following are several more specific strategies for promoting conceptual understanding of classroom subject matter:

- Organize units around a few core ideas or issues, always relating specific content back to this core.
- Explore each topic in depth—for example, by considering many examples, examining cause–and–effect relationships, and discovering how specific details relate to more general principles.
- Regularly connect new ideas to students' personal experiences and to things students have previously learned at school.
- Show students—through the statements made, the questions asked, the assignments given, and the criteria used to evaluate achievement—that conceptual understanding is far more important than knowledge of specific facts.
- Ask students to teach what they've learned to others. Teaching others encourages them to focus on and pull together main ideas in ways that make sense. (Brophy, 2004; Brophy, Alleman, & Knighton, 2009; Hatano & Inagaki, 1993; Middleton & Midgley, 2002; Perkins & Ritchhart, 2004; Roscoe & Chi, 2007; VanSledright & Brophy, 1992; J. J. White & Rumsey, 1994)

## USING MNEMONICS IN THE ABSENCE OF RELEVANT PRIOR KNOWLEDGE

Some things are hard to make sense of—that is, hard to learn meaningfully. For instance, why do bones in the human body have such names as *fibula, humerus,* and *ulna?* Why is *Au* the chemical symbol for gold? Why is Augusta the capital of Maine? From most students' perspectives, there is no rhyme or reason to such facts.

**meaningful learning set** Attitude that one can make sense of the information one is studying.

**conceptual understanding** Meaningfully learned and well-integrated knowledge about a topic, including many logical connections among specific concepts and ideas.

**FIGURE 6.8** **Common mnemonic techniques**

## Verbal Mediation

A **verbal mediator** is a word or phrase that creates a logical connection, or bridge, between two pieces of information. Verbal mediators can be used for paired pieces of information such as foreign language words and their English meanings, countries and their capitals, chemical elements and their symbols, and words and their spellings. Following are examples:

| Information to Be Learned | Verbal Mediator |
|---|---|
| *Handschuh* is German for "glove." | A glove is a *shoe* for the *hand*. |
| Quito is the capital of Ecuador. | *Mosquitoes* are at the *equator*. |
| *Au* is the symbol for gold. | *Ay, you* stole my *gold* watch! |
| The word *principal* (a school administrator) ends with the letters *pal* (not *ple*). | The *principal* is my *pal*. |
| The *humerus* bone is the large arm bone above the elbow. | The *humorous* bone is just above the *funny* bone. |
| Amendment *2* to the U.S. Constitution is the right to *bear arms*. | A *bear* has *two arms*. |

## Keyword Method

Like verbal mediation, the **keyword method** aids memory by making a connection between two things. This technique is especially helpful when there is no logical verbal mediator to fill the gap—for example, when there is no obvious sentence or phrase to relate a foreign language word to its English meaning. The keyword method involves two steps, which we can illustrate using the Spanish word *amor* and its English meaning, "love":

1.  Identify a concrete object to represent each piece of information. The object can be either a commonly used symbol (e.g., a heart to symbolize *love*) or a sound-alike word (e.g., a suit of armor to represent *amor*). Such objects are *keywords*.

2.  Form a mental picture—that is, a visual image—of the two objects together. For example, to remember that *amor* means *love*, we might picture a knight in a suit of armor with a huge red heart painted on his chest.

You used the keyword method when you completed the "Five Chinese Words" exercise earlier in the chapter. Here are additional examples:

| Information to Be Learned | Visual Image |
|---|---|
| *Das Pferd* is German for *horse*. | Picture a *horse* driving a *Ford*. |
| Augusta is the capital of Maine. | Picture a *gust of* wind blowing through a horse's *mane*. |
| Tchaikovsky composed the ballet *Swan Lake*. | Picture a *swan* swimming on a *lake*, wearing a *tie* and *cough*ing. |

## Superimposed Meaningful Structure

A larger body of information, such as a list of items, can often be learned by superimposing a meaningful visual or verbal organizational structure on it—for instance, a familiar shape, word, sentence, rhythm, poem, or story. The following are examples of such **superimposed meaningful structures**:

| Information to Be Learned | Superimposed Meaningful Structure |
|---|---|
| The shape of Italy | A boot |
| The five Great Lakes (Huron, Ontario, Michigan, Erie, Superior) | HOMES |
| Lines on the treble clef (E G B D F) | Elvis's Guitar Broke Down Friday, *or* Every Good Boy Does Fine. |
| The distinction between stalagmites and stalactites | When the "mites" go up, the "tites" come down. |
| The number of days in each month | Thirty days has September, . . . |

Superimposed meaningful structures can be used to remember procedures as well as declarative information. Here are three examples:

| Procedure to Be Learned | Superimposed Meaningful Structure |
|---|---|
| Shooting a free throw in basketball | BEEF: Balance the ball, Elbows in, Elevate the arms, Follow through. |
| Simplifying a complex algebraic expression | Please Excuse My Dear Aunt Sally: First, simplify terms within **p**arentheses, then terms with an **e**xponent, then terms to be **m**ultiplied or **d**ivided, and finally terms to be **a**dded or **s**ubtracted. |
| Turning a screw (clockwise to tighten, counterclockwise to loosen) | Righty, tighty, lefty, loosey. |

When students have trouble finding relationships between new material and their prior knowledge, or when a body of information seemingly has no organizational structure (as is true for many lists), special memory tricks known as mnemonics can help students remember classroom material more effectively. Three commonly used mnemonics—verbal mediation, the keyword method, and superimposed meaningful structures—are described in Figure 6.8.

Research consistently supports the effectiveness of using mnemonics in learning (e.g., R. K. Atkinson et al., 1999; M. S. Jones, Levin, Levin, & Beitzel, 2000; Pressley, Levin, & Delaney, 1982). Their effectiveness lies in their conformity with a basic principle of long-term memory storage: Learners find some sort of meaning—even if that "meaning" is a bit contrived—in what might otherwise be nonsensical information. The artificial organization structure that some mnemonics provide is an additional plus. Imposing rhythm on a body of information—for instance, embedding the information in a song or hip-hop lyrics—is one way of giving it structure and can be especially beneficial when music is a significant part of students' cultures (B. A. Allen & Boykin, 1991; Barton, Tan, & Rivet, 2008; Tyler et al., 2008).

Mnemonics are helpful for remembering seemingly arbitrary bits of information. Watch two examples in "Using Mnemonics."

# When Knowledge Construction Goes Awry: Addressing Learners' Misconceptions

When learners construct their own understandings, there is, of course, no guarantee that they'll construct accurate ones. Occasionally they may instead construct misconceptions—beliefs that are inconsistent with commonly accepted and well-validated explanations of phenomena or events. In science, for example, some of students' beliefs might be at odds with data collected over the course of decades or centuries of scientific research. And in history, students' understandings of certain events might be inconsistent with existing historical records and artifacts from the time period in question. Figure 6.9 presents misconceptions that researchers have often observed in students—not only in children and adolescents, but occasionally in college students as well.

In many instances students' misconceptions arise out of their own well-intended efforts to make sense of the things they see—for instance, a sun and moon that seem to "travel" across the sky. But society and culture can foster misconceptions as well. Sometimes common expressions in language misrepresent the true nature of physical events. For instance, when we talk about the sun "rising" and "setting," children may easily conclude that the sun revolves around the earth, rather than vice versa. In addition, fairy tales and television cartoon programs may misrepresent what we know to be true in, say, physics or paleontology—as examples, you've probably seen cartoon bad guys run off cliffs and remain suspended in the air until they realize there's nothing holding them up, and perhaps you've watched cartoon caveman Fred Flintstone riding a brontosaurus to work. Unfortunately, students can also acquire erroneous ideas from other people, occasionally including teachers and textbook authors (Brophy et al., 2009; Glynn, Yeany, & Britton, 1991; M. C. Linn & Eylon, 2011; Wiser & Smith, 2008).

Regardless of how students' misconceptions originate, they can wreak havoc on new learning. As a result of elaborating on new information—a process that usually facilitates learning—students may interpret or distort the information to be consistent with what they already "know" and thus continue to believe what they've always believed. For example, one eleventh-grade physics class was studying the idea that an object's mass and weight do *not*, by themselves, affect the speed at which the object falls. Students were asked to build egg containers that would keep eggs from breaking when dropped from a third-floor window. They were told that on the day of the egg drop, they would record the time it took for the eggs to reach the ground. Convinced that heavier objects fall faster, a student named Barry added several nails to his egg's container. Yet when he dropped it, classmates timed its fall at 1.49 seconds—a time very similar to that for other students' lighter containers. Rather than acknowledge that light and heavy objects fall at the same rate, Barry explained the result by rationalizing that "the people weren't timing real good" (Hynd, 1998a, p. 34).

When students have misunderstandings such as Barry's, we must work hard to promote conceptual change, a process of revising or overhauling an existing theory or belief system in such a way that new, discrepant information can be better understood and explained. Don't let the term *conceptual* mislead you here: For the most part, we're talking about changing tightly interconnected sets of ideas rather than changing single, isolated concepts.

If you took the OOPS test in Chapter 1, you may have discovered some of your own misconceptions about human learning and development.

**mnemonic** Memory aid or trick designed to help students learn and remember one or more specific pieces of information.

**verbal mediator** Word or phrase that forms a logical connection, or cognitive "bridge," between two pieces of information.

**keyword method** Mnemonic technique in which an association is made between two ideas by forming a visual image of one or more concrete objects (*keywords*) that either sound similar to or symbolically represent those ideas.

**superimposed meaningful structure** Familiar shape, word, sentence, poem, or story imposed on information to facilitate recall.

**misconception** Belief that is inconsistent with commonly accepted and well-validated explanations of phenomena or events.

**conceptual change** Significant revision of an existing theory or belief system, enabling new and discrepant information to be better understood and explained.

**FIGURE 6.9  Common student beliefs and misconceptions**

### In Biology

- Plants use their roots to take in "food" (e.g., water, nutrients) from the soil. (From the perspective of biology, plants produce their own food through photosynthesis.)

- Vision involves something moving outward from the eye toward the object being seen. (In reality, the opposite is true: Light rays bounce off the object to the eye.)

### In Astronomy

- The sun revolves around the earth. It "rises" in the morning and "sets" in the evening, at which point it "goes" to the other side of the earth.

- The earth is shaped like a round, flat disk, with people living on its top, or a hollowed-out sphere, with people living on a horizontal surface in its middle.

- Space has an absolute "up" and "down"; people standing at the South Pole will fall off the earth.

### In Climatology

- The four seasons are the result of the earth's distance from the sun; the earth is closer to the sun in the summer, farther away in the winter. (In fact, distance from the sun is largely irrelevant; seasons are the result of the angle at which the sun's rays hit different parts of the earth's surface.)

### In Physics

- Objects exist for a purpose; for example, some rocks are pointy so that animals that live nearby can scratch themselves when they have an itch.

- Any moving object has a force acting on it. For example, a ball thrown in the air continues to be pushed upward by the force of the throw until it begins its descent. (In reality, force is needed only to change the direction or speed of an object; otherwise, *inertia* is at work.)

- If an astronaut were to open the hatch while traveling in outer place, he or she would be "sucked out" by the vacuum in space. (In reality, the astronaut would be blown out by the air inside the spacecraft.)

### In Mathematics

- Multiplication always leads to a bigger number. (This principle holds true only when the multiplier is larger than 1.)

- Division always leads to a smaller number. (This principle holds true only when the divisor is larger than 1.)

- Parallelograms must be slanted; rectangles must have widths different from their lengths. (In reality, parallelograms can have right angles, in which case they're also rectangles; rectangles can have four equal sides, in which case they're also squares.)

### In History

- Early human beings lived at the same time that dinosaurs did.

- Christopher Columbus was the first person to believe that the world is round rather than flat.

### In Geography and Social Studies

- The lines separating countries or states are marked on the earth.

- Erosion is largely something that happened in the past; for example, the Grand Canyon is no longer eroding.

- People are poor only because they don't have enough money to "buy" a job; giving a poor person a small amount of money will make the person rich.

*Sources:* Brewer, 2008; Brophy et al., 2009; Chi, 2008; De Corte, Greer, & Verschaffel, 1996; Delval, 1994; diSessa, 1996; H. Gardner, Torff, & Hatch, 1996; Haskell, 2001; Hynd, 2003; Kelemen, 1999, 2004; V. R. Lee, 2010; Martínez, Bannan-Ritland, Kitsantas, & Baek, 2008; Masters et al., 2010; K. J. Roth & Anderson, 1988; Sneider & Pulos, 1983; Tirosh & Graeber, 1990; Vosniadou & Brewer, 1987; Vosniadou, Vamvakoussi, & Skopeliti, 2008; Winer & Cottrell, 1996.

## OBSTACLES TO CONCEPTUAL CHANGE

Teachers often present new information with the expectation that it will easily replace students' erroneous beliefs about a topic. And in fact some misconceptions are easily corrected. Yet students of all ages can hold quite stubbornly to certain counterproductive beliefs about the world, even after considerable instruction that explicitly contradicts those beliefs. Theorists have offered several possible explanations about why students' misconceptions can be so resistant to change:

- *Most children and adolescents have a confirmation bias.* Learners of all ages (even college students!) tend to look for information that confirms their existing beliefs and to ignore or discredit contradictory evidence—a phenomenon known as confirmation bias (e.g., De Lisi & Golbeck, 1999; Hynd, 1998b; P. K. Murphy & Mason, 2006). For example, when students in a high school science lab observe results that contradict what they expected to happen, they might complain, "Our equipment isn't working right" or "I can never do science right anyway" (Minstrell & Stimpson, 1996, p. 192).

- *Students may believe that their existing beliefs better explain their everyday experiences.* Well-established scientific theories are often fairly abstract and sometimes seem to contradict everyday reality (D. B. Clark, 2006; M. C. Linn, 2008; Wiser & Smith, 2008). For example, in physics, although the law of inertia tells us that force is needed to *start* an object in motion but not to *keep* it in motion, we know from experience that if we want to move a heavy object across the floor, we must continue to push it until we get it where we want it (Driver, Asoko, Leach, Mortimer, & Scott, 1994). And although virtually any piece of matter has some weight, a very small piece of Styrofoam may feel weightless in our hands (C. L. Smith, 2007).

- *Some beliefs are integrated into cohesive theories, with many interrelationships existing among various ideas.* In such circumstances, changing misconceptions involves changing an entire organized body of knowledge rather than a single belief (Sinatra & Pintrich, 2003; C. L. Smith, Maclin, Grosslight, & Davis, 1997; Vosniadou, 2008). For example, the belief that the sun revolves around the earth may be part of a more general earth-centered view of things, perhaps one that includes the moon, stars, and other heavenly bodies revolving around the earth as well. In reality, of course, the moon revolves around the earth, the earth revolves around the sun, and other stars aren't directly involved with the earth in one way or another. Yet the earth-centered view is a much easier one to understand and accept (on the surface, at least), and everything fits so nicely together.

- *Students may fail to notice an inconsistency between new information and their existing beliefs.* Sometimes this happens because students learn the new information in a rote manner, without relating it to things they already know and believe. In other instances it occurs because existing misconceptions take the form of *implicit knowledge*—knowledge that students aren't consciously aware of. In either case, students don't realize that the material they're studying contradicts their current understandings, and thus they may continue to apply their misconceptions when interpreting new situations (Hynd, 2003; M. C. Linn & Eylon, 2011; P. K. Murphy, 2007; Ohlsson, 2009; Strike & Posner, 1992).

- *Students have a personal or emotional investment in their existing beliefs.* For one reason or another, students may be especially committed to certain beliefs, perhaps insisting "This theory is what I believe in! Nobody can make me change it!" (Mason, 2003, p. 228). In some instances their beliefs may be an integral part of their religion or culture (Mosborg, 2002; Porat, 2004; Sinatra & Mason, 2008). In other cases students may interpret information that contradicts their existing understandings as a threat to their self-esteem (Linnenbrink & Pintrich, 2003; Minstrell & Stimpson, 1996; Sherman & Cohen, 2002).

## PROMOTING CONCEPTUAL CHANGE

For the reasons just identified, promoting conceptual change can be quite a challenge. Not only must we help students learn new things, but we must also help them *un*learn—or at least *inhibit*—their existing beliefs (Hynd, 2003). Following are strategies that seem to have an impact, especially when used in combination.

**confirmation bias** Tendency to seek information that confirms rather than discredits current beliefs.

Novice researchers often "prove" what they expect to find, a phenomenon known as *confirmation bias*. Watch "Designing Experiments."

Students' culturally based *worldviews* also come into play here, as you'll discover in Chapter 8.

🍏 *Identify existing misconceptions before instruction begins.* As teachers, we can more easily address students' misconceptions when we know what they *are* (P. K. Murphy & Alexander, 2004, 2008; Putnam, 1992). Thus, we should probably begin any new topic by assessing students' current beliefs about the topic—perhaps simply by asking a few informal questions and probing further if students' initial explanations are vague. As an example, an 11-year-old once described rain as "water that falls out of a cloud when the clouds evaporate." The response has an element of truth— evaporation is an essential process in cloud formation—but not quite on target: In fact, rain results a bit later in the water cycle as a result of *condensation*. A series of follow-up questions eventually revealed a rather unique understanding: The water "comes down at little times like a salt shaker when you turn it upside down. It doesn't all come down at once 'cause there's little holes [in the cloud] and it just comes out" (Stepans, 1991, p. 94). This conception of a cloud as a salt shaker is hardly consistent with scientific views of rain and should definitely be addressed during instruction.

Informal preassessments of students' current understandings will be especially important in your first few years of teaching. As you gain experience teaching a particular topic year after year, you may eventually find that you can anticipate what students' prior beliefs and misbeliefs about the topic are likely to be.

🍏 *Look for—and then build on—kernels of truth in students' existing understandings.* Often students' current understandings have a partly-right-and-partly-wrong quality (diSessa, 1996, 2006; Vosniadou, 2008). For example, the 11-year-old with the salt-shaker explanation of rain correctly knew that evaporation is somehow involved in the water cycle, and such knowledge would be a good starting point for further instruction. Among other things, a teacher might (1) help the child understand how evaporation and condensation are essentially opposite processes that involve either changing from liquid form to vapor form (evaporation) or vice versa (condensation); and (2) explain how a cloud actually is *water itself* rather than a shakerlike water container.

🍏 *Convince students that their existing beliefs need revision.* We can more effectively promote conceptual change when we show students how new information contradicts what they currently believe and when we demonstrate why their existing conceptions are inadequate. In Jean Piaget's terminology, we need to create *disequilibrium,* perhaps with strategies such as these:

🍏 Present phenomena and ask questions that lead students to find weaknesses in their current understandings.

🍏 Have students conduct experiments to test various hypotheses and predictions.

🍏 Ask students to provide several explanations for puzzling phenomena and to discuss the pros and cons of each one.

🍏 Show how one explanation of an event or phenomenon is more plausible (i.e., makes more sense) than others.

🍏 Have students apply the new ideas to real-life situations and problems. (Chinn & Malhotra, 2002; Chinn & Samarapungavan, 2009; D. B. Clark, 2006; M. C. Linn & Eylon, 2011; P. K. Murphy & Mason, 2006; Pine & Messer, 2000; G. J. Posner, Strike, Hewson, & Gertzog, 1982; K. J. Roth, 2002; Sinatra & Pintrich, 2003; C. L. Smith, 2007; Vosniadou, 2008)

Such strategies might encompass a wide variety of instructional methods, including demonstrations, hands-on activities, teacher explanations, small-group or whole-class discussions, and writing assignments. But all of these strategies have one thing in common: a focus on meaningful learning rather than rote memorization.

🍏 *Motivate students to learn correct explanations.* Students will be most likely to engage in meaningful learning and undergo conceptual change when they're motivated to do so. At a minimum, they must be interested in the subject matter, see it as useful in helping them achieve their personal goals, set their sights on mastering it, and have sufficient self-confidence to believe they *can* master it. Furthermore, the classroom should be socially and emotionally *supportive* of conceptual change. For example, students must feel confident that (1) their teacher and classmates won't ridicule them for their initially erroneous or partly-right-but-partly-wrong ideas and (2) the ultimate goal of a lesson is understanding the subject matter rather than simply performing well on a quiz or assignment (Hatano & Inagaki, 2003; Pintrich, Marx, & Boyle, 1993; Sinatra & Mason, 2008).

To promote conceptual change, teachers must bring students' current misconceptions into focus. For example, watch "Properties of Air."

Chapter 11 describes many strategies for motivating students to master classroom subject matter.

🍏 *Monitor what students say and write for signs of persistent misconceptions.* Some misconceptions and only-partly-correct understandings may persist despite our best efforts. Throughout a lesson, then, we should often check students' beliefs about the topic at hand, looking for subtle signs that their understanding isn't completely on target and giving corrective feedback when necessary. As an illustration, imagine a lesson about human vision that includes the following general principles:

- The retina of the human eye detects light rays that reach it; the eye sends information about these light rays to the brain for interpretation.

- A person sees an object when (1) light rays travel from the sun or other light source to the object, (2) bounce off of the object, and then (3) travel to the retina.

- Light rays bounce off of some (opaque) objects but go through other (transparent) objects.

A common misconception in both children and adults is that vision involves something going *out from the eye to the object,* rather than vice versa (K. J. Roth & Anderson, 1988; Winer & Cottrell, 1996; Winer, Cottrell, Gregg, Fournier, & Bica, 2002). Therefore, this misconception is something we would want to be on the lookout for throughout the lesson. For instance, we might show students the drawing in Figure 6.10 and ask them whether the girl can see the car. Several of them might respond, "No, she can't see through it" or "It's opaque." The phrase *see through* is one that people often use when talking about transparent objects, but it implies that something is traveling from—not *to*—the eye. We would thus want to ask follow-up questions to pin down their reasoning: "What do you mean, she can't see *through* it?" "What does *opaque* mean?" and "What are the light rays doing?"

Assessment of students' comprehension is important *after* a lesson as well. We're more likely to detect and correct misconceptions when we ask students to *explain* and *apply* what they've learned, rather than just spitting back memorized facts, definitions, and formulas (D. B. Clark, 2006; Pine & Messer, 2000; K. J. Roth, 1990). Even so, we must remember that true and lasting conceptual change may take considerable time and instruction—perhaps several years' worth—especially if it involves overhauling a complex, interrelated set of student-constructed ideas (Vosniadou, 2008).

**FIGURE 6.10** **Can the girl see the car? If not, why not?**

🍏 Remember that true and lasting conceptual change about complex phenomena can take considerable time and instruction.

# Long-Term Memory Retrieval

As you've already discovered, some of the information stored in long-term memory is easily retrieved later on. Other pieces of information are harder to find, and still others may never be found at all. Retrieving information from long-term memory appears to involve following a pathway of associations; it's a process of mentally going down Memory Lane. One idea reminds us of another idea—that is, one idea *activates* another—the second idea reminds us of a third idea, and so on. The process is similar to what happened when you followed your train of thought from the word *horse* earlier in the chapter. If the pathway of associations eventually leads us to what we're trying to remember, we do indeed remember it. If the path takes us in another direction, we're out of luck.

Learners are more likely to remember something later on if, in the process of storing it, they connect it with something else in long-term memory. Ideally, the new and the old have a logical relationship. To illustrate this idea, let's return once again to all that mail you routinely get in your mail and e-mail boxes. Imagine that, on average, you receive five important items—five things you really want to save—each day. That adds up to more than 1,800 items a year. Over the course of 15 years, you would have more than 27,000 important things stashed somewhere in your home, on your computer, or on a flash drive or other back-up storage device.

Imagine that one day you hear that stock in a clothing company (Mod Bod Jeans) has tripled in value. You remember that your wealthy Aunt Agnes bought you some Mod Bod stock for your birthday several years ago, and you presumably decided that the paperwork documenting her purchase was important enough to save. But where in the world did you put it? How easily you find it—in fact, whether you find it at all—depends on how you've been storing your mail as you've accumulated it. If you've been storing it in a logical, organized fashion—for instance, all the bills you've paid by regular mail on a closet shelf, all banking and investment paperwork in alphabetical order in a file drawer, and all electronic documents from family and friends in labeled folders on your computer—you should quickly find Aunt Agnes's gift. But if you simply tossed each day's mail and e-mail randomly about, you'll be searching for a long, long time, possibly without ever finding a trace of the Mod Bod stock.

Like a home with 15 years' worth of mail, long-term memory contains a great deal of information. And like your search for the Mod Bod purchase, the ease with which information is retrieved from long-term memory depends somewhat on whether the information has been stored in a logical place—that is, whether it's connected to related ideas. By making connections to existing knowledge—that is, by engaging in meaningful learning—we'll know where to look for information when we need it. Otherwise, we may never retrieve it again.

## FACTORS AFFECTING RETRIEVAL

Even when people connect new information to their existing knowledge base, they can't always find it when they need it. We now look at several factors affecting retrieval from long-term memory.

### MULTIPLE CONNECTIONS WITH EXISTING KNOWLEDGE AND A VARIETY OF CONTEXTS

Sometimes learners acquire and practice certain behaviors and ways of thinking in a very limited set of environments—say, in their math classes or science labs. When this happens, the learners may associate those behaviors and ways of thinking *only* with those particular environments and therefore fail to retrieve what they've learned when they're in other contexts. This tendency for some responses and cognitive processes to be associated with and retrieved only in a very limited range of circumstances is known as situated learning or situated cognition (e.g., J. S. Brown, Collins, & Duguid, 1989; Lave & Wenger, 1991; Robbins & Aydede, 2009). For example, if students associate principles of geometry only with math classes, they may not retrieve those principles at times when geometry would come in handy—say, when trying to determine whether a 10-inch pizza that costs eight dollars is a better value than an 8-inch pizza that costs six dollars.

In general, learners are more likely to retrieve information when they have *many* possible pathways to it—in other words, when they've associated the information with many other things they know and with many different contexts in which they might use it. Making multiple connections is like using cross-references in your mail storage system. You may have filed the Mod Bod paperwork in the banking/investments file drawer, but you may also have written its location on notes-to-self you've put in other places—perhaps with your birth certificate (after all, you received the stock on your birthday) and in a computer folder of family documents and photos (because a family member gave you the stock). By looking in one of these logical places, you'll discover where to find the Mod Bod documentation.

As teachers, we can help students more effectively remember classroom subject matter over the long run if we show how it relates to *many* other things they already know. For example, we can show them how new material relates to one or more of the following:

- Concepts and ideas within the same subject area (e.g., showing how multiplication is related to addition)
- Concepts and ideas in other subject areas (e.g., talking about how scientific discoveries have affected historical events)
- Students' general knowledge of the world (e.g., relating the concept of *inertia* to how passengers are affected when a car quickly turns a sharp corner)
- Students' personal experiences (e.g., finding similarities between the family feud in *Romeo and Juliet* and students' own interpersonal conflicts)
- Students' current activities and needs outside the classroom (e.g., showing how persuasive writing skills might be used to craft an essay for a college application)

Help students connect important ideas to a variety of disciplines and real-world situations.

**situated learning and cognition** Knowledge, behaviors, and thinking skills acquired and used primarily within certain contexts, with limited or no retrieval and use in other contexts.

### DISTINCTIVENESS

Learners are more likely to remember things that are unique in some way—for instance, things that are new, unusual, or a bit bizarre (R. R. Hunt & Worthen, 2006). For example, second graders are more likely to remember a visit to the local firehouse than, say, their teacher's explanation of what a *noun* is. And when U.S. high school students recall what they've learned about events leading up to the American Revolution, they're more likely to remember the Boston Tea Party—a unique and colorful illustration of colonists' dissatisfaction with British taxation policies—than, say, the Quartering Act or the publication of Thomas Paine's *Common Sense*. Certainly, learners are more likely to *pay attention* to distinctive information, increasing the odds that they store it in long-term memory in the first place. But even when attention and initial learning have been the same, distinctive information is easier to retrieve than dull-and-ordinary information (Craik, 2006; Mather & Sutherland, 2011).

### EMOTIONAL OVERTONES

As learners pay attention to and think about new information, their thoughts and memories sometimes become emotionally charged—a phenomenon called hot cognition. For example, learners might get excited when they read about advances in science that could lead to effective treatments for cancer, spinal cord injuries, or mental illness. Or they might feel quite sad when they read about living conditions in certain parts of the world. And they will, we hope, get angry when they learn about atrocities committed against African American slaves in the pre-Civil War days of the United States or about large-scale genocides carried out in more recent times in Europe, Africa, and Asia.

When information is emotionally charged in such ways, learners are more likely to pay attention to it, continue to think about it for an extended period, and repeatedly elaborate on it (Bower, 1994; Heuer & Reisberg, 1992; Zeelenberg, Wagenmakers, & Rotteveel, 2006). And over the long run, learners can usually retrieve material with high emotional content more easily than they can recall relatively nonemotional information (LaBar & Phelps, 1998; Phelps & Sharot, 2008; Reisberg & Heuer, 1992).[1] It appears that students' emotional reactions to classroom topics become integral parts of their network of associations in long-term memory (Bower & Forgas, 2001; Siegel, 2012).

Academic subject matter certainly doesn't need to be dry and emotionless. In addition to presenting subject matter that evokes strong emotions, we can promote hot cognition by revealing our own feelings about a topic. For instance, we might bring in newspaper articles and other outside materials about which we're excited, or we might share the particular questions and issues about which we ourselves are concerned (Brophy, 2004; R. P. Perry, 1985).

### REGULAR PRACTICE

As noted earlier, rehearsal—mindlessly repeating information over and over within the course of a few seconds or minutes—is a relatively *in*effective way of getting information into long-term memory. But by "regular practice," I mean repetition over a lengthy time span: reviewing and using information and skills at periodic intervals over the course of a few weeks, months, or years. When practice is spread out in this manner—ideally in a variety of contexts—people of all ages learn something better and remember it longer (Dempster, 1991; Proctor & Dutta, 1995; Rohrer & Pashler, 2010).

When learners continue to practice things they've already mastered, they eventually achieve automaticity: They can retrieve what they've learned quickly and effortlessly and can use it almost without thinking (J. R. Anderson, 2005; Pashler, Rohrer, Cepeda, & Carpenter, 2007; Proctor & Dutta, 1995). As an example, think of driving a car, a complicated skill that you can probably perform easily. Your first attempts at driving many years ago may have required a great deal of mental effort. But perhaps now you can drive without having to pay much attention to what you're doing. Even if your car has a standard transmission that frequently requires stepping on a clutch and shifting gears, driving is, for you, an automatic activity.

Learning some knowledge and skills to a level of automaticity has a second advantage as well. Remember that working memory has a limited capacity: The active, consciously-thinking

Make important ideas distinctive in some way, perhaps by illustrating them with vivid examples or engaging hands-on experiences.

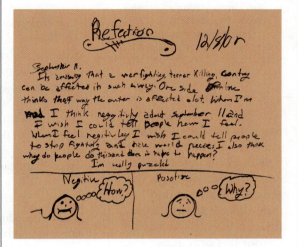

Information and events that evoke strong emotional reactions often remain vivid in memory for quite some time. In this reflection in a class journal, written more than a year after the 9/11 terrorist attacks on the World Trade Center and Pentagon, 12-year-old Amaryth still has strong feelings about the attacks.

Convey your own enthusiasm for a topic.

**hot cognition** Learning or cognitive processing that is emotionally charged.

**automaticity** Ability to respond quickly and efficiently while mentally processing or physically performing a task.

---

[1]Occasionally people may have trouble retrieving highly anxiety-arousing memories. This phenomenon, known as *repression*, is most likely to occur with traumatic personal events (M. C. Anderson et al., 2004; Erdelyi, 2010; Pezdek & Banks, 1996). It's unlikely to be a factor in the retrieval of classroom subject matter.

part of the human memory system can handle only so much at a time. When much of its capacity must be used for recalling isolated facts or carrying out simple procedures, little room is left for addressing more complex situations or tasks. One key reason for learning some facts and procedures to the point of automaticity, then, is to free up working memory capacity for complex tasks and problems that require those simpler facts and procedures (De La Paz & McCutchen, 2011; Kalyuga, 2010; Stanovich, 2000). For example, second graders who are reading a story can better focus their efforts on understanding it if they don't have to sound out words like *before* and *after*. High school chemistry students can more easily interpret the expression $Na_2CO_3$ (sodium carbonate) if they don't have to stop to think about what the symbols *Na, C,* and *O* represent.

Unfortunately, automaticity is achieved in only one way: practice, practice, and more practice. Practice doesn't necessarily make perfect, but it does make knowledge more durable and more easily retrievable. When learners use information and skills frequently, they essentially pave their retrieval pathways—in some cases creating superhighways. This is *not* to say that we should continually assign drill-and-practice exercises involving isolated facts and procedures (e.g., see Figure 6.11). Such activities promote rote (rather than meaningful) learning, are often boring, and are unlikely to convince students of the value of the subject matter (Mac Iver, Reuman, & Main, 1995). A more effective approach is to routinely incorporate basic knowledge and skills into a variety of meaningful and enjoyable activities—problem-solving tasks, group projects, games, brainteasers, and so on.

### RELEVANT RETRIEVAL CUES

If you were educated in North America, then at one time or another you probably learned the names of the five Great Lakes. Yet at any given moment you may have trouble retrieving all five, even though they're all still stored somewhere in your long-term memory. Perhaps Lake Michigan doesn't come to mind when you retrieve the other four. The *HOMES* mnemonic presented in Figure 6.8 provides a retrieval cue—a hint about where to "look" in long-term memory. The mnemonic tells you that one lake begins with the letter *M,* prompting you to search among the *M* words you know until (we hope) you find *Michigan.* Learners are more likely to retrieve information when relevant retrieval cues are present to start their search of long-term memory in the right direction (e.g., Morris, Bransford, & Franks, 1977; Tulving & Thomson, 1973).

Providing retrieval cues is often useful in the classroom, especially when students have trouble recalling information that might help them remember or apply *other* information. For example, if a student asks what the symbol *Au* stands for, we might respond by saying "One day we talked about how *Au* comes from the Latin word *aurum.* Can you remember what *aurum* means?" Another example comes from one of my former teacher interns, Jess Jensen. A student in her eighth-grade history class had been writing about the Battle of New Orleans, which was a decisive victory for the United States in the War of 1812. The following exchange took place:

> *Student:* Why was the Battle of New Orleans important?
>
> *Jess:* Look at the map. Where is New Orleans?
>
> [The student finds New Orleans.]
>
> *Jess:* Why is it important?
>
> *Student:* Oh! It's near the mouth of the Mississippi. It was important for controlling transportation up and down the river.

In the early grades, teachers typically provide many retrieval cues for their students; for instance, they remind students about tasks they need to do at certain times ("I hear the fire alarm. Remember, we must all walk quietly during a fire drill"). But as students grow older, they must develop greater independence, relying more on themselves and less on their teachers for the things they need to remember. At all grade levels we can teach students ways of providing retrieval cues for *themselves.* For example, if we expect first graders to get a permission slip signed, we might ask them to write a reminder on a piece of masking tape that they put on their jacket or backpack. If we give junior high school students a major assignment due in several weeks, we might suggest that they tape a note with the due date to their bedside table or add an appropriate

Occasionally conduct activities in which students review and practice things they've learned in previous weeks, months, or years.

**FIGURE 6.11** Occasional rote practice of numerals and letters can be helpful in promoting automaticity, but too much conveys the message that learning basic skills is boring and tedious. Here 5-year-old Gunnar has practiced writing numerals 1 through 9. Notice that he got practice in writing 9 backward!

**retrieval cue** Stimulus that provides guidance about where to "look" for a piece of information in long-term memory.

reminder to their cell phone calendar. One tenth grader developed several effective retrieval cues, each appropriate for certain situations:

> Homework is written down in my agenda book. If it is something to do when I get home, I will write it on my hand. If I have something to do in the next few days, I write it on a note card in my wallet, and whenever I go to get money, I will think to do it.

## WAIT TIME

**Wait time** is the length of time a teacher allows to pass after the teacher or a student says something before the teacher says something else. In many classrooms, wait time is insufficient for most students to retrieve information that might be relevant to a teacher's or classmate's question or comment. For instance, when teachers ask students a question, many wait for only a very short time—perhaps a second or less—and if they don't get a response, they ask another student the same question, rephrase the question, or answer the question themselves. Many teachers are equally reluctant to let much time elapse after students answer questions or make comments in class; on average, teachers allow one second or less of silence before responding to a statement or asking another question (Jegede & Olajide, 1995; M. B. Rowe, 1974, 1987).

Students benefit tremendously simply from being given a little time to think. When teachers instead allow at least *three seconds* of wait time, more students participate in class—this is especially true for females and minority-group members—and students begin to respond to one another's comments and questions. In addition, students are more likely to support their reasoning with evidence or logic and more likely to speculate when they don't know an answer. Furthermore, they're more motivated to learn classroom subject matter, thereby increasing actual learning and decreasing behavior problems. Such changes are due, in part, to the fact that with increased wait time, *teachers'* behaviors change as well. Teachers ask fewer simple questions (e.g., those requiring recall of facts) and more thought-provoking ones (e.g., those requiring elaboration). They also modify the direction of discussion to accommodate students' comments and questions, and they allow their classes to pursue a topic in greater depth than they had originally anticipated. Moreover, their expectations for many students, especially low-achieving ones, begin to improve (Castagno & Brayboy, 2008; Giaconia, 1988; M. B. Rowe, 1974, 1987; Tharp, 1989; Tobin, 1987).

When our objective is simple recall—when students need to retrieve classroom material very quickly, to "know it cold"—then wait time should be short. Students may sometimes benefit from rapid-fire drill and practice to learn information and skills to automaticity. But when our instructional goals include more complex processing of ideas and issues, a longer wait time may give both our students and us the time needed to think things through.

## WHY LEARNERS SOMETIMES FORGET

Fortunately, people don't need to remember everything they've stored. For instance, you may have no reason to remember the Internet address of a website you looked at yesterday, the plot of last week's episode of a certain television show, or the due date of an assignment you turned in last semester. Much of the information learners encounter is, like junk mail, not worth keeping, and forgetting it enables learners to get rid of needless clutter (Schacter, 1999). But sometimes learners have trouble recalling what they *do* need to remember. Here we look at several possible explanations for why students may sometimes forget important information.

### FAILURE TO STORE OR CONSOLIDATE INFORMATION IN LONG-TERM MEMORY

As we've seen, a great deal of the information students encounter never reaches long-term memory. Perhaps students didn't pay attention in the first place, so the information never went beyond the sensory register. Or perhaps after attending to it, students didn't continue to process it, so it went no further than working memory.

Even when information does reach long-term memory, it needs some time to "firm up" in the brain—a process called **consolidation**. A good night's sleep after learning something new seems to facilitate this process (see the earlier Applying Brain Research feature). And an event

 Provide retrieval cues when appropriate. Also, teach students to develop their own retrieval cues for things they must remember to do.

 Give students time to think about and formulate responses to challenging questions.

**wait time**  Length of time a teacher pauses, either after asking a question or hearing a student's comment, before saying something further.

**consolidation**  Neurological process in which newly acquired knowledge is firmed up in the brain; often takes several hours, sometimes even longer.

that interferes with consolidation—such as a serious brain injury—may cause a student to forget things that happened several seconds, minutes, hours, or even longer prior to the event (Bauer, DeBoer, & Lukowski, 2007; Wixted, 2005).

### DECAY

Historically, many psychologists believed that once information is stored in long-term memory, it remains there permanently in some form (Loftus & Loftus, 1980). More recently, however, some psychologists have come to the conclusion that information can slowly weaken and eventually disappear—that is, it can **decay**—especially if it isn't used regularly (e.g., Altmann & Gray, 2002; Brainerd & Reyna, 2005; Schacter, 1999).

### INSUFFICIENT SEARCH OF LONG-TERM MEMORY

A man at the supermarket looks familiar, but you can't remember who he is or where you met him. He smiles at you and says, "Nice to see you again." Gulp! You desperately search your long-term memory for his name, but you've clearly forgotten who he is. A few days later you have a bowl of chili for dinner. The chili reminds you of the Chili for Charity supper at which you worked a few months back. Of course! You and the man at the supermarket had stood side by side serving chili to hundreds of people that night. Oh yes, you now recall, his name is Melville Herman.

Like you, students often have retrieval difficulties: They simply can't find something that's actually in long-term memory (e.g., Schacter, 1999). Sometimes they may stumble on the information later, while looking for something else. But at other times they never do retrieve it, perhaps because they've learned it by rote or don't have sufficient retrieval cues to guide their memory search.

### INTERFERENCE

Sometimes people can easily retrieve things they've learned but don't know what goes with what. To experience this phenomenon yourself, try the following exercise.

### EXPERIENCING FIRSTHAND
### SIX CHINESE WORDS

Following are six more Mandarin Chinese words and their English meanings (for simplicity I've omitted the pronunciation marks over the words). Read the words two or three times, and try to store them in your long-term memory. But don't do anything special to learn the words—for instance, don't intentionally develop mnemonics to help you remember them.

| Chinese | English |
| --- | --- |
| jung | middle |
| ting | listen |
| sung | deliver |
| peng | friend |
| ching | please |
| deng | wait |

Now cover up the list of words and test yourself. What is the Chinese word for *friend?* For *please?* For *listen?* For *wait?*

Did you find yourself getting confused, perhaps forgetting which English meaning went with each Chinese word? If you did, you were the victim of **interference**. The various pieces of information you stored in memory were interfering with one another—essentially, they were getting mixed up in your head. Interference is especially likely to occur when items are similar to one another and when they're learned in a rote rather than meaningful or mnemonic-based fashion (Dempster, 1985; Healey, Campbell, Hasher, & Ossher, 2010; Lustig, Konkel, & Jacoby, 2004). Interference was probably at work when Kanesha struggled to remember *tibia* and *fibula*—two similar-sounding bones in the lower leg—in the opening case study.

**decay** Gradual weakening of information stored in long-term memory, especially if the information is used infrequently or not at all.

**interference** Phenomenon whereby something stored in long-term memory inhibits one's ability to remember something else correctly.

## RECONSTRUCTION ERROR

Have you and a friend ever remembered the same event quite differently, even though the two of you were equally active participants at the time? Were you and your friend both certain of the accuracy of your own memories and convinced that the other person remembered incorrectly? Constructive processes in retrieval might explain this difference of opinion. Retrieval isn't necessarily an all-or-nothing phenomenon. Sometimes learners retrieve part of the information they're seeking but can't recall the rest. They may logically but incorrectly fill in the gaps using their general knowledge and assumptions about the world—a form of forgetting called reconstruction error (Levstik, 2011; Roediger & McDermott, 2000; Schacter, 1999). If certain details are important to remember, then, we must help students study and learn them in a memorable fashion.

When important details are difficult to fill in logically or might easily be confused with one another, make sure students learn them well.

All of these explanations of forgetting underscore the importance of instructional strategies presented earlier: We must make sure students are paying attention, help them relate new material to things they already know, and give them frequent opportunities to review, practice, and apply the material.

# Diversity in Cognitive Processes

Children and adolescents differ considerably in the various factors that influence their ability to learn and remember in the classroom—attention, long-term memory storage processes, knowledge base, and so on. For example, on average, girls have a slight edge over boys in keeping their attention focused on classroom activities and in performing certain kinds of memory tasks, such as remembering lists and specific life events (Das, Naglieri, & Kirby, 1994; Halpern, 2006; Halpern & LaMay, 2000). And students of both genders vary in their general ability to think about, encode, and respond to new events and ideas quickly and easily (Coyle, Pillow, Snyder, & Kochunov, 2011; Danthiir, Roberts, Schulze, & Wilhelm, 2005; Demetriou, Christou, Spanoudis, & Platsidou, 2002). Some of this variability is the result of differences in working memory capacity. Students with a smaller overall capacity can have trouble remembering instructions, tackling complex problems, and staying on task; they're also more likely than their classmates to make careless mistakes and monitor the quality of their work (Alloway, Gathercole, Kirkwood, & Elliott, 2009; Gathercole, Lamont, & Alloway, 2006). Working memory difficulties are especially common in children who have grown up in chronically stressful living conditions, often as a result of living in extreme poverty (G. W. Evans & Schamberg, 2009; Noble, McCandless, & Farah, 2007).

Another important source of diversity in cognitive processing is cultural background. Different cultures foster somewhat different ways of looking at physical and social events—different *worldviews*—that influence how students interpret classroom subject matter. For example, students whose cultures have taught them to strive to live in harmony with their natural environment may struggle with a science curriculum that urges them to *change* their environment in some way (Atran, Medin, & Ross, 2005; Medin, 2005). And whereas students of European ancestry are apt to view the Europeans' migration to North America in the 1600s and 1700s as a process of *settlement,* students with Native American backgrounds might instead view it as increasing *invasion* (Banks, 1991; VanSledright & Brophy, 1992).

Chapter 8 examines worldviews in greater depth.

Children's varying cultural backgrounds may also have prepared them to handle different kinds of learning environments and tasks. For instance, African American and Hispanic students are more likely than European American students to be comfortable in environments in which several activities are going on at once and can more easily shift their attention from one activity to another (Correa-Chávez, Rogoff, & Mejía Arauz, 2005; Tyler et al., 2008). Students from North American, East Asian, and Middle Eastern cultures are apt to have had experience rote-memorizing specific facts and written materials (perhaps in the form of multiplication tables, poems, or religious teachings), whereas students from certain cultures in Africa, Australia, and Central America may have been encouraged to remember oral histories or particular landmarks in the local terrain (Purdie & Hattie, 1996; Rogoff, 2001, 2003; Rogoff et al., 2007; Q. Wang & Ross, 2007).

Expose students to multiple and possibly equally valid perspectives of historical and current events.

The importance of wait time depends partly on students' cultural backgrounds as well. For example, some Native American students may wait several seconds before responding to a

**reconstruction error** Construction of a logical but incorrect "memory" by combining information retrieved from one's long-term memory with one's general knowledge and beliefs about the world.

Chapter 4 describes cultural differences in wait time.

question as a way of showing respect for an adult (Castagno & Brayboy, 2008; Gilliland, 1988). And English language learners—students who have grown up in a non-English-speaking environment and are still developing their proficiency in English—are apt to require more mental translation time than their native-English-speaking peers (Igoa, 2007).

To maximize each student's learning and achievement in the classroom, we must take such individual and group differences into account. For example, we should be especially careful to engage the interest of—and also minimize distractions for—those students whose attention easily wanders. In addition, in our attempts to promote meaningful learning and other effective storage processes, we should relate classroom subject matter to the diverse background experiences that students have had. And we must allow sufficient wait time after questions and comments so that all students can actively think about and elaborate on topics of discussion.

## FACILITATING COGNITIVE PROCESSING IN STUDENTS WITH SPECIAL NEEDS

Some diversity in learning and cognitive processes is the result of certain disabilities, on the one hand, or giftedness, on the other. For example, some students with disabilities have particular trouble attending to and effectively processing classroom subject matter. This is certainly true for students with learning disabilities (who, by definition, have deficits in certain cognitive processes), and it's often true for students with attention-deficit hyperactivity disorder (ADHD) and general intellectual disabilities as well. In contrast, many children with autism spectrum disorders can be *very* attentive, sometimes to the point that they have trouble shifting to new tasks. And on average, gifted students have a longer attention span and can process new ideas more rapidly and elaboratively than many of their classmates. Table 6.5 identifies commonly observed cognitive processing differences in students who have special educational needs.

Chapter 5 identifies specific categories of special needs that fall within the five general categories listed in Table 6.5.

As teachers, we must keep in mind that students with disabilities almost invariably have strengths as well as weaknesses. For example, some students with ADHD have a keen memory for events they've personally experienced and may generate more detailed narratives than their nondisabled classmates (Skowronek, Leichtman, & Pillemer, 2008). And some students with autism spectrum disorders notice and remember many subtle nuances in the things they see and may produce highly detailed and skillful drawings that are unusual for their age-group (I. L. Cohen, 2007; S. Moran & Gardner, 2006).

The far-right column of Table 6.5 presents many useful strategies for working with students who have special educational needs. The first of these—analyzing students' errors for clues about possible processing difficulties—is illustrated in 9-year-old Nicholas's lab report in Figure 6.12. Nick's description of what he observed can be translated as "We poured so many cubes [that] the cup overflowed. The blocks took up all the room." We can only speculate about why Nick wrote up the left side of the glass, across the top, and then down the other side. One possible explanation is that, with his limited language skills, Nick hadn't yet mastered the conventional direction of written English. This hypothesis seems unlikely, however, as other samples of Nick's writing (not shown here) correctly begin at the top of the page and proceed downward. Another possibility is that Nick was thinking about the direction of the water flow (up and out) as he wrote and either intentionally or unintentionally followed the water's direction in his writing. His limited working memory capacity may have been a factor here: Perhaps he had insufficient mental "room" to think simultaneously about his observations plus the spellings of words and conventions of written English.

Virtually all students occasionally have difficulty learning or remembering class material. Accordingly, many of the instructional strategies in Table 6.5 need not be limited to use with students with special needs. *All* students can benefit from guidance and support that enable them to process information more effectively.

**FIGURE 6.12** In a science activity in his third-grade class, 9-year-old Nicholas copied the scientific principle "No two pieces of matter can occupy the same space at the same time" onto a sheet of paper. He and a lab partner then filled a cup with water and dropped, one at a time, more than a dozen small metal cubes into the cup. Here Nick recorded his observations with both words and a drawing.

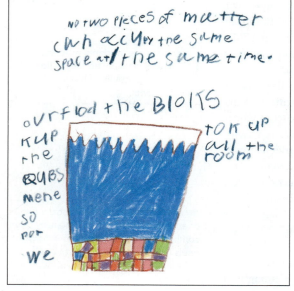

# STUDENTS IN INCLUSIVE SETTINGS

**TABLE 6.5 • Facilitating Cognitive Processing in Students with Special Educational Needs**

| CATEGORY | CHARACTERISTICS YOU MIGHT OBSERVE | SUGGESTED STRATEGIES |
|---|---|---|
| Students with specific cognitive or academic difficulties | • Deficiencies in one or more specific cognitive processes (e.g., perception, organization of related ideas into an integrated whole)<br>• Distractibility, inability to sustain attention for some students<br>• Difficulty screening out irrelevant stimuli<br>• Less working memory capacity or less efficient use of working memory<br>• Impulsivity in responding to classroom tasks<br>• Exceptionally detailed memory for personally experienced events (for some students with ADHD) | • Analyze students' errors as a way of identifying possible processing difficulties.<br>• Identify weaknesses in specific cognitive processes, and provide instruction that enables students to compensate for these weaknesses.<br>• Minimize distracting stimuli, and make sure you have students' attention before beginning instruction.<br>• Intersperse activities requiring sustained attention with opportunities for physical exercise.<br>• Encourage greater reflection before responding—for instance, by reinforcing accuracy rather than speed.<br>• Present information in an organized fashion and make frequent connections to students' prior knowledge.<br>• Teach mnemonics to aid long-term memory storage and retrieval.<br>• When appropriate, provide concrete memory aids that remind students of what they've learned.<br>• Capitalize on students' strengths (e.g., detailed knowledge about certain topics). |
| Students with social or behavioral problems | • Limited ability to focus attention because of off-task thoughts and behaviors (for some students with emotional and behavioral disorders)<br>• Difficulty shifting attention quickly (for students with autism)<br>• Exceptional ability to attend to small details; may be reflected in unusually detailed memory and drawings (for some students with autism)<br>• Impulsivity; less ability to inhibit inappropriate social behaviors (sometimes due to neurological deficits)<br>• Possible difficulties in other cognitive processes (e.g., undiagnosed learning disabilities) | • Capture students' attention by relating instruction to their personal interests.<br>• Nurture and capitalize on the visual-memory and artistic strengths that some students with autism may have.<br>• Refer students to a school psychologist for evaluation and diagnosis of possible learning disabilities.<br>• As appropriate, use strategies listed above for students with specific cognitive or academic difficulties. |
| Students with general delays in cognitive and social functioning | • Slower cognitive processing<br>• Difficulty with attention to task-relevant information<br>• Reduced working memory capacity or less efficient use of working memory<br>• Less intentional control of cognitive processes<br>• Smaller knowledge base on which to build new learning<br>• Greater difficulty retaining information for long time periods | • Keep instructional materials simple, emphasizing relevant stimuli and minimizing irrelevant stimuli.<br>• Provide clear instructions that focus students' attention on desired behaviors (e.g., "Listen," "Write," "Stop").<br>• Pace instruction to allow students enough time to think about and process information adequately (e.g., provide ample wait time after questions).<br>• Assume little prior knowledge about new topics (i.e., begin at the beginning). |
| Students with physical or sensory challenges | • Normal cognitive processing ability in most students<br>• Less-developed knowledge base to which new information can be related, due to limited experiences in the outside world<br>• Better than average ability to recall details of abstract shapes (for older students who are deaf but proficient with sign language) | • Assume equal ability for acquiring new information and skills, but consider how students' physical or sensory challenges may interfere with some learning processes.<br>• Provide basic life experiences that students may have missed because of their disabilities. |
| Students with advanced cognitive development | • Greater ability to attend to tasks for extended periods<br>• More rapid cognitive processing<br>• Greater intentional control of cognitive processes<br>• Larger knowledge base, with specific contents dependent on students' cultural backgrounds<br>• More interconnections among ideas in long-term memory; greater conceptual understanding of classroom material<br>• More rapid retrieval of information from long-term memory | • Proceed through topics more quickly or in greater depth.<br>• Create interdisciplinary lessons to foster integration of material in long-term memory. |

*Sources:* Barkley, 2006; Beirne-Smith, Patton, & Kim, 2006; Bulgren, Schumaker, & Deshler, 1994; Cattani, Clibbens, & Perfect, 2007; B. Clark, 1997; Courchesne et al., 1994; Fletcher, Lyon, Fuchs, & Barnes, 2007; Gathercole et al., 2006; Geary, Hoard, Byrd-Craven, Nugent, & Numtee, 2007; Grandin & Johnson, 2005; N. Gregg, 2009; Heward, 2009; J. Johnson, Im-Bolter, & Pascual-Leone, 2003; G. R. Lyon & Krasnegor, 1996; Meltzer, 2007; Mercer & Pullen, 2005; S. Moran & Gardner, 2006; Piirto, 1999; M. I. Posner & Rothbart, 2007; Rabinowitz & Glaser, 1985; Skowronek, Leichtman, & Pillemer, 2008; H. L. Swanson, 1998; Turnbull, Turnbull, & Wehmeyer, 2010.

# 6 What Have You Learned?

As a way of summing up our discussion of learning and cognitive processes in this chapter, we now return to the chapter's learning outcomes.

**6.1: Distinguish among four distinct approaches to the study of human learning, and summarize one of these approaches—cognitive psychology—in terms of five basic assumptions.** In general, *learning* is a long-term change in mental representations or associations as a result of experience. Over the past century, psychologists have offered a variety of perspectives on human learning, many of which fall into one of four general categories: behaviorism, social cognitive theory, cognitive psychology, and contextual theories. As teachers, we can be most effective when we're theoretically eclectic—that is, when we draw from all of these perspectives to maximally facilitate students' learning and achievement.

Cognitive psychologists propose that the things learners do *mentally* with new subject matter determine how effectively they learn and remember it. Learners' cognitive processes can often be inferred from overt behaviors—for instance, from the ways in which learners recall information they've previously encountered. Learners must be selective about the information they process in any depth, and they use the information they've focused on to construct their own, somewhat idiosyncratic understandings of physical and social phenomena. To some degree, the sophistication and effectiveness of learners' cognitive processes depends on brain maturation over the course of childhood and adolescence.

Evaluate and apply your knowledge related to this learning outcome in MyEducationLab™.

**6.2: Describe and illustrate the key components that many researchers believe may characterize the human memory system.** Many cognitive theorists propose that human memory has three components. The *sensory register* provides temporary storage for incoming information, holding new input for two or three seconds at most. By paying attention to information, learners move it to *working memory*, where they actively think about and make sense of it. Attention and working memory have a limited capacity; hence, students can pay attention to and think about only a small amount of information at any one time. Furthermore, information stored in working memory has a short duration (typically less than half a minute) and so must be processed further to promote storage in *long-term memory*. Long-term memory has an extremely large capacity and an indefinitely long duration. This particular model of memory has its flaws—for example, some brain research indicates that working memory and long-term memory aren't as distinctly different as the model suggests—but it can help us remember many aspects of learning and memory that we should take into account when designing and delivering instruction.

Evaluate and apply your knowledge related to this learning outcome in MyEducationLab™.

**6.3: Apply your knowledge of long-term memory storage in identifying effective strategies for enhancing students' learning.** Long-term memory contains both information (*declarative knowledge*) and skills (*procedural knowledge*). A good deal of it is organized, often as concepts that are, in turn, integrated into more general schemas, scripts, and theories. To effectively acquire the kinds of declarative knowledge the school curriculum encompasses, learners should ideally engage in meaningful learning, perhaps by elaborating on or organizing new information or perhaps by engaging in visual imagery. In some cases, acquiring procedural knowledge involves learning and refining various physical behaviors; in other cases, it involves gradually converting declarative knowledge into either physical or mental actions. How effectively learners store new information and skills depends, in part, on how much they already know about the topic at hand. In the absence of relevant prior knowledge, mnemonics can enhance learners' memory for things that are important for them to remember.

Evaluate and apply your knowledge related to this learning outcome in MyEducationLab™.

**6.4: Explain how students' self-constructed beliefs can sometimes interfere with effective learning, and identify several ways of helping students productively revise such beliefs.** Although meaningful learning is usually beneficial, it can occasionally lead students to misinterpret classroom material, especially if they have currently erroneous or only-partly-correct beliefs about the topic or phenomenon they're studying. Some misconceptions may persist despite lessons and activities that present information to the contrary, in part because students are cognitively and emotionally predisposed to confirm (rather than discredit) what they currently believe and in part because students' current beliefs may be integrated into cohesive theories that can't easily be unraveled and revised. As teachers, we're more likely to promote conceptual change when we determine what misconceptions students have before instruction begins, build on kernels of truth in students' existing understandings, convince students that revision is both warranted and within their grasp, and monitor what students say and write for especially persistent misunderstandings.

Evaluate and apply your knowledge related to this learning outcome in MyEducationLab™.

**6.5: Describe six different factors that influence students' ability to recall what they have previously learned; also describe five possible reasons why students may either forget or incorrectly remember what they have learned.** Retrieving information from long-term memory appears to be a process of following pathways of associations. In general, classroom subject matter is more memorable if it has elements that are emotionally laden or in some other way unique and distinctive. Furthermore, students are more likely to be successful in recalling what they've learned if they've connected it with numerous other things they know, if they've used it frequently (and perhaps learned it to automaticity), if their environment provides retrieval cues that send them down the right memory "path," and if they're given sufficient wait time to conduct a successful long-term memory search. Even under the best of circumstances, however, students sometimes forget or misremember what they've studied, perhaps as a result of insufficient consolidation, lack of use (resulting in gradual decay), restricted memory search, interference from competing memories, or reconstruction error.

*Evaluate* and *apply* your knowledge related to this learning outcome in MyEducationLab™.

■ **6.6: Give examples of the diversity in cognitive processes you are likely to see in students, in some cases as a result of their cultural background or special educational needs.** Many components of the human memory system—attention span, working memory capacity, prior knowledge, and so on—can vary significantly from one student to another, and as a result students have varying abilities to learn and remember classroom subject matter. Students' cognitive processes differ, in part, as a function of their cultural worldviews, the kinds of learning tasks and environments

to which they're accustomed, and their proficiency with the language in which instruction is being conducted. In addition, some diversity may be the result of certain disabilities. For example, students with attention-deficit hyperactivity disorder have difficulty keeping their attention on any single task for lengthy periods, whereas some students with autism spectrum disorders may have trouble shifting their attention to new tasks. Yet at one time or another, all students are likely to have trouble understanding and mastering particular topics. By identifying and facilitating cognitive processes that are most likely to lead to effective learning, teachers can better help *all* students achieve classroom success.

*Evaluate* and *apply* your knowledge related to this learning outcome in MyEducationLab™.

## Practice For Your Licensure Exam

### Vision Unit

Ms. Kontos is teaching a unit on human vision to her fifth-grade class. She shows her students a diagram of the various parts of the human eye: lens, cornea, retina, and so on. She then explains that people can see objects because light from the sun or another light source bounces off those objects and into their eyes. To illustrate this idea, she shows them Picture A.

**A**

"Do you all understand how our eyes work?" she asks. Her students nod that they do.

The next day Ms. Kontos gives her students Picture B. She asks students to draw one or more arrows on the picture to show how light enables

**B**

the child to see the tree. More than half of the students draw arrows something like the one shown in Picture C.

**C**

*Source:* Case based on a study by J. F. Eaton, Anderson, & Smith, 1984.

1. **Constructed-response question:**

   Obviously, most of Ms. Kontos's students have not learned what she thought she had taught them about human vision.

   **A.** Explain why many students believe the opposite of what Ms. Kontos has taught them. Base your response on contemporary principles and theories of learning and cognition.

   **B.** Describe two different ways in which you might improve on this lesson to help students gain a more accurate understanding of human vision. Base your strategies on contemporary principles and theories of learning and cognition.

2. **Multiple-choice question:**

   Many elementary school children think of human vision in the way that Ms. Kontos's fifth graders do—that is, as a process that originates in the eye and goes outward toward objects that are seen. When students revise their thinking to be more consistent with commonly accepted scientific explanations, they are said to be

   a. acquiring a new script

   b. revising their worldview

   c. undergoing conceptual change

   d acquiring procedural knowledge

**PRAXIS** Go to Appendix C, "Matching Book and MyEducationLab™ to the Praxis Principles of Learning and Teaching Tests," to discover sections of this chapter that may be especially applicable to the Praxis tests.

# 7 Complex Cognitive Processes

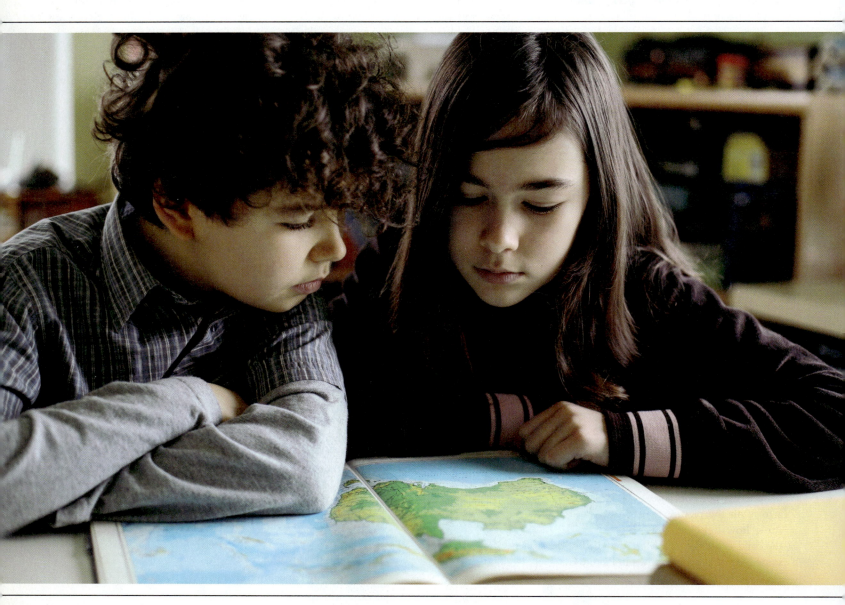

## LEARNING OUTCOMES

**7.1:** Explain how learners' metacognitive knowledge and skills influence their learning and academic achievement; also explain how you can promote metacognitive development in your own students.

**7.2:** Describe various forms that transfer might take and the conditions in which transfer is most likely to occur, and apply research findings about transfer to your classroom practices.

**7.3:** Describe four general factors that influence problem-solving performance; also describe teaching strategies you can use to help students successfully solve both well-defined and ill-defined problems.

**7.4:** Identify several instructional strategies that can encourage students to think creatively as they tackle new tasks and problems.

**7.5:** Describe several different forms that critical thinking can take, and explain how you can help students critically evaluate what they see, hear, and read both inside and outside the classroom.

**7.6:** Give examples of diversity you might see in creativity, critical thinking, and other complex thinking processes as a result of students' cultural backgrounds, disabilities, or advanced cognitive development.

## CASE STUDY: TAKING OVER

When an eighth-grade math teacher goes on maternity leave in March, substitute teacher Ms. Gaunt takes over her classes. In accordance with Massachusetts state standards, the students are expected to master numerous mathematical concepts and procedures, including working with exponents and irrational numbers, graphing linear equations, and applying the Pythagorean theorem. But many of the students haven't yet mastered more basic concepts and operations, such as percentages, negative numbers, and long division. A few haven't even learned such number facts as 6 x 3 = 18 and 7 x 8 = 56.

Before long, Ms. Gaunt discovers that many students have beliefs and attitudes that also impede their learning progress. For instance, some think that a teacher's job is to present material in such a way that they "get it" immediately and will remember it forever. Thus they neither work hard to understand the material nor take notes during classroom explanations. And most students are concerned only with getting the right answer as quickly as possible. They depend on calculators to do their mathematical thinking for them and complain when Ms. Gaunt insists that they solve a problem with pencil and paper rather than a calculator. Students rarely check to see whether their solutions make logical sense. For instance, in a problem such as

> Louis can type 35 words a minute. He needs to type a final copy of his English composition, which is 4,200 words long. How long will it take Louis to type his paper?

a student might submit an answer of 147,000 minutes—an answer that translates into more than 100 days of around-the-clock typing—and not give the outlandishness of the solution a second thought. (It would actually take two hours to type the paper.)

In mid-April, Ms. Gaunt begins moving through lessons more rapidly so that she can cover the mandated eighth-grade math curriculum before the upcoming statewide math competency exam. "Students can't do well on the exam if they haven't even been exposed to some of the required concepts and procedures," she reasons. "Mastery probably isn't possible at this point, but I should at least *present* what students need to know. Maybe this will help a few of them with some of the test items."

- Why are the students having difficulty mastering the eighth-grade math curriculum? Can you identify at least three different factors that appear to be interfering with students' learning?

*Source:* Case used courtesy of a friend who wishes to be anonymous; "Ms. Gaunt" is a pseudonym.

Two key ingredients of metacognition
are theory of mind and self-regulation,
described in Chapter 3 and Chapter 10,
respectively.

**complex cognitive processes**
Cognitive process that involves going
well beyond information specifically
learned (e.g., by analyzing, applying, or
evaluating it).

**metacognition** Knowledge and beliefs
about the nature of human cognitive
processes (including one's own), as well
as conscious attempts to engage in
behaviors and thought processes that
increase learning and memory.

**learning strategy** One or more
cognitive processes used intentionally
for a particular learning task.

One factor, of course, is students' lack of prerequisite knowledge and skills on which the eighth-grade curriculum depends. For instance, if students haven't learned basic number facts—let alone achieved automaticity for them—even fairly simple word problems may exceed their working memory capacity. But students' beliefs about learning and problem solving are also coming into play. In their minds, learning should come quickly and easily if the teacher does her job. They seem not to understand that understanding classroom subject matter is an active, constructive process involving considerable effort on their part and that certain strategies (e.g., taking notes) can enhance their learning. And they view mathematical problem solving as a quick, mindless enterprise that involves plugging numbers into a calculator and writing down the result, rather than a step-by-step process that requires logical reasoning and frequent self-checking.

Study skills and problem solving are examples of complex cognitive processes, processes in which learners go far beyond the specific information they're studying, perhaps to apply it to a new situation, use it to solve a problem or create a product, or critically evaluate it. Mastering basic facts and skills is important, to be sure. But learners gain little if they can't also *do something* with what they've learned. In this chapter we'll look at a variety of complex cognitive processes, including transfer, problem solving, creativity, and critical thinking. But we'll begin with a particular set of complex processes that in one way or another influence all of the others: metacognition.

# Metacognition and Learning Strategies

The term metacognition literally means "thinking about thinking." It encompasses knowledge and beliefs about the general nature of human cognitive processes, reflection on one's *own* cognitive processes, and intentional engagement in behaviors and thought processes that enhance learning and memory. For example, you've undoubtedly learned by now that you can acquire only so much information so fast—you can't possibly absorb the contents of an entire textbook in an hour. You've also discovered that you can learn information more quickly and recall it more easily if you put it into some sort of organizational framework. Perhaps, too, you've learned that you need to periodically check yourself to make sure you remember and understand what you've read.

The more learners know about thinking and learning—that is, the greater their *metacognitive awareness*—the better their learning and achievement is likely to be (B. Hofer & Pintrich, 2002; Schneider, 2010). Furthermore, students who have a more advanced understanding of learning and thinking—for instance, students who realize that one's knowledge of a topic continues to evolve over time—are more likely to undergo conceptual change when it's warranted (Mason, 2010; Sinatra & Pintrich, 2003).

As children grow older, they become increasingly aware of their own thinking and learning processes and increasingly realistic about what they can learn and remember in a given time period (see Table 7.1). With this growing self-awareness come more sophisticated study strategies. Truly effective strategies emerge quite slowly, however, especially if young learners don't get guidance from teachers, parents, or other adults about how to study and learn (J. E. Barnett, 2001; Schneider, 2010; Schommer, 1994a; Veenman, 2011).

## EFFECTIVE LEARNING STRATEGIES

An important component of metacognition is *controlling* one's own thinking and learning to some degree. Thanks, in part, to maturational changes in the brain, children and adolescents gradually become more capable of controlling and directing their cognitive processes in their efforts to learn something new (Eigsti et al., 2006; Kuhn & Franklin, 2006). When learners *intentionally* use a certain approach to learning and remembering something, they're using a learning strategy.

# DEVELOPMENTAL TRENDS

## TABLE 7.1 • Metacognition at Different Grade Levels

| GRADE LEVEL | AGE-TYPICAL CHARACTERISTICS | EXAMPLE | SUGGESTED STRATEGIES |
|---|---|---|---|
|  **K–2** | • Awareness of thought in oneself and others, albeit in a simplistic form; limited ability to reflect on the specific nature of one's own thought processes<br>• Considerable overestimation of what has been learned and how much can be remembered in the future<br>• Belief that learning is a relatively passive activity<br>• Belief that the absolute truth about any topic is "out there" somewhere, waiting to be discovered | An adult tells 6-year-old Brent that she will read him a list of 12 words; she then asks him to predict how many he'll be able to remember. Brent predicts "about 8 or 9 . . . maybe all of them," but in fact recalls only 6. Later, when the adult asks him what he did to try to remember the words, he says only "Think" and "Holded it, hold it in my brain." (You can see this example in the video "Memory and Cognition: Early Childhood.")  | • Talk often about thinking processes (e.g., "I *wonder* if . . ." "How might you *remember* to . . .?").<br>• Provide opportunities for students to experiment with their memories (e.g., playing "I'm going on a trip and I'm going to pack ___," in which each student repeats items previously mentioned and then adds another item to the list).<br>• Introduce simple learning strategies (e.g., rehearsal of spelling words, repeated practice of motor skills). |
|  **3–5** | • Increasing ability to reflect on the nature of one's own thought processes<br>• Some overestimation of memory capabilities<br>• Emerging realization that learning is an active, constructive process and that people may misinterpret what they observe<br>• Continuing belief in an absolute truth "out there" | After reading several explanations of how ancient humans migrated from Asia to North America, a cooperative learning group in a combined fifth- and sixth-grade classroom includes the following points in its summary of what it has learned: "The more that we learn, the more we get confused about which is fact and which is fiction . . . We have made [our] own theories using information we found and trying to make sense of it." | • Provide simple techniques (e.g., self-test questions) that enable students to monitor their learning progress.<br>• Examine scientific phenomena through hands-on activities and experimentation; ask students to make predictions about what will happen and to defend their explanations for what they observe. |
|  **6–8** | • Few and relatively ineffective study strategies (e.g., poor note-taking skills, little or no self-monitoring of comprehension)<br>• Belief that knowledge about a topic consists largely of a collection of discrete facts<br>• Increasing realization that knowledge can be subjective and that conflicting perspectives may all have some validity (e.g., "people have a right to form their own opinions")<br>• Increasing differentiation among the underlying natures of various content domains (e.g., thinking that math involves right vs. wrong answers whereas social studies allows for diverse opinions) | The students in Ms. Gaunt's eighth-grade math class rarely take notes to help them remember new concepts and procedures, and most are more concerned about getting correct answers than about making sense of mathematical operations (see the opening case study). | • Teach and model effective strategies within the context of various subject areas.<br>• Scaffold students' studying efforts (e.g., provide a structure for note taking, give students questions to answer as they study).<br>• Introduce multiple perspectives about topics (e.g., asking whether Christopher Columbus was a brave explorer in search of new knowledge or, instead, an entrepreneur in search of personal wealth).<br>• Explicitly ask students to reflect on their beliefs about the nature of various academic disciplines (e.g., "Can a math problem sometimes have two different right answers?"). |
|  **9–12** | • Growing (but incomplete) knowledge of study strategies that are effective in different situations; persistent use of rehearsal by some students<br>• Increasing mastery of covert learning strategies (e.g., intentional use of elaboration, comprehension monitoring)<br>• Increasing recognition that knowledge involves understanding interrelationships among ideas<br>• Increasing recognition that mastering a topic or skill takes time and practice (rather than happening quickly as a result of innate ability)<br>• Emerging understanding that conflicting perspectives should be evaluated on the basis of evidence and logic (seen in a small minority of high school students) | When 16-year-old Hilary is asked to describe the things she does to help her remember school subject matter, she says, "When I'm trying to study for tests, I try to associate the things I'm trying to learn with familiar things . . . with the Spanish words, I'll try to think of the English word that it sounds like . . . sometimes if I can't find any rule, then I just have to memorize it, just try to remember it, just go over it a lot. (You can see this example in the video "Memory and Cognition: Late Adolescence.")  | • Continue to teach and model effective learning strategies; ask students to describe their strategies to one another.<br>• Design classroom assignments and assessments that emphasize understanding, integration, and application, rather than recall of discrete facts.<br>• Present various subject areas as dynamic entities that continue to evolve with new discoveries and theories.<br>• Have students weigh pros and cons of various explanations and documents using objective criteria (e.g., hard evidence, logical reasoning processes). |

*Sources:* Andre & Windschitl, 2003; Astington & Pelletier, 1996; J. E. Barnett, 2001; Bendixen & Feucht, 2010; Buehl & Alexander, 2006; Chandler, Hallett, & Sokol, 2002; Elder, 2002; Flavell, Friedrichs, & Hoyt, 1970; Flavell, Miller, & Miller, 2002; Hatano & Inagaki, 2003; Hewitt, Brett, Scardamalia, Frecker, & Webb, 1995, p. 7 (migration example); P. M. King & Kitchener, 2002; Ku, Chan, Wu, & Chen, 2008; Kuhn, 2009; Kuhn, Garcia-Mila, Zohar, & Andersen, 1995; Kuhn & Park, 2005; Kuhn & Weinstock, 2002; Lovett & Flavell, 1990; McCrudden & Schraw, 2007; Meltzer, Pollica, & Barzillai, 2007; Muis, Bendixen, & Haerle, 2006; P. A. Ornstein, Grammer, & Coffman, 2010; Schneider, 2010; Schommer, 1994a, 1997; Short, Schatschneider, & Friebert, 1993; J. W. Thomas, 1993a; vanSledright & Limón, 2006; Wellman, 1985, 1990; J. P. Williams, Stafford, Lauer, Hall, & Pollini, 2009.

**overt strategy** Learning strategy that is at least partially evident in a learner's behavior (e.g., taking notes during a lecture).

**covert strategy** Learning strategy that is strictly mental (rather than behavioral) in nature and thus cannot be directly observed by others.

Chapter 6 describes the development of basic long-term memory storage processes (e.g., see Table 6.4).

Information processing theorists have described several processes that may facilitate long-term memory storage, including rehearsal, elaboration, organization, and visual imagery. As children grow older, they increasingly discover the benefits of these processes and use them more frequently (P. A. Ornstein, Grammer, & Coffman, 2010; Pressley & Hilden, 2006). Children gradually acquire additional strategies as well. For example, consider the simple idea that you need to devote more study time to more difficult material; children don't use this seemingly obvious strategy until the fourth or fifth grade (Schneider, 2010). With age and experience, children also become more aware of which strategies are effective in different situations. Even so, many students of all ages (college students included!) seem relatively uninformed about effective learning strategies (Lovett & Flavell, 1990; Schneider, 2010; Schommer, 1994a; Short, Schatschneider, & Friebert, 1993).

Some learning strategies are **overt strategies**; in other words, they're behaviors we can actually see. Others, such as elaborating and forming visual images, are **covert strategies**; they're internal mental processes we often *can't* see (Kardash & Amlund, 1991).

## OVERT STRATEGIES

To some degree, successful learning and classroom achievement are the result of certain behaviors, such as asking questions in times of confusion, keeping a calendar for assignments and due dates, devoting part of every evening to schoolwork, and so on. One especially effective overt strategy is *writing* about classroom subject matter (Bangert-Drowns, Hurley, & Wilkinson, 2004; P. D. Klein, 1999; Shanahan, 2004). Here we look at research on two writing-based learning strategies: taking notes and creating summaries.

**Taking notes** By the time students reach the upper elementary or middle school grades, note-taking skills begin to play a role in their classroom achievement. In general, students who take more notes learn and remember classroom subject matter better. However, the *quality* of the notes is equally important. Useful notes typically reflect the main ideas of a lesson or reading assignment (A. L. Brown, Campione, & Day, 1981; Kiewra, 1985, 1989; J. Lee & Shute, 2010).

Despite the advantages of note taking, many young adolescents take few or no class notes unless specifically instructed to take them (recall the infrequent note taking in Ms. Gaunt's eighth-grade math class). And the notes they do take differ considerably in quality. For example, Figure 7.1 shows

**FIGURE 7.1** Two students' class notes on King Midas, taken in a seventh-grade language arts unit on Greek mythology the notes that two students took about King Midas in a Greek mythology unit in their seventh-grade language arts class. The notes on the left provide a good overall synopsis of the King Midas story and might reasonably help the student remember the story fairly accurately. In contrast, the notes on the right are probably too brief and disjointed to be useful.

Especially when students are first learning how to take notes in class, we should scaffold their efforts by giving them an idea about which things are most important to include (Meltzer, Pollica, & Barzillai, 2007; Pressley, Yokoi, van Meter, Van Etten, & Freebern, 1997). One approach is to provide a specific structure to use, such as the one shown in Figure 7.1. Another strategy, especially if students are novice note takers, is to occasionally check their notebooks for accuracy and appropriate emphasis and give constructive feedback.

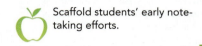 Scaffold students' early note-taking efforts.

**Creating summaries**    Research consistently indicates that writing a summary of material being studied can enhance learning and memory (A. King, 1992; R. E. Mayer, 2010b; Wade-Stein & Kintsch, 2004). Creating a good summary is a fairly complex process, however. At a minimum it includes distinguishing between important and unimportant information, synthesizing details into more general ideas, and identifying critical interrelationships. It's not surprising, then, that even many high school students have trouble writing a good summary (Hidi & Anderson, 1986).

Probably the best way of helping students acquire this strategy is to ask them frequently to summarize what they hear and read (e.g., see Figure 7.2). Initially we should scaffold the process for them—for example, by providing compare–contrast tables they can fill in as they read or having them develop summaries in collaboration with peers (Spörer & Brunstein, 2009; J. P. Williams, Stafford, Lauer, Hall, & Pollini, 2009). Computer software is also available to scaffold the summarizing process (e.g., Wade-Stein & Kintsch, 2004).

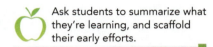 Ask students to summarize what they're learning, and scaffold their early efforts.

## COVERT STRATEGIES

Students' overt strategies—allocating time for studying, taking notes, summarizing, and so on—are probably valuable only to the extent that effective cognitive processes, or *covert strategies,* underlie them (Kardash & Amlund, 1991). For example, high-achieving students tend to benefit more from note taking than low-achieving students, perhaps because the high-achieving students are more likely to elaborate on and organize what they're learning as they take notes (Kiewra, Benton, & Lewis, 1987; Ku, Chan, Wu, & Chen, 2008). In addition to engaging in meaningful learning processes (e.g., elaboration, organization), two covert strategies that may be especially critical for effective classroom learning and achievement are (1) accurately identifying important information and (2) regularly self-monitoring learning.

**FIGURE 7.2** **Eight-year-old Neville summarizes a lesson about glaciers**

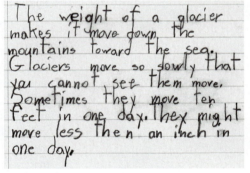

**Identifying important information**    The human memory system isn't set up to remember *all* the information a typical classroom curriculum presents; thus, students must be selective when studying classroom material. The things they choose to study—whether main ideas and essential supporting details or, instead, isolated facts and trivia—inevitably affect their learning and school achievement (Dee-Lucas & Larkin, 1991; J. A. Dole, Duffy, Roehler, & Pearson, 1991; R. E. Reynolds & Shirey, 1988).

Students often have trouble identifying the most important information in a lesson or reading assignment, especially when they don't know very much about the topic. Many use relatively superficial strategies in choosing what to focus on—for instance, zeroing in on definitions and formulas, taking notes only on things their teacher writes on the board, or reading only the first sentence of each paragraph of a textbook—and miss critical ideas as a result.

As teachers, we can, of course, simply tell students exactly what they should study. But we can also highlight important ideas through more subtle means:

-  Provide a list of learning objectives for a lesson.
- Write key concepts and relationships on the board.
- Ask questions that focus students' attention on central ideas.

Students—low-achieving ones especially—are more likely to learn the essential points of a lesson when such prompts are provided for them (Kiewra, 1989; McCrudden & Schraw, 2007;

Let students know what things are most important to learn and remember.

**comprehension monitoring**
Process of checking oneself to verify understanding and memory of newly acquired information.

**illusion of knowing**  Thinking that one knows something that one actually does *not* know.

**self-explanation**  Process of occasionally stopping to verbalize to oneself (and hence to better understand) material being read or studied.

**self-questioning**  Process of asking oneself questions as a way of checking understanding of a topic.

R. E. Reynolds & Shirey, 1988; Schraw, Wade, & Kardash, 1993). As students become better able to distinguish between important and unimportant information on their own, we can gradually phase out our guidance.

**Regularly monitoring learning**    One powerful learning strategy is **comprehension monitoring**, a process of periodically checking oneself for recall and understanding. How well do *you* monitor your comprehension? The following exercise can help you find out.

### ■■ EXPERIENCING FIRSTHAND
### LOOKING BACK

Stop for a minute and ask yourself this question:

What have I learned from the last five pages of this book?

Quickly jot down what you can recall.

Now go back and look at the five pages preceding this one. Do the notes you've just written include all of the major points? Is there something you thought you understood but realize now that you don't? Is there something you never learned at all—perhaps something you were supposedly "reading" when your mind was someplace altogether different?

Successful learners continually monitor their comprehension both *while* they study something and at some point *after* they've studied it (Hacker, Dunlosky, & Graesser, 2009b). Furthermore, when they realize they don't understand, they take steps to correct the situation, perhaps by rereading a section of a textbook or asking a question in class. In contrast, low achievers rarely check themselves or take appropriate action when they don't comprehend something. For example, they're unlikely to reread paragraphs they haven't understood the first time around (L. Baker & Brown, 1984; Haller, Child, & Walberg, 1988; Veenman, 2011).

Many children and adolescents engage in little or no comprehension monitoring (J. A. Dole et al., 1991; McKeown & Beck, 2009; Nokes & Dole, 2004). When they don't monitor their learning and comprehension, they don't know what they know and what they don't know; consequently, they may think they've mastered something when they really haven't. Although this **illusion of knowing** is especially common in young children, it's seen in learners at all levels, even college students. As paper-and-pencil exams become increasingly prevalent at upper grade levels, an illusion of knowing can lead students to overestimate how well they'll perform on these assessments (Hacker, Bol, Horgan, & Rakow, 2000; Stone, 2000; Zimmerman & Moylan, 2009). My own students occasionally come to me expressing frustration with low test scores. "I knew the material so well!" they tell me. But when we begin to talk about the exam material, it usually becomes clear that they have only vague understandings of some ideas and incorrect understandings of others.

Comprehension monitoring doesn't have to be a solitary activity, of course. If students work in small study groups, they can easily test one another on classroom material and may detect gaps or misconceptions in one another's understandings (Dunning, Heath, & Suls, 2004; Hacker, 1998; Vaughn et al., 2011). Ideally, the questions they ask one another should encourage them to elaborate on rather than simply recall what they're studying. For example, we might teach them to ask questions beginning with such phrases as *Explain why, What do you think would happen if,* and *What is the difference between* (A. King, 1992, p. 309).

Yet to be truly effective learners, students must ultimately learn how to test *themselves* as well. One effective strategy is **self-explanation**, in which students frequently stop to explain to themselves what they're studying (Berthold & Renkl, 2009; Fonseca & Chi, 2011; McNamara & Magliano, 2009). Another, similar approach is **self-questioning**, in which students periodically stop to ask themselves questions—essentially internalizing the mutual question-asking process they've previously used in small-group study sessions (Dunning et al., 2004; Martínez, Bannan-Ritland, Kitsantas, & Baek, 2008; Wong, 1985). Their self-questions should, of course, include not only simple, fact-based questions but also elaborative ones.

  Teach students strategies for monitoring their own and others' learning progress.

This internalization of the question-asking process should remind you of Vygotsky's theory of cognitive development (see Chapter 2).

## FACTORS AFFECTING STRATEGY USE

As we've seen, students become increasingly capable of using effective learning strategies as they grow older, in part because they can better control and direct their cognitive processes. With age, too, comes an ever-expanding knowledge base that supports students' efforts to engage in elaboration, identify important information, and effectively monitor their comprehension. Several other factors also influence students' choice and use of various strategies, as reflected in the following principles.

- *Learning strategies depend partly on the learning task at hand.* In some situations teachers may assign tasks for which truly effective learning strategies are either counterproductive or impossible. For instance, if we insist that facts and definitions be learned verbatim, students will understandably be reluctant to engage in elaboration and other meaningful learning processes (Turner, 1995; Van Meter, Yokoi, & Pressley, 1994). And if we expect students to master a great deal of material for a single exam, they may have to devote their limited study time to getting only a superficial impression of everything or to studying only the easy material they're confident they can master (Son & Schwartz, 2002; J. W. Thomas, 1993b). Sometimes working memory's limited capacity discourages metacognitive processing: If a learning task involves thinking about a lot of information all at once—that is, if it imposes a heavy cognitive load—students may have insufficient "room" in working memory to use strategies that might otherwise be effective (Kalyuga, 2010; H. S. Waters & Kunnmann, 2010).

- *Students are likely to acquire and use new, more effective strategies only if they realize that their current strategies aren't working.* Students will come to such a conclusion only if they've been regularly monitoring their comprehension in previous learning tasks and become aware of their learning difficulties. Comprehension monitoring, then, doesn't just affect students' understanding of classroom subject matter, it also plays a pivotal role in the development of *other* metacognitive strategies (Kuhn, Garcia-Mila, Zohar, & Andersen, 1995; Lodico, Ghatala, Levin, Pressley, & Bell, 1983; Loranger, 1994). In some cases, too, feedback that students haven't yet mastered a learning task will spur them to adopt more effective strategies, at least for the short run (Starr & Lovett, 2000).

- *Students' beliefs about the nature of knowledge and learning influence their strategy choices.* I once had a conversation with my son Jeff, then an eleventh grader, about the Canadian Studies program that a local university had just added to its curriculum. Jeff's comments revealed a very simplistic view of what history is:

*Jeff:* The Canadians don't have as much history as we [Americans] do.

*Me:* Of course they do.

*Jeff:* No they don't. They haven't had as many wars.

*Me:* History's more than wars.

*Jeff:* Yeah, but the rest of that stuff is really boring.

Once Jeff reached college, he discovered that history is a lot more than wars and other, "really boring" stuff. In fact, he majored in history and now, as a middle school teacher, actually *teaches* history. But it's unfortunate that he had to wait until college to discover the true nature of history as an academic discipline.

Children and adolescents have misconceptions about other subject areas as well. For example, in the opening case study, Ms. Gaunt's students think that math consists of nothing more than a collection of procedures that yield single right answers. Furthermore, many students have misconceptions about the general nature of learning. For instance, Ms. Gaunt's students think they should be able to learn mathematical concepts and procedures quickly and easily—with little or no effort on their part—as long as their teacher does her job.

Students' beliefs about the nature of knowledge and learning are collectively known as epistemic beliefs (you may also see the term *epistemological* beliefs). Such beliefs often influence studying and learning (Bendixen & Feucht, 2010; B. Hofer & Pintrich, 1997; Muis, 2007). For example, when students believe that learning happens quickly in an all-or-none fashion (as Ms. Gaunt's students apparently do), they're apt to believe they've mastered something before they really have. Furthermore, they tend to give up quickly in the face of failure and express discouragement or dislike regarding the topic they're studying. In contrast, when students believe that

**cognitive load** Cognitive burden that a particular learning activity places on working memory at any one time; includes both the amount of information students must simultaneously think about and the specific cognitive processes students must engage in to understand what they're studying.

**epistemic belief** Belief about the nature of knowledge or knowledge acquisition.

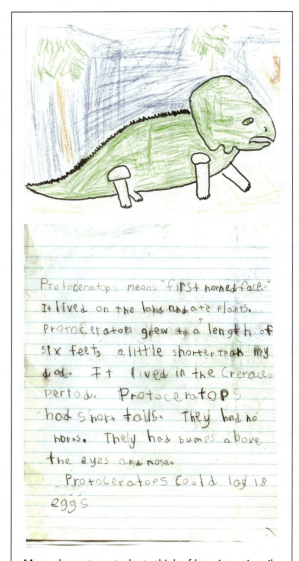

Many elementary students think of learning primarily as a process of acquiring specific, isolated facts, as illustrated in 8-year-old David's "Protoceratops" composition. Notice that David makes one meaningful connection: how a protoceratops's length compared to his own father's height.

Communicate that genuinely useful knowledge tends to be complex rather than simple and that learning requires considerable thought and effort.

The discussion of motivation in Chapter 11 identifies many things teachers can do to overcome such impediments to successful learning and achievement.

learning is a gradual process that often takes time and effort, they're likely to use a wide variety of learning strategies as they study and to persist until they've made sense of the material (D. L. Butler & Winne, 1995; Kardash & Howell, 2000; Muis, 2007; Schommer, 1990, 1994b).

As another example of variability in learners' epistemic beliefs, some students believe that when they read a textbook, they're passively absorbing information—often in the form of isolated facts—directly from the page to their minds. In contrast, other students recognize that learning from reading requires them to construct their own meanings by actively interpreting, organizing, and applying the information. Learners who realize that reading is a constructive, integrative process are more likely to engage in meaningful learning as they read and to undergo conceptual change when they encounter ideas that contradict their existing understandings (Mason, Gava, & Boldrin, 2008; Muis, 2007; Schommer-Aikins, 2002; Sinatra & Pintrich, 2003).

Epistemic beliefs tend to evolve over the course of childhood and adolescence (Kuhn & Park, 2005; Muis, Bendixen, & Haerle, 2006; Schommer, Calvert, Gariglietti, & Bajaj, 1997). Children in the elementary grades typically believe in the certainty of knowledge: They think that for any topic there's an absolute truth "out there" somewhere. As they reach high school, some (but by no means all) of them begin to realize that knowledge is a subjective entity and that different perspectives on a topic are sometimes equally valid. Additional changes may occur over the course of the high school grades. For example, twelfth graders are more likely than ninth graders to believe that knowledge consists of complex interrelationships rather than discrete facts and that learning happens slowly rather than quickly. And throughout adolescence, students' epistemic beliefs become increasingly domain specific (Buehl & Alexander, 2006; Muis et al., 2006). For example, students may believe that, in math, answers are always either right or wrong (recall the students in the opening case study) but that in social studies conflicting perspectives may all have some validity. Such developmental trends are reflected in some of the entries in Table 7.1.

As teachers, we must communicate to students what we ourselves know to be true about knowledge and learning:

- Knowledge involves not only knowing facts, concepts, and ideas but also understanding interrelationships among these things.
- Learning involves active construction of knowledge, rather than just a passive absorption of it.
- Knowledge doesn't always mean having clear-cut answers to difficult, complex issues, and in some cases it involves critically evaluating available evidence relative to a particular point of view.
- Mastering a body of information or a complex skill sometimes requires persistence and hard work.

In communicating such messages—not only in what we say but also in what we *do*, such as in the questions we ask, the activities we assign, and the ways in which we assess students' learning—we increase the likelihood that students will apply effective learning strategies, critically evaluate classroom subject matter, and undergo conceptual change when appropriate (Bendixen & Feucht, 2010; B. Hofer & Pintrich, 2002; Sinatra & Pintrich, 2003).

• *Different motives and goals call for different strategies.* Motivational factors clearly influence the extent to which students use effective strategies to learn and study. Some students may be more interested in getting by with a passing grade than truly mastering classroom material. Others may think that meaningful learning and other effective strategies involve too much time and effort to be worthwhile. Still others may have so little faith in their learning ability that they expect to do poorly regardless of the strategies they use (P. A. Alexander, Graham, & Harris, 1998; Mason, 2010; Nolen, 1996; Palmer & Goetz, 1988).

• *Ongoing instruction and guidance about effective strategies enhances learning and achievement.* With every transition to a higher educational level, teachers expect students to learn more

## Into the Classroom

### Promoting Effective Learning and Study Strategies

🍏 **When teaching academic content, simultaneously teach students how to effectively study and remember it.**
When a second-grade teacher presents the new spelling words for the week, he asks students to practice writing each word once by itself and once in a sentence. He also asks students to think about how some of the words are spelled similarly to words they already know (e.g., "The word *clown* ends in the letters *o-w-n*. What other words have you learned that end with those letters?"). And he teaches his students the mnemonic "*I before E* except after *C* . . ." to help them remember the spellings of such words as *believe* and *receive*.

🍏 **Suggest a wide variety of strategies—taking notes, thinking of new examples, forming mnemonics, summarizing, taking self-check quizzes, and so on—each of which is apt to be useful in different situations and for different purposes.**
A high school social studies teacher acknowledges that some aspects of geography, such as the names of European capital cities, can be hard to remember. She suggests the keyword mnemonic and illustrates this process with the capital of Belgium, which is Brussels: "Think of a large *bell* with eyes and a mouth, and picture it eating some *Brussels* sprouts." But in addition, the teacher points out that many aspects of geography make sense and should be understood rather than memorized. For example, when presenting a map of Europe one day, she says, "Notice how most European capitals—for instance, Paris, Rome, Brussels, Prague—are on major rivers. Why do you suppose this is the case?"

🍏 **Scaffold students' attempts to use new strategies— for instance, by modeling the strategies, giving clues about when to use them, and providing feedback on appropriate and inappropriate strategy use.**
A seventh-grade language arts teacher gives her students note-taking forms they can use to take notes in a unit on Greek mythology (see Figure 7.1).

🍏 **Explain the usefulness of various strategies in an age-appropriate way.**
A ninth-grade history teacher asks his class, "Who can tell me why the American colonists were so upset about the Quartering Act of 1765? We talked about that last week. Does anyone remember?" When no one responds, the teacher continues, "A lot of kids don't

realize this, but we human beings can't always remember everything we're taught. It's time we started getting serious about taking notes in this class." The teacher gives some initial pointers on how and when to take notes and continues to scaffold the students' note taking over the course of the school year, sometimes simply by saying, "This is an important point, so you should be sure to include it in your notes."

🍏 **Occasionally ask students to study instructional material in pairs or small cooperative learning groups.**
In a unit on the human muscular system, seventh graders are given "starters" (e.g., "Describe ___ in your own words"; "Compare ___ with respect to ___") to help them formulate elaboration-promoting questions to ask a study partner. The students then break into pairs to study together. Many of them generate and are able to answer such elaborative questions as "Why are muscles important?" and "How are the skeletal muscles and the cardiac muscles the same?"

🍏 **Ask students to share their strategies with one another.**
At a school that serves a large number of minority-group students who are at risk for academic failure, faculty and students create a Minority Achievement Committee (MAC) program designed to make academic achievement a high priority. Participation in the program is selective (i.e., students must show a commitment to academic improvement) and prestigious. In regular meetings, high-achieving eleventh and twelfth graders describe, model, and encourage many effective strategies, and they help younger students who are struggling with their schoolwork.

🍏 **Make use of software that enhances students' awareness of effective metacognitive strategies.**
Students in an eighth-grade science class are learning about global climate change. As part of the unit, the students interact with a computer-based learning environment called *Betty's Brain*, in which they must teach a virtual "student" (Betty) what they've been learning and assess her understanding. Betty sometimes tells the students that their explanations don't make sense to her, and she answers some quiz questions incorrectly. On such occasions, a virtual "mentor" teacher (Mr. Davis) offers gentle guidance that encourages students to improve their explanations—and so indirectly also encourages them to monitor and improve their own understandings. As a result of "teaching" Betty and learning from their mistakes while doing so, the students gain considerable knowledge about cause–and–effect relationships affecting climate change.

*Sources:* P. A. Alexander et al., 1998; Azevedo & Witherspoon, 2009; J. E. Barnett, Di Vesta, & Rogozinski, 1981; Bulgren, Marquis, Lenz, Deshler, & Schumaker, 2011; Hacker et al., 2009b; Hattie et al., 1996; Kahl & Woloshyn, 1994; A. King, Staffieri, & Adelgais, 1998 (muscular system example, pp. 139, 141); Kinnebrew & Biswas, 2011 (*Betty's Brain* example); Kucan & Beck, 1997; Kuhn et al., 1995; McCrudden & Schraw, 2007; McGovern, Davis, & Ogbu, 2008 (Minority Achievement Club example); Meltzer et al., 2007; Nokes & Dole, 2004; S. G. Paris & Winograd, 1990; Pressley, Borkowski, & Schneider, 1987; Pressley, Harris, & Marks, 1992; Pressley & Hilden, 2006; Rosenshine, Meister, & Chapman, 1996; Starr & Lovett, 2000; J. W. Thomas, 1993a; Vaughn et al., 2011; Veenman, 2011; Vygotsky, 1978; C. E. Weinstein, Goetz, & Alexander, 1988; C. E. Weinstein & Hume, 1998; Wentzel, 2009; E. Wood et al., 1999.

material and to think about it in more sophisticated ways. Thus, the simple learning strategies children acquire in elementary school (e.g., rehearsal) become less and less effective with each passing year. All too often, however, teachers teach academic content areas—history, biology, math, and so on—without also teaching students how to *learn* in those content areas. When left to their own devices, most students develop effective strategies very slowly (if at all) and thus, over the years, encounter increasing difficulty in their attempts to master classroom subject matter. And when they *don't* master it, they may not know why they've failed or how to improve their chances of succeeding the next time around (Hacker et al., 2000; Hamman, Berthelot, Saia, & Crowley, 2000; Nokes & Dole, 2004; O'Sullivan & Joy, 1994).

Using effective learning strategies makes such a difference in students' classroom achievement that we mustn't leave the development of these strategies to chance. How can we help students *learn how to learn?* The Into the Classroom feature "Promoting Effective Learning and Study Strategies" presents several research-based strategies. The most important of the strategies presented there is the first one: *When teaching academic content, simultaneously teach students how to effectively study and remember it.* Students are more likely to use effective learning and study strategies when those strategies are taught not in separate study skills classes but rather as integral parts of everyday instruction about specific academic topics (Hattie, Biggs, & Purdie, 1996; S. G. Paris & Paris, 2001; Pressley, Harris, & Marks, 1992; Veenman, 2011).

## DIVERSITY, DISABILITIES, AND EXCEPTIONAL ABILITIES IN METACOGNITION

Researchers have observed cultural differences in students' epistemic beliefs—in particular, their beliefs about what it means to *learn* something. From the perspective of mainstream Western culture, learning is largely a mental enterprise: People learn in order to understand the world and acquire new skills and abilities. But for many people in China, learning also has moral and social dimensions: It enables an individual to become increasingly virtuous and honorable and to contribute in significant ways to the betterment of society. From a traditional East Asian perspective, true learning isn't a quick-and-easy process; rather, it comes only with a great deal of diligence, concentration, and perseverance (Dahlin & Watkins, 2000; H. Grant & Dweck, 2001; J. Li, 2005; J. Li & Fischer, 2004).

Learning strategies, too, may differ somewhat from culture to culture. Consistent with a belief that learning requires diligence and perseverance, many East Asian parents and teachers encourage frequent use of rehearsal and rote memorization as learning strategies that supplement students' efforts to make sense of material (Dahlin & Watkins, 2000; Ho, 1994; Purdie & Hattie, 1996). Rehearsal and memorization are also common in cultures that value verbatim learning of oral histories or passages of sacred text (e.g., the Bible, the Koran) (MacDonald, Uesiliana, & Hayne, 2000; Rogoff et al., 2007; Q. Wang & Ross, 2007). In contrast, many schools in mainstream Western culture are increasingly conducting activities and encouraging strategies that foster meaningful learning and conceptual understanding. Even so, Western schools typically insist that students learn certain things—such as multiplication tables and word spellings—by heart (Q. Wang & Ross, 2007).

> Remember that students' learning strategies and beliefs about learning may be partly the result of their cultural backgrounds.

### ACCOMMODATING STUDENTS WITH SPECIAL NEEDS

We're especially likely to see diversity in metacognition in students who have special educational needs. Table 7.2 presents characteristics you might see in these students. Notice that many students with cognitive disabilities—and some with emotional and behavioral disorders as well—may exhibit little knowledge and use of effective learning strategies. In contrast, students who are gifted typically have more sophisticated learning strategies than their peers do.

For many students with disabilities, we may have to teach metacognitive skills explicitly and with considerable scaffolding—that is, with close guidance and assistance in the use of specific learning strategies (Meltzer, 2007). For example, we might provide partially filled-in outlines to guide students' note taking (e.g., see Figure 7.3). We might also tell students when particular strategies (e.g., elaboration, comprehension monitoring) are appropriate and model the use of such strategies with specific classroom subject matter. Finally, we must give students opportunities to practice their newly acquired strategies, along with feedback about how effectively they are using each one.

> Keep in mind that your students are apt to be less effective learners than you are.

As teachers, we must remember that our students are likely to learn differently—and often less efficiently and successfully—than we do. Almost all of them can benefit from acquiring more sophisticated understandings of what knowledge and learning involve and from regularly practicing effective strategies for mastering school subject matter.

# STUDENTS IN INCLUSIVE SETTINGS

**TABLE 7.2 • Promoting Metacognitive Development in Students with Special Educational Needs**

| CATEGORY | CHARACTERISTICS YOU MIGHT OBSERVE | SUGGESTED STRATEGIES |
|---|---|---|
| Students with specific cognitive or academic difficulties | • Less metacognitive awareness or control of learning<br>• Use of few and relatively inefficient learning strategies<br>• Increased strategy use after explicit instruction in strategies | 🍏 Teach effective learning and reading strategies (e.g., taking notes, using mnemonics, identifying main ideas and general themes) within the context of lessons about particular topics.<br>🍏 Model effective strategies and scaffold students' efforts to use them (e.g., provide outlines to guide note taking, ask questions that encourage activation of prior knowledge). |
| Students with social or behavioral problems | • Limited metacognitive awareness of one's processing difficulties (for some students)<br>• Few effective learning strategies (for some students) | 🍏 Provide guidance in using effective learning and study strategies (e.g., verbally model strategies, give outlines that guide note taking). |
| Students with general delays in cognitive and social functioning | • Lack of metacognitive awareness or control of learning<br>• Lack of learning strategies, especially in the absence of strategies training | 🍏 Teach relatively simple learning strategies (e.g., rehearsal, specific mnemonics), and give students ample practice in using them. |
| Students with physical or sensory challenges | • No consistently observed deficits in metacognitive knowledge or strategies; specific deficits sometimes due to sensory impairments | 🍏 Address any deficits in metacognition with strategies you would use with nondisabled students, making appropriate accommodations for physical and sensory limitations. |
| Students with advanced cognitive development | • Use of relatively sophisticated learning strategies in comparison with peers | 🍏 Don't assume that students have adultlike learning strategies; assess their existing strategies and, as appropriate, encourage more effective strategies (e.g., elaboration, comprehension monitoring).<br>🍏 Provide opportunities for self-directed learning if students clearly have effective learning strategies they can use with little teacher guidance. |

*Sources:* Beirne-Smith, Patton, & Kim, 2006; Campione, Brown, & Bryant, 1985; B. Clark, 1997; Edmonds et al., 2009; E. S. Ellis & Friend, 1991; Graham & Harris, 1996; N. Gregg, 2009; Grodzinsky & Diamond, 1992; Heward, 2009; Mastropieri & Scruggs, 2007; McGlynn, 1998; Meltzer, 2007; Mercer & Pullen, 2005; Piirto, 1999; Pressley, 1995; Scruggs & Mastropieri, 1992; H. L. Swanson, 1993; Turnbull, Turnbull, & Wehmeyer, 2010; Waber, 2010; Wong, 1991.

**FIGURE 7.3** Example of a partially filled-in outline that can guide students' note

MUSCLES

A. Number of Muscles

   1. There are approximately _____ muscles in the human body.

B. How Muscles Work

   1. Muscles work in two ways:

     a. They _____ , or shorten.

     b. They _____ , or lengthen.

C. Kinds of Muscles

   1. _____ muscles are attached to the bones by _____ .

     a. These muscles are _____ (voluntary/involuntary).

     b. The purpose of these muscles is to _____ .

   2. _____ muscles line some of the body's _____ .

     a. These muscles are _____ (voluntary/involuntary).

     b. The purpose of these muscles is to _____ .

   3. The _____ muscle is the only one of its kind.

     a. This muscle is _____ (voluntary/involuntary).

     b. The purpose of this muscle is to _____ .

# Transfer

How students think about and study school subject matter has implications not only for how well they can understand and remember it but also for how effectively they can *use and apply* it on later occasions. Here we're talking about transfer: the extent to which knowledge and skills acquired in one situation affect a person's learning or performance in a subsequent situation. Following are examples:

- Elena speaks both English and Spanish fluently. When she begins a French course in high school, she immediately recognizes many similarities between French and Spanish. "Aha," she thinks, "what I know about Spanish will help me learn French."
- In her middle school history class, Stella discovers that she does better on quizzes when she takes more notes. She decides to take more notes in her chemistry class as well, and once again the strategy pays off.
- Ted's fifth-grade class has been working with decimals for several weeks. His teacher asks, "Which number is larger, 4.4 or 4.14?" Ted recalls something he knows about whole numbers: Numbers with three digits are larger than numbers with only two digits. "The larger number is 4.14," he mistakenly concludes.

In most cases prior learning *helps* learning or performance in another situation. Such positive transfer takes place when Elena's Spanish helps her learn French and when Stella's practice with note taking in history class improves her performance in chemistry class. In some instances, however, existing knowledge or skills *hinder* later learning. Such negative transfer is the case for Ted, who transfers a principle related to whole numbers to a situation in which it doesn't apply: comparing decimals.

Sometimes we see specific transfer, in which the original learning task and the transfer task overlap in content. For example, Elena should have an easy time learning to count in French because the numbers *(un, deux, trois, quatre, cinq . . .)* are very similar to the Spanish ones she already knows *(uno, dos, tres, cuatro, cinco . . .)*. At other times we may see general transfer, in which learning in one situation affects learning and performance in a somewhat dissimilar situation. Consider, for example, Stella's strategy of taking more notes in chemistry because of her success with note taking in history. History and chemistry don't necessarily overlap in content, but a strategy acquired in one class helps with learning in the other.

Historically, research studies have indicated that when application of academic subject matter is involved, specific transfer occurs far more often than general transfer (S. M. Barnett & Ceci, 2002; W. D. Gray & Orasanu, 1987). In fact, the question of whether general transfer occurs at all has been the subject of considerable debate over the years. Many early educators believed that certain subjects (e.g., math, Latin, formal logic) have great potential for general transfer: Because these subjects require considerable attention to precision and detail, they might strengthen students' minds and thereby enable students to tackle other, unrelated tasks more easily. This formal discipline perspective of transfer persisted throughout the first several decades of the twentieth century. For instance, when I was in high school in the mid-1960s, most college-bound students at my school were encouraged to take both French and Latin—the only two languages my school offered. Taking French made a great deal of sense: Living in Massachusetts, we were within a day's drive of French-speaking Quebec. "But why should I take Latin?" I asked. "I can use it only if I attend Catholic mass or run across phrases like 'caveat emptor' or 'e pluribus unum.' " My guidance counselor pursed her thin red lips and gave me a look suggesting that she knew best. "Latin will discipline your mind," she told me. "It will help you learn better."

Most research has discredited this mind-as-muscle notion of transfer (Haskell, 2001; Perkins & Salomon, 1989; E. L. Thorndike, 1924). For example, practice in memorizing poems doesn't necessarily make one a faster poem memorizer (James, 1890). And studying computer programming, though often a worthwhile activity in its own right, doesn't necessarily help a person with dissimilar kinds of logical tasks (R. E. Mayer & Wittrock, 1996; Perkins & Salomon, 1989).

We're more likely to see general transfer when we broaden our notion of transfer to include application of general academic skills (e.g., reading comprehension, persuasive writing) and general learning strategies (e.g., taking notes) that can be applied to a wide variety of topics and contexts (J. R. Anderson, Greeno, Reder, & Simon, 2000; S. M. Barnett & Ceci, 2002; Perkins, 1995; M. I. Posner & Rothbart, 2007). Furthermore, general beliefs, attitudes, and dispositions

**transfer** Phenomenon in which something a person has learned at one time affects how the person learns or performs in a later situation.

**positive transfer** Phenomenon in which something learned at one time facilitates learning or performance at a later time.

**negative transfer** Phenomenon in which something learned at one time interferes with learning or performance at a later time.

**specific transfer** Instance of transfer in which the original learning task and the transfer task overlap in content.

**general transfer** Instance of transfer in which the original learning task and the transfer task are different in content.

**formal discipline** View of transfer suggesting that the study of rigorous subject matter enhances one's ability to learn other, unrelated things.

Teachers
↳ misconception

related to learning and thinking—for instance, recognition that learning often requires hard work, as well as open-mindedness to diverse viewpoints—can have a profound impact on later learning and achievement across multiple domains and so clearly illustrate general transfer at work (Cornoldi, 2010; De Corte, 2003; K. J. Pugh & Bergin, 2006; D. L. Schwartz, Bransford, & Sears, 2005). And some students develop a general desire to apply what they learn in the classroom—that is, they have a *spirit of transfer*—that consistently resurfaces in later instructional contexts (Haskell, 2001; Volet, 1999).

## FACTORS AFFECTING TRANSFER

Ideally, *positive* transfer to real-world contexts should be a major objective in classrooms at all grade levels. When learners can't use their basic math skills to compute correct change or balance a checkbook, when they can't use their knowledge of English grammar in a job application or business report, and when they can't apply their knowledge of science to an understanding of personal health or environmental problems, then we have to wonder whether the time spent learning these things might have been better spent doing something else.

Although both specific and general transfer do occur, students often *don't* apply the academic content they learn in particular classes to other classes or to out-of-school situations (Levstik, 2011; R. E. Mayer & Wittrock, 1996; Perkins, 1992; Renkl, Mandl, & Gruber, 1996). Learners are, of course, more likely to transfer what they learn at school when they approach each classroom topic with a deliberate intention to apply it. But several other factors also influence the probability of transfer, often because they influence learners' ability to *retrieve* what they've learned when they need to use it:

> • *Meaningful learning promotes better transfer than rote learning.* Instructional time is clearly an important variable affecting transfer: The more time students spend studying a particular topic, the more likely they are to apply what they've learned on future occasions (P. A. Alexander & Judy, 1988; Haskell, 2001; Schmidt & Bjork, 1992; Voss, 1987). Ideally, students should gain a *conceptual understanding* of the topic—that is, they should have the many things they've learned appropriately organized and interrelated. Here we see an example of the general principle *Less is more*: Students are more likely to transfer their school learning to new situations, including those beyond the classroom, when they study a few things in depth and learn them meaningfully instead of studying many topics superficially (Bereiter, 1995; Brooks & Dansereau, 1987; R. E. Mayer & Wittrock, 1996; Schwamborn, Mayer, Thillmann, Leopold, & Leutner, 2010).

The *less-is-more* principle is clearly being violated in the opening case study. Ms. Gaunt realizes that she must move quickly in order to cover the entire eighth-grade math curriculum, even if it means that few students will master any particular topic or procedure. Given the upcoming statewide competency exam, she may have little choice about the matter, but her students are unlikely to *use* what they're learning on future occasions.

> • *Both positive and negative transfer are more common when a new situation is similar—or at least appears to be similar—to a previous one.* Perceived similarity increases the chances that a new situation will provide retrieval cues that point learners in the right direction as they search long-term memory for potentially relevant knowledge and skills (Bassok, 2003; Di Vesta & Peverly, 1984; Haskell, 2001). For instance, when Elena first encounters number words in her French class *(un, deux, trois)*, the words should quickly trigger recall of similar-sounding Spanish words *(uno, dos, tres)*.

However, we should note that the similarity of two situations, although usually promoting positive transfer, can sometimes lead to negative transfer instead (e.g., Sun-Alperin & Wang, 2008). To see what I mean, try the following exercise.

### EXPERIENCING FIRSTHAND
### A DIVISION PROBLEM

Quickly estimate an answer to this division problem:

$$60 \div 0.38$$

*Chapter 5 describes open-mindedness and other general dispositions that positively influence students' learning and achievement.*

*You have previously seen this less-is-more principle in Chapter 6.*

Teach important topics in depth, with a focus on true understanding rather than rote memorization.

For tonight's homework assignment, memorize all 50 states in the U.S.A. in reverse alphabetical order.

Meaningless mental "exercises" such as this one have little or no benefit. Not only do they *not* "strengthen" students' minds, but in fact they're likely to communicate the message that schoolwork is often a waste of time.

Is your answer larger or smaller than 60? If you applied your knowledge of division by whole numbers, you undoubtedly concluded that the answer is smaller than 60. In fact, the answer is approximately 158, a number much *larger* than 60. Does this exercise remind you of Ted's erroneous conclusion—that 4.14 is larger than 4.4—based on his knowledge of how whole numbers can be compared? Many students at all levels, even in college, show negative transfer of whole-number principles to situations involving decimals and fractions (M. Carr, 2010; Ni & Zhou, 2005; Tirosh & Graeber, 1990). Working with decimals appears, on the surface, to be similar to working with whole numbers. The only difference—a very important one, as it turns out—is a tiny decimal point.

To minimize negative transfer, we teachers must be sure to point out differences between two superficially similar topics. For example, Ted's teacher might have identified some of the specific ways in which decimals are different from whole numbers. As another example, I find that students in my educational psychology classes often have trouble correctly understanding certain concepts (e.g., *maturation, socialization, short-term memory, reinforcement*) because the meanings of these words in psychology are quite different from their meanings in everyday conversation. So when I first introduce one of these concepts, I take great pains to contrast the different meanings. Even so, the everyday meanings regularly intrude into some students' thinking about course content, especially if the students don't continually monitor their own thinking and understanding.

When concepts might be easily confused, explicitly point out their differences.

Emphasize general principles more than discrete facts.

• *Principles and theories are more easily transferred than discrete facts.* Specific facts certainly have an important place in the classroom. For instance, students should know what 2 + 3 equals, what the Berlin Wall signified, and where to find Africa on a globe. Yet by themselves, facts have limited usefulness in new situations. On average, general principles, rules, and theoretical explanations are more widely applicable than specific facts and information (S. M. Barnett & Ceci, 2002; Bransford & Schwartz, 1999; Haskell, 2001; M. Perry, 1991). The more we can emphasize general principles—for example, that adding two positive whole numbers always yields a larger number, that a country's citizens sometimes revolt when their government officials act unjustly, and that the cultures of various nations are influenced by their locations and climates—the more we facilitate students' ability to transfer what they learn.

Especially as they get older, some students acquire an ability to apply general principles to topics quite different from those they've previously studied. For example, in one research study, fifth graders and college students were asked to develop a plan for increasing the population of bald eagles, an endangered species in their state (Bransford & Schwartz, 1999). None of the students in either age-group had previously studied strategies for eagle preservation, and the plans that both groups developed were largely inadequate. Yet in the process of developing their plans, the college students addressed more sophisticated questions than the fifth graders did. In particular, the fifth graders focused on the eagles themselves (e.g., How big are they? What do they eat?), whereas the college students looked at the larger picture (e.g., What type of ecosystem supports eagles? What about predators of eagles and eagle babies?) (Bransford & Schwartz, 1999, p. 67). Thus, the college students were drawing on an important principle they had acquired in their many years of science study: Living creatures are more likely to survive and thrive when their habitat supports rather than threatens them.

• *Transfer is more common when information and skills are perceived as being relevant to diverse disciplines and real-world situations.* Unfortunately, many students tend to think of academic subject areas as *context bound*—that is, as being distinct disciplines that are completely separate from one another and from real-world concerns (P. A. Alexander & Judy, 1988; S. M. Barnett & Ceci, 2002; Perkins & Simmons, 1988; Renkl et al., 1996). For example, when baking cookies, an 11-year-old might ask a parent, "Do two one-quarters make two fourths? I know it does in math but what about in cooking?" (K. J. Pugh & Bergin, 2005, p. 16).

The context-bound nature of some school learning may prevent students from retrieving what they've learned in situations where it might be useful. A study with high school students (Saljo & Wyndhamn, 1992) provides an illustration. Students were asked to figure out how much postage they should put on an envelope that weighed a particular amount, and they were given a table of postage rates that would enable them to determine the correct amount. When students were given the task in a social studies class, most used the postage table to find the answer. But when students were given the task in a math class, most of them ignored the postage table and tried to calculate the postage, in some cases figuring it to several decimal places. Thus, the students in the social studies class were more likely to solve the problem correctly—as a former social studies teacher myself, I suspect that, in that context, they were well accustomed to looking for information in tables and charts. In contrast, many of the students in the math class drew on strategies they associated with math, using formulas and performing calculations, and thus overlooked the more efficient and accurate approach.

Fortunately, not all school learning remains "stuck" in school or in a particular classroom. People regularly use some of the skills they've learned in their daily lives—reading, arithmetic, map interpretation, and so on. But we can increase the transferability of school subject matter by regularly relating it to other disciplines and to the outside world (R. E. Clark & Blake, 1997; Perkins, 1992; J. F. Wagner, 2010). For instance, we might show students how human digestion provides a justification for categorizing food into several basic food groups or how principles of economics have indirect impacts on global climate change.

• *Numerous and varied opportunities for practice increase the probability of transfer.* The more that students practice using what they've learned to address real-world tasks and problems—and the more *diverse* those tasks and problems are—the greater the probability that students will apply school subject matter in future situations, including those outside the classroom (Gijbels, Dochy, Van den Bossche, & Segers, 2005; Gresalfi & Lester, 2009; J. F. Wagner, 2010). Especially important are authentic activities—activities similar or identical to those that students will eventually encounter in the outside world. For example, when students are learning basic arithmetic principles, they might be asked to apply those principles in determining best buys at a discount store, dividing items equitably among friends, running a school book sale, and so on. Arithmetic will then be associated in long-term memory with all these situations, and when the need arises to determine which of two purchases yields the most for the money, relevant arithmetic procedures should be readily retrieved. Ideally, students should discover that much of what they learn at school truly has wide applicability—in other words, school topics become *context free* (A. Collins, Brown, & Newman, 1989; Cox, 1997; Perkins & Salomon, 1989).

• *Transfer increases when the cultural environment encourages and expects transfer.* All too often, it seems, students are encouraged to acquire school subject matter for mysterious purposes — for example, "You'll need to know this in college" or "It will come in handy later in life." Ideally, we should instead create a culture of transfer—a learning environment in which applying school subject matter to new situations, cross-disciplinary contexts, and real-world problems is both the expectation and the norm. For instance, we might regularly encourage students to ask themselves, "How might I use this information?" as they listen, read, and study (R. A. Engle, 2006; Haskell, 2001; M. C. Linn, 2008; Pea, 1987; Sternberg & Frensch, 1993).

---

**authentic activity** Classroom activity similar to an activity that students are apt to encounter in the outside world.

**culture of transfer** Learning environment in which applying school subject matter to new situations, cross-disciplinary contexts, and real-world problems is both the expectation and the norm.

The context-bound nature of some knowledge and skills learned in schools should remind you of the discussion of *situated learning and cognition* in Chapter 6.

 Regularly relate topics in one academic discipline to other academic disciplines and to the nonacademic world.

 Provide numerous opportunities to apply classroom content to authentic, real-world tasks.

Chapter 8 discusses authentic activities in more detail.

 Create a classroom culture in which transfer is both the expectation and the norm.

# Problem Solving

**Problem solving** involves using—that is, *transferring*—existing knowledge and skills to address an unanswered question or troubling situation. The world presents innumerable problems that differ widely in content and scope, as illustrated in the next exercise.

Sometimes problems are straightforward and easy to solve. Problem 1 requires only simple addition and subtraction procedures, which easily yield a correct solution: 10 cents. Problem 2

**FIGURE 7.4** How long do the roof planks of this treehouse need to be?

5ft.

2ft.

4ft.

?

### EXPERIENCING FIRSTHAND
## FOUR PROBLEMS

How many of these problems can you solve?

1. You buy two apples for 25 cents each and one pear for 40 cents. How much change will you get back from a dollar bill?

2. You're building a treehouse with the shape and dimensions illustrated in Figure 7.4. You need to buy planks for a slanted roof. How long must the roof planks be to reach from one side of the treehouse to the other?

3. As a teacher, you want to illustrate the idea that metal battleships float even though metal is denser (and thus heavier) than water. You don't have a toy boat made of metal. What can you use instead to demonstrate that a metal object with a hollow interior can float on water?

4. Tropical rainforests provide homes for many species of animals and plants (including some plants useful in modern medicine), and they help to reduce the rapid increase in carbon dioxide in the earth's atmosphere. Yet each day tens of thousands of acres of tropical rainforest disappear, largely as a result of farmers' efforts to create new farmland by slashing and burning existing vegetation. What steps might be taken to curtail this alarming rate of deforestation?

(Figure 7.4) is more difficult, partly because you probably don't encounter such problems very often. But if you've studied geometry, you've almost certainly learned the Pythagorean theorem: In any right triangle, the square of the hypotenuse equals the sum of the squares of the other two sides. Looking at the top part of the treehouse (from the dashed line upward) as a triangle, we can find the length for the roof planks ($x$) this way:

$$(\text{Slanted side})^2 = (\text{Horizontal side})^2 + (\text{Vertical side})^2$$
$$x^2 = 4^2 + (5 - 2)^2$$
$$x^2 = 16 + 9$$
$$x^2 = 25$$
$$x = 5$$

Problems don't always have a single correct solution, of course. A variety of objects (e.g., a metal pie plate, bucket, or thimble) might be used to solve Problem 3. And you might identify several possible ways of addressing Problem 4, but you probably wouldn't know which ones could successfully curtail rainforest destruction until you actually implemented them.

Problems differ considerably in the extent to which they're clearly specified and structured. At one end of this clarity-and-structure continuum is the **well-defined problem**, in which the goal is clearly stated, all information needed to solve the problem is present, and only one correct answer exists. Calculating correct change after a purchase (Problem 1) and determining the length of planks needed for a treehouse roof (Problem 2) are well-defined problems. At the other end of the continuum is the **ill-defined problem**, in which the desired goal is unclear, information needed to solve it is missing, or several possible solutions exist. Finding a suitable

**problem solving** Using existing knowledge and skills to address an unanswered question or troubling situation.

**well-defined problem** Problem in which the goal is clearly stated, all the information needed to solve the problem is present, and only one correct answer exists.

substitute for a metal ship (Problem 3) is somewhat ill defined: Many objects might serve as a ship substitute, and some might work better than others. The rainforest destruction problem (Problem 4) is even less defined: The goal (curtailing deforestation) is ambiguous, we're missing a lot of information that would help us solve the problem (e.g., what alternatives might replace farmers' slash-and-burn practices?), and there's no single correct solution. On average, ill-defined problems are harder to solve than well-defined ones.

Most problems presented in school are well defined. As an example, let's return to the typing problem in the opening case study:

> Louis can type 35 words a minute. He needs to type a final copy of his English composition, which is 4,200 words long. How long will it take Louis to type his paper?

Notice that all the information needed to solve the problem is provided, and there's no irrelevant information to lead students astray. And there's only one correct answer, with no room for debate. Yet the real world presents ill-defined problems far more often than well-defined ones, and students need practice in dealing with them. Furthermore, when students regularly encounter ill-defined problems in the school curriculum, they may acquire more sophisticated epistemic beliefs—in particular, they may begin to realize that many topics and issues don't have easy, clear-cut right and wrong answers (Rule & Bendixen, 2010).

Taking the perspective of cognitive psychology (especially information processing theory), you might think of problem solving as involving five basic steps:

1. Encoding the problem
2. Retrieving one or more strategies that might be useful in solving the problem
3. Choosing the most appropriate strategy or set of strategies
4. Carrying out the chosen strategy or strategies
5. Evaluating the quality of the problem solution obtained (steps based loosely on Polya, 1957)

Cognitive factors we've previously identified as affecting transfer—thorough understanding of a topic, perception of relevance to diverse academic disciplines and to real-world situations, and so on—certainly affect learners' ability to carry out these steps successfully. Researchers have identified additional factors related to four general categories: problem encoding, problem-solving strategies, working memory capacity, and metacognition.

## PROBLEM ENCODING

At Step 1 in the problem-solving process, learners might mentally represent a problem—that is, they might *encode* it—in a variety of ways. As an example, see whether you can solve the problem in the following exercise.

**EXPERIENCING FIRSTHAND**

## PIGS AND CHICKENS

Consider this problem:

> Old MacDonald has a barnyard full of pigs and chickens. Altogether there are 21 heads and 60 legs in the barnyard (not counting MacDonald's own head and legs). How many pigs and how many chickens are running around the barnyard?

Can you figure out the answer? If you're having trouble, think about the problem this way:

> Imagine the pigs standing upright on their two hind legs, with their front two legs raised over their heads. Therefore, both the pigs and the chickens are standing on two legs. Figure out how many legs are on the ground and how many must be in the air. From this information, can you determine the number of pigs and chickens in the barnyard?

---

*Margin notes:*

**ill-defined problem** Problem in which the desired goal is unclear, some information needed to solve the problem is missing, and/or several possible solutions to the problem exist.

 Give students guidance and practice in dealing with ill-defined problems.

Some ways of encoding a problem enable more successful problem solving than others do.

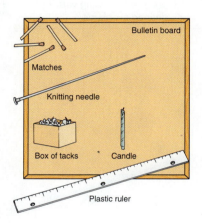

Bulletin board
Matches
Knitting needle
Box of tacks     Candle
Plastic ruler

Because there are 21 heads, there must be 21 animals. Thus there must be 42 legs on the ground (21 × 2), which leaves 18 pigs' legs in the air (60 − 42). There must therefore be 9 pigs (18 ÷ 2) and 12 chickens (21 − 9).

There are, of course, several ways you might approach the pigs-and-chickens problem. But if you initially had trouble solving it—perhaps because your algebra skills are rusty—you may have struggled to encode it in a way that led you to an easy solution. Students often have difficulty solving mathematical word problems because they don't know how to translate the problems into the procedures they've learned (K. Lee, Ng, & Ng, 2009; R. E. Mayer, 1992; Walkington, Sherman, & Petrosino, 2010).

At other times students may encode a problem in a seemingly logical way that nevertheless fails to yield a workable result. As an example, take a stab at the next problem.

## EXPERIENCING FIRSTHAND
### CANDLE PROBLEM

How might you stand a candle upright in front of a bulletin board attached to the wall? You don't want the candle to touch the bulletin board, because the flame might singe the board. Instead, you need to place the candle about a centimeter away from the board. How can you accomplish the task using some or all of the following materials: a small candle (birthday cake size), a metal knitting needle, matches, a box of thumbtacks, and a 12-inch ruler?

*Source:* Based on Duncker, 1945.

As it turns out, the ruler and knitting needle are useless in solving the problem. Piercing the candle with the knitting needle will probably break the candle, and you're unlikely to have much luck balancing the ruler on a few tacks. (I speak from experience here, as my own students have unsuccessfully tried both strategies.) The easiest solution is to turn the thumbtack box upside down or sideways, attach it to the bulletin board with tacks, and then attach the candle to the top of the box with either a tack or melted wax. Many people don't consider this possibility because they encode the box only as a *container of tacks* and so overlook its potential use as a candle stand. When learners encode a problem in a way that limits possible solutions, they're the victims of a **mental set**. Mental sets, then, interfere with Step 2 in the problem-solving process: retrieving potentially useful strategies from long-term memory.

Mental sets sometimes emerge when learners practice solving a particular kind of problem (e.g., doing subtraction problems in math or applying the formula $E = mc^2$ in physics) without also practicing other kinds of problems at the same time. Such repetitive practice can lead students to encode problems in a particular way without really thinking about them—in other words, it can lead to automaticity in encoding. Although automaticity in the basic information and skills needed for problem solving is often an advantage because it frees up working memory capacity (more about this point shortly), automaticity in *encoding* problems can lead students to solve them incorrectly (E. J. Langer, 2000; Luchins, 1942; Rohrer & Pashler, 2010).

Several teaching strategies can help students effectively encode problems, without falling victim to counterproductive mental sets:

- Present problems in a concrete form; for example, provide real objects that students can manipulate, or present an illustration of a problem's components.
- Encourage students to make problems concrete *for themselves;* for example, encourage them to draw a picture or diagram.
- Highlight aspects of problems that students can competently solve, and when those elements appear again in a different problem, point out that the same information can be applied or the same approach to problem solution can be used.
- Give problems that look different on the surface yet require the same or similar problem-solving procedures.
- Mix the kinds of problems that students tackle in any single practice session.

**mental set** Inclination to encode a problem in a way that excludes potential solutions.

🍏 Have students work in cooperative groups to identify several ways of representing a single problem—perhaps as a formula, a table, and a graph. (Anzai, 1991; Brenner et al., 1997; Z. Chen, 1999; L. S. Fuchs et al., 2003; R. E. Mayer, 1992; Mayfield & Chase, 2002; Prawat, 1989; Rohrer & Pashler, 2010; Sherman & Bisanz, 2009; Turner, Meyer, et al., 1998)

## PROBLEM-SOLVING STRATEGIES: ALGORITHMS AND HEURISTICS

At the heart of successful problem solving, of course, are the *strategies* learners have available to them, as reflected in Steps 2, 3, and 4 of the problem-solving process described earlier. Some problems can be successfully solved with an algorithm, a specific sequence of steps that guarantees a correct solution. For example, by dividing 4,200 by 35, we can easily determine that Louis will need 120 minutes (2 hours) to type his English composition. And by using the Pythagorean theorem and simple algebra, we can correctly calculate the length of a treehouse's slanted roof.

Yet the world presents many problems for which no algorithms exist. There are no rules we can follow to identify a substitute metal ship, no set of instructions to help us address worldwide rainforest destruction. In fact, few algorithms exist for solving problems outside the domains of mathematics and science. In the absence of an algorithm, learners must use one or more heuristics, general problem-solving strategies that may or may not yield a successful outcome. For example, one heuristic we might use in solving the deforestation problem is this: Identify a new behavior that adequately replaces the problem behavior (i.e., identify another way that rainforest farmers can meet their survival needs).

Both types of problem-solving strategies—algorithms and heuristics alike—are often specific to particular content domains. But here are several general problem-solving heuristics that can be helpful in a variety of contexts:

- *Identify subgoals.* Break a large, complex task into two or more specific subtasks that can be more easily addressed.
- *Round complex numbers up or down.* Estimate mathematical solutions by converting hard-to-work-with numbers to simpler ones.
- *Use paper and pencil.* Draw a diagram, list a problem's components, or jot down potential solutions or approaches.
- *Draw an analogy.* Identify a situation analogous to the problem situation, and derive potential solutions from the analogy.
- *Brainstorm.* Generate a wide variety of possible approaches or solutions—perhaps including some that might seem outlandish or absurd—without initially evaluating any of them. After a lengthy list has been created, evaluate each item for its potential relevance and usefulness.
- *"Incubate" the situation.* Let a problem remain unresolved for a few hours or days, allowing time for a broad search of long-term memory for potentially productive approaches. (J. E. Davidson & Sternberg, 1998, 2003; De Corte, Op't Eynde, Depaepe, & Verschaffel, 2010; Halpern, 1997; Minsky, 2006; Sweller, 2009a; Zhong, Dijksterhuis, & Galinsky, 2008)

### TEACHING PROBLEM-SOLVING STRATEGIES

Occasionally students develop problem-solving strategies on their own. For instance, many children invent simple addition and subtraction strategies long before they encounter arithmetic at school (Bermejo, 1996; Ginsburg, Cannon, Eisenband, & Pappas, 2006; Siegler & Jenkins, 1989). But without some formal instruction in effective strategies, even the most inventive students may occasionally resort to unproductive trial and error to solve problems. Following are research-based recommendations for teaching problem-solving strategies:

**For Teaching Algorithms**

🍏 Describe and demonstrate specific procedures and the situations in which each can be used.

🍏 Provide worked-out examples of algorithms being applied, and ask students to explain what's happening at each step.

**algorithm** Prescribed sequence of steps that guarantees a correct problem solution.

**heuristic** General strategy that facilitates problem solving but doesn't always yield a solution.

**FIGURE 7.5** Thirteen-year-old Malika incorrectly simplifies the expression $6(2x + y) + 2(x + 4y)$ as $14x + 10y$. The correct answer is $14x + 14y$. Where did Malika go wrong?

- Help students understand why particular algorithms are relevant and effective in certain situations.
- When a student's application of an algorithm yields an incorrect answer, look closely at what the student has done, and locate the trouble spot (e.g., see Figure 7.5).

### For Teaching Both Algorithms and Heuristics

- Teach problem-solving strategies within the context of specific subject areas—*not* as a topic separate from academic content.
- Have students tackle problems within the context of authentic activities. For example, in problem-based learning, students acquire new knowledge and skills while working on a complex problem similar to one that might exist in the outside world.
- Engage in joint problem-solving activities with students, modeling effective strategies and guiding students' initial efforts.
- Provide scaffolding for difficult problems (e.g., break them into smaller and simpler problems, give hints about possible strategies, or provide partial solutions).
- Have students solve problems in pairs or small groups, in which they share ideas about problem-solving strategies, model various approaches for one another, and discuss the merits of each approach. (Barron, 2000; M. Carr, 2010; Crowley & Siegler, 1999; Hmelo-Silver, 2004; Hmelo-Silver, Duncan, & Chinn, 2007; Hung, Jonassen, & Liu, 2008; Kirschner, Sweller, & Clark, 2006; R. E. Mayer, 1985; Renkl, 2011; Rittle-Johnson, 2006; D. L. Schwartz, Lindgren, & Lewis, 2009; Wentzel & Watkins, 2011)

## WORKING MEMORY AND PROBLEM SOLVING

You may recall from an exercise in Chapter 6 just how difficult it can be to solve a long division problem in your head.

Remember, working memory has a limited capacity: At any one time it can hold only a few pieces of information and accommodate only so much cognitive processing. If a problem requires dealing with a lot of information at once or manipulating that information in a very complex way—when the *cognitive load* is high—working memory capacity may be insufficient for effective problem processing (K. Lee et al., 2009; Moreno & Park, 2010; H. L. Swanson, Jerman, & Zheng, 2008). Thus, working memory places an upper limit on Step 4 in the problem-solving process: successfully carrying out chosen strategies.

 Encourage students to write parts of a problem on paper.

 Make sure students learn basic problem-solving skills to a level of automaticity.

Learners can overcome the limits of working memory in at least two ways. One obvious way is to create an external record of needed information—for example, by writing it on a piece of paper (as we often do with long division problems). Another approach is to learn some skills to automaticity—in other words, to learn them so well that they can be retrieved quickly and easily (N. Frederiksen, 1984a; R. E. Mayer & Wittrock, 2006; Sweller, 1994).

## METACOGNITION IN PROBLEM SOLVING

Successful problem solving often involves considerable metacognition. Especially when problems are fairly complex and challenging, effective problem solvers tend to engage in metacognitive process at all five steps of the problem-solving process—for example, by doing the following:

- Identifying one or more goals that must be accomplished to solve the problem
- Breaking the problem into two or more subproblems
- Planning a systematic, sequential approach to solving the problem and its subproblems
- Continually monitoring and evaluating their progress toward the problem-solving goal(s)
- Identifying obstacles that may be impeding their progress
- Changing to a new strategy if the current one isn't working
- Scrutinizing the final solution to make sure it's logical and realistic (M. Carr, 2010; J. E. Davidson & Sternberg, 1998, 2003; Dominowski, 1998; Kirsh, 2009)

**problem-based learning** Classroom activity in which students acquire new knowledge and skills while working on a complex problem similar to one that might exist in the outside world.

Such actions enable learners to use problem-solving strategies flexibly and to determine when particular strategies aren't appropriate. In contrast, *in*effective problem solvers tend to apply problem-solving procedures mindlessly, without any real understanding of what they're doing or why they're doing it. In the opening case study, Ms. Gaunt's students rarely critique their problem solutions for logical sense; thus, they may not recognize that typing a 4,200-word paper is unlikely to take 100 days.

To some extent, students' metacognitive problem-solving processes depend on their conceptual understanding of the subject matter (M. Carr & Biddlecomb, 1998; J. E. Davidson & Sternberg, 1998; Rittle-Johnson & Star, 2009). Yet students also benefit from instruction and guidance in metacognitive strategies. For example, we can do the following:

- Ask students to explain what they're doing and why they're doing it as they work on a problem.
- Give students questions they can ask themselves as they work on a problem (e.g., "Are we getting closer to our goal?" "Why is this strategy most appropriate?").
- Help students to identify common errors in their problem solving and to check regularly for these errors.
- Ask students to reflect on their problem solutions to determine whether the solutions make sense within the context of the original problems. (M. Carr, 2010; Dominowski, 1998; Johanning, D'Agostino, Steele, & Shumow, 1999; A. King, 1999, p. 101; Kramarski & Mevarech, 2003, p. 286; Roditi & Steinberg, 2007; Siegler, 2002)

Such approaches can be especially effective when students work on challenging problems with one or more classmates and must explain and defend their reasoning to each other.

## USING COMPUTER TECHNOLOGY TO TEACH PROBLEM-SOLVING SKILLS

The strategies we've considered thus far have been largely "low tech." But we can also capitalize on computer technology to foster problem-solving skills. Following are several possibilities:

- Use computer-based **intelligent tutoring systems**—software that provides individualized instruction and guidance related to a particular topic and set of skills—to teach mathematical and scientific reasoning and problem solving (e.g., see Figure 7.6).
- Show students how to use spreadsheets to analyze complex sets of data.
- Use computer simulations that allow students to formulate hypotheses, design experiments to test the hypotheses, and interpret the virtual results.
- Present complex real-world problems (i.e., authentic activities) that students must solve. (Beal, Arroyo, Cohen, & Woolf, 2010; Cognition and Technology Group at Vanderbilt, 1990, 1996; Kuhn & Dean, 2005; Vye et al., 1998)

Numerous software packages and Internet resources can help us with the last of these strategies: presenting complex real-world problems. Here are three examples:

- *Gary Gadget: Building Cars.* Students assemble a car and drive to various destinations using a map; they occasionally encounter obstacles (e.g., a muddy road, a steep hill) that require making adjustments to the car.
- *Crazy Machines: The Wacky Contraptions Game.* Students use a collection of three-dimensional parts (e.g., pumps, pipes, generators, balls) to construct machines for various purposes (e.g., driving nails, moving heavy objects, shooting cannons).
- *Animal Hospital: Pet Vet 3D.* Students play the role of a veterinarian who must diagnose and treat a variety of sick pets and also handle the business side of a veterinary office (e.g., purchasing supplies, maintaining a reasonable workload).

Many Internet websites also provide both traditional and authentic problem-solving activities appropriate for children and adolescents. For example, you might look at the websites for the National Science Foundation (www.nsf.gov) and Discover Education (school.discovery-education.com).

**intelligent tutoring system**
Computer software program that provides individually tailored instruction and practice, plus ongoing guidance and feedback, related to a particular topic and set of skills.

**creativity** New and original behavior that yields a productive and culturally appropriate result.

**convergent thinking** Process of pulling together several pieces of information to draw a conclusion or solve a problem.

**divergent thinking** Process of mentally moving in a variety of directions from a single idea.

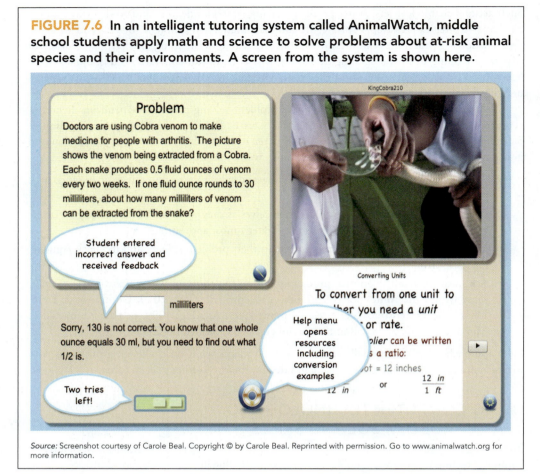

**FIGURE 7.6** In an intelligent tutoring system called AnimalWatch, middle school students apply math and science to solve problems about at-risk animal species and their environments. A screen from the system is shown here.

*Source:* Screenshot courtesy of Carole Beal. Copyright © by Carole Beal. Reprinted with permission. Go to www.animalwatch.org for more information.

**FIGURE 7.7 Convergent versus divergent thinking**

Convergent Thinking

Divergent Thinking

# Creativity

**Creativity**, like problem solving, is a form of transfer, because it involves applying previously learned knowledge or skills to a new situation. Psychologists have offered varying opinions about the nature of creativity, but in general it has two components:

- *New and original behavior:* Behavior not specifically learned from someone else
- *A productive result:* An outcome appropriate for, and in some way valuable to, one's culture (e.g., Beghetto & Kaufman, 2010; Runco & Chand, 1995; R. K. Sawyer, 2003)

To illustrate these two components, let's say that I'm giving a lecture on creativity and want a creative way of keeping my students' attention. One possible approach would be to come to class stark naked. This approach certainly meets the first criterion for creativity (it's new and original) but not the second criterion (it isn't appropriate in our culture). An alternative strategy might be to give my students several challenging problems that require creative thinking. This approach is more likely to meet both criteria: Not only is it a relatively original way of teaching, but it's also appropriate and productive for students to learn about creativity by exploring the process firsthand.

Many complex tasks involve both problem solving and creativity. But the two processes differ somewhat in the extent to which they involve convergent versus divergent thinking (see Figure 7.7). To successfully tackle a problem, we typically pull together two or more pieces of information into an integrated whole that resolves the problem. This combining of information into a single idea or product is known as **convergent thinking**. In contrast, when we engage in creativity, we often begin with a single idea and take it in a variety of directions, at least one of which leads to something that's new, original, and culturally appropriate. This process of generating many different ideas from a single starting point is known as **divergent thinking**. To see the difference firsthand, try the next exercise.

## EXPERIENCING FIRSTHAND
## CONVERGENT AND DIVERGENT THINKING

On a sheet of paper, write your responses to each of the following:

1. Why are houses more often built with bricks than with stones?

2. What are some possible uses of a brick? Try to think of as many different and unusual uses as you can.

3. Add improvements to the wagon drawing so that the object will be more fun to play with.

*Source:* Items 2 and 3 modeled after Torrance, 1970.

To answer the first question, you must use convergent thinking to pull together the things you know about bricks, stones, and building construction. But the other two items require divergent thinking about a single object: You must consider how a brick might be used in different contexts and how different parts of the wagon might be embellished—with some of your responses being novel and unique.

Contrary to popular belief, creativity is *not* a single entity that people either have or don't have. Rather, it's probably a combination of many specific thinking processes, motives, and behaviors. Among other things, creative individuals tend to have the following characteristics:

• Considerable knowledge relevant to the task at hand

• An ability to interpret problems and situations in a flexible, open-minded manner and to combine existing information and ideas in new ways

• A passion for—and therefore a willingness to invest much time and effort in—what they're doing (Amabile, 1996; Csikszentmihalyi, 1996; Leung, Maddux, Galinsky, & Chiu, 2008; Runco & Chand, 1995; Russ, 1993; Simonton, 2004; Weisberg, 1993)

Furthermore, creativity is often specific to particular situations and content areas (Dai, 2010; Glover, Ronning, & Reynolds, 1989; Runco, 2004). For example, students might show creativity in art, writing, or science but won't necessarily be creative in all of these areas.

## FOSTERING CREATIVITY

Certain aspects of creative thinking may have their roots in hereditary factors, but environmental factors play an equally important role in the development of creativity (Esquivel, 1995; Ripple, 1989; Simonton, 2000). In fact, because creativity requires considerable expertise and fairly sophisticated thought processes, learners are apt to become increasingly creative as they grow older, gain diverse experiences and perspectives—ideally including *multicultural* experiences and perspectives—and have numerous opportunities to experiment with objects and ideas (Hatano & Oura, 2003; Leung et al., 2008; Simonton, 2004).

Research studies suggest several strategies for promoting creativity in the classroom:

🍏 *Show students that creative thoughts and behaviors are valued.* One way to do this is to encourage and reward unusual ideas and responses. For example, we can assign activities that require students to generate a wide variety of ideas, and we can express excitement when students complete a project or assessment task in a unique and unusual manner. Engaging in creative activities ourselves also shows that we value creativity (Beghetto & Kaufman, 2010; Lubart & Mouchiroud, 2003; Runco, 2004; Sternberg, 2010).

🍏 *Focus students' attention on internal rather than external rewards.* Students are more creative when they engage in activities they enjoy and when they have reason to take pride in their accomplishments (B. A. Hennessey, 2010; Lubart & Mouchiroud, 2003). To foster creativity, then, we should occasionally give students opportunities to explore their own interests—those they'll gladly pursue without having to be prodded. We can also foster creativity by downplaying the importance of grades, focusing students' attention instead on the internal satisfaction their creative efforts bring (B. A. Hennessey, 2010; Perkins, 1990). For instance, we might say this to students in an art class:

Please don't worry too much about grades. As long as you use the materials appropriately and give each assignment your best shot, you will do well in this class. The important thing

Such a statement is intended to encourage *intrinsic motivation*, a concept discussed in depth in Chapter 11.

is to find an art form that you enjoy and through which you can effectively express your perceptions and feelings.

🍏 *Promote mastery of a subject area.* Creativity in a particular subject area is more likely to occur when students have considerable mastery and conceptual understanding of a topic (Amabile & Hennessey, 1992; Haskell, 2001; Simonton, 2000). For example, if we want students to apply scientific principles in a creative manner—perhaps as they complete a science fair experiment or develop a solution to an environmental problem—we should make sure that they know those principles *well*.

🍏 *Ask thought-provoking questions.* Students are more likely to think creatively when we pose higher-level questions—questions that require them to use previously learned information in new ways. Questions that require divergent thinking can be particularly helpful (Perkins, 1990; Sternberg, 2010). For example, in history lessons we might ask questions such as the following:

- *In a lesson on the Pony Express as a method of U.S. mail delivery in the 1860s:* "In what different ways might people have carried mail across the country at that time?" (Feldhusen & Treffinger, 1980)

- *In a lesson on Angkor Wat, an enormous stone temple complex built in the 12th century in what is now Cambodia:* "How might the Khmer people have built these temples using massive blocks (400 pounds each) with no cement?" (Courtesy of Jeffrey Ormrod)

🍏 *Teach and encourage cognitive and metacognitive strategies that support creative thinking.* Explicit instruction in some of the strategies that creativity requires can definitely have an impact (Hattie, 2009). Following are several examples of such strategies:

- Brainstorming ideas, perhaps in collaboration with peers; deferring judgment until after a lengthy list has been generated

- Focusing attention on gradual progress toward a goal, rather than expecting an immediate solution

- Identifying and addressing specific obstacles that may be impeding progress (Baer & Garrett, 2010; Beghetto & Kaufman, 2010; Sternberg, 2010)

🍏 *Give students the freedom and security they need to take risks.* To be creative, students must be willing to take risks—something they're unlikely to do if they're afraid of failing (Amabile, 1996; Houtz, 1990; Sternberg, 2010). To encourage risk taking, we can allow students to engage in certain activities without evaluating their performance. For example, in response to the question presented earlier about how 12th-century Khmer people might have built large stone temples at Angkor Wat, a student at an English-speaking school in Thailand was quite creative in his response, as his teacher reported:

> Several students drew a long wooden ramp on which they would drag the giant blocks. I asked them what would probably happen as soon as they started dragging the block up this ramp (i.e., the block would break the ramp and come crashing down). So one student drew poles under his ramp to support it. I pointed out that this would work only at very low levels because the trees in the area were small and weak. His next idea was to use wood and bamboo to make the ramp stronger, but I suggested that the structure still wouldn't be strong enough to bear the load. He came back a few minutes later with another idea. He still had the ramp, but underneath it for support he had drawn in a few elephants. I urged him to reflect on his new idea: "Even if you can get the elephants to stand still and put a ramp on their backs, elephants are only about this tall. [I showed their height with my hand.] Angkor Wat is 213 feet tall. How are you going to support the ramp between about 6 feet and 213 feet?" His response was to stack the elephants on top of each other. (Excerpt by Jeffrey Ormrod. Copyright © by Jeffrey Ormrod. Reprinted by permission.)

*provoking question*

**higher-level question** Question that requires students to use previously learned information in a new way—that is, to engage in complex cognitive processes.

Granted, the student's ultimate solution wasn't realistic, but he was definitely thinking in an innovative, divergent manner— "outside the box"—and his teacher had created a classroom atmosphere in which he felt comfortable doing so.

We can further encourage risk taking by urging students to think of their mistakes and failures as an inevitable—but usually temporary—aspect of the creative process (B. A. Hennessey & Amabile, 1987; J. C. Kaufman & Beghetto, 2009). For example, when students are writing a short story, we might give them several opportunities to get our feedback and perhaps also the feedback of their peers before they turn in a final product.

🍎 *Provide the time and resources that creativity requires.* Students need time to experiment with new materials and ideas, think in divergent directions, and make mistakes. And in many instances they can be more creative if they have a variety of physical and social resources on which to draw—perhaps paper and pencil, the Internet, ample space in which to work, and the ideas and support of classmates. Occasional gentle guidance from a teacher can also boost creative thinking (Fairweather & Cramond, 2010; Sternberg, 2010).

Ideally, students should reflect on and carefully evaluate the results of their creative thinking (Dai, 2010; Fairweather & Cramond, 2010). In other words, truly productive creative thinking also requires critical thinking—our next topic.

# Critical Thinking

Critical thinking involves evaluating the accuracy, credibility, and worth of information and lines of reasoning (Beyer, 1985; Heyman, 2008). It can take a variety of forms, depending on the context. The following exercise presents four possibilities.

## EXPERIENCING FIRSTHAND
### COLDS, CARS, CHANCE, AND CHEER

Read and respond to each of the following situations:

1. It's autumn, and the days are becoming increasingly chilly. You see the following advertisement:

   Aren't you tired of sniffles and runny noses all winter? Tired of always feeling less than your best? Get through a whole winter without colds. Take Eradicold Pills as directed. (R. J. Harris, 1977, p. 605)

   Should you go out and buy a box of Eradicold Pills?

2. You have a beat-up old car and have invested several thousand dollars to get it in working order. You can sell the car in its present condition for $1,500, or you can invest a couple of thousand dollars more on repairs and then sell it for $3,000. What should you do? (modeled after Halpern, 1998)

3. You have been rolling a typical six-sided die (i.e., one member of a pair of dice). You know that the die isn't heavier on one side than another, and yet in the past 30 rolls you haven't rolled a number 4 even once. What are the odds that you'll get a 4 on the next roll?

4. This research finding was presented by Dr. Edmund Emmer at the annual conference of the American Educational Research Association in 1994:

   Teachers who feel happy when they teach are more likely to have well-behaved students (Emmer, 1994).

   If you're a teacher, do such results suggest that you should try to feel happy when you enter the classroom each morning?

In each of these situations, you had to evaluate information and make some sort of judgment. In Item 1, I hope you weren't tempted to buy Eradicold Pills, because the advertisement provided no proof that they reduce cold symptoms. It simply included the suggestion to "Take Eradicold Pills as directed" within the context of a discussion of undesirable symptoms—a common ploy in persuasive advertising.

As for Item 2, it makes more sense to sell the car now. If you sell the car for $3,000 after making $2,000 worth of repairs, you'll make $500 less than you would otherwise. Many people

**critical thinking** Process of evaluating the accuracy, credibility, and worth of information and lines of reasoning.

mistakenly believe that their past investments justify making additional ones, when in fact past investments are irrelevant to the present circumstances (Halpern, 1998).

In Item 3, the chance of rolling a 4 on an evenly balanced die is—as always—one in six. The outcomes of previous rolls are irrelevant, because each roll is independent of the others. But when a 4 hasn't shown up even once in 30 rolls, many people believe that a 4 is long overdue and so greatly overestimate its probability—a misconception known as the *gambler's fallacy*.

Now what about making sure you're happy each time you enter the classroom (Item 4)? One common mistake people make in interpreting research results is to think that an association *(correlation)* between two things means that one of those things must *cause* the other. In fact, however, a correlation between two variables doesn't necessarily indicate a cause–and–effect relationship. Possibly teacher happiness does improve students' classroom behavior, but there are other potential explanations for the correlation as well. For instance, perhaps good student behavior makes teachers feel happy (rather than vice versa), or perhaps teachers who feel upbeat use more effective teaching techniques and can better keep students on task as the result of using those techniques (Emmer, 1994).

The four situations presented in the preceding exercise illustrate several forms that critical thinking can take (Halpern, 1997, 1998, 2008; Nussbaum, 2008):

- *Verbal reasoning:* Understanding and evaluating persuasive techniques found in oral and written language. You engaged in verbal reasoning when deciding whether to purchase Eradicold Pills.

- *Argument analysis:* Discriminating between reasons that do and don't support a conclusion. You engaged in argument analysis when you considered possible pros and cons of investing an additional $2,000 in car repairs.

- *Probabilistic reasoning:* Determining the likelihood and uncertainties associated with various events. You engaged in probabilistic reasoning when you determined the probability of rolling a 4 on the die.

- *Hypothesis testing:* Judging the value of data and research results in terms of the methods used to obtain them and their potential relevance to certain conclusions. When hypothesis testing includes critical thinking, it involves considering questions such as these:

  - Was an appropriate instrument used to measure a particular outcome?

  - Have other possible explanations or conclusions been eliminated?

  - Can the results obtained in one situation be reasonably generalized to other situations?

  - You engaged in hypothesis testing when you evaluated Dr. Emmer's findings about teacher happiness.

Some theorists have argued that critical thinking involves a general set of cognitive skills that learners can apply broadly in many different contexts (e.g., Ennis, 1996). But in fact, the nature of critical thinking is somewhat specific to various content domains. In writing, critical thinking may involve reading the first draft of a persuasive essay to look for errors in logical reasoning or for situations in which opinions haven't been sufficiently justified. In science, it may involve revising existing theories or beliefs to account for new evidence—that is, it may involve conceptual change. In history, it may involve drawing inferences from historical documents, attempting to determine whether things *definitely* happened a particular way or only *maybe* happened that way.

As you might guess, critical thinking skills emerge gradually over the course of childhood and adolescence (Amsterlaw, 2006; Kuhn & Franklin, 2006; Pillow, 2002). Yet all too often, students at all grade levels—and even many well-educated adults—take the information they see in textbooks, news reports, on the Internet, and elsewhere at face value. In other words, they engage in little or no critical thinking as they consider the accuracy, credibility, and worth of the information they encounter (Kuhn, 2009; G. Marcus, 2008; M. J. Metzger, Flanagin, & Zwarun, 2003).

Students are more likely to look analytically and critically at new information if they believe that even experts' understanding of a topic continues to evolve as new evidence accumulates. They're *less* likely to engage in critical thinking if they believe that knowledge is an absolute, unchanging entity (Kardash & Scholes, 1996; Kuhn, 2001a; Moon, 2008; Schommer-Aikins, 2002). Thus, students' *epistemic beliefs* enter into the critical thinking process.

My analysis of Item 4 might remind you of the discussion of correlation versus causation in Chapter 1.

# FOSTERING CRITICAL THINKING

Critical thinking is a general disposition as well as a set of sophisticated, evaluative thinking processes. In other words, some learners are more inclined than others to approach new ideas in a thoughtful, analytical manner (Halpern, 2008; Perkins, Tishman, Ritchhart, Donis, & Andrade, 2000). Yet researchers have had some success in *nurturing* critical thinking in children and adolescents (Abrami et al., 2008; Kuhn & Franklin, 2006). Perhaps because critical thinking encompasses such a variety of cognitive skills, strategies for encouraging it are many and varied. Following are several theory- and research-based recommendations:

- Teach fewer topics, but in greater depth—the *less-is-more* principle once again.
- Encourage some intellectual skepticism—for instance, by urging students to question and challenge the ideas they read and hear—and communicate the epistemic belief that people's knowledge and understanding of any single topic will continue to change over time.
- Model critical thinking—for instance, by thinking aloud while analyzing a persuasive argument or scientific report.
- Give students many opportunities to practice critical thinking—for instance, by identifying flaws in the arguments of a persuasive essay, evaluating the quality and usefulness of a scientific finding, and using evidence and logic to support a particular viewpoint.
- Ask questions such as these to encourage critical thinking:
  - What biases might the author of this document have?
  - Do some ideas contradict information I've seen elsewhere?
  - What reasons support the conclusion? What reasons *don't* support it?
  - How might the design of this research study be improved?
- Have students debate controversial issues from several perspectives, and occasionally ask them to defend a perspective quite different from their own.
- Help students understand that critical thinking involves considerable mental effort but that its benefits make the effort worthwhile.
- Embed critical thinking skills within the context of authentic, real-world activities as a way of helping students retrieve those skills later on, both in the workplace and in other aspects of adult life. (Afflerbach & Cho, 2010; Bonney & Sternberg, 2011; Chinn, Anderson, & Waggoner, 2001; De La Paz & Felton, 2010; Derry, Levin, Osana, & Jones, 1998; Halpern, 1998; Heyman, 2008; Kardash & Scholes, 1996; Kuhn & Pease, 2008; Monte-Sano, 2008; Moon, 2008; Nussbaum, 2008; Nussbaum & Edwards, 2011; S. A. Stahl & Shanahan, 2004; Yang & Tsai, 2010)

The Into the Classroom feature "Fostering Critical Thinking" presents examples of what teachers might do in language arts, history, and science.

Using an Internet search engine such as Google or Bing, you can find numerous computer software programs allegedly designed to promote critical thinking skills. Some of these programs may be effective, whereas others may not be. When considering them for possible use in your classroom, keep in mind that like all complex cognitive processes, critical thinking skills are probably most effectively learned—and most likely to be transferred to new situations—when they're practiced within the context of specific academic topics (e.g., De La Paz & Felton, 2010; Kuhn & Franklin, 2006; Yang & Tsai, 2010).

It's important that students think critically not only about what they read and hear in the classroom but also about what they see online. People with a variety of motives and ideologies post their ideas on websites, and students must learn to scrutinize each posting with a skeptical eye. One good resource for teachers is a website maintained by the Center for Media Literacy (www.medialit. org), where you can find free software that teaches students to ask themselves questions such as these:

- Who created this message?
- What values, lifestyles and points of view are represented in, or omitted from, this message?
- Why is this message being sent? (Center for Media Literacy, n.d.)

In this age of widespread access to the Internet, critical thinking skills are now more *critical* than ever.

Teach and encourage critical thinking skills in diverse disciplines across the school curriculum.

## Into the Classroom

### Fostering Critical Thinking

🍏 **Teach elements of critical thinking.**
In a unit on persuasion and argumentation, a junior high school language arts teacher explains that a sound argument meets three criteria: (1) The evidence presented to justify the argument is accurate and consistent; (2) the evidence is relevant to and provides sufficient support for the conclusion; and (3) little or no information has been omitted that, if present, would lead to a contradictory conclusion. The teacher then has students practice applying these criteria to a variety of persuasive and argumentative essays.

🍏 **Foster epistemic beliefs that encourage critical thinking.**
Rather than teaching history as a collection of facts to be memorized, a high school history teacher portrays the discipline as an attempt by informed but inevitably biased scholars to interpret and make sense of historical events. On several occasions he asks his students to read two or three different historians' accounts of the same incident and to look for evidence of personal bias in each one.

🍏 **Embed critical thinking skills within the context of authentic activities.**
In a unit on statistical and scientific reasoning, an eighth-grade science class studies concepts related to probability, correlation, and experimental control. Then, as part of a simulated legislative hearing, the students work in small groups to develop arguments for or against a legislative bill concerning the marketing and use of vitamins and other dietary supplements. To find evidence to support their arguments, the students apply what they've learned about statistics and experimentation as they read journal articles and government reports regarding the possible benefits and drawbacks of nutritional supplements.

🍏 **Teach students how to evaluate the accuracy of information posted on Internet websites.**
On an educational website called "All About Explorers," elementary students practice distinguishing between credible and questionable information while searching for facts about well-known early explorers. For example, as students look for information about Christopher Columbus, they visit a bogus "website" that describes Columbus as having been born in 1951 but dying in 1906—a timeline that obviously makes no sense—and asserts that the King and Queen of Spain called Columbus on his toll-free number.

*Sources:* Derry et al., 1998 (statistics example based on this study); Halpern, 1997 (criteria for a sound argument); Paxton, 1999 (bias in history example). "All about Explorers," is a teacher-created website at www.allaboutexplorers.com.

## Diversity in Creativity, Critical Thinking, and Other Complex Cognitive Processes

We might reasonably speculate that Western schools' focus on meaningful learning and conceptual understanding enhances students' ability to be creative: One recent study with college students found students from a European American background to be especially proficient in solving math problems requiring creative thinking (Schommer-Aikins & Easter, 2008). Perhaps more significant, however, was the finding that experiences in *two or more cultures* enhance creative thinking and behaviors. Quite possibly, such a multicultural background exposes learners to a broader range of concepts, ideas, and perspectives from which to draw when trying to think about a topic or problem in nontraditional ways (Leung et al., 2008).

Critical thinking is another complex cognitive process that seems to depend somewhat on students' cultural backgrounds. Some cultures place high value on respecting one's elders or certain religious leaders, and in doing so, they may foster the belief that "truth" is a cut-and-dried entity that is best gained from authority figures (Losh, 2003; Qian & Pan, 2002; Tyler et al., 2008). Furthermore, a cultural emphasis on maintaining group harmony may discourage children from hashing out differences in perspectives, which critical thinking often entails (Kağitçibaşi, 2007; Kuhn & Park, 2005). Perhaps as a result of such factors, critical thinking may be less common in some groups (e.g., in some traditional Asian and Native American communities and in some fundamentalist religious groups) than in others (Kuhn, Daniels, & Krishnan, 2003; Kuhn & Park, 2005; Tyler et al., 2008). In some situations, then, we must walk a fine line between teaching students to critically evaluate persuasive arguments and scientific evidence, on the one hand, and to show appropriate respect and strive for group harmony in their community and culture, on the other. One potentially effective approach is to suggest that students pose questions in a nonthreatening way, perhaps like this: "What if someone were to criticize your idea by saying _____? How might you respond?"

🍏 Teach students tactful and respectful ways of critiquing other people's arguments and viewpoints.

# STUDENTS IN INCLUSIVE SETTINGS

## TABLE 7.3 • Promoting Advanced Thinking Skills in Students with Special Educational Needs

| CATEGORY | CHARACTERISTICS YOU MIGHT OBSERVE | SUGGESTED STRATEGIES |
|---|---|---|
| **Students with specific cognitive or academic difficulties** | • Difficulty in transferring learned information to new situations<br>• Difficulties in problem solving, perhaps because of limited working memory capacity, inability to identify important aspects of a problem, inability to retrieve appropriate problem-solving strategies, or limited metacognitive problem-solving skills | • Encourage and scaffold transfer of school topics.<br>• Model effective problem-solving strategies and scaffold students' efforts to use them (e.g., teach questions that students should ask themselves as they work their way through problems).<br>• Present simple problems at first, then gradually move to more difficult problems as students gain proficiency and self-confidence.<br>• Teach techniques for minimizing the load on working memory during problem solving (e.g., writing parts of a problem on paper, drawing a diagram of the problem). |
| **Students with social or behavioral problems** | • Deficiencies in social problem-solving skills | • Teach strategies for solving social problems (e.g., taking a multistep approach that includes defining the specific problem, identifying several possible solutions, and predicting the likely outcomes of each one). |
| **Students with general delays in cognitive and social functioning** | • Difficulty in transferring information and skills to new situations<br>• Few effective problem-solving strategies<br>• Little, if any, ability to think creatively or critically about classroom topics | • Teach new information and skills in the specific contexts and situations in which students should be able to use them.<br>• Present simple problems and guide students through each step needed to solve them. |
| **Students with physical or sensory challenges** | • No consistent deficits in complex cognitive processes; deficits sometimes due to students' limited experiences with tasks that require such processes | • Address any deficits in complex processes using strategies you would use with nondisabled students, making appropriate accommodations for physical and sensory limitations. |
| **Students with advanced cognitive development** | • More frequent transfer of learning to new situations<br>• Greater effectiveness in problem solving, more sophisticated problem-solving strategies, greater flexibility in strategy use, and less susceptibility to mental sets<br>• Interest in addressing general problems of society<br>• Divergent thinking (e.g., asking unusual questions, giving novel responses)<br>• Greater facility with critical thinking | • Place greater emphasis on complex processes (e.g., transfer, problem solving) within the curriculum.<br>• Teach advanced thinking skills within the context of specific classroom topics rather than in isolation from academic content.<br>• Accept and encourage divergent thinking, including unanticipated yet appropriate responses.<br>• Encourage critical analysis of ideas, opinions, and evidence. |

*Sources:* Beirne-Smith et al., 2006; Brownell, Mellard, & Deshler, 1993; B. Clark, 1997; DuPaul & Eckert, 1994; E. S. Ellis & Friend, 1991; N. R. Ellis, 1979; S. Goldstein & Rider, 2006; K. R. Harris, 1982; Heward, 2009; M. C. Linn, Clement, Pulos, & Sullivan, 1989; Maker, 1993; Mastropieri & Scruggs, 2007; Meichenbaum, 1977; Mendaglio, 2010; Mercer & Pullen, 2005; Piirto, 1999; Pulos & Linn, 1981; Slife, Weiss, & Bell, 1985; Stanley, 1980; Torrance, 1989; Turnbull et al., 2010; Weissberg, 1985.

## ACCOMMODATING STUDENTS WITH SPECIAL NEEDS

In addition to differences that may be a function of cultural background, researchers have observed differences in complex thinking skills for students with various disabilities and for students who have advanced cognitive abilities. Table 7.3 presents some of the characteristics you're likely to see in students with special educational needs, along with recommendations for working with these students.

Chapter 5 identifies specific categories of special needs that fall within the five general categories listed in Table 7.3.

 7  ## What Have You Learned?

If we focus classroom activities on learning isolated facts and if we also use assessment techniques that emphasize knowledge of those facts, students will naturally begin to believe that school learning is a process of absorbing information in a rote fashion and regurgitating it later on. But if we instead focus class time and activities on *doing things with* information—for instance, applying, analyzing, and critically evaluating it—then students should acquire the cognitive processes and skills that will serve them well in the world beyond the classroom. With these points in mind, let's return to the learning outcomes presented at the beginning of the chapter.

■ **7.1: Explain how learners' metacognitive knowledge and skills influence their learning and academic achievement; also explain how you can promote metacognitive development in your own students.** *Metacognition* includes both the beliefs students have about their own cognitive processes and their attempts to strategically regulate those processes to maximize learning and memory. Some effective learning strategies, such as taking notes and writing summaries, are overt ones easily seen in students' behaviors. Others, such as identifying important ideas and self-monitoring comprehension, are covert ones that take place largely or entirely inside students' heads. Students' use or nonuse of effective strategies depends, in part, on the particular learning task at hand and also, in part, on (1) students' ability to reflect on the effectiveness of previous strategies, (2) their beliefs about the nature of knowledge and learning (i.e., their *epistemic beliefs*), and (3) their ultimate goals for learning and classroom performance. As teachers, we should promote students' metacognitive development at the same time that we teach them academic subject matter—for example, by providing guidance and scaffolding in note taking, elaborative processing, and summarizing, and by having students use new strategies in small-group activities.

Evaluate and apply your knowledge related to this learning outcome in MyEducationLab™.

**7.2: Describe various forms that transfer might take and the conditions in which transfer is most likely to occur, and apply research findings about transfer to your classroom practices.** Transfer occurs when something learned in one situation either helps or hinders learning or performance in another situation; these two phenomena are known as *positive transfer* and *negative transfer*, respectively. Some instances of transfer involve applying specific facts to a similar situation; for example, a student might apply her knowledge of French vocabulary words in a Spanish class. Other instances involve general transfer of knowledge, skills, or attitudes to a very different situation; for example, a student might apply study strategies learned in a history class to a science class and, after gaining self-confidence in one class, might bring that self-confidence to other classes as well. Students are more likely to transfer what they learn when they engage in meaningful learning (rather than rote learning), when they see the relevance of classroom material to diverse disciplines and real-world situations (rather than seeing it as context-bound), and when they have many opportunities to use the material in new ways.

Evaluate and apply your knowledge related to this learning outcome in MyEducationLab™.

**7.3: Describe four general factors that influence problem-solving performance; also describe teaching strategies you can use to help students successfully solve both well-defined and ill-defined problems.** Schools have traditionally focused attention on solving well-defined problems, yet the outside world presents many ill-defined problems that students must also learn how to tackle. To be successful problem solvers, students must (1) encode problems in ways that lead them in potentially useful directions in long-term memory, (2) master both step-by-step procedures for particular situations (algorithms) and more general problem-solving strategies (heuristics), (3) compensate for the limits of working memory (e.g., by learning basic skills to mastery), and (4) consciously self-direct and self-monitor the overall problem-solving process. As teachers, we can help students become more effective problem solvers in a number of ways—for example, by scaffolding their attempts

to solve new and complex problems (perhaps in technology-based simulations), mixing up the kinds of problems we ask them to solve in any single lesson or unit, and asking them to explain what they're doing as they work through a problem.

Evaluate and apply your knowledge related to this learning outcome in MyEducationLab™.

**7.4: Identify several instructional strategies that can encourage students to think creatively as they tackle new tasks and problems.** Creativity involves new and original behavior that leads to an appropriate and productive result; it's probably a combination of many thinking processes and behaviors that each may or may not come into play in different situations and content areas. We're more likely to see creative thinking and behavior when we show students that we value creativity, focus their attention on internal rather than external rewards, help them master essential knowledge and skills, teach them metacognitive strategies that support creative thinking, ask thought-provoking questions, encourage risk taking, and provide the time and resources that creativity requires.

Evaluate and apply your knowledge related to this learning outcome in MyEducationLab™.

**7.5: Describe several different forms that critical thinking can take, and explain how you can help students critically evaluate what they see, hear, and read both inside and outside the classroom.** Critical thinking involves evaluating the accuracy, credibility, and worth of information and lines of reasoning. It takes a variety of forms, depending on the situation, and requires not only a number of cognitive skills (e.g., argument analysis, probabilistic reasoning) but also a general disposition to approach new ideas in a thoughtful, evaluative manner and a belief that humankind doesn't have all the answers to many important topics. As teachers, we should encourage and model a certain amount of intellectual skepticism, give students many opportunities to engage in critical analysis of classroom subject matter, and ask questions that encourage students to carefully scrutinize and evaluate the ideas they encounter in written documents, classroom discussions, and Internet websites.

Evaluate and apply your knowledge related to this learning outcome in MyEducationLab™.

**7.6: Give examples of diversity you might see in creativity, critical thinking, and other complex thinking processes as a result of students' cultural backgrounds, disabilities, or advanced cognitive development.** Students exhibit considerable diversity in the extent and nature of their complex cognitive thinking processes. For example, students from some cultural backgrounds may be unaccustomed to thinking in divergent, creative ways about complex problems. Students from other backgrounds may have been discouraged from critically evaluating what their elders tell them. And many students with special needs may have acquired few, if any, effective learning strategies and thus may need considerable scaffolding in their early attempts at using such strategies.

Evaluate and apply your knowledge related to this learning outcome in MyEducationLab™.

# Practice for Your Licensure Exam

## Interview with Charlie

Seventeen-year-old Charlie has been earning As in his high school classes; now, at the end of his eleventh-grade year, he has a 4.0 grade point average. He has particular interests in science and technology; in fact, in addition to challenging coursework at school, Charlie has taken several computer courses at a local community college. His mother says, "He invests a lot of time in projects (writing papers, reports, etc.) but doesn't crack open a book to read or study often."

One afternoon Charlie has the following discussion with an adult:

*Adult:* Why do you think your grades have been so good?
*Charlie:* I do the homework, and I do well on the tests. I don't really study—I just make sure to focus on the homework and make sure it makes sense to me. . . . What I do depends on the circumstances. For math and chemistry, just doing homework and going over it with friends during lunch or something helps. That's about all I do for studying.
*Adult:* What do you mean, "make sure it makes sense"?
*Charlie:* If I look at the problem and I know the process of how to do it, like in math and chemistry.
*Adult:* Let's say that a teacher assigns a textbook chapter for you to read sometime in the next three days. What things would you do—in your head, that is—when you read the chapter?
*Charlie:* Depends on the book and the class. Probably just skim it. Is the teacher just telling us to read it, or are there questions with it? I think about those things. We have a textbook in my computer programming class. I go through the chapter, look at examples and the [computer] code. I don't look at the other stuff.
*Adult:* I haven't heard you talk about trying to memorize anything.
*Charlie:* We do have to memorize. If I write it down once—a formula or something—and can use it in a few problems, I get it.
*Adult:* Do you ever use flashcards?
*Charlie:* Flashcards wouldn't work for what I do.
*Adult:* How do you know when you've really learned something—I mean, *really* learned it—and will remember it for a long time?
*Charlie:* When I do a couple of problems and they don't seem as hard . . . when I can get the right answer every time.

*Adult:* Your teachers probably expect you to do a lot of things outside of class, right? How do you make sure you get them all done?
*Charlie:* Making lists is really helpful, of everything that's due.
*Adult:* So what do you do with the lists?
*Charlie:* I either do things as soon as possible or else procrastinate, do it the night before. Sometimes I have a free block at the end of the day to do it. Or I go home and do my chemistry right away. Or I might wait until the last minute. It depends on whether I'm hanging out with friends.

1. **Multiple-choice question:**

   Charlie says, "I don't really study—I just make sure to focus on the homework and make sure it makes sense to me." Which one of the following terms most accurately describes the nature of this statement?

   a. Algorithm
   b. Metacognition
   c. Critical thinking
   d. Divergent thinking

2. **Multiple-choice question:**

   Which one of the following statements is the best example of *comprehension monitoring?*

   a. "Depends on the book and the class. Probably just skim it."
   b. "I go through the chapter, look at examples and the [computer] code. I don't look at the other stuff."
   c. "When I do a couple of problems and they don't seem as hard . . . when I can get the right answer every time."
   d. "I either do things as soon as possible or else procrastinate, do it the night before. Sometimes I have a free block at the end of the day to do it."

3. **Constructed-response question:**

   Would you characterize Charlie's learning strategies as involving *rote learning* or *meaningful learning?* Use excerpts from the interview to support your answer.

---

**PRAXIS**   Go to Appendix C, "Matching Book and MyEducationLab™ to the Praxis Principles of Learning and Teaching Tests," to discover sections of this chapter that may be especially applicable to the Praxis tests.

# 8 Learning and Cognition in Context

## LEARNING OUTCOMES

**8.1:** Describe five basic assumptions underlying contextual theories of learning, and apply these assumptions to classroom practice.

**8.2:** Contrast the benefits of interacting with more advanced individuals versus the benefits of interacting with peers; explain how you might enhance students' learning through both kinds of interactions.

**8.3:** Explain how learners' cultural backgrounds can influence their interpretations of new information and experiences; also explain how learners can effectively begin to participate in one or more communities of practice.

**8.4:** Describe key elements of society that impact learning, and explain how authentic activities can enhance learners' performance in their out-of-school world.

**8.5:** Describe the unique roles that digital technologies and the Internet can play in classroom instruction.

**8.6:** Apply your knowledge of learning, cognition, and effective instructional practices to various academic content domains.

## CASE STUDY: IT'S ALL IN HOW YOU LOOK AT THINGS

In a research study by Susan Mosborg (2002), high-achieving 12th-grade history students learned about a 1996 court case involving a school district that had been regularly broadcasting prayers and Bible classes over the high school's loudspeaker system. The students read two newspaper articles about the case. One article, a front-page news story, presented the opposing perspectives of the mother who was suing the school district (she argued that the practice violated her daughter's right to religious freedom) and the school superintendent (he argued that the broadcasts legitimately manifested the school's right to free speech). The second article, an editorial, lamented the court's decision to rule in favor of the mother and suggested that the decision would force people to practice their religion behind closed doors, "in the closet."

When students reflected on the articles in light of what they'd previously learned about American history, they reached varying conclusions. For example, a student named Jacob thought the decision reflected society's general moral decline:

> The nation's Christian heritage to me says a lot about the decline of a lot of things in our country. Over the last century, in particular, morals and beliefs have changed quite a bit and fragmented lots of different groups. And I think a lot of that can be attributed to the fact that we've kind of forgotten and strayed away from Christian belief, from prayer. (Mosborg, 2002, p. 333)

Meanwhile, a student named Howard interpreted the court decision as reflecting progress toward greater religious choice:

> Despite the assertion that the government was never linked to the church, it really was a lot more back in colonial times. . . . If you didn't believe in Puritanism, if you did something that was against their morals, but not yours, you were put in jail for it . . . . And I think we've come a long way since then. (Mosborg, 2002, p. 333)

- Why might the two boys have interpreted the same information in such radically different ways? What principles of learning and cognition might you draw on to help you make sense of their diverging perspectives?

---

As cognitive psychologists have explained, <u>human learning typically involves *meaningful learning*—connecting new information and experiences to existing knowledge and beliefs about the world.</u> Often, in fact, learners engage in *elaboration,* embellishing on and sometimes distorting new input so that it's a good fit with their current understandings. To the extent that different learners retrieve different knowledge and beliefs in any given situation, they're likely to interpret that situation in very different ways. For example, Jacob may have retrieved information about undesirable behaviors in the early decades of the twentieth century—perhaps the rise of organized crime in the 1920s or the increasing popularity of illegal drugs beginning in the late 1960s. In contrast, Howard apparently retrieved his knowledge of the rigidity and intolerant religious practices of many Puritans in the Massachusetts Bay Colony of the seventeenth century.

But *why* did the boys retrieve different prior knowledge and elaborate on the information is distinctly different ways? In her study, Mosborg discovered one important factor that seemed to make a difference: the broader social context in which students had grown up. Some students in the study were, like Jacob, attending an interdenominational religious school that stressed

Cognitive psychology is described in Chapter 6.

**contextual theory** Theory of learning that focuses on how people's general physical, social, and/or cultural surroundings support their learning, development, and behavior.

**situated learning and cognition** Knowledge, behaviors, and thinking skills acquired and used primarily within certain contexts, with limited or no retrieval and use in other contexts.

**distributed cognition and intelligence** Enhancement of thinking through the use of physical objects and technology, concepts and symbols of one's culture, and/or social collaboration and support.

adherence to certain principles of Christianity. Other students, like Howard, attended a more secular private school that focused only on traditional academic disciplines. Presumably the students' schools reflected their parents' priorities, beliefs, and values—all of which parents wanted to pass along to their children.

Learning always take place within particular *contexts*—for instance, within a particular classroom environment, social group, culture, and society. Furthermore, in those societies where children attend school, instruction is typically divided into discrete content domains—reading, math, science, and so on—that involve somewhat idiosyncratic kinds of knowledge and skills. Such social and content-specific contexts for learning are the subject of this chapter.

# Basic Assumptions of Contextual Theories

Cognitive theories of learning—such as information processing theory and individual constructivism—tell us a great deal about how human beings learn and develop. But in recent years psychologists have become increasingly aware that people's learning and development are inextricably dependent on and bound to various physical, social, and cultural contexts. Contextual theories of learning vary considerably in the particular contexts they emphasize. Even so, they tend to share most or all of the following assumptions.

• *The brain functions in close collaboration with—rather than in relative isolation from—the rest of the body.* Obviously the brain can't function without the nutrition and health of the rest of the body, and it gets new information from the eyes, ears, and other sensory organs. But in addition, thinking and learning are often intimately intertwined with a learner's physical actions and reactions. For example, when we think about throwing a baseball, we activate parts of the brain that control arm and hand muscles involved in throwing even if we aren't actually moving those muscles (Spunt, Falk, & Lieberman, 2010). And when we're pondering complex situations—perhaps math problems or perhaps the shapes and locations of various objects in space—gestures with our hands or arms can sometimes help us think and talk about the situations more effectively (Alibali, Spencer, Knox, & Kita, 2011; Goldin-Meadow & Beilock, 2010).

• *Acquired knowledge and skills are often tied to a limited set of activities and environments.* When learners acquire new information, behaviors, and ways of thinking in a particular situation—for instance, during a particular kind of activity or in a particular kind of environment—they may use the things they've learned only when they're in the same situation once again. This tendency for some responses and cognitive processes to be rooted in particular activities and environments is known as situated learning or situated cognition.

• *Learners often think and perform more effectively when they can offload some of the cognitive burden onto something or someone else.* As you should recall from information processing theory, active cognitive processing takes place in working memory, which—by itself—can handle only a small amount of information at any one time. For complex tasks, then, it's helpful to shift some of the cognitive load elsewhere—an idea that's sometimes referred to as distributed cognition or distributed intelligence (e.g., Pea, 1993; Salomon, 1993; E. R. Smith & Conrey, 2009). One way to "distribute" the cognitive load is to use physical objects—for instance, by writing parts of a problem on paper or using a calculator to carry out multistep computations. A second way is to organize and interpret the specific, concrete facts of a situation—the "raw data," as it were—using concepts, principles, strategies, and other cognitive tools that one's cultural group has developed to address common problems. For example, we might use a *calendar* to keep track of upcoming appointments and other commitments, or we might draw a *line graph* to see if a particular region's average annual rainfall has substantially increased or decreased over the past few decades.

Still a third way to distribute the cognitive load is to share it with other individuals. When learners spread a challenging task or problem across many minds, they can draw on multiple knowledge bases and ideas. For example, we might convene a group of people to brainstorm possible solutions to a local, national, or international problem. Furthermore, in virtually any social group, different people gain expertise in different topics—some become medical doctors, others become engineers, and so on—thereby distributing the group's collective knowledge base.

• *Learners sometimes learn more effectively when they collaborate with others to co-construct meaning.* I've just mentioned how learners can reduce their own cognitive burden, in part, by sharing a task or problem with others. An additional advantage of multilearner collaboration is that, as a group, learners can often make better sense of a situation than they might do on their own. For example, think about times when you've worked cooperatively with classmates to make sense of confusing classroom material. Quite possibly, by sharing various possible interpretations, your group jointly constructed a better understanding of the material than any one of you could have constructed on your own. Unlike individually constructed knowledge, which might differ considerably from one individual to another, socially constructed knowledge is shared by two or more people simultaneously. A perspective known as social constructivism focuses on such collective efforts to impose meaning on the world.

Joint meaning-making doesn't necessarily have to occur in a single learning session, however. In some cases it proceeds gradually over the course of several days or weeks—or even over the course of many decades or centuries. For example, such academic disciplines as mathematics, science, history, economics, and psychology have evolved as the result of long-term collaborations among many individuals. Through these disciplines people have developed concepts (e.g., *pi* [$\pi$], *molecule*, and *revolution*) and principles (e.g., *Pythagorean theorem, supply-and-demand,* and the *limited capacity of working memory*) to simplify, organize, and explain certain aspects of the world or its inhabitants. Literature, music, and the fine arts help us impose meaning on the world as well—for example, by trying to portray the thoughts and feelings that characterize human experience. Here we see the very critical role that *culture* plays in knowledge construction: To the extent that different groups of people use different concepts and principles to explain their physical experiences and to the extent that they have unique bodies of literature, music, and art to capture their psychological experiences, they'll inevitably see the world in diverse ways.

• *With the help and guidance of more knowledgeable individuals, learners benefit from the accumulated wisdom of their cultural group.* Through its ongoing co-construction of meanings and development of new tools and strategies, any long-standing social group becomes increasingly effective and efficient in tackling challenging tasks and problems. As the group gains new members—in many cases by giving birth to a new generation—it maintains its effectiveness and efficiency by indoctrinating the new members into its typical ways of interpreting and responding to various situations. Contextual perspectives that emphasize the role of society and culture in promoting learning and development are collectively known as sociocultural theory.

In virtually any culture, adults and other more experienced individuals continually help growing children make sense of and respond to new situations in ways the culture deems to be appropriate and productive. In other words, adults *mediate* new situations for children. Over time, children gradually internalize adults' ways of interpreting and addressing day-to-day events until they themselves become the experts who guide future generations.

A sociocultural perspective can help us understand Jacob's and Howard's differing interpretations of the school prayer issue in the opening case study. Although both boys had grown up in the United States—and, in fact, in the same geographic part of the country—their parents and schools had probably passed along somewhat different ways of looking at religion and its role in human society. For Jacob, prayer and other Christian traditions provided essential foundations for people's overall well-being, whereas for Howard, legitimate religious beliefs and practices might take a wide variety of forms.

Table 8.1 summarizes the five assumptions, along with some of their implications for instruction. Taken together, the assumptions involve three general layers of context. In particular, people think and learn within the contexts of (1) their physical bodies, (2) their immediate

Here we are revisiting concepts discussed in previous chapters, including *working memory* and *cognitive load* (Chapter 6), *distributed intelligence* (Chapter 5), and *cognitive tools* (Chapter 2).

Chapter 2 describes Lev Vygotsky's early sociocultural theory, including the processes of mediation and internalization.

**social constructivism**  Theoretical perspective that focuses on people's collective efforts to impose meaning on the world.

**sociocultural theory**  Theoretical perspective emphasizing the importance of society and culture in promoting learning and development.

# PRINCIPLES/ASSUMPTIONS

## TABLE 8.1 • Basic Assumptions of Contextual Theories and Their Educational Implications

| ASSUMPTION | EDUCATIONAL IMPLICATION | EXAMPLE |
|---|---|---|
| Brain–body interdependence | 🍎 Encourage students to use their bodies to help them think about and remember classroom subject matter. | 🍎 As students try to understand the difference between folded and fault-block mountains, suggest that they use their hands to simulate what the earth's shifting tectonic plates do to create these two different types of mountains. |
| Situated nature of learning and cognition | 🍎 Have students apply new knowledge and skills to real-world, authentic tasks. | 🍎 Ask students to design and conduct an experiment in which they apply scientific procedures (e.g., isolation and control of variables) to a question relevant to their personal lives and interests. |
| Distributed nature of learning and cognition | 🍎 Teach students how to use various physical and cognitive tools (e.g., technology, scientific research skills) to help them more effectively gain new knowledge and solve new problems. Also, teach them how they can productively collaborate with others and draw on the wisdom of experts. | 🍎 Teach students how to use a search engine such as Google or Bing to find information relevant to a particular topic. Also teach them how to distinguish between websites that present valid, well-documented information and websites that present erroneous "facts" or highly biased opinions. |
| Collaborative co-construction of meaning | 🍎 Convene small groups in which students discuss complex issues with no obvious right and wrong answers. | 🍎 Assign students to four-member groups that discuss the pros and cons of increasing taxes in their community. Ask each group to (1) divide into pairs, with one pair identifying pros and the other identifying cons; (2) make a combined list of the pros and cons; and (3) develop a tax policy that takes both pros and cons into account. |
| Guidance from more advanced individuals | 🍎 Teach concepts and principles that can help students make better sense of new and potentially puzzling situations. | 🍎 Use principles of chemistry to explain why water expands when it freezes—a phenomenon that has implications for food storage, road construction, and other important aspects of human society. |

Chapter 2 explains how children's long-term development also involves several layers of context; for example, see the discussion of Bronfenbrenner's theory.

physical and social environments, and (3) the broader cultures and societies in which they live (see Figure 8.1). Keep in mind, however, that the three layers of context *interact and influence one another,* as reflected in the two way-arrows in the figure. Furthermore, all of them *change over time*—for instance, the body's physical capabilities change, availability of immediate resources and potential social collaborators change, new technological innovations become available in society, and so on.

Our focus in the rest of the chapter will be on Layers 2 and 3—more specifically, on how thinking and learning are influenced by learners' immediate social environments and broader culture and society, as well as by the various tools and knowledge bases that culture and society have created to enhance human performance. As we look at such topics, we mustn't throw our knowledge of learners' internal cognitive processes out the window. Instead we must simply recognize that learners' cognitive processes—processes related to long-term memory storage, metacognition, problem solving, and so on—work *in conjunction with* contextual factors (e.g., Kirsh, 2009; Sawyer & Greeno, 2009; Zusho & Clayton, 2011).

## Social Interactions as Contexts

Certainly people sometimes learn new things on their own, perhaps by experimenting with the physical objects around them or perhaps simply by thinking and *re*thinking about things they've previously observed. Yet most human learning is in one way or another a very social enterprise, involving interaction with more advanced individuals, with equal-ability peers, or both.

### INTERACTIONS WITH MORE ADVANCED INDIVIDUALS

Young learners are most likely to construct a productive understanding of the world when adults and other advanced individuals share with them the many concepts, principles, theories, and so on that society has developed to explain the physical and psychological aspects of human

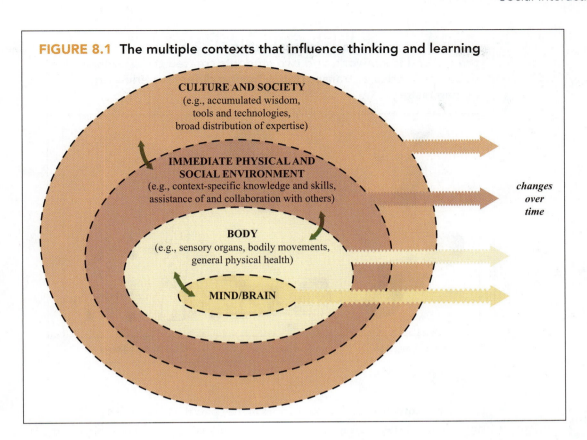

**FIGURE 8.1** The multiple contexts that influence thinking and learning

experience (R. Driver, 1995; Sweller, Kirschner, & Clark, 2007; Vygotsky, 1934/1986). For example, children can learn a great deal about various biological species and fragile ecosystems—and are likely to acquire positive attitudes toward science—when firsthand observations in class or on field trips are accompanied by scientific explanations of the phenomena at hand (e.g., Patrick, Mantzicopoulos, & Samarapungavan, 2009; Zaragoza & Fraser, 2008). Any explanation that helps learners relate what they're observing to particular concepts, principles, or theories is a **mediated learning experience**.

Adults and other advanced individuals help young learners in another important way as well: They introduce new cognitive and metacognitive strategies and guide learners in how to use these strategies, perhaps in a group instructional setting or perhaps in a one-on-one apprenticeship. For instance, in the elementary grades a teacher and students might co-construct a timeline that organizes information about different modes of transportation over the course of human history (Brophy, Alleman, & Knighton, 2009); Figure 8.2 is an example of such a co-constructed timeline. In the secondary grades a teacher and students might collaboratively create two-dimensional charts to help them compare and contrast what they're learning about the climate, geography, and economic resources of various states or countries. Through joint discussions and use of strategies—typically with considerable adult guidance and scaffolding at first—learners gradually internalize the strategies and begin using them independently (A. Collins, 2006; Dennen & Burner, 2008; Rogoff, 1990).

## INTERACTIONS WITH PEERS

Learners benefit in somewhat different ways from interacting with equal-ability peers—in particular, from sharing their ideas and perspectives with one another:

- They must clarify and organize their thoughts well enough to explain and justify them to others.

- They tend to elaborate on what they've learned—for example, by drawing inferences, generating hypotheses, and formulating questions to be answered.

- They're exposed to the views of others, who may have more accurate understandings or culturally different—and yet equally valid—perspectives.

Teach concepts, principles, and theories that help students make sense of their observations and experiences.

Chapter 2 discusses apprenticeships.

One effective strategy for organizing new material is to create a compare-and-contrast table. Observe a teacher co-construct such a table with her students in "Cause–Effect in Geography."

**mediated learning experience**
Discussion between an adult and a child in which the adult helps the child make sense of an event they are mutually experiencing.

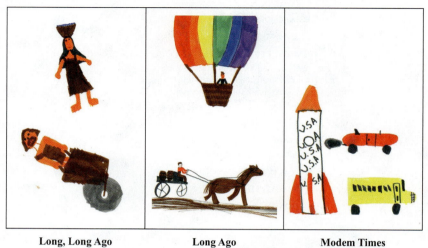

**FIGURE 8.2** In this co-constructed time line, a teacher provided the general framework, and two students created the drawings depicting modes of transportation during different periods in human history.

Long, Long Ago | Long Ago | Modem Times

Regularly engage students in small-group or whole-class discussions that encourage them to exchange views and build on one another's ideas.

- They may discover flaws and inconsistencies in their own thinking.
- They can model effective ways of thinking about and studying academic subject matter for one another.
- With the support of their peers, they can gain practice in more sophisticated learning and reasoning skills, which they can eventually begin to use on their own.
- They can also gain practice in the argumentation skills that experts in various disciplines use to advance the frontiers of knowledge—for instance, presenting evidence in support of conclusions and examining the strengths and weaknesses of various explanations.
- They may acquire more advanced *epistemic beliefs*—more sophisticated views of the nature of knowledge and learning. For example, they may begin to realize that genuine understanding involves acquiring an integrated set of ideas about a topic and that such knowledge is likely to evolve gradually over time. (Andriessen, 2006; Banks, 1991; Bendixen & Rule, 2004; M. Carr & Biddlecomb, 1998; Chinn, 2006; Hatano & Inagaki, 2003; K. Hogan, Nastasi, & Pressley, 2000; D. W. Johnson & Johnson, 2009b; A. King, 1999; Kuhn & Crowell, 2011; P. K. Murphy, Wilkinson, & Soter, 2011; Nussbaum, 2008; B. B. Schwarz, Neuman, & Biezuner, 2000; Sinatra & Pintrich, 2003; C. L. Smith, 2007; Vygotsky, 1978; N. M. Webb & Palincsar, 1996; Wentzel & Watkins, 2011)

Chapter 7 describes epistemic beliefs in greater depth.

Peer-group discussions about academic subject matter have social and motivational benefits as well as cognitive ones. Discussing a topic with classmates can help students acquire more effective interpersonal skills (Certo, 2011; Y. Li et al., 2007; N. M. Webb & Farivar, 1994). It can also have an energizing effect on students and instill a genuine desire to understand a topic better (Hacker & Bol, 2004; P. K. Murphy & Mason, 2006). Controversial topics can be especially motivating because students may be eager to resolve conflicting viewpoints, provided that they can effectively do so without alienating their peers (Chinn, 2006). Clearly, then, students have a great deal to gain from conversing with one another regularly about classroom subject matter.

## CREATING A COMMUNITY OF LEARNERS

With the benefits of student dialogue in mind and with a goal of promoting social co-construction of meaning, some psychologists and educators suggest that we create a community of learners, a class in which teachers and students collaborate to build a body of knowledge about a topic and help one another learn about it. A class that operates as a community of learners is likely to have characteristics such as these:

**community of learners** Class in which teachers and students actively and collaboratively work to create a body of knowledge and help one another learn.

- All students are active participants in classroom activities.
- The primary goal is to acquire a body of knowledge on a specific topic, with students contributing to and building on one another's efforts.
- Students draw on many resources—textbooks, the school library, the Internet, and one another—in their efforts to learn about the topic.
- Discussion and collaboration among two or more students are common occurrences and play a key role in learning.
- Diversity in students' interests and rates of progress is expected and respected.
- Students and teacher coordinate their efforts in helping one another learn; no one has exclusive responsibility for teaching others.
- Everyone is a potential resource for others; different individuals are likely to serve as resources on different occasions, depending on the topics and tasks at hand. In some cases individual students focus on particular topics and become local experts on them. Occasionally people outside the classroom share their expertise as well.
- The teacher provides some guidance and direction for classroom activities, but students also contribute guidance and direction.
- Mechanisms are in place through which students can share what they've learned with others; students regularly critique one another's work.
- The process of learning is emphasized as much as—and sometimes more than—the finished product. (Bielaczyc & Collins, 2006; A. L. Brown & Campione, 1994; Campione, Shapiro, & Brown, 1995; A. Collins, 2006; R. A. Engle, 2006; Rogoff, Matusov, & White, 1996; Scardamalia & Bereiter, 2006)

> Create a community atmosphere in which peer collaboration and mutual support are integral parts of classroom learning and achievement.

In one example of how a community of learners can be structured (A. L. Brown & Campione, 1994), students are divided into small groups to study different subtopics falling under a general theme; for instance, subtopics for the theme *changing populations* might be *extinct, endangered, artificial, assisted,* and *urbanized.* Each group conducts research and prepares teaching materials related to its subtopic. The class then reassembles into new groups that include at least one representative from each of the previous groups. Within these new groups, the students teach one another what they've learned.

Another approach is to use a computer network to promote a community of learners (Bereiter & Scardamalia, 2006; G. Stahl, Koschmann, & Suthers, 2006; J. Zhang, Scardamalia, Reeve, & Messina, 2009). In this electronic environment, students create a variety of documents—perhaps brief notes, lengthier reports, problem solutions, diagrams, or short stories—and post their work as computer files that their classmates can read, react to, and possibly modify or build on. Students also interact in an ongoing computer-based chat room in which they present questions or issues to which their classmates respond. For example, students might jointly wrestle with the fact that heat melts some solids but burns others, or they might critique various theories about how human beings first migrated to and then spread throughout North and South America (e.g., Hewitt, Brett, Scardamalia, Frecker, & Webb, 1995; Hewitt & Scardamalia, 1998).

Working in communities of learners can give students a sense of the strategies scientists and other scholars use to advance the frontiers of knowledge: They conduct individual and collaborative research, share ideas, build on one another's findings, and so on. And in fact, participating in such communities appears to promote fairly complex thinking and knowledge-building processes, often for extended time periods (A. L. Brown & Campione, 1994, 1996; R. A. Engle, 2006; R. A. Engle & Conant, 2002; Scardamalia & Bereiter, 2006). Participating in a community of learners is also highly motivating for students, who may insist on going to school even when they're sick and may express regret when the school year ends (Rogoff, 1994; Turkanis, 2001).

In addition to the cognitive and motivational benefits, working in a community of learners can foster effective peer relationships and social skills. It can also help create a *sense of community* in the classroom—a sense that teachers and students have shared goals, are mutually respectful and supportive of one another's efforts, and believe that everyone makes an important contribution to classroom learning.

> You can learn more about creating a sense of community in Chapter 13.

A community of learners can be especially useful when we have a diverse student population (Kincheloe, 2009; Ladson-Billings, 1995b; Rothstein-Fisch & Trumbull, 2008). Such a community values the contributions of all students, using everyone's individual backgrounds, cultural perspectives, and unique abilities to enhance the overall learning and achievement of the

**culture** Behaviors and belief systems of a long-standing social group.

**schema** Tightly organized set of facts about a specific topic.

**script** Schema that involves a predictable sequence of events related to a common activity.

class. It also provides a context in which students can form friendships across the lines of ethnicity, gender, socioeconomic status, and disability—friendships that are critical for students' social development and multicultural understandings.

However, we must also note potential weaknesses of communities of learners, as well as of peer-group discussions more generally. Some students may dominate interactions, and others (e.g., English language learners) may participate little or not at all (Walshaw & Anthony, 2008; T. White & Pea, 2011). Furthermore, what students learn is inevitably limited to the knowledge they personally acquire and share with one another, and students may occasionally pass along their biases, misconceptions, and ineffective strategies (A. L. Brown & Campione, 1994; Hynd, 1998b; E. R. Smith & Conrey, 2009). Obviously, then, when we conduct classroom discussions or structure our classrooms as communities of learners, we must carefully monitor student interactions to make sure that everyone is meaningfully participating and that students ultimately acquire *accurate* understandings of the topic they're studying.

## Cultures as Contexts

Almost any long-standing social group develops some sort of culture, which includes both behaviors and beliefs that are passed from old members to new ones, from generation to generation. Culture is a phenomenon that is largely—although not exclusively—unique to the human species (M. Cole & Hatano, 2007). Through its culture a human social group ensures that each new generation acquires and presumably benefits from the wisdom that preceding generations have accumulated. By passing along this collective knowledge base, a cultural group increases the chances that it will survive and thrive over the long run.

Especially in large, complex societies, learners typically have exposure to and involvement in two or more cultural groups simultaneously. For example, in North America most learners are immersed in *mainstream Western culture,* which encourages literacy, knowledge of various academic disciplines, and, in its twenty-first-century form, proficiency in digital technologies. But North American learners are likely to be active participants in other cultures as well, such as those associated with particular ethnic or religious groups.

Some aspects of cultural knowledge are concrete and easily observable. This is the case, for example, when people use paper and pencil, equations, diagrams, or computers to help them analyze data or solve problems. But other aspects of cultural knowledge are so abstract and pervasive that they're taken for granted and easily overlooked as contextual factors affecting learning. Consider, for example, the concepts *north, south, east,* and *west.* You've probably used these concepts frequently to help you find your way around the countryside or on a map. Despite their seemingly obvious relationship to Mother Earth, these concepts are creations that some cultures—and only some cultures—provide. Culture's influence on learning and thinking is so strong that researchers have observed cultural differences—small, subtle ones, to be sure—in brain organization and functioning (Park & Huang, 2010).

As culturally experienced individuals explain various phenomena to newer members of a cultural group, they must inevitably focus on certain aspects of the phenomena and not on others. In the process of doing so, young learners discover that certain things are especially important to think about and remember, and these things typically reflect the cultural group's perspectives and priorities. For example, recall once again Jacob's and Howard's differing interpretations of a court case regarding school prayer—interpretations that presumably reflected the boys' different religious backgrounds. As another example, when European American mothers recall past events with their children, they often speculate about the thoughts and feelings of the participants. In contrast, Asian mothers are more likely to talk about social norms and expectations, such as how someone might have behaved more appropriately. Such differences are consistent with the priorities and values of these two cultures (MacDonald, Uesiliana, & Hayne, 2000; Mullen & Yi, 1995; Q. Wang & Ross, 2007).

### SCHEMAS, SCRIPTS, AND WORLDVIEWS AS ASPECTS OF CULTURE

Schemas and scripts are introduced in Chapter 6.

As cognitive psychologists have suggested, developing learners draw on their experiences to construct schemas and scripts—general understandings of what things are typically like and how common activities typically unfold. Many schemas and scripts are unique to particular cultures. The following exercise illustrates this point.

## EXPERIENCING FIRSTHAND
## THE WAR OF THE GHOSTS

Read the following story *one time only:*

> One night two young men from Egulac went down to the river to hunt seals, and while they were there it became foggy and calm. Then they heard war-cries, and they thought, "Maybe this is a war-party." They escaped to the shore, and hid behind a log. Now canoes came up, and they heard the noise of paddles, and saw one canoe coming up to them. There were five men in the canoe, and they said:
>
> "What do you think? We wish to take you along. We are going up the river to make war on the people."
>
> One of the young men said: "I have no arrows."
>
> "Arrows are in the canoe," they said.
>
> "I will not go along. I might be killed. My relatives do not know where I have gone. But you," he said, turning to the other, "may go with them."
>
> So one of the young men went, but the other returned home.
>
> And the warriors went on up the river to a town on the other side of Kalama. The people came down to the water, and they began to fight, and many were killed. But presently the young man heard one of the warriors say, "Quick, let us go home: that Indian has been hit." Now he thought: "Oh, they are ghosts." He did not feel sick, but they said he had been shot.
>
> So the canoes went back to Egulac, and the young man went ashore to his house, and made a fire. And he told everybody and said, "Behold I accompanied the ghosts, and we went to fight. Many of our fellows were killed, and many of those who attacked us were killed. They said I was hit, and I did not feel sick."
>
> He told it all, and then he became quiet. When the sun rose he fell down. Something black came out of his mouth. His face became contorted. The people jumped up and cried.
>
> He was dead. (F. C. Bartlett, 1932, p. 65)

Now cover the story, and write down as much of it as you can remember.

---

Compare your own rendition of the story with the original. What differences do you notice? Your version is almost certainly the shorter of the two, and you probably left out many details. But did you also find yourself distorting certain parts of the story so that it made more sense to you?

As a Native American ghost story, "The War of the Ghosts" may be inconsistent with some of the schemas and scripts you've acquired, especially if you were raised in a non-Native American culture. In an early study of long-term memory (F. C. Bartlett, 1932), students at England's Cambridge University were asked to read the story twice and then to recall it at various times later on. Students' recollections of the story often included additions and distortions that made the story more consistent with English culture. For example, people in England rarely go "to the river to hunt seals" because seals are saltwater animals and most rivers have fresh water. Students might therefore say that the men went to the river to *fish.* Similarly, the ghostly element of the story didn't fit comfortably with the religious beliefs of most Cambridge students and so was often modified. When one student was asked to recall the story six months after he had read it, he provided the following account:

> Four men came down to the water. They were told to get into a boat and to take arms with them. They inquired, "What arms?" and were answered "Arms for battle." When they came to the battle-field they heard a great noise and shouting, and a voice said: "The black man is dead." And he was brought to the place where they were, and laid on the ground. And he foamed at the mouth. (F. C. Bartlett, 1932, pp. 71–72)

Notice how the student's version of the story leaves out many of its more puzzling aspects—puzzling, at least, from his own cultural perspective.

When students from diverse cultural backgrounds come to school with somewhat different schemas and scripts, they may interpret the same classroom materials or activities differently and in some cases may have trouble making sense of a particular lesson or reading assignment

Determine whether students have appropriate schemas and scripts to understand the topic at hand.

(e.g., Lipson, 1983; R. E. Reynolds, Taylor, Steffensen, Shirey, & Anderson, 1982; Steffensen, Joag-Dev, & Anderson, 1979). As teachers, then, we need to find out whether students have the appropriate schemas and scripts to understand whatever topic we're teaching. When students *don't* have such knowledge, we may sometimes need to back up and help them acquire it before we forge ahead with new material.

Learners' schemas and scripts tend to be specific to particular topics. In contrast, their worldviews—their general beliefs and assumptions about reality—can influence their meaning-making in a great many domains (Koltko-Rivera, 2004). Following are examples of assumptions that a worldview might encompass:

- Life and the universe came into being through random acts of nature *or* as part of a divine plan and purpose.

- Objects in nature (rocks, trees, etc.) have some degree of consciousness *or* are incapable of conscious thought.

- Human beings are at the mercy of the forces of nature *or* should strive to master the forces of nature *or* must learn to live in harmony with nature.

- People are most likely to enhance their well-being by relying on scientific principles and logical reasoning processes *or* by seeking guidance and support from sources beyond the realm of scientific and logical thought.

- People's successes and failures in life are the result of their own actions *or* divine intervention *or* fate *or* random occurrences.

- The human world is fair and just—good deeds ultimately bring rewards, misdeeds are eventually punished—*or* is not necessarily fair and just. (M. Cole & Hatano, 2007; Furnham, 2003; Keil & Newman, 2008; Koltko-Rivera, 2004; Medin, 2005)

To a considerable degree, such beliefs and assumptions are culturally transmitted, with different cultures communicating somewhat different beliefs and assumptions either explicitly through their words or implicitly through their actions (Berti, Toneatti, & Rosati, 2010; M. Cole & Hatano, 2007; Kitayama, 2002; Losh, 2003).

Worldviews are often such an integral part of everyday thinking that learners take them for granted and usually aren't consciously aware of them. In many cases, then, worldviews encompass *implicit knowledge* rather than explicit knowledge. Nevertheless, they influence learners' interpretations of current events and classroom subject matter. For example, if students believe that the world and its inhabitants are guided and protected by a an omniscient and benevolent Greater Being, they're unlikely to believe that global climate change is real or poses a significant threat to human society (Feinberg & Willer, 2011). And if students' culture consistently emphasizes the importance of accepting and living in harmony with nature as it is, they might struggle with a science curriculum that explores how human beings might manipulate and gain control over natural events (Atran, Medin, & Ross, 2005; Medin, 2005).

When students' worldviews are central to their sense of identity, recognize that they may steadfastly hold on to their existing beliefs. In such cases, focus on helping them understand—rather than accept—experts' explanations and lines of reasoning.

In some cases, academic subject matter may conflict with students' most core beliefs, and ultimately with the very essence of who they are as individuals. For example, students who strongly believe in the divine creation of humankind may readily dismiss any suggestion that the human race has evolved from more primitive species (E. M. Evans, 2008; Southerland & Sinatra, 2003). And students whose cultures view certain historical battles as involving good guys triumphing over bad guys—or vice versa—may disregard more balanced perspectives in which each side has had legitimate needs and concerns (K. Jacoby, 2008; Levstik, 2011; Porat, 2004). Hence, students' worldviews can sometimes interfere with their ability to undergo legitimate conceptual change. Under such circumstances a more achievable goal may be to help students *understand* (rather than *accept*) academic scholars' explanations and lines of reasoning (Feinberg & Willer, 2011; Southerland & Sinatra, 2003).

See Chapter 6 for an in-depth discussion of conceptual change.

## COMMUNITIES OF PRACTICE AS ASPECTS OF CULTURE

Any cultural group passes along not only certain ways of interpreting the world but also certain ways of doing things. In other words, different cultures foster somewhat different kinds of *procedural knowledge*. Some procedural knowledge is task- or topic-specific and is conveyed directly and explicitly—for example, "Here's how to write a cursive *A*," and "Let me show you how to

**worldview** General, culturally based set of assumptions about reality that influence understandings of a wide variety of phenomena.

do long division." But cultures typically also pass along a good deal of procedural knowledge within the context of communities of practice—groups of people who share common interests and goals and regularly interact and coordinate their efforts in pursuit of those interests and goals (e.g., Lave, 1991; Sawyer & Greeno, 2009; Wenger, 1998). Communities of practice tend to adhere to certain standards for action and interaction—standards that are often unwritten understandings rather than explicitly stated rules. For example, in the adult world of mainstream Western culture, people in various professions—medicine, law, scientific research, and so on—tend to communicate regularly with one another and to support one another in particular ways. In most cases, new members of a community of practice learn the acceptable ways of doing things primarily by actively *participating* in the group. Often a learner begins by participating only at the fringe of the group, perhaps by doing menial chores or by assisting or apprenticing with a more experienced group member. In other words, a novice is gradually introduced to the ways of the group through legitimate peripheral participation (Lave & Wenger, 1991). Participation is *legitimate* in the sense that the novice contributes in genuine, authentic ways to the group's overall effort. It's *peripheral* in that it involves only small tasks at the outer edge, or periphery, of the action.

Communities of practice are hardly limited to adult professional groups. For example, volunteer organizations (e.g., the American Red Cross) and organized youth groups (e.g., Boy Scouts and Girl Scouts) are essentially communities of practice as well. Schools, too, are communities of practice, in that they have certain prescribed ways of doing things in order to accomplish particular goals—for example, following schedules, completing assignments, and meeting deadlines.

As teachers, we must certainly help students learn the expectations of their educational community. But in addition, we can help students learn the ways of various adult professional communities, as well as of the adult world more generally, by having students actually participate in adult activities—for example, by encouraging part-time internships with local businesses or collaborative efforts with public service organizations. Initially their participation might involve only easy tasks that are closely guided and supported, but as students gain more knowledge and skills they should also gain more responsibility and independence.

**community of practice** Group of people who share common interests and goals and regularly interact and coordinate their efforts in pursuit of those interests and goals.

**legitimate peripheral participation** Initially participating at the fringe of a community of practice as a way of gaining knowledge and skills related to the group's typical ways of doing things.

**society** Very large, enduring social group that has fairly explicit social and economic structures and collective institutions and activities.

**distributed knowledge** Possession of different areas of expertise by various members of a social group, such that group members must rely on one another to maximize their personal and collective performance and success.

Encourage involvement in local businesses and public service organizations as a way of introducing students to the skills and commonly accepted practices of the adult world.

## Society and Technology as Contexts

A concept related to culture, but also somewhat distinct from it, is society: a very large, enduring social group that has fairly explicit social and economic structures, as well as collective institutions and activities. For instance, virtually any nation is a society, in that it has a government that regulates some of its activities, a set of laws identifying permissible and unacceptable behaviors, a monetary system that allows members to exchange goods and services, and so on.

A society influences its members' learning in a variety of ways, including through the resources it provides, the activities it supports, and the general messages it communicates (e.g., Bronfenbrenner, 2005; Gauvain & Munroe, 2009). For example, a society's infrastructure—such as its roads, power plants, and telephone and cable lines—enables the movement of people and goods over great distances and regular collaboration among its residents. Various media (newspapers, television, the Internet, etc.) convey information, ideas, opinions, and messages (often subtle ones) about desired behaviors and group stereotypes. And, of course, schools provide formal structures through which children and adults alike acquire knowledge and skills that will presumably enhance their personal and professional success.

One noteworthy aspect of any society is its distributed knowledge: Different people have expertise in different topics, and so society members must rely on one another in order to maximize both their individual success and the success of the overall group. To be truly effective participants in society, then, people must learn how to seek out the expertise they may occasionally need to tackle challenging problems and to distinguish between true experts, on the one hand, and individuals who only *claim* to be experts, on the other (Bromme, Kienhues, & Porsch, 2010).

As teachers, virtually anything we do with students should in one way or another enhance their long-term success in adult society. But here we focus on two particular topics about which educational psychologists have had a great deal to say in recent years: authentic activities and technological innovations.

Advanced societies provide many services that either directly or indirectly promote learning. Watch an elementary school class discuss some of these services in "Production, Distribution, and Consumption."

## AUTHENTIC ACTIVITIES

In industrialized societies, children are largely separated from the adult workplace, and thus they have little exposure to the kinds of tasks they'll eventually need to perform when they themselves reach adulthood (Rogoff, 2003). Accordingly, many learning theorists recommend that teachers make frequent use of authentic activities—activities similar or identical to those that students will eventually encounter in the outside world (e.g., Barab & Dodge, 2008; Edelson & Reiser, 2006; Greeno, Collins, & Resnick, 1996; Hickey, 1997). Such activities are likely to have several benefits. For one thing, when students work in a naturalistic context, using the physical and social resources that such a context offers (e.g., tools, other people), students should be able to accomplish more than they might accomplish in relatively artificial and simplistic classroom tasks. Second, complex authentic tasks are likely to promote meaningful learning rather than rote memorization of new information and procedures. Finally, because authentic activities resemble real-world tasks and problems, they should help students make mental connections between school subject matter and out-of-school situations, and these connections should help them retrieve and apply—that is, *transfer*—what they've learned in appropriate contexts.

Numerous research studies have confirmed the effectiveness of authentic activities (e.g., Gijbels, Dochy, Van den Bossche, & Segers, 2005; Hung, Jonassen, & Liu, 2008). For example, students' writing skills may show greater improvement in both quality and quantity when, instead of completing traditional workbook writing exercises, they write stories, essays, and letters to real people (E. H. Hiebert & Fisher, 1992). Students gain a more complete understanding of how to use and interpret maps when, instead of answering workbook questions about maps, they construct their *own* maps (M. Gregg & Leinhardt, 1994a). And students are more likely to check their solutions to math problems—in particular, to make sure their solutions make logical sense—when they use math for real-life tasks (Cognition and Technology Group at Vanderbilt, 1993; De Corte, Greer, & Verschaffel, 1996).

Authentic activities can also be highly motivating for students (M. Barnett, 2005; Marks, 2000; Wirkala & Kuhn, 2011). As an example, consider one high school student's recollection of a ninth-grade moon-tracking activity:

> It was the first time I can remember in school doing something that wasn't in the textbook . . . like we were real scientists or something. We had to keep data sheets, measure the time and angle of the moonrise every day for a month. It drove my mom nuts because sometimes we'd be eating dinner, and I'd look at my watch and race out the door! We had to measure the river near us to see how it was affected by the moon. . . . I went down to the river more than I have in my whole life, I think. Then we had to do the calculations, that was another step, and we had to chart our findings. The test was to analyze your findings and tell what they meant about the relationship of the tides and the moon. . . . I felt that I did something real, and I could see the benefit of it. (Wasley, Hampel, & Clark, 1997, pp. 117–118)

By placing classroom activities in real-world contexts, we help students discover the reasons that they're learning academic subject matter. Accordingly, authentic activities may be especially valuable in working with students who are at risk for academic failure (L. W. Anderson & Pellicer, 1998; Christenson & Thurlow, 2004; Tate, 1995).

Authentic activities can be developed for virtually any area of the curriculum. For example, we might ask students to do the following:

- Write an editorial
- Participate in a debate
- Design an electrical circuit
- Conduct an experiment
- Construct a map

- Make a video
- Plan a family budget
- Perform in a concert
- Converse in a foreign language
- Develop an Internet home page

In some instances authentic activities take the form of problem-based learning or project-based learning, in which students acquire new knowledge and skills as they work on complex problems or projects similar to those they might find in the outside world (Hmelo-Silver, 2004, 2006; Krajcik & Blumenfeld, 2006; Wirkala & Kuhn, 2011). Occasionally authentic activities may also involve service learning—that is, they involve projects that directly or indirectly enhance the

See Chapter 7 for a discussion of factors affecting transfer.

Incorporate classroom subject matter into real-world tasks.

**authentic activity**   Classroom activity similar to an activity that students are apt to encounter in the outside world.

**problem-based learning**   Classroom activity in which students acquire new knowledge and skills while working on a complex problem similar to one that might exist in the outside world.

**project-based learning**   Classroom activity in which students acquire new knowledge and skills while working on a complex, multifaceted project that yields a concrete end product.

**service learning**   Activity that promotes learning and development through contributing to the betterment of others and the outside community.

quality of life in the outside community. To be effective in enhancing students' learning—and to be sources of pleasure and success rather than sources of frustration and failure—most complex authentic activities require considerable teacher guidance and support (Hmelo-Silver, Duncan, & Chinn, 2007; Mergendoller, Markham, Ravitz, & Larmer, 2006).

Authentic activities are possibly most beneficial when they promote complex thinking skills—for instance, synthesizing information, forming and testing hypotheses, or solving problems—and when their final outcomes are multifaceted and somewhat unpredictable (Newmann & Wehlage, 1993; S. G. Paris & Turner, 1994). Nevertheless, they should be sufficiently simple that they don't impose an unmanageable cognitive load—in other words, they shouldn't be so complex that students find them too overwhelming (Kester, Paas, & van Merriënboer, 2010; Plass, Kalyuga, & Leutner, 2010). The Into the Classroom feature "Conducting Authentic Activities" offers several strategies that researchers and experienced educators have found to be effective.

## TECHNOLOGICAL INNOVATIONS

Strictly speaking, *technology* includes any humanmade application of scientific knowledge for a practical purpose. But the focus here will be on *digital technologies*—those that enable us to electronically store, manipulate, and transmit information. (The word *digital* refers to the fact that the information is stored in the form of many, many 0s and 1s, collectively known as *bits*.) Computer hardware and software, cell phones, video cameras, video game systems, and the Internet are all examples of digital technologies.

As these technologies have become more widely available and affordable, they've also become more pervasive in modern-day societies. For example, although precise statistics on cell

## Into the Classroom

### Conducting Authentic Activities

🍎 **Simplify the task sufficiently to be appropriate for students' age levels and cognitive abilities.**

At a school in Seattle, Washington, students in kindergarten and the first and second grades work cooperatively with researchers to monitor dog "poop" along a nature trail in an important watershed area. Once every two months, the students and several adult volunteers count and map the various dog deposits they find on the trail and within seven feet to either side. Midway through the school year, the students place plastic-bag dispensers at various locations near the trail and continue their bimonthly monitoring in order to determine whether the dispensers and bags have any effect. Not only do the students gain an awareness of the harmful effects of pollution on natural resources, but they also gain confidence in their ability to have a positive impact on the health of their local environment.

🍎 **Choose a task that requires students to integrate and apply what they've learned in two or more subject areas.**

A third-grade class creates a "publishing company" that provides various printed materials (announcements, programs, banners, etc.) for activities and performances throughout their school. Students engage in many typical business activities; for instance, they interview for various jobs in the company, make sales calls to solicit business from other classes, design customer order forms, edit and proofread their work, and conduct customer satisfaction surveys.

🍎 **Communicate that there is no single best or right approach or solution for a task.**

A teacher of a high school Life Skills class gives students a list of prices of many items (meats, fruits, vegetables, milk, etc.) available at the local grocery store. Using the list, the food pyramid, and a budget of $30, students must plan a healthful breakfast, lunch, and dinner for a family of four for one day.

🍎 **Encourage students to experiment with new ideas and strategies.**

A fifth-grade class has been studying a number of common plants and animals indigenous to their area. The students work in groups of two or three to create informational displays about several species for the city museum. Their teacher helps each group brainstorm ideas about how it might effectively portray a particular plant or animal for the general public.

🍎 **Communicate high expectations for students' performance but provide enough scaffolding to ensure students' success.**

All 92 eighth graders at a middle school are required to contribute in a meaningful way to the annual eighth-grade musical. Some students are members of the cast, whereas others are involved in scenery construction, costume design, or lighting. Faculty members supervise each aspect of the project and provide guidance and assistance as needed, but the students are largely responsible for the quality of the production. As students from different social groups work with one another, social barriers and ill feelings between popular and unpopular students begin to break down. By opening night the class has acquired a sense of cohesiveness and overall class spirit, and collectively the students take much pride in their successful production.

*Sources:* Edelson & Reiser, 2006; Hmelo-Silver et al., 2007; Kester et al., 2010; Kornhaber, Fierros, & Veenema, 2004 (publishing business example); Mergendoller et al., 2006; Newmann & Wehlage, 1993; S. G. Paris & Turner, 1994; Pickens, 2006 (dog poop example); Plass et al., 2010; M. Thompson & Grace, 2001 (class play example).

**e-learning** Instruction and learning that occur largely or entirely within the context of digital technologies.

**distance learning** Technology-based instruction in which students are at a location physically separate from that of their instructor.

**intelligent tutoring system** Computer software program that provides individually tailored instruction and practice, plus ongoing guidance and feedback, related to a particular topic and set of skills.

phone usage are virtually impossible to obtain, the majority of middle school and high school students in North America and western Europe appear to have their own cell phones, and many of them are proficient in using their phones not only to make calls but also to send text messages, take and send photographs, and post opinions and photographs on social networking sites such as Facebook. For most adolescents, the primary motive for using cell phones and other new technologies is to initiate and maintain social relationships, especially with peers (Ito et al., 2009; Valkenburg & Peter, 2009; Warschauer, 2011).

In large, complex societies, recent technological innovations have increasingly enabled people to access that *distributed knowledge* of which I spoke earlier. Gone are the days when quick access to important information required people to either (1) effectively store it in their own long-term memories or on personal bookshelves or (2) travel to a public library or other physical source of knowledge about a particular topic. Instead, people can gain needed information about almost any subject area—and sometimes they gain *mis*information—with a few simple keystrokes on an Internet search engine such as Google, Bing, or Yahoo! The overall learning environment of the early twenty-first century is indeed a very different one from that of the mid-twentieth century.

## TECHNOLOGY IN LEARNING AND INSTRUCTION

When learning takes place in an electronic environment, it's sometimes called e-learning. But regardless of what we call it, the many technologies available in twenty-first-century societies can enhance it in numerous ways:

- *Instruction can seamlessly integrate several media and multiple pedagogical strategies.* For example, instructional software programs often integrate written text with graphics, videos, simulations, exercises, and assessments. And interactive *smartboards*—large wall-mounted displays connected to a computer and projector—are increasingly replacing traditional chalkboards and whiteboards. Not only can these boards display the contents of a computer screen—perhaps a video, a set of instructions, or an Internet website—but in addition, class members can electronically write and draw on them, with the products being transmitted to and saved on the computer.

Even many textbooks (including this one!) can take a digital form these days. Digital textbooks might include not only traditional text and graphics but also audio recordings, videos, and links to dictionary and glossary entries. Students can electronically "search" for particular words or concepts, highlight sections of particular interest or importance, and write notes related to the content.

- *Instruction itself can be delivered from afar.* For example, students can participate in classroom activities when they must be absent from school for extended periods, perhaps because of a chronic illness or significant injury. Also, students can take courses that aren't available in their local school districts—perhaps Advanced Placement high school courses or college coursework appropriate for their ability levels. Collectively, such forms of instruction are known as distance learning.

Figure 7.6 in Chapter 7 presents an example of an intelligent tutoring system.

- *Instruction can more easily be individualized to accommodate students' unique needs.* For example, Internet-based research projects allow students to pursue topics of personal interest in considerable depth. And software programs known as intelligent tutoring systems help students master knowledge and skills in various content domains—for instance, in reading, math, and science—by giving them ongoing, individually tailored guidance, hints, and feedback as they study new concepts and procedures. When well designed, these software programs can be as effective as one-on-one human tutors in helping students learn (VanLehn, 2011; Woolf, 2009).

Consider the many ways in which technology might help students think more creatively and resourcefully about complex issues and problems.

- *Learners can manipulate data in a variety of ways while also keeping their cognitive load within reasonable limits.* As teachers, we must remember that complex thinking tasks can impose a significant burden on working memory. In line with the notion of *distributed cognition,* digital technologies can carry some of the cognitive burden and free up some working memory capacity for problem solving and creativity. For example, students can use computer spreadsheets and graphing software to explore and examine the effects of different values of $x$ in an algebraic equation. And they can use concept mapping software (e.g., Kidspiration, MindMapper Jr. for Kids) to try out various ways of organizing and interrelating new material. Ideally, technology can provide an electronic "playground" in which students can experiment with and expand on ideas (J. A. Langer, 2011; Spiro & DeSchryver, 2009).

• *Diverse bodies of knowledge are within easy reach, especially on the Internet, and can be searched on an as-needed basis.* Most schools in mainstream Western culture have computers with Internet connections, either in individual classrooms or in separate computer resource rooms. Some schools also provide laptops or computer tablets (e.g., iPads) that students can use as individuals or in small groups. Outside of school, many students can find computers at libraries and other public places. And as their cell phones increasingly become multifunction *smartphones,* they can access the Internet wirelessly (i.e., through *wifi*) at libraries, coffee shops, and many other wireless "hotspots."

• *Teachers and learners can easily communicate and collaborate with one another.* Technology can certainly enhance communication and collaboration within a single classroom. For instance, course management systems such as Blackboard and Moodle provide means through which teachers can post materials and assignments, students can upload their work for feedback or evaluation, and all class members can regularly interact through classroom discussion boards or chat rooms. Another good resource is Google Apps for Education, through which schools can create a separate e-mail account for every student, post school and classroom calendars with scheduled activities and due dates, and upload documents to which teachers and students alike can contribute. In addition, teachers and their students can create class-specific *wikis,* websites on which individual class members can add to, edit, or rearrange material previously contributed by other members. Popular wiki-creation websites include pbworks.com, wikisineducation.wetpaint.com, and wiki-spaces.com.

Set up Internet websites that foster ongoing classroom communication both in and outside of school.

Thanks to the Internet, individual students or entire classes can also communicate and collaborate with students or classes in other locations—even in other nations (e.g., see iearn.org). One vehicle for doing so is Skype (www.skype.com), through which people at two different locations can both see and hear each other on any computer, tablet, or smartphone that has a built-in video camera and microphone. As I write this book, setting up and using a Skype account is free and easy, allowing me to talk regularly with my son Jeff, who is now a middle school teacher in Shanghai, China.

Finally, teachers are increasingly communicating and collaborating with *one another* via the Internet. For example, many teachers share lesson plans and other instructional strategies they've found to be effective (e.g., see www.tappedin.org or www.oercommons.org). Some teachers have even written electronic textbooks that other teachers can use and modify for their own purposes (e.g., see www.ck12.org).

Computers and the Internet facilitate cross-class communication. For example, watch high school history classes in Hawaii and New Hampshire share their knowledge and perspectives in "Distance Education."

• *Technology offers many means of providing authentic activities.* For example, students can create their own videos, websites, or video games (e.g., see sploder.com or arisgames.org). They can post their poems and short stories for others to read and critique (e.g., see fanfiction.net). And through well-designed simulations, they can design and carry out virtual scientific "experiments" to test their theories about cause-and-effect relationships in the physical world.

• *Some technology-based instructional strategies effectively blur the lines between "work" and "play."* Well-designed technology-based instruction is highly interactive and can keep students motivated and engaged for lengthy periods. And some educators and software developers are now developing challenging video games that electronically immerse students in simulated environments in which they act as tribal chiefs in 4000 BC, pirates in the 1600s, or twentieth-century urban planners (in *Civilization, Pirates!,* and *SimCity,* respectively). In the process of playing these games, students can learn a great deal about history, geography, and other academic content domains (Barab & Dodge, 2008; Squire, 2011).

As we incorporate digital technologies and the Internet into instruction, however, we must give students the guidance they need to use these things effectively. Following are general suggestions:

🍏 Don't assume that instruction is better only because it involves technology. Instead, make sure that the technological tools you use *enhance* students' thinking and learning in some way.

🍎 Remember that some students may have had little or no experience with technology. As needed, teach them any basic skills they haven't yet mastered—perhaps how to send an e-mail message, how to conduct a simple Internet search, or how to create, edit, and save a word processing document.

🍎 Teach and insist on appropriate social etiquette for cross-communication, and monitor students' entries for content; especially be on the lookout for bullying and other antisocial messages. (Bellanca & Stirling, 2011; R. E. Clark, Yates, Early, & Moulton, 2009; Rivers, Chesney, & Coyne, 2011; Warschauer, 2011)

In addition, we must remember that use of the Internet requires literacy skills far beyond those necessary for more traditional reading and writing tasks, as we'll discover in an upcoming section on technological literacy.

## Academic Content Domains as Contexts

In the early millennia of human civilization, cultures and societies focused largely on teaching children knowledge and skills related to basic survival (hunting, growing crops, cooking, etc.), and experts in such areas as woodworking, metalwork, and medicine often taught their knowledge to new generations through one-on-one apprenticeships. But as cultural groups developed writing systems and constructed increasingly complex understandings of their physical, biological, and social worlds, they began to establish formal schools that could more efficiently pass their cultural creations along to future generations. One way in which schools made the ever-expanding knowledge base more manageable for instruction was to subdivide it into various academic disciplines: reading, writing, mathematics, science, and so on.

To some degree, different academic content domains require different thinking skills. For example, effective reading requires automatic retrieval of the meanings of thousands of words in one's language, whereas mathematical problem solving requires precisely thinking about quantities and flexibly manipulating symbols that represent them. Furthermore, various subject areas may depend more or less heavily on different parts of the brain (Dehaene, 2007; Katzir & Paré-Blagoev, 2006; Norton, Kovelman, & Pettito, 2007; Plumert & Spencer, 2007; Posner & Rothbart, 2007).

In a very real way, then, different content domains are additional *contexts* in which students learn, and strategies for effectively teaching the subject matter can vary significantly from one domain to another. In upcoming sections we'll consider four general content domains: literacy, mathematics, science, and social studies. By no means do these topics cover all of the academic curriculum; for example, physical education, music, and the visual and performing arts are also disciplines in their own rights and enhance children's development and general well-being in many ways (e.g., J. H. Davis, 2008).

In discussing the four domains separately, I don't mean to imply that we should consistently teach each domain in isolation from the others. On the contrary, instruction is often more effective when it simultaneously incorporates two or more domains—perhaps teaching reading in conjunction with science or teaching writing in conjunction with history (e.g., Martínez, Bannan-Ritland, Kitsantas, & Baek, 2008; Monte-Sano, 2008). Furthermore, several general principles of learning apply to *all* domains:

🍏 Regularly consider how you might integrate two or more content domains in instruction, perhaps in collaboration with other teachers.

- Learners use the information they receive from various sources to construct their own, unique understandings.

- Learners' interpretations of new information and events are influenced by what they already know and believe about the world.

- With age and development, learners acquire metacognitive strategies and epistemic beliefs that influence their thinking and performance within a domain.

- Learners often gain greater understanding and greater metacognitive sophistication in a domain when they work collaboratively with peers.

Table 8.2 illustrates how each of these principles can be seen in each of the domains we'll consider in this chapter.

# COMPARE/CONTRAST

## TABLE 8.2 • Applying General Principles of Learning in Different Content Domains

| PRINCIPLE | LITERACY | MATHEMATICS | SCIENCE | SOCIAL STUDIES |
|---|---|---|---|---|
| **Constructive processes in learning** | Good readers go beyond the information explicitly presented on the page—for example, by drawing inferences, making predictions, and identifying underlying themes. Effective writing involves more than simply transcribing one's knowledge and beliefs on paper; rather, it involves constructively recasting ideas in such a way that others can more readily understand them. | Beginning with a basic understanding of quantity, numbers, and counting, learners build an increasingly complex and integrated understanding of mathematical concepts and principles. | Learning science effectively involves constructing general theories and models that integrate many concepts and principles related to particular topics. | Mastery of history, geography, and related domains involves reading maps and historical documents to construct integrated understandings of cause–and–effect relationships among people, events, and features of the physical environment. |
| **Influence of prior knowledge and beliefs** | Learners use what they already know about a topic to help them construct meaning from text, and they write more effectively about topics they know well. | Mathematics is an especially hierarchical discipline in which many advanced concepts and principles build on ideas learned in earlier years. | Learners often construct their own theories about natural phenomena long before they have formal instruction about these phenomena. Such theories sometimes interfere with their ability to learn more scientifically acceptable explanations. | Learners learn social studies more effectively when they can relate historical events and geographical phenomena to their own personal experiences. |
| **Metacognitive strategies and epistemic beliefs** | Good readers understand that reading involves active meaning making; they monitor their comprehension and engage in processes that are likely to increase it (setting goals, asking questions they try to answer, etc.). Good writers set goals for their writing, consider what their audience is likely to know about a topic, and focus on enhancing organization and clarity as they revise what they've written. | Effective problem solvers monitor their progress toward problem solutions. They also have epistemic beliefs conducive to problem-solving success; for example, they recognize that mathematical procedures make logical sense and know that they may need to try several different approaches before they're successful. | Learners' beliefs about the nature of science influence how they study and learn science; for example, those who believe that science consists of isolated facts are likely to focus on meaningless memorization. Furthermore, learners' ability to conduct meaningful experiments is influenced by the extent to which they ask themselves questions about their observations and interpretations (e.g., "Have I confirmed my prediction?"). | A true understanding of history involves the recognition that a great deal of historical "knowledge" is interpretive rather than factual. A true understanding of geography involves the recognition that locations of various physical features and human creations are not random—rather, that human settlement and activity patterns are largely a function of local environmental conditions. |
| **Collaboration with peers** | Learners more effectively construct meaning from what they read when they discuss reading material with their classmates. They write more effectively when their peers read and critique their work and when they collaborate on writing projects. | Learners gain a better understanding of math when they tutor classmates or younger children. They gain greater metacognitive awareness of their strategies—and may also modify inappropriate ones—when they must explain and justify their reasoning to others. | Learners often revise misconceptions about scientific phenomena and acquire more sophisticated scientific reasoning processes when they jointly wrestle with puzzling findings and critique one another's conclusions. | Learners can more effectively practice advanced reasoning skills (e.g., evaluating and integrating information presented in multiple historical documents) when they work in partnership with peers. |

## LITERACY

The word *literacy* has two distinct meanings. In its narrower sense, it refers to one's reading and writing abilities. In its broader sense, it refers to one's general ability to understand and communicate meanings using the various concepts and symbols of a particular community of practice—perhaps that of physicists, musicians, or computer programmers. For now we'll be focusing on the narrower sense of the word: reading and writing. But we must remember that success in virtually any academic discipline requires mastery of its discipline-specific concepts and symbols.

**emergent literacy** Knowledge and skills that lay a foundation for reading and writing; typically develops from early experiences with written language.

**phonological awareness** Ability to hear the distinct sounds of which spoken words are comprised.

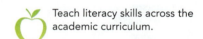

Teach literacy skills across the academic curriculum.

Children's reading and writing skills obviously build on their knowledge of spoken language. But in addition, children must learn the relationships between how words sound and are produced in speech, on the one hand, and how they look and are written on paper, on the other. Children must also master nuances of the written symbol system that have no counterparts in spoken language, such as punctuation marks and appropriate uses of uppercase and lowercase letters.

Through storybook reading and other activities at home, many children—but not all of them—come to school knowing a few things about written language. For example, they may know that spoken language is represented in a consistent fashion in writing, that reading proceeds from left to right and from the top of the page to the bottom, and that each alphabet letter is associated with particular sounds in spoken language. They may be able to write part or all of their own name, and they may recognize logos of popular products and commercial establishments, such as Coke and McDonald's. Taken together, such knowledge and skills—collectively known as emergent literacy—lay a basic foundation for reading and writing (Oliver, Dale, & Plomin, 2005; Serpell, Baker, & Sonnenschein, 2005). And reading and writing, in turn, provide important foundations for learning most other academic disciplines, especially in the middle and secondary school grades (E. Fox & Alexander, 2011; Martínez et al., 2008; C. Shanahan, 2004; H. L. Swanson, 2006).

As a topic of formal instruction, reading is taught primarily in elementary school. Writing instruction continues in secondary school language arts classes. Yet effective reading and writing strategies tend to take somewhat different forms in different academic disciplines—for example, reading a textbook in a math class is quite different from reading a newspaper article in a social studies class (recall the opening case study), and writing a short story is quite different from writing a science lab report. As teachers, then, we should teach reading and writing within the context of a variety of content domains—not only in language arts classes but also in math, science, and social studies classes.

## THE NATURE OF SKILLED READING

Reading is a multifaceted process that involves considerable knowledge and abilities:

- *Sound and letter recognition:* A large body of research indicates that phonological awareness—hearing distinct sounds, or *phonemes,* within a spoken word (e.g., detecting the sounds "guh," "ay," and "tuh" in the word *gate*)—is an essential element of successful reading, especially in the beginning stages of learning to read. And, of course, learners must be able to recognize alphabet letters in various fonts and in both uppercase and lowercase forms (Anthony & Francis, 2005; Boscardin, Muthén, Francis, & Baker, 2008; Schatschneider, Fletcher, Francis, Carlson, & Foorman, 2004).

- *Word decoding skills:* Readers inevitably encounter words they don't recognize. In such instances they must draw on letter–sound relationships, familiar prefixes and root words, common spelling patterns, and context clues to decipher the words (Goswami, 2007; Nagy, Berninger, & Abbott, 2006; Rayner, Foorman, Perfetti, Pesetsky, & Seidenberg, 2001).

- *Automatic word recognition:* When learners must use their limited working memory capacity to decode and interpret *many* individual words, they have little or no mental "room" left to use in gaining an overall understanding of what they're reading. Ultimately, word recognition must become automatic in two ways: Learners must be able to (1) identify most words in a split second, without having to decode them letter by letter; and (2) immediately retrieve the words' meanings (Betjemann & Keenan, 2008; Curtis, 2004; Klauda & Guthrie, 2008).

- *Meaning construction:* Effective reading is a constructive process: Good readers go far beyond the words themselves, identifying main ideas, drawing inferences, deriving applications, and so on. Sophisticated readers also find symbolism in works of fiction, evaluate the quality of evidence in persuasive essays, and identify assumptions or philosophical perspectives that underlie editorials. Meaning construction can be especially challenging when learners must integrate what they read from two or more distinct texts, as Jacob and Howard must do in the opening case study (Cromley & Azevedo, 2007; E. Fox & Alexander, 2011; Gaskins, Satlow, & Pressley, 2007; Kintsch, 2009).

- *Metacognitive oversight:* Good readers metacognitively "supervise" their own reading. For example, they set goals regarding what they want to learn, focus attention on parts they deem to be important, and continually self-assess their understanding and memory of what they've read. And ultimately, good readers understand that reading involves actively *making* meaning, rather than mindlessly "absorbing" meaning from the page (Bråten, Britt, Strømsø, & Rouet, 2011; Gaskins et al., 2007; Pressley & Harris, 2006).

Effective meaning construction in reading is, of course, enhanced by the amount of knowledge learners already have about a topic (Beck, McKeown, Sinatra, & Loxterman, 1991; Britton, Stimson, Stennett, & Gülgöz, 1998; Vidal-Abarca, Martínez, & Gilabert, 2000). For example, second graders who already know a lot about spiders remember more when they read a passage about spiders and can draw inferences more readily than their less knowledgeable classmates (Pearson, Hansen, & Gordon, 1979). Helpful, too, is knowledge about the structures that various types of literature typically follow; for example, the events described in works of fiction usually follow a chronological sequence, and persuasive essays usually begin with a main point and then present evidence to support it (Byrnes, 1996; Cain, Oakhill, & Bryant, 2004; Leon, 2008).

As learners grow older and gain more experience as readers, they become increasingly able to understand what they read, in part because they (1) gain automaticity in word recognition, (2) acquire more effective learning strategies and metacognitive processes, and (3) have a larger knowledge base on which to draw as they read. Table 8.3 lists typical characteristics of readers at different grade levels. Nevertheless, we must keep in mind that students at any single grade level differ widely in their reading skills; for example, some high school students have poor word decoding skills and little ability to make sense of what they read (Curtis, 2004; Felton, 1998; N. Gregg, 2009). As teachers, then, we should nurture students' reading development at *all* grades.

Teach and scaffold reading skills even in the secondary grades.

## THE NATURE OF SKILLED WRITING

As you might guess, learners who are better readers also tend to be better writers. This correlation is partly due to the fact that general language ability—knowledge and effective use of vocabulary, syntax, and so on—provides a foundation for both reading and writing. Furthermore, practice in reading promotes vocabulary development and greater awareness of how words are spelled. And regular reading familiarizes learners with common ways in which fiction and nonfiction texts are structured (De La Paz & McCutchen, 2011; Rayner et al., 2001; T. Shanahan & Tierney, 1990). But effective writing involves additional processes as well:

- *Goal setting:* Good writers determine what they want to accomplish in their writing—perhaps to entertain, describe, report, or persuade—and have a good sense of the audience for whom they're writing (Graham, 2006; Scardamalia & Bereiter, 1986; Sitko, 1998).

- *Identification and organization of relevant knowledge:* Whether they're writing fiction or nonfiction, good writers identify what they know about a topic—knowledge that they've acquired through either personal experience or formal instruction—and then, if necessary, supplement it with additional research. Typically they also spend a fair amount of time organizing their ideas before they write (Benton, 1997; Berninger, Fuller, & Whitaker, 1996; R. T. Kellogg, 1994).

- *Focus on communication rather than mechanics:* Good writers have typically learned the basic mechanics of writing (handwriting, spelling, punctuation, etc.) to automaticity, thereby leaving "room" in working memory to focus on effectively communicating their intended message (Benton, 1997). In their initial drafts, skilled writers focus on conveying their ideas in ways that will help readers readily grasp their meaning; for example, they begin with what they think readers are likely to know and systematically lead readers toward better understandings. In other words, good writers engage in knowledge transforming. In contrast, less skilled writers engage in knowledge telling, writing thoughts in the order in which they retrieve them from long-term memory, with little concern for helping readers understand and learn (Bereiter & Scardamalia, 1987; Graham, Harris, & Olinghouse, 2007; McCutchen, 1996). The essays in Figure 8.3 illustrate the difference.

- *Revision:* Good writers almost invariably revise what they've written, often several times. Although they certainly look for problems related to spelling and grammar, they focus on enhancing organization and clarity while keeping in mind the overall goals of their writing (De La Paz & McCutchen, 2011; Fitzgerald, 1992; K. R. Harris, Santangelo, & Graham, 2010).

**knowledge transforming** Writing about ideas in a manner that intentionally helps the reader comprehend them.

**knowledge telling** Writing ideas in whatever order they come to mind, with little regard for communicating the ideas effectively.

# DEVELOPMENTAL TRENDS

## TABLE 8.3 • Typical Reading Skills at Different Grade Levels

| GRADE LEVEL | AGE-TYPICAL CHARACTERISTICS | EXAMPLE | SUGGESTED STRATEGIES |
|---|---|---|---|
| K–2 | • Before school entry, considerable differences in emergent literacy skills; for some students, lack of understanding that true reading involves constructing meaning from text<br>• Increasing knowledge of letters and letter–sound correspondences; increasing ability to hear individual phonemes within words (phonological awareness)<br>• Increasing focus on gaining meaning from text<br>• Beginning of silent reading (around grade 2) | When asked if something she's just read makes sense to her, 6-year-old Marissa replies, "What I read never makes sense. The teacher just gives us books so we can practice reading words—they don't have to make sense." | • Emphasize that written language is intended to communicate ideas and that true reading involves making sense of print; for example, ask students questions about what they've read.<br>• Jointly read a variety of storybooks, including some that tell stories with which students are familiar.<br>• Teach letter–sound correspondences through storybooks, games, rhymes, and enjoyable writing activities.<br>• Have students listen to or read animated multimedia storybooks on a desktop or tablet computer. |
| 3–5 | • Growing sight-word vocabulary, leading to greater reading fluency<br>• Increasing ability to draw inferences from text<br>• Increasing ability to learn from nonfiction, but with only limited metacognitive awareness and use of effective learning strategies<br>• Tendency to take things in print at face value, without critically evaluating the content | As 10-year-old Gerrit reads about the Industrial Revolution in his history textbook, he focuses on specific facts. In doing so, he doesn't grasp the big picture—how people's entire way of life changed as a result of technological innovations at the time. | • Encourage students to read for meaning.<br>• Assign well-written trade books (e.g., children's paperback novels) appropriate for students' reading levels.<br>• Provide explicit instruction in how to read textbooks effectively.<br>• Engage students in small-group or whole-class discussions of what they're reading. Focus on interpretation, drawing inferences, and speculation.<br>• For students who continue to struggle with reading, explicitly teach word decoding skills within the context of meaningful reading activities. |
| 6–8 | • Automaticity in recognizing most common words<br>• Increasing ability to identify main ideas in text<br>• Emerging ability to go beyond the literal meanings of text<br>• Increasing involvement of metacognitive processes that enhance understanding (e.g., comprehension monitoring) | When 12-year-old Dominic reads Harper Lee's To Kill a Mockingbird, he is appalled by the blatantly racist attitudes of some of the characters in the book. | • Assign age-appropriate reading materials in various content domains; provide scaffolding (e.g., questions to answer) to guide students' thinking and learning as they read.<br>• Continue explicit instruction in effective reading strategies, with an emphasis on metacognitive processes (e.g., identifying important information, monitoring comprehension).<br>• Begin to explore classic works of poetry and literature.<br>• Seek the advice and assistance of specialists to help promote the reading skills of low-ability readers. |
| 9–12 | • Automaticity in recognizing many abstract and discipline-specific words<br>• Ability to consider multiple viewpoints about a single topic<br>• Some ability to critically evaluate the content of text, but often without all the knowledge and skills necessary to evaluate it appropriately<br>• Considerable individual differences in sophistication of metacognitive reading strategies | For a high school science assignment, 16-year-old Lily searches the Internet for websites about global climate change. The websites she finds present conflicting results: Some stress that climate change is significant and the result of human activity, whereas others reject such claims. Lily knows that the websites can't all be right, but she doesn't have the expertise to distinguish between well-controlled research studies and poorly executed ones. | • Expect that many students can learn effectively from textbooks and other reading materials, but continue to scaffold reading assignments, especially for poor readers.<br>• Ask students to read multiple paper and/or Internet sources on a single topic; guide them in their efforts to compare, contrast, and synthesize what they read.<br>• Jointly discuss and interpret classic works of poetry and literature. |

Sources: Afflerbach & Cho, 2010; Anthony & Francis, 2005; Chall, 1996; Gaskins et al., 2007 (Marissa example, pp. 196–197); Jetton & Dole, 2004; Nagy, Berninger, Abbott, Vaughan, & Vermeulen, 2003; Nokes, Dole, & Hacker, 2007; R. E. Owens, 2008; Pressley & Harris, 2006; Serpell et al., 2005; Slavin, Lake, Chambers, Cheung, & Davis, 2009; Stuebing, Barth, Cirino, Francis, & Fletcher, 2008; van den Broek, Lynch, Naslund, Ievers-Landis, & Verduin, 2003; Verhallen, Bus, & de Jong, 2006.

**FIGURE 8.3** Working in small groups, fourth graders wrote these two essays to help younger children learn about electric circuits. Notice how the first group's untitled piece simply presents a series of facts. In contrast, the second group's piece anticipates what young children might and might not already know about circuits, uses language appropriate for young children, and gives a concrete example.

**Example of knowledge telling:**

Electric circuits are wires that when it's closed electricity flows through and it's circular. A generator is a magnet that spins around in coils. It powers up a city or town. A conductor is what makes electricity. It powers up electrical things.

**Example of knowledge transforming:**

### Electric Circuits They'll Shock You

You have energy inside of you that allows you to walk, run, jump, etc. There's also another source of energy, electrical energy. It lets you turn on your light, run your computer, listen to the radio, and many other things.

But before you experiment let us caution you that electricity can be very dangerous so don't experiment without adult supervision. Here are some safety precautions for when you experiment: Never touch the copper part of a wire. Do NOT leave liquid substances near electrical equipment. Do not open a battery without protection (it contains acid).

Now that you know the rules let me tell you about electricity. When you turn on your light that means you have made a circuit flow, when you turn off the light that means you broke the circuit. How does a light bulb light you ask? Well you have to have a complete circuit. Let all the equipment touch each other. The wires must touch the battery. The battery must touch the light. The light must touch the battery.

If you don't understand how the circuit breaks, here is an example. When you are using the refrigerator, you open it, and all the air comes out. When you are not using the refrigerator, you close it, and the air no longer comes out.

Now that you know about electricity it won't shock you the way it works.

*Source:* Excerpts from "Children as Thinkers Composing Scientific Explanations" by Marilyn J. Chambliss, paper presented at the annual meeting of the American Educational Research Association, April 1998. Copyright © 1998 by Marilyn J. Chambliss. Reprinted with permission of the author.

- *Metacognitive regulation of the overall writing effort:* Throughout the writing process, good writers are metacognitively active: They monitor their progress and the effectiveness of what they've written, addressing questions such as these:

  - Am I achieving my goal(s) for writing this piece?
  - Am I following a logical train of thought?
  - Am I giving examples to illustrate my ideas?
  - Am I supporting my opinions with valid arguments?

The answers to such questions influence their subsequent courses of action (Hacker, Keener, & Kircher, 2009; K. R. Harris et al., 2010).

The nature and quality of students' writing evolve in many ways throughout the elementary and secondary school years. In the early elementary grades, writing projects typically involve narratives: Students write about their personal experiences and create short, fictional stories. They have a hard time writing for an imagined audience and, as a result, engage almost exclusively in knowledge telling rather than knowledge transforming. And of course, they're still working on basic skills in spelling, punctuation, and grammar—skills that can consume much or all of their working memory capacity (Graham et al., 2007; Hemphill & Snow, 1996; McCutchen, 1996).

In the upper elementary grades, writing mechanics are becoming automatic, enabling students to devote more effort to communicating their thoughts effectively. Furthermore, students begin to think about how their readers might respond to what they've written and so are more apt to proofread and revise their work. At this point, however, they do little planning before they begin to write, and their writing continues to involve more knowledge telling than knowledge transforming (Graham, 2006; R. E. Owens, 2008).

In the secondary grades, students are better able to analyze and synthesize their thoughts as they write, and thus they're more skillful in writing research papers and argumentative essays. At this point, too, although many students continue to engage in knowledge telling, knowledge transforming becomes more common. And students become more metacognitively involved in the writing process, especially when given instruction and guidance in effective metacognitive writing strategies (Graham & Perin, 2007; K. R. Harris et al., 2010; Spivey, 1997).

## PROMOTING READING AND WRITING DEVELOPMENT

Explicit instruction in basic reading skills—relating letters to sounds, identifying common words, finding main ideas, and so on—facilitates reading development, especially for poor readers (Ehri, Dreyer, Flugman, & Gross, 2007; Elbro & Petersen, 2004; Rayner et al., 2001). To become truly effective readers, students must master the most basic components of reading, such as word recognition, to a level of automaticity—something that comes primarily through practice, practice, practice (Ehri, Nunes, Stahl, & Willows, 2001; Stanovich, 2000). One approach, of course, is to provide drill-and-practice activities—workbook exercises, flash cards, and so on—but many students find such activities dull and boring (E. H. Hiebert & Raphael, 1996; J. C. Turner, 1995). Better are basic-skills activities that genuinely engage and challenge students. For example, to promote phonological awareness in young children, we might conduct a game of "Twenty Questions" (e.g., "I'm thinking of something in the room that begins with the letter *B*") or ask children to bring something from home that begins with the letter *T*. And to foster greater automaticity in word recognition, we might simply engage students in a variety of authentic reading activities (Ehri, 1998; Share, 1995).

Under no circumstances should we postpone teaching reading comprehension until basic skills are automatic. To do so would be to communicate the message that reading is a meaningless, tedious task, rather than a source of enlightenment and pleasure (Serpell et al., 2005). In an approach known as *whole-language instruction,* some educators have suggested that virtually all basic literacy skills—knowledge of letter–sound relationships, root words, common spelling patterns, and so on—be taught entirely within the context of reading children's books and other authentic written materials. Whole-language approaches are often quite effective in promoting emergent literacy—familiarity with the nature and purposes of books, letter recognition, and so on (Purcell-Gates, MyIntyre, & Freppon, 1995; Sacks & Mergendoller, 1997; S. A. Stahl & Miller, 1989). On the downside, however, letter–sound relationships and phonological awareness are often shortchanged in strictly whole-language instruction (Juel, 1998; Rayner et al., 2001; T. A. Roberts & Meiring, 2006). When working with novice readers, then, we probably need to strike a balance between whole-language and basic-skills activities (Cummins, 2007; Rayner et al., 2001; Xue & Meisels, 2004).

Authenticity is important in writing assignments as well. Students write more frequently, and in a more organized and communicative (i.e., knowledge-transforming) manner, when they can write for a real audience—perhaps their classmates or perhaps peers on the Internet—and when they're interested in their topic (Benton, 1997; Garner, 1998; Graham, 2006).

We must remember, too, that skilled reading and writing are both complex activities that involve considerable scaffolding. Following are examples of what we might do:

Maximize the authenticity of reading and writing tasks, but teach basic skills separately if students might not otherwise master them.

### For Reading

- Especially for novice readers, provide multimedia books to which students can listen while reading along.
- Remind students of things they already know about a topic.
- Have students meet in pairs to retell or summarize short sections of what they've just read.
- Have students ask one another teacher-like questions about something they've all read (e.g., "Why do you think she did that?" "What do you think the author might talk about in the next section?").
- Provide outlines or graphics that students can use to organize what they're reading.
- Explicitly teach strategies for comparing, contrasting, and evaluating multiple texts that give competing messages. (Alfassi, 2004; De La Paz, 2005; D. Fuchs, Fuchs, Mathes, & Simmons,

## Into the Classroom

### Promoting Reading and Writing Development

🍏 **Help students develop phonological awareness.**
A kindergarten teacher suggests to his class, "Let's see how many words we can think of that rhyme with the word *gate*. I'll write the words on the board. Let's see if we can think of at least eight words that rhyme with *gate*."

🍏 **Help students develop automaticity in word recognition and spelling, but do so within the context of authentic reading and writing activities as much as possible.**
A second-grade teacher has several poor readers read Dr. Seuss's *The Cat in the Hat,* a book that repeatedly uses many of the same words (e.g., *cat, hat, thing*).

🍏 **Give students some choices in what they read and write about.**
A fourth-grade teacher gives students several options of paperback books they might read during their free time, being sure to include books that address students' diverse interests (e.g., animals, mysteries, science fiction).

🍏 **Have students discuss with peers the things they are reading and writing.**
A middle school teacher has students meet in small groups to read aloud the short stories they've written. As each student reads his or her story, other group members ask questions for clarification and make suggestions about how to make the story better. Later, students revise their stories with their peers' comments in mind.

🍏 **Scaffold students' efforts as they work on increasingly challenging reading and writing tasks.**
A high school English teacher gives students a format to follow when writing a research paper: an introductory paragraph that describes the topic of the paper, at least three different sections within the paper that address different aspects of the topic (each one beginning with a new heading), and a "Conclusion" section that summarizes and integrates the main ideas of the paper.

🍏 **Address reading and writing skills in all areas of the curriculum.**
An eighth-grade social studies teacher gives students an article to read from *Time* magazine. Knowing that the reading level of the article may be challenging for many of her students, she gives them specific questions to answer as they read the article.

*Sources:* Botelho, Cohen, Leoni, Chow, & Sastri, 2010; Cromley & Azevedo, 2007; J. T. Guthrie et al., 2004; K. R. Harris et al., 2010; Jetton & Dole, 2004; Monte-Sano, 2008; Reis, McCoach, Little, Muller, & Kaniskan, 2011; Slavin, Lake, Chambers, Cheung, & Davis, 2009; Stuebing, Barth, Cirino, Francis, & Fletcher, 2008; J. P. Williams, Stafford, Lauer, Hall, & Pollini, 2009.

---

1997; J. T. Guthrie et al., 2004; Hacker, Dunlosky, & Graesser, 2009b; Palincsar & Brown, 1984; Spörer & Brunstein, 2009; Verhallen, Bus, & de Jong, 2006)

### For Writing

🍏 Ask students with limited writing skills—especially young children—to dictate rather than write their stories.

🍏 Ask students to set specific goals for their writing, and help them organize their thoughts before beginning to write.

🍏 Help students brainstorm ideas for communicating effectively.

🍏 Provide an explicit structure for students to follow as they write (e.g., for a persuasive essay, ask students to include a main argument, supporting arguments, and rebuttals to possible counterarguments).

🍏 Suggest that children initially focus on communicating clearly and postpone attention to writing mechanics (e.g., spelling, punctuation) until later drafts.

🍏 Provide specific questions that students should ask themselves as they critique their writing (e.g., "Do I follow a logical train of thought?").

🍏 Encourage use of word processing programs, voice recognition software, and other writing software that can support effective writing.

🍏 Have students work in small groups to either (1) critique one another's work or (2) co-write stories and essays. (Benton, 1997; L. K. Clarke, 1988; Ferretti, Lewis, & Andrews-Weckerly, 2009; Graham & Perin, 2007; K. R. Harris et al., 2010; Larkin, 2008; McLane & McNamee, 1990; Quinlan, 2004; Sitko, 1998)

The Into the Classroom feature "Promoting Reading and Writing Development" illustrates some of these strategies.

## TECHNOLOGICAL LITERACY

Use of digital technologies and the Internet requires literacy knowledge and skills beyond those involved in traditional paper-based reading and writing tasks, including the following:

- *Use of common functions:* Some functions are essential in using a wide variety of computer applications. For example, learners must know how to "open," "cut," "paste," and "save" and how to search for desired information or locations in a document.

- *Use of device-specific operating systems:* Most learners who have cell phones know such basics as how to make a telephone call, send a text message, or add a friend's contact information to an address book. But to be technologically literate in the twenty-first century—especially as electronic books (e-books) become increasingly common—learners must also be able to find their way around the various applications of personal computers and tablets (iPads, Kindles, etc.).

- *Use of specific computer applications:* For example, word processing software, spreadsheets, and presentation software (e.g., PowerPoint) are now commonplace in many elementary and secondary school classrooms. And various Internet-based communication applications—e-mail, chat rooms, discussion boards, wikis, and so on—all involve not only basic reading and writing skills but also application-specific knowledge.

- *Effective search for relevant and credible Internet websites:* Learners must know how to use Internet browsers (e.g., Google, Bing, Yahoo!) and identify appropriate keywords to initiate a search. They must be able to determine whether particular Internet websites are relevant or irrelevant to particular tasks and questions. They must critically evaluate each website in order to make reasonable judgments about the validity of its content. And they must often pull together what they learn from various sources into an integrated, organized whole.

Remember that some students may lack basic skills related to digital technologies.

Some of these skills involve *critical thinking* (see Chapter 7). The final one—stick-to-it-iveness—involves *self-regulation* (see Chapter 10).

Perhaps through past experiences with cell phones, video games, or home computers, many students come to school with some of these skills. Others, of course, don't have the basics—for example, they may not know how to turn a particular device on and off—and so we must certainly teach them what they don't know. Yet even students who seem to be technologically sophisticated may lack all the cognitive skills they need to *learn* effectively from technology. Learning from Internet websites can be especially problematic for them, for several reasons. First, they may have trouble sorting through the hundreds of sites that an Internet search yields in order to determine which ones are truly relevant to their questions and needs. Second, they may not have the knowledge and skills they need to discriminate between sites that present objective information, on the one hand, and those that convincingly offer biased social or political propaganda, on the other. Third, they may not know how to organize and synthesize the separate bits of information they've found on various sites. Finally, they may not have the self-motivating "stick-to-it-iveness" that lengthy and occasionally frustrating Internet searches can involve (Afflerbach & Cho, 2010; K. Hartley & Bendixen, 2001; Leu, O'Byrne, Zawilinski, McVerry, & Everett-Cacopardo, 2009; Manning, Lawless, Goldman, & Braasch, 2011).

Clearly, then, students often need considerable scaffolding as they conduct online research about classroom topics. Following are a few suggestions:

- Use a database or search engine that restricts the websites to which students have access (e.g., EBSCO Information Services's "Searchasaurus" search engine).

- Provide specific questions students should try to answer as they read (e.g., see Figure 8.4).

- Also provide questions students should consider in evaluating the credibility of a website's content (e.g., "Does a reputable organization sponsor the website?" "What evidence supports this point of view?").

- Give students structured practice in comparing and contrasting websites that present diverse and possibly contradictory perspectives.

- Ask students to write summaries of what they've learned from multiple websites, perhaps in collaboration with peers. (Afflerbach & Cho, 2010; Bromme et al., 2010; Gil, Bråten, Vidal-Abarca, & Strømsø, 2010; Manning et al., 2011; Wiley et al., 2009)

**FIGURE 8.4** Students may need some scaffolding to develop their online literacy skills—for instance, specific questions to answer as they look at a website about maple sugaring.

*Website*
- What is sucrose? _____
- What percent of sap is sucrose? _____
- How many gallons of sap does it take to make ONE gallon of syrup? _____
- Name one of the types of maple tree that yields the best syrup. _____
- How many links are on this website? _____

*Source:* Used courtesy of Carol Lincoln.

In doing these things, we enhance students' general information literacy—their knowledge and skills related to finding, using, evaluating, organizing, and presenting information acquired from diverse sources.

Scaffold students' early research on the Internet, and monitor their explorations to ensure that they don't venture into inappropriate websites and subject matter.

## MATHEMATICS

Mathematics includes several subdomains (e.g., arithmetic, algebra, geometry, calculus, statistics) that use various methods for representing and solving quantitative problems. Central to all of them are the following knowledge and skills:

- *Understanding numbers and counting:* Obviously learners must know number words (*one, two, three . . .* ), the written symbols that represent them (*1, 2, 3 . . .* ), and their correct sequence. In addition, they must understand that, when counting objects, you must count each object once—and only once—until all objects have been included in the count. Learners eventually construct the mental equivalent of a *number line* on which positive whole numbers and then, later, negative whole numbers are spaced at equidistant intervals (see Figure 8.5). Such understandings provide the basic foundation on which virtually all other mathematical concepts, principles, and procedures rest (Case & Okamoto, 1996; Edwards, Esmonde, & Wagner, 2011; Gallistel & Gelman, 1992).

> **FIGURE 8.5** **A genuine understanding of numbers and mathematics requires constructing a mental number line on which all numbers are spaced at equidistant intervals.**
>
> -5  -4  -3  -2  -1   0   1   2   3   4   5

- *Understanding central concepts and principles:* For example, learners must master such concepts as *negative number, right angle,* and *variable* and such principles as "A negative times a negative equals a positive" and "The three angles of a triangle always equal 180°."

- *Mastering problem-solving procedures:* Many of these procedures are specific algorithms that, when correctly applied, always yield an accurate solution. Such is the case, for example, for doing long division, multiplying and dividing fractions, and solving for *x* in algebraic equations. But general problem-solving heuristics (e.g., identifying subgoals, drawing diagrams, rounding complex numbers up or down) often come into play as well. To be truly proficient mathematicians, learners can't simply apply such procedures in a rote, meaningless fashion; rather, they must *make sense* of the procedures so that they can use them in appropriate circumstances (M. Carr, 2010; Hecht & Vagi, 2010; Rittle-Johnson, Siegler, & Alibali, 2001).

See Chapter 7 for a more detailed discussion of algorithms and heuristics in problem solving.

- *Encoding problems appropriately:* An essential step in solving a problem is to encode it—to think of it as being a certain *kind* of problem and then represent it with relevant mathematical symbols. For example, a learner might identify one problem as requiring simple addition and another as requiring solving for an unknown variable in a quadratic equation. Ideally, learners apply their mathematical knowledge and skills in encoding and solving real-world problems as well as the more traditional word problems they typically encounter in school (De Corte et al., 1996; Geary, 2006).

- *Metacognitive oversight and regulation of problem solving:* Like virtually any other complex cognitive task, successful mathematical problem solving involves metacognitive processes. The learner must set one or more goals for a problem-solving task, monitor the effectiveness of various problem-solving strategies, and carefully scrutinize final solutions to determine whether they're logical ones (M. Carr, 2010; De Corte, Op't Eynde, Depaepe, & Verschaffel, 2010; L. S. Fuchs et al., 2003).

Students are far more likely to enjoy math when they understand it. For example, listen to 12-year-old Claudia in "Motivation: Early Adolescence."

Even as young infants, we human beings seem to have a basic ability to think in terms of quantities and relative proportions, but our systematic ways of counting, measuring, and symbolically manipulating quantities are cultural creations that not all cultural groups share (Halford & Andrews, 2006; McCrink & Wynn, 2007; Saxe & Esmonde, 2005). When children are regularly exposed to numbers and counting, many of them come to school knowing how to count—at least to 10, and often well beyond (Ginsburg, Cannon, Eisenband, & Pappas, 2006). They may also have self-constructed simple procedures for adding and subtracting small quantities of objects. For example, if they want to add three objects to a group of five objects they might begin with *five* and then count the smaller group: "Five, six, seven, eight" (Bermejo, 1996; Siegler & Jenkins, 1989). By and large, however, more sophisticated mathematical knowledge and skills come from formal instruction, especially at school.

**information literacy** Knowledge and skills that help a learner find, use, evaluate, organize, and present information about a particular topic.

Despite ongoing math instruction throughout the elementary and secondary grades, many students seem to have particular difficulty with mathematics as a content domain. To some degree, their difficulty may lie in their limited ability to think about proportions (e.g., decimals, ratios) and abstract concepts removed from everyday reality (e.g., *pi, infinity*) (Byrnes, 1996; Tourniaire & Pulos, 1985). Encoding problems mathematically can pose an additional challenge, especially if students have learned concepts and procedures only in a rote, meaningless manner (M. Carr, 2010; Clement, 1982; Geary, 2006). For example, students of all ages tend to have trouble encoding relational problems—problems in which only comparative numbers are given—and hence are often unable to solve problems such as this one:

> Laura is 3 times as old as Maria was when Laura was as old as Maria is now. In 2 years Laura will be twice as old as Maria was 2 years ago. Find their present ages. (R. E. Mayer, 1982, p. 202)

Even college students have trouble encoding and solving this problem (R. E. Mayer, 1982). (Laura is 18 and Maria is 12.)

Unfortunately, too, many elementary and secondary school students don't metacognitively reflect on what they're doing as they work on mathematical problems (M. Carr, 2010; Roditi & Steinberg, 2007). To see how metacognitively reflective *you* are when you do math problems, try the next exercise.

## EXPERIENCING FIRSTHAND
### BUSING THE BAND

Take a minute to solve this problem. Feel free to use a calculator if you have one handy.

> The Riverdale High School marching band is traveling to Hillside High School to perform in the half-time show at Saturday's football game. The school buses owned by the Riverdale School District can transport 32 passengers each. There are 104 students in the Riverdale band. How many buses will the band director need in order to transport the band to Hillside on Saturday?

Is your answer 3.25? If so, think about that for a moment. How is it possible to have 3.25 *buses*? The band director must actually request four buses for Saturday's game. If you fell into my trap, you're not alone. Many students develop the habit of solving word problems based on the numbers alone and overlook the realities with which they're dealing (De Corte et al., 1996).

Compounding the issue is that students are apt to have fairly naive epistemic beliefs about the nature of mathematics. The following misconceptions are common:

- Mathematics is a collection of meaningless procedures that must simply be memorized and recalled as needed.
- Math problems always have one and only one right answer.
- There's only one correct way to solve any particular math problem.
- Mathematical ability is largely a genetically endowed gift: Some people are naturally good at math, whereas others are not. (De Corte et al., 2010; Muis, 2004; Schoenfeld, 1988, 1992)

### PROMOTING LEARNING IN MATHEMATICS

Unfortunately, many students focus largely on rote memorization of concepts and procedures when they study math (M. Carr, 2010; De Corte et al., 2010). Following are general strategies for promoting more meaningful learning and conceptual understanding:

- When formally introducing addition and subtraction, encourage students to use effective strategies they've already constructed on their own (e.g., counting on fingers), but also foster gradual automaticity for addition and subtraction facts.
- Have students apply fundamental concepts and procedures in working with concrete objects and computer simulations.

- Use a number line to help students understand how numbers relate to one another.
- Combine problems requiring different strategies (e.g., subtraction, multiplication) into a single practice set.
- Present problems that include irrelevant as well as relevant information.
- Present complex, real-world problems with multiple possible answers; have students work on them in small groups and explain their reasoning to one another.
- Encourage students to use calculators and computers to assist them in solving problems, especially after they've mastered the basic skills and procedures they're now offloading onto technology (e.g., adding a lengthy set of numbers).
- Present worked-out examples to illustrate multistep problem-solving procedures (e.g., solving for *x* in a quadratic equation).
- Teach and scaffold effective metacognitive processes (e.g., have students ask themselves such questions as "Am I closer to my goal?" and "Does this solution make sense?").
- Have students tutor classmates or younger children in math, thereby encouraging the tutors to elaborate on and better clarify *for themselves* what they've learned. (M. Carr, 2010; B. Clarke, Gersten, & Newman-Gonchar, 2010; De Corte et al., 2010; L. S. Fuchs, Fuchs, et al., 2008; Geary, 2006; Greeno et al., 1996; S. Griffin & Case, 1996; J. Hiebert et al., 1996; Inglis & Biemiller, 1997; Lampert, Rittenhouse, & Crumbaugh, 1996; R. E. Mayer, 1999; Renkl & Atkinson, 2010; Rittle-Johnson, 2006; Rittle-Johnson & Star, 2009; Roditi & Steinberg, 2007; Rohrer & Pashler, 2010; Sarama & Clements, 2009; Siegler, 1989)

Concrete manipulatives can foster conceptual understanding of mathematical concepts and procedures. For example, watch "Manipulative Strategies."

## SCIENCE

As a discipline, science has two major goals: to both (1) describe and (2) explain what people observe in nature. At its core is the basic assumption that the world is somewhat predictable—that the phenomena we human beings observe are various manifestations of general cause–and–effect relationships. Also central is the *scientific method,* which includes a number of more specific cognitive processes with a common element: a conscious intention to both acquire and evaluate new knowledge and explanations.

Key to scientific reasoning are the following:

- *Hypothesis formation and testing:* Scientists begin with tentative conjectures—hypotheses—about the nature of the world, its inhabitants, and the broader universe. Then, to the extent possible, they systematically test their hypotheses by separating and controlling variables that may possibly influence other variables. Good scientists look not only for evidence that confirms a particular hypothesis but also for evidence that might *disconfirm* it.

- *Careful, objective documentation of observations:* Scientists keep careful records of their observations. Ideally, they categorize and/or measure the things they observe in consistent, objective ways.

- *Construction of theories and models:* Scientific inquiry is a very constructive process. Often it involves constructing theories—organized bodies of concepts and principles intended to explain certain phenomena. It may also involve constructing models—physical or symbolic representations that show how certain entities might be interrelated parts of a larger system. (For example, you've probably seen physical models of the sun and planets in our solar system, and you've undoubtedly seen graphic models of various phenomena in textbooks; Figure 8.1 in this chapter is an example.)

- *Metacognitive reflection:* Good scientists think not only about the nature of things but also about the *nature of their thinking about things.* For example, they continually ask themselves whether they're being objective in their observations, whether their evidence adequately supports their hypotheses and conclusions, and where there might be holes or inconsistencies in their theories and models (Kuhn & Pearsall, 2000; M. C. Linn & Eylon, 2011; Metz, 2004; B. White, Frederiksen, & Collins, 2009).

- *Advanced epistemic beliefs about the nature of scientific knowledge:* Good scientists understand that theories and models are, at best, incomplete and somewhat flawed constructions

The "Pendulum Problem" exercise in Chapter 2 can give you a firsthand experience with separating and controlling variables.

**theory** Integrated set of concepts and principles developed to explain a particular phenomenon.

**model** Physical or symbolic representation of a phenomenon or system that depicts its key components and important interrelationships.

of reality and that, more generally, scientific understandings must continue to change and evolve as new evidence comes in (Kuhn, 2009; M. C. Linn, Songer, & Eylon, 1996; Wiser & Smith, 2008).

- *Conceptual change when warranted:* Good scientists continually revise their beliefs and understandings as credible new evidence and theories appear on the scene. In general, they keep open minds about the nature of phenomena and cause–and–effect relationships.

Children begin to construct theories about their physical and biological worlds long before they reach school age, but these early, self-constructed theories don't necessarily jibe with contemporary scientific thinking (Goldberg & Thompson-Schill, 2009; Vosniadou, 2008). For example, consider 7-year-old Rob's theory about mountain formation:

*Adult:* How were the mountains made?

*Rob:* Some dirt was taken from outside and it was put on the mountain and then mountains were made with it.

*Adult:* Who did that?

*Rob:* It takes a lot of men to make mountains, there must have been at least four. They gave them the dirt and then they made themselves all alone.

*Adult:* But if they wanted to make another mountain?

*Rob:* They pull one mountain down and then they could make a prettier one. (Piaget, 1929, p. 348)

Perhaps as a result of traditional science instruction, many students think of learning science more as a process of memorizing facts than as a process of developing scientific reasoning skills. For example, listen to 12-year-old Colin in "Memory: Early Adolescence."

See Chapter 6 for more detailed information on children's early theories and common misconceptions.

Sometimes children's early theories are the results of their day-to-day observations; for instance, construction workers have probably brought about many visible changes in young Rob's local environment. In other instances their theories emerge from explicit teachings or more implicit worldviews of their cultures. In any case, children rarely come to school as "blank slates" when it comes to science. With formal instruction and informal learning experiences, their scientific knowledge gradually aligns itself with that of the adult scientific community, but misconceptions persist, especially when scientists' explanations are exceptionally abstract or seemingly conflict with children's personal experiences or cultural worldviews.

So, too, do children's scientific reasoning abilities change with age, experience, and formal instruction. For example, elementary school students can often distinguish between experiments that do and don't adequately control variables, yet they're apt to have trouble controlling variables in their *own* experiments—a task that requires them to keep track of several things simultaneously and thus may tax their limited working memory capacity (Barchfeld, Sodian, Thoermer, & Bullock, 2005; Bullock & Ziegler, 1999; Metz, 2004, 2011). Middle school and high school students are better able to separate and control variables than elementary school children, but even they occasionally have trouble doing so. Furthermore, in their hypothesis testing, they tend to focus on and test hypotheses they think are correct and to ignore evidence that contradicts their hypotheses. Such *try-to-prove-what-I-already-believe* thinking is known as confirmation bias (Barchfeld et al., 2005; Kuhn & Franklin, 2006; Minstrell & Stimpson, 1996; Schauble, 1996).

And as you might guess, students' metacognitive sophistication in scientific thinking improves with age and instruction (Kuhn, 2009; Kuhn & Franklin, 2006). For example, students become increasingly aware of the tentativeness of science—an idea clearly evident in this explanation by Giulana, an eighth grader:

We can say it's true now, but tomorrow another scientist may say "I've found another document that proves something else" and then we'll have two different things and we'll no longer know which is true and which is false. When the atom was discovered, it was considered the smallest particle, but now the quark's been discovered. What we believed before, now we don't believe anymore because the quark is smaller. Perhaps in fifty years' time an even smaller particle will turn up and then we'll be told that what we believed in before was false. It's really something to do with progress. (Mason, 2003, p. 223)

**confirmation bias**  Tendency to seek information that confirms rather than discredits current beliefs.

## Into the Classroom

### Promoting Mathematical and Scientific Reasoning Skills

🍏 **Take students' general cognitive development into account when teaching concepts and principles.**

A fourth-grade teacher asks students to conduct experiments to find out what conditions influence the growth of sunflower seeds. He knows that his students probably have only a limited ability to separate and control variables, so he asks them to study the effects of just two things: the amount of water and the kind of soil. He has the students keep their growing plants on a shelf by the window, where temperature and amount of sunlight will be the same for all the plants.

🍏 **Use concrete manipulatives, analogies, and computer simulations to illustrate abstract ideas.**

A high school physics teacher has learned from experience that, even though her students are, in theory, capable of abstract thought, they're still apt to have trouble understanding this principle: *When an object rests on a surface, the object exerts a force on the surface, and the surface also exerts a force on the object.* To illustrate the principle, she places a book on a large spring. The book compresses the spring somewhat, but not completely. "So you see, class," she says, "the book pushes downward on the spring, and the spring pushes upward on the book. An object compresses even a hard surface, such as a table, a little bit, and the surface pushes back in response."

🍏 **Ask students to apply math and science to real-world problems.**

With the help of a local scientist, a fifth-grade class conducts a study of its town's drinking water, taking small samples from various sources, examining the contents under a microscope, tabulating the results, and comparing its findings to recommended safety standards.

🍏 **Ask students to identify several strategies or hypotheses regarding a particular task or problem and to explain and justify their ideas to one another.**

A middle school math teacher is beginning a unit on how to divide numbers by fractions. After students convene in small groups, she says, "You've already learned how to multiply one fraction by another. For example, you've learned that when you multiply $1/3$ by $1/2$, you get $1/6$. But now imagine that you want to *divide* $1/3$ by $1/2$. Do you think you'll get a number smaller than $1/3$ or larger than $1/3$? And what kind of number might you get? Discuss these questions within your groups. In a few minutes we'll all get back together to talk about the ideas you've come up with."

🍏 **Foster metacognitive strategies that students can use to regulate their experimentation and problem solving.**

When a high school science teacher has students conduct lab experiments, he always has them keep three questions in mind as they work: (1) As I test the effects of one variable, am I controlling for possible effects of other variables? (2) Am I seeing anything that supports my hypothesis? (3) Am I seeing anything that contradicts my hypothesis?

🍏 **Have students use mathematics and scientific methods in other content domains.**

A junior high school social studies teacher asks students to work in small groups to conduct experiments regarding the effects of smiling on other people's behavior. As the groups design their experiments, he reminds them about the importance of separating and controlling variables, and he insists that each group identify an objective means of measuring the specific behavior or behaviors that it intends to study. Later, he has the groups tabulate their results and report their findings to the rest of the class.

*Sources:* Boxerman, 2009; D. E. Brown & Clement, 1989 (book-on-spring example); M. Carr, 2010; Clement, 2008; De Corte et al., 2010; Graesser et al., 2005; Kuhn & Dean, 2005; Lampert et al., 1996; Lehrer & Schauble, 2006; M. C. Linn & Eylon, 2011; Metz, 2011; Morra, Gobbo, Marini, & Sheese, 2008; Sarama & Clements, 2009; Singer, Marx, Krajcik, & Chambers, 2000; C. L. Smith, 2007; Snir, Smith, & Raz, 2003.

### PROMOTING LEARNING IN SCIENCE

Certainly science instruction should introduce students to the many fundamental concepts, principles, and theories the discipline has developed to explain everyday experiences—for instance, why people get sick, why water expands when it freezes, and why (thanks to a solar eclipse) the sky might suddenly turn dark in the middle of the day. But in addition, we must attune students to the dynamic, ever-changing nature of science and foster the reasoning skills that will enable them both to draw appropriate conclusions from others' research findings and to conduct valid research studies themselves. Educated individuals understand that science isn't undisputed fact—that, instead, it simply reflects society's best efforts to make sense of the world—and that almost anyone can make significant contributions to humankind's collective knowledge base.

The Into the Classroom feature "Promoting Mathematical and Scientific Reasoning Skills" presents several general strategies useful in both math and science instruction. Following are additional strategies that researchers have found to be effective in teaching science:

🍏 Ask students to explain their current beliefs and theories about a phenomenon; listen carefully both for elements of truth on which you can build and for unproductive misconceptions that require revision.

🍏 Illustrate relationships among concepts and principles using live demonstrations, physical models, paper-and-pencil diagrams, or computer simulations.

In this pencil drawing, 9-year-old Corey portrays his science lab as one in which his teacher prescribes particular steps to follow. Ultimately, however, students should be able to conduct their *own* experiments—separating and controlling variables, systematically measuring and recording their observations, and so on.

You can find additional strategies for promoting conceptual change in Chapter 6.

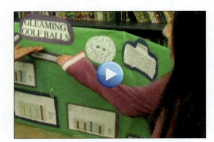

Students can learn a great deal about science when, with age-appropriate scaffolding, they conduct their own experiments about self-chosen topics. For example, watch "Science Fair Projects."

- Present phenomena that are inconsistent with students' current understandings—for example, by showing how a wool blanket (something students associate with warmth) can actually help keep a cold drink cool.

- Have students design and carry out experiments to test various hypotheses about cause–and–effect relationships.

- When experiments with real-world objects and events are impractical or impossible, have students test their hypotheses in computer-simulated environments.

- Scaffold students' efforts to separate and control variables and to draw appropriate conclusions. For example, ask questions that focus their attention on critical aspects of what they're observing and nudge their thinking in appropriate directions.

- Explicitly draw students' attention to results that contradict their predictions and expectations; ask students to explain and in other ways make sense of those results. (Boxerman, 2009; D. B. Clark, 2006; Clement, 2008; Eberbach & Crowley, 2009; Graesser, McNamara, & VanLehn, 2005; Gustafson, Mahaffy, Martin, & Gentilini, 2011; M. C. Linn & Eylon, 2011; R. E. Mayer, 2008; Metz, 2011; C. L. Smith, 2007; Snir, Smith, & Raz, 2003; Zohar & Aharon-Kraversky, 2005)

Such strategies not only help students gain new understandings about their physical and biological worlds but can also help them revise certain *mis*understandings. In other words, such strategies can promote conceptual change.

## SOCIAL STUDIES

The term *social studies* encompasses content domains concerned with the nature of human societies and social relationships, both past and present. Our focus here will be on two domains that are especially prominent in elementary and secondary school curricula: history and geography.

### THE NATURE OF HISTORICAL KNOWLEDGE AND THINKING

At its core, history is very much a socioculturally transmitted body of knowledge. Furthermore, as the opening case study illustrates, different cultural groups are likely to put their own spins on history, portraying past events in ways that are consistent with their beliefs and worldviews. For example, European American students tend to view U.S. history as being guided by principles of freedom and democracy, whereas African American students are more likely to view American history as being marked by racism and violations of basic human rights (T. Epstein, 2000; T. Epstein & Shiller, 2009). Such diverse interpretations are almost certainly the result of how various people and media in one's cultural group and larger society have described historical events (J. M. Hughes, Bigler, & Levy, 2007; Levstik, 2011; Porat, 2004; vanSledright & Limón, 2006).

A solid mastery of history, both as a body of knowledge and as an academic discipline, requires several abilities and processes:

- *Comprehending the nature of historical time:* Constructing legitimate understandings of history requires an abstract comprehension of the lengthy time span across which human events may have occurred—a time span far beyond any individual's personal experience.

- *Perspective taking:* Truly making sense of history requires recognizing that even highly influential and respected people (e.g., George Washington, Martin Luther King, Jr.) weren't perfect: They had their own foibles and fallibilities, and they made mistakes. Furthermore, historical figures lived in particular cultural and social contexts that profoundly influenced their thoughts and actions. Good historians try to put themselves in historical figures' shoes—to perceive events as those individuals might reasonably have perceived them (P. Lee & Ashby, 2001).

- *Drawing inferences from historical documents:* History textbooks often describe historical events in a matter-of-fact manner, communicating the message that "This is what happened." In reality, however, historians often don't know exactly how particular events occurred. Instead, they construct reasonable interpretations of events after looking at a variety of historical documents that might offer conflicting accounts of what transpired (Leinhardt, Beck, & Stainton, 1994; Paxton, 1999; vanSledright & Limón, 2006).

- *Identifying possible cause–and–effect relationships among events.* Mastery of history includes not only knowledge and interpretations of events but also a sense of how some events—perhaps certain political decisions, religious movements, or economic conditions—may have directly or indirectly led to *other* events (van Drie, van Boxtel, & van der Linden, 2006).

- *Evaluating the credibility of various documents and interpretations:* Some documents are reasonably objective and accurate accounts of historical events and trends; government census records from past decades are an example. But many other historical documents—newspaper articles, personal diaries, and the like—reflect the opinions and biases of their authors. Competent historians take such biases into account when drawing their conclusions about events, but they also understand—metacognitively—that their own and others' interpretations aren't necessarily the best or only ones (Paxton, 1999; van Drie et al., 2006; vanSledright & Limón, 2006).

By and large, such abilities and processes require a fair amount of abstract thinking, and so learners acquire them only gradually over the course of development. For instance, children in the early elementary grades have little understanding of historical time and the complexity of historical changes (Barton & Levstik, 1996; Ormrod, Jackson, Kirby, Davis, & Benson, 1999). They might refer to events that happened "a long, long time ago" or "in the old days" but have virtually no conception of the time span in question. And they tend to lump historical events into two general categories: those that happened very recently and those that happened many years ago. Not until about fifth grade do students show a reasonable ability to sequence historical events and to attach them to particular time periods (Barton & Levstik, 1996).

Other abstract notions continue to challenge students even in adolescence. Many high school students struggle with the ideas that history involves perspectives as well as facts and that historical figures may have been influenced by social and cultural factors very different from their own. And without explicit instruction and guidance, they have trouble effectively reconciling conflicting data that various historical accounts yield (Levstik, 2011; Nokes et al., 2007; S. A. Stahl & Shanahan, 2004).

## THE NATURE OF GEOGRAPHICAL KNOWLEDGE AND THINKING

The discipline of geography is concerned not only with where various natural features and cultural groups are located but also with why and how they got there. For example, geographers study how rivers and mountain ranges end up where they do, why people are more likely to settle in some locations than in others, and how people in various locations make their livings and interact with one another.

The following abilities are key elements of knowledge and thinking in geography:

- *Understanding maps as symbolic representations:* An essential cognitive tool in geography is, of course, the *map*. Learners must understand that maps symbolically depict spatial relationships among various physical and/or humanmade features in a given geographic area. They must also understand that different maps are drawn to different scales, reflecting various proportions between graphic representations and reality.

- *Identifying interrelationships among people and their environments:* For example, skilled geographers recognize that people tend to migrate from places with limited or decreasing resources to places with more plentiful resources. And people are more likely to settle in areas that are easily accessible by water or land—perhaps those along navigable rivers or near major roadways.

- *Acknowledging cultural differences and their implications for human behavior patterns:* Geographers are acutely aware of how cultural beliefs and practices can have widespread influences on people's behavior. For example, a group's beliefs about forbidden foods can put limitations on the crops and livestock they raise. And the Chinese concept of *feng shui* directs some individuals to locate and orient buildings in ways that effectively align with certain spiritual forces.

Learners' facility in interpreting and using maps depends in part on the sociocultural context in which they've been raised. Maps are commonplace in some cultures, nonexistent in others. Even in a society that uses maps extensively, children have varying degrees of experience with geography and maps. For instance, children whose families travel extensively tend to have greater appreciation of distance, more familiarity with diverse landscapes, and a better understanding of how maps are used (Liben & Myers, 2007; Trawick-Smith, 2003).

When children in the early elementary grades look at larger-scale maps—perhaps those depicting a state or country—they tend to take what they see somewhat literally. For example, they may think that lines separating states and countries are actually painted on the earth or that an airport denoted by a picture of an airplane has only one plane. Young children also have trouble maintaining a sense of scale and proportion when interpreting maps. For example, they might deny that a road could actually be a road because "it's not fat enough for two cars to go on" or insist that a mountain depicted on a three-dimensional relief map can't possibly be a mountain because "it's not high enough" (Liben & Myers, 2007, p. 202). As children get older, and especially as they reach adolescence, they become more proficient in dealing with the symbolic and proportional nature of maps (Forbes, Ormrod, Bernardi, Taylor, & Jackson, 1999; Liben & Myers, 2007; L. J. Myers & Liben, 2008).

Despite their growing proficiency with maps, children and adolescents alike tend to have somewhat narrow epistemic beliefs about geography as a discipline. Typically, they conceive of geography as being little more than the names and locations of various countries, capital cities, rivers, mountain ranges, and so on—perhaps, in part, because teachers often present geography this way (Bochenhauer, 1990; vanSledright & Limón, 2006). Even in the high school years, students rarely reflect on why various locations have the physical features they do or on how the economic and cultural practices of various social groups might be partly the result of their physical environments.

## PROMOTING LEARNING IN SOCIAL STUDIES

The Into the Classroom feature "Facilitating Learning in History and Geography" presents several general strategies for teaching these two disciplines. Following are more specific instructional strategies to keep in mind:

### For History

🍏 In the early elementary grades, focus instruction on students' own personal histories and on events that have occurred locally and in the recent past.

## Into the Classroom

### Facilitating Learning in History and Geography

🍏 **Help students organize and integrate the things they are learning.**
During a unit on ancient civilizations (e.g., Mesopotamia, Egypt, Greece, Rome), a middle school social studies teacher has students mark the location of each civilization on a map of the Eastern Hemisphere. She also has them develop a time line that depicts the rise and fall of various civilizations.

🍏 **Ask students to draw inferences from maps and historical documents and to support their inferences with evidence.**
A high school geography teacher displays a map showing European countries and their capital cities. "Notice how almost all of the capital cities are located either by seaports or on major rivers," he points out. "Why do you suppose that is?"

🍏 **Identify cause–and–effect relationships.**
A high school history teacher asks students to consider the questions, "Why was Pearl Harbor such an important location to control?" and "What effects did the Japanese bombing of Pearl Harbor have on the course and final outcome of World War II?"

🍏 **Encourage empathy for people from diverse cultures and different time periods.**
A third-grade teacher encourages students to imagine themselves as Native Americans who are seeing Europeans for the first time.

"You see some strange-looking men sail to shore on big boats—boats much larger than the canoes your own people use. As the men get out of their boats and approach your village, you see that they have very light skin; in fact, it's almost white. Furthermore, some of them have yellow hair and blue eyes. 'Strange colors for hair and eyes,' you think to yourself. How might you feel as these people approach you?"

🍏 **Scaffold productive metacognitive processes.**
An eighth-grade history teacher has students read several historical documents related to European Americans' westward expansion during the 1800s. The teacher gives students several questions to consider as they read and compare the documents—for example, "What was each author's purpose?" "Do you find evidence of bias?" "Is an event described differently in different documents?"

🍏 **Have students tackle challenging tasks in pairs or small groups.**
Students in an advanced high school history class work in pairs to (1) read multiple documents related to a historical event and then (2) write an essay evaluating the trustworthiness of the documents and defending a particular narrative about the event itself.

*Sources:* Brophy et al., 2009; Davison, 2011; De La Paz, 2005 (westward expansion example, p. 145); Enyedy, 2005; M. Gregg & Leinhardt, 1994b; J. M. Hughes et al., 2007; Liben & Downs, 1989a; Monte-Sano, 2008; Nokes et al., 2007; S. A. Stahl & Shanahan, 2004; van Drie et al., 2006; Wolfe & Goldman, 2005; Yeager et al., 1997.

- In the upper elementary grades, introduce students to primary historical sources—diaries, letters, newspaper articles, and so on.

- In the middle school and secondary grades, have students read multiple accounts of significant historical events and then draw conclusions both about what *definitely* happened and about what *might* have happened.

- Have "journalists" (two or three students) interview people (other students) who "participated" in various ways in a historical event.

- Role-play family discussions and decision making during critical times (e.g., British soldiers demand to be housed in American colonists' homes, or a 14-year-old son wants to enlist and go off to war).

- Have students write fictional diary or journal entries from the perspective of a particular time period or historical figure.

- Ask students to consider how things might have been different if certain events had *not* taken place. (Afflerbach, VanSledright, & Dromsky, 2003; Brophy & Alleman, 1996; Brophy et al., 2009; Byrnes, 1996; Leinhardt et al., 1994)

Figure 3.4 in Chapter 3 presents a student's fictional journal entries written from the perspective of a slave owner in the pre-Civil War United States.

## For Geography

- Have students create maps of their school building or local neighborhood (e.g., see Figure 8.6).

- Provide explicit instruction in common map symbols (e.g., compass rose, special dots designating capital cities, contour lines depicting elevation).

- In the middle school grades, introduce the concept of *scale* in maps (e.g., one inch per mile, one centimeter per ten kilometers).

- Emphasize the complex, dynamic interrelationships among the earth's physical features and human activity (e.g., why towns and roads were constructed in particular locations).

- Teach students how to use age-appropriate mapping websites and software (e.g., Google Earth). (Brophy et al., 2009; Egbert, 2009; Enyedy, 2005; M. Gregg & Leinhardt, 1994a; Liben & Downs, 1989a, 1989b; National Geographic Education Project, 1994)

## For Social Studies in General

- Focus on key principles—*big ideas*—that underlie social studies (e.g., basic human needs and motives, adaptation, interdependence, globalization).

- Relate concepts and principles to students' everyday experiences.

- Avoid characterizing individuals and groups as simplistic, one-dimensional figures, and vigorously combat stereotypes of any particular group in history or the modern-day world.

- Assign works of fiction that realistically depict people living in particular times and places.

- Engage students in authentic activities related to what they're learning (e.g., creating a museum display, analyzing political attack ads on television). (Brayboy & Searle, 2007; Brophy et al., 2009; A. Collins, Hawkins, & Carver, 1991; M. McDevitt & Chaffee, 1998; NCSS, 1994; Olsen, 1995)

**FIGURE 8.6** Twelve-year-old Mary Lynn constructed this local map for an assignment in her social studies class.

## TAKING STUDENT DIVERSITY INTO ACCOUNT

As we teach reading and writing, we must remember that students will have had varying experiences with literacy at home. For example, the lives of some students may have been filled with storybooks and bedtime reading, whereas the lives of others may have involved more oral storytelling. Especially in the primary grades, then, we must not assume that children have mastered alphabet letters and other basics of written language. In addition, of course, some children's families speak a language other than English at home, and other children's families speak a dialect of English quite different from the Standard English that's typically used in classrooms. Effective reading and writing instruction—and, in fact, literate activities in any content domain—takes such backgrounds into account (Janzen, 2008; Klingner & Vaughn, 2004; Serpell et al., 2005).

When teaching math and science, we must keep in mind that these two disciplines have, historically, been considered "male" domains. As a result, the boys in our classes are, on average, more likely to believe they can be successful in these areas; this tends to be the case even though there are no substantial gender differences in *ability* in math and science (Herbert & Stipek, 2005; Leaper & Friedman, 2007; Wigfield, Byrnes, & Eccles, 2006). We must regularly convey the message that both content domains are important for girls as well as boys. We should also use instructional strategies—small-group discussions, hands-on activities, and so on—that encourage males and females alike to become actively involved in talking about, applying, and mastering math and science.

Traditionally, too, females have been given short shrift in history—as have most minority groups—in the sense that history textbooks focus largely on the activities and accomplishments of European American males (Berkin, Crocco, & Winslow, 2009; Levstik, 2011). Accordingly, we may often need to supplement texts with materials that paint a more inclusive picture of our multicultural heritage. Furthermore, we must remember that students' meaning making in social studies will, in part, be a function of the cultures in which they've been raised and the early family experiences they've had. For example, students with Japanese ancestry are likely to have a very different perspective on President Harry Truman's decision to bomb Hiroshima than students with European ancestry. And, of course, some students have had little or no experience with diverse cultural environments and far-away places. A friend of mine once took students from a lower-income, inner-city Denver neighborhood on a field trip to the Rocky Mountains. Even though these children had seen the Rockies many times from downtown Denver, on seeing them up close for the first time some of them were amazed at how big they were. And a few of them were surprised to discover that the white stuff on the mountaintops was snow!

### ACCOMMODATING STUDENTS WITH SPECIAL NEEDS

Many students with special needs have difficulties with reading and writing. The majority of poor readers, whether they've been identified as having a learning disability, attention-deficit hyperactivity disorder (ADHD), or some other disability, appear to have a significant deficit in phonological awareness: They have trouble hearing the individual sounds in words and connecting those sounds with letters. A few poor readers have other cognitive processing deficits; for example, they may have greater-than-average difficulty retrieving words and word meanings based on what they see on the page. In extreme forms, such reading difficulties are known as dyslexia, a disability that often has biological roots (Goswami, 2007; Shaywitz, Mody, & Shaywitz, 2006; Snowling, Gallagher, & Frith, 2003; Stanovich, 2000; Wimmer, Landerl, & Frith, 1999).

Chronic difficulties with literacy can have wide-ranging effects, not only for success in other academic disciplines but also for self-esteem. Tom, a second grader, describes his feelings when first trying to learn how to read in first grade:

> I falt like a losr. Like nobad likde me. I was afrad then kais wod tec me. Becacz I wased larning wale . . . I dan not whet to raed. I whoe whte to troe a book it my mom.
> *(I felt like a loser. Like nobody liked me. I was afraid that kids would tease me. Because I wasn't learning well ... I did not want to read. I would want to throw a book at my mom.)* (Knapp, 1995, p. 9)

To minimize the academic and psychological damage, we should address students' reading and writing deficits as early as possible, ideally with deliberate and intensive training in both basic skills (e.g., letter recognition, phonological awareness) and more complex processes (e.g., metacognitive skills in reading, composition skills in writing) (e.g., Elbro & Petersen, 2004; N. Gregg, 2009; Meltzer, 2007; Vadasy, Sanders, & Peyton, 2006). In addition, students with chronic literacy difficulties must find *joy* in reading and writing. For example, one especially popular series

---

*Address any missing emergent literacy skills within the context of engaging activities, such as alphabet games and high-interest storybook reading. Encourage students to write in their native dialect in appropriate contexts, such as in poems and short stories.*

Chapter 2 offers strategies for working with English language learners. Chapter 4 describes the nature of dialects and Standard English; it also summarizes research regarding gender differences in various content domains.

*Take extra steps to motivate and encourage females to achieve in math and science, and include the important roles of women and minority groups in history lessons.*

*Remember that students' differing cultural backgrounds and early experiences may influence their understanding of both history and geography.*

**dyslexia** Inability to master basic reading skills in a developmentally typical time frame despite normal reading instruction; often has biological roots.

of paperback novels, Rick Riordan's "Percy Jackson and the Olympians," features a boy with dyslexia and attention-deficit hyperactivity disorder whose disabilities actually work in his favor in his adventures with various god-like characters based on ancient Greek mythology.

Students' exceptional difficulties aren't always limited to reading and writing, of course; for instance, some students with learning disabilities have difficulty with mathematics as well (Price, Holloway, Räsänen, Vesterinen, & Ansari, 2007; A. J. Wilson & Dehaene, 2007). So when we teach various content domains, we must often make special accommodations for those students who have special educational needs. Table 8.4 presents specific strategies that may be helpful as we work with these students.

Help students with disabilities find joy in literacy activities— ideally with authentic reading and writing activities.

Chapter 5 identifies specific categories of special needs that fall within the five general categories listed in Table 8.4.

# STUDENTS IN INCLUSIVE SETTINGS

**TABLE 8.4 • Facilitating Learning in Various Content Domains in Students with Special Educational Needs**

| CATEGORY | CHARACTERISTICS YOU MIGHT OBSERVE | SUGGESTED STRATEGIES |
|---|---|---|
| **Students with specific cognitive or academic difficulties** | • Difficulties in word recognition and reading comprehension, often as a result of poor phonological awareness<br>• Difficulties in handwriting and spelling; possible difficulties in composition skills as well<br>• Less proficiency in learning from the Internet, due to poor literacy skills<br>• Tendency to focus on mechanics (rather than meaning) when revising written work<br>• Greater-than-average difficulty learning basic facts in math, science, and social studies | • Explicitly teach sound–print relationships.<br>• Assign reading materials appropriate for students' reading skills.<br>• Provide extra scaffolding for paper-based and electronic reading assignments (e.g., shorten assignments, identify main ideas, have students look for answers to specific questions).<br>• Provide extra scaffolding for writing activities (e.g., ask students to set goals for their writing, give students a specific structure to follow as they write, encourage use of word processing programs with grammar and spell checkers).<br>• Use concrete manipulatives to teach math and science.<br>• Use mnemonics to help students remember basic facts. |
| **Students with social or behavioral problems** | • Less motivation to achieve academic success in some or all content domains<br>• In some instances, achievement two or more years below grade level in one or more content domains | • Have students read and write about topics of personal interest.<br>• Ask students to apply math, science, and social studies to situations relevant to their own lives.<br>(Also use strategies listed for students with specific cognitive or academic difficulties.) |
| **Students with general delays in cognitive and social functioning** | • Delayed language development, with resulting delays in literacy skills<br>• Smaller-than-average knowledge base to which new information can be related<br>• Difficulty remembering basic facts<br>• Lack of learning strategies such as rehearsal or organization<br>• Reasoning abilities characteristic of younger children (e.g., inability to think abstractly in the secondary grades) | • Minimize reliance on reading materials as a way of presenting new information.<br>• Provide experiences that help students learn the basic knowledge and skills that other students may have already learned on their own.<br>• Have students conduct simple scientific experiments in which they need to consider only one or two variables at a time.<br>(Also use strategies listed for students with specific cognitive or academic difficulties.) |
| **Students with physical or sensory challenges** | • Less advanced reading and writing skills, especially if students have hearing loss<br>• Less awareness of the conventions of written language, especially if students have visual impairments<br>• Fewer outside experiences and less general world knowledge upon which instruction in math, science, and social studies can build | • Locate Braille or audio texts for students with visual impairments; also encourage use of text-to-speech software.<br>• When students have difficulty with motor coordination, allow them to dictate their stories and compositions.<br>• Conduct demonstrations and experiments to illustrate basic scientific concepts and principles.<br>• Use drama and role-playing to illustrate historical events.<br>• If students have limited vision, enlarge images on a computer screen; if they are blind, use three-dimensional relief maps and embellish two-dimensional maps with dried glue or nail polish. |
| **Students with advanced cognitive development** | • Development of reading at an early age<br>• Advanced reading comprehension skills<br>• More sophisticated writing abilities<br>• Greater ability to construct abstract and integrated understandings | • Provide challenging tasks (e.g., higher-level reading assignments, more advanced writing assignments).<br>• Form study groups in which students can pursue advanced topics in particular domains. |

*Sources:* Bassett et al., 1996; Curtis, 2004; De La Paz & McCutchen, 2011; Ferretti, MacArthur, & Dowdy, 2000; Garner, 1998; N. Gregg, 2009; Hallenbeck, 1996; Hulme & Joshi, 1998; Mastropieri & Scruggs, 1992, 2000; Page-Voth & Graham, 1999; Piirto, 1999; Rayner et al., 2001; Salend & Hofstetter, 1996; Sampson, Szabo, Falk-Ross, Foote, & Linder, 2007; H. L. Swanson, Cooney, & O'Shaughnessy, 1998; Tompkins & McGee, 1986; Turnbull, Turnbull, & Wehmeyer, 2010; D. K. Wood, Frank, & Wacker, 1998.

# 8 What Have You Learned?

Let's now review and summarize our discussions of the various contexts for learning by returning to the chapter's learning outcomes.

■ **8.1: Describe five basic assumptions underlying contextual theories of learning, and apply these assumptions to classroom practice.** Thinking and learning always take place within certain contexts; in particular, they're inextricably intertwined with the learner's physical body, immediate physical and social environment, and broader culture and society. Taken as a whole, contextual theories rest on at least five assumptions. First, the brain functions in close conjunction with the rest of the body—for instance, with the sensory systems, overt physical actions, and general bodily well-being. Second, acquired knowledge and skills are often linked to, or *situated* in, specific activities and environments. Third, learners often think and perform more effectively when they can offload, or *distribute,* some of their cognitive burden onto physical objects, symbolic systems, or other people. Fourth, learners are sometimes more effective when they collaborate with other people in thinking and learning tasks; such collaborative efforts can take place either at a single point in time or sequentially over a lengthy period. And fifth, learners benefit greatly from the collective wisdom of their culture and society.

Evaluate and apply your knowledge related to this learning outcome in MyEducationLab™.

■ **8.2: Contrast the benefits of interacting with more advanced individuals versus the benefits of interacting with peers; explain how you might enhance students' learning through both kinds of interactions.** Learners benefit in numerous ways from the guidance of teachers and other more advanced individuals. Such individuals can *mediate* new experiences for learners, helping them attach meaningful concepts, principles, and other interpretations to what they see and hear. These individuals also introduce learners to new cognitive and metacognitive strategies and scaffold learners' efforts to use them effectively.

Interactions with peers have a different set of advantages. For example, when learners collaboratively discuss and apply new subject matter, they must clarify, organize, and elaborate on what they've learned sufficiently that they can explain it to others. Furthermore, when they encounter conflicting ideas coming from peers, they may reexamine their own perspectives and possibly revise their views to achieve more accurate and complete understandings. And active discussions of classroom subject matter provide a means through which learners can observe and acquire more advanced ways of thinking and more sophisticated views of the nature of knowledge.

One classroom strategy gaining research support is to create a *community of learners*—a class in which teachers and students collaborate to build a body of knowledge about a topic and help one another learn about it. In such a context, face-to-face and online interactions and feedback are common, as are collective efforts at meaning making.

Evaluate and apply your knowledge related to this learning outcome in MyEducationLab™.

■ **8.3: Explain how learners' cultural backgrounds can influence their interpretations of new information and experiences; also explain how learners can effectively begin to participate in one or more communities of practice.** Any long-standing social group has a *culture,* which includes behaviors and beliefs that older, more experienced group members pass along to newer members. A learner's culture influences the ways in which the learner thinks about and interprets virtually any new situation. From day-to-day experiences and interactions within the culture, the learner acquires general schemas and scripts regarding what things are typically like and how common activities typically unfold. In addition, a culture passes along certain worldviews—all-encompassing sets of beliefs and assumptions about the very nature of reality and human existence. Occasionally students from certain cultural backgrounds may not have the schemas and scripts they need to effectively make sense of classroom material; at other times students may hold certain worldviews that are inconsistent with scientific theories or that distort their understandings of historical events.

Cultures typically include *communities of practice*—groups of people who share common interests and goals (e.g., making sick people well, creating Internet websites) and regularly interact and coordinate their efforts in pursuit of those interests and goals. In general, people best gain competence in a community of learners by actively participating in it, usually at the fringe of an activity at first and then gradually becoming more centrally involved as competence increases.

Evaluate and apply your knowledge related to this learning outcome in MyEducationLab™.

■ **8.4: Describe key elements of society that impact learning, and explain how authentic activities can enhance learners' performance in their out-of-school world.** A *society* is a very large, enduring social group that has fairly explicit social and economic structures, as well as collective institutions and activities. Any society influences learning in a number of ways—for instance, through the resources it provides, the activities it supports, and the general messages it communicates. Furthermore, different members of society have different areas of expertise, and so its members must rely on one another for their individual and collective success.

One critical way of preparing students for their eventual participation in adult society is engaging them in *authentic activities*—those that resemble tasks in the outside world. For example, authentic activities may involve solving complex, real-world problems, working on multifaceted projects, or engaging in community service. Such activities foster meaningful learning of classroom subject matter and increase the odds that students will eventually apply what they've learned to future tasks and problems outside of school.

Evaluate and apply your knowledge related to this learning outcome in MyEducationLab™.

■ **8.5: Describe the unique roles that digital technologies and the Internet can play in classroom instruction.** Recent technological advancements (especially those based on digital technologies) offer numerous benefits for instructional practice. They enable seamless integration of multiple media and pedagogical strategies into instruction, which can be simultaneously delivered to students in distant locations and individualized for different students' unique abilities and needs. Also, appropriately designed and scaffolded software can provide mechanisms through which students can manipulate complex data sets and bodies of information without being overwhelmed by the cognitive load. Furthermore, the Internet puts information about many topics within easy reach and allows teachers and students to communicate and collaborate easily and frequently. Finally, some technology-based instructional programs simulate real-world or fantasy environments that engage students in highly motivating learning and problem-solving tasks.

Evaluate and apply your knowledge related to this learning outcome in MyEducationLab™.

■ **8.6: Apply your knowledge of learning, cognition, and effective instructional practices to various academic content domains.** Different content domains involve somewhat different kinds of knowledge; for example, reading and writing involve knowledge related to verbal language, whereas mathematics involves knowledge related to counting and measurement. The various domains also require different kinds of thinking and reasoning skills; for example, scientific investigations require forming hypotheses and testing them through careful separation and control of variables, whereas historical research involves critically evaluating and comparing potentially biased accounts of events and then constructing defensible explanations of what may have transpired.

The chapter offers many strategies for teaching reading, writing, math, science, and social studies; underlying a good number of them are some common themes. First, we must scaffold students' efforts to construct reasonable meanings from various sources—from textbooks, Internet websites, historical documents, maps, and so on. Second, we must help students acquire the metacognitive processes and epistemic beliefs that will enhance their competencies in various content domains. For example, students must learn how to set goals and monitor their progress in reading, writing, and mathematical problem solving, and they must come to understand that science and social studies are evolving disciplines in which theories (and sometimes even basic "facts") may continue to change as new evidence comes in. And third, we can often help students acquire more sophisticated understandings, reasoning processes, and metacognitive skills by having them work collaboratively with peers to tackle complex issues and tasks.

Evaluate and apply your knowledge related to this learning outcome in MyEducationLab™.

## Practice for Your Licensure Exam

### The Birth of a Nation

Ms. Jackson has asked her second graders to write an answer to this question: *The land we live on has been here for a very long time, but the United States has been a country for only a little more than 200 years. How did the United States become a country?* Following are some of the children's responses:

> *Meg:* The United States began around two hundred years ago. The dinosors hav ben around for six taosine years ago. Christfer klumbis salde the May flowr.
>
> *Sue:* The pilgrums we're sailing to some place and a stome came and pushed them off track and they landed we're Amaraca is now and made friends with the indens and coled that spot AMARACA!
>
> *Matt:* It all staredid in eginggind they had a wore. Thein they mad a bet howeevery wone the wore got a ney country. Called the united states of amarica and amaricins wone the wore. So they got a new country.
>
> *Lisa:* We wone the saver wore. It was a wore for fradam and labrt. One cind of labraty is tho stashow of labrt. We got the stashew of labraty from england. Crastaver calbes daskaved Amaraca.

**1. Multiple-choice question:**

Which one of the following pairs of word spellings best reflects possible difficulty with *phonological awareness,* especially with regard to consonants?

a. Meg spells *sailed* as "salde" and *flower* as "flowr."

b. Sue spells *Pilgrims* as "pilgrums" and *called* as "coled."

c. Matt spells *started* as "staredid" and *war* as "wore."

d. Lisa spells *civil* as "saver" and *discovered* as "daskaved."

**2. Multiple-choice question:**

Which one of the following statements best characterizes the content of these writing samples?

a. The children have set clear goals for their writing efforts.

b. The children appear to have a good sense of the audience for whom they're writing.

c. The children have engaged in knowledge telling rather than knowledge transforming.

d. The children have pulled together what they have learned about American history into coherent understandings.

**3. Constructed-response question:**

Despite the many misspellings, the children have clearly learned some things about written language. Identify at least three aspects of written language that most or all of the students appear to have mastered.

**PRAXIS** Go to Appendix C, "Matching Book and MyEducationLab™ to the Praxis Principles of Learning and Teaching Tests," to discover sections of this chapter that may be especially applicable to the Praxis tests.

# 9 Behaviorist Views of Learning

## LEARNING OUTCOMES

**9.1:** Describe five basic assumptions underlying behaviorist views of learning, and apply these assumptions to classroom practice.

**9.2:** Explain how learners can acquire involuntary responses through classical conditioning and how you might help a student overcome classically conditioned emotional responses that interfere with classroom performance.

**9.3:** Describe the effects that various kinds of consequences can have on behavior.

**9.4:** Apply behaviorist principles to encourage productive student behaviors and discourage undesirable ones.

**9.5:** Accommodate students' personal and cultural backgrounds and special needs in your application of behaviorist principles.

**9.6:** Describe circumstances in which behaviorist techniques might not be helpful.

## CASE STUDY: THE ATTENTION GETTER

James is the sixth child in a family of nine children. He likes many things; for instance, he likes rock music, comic books, basketball, and strawberry ice cream. But more than anything else, James likes attention.

James is a skillful attention getter. He gets his teacher's attention by making outrageous remarks in class, throwing paper airplanes across the room, and refusing to turn in assignments. He gets his classmates' attention by teasing them, poking them, and writing obscenities on the restroom walls. And by the middle of the school year, James's antics are regularly earning him trips to the school office, where he gets the assistant principal's attention at least once a week.

- Why might James be choosing inappropriate behaviors, rather than more productive ones, in order to get attention? What general principle of learning might explain his behavior?

As you consider James's situation, think back to your own experiences as a student in elementary and secondary school. Which students received the most attention: those who behaved well or those who behaved poorly? Chances are, your teachers and classmates paid the most attention to *mis*behaving students (Landrum & Kauffman, 2006; J. C. Taylor & Romanczyk, 1994). James has undoubtedly learned that if he wants to be noticed—if he wants to stand out in a crowd—he must behave in ways that are hard to ignore.

Throughout our lives we learn many, many new behaviors—how to sharpen a pencil, dribble a basketball, make and fly a paper airplane, and so on. In this chapter we'll examine a theoretical perspective known as behaviorism, which focuses on how people's immediate environments bring about changes in their behavior. We'll also use behaviorist ideas to understand how, as teachers, we can help students acquire behaviors that are more complex, productive, or prosocial than the ones they exhibit when they first enter our classrooms.

# Basic Assumptions of Behaviorism

When psychologists first began systematically studying human learning and behavior in the late 1880s, much of their work involved asking people to "look" inside their heads and describe what they were mentally doing (e.g., Ebbinghaus, 1885/1913; Galton, 1880; James, 1890). But beginning in the early 1900s, some psychologists criticized this approach as being subjective and scientifically unsound. In their minds, the human mind was a *black box* that couldn't be opened for inspection. Instead, these psychologists began to focus on two things that could be observed and objectively measured: local conditions and events—that is, environmental stimuli (sometimes abbreviated as S)—and learners' behaviors, or responses (sometimes abbreviated as R). This focus gave rise to the behaviorist movement, which dominated much of psychology in the middle decades of the twentieth century, especially in North America. In later decades, psychologists became increasingly inventive in their effects to study thinking processes with scientific rigor, and many left the behaviorist approach behind for more cognitively oriented approaches. Nevertheless, behaviorism is still very much alive and well, in large part because behaviorist concepts and principles can be quite useful in helping people of all ages acquire productive behaviors in classrooms and other settings.

Underlying the behaviorist perspective are several key assumptions:

- *People's behaviors are largely the result of their experiences with stimuli in their immediate environments.* Many early behaviorists suggested that, with the exception of a few simple reflexes, a person is born as a "blank slate" (or in Latin, *tabula rasa*), with no inherited tendency to behave one way or another. Over the years the environment "writes" on this slate, slowly molding, or conditioning, the person into someone who has unique characteristics and ways of behaving.

As teachers, we must keep in mind the very significant effect that students' past and present environments are likely to have on their behaviors. We can often use this basic principle to

**behaviorism** Theoretical perspective in which learning and behavior are described and explained in terms of stimulus–response relationships.

**stimulus (S)** Specific object or event that influences an individual's learning or behavior.

**response (R)** Specific behavior that an individual exhibits.

**conditioning** Term commonly used by behaviorists for *learning*; typically involves specific environmental events leading to the acquisition of specific responses.

our advantage: By changing the classroom environment, we may also be able to change how students behave.

• *Learning involves a behavior change.* Whereas most contemporary psychologists think of *learning* as a mental phenomenon, many behaviorists define it as a behavior change—in particular, learning is a *change in behavior as a result of experience.* Such a view of learning can often be useful in the classroom. Consider this scenario:

> Your students look at you attentively as you explain a difficult concept. When you finish, you ask, "Any questions?" You look around the room, and not a single hand is raised. "Good," you think, "everyone understands."

But *do* your students understand? On the basis of what you've just observed, you really have no idea whether they do or don't. Only observable behavior changes—perhaps an improvement in achievement test scores, a greater frequency of independent reading, or a reduction in off-task behaviors—can ultimately tell us that learning has occurred.

• *Learning involves forming associations among stimuli and responses.* By and large, behaviorist principles focus on relationships among observable events. For example, the opening case study illustrates one important behaviorist principle: People are likely to learn and exhibit behaviors that bring about certain kinds of consequences. For example, in the opening case study, James has formed an association between his own disruptive behaviors *(responses)* and attention from other people (which is an environmental event, or *stimulus,* for James).

If we were to take a strict black-box perspective here, we wouldn't concern ourselves with what's going on inside James's head at all. But in recent decades, it has become increasingly evident, even to behaviorists, just how difficult it is to omit thinking from explanations of learning and behavior. Accordingly, some behaviorists have begun to incorporate cognitive processes and other internal phenomena into their theoretical explanations (e.g., DeGrandpre, 2000; Rescorla, 1988). As you read this chapter, you'll find that I occasionally allude to internal phenomena in my discussion of behaviorist principles. In doing so, I'm revealing my own bias as a cognitive psychologist, and pure behaviorists might object.

• *Learning is most likely to take place when stimuli and responses occur close together in time.* When two events occur at more or less the same time—perhaps two stimuli or perhaps a stimulus and a response—there is contiguity between them. The following examples illustrate contiguity:

- One of your instructors (Professor X) scowls at you as she hands back an exam she has just corrected. You discover that you've gotten a D– on the exam, and your entire body tenses up. The next time Professor X scowls at you, that same bodily tension returns.

- Another instructor (Professor Y) calls on you every time you raise your hand. Although you're fairly quiet in your other classes, you find yourself raising your hand and speaking up more frequently in this one.

In the first situation, Professor X's scowl and the D– on your exam are presented more or less simultaneously. Here we see contiguity between two stimuli. In the second situation, your hand-raising response is followed immediately by Professor Y's request for your input. In this case we see contiguity between a response and a subsequent stimulus (although calling on you is a response that Professor Y makes, it's a *stimulus* for *you*). In both situations a behavior has changed: You've learned to tighten your muscles every time one instructor scowls, and you've learned to raise your hand and speak up more frequently in another instructor's class.

• *Many species, including human beings, learn in similar ways.* Many behaviorist principles have been derived from research with nonhuman animals. For instance, as you'll see in a moment, our knowledge about classical conditioning first emerged from Ivan Pavlov's early work with dogs. And another well-known behaviorist, B. F. Skinner, worked almost exclusively with rats and pigeons.

# PRINCIPLES/ASSUMPTIONS

## TABLE 9.1 • Basic Assumptions of Behaviorism and Their Educational Implications

| ASSUMPTION | EDUCATIONAL IMPLICATION | EXAMPLE |
|---|---|---|
| Influence of the environment | Create a classroom environment that fosters desirable student behaviors. | When a student consistently has trouble working independently, praise her inconspicuously every time she completes an assignment without having to be prompted. |
| Learning as a behavior change | Conclude that learning has occurred only when students exhibit a change in classroom performance. | Regularly assess students' learning, and look for ongoing progress in what they know and can do. |
| Focus on observable events (stimuli and responses) | Identify specific stimuli (including your own actions as a teacher) that may be influencing students' behaviors. | If a student frequently engages in disruptive classroom behavior, consider whether you might be encouraging such behavior by giving him attention every time he misbehaves. |
| Contiguity of events | If you want students to associate two events (stimuli, responses, or stimulus and response), make sure those events occur close together in time. | Include enjoyable yet educational activities in each day's schedule as a way of helping students associate school subject matter with pleasurable feelings. |
| Similarity of learning principles across species | Remember that research with nonhuman species often has relevance for classroom practice. | Reinforce a hyperactive student for sitting quietly for successively longer time periods—a *shaping* process based on early research studies with rats and pigeons. |

Students in my own educational psychology classes sometimes resent having human learning compared to that of laboratory rats. But, in fact, behaviorist principles developed from the study of nonhuman animals are often quite helpful in explaining human behavior.

Table 9.1 summarizes the five assumptions just described and draws general implications for classroom practice.

# Building on Existing Stimulus–Response Associations: Classical Conditioning

Consider this situation:

> Alan has always loved baseball. But in a game last year, he was badly hurt by a wild pitch while he was up at bat. Now, although he still plays baseball, he gets anxious whenever it's his turn at bat, to the point that his heart rate increases and he often backs away from the ball instead of swinging at it.

One possible explanation of Alan's behavior is classical conditioning, a theory that explains how we sometimes learn new responses as a result of two stimuli being presented at approximately the same time. Alan experienced two stimuli—an oncoming baseball and its painful impact—almost simultaneously. The ways in which Alan now responds to a pitched ball—his physiological reactions and his backing away—are ones he didn't exhibit before his painful experience with the baseball. Thus, learning has occurred.

Classical conditioning was first described by Ivan Pavlov (e.g., 1927), a Russian physiologist who was conducting research about salivation. Pavlov often used dogs in his research projects and presented meat to get them to salivate. He noticed that the dogs frequently began to salivate as soon as they heard the lab assistant coming down the hall, even though they couldn't yet smell the meat that the assistant was bringing. Curious about this phenomenon, Pavlov conducted an experiment to examine more systematically how a dog learns to salivate in response to a new stimulus. His experiment went something like this:

1. Pavlov flashes a light and observes that the dog doesn't salivate. Using the letters S for stimulus and R for response, we can symbolize Pavlov's first observation like this:

    S (light) ➔ R (none)

**contiguity**  Occurrence of two or more events (e.g., two stimuli, or a stimulus and a response) at approximately the same time.

**classical conditioning**  Form of learning in which a new, involuntary response is acquired as a result of two stimuli being presented close together in time.

**2.** Pavlov flashes the light again and presents meat immediately afterward. He repeats this procedure several times, and the dog salivates each time. The dog is demonstrating something it already knows how to do—salivate to meat—and hasn't yet learned anything new. We can symbolize Pavlov's second observation like so:

S (light) ⎤
S (meat) ⎦ → R (salivation)

**3.** Pavlov flashes the light once more, but this time without any meat. The dog salivates; in other words, it has learned a new response to the light stimulus. We can symbolize Pavlov's third observation this way:

S (light) → R (salivation)

In more general terms, classical conditioning proceeds as follows:

**1.** It begins with a stimulus–response association that already exists—in other words, an *unconditioned* stimulus–response association. Pavlov's dog salivates automatically whenever it smells meat, and Alan becomes upset and backs away whenever he encounters a painful stimulus. No learning is involved in either case. When a stimulus leads to a particular response without prior learning, we say that an unconditioned stimulus (UCS) elicits an unconditioned response (UCR).[1] The unconditioned response is typically an automatic, involuntary one over which the learner has little or no control.

**2.** Conditioning occurs when a neutral stimulus—one that doesn't elicit any particular response—is presented immediately before the unconditioned stimulus. In the case of Pavlov's dog, a light is presented immediately before the meat. In the case of Alan, a baseball is pitched immediately before the painful impact. Conditioning is especially likely to occur when both stimuli are presented together on several occasions and when the neutral stimulus occurs *only* when the unconditioned stimulus is about to follow (R. R. Miller & Barnet, 1993; Rachlin, 1991; Rescorla, 1967). Sometimes one pairing is enough, especially if the unconditioned stimulus is a very painful or frightening one.

**3.** Before long, the new stimulus also elicits a response, usually one very similar to the unconditioned response. The neutral stimulus has become a conditioned stimulus (CS), and the response to it has become a conditioned response (CR). For example, Pavlov's dog acquires a conditioned response of salivation to a new, conditioned stimulus—the light. Likewise, Alan acquires conditioned responses of increased heart rate and backing away—both of which reflect *anxiety*—to a pitched baseball. Like the unconditioned response, the conditioned response is an involuntary one: It occurs automatically every time the conditioned stimulus is presented.

## CLASSICAL CONDITIONING OF INVOLUNTARY EMOTIONAL RESPONSES

Classical conditioning can help us understand how people learn a variety of involuntary responses, especially responses associated with physiological processes, emotions, and other relatively "thoughtless" aspects of human functioning (Mineka & Zinbarg, 2006; J. B. Watson & Rayner, 1920). Following are three examples of how unpleasant emotional responses might be learned through classical conditioning. Notice that in each case two stimuli are presented together: One stimulus already elicits a response, and the second stimulus begins to elicit a similar response as a result of the pairing.

- Bernard falls into a swimming pool and almost drowns. A year later, when his mother takes him to the local recreation center for a swimming lesson, he cries hysterically as she tries to drag him to the side of the pool.

**unconditioned stimulus (UCS)** Stimulus that elicits a particular response without prior learning.

**unconditioned response (UCR)** Response that is elicited by a particular (unconditioned) stimulus without prior learning.

**neutral stimulus** Stimulus that does not elicit any particular response.

**conditioned stimulus (CS)** Stimulus that begins to elicit a particular response through classical conditioning.

**conditioned response (CR)** Response that begins to be elicited by a particular (conditioned) stimulus through classical conditioning.

---

[1]In discussions of classical conditioning, behaviorists often use the word *elicit* (meaning "draw forth or bring out"), as I do here. The word conveys the idea that learners have little or no control over their classically conditioned responses.

UCS: inability to breathe  →  UCR: fear of asphyxiation
CS: swimming pool  →  CR: fear of the pool

- Bobby misses a month of school because of illness. When he returns to school, he doesn't know how to do the long division problems his teacher is now assigning. After a number of frustrating experiences with the assignments, he begins to feel anxious whenever he encounters a division task.

  UCS: failure/frustration  →  UCR: anxiety about failure
  CS: long division  →  CR: anxiety about long division

- Beth's teacher catches her writing a note to a friend during class. The teacher reads the note to the entire class, revealing some very personal, private information that embarrasses her. Beth now feels extremely uncomfortable whenever she goes into that teacher's classroom.

  UCS: humiliation  →  UCR: embarrassment in response to humiliation
  CS: teacher/classroom  →  CR: emotional discomfort in response to teacher/classroom

As teachers, we should create a classroom environment in which stimuli—including our own behaviors—are likely to elicit such responses as enjoyment or relaxation, *not* fear or anxiety. When students associate school with pleasant circumstances (e.g., positive feedback, enjoyable activities), they soon learn that school is a place they want to be. But when they encounter unpleasant stimuli in school—such as public humiliation or constant frustration and failure—they may eventually learn to fear or dislike a particular activity, subject area, teacher, or school in general.

## COMMON PHENOMENA IN CLASSICAL CONDITIONING

Two common phenomena in classical conditioning are generalization and extinction. As you'll discover later in the chapter, variations of these phenomena occur in instrumental conditioning as well.

### GENERALIZATION

When people learn a conditioned response to a new stimulus, they may respond in the same way to similar stimuli—a phenomenon known as generalization. For example, a boy who learns to feel anxious about long division problems may generalize the anxiety response to other kinds of math problems. And a girl who experiences humiliation in one classroom may generalize her feelings of embarrassment to other classrooms as well. Thus, we see a second reason that students should associate pleasant feelings with school subject matter: Students' reactions to a particular topic, activity, or context may generalize—that is, they may *transfer*—to other topics, activities, or contexts.

### EXTINCTION

Pavlov discovered that conditioned responses don't necessarily last forever. By pairing a light with meat, he conditioned a dog to salivate to the light alone. But later, when he repeatedly flashed the light without following it with meat, the dog salivated less and less. Eventually, the dog no longer salivated to the light flash. When a conditioned stimulus occurs repeatedly *in the absence of* the unconditioned stimulus—for example, when math is never again associated with failure or when a teacher is never again associated with humiliation—the conditioned response may decrease and eventually disappear. In other words, extinction can occur.

Many conditioned responses do fade over time. Unfortunately, many others do not. A child's fear of water or anxiety about mathematics can persist for years. One reason that fears and anxieties persist is that learners tend to avoid situations that elicit negative emotional reactions. But if they stay away from a stimulus that makes them fearful, they never have a chance to experience the stimulus in the absence of the unconditioned stimulus with which it was originally paired. As a result, they have no opportunity to learn to be *un*afraid—no opportunity for the response to undergo extinction.

---

*The best part of third grade was*

division
algebra
multiplication
math
reading

In a personal "yearbook," Ashton identifies math and reading as being the best part of his third-grade year. He clearly associates these subjects with pleasure rather than discomfort.

🍏 Create a classroom atmosphere in which students feel physically and psychologically safe and secure.

🍏 Remember that the feelings students develop in response to you, your classroom, or specific academic topics may generalize to other situations.

**generalization** Phenomenon in which a person learns a response to a particular stimulus and then makes the same response to a similar stimulus; in classical conditioning, involves making a conditioned response to a stimulus similar to a conditioned stimulus.

**extinction** Gradual disappearance of an acquired response; in classical conditioning, results from repeated presentation of a conditioned stimulus in the absence of the unconditioned stimulus.

## ADDRESSING COUNTERPRODUCTIVE EMOTIONAL RESPONSES

As teachers, how can we reduce conditioned responses that interfere with students' learning and performance? One effective way to extinguish a negative emotional reaction to a particular conditioned stimulus is to introduce the stimulus *slowly and gradually* while a student is happy, relaxed, or in some other way feeling good (M. C. Jones, 1924; Ricciardi, Luiselli, & Camare, 2006; Wolpe & Plaud, 1997). For example, if Bernard is afraid of water, we might begin his swimming lessons someplace where he feels at ease—perhaps on dry land or in the wading pool—and move to a deeper pool only as he begins to feel more comfortable. And if Bobby gets overly anxious every time he encounters a math problem, we might revert to very easy problems—those he can readily solve—and gradually increase the difficulty of his assignments only as he demonstrates greater competence and self-confidence.

There's nothing like success to help students feel good about being in the classroom. One way to promote student success is to structure the classroom environment so that appropriate behaviors lead to desirable consequences and inappropriate behaviors do not. Such *reinforcement* plays a central role in instrumental conditioning.

When students associate classroom tasks with pleasant feelings, they learn that school is a place where they want to be. For example, notice how engaged the students are in "Water Wheels Activity."

> When a particular subject matter or task arouses anxiety, present it slowly and gradually while the learner is happy and relaxed.

## Learning from Consequences: Instrumental Conditioning

Mark is a student in Ms. Ferguson's geography class. Let's look at what happens to him during the first week in October:

- *Monday:* Ms. Ferguson asks students where Colombia is. Mark knows that Colombia is the northern part of South America. He sits smiling, with his hands in his lap, hoping to be called on. Instead Ms. Ferguson calls on another student.
- *Tuesday:* Ms. Ferguson asks the class where Colombia got its name. Mark reasonably guesses that it was named after Christopher Columbus, so he raises his hand a few inches. Ms. Ferguson calls on another student.
- *Wednesday:* Ms. Ferguson asks the class why Colombia's official language is Spanish rather than, say, English or French. Mark knows that Colombians speak Spanish because many of the country's early European settlers came from Spain. He raises his hand high in the air. Ms. Ferguson calls on another student.
- *Thursday:* Ms. Ferguson asks the class why Colombia grows coffee but Canada doesn't. Mark knows that coffee can grow only in certain climates. He raises his hand high and waves it wildly back and forth. Ms. Ferguson calls on him.
- *Friday:* Whenever Ms. Ferguson asks a question Mark can answer, he raises his hand high and waves it wildly about.

Several of Mark's behaviors bring no results. But waving his hand wildly brings Mark the outcome he wants—a chance to speak in class—and so it increases in frequency.

When learners' behaviors either increase or decrease as a result of the consequences those behaviors bring about, **instrumental conditioning** is at work. Consequences that *increase* the behaviors they follow are **reinforcers**, and the act of following a particular response with a reinforcer is known as **reinforcement**. Conversely, consequences that *decrease* the behaviors they follow constitute **punishment**. Both reinforcers and punishments are environmental *stimuli* that influence behavior.

In his research with animals, one highly influential early behaviorist, B. F. Skinner, found consistent evidence that reinforcers increased the behaviors they followed but little evidence for the influence of punishing consequences (e.g., B. F. Skinner, 1938, 1953, 1954). Skinner used the term **operant conditioning** to refer to *reinforcement-based learning*—a term that essentially captures the *increase-in-behavior* half of our instrumental conditioning definition—and many behaviorists continue to use that term today. However, many other behaviorists have found that punishment can, under certain conditions, be quite effective in reducing inappropriate behaviors. Accordingly, we'll use the more inclusive term *instrumental conditioning* in the rest of the chapter.

**instrumental conditioning**  Learning process in which a response either increases or decreases as a result of being followed by either reinforcement or punishment, respectively.

**reinforcer**  Consequence (stimulus) of a response that increases the frequency of the response it follows; the act of following a response with a reinforcer is known as **reinforcement**.

**punishment**  Consequence (stimulus) that decreases the frequency of the response it follows.

**operant conditioning**  Learning process in which a response increases as a result of being followed by reinforcement; is one form of *instrumental conditioning*.

Notice that I've defined both *reinforcer* and *punishment* in terms of their effects on behavior, rather than in terms of their relative pleasantness and desirability. Some learners increase certain behaviors for consequences that most of us would think of as unpleasant—consequences that we certainly wouldn't think of as "rewards." As an example, let's return to the opening case study. When James throws objects, makes outrageous comments, and so on, we can assume that his teacher is probably frowning at or scolding him, which we don't usually think of as desirable outcomes. Yet those consequences are leading to an increase in James's misbehaviors; thus, they're apparently reinforcing for him. Other people's attention, regardless of the form it might take, can be highly reinforcing for some students and often serves to maintain counterproductive classroom behaviors (McGinnis, Houchins-Juárez, McDaniel, & Kennedy, 2010; Mueller, Nkosi, & Hine, 2011; N. M. Rodriguez, Thompson, & Baynham, 2010).

Punishment, too, seems to be in the eye of the beholder. For example, some seemingly very desirable forms of attention, such as teacher praise, can be a must-to-avoid—and hence punishing—for adolescents who don't want their peers to think of them as a "goodie-two-shoes" or teacher's pet (Burnett, 2001; Pfiffner, Rosen, & O'Leary, 1985).

## CONTRASTING CLASSICAL CONDITIONING AND INSTRUMENTAL CONDITIONING

Classical conditioning and instrumental conditioning both involve stimuli and responses. But instrumental conditioning is different from classical conditioning in two important ways:

- *The response is voluntary rather than involuntary.* In classical conditioning, the response is involuntary: When a particular (conditioned) stimulus is present, the response usually follows automatically, with little choice on the learner's part. In instrumental conditioning, however, the response is typically voluntary: The learner can control whether or not to make it. For example, in the opening case study, James can choose whether to make inappropriate comments, toss paper airplanes, or tease classmates; nothing in the classroom environment is forcing him to do these things.

The voluntary nature of responses in instrumental conditioning is an important one for teachers to keep in mind. In order for such conditioning to occur, *learners must first make a response.* Many educational applications of behaviorist principles, then, involve getting students physically and actively engaged in working with academic subject matter.

 Get students physically and actively engaged in working with classroom topics.

- *Learning occurs as a result of a stimulus that comes after, rather than before, the response.* Classical conditioning results from the pairing of two stimuli, one (the UCS) that initially elicits a response and another (the CS) that begins to elicit the same or a similar response. Thus, these two stimuli *lead to* certain responses. In instrumental conditioning, however, the learner makes the first move, and an environmental stimulus (either a reinforcer or punishment) follows. Typically there's a contingency between the response and the consequence: The consequence almost always follows the response and seldom occurs when the response hasn't been made. For example, a teacher who praises students only when they behave appropriately is making reinforcement contingent on desired behavior. In contrast, a teacher who laughs at the antics of a chronically misbehaving student is providing reinforcement even when an acceptable response hasn't occurred; consequently, the student's behavior is unlikely to improve.

Don't confuse *contingency* with the term *contiguity* introduced near the beginning of the chapter. Contingency involves an if-this-happens-then-that-happens relationship. In contrast, contiguity simply involves two things happening at about the same time. Effective instrumental conditioning usually involves contiguity as well as contingency; that is, the consequence occurs almost immediately after the response (J. A. Kulik & Kulik, 1988; Rachlin, 1991). The immediacy of reinforcement or punishment after a response is especially important when working with young children. It's less critical for older children and adolescents, who are better able to make a mental connection between what they do *now* with what happens to them *later* (more on this point shortly).

## THE VARIOUS FORMS THAT REINFORCEMENT CAN TAKE

Reinforcers come in all shapes and sizes, and different ones are effective for different learners. We explore a few possibilities in the following exercise.

**contingency**  Situation in which one event happens only after another event has already occurred; one event is *contingent* on the other's occurrence.

## EXPERIENCING FIRSTHAND
## WHAT WOULD IT TAKE?

1. Imagine that you're currently enrolled in my educational psychology class. As your instructor, I ask you if you'd be willing to spend an hour after class tutoring two classmates who are having trouble understanding course material. You have no other commitments for that hour, but you'd really like to spend the time at a nearby coffee shop where several friends are having lunch. What would it take for you to spend the hour tutoring your classmates instead of joining your friends? Would you do it to gain my approval? Would you do it for a candy bar? How about if I gave you five dollars? Would you do it simply because it made you feel good to be helping someone else? Write down a consequence—perhaps one I've just listed or perhaps a different one altogether—that would persuade you to help your classmates instead of meeting your friends.

2. A few weeks later, I ask you to spend the weekend (eight hours a day on both Saturday and Sunday) tutoring the same two struggling classmates. What would it take this time to convince you to do the job? Would my approval do the trick? A candy bar? Five dollars? Five *hundred* dollars? Or would your internal sense of satisfaction be enough? Once again, write down what it would take for you to agree to help your classmates.

There are no right or wrong answers to this exercise. Different people would agree to tutor classmates for different reasons. But you were probably able to identify at least one consequence in each situation that would entice you to give up your free time to help others.

### PRIMARY VERSUS SECONDARY REINFORCERS

Some reinforcers, such as a candy bar, are primary reinforcers, because they address a basic biological need. Food, water, sources of warmth, and oxygen are all primary reinforcers. To some extent, physical affection and cuddling seem to address built-in biological needs as well, and for an adolescent addicted to an illegal substance, the next "fix" is also a primary reinforcer (Harlow & Zimmerman, 1959; Lejuez, Schaal, & O'Donnell, 1998; Vollmer & Hackenberg, 2001).

Other reinforcers, known as secondary reinforcers, don't satisfy any physiological need. Praise, money, good grades, and trophies are examples. Such stimuli may become reinforcing over time through their association with other stimuli that already have a reinforcing effect. For example, if praise is occasionally associated with a special candy treat from Mother, and if money often comes with a hug from Father, the praise and money eventually become reinforcing in and of themselves. In this way, seemingly unpleasant stimuli can become reinforcers. For instance, if James regularly associates a teacher's scolding with something he wants—more attention—then a scolding may indeed become a reinforcer in its own right.

Secondary reinforcers are far more common in classrooms than primary reinforcers. In fact, making primary reinforcers (e.g., lunch, restroom breaks) contingent on certain levels of performance is generally *not* good teaching practice. When we use secondary reinforcers, however, we must remember that they're *learned* reinforcers, and not everyone has come to appreciate them. Although most students respond positively to such consequences as praise and good grades, a few students may not.

### POSITIVE VERSUS NEGATIVE REINFORCEMENT

Up to this point, we've been talking about reinforcement as the *presentation* of a particular reinforcing stimulus. But in some cases we can also reinforce a behavior through the *removal* of a stimulus. Behaviorists use the terms *positive reinforcement* and *negative reinforcement*, respectively, for these two situations.

**Positive reinforcement** Whenever a particular stimulus is *presented* after a behavior and the behavior increases as a result, positive reinforcement has occurred. Don't be misled by the word *positive*, which in this case has nothing to do with the pleasantness or desirability of the stimulus being presented. Positive reinforcement can occur even when the presented stimulus is one that others might think is *un*pleasant or *un*desirable. The word *positive* here simply means *adding* something to the situation. For instance, some students may make a response to get a teacher's

---

Keep in mind that not all students have learned to appreciate such secondary reinforcers as praise and good grades.

---

**primary reinforcer** Consequence that satisfies a biologically built-in need.

**secondary reinforcer** Consequence that becomes reinforcing over time through its association with another reinforcer.

**positive reinforcement** Consequence that brings about the increase of a behavior through the presentation (rather than the removal) of a stimulus.

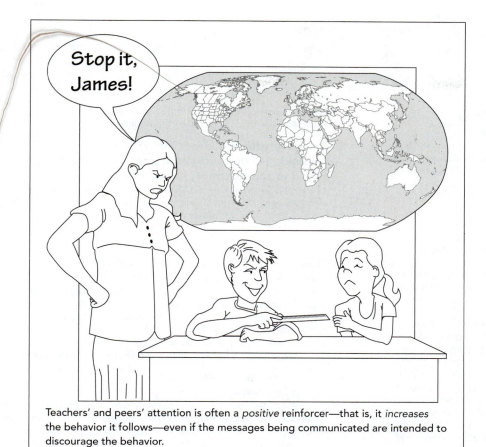

Teachers' and peers' attention is often a *positive* reinforcer—that is, it *increases* the behavior it follows—even if the messages being communicated are intended to discourage the behavior.

praise, but others (like James in the opening case study) may behave in a way that gets them a scolding. Most students will work for As, but a few may actually prefer Cs or even Fs. (As a school psychologist, I once worked with a high school student who used Fs as a way to get revenge on his overly controlling parents.) Depending on the individual, any one of these stimuli—praise, a scolding, an A, or an F—can be a positive reinforcer. Following are examples of the forms that positive reinforcement can take:

- A *concrete reinforcer* is an actual object—something that can be touched (e.g., a snack, sticker, or toy).

- A *social reinforcer* is a gesture or sign (e.g., a smile, attention, or praise) that one person gives another, often to communicate positive regard.

- An *activity reinforcer* is an opportunity to engage in a favorite pastime. Learners often do one thing—even something they don't like to do—if it enables them to do something they enjoy. This phenomenon is sometimes called the Premack principle (Premack, 1959, 1963). For example, children with attention-deficit hyperactivity disorder (ADHD) are more likely to sit quietly during a lesson if they know that doing so will enable them to engage in a physically more lively activity afterward (Azrin, Vinas, & Ehle, 2007).

- A *token reinforcer* is a small, insignificant item (e.g., poker chip, specially marked piece of colored paper) that a learner can later use to "purchase" a desired object or privilege. It's often used in a *token economy,* a strategy to be described a bit later.

- Sometimes the simple message that an answer is correct or that a task has been done well—*positive feedback*—is reinforcement enough. In fact, sometimes even *negative* feedback can be reinforcing if the overall message is a positive one. The Creating a Productive Classroom Environment feature "Using Feedback to Improve Learning and Behavior" offers suggestions based on research by behaviorists, cognitive psychologists, and motivation theorists.

Be aware that certain consequences that seem "negative" (e.g., scoldings, bad grades) may nevertheless be *positively* reinforcing for some students.

**Premack principle** Phenomenon in which learners do less-preferred activities in order to engage in more-preferred activities.

## Creating a Productive Classroom Environment

### Using Feedback to Improve Learning and Behavior

🍎 **Be explicit about what students are doing well—ideally, at the time they are doing it.**

When praising her students for appropriate classroom behavior, a second-grade teacher is quite specific about the actions for which she's commending them. For example, she says, "I like the way you're working quietly" and "You should see Ricky being so polite. Thank you, Ricky, for not disturbing the rest of the class."

🍎 **Give concrete guidance about how students can improve their performance.**

A high school physical education teacher tells a student, "Your time in the 100-meter dash wasn't as fast as it could have been. It's early in the season, though, and if you work on your endurance, I know you'll improve. Also, I think you might get a faster start if you stay low when you first come out of the starting blocks."

🍎 **Communicate optimism that students can improve.**

When a student in a middle school geography class gives her oral report on Mexico, she goes on at length about her family's recent trip to Puerto Vallarta, showing many photos, postcards, and souvenirs to illustrate her remarks. The other students soon become bored and communicate their displeasure through body language and occasional whispers across the aisles. At the end of class, the student is devastated that her report has been so poorly received. Her teacher takes her aside and gently says, "You included many interesting facts in your report, Julie, and all your pictures and artifacts really helped us understand Mexican culture. But you know how young teenagers are—they can have a pretty short attention span at times. I'll be assigning oral reports again next semester.

Before you give yours, let's sit down and plan it so that your classmates will think, 'Wow, this is really interesting!'"

🍎 **Don't overwhelm students with too much feedback; tell them only what they can reasonably attend to and remember at the time.**

As a kindergarten teacher watches one of his students practice writing several alphabet letters, he helps the student hold her pencil in a way that gives her better control. He doesn't mention that she's writing her Bs and Ds backward; he'll save this information for a later time, after she has mastered her pencil grip.

🍎 **Minimize feedback when students already know exactly what they've done well or poorly.**

A high school math teacher has a student who has been getting poor grades in large part because of insufficient effort. When the student begins to buckle down and do his homework regularly, his quiz scores improve tremendously. As his teacher hands back his first quiz after his newfound diligence—a quiz on which he's earned a score of 96%—she says nothing but smiles and gives him a private thumbs-up.

🍎 **Teach students strategies for appropriately asking for teacher feedback.**

A fourth-grade teacher has two students with intellectual disabilities in her class. She knows that these students may need more frequent feedback than their classmates. She teaches them three steps to take when they need her assistance: (1) They should raise their hands or walk quietly to her desk; (2) they should wait patiently until she has time to speak with them; and (3) they should make their needs known (e.g., "How am I doing?" "What do I do next?").

*Sources:* Bangert-Drowns, Kulik, Kulik, & Morgan, 1991; Boyanton, 2010; D. L. Butler & Winne, 1995; Craft, Alberg, & Heward, 1998, p. 402 (fourth-grade example); Feltz, Chase, Moritz, & Sullivan, 1999; Hattie & Gan, 2011; Hattie & Timperley, 2007; K. A. Meyer, 1999; Narciss, 2008; Pintrich & Schunk, 2002; Schunk & Pajares, 2005; Shute, 2008; J. V. Stokes, Luiselli, Reed, & Fleming, 2010; Tunstall & Gipps, 1996.

One form of intrinsic reinforcement is students' sense of pride about a job well done. For example, watch "Science Fair Projects."

The reinforcers just listed are **extrinsic reinforcers**, those provided by the external environment (often by other people). Yet some positive reinforcers are **intrinsic reinforcers**, those supplied by learners themselves or inherent in tasks being performed. When students perform certain behaviors in the absence of any observable reinforcers—when they read an entire book without putting it down, do extra classwork without being asked, or practice with a neighborhood rock group into the wee hours of the morning—they're probably working for the intrinsic reinforcement that such behaviors yield. Intrinsic reinforcers are *not* observable events and thus don't fit comfortably within traditional behaviorist theory. Yet students clearly do engage in some behaviors solely for the intrinsic satisfaction their behaviors bring. For instance, in the earlier "What Would It Take?" exercise, if you agreed to help your classmates simply because doing so would make you feel good, you'd be working for an intrinsic reinforcer.

From our perspective as teachers, positive feedback (an extrinsic reinforcer) and the feelings of pleasure and satisfaction that such feedback can bring (intrinsic reinforcers) are probably the most desirable forms of classroom reinforcement. But we must remember that the classroom successes that yield such forms of reinforcement can occur only when instruction has been carefully tailored to individual skill levels and abilities and only when students have learned to value academic achievement. When students aren't motivated to achieve academic success for whatever reasons, then social reinforcers, activity reinforcers, and occasionally even concrete reinforcers can be used to increase desired classroom behaviors.

**Negative reinforcement**    Whereas positive reinforcement involves the presentation of a stimulus, negative reinforcement brings about the increase of a behavior through the *removal* of a stimulus—typically an unpleasant one, at least from the learner's perspective. The word *negative* here isn't a value judgment. It simply refers to the act of *taking away*, rather than adding, a stimulus.[2] When people make a response in order to get rid of something and the frequency of the response increases as a result, they're being negatively reinforced.

Imagine, for example, that you have a difficult assignment to do for one of your classes. Because you don't like the assignment hanging over your head, you complete it and give it to your instructor well before its due date. After you turn it in, you feel much better: You've gotten rid of that annoying *worry* feeling. If you find yourself completing future assignments early as well, then you've been negatively reinforced for your complete-something-before-due-date behavior.

We can see another possible example of negative reinforcement in the opening case study. When James misbehaves, his teacher sometimes sends him to the assistant principal's office. By doing so, the teacher may be negatively reinforcing his troublesome behavior. In particular, James *gets out of class*, thereby removing a stimulus—some aspect of the classroom environment—that may be aversive for him. (If James likes spending time with the assistant principal, he's receiving positive reinforcement as well.) Whereas some students misbehave in class primarily to get attention (a positive reinforcer), others often misbehave to escape something they don't want to do, such as a difficult assignment, and their escape behavior is negatively reinforced (McComas, Thompson, & Johnson, 2003; K. A. Meyer, 1999; Mueller et al., 2011). Students may learn other escape behaviors as well, as one student with a learning disability revealed:

> When it comes time for reading I do everything under the sun I can to get out of it because it's my worst nightmare to read. I'll say I have to go to the bathroom or that I'm sick and I have to go to the nurse right now. My teacher doesn't know that I'll be walking around campus. She thinks I am going to the bathroom or whatever my lame excuse is. All I really want to do is get out of having to read. (Zambo & Brem, 2004, p. 5)

As teachers, we should use negative reinforcement rarely, if at all. Ideally, we want to create a classroom environment in which there are few stimuli that students want to escape. Nevertheless, we should recognize that negative reinforcement *does* have an effect on behavior. Some students may finish an assignment more to get it out of the way than for any intrinsic satisfaction the assignment brings. Others may engage in a variety of responses—perhaps misbehaving or identifying imaginary reasons for leaving the classroom—as a way of avoiding the assignment altogether. When certain responses enable students to eliminate or escape unpleasant stimuli, those responses will increase in frequency.

> When students consistently behave in ways that enable them to avoid or escape certain activities, identify and address possible reasons that students find the activities aversive.

## LOOKING AT REINFORCEMENT FROM A DEVELOPMENTAL PERSPECTIVE

Children's preferences for various kinds of reinforcers tend to change with age. For example, concrete reinforcers (e.g., scratch-and-sniff stickers, small trinkets) can be effective with young children, but teenagers are more likely to appreciate opportunities to interact with friends. Table 9.2 presents forms of reinforcement that may be especially effective at various grade levels.

An important developmental trend is evident in Table 9.2 as well: As children get older, they become better able to handle delay of gratification. That is, they can forego small, immediate reinforcers for the larger reinforcers that their long-term efforts may bring down the road (Atance, 2008; L. Green et al., 1994; Steinberg, Graham, et al., 2009). Whereas a preschooler or kindergartner is apt to choose a small reinforcer available *now* rather than a larger and more attractive reinforcer she can't get until tomorrow, an 8-year-old may be willing to wait a day or two for the more appealing item. Many adolescents can delay gratification for several weeks or even longer. For instance, as a 16-year-old, my son Jeff worked long hours stocking shelves at the

**extrinsic reinforcer**  Reinforcer that comes from the outside environment, rather than from within the learner.

**intrinsic reinforcer**  Reinforcer that is provided by the learner or inherent in the task being performed.

**negative reinforcement**  Consequence that brings about the increase of a behavior through the removal (rather than the presentation) of a stimulus.

**delay of gratification**  Ability to forego small, immediate reinforcers in order to obtain larger ones later on.

---

[2]You might draw an analogy between positive versus negative reinforcement and positive versus negative numbers. Positive numbers and positive reinforcement both *add* something to a situation. Negative numbers and negative reinforcement both *subtract* something from a situation.

# DEVELOPMENTAL TRENDS

## TABLE 9.2 • Effective Reinforcers at Different Grade Levels

| GRADE LEVEL | AGE-TYPICAL CHARACTERISTICS | EXAMPLE | SUGGESTED STRATEGIES |
|---|---|---|---|
| K–2 | • Preference for small, immediate reinforcers over larger, delayed ones<br>• Examples of effective reinforcers:<br>  • Concrete reinforcers (e.g., stickers, crayons, small trinkets)<br>  • Teacher approval (e.g., smiles, praise)<br>  • Privileges (e.g., going to lunch first)<br>  • "Grown-up" responsibilities (e.g., taking absentee forms to the main office) | When a kindergarten teacher asks children to choose between a small snack before morning recess or a larger one after recess, most of them clamor for the smaller, immediate snack. | • Give immediate praise for appropriate behavior.<br>• Describe enjoyable consequences that may come later as a result of students' current behaviors.<br>• Use stickers, handwritten smiley faces, and the like to reinforce students' written work.<br>• Have students line up for recess, lunch, or dismissal based on desired behaviors (e.g., "Table 2 is the quietest and can line up first").<br>• Rotate opportunities to perform classroom duties (e.g., feeding the goldfish, watering plants); make such duties contingent on appropriate behavior. |
| 3–5 | • Increasing ability to delay gratification (i.e., to put off small reinforcers in order to gain larger ones later on)<br>• Examples of effective reinforcers:<br>  • Concrete reinforcers (e.g., snacks, pencils, small toys)<br>  • Teacher approval and positive feedback<br>  • "Good citizen" certificates<br>  • Free time (e.g., to draw or play games) | Nine-year-old Li-Mei glows with pride when her teacher praises her for helping a classmate with a challenging writing assignment | • Use concrete reinforcers only occasionally, perhaps to add novelty to a classroom activity.<br>• Award a certificate to a Citizen of the Week, explicitly identifying things the recipient has done especially well; be sure that every student gets at least one certificate during the school year.<br>• Plan a trip to a local amusement park for students with good attendance records (especially useful for students at risk for academic failure). |
| 6–8 | • Increasing desire to have social time with peers<br>• Examples of effective reinforcers:<br>  • Free time with friends<br>  • Acceptance and approval from peers<br>  • Teacher approval and emotional support (especially critical after the transition to middle school or junior high)<br>  • Specific positive feedback about academic performance (preferably given in private) | Students in a sixth-grade science class work diligently on an assigned lab activity, knowing that if they complete it before the end of the class session they can have a few minutes to talk with their friends. | • Make short periods of free time with peers (e.g., five minutes) contingent on accomplishing assigned tasks.<br>• Spend one-on-one time with students, especially those who appear to be socially isolated.<br>• Provide explicit feedback about what things students have done well (e.g., their use of colorful language in an essay or their prosocial behaviors with classmates). |
| 9–12 | • Increasing ability to postpone immediate pleasures in order to gain desired long-term outcomes<br>• Concern about getting good grades (especially for students who are applying to selective colleges)<br>• Examples of effective reinforcers:<br>  • Opportunities to interact with friends<br>  • Specific positive feedback about academic performance<br>  • Public recognition for group performance (e.g., newspaper articles about a club's public service work)<br>  • Positions of responsibility (e.g., being student representative to the Faculty Senate) | When 16-year-old Deon's friends ask him to go to the movies on a Thursday evening, he declines. "I have to study for tomorrow's history test," he tells them. "If I keep my grades up, I'll have a better chance of getting a good college scholarship." | • Acknowledge students' concerns about earning good grades, but focus their attention on the value of learning school subject matter for its own sake.<br>• Be sure that good grades are contingent on students' own work; take precautions to ensure that cheating and plagiarism are *not* reinforced.<br>• Publicize accomplishments of extracurricular groups and athletic teams in local news media.<br>• Provide opportunities for independent decision making and responsibility, especially when students show an ability to make wise decisions. |

*Sources:* E. M. Anderman & Mueller, 2010; L. H. Anderman, Patrick, Hruda, & Linnenbrink, 2002; Atance, 2008; Cizek, 2003; S. A. Fowler & Baer, 1981; L. Green, Fry, & Myerson, 1994; Hine & Fraser, 2002; Krumboltz & Krumboltz, 1972; Rimm & Masters, 1974; Rotenberg & Mayer, 1990; M. G. Sanders, 1996; Steinberg, Graham, et al., 2009; Urdan & Mestas, 2006; M.-T. Wang & Holcombe, 2010.

local grocery store (hardly an intrinsically reinforcing activity!) to earn enough money to pay half the cost of a $400-a-night limousine for his high school prom.

Some children and adolescents are better able to delay gratification than others. Those who are willing and able to postpone reinforcement are less likely to yield to temptation, more carefully plan their future actions, and achieve at higher levels at school (Bembenutty & Karabenick, 2004; Rothbart, 2011; Shoda, Mischel, & Peake, 1990). However, even 4- and 5-year-olds can learn to delay gratification for a few hours if their teachers tell them that rewards for desired behaviors (e.g., sharing toys with peers) will be coming later in the day (S. A. Fowler & Baer, 1981). Teaching children effective waiting strategies—for instance, focusing attention on something else during the delay and using such self-talk as "If I wait a little longer, I'll get something better"—enhances their ability to postpone gratification as well (Binder, Dixon, & Ghezzi, 2000).

When working with young children, try to reinforce desired behaviors immediately, even if only by pointing out that a desired consequence will come later.

## THE VARIOUS FORMS THAT PUNISHMENT CAN TAKE

Historically, the use of punishment in the classroom has been controversial, and in fact some forms of punishment do a great deal of harm. But under certain conditions, punishment can be both effective and appropriate, especially when students seem to have little motivation to change their behavior for the better.

All punishing consequences fall into one of two categories. **Presentation punishment** involves presenting a new stimulus, presumably something that a learner finds unpleasant and doesn't want. Scoldings and teacher scowls—*if* they lead to a reduction in the behavior they follow—are instances of presentation punishment. **Removal punishment** involves removing an existing stimulus or state of affairs, presumably one that a learner finds desirable and doesn't want to lose. Loss of a privilege, a fine or penalty (involving the loss of money or previously earned points), and grounding (i.e., restriction from certain pleasurable outside activities) are all examples of removal punishment.[3]

Over the years I've often seen or heard people use the term *negative reinforcement* when they're really talking about punishment. Remember, negative reinforcement is *reinforcement*, which increases a response, whereas punishment has the opposite effect. Table 9.3 can help you understand the distinction.

### CONSEQUENCES THAT SERVE AS EFFECTIVE PUNISHMENTS

As a general rule, we should use only mild forms of punishment in the classroom. Researchers and educators have identified several mild consequences that can be effective in reducing classroom misbehaviors.

**Verbal reprimands (scolding)**  As is true for James in the opening case study, some students seem to thrive on teacher scolding because it brings them the attention they can't seem to get in other ways. But most students find verbal reprimands to be unpleasant and punishing (Landrum & Kauffman, 2006; Pfiffner & O'Leary, 1993; Van Houten, Nau, MacKenzie-Keating, Sameoto, & Colavecchia, 1982). In general, reprimands are most effective when they're immediate, brief, unemotional, and given in a quiet tone of voice. Whenever possible, we should reprimand students privately rather than publicly. When students are scolded in front of classmates, some may relish the peer attention, and others (e.g., many Native American and Hispanic students) may feel totally humiliated (Fuller, 2001).

**Response cost**  The loss either of a previously earned reinforcer or of an opportunity to obtain reinforcement is known as **response cost**. A form of *removal punishment*, response cost is especially effective when used in combination with reinforcement of appropriate behavior and when learners who make a few missteps within an overall pattern of desirable behavior lose only a *little* of what they've earned (Conyers et al., 2004; Landrum & Kauffman, 2006; E. L. Phillips, Phillips, Fixsen, & Wolf, 1971).

**presentation punishment**
Punishment involving presentation of a new stimulus, presumably one a learner finds unpleasant.

**removal punishment**  Punishment involving removal of an existing stimulus, presumably one a learner doesn't want to lose.

**response cost**  Loss either of a previously earned reinforcer or of an opportunity to obtain reinforcement.

---

[3]You may sometimes see the terms *positive punishment* and *negative punishment* used instead of *presentation punishment* and *removal punishment*, respectively. But in my experience, such terms can lead to the same value-judgment misinterpretation problem that exists for negative reinforcement: Many people mistakenly believe that positive punishment is somehow more desirable than negative punishment, which isn't necessarily the case.

## COMPARE/CONTRAST

### TABLE 9.3 • Distinguishing among Positive Reinforcement, Negative Reinforcement, and Punishment

| CONSEQUENCE | EFFECT | EXAMPLES |
|---|---|---|
| **Positive reinforcement** | Response *increases* when a new stimulus (presumably one the learner finds desirable) is *presented*. | • A student *is praised* for writing an assignment in cursive. She begins to write other assignments in cursive as well.<br>• A student *gets lunch money* by bullying a girl into surrendering hers. He begins bullying his classmates more frequently. |
| **Negative reinforcement** | Response *increases* when a previously existing stimulus (presumably one the learner finds undesirable) is *removed*. | • A student *no longer has to worry* about a research paper that he completed several days before the due date. He begins to do his assignments ahead of time whenever possible.<br>• A student *escapes the principal's wrath* by lying about her role in recent school vandalism. After this incident she begins lying to school faculty whenever she finds herself in an uncomfortable situation. |
| **Presentation punishment** | Response *decreases* when a new stimulus (presumably one the learner finds undesirable) is *presented*. | • A student *is scolded* for taunting other students. She taunts others less frequently after that.<br>• A student *is ridiculed by classmates* for asking what they perceive to be a stupid question during a lesson. He stops asking questions in class. |
| **Removal punishment** | Response *decreases* when a previously existing stimulus (presumably one the learner finds desirable) is *removed*. | • A student *is removed from the softball team for a week* for showing poor sportsmanship. She rarely shows poor sportsmanship in future games.<br>• A student *loses points on a test* for answering a question in a creative but unusual way. He takes fewer risks on future tests. |

**Logical consequences** A logical consequence is something that follows naturally or logically from a student's misbehavior; in other words, it's punishment that fits the crime. For example, if a student destroys a classmate's possession, a reasonable consequence is for the student to replace it or pay for a new one. If two close friends talk so much that they aren't completing assignments, a reasonable consequence is for them to be separated. The use of logical consequences makes logical sense, and research vouches for its effectiveness (Dreikurs, 1998; Landrum & Kauffman, 2006; Nucci, 2001).

**Positive-practice overcorrection** One desired result of administering punishment, of course, is that students learn more appropriate behavior in the process. Positive-practice overcorrection involves having a student repeat an action, but doing it correctly, perhaps in an exaggerated form. For example, a student who runs dangerously down the school corridor might be asked to back up and then *walk*—perhaps at a normal pace, or perhaps very slowly—down the hall. Similarly, a student in a drivers' education class who neglects to stop at a stop sign might be asked to drive around the block, return to the same intersection, and come to a complete stop (perhaps counting aloud to five) before proceeding. In general, positive-practice overcorrection is most likely to be effective when its duration is relatively short and when teachers portray it as a means for helping students acquire appropriate behavior rather than simply as punishment per se (Alberto & Troutman, 2013; R. G. Carey & Bucher, 1983; M. D. Powers & Crowel, 1985).

**Time-out** A misbehaving student given a time-out is placed in a dull, boring (but not scary) situation—perhaps a separate room designed especially for time-outs, a little-used office, or a remote corner of the classroom. A student in time-out has no opportunity to interact with classmates and no opportunity to get reinforcement. The length of the time-out is typically quite short (perhaps 2 to 10 minutes, depending on the student's age), but the student isn't released until any inappropriate behavior (e.g., screaming, kicking) has stopped.

Time-outs have been used successfully to reduce a variety of noncompliant, disruptive, and aggressive behaviors. Keep in mind, however, that a time-out is apt to be effective only if ongoing classroom activities are a source of pleasure and reinforcement for a student. If a time-out allows a student to escape difficult tasks or an overwhelming amount of noise and stimulation, it might actually be a form of negative reinforcement and thus *increase* undesirable

**logical consequence** Unpleasant consequence that follows naturally or logically from a student's misbehavior.

**positive-practice overcorrection** Consequence of a poorly performed response in which a learner must repeat the response correctly and appropriately, perhaps in an exaggerated manner.

**time-out** Consequence for misbehavior in which a learner is placed in a dull, boring situation with no opportunity for reinforcement or social interaction.

behavior (J. M. Donaldson & Vollmer, 2011; McClowry, 1998; Pfiffner, Barkley, & DuPaul, 2006; Rortvedt & Miltenberger, 1994; A. G. White & Bailey, 1990).

**In-school suspension**   Like time-out, in-school suspension involves placing a student in a quiet, boring room within the school building. However, it often lasts one or more school days and involves close adult supervision. Students receiving in-school suspension spend the day working on their class assignments, enabling them to keep up with their schoolwork. But they have no opportunity for interaction with peers—an aspect of school that's reinforcing for most students.

Although in-school suspension programs haven't been systematically investigated through controlled research studies, educators report that these programs are often effective in reducing chronic behavior problems. They're typically most effective when suspension sessions include instruction in appropriate behaviors and missing academic skills and when the supervising teacher acts as a supportive resource rather than a punisher (Gootman, 1998; Huff, 1988; Pfiffner et al., 2006; J. S. Sullivan, 1989).

## CONSEQUENCES THAT MAY UNDERMINE DESIRED BEHAVIOR CHANGES

Several forms of punishment are typically *not* recommended because they have adverse side effects, convey a counterproductive message, or actually serve as reinforcers for some students.

**Physical punishment**   Most experts advise against physical punishment for school-age children (e.g., W. Doyle, 1990; Hyman et al., 2006; Landrum & Kauffman, 2006). Furthermore, its use in the classroom is *illegal* in many places. Even mild physical punishment, such as a spank or slap with a ruler, can lead to such undesirable outcomes as resentment of the teacher, avoidance of school tasks, lying, aggression, vandalism, and truancy. When carried to extremes, physical punishment constitutes child abuse and can cause long-term physical damage, psychological problems, or both.

**Psychological punishment**   Any consequence that seriously threatens a student's sense of self-worth is psychological punishment and isn't recommended. Fear tactics, embarrassing remarks, and public humiliation can lead to some of the same side effects as physical punishment can—for instance, resentment, distraction from schoolwork, and truancy—and can inflict long-term psychological harm. By deflating students' sense of self, psychological punishment can also dampen their interest in classroom subject matter and expectations for future performance (Brendgen, Wanner, Vitaro, Bukowski, & Tremblay, 2007; J. Ellis, Fitzsimmons, & Small-McGinley, 2010; Hyman et al., 2006).

**Extra classwork**   Asking a student to complete makeup work for time missed in school is a reasonable and justifiable request. But assigning extra classwork or homework beyond that required for other students is inappropriate if it's assigned simply to punish a student for wrongdoing (H. Cooper, 1989; Corno, 1996). Such punishment has a very different side effect: It communicates the message that schoolwork is unpleasant.

**Out-of-school suspension**   Teachers and administrators are negatively reinforced when they suspend a problem student. After all, they get rid of something they don't want—a problem! But out-of-school suspension is usually *not* an effective means of changing a student's behavior. For one thing, being suspended from school may be exactly what the student wants, in which case inappropriate behaviors are being reinforced rather than punished. Also, because many students with chronic behavior problems tend to do poorly in their schoolwork, suspension involves a loss of valuable instructional time and interferes with any psychological attachment to school. Thus, it decreases students' chances for academic and social success even further and increases the probability that students will drop out before graduation (American Psychological Association Zero Tolerance Task Force, 2008; Christenson & Thurlow, 2004; Gregory, Skiba, & Noguera, 2010; Osher, Bear, Sprague, & Doyle, 2010).

## CONSEQUENCES WITH MIXED REVIEWS

Two additional forms of punishment get mixed reviews regarding effectiveness. In some situations *missing recess* is a logical consequence for students who fail to complete their schoolwork during regular class time because of off-task behavior. Yet research indicates that, especially at

**in-school suspension**   Consequence for misbehavior in which a student is placed in a quiet, boring room within the school building, typically to do schoolwork under close adult supervision.

**psychological punishment**   Consequence that seriously threatens self-esteem and general psychological well-being.

Do *not* use physical punishment, public humiliation, or extra classwork to discourage undesirable behaviors.

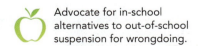
Advocate for in-school alternatives to out-of-school suspension for wrongdoing.

the elementary level, students can more effectively concentrate on school tasks if they have frequent breaks and opportunities to release pent-up energy (Maxmell, Jarrett, & Dickerson, 1998; Pellegrini & Bohn, 2005; Pellegrini, Huberty, & Jones, 1995). And although imposing *after-school detention* for serious misbehavior is common practice at many schools, some students simply can't stay after school hours, perhaps because they have transportation issues, must take care of younger siblings at home, or are justifiably afraid to walk through certain neighborhoods after dark (J. D. Nichols, Ludwin, & Iadicola, 1999). Unless we can address such concerns, imposing after-school detention isn't logistically feasible.

Keep in mind the downsides of having students miss recess and imposing after-school detention.

# Strategies for Encouraging Productive Behaviors

As a prominent early behaviorist, B. F. Skinner was quite vocal in advocating for the application of behaviorist principles in classroom settings. He argued that punishment was a relatively *in*effective means of changing behavior—it might temporarily suppress a response but could never eliminate it—and thus urged teachers to focus their efforts on reinforcing desirable behaviors rather than punishing undesirable ones (e.g., B. F. Skinner, 1954, 1968; B. F. Skinner & Epstein, 1982). Following Skinner's lead, most contemporary behaviorists suggest that we emphasize the positive, looking for and reinforcing what's *right* with student behavior.

As teachers, we must be sure that productive student behaviors—contributing to class discussions, keeping work areas tidy, working cooperatively with peers, and so on—are reinforced in some way. At the same time, we should be careful *not* to reinforce counterproductive behaviors. If we repeatedly allow Carol to turn in assignments late because she says she forgot her homework and if we often let Caleb get his way by bullying his peers, then we're reinforcing—and hence increasing—Carol's irresponsibility and Caleb's aggressiveness.

Be careful that you don't inadvertently reinforce undesirable behaviors.

## USING REINFORCEMENT EFFECTIVELY

The following strategies are consistent with behaviorist principles and research findings:

 *Specify desired behaviors at the outset.* Before beginning a lesson or behavioral intervention, behaviorists identify the desired end results—the terminal behaviors—in specific, concrete, observable terms. Rather than talk about the need for students to "Learn world history," we might instead talk about them being able to "Describe the antecedents and outcomes of World War II." Rather than say that students should "Learn responsibility," we might instead talk about their need to "Follow instructions, bring the necessary books and supplies to class each day, and turn in assignments by the due dates." By specifying terminal behaviors up front, we give both ourselves and our students targets to shoot for, and we can better determine whether everyone is making progress toward them.

Educators are increasingly recognizing the importance of spelling out in advance the most important things that students should learn and achieve. You're apt to see a variety of terms for this idea—perhaps *instructional goals, objectives, outcomes, competencies, benchmarks,* and *standards.*

 *Make sure that all students regularly receive reinforcement for desired behaviors.* In the opening case study, James engages in a variety of inappropriate behaviors in order to gain other people's attention. We might reasonably guess that James would prefer more pleasant interactions with adults and peers, yet for whatever reasons he seldom has such interactions—perhaps because his academic performance rarely gains his teacher's praise or perhaps because he lacks the social skills to make and maintain friendships. In working with James, then, his teacher should identify the academic and social skills he might be missing, help him acquire those skills, and then, of course, reinforce him for using the skills.

In our attempts to improve the behaviors of some students, however, we must be careful that we don't unintentionally slight other, equally deserving students. Furthermore, we must keep in mind that some students may be unable to exhibit particular behaviors through little or no fault of their own. Consider the case of an immigrant student who had to adjust very quickly from a 10:00–5:00 school day in Vietnam to a 7:45–3:45 school day in the United States:

**terminal behavior** Form and frequency of a desired response that a teacher hopes to foster through reinforcement.

Every week on Friday after school, the teacher would give little presents to kids that were good during the week. And if you were tardy, you wouldn't get a present. . . . I would never get one because I would always come to school late, and that hurt at first. I had a terrible time. I didn't look forward to going to school. (Igoa, 1995, p. 95)

Ultimately school should be a place where *all* students can, in one way or another, earn reinforcement for appropriate behaviors and academic progress.

🍏 *Use extrinsic reinforcers only when desired behaviors will not otherwise occur.* It's neither possible nor necessary to reinforce every good deed. Furthermore, many extrinsic reinforcements lose their effectiveness when used repeatedly (Michael, 2000; Murphy, McSweeney, Smith, & McComas, 2003). The best reinforcers are intrinsic ones, such as the pleasure one gets from reading, the pride one feels after completing a challenging task, and the internal satisfaction one feels while helping others. Students willingly engage in activities that are enjoyable or pique their curiosity, and they'll readily behave in ways that lead to feelings of mastery and accomplishment.

Yet many of the tasks students tackle in school—writing persuasive essays, solving mathematical word problems, playing a musical instrument, and so on—can be difficult and frustrating, especially at first. When students struggle with a task and encounter frequent failure, we should probably provide some extrinsic reinforcement (praise, free time, etc.) for small improvements. And when we find that we must break a complex task into small pieces that are easier to accomplish but less fulfilling in their own right—for instance, drill-and-practice activities that foster automaticity for basic math facts—we'll probably need to reinforce students' many seemingly meaningless successes. However, once students have mastered tasks and skills to a level that brings them feelings of genuine accomplishment, extrinsic reinforcers may no longer be necessary (J. Cameron, 2001; Covington, 1992; Deci, Koestner, & Ryan, 2001; Hidi & Harackiewicz, 2000).

🍏 *Determine whether particular "reinforcers" are truly reinforcing for students.* Different students have different needs and desires—factors that underlie their *motivation*—that influence the effectiveness of various reinforcers (McGill, 1999; Michael, 2000; Rispoli et al., 2011). Accordingly, the use of reinforcement is far more effective when reinforcers are tailored to individual students. In some cases we can let students choose their *own* reinforcers and perhaps choose different reinforcers on different occasions. Children seem to prefer having some choice in the reinforcers for which they work (Geckeler, Libby, Graff, & Ahearn, 2000; Sran & Borrero, 2010; Tiger, Hanley, & Hernandez, 2006; Ulke-Kurcuoglu & Kircaali-Iftar, 2010).

One useful strategy for a class with many chronic misbehavers is a **token economy**, in which students who exhibit desired behaviors receive tokens—perhaps specially printed "class dollars" or teacher-initialed checkmarks on a slip of paper—that they can collect and later use to "purchase" a variety of *backup reinforcers*—perhaps small treats, free time in the reading center, or a prime position in the lunch line. In such instances the tokens often become effective reinforcers in and of themselves. Perhaps they become secondary reinforcers through repeated association with other reinforcing objects and events, or perhaps they're effective simply because they provide feedback that students are doing something well.

By and large, however, we should stay away from concrete reinforcers (e.g., toys and candy) as much as possible. Such reinforcers can be expensive and distract students' attention away from their schoolwork. Fortunately, many less tangible reinforcers—such as positive feedback, special privileges, and favorite activities—and reinforcement at home for school behaviors can be quite effective with school-age children and adolescents (e.g., Feltz et al., 1999; Homme, deBaca, Devine, Steinhorst, & Rickert, 1963; Kelley & Carper, 1988). The Creating a Productive Classroom Environment feature "Identifying Effective Reinforcers for Different Students" offers some widely recommended strategies.

🍏 *Make response–consequence contingencies explicit.* Reinforcement is typically more effective when students know exactly which behaviors will lead to which consequences. For example, kindergarten students are more likely to respond appropriately if they're told, "The quietest group will be first to get in line for recess." And high school students are more likely to complete their Spanish assignments if they know that regularly doing so will earn them a field trip to a local Cinco de Mayo festival.

**token economy** Technique in which desired behaviors are reinforced by small, insignificant items (tokens) that learners can use to "purchase" a variety of other, more desirable reinforcers.

Chapter 11 explores motivation in depth.

Use concrete reinforcers (e.g., toys, candy) only if less tangible reinforcers are ineffective.

## Creating a Productive Classroom Environment

### Identifying Effective Reinforcers for Different Students

🍎 **Give students choices among two or more alternatives.**

A high school teacher is working with a boy who has a significant intellectual disability and chronic behavior problems. On various occasions, she gives him different choices about which of two things he'd prefer to do. For example, she might give him a choice between (1) talking with her versus playing alone with favorite items, (2) working with her on an assigned task versus sitting by himself with nothing to do, or (3) working with her on an assigned task versus playing alone with favorite items. From the student's pattern of choices, the teacher concludes that her attention is an effective reinforcer for the student.

🍎 **Ask students (or perhaps their parents) about consequences they would find especially appealing.**

A first-grade teacher always includes his students in parent–teacher conferences. At one such conference, the teacher expresses his delight about the progress a student has made in the last few weeks but adds, "I've seen a lot of inconsistency in Janie's performance. Sometimes she works very hard, but at other times she doesn't put much effort into her schoolwork, and occasionally she doesn't complete assignments at all." Together the teacher, Janie, and her parents agree that successfully completed assignments will earn her points toward the bicycle she has been asking her parents for.

🍎 **Make use of the Premack principle: Students will often engage in behaviors they don't especially enjoy so that they can do something else they *do* enjoy.**

After class one day, a ninth-grade teacher commends a student for his desire to make other people laugh. Then she points out the downside of his sense of humor: "Unfortunately, your jokes can distract your classmates from what they're supposed to be doing, and sometimes I have a hard time getting class discussions back on topic." She promises the student that if he can keep his attention and remarks focused on classroom subject matter throughout a class period, she'll give him the last two or three minutes of the period to tell the class a joke or two.

*Source:* W. K. Berg et al., 2007 (student with intellectual disability example).

🍎 **Provide a small amount of free time contingent on desired behaviors.**

A fifth-grade teacher allows students to engage in favorite activities during the free time they earn each day. Some students work on the classroom computer, others work on art projects, and still others talk with friends.

🍎 **Observe students' behaviors and written work, keeping a lookout for activities and consequences that students seem to appreciate.**

At home one night, 11-year-old Amie writes the entry below in the class journal that she and her teacher regularly use to communicate. The entry reveals that Amie clearly enjoys playing soccer; in other words, soccer is intrinsically reinforcing for her. It appears, too, that Amie appreciates attention from her coach, probably because (1) he might have her play more and (2) she would like feedback about what she's doing well and how she might improve her skills.

> Today I had a soccer game to see who would go to the state finals. Unfortunly we lost. I was very dis apontated, not because we lost, but because my coach only put me in for 10 mins. I feel that the coach was ignoring me and was just focused on winning. I wish the coach would take notice of me on the side lines and not just focuse on winning.

---

Some students need explicit and frequent information about response–consequence contingencies. For example, watch "Incentive Systems for Academic Performance."

One concrete way of communicating both behavioral expectations and response–reinforcement contingencies is a **contingency contract**. To develop such a contract, the teacher meets with a student to discuss a problem behavior (e.g., talking to friends during independent seatwork or speaking disrespectfully to classmates). The teacher and the student then identify and agree on desired behaviors that the student will demonstrate (e.g., completing seatwork assignments within a certain time frame or speaking with classmates in a friendly, respectful manner). The two also agree on one or more reinforcers (e.g., a certain amount of free time or points earned toward a particular privilege or prize). Together the teacher and the student write and sign a contract that describes the desired behaviors and contingent reinforcers. Contingency contracts can be highly effective in improving a variety of academic and social behaviors (K. L. Lane, Menzies, Bruhn, & Crnobori, 2011; D. L. Miller & Kelley, 1994).

🍏 *When you want to encourage the same behavior in a group of students, consider using a group contingency.* In a **group contingency**, students are reinforced only when *everyone* in a particular group—perhaps even an entire class—achieves at a certain level or behaves appropriately. Following are two examples of whole-class contingencies:

- A class of 32 fourth graders was doing poorly on weekly spelling tests, with an average of only 12 students (38%) earning perfect test scores in any given week. Hoping for improvement, the teacher announced that any student with a perfect score would get free time later in the week, and the average number of perfect spelling tests rose to 25 (78%) a week. But then the teacher added a group contingency: Whenever the entire class achieved perfect spelling tests by Friday, the class could listen to the radio for 15 minutes. The group contingency produced an average of 30 perfect spelling tests (94%) a week (Lovitt, Guppy, & Blattner, 1969).

- Another fourth-grade teacher was dealing with an especially unruly class: In any given minute, chances were good that one or more students would be talking out of turn or getting out of their seats. In a desperate move, the teacher divided the class into two teams that competed in a "good behavior game." Every time that a student was observed talking out of turn or getting out of his or her seat, the student's team received a mark on the chalkboard. The team receiving fewer marks during a lesson won special privileges (e.g., having some free time or being first in the lunch line). If both teams had five marks or fewer, everyone won privileges. Misbehaviors dropped almost immediately to less than 20% of their initial frequency (Barrish, Saunders, & Wolf, 1969; also see J. M. Donaldson, Vollmer, Krous, Downs, & Berard, 2011; Taub & Pearrow, 2006).

Group contingencies are an important component of many cooperative learning activities. For example, watch "Cooperative Learning."

Group contingencies are clearly effective in improving academic achievement and classroom behavior *if* everyone in the group is capable of making the desired responses (Heck, Collins, & Peterson, 2001; Kellam, Rebok, Ialongo, & Mayer, 1994; S. L. Robinson & Griesemer, 2006). Peer pressure and social reinforcers seem to play a role here. Many students encourage misbehaving classmates to behave appropriately and then reinforce those who do so. Furthermore, when students' own success is riding on the success of their peers, students who have mastered a topic begin to tutor students who are struggling (D. W. Johnson & Johnson, 1987; Pigott, Fantuzzo, & Clement, 1986; Slavin, 1983). Whenever we use group contingencies, however, we must closely monitor students' behaviors to make sure that any peer pressure is socially appropriate—for instance, that students aren't ridiculing or bullying their low-performing classmates.

When imposing a group contingency, make sure that everyone in the group is capable of making the desired response.

🍎 *Monitor students' progress.* Whenever we use reinforcement as a primary strategy for increasing desired behaviors—especially with students who have been performing poorly—we should ideally determine whether our efforts are bringing about the desired results. In particular, we should assess the frequency of the desired terminal behavior both before and during our attempts to increase it. The frequency of a behavior *before* we intentionally begin reinforcement is its baseline level. Some behaviors occur frequently even when they're not being explicitly reinforced; others occur rarely or not at all.

By comparing the baseline frequency of a response with its frequency after we begin reinforcing it, we can determine whether our strategy is actually having an effect. As an example, let's look once again at James in the opening case study. He rarely turns in classroom assignments; this is a behavior with a low baseline. An obvious reinforcer to use with James is attention—a consequence that, until now, has effectively reinforced such counterproductive behaviors as making inappropriate comments in class and throwing objects across the room. When we make our attention contingent on James's turning in assignments, rather than on his refusing to do so, we might see an almost immediate increase in the number of assignments we receive from James. But if we see no significant change, we might need to consider alternative reinforcers. We should also consider and address possible reasons—perhaps poor reading skills—why he might be trying to avoid his schoolwork.

**contingency contract** Formal agreement between a teacher and a student that identifies behaviors the student will exhibit and the reinforcers that will follow.

**group contingency** Situation in which everyone in a group must make a particular response before reinforcement occurs.

**baseline** Frequency of a response before it is intentionally and systematically reinforced.

🍎 *Administer reinforcement consistently until the desired behavior occurs at a desired rate.* As you might guess, desired responses increase more quickly when they're reinforced every time they occur—that is, when the responses lead to continuous reinforcement. Continuous reinforcement is most important when students are first learning new behaviors, perhaps when they begin a new school year or perhaps when they must tackle a challenging new task. In some instances we may need to begin by reinforcing *effort* (e.g., time on task) and switch to reinforcing *accuracy* only after students have gained some proficiency (Lannie & Martens, 2004).

**continuous reinforcement** Reinforcement of a response every time it occurs.

🍎 *Once a behavior is well established, gradually—but only gradually—wean students from extrinsic reinforcement.* Just as reinforced behaviors increase in frequency, nonreinforced behaviors

**extinction (in instrumental conditioning)** Gradual disappearance of an acquired response as a result of repeated lack of reinforcement.

**intermittent reinforcement** Reinforcement of a response only occasionally, with some occurrences of the response *not* being reinforced.

**shaping** Process of reinforcing successively closer and closer approximations to a desired terminal behavior.

Different patterns of intermittent reinforcement—different *schedules of reinforcement*—have somewhat different effects on learning and extinction. Learn more about their varying effects in "Schedules of Reinforcement."

After students have begun to exhibit a desired behavior regularly, continue to reinforce it intermittently to encourage persistence and prevent extinction.

often *decrease* in frequency and may eventually disappear altogether. Like the decrease of a conditioned response in classical conditioning, the decrease and eventual disappearance of a nonreinforced response in instrumental conditioning is known as extinction.

Intrinsic reinforcement can, of course, maintain many productive behaviors over the long run, both in the classroom and in the outside world. But as previously noted, students don't necessarily find *all* desired behaviors enjoyable in and of themselves. When certain behaviors have no intrinsic appeal, intermittent reinforcement—reinforcing a behavior on some occasions but not others—provides a viable alternative.

As an example, let's consider Molly and Maria, two students who rarely participate in class discussions. Their teacher, Mr. Oliver, decides to reinforce the girls for raising their hands. Each time Molly raises her hand, Mr. Oliver calls on her and praises her response. But when Maria raises her hand, Mr. Oliver isn't always looking in her direction; hence he calls on her on some occasions but not others. Thus, Molly is getting continuous reinforcement and Maria is getting intermittent reinforcement. Other things being equal, Molly's hand raising should increase more rapidly than Maria's.

Now let's move ahead a few weeks. Thanks to Mr. Oliver's attentiveness to Molly and Maria, both girls are regularly volunteering in class. Consequently, Mr. Oliver turns his attention to other quiet students and no longer reinforces Molly and Maria when they raise their hands. As you might expect, the girls begin to participate less often; in other words, we see signs of extinction. But which girl's class participation will extinguish more quickly?

If you predicted that Molly's volunteering will decrease more rapidly than Maria's, you're right. Responses that have previously been continuously reinforced tend to extinguish quickly once reinforcement stops. But because Maria has been receiving intermittent reinforcement, she's accustomed to being occasionally ignored and may not realize that reinforcement has stopped altogether. Behaviors that have been reinforced only intermittently decrease slowly, if at all, after reinforcement ceases. In other words, these behaviors can be more *resistant to extinction* (e.g., Ferster & Skinner, 1957; Freeland & Noell, 1999; Pipkin & Vollmer, 2009).

Once students have mastered a desired behavior and are using it regularly, then, we should continue to reinforce it intermittently, especially if it has no intrinsically reinforcing effect. Mr. Oliver doesn't need to call on Molly and Maria every time they raise their hands, but he should certainly call on them once in a while. In a similar manner, we might occasionally reinforce diligent study habits, completed homework assignments, prosocial behaviors, and so on—even for the best of students—as a way of encouraging these responses to continue.

## SHAPING NEW BEHAVIORS

What if a desired behavior has a baseline level of *zero?* How can we encourage a behavior that a student never exhibits at all, at least not in its ideal form? In such cases behaviorists suggest gradually shaping the behavior: reinforcing a series of responses—known as *successive approximations*—that increasingly resemble the terminal behavior. Shaping involves these steps:

1. Reinforce any response that in some way resembles the terminal behavior.
2. Reinforce a response that more closely approximates the terminal behavior (while no longer reinforcing the previously reinforced response).
3. Reinforce a response that resembles the terminal behavior even more closely.
4. Continue reinforcing closer and closer approximations to the terminal behavior.
5. Reinforce only the terminal behavior.

Shape a low-frequency behavior by reinforcing closer and closer approximations over time.

Each response in the sequence is continuously reinforced until it occurs regularly. Only at that point do we begin reinforcing a behavior that more closely approaches the desired end result. As an example, imagine that we have a second grader who can't seem to sit still long enough to get much of anything done. We'd ultimately like her to sit still for 20-minute periods, but we may first have to reinforce her for staying in her seat for just 2 minutes, gradually increasing the required sitting time as she makes progress.

**FIGURE 9.1** As Jeff moved through the elementary grades, his teachers gradually shaped his handwriting, in part by reducing the spacing between lines and, later, omitting some of the lines.

Grade 1    I like to riyt.

Grade 2    One day Lonely was eating his brefisk

Grade 4    When we left Greeley. I didn't want to go. On the same day we stoped at a restrant. Then we went on. In the ernen

---

antecedent stimulus  Stimulus that influences the probability that a particular response will follow.

antecedent response  Response that influences the probability that a certain other response will follow.

cueing  Use of a verbal or nonverbal signal to indicate that a certain behavior is desired or that a certain behavior should stop.

---

We can often use shaping to help students acquire complex physical and psychomotor skills. For example, in the early elementary grades teachers gradually shape students' handwriting skills—for instance, expecting increasingly small and well-shaped letters (see Figure 9.1). And in secondary schools, physical education teachers and coaches may teach and expect increasingly proficient athletic skills (e.g., J. V. Stokes, Luiselli, & Reed, 2010).

In much the same way, we can use shaping—and teachers often do so—to teach students to work independently on assignments. We begin by giving first graders structured tasks that may take only 5 to 10 minutes to complete. As students move through the elementary school years, we expect them to work independently for longer periods and begin to give them short assignments to do at home. By the time students reach high school, they have extended study halls and complete lengthy assignments on their own after school hours. In the college years, student assignments require a great deal of independence and self-direction.

## BRINGING ANTECEDENT STIMULI AND RESPONSES INTO THE PICTURE

In our discussion of instrumental conditioning so far, we've focused on the *consequences* of behaviors. But stimuli and responses that *precede* a desired behavior—antecedent stimuli and antecedent responses—can have effects as well. Here we'll look at several phenomena that involve antecedent stimuli, as well as one phenomenon (behavioral momentum) that involves antecedent responses.

### CUEING

Students are more likely to behave appropriately when they're given reminders—often called *cues* or *prompts*—that certain behaviors are expected (e.g., Northup et al., 1995; Shabani et al., 2002). Such cueing sometimes involves a nonverbal signal, such as flicking overhead lights off and on to remind students to use their "indoor voices." At other times it involves a verbal reminder about what students should be doing. Subtle hints are often effective for older students (e.g., "I see some art supplies that still need to be put away"), whereas more explicit hints may be necessary for younger children (e.g., "Table 3 needs to clean up its art supplies before it can go to lunch").

Quickly and unobtrusively cue students about appropriate behaviors, perhaps through a flick of the light switch or short verbal reminder.

setting event  Complex environmental condition that is likely to evoke certain voluntary behaviors.

generalization (in instrumental conditioning)  Phenomenon in which a person makes a voluntary response to a stimulus that is similar to one previously associated with a response–reinforcement contingency.

discrimination  Phenomenon in which a student learns that a response is reinforced in the presence of one stimulus but not in the presence of another, similar stimulus.

behavioral momentum  Increased tendency for a learner to make a particular response immediately after making similar responses.

Create an environment that naturally evokes desired behaviors, and provide opportunities for students to practice desired behaviors in a variety of settings.

Describe conditions under which certain behaviors are appropriate, and reinforce the behaviors only when they *are* appropriate.

Take advantage of behavioral momentum, assigning easy tasks as a lead-in to similar but more challenging ones.

## SETTING EVENTS

In cueing we use specific stimuli to prompt students to behave in particular ways. An alternative approach is to create an overall environment—a setting event—that's apt to evoke desired behaviors. For example, young children are more likely to interact with peers during free-play time if they have a relatively small area in which to play and if the toys available to them (e.g., balls, puppets) encourage cooperation and group activity (W. H. Brown, Fox, & Brady, 1987; Frost, Shin, & Jacobs, 1998; S. S. Martin, Brady, & Williams, 1991). Similarly, the nature of the games children are asked to play influences the behaviors they exhibit: Cooperative games promote cooperative behavior, whereas competitive games promote aggressive behavior (Bay-Hinitz, Peterson, & Quilitch, 1994).

## GENERALIZATION

Once children have learned that a response is likely to be reinforced in one set of circumstances (which serve as antecedent stimuli), they're apt to make the same response in a similar situation. In other words, they show generalization. For example, after an especially fidgety student has learned to sit quietly and attentively for 20-minute periods in her second-grade classroom, she may generalize that behavior to her third-grade classroom the following year. And once a student has learned cursive writing at school, he's apt to use cursive in his out-of-school writing tasks. Generalization of newly acquired behaviors is most likely to occur when students have opportunities to practice them in diverse settings (Haring & Liberty, 1990; B. M. Johnson et al., 2006; T. F. Stokes & Baer, 1977).

This process of generalization should remind you of the generalization that occurs in classical conditioning: In both cases an individual learns a response to one stimulus and then responds in the same way to a similar stimulus. The major difference is one of learner control: Generalization involves an automatic, involuntary response in classical conditioning but a voluntary response in instrumental conditioning.

## DISCRIMINATION

Sometimes responses are reinforced only when certain environmental conditions (i.e., certain antecedent stimuli) are present. This ability to distinguish between conditions in which a particular behavior will and won't be reinforced is known as discrimination. For example, teenage boys should certainly learn that slapping a peer on the fanny may be quite acceptable when celebrating an athletic victory with teammates but is *not* acceptable when greeting a female classmate in the hall. Some students may need explicit guidance about the circumstances in which particular behaviors are and are not likely to be reinforced.

It's occasionally helpful to use cueing to help students determine when certain behaviors are allowed. For example, in one recent study, children in three elementary classrooms were having trouble determining when they could and could not request a teacher's assistance. Their teachers began to wear green and red leis at different times and told them, "While I am wearing the green lei, I will be able to answer your questions. While I am wearing the red lei, I will not be able to answer your questions." This simple procedure minimized student requests at inopportune moments (Cammilleri, Tiger, & Hanley, 2008, p. 301).

## BEHAVIORAL MOMENTUM

In many cases students are more likely to make desired responses if they're already making similar responses—a phenomenon known as behavioral momentum (Ardoin, Martens, & Wolfe, 1999; Belfiore, Lee, Vargas, & Skinner, 1997; Mace et al., 1988). For example, imagine that we have low-achieving high school students with a history of refusing to do math assignments. Such students are more likely to attempt difficult three-digit multiplication problems after they've first worked on a few simple one-digit problems (Belfiore et al., 1997). Similarly, we might ask students to tidy up a messy classroom after they've already cleaned their own desktops or to try a backward roll after they've successfully executed a forward roll. In general, we can promote behavioral momentum by assigning relatively easy or enjoyable tasks that lead naturally into more complex and potentially frustrating ones.

# Strategies for Discouraging Undesirable Behaviors

Our focus so far has been primarily on promoting desirable behaviors. But we must also actively discourage *un*desirable behaviors—those that jeopardize students' classroom success or their class-mates' well-being. Behaviorists offer several possible approaches that we look at now.

## CREATING CONDITIONS FOR EXTINCTION

One way to reduce the frequency of an inappropriate response is simply to make sure it's never reinforced. For instance, a class clown whose antics are ignored might stop distracting his class-mates, and a child who never gets what she wants by insulting others may begin to speak to them more respectfully.

There are several points to keep in mind about extinction, however. First, once rein-forcement stops, a previously reinforced response may initially *increase* for a short time (Lerman & Iwata, 1995; McGill, 1999). For example, imagine you have a television set that works only when you bang on it once or twice. At some point something changes inside your TV that makes the banging ineffective, but you don't realize this at first, so you bang it *many times and very hard* before you finally give up. In much the same way, students whose inappropriate behaviors have previously been reinforced may begin to behave even *less* appropriately once their original behaviors are no longer working for them. Fortunately, such increases in misbehavior are usually temporary, but they can certainly try our patience and perhaps tempt us into paying attention to—and thereby inadvertently reinforcing—the more extreme responses.

Second, if we ignore a student's misbehavior in an effort to extinguish it, we must be sure that we don't ignore the student altogether. Instead, we should give a misbehaving student atten-tion for doing things *well* and also at random intervals throughout the school day (Austin & Soeda, 2008).

Third, we may sometimes have situations in which removing a reinforcer has no notice-able effect on a student's counterproductive behavior. Perhaps the behavior has previously been reinforced only intermittently, thus making it fairly resistant to extinction (recall the earlier Molly/Maria example). Or perhaps the behavior is being reinforced in other ways—say, by class-mates' attention or the release of pent-up energy. In such cases, one or more of the strategies that follow are called for.

 Identify and try to remove reinforcers that may be maintaining an undesirable behavior.

## CUEING INAPPROPRIATE BEHAVIORS

Just as we can use cueing to remind students about what they should be doing, we can also cue them about what they should *not* be doing (Emmer, 1987; Northup et al., 1995; Woolfolk & Brooks, 1985). For example, we might use *body language*—perhaps making eye contact and rais-ing an eyebrow—or *physical proximity*—moving closer to the student and standing there until the problem behavior stops. When subtlety doesn't work, a brief *verbal cue* may be in order—perhaps stating a student's name or (if necessary) pointing out an inappropriate behavior (e.g., "Lucy, put away your cell phone").

Use physical or verbal cues to discourage inappropriate behavior.

## REINFORCING INCOMPATIBLE BEHAVIORS

Often we can reduce the frequency of an unproductive behavior simply by reinforcing an *alterna-tive* behavior. Ideally, the two behaviors are incompatible behaviors, which can't be performed simultaneously. For example, try the following exercise.

### EXPERIENCING FIRSTHAND
### ASLEEP ON YOUR FEET

Have you ever tried to sleep while standing up? Horses can do it, but most of us humans really can't. In fact, there are many pairs of responses that are impossible to perform simultaneously.

**incompatible behaviors** Two or more behaviors that cannot be performed simultaneously.

Take a minute to identify something you can't possibly do when you perform each of these activities:

| *When you . . .* | *You cannot simultaneously . . .* |
|---|---|
| Sit down | _____ |
| Eat crackers | _____ |
| Take a walk | _____ |

Obviously there are many possible right answers. For instance, sitting is incompatible with standing. Eating crackers is incompatible with singing—or at least with singing *well.* Taking a walk is incompatible with taking a nap. In each case it's physically impossible to perform both activities at exactly the same time.

When our attempts at extinction or cueing are unsuccessful, reinforcement of one or more behaviors that are incompatible with a problem behavior is often quite effective (K. Lane, Falk, & Wehby, 2006; Lerman, Kelley, Vorndran, Kuhn, & LaRue, 2002; Pipkin, Vollmer, & Sloman, 2010). This is the approach we're taking when we reinforce a hyperactive student for sitting quietly: Sitting is incompatible with getting-out-of-seat and roaming-around-the-room behaviors. It's also an approach we might use to deal with forgetfulness (we reinforce students when they remember to do what they're supposed to do), being off-task (we reinforce on-task behavior), and verbal abusiveness (we reinforce prosocial statements). And consider how we might deal with a chronic litterbug (Krumboltz & Krumboltz, 1972):

Encourage and reinforce responses that are incompatible with undesirable behaviors.

> Walt often leaves banana peels, sunflower seed shells, and other garbage in and outside the school building. When the school faculty establishes an Anti-Litter Committee, it puts Walt on the committee, and the committee eventually elects him as its chairman. Under Walt's leadership, the committee institutes an anti-litter campaign, complete with posters and lunchroom monitors, and Walt receives considerable recognition for the campaign's success. Subsequently, school personnel no longer find Walt's garbage littering the building and school grounds.

## USING PUNISHMENT WHEN NECESSARY

Some misbehaviors require an immediate remedy—for instance, they might interfere significantly with classroom learning or reflect total disregard for other people's rights and welfare. Consider this example:

> Bonnie doesn't handle frustration well. Whenever she encounters an obstacle she can't immediately overcome, she hits, punches, kicks, or breaks something. Once, during a class Valentine's Day party, she accidentally drops her cupcake. When she discovers that it's no longer edible, she throws her milk carton across the room, hitting another child on the head.

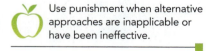

Use punishment when alternative approaches are inapplicable or have been ineffective.

Bonnie's troublesome behaviors are hard to extinguish because they aren't being reinforced to begin with—at least not extrinsically. Also, there are no obvious incompatible responses that might be reinforced instead. And presumably Bonnie's teacher has often cued her about her inappropriate behaviors. When other strategies are inapplicable or ineffective, punishment is a potentially viable alternative.

A frequent criticism of punishment is that it's inhumane, or somehow cruel and barbaric. Indeed, certain forms of punishment, such as physical abuse and public humiliation, do constitute inhumane treatment. We must be *extremely careful* when we use punishment in the classroom. If administered judiciously, however, some forms of mild punishment can lead to rapid reductions in misbehavior without causing physical or psychological harm. And when we can decrease counterproductive classroom behaviors quickly and effectively—especially when those behaviors are harmful to self or others—punishment may, in fact, be one of the most humane approaches we can take (Lerman & Vorndran, 2002). Following are several guidelines for using punishment effectively and humanely.

🍏 *Choose a consequence that is truly punishing without being overly severe.* Any unpleasant consequence must be strong enough to discourage students from engaging further in the punished behavior (Boyanton, 2010; Landrum & Kauffman, 2006; Lerman & Vorndran, 2002). But unnecessarily harsh punishments—those that far surpass the severity of the crime—are apt to lead to such undesirable side effects as resentment, hostility, aggression, and escape behavior. Furthermore, although severe punishment can quickly suppress a response, that response may reappear at its original level once the punisher has left the scene (Appel & Peterson, 1965; Azrin, 1960; Landrum & Kauffman, 2006). The ultimate purpose of administering punishment is to communicate that the limits of acceptable behavior have been exceeded, *not* to exact revenge and retaliation.

🍏 *Inform students ahead of time that certain behaviors will be punished, and explain how those behaviors will be punished.* When students are informed of response–punishment contingencies ahead of time, they're less likely to engage in forbidden behaviors, and they're less likely to be surprised or resentful if punishment must be administered (Boyanton, 2010; Moles, 1990). Ultimately, students must learn that their behaviors influence the consequences they experience— that they have some control over what happens to them.

🍏 *Follow through with specified consequences.* A mistake some teachers make is to continually threaten punishment without ever following through. One warning is desirable, but repeated warnings are not. Consider the teacher who says, "If you bring that rubber snake to class one more time, I'll take it away!" but never does take away the snake. This teacher is giving the message that no response–punishment contingency really exists.

🍏 *Administer punishment privately, especially when other students are not aware of the transgression.* By administering punishment in private, we protect students from public embarrassment and humiliation. We also eliminate the possibility that the punishment will draw classmates' attention—a potential reinforcer for the very behavior we're trying to eliminate.

🍏 *Emphasize that it is the behavior—not the student—that is unacceptable, and explain why it is unacceptable.* We must explain exactly why a certain behavior can't be tolerated in the classroom—perhaps because it interferes with learning, threatens other students' safety or self-esteem, or damages school property. In other words, punishment should be accompanied by induction. Punishment is far more effective when accompanied by one or more reasons that the punished behavior is unacceptable (Hoffman, 1975, 2000; Parke, 1974; D. G. Perry & Perry, 1983).

🍏 *Administer punishment within the context of a warm, supportive interpersonal relationship.* Punishment is more effective when the person administering it has previously established a good working relationship with the student (Landrum & Kauffman, 2006; Nucci, 2001). The message should ultimately be this: "I care for you and want you to succeed, and your current behavior is interfering with your success."

🍏 *Simultaneously teach and reinforce desirable alternative behaviors.* Punishment of misbehavior is almost always more effective when appropriate behaviors are being reinforced at the same time (Landrum & Kauffman, 2006; Lerman & Vorndran, 2002). Furthermore, by reinforcing desirable responses as well as punishing undesirable ones, we give students the positive, optimistic message that, yes, behavior can and will improve. Ultimately, the overall classroom atmosphere we create must be a positive one that highlights the *good* things students do.

🍏 *Monitor the punishment's effectiveness.* Remember that punishment is defined by its effect on behavior. True punishment decreases the response it follows, typically quite rapidly (R. V. Hall et al., 1971; Landrum & Kauffman, 2006). If a given consequence doesn't decrease the response it's intended to punish, the consequence may not be aversive to the individual being "punished." In fact, it may even be reinforcing.

**induction** Explanation of why a certain behavior is unacceptable, often with a focus on the pain or distress that someone has caused another.

Understanding that one's own behaviors influence consequences is an example of an *attribution* (see Chapter 11).

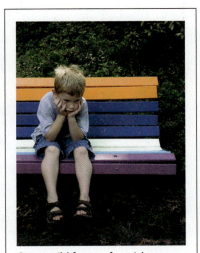

Some mild forms of punishment, such as a brief time-out in a quiet corner away from peers, can reduce counterproductive behaviors, but we must monitor their effectiveness for different students.

**applied behavior analysis (ABA)**
Systematic application of behaviorist principles in educational and therapeutic settings.

**functional analysis** Examination of inappropriate behavior and its antecedents and consequences to determine one or more purposes (functions) that the behavior might serve for the learner.

# Addressing Especially Difficult Classroom Behaviors

Behaviorist principles can be extremely helpful in tackling difficult and chronic behavior problems. In this section we consider three related approaches for addressing especially challenging behaviors. Often they're planned and carried out by one or more teachers in consultation with a school psychologist or other specialist.

## APPLIED BEHAVIOR ANALYSIS

**Applied behavior analysis**, or **ABA**, is a group of procedures that systematically apply behaviorist principles in changing behavior. (You might also see such terms as *behavior modification, behavior therapy,* and *contingency management.*) Applied behavior analysis is based on the assumptions that (1) behavior problems result from past and present environmental conditions and (2) modifying a learner's present environment will promote more productive responses. When teachers and therapists use ABA to help a student acquire more appropriate classroom behavior, they typically use strategies such as these:

- Describe both the present behaviors and the desired terminal behaviors in objectively measurable terms.
- Identify one or more effective reinforcers.
- Develop a specific intervention or treatment plan, which may involve reinforcement of desired behaviors, shaping, extinction, reinforcement of incompatible behaviors, punishment, or some combination of these.
- Give explicit instruction related to desired behaviors.
- Measure the frequency of desired and undesired behaviors both before the intervention (i.e., at baseline level) and during the intervention in order to monitor the intervention's effectiveness; modify the program if necessary.
- Take steps to promote generalization of new behaviors (e.g., through practice in various realistic situations).
- Gradually phase out the treatment (e.g., through intermittent reinforcement) after desired behaviors are occurring regularly.

The systematic use of behaviorist strategies such as these can lead to significant improvements in academic performance and classroom behavior. For example, when we reinforce students for academic accomplishments, we're apt to see noticeable progress in such areas as reading, spelling, creative writing, and math. And when we reinforce appropriate classroom behaviors—paying attention, interacting cooperatively and prosocially with classmates, and so on—misbehaviors decrease (S. N. Elliott & Busse, 1991; Evertson & Weinstein, 2006; Piersel, 1987).

One likely reason that ABA often works so well is that it gives students clear and consistent messages about which behaviors are acceptable and which are not. Another likely reason is that through the gradual process of *shaping,* students begin to practice new behaviors only when they're truly ready to acquire them; thus, their probability of achieving success and reinforcement is quite high.

## FUNCTIONAL ANALYSIS AND POSITIVE BEHAVIOR SUPPORT

Traditional ABA focuses largely on changing response–reinforcement contingencies to bring about more appropriate behavior. Some behaviorists suggest that we also consider the purposes, or *functions,* that students' inappropriate behaviors may serve. Such an approach is known as **functional analysis** (you might also see the terms *functional assessment* and *functional behavioral assessment*). Functional analysis involves collecting data regarding the specific conditions (i.e., antecedent stimuli) in which students tend to misbehave and also the consequences (i.e., reinforcers, punishments, or both) that typically follow the misbehaviors. Thus, we would collect data related to the three parts of a stimulus–response–stimulus sequence:

Antecedent → Behavior → Consequence

For example, we've speculated that in the opening case study, James misbehaves in order to get the attention he apparently can't get in more productive ways and possibly also to escape certain classroom tasks. Functional analyses have shown that students with chronic classroom behavior problems often misbehave when they're asked to do difficult or unpleasant tasks (this is the *antecedent*) and that their misbehavior either allows them to escape these tasks or gains them the attention of others (these are possible *consequences*) (McComas et al., 2003; Mueller et al., 2011; Van Camp et al., 2000).

Positive behavior support (PBS) takes the process a step further: After identifying the purposes that inappropriate behaviors might serve, a teacher—or, more often, a team of teachers and other professionals—develops and carries out a plan to encourage appropriate behaviors. In particular, positive behavior support involves strategies such as these:

- Teach behaviors that can serve the same purpose as—and can therefore replace—inappropriate behaviors.
- Modify the classroom environment to minimize conditions that might trigger inappropriate behaviors.
- Establish a predictable daily routine as a way of minimizing anxiety and making the student feel more comfortable and secure.
- Give the student opportunities to make choices; in this way the student can often gain desired outcomes without having to resort to inappropriate behavior.
- Make adaptations in the curriculum, instruction, or both to maximize the likelihood of academic success (e.g., build on the student's interests, present material at a slower pace, or intersperse challenging tasks among easier and more enjoyable ones).
- Monitor the frequency of various behaviors to determine whether the intervention is working or, instead, requires modification. (Crone & Horner, 2003; Ruef, Higgins, Glaeser, & Patnode, 1998; Wheeler & Richey, 2010)

The following case study (summarized from DeVault, Krug, & Fake [1996]) provides an example of how functional analysis and positive behavior support might be used in combination:

> Nine-year-old Samantha had been identified as having a mild form of autism and moderate speech disabilities. She frequently ran out of her third-grade classroom, damaging school property and classmates' belongings in her flight. When an adult tried to intervene, she would fight back by biting, hitting, kicking, or pulling hair. On such occasions school personnel often asked her parents to take her home.
>
> By systematically collecting data on Samantha's classroom performance, a team of teachers and specialists discovered that her misbehaviors typically occurred when she either was given or was expecting a difficult assignment. Departures from the regular schedule or the absence of favorite teachers further increased the frequency of misbehaviors.
>
> The team hypothesized that Samantha's undesirable behaviors served two purposes: They (1) helped her escape unpleasant academic tasks and (2) enabled her to gain the attention of valued adults. The team suspected, too, that Samantha felt as if she had little or no control over classroom activities and that she yearned for more social interaction with her teachers and classmates.
>
> Armed with this information, the team took several steps:
>
> - Samantha was given a consistent and predictable daily schedule that included frequent breaks from potentially challenging academic tasks and numerous opportunities to interact with others.
> - Samantha was given goal sheets from which she could choose the academic tasks she would work on, the length of time she would work on them, and the reinforcer she would receive for achieving each goal.
> - Samantha was taught how to ask for help on challenging tasks.
> - When Samantha felt she needed a break from academic work, she could ask to spend some time in the "relaxation room," a quiet and private space where she could sit in a beanbag chair and listen to soothing audiotapes.

When a student's problem behavior persists, try to identify functions that the behavior might serve for the student.

**positive behavior support** Variation of traditional applied behavior analysis that involves identifying the purposes of undesirable behaviors and encouraging alternative behaviors that more appropriately accomplish those purposes.

**schoolwide positive behavior support** Systematic use of behaviorist principles to encourage and reinforce productive behaviors in all students; typically involves multiple layers of support in order to accommodate the varying needs and behavior patterns of different students.

- If Samantha tried to leave the classroom, an adult would place her immediately in the relaxation room, where she could calm down without a lot of adult attention.
- Samantha was given explicit instruction in how to interact appropriately with classmates. Initially, she earned points for appropriate social behaviors and could trade them for special treats (e.g., a family trip to Dairy Queen or a video store). Eventually, her new social skills led to natural consequences—friendly interactions with peers—that made extrinsic reinforcers unnecessary (DeVault et al., 1996).

Samantha's problem behaviors didn't disappear overnight, but they showed a dramatic decline over the next few months. By the time Samantha was 12 years old and in sixth grade, her grades consistently earned her a place on the honor roll, and she had a group of friends with whom she participated in extracurricular activities. Her teachers described her as being sociable, inquisitive, and creative. Her principal called her a "model student" (DeVault et al., 1996).

In recent years some schools have successfully instituted schoolwide positive behavior support programs that encourage productive behaviors in *all* students. These programs typically include most or all of the following:

Positive behavior support is sometimes use on a schoolwide basis. For example, watch "Principals 200 Club."

- Explicitly defining and teaching appropriate behaviors, including productive ways of getting desired outcomes (e.g., teacher attention)
- Designing a curriculum and implementing instructional practices tailored to students' current needs and ability levels
- Giving students opportunities to make choices
- Regularly reinforcing students for behaving appropriately, almost always with praise but often also with token reinforcers that can be traded for special prizes and privileges
- Providing considerable guidance and support (sometimes including individualized interventions) for students who need them
- Continually monitoring the program's effectiveness by examining office referrals, disciplinary actions, and other relevant data

Such steps often lead to dramatic changes in students' behavior and are especially helpful in schools that have historically had many discipline problems. Furthermore, teachers become more optimistic that they can truly make a difference in improving students' classroom behavior and academic achievement (Ihlo & Nantais, 2010; T. J. Lewis, Newcomer, Trussell, & Richter, 2006; Osher et al., 2010; Warren et al., 2006).

The importance of doing such things will become clearer in the discussions of motivation and affect in Chapter 11.

Positive behavior support clearly has elements of behaviorist theory, including its focus on structuring an environment that reinforces desired behaviors and extinguishes undesirable ones. At the same time, it also incorporates contemporary theories of motivation, as reflected in its attempts to minimize anxiety, provide opportunities for choice making, and promote mastery of classroom tasks.

## Diversity in Student Behaviors and Reactions to Consequences

When we take a behaviorist perspective, we realize that every student brings a unique history of environments and experiences to the classroom, and such diversity is a key reason for the different behavior patterns we see. Some students may have associated particular stimuli with anxiety-arousing events (classical conditioning), and various students have undoubtedly been reinforced and punished—by parents, previous teachers, peers, and so on—for different kinds of behaviors (instrumental conditioning). For example, some students may have been reinforced for completing tasks carefully and thoroughly, whereas others may have been reinforced for completing them quickly and with little regard for quality. Likewise, some students may have been reinforced for initiating interactions with age-mates, whereas others may have been punished (e.g., by peer rejection) for similar outgoing behavior. In some instances, diversity in students' behaviors is the result of the different behaviors that various cultures encourage (i.e., reinforce) and discourage (i.e., punish) in children.

Differences also exist in the consequences students find reinforcing, to some degree as a result of the cultures in which they've grown up. For instance, although students from mainstream Western culture are apt to appreciate praise for their personal accomplishments, many students from Asian cultures are unaccustomed to public praise, preferring instead to have simple compliments given in private along with feedback that helps them improve on their weaknesses. And many Native American students may feel uncomfortable when praised for their work as individuals yet feel quite proud when they receive praise for group success—a preference that's consistent with the cooperative spirit of most Native American groups (Fuller, 2001; Hattie & Gan, 2011; Jiang, 2010; Kitayama, Duffy, & Uchida, 2007).

In some cultures reprimands are often used to communicate concern and affection. For example, on one occasion a teacher in Haiti was reprimanding students for proceeding across a parking lot without her:

*Teacher:* Did I tell you to go?

*Children:* No.

*Teacher:* Can you cross this parking lot by yourselves?

*Children:* No.

*Teacher:* That's right. There are cars here. They're dangerous. I don't want you to go alone. Why do I want you to wait for me, do you know?

*Claudette:* Yes . . . because you like us. (Ballenger, 1992, p. 205)

## ACCOMMODATING STUDENTS WITH SPECIAL NEEDS

The structured, systematic use of behaviorist principles—such as those manifested in positive behavior support—can be especially effective with students who have cognitive, social, or behavioral disabilities. Table 9.4 offers specific recommendations for working with students who have various special needs.

> Keep in mind that students from some cultures are unaccustomed to public praise for their individual accomplishments.

> Chapter 5 identifies specific categories of special needs that fall within the five general categories listed in Table 9.4.

# Strengths and Potential Limitations of Behaviorist Approaches

Behaviorist techniques are especially helpful when we need to address chronic and challenging behavior problems, and in such cases they're often effective when other approaches have failed. However, psychologists have had mixed feelings about the value of behaviorist techniques in addressing *academic* problems. Reinforcement and other behaviorist strategies often do lead to improved academic performance, but we should keep the following drawbacks in mind:

• *Attempts to change behaviors ignore cognitive factors that are potentially interfering with learning.* When cognitive deficiencies (e.g., limited background knowledge, poor study strategies) hinder students' ability to master certain topics or skills, reinforcement alone may be insufficient to bring about significant improvement. For example, let's return one final time to the opening case study. Perhaps James has poor reading skills that, because of shame or embarrassment, he wants to hide from his teacher and classmates. If so, he may sometimes misbehave to escape tasks that, to him, seem impossible. For those students who have significant weaknesses in their knowledge or cognitive abilities, instructional strategies based on cognitive, contextual, or social cognitive theories of learning may be more effective.

• *Reinforcement for accomplishing academic tasks may encourage students to do things quickly rather than well.* In general, reinforcement solely for accomplishing a particular task, perhaps at a minimally acceptable level, focuses students' attention and effort more on completing the activity than on *learning* from it. Especially if we want students to engage in complex cognitive processes—for example, to think critically and creatively about a topic—then extrinsic reinforcement simply for task accomplishment may be counterproductive (E. M. Anderman & Anderman, 2010; Deci & Ryan, 1985; McCaslin & Good, 1996).

• *Extrinsic reinforcement of an activity that students already find intrinsically reinforcing may undermine their enjoyment of the activity.* Students often engage in behaviors because of the

# STUDENTS IN INCLUSIVE SETTINGS

**TABLE 9.4 • Encouraging Appropriate Behaviors in Students with Special Educational Needs**

| CATEGORY | CHARACTERISTICS YOU MIGHT OBSERVE | SUGGESTED STRATEGIES |
|---|---|---|
| **Students with specific cognitive or academic difficulties** | • Inappropriate classroom behaviors (for some students)<br>• Less ability to delay gratification (for students with ADHD)<br>• Avoidance behaviors common when confronting challenging tasks<br>• Difficulty discriminating among similar stimuli, especially when perceptual deficits exist | • Be explicit about and consistently reinforce desired classroom behaviors.<br>• Emphasize differences among similar stimuli (e.g., the letters b, d, p, and q), and provide opportunities to practice making subtle discriminations.<br>• Promote generalization of new responses (e.g., by pointing out similarities among different situations and by teaching skills in real-world contexts).<br>• Have students work on assignments with classmates who are good role models and can encourage on-task behaviors. |
| **Students with social or behavioral problems** | • Inappropriate responses, especially in social situations; difficulty determining when and where particular responses are appropriate<br>• A history of inappropriate behaviors being reinforced (e.g., intrinsically or by teacher attention)<br>• Responsiveness to teacher praise if given in private (for students with emotional and behavioral disorders)<br>• Little or no appreciation of others' praise and approval (for some students with autism)<br>• Difficulty generalizing appropriate responses to new situations | • Explicitly and concretely describe desired behaviors.<br>• Give precise feedback regarding students' behavior.<br>• Reinforce desired behaviors using teacher attention, private praise, activity reinforcers, and group contingencies (for students with emotional and behavioral disorders).<br>• Reinforce accomplishments immediately, using concrete reinforcers or activity reinforcers; combine them with praise so that praise eventually becomes reinforcing in and of itself (for students with more severe forms of autism).<br>• Shape desired behaviors over time; expect gradual improvement rather than immediate perfection.<br>• Punish inappropriate behaviors (e.g., using time-out or response cost); consider applied behavior analysis or positive behavior support for persistently challenging behaviors.<br>• Promote generalization of new responses to appropriate situations (e.g., by teaching skills in real-world contexts and providing opportunities to role-play new responses). |
| **Students with general delays in cognitive and social functioning** | • Appreciation of and responsiveness to extrinsic reinforcers<br>• Difficulty delaying gratification; behavior more likely to improve when reinforcement is immediate rather than delayed<br>• Inappropriate responses in social situations<br>• Difficulty discriminating between important and unimportant stimuli<br>• Difficulty generalizing responses from one situation to another | • Explicitly teach and cue appropriate behaviors.<br>• Reinforce accomplishments immediately (e.g., using concrete reinforcers, activity reinforcers, praise).<br>• Use continuous reinforcement during the acquisition of new responses.<br>• Shape complex behaviors slowly over time; expect gradual improvement rather than immediate perfection.<br>• Reprimand minor misbehaviors; use time-out or response cost for more serious and chronic misbehaviors.<br>• Emphasize the stimuli to which you want students to attend.<br>• Promote generalization of new responses (e.g., by teaching skills in real-world contexts and by reinforcing generalization). |
| **Students with physical or sensory challenges** | • Loss of some previously learned behaviors if students have had traumatic brain injury | • Shape desired behaviors slowly over time; expect gradual improvement rather than immediate perfection. |
| **Students with advanced cognitive development** | • Unusual and sometimes creative responses to classroom tasks | • Keep an open mind about acceptable responses to classroom assignments.<br>• Encourage and reinforce creative responses. |

*Sources:* Barbetta, 1990; Barbetta, Heward, Bradley, & Miller, 1994; Beirne-Smith, Patton, & Kim, 2006; Buchoff, 1990; J. O. Cooper, Heron, & Heward, 2007; Cuskelly, Zhang, & Hayes, 2003; E. S. Ellis & Friend, 1991; S. Goldstein & Rider, 2006; Grauvogel-MacAleese & Wallace, 2010; Heward, 2009; Hobson, 2004; Hoerger & Mace, 2006; Landau & McAninch, 1993; Mercer & Pullen, 2005; Mueller et al., 2011; Neef et al., 2005; Patton, Blackbourn, & Fad, 1996; Pfiffner et al., 2006; Piirto, 1999; Pressley, 1995; Turnbull, Turnbull, & Wehmeyer, 2010.

personal satisfaction and other intrinsic reinforcers that those behaviors bring. Some research studies indicate that enjoyable activities can be increased through extrinsic reinforcement but will then *decrease* to a below-baseline frequency once the reinforcers are removed. Extrinsic reinforcers are most likely to have this adverse effect when students perceive them as being controlling or manipulative, rather than as promoting improvement and mastery (Deci & Moller, 2005; Lepper & Hodell, 1989; Reeve, 2006).

Before using extrinsic reinforcers, then, we should be sure that such reinforcers are truly necessary—that students have little or no intrinsic desire to acquire the academic skills and classroom behaviors essential for their school success. As they gain competence and self-confidence, however, they may begin to find certain activities and behaviors worth engaging in for their own sake.

> Communicate genuine appreciation for what students have done. Try not to come across as controlling or manipulative.

> Extrinsic reinforcement for students who don't need it can undermine their sense of *self-determination* (see Chapter 11).

# 9 What Have You Learned?

As a way of recapping our discussion of behaviorist principles, we now return to the chapter's learning outcomes.

**9.1: Describe five basic assumptions underlying behaviorist views of learning, and apply these assumptions to classroom practice.** Historically behaviorists have argued that internal mental processes can't be studied objectively, and thus they have focused largely on stimuli in a learner's immediate environments (both past and present) and on a learner's responses to those stimuli. Behaviorists view learning as a change in behavior (rather than a mental change) and explain it in terms of specific stimulus–response associations. Key to forming such associations is close proximity in time (contiguity) between the stimuli and responses involved. Many behaviorist principles of learning apply equally to human beings and other animal species.

Evaluate and apply your knowledge related to this learning outcome in MyEducationLab™.

**9.2: Explain how learners can acquire involuntary responses through classical conditioning and how you might help a student overcome classically conditioned emotional responses that interfere with classroom performance.** Classical conditioning occurs when (1) one stimulus (the unconditioned stimulus) already elicits a particular response (the unconditioned response) and (2) that stimulus is presented in conjunction with another stimulus, usually on several occasions. Under these circumstances, the second (conditioned) stimulus begins to elicit a (conditioned) response as well. Classical conditioning is one possible explanation for why students may have unproductive emotional reactions in certain learning environments—say, in a math class or on the athletic field. As teachers, we should strive to create an instructional environment that conditions pleasure and relaxation responses to new tasks and activities, not an environment that elicits fear and anxiety.

Evaluate and apply your knowledge related to this learning outcome in MyEducationLab™.

**9.3: Describe the effects that various kinds of consequences can have on behavior.** By definition, a *reinforcing* stimulus increases the behavior it follows, whereas a *punishing* stimulus decreases the behavior. Taken together, these two effects are known as *instrumental conditioning,* although you may also see the term *operant conditioning* used in reference to the effects of a reinforcer.

Positive reinforcement is at work when a response increases after previously being followed by the presentation of a particular stimulus or event (e.g., a compliment or opportunity to engage in a favorite activity). Negative reinforcement is at work when a response increases after previously being followed by the *removal* of an *unpleasant* stimulus (e.g., a frustrating task or feeling of anxiety).

Negative reinforcement—which *increases* the behavior—shouldn't be confused with punishment, which can involve either the presentation of a stimulus (presumably one that a learner finds desirable) or the removal of a stimulus (presumably one that a learner wants to get rid of). Some forms of punishment (e.g., mild reprimands, time-outs) can be quite effective when used judiciously, whereas others (e.g., public humiliation, out-of-school suspension) are usually counterproductive.

Evaluate and apply your knowledge related to this learning outcome in MyEducationLab™.

**9.4: Apply behaviorist principles to encourage productive student behaviors and discourage undesirable ones.** We can increase the frequency of desired student behaviors either by reinforcing the behaviors whenever they occur or by gradually shaping them over time. Our use of reinforcement is more likely to be effective when we make response–consequence contingencies explicit and when we individualize reinforcers to match students' preferences. We must also be careful that we *don't* reinforce inappropriate behaviors.

Students' behaviors are influenced not only by their consequences but also by antecedent events. For example, once students have learned a particular response to a particular stimulus, they'll tend to generalize the same response to similar stimuli. Seemingly similar situations occasionally call for very different behaviors, however, and so we must help students discriminate between occasions when certain responses are and are not appropriate. It's important, too, to create environments that readily evoke desired student behaviors and to introduce challenging tasks only after students have become comfortable performing similar but slightly easier ones.

Behaviorist principles offer several strategies for reducing nonproductive or counterproductive classroom behaviors. As teachers, we might remove the consequences that reinforce an unwanted behavior (possibly resulting in extinction), cue students about inappropriate behavior, or reinforce responses that are incompatible with those we want to eliminate. In some cases, we may need to resort to punishment, especially if students' behaviors significantly interfere with classroom learning or jeopardize one or more students' welfare. We must abide by strict guidelines in the use of punishment; for example, we should tell students ahead of time which behaviors are unacceptable and what the particular consequences will be, and we should administer punishment within the context of a warm, supportive relationship—one that communicates a genuine concern for students' well-being.

Applied behavior analysis, functional analysis, and positive behavior support are three approaches through which we can apply behaviorist principles in a systematic fashion. Such techniques are often effective in promoting academic achievement and appropriate classroom behavior, even in cases where other approaches haven't worked. In fact, positive behavior support can be effectively applied on a schoolwide basis to reduce discipline problems and enhance student achievement across the board.

**Evaluate** and **apply** your knowledge related to this learning outcome in MyEducationLab™.

■ **9.5: Accommodate students' personal and cultural backgrounds and special needs in your application of behaviorist principles.** The students in any single classroom have had different histories of reinforcement and different prior experiences with the stimuli they encounter at school; hence, they'll inevitably have varying reactions to the same tasks and situations. Students' cultural backgrounds may also have contributed to their diversity; for example, some students may appreciate praise only when it's given in private, and others may prefer reinforcement for group achievement rather than individual accomplishments.

Students with cognitive, social, or behavioral disabilities can especially benefit from the structured, consistent learning environments that behaviorists advocate. For example, a functional analysis can help us understand why a certain student is frequently aggressive or noncompliant and then enable us to plan an intervention that promotes more productive classroom behaviors. And consistent, explicit, and immediate use of reinforcement to shape increasingly complex behaviors can help students with cognitive disabilities acquire many new skills.

**Evaluate** and **apply** your knowledge related to this learning outcome in MyEducationLab™.

■ **9.6: Describe circumstances in which behaviorist techniques might not be helpful.** Behaviorist techniques are most applicable when students have the *ability* to behave appropriately. If cognitive factors interfere with learning or behavior, however, behaviorist approaches alone may be ineffective. Furthermore, we must be careful that we don't provide extrinsic reinforcement unnecessarily; in doing so, we may encourage students to do things *quickly* rather than *well,* and we may undermine students' intrinsic enjoyment of certain activities.

**Evaluate** and **apply** your knowledge related to this learning outcome in MyEducationLab™.

## Practice for Your Licensure Exam

### Hostile Helen

Mr. Washington has a close-knit group of friends in one of his high school vocational education classes. He is concerned about one particular student in this group, a girl named Helen. Helen uses obscene language in class. She's also rude and disrespectful to Mr. Washington, and she taunts and insults classmates outside her own circle of friends. In addition, Helen is physically aggressive toward school property; she defaces furniture, kicks equipment, punches walls, and so on.

At first, Mr. Washington tries to ignore Helen's hostile and aggressive behaviors, but this strategy doesn't lead to any improvement in her behavior. He then tries praising Helen on those rare occasions when she does behave appropriately, but this strategy doesn't seem to work either.

1. **Multiple-choice question:**

   Mr. Washington initially tries to ignore Helen's inappropriate behavior. This approach best reflects which one of the following concepts from behaviorism?

   a. Extinction

   b. Response cost

   c. Functional analysis

   d. Negative reinforcement

**2. Multiple-choice question:**

Later, Mr. Washington tries praising Helen for appropriate behaviors. This approach best reflects which one of the following behaviorist concepts?

a. Setting event

b. Discrimination

c. Positive behavior support

d. Reinforcement of incompatible behaviors

**3. Constructed-response question:**

Many research studies indicate that behaviorist principles *can* be effective in bringing about significant improvements in students' classroom behavior, yet neither of Mr. Washington's strategies has an effect on Helen's classroom behavior.

A. Suggest at least three different reasons that Mr. Washington's strategies might not be having much effect.

B. Describe how *you* might use behaviorist learning principles to bring about a behavior change in Helen. Be specific about what you would do.

**PRAXIS**  Go to Appendix C, "Matching Book and MyEducationLab™ to the Praxis Principles of Learning and Teaching Tests," to discover sections of this chapter that may be especially applicable to the Praxis tests.

# 10 Social Cognitive Views of Learning

## LEARNING OUTCOMES

**10.1:** Describe five basic assumptions of social cognitive theory and their classroom implications.

**10.2:** Use a social cognitive perspective to explain how mental processes can influence the effects of reinforcement and punishment.

**10.3:** Describe the potential effects of modeling on learners' behaviors, and explain how you can productively use modeling in instruction.

**10.4:** Describe the nature and origins of self-efficacy, and explain how you might enhance self-efficacy both in

your students as developing learners and in yourself as a teacher.

**10.5:** Identify important components of self-regulated behavior and self-regulated learning, and apply your knowledge of self-regulation to help diverse learners effectively control their behavior, master academic subject matter, and address interpersonal problems.

**10.6:** Compare and contrast perspectives of learning associated with cognitive psychology, contextual theories, behaviorism, and social cognitive theory.

## CASE STUDY: PARLEZ-VOUS FRANÇAIS?

Nathan is in French I only because his mother insisted that he take it. On the first day of class, Nathan notices that most of his classmates are girls and the few boys are students he doesn't know very well. He sits sullenly in the back, recalling that three male friends who took French last year got mostly Ds and Fs on quizzes and homework and that two of them dropped the class after one semester. "I do great in math and science," he tells himself, "but I'm just no good at learning languages. Besides, learning French is a *girl* thing."

Although Nathan comes to class every day, his mind often wanders as his teacher demonstrates correct pronunciations and explains simple syntactical structures. He makes feeble attempts at homework assignments but quickly puts them aside whenever he encounters something he doesn't immediately understand.

Sure enough, Nathan is right: He's no good at French. He gets a D– on the first exam.

- What things has Nathan learned from observing the people around him? What things has he *not* learned, and why?
- In what general ways might observing other individuals influence learning?

---

Although Nathan hasn't learned much from his French teacher—partly because he hasn't been paying attention during lessons and partly because he hasn't put much effort into assignments—he's learned a few things from observing his *peers*. Knowing what happened to three male friends and seeing mostly girls in his class, he concludes that, as a boy, he's doomed to failure. We human beings learn a wide variety of behaviors by observing the people in our lives and in the media. We also learn which behaviors are likely to get us ahead—and which are not—by seeing their consequences for others. In part by watching what others do, we develop a sense of what our own capabilities are likely to be, and we begin to direct our behavior toward goals we think we can achieve.

In this chapter we explore social cognitive theory, a perspective that can help us understand what and how people learn by observing others and how, in the process, they begin to take control of their own behavior. Originally called *social learning theory,* social cognitive theory has its early roots in behaviorism and thus addresses the effects of reinforcement and punishment. Over the past few decades, however, it has increasingly incorporated cognitive processes into its explanations of learning and now includes a blend of ideas from behaviorism and cognitive psychology.

Social cognitive theory has developed in large part through the research efforts of Albert Bandura at Stanford University. You'll find references to Bandura and others who have built on his ideas (e.g., Dale Schunk, Barry Zimmerman) throughout the chapter.

Chapter 9 presents behaviorist perspectives of learning.

# Basic Assumptions of Social Cognitive Theory

Several basic assumptions underlie social cognitive theory:

- *People can learn by observing others.* From the perspective of behaviorism, learning is often a process of trial and error: Learners try many different responses, keep those that bring desired consequences, and leave unproductive ones behind. Social cognitive theorists argue that learners don't necessarily have to experiment in such a trial-and-error manner. Instead learners acquire many new responses simply by observing the behaviors of other individuals, or *models.*

**social cognitive theory** Theoretical perspective that focuses on how people learn by observing others and how they eventually assume control over their own behavior.

Children learn many new behaviors simply by watching adults or peers perform them successfully.

For example, a student might learn how to solve a long division problem, spell the word *synonym* correctly, or mouth off at a teacher simply by watching someone else do these things first.

• *Learning is an internal process that may or may not lead to a behavior change.* Rather than define learning as a change in behavior (as many behaviorists do), social cognitive theorists (like cognitive psychologists) view learning as a mental change that may or may not be reflected in the learner's present or future behavior. For example, you might try to dribble a basketball as soon as you watch someone else do it. You probably won't demonstrate that you've learned how to apologize tactfully until a later time when an apology is necessary. And you might *never* walk through campus nude, no matter how many times you see someone else do it.

• *Cognitive processes influence motivation as well as learning.* Like cognitive psychologists, social cognitive theorists recognize the importance of cognitive processes (e.g., attention, encoding) for learning and remembering new information. But they point out that cognition is also an important ingredient in *motivation*. For example, people set mental *goals* toward which they direct their behavior, and their goals are based to some degree on their *expectations* about what they might reasonably accomplish. People's beliefs about their own ability to execute certain behaviors or reach certain goals—their *self-efficacy*—influence how hard they try, how long they persist at challenging tasks, and ultimately how much they learn and achieve.

• *People and their environments mutually influence each other.* Some learning theorists, especially behaviorists, focus primarily on how environmental variables can influence learners. But the reverse is true as well: Learners influence their environments, often quite deliberately. To some degree learners influence their environments through their *behaviors*. For example, the responses they make (e.g., the classes they choose, the extracurricular activities they pursue, the company they keep) affect the learning opportunities they have and the consequences they experience. Mental processes, personality characteristics, and other things that learners "own" in some way—social cognitive theorists call these things *person* variables—come into play as well. For example, learners are apt to focus their attention on—and thus learn from—only certain aspects of their environment, and their idiosyncratic interpretations of why they've been reinforced or punished influence the specific effects that such consequences have.

Ultimately, all three of these factors—environment, behavior, and person—influence one another in the manner shown in Figure 10.1. Social cognitive theorists use the term reciprocal causation when referring to this constant interplay among environment, behavior, and person variables (e.g., Bandura, 1989, 2008).

**reciprocal causation**
Interdependence of environmental, behavioral, and personal variables in influencing learning and development.

• *Behavior becomes increasingly self-regulated.* In the first few years of life, children's actions are controlled and guided to a considerable degree by others—by parents, older siblings, child care providers, teachers, and so on. But as children grow older, most of them increasingly take charge of their lives, not only identifying particular goals toward which to strive but also directing and monitoring their behaviors and thought processes to accomplish their goals. In other words, most children increasingly engage in *self-regulation.*

**FIGURE 10.1** In social cognitive theory, environmental, behavioral, and personal variables mutually influence one another.

Table 10.1 summarizes the assumptions just listed and offers examples of their implications for classroom practice.

# The Social Cognitive View of Reinforcement and Punishment

Reinforcement and punishment are less critical in social cognitive theory than they are in behaviorism, but they do have several indirect effects on learning and behavior (e.g., Bandura, 1977, 1986; T. L. Rosenthal & Zimmerman, 1978). Cognitive factors come into play in these indirect effects, as reflected in the following ideas:

• *Consequences influence behavior only if learners are aware of the response–consequence contingency.* From a social cognitive perspective, reinforcement and punishment influence learners' behaviors only if the learners connect these consequences to specific things they've done (Bandura, 1986). As teachers, then, we should be very clear about what we're reinforcing and punishing, so that students know the real response–reinforcement contingencies operating in the classroom. For instance, if we give Sam an A on an essay but we don't tell him *why* he's earned that grade, he won't necessarily know how to get an A the next time. Thus we might accompany the A grade with feedback such as "You followed a logical train of thought and gave three good examples." And rather that simply tell Sandra "Good job!" after a basketball game, we might tell her that we were pleased with her high energy level and passing accuracy.

 Be explicit about which behaviors have led to which consequences.

## PRINCIPLES/ASSUMPTIONS

| TABLE 10.1 • Basic Assumptions of Social Cognitive Theory and Their Educational Implications | | |
|---|---|---|
| **ASSUMPTION** | **EDUCATIONAL IMPLICATION** | **EXAMPLE** |
| Learning by observation | Help students acquire new behaviors more quickly by demonstrating those behaviors yourself. | Demonstrate appropriate ways to deal with and resolve interpersonal conflicts. Then ask students to role-play conflict resolution in small groups, and compliment those who use prosocial strategies. |
| Learning as an internal process that may or may not be reflected in behavior | Remember that new learning doesn't always reveal itself immediately but may instead be reflected in students' behaviors at a later time. | When one student engages in disruptive classroom behavior, take appropriate steps to discourage it. Otherwise, classmates who have witnessed the misbehavior may be similarly disruptive in the future. |
| Cognitive processes in motivation | Encourage students to set productive goals for themselves, especially goals that are challenging yet achievable. | When teaching American Sign Language to help students communicate with a classmate who is deaf, ask them to predict how many new words and phrases they can learn each week. |
| Reciprocal influences among environmental, behavioral, and personal variables | Encourage students to make choices that will lead to valuable learning experiences. | Describe the benefits of taking an advanced writing course both as a means of enhancing writing skills and as a way of exploring writing as a possible career path. |
| Increasing self-regulation with age | Teach students strategies through which they can better control their own behavior and direct their own learning. | Give students concrete suggestions about how they can remind themselves to bring needed supplies to school each day. |

**outcome expectation** Prediction regarding the consequence that a particular behavior is likely to yield.

**incentive** Hoped-for, but not guaranteed, future consequence of behavior.

• *Learners form expectations about the likely consequences of future actions and then behave in ways they think will maximize desired results.* Learners often base such outcome expectations on existing patterns of reinforcement, nonreinforcement, and punishment. For example, perhaps you've taken a course in which all exam questions came from the textbook, without a single question coming from class lectures. After the first exam, did you find yourself reading the textbook carefully but skipping class a lot? And perhaps you've taken a course in which exams were based almost entirely on lectures. In that situation, did you go to class regularly but hardly ever open your textbook? When a particular response is reinforced every time it's made, learners typically expect to be reinforced for behaving the same way in the future. In a similar manner, when a response frequently leads to punishment—as insulting an instructor or skipping class on a test day might—learners will probably expect that response to be punished on later occasions as well.

Sometimes, however, learners form expectations about future consequences on the basis of little or no hard data. For example, a high school student might erroneously believe that bragging about perfect test scores will gain him the admiration of his classmates (i.e., a reinforcer). Another student might believe that her classmates will ridicule and reject (i.e., punish) her for being smart, even though they wouldn't actually do so.

Expectations about future contingencies certainly affect learners' behaviors. They may or may not influence learning itself, as the following exercise can show you.

### ■▪ EXPERIENCING FIRSTHAND
### DR. X

Think about a class you're taking now or have taken recently—not an online class but one that involves an instructor and students regularly convening in a single room. How many of the following questions can you answer about your instructor, whom I'll call "Dr. X"?

1. Is Dr. X right handed or left handed?
2. Is Dr. X a flashy dresser or more conservative one?
3. What kind of shoes does Dr. X wear to class?
4. Does Dr. X wear a wedding ring?
5. Does Dr. X bring a briefcase to class each day?

If you've attended class regularly, you can probably answer at least two of these questions and possibly all five. But I'm guessing that you've never mentioned what you've learned to anyone else, because you've had no reason to believe that demonstrating your knowledge about these matters would be reinforced. When learners *do* expect reinforcement for such knowledge, it suddenly surfaces. For example, every time I teach educational psychology, I take a minute sometime during the semester to hide my feet behind the podium and ask my students what my shoes look like. They first look at me as if I have two heads, but after a few seconds of awkward silence, at least a half dozen of them (usually those who regularly sit in the first two rows) begin to describe my shoes, right down to the rippled soles, scuffed leather, and beige stitching.

Students learn many things in the classroom. They learn facts and figures, they learn ways of getting their teacher's attention, and they may even learn which classmate stores M&Ms in his desk or what kind of shoes their teacher wears to class. Of all the things they learn, they're most likely to demonstrate the things they think will bring reinforcement.

When learners choose to behave in a way that might bring future reinforcement, they're working for an incentive, which is never guaranteed. For instance, students never know that they're going to get an A on a test when they study for it or that they'll win a position on the Student Council simply because they run for office. An incentive is an expected or hoped-for consequence that may or may not actually occur.

• *Learners' expectations are influenced by what happens to other people as well as to themselves.* When I was in the third grade, I entered a Halloween costume contest dressed as Happy Tooth, a character in several toothpaste commercials at the time. I didn't win the contest; a witch won first

🍎 Be explicit about *future* response–reinforcement and response–punishment contingencies as well.

prize. So the following year I entered the same contest dressed as a witch, figuring I was a shoo-in for first place. I had experienced reinforcement *vicariously* rather than directly—that is, through watching what happened to someone else.

Learners who observe someone else being reinforced for a behavior are likely to exhibit that behavior more frequently themselves—a phenomenon known as vicarious reinforcement. For example, by watching the consequences their classmates experience, students might learn that studying hard leads to good grades, that being elected to class office brings status and popularity, or that neatness counts. Conversely, when learners see someone else get punished for a behavior, they're *less* likely to behave that way themselves—a phenomenon known as vicarious punishment. For example, when a coach benches a football player for unsportsmanlike conduct, other players are unlikely to behave similarly. Unfortunately, vicarious punishment can suppress desirable behaviors as well as undesirable ones. For instance, when a teacher belittles a student's question by calling it "silly," other students may be reluctant to ask questions of their own.[1]

As teachers, we must be extremely careful that we don't vicariously reinforce undesirable behaviors or vicariously punish desirable ones. If we give too much attention to a misbehaving student, others who want our attention may misbehave as well. Or if we ridicule a student who volunteers an incorrect answer or erroneous belief, classmates will hardly be eager to voice their own ideas.

• *Expectations about future consequences affect how thoroughly and in what ways learners cognitively process new information.* To get a sense of how this might happen, try the next exercise.

### EXPERIENCING FIRSTHAND
## PLANNING AHEAD

Quickly skim the contents of the upcoming section on modeling to get a general idea of the topics it includes. Once you've done so, imagine yourself in each of these situations:

1. Your instructor announces, "The section on modeling won't be on your test, but please read it anyway." How thoroughly and carefully will you read that section?
2. The next day your instructor announces, "I misled you yesterday. Actually, half of next week's test will be on modeling." *Now* how thoroughly and carefully will you read that section?

If you don't expect to be reinforced for knowing about modeling, you may very well *not* read the chapter's discussion of it. (Perhaps you'll read it later, you tell yourself, but you have other things you need to do right now.) If, instead, you discover that getting an A in your educational psychology class depends on knowing the material about modeling really well, you're apt to read the material slowly and attentively, possibly trying to remember every detail.

When learners believe they'll be reinforced for learning something, they're more likely to pay attention to it and perhaps engage in elaboration, comprehension monitoring, and other effective cognitive processes. When they *don't* expect to be reinforced for learning something, they're far less likely to process it in any significant way. As an example of the latter situation, let's return to the opening case study. Nathan is convinced he can't learn French, thanks in part to his friends' low French grades (which served as vicarious punishment for him). As a result, Nathan pays little attention to what his teacher says in class, and he makes only halfhearted attempts to complete assignments. His low expectations almost guarantee poor performance—a self-fulfilling prophecy.

• *The [lack of] nonoccurrence of an expected consequence—whether for oneself or for someone else—can have a reinforcing or punishing effect in and of itself.* What happens when learners' expectations aren't met—say, when an expected reinforcement never comes? When, as a fourth grader, I entered the Halloween costume contest as a witch, I lost once again—this time to a girl wearing a metal colander on her head and claiming to be *Sputnik,* the first satellite launched into space by what

**vicarious reinforcement**
Phenomenon in which a response increases in frequency when another person is observed being reinforced for that response.

**vicarious punishment** Phenomenon in which a response decreases in frequency when another person is observed being punished for that response.

---

[1] The effects of vicarious reinforcement and vicarious punishment are sometimes referred to as the *response facilitation effect* and *response inhibition effect,* respectively.

was then the Soviet Union. That was the last time I entered a Halloween contest. I had expected reinforcement and felt cheated because I didn't get it. Social cognitive theorists propose that the nonoccurrence of expected reinforcement is a form of punishment (e.g., Bandura, 1986). When people think that a certain response is going to be reinforced but the response *isn't* reinforced, they're less likely to exhibit the response in the future.

Just as the nonoccurrence of expected reinforcement is a form of punishment, the nonoccurrence of expected punishment is a form of reinforcement (Bandura, 1986). Perhaps you can think of a time when you broke a rule, expecting to be punished, but you got away with your crime. Or perhaps you can remember seeing someone else break a rule without being caught. When nothing bad happens after a forbidden behavior, people may actually feel as if the behavior has been reinforced.

Thus, when students work hard to achieve a desired result—perhaps a compliment, a high grade, or a special privilege—and the anticipated result doesn't materialize, they'll be unlikely to work as hard the next time around. And when students break school rules but aren't punished for doing so, they're likely to break the rules again—and so are other students who are aware that the behavior has gone unpunished.[2] It's important that we, as teachers, follow through with promised reinforcements for desirable student behaviors. It's equally important that we impose any reasonable consequences students have come to expect for inappropriate behaviors.

Follow through with the consequences students have been led to expect for certain behaviors.

See Chapter 9 for guidelines and cautions in the use of punishment.

# Modeling

As human beings, we have some ability to imitate others beginning early in infancy (S. S. Jones, 2007; Meltzoff, 2005; Nielsen & Tomaselli, 2010). In fact, the brain seems to be specially equipped for imitation. Certain neurons in the brain, appropriately called **mirror neurons**, become active either (1) when learners observe others engaging in a particular behavior or (2) when learners engage in that same behavior themselves. It appears, then, that our brains are prewired to make connections between observing and doing, thus enhancing our ability to learn new skills from our social and cultural surroundings (Arbib, 2005; Gallese, Gernsbacher, Heyes, Hickok, & Iacoboni, 2011; Iacoboni & Woods, 1999).

In general, a **model** can take one of three forms (Bandura, 1977, 1986). One form, of course, is a *live model*—an actual person demonstrating a particular behavior. But we can also learn from a *symbolic model*—a person or character portrayed in a book, film, television show, video game, or other medium. For example, many children model their behavior after football players, rock singers, or such fictional characters as Harry Potter and Dora the Explorer. Finally, we can learn from *verbal instructions*—descriptions of how to successfully execute certain behaviors—without another human being, either live or symbolic, being anywhere in sight.

Social cognitive theorists sometimes use the term **modeling** to describe what a model does (i.e., demonstrate a behavior) and at other times to describe what the observer does (i.e., imitate the behavior). To minimize confusion, I'll often use the verb *imitate* rather than *model* when referring to what the observer does.

## BEHAVIORS AND SKILLS THAT CAN BE LEARNED THROUGH MODELING

By observing what other people do, learners can, of course, acquire a wide variety of psychomotor skills, from relatively simple actions (e.g., brushing teeth) to far more complex ones (e.g., performing dance routines or gymnastics skills) (Boyer, Miltenberger, Batsche, & Fogel, 2009; Poche, McCubbrey, & Munn, 1982; Vintere, Hemmes, Brown, & Poulson, 2004). But observations of other people also enable learners to acquire many behaviors with cognitive or emotional components. For example, learners are apt to do the following:

- Develop more sophisticated drawing skills when others demonstrate such skills, either in person or on videotape (Geiger, LeBlanc, Dillon, & Bates, 2010)

**mirror neuron** Neuron in the brain that fires either when a person is performing a particular behavior or when the person sees someone else perform the behavior.

**model** Real or fictional individual who demonstrates a behavior that learners might emulate; alternatively, a set of instructions for successfully executing the behavior.

**modeling** Demonstrating a behavior for another person *or* observing and imitating another person's behavior.

---

[2]The tendency for learners to engage in forbidden behavior when they see others incur no adverse consequences for behaving that way is known as the *response disinhibition effect*. In this situation, the learners have presumably already mastered the behavior but the expectation of punishment has previously inhibited it. With the expectation no longer present, the behavior is disinhibited and may increase in frequency.

- Learn to fear particular stimuli or situations if others show fear in those circumstances (Mineka & Zinbarg, 2006)
- Better resist the enticements of a stranger when a peer has modeled resistance strategies (Poche, Yoder, & Miltenberger, 1988)
- Be less likely to tolerate racist statements if people around them refuse to tolerate such statements (Blanchard, Lilly, & Vaughn, 1991)

Considerable research has been conducted concerning the impact of models in three areas: academic skills, aggression, and productive interpersonal behaviors.

## ACADEMIC SKILLS

Learners acquire many academic skills, at least in part, by observing what others do. For instance, they may learn how to solve long division problems or write a cohesive composition partly by observing how adults or peers do these things (Braaksma, Rijlaarsdam, & van den Bergh, 2002; K. R. Harris, Graham, Brindle, & Sandmel, 2009; Schunk & Hanson, 1985). Modeling of academic skills can be especially effective when the model demonstrates not only how to *do* a task but also how to *think about* the task—in other words, when the model engages in cognitive modeling (Schunk, 1998; Schunk & Swartz, 1993; Zimmerman, 2004). As an example, consider how a teacher might model the thinking processes involved in the long division problem in the margin:

Students who are prominent members of the school community can be powerful models for many of their peers—perhaps for the better or perhaps for the worse, depending on the specific behaviors being modeled.

First I have to decide what number to divide 4 into. I take 276, start on the left and move toward the right until I have a number the same as or larger than 4. Is 2 larger than 4? No. Is 27 larger than 4? Yes. So my first division will be 4 into 27. Now I need to multiply 4 by a number that will give an answer the same as or slightly smaller than 27. How about 5? 5 × 4 = 20. No, too small. Let's try 6. 6 × 4 = 24. Maybe. Let's try 7. 7 × 4 = 28. No, too large. So 6 is correct.[3]

$$4{\overline{\smash{)}276}}$$

## AGGRESSION

Numerous research studies have indicated that children become more aggressive when they observe aggressive or violent models (Bandura, 1965; N. E. Goldstein, Arnold, Rosenberg, Stowe, & Ortiz, 2001; Guerra, Huesmann, & Spindler, 2003). Children learn aggression not only from live models but also from the symbolic models they see in films, on television, and in video games—and possibly also from aggressive lyrics they hear in popular music (C. A. Anderson et al., 2003; Carnagey, Anderson, & Bartholow, 2007; Wartella, Caplovitz, & Lee, 2004). Furthermore, young learners' aggressive behaviors tend to take the same *forms* as the aggression they witness. Boys in particular are apt to copy other people's aggressive actions (Bandura, Ross, & Ross, 1963; Bushman & Anderson, 2001; Lowry, Sleet, Duncan, Powell, & Kolbe, 1995).

A classic study by Bandura, Ross, and Ross (1961) dramatically illustrates the power of modeling for both encouraging and *dis*couraging aggressive behavior. Preschoolers were taken, one at a time, to a playroom containing a variety of toys and were seated at a table where they could draw pictures. While in the playroom, some of the children saw an aggressive model: An adult came in and behaved aggressively toward an inflatable punching doll—for example, kicking

---

[3]Extract from "Teaching Elementary Students to Self-Regulate Practice of Mathematical Skills with Modeling" by Dale H. Schunk, from *Self-Regulated Learning: From Teaching to Self-Reflective Practice,* edited by Dale H. Schunk and Barry J. Zimmerman, p. 146. Copyright © 1998 by Guilford Publications, Inc. Reprinted with permission.

cognitive modeling  Demonstrating how to think about as well as how to do a task.

the doll in the air, hitting its head with a wooden mallet, and making statements such as "Pow!" and "Punch him in the nose." Other children instead observed a nonaggressive model: An adult came in and played constructively with building blocks. Still other children saw no model at all in the playroom. The children were then led to another room where they were mildly frustrated: Just as they began to play with some attractive, entertaining toys, the toys were taken away. Finally, the children were taken to a third room that contained both nonaggressive and aggressive toys (including the punching doll and mallet). Children who had seen the aggressive model were the most aggressive of the three groups; in fact, they mimicked many of the behaviors they'd seen the aggressive model display. Children who had observed a nonaggressive model were even less aggressive than the no-model group. With regard to aggression, then, models can have an impact either way: Aggressive models lead to increased aggression in children, and nonaggressive models lead to decreased aggression.

### PRODUCTIVE INTERPERSONAL BEHAVIORS

Learners acquire many interpersonal skills by observing and imitating others. For example, when they talk about literature in small groups, children may adopt one another's strategies for conducting discussions, perhaps learning how to solicit one another's opinions ("What do you think, Jalisha?"), express agreement or disagreement ("I agree with Kordell because . . ."), and justify a point of view ("I think it shouldn't be allowed, because . . .") (R. C. Anderson et al., 2001, pp. 14, 16, 25). And children with mild or moderate forms of an autism spectrum disorder are apt to play more effectively with age-mates after watching a videotape of a nondisabled peer using good social skills in play activities (Nikopoulos & Keenan, 2004).

You can learn more about the development of prosocial behaviors in Chapter 3.

Learners can also acquire prosocial behaviors in part through observation and modeling (R. Elliott & Vasta, 1970; Jordan, 2003; Radke-Yarrow, Zahn-Waxler, & Chapman, 1983). In one research study (Rushton, 1980), children observed an adult playing a game and reinforcing himself with tokens for good performance. Some children saw the adult donate half of his earned tokens to a poor boy named Bobby pictured on a poster in the room; other children observed the adult keep all his winnings for himself. After that, the children played the game and could reward themselves with tokens. The more tokens they earned, the better the prize they could purchase. They could make a donation to Bobby, but doing so meant lesser purchasing power for themselves. Children who had seen a generous model were more likely to give some tokens to Bobby than were children who had seen a selfish model—not only at that time but also in a follow-up session two months later.

Regularly expose students to prosocial models in literature, history, and other academic subject areas.

Benevolent models in popular media can have a positive impact as well. Rather than encouraging aggression, some characters in books, television programs, and other popular media promote prosocial behaviors—those aimed at helping others rather than at enhancing personal well-being—and such models can prompt children and adolescents to behave similarly (D. R. Anderson, 2003; Huston, Watkins, & Kunkel, 1989; Jordan, 2003; Nucci, 2001; Rushton, 1980).

## CHARACTERISTICS OF EFFECTIVE MODELS

Learners don't always imitate the people they see around them and in the media. Influential models typically have several characteristics (Bandura, 1986; T. L. Rosenthal & Bandura, 1978; Schunk, 1987). First, they're *competent* at the behavior or skill in question. Learners usually want to behave like people who do something well rather than poorly. For instance, children may try to imitate the basketball skills of a professional basketball player, and adolescents may make note of especially effective techniques they observe in art or literature (see Figure 10.2). Even preschoolers have some ability to discriminate between competent and incompetent models (P. L. Harris & Want, 2005).

Second, influential models typically have *prestige and power*. Some effective models—a world leader, a renowned athlete, a popular rock star—are famous at a national or international level. The prestige and power of other models—a head cheerleader, the captain of the high school hockey team, a gang leader—may be more localized. As an example of such local influence, children are more likely to interact with students who have disabilities when they see popular classmates (rather than unpopular ones) initiating such interactions (Sasso & Rude, 1987).

Third, and perhaps most importantly, influential models exhibit *behaviors relevant to learners' own circumstances*. Learners are most likely to adopt behaviors they believe will be useful for

**FIGURE 10.2** Seventh graders in a language arts class chose these examples of figurative writing to serve as models for their own writing efforts.

"The blackness of the night came in, like snakes around the ankles."
—Caroline Cooney, *Wanted*, p. 176

"Flirtatious waves made passes at the primly pebbled beach."
—Lilian Jackson Braun, *The Cat Who Saw Stars*, p. 120

"Water boiled up white and frothy, like a milkshake."
—Lurlene McDaniel, *For Better, for Worse, Forever*, p. 60

"I try to swallow the snowball in my throat."
—Laurie Halse Anderson, *Speak*, p. 72

themselves and are within their own ability levels (Braaksma et al., 2002; Schunk & Hanson, 1985). And remember Nathan's belief that French is a "girl thing"? Learners must believe that a particular behavior is appropriate for their gender, with different individuals having varying views about which activities are "gender appropriate" (Grace, David, & Ryan, 2008; Leaper & Friedman, 2007).

As classroom teachers, we're likely to be perceived by most students as competent, prestigious, and powerful—that is, we're likely to be influential models. Thus, we "teach" not only by what we say but also by what we do. It's critical, then, that we model appropriate behaviors—for instance, showing enthusiasm about classroom topics and fairness in our dealings with all students—and *don't* model inappropriate ones. Our actions will often speak louder than our words (e.g., J. H. Bryan, 1975).

Yet our students won't always perceive our behaviors as being relevant to their own circumstances. For instance, students from cultures and socioeconomic groups very different from our own may think that certain topics have little value in their own lives and communities. Students of both genders may view certain content domains and careers as being only for males or "girl things." And students with disabilities may believe they're incapable of performing the skills that a nondisabled teacher demonstrates. Ideally, students need to see successful models who are similar to themselves in obvious ways—for instance, in race, cultural background, socioeconomic status, gender, and (if applicable) disability (C. L. Martin & Ruble, 2004; Pang, 1995; L. E. Powers, Sowers, & Stevens, 1995).

Expose students to successful male and female models from diverse cultural and socioeconomic backgrounds. Also expose them to models who have achieved success despite disabilities.

## ESSENTIAL CONDITIONS FOR SUCCESSFUL MODELING

Even with the presence of influential models, however, learners don't always acquire the behaviors and skills they see others demonstrate. Social cognitive theorists suggest that four conditions are necessary for successful learning from models: attention, retention, motor reproduction, and motivation (e.g., Bandura, 1986).

### ATTENTION

To learn effectively, *the learner must pay attention to the model* and, in particular, to critical aspects of the modeled behavior. For instance, students must observe carefully as we show proper procedures in the science lab or demonstrate the elementary backstroke, and they must listen attentively as we pronounce *Comment allez-vous?* in a French class—something Nathan didn't do in the opening case study.

Chapter 6 presents many strategies for enhancing students' attention and retention.

### RETENTION

After paying attention, *the learner must remember what the model does.* As cognitive psychologists have discovered, students are more likely to recall information they've encoded in memory in more than one way—perhaps as both a visual image and a verbal representation (R. E. Mayer, 2011b; Moreno, 2006). As teachers, then, we may often want to describe what we're doing as we demonstrate behaviors. We may also want to give descriptive labels to complex behaviors that might otherwise be hard to remember (Vintere et al., 2004; Ziegler, 1987). For example, in

**FIGURE 10.3** Often learners can more easily remember a complex, multifaceted behavior—such as the sequence of arm movements in the elementary backstroke—when the various components have verbal labels.

"Chicken"          "Airplane"          "Soldier"

teaching swimming, an easy way to help students remember the sequence of arm positions in the elementary backstroke is to teach them the labels *chicken, airplane,* and *soldier* (see Figure 10.3).

### MOTOR REPRODUCTION

In addition to attending and remembering, *the learner must be physically capable of reproducing the modeled behavior.* When a student lacks the ability to reproduce an observed behavior, motor reproduction obviously can't occur. For example, first graders who watch a teenager throw a softball don't have the muscular coordination to mimic the throw. And high school students who haven't yet learned to roll their *r*s will have trouble repeating the Spanish teacher's tongue twister: *Erre con erre cigarro, erre con erre barril. Rápido corren los carros del ferrocarril.*

It's often useful to have students imitate a desired behavior immediately after they see it modeled and to give them guidance and feedback that can help them improve their performance. This approach—sometimes known as *coaching*—is often more effective than modeling alone (S. N. Elliott & Busse, 1991; Kitsantas, Zimmerman, & Cleary, 2000; Schunk & Swartz, 1993). When considering this approach, however, we must keep in mind that students from some ethnic groups (e.g., many Native Americans) may prefer to practice new behaviors in private at first and show us what they've learned only after they've achieved reasonable mastery (Castagno & Brayboy, 2008; Suina & Smolkin, 1994).

### MOTIVATION

Finally, *the learner must be motivated to demonstrate the modeled behavior.* Some students may be eager to show what they've observed and remembered; for example, they may have seen the model reinforced for a certain behavior and thus have already been vicariously reinforced. But other students may not have any motivation to demonstrate something they've seen a model do, perhaps because they don't see the model's actions as being appropriate for themselves.

When all four factors—attention, retention, motor reproduction, and motivation—are present, modeling can be an extremely effective teaching technique. The Into the Classroom feature "Promoting Learning through Modeling" offers several strategies that can maximize its effectiveness.

## Self-Efficacy

One important aspect of the fourth condition—motivation—is self-efficacy, and in this respect learners often differ considerably. In general, self-efficacy is a learner's self-constructed judgment about his or her ability to execute certain behaviors or reach certain goals. To get a sense of your own self-efficacy for various activities, try the following exercise.

### EXPERIENCING FIRSTHAND
### SELF-APPRAISAL

Take a moment to answer the following questions:

1. Do you believe you'll be able to understand and apply educational psychology by reading this book and thinking carefully about its content? Or do you believe you're going to have trouble with the material regardless of how much you study?

2. Do you think you could learn to execute a reasonable swan dive from a high diving board if you were shown how to do it and given time to practice? Or do you think you're such a klutz that no amount of training and practice would help?

3. Do you think you could walk barefoot over hot coals unscathed? Or do you think the soles of your feet would be burned to a crisp?

**self-efficacy** Belief that one is capable of executing certain behaviors or achieving certain goals.

## Into the Classroom

### Promoting Learning Through Modeling

🍏 **Make sure you have students' attention when modeling a desired behavior.**

A middle school science teacher wants to show his class how to prepare a slide of swamp water for inspection under a microscope. He meets with students in groups of three or four so that everyone can closely observe what he does.

🍏 **Describe what you are doing as you model a desired behavior.**

As a fourth-grade teacher shows students how to use word processing software to edit their compositions, she explains every step she takes to insert new text, cut unwanted text, use the thesaurus and spell-check functions, and so on. She also distributes a handout that describes, step by step, how to perform each of these procedures, and she shows where to find important commands and functions on the computer screen.

🍏 **When teaching a complex behavior or sequence or behaviors, provide descriptive labels that students can repeat to themselves to help them remember what they need to do.**

To help students remember the new dance steps she demonstrates, a dance teacher instructs them to say such things as "One, two, gallop, gallop" and "One leg, other leg, turn, and turn" while performing the steps.

🍏 **Have students perform a desired behavior immediately after you model it; give them guidance and feedback to help them improve their performance.**

After an elementary art teacher shows students how to work effectively with watercolor paints, she walks around the classroom, giving pointers on how to blend colors for desired shades and how to keep differently colored areas from bleeding into one another.

🍏 **Show students how the skills you model can help them in their own lives.**

After demonstrating how to use rounding to estimate sums, a middle school math teacher presents examples of how students might quickly estimate the total cost of several purchases at a local discount store.

🍏 **Invite respected professionals to the classroom to demonstrate skills in their areas of expertise.**

A high school journalism teacher invites a local newspaper reporter to show students how he determines the sequence in which he presents information in a newspaper article.

🍏 **Show videos of skilled individuals performing complex psychomotor skills.**

A gymnastics coach shows an aspiring young gymnast a video in which an expert performs a particular gymnastics skill. The coach also videotapes the child's execution of the skill. The coach and child then watch the two videos—sometimes pausing the videos at particular frames—to identify components of the skill in which the child could benefit from further practice.

🍏 **Have students read about or observe positive role models in such media as books and films.**

In a unit on civic responsibility and community service, a high school social studies teacher has students read excerpts from Barack Obama's *Dreams from My Father*.

🍏 **Introduce students to models who have successfully crossed traditional gender boundaries in certain professions.**

When exploring various professions over the course of the school year, a second-grade teacher invites several adults in the community—including a female police officer and a male nurse—to come to class and describe what they do in their jobs.

🍏 **Include competent children as well as adults in the role models you present.**

Once a week, a kindergarten teacher invites one or two third graders to come and read storybooks to his class. The older children delight in their ability to show off their reading skills and work especially hard to make the stories lively and entertaining.

*Sources:* Boyer et al., 2009 (gymnastics example); R. L. Cohen, 1989; S. N. Elliott & Busse, 1991; Féry & Morizot, 2000; Gerst, 1971; Kitsantas et al., 2000; Mace, Belfiore, & Shea, 1989; Obama, 2004; T. L. Rosenthal, Alford, & Rasp, 1972; Schunk, 1989c; Schunk & Hanson, 1985; Schunk & Swartz, 1993; Shute, 2008; Vintere et al., 2004, p. 309 (dance example); Ziegler, 1987.

Learners are more likely to engage in certain behaviors when they believe they'll be able to execute the behaviors successfully—that is, when they have high *self-efficacy* for the behaviors (e.g., Bandura, 1997). For example, I hope you have high self-efficacy for learning educational psychology, believing that with careful thought about what you read, you'll be able to understand and apply its key principles. You may or may not believe that with instruction and practice, you could eventually execute a passable swan dive. You're probably quite skeptical that you could ever walk barefoot over hot coals, so my guess is that you have low self-efficacy regarding this endeavor. Obviously, then, self-efficacy plays a key role in learners' *outcome expectations* for various courses of action.

Self-efficacy is a component of one's overall sense of self. It may seem similar to such concepts as *self-concept* and *self-esteem*, but it's different from these other two concepts in important ways (Bong & Skaalvik, 2003; Pietsch, Walker, & Chapman, 2003; Schunk & Pajares, 2005). When psychologists talk about self-concept and self-esteem, they're typically describing a fairly general self-view that pervades a broad range of activities (e.g., "Am I a good student?") and may encompass feelings as well as beliefs (e.g., "How proud am I of my classroom performance?").

See Chapter 3 for a discussion of other aspects of a learner's sense of self (e.g., self-concept, identity).

Students tend to choose and enjoy topics for which they have high self-efficacy. Hear 12-year-old Claudia express her high self-efficacy for math in "Motivation: Early Adolescence." ■

Chapter 11 examines the development of value in greater detail. ■

Interpret reluctance and lack of persistence as possible indicators of low self-efficacy. ■

In contrast, self-efficacy is more task or situation specific and involves judgments (rather than feelings) almost exclusively (e.g., "Can I learn how to solve quadratic equations?").

## HOW SELF-EFFICACY AFFECTS BEHAVIOR AND COGNITION

Learners' sense of self-efficacy affects their choice of activities, their goals, and their effort and persistence in classroom activities. Ultimately, then, it also affects their learning and achievement (Bandura, 1982, 2000; Pajares, 2009; Schunk & Pajares, 2005).

**Choice of activities**    Imagine yourself on registration day, perusing the hundreds of courses in the semester schedule. You fill most of your schedule with required courses, but you have room for an elective. Only two courses are offered at the time slot you want to fill. Do you sign up for Advanced Psychoceramics, a challenging seminar taught by the world-renowned Dr. Josiah S. Carberry? Or do you sign up for an English literature course known across campus as being an "easy A"? Perhaps you find the term *psychoceramics* a bit intimidating, and you think you can't possibly pass such a course, especially if Dr. Carberry is as demanding as everyone claims. So you settle for the literature course, knowing it's one in which you can succeed.

Learners tend to choose tasks and activities at which they believe they can succeed and to avoid those at which they think they'll fail. Eventually they also place greater *value* on activities in which they think they'll do well (Bandura, 1986; Pajares, 2009).

**Goals**    Learners set higher goals for themselves when they have high self-efficacy in a particular domain. For example, adolescents' choices of careers and occupational levels reflect subject areas in which they have high rather than low self-efficacy. On average, their choices tend to be consistent with traditional gender stereotypes: Boys are more likely to have high self-efficacy for (and so choose) careers in science and technology, whereas girls are more likely to have high self-efficacy for (and so choose) careers in education, health, and social services (Bandura, Barbaranelli, Caprara, & Pastorelli, 2001; Plante & O'Keefe, 2010).

**Effort and persistence**    Learners with a high sense of self-efficacy are more likely to exert effort when attempting a new task, and they're more likely to persist—to "try, try again"—when they confront obstacles. In contrast, learners with low self-efficacy about a task will put in little effort and give up quickly in the face of difficulty. For example, in the opening case study, Nathan is convinced he can't learn French, and so he quickly abandons assignments when he encounters something he doesn't immediately understand.

**Learning and achievement**    Learners with high self-efficacy tend to learn and achieve more than those with low self-efficacy, even when the two groups initially have similar ability levels (Bandura, 1986; Klassen, 2002; T. Williams & Williams, 2010). Learners with high self-efficacy may achieve at superior levels partly because they're more likely to engage in cognitive processes that promote learning—paying attention, elaborating, organizing, and so on (Berger & Karabenick, 2010; Bong & Skaalvik, 2003; Liem, Lau, & Nie, 2008; Schunk & Pajares, 2005).

## SOME OVERCONFIDENCE—BUT NOT TOO MUCH—CAN BE BENEFICIAL

Most 4- to 6-year-olds are quite confident about their ability to perform various tasks (R. Butler, 1990, 2005; Eccles et al., 1998). As they move through the elementary grades, however, they can better recall their past successes and failures, and they become increasingly aware of and concerned about how their performance compares with that of their peers. Presumably as a result of these changes, students gradually become less confident—although usually more realistic—about what they can and can't do (R. Butler, 2005; Dijkstra, Kuyper, van der Werf, Buunk, & van der Zee, 2008; Wigfield & Wagner, 2005).

Ideally learners should have a reasonably accurate sense of what they can and cannot accomplish, putting them in a good position to capitalize on their strengths and address their weaknesses (P. P. Chen, 2003; Försterling & Morgenstern, 2002; J. Wang & Lin, 2005). However, a tad of overconfidence can often be beneficial, because it may entice learners to take on challenging activities that will help them develop new skills and abilities (Assor & Connell, 1992; Bandura, 1997; Pajares, 2009). Within this context it's useful to distinguish between *self-efficacy for learning*

("I can learn this if I put my mind to it") and *self-efficacy for performance* ("I already know how to do this") (Lodewyk & Winne, 2005; Schunk & Pajares, 2004). Self-efficacy for learning—for what one can *eventually* do with effort—should be on the optimistic side, while self-efficacy for performance should be more in line with current ability levels.

Sometimes students—especially girls—*under*estimate their chances of success, perhaps because they've had a few bad experiences or are especially attuned to how their own performance falls short relative to that of peers (D. A. Cole, Martin, Peeke, Seroczynski, & Fier, 1999; Dijkstra et al., 2008; Schunk & Pajares, 2005). For example, a girl who gets a C in science from a teacher with exceptionally strict grading criteria may erroneously believe that she's "no good" in science. Or a new boy at school whose attempts at being friendly are rejected by two or three thoughtless classmates may erroneously believe that "no one" likes him. In such circumstances students set unnecessarily low goals for themselves and give up easily in the face of small obstacles.

But it's also possible to have too much of a good thing. When learners are *too* overconfident, they can set themselves up for failure by forming unrealistically high expectations or exerting insufficient effort to succeed. Moreover, students will hardly be inclined to address weaknesses they don't realize they have (Bandura, 1997; Sinatra & Mason, 2008; Sweeny, Carroll, & Shepperd, 2006; Zimmerman & Moylan, 2009).

## FACTORS IN THE DEVELOPMENT OF SELF-EFFICACY

At least five distinct factors affect learners' self-efficacy: their previous successes and failures, their current emotional state, other people's messages, other people's successes and failures, and successes and failures that learners experience as members of a particular group (Bandura, 1986, 1997; Usher & Pajares, 2009).

### PREVIOUS SUCCESSES AND FAILURES

Without a doubt, the most important factor affecting learners' self-efficacy for an activity is the extent to which they've previously succeeded at that activity or similar ones (Bandura, 1986; Usher & Pajares, 2008; T. Williams & Williams, 2010). For example, Edward is more likely to believe he can learn to divide fractions if he has previously mastered fraction multiplication, and Elena will be more confident about learning to play rugby or field hockey if she's already acquired reasonable soccer skills. However, learners show developmental differences in *how far back* they look when they consider their prior successes and failures. Perhaps because of more limited cognitive abilities, children in the early elementary grades typically recall only their most recent experiences when predicting the likelihood of future success. In contrast, older children and adolescents are apt to consider a long-term pattern of prior successes and failures (Eccles et al., 1998).

As you can see, then, one important strategy for enhancing students' self-efficacy is to help them be successful at a variety of tasks in different content domains. Ideally we should tailor task difficulty to students' current self-efficacy levels: Students with little or no confidence in their ability to perform in a particular domain may initially respond more favorably if we give them tasks at which they'll almost certainly do well. But ultimately, students develop higher self-efficacy when they can successfully accomplish *challenging* tasks, perhaps initially with some degree of structure—that is, *scaffolding*—to increase the likelihood of successful performance (Falco, 2008; Lodewyk & Winne, 2005).

Nonetheless, mastery of important knowledge and skills, even fairly basic ones, often comes only slowly over time. Consequently, it's often important to define success in terms of *improvement* rather than mastery (R. Butler, 1998a; M.-T. Wang & Holcombe, 2010). In such instances we may need to provide concrete mechanisms that highlight day-to-day progress—for instance, giving students progress charts they can fill in themselves (e.g., see Figure 10.4) and providing frequent verbal or written feedback about the little things students are doing well.

Once students have developed a high sense of self-efficacy, an occasional failure is unlikely to dampen their optimism much. In fact, when these students encounter small setbacks, they know they *can* succeed if they try, and they also develop a realistic attitude about failure—that at worst it's a temporary setback and at best it can give them useful information about how to improve their performance. In other words, students develop resilient self-efficacy (Bandura, 1989, 2008; Dweck, 2000).

**FIGURE 10.4** Nine-year-old Sophie has been charting her monthly progress in remembering multiplication facts. Although she has had minor setbacks, her general progress is upward. (She was absent for February's assessment.)

Adjust the initial difficulty of tasks to students' existing self-efficacy levels. Then gradually increase the challenge, providing structure to guide students' efforts.

**resilient self-efficacy** Belief that one can perform a task successfully even after experiencing setbacks.

## CURRENT EMOTIONAL STATE

Learners' current emotional state—for instance, their general mood and the extent to which they feel anxious or stressed—can significantly affect their self-efficacy for the task at hand. For example, a student who feels excessively anxious or agitated during an important academic task may interpret that feeling as a sign of low ability for the task, even if the feeling has come from an unrelated source (Bandura, 1997; Schunk & Pajares, 2005; Usher & Pajares, 2009). The resulting low self-efficacy will, of course, undermine the student's performance, perhaps to the point that the task itself subsequently evokes anxiety and stress.

## MESSAGES FROM OTHERS

When learners' successes aren't obvious, we can enhance their self-efficacy by explicitly pointing out ways in which they've previously done well or are now excelling. Occasionally we may also be able to boost their self-efficacy by giving them reasons to believe they can be successful in the future (Usher & Pajares, 2008). Statements such as "You can do this problem if you work at it" and "I bet Judy will play with you if you ask her" might give students a slight boost in self-confidence. The effects of optimistic predictions will be modest and short lived, however, unless learners' efforts at a task ultimately *do* meet with success (Schunk, 1989a; Valentine, DuBois, & Cooper, 2004).

Even negative feedback can promote high self-efficacy *if* it gives guidance about how to improve and communicates confidence that improvement is likely—in other words, if it boosts *self-efficacy for learning* (Deci & Ryan, 1985; Narciss, 2008; Pintrich & Schunk, 2002). For example, consider the following statement:

> In the first draft of your research paper, many of your paragraphs don't lead logically to the ones that follow. A few headings and transitional sentences would make a world of difference. Let's find a time to discuss how you might use these techniques to improve the flow of your paper.

The statement indirectly communicates the message "With a little effort and new strategies, I know you can do better."

In some cases we communicate our beliefs about learners' competence through our actions rather than our words. For example, if we offer after-school assistance to students who are struggling to master a particular mathematical procedure or musical technique, we're communicating that with a little persistence, improvement is possible. We must be careful not to go overboard, however. If we give struggling students more assistance than they really need, we may inadvertently communicate the message "I don't think you can do this on your own" (Schunk, 1989b).

## SUCCESSES AND FAILURES OF OTHER INDIVIDUALS

We often form opinions about our probability of success by observing the successes and failures of other people, especially those whose ability levels are seemingly similar to our own (Dijkstra et al., 2008; Usher & Pajares, 2008; Zeldin & Pajares, 2000). For example, you're more likely to enroll in Dr. Carberry's Advanced Psychoceramics class if most of your friends have done well in the course, but if, instead, numerous friends have dropped the course in frustration, you may suspect that your own chances of succeeding are pretty slim. Likewise, recall Nathan's pessimism about learning French in the opening case study—pessimism based largely on the experiences of three low-achieving friends.

Another way of enhancing learners' self-efficacy, then, is to point out that others like them have mastered the knowledge and skills at hand (Schunk, 1983, 1989c). For example, a class of chemistry students who seem overwhelmed by the many chemical symbols they must learn might be reassured with a statement such as this:

> I know it seems like a lot to learn in such a short time. My students last year thought so, too, but they found that they could learn the symbols within three weeks if they studied a few new symbols each day.

But even more than *telling* learners about others' successes, *seeing* is believing. Learners who actually observe similar-ability peers successfully reach a goal are especially likely to believe that

Teacher messages can have a big impact on students' self-efficacy for literacy skills. Observe examples of efficacy-enhancing feedback in "Author's Chair."

Communicate your confidence in students' abilities even in your feedback about students' weaknesses.

Try not to give students more help than they actually need to succeed.

they, too, can achieve the goal. Hence, students sometimes develop greater self-efficacy when they see a classmate model a behavior than when they see their teacher model it. In one study (Schunk & Hanson, 1985), elementary school students who were having trouble with subtraction were given 25 subtraction problems to complete. Students who had seen another student successfully complete the problems got an average of 19 correct, whereas those who saw a teacher complete the problems got only 13 correct, and those who saw no model at all solved only 8! It may be even more beneficial for students to see one or more peers struggling with a task or problem at first—as they themselves might do—and then eventually mastering it (Kitsantas et al., 2000; Schunk, Hanson, & Cox, 1987; Schunk & Pajares, 2005). Presumably observing such a coping model shows learners that success doesn't necessarily come easily—that they must work and practice to achieve success—and allows them to observe the strategies the model uses to gain proficiency.

What we *don't* want to do, however, is to *define* success in terms of how students' performance compares with that of their peers—perhaps identifying the "best" writer, science student, or basketball player. Such comparison sets up a competitive situation in which the majority of students must inevitably lose. Most students have higher self-efficacy and achieve at higher levels if they *don't* evaluate their own performance in terms of how they stack up against others (Graham & Golen, 1991; Shih & Alexander, 2000; Stipek, 1996).

### SUCCESSES AND FAILURES AS PART OF A GROUP

Learners can often think more intelligently and acquire a more complex understanding of a topic when they collaborate with peers to master and apply classroom subject matter (e.g., D. W. Johnson & Johnson, 2009a; Pea, 1993; Slavin, 2011). Collaboration with peers has a possible additional benefit: Learners may have greater self-efficacy when they work in a group rather than alone. Such collective self-efficacy depends not only on students' perceptions of their own and others' capabilities but also on their perceptions of how effectively they can work together and coordinate their roles and responsibilities (Bandura, 1997, 2000; George & Feltz, 1995; Klassen & Usher, 2010).

Whether we ask students to tackle challenging tasks as individuals or in small groups, we must keep in mind that the school day shouldn't necessarily pose one challenge after another. Such a state of affairs would be absolutely exhausting, and probably quite discouraging as well. Instead, we should strike a balance between easy tasks, which will boost students' self-confidence over the short run, and the challenging tasks so critical for an optimistic sense of self-efficacy for the long term (Spaulding, 1992; Stipek, 1996). The Into the Classroom feature "Fostering Productive Self-Efficacy Levels" presents several research-based strategies.

## TEACHER SELF-EFFICACY

Not only should our students have high self-efficacy about their ability to succeed in the classroom but so, too, should we teachers have high self-efficacy about our ability to *help* them succeed. Students are more likely to achieve at high levels when their teachers have confidence that they can help students master classroom topics (Skaalvik & Skaalvik, 2008; Tschannen-Moran, Woolfolk Hoy, & Hoy, 1998; Ware & Kitsantas, 2007). Some of this teacher confidence may take the form of collective self-efficacy: When teachers at a school believe that, as a group, they can make a significant difference in the lives of children and adolescents, their students, too, have higher self-efficacy themselves and are more likely to achieve at high levels (Goddard, 2001; Goddard, Hoy, & Woolfolk Hoy, 2000; Tschannen-Moran et al., 1998).

When teachers have high self-efficacy about their effectiveness in the classroom—both individually and collectively—they influence students' achievement in several ways:

- They are more willing to experiment with new teaching strategies that can better help students learn.
- They set higher goals for students' performance.
- They put more effort into their teaching and are more persistent in helping students learn. (Bandura, 1997; Roeser, Marachi, & Gehlbach, 2002; Skaalvik & Skaalvik, 2008; Tschannen-Moran et al., 1998)

Such effects should look familiar: Just as self-efficacy affects students' choice of activities, goals, effort, and persistence, so, too, does it affect *teachers'* choices, goals, effort, and persistence.

**coping model** Model who initially struggles with a task but successfully overcomes obstacles.

**collective self-efficacy** People's beliefs about their ability to be successful when they work together on a task.

 Minimize students' awareness of classmates' performance levels.

See Chapter 8 and Chapter 12 for discussions of the benefits of cooperative learning activities.

Collaborate with colleagues to identify effective ways of fostering *all* students' academic and social success at school.

## Into the Classroom

### Fostering Productive Self-Efficacy Levels

🍏 **Teach basic knowledge and skills to mastery.**
A biology teacher makes sure all students clearly understand the basic structure of DNA before moving to mitosis and meiosis, two topics that require a knowledge of DNA structure.

🍏 **Assure students that they can be successful at challenging tasks, and point out that others like them have been successful in the past.**
Early in the school year, students in beginning band express frustration in learning to play their instruments. Their teacher reminds them that, like themselves, students in last year's beginning band started out with little knowledge but eventually mastered their instruments. A few weeks later, the beginning band class attends a concert at which the school's advanced band (last year's beginning band class) play a medley from the Broadway musical *Wicked*.

🍏 **Have students see peers with similar ability successfully accomplishing challenging tasks.**
To convince his students from low-income, minority-group families that they can do almost anything if they put their minds to it, a high school math teacher shows his class the film *Stand and Deliver*. The film depicts the true story of 18 Mexican American high school students from a low-income neighborhood in East Los Angeles who, through hard work and perseverance, earned college credit by passing the national Advanced Placement (AP) calculus exam.

🍏 **Help students track their progress on challenging tasks.**
As first graders are learning how to weave on small circular looms, one student approaches her teacher in tears, frustrated that her first few rows are full of mistakes. The teacher responds, "Look, Dorothy, this is the history, your own history, of learning to weave. You can look at this and say, 'Why, I can see how I began, here I didn't know how very well, I went over two instead of one; but I learned, and then—it is perfect all the way to the end!'" The student returns to her seat, very much comforted, and finishes her piece. She follows it with another, flawless one and proudly shows it to her teacher.

🍏 **After students have mastered basic skills, present some tasks at which they can succeed only with effort and perseverance.**
A physical education teacher tells his students, "Today we've determined how far each of you can go in the broad jump. We'll continue to practice good form a little bit each week. Some of your future efforts will be more successful than others, but let's see if every one of you can jump at least two inches farther when I test you again at the end of the month."

🍏 **Have students tackle especially challenging tasks in small, cooperative groups.**
A fifth-grade teacher has students work in groups of three or four to write research papers about early colonial life in North America. The teacher makes sure that the students in each group collectively have the skills in library research, writing, word processing, and art necessary to complete the task. She also makes sure that every student has some unique skills to contribute to the group effort.

🍏 **If students are unrealistically overconfident—so much so that they don't exert the effort and strategies needed to master the material—help them learn how to accurately evaluate their current knowledge and skill levels.**
Many students in math classes at a technical school are quite confident that they're solving problems correctly, even though their past grades in the class have been poor. To help them more realistically assess their current understandings, a teacher in one of the classes begins giving frequent short quizzes in which students have to predict their ability to correctly solve each problem before actually trying to solve it; they must also evaluate the accuracy of their problem solutions. Then, when they get back their graded quizzes, they get extra points for critiquing the accuracy of their problem-specific self-evaluations and for explaining and correcting their errors. Students in this class begin to achieve at higher levels than their peers in other classes.

*Sources:* Bandura, 1986, 1989, 1997, 2000; R. Butler, 1998a; Eccles et al., 1998; Hawkins, 1997, p. 332 (weaving example); Lodewyk & Winne, 2005; Mathews, 1988; Menéndez, 1988 (*Stand and Deliver* example); Schunk, 1983, 1989a, 1989c; Usher & Pajares, 2008; Zeldin & Pajares, 2000; Zimmerman & Moylan, 2009 (math example).

As is true for students, however, it's possible for teachers to have too much of a good thing. Occasionally teachers have so much confidence in their existing knowledge and skills that they find little benefit in professional development activities that would enhance their effectiveness (Guskey, 1988; Middleton & Abrams, 2004; Tschannen-Moran et al., 1998). We teachers are *learners* as well, and we'll always have room for improvement in our classroom strategies.

## Self-Regulation

**self-regulation** Process of setting goals for oneself and engaging in behaviors and cognitive processes that lead to goal attainment.

Although high self-efficacy can certainly enhance students' classroom performance, it's by no means the only thing that affects their performance. Students must also master the knowledge and skills that make high performance levels possible. Some knowledge and skills are specific to particular topics and academic domains, but one set of skills—those related to self-regulation—can have a pervasive influence on students' achievement across the board. To get a sense of your own self-regulation skills, try the following exercise.

## EXPERIENCING FIRSTHAND
## SELF-REFLECTION ABOUT SELF-REGULATION

For each of the following situations, choose the alternative that most accurately describes your attitudes, thoughts, and behaviors as a college student. No one will see your answers except you, so be honest!

1. With regard to my final course grades, I'm trying very hard to
   a. Earn all As.
   b. Earn all As and Bs.
   c. Keep my overall grade point average at or above the minimally acceptable level at my college.

2. As I'm reading or studying a textbook,
   a. I often notice when my attention is wandering, and I immediately get my mind back on my work.
   b. I sometimes notice when my attention is wandering, but not always.
   c. I often get so lost in daydreams that I waste a lot of time.

3. Whenever I finish a study session,
   a. I write down how much time I've spent on my schoolwork.
   b. I make a mental note of how much time I've spent on my schoolwork.
   c. I don't really think much about the time I've spent on my schoolwork.

4. When I turn in an assignment,
   a. I usually have a good idea of the grade I'll get on it.
   b. I'm often surprised by the grade I get.
   c. I don't think much about the quality of what I've done.

5. When I do exceptionally well on an assignment,
   a. I feel good about my performance and might reward myself in some way.
   b. I feel good about my performance but don't do anything special for myself afterward.
   c. I don't feel much different than I did before I received my grade.

Regardless of how you answered Item 1, you could probably identify a particular goal toward which you're striving. Your response to Item 2 should give you an idea of how much you monitor and try to control your thoughts when you're studying. Your responses to Items 3 and 4 tell you something about how frequently and accurately you evaluate your performance. And your response to Item 5 indicates whether you're likely to reinforce yourself for desired behaviors. To the extent that we establish our own priorities and goals, take charge of our own thoughts and actions, and reflect on and evaluate our own behaviors, we are self-regulating individuals (e.g., Bandura, 2008).

Thanks, in part, to brain maturation over the course of childhood and adolescence, most learners become increasingly self-regulating as they grow older (more on this point in an Applying Brain Research feature later in the chapter). Table 10.2 presents typical advancements in the elementary and secondary school years. Some of the entries in the table, such as self-instructions and self-evaluation of actions, reflect self-regulation in *behavior*. Others, such as ability to control attention and self-motivation, reflect self-regulation in *learning*. We'll look here at both self-regulated behavior and self-regulated learning, as well as at self-regulated problem solving.

## SELF-REGULATED BEHAVIOR

When we behave in particular ways and observe how our environment reacts—reinforcing some behaviors and punishing or otherwise discouraging others—we begin to distinguish between productive and unproductive responses, and most of us increasingly control and monitor our own actions (Bandura, 1986, 2008). In other words, we engage in self-regulated behavior. Self-regulated behavior has at least six important components, which are summarized in Figure 10.5. As you'll see, all six of them have cognitive elements as well as behavioral ones.

**FIGURE 10.5 Components of self-regulated behavior**

**Before the Response:**
• Self-Determined Standards and Goals

**During the Response:**
• Emotion Regulation
• Self-Instructions
• Self-Monitoring

**After the Response:**
• Self-Evaluation
• Self-Imposed Contingencies

# DEVELOPMENTAL TRENDS

## TABLE 10.2 • Self-Regulation at Different Grade Levels

| GRADE LEVEL | AGE-TYPICAL CHARACTERISTICS | EXAMPLE | SUGGESTED STRATEGIES |
|---|---|---|---|
| K–2 | • Some internalization of adults' standards for behavior<br>• Emerging ability to set self-chosen goals for learning and achievement<br>• Some use of self-instructions (self-talk) to guide behavior<br>• Some self-evaluation of effectiveness and appropriateness of actions; feelings of guilt about wrongdoings<br>• Individual differences in self-control of impulses, emotions, and attention; peer relationships and classroom performance affected by amount of self-control in these areas | Most of the children in a kindergarten class can sit quietly and listen when their teacher reads a storybook. But a few of them squirm restlessly and occasionally poke or otherwise distract their classmates. | • Discuss rationales for classroom rules.<br>• Show students how some behaviors can help them reach their goals and how other behaviors interfere with goal attainment.<br>• Organize the classroom so that students can carry out some activities on their own (e.g., have reading centers where children can listen to storybooks on tape).<br>• When students show impulsiveness or poor emotion control, provide guidelines and consistent consequences for behavior. |
| 3–5 | • Improving ability to self-assess performance and progress<br>• Guilt and shame about unsatisfactory performance and moral transgressions<br>• Emerging self-regulated learning strategies (e.g., conscious attempts to focus attention, ability to do short assignments independently at home)<br>• Persistent difficulties with self-control for some students | Every Thursday evening, 8-year-old Logan studies for the weekly spelling test his teacher will give his class the following day. Sometimes he asks his father or older brother to test him on especially difficult words. | • Have students set specific, concrete goals for their learning.<br>• Encourage students to assess their own performance; provide criteria they can use to evaluate their work.<br>• Ask students to engage in simple, self-regulated learning tasks (e.g., small-group learning activities, short homework assignments); provide some structure to guide students' efforts.<br>• Encourage students to use their peers as resources when they need help.<br>• If students have continuing difficulty with self-control, teach self-instructions that can help them control their behavior. |
| 6–8 | • Increasing ability to plan future actions, due in part to increased capacity for abstract thought<br>• Increasing mastery of some self-regulating learning strategies, especially those that involve overt behaviors (e.g., keeping a calendar of assignments and due dates)<br>• Self-motivational strategies (e.g., minimizing distractions, devising ways to make a boring task more interesting and enjoyable, reminding oneself about the importance of doing well)<br>• Decrease in help-seeking behaviors during times of confusion, especially if teachers appear to be aloof and nonsupportive | For fear of looking "stupid" in her math class, 13-year-old Katherine rarely asks questions when she doesn't understand a new concept or procedure. | • Assign homework and other tasks that require age-appropriate independent learning.<br>• Provide concrete strategies for keeping track of learning tasks and assignments (e.g., provide monthly calendars on which students can write due dates).<br>• Provide concrete guidance about how to learn and study effectively (e.g., give students questions they should answer as they complete reading assignments at home).<br>• Give students frequent opportunities to assess their own learning; have them compare your evaluations with theirs. |
| 9–12 | • More long-range goal setting<br>• Continuing development of strategies for emotion regulation, especially in contexts that can evoke strong emotions (e.g., sports, theater productions)<br>• Wide variability in ability to self-regulate learning, especially when out-of-school assignments conflict with attractive leisure activities; few self-regulating learning strategies among many low-achieving high school students<br>• For a small number of older adolescents, persistent difficulties in self-control that can adversely affect classroom behavior and peer relationships | After moving from fairly small middle schools to a much larger, consolidated high school, some students diligently complete their homework each night. But many others are easily enticed into more enjoyable activities with friends—hanging out at a local fast-food restaurant, instant-messaging on cell phones, and so on—and their grades decline significantly as a result. | • Relate classroom learning tasks to students' long-range personal and professional goals.<br>• Encourage students to experiment with various emotions and emotion-control strategies through role-playing and drama.<br>• Assign complex independent learning tasks, providing the necessary structure and guidance for students who are not yet self-regulating learners.<br>• Have high-achieving students describe their strategies for resisting attractive alternatives and keeping themselves on task when doing homework. |

*Sources:* Blair, 2002; Bronson, 2000; Corno & Mandinach, 2004; Damon, 1988; Dunning, Heath, & Suls, 2004; Eccles, Wigfield, & Schiefele, 1998; Fries, Dietz, & Schmid, 2008; Hampson, 2008; M. Hofer, 2010; M. H. Jones, Estell, & Alexander, 2008; Kochanska, Gross, Lin, & Nichols, 2002; Larson & Brown, 2007; Marchand & Skinner, 2007; J. S. Matthews, Ponitz, & Morrison, 2009; Meichenbaum & Goodman, 1971; Meltzer et al., 2007; S. D. Miller, Heafner, Massey, & Strahan, 2003; S. G. Paris & Paris, 2001; Posner & Rothbart, 2007; Schneider, 2010; Valiente, Lemery-Calfant, Swanson, & Reiser, 2008; Wolters & Rosenthal, 2000.

## SELF-DETERMINED STANDARDS AND GOALS

As self-regulating human beings, we tend to have general standards for our behavior—standards that serve as criteria for evaluating our performance in specific situations. We also establish certain goals that guide our actions and activity choices. Meeting our standards and reaching our goals give us considerable self-satisfaction, enhancing our self-efficacy and spurring us on to greater heights (Bandura, 1986, 1989).

Different individuals adopt different standards and goals for themselves, of course. Often their standards and goals are modeled after those of other people (Fitzsimmons & Finkel, 2010; E. A. Locke & Latham, 1990; R. B. Miller & Brickman, 2004). For example, at the high school I attended, many students wanted to go to the best college they possibly could, and their academic aspirations were contagious. But at a different high school, getting a job after graduation—or perhaps *instead* of graduation—might have been the goal more commonly modeled by peers.

Students are typically more motivated to work toward goals they've chosen for themselves, rather than goals that others have imposed on them (e.g., Deci & Ryan, 1992; Fitzsimmons & Finkel, 2010; M. E. Ford, 1992). One way to help students develop self-regulation, then, is to provide situations in which they set their own goals. For example, we might ask them to decide how many addition facts they're going to learn by Friday, what topic they want to study for a research project, or which gymnastic skills they'd like to master.

Ideally we should encourage students to establish standards and goals that are challenging yet realistic. We might even want to provide incentives that encourage students to set and achieve challenging goals (Stipek, 1996). At the same time, we must caution students that constant perfection is *not* a realistic goal—that occasional errors are inevitable in the pursuit of new and difficult tasks. Students who are satisfied only with flawless performance can't possibly live up to such an impossible standard and, as a result, may become excessively anxious or depressed (Bandura, 1986; Covington, 1992; Parker, 1997).

## EMOTION REGULATION

A second important aspect of self-regulated behavior is emotion regulation, keeping in check or modifying any feelings that might lead to counterproductive responses—perhaps anger, resentment, or excessive excitement. Effective emotion regulation often involves a two-pronged approach (Buckley & Saarni, 2009; Pekrun, 2006; J. M. Richards, 2004). First, learners control the extent to which they *express their feelings*. In addition, self-regulating individuals often *reinterpret events* in order to put a positive spin on what might otherwise be anger- or sadness-inducing circumstances. For instance, a student who gets an unexpectedly low quiz score might treat it as a wake-up call to study more diligently in the future. And a student who doesn't make the varsity soccer team might think, "Maybe this is a blessing in disguise, because it gives me more time to help out at the Boys' Club after school."

On average, children and adolescents who can effectively control their emotions have more friends and better social skills (Aikins & Litwack, 2011; Eisenberg, Vaughan, & Hofer, 2009). In contrast, those who have trouble keeping their feelings in check are likely to be lonely and depressed; some exhibit behavior problems at school, and others become chronic victims of school bullies (Buckley & Saarni, 2009; Silk, Steinberg, & Morris, 2003).

## SELF-INSTRUCTIONS

Sometimes learners simply need reminders of how to behave in particular situations. By teaching them how to use self-instructions to guide themselves through complex situations, we provide them with a means through which *they remind themselves* about appropriate actions. One effective approach involves five steps (Meichenbaum, 1977):

1. *Cognitive modeling:* The teacher models self-instruction by repeating instructions aloud while simultaneously performing the activity.
2. *Overt, external guidance:* The teacher repeats the instructions aloud while the learner performs the activity.
3. *Overt self-guidance:* The learner repeats the instructions aloud while performing the activity.
4. *Faded, overt self-guidance:* The learner whispers the instructions while performing the activity.
5. *Covert self-instruction:* The learner silently thinks about the instructions while performing the activity.

**emotion regulation** Process of keeping in check or intentionally altering feelings that might lead to counterproductive behavior.

**self-instructions** Instructions that one gives oneself while performing a complex behavior.

Self-chosen rather than other-chosen goals enhance one's sense of *self-determination*, an important prerequisite for intrinsic motivation (see Chapter 11).

Have students set some of their own goals in the classroom. Encourage them to set challenging yet realistic goals; caution them against always striving for perfection.

As children grow older, most develop strategies for regulating their emotions. For example, listen to 10-year-old Daniel, 13-year-old Crystal, and 15-year-old Greg in "Emotions."

Teach students instructions they can use to guide themselves through difficult tasks.

Vygotsky's theory is presented in Chapter 2.

As you can see in these steps, the teacher initially serves as a model both for the behavior and for the self-instructions and then gradually transfers responsibility to the learner. Steps 3 through 5 in the process may remind you of Vygotsky's concepts of *self-talk* and *inner speech*.

Teaching self-instructions can be useful in helping students acquire and improve complex athletic skills (Hatzigeorgiadis, Zourbanos, Galanis, & Theodorakis, 2011). It can also be quite effective in working with students who consistently exhibit behavior problems, such as chronic impulsivity or dishonesty (Carter & Doyle, 2006; W. M. Casey & Burton, 1982; Meichenbaum, 1985). Furthermore, applications are now available for programming individualized self-instructions into a smartphone (e.g., search the Internet for "self-talk apps").

## SELF-MONITORING

Another important aspect of self-regulation is to observe oneself in action—a process known as self-monitoring (or *self-observation*). To make progress toward important goals, learners must be aware of how well they're currently doing. And when they see themselves making progress, they're more likely to continue with their efforts (Schunk & Zimmerman, 1997).

Learners aren't always astute monitors of their own behavior, however. For instance, they may not be aware of how frequently they do something incorrectly or ineffectively or of how *infre*quently they do something well. Specific, concrete mechanisms can often enhance their self-monitoring. For example, if Raymond too often speaks out of turn, we can ask him to make a checkmark on a sheet of paper every time he catches himself talking at inappropriate times. And if Hillary has trouble staying on task during assigned activities, we can ask her to stop and reflect on her behavior every few minutes (perhaps with the aid of an egg timer or electronic beeper) to determine whether she was staying on task during each interval. Figure 10.6 illustrates the type of form we might give Hillary to record her observations.

Such self-focused observation and recording can bring about noticeable changes—sometimes quite dramatic ones—in learners' behavior. For example, self-monitoring can be used to increase students' participation in class and diligence in completing assignments. It's also effective in reducing aggression and such disruptive behaviors as talking out of turn and getting out of one's seat (Belfiore & Hornyak, 1998; Plavnick, Ferreri, & Maupin, 2010; Prater, Carter, Hitchcock, & Dowrick, 2011; Reid, Trout, & Schartz, 2005; Webber, Scheuermann, McCall, & Coleman, 1993).

Use of video technology can further enhance learners' self-monitoring capabilities (Bear, Torgerson, & Dubois-Gerchak, 2010; Hitchcock, Dowrick, & Prater, 2003; Prater et al., 2011). Consider, for example, the case of Charles, a highly intelligent fifth grader whose classroom behaviors—aggression, temper tantrums, regular refusals to complete schoolwork—had his parents and teachers totally exasperated. Nothing had worked with Charles—not traditional behaviorist techniques (e.g., systematic praise, time-outs, a token economy), counseling, or paper-and-pencil self-monitoring sheets. But when his special education teacher began videotaping and then showing him his behaviors in math class, he was appalled at what he saw: "Do I really look like that?" "Did I really say that?" "Turn it off!" Charles expressed a strong desire to be "normal," his classroom behaviors became noticeably more compliant and respectful, and he began to appreciate the praise, tokens, and other reinforcers he'd previously shunned (Bear et al., 2010, p. 83).

## FIGURE 10.6 Example of a self-monitoring sheet for staying on task

Self-Observation Record for ___Hillary___

Every ten minutes, put a mark to show how well you have been staying on task.

+   means you were almost always on task
1/2 means you were on task about half the time
−   means you were hardly ever on task

| 9:00-9:10 | 9:10-9:20 | 9:20-9:30 | 9:30-9:40 | 9:40-9:50 | 9:50-10:00 |
|---|---|---|---|---|---|
| + | + | − | + | $\frac{1}{2}$ | − |

| 10:00-10:10 | 10:10-10:20 | 10:20-10:30 | 10:30-10:40 | 10:40-10:50 | 10:50-11:00 |
|---|---|---|---|---|---|
| $\frac{1}{2}$ | − | *recess* | | + | $\frac{1}{2}$ |

| 11:00-11:10 | 11:10-11:20 | 11:20-11:30 | 11:30-11:40 | 11:40-11:50 | 11:50-12:00 |
|---|---|---|---|---|---|
| | | | | | |

Have students observe and record information about their own behavior.

**self-monitoring** Process of observing and recording one's own behavior.

**self-evaluation** Process of judging one's own performance or behavior.

## SELF-EVALUATION

To be truly self-regulating, learners must not only monitor but also *judge* their own behavior, as Charles obviously did when he watched the videotapes. In other words, they must engage in self-evaluation. Reasonably accurate self-evaluation depends on having appropriate standards

**FIGURE 10.7** After a cooperative group activity with three classmates, Rochelle and her teacher used the same criteria to rate Rochelle's performance and that of her group. With the two sets of ratings side by side, Rochelle could evaluate the accuracy of her self-assessments.

Project description ___*Travel Guide*_____

Evaluate with a 1 for weak, a 2 for fair, a 3 for good, a 4 for very good, and a 5 for excellent.

| Student | Teacher | |
|---|---|---|
| 4 | 4 | 1. The task was a major amount of work in keeping with a whole month of effort. |
| 5 | 4 | 2. We used class time quite well. |
| 4 | 5 | 3. The workload was quite evenly divided. I did a fair proportion. |
| 4 | 5 | 4. I showed commitment to the group and to a quality project. |
| 5 | 4 | 5. My report went into depth; it didn't just give the obvious, commonly known information. |
| 5 | 5 | 6. The project made a point: a reader (or viewer) could figure out how all of the details fitted together to help form a conclusion. |
| 5 | 5 | 7. The project was neat, attractive, well assembled. I was proud of the outcome. |
| 4 | 5 | 8. We kept our work organized; we made copies; we didn't lose things or end up having to redo work that was lost. |
| 5 | 4 | 9. The work had a lot of original thinking or other creative work. |
| 4 | 4 | 10. The project demonstrated mastery of basic language skills—composition, planning, oral communication, writing. |
| 45 | 45 | Total |

for behavior, of course, and also on having relatively objective techniques for self-monitoring one's own actions. When learners have such prerequisites, we can use strategies such as the following:

- Have students write in daily or weekly journals in which they address the strengths and weaknesses of their performance.
- Arrange small-group peer conferences in which several students discuss their reactions to one another's work.
- Have students assemble portfolios of what they consider their best work, with a self-evaluation of each entry. (S. G. Paris & Ayres, 1994; S. G. Paris & Paris, 2001)

In addition, we can provide self-assessment instruments that show students what to look for as they evaluate their work, and we can occasionally have them compare their self-assessments with others' independent judgments of their performance (DuPaul & Hoff, 1998; Mitchem & Young, 2001; Reid et al., 2005; D. J. Smith, Young, West, Morgan, & Rhode, 1988). Figure 10.7 presents a form one teacher has used to help her students learn to evaluate their performance in a cooperative group activity.

## SELF-IMPOSED CONTINGENCIES

**Self-imposed contingencies** involve giving oneself reinforcement or punishment for one's behavior. For example, how do you feel when you accomplish a difficult task—perhaps earning an A in a challenging course or making a three-point shot in a basketball game? And how do you feel when you fail in your endeavors—perhaps getting a D on an important exam or thoughtlessly hurting a friend's feelings? When you accomplish something you've set out to do, especially if the task is complex and challenging, you probably feel quite proud of yourself

Once students have set appropriate standards and objective methods of self-observation, ask them to evaluate their own performance.

Chapter 15 offers recommendations for helping students create portfolios.

**self-imposed contingency**
Self-reinforcement or self-punishment that follows a behavior.

**self-regulated learning** Regulation of one's own cognitive processes and studying behaviors in order to learn successfully.

and give yourself a mental pat on the back. In contrast, when you fail to accomplish a task, you're probably unhappy with your performance; you may also feel guilty, regretful, or ashamed (Harter, 1999; Krebs, 2008).

As children and adolescents become increasingly self-regulating, they, too, begin to reinforce themselves when they accomplish their goals—perhaps by feeling proud or telling themselves they did a good job. And they may punish themselves when they do something that doesn't meet their own performance standards—perhaps by feeling sorry, guilty, or ashamed. But self-imposed contingencies aren't necessarily confined to emotional reactions. Many self-regulating individuals reinforce themselves in far more concrete ways when they do something well (Bandura, 1977). I once had a colleague who went shopping every time she completed a research article or report (she had one of the best wardrobes in town). I'm more frugal: When I finish writing each major section of a chapter, I either help myself to a piece of chocolate or take time to watch one of my favorite television game shows. As a result, I'm chubbier than my colleague, but I have a wealth of knowledge of game-show trivia and would almost certainly beat her in a game of Trivial Pursuit.

Teach students to reinforce themselves for productive behavior.

Thus, an additional way to help students become more self-regulating is to teach them self-reinforcement. When students begin to reinforce themselves for appropriate responses—perhaps giving themselves some free time, allowing themselves to engage in a favorite activity, or simply praising themselves—their study habits and classroom behavior can improve significantly (K. R. Harris, 1986; Hayes et al., 1985; Reid et al., 2005). In one research study, students who were performing poorly in arithmetic were taught to give themselves points when they did well on assignments; they could later use the points to "buy" a variety of items and privileges. Within a few weeks, these students were doing as well as their classmates on both in-class assignments and homework (H. C. Stevenson & Fantuzzo, 1986).

Some students need considerable scaffolding to help them acquire self-regulation skills. Observe how one teacher uses technology to provide such scaffolding in "Self-Management: Brandon's MotivAider and Picture Schedule."

The most diligent workers and highest achievers in the classroom, on the athletic field, and elsewhere are likely to be individuals who can effectively self-regulate their behavior (Duckworth & Seligman, 2005; Trautwein, Lüdtke, Kastens, & Köller, 2006; Zimmerman & Kitsantas, 2005). But we certainly don't have to leave the development of self-regulated behavior to chance. As we teach students strategies for taking charge of their own actions, we should keep several points in mind:

- Students must be physically and cognitively capable of achieving the goals they've set.
- Students must be motivated to change their behavior.
- Students' expectations for change must be realistic and practical; dramatic overnight improvements are rare.
- Students must have high self-efficacy for making the necessary changes.

Acquiring effective self-regulation skills is often a slow, gradual process, but with reasonable guidance and scaffolding, virtually all students can master them.

## SELF-REGULATED LEARNING

See Chapter 7 for other aspects of metacognition.

To be truly self-regulating, learners must direct and monitor their learning as well as their behavior. In particular, self-regulated learning includes the following processes, many of which clearly involve metacognition:

- *Goal setting:* Self-regulating learners know what they want to accomplish when they read or study—perhaps to learn specific facts, gain a broad conceptual understanding of a topic, or simply acquire enough knowledge to do well on a classroom exam. Typically they tie their goals for a particular learning activity to longer-term goals and aspirations (Nolen, 1996; Winne & Hadwin, 1998; Wolters, 1998; Zimmerman & Moylan, 2009).
- *Planning:* Self-regulating learners determine ahead of time how best to use the time and resources they have available for learning tasks (Zimmerman & Moylan, 2009).
- *Self-motivation:* Self-regulating learners typically have high self-efficacy regarding their ability to accomplish a learning task successfully. They use a variety of strategies to keep themselves on task—perhaps embellishing the task to make it more fun, reminding themselves of the importance of doing well, or promising themselves a reward when they're finished (Pajares, 2009; Usher, 2009; Wolters, 2003).

- *Attention control:* Self-regulating learners try to focus their attention on the subject matter at hand and to clear their minds of potentially distracting thoughts and emotions (Harnishfeger, 1995; J. Kuhl, 1985; Winne, 1995).

- *Flexible use of learning strategies:* Self-regulating learners choose different learning strategies depending on the specific goals they hope to accomplish. For example, how they read a magazine article depends on whether they're reading it for entertainment or studying for an exam (Meltzer et al., 2007; van den Broek, Lorch, Linderholm, & Gustafson, 2001; Winne, 1995).

- *Self-monitoring:* Self-regulating learners continually monitor their progress toward their goals for studying—for instance, by frequently checking their understanding of and memory for what they're reading (i.e., monitoring comprehension). In addition, they change their learning strategies or modify their goals as necessary (D. L. Butler & Winne, 1995; Carver & Scheier, 1990; Zimmerman & Moylan, 2009).

- *Appropriate help-seeking:* Truly self-regulating learners don't necessarily try to do everything on their own. On the contrary, they recognize when they need other people's help and actively seek it out. They're especially likely to ask for the kinds of help that will enable them to work more independently in the future (R. Butler, 1998b; J. Lee & Shute, 2010; R. S. Newman, 2008; Zusho & Barnett, 2011).

- *Self-evaluation:* Self-regulating learners determine whether the things they've learned have helped them meet their goals. Ideally, they also use their self-evaluations to adjust their use of various learning strategies on future occasions (Schraw & Moshman, 1995; Winne & Hadwin, 1998; Zimmerman & Moylan, 2009).

As noted in Table 10.2, a few elements of self-regulated learning (e.g., conscious efforts to focus attention and completing short learning tasks independently) emerge in the upper elementary grades, and additional ones (e.g., planning, self-motivation) appear in the middle school and high school years. To some extent, self-regulated learning probably develops from opportunities to engage in age-appropriate independent learning activities and to observe other people modeling effective self-regulation strategies (S. G. Paris & Paris, 2001; Vye et al., 1998; Zimmerman, 2004). But if we take Vygotsky's perspective for a moment, we might suspect that self-regulated learning also has roots in socially regulated learning (Stright, Neitzel, Sears, & Hoke-Sinex, 2001; Vygotsky, 1934/1986; Zimmerman, 1998). At first, a teacher or parent might help children learn by setting goals for a learning activity, keeping the children's attention focused on the learning task, suggesting effective learning strategies, monitoring learning progress, and so on. Then, in co-regulated learning, the adult and children share responsibility for directing the various aspects of the learning process (McCaslin & Good, 1996; McCaslin & Hickey, 2001; Zimmerman, 2004). For example, a teacher and students might agree on the specific goals of a learning endeavor, or the teacher might prescribe criteria that students might use to self-evaluate their performance. The teacher might initially provide considerable scaffolding for the students' learning efforts and then gradually remove it as students become more proficient self-regulators. Alternatively, several learners of *equal ability* might collectively regulate a learning task, perhaps in a cooperative group activity (Hickey, 2011; Volet, Vaura, & Salonen, 2009). In such a situation, different learners can take on different responsibilities and monitor one another's progress.

When children and adolescents are self-regulating learners, they set more ambitious academic goals for themselves, learn more effectively, and achieve at higher levels in classrooms and computer-based learning environments (D. L. Butler & Winne, 1995; Corno et al., 2002; Greene & Azevedo, 2009; Zimmerman & Risemberg, 1997). Self-regulation becomes increasingly important in adolescence and adulthood, when many learning activities—reading, doing homework, seeking needed resources on the Internet, and so on—occur in isolation from other people and thus require considerable self-direction (Trautwein et al., 2006; Winne, 1995; Zimmerman & Kitsantas, 2005). Even at advanced grade levels, however, many students have few self-regulated learning skills, perhaps in part because traditional instructional practices do little to encourage them (S. G. Paris & Ayres, 1994; Winters, Greene, & Costich, 2008; Zimmerman & Risemberg, 1997).

**co-regulated learning** Process through which an adult and child share responsibility for directing various aspects of the child's learning; alternatively, collaborative process in which one or more learners jointly support and monitor one another's learning progress.

**self-regulated problem solving** Use of self-directed strategies to address complex problems.

## PROMOTING SELF-REGULATED LEARNING

To promote self-regulated learning, we must, of course, teach students the kinds of cognitive processes that facilitate learning and memory—comprehension monitoring, elaborative self-questioning, and so on. In addition, researchers have suggested the following strategies:

- Encourage students to set some of their own goals for learning and then to monitor their progress toward those goals.
- Give students opportunities to work without teacher direction or assistance; include both independent learning activities in which students study by themselves (e.g., seatwork assignments, homework) and small-group activities in which students help one another learn (e.g., peer tutoring, cooperative learning).
- Occasionally assign activities in which students have considerable leeway regarding goals and use of time (e.g., research papers, creative projects).
- Teach time management strategies (e.g., setting aside specific times to study at home, prioritizing assignments based on difficulty and due dates).
- Provide the scaffolding students need to acquire self-regulation skills (e.g., give them checklists they can use to identify what they need to do each day and to determine when they've completed all assigned work).
- Model self-regulating cognitive processes by thinking aloud while using such processes, and then give students constructive feedback as they engage in similar processes.
- Encourage students to seek short-term, focused help to overcome temporary difficulties in understanding.
- Consistently ask students to evaluate their own performance, and have them compare their self-assessments to teacher assessments. (Belfiore & Hornyak, 1998; Bronson, 2000; Falco, 2008; A. King, 1997; McCaslin & Good, 1996; McMillan, 2010; Meltzer et al., 2007; R. S. Newman, 2008; S. G. Paris & Paris, 2001; N. E. Perry, 1998; N. E. Perry, VandeKamp, Mercer, & Nordby, 2002; Schunk & Zimmerman, 1997; J. W. Thomas, 1993b; Winne & Hadwin, 1998; Wong, Hoskyn, Jai, Ellis, & Watson, 2008; Zimmerman & Risemberg, 1997)

## SELF-REGULATED PROBLEM SOLVING

Effectively directing one's own efforts in tackling complex problems—that is, **self-regulated problem solving**—involves many of the same components as self-regulated learning: goal setting, self-motivation, attention control, self-monitoring, self-evaluation, and so on (Zimmerman & Campillo, 2003). And just as teacher scaffolding facilitates the development of self-regulated learning skills, so, too, does it facilitate the acquisition of self-regulated problem-solving strategies. For example, to encourage brainstorming and creativity in solving problems, we might suggest that students give themselves instructions such as these:

> I want to think of something no one else will think of, something unique. Be freewheeling, no hang-ups. I don't care what anyone thinks; just suspend judgment. I'm not sure what I'll come up with; it will be a surprise. The ideas can just flow through me. (Meichenbaum, 1977, p. 62)

Teach students the mental steps they can follow to solve complex problems more effectively.

We might also provide a general structure for students to follow as they approach complex problems—for example, by encouraging them to ask themselves such questions as "Why am I using this strategy?" and "Am I sure this answer makes sense?" (Berardi-Coletta, Buyer, Dominowski, & Rellinger, 1995; Desoete, Roeyers, & De Clercq, 2003).

Self-regulated problem solving is important not only for solving academic problems but for solving social problems as well. For instance, to help students deal more effectively with interpersonal conflicts, we might teach them to take these steps:

1. Define the problem.
2. Identify several possible solutions.
3. Predict the likely consequences of each solution.
4. Choose the best solution.
5. Identify the steps required to carry out the solution.

6. Carry out the steps.

7. Evaluate the results. (S. N. Elliott & Busse, 1991; Meichenbaum, 1977; Weissberg, 1985; Yell, Robinson, & Drasgow, 2001)

Following such steps often helps students who have interpersonal problems—for instance, students who are either socially withdrawn or overly aggressive—to develop more effective social skills (K. R. Harris, 1982; Meichenbaum, 1977; Yell et al., 2001).

Another approach is to provide training in peer mediation, in which students *help one another* solve interpersonal problems. In this approach, students learn how to mediate conflicts among classmates by asking opposing sides to express their differing points of view and then work together to devise a reasonable resolution (M. Deutsch, 1993; D. W. Johnson & Johnson, 1996, 2006; Stevahn, Johnson, Johnson, Oberle, & Wahl, 2000). In one study involving several second-through fifth-grade classrooms (D. W. Johnson, Johnson, Dudley, Ward, & Magnuson, 1995), students were trained to help peers resolve interpersonal conflicts by asking the opposing sides to do the following:

1. Define the conflict (the problem).

2. Explain their own perspectives and needs.

3. Explain the other person's perspectives and needs.

4. Identify at least three possible solutions to the conflict.

5. Reach an agreement that addresses the needs of both parties.

Students took turns serving as mediator for their classmates, such that everyone had experience resolving the conflicts of others. As a result, the students more frequently resolved their *own* interpersonal conflicts in ways that addressed the needs of both parties, and they were less likely than students in an untrained control group to ask for adult intervention.

Teach students strategies for effectively mediating classmates' interpersonal conflicts.

In peer mediation, then, we see another example of Vygotsky's notion that many effective cognitive processes have their roots in social interactions. In a peer mediation session, students model effective conflict resolution skills for one another, and they may eventually internalize the skills they use in solving others' problems to solve their *own* problems.

Peer mediation is most effective when students of diverse ethnic backgrounds, socioeconomic groups, and achievement levels all serve as mediators (Casella, 2001a; K. M. Williams, 2001b). It's appropriate primarily for small, short-term interpersonal problems, such as hurt feelings or conflicts over use of limited academic resources. Even the most proficient of peer mediators may be ill prepared to handle conflicts that involve deep-seated and emotionally charged attitudes and behaviors, such as homophobia and sexual harassment (Casella, 2001a). In such cases the guidance and intervention of teachers and other school personnel is probably necessary.

## DIVERSITY IN SELF-REGULATION

Some diversity in self-regulation—especially diversity related to effortful control—is the result of maturational changes in the brain (see the Applying Brain Research feature "Understanding and Accommodating Individual Differences in Self-Regulation"). Brain development progresses somewhat more quickly in females than in males—a trend that might partly explain girls' tendency to be more self-regulating than boys as early as kindergarten (Lenroot et al., 2007; Matthews, Ponitz, & Morrison, 2009).

But culture, too, seems to make a difference. Some cultural groups—for instance, many East Asian cultures—place particular importance on emotional restraint and self-discipline. Children growing up in these cultures are apt to be hard workers who can focus their attention and work independently on assigned tasks for long periods (X. Chen & Wang, 2010; P. M. Cole, Tamang, & Shrestha, 2006; Morelli & Rothbaum, 2007).

### PROMOTING SELF-REGULATION IN STUDENTS AT RISK

Some students have few outside role models for effective study habits—few people in their out-of-school lives who can model the self-regulated learning skills they'll need to succeed in high school and postsecondary education (J. Chen & Morris, 2008). As a result, these students may have little knowledge about how to accomplish goals such as graduating from high school, attending college, and eventually becoming successful professionals (Belfiore & Hornyak, 1998; B. L. Wilson & Corbett, 2001). For example, in a study with low-income, inner-city middle school students

**peer mediation** Approach to conflict resolution in which a student (serving as a *mediator*) asks peers in conflict to express their differing viewpoints and then work together to devise a reasonable resolution.

**effortful control** Ability to inhibit dominant responses in favor of other, less dominant ones that might be more productive; an aspect of temperament that is influenced by biology and brain maturation.

(B. L. Wilson & Corbett, 2001), researchers found that many of the students aspired to professional careers (doctor, lawyer, teacher, etc.) yet misbehaved in class, inconsistently completed homework, and often skipped school. They had little idea about what it would take to do well in their studies, as this interview with one of the students reveals:

> *Adult:* Are you on track to meet your goals?
>
> *Student:* No. I need to study more.
>
> *Adult:* How do you know that?
>
> *Student:* I just know by some of my grades. [mostly Cs]
>
> *Adult:* Why do you think you will be more inclined to do it in high school?
>
> *Student:* I don't want to get let back. I want to go to college.
>
> *Adult:* What will you need to do to get better grades?
>
> *Student:* Just do more and more work. I can rest when the school year is over.[4]

Motivation and effort are important, to be sure, but so are planning, time management, regular self-monitoring and self-evaluation, and appropriate help-seeking—things about which this student seemed to have little knowledge (B. L. Wilson & Corbett, 2001).

_____

[4]Dialogue from *Listening to Urban Kids: School Reform and the Teachers They Want* by Bruce L. Wilson and Dick Corbett, p. 23. Copyright © 2001 by the State University of New York Press, State University of New York. Reprinted with permission. All rights reserved.

## Applying Brain Research

### Understanding and Accommodating Individual Differences in Self-Regulation

Learners' ability to regulate their behaviors and emotions depend largely on two areas in the front part of the brain—the *prefrontal cortex* and the *anterior cingulate cortex*—that continue to develop over the course of childhood, adolescence, and early adulthood (Velanova, Wheeler, & Luna, 2008). In normal brain development, these two areas gradually gain some control over a set of structures in the middle of the brain—including the *amygdala*—that are heavily involved in feeling and responding to emotions. To some degree, then, effective self-regulation requires maturational changes that come only slowly with development (M. D. Lewis & Stieben, 2004; Rothbart, 2011; Steinberg, 2009; Wisner Fries & Pollak, 2007).

Compounding the problem for adolescents is that the changing hormone levels accompanying puberty can increase their sensitivity and reactions to high-stress situations. For example, the increasing testosterone levels in teenage boys make some of them especially prone to impulsive aggressive responses (S. Moore & Rosenthal, 2006; E. Walker, Shapiro, Esterberg, & Trotman, 2010).

Yet in any single age-group, learners seem to differ considerably in their ability to regulate their behaviors, emotions, and cognitive processes. Some of this variability is the result of differences in an aspect of temperament known as effortful control, which appears to have its basis in the brain. In particular, some learners are better able than others to consciously restrain themselves from making impulsive responses when other, less dominant responses might be more productive (Bates & Pettit, 2007; Rothbart, 2011; Rothbart et al., 2007). Students who show high levels of effortful control can better plan ahead, focus their attention where they need to, and keep inappropriate emotional reactions in check. Such students also tend to be better behaved in class and to achieve at higher levels than their classmates with less self-control (Blair & Razza, 2007; Liew, McTigue, Barrois, & Hughes, 2008; Valiente, Lemery-Calfant, Swanson, & Reiser, 2008).

As you can see, then, some students may need more guidance and support than others in acquiring self-regulation skills. With this point in mind, I offer two suggestions:

🍎 **Individualize the scaffolding students need to regulate their behaviors.** Some students are likely to need considerable structure to help them keep unproductive behaviors in check; for example,

this will be true for many students who have been identified as having emotional and behavioral disorders. Clear rules for behavior, explicit response–consequence contingencies, and concrete mechanisms for self-monitoring and self-evaluation are often in order. Also useful are simple technological devices—such as small buzzers that a teacher or other adult can remotely activate—that either remind students of things they should be doing or give them feedback that they're doing something well (J. O. Cooper, Heron, & Heward, 2007).

🍎 **Teach strategies for keeping counterproductive emotions in check.** Especially when working with students who are prone to emotional volatility, we can provide concrete guidance about how they might control feelings that would lead them to behave in ways they'd later regret. For instance, we might suggest that they count to 10 and take a few deep breaths in order to calm down before responding to a provocation on the playground. And we can help them brainstorm possible "silver linings" in disappointing circumstances (K. L. Fletcher & Cassady, 2010; Silk et al., 2003).

Fortunately, explicit instruction in self-regulating strategies can help students at risk begin to acquire more effective study habits (Cosden et al., 2001; Eilam, 2001; Graham & Harris, 1996; S. D. Miller et al., 2003). Sometimes instruction can take place in structured after-school homework programs, in which students have considerable scaffolding for such basic skills as keeping track of homework assignments and due dates, developing plans to complete all assignments in a timely manner, and locating helpful resources. But we can also provide scaffolding for self-regulated activities during regular school hours—for instance, distributing forms that students can use to keep track of what they've already done and still need to do. A daily log sheet, such as that presented in Figure 10.8, can help middle school students keep track of their math assignments and monitor their performance. The form has its limits, because it provides no place for students to record the types of problems they get wrong, the kinds of errors they make, or any other

**FIGURE 10.8** On this daily log sheet, 13-year-old Lea has kept track of her math assignments, their due dates, and her performance on them.

information that might help them improve. For students with few self-regulation strategies, however, using such a form can start them on the road to effective self-monitoring.

## SUPPORTING STUDENTS WITH SPECIAL NEEDS

Students with disabilities often grow up in tightly controlled and structured environments, and some of them have brain abnormalities that make self-regulation difficult. Thus many of these students may especially benefit from explicit instruction in self-regulation strategies and scaffolded opportunities to self-regulate some of their own activities (Coch, Dawson, & Fischer, 2007; Wehmeyer et al., 2007). For instance, we might encourage students with disabilities to set and strive for their own goals, especially goals that are concrete, specific, and accomplishable within a short time period. These students are also well served when we teach them self-monitoring, self-reinforcement, and self-regulated problem-solving skills (Cunningham & Cunningham, 2006; Mithaug & Mithaug, 2003; Reid et al., 2005; J. R. Sullivan & Conoley, 2004).

Table 10.3 presents a social cognitive perspective of characteristics commonly seen in students with special needs, as well as strategies for promoting the academic and social success of these students.

Chapter 5 identifies specific categories of special needs that fall within the five general categories listed in Table 10.3.

## REVISITING RECIPROCAL CAUSATION

We return now to a concept introduced at the beginning of the chapter: reciprocal causation. As we've explored social cognitive theory, we've identified how environmental factors (e.g., reinforcement, teacher scaffolding) can influence learners' behaviors. We've also identified personal factors (e.g., self-efficacy, self-determined standards and goals) that learners bring with them to new tasks, and those, too, affect learners' behaviors. From a social cognitive perspective, all three of these factors—environment, behavior, and person—mutually influence one another (e.g., Bandura, 2008). Several examples of these reciprocal influences are presented in the "General Examples" column in Table 10.4.

# STUDENTS IN INCLUSIVE SETTINGS

**TABLE 10.3 • Applying Social Cognitive Theory with Students Who Have Special Educational Needs**

| CATEGORY | CHARACTERISTICS YOU MIGHT OBSERVE | SUGGESTED STRATEGIES |
|---|---|---|
| **Students with specific cognitive or academic difficulties** | • Difficulty predicting the consequences of specific behaviors<br>• Low self-efficacy for academic tasks in areas where there has been a history of failure<br>• Less self-regulation of learning and behavior | • Help students form more realistic expectations about the consequences of their behaviors.<br>• Scaffold students' efforts on academic tasks to increase the probability of success.<br>• Identify students' areas of strength, and give them opportunities to tutor peers in those areas.<br>• Teach self-regulation strategies (e.g., goal setting and planning, self-monitoring, self-instructions, self-reinforcement). |
| **Students with social or behavioral problems** | • Unusual difficulty in learning from models and other aspects of the social environment (for many students with autism spectrum disorders)<br>• Difficulties in planning a productive course of action and in predicting the likely consequences of specific behaviors<br>• Friendships with peers who are poor models of effective social skills and prosocial behavior (for some students with emotional and behavioral disorders)<br>• Less self-regulation of emotions and behaviors<br>• Deficits in social problem solving | • Model appropriate classroom behaviors; combine modeling with explicit verbal instruction, and use visual aids to communicate desired behaviors.<br>• Discuss possible consequences of various courses of action when social conflicts arise.<br>• Provide opportunities for students to interact with peers who model effective social and prosocial behaviors.<br>• Videotape students as they exhibit appropriate and inappropriate behaviors; use videos of their appropriate behaviors as models for future actions.<br>• Teach self-regulation strategies (e.g., self-monitoring, self-instructions, self-regulated problem solving).<br>• Help students recognize and interpret other people's body language and other social cues. |
| **Students with general delays in cognitive and social functioning** | • Low self-efficacy for academic tasks<br>• Tendency to watch others for guidance about how to behave<br>• Low goals for achievement (possibly as a way of avoiding failure)<br>• Little or no self-regulation of learning and behavior | • Scaffold students' efforts on academic tasks to increase the probability of success.<br>• Model desired behaviors; identify peers who can also serve as good models.<br>• Encourage students to set high yet realistic goals for achievement.<br>• Promote self-regulation (e.g., by teaching self-monitoring, self-instructions, self-reinforcement). |
| **Students with physical or sensory challenges** | • Few opportunities to develop self-regulation skills because of health limitations and/or a tightly controlled environment | • Teach skills that promote self-sufficiency and independence.<br>• Teach students to make positive self-statements (e.g., "I can do it!") to enhance their self-efficacy for acting independently. |
| **Students with advanced cognitive development** | • High self-efficacy for academic tasks<br>• High goals for performance<br>• More effective self-regulated learning<br>• A history of easy successes and, hence, little experience dealing productively with failure (for some students) | • Provide the academic support that students need to reach high goals.<br>• Provide opportunities for independent study.<br>• Provide challenging tasks, including some at which students may initially fail; teach constructive strategies for dealing with failure (e.g., persistence, using errors to guide future practice efforts). |

*Sources:* Bandura, 1989; Bear et al., 2010; Beirne-Smith, Patton, & Kim, 2006; Biemiller, Shany, Inglis, & Meichenbaum, 1998; Coch et al., 2007; Cunningham & Cunningham, 2006; Dapretto et al., 2006; E. S. Ellis & Friend, 1991; Fletcher, Lyons, Fuchs, & Barnes, 2007; Kehle, Clark, Jenson, & Wampold, 1986; Meltzer, 2007; Mercer & Pullen, 2005; Mithaug & Mithaug, 2003; J. R. Nelson, Smith, Young, & Dodd, 1991; Nikopoulos & Keenan, 2004; Piirto, 1999; Reid et al., 2005; Sands & Wehmeyer, 1996; Schumaker & Hazel, 1984; Schunk et al., 1987; Silk et al., 2003; J. R. Sullivan & Conoley, 2004; Turnbull, Turnbull, & Wehmeyer, 2010; Usher & Pajares, 2008; Webber & Plotts, 2008; Yell et al., 2001; Zimmerman, 2004.

# COMPARE/CONTRAST

| TABLE 10.4 • Mutual Influences (Reciprocal Causation) among Environment, Behavior, and Person | | | | |
|---|---|---|---|---|
| | | **GENERAL EXAMPLES** | **EXAMPLES IN LORI'S CASE: SCENE 1** | **EXAMPLES IN LORI'S CASE: SCENE 2** |
| **Effect of Environment** | On behavior | Reinforcement and punishment affect future behavior. | Teacher's ignoring Lori leads to future classroom failure. | New instructional methods lead to improved academic performance. |
| | On person | Feedback from others affects sense of self-efficacy. | Teacher's ignoring Lori perpetuates low self-efficacy. | New instructional methods capture Lori's interest and attention. |
| **Effect of Behavior** | On environment | Specific behaviors affect the amount of reinforcement and punishment received. | Poor classroom performance leads the teacher to meet privately with Lori and then eventually to ignore her. | Increasing self-regulation and better academic performance lead to more reinforcement from the teacher. |
| | On person | Success and failure affect expectations for future performance. | Poor classroom performance leads to low self-efficacy. | Increasing self-regulation and better academic performance lead to higher self-efficacy. |
| **Effect of Person** | On environment | Self-efficacy affects choices of activities and therefore also affects the specific environment encountered. | Attention to classmates rather than classroom activities affects the specific environmental stimuli and events perceived and experienced. | Attention to classroom activities leads to greater benefits derived from teacher's instruction. |
| | On behavior | Attention, retention, and motivation affect the degree to which a learner imitates behaviors modeled by others. | Attention to classmates rather than classroom activities leads to academic failure. | Greater self-efficacy and increased motivation lead to more persistent study habits. |

As a concrete illustration of how environment, behavior, and personal factors are continually intertwined, let's consider Scene 1 in the case of a student named Lori:

**Scene 1**

Lori often comes late to Mr. Broderick's seventh-grade social studies class, and she's usually ill prepared for the day's activities. In class she spends more time interacting with friends (e.g., whispering, passing notes) than engaging in assigned tasks. Lori's performance on most exams and assignments is unsatisfactory—when she turns in her work at all.

In mid-October Mr. Broderick takes Lori aside to express his concern about her lack of classroom effort. He suggests that she could do better if she paid more attention in class. He also offers to work with her twice a week after school to help her understand class material. Lori is less optimistic, describing herself as "not smart enough to learn this stuff."

For a week or so after meeting with Mr. Broderick, Lori seems to buckle down and exert more effort, but she never does stay after school for extra help. And before long she's back to her old habits. Mr. Broderick eventually concludes that Lori is a lost cause and decides to devote his time and effort to helping more motivated students.

Lori's low self-efficacy (a *person* factor) is probably one reason she spends so much class time engaged in task-irrelevant activities *(behaviors).* The fact that she devotes her attention (another *person* factor) to her classmates rather than to her teacher affects the particular stimuli she experiences (her *environment*). Lori's non-self-regulating behaviors and resulting poor performance on assignments and exams *(behaviors)* affect both her self-efficacy *(person)* and Mr. Broderick's treatment of her *(environment).* By eventually concluding that Lori is a lost cause, Mr. Broderick begins to ignore Lori *(environment),* contributing further to her failure *(behavior)* and even lower self-efficacy *(person)*. The "Scene 1" column in Table 10.3 presents examples of such interactive effects. In general, Lori is showing signs of being at risk for long-term academic failure.

Now imagine that Mr. Broderick reads several research articles describing effective strategies for working with students like Lori. Midway through the school year, he makes the following changes in his classroom:

- He communicates clearly and consistently that he expects all his students to succeed.
- He incorporates students' personal experiences and interests into the study of social studies.
- He identifies specific, concrete tasks that students will accomplish each week.
- He provides explicit guidance for accomplishing each task.
- To teach simple self-regulation strategies, he asks students to set goals for each learning task, suggests that they reinforce themselves with 15 minutes of a favorite activity after finishing a homework assignment, and shows them how to track their progress on graph paper.
- After consulting with the school's reading specialist and school psychologist, he helps students develop more effective reading and learning strategies.
- He gives a quiz every Friday so that students can self-assess what they've learned each week.
- When students perform well on weekly quizzes, he reminds them that they themselves are responsible for their performance.

Let's see what happens next, as we consider Scene 2:

### Scene 2

By incorporating students' personal experiences and interests into daily lesson plans, Mr. Broderick captures Lori's interest and attention. She begins to realize that social studies has implications for her own life, and she becomes more involved in class activities. With the more structured assignments, better guidance about how to study class material, and frequent quizzes, Lori finds herself succeeding in a subject in which she previously experienced only failure. Mr. Broderick is equally pleased with her performance, and he frequently communicates his pleasure through his facial expressions, verbal feedback, and willingness to provide help whenever she needs it.

By the end of the school year, Lori is studying course material more effectively and completing her assignments regularly. She's actually looking forward to next year's social studies class, confident that she'll continue to do well.

Once again, we see the interplay among environment, behavior, and person. Mr. Broderick's new instructional methods *(environment)* engage Lori's attention *(person)*, foster self-regulation, and enhance academic performance *(behaviors)*. Lori's improved classroom performance, in turn, influences Mr. Broderick's treatment of her *(environment)* and her own self-efficacy *(person)*. Her improved self-efficacy, her greater attention to classroom activities, and her increased motivation to succeed (all *person* variables) affect her ability to benefit from Mr. Broderick's instruction *(environment)* and her classroom success *(behavior)*. The "Scene 2" column in Table 10.4 presents examples of such interactive effects.

## Comparing Theoretical Perspectives of Learning

At this point in your study of human learning, you may have examined four general theoretical perspectives: cognitive psychology, contextual theories, behaviorism, and social cognitive theory. Table 10.5 identifies central ways in which these perspectives are similar and different. But I urge you to keep this point in mind: *Diverse perspectives of learning often complement rather than contradict one another, and together they give us a richer, more multifaceted picture of human learning than any single perspective can give us by itself.* All four perspectives provide valuable guidance about how we can help students achieve in classroom settings.

For detailed discussions of the other three theoretical perspectives, see Chapter 6 and Chapter 7 (cognitive psychology), Chapter 8 (contextual theories), and Chapter 9 (behaviorism).

# ⭐ COMPARE/CONTRAST

## TABLE 10.5 • Comparing the Four Perspectives of Learning

| ISSUE | COGNITIVE PSYCHOLOGY | CONTEXTUAL THEORIES | BEHAVIORISM | SOCIAL COGNITIVE THEORY |
|---|---|---|---|---|
| Learning is defined as… | An internal mental phenomenon that may or may not be reflected in behavior | A phenomenon that is often situated within a particular physical or social context | A behavior change | An internal mental phenomenon that may or may not be reflected in behavior |
| The focus of investigation is on… | Cognitive processes | Various layers of context (e.g., small groups, culture, society) that support learning and development | Stimuli and responses that can be readily observed | Both behavior and cognitive processes |
| Principles of learning describe how… | People mentally process new information and construct knowledge from their experiences | Physical, social, and cultural mechanisms influence learning and cognition | People's behaviors are affected by environmental stimuli | People's observations of those around them affect their behavior and cognitive processes |
| Consequences of behavior… | Are not a major focus of consideration | Are not a major focus of consideration | Must be experienced directly if they are to affect learning | Can be experienced either directly or vicariously |
| Learning and behavior are influenced… | Primarily by cognitive processes within the individual | Both by local environmental conditions and by broader cultural and social factors | Primarily by local environmental conditions | Partly by the environment and partly by cognitive processes (people become increasingly self-regulating—and therefore less controlled by the environment—over time) |
| Educational implications focus on how we can help students… | Process information in effective ways and construct accurate and complete knowledge about classroom topics | Acquire complex knowledge and skills within authentic, real-world contexts | Acquire more productive classroom behaviors | Learn by observing others and acquire effective self-regulation skills |

# 🧩 10  What Have You Learned?

We now return to the chapter's learning outcomes to summarize key concepts, principles, and applications of social cognitive theory.

■ **10.1: Describe five basic assumptions of social cognitive theory and their classroom implications.** As a perspective that focuses on how people learn by observing others, social cognitive theory has built on ideas from both behaviorism and cognitive psychology. Social cognitive theorists view learning as an internal mental process (as cognitive psychologists do), but it also stresses the important influences of response–consequence contingencies (as behaviorists do). Furthermore, the interplay of mental processes and environmental consequences has implications not only for learning but also for motivation. Ultimately environmental, behavioral, and personal factors all interact with one another in their effects on learning—a three-way interdependence known as *reciprocal causation*. With age, experience, and appropriate scaffolding, many learners can increasingly take charge of their own behaviors, academic learning, and interpersonal problems.

**Evaluate** and **apply** your knowledge related to this learning outcome in MyEducationLab™.

■ **10.2: Use a social cognitive perspective to explain how mental processes can influence the effects of reinforcement and punishment.** Social cognitive theorists' beliefs about how reinforcement influences learning and behavior are quite different from those of behaviorists. From a social cognitive perspective, reinforcement and punishment affect learning indirectly rather than directly, and consequences to one learner vicariously influence the behaviors of other learners as well. For example, students who observe a classmate being reinforced or punished for a particular behavior may conclude that engaging in that behavior will yield similar consequences for themselves. Furthermore, the nonoccurrence of expected reinforcement is punishing, and the nonoccurrence of expected punishment is reinforcing. As teachers, we should recognize that the consequences of students' behaviors are likely to influence the expectations students form, the ways in which they process information, and the choices they make.

**Evaluate** and **apply** your knowledge related to this learning outcome in MyEducationLab™.

■ **10.3: Describe the potential effects of modeling on learners' behaviors, and explain how you can productively use

**modeling in instruction.** Effective models can take one of three forms: living people, real or fictional characters portrayed in various media, or verbal instructions regarding how to successfully execute desired behaviors. Such models can encourage either productive behaviors and skills (e.g., math and writing competencies, interpersonal skills) or inappropriate ones (e.g., aggression). Four conditions are essential if students are to learn from models: attention to the model, retention (memory) of what the model does, capacity for motor reproduction of the modeled behavior, and motivation to exhibit the modeled behavior. Students often benefit more from models who are not only competent and prestigious but also similar to themselves in cultural background, socioeconomic status, gender, and (if applicable) disability.

Evaluate and apply your knowledge related to this learning outcome in MyEducationLab™.

■ **10.4: Describe the nature and origins of self-efficacy, and explain how you might enhance self-efficacy both in your students as developing learners and in yourself as a teacher.** Learners are more likely to engage and persist in certain activities when they believe they can perform or learn the activities successfully—that is, when they have high *self-efficacy*. As teachers, we can enhance students' self-efficacy by giving them reasons to believe they can master school subject matter (e.g., by having them observe successful peer models) and by providing many opportunities to experience success working either as individuals or as part of a group. At the same time, we must remember that our *own* self-efficacy—our belief that with effort and effective instructional strategies we can definitely make a difference in students' lives—is an important factor in students' success.

Evaluate and apply your knowledge related to this learning outcome in MyEducationLab™.

■ **10.5: Identify important components of self-regulated behavior and self-regulated learning, and apply your knowledge of self-regulation to help diverse learners effectively control their behavior, master academic subject matter, and address interpersonal problems.** As children grow older, most of them become increasingly self-regulating. For example, they begin to set standards and goals for themselves, try to keep counterproductive emotions in check, and monitor and evaluate their

own behaviors. With development, too, many children gradually acquire strategies for regulating their learning efforts. For example, they conscientiously plan how they might best use their time and resources, motivate themselves to stay on task as they work, apply and evaluate various study strategies, and seek help when they need it. They can be equally self-regulating in addressing interpersonal problems, identifying various possible solutions and evaluating the end result of whatever solution they choose.

As teachers, we can foster the development of self-regulation skills in many ways—for instance, by asking students to set some of their own goals, providing explicit criteria with which they can evaluate their performance, and giving them age-appropriate independence in various situations and tasks. However, we must keep in mind that students in any single age-group vary considerably in their ability to control their behaviors and emotions, in part as a result of differences in brain maturation and temperament. Furthermore, some students may have had few outside role models for effective study habits. Some of our students, then, may need considerable guidance and support in their development of self-regulation skills.

Evaluate and apply your knowledge related to this learning outcome in MyEducationLab™.

■ **10.6: Compare and contrast perspectives of learning associated with cognitive psychology, contextual theories, behaviorism, and social cognitive theory.** Cognitive psychology, contextual perspectives, behaviorism, and social cognitive learning sometimes share and build on one another's ideas, but in other respects they offer competing views of how human beings learn. Key differences among the four perspectives include their definitions of learning; the nature of their research; their emphases on mental processes, influences of stimuli and consequences in one's immediate environment, or broader social and cultural contexts; and the specific implications they derive for instruction. As teachers, we must keep in mind that all four perspectives have useful applications for classroom practice.

Evaluate and apply your knowledge related to this learning outcome in MyEducationLab™.

## Practice for Your Licensure Exam

### Teacher's Lament

"Sometimes a teacher just can't win," complains Mr. Adams, a sixth-grade teacher. "At the beginning of the year, I told my students that homework assignments would count for 20% of their grades. Yet some students hardly ever turned in any homework, even though I continually reminded them about their assignments. After reconsidering the situation, I decided that I probably shouldn't use

homework as a criterion for grading. After all, in this low-income neighborhood, many kids don't have a quiet place to study at home. "So in November I told my class that I wouldn't be counting homework assignments when I calculated grades for the first report card. Naturally, some students—the ones who hadn't been doing their homework—seemed relieved. But the students who *had* been doing it were absolutely furious! And now hardly anyone turns in homework anymore."

1. **Multiple-choice question:**

Which one of the following statements best uses principles from social cognitive theory to explain why the students who had regularly been doing their homework were so upset?

a. Switching grading policies midstream, as Mr. Adams did, was a form of negative reinforcement.

b. The nonoccurrence of expected reinforcement for completing homework was a form of punishment.

c. By not giving credit for homework assignments, Mr. Adams significantly reduced students' self-efficacy regarding academic subject matter.

d. Reciprocal causation was at work: The students were essentially retaliating against their teacher for his unexpected change in grading policy.

2. **Constructed-response question:**

What might Mr. Adams do to encourage and help all students to complete homework assignments? Basing your discussion on principles of self-regulation, describe at least three different strategies in specific, concrete terms.

---

**PRAXIS**  Go to Appendix C, "Matching Book and MyEducationLab™ to the Praxis Principles of Learning and Teaching Tests," to discover sections of this chapter that may be especially applicable to the Praxis tests.

# 11 Motivation and Affect

## LEARNING OUTCOMES

**11.1:** Draw on diverse theoretical perspectives to describe the multifaceted nature of motivation.

**11.2:** Describe several basic needs that seem to drive much of human behavior, and identify numerous strategies for helping students address these needs at school.

**11.3:** Explain how learners' cognitive processes and sociocultural environments can have significant impacts on their motivation, and apply your knowledge of these factors to classroom practice.

**11.4:** Describe how various forms of affect are intertwined with motivation, learning, and cognition, and explain how you might promote productive affective states in students.

## CASE STUDY: PASSING ALGEBRA

Fourteen-year-old Michael has been getting failing grades in his eighth-grade algebra class, prompting his family to ask graduate student Valerie Tucker to tutor him. In the first tutoring session, Michael tells Ms. Tucker that he probably won't pass the course because he has little aptitude for math and his teacher doesn't explain the subject matter very well. In his mind, he's powerless to change either his own ability or his teacher's instructional strategies, making continuing failure inevitable.

As Ms. Tucker works with Michael over the next several weeks, she encourages him to think more about what *he* can do to master algebra and less about what his teacher may or may not be doing to help him. She points out that he did well in math in earlier years and so certainly has the ability to learn algebra if he puts his mind to it. She also teaches him some strategies for understanding and applying algebraic principles. Michael takes a giant step forward when he finally realizes that his own efforts play a role in his classroom success:

> Maybe I can try a little harder. . . . The teacher is still bad, but maybe some of this other stuff can work. (Tucker & Anderman, 1999, p. 5)

When Michael sees gradual improvement on his algebra assignments and quizzes, he becomes increasingly aware that the specific strategies he uses are just as important as his effort:

> I learned that I need to understand information before I can hold it in my mind. . . . Now I do things in math step by step and listen to each step. I realize now that even if I don't like the teacher or don't think he is a good teacher, it is my responsibility to listen. I listen better now and ask questions more. (Tucker & Anderman, 1999, p. 5)

As Michael's performance in algebra continues to improve in later weeks, he gains greater confidence that he *can* master algebra after all, and he comes to realize that his classroom success is ultimately up to him:

> The teacher does most of his part, but it's no use to me unless I do my part. . . . Now I try and comprehend, ask questions and figure out how he got the answer. . . . I used to just listen and not even take notes. I always told myself I would remember but I always seemed to forget. Now I take notes and I study at home every day except Friday, even if I don't have homework. Now I study so that I know that I have it. I don't just hope I'll remember.[1]

- On what factors does Michael initially blame his failure? To what factors does he later attribute his success? How do his changing beliefs affect his learning strategies?
- What inferences about motivation might you draw from the case study? How might learners' cognitive processes influence their motivation? How might teachers' behaviors also have an impact?

---

[1]This and preceding extracts from "Cycles of Learning: Demonstrating the Interplay between Motivation, Self-Regulation, and Cognition" by Valerie G. Tucker and Lynley H. Anderman, paper presented at the annual meeting of the American Educational Research Association, April 1999, pp. 5-6. Copyright © 1999 by Valerie G. Tucker and Lynley H. Anderman. Reprinted with permission of the authors.

Michael initially believes he's failing algebra because of two things he can't control—his teacher's poor instruction and his own low ability—and so exerts little effort in the class. But with Ms. Tucker's guidance, he discovers that increased effort and better strategies can make a big difference in his classroom performance. Suddenly Michael himself—not his teacher and not some genetically predetermined inability that lurks within him—is in control of the situation, and his confidence skyrockets.

In this chapter we'll discover that learners' beliefs and goals play key roles in their motivation—or apparent lack of it—to master classroom subject matter. We'll discover, too, that teachers' behaviors and the overall classroom environment can either enhance learners' motivation (perhaps by facilitating mastery, as Ms. Tucker does) or discourage it (perhaps by using ineffective instructional strategies, as Michael's teacher seemingly does). Later in the chapter we'll also look at the nature of emotions—which psychologists often refer to as *affect*—and consider how they come into play in both learning and motivation.

# The Nature of Motivation

Learning theorists focus primarily on the question "What can people do and learn?" Motivation theorists focus on a somewhat different question: "How *likely* are people to do what they're capable of doing and to learn what they're capable of learning?" In general, motivation is something that energizes, directs, and sustains behavior; it gets people moving, points them in a particular direction, and keeps them going. More specifically, motivation has several effects:

- It directs behavior toward particular goals.
- It leads to increased effort and energy in pursuit of those goals.
- It increases initiation of and persistence in certain activities, even in the face of occasional obstacles and interruptions.
- It affects cognitive processes, such as what learners pay attention to and how much they think about and elaborate on it.
- It determines which consequences are reinforcing and punishing.

We often see students' motivation reflected in *personal investment* and in cognitive, emotional, and behavioral *engagement* in certain activities. In general, then, motivation increases students' physical and cognitive time on task, an important factor affecting their learning and achievement in a particular domain (Fredricks, Blumenfeld, & Paris, 2004; Ladd & Dinella, 2009; J. Lee & Shute, 2010; Maehr & McInerney, 2004; E. Skinner, Furrer, Marchand, & Kindermann, 2008).

Researchers have approached the study of motivation from several angles, which are summarized in Table 11.1. Each of these theoretical perspectives provides pieces of the motivation "puzzle," offering useful ideas about how we can motivate students in classroom settings, and so we'll draw from all of them in the pages ahead. But three general principles of motivation will underlie much of our discussion:

- *All children and adolescents are motivated in one way or another.* Occasionally I hear educators, policy makers, or the public at large talking about "unmotivated" students. In reality, all students have needs and desires they're motivated to satisfy. One student may be keenly interested in classroom topics and seek out challenging coursework, participate actively in class discussions, and earn high marks on assigned projects. Another student may be more concerned with the social side of school, interacting frequently with classmates, attending many extracurricular activities, and perhaps running for a student government office. Still another may be focused on athletics, excelling in physical education classes, playing or watching sports most afternoons and weekends, and faithfully following a physical fitness regimen. Yet another student—perhaps because of an undetected

# COMPARE/CONTRAST

## TABLE 11.1 • General Theoretical Approaches to the Study of Motivation

| THEORETICAL PERSPECTIVE | GENERAL DESCRIPTION |
|---|---|
| **Trait theories** | Relatively enduring characteristics and personality traits play a significant role in motivation. For example, learners have different *temperaments* that predispose them to either seek or avoid novel experiences and social situations. Furthermore, significant *individual differences* exist in learners' motives—for instance, in their desires to achieve at high levels, to interact frequently with other people, and to obtain other people's approval for their achievements and behaviors. |
| **Behaviorist theories** | Motivation is often the result of *drives:* internal states caused by a lack of something necessary for optimal functioning. Consequences of behavior (reinforcement, punishment) are effective to the extent that they either decrease or increase these drive states. In recent years some behaviorists have added a *purposeful* element to the behaviorist perspective: They suggest that learners intentionally behave in order to achieve certain end results. |
| **Humanism** | Learners have within themselves a tremendous *potential for psychological growth* and continually strive to fulfill this potential. When given a caring and supportive environment, learners strive to understand themselves, to enhance their abilities, and to behave in ways that benefit both themselves and others. Initially, humanism arose largely in reaction to behaviorists' environment-driven portrait of human motivation and was grounded largely in philosophy rather than in research findings. In recent years, however, a more research-based perspective known as **positive psychology** has begun to emerge. |
| **Social cognitive theories** | In the first few years of life, learners are motivated largely by the consequences that follow either their own behaviors or the behaviors of other people. With age and experience, they acquire *self-efficacy beliefs*—beliefs about their ability to achieve desired results in different domains. As many learners become increasingly self-regulating over time, they begin to set *goals* for themselves, and much of their motivation comes from within rather than from external consequences. |
| **Cognitive theories** | A variety of cognitive factors—sometimes in combination with emotional factors—affect learners' perceptions of themselves, of various topics, and of the world at large. Such perceptions, in turn, influence learners' inclinations to engage or not engage in particular tasks and activities. For example, learners tend to be more intrinsically motivated when they believe they have some control and choice in their activities—in other words, when they have a sense of *self-determination*. Also, learners identify what are, in their minds, the likely causes of their successes and failures, and these *attributions* influence their subsequent behaviors. |
| **Contextual theories** | Many aspects of motivation are the result of social and cultural factors, such as the behavioral norms that a peer group or overall culture endorses (which learners might gradually internalize) and the many formal and informal learning opportunities that learners' local community and broader society provide. Furthermore, motivation is often *situated* in particular contexts and content domains; for example, learners might be eager to learn technology skills when texting or playing video games with friends but have little interest in mastering math or science at school. Ultimately learners and the contexts in which they live and work dynamically influence each other, with learners choosing and changing their environments, and their environments, in turn, nurturing and in other ways influencing learners' specific interests and motives. |

learning disability, shy temperament, or seemingly uncoordinated body—may be motivated to *avoid* academics, social situations, or athletic activities.

• *Motivation to do well in school is grounded in a variety of cognitive and sociocultural factors that evolve over time.* A common misconception is that students can turn their motivation "on" or "off" at will, much as one would flip a light switch. In fact, students' motivation to achieve—or *not* achieve—in a traditional academic curriculum is the result of many factors that don't easily change overnight. Some of these factors are cognitive in nature, such as students' short-term and long-term goals and their self-efficacy for learning academic topics. Others have social or cultural origins, such as the activities and values that students' families and local communities endorse. In the opening case study, Michael's self-efficacy for mastering math improves—but only *gradually*— as he discovers that by applying effort and good strategies, he can be successful in the class.

• *Conditions in the classroom play a major role in students' motivation to learn and achieve.* Motivation isn't necessarily something that learners bring *to* school; it can also arise from environmental conditions *at* school. When we talk about how the environment can enhance a learner's motivation to learn particular things or behave in particular ways, we're talking about situated motivation (S. G. Paris & Turner, 1994; Rueda & Moll, 1994; Turner & Patrick, 2008). As you'll see throughout the chapter, we teachers can do many things to motivate students to learn

**motivation** Inner state that energizes, directs, and sustains behavior.

**time on task** Amount of time that students are both physically and cognitively engaged in a learning activity.

**situated motivation** Phenomenon in which aspects of the immediate environment enhance motivation to learn particular things or behave in particular ways.

and achieve in ways that promote their long-term success and productivity. Sometimes even the seemingly "little" things we do—for instance, communicating genuine concern about students' academic and personal well-being and ensuring that their peers treat them respectfully—can have a significant long-term impact (Yeager & Walton, 2011).

## EXTRINSIC VERSUS INTRINSIC MOTIVATION

Not all forms of motivation have exactly the same effects on human learning and performance. Consider these two students in an advanced high school writing class:

- Sheryl is taking the class for only one reason: Earning an A or B in the class will help her earn a scholarship at State University, which she desperately wants to attend.
- Shannon has always liked to write. Doing well in the class will certainly help her get a scholarship at State University, but more importantly, she wants to become a better writer and knows that the skills she can gain will be useful in her future profession as a journalist. An additional bonus is that she's learning many new techniques for making her writing more vivid and engaging.

Sheryl has **extrinsic motivation**: She's motivated by factors external to herself and unrelated to the task at hand. Extrinsically motivated learners perform a task as a means to an end—perhaps the good grades, money, or recognition that particular activities and accomplishments bring—rather than as an end in itself. In contrast, Shannon shows **intrinsic motivation**: She's motivated by factors within herself and inherent in the task she's performing. Intrinsically motivated learners may engage in an activity because it gives them pleasure, helps them develop an important skill, or seems to be the ethically and morally right thing to do. Some learners with high levels of intrinsic motivation become so focused on and absorbed in an activity that they lose track of time and completely ignore other tasks—a phenomenon known as **flow** (Csikszentmihalyi, 1990, 1996; Csikszentmihalyi, Abuhamdeh, & Nakamura, 2005; Shernoff & Csikszentmihalyi, 2009).

Learners are most likely to show the beneficial effects of motivation when they're *intrinsically* motivated to engage in classroom activities. Intrinsically motivated learners willingly tackle assigned tasks and are eager to learn classroom material, are more likely to process information in effective ways (e.g., by engaging in meaningful learning), and are more likely to achieve at high levels. In contrast, extrinsically motivated learners may have to be enticed or prodded, may process information only superficially, and may be interested in performing only easy tasks and meeting minimal classroom requirements (M. Becker, McElvany, & Kortenbruck, 2010; Reeve, 2006; Schiefele, 1991).

In the early elementary grades, students are eager and excited to learn new things at school. But sometime between grades 3 and 9, their intrinsic motivation to master school subject matter declines (A. E. Gottfried, Fleming, & Gottfried, 2001; Lepper, Corpus, & Iyengar, 2005; Otis, Grouzet, & Pelletier, 2005). This decline is probably the result of several factors. As students get older, they're increasingly reminded of the importance of good grades (extrinsic motivators) for promotion, graduation, and college admission, causing them to focus their efforts on earning high grade point averages. In addition, they become more cognitively capable of setting and striving for long-term goals, and they begin to evaluate school subjects in terms of their usefulness in meeting such goals. Furthermore, they may grow increasingly impatient with the overly structured, repetitive, and boring activities they often encounter at school (Battistich, Solomon, Kim, Watson, & Schaps, 1995; Larson, 2000; Shernoff, Csikszentmihalyi, Schneider, & Shernoff, 2003).

Extrinsic motivation isn't necessarily a bad thing. Often learners are simultaneously motivated by *both* intrinsic and extrinsic factors (J. Cameron & Pierce, 1994; Covington, 2000; Lepper et al., 2005). For example, although Shannon enjoys her writing course, she also knows that getting a good grade will help her get a scholarship at State U. And good grades and other external rewards for high achievement may confirm for her that she's mastering school subject matter (Hynd, 2003). Furthermore, in some situations, extrinsic motivation—perhaps in the form of extrinsic reinforcers for academic achievement or desired behavior—may be the only thing that can get students on the road to successful classroom learning and productive behavior. Yet ultimately motivation from *within* is what will sustain students over the long run.

**extrinsic motivation** Motivation resulting from factors external to the individual and unrelated to the task being performed.

**intrinsic motivation** Motivation resulting from internal personal characteristics or inherent in the task being performed.

**flow** Intense form of intrinsic motivation, involving complete absorption in and concentration on a challenging activity.

# Basic Human Needs

**need for arousal** Ongoing need for either physical or cognitive stimulation.

Obviously learners have certain needs they must address related to their physical survival; for example, they must regularly have food, water, and shelter. But some motivation theorists have speculated that fulfilling certain other needs may be important for psychological well-being and that these needs might be key ingredients in intrinsic motivation. Here we'll look at four such psychological needs: the needs for arousal, competence, self-determination, and relatedness.

## AROUSAL

Human beings appear to have a need for arousal—a need for some degree of stimulation (E. M. Anderman, Noar, Zimmerman, & Donohew, 2004; Berlyne, 1960; Heron, 1957; Labouvie-Vief & González, 2004). As an example, try the following exercise.

### EXPERIENCING FIRSTHAND
### TAKE FIVE

For the next five minutes, you're going to be a student who has nothing to do. *Remain exactly where you are,* put your book aside, and *do nothing.* Spend at least five minutes on this "task."

What kinds of responses did you make during your five-minute break? Did you fidget a bit, perhaps wiggling tired body parts or scratching newly detected itches? Did you interact in some way with something or someone else, perhaps tapping on a table or talking to another person in the room? Did you get out of your seat altogether—something I specifically asked you *not* to do? The exercise has, I hope, shown you that you tend to feel better when *something,* rather than nothing at all, is happening to you.

Not only do people seem to have a basic need for arousal but they also strive for a certain *optimal level* of arousal at which they feel best (E. M. Anderman et al., 2004; Berlyne, 1960; Hsee, Yang, & Wang, 2010). Too little stimulation is unpleasant, but so is too much. You might enjoy watching a television game show or listening to music, but you'd probably rather not have three TV sets, five CD players, and a live rock band all blasting at you at once. Different people have different optimal levels: Some individuals are *sensation seekers* who thrive on physically thrilling and possibly dangerous experiences (Cleveland, Gibbons, Gerrard, Pomery, & Brody, 2005; V. F. Reyna & Farley, 2006). Others prefer a quieter existence. I, for one, like physical stimulation a bit on the dull side: You'll never catch me hang-gliding or bungee-jumping. Yet I like a lot of *cognitive* stimulation in the form of regular exposure to new ideas, occasional debates about controversial issues, and so on (e.g., see Cacioppo, Petty, Feinstein, & Jarvis, 1996).

The need for arousal explains some of the things students do in the classroom. For instance, it explains why many students happily pull out a favorite book and read if they finish an in-class assignment before their classmates. But it also explains why students sometimes engage in off-task behaviors—for instance, passing notes and playing practical jokes—during boring lessons (Pekrun, Goetz, Daniels, Stupnisky, & Perry, 2010).

All human beings have a basic need for arousal. Students who don't find classroom activities reasonably stimulating will satisfy their need for arousal in other ways.

Plan classroom activities that keep students continually active, either physically or cognitively.

Obviously, students are most likely to stay *on* task when classroom activities keep them sufficiently aroused that they have little need to look elsewhere for stimulation.

## COMPETENCE AND SELF-WORTH

Human beings also appear to have a basic need for competence—a need to believe they can deal effectively with their environment (Boggiano & Pittman, 1992; Elliot & Dweck, 2005; Reeve, Deci, & Ryan, 2004; R. White, 1959). To achieve this sense of competence, children spend a great deal of time exploring and trying to gain mastery over various aspects of their world.

One motivation theorist has proposed that a high priority for most people is *protecting* their general belief that, overall, they're good, capable individuals—something he calls self-worth (Covington, 1992). Occasionally some individuals seem more concerned about maintaining *consistent* self-perceptions, even if those self-perceptions are negative (J. Cassidy, Ziv, Mehta, & Feeney, 2003; Hay, Ashman, van Kraayenoord, & Stewart, 1999). By and large, however, viewing oneself favorably and demonstrating competence for others do appear to be high priorities (Rhodewalt & Vohs, 2005; Sedikides & Gregg, 2008; T. D. Wilson & Gilbert, 2008).

Other people's judgments and approval play a key role in children's development of a sense of competence and self-worth, especially in the early years (Harter, 1999; Rudolph, Caldwell, & Conley, 2005). Regularly achieving success in new and challenging activities—as Michael eventually does in the opening case study—is another important way of maintaining, perhaps even enhancing, a sense of competence and self-worth (Deci & Moller, 2005; N. E. Perry, Turner, & Meyer, 2006; Reeve et al., 2004).

But consistent success isn't always possible, especially when learners must undertake especially difficult tasks. In the face of such tasks, an alternative way to maintain self-worth is to *avoid failure,* because failure gives the impression of low ability (Covington & Müeller, 2001; Urdan & Midgley, 2001). Failure avoidance manifests itself in a variety of ways: Learners might refuse to engage in a task, minimize the task's importance, or set exceedingly low expectations for performance (Covington, 1992; Harter, 1990; Rhodewalt & Vohs, 2005).

When learners *can't* avoid tasks at which they expect to do poorly, they have several strategies at their disposal. They may make excuses that seemingly justify their poor performance (Covington, 1992; Urdan & Midgley, 2001). They may also do things that actually *undermine* their chances of success—a phenomenon known as self-handicapping. Self-handicapping takes a variety of forms, including the following:

- *Reducing effort:* Putting forth an obviously insufficient amount of effort to succeed
- *Setting unattainably high goals:* Working toward goals that even the most capable individuals couldn't achieve
- *Taking on too much:* Assuming so many responsibilities that no one could possibly accomplish them all
- *Procrastinating:* Putting off a task until success is virtually impossible
- *Cheating:* Presenting others' work as one's own
- *Using alcohol or drugs:* Taking substances that will inevitably reduce performance (E. M. Anderman, Griesinger, & Westerfield, 1998; Covington, 1992; Hattie, 2008; Riggs, 1992; Urdan, Ryan, Anderman, & Gheen, 2002)

It might seem paradoxical that learners who want to be successful would actually try to undermine their own success. But if they believe they're unlikely to succeed no matter what they do—and especially if failure will reflect poorly on their intelligence and ability—such behaviors increase their chances of *justifying* the failure and thereby protecting their self-worth. Self-handicapping is seen as early as elementary school and becomes increasingly common in the high school and college years (Urdan, 2004; Urdan & Midgley, 2001; Wolters, 2003).

> A Book That canged me
>
> The Book that canged me was At The Plat With Ken Jriffey Jr. This Book canged me becouse it was my first book that had over onehondred pagis after that I read On The Cort With Mikeol Jorden. I asow liked it becouse it was by Matt Crister the Frst spotswiter for Kids.

Mastering new challenges is one important means of gaining a sense of competence and self-worth. In writing about "A Book That C(h)anged Me," 8-year-old Anthony expresses pride in reading his first 100-page book. Notice Anthony's personal interest in sports: *At the Plat(e)* is about baseball, and *On the Co(u)rt* is about basketball.

need for competence  Basic need to believe that one can deal effectively with one's overall environment.

self-worth  General belief about the extent to which one is a good, capable individual.

self-handicapping  Behavior that undermines one's own success as a way of protecting self-worth during potentially difficult tasks.

## REVISITING SELF-EFFICACY

On the surface, the concepts of competence and self-worth are similar to the concept of *self-efficacy*. In theory, however, there's a key difference between the need for competence and self-worth, on the one hand, and self-efficacy, on the other. Having a sense of competence and self-worth may be a basic human need. In contrast, social cognitive theorists have suggested that self-efficacy is certainly a *good* thing, but they don't go so far as to speculate that it's an essential driving force of human nature. However, one point on which virtually all motivation theorists agree is that students' confidence about their ability to handle day-to-day tasks is an important variable influencing motivation—especially *intrinsic* motivation—in the classroom (Boggiano & Pittman, 1992; Elliot & Dweck, 2005; Reeve et al., 2004; Zimmerman, 2010).

Self-efficacy is a key component of social cognitive theory, discussed in Chapter 10.

## ENHANCING STUDENTS' SENSE OF COMPETENCE AND SELF-WORTH

Strategies for enhancing students' general sense of self and more domain-specific self-efficacy should, of course, increase their sense of competence and self-worth. Following are three widely recommended strategies:

Chapter 3 and Chapter 10 describe these strategies in more detail.

- 🍎 Help students achieve success, especially on challenging tasks.
- 🍎 Give students concrete mechanisms through which they can track their progress over time.
- 🍎 Minimize competitions and other situations in which students might judge themselves unfavorably in comparison with peers.

Ideally, learners' sense of competence and self-worth should be based on a reasonably accurate appraisal of what they can and cannot accomplish. Learners who underestimate their abilities set unnecessarily low goals for themselves and give up easily after only minor setbacks. Those who overestimate their abilities—perhaps because they've been lavished with praise by parents or teachers or perhaps because school assignments have been consistently easy and unchallenging—may set themselves up for failure by forming unrealistically high expectations, exerting insufficient effort, or not addressing their weaknesses (Försterling & Morgenstern, 2002; Hattie & Gan, 2011; S. G. Paris & Cunningham, 1996; H. W. Stevenson, Chen, & Uttal, 1990).

As teachers, we're more likely to encourage students to tackle realistically challenging tasks—and thus enhance their sense of competence and intrinsic motivation—when we create an environment in which they feel comfortable taking risks and making mistakes (Clifford, 1990; Fredricks et al., 2004). We can also provide greater rewards for succeeding at challenging tasks than for achieving easy successes; for example, we might give students a choice between doing an easy task or a more difficult one but give them more points for accomplishing the difficult one (Clifford, 1990; Lan, Repman, Bradley, & Weller, 1994). Once students are intrinsically motivated, they seem to *prefer* challenges rather than easy tasks (Csikszentmihalyi et al., 2005; Reeve, 2006; Shernoff & Csikszentmihalyi, 2009). In general, challenges and intrinsic motivation mutually enhance one another, leading to a "vicious cycle" of the most desirable sort.

Most learners are motivated by realistically challenging tasks—those they can successfully accomplish with reasonable effort. Listen to 9-year-old Elena and 15-year-old Greg in "Motivation: Middle Childhood" and "Motivation: Late Adolescence."

To date, most research on competence, self-worth, and self-handicapping has focused on academic tasks and accomplishments. We must keep in mind, however, that academic achievement isn't always the most important thing affecting students' sense of competence and self-worth. For many students such factors as physical appearance, peer approval, and social success are more influential (Eccles, Wigfield, & Schiefele, 1998; Rudolph et al., 2005). To the extent that we can, then, we should support students' successes in the nonacademic as well as the academic aspects of their lives.

🍏 Create an environment that encourages students to take risks—for instance, through the kinds of feedback you give and the criteria you use to assign grades.

🍏 Help students achieve a sense of competence in social as well as academic activities.

## SELF-DETERMINATION

Some theorists suggest that in addition to a need for competence, human beings may also have a **need for self-determination**—a desire for autonomy and self-direction regarding the things they do and the courses their lives take (d'Ailly, 2003; deCharms, 1972; Reeve et al., 2004; R. M. Ryan & Deci, 2000). When we think, "I *want* to do this" or "I'd *find it valuable* to do that," we have a high sense of self-determination. In contrast, when we think, "I *have to*" or "I *should,*" we're telling ourselves that someone or something else is making decisions for us. The following exercise provides an example.

**need for self-determination** Basic need to believe that one has some autonomy and control regarding the course of one's life.

## PAINTING BETWEEN THE LINES

Imagine that I give you a paintbrush, a set of watercolor paints, two sheets of paper (a fairly small one glued on top of a larger one), and some paper towels. I ask you to paint a picture of your house, apartment building, or dormitory and then give you the following instructions:

> You have to keep the paints clean. You can paint only on this small sheet of paper, so don't spill any paint on the big sheet. And you must wash out your brush and wipe it with a paper towel before you switch to a new color of paint, so that you don't get the colors all mixed up. In general, don't make a mess with the paints. (Koestner, Ryan, Bernieri, & Holt, 1984, p. 239)

How much fun do you think your task would be? After reading my rules, how eager are you to begin painting?

My rules about painting are quite *controlling:* They make it clear that I'm in charge of the situation and that you, as the artist, have little choice about how to go about your task. By diminishing your sense of self-determination, my rules would undermine any intrinsic motivation you might have to paint the picture, and you'd probably be less creative in your painting than you might be otherwise (Amabile & Hennessey, 1992; Koestner et al., 1984; Reeve, 2006).

Students with a sense of self-determination are more likely to be intrinsically motivated during classroom activities, to achieve at high levels, and to complete high school (Hardré & Reeve, 2003; Reeve, Bolt, & Cai, 1999; Shernoff, Knauth, & Makris, 2000; Vansteenkiste, Lens, & Deci, 2006). Even kindergartners seem to prefer classroom activities of their own choosing (E. J. Langer, 1997; Paley, 1984). For example, when students in Ms. Paley's kindergarten class are asked whether activities at the class painting table are "work" or "play," two of them respond as follows:

> ***Clarice:*** If you paint a real picture, it's work, but if you splatter or pour into an egg carton, then it's play.
>
> ***Charlotte:*** It's mostly work, because that's where the teacher tells you how to do stuff. (Paley, 1984, p. 31)

### ENHANCING STUDENTS' SENSE OF SELF-DETERMINATION

As teachers, we can't always give students total freedom about what they will and won't do in the classroom. And it's neither realistic nor helpful to suggest that all assigned tasks are just "play," because many tasks will—or at least *should*—require hard work and persistence in the face of obstacles. Nevertheless, we can do several things to enhance students' sense of self-determination at school:

🍎 *Provide opportunities for independent work and decision making.* Opportunities to work and make decisions independently not only foster the development of self-regulation skills but also enhance learners' sense of self-determination. For instance, we might have students study new topics through instructional software programs or tackle challenging tasks through small-group work, and we can give students considerable autonomy in the extracurricular activities we supervise (Larson, 2000; Stefanou, Perencevich, DiCintio, & Turner, 2004; Swan, Mitrani, Guerrero, Cheung, & Schoener, 1990).

Providing autonomy in activities doesn't mean removing all structure, however. Some scaffolding—tailored to students' developmental levels, of course—can further increase students' sense of self-determination. For example, we can establish general routines and procedures that students should follow as they work, thereby minimizing the need to give explicit instructions for every assignment. And we should describe our evaluation criteria in advance so that students know exactly what they'll need to do to be successful (Clani, Middleton, Summers, & Sheldon, 2010; Jang, Reeve, & Deci, 2010; Spaulding, 1992; M.-T. Wang & Holcombe, 2010).

🍎 *Present rules and instructions in an informational rather than controlling manner.* Virtually every classroom needs a few rules and procedures to ensure that students act appropriately and

Chapter 10 describes the nature and development of self-regulation skills.

activities run smoothly. The challenge is to present these rules and procedures without communicating a message of *control*. Instead, we can present them as *information*—for instance, as conditions that can help students accomplish classroom objectives (Deci, 1992; Koestner et al., 1984; Reeve, 2009). Here are two examples:

- "We can make sure everyone has an equal chance to speak and be heard if we listen without interrupting and if we raise our hands when we want to contribute to the discussion."
- "I'm giving you a particular format to follow when you do your math homework. If you use this format, it will be easier for me to find your answers and to figure out how I can help you improve."

Yet we should also acknowledge students' feelings about things they must do but would rather *not* do—thus communicating the message that their opinions matter (Deci & Ryan, 1985; Reeve, 2009).

🍎 *Give some choices about how to accomplish classroom goals.* Sometimes a variety of routes will lead to the same destination. For example, we might encourage students to make choices, either individually or as a group—and within reasonable limits—about some or all of the following:

- Rules and procedures to make the class run more smoothly
- Specific topics for reading or writing projects
- Sequencing or due dates of assigned tasks
- Ways of achieving or demonstrating mastery of a particular skill (e.g., see Figure 11.1)
- Criteria by which some assignments will be evaluated (Clani et al., 2010; Fairweather & Cramond, 2010; Meece, 1994; Patall, Cooper, & Wynn, 2010; Reed, Schallert, Beth, & Woodruff, 2004; A. C. Schmidt, Hanley, & Layer, 2009)

**FIGURE 11.1** In this assignment, a sixth-grade language arts teacher enhances students' sense of self-determination by offering several options for demonstrating understanding of a science fiction book.

*Choose One!*

### SCIENCE FICTION BOOK PROJECTS

_____ Write a "Dear Abby" letter from one of the main characters, in which he or she asks for advice on solving his or her main problem. Then answer the letter.

_____ Draw a time line of the main events of the book.

_____ Create a comic book or a comic strip page that features a major scene from the book in each box.

_____ Make a collage of objects and printed words from newspapers and magazines that give the viewer a feeling for the mood of the book.

_____ Your book probably takes place in an unusual or exotic setting, so illustrate and write a travel brochure describing that location.

_____ Imagine yourself as a scientist who has been asked to explain the unusual events in the book. Write up a report in scientific style.

_____ With other students who have read the same book, plan a bulletin board display. Write a plot summary; character and setting descriptions; discussions of special passages. Each group member must contribute one artistic piece—for example, new book cover, bookmark, poster, banner, some of the ideas listed above. Arrange the writing and artwork under a colorful heading announcing the book.

Evaluative feedback is more likely to promote intrinsic motivation when it's presented in an informational, noncontrolling manner. Observe examples in "Author's Chair."

See Chapter 9 if you need a refresher on the distinction between extrinsic and intrinsic reinforcers.

When students can make choices about such matters, they gain a sense of ownership about classroom activities, are more likely to be interested and engaged in what they're doing, and take genuine pride in their work (Deci & Ryan, 1992; Nolen, 2011; Patall et al., 2010; Schraw, Flowerday, & Lehman, 2001; Stefanou et al., 2004).

🍎 *Evaluate students' performance in a noncontrolling way.* As teachers, we must regularly evaluate students' accomplishments. But external evaluations can undermine students' intrinsic motivation, especially if they're communicated in a controlling manner (E. M. Anderman & Dawson, 2011; Deci & Moller, 2005). Ideally, we should present evaluations of students' work not as judgments to remind students of how they *should* perform but as information that can help them improve their knowledge and skills. And, of course, we can give students criteria by which they can evaluate *themselves.*

🍎 *Be selective about when and how you use extrinsic reinforcers.* Ideally we should rely on intrinsic reinforcers—such as students' own feelings of pride and satisfaction about their accomplishments—as often as possible. One problem with *extrinsic* reinforcers (e.g., praise, good grades) is that they can undermine self-determination and intrinsic motivation, especially if students perceive them as controlling behavior and limiting choices (Deci & Moller, 2005; Lepper & Hodell, 1989; Reeve, 2006). Extrinsic reinforcers may also communicate the message that classroom tasks are unpleasant chores—why else would a reinforcer be necessary?—rather than activities to be carried out and enjoyed for their own sake (B. A. Hennessey, 1995; Stipek, 1993).

Extrinsic reinforcers appear to have no adverse effects when they're unexpected—for example, when students get special recognition for a community service project—or when the reinforcers aren't contingent on specific behaviors—for example, when they're used simply to make an activity more enjoyable. They can even be beneficial if used to encourage students not only to do something but also to do it *well.* And if they communicate that students *have* done something well (as a high grade might indicate) or have made considerable improvement, they can enhance students' sense of competence and focus students' attention on mastering the subject matter (E. M. Anderman & Dawson, 2011; J. Cameron, 2001; Deci & Moller, 2005; Reeve, 2006).

Sometimes students may initially find a new topic or skill boring or frustrating and thus may need external encouragement to continue (J. Cameron, 2001; Deci, Koestner, & Ryan, 2001; Hidi & Harackiewicz, 2000). On such occasions, one effective strategy is to praise students in a manner that communicates information but doesn't show an intent to control behavior (Deci, 1992; R. M. Ryan, Mims, & Koestner, 1983). Following are examples:

- "Your description of the main character in your short story is so detailed and vivid! It really makes her come alive."
- "Your poster clearly describes every step you took in your experiment. Your use of a bar graph makes your results easy to see and interpret."

Self-imposed reinforcement is an important aspect of self-regulated behavior (see Chapter 10).

Another strategy is to teach students to reinforce *themselves* for their accomplishments, a practice that clearly keeps control in students' hands.

## RELATEDNESS

To some degree we're all social creatures: We live, work, and play with our fellow human beings. Some psychologists have proposed that people of all ages have a fundamental need for relatedness—a need to feel socially connected and to secure the love and respect of others (Connell & Wellborn, 1991; Fiske & Fiske, 2007; Reeve et al., 2004; R. M. Ryan & Deci, 2000). The need for relatedness seems to be especially strong in adolescence: Most teenagers spend a great deal of time interacting with peers, perhaps through face-to-face activities, instant messaging on cell phones, or social networking sites such as Facebook (Barron, 2006; Ito et al., 2009; A. M. Ryan & Patrick, 2001; Valkenburg & Peter, 2009).

At school the need for relatedness manifests itself in a variety of behaviors. Some students place a higher priority on interacting with friends than on getting schoolwork done (Dowson & McInerney, 2001; W. Doyle, 1986a; Wigfield, Eccles, Mac Iver, Reuman, & Midgley, 1991). They may also be concerned about projecting a favorable public image—that is, looking smart, popular, athletic, or cool. By looking good in the eyes of others, students not only satisfy their need for relatedness but also enhance their sense of self-worth (Harter, 1999; Juvonen, 2000).

**need for relatedness** Basic need to feel socially connected to others and to secure others' love and respect.

Yet another way in which they might address the need for relatedness is to work for the betterment of others—for example, by helping peers who are struggling with classroom assignments (Dowson & McInerney, 2001; Lawlor & Schonert-Reichl, 2008; Thorkildsen, Golant, & Cambray-Engstrom, 2008).

### ENHANCING STUDENTS' SENSE OF RELATEDNESS

Students are more likely to be academically motivated and successful—and more likely to stay in school rather than drop out—when they believe that their peers and teachers like and respect them (Christenson & Thurlow, 2004; Furrer & Skinner, 2003; Roorda, Koomen, Spilt, & Oort, 2011; A. M. Ryan & Patrick, 2001). Ideally we should find ways to help students simultaneously learn academic subject matter *and* address their eagerness to interact with peers. Group-based activities—such as cooperative learning tasks, role-playing, and playful game-show contests among two or more teams of equal ability—all provide the means through which students can satisfy their need for relatedness while also acquiring new knowledge and skills (Blumenfeld, Kempler, & Krajcik, 2006; D. W. Johnson & Johnson, 2009a; Wentzel & Wigfield, 1998).

Give students frequent opportunities to interact as they study classroom topics.

Students' relationships with their teachers are just as important. Thus, we should show students that we enjoy being with them and are concerned about their academic achievement and personal well-being (M.-L. Chang & Davis, 2009; D. K. Meyer & Turner, 2006; Roorda et al., 2011). We can communicate our fondness and concern for them in numerous ways—for example, by expressing interest in their outside activities, providing extra help when they need it, and lending a sympathetic ear in stressful times. Such caring messages are especially important for students who are at risk for academic failure and dropping out of school (Christenson & Thurlow, 2004; Hamre & Pianta, 2005; Pianta, 1999).

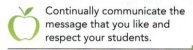
Continually communicate the message that you like and respect your students.

## UNIVERSALITY AND DIVERSITY IN BASIC NEEDS

The four basic needs just described are probably universal among people throughout the world (e.g., Bao & Lam, 2008; Berlyne, 1960; Deci & Moller, 2005; Fiske & Fiske, 2007). However, researchers have identified distinct cultural differences in how people strive to address three of them—in particular, the needs for competence, self-determination, and relatedness.

**Achieving a sense of competence and self-worth** In mainstream Western culture, achieving a sense of self-worth often involves *being good at* certain things and also *thinking* that one is good at these things. In such a context, learners are likely to engage in self-handicapping as a means of justifying poor performances. But not all cultures stress the importance of positive self-evaluations. For instance, many people in East Asian cultures place greater importance on how well other people view an individual as living up to society's standards for behavior. In such cultures the focus is more likely to be on correcting existing weaknesses—that is, on *self-improvement*—than on demonstrating current strengths (Heine, 2007; J. Li, 2005; Sedikides & Gregg, 2008).

**Achieving a sense of self-determination** The amounts and forms of autonomy and self-determination may differ considerably from group to group (d'Ailly, 2003; Fiske & Fiske, 2007; Rogoff, 2003). For example, adults in some Native American groups (e.g., those living in the Navajo Nation in the southwestern United States) give children more autonomy and control over decision making than do many adults in mainstream Western culture (Deyhle & LeCompte, 1999). In contrast, many Asian and African American parents give children *less* autonomy than other American adults, in some cases as a way of ensuring children's safety in potentially hostile environments (McLoyd, 1998; L. Qin, Pomerantz, & Wang, 2009; Tamis-Lemonda & McFadden, 2010).

Cultural differences have also been observed in one important aspect of self-determination: opportunities to make choices. In particular, although young people around the world find choice-making opportunities highly motivating, those from Asian cultures often prefer that people they trust (e.g., parents, teachers, respected peers) make the choices for them (Bao & Lam, 2008; Hufton, Elliott, & Illushin, 2002; Iyengar & Lepper, 1999).

Passing notes in class is one way that some students regularly address their need for relatedness.

Perhaps Asian children see trusted others as people who can make *wise* choices, which will ultimately lead to greater learning and competence.

**Achieving a sense of relatedness** Researchers have found several cultural differences in how children and adolescents address their need for relatedness. In comparison to other groups, Asian children spend less time with peers and place greater importance on excelling in schoolwork and gaining others' approval (Dien, 1998; J. Li, 2005; Steinberg, 1996). Furthermore, whereas Asian students are apt to have friends who encourage academic achievement, some students from certain other ethnic groups (boys especially) may feel considerable peer pressure *not* to achieve at high levels, perhaps because high achievement reflects conformity to mainstream Western culture (Bergin & Cooks, 2008; B. B. Brown, 1993; Ogbu, 2008b).

An additional factor is family ties: Students from many cultural and ethnic groups have especially strong loyalties to family and may have been brought up to achieve for their respective communities, rather than just for themselves as individuals. Motivating statements such as "Think how proud your family will be!" and "If you get a college education, you can really help your community!" are likely to be especially effective for such students (C.-Y. Chiu & Hong, 2005; Fiske & Fiske, 2007; Kağitçibaşi, 2007; Timm & Borman, 1997).

The need for relatedness can sometimes be at odds with the need for self-determination. In particular, achieving relatedness can involve doing what *others* want one to do, whereas achieving self-determination involves doing what one *personally* wants to do. Many people from Asian cultures resolve this apparent conflict by willingly agreeing to adjust personal behaviors and goals to meet social demands and maintain overall group harmony (Iyengar & Lepper, 1999; Kağitçibaşi, 2007; J. Li & Fischer, 2004; Savani, Markus, Naidu, Kumar, & Berlia, 2010).

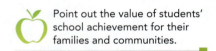 Point out the value of students' school achievement for their families and communities.

## A POSSIBLE HIERARCHY OF NEEDS: MASLOW'S THEORY

What happens when people have trouble reconciling their various needs? One early humanist, Abraham Maslow, suggested that people tend to prioritize their needs in a fairly consistent manner (e.g., Maslow, 1943, 1973, 1987). His theory predates much of the research on the four basic needs we've examined in this chapter, but at least two of them—and possibly three—are reflected in the five central needs he identified:

1. *Physiological:* Needs related to physical survival (food, water, shelter, etc.)
2. *Safety:* The need to feel safe and secure in one's environment
3. *Love and belonging:* The need to have affectionate relationships with others and to be accepted as part of a group
4. *Esteem:* The need to feel good about oneself (*self-esteem*) and also to believe that others also perceive oneself favorably (*esteem from others*)
5. *Self-actualization:* The need to reach one's full potential—to become all that one is capable of becoming

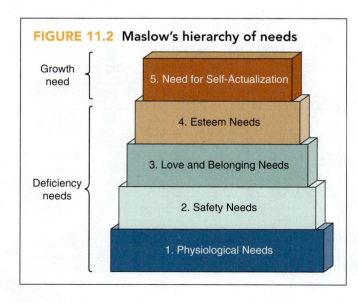

**FIGURE 11.2** **Maslow's hierarchy of needs**

Growth need
5. Need for Self-Actualization

Deficiency needs
4. Esteem Needs
3. Love and Belonging Needs
2. Safety Needs
1. Physiological Needs

We can reasonably speculate that the need for relatedness underlies Maslow's love-and-belonging and esteem-from-others needs and that the need for competence underlies his self-esteem and self-actualization needs. Furthermore, the need for arousal may sometimes have a physiological basis—perhaps simply in the form of a need to release pent-up energy.

Maslow proposed that the five needs form a hierarchy, as illustrated in Figure 11.2. Specifically, learners try to satisfy their physiological needs first, then their need for safety, and still later their needs for love, belonging, and esteem. Only when such needs have been met do they strive for self-actualization, exploring areas of interest, learning simply for the sheer pleasure of it, and so on. For example, a boy with a need for releasing pent-up energy (a physiological need) may become excessively restless in class even though his teacher scolds him for his hyperactivity (and thereby doesn't satisfy his need for esteem from others). A girl with an unfulfilled need for love and belonging may decide not to enroll in intermediate algebra—a class that would satisfy her desire to learn more math—if the peers whose friendships she most values tell her the class is only for nerds and dweebs. I once knew a boy living in a Philadelphia ghetto who was eager to go to school but often stayed home to avoid the violent gangs that hung out on the local street corner. This boy's need for safety took precedence over any need for self-actualization he might have had.

The first four needs in the hierarchy—physiological, safety, love and belonging, and esteem—result from things a learner *lacks;* thus Maslow called them *deficiency needs.* Deficiency needs can be met only by external sources—by people and events in one's environment. And once these needs are fulfilled, there's no reason to satisfy them further. In contrast, self-actualization is a *growth need:* It enhances the learner's development and is rarely satisfied completely. Self-actualizing activities tend to be intrinsically motivating: Learners engage in them because doing so gives them pleasure and satisfies their desire to know and grow. In Maslow's view total self-actualization is rarely, if ever, achieved, and then typically only by mature adults.

Unfortunately, Maslow's hierarchy of needs was based on very little hard evidence; thus, many theorists continue to regard his theory as being more conjecture than fact. Yet aspects of Maslow's theory clearly have some merit. It makes sense that learners will worry about their physical well-being and personal safety before trying to address more social needs (e.g., Kenrick, Griskevicius, Neuberg, & Schaller, 2010). And many people do seem to be eager to gain wisdom or creatively express themselves, consistent with Maslow's idea of self-actualization (Kesebir, Graham, & Oishi, 2010; C. Peterson & Park, 2010).

> Remember that students will be more eager to learn and master academic subject matter if they have met their more basic physiological and psychological needs.

# Cognitive and Sociocultural Factors in Motivation

Let's return to the opening case study, in which Michael changes from a student who is failing algebra to one who pays close attention in class, regularly does his homework, and seeks help with things he doesn't understand. Michael's initial beliefs about his math ability (i.e., his self-efficacy) and his explanations for his poor performance (low ability and poor instruction) contribute to a lackadaisical attitude: He simply *hopes* he'll remember—but usually forgets—his teacher's explanations. Later, when Michael's appraisal of the situation changes, he's a much more engaged and proactive learner.

Michael's dramatic turnaround illustrates both that *cognitive processes affect motivation* and that *motivation affects cognitive processes.* Yet the turnaround requires a significant change in Michael's social environment—in particular, a new tutor who helps him think in more productive ways both about mathematics as a content domain and about his ability to do well in that domain. As we explore various elements of motivation in the upcoming sections, we'll see how cognition and motivation often interact in their effects on learning and behavior and how numerous sociocultural factors enter into the picture as well.

## INTERESTS

When we say that learners have **interest** in a particular topic or activity, we mean that they find the topic or activity intriguing and engaging. Interest, then, is a form of intrinsic motivation. Interest is typically accompanied by cognitive arousal and such feelings as enjoyment and excitement (Ainley & Ainley, 2011; M. Hofer, 2010; Renninger, 2009).

Learners who are interested in a topic devote more time and attention to it and become more cognitively engaged in it—often both in and outside of school (Barron, 2006; Hidi & Renninger, 2006; M. A. McDaniel, Waddill, Finstad, & Bourg, 2000). They're also likely to learn it more meaningfully—for instance, by interconnecting ideas, drawing inferences, and identifying potential applications (Pintrich & Schrauben, 1992; Schraw & Lehman, 2001; Tobias, 1994). And unless they're emotionally attached to their current beliefs, learners who are interested in what they're studying are more likely to undergo conceptual change when

**interest** Perception that an activity is intriguing and enticing; typically accompanied by both cognitive engagement and positive affect.

**situational interest** Interest evoked temporarily by something in the environment.

**personal interest** Long-term, relatively stable interest in a particular topic or activity.

Hands-on activities often evoke situational interest. For example, watch "Investigating Particles: Part 1."

Ask students to apply newly acquired skills to areas of personal interest.

it's warranted (Andre & Windschitl, 2003; Linnenbrink & Pintrich, 2003; Mason, Gava, & Boldrin, 2008). As you might guess, then, students who are interested in what they study show higher academic achievement and are more likely to remember the subject matter over the long run (Garner, Brown, Sanders, & Menke, 1992; Hidi & Harackiewicz, 2000; Renninger, Hidi, & Krapp, 1992).

Psychologists distinguish between two general types of interest. Situational interest is evoked by something in the immediate environment. Things that are new, different, or unexpected often generate interest, as do things with a high activity level or intense emotions. Children and adolescents also tend to be intrigued by topics related to people and culture (e.g., diseases, holidays), nature (e.g., dinosaurs, the sea), and popular media (e.g., television shows, video games, contemporary music). Works of fiction and fantasy are more engaging when they include themes and characters with which readers can personally identify. Textbooks and other works of nonfiction are more interesting when they're easy to understand and when relationships among ideas are clear. And challenging tasks are often more interesting than easy ones—a fortunate state of affairs if, as Lev Vygotsky proposed, challenges promote cognitive growth (Ainley, 2006; J. M. Alexander, Johnson, Leibham, & Kelley, 2008; Hidi & Renninger, 2006; M. Hofer, 2010; Schraw & Lehman, 2001; Shernoff & Csikszentmihalyi, 2009; Zahorik, 1994).

Other interests lie within: Learners tend to have personal preferences about the topics they pursue and the activities in which they engage. Such personal interests are relatively stable over time and lead to consistent patterns in the choices learners make (J. M. Alexander et al., 2008; Nolen, 2007; Y.-M. Tsai, Kunter, Lüdtke, Trautwein, & Ryan, 2008). Even in the early elementary grades, many children have specific interests that persist over time—perhaps about reptiles, ballet, or computer technology. Often personal interest and knowledge perpetuate each other: Interest in a topic fuels a quest to learn more about it, and the increased knowledge and skills gained, in turn, promote greater interest (Barron, 2006; Blumenfeld et al., 2006; Nolen, 2007). And especially in adolescence, long-standing personal interests can be important components of a learner's sense of identity (Barron, 2006; M. Hofer, 2010).

Ultimately, personal interest is more beneficial than situational interest because it sustains engagement, effective cognitive processing, and improvement over the long run. Yet situational interest is important as well, because it captures learners' attention and often provides a seed from which a personal interest can grow (P. A. Alexander, Kulikowich, & Schulze, 1994; Durik & Harackiewicz, 2007; Hidi & Renninger, 2006; M. Mitchell, 1993).

**FIGURE 11.3** Students' personal interests can provide a motivating context in which to practice basic skills. Here, 12-year-old Connor practiced research and graphing skills by surveying peers about a favorite topic: cars.

## PROMOTING INTEREST IN CLASSROOM SUBJECT MATTER

As teachers, we can certainly capitalize on students' personal interests by allowing some flexibility in the topics about which they read, learn, write, and study (e.g., see Figure 11.3). On other occasions we can temporarily pique students' interest, and perhaps also stimulate the beginnings of more enduring personal interests, through the activities we develop and the ways we present information. Following are several strategies that often evoke interest in classroom topics:

- Model excitement and enthusiasm about classroom topics and healthful physical activities.
- Occasionally incorporate novelty, variety, fantasy, or mystery into lessons and procedures.
- Encourage students to identify with historical figures or fictional characters and to imagine what these people might have been thinking or feeling.
- Provide opportunities for students to respond actively to the subject matter—perhaps by manipulating physical objects, creating new inventions, debating controversial issues, representing ideas in art or drama, or teaching something they've

---

**FIGURE 11.4** **Examples of strategies for generating interest in various content domains**

🍎 **Art:** Have students make a mosaic from items they've found on a scavenger hunt around the school building.

🍎 **Biology:** Hold a class debate about the ethical implications of conducting medical research on animals.

🍎 **Geography:** Present household objects not found locally, and ask students to guess where they might be from.

🍎 **Health education:** In a lesson about alcoholic beverages, have students role-play being at a party and being tempted to have a beer or wine cooler.

🍎 **History:** Have students read children's perspectives of historical events (e.g., Anne Frank's diary during World War II, Zlata Filipovic's diary during the Bosnian War).

🍎 **Language arts:** Examine lyrics in popular hip hop music, looking for grammatical patterns and literary themes.

🍎 **Mathematics:** Have students apply their math skills in computer software programs that enable them to create fantasy sports teams or to solve authentic, real-world problems.

🍎 **Music:** In a unit on musical instruments, let students experiment with a variety of simple instruments.

🍎 **Physical education:** Incorporate steps from hip hop, swing, or country line dancing into an aerobics workout.

🍎 **Physical science:** Challenge students to design and construct model airplanes (e.g., out of lightweight balsa wood strips) that will be able to fly a certain distance.

🍎 **Reading:** Turn a short story into a play, with each student taking a part.

🍎 **Spelling:** Occasionally depart from standard word lists, instead asking students to learn how to spell the names of favorite television shows or classmates' surnames.

🍎 **Writing:** Ask students to create children's storybooks related to their own personal interests and experiences.

*Sources:* Some ideas derived from Alim, 2007; Barab, Gresalfi, & Ingram-Goble, 2010; Botelho, Cohen, Leoni, Chow, & Sastri, 2010; Brophy, 1986; A. Collins & Halverson, 2009; Lepper & Hodell, 1989; W.-M. Roth, 2011; Spaulding, 1992; Stipek, 1993; Wlodkowski, 1978.

---

learned to peers. (Ainley, 2006; Andre & Windschitl, 2003; Brophy, Alleman, & Knighton, 2009; Certo, Cauley, & Chafin, 2003; Chinn, 2006; Hidi & Renninger, 2006; Hidi, Weiss, Berndorff, & Nolan, 1998; Kunter, Frenzel, Nagy, Baumert, & Pekrun, 2011; Pool, Dittrich, & Pool, 2011; Radel, Sarrazin, Legrain, & Wild, 2010; Zahorik, 1994)

Figure 11.4 presents examples of how we might promote intrinsic motivation in a variety of content domains.

## EXPECTANCIES AND VALUES

Some theorists have proposed that motivation for performing a particular task depends on two variables, both of which are fairly subjective (e.g., Feather, 1982; Nagengast et al., 2011; Wigfield & Eccles, 2000). First, learners must have a high expectation, or **expectancy**, that they'll be successful. Certainly their prior history of success and failure at a particular task—and thus their self-efficacy—has a strong influence. But other factors also affect expectancy level, including the perceived difficulty of a task, the availability of resources and support, the quality of instruction (recall Michael's complaint about his algebra teacher), and the amount of effort that will be necessary (Dweck & Elliott, 1983; Wigfield & Eccles, 1992; Zimmerman, Bandura, & Martinez-Pons, 1992). From such factors learners come to conclusions—perhaps accurate, perhaps not—about their chances of success.

Equally important and equally subjective is value: Learners must believe there are direct or indirect benefits in performing a task. Theorists have suggested four possible reasons that value might be high or low: importance, utility, interest, and cost (Eccles, 2009; Wigfield & Eccles, 2000). Some activities are valued because they're associated with desirable personal qualities; that is, they're viewed as *important*. For example, a boy who wants to be smart and thinks that smart people do well in school will place a premium on academic success. Other activities have high value because they're seen as a means to a desired goal; that is, they have *utility*. For example, although my daughter Tina found mathematics confusing and frustrating, she struggled through four years of high school math because many colleges require that much math. Still other activities are valued simply because they bring pleasure and enjoyment; in other words, they're *interesting*.

However, we can also envision circumstances in which learners probably won't value an activity very much. Some activities may require a lot more effort than they're worth; this is the *cost* factor. For example, although you could eventually become an expert on some little-known

**expectancy** Belief about the likelihood of success in an activity, given present ability levels and external circumstances that may either help or hinder performance.

**value** Belief regarding the extent to which an activity has direct or indirect benefits.

**internalized motivation** Adoption of other people's priorities and values as one's own.

topic (e.g., the nature of rats' dreams, animal-eating plants of Borneo), gaining expertise might require far more time and energy than you're willing to expend. Other activities might seem costly as a result of their association with bad feelings. For example, if learners become frustrated often enough in their efforts to understand math, they may eventually try to avoid it whenever they can. And of course, anything likely to threaten a learner's sense of self-worth is a "must" to avoid.

Students are likely to engage in a particular behavior only if they have some expectancy of success *and* find some value in the behavior. Aside from this both-are-necessary condition, expectancies and values are related to different aspects of students' behavior and performance. Values affect the choices students make—for instance, which courses they select and whether they participate in extracurricular activities. In contrast, expectancies are related to students' effort and achievement—for instance, their grade point average (Durik, Vida, & Eccles, 2006; Mac Iver, Stipek, & Daniels, 1991; Wigfield, Tonks, & Eccles, 2004).

In the early elementary years, students often pursue activities they find interesting and enjoyable, regardless of their expectancies for success (Wigfield, 1994). As they get older, however, their values and expectancies become somewhat interdependent. In particular, they increasingly attach value to activities for which they have high expectancy for success and which they think will help them meet long-term goals. At the same time, they begin to *devalue* the things they do poorly (Jacobs, Lanza, Osgood, Eccles, & Wigfield, 2002; Wigfield, 1994). Sadly, the value students find in many school subjects declines markedly over the school years (Archambault, Eccles, & Vida, 2010; Jacobs et al., 2002; Wigfield et al., 2004). As one 16-year-old put it, "School's fun because you can hang out with your friends, but I know I won't use much of this stuff when I leave here" (Valente, 2001).

## INTERNALIZING VALUES OF ONE'S SOCIAL AND CULTURAL GROUPS

As children grow older, they tend to adopt many of the priorities and values of the people around them. Such internalized motivation typically develops gradually over the course of childhood and adolescence, perhaps in the sequence depicted in Figure 11.5 (Deci & Moller, 2005; Deci & Ryan, 1995; R. M. Ryan & Deci, 2000). Initially children may engage in certain activities primarily because of the external consequences that result. For instance, they may do schoolwork to earn praise or to avoid being punished for poor grades. With time other people's approval becomes increasingly important for children's sense of self. Eventually children begin to internalize the pressure to perform certain activities and to see these activities as important in their own right. Such internalization of values is most likely to occur if adults who espouse those values (parents, teachers, etc.) do the following:

---

**FIGURE 11.5 Sequence in which internalized motivation may develop**

1. **External regulation:** Learners are initially motivated to behave in certain ways, based primarily on the external consequences that will follow the behaviors; that is, the learners are extrinsically motivated.

2. **Introjection:** Learners begin to behave in ways that gain the approval of others, partly as a way of protecting and enhancing their sense of self. They feel guilty when they violate certain standards for behavior but do not fully understand the rationale behind these standards.

3. **Identification:** Learners now see some behaviors and activities as being personally important or valuable for them.

4. **Integration:** Learners integrate certain behaviors and activities into their overall system of motives and values. In essence, these behaviors become a central part of their identity and general sense of self.

*Source:* Based on Deci & Moller, 2005; Deci & Ryan, 1995.

---

- Engage in and thereby model valued activities themselves.

- Provide a warm, responsive, and supportive environment (addressing children's need for relatedness).

- Offer some autonomy in decision making (addressing children's need for self-determination).

- Set reasonable limits for behavior and provide information about why certain behaviors are important. (Deci & Moller, 2005; Eccles, 2007; Jacobs et al., 2005; R. M. Ryan, Connell, & Grolnick, 1992; R. M. Ryan & Deci, 2000)

Find a reasonable balance between giving students autonomy in their actions and imposing reasonable limits on their behavior.

Fostering the development of internalized motivation, then, involves striking a delicate balance between giving students opportunities to experience self-determination and providing guidance about desired behaviors.

In one respect, internalized motivation is similar to intrinsic motivation: Both forms of motivation arise from inside the learner rather than from outside factors in the immediate, here-and-now environment. But there's an important difference: Because intrinsic motivation seems to arise spontaneously within the learner, it can increase or decrease somewhat unpredictably. In contrast, because internalized motivation is a product of ongoing social and cultural factors and eventually becomes an integral part of learners' sense of self, it has considerable stability and is therefore fairly dependable over time (Otis et al., 2005; Reeve et al., 2004).

The more students have internalized the value of learning and academic success, the more cognitively engaged they become in school subject matter and the better their overall classroom achievement is likely to be. Internalized motivation is also an important aspect of self-regulated learning: It underlies a general work ethic in which learners spontaneously engage in activities that, although not always fun or immediately gratifying, are essential for reaching long-term goals (Assor, Vansteenkiste, & Kaplan, 2009; La Guardia, 2009; Ratelle, Guay, Vallerand, Larose, & Senécal, 2007; R. M. Ryan et al., 1992; Walls & Little, 2005).

## FOSTERING EXPECTANCIES AND VALUES IN THE CLASSROOM

As teachers, we must certainly give students reasons to expect success with classroom tasks—for instance, by providing the necessary resources, support, and strategies, as Ms. Tucker did in the opening case study. But we must also help students find value in school activities. Motivation theorists and experienced teachers have offered several suggestions for fostering genuine appreciation for academic subject matter:

*Enhance students' expectancies for success by providing the necessary resources, strategies, and support.*

- Clearly identify the particular knowledge and skills that students will gain from lessons.
- Convey how certain concepts and principles can help students make better sense of the world around them.
- Help students relate information and skills to their present concerns and long-term goals.
- Embed the use of new skills within the context of real-world (i.e., authentic) and personally meaningful activities.
- Model how you yourself value academic activities—for example, by describing how you apply the things you've learned in school.
- Above all, refrain from asking students to engage in activities with little long-term benefit—for instance, having them memorize trivial facts for no good reason or requiring them to read material that is clearly beyond their comprehension levels. (Ames, 1992; Brophy et al., 2009; G. L. Cohen, Garcia, Purdie-Vaughns, Apfel, & Brzustoski, 2009; Eccles, 2009; Ferrari & Elik, 2003; Hulleman, Godes, Hendricks, & Harackiewicz, 2010; Newmann & Wehlage, 1993; W.-M. Roth, 2011; Stefanou et al., 2004)

# GOALS

Much of human behavior is directed toward particular goals. Some goals are short term and transitory (e.g., "I want to finish reading my dinosaur book"); others are long term and relatively enduring (e.g., "I want to be a paleontologist"). Children and adolescents typically have a wide variety of goals: Being happy and healthy, doing well in school, gaining popularity with peers, winning athletic competitions, and finding a long-term mate are just a few of the many possibilities (M. E. Ford & Smith, 2007; Schutz, 1994). Here we'll look at research related to several types of goals especially relevant to instructional settings.

## ACHIEVEMENT GOALS

Early motivation theorists proposed that *achievement motivation* is a general trait that learners consistently exhibit in a wide variety of contexts. In contrast, most contemporary theorists believe that achievement motivation may be somewhat specific to particular tasks and occasions. It can also take different forms, depending on learners' specific goals. For example, let's consider what three different boys might be thinking during the first day of a basketball unit in Mr. Wesolowski's physical education class:

> *Tim:* I'd like to show everyone what a great basketball player I am. If I stay near the basket, Travis and Tony will keep passing to me, and I can make a bunch of baskets.

> *Travis:* I hope I don't screw this up. If I shoot at the basket and miss, I'll look like a real loser. Maybe I should just stay outside the three-point line and keep passing to Tim and Tony.

> *Tony:* I really want to become a better basketball player. I'll ask Wesolowski to give me feedback about how I can improve my game. Maybe some of my friends will have suggestions as well.

All three boys want to play basketball well—that is, they all have *achievement goals*. But they have different reasons for wanting to play well. Tim is concerned mostly about impressing his teacher and classmates and so wants to maximize opportunities to demonstrate his skills. Travis, too, is concerned about the impression he'll make, but he just wants to make sure he doesn't look *bad*. In contrast, Tony isn't thinking about how his performance will appear to others. Instead, he's interested mainly in developing his basketball skills and doesn't expect immediate success. For Tony, making mistakes is an inevitable part of learning a new skill, not a source of embarrassment or humiliation.

Tony's approach to basketball illustrates a mastery goal, a desire to acquire additional knowledge or master new skills. Tim and Travis each have a performance goal, a desire to present themselves as competent in the eyes of others. More specifically, Tim has a performance-approach goal: He wants to look good and receive favorable judgments from others. In contrast, Travis has a performance-avoidance goal: He wants to avoid looking bad and receiving unfavorable judgments. Sometimes achievement goals—especially performance goals—have an element of social comparison, with learners being concerned about how their accomplishments compare to those of their peers (Elliot, Murayama, & Pekrun, 2011; Régner, Escribe, & Dupeyrat, 2007; Senko, Hulleman, & Harackiewicz, 2011).

Mastery goals, performance-approach goals, and performance-avoidance goals aren't necessarily mutually exclusive. Learners may simultaneously have two kinds or even all three (Luo, Paris, Hogan, & Luo, 2011; Murayama, Elliot, & Yamagata, 2011; Senko et al., 2011). Returning to our basketball example, we could imagine a fourth boy, Trey, who wants to improve his basketball skills *and* look good in front of his classmates *and* not come across as a klutz.

### Effects of mastery and performance goals

In most instances, having mastery goals is the optimal situation. As Table 11.2 illustrates, learners with mastery goals tend to engage in the very activities that will help them learn: They pay attention in class, process information in ways that promote effective long-term memory storage, and learn from their mistakes. Furthermore, they have a healthy perspective about learning, effort, and failure: They realize that learning is a process of trying hard and continuing to persevere in the face of temporary setbacks. Consequently, these learners are the ones who are most likely to stay on task and who benefit the most from their classroom experiences (Elliot et al., 2011; Kumar, Gheen, & Kaplan, 2002; Sins, van Joolingen, Savelsbergh, & van Hout-Wolters, 2008).

In contrast, learners with performance goals—especially those with performance-*avoidance* goals—tend to steer clear of the challenges so important for learning, give up easily in the face of failure, and are apt to engage in self-handicapping when they expect to do poorly. Performance-*approach* goals are a mixed bag: They sometimes have positive effects, especially in combination with mastery goals, spurring learners to achieve at high levels (Linnenbrink, 2005; Rawsthorne & Elliot, 1999; Wolters, 2004). Yet by themselves, performance-approach goals may be less beneficial than mastery goals: Learners may exert only the minimum effort necessary, use relatively superficial learning strategies (e.g., rote memorization), and occasionally cheat on assessments. Performance-approach goals appear to be most detrimental when learners are younger (e.g., in the elementary grades) and have low self-efficacy for classroom tasks (E. M. Anderman et al., 1998; Midgley, Kaplan, & Middleton, 2001; M.-T. Wang & Holcombe, 2010).

### Developmental trends in achievement goals

In the preschool and early elementary years, children seem to focus largely on mastery goals, but performance goals become increasingly prevalent at more advanced grade levels (Bong, 2009: Dweck & Elliott, 1983; Harter, 1992). By the time students reach high school, they may find pleasure in learning new things, but many are concerned primarily about getting good grades and prefer short, easy tasks to lengthier, more challenging ones. Performance goals are also common in team sports, where the focus often is more on winning and gaining public recognition than on developing new skills (G. C. Roberts, Treasure, & Kavussanu, 1997).

When children begin school at age 5 or 6, two things happen that gradually orient them more toward performance goals (Dweck & Elliott, 1983). For one thing, they now have many peers with whom to compare their own behaviors, and they may sometimes see themselves coming up short. In addition, children may have trouble evaluating their progress on complex academic skills and thus must rely on others (e.g., teachers) to make judgments about their competence.

Students with mastery goals recognize that competence comes from effort and practice. For example, listen to 8-year-old Keenan in "Portfolio."

**mastery goal** Desire to acquire new knowledge or master new skills.

**performance goal** Desire to demonstrate high ability and make a good impression.

**performance-approach goal** Desire to look good and receive favorable judgments from others.

**performance-avoidance goal** Desire not to look bad or receive unfavorable judgments from others.

# COMPARE/CONTRAST

| TABLE 11.2 • Typical Differences between Learners with Mastery versus Performance Goals | |
|---|---|
| **LEARNERS WITH MASTERY GOALS** | **LEARNERS WITH PERFORMANCE GOALS (ESPECIALLY THOSE WITH PERFORMANCE-AVOIDANCE GOALS)** |
| Are more likely to be actively engaged in classroom activities and intrinsically motivated to learn course material | Are more likely to be extrinsically motivated and more likely to cheat to obtain good grades |
| Believe that competence develops over time through practice and effort; persist in the face of difficulty | Believe that competence is a stable characteristic (people either have talent or they don't); think that competent people shouldn't have to try very hard; give up quickly when facing difficulty |
| Choose tasks that maximize opportunities for learning; seek out challenges | Choose tasks that maximize opportunities for showing competence; avoid tasks and actions that might reveal incompetence (e.g., asking for help) |
| Exhibit more self-regulated learning and behavior | Exhibit less self-regulation |
| Use learning strategies that promote true understanding and complex cognitive processes (e.g., elaboration, comprehension monitoring, transfer) | Use learning strategies that promote only rote learning (e.g., word-for-word memorization); may procrastinate on assignments |
| Are more likely to undergo conceptual change when confronted with convincing evidence that contradicts current beliefs | Are less likely to undergo conceptual change, in part because they are less likely to notice the discrepancy between new information and existing beliefs |
| React to easy tasks with feelings of boredom or disappointment | React to success on easy tasks with feelings of pride or relief |
| Seek feedback that accurately describes their ability and helps them improve | Seek feedback that flatters them |
| Have friends with whom they often collaborate to address academic or social problems | Collaborate with peers primarily when doing so can help them look competent or enhance their social status |
| Evaluate their own performance in terms of the progress they make | Evaluate their own performance in terms of how they compare with others |
| View errors as a normal and useful part of the learning process; use errors to improve performance | View errors as a sign of failure and incompetence; engage in self-handicapping to provide apparent justification for errors and failures |
| Are satisfied with their performance if they try hard and make progress | Are satisfied with their performance only if they succeed; are apt to feel ashamed and depressed when they fail |
| View a teacher as a resource and guide to help them learn | View a teacher as a judge and as a rewarder or punisher |
| Remain relatively calm during tests and other classroom assessments | Are often quite anxious about tests and other assessments |
| Are more likely to be enthusiastic about and become actively involved in school activities | Are more likely to distance themselves from the school environment |

*Sources:* Ablard & Lipschultz, 1998; E. M; E. M. Anderman & Maehr, 1994; L. H. Anderman & Anderman, 2009; Corpus, McClintic-Gilberg, & Hayenga, 2009; Dweck, 1986; Dweck & Elliott, 1983; Dweck, Mangels, & Good, 2004; Elliot et al., 2011; Gabriele, 2007; Gabriele & Boody, 2001; Graham & Weiner, 1996; Hardré, Crowson, DeBacker, & White, 2007; Jagacinski & Nicholls, 1984, 1987; Kaplan & Midgley, 1999; Lau & Nie, 2008; Levy-Tossman, Kaplan, & Assor, 2007; Liem, Lau, & Nie, 2008; Linnenbrink & Pintrich, 2002, 2003; E. A. Locke & Latham, 2006; McGregor & Elliot, 2002; Meece, 1994; Middleton & Midgley, 1997; P. K. Murphy & Alexander, 2000; Newman & Schwager, 1995; Nolen, 1996; Pekrun, Elliot, & Maier, 2006; Poortvliet & Darnon, 2010; Pugh & Bergin, 2006; Rawsthorne & Elliot, 1999; A. M. Ryan, Pintrich, & Midgley, 2001; Schiefele, 1991; Senko et al., 2011; Shernoff & Hoogstra, 2001; Shim, Ryan, & Anderson, 2008; Sideridis, 2005; Sinatra & Mason, 2008; Sins et al., 2008; Skaalvik, 1997; Steuer & Dresel, 2011; Turner, Thorpe, & Meyer, 1998; Urdan, 2004; Urdan & Midgley, 2001; Urdan, Midgley, & Anderman, 1998; Wolters, 2004

As children reach adolescence, two more factors kick in: They become increasingly concerned about what other people think of them, and they realize that performing at high levels—for instance, getting good grades—is critical for their future educational and professional opportunities (Covington & Müeller, 2001; Juvonen, 2000; Midgley, 1993).

Many teaching and coaching practices also contribute to the development of performance goals. Consider these common practices:

- Reinforcing students only for correct answers
- Posting only the "best" work on a bulletin board
- Grading tests on a curve
- Reminding students of the importance of good grades for college admissions
- Giving special recognition to sports teams that consistently defeat their rivals

All of these strategies are undoubtedly well intentioned, but they encourage students to focus their attention more on *demonstrating* competence than on *acquiring* it (E. M. Anderman & Mueller, 2010; Midgley, 2002).

Adolescents' increasing concern about other people's opinions of them may remind you of the *imaginary audience*, a concept presented in Chapter 3.

**Fostering productive achievement goals** To some degree, performance goals are probably inevitable in today's schools and in society at large. Learners may quite legitimately use their peers' performance as a criterion for evaluating their own ability levels, many colleges look at grade point averages and test scores when screening applicants, and many aspects of the adult world are inherently competitive in nature. Ultimately, however, mastery goals are the ones most likely to lead to effective learning and performance over the long run.

Sometimes mastery goals come from within, especially when students both value and have high self-efficacy for learning a topic (Liem, Lau, & Nie, 2008; P. K. Murphy & Alexander, 2000; Pajares, 2009). But the following classroom practices can also encourage mastery goals:

- Show how mastery of certain topics is relevant to students' long-term personal and professional goals.
- Insist that students *understand*, rather than simply memorize, classroom material.
- Communicate the belief that effective learning requires exerting effort and making mistakes.
- Give students short-term, concrete goals—known as proximal goals—toward which to work; identify goals that are challenging yet accomplishable with reasonable effort.
- Ask students to set some of their *own* short-term and long-term goals for learning (e.g., see Figure 11.6).
- Provide regular feedback that enables students to assess their progress toward goals.
- Offer specific suggestions about how students can improve.
- Give praise that focuses on mastery of content rather than on comparison with classmates.
- Encourage students to use their peers not as reference points for their own progress but rather as a source of ideas and assistance. (E. M. Anderman & Maehr, 1994; Brophy, 2004; Corpus, Tomlinson, & Stanton, 2004; E. A. Locke & Latham, 2006; Middleton & Midgley, 2002; R. B. Miller & Brickman, 2004; Page-Voth & Graham, 1999; N. E. Perry & Winne, 2004; Schunk & Pajares, 2005; Turner, Meyer, et al., 1998; Urdan et al., 2002; M.-T. Wang & Holcombe, 2010)

Focusing on mastery goals, especially when these goals relate to students' own lives and needs, may especially benefit students from diverse ethnic backgrounds and students at risk for academic failure (E. S. Alexander, 2008; García, 1992; Wlodkowski & Ginsberg, 1995).

## WORK-AVOIDANCE AND DOING-JUST-ENOUGH GOALS

As we've seen, learners sometimes want to avoid looking bad as they perform classroom tasks. But on other occasions they may want to avoid doing classroom tasks *at all,* or at least to invest as little effort as possible in them. In other words, learners may have a work-avoidance goal, often because they have low self-efficacy for the tasks at hand (Coddington & Guthrie, 2008; Dowson & McInerney, 2001; Urdan et al., 2002). Students use a variety of strategies to avoid classroom tasks—for instance, they might engage in disruptive behaviors, complain loudly about challenging assignments, or refuse to contribute to small-group learning activities (Dowson & McInerney, 2001; Gallini, 2000; Hemmings, 2004).

A similar goal—but for a very different reason—is a doing-just-enough goal (McClure et al., 2011). In particular, students want to get reasonable school grades through the easiest possible routes, perhaps by rote-memorizing isolated facts, copying classmates' homework, or submitting research papers downloaded from the Internet. A doing-just-enough goal is in some respects a performance goal, but the focus isn't on demonstrating competence or hiding a lack of it. Instead, students simply have other priorities for their time—perhaps pursuing nonacademic interests or enhancing their relationships with peers (Hickey, 2011; M. Hofer, 2010; Wells, 2011). As you might guess, students with doing-just-enough goals have relatively low achievement levels (McClure et al., 2011; Tuominin-Soini, Salmela-Aro, & Niemivirta, 2011).

**FIGURE 11.6** With this handout, a middle school information technology teacher asks students to reflect on their current strengths and identify specific goals for improvement. This handout is for girls; boys get one with shorter hair.

Things I need to improve are . . .

By the end of the term I will . . .

Things I am good at are . . .

By the end of the year I will . . .

*Source:* Figure by Jeffrey Ormrod. Copyright © by Jeffrey Ormrod. Reprinted with permission of the author.

**proximal goal** Concrete goal that can be accomplished within a short time period; may be a stepping stone toward a long-term goal.

**work-avoidance goal** Desire either to avoid classroom tasks or to complete them with minimal effort, often because of low self-efficacy for the tasks.

**doing-just-enough goal** Desire to get reasonable school grades through the easiest possible routes—routes that may or may not involve actually learning classroom material.

When students actively avoid assigned tasks because of low self-efficacy, obviously the most effective strategy is to give them the guidance and support they need to improve their performance, as Ms. Tucker does in the opening case study. When, instead, they have doing-just-enough goals, we must help them find relevance in classroom subject matter and tie it to things that are important to them. For example, they might enhance their writing skills by writing about their own lives and exchanging their stories with peers on the Internet (Garner, 1998). Or they might apply scientific and mathematical concepts to document the ecological decline of their local environment and report their findings to the adult community (W.-M. Roth, 2011). Students with work-avoidance goals and doing-just-enough goals may ultimately be our biggest challenges, and we'll probably need to use a variety of motivational strategies—extrinsic reinforcement as well as strategies that promote interest and mastery goals—to get them genuinely engaged in academic subject matter (Brophy, 2004).

Use multiple strategies—including extrinsic reinforcement if necessary—to engage students who have work-avoidance and doing-just-enough goals.

## SOCIAL GOALS

Earlier we noted that virtually all people have a need for relatedness—a need to feel socially connected with their fellow human beings. Consistent with this fundamental need, children and adolescents are apt to have a variety of social goals as they interact with other people. Such goals typically include some or all of the following:

- Forming and maintaining friendly or intimate social relationships
- Gaining other people's approval
- Achieving status, popularity, and prestige among peers
- Becoming part of a cohesive, mutually supportive group; gaining a sense of belonging in the classroom
- Adhering to the rules and conventions of the group (e.g., being a good "class citizen")
- Meeting social obligations and keeping interpersonal commitments
- Assisting and supporting others and ensuring their welfare (Dowson & McInerney, 2001; M. E. Ford & Smith, 2007; Hinkley, McInerney, & Marsh, 2001; Kiefer & Ellerbrock, 2011; Patrick, Anderman, & Ryan, 2002; Schutz, 1994; Wentzel, Filisetti, & Looney, 2007)

The specific nature of students' social goals affects their classroom behavior and academic performance—sometimes for the better but sometimes for the worse. If students are seeking friendly relationships with classmates or are concerned about others' welfare, they may eagerly engage in such activities as cooperative learning and peer tutoring (Dowson & McInerney, 2001; Wentzel et al., 2007). But if they're more concerned about gaining the *approval* of their peers, they may go out of their way to behave in ways they think will please others, possibly compromising their own standards for behavior in the process and possibly also alienating peers because they're trying too hard to be liked (M. Bartlett, Rudolph, Flynn, Abaied, & Koerber, 2007; Boyatzis, 1973; Rudolph et al., 2005).

Meanwhile, of course, many students are also eager to form productive social relationships with their teachers. Ideally, we would hope that they see us teachers primarily as sources of support and guidance who can help them master academic subject matter and adjust comfortably to the school environment. But some may be more concerned with gaining our approval, in which case they're likely to shoot for performance goals and may self-handicap in activities at which they expect to do poorly (H. A. Davis, 2003; Hinkley et al., 2001; S. C. Rose & Thornburg, 1984).

## LONG-TERM LIFE GOALS

Many children and adolescents give considerable thought to the kinds of lives they want to lead and set goals consistent with those hoped-for lives (J. Q. Lee, McInerney, Liem, & Ortiga, 2010; Oyserman, 2008). Key among these long-term goals, of course, are career goals. Young children set such goals with little thought and change them frequently; for instance, a 6-year-old may want to be a firefighter one week and a professional baseball player the next. But by late adolescence many young people have reached tentative and relatively stable decisions about the career paths they want to pursue (Lapan, Tucker, Kim, & Kosciulek, 2003; Marcia, 1980). Often their choices are based on a strong sense of competence in a particular domain and on personal and cultural values regarding important life pursuits (Plante & O'Keefe, 2010).

Many children begin thinking about long-term goals as early as the preschool and early elementary years. Here, 7-year-old Ashton explains why he wants to be a surgeon. His explanation reflects social goals as well as a career goal.

Students' long-term goals can certainly direct them toward particular curricular and extra-curricular activities at school—perhaps in science, music, or athletics. Three teaching strategies can capitalize on those goals:

- Have students brainstorm the kinds of knowledge and abilities they're likely to need to accomplish their goals.
- Also have students brainstorm possible obstacles they might encounter in pursuit of their goals, along with specific ways they might overcome those obstacles.
- Regularly tie school subject matter to students' personal goals; for example, conduct activities in which they can authentically apply classroom topics to tasks related to their chosen professions. (Gay, 2010; Nolen, 2011; Oyserman, 2008)

But in addition, we must keep in mind that many students don't have the self-regulation skills to keep themselves on track toward meeting their long-term goals, perhaps because they have few self-regulating role models in their outside lives (R. B. Miller & Brickman, 2004; Oyserman, 2008; B. L. Wilson & Corbett, 2001). Another key strategy, then, is to teach and scaffold such skills—scheduling sufficient time for studying, saying "no" to appealing but nonproductive leisure-time activities, self-imposing reinforcement for completing specific tasks, and so on. At the same time, students will probably have greater stick-to-itiveness if they also build enjoyable leisure activities into their schedules. Expecting them to totally deny themselves life's little pleasures isn't likely to be either productive or realistic (M. Hofer, 2010).

*Urge students to build enjoyable leisure activities into their daily schedules, perhaps by making those activities contingent on completing specific academic tasks.*

## COORDINATING MULTIPLE GOALS

Most students have numerous goals and use a variety of strategies to juggle them (Covington, 2000; Dodge, Asher, & Parkhurst, 1989; Urdan & Maehr, 1995). Sometimes students find activities that allow them to address two or more goals simultaneously; for example, they can address both achievement goals and social goals by forming a study group to prepare for a test. Sometimes students pursue one goal while temporarily putting others on the back burner; for example, they might complete a required reading assignment while bypassing more interesting but unassigned material. And occasionally students may modify their idea of what it means to achieve a particular goal; for instance, an ambitious high school student who initially hopes to earn all As in three advanced classes may eventually concede that earning Bs in two of them may be more realistic.

In other situations students may entirely abandon one goal in order to satisfy another, conflicting one (M. Hofer, 2010; McCaslin & Good, 1996; Phelan et al., 1994). For example, students who want to do well in school may choose *not* to perform at their best in order to maintain relationships with peers who don't value academic achievement (B. B. Brown, 1993; Ogbu, 2008b). And students with mastery goals in particular content domains may find that the multiple demands of school coerce them into focusing on performance goals (e.g., getting good grades) rather than studying the subject matter as thoroughly as they'd like. Brian, a junior high school student, expresses his concern about leaving his mastery goals behind as he strives for performance goals:

> I sit here and I say, "Hey, I did this assignment in five minutes and I still got an A+ on it." I still have a feeling that I could do better, and it was kind of cheap that I didn't do my best and I still got this A. . . . I think probably it might lower my standards eventually, which I'm not looking forward to at all. . . . I'll always know, though, that I have it in me. It's just that I won't express it that much. (S. Thomas & Oldfather, 1997, p. 119)

*Consider how your classroom practices might help students address multiple goals simultaneously.*

Naturally, our students will be most successful when their multiple goals all lead them in the same direction (M. E. Ford, 1992; Wentzel, 1999). For example, students might work toward mastery goals by learning and practicing new skills within the context of group projects (thus meeting their social goals) and with evaluation criteria that allow for taking risks and making mistakes (thus also meeting their performance goals). Students are *un*likely to strive for mastery goals when assignments ask little of them (recall Brian's concern about the minimal requirements for an A), when we insist that they compete with one another for resources or high test scores (thereby interfering with their social goals), or when any single failure has a significant impact on their final grades (thereby thwarting their progress toward performance goals).

# ATTRIBUTIONS

**Attributions** are learners' self-constructed explanations of their successes and failures—their beliefs about *what causes what* in their personal lives. Learners are often eager to identify the probable causes of things that happen to them, especially when events are unexpected—for instance, when they get a low score on a class assignment after thinking they've done a good job. Forming attributions is just one of the many ways in which learners try to make better sense of their world (Stupnisky, Stewart, Daniels, & Perry, 2011; Tollefson, 2000; Weiner, 1986, 2000).

To gain insight into the kinds of attributions you yourself might form, try the following exercise.

■■ ■ **EXPERIENCING FIRSTHAND**
## CARBERRY AND SEVILLE #1

1. Professor Josiah S. Carberry has just returned the first set of exams in your advanced psychoceramics class. You've gotten one of the few high test scores in the class: an A–. Why did you do so well when most of your classmates did poorly? Jot down several possible explanations for your high grade in Carberry's class.

2. An hour later you get the results of the first test in Professor Barbara F. Seville's sociocosmetology class, and you learn that you *failed* it! Why did you do so poorly? Jot down several possible reasons for your F on Seville's test.

3. You'll be taking second exams in both psychoceramics and sociocosmetology in about three weeks. How much will you study for each exam?

Here are some possible explanations for your A– in Carberry's class:

- You studied hard.
- You're a very intelligent human being.
- You have a natural talent for psychoceramics in particular.
- You were lucky that Carberry chose questions you could correctly answer.
- All those hours you spent brown-nosing Carberry in his office, asking questions about psychoceramics and requesting copies of the articles he's written (which you never actually read), really paid off.

In contrast, here are some possible reasons you failed the exam in Seville's class:

- You didn't study enough.
- You studied the wrong things.
- You've never had a knack for sociocosmetology.
- The student next to you was constantly distracting you with his wheezing and coughing.
- You were unlucky. If Seville had asked different questions, you'd have done better.
- It was a bad test: The questions were ambiguous and tested knowledge of trivial facts.

How much time you spend studying for the next exams will depend to some degree on how you've interpreted your previous test grades. Let's first consider your A– on Professor Carberry's exam. If you think you did well because you studied hard, you'll probably spend a lot of time studying for the second test as well. If you think you did well because you're smart or a natural whiz at psychoceramics, you may not study quite as much. If you believe your success was a matter of luck, you may hardly study at all, but you might wear your lucky sweater when you take the next exam. And if you think the A– reflects how much Carberry likes you, you may decide that time spent flattering him is more important than time spent studying.

Now let's consider your failing grade on Professor Seville's exam. Once again, your explanation of the grade will influence the ways in which you prepare for the second exam—if, in fact, you prepare at all. If you believe you didn't study enough or didn't study the right things, you may spend more time studying the next time. If you think your poor grade was due to a temporary situation—the student sitting next to you was distracting, or Seville asked the wrong questions— you may study in much the same way you did before, hoping you'll do better the second time

**attribution** Self-constructed causal explanation for a personally experienced or observed event, such as one's own or another person's success or failure.

around. If you believe your failure was due to your low aptitude for sociocosmetology or to the fact that Seville writes lousy tests, you may study even less than you did the first time. What good will it do to study when your poor test performance is beyond your control?

Learners form attributions for many events in their daily lives—not only about why they do well or poorly on tests and assignments but also about why they're popular or unpopular with peers, why they're skilled athletes or total klutzes, and so on. Their attributions vary in three primary ways (Weiner, 1986, 2000, 2004, 2005):

- *Locus: Internal versus external.*[2] Learners sometimes attribute the causes of events to *internal* things—to factors within themselves. Thinking that a good grade is due to your hard work and believing that a poor grade is due to your lack of ability are examples of internal attributions. At other times learners attribute events to *external* things—to factors outside themselves. Concluding that you received a scholarship because you were lucky and interpreting a classmate's scowl as a sign of her bad mood (rather than a response to something you might have done to deserve it) are examples of external attributions.

- *Stability: Stable versus unstable.* Sometimes learners believe that events are due to *stable* factors—to things that probably won't change much in the near future. For example, if you believe that you do well in science because of your innate intelligence or that you have trouble making friends because you're overweight, you're attributing events to stable, relatively long-term causes. But sometimes learners believe that events result from *unstable* factors—things that can change from one time to the next. Thinking that winning a tennis game was a lucky break and believing you got a bad test grade because you were exhausted when you took the test are examples of attributions involving unstable factors.

- *Controllability: Controllable versus uncontrollable.* On some occasions learners attribute events to *controllable* factors—things they can influence and change. For example, if you think a classmate invited you to a party because you often smile at him and if you think you failed a test simply because you didn't study the right things, you're attributing these events to controllable factors. On other occasions learners attribute events to *uncontrollable* factors—to things over which they have no influence. If you think that you were chosen for the lead in the school play only because you look "right" for the part or that you played a lousy game of basketball because you were sick, you're attributing these events to uncontrollable factors.

Attributions are an excellent example of knowledge construction in action: Learners interpret new events in light of existing knowledge and beliefs about themselves and the world and then develop what seems to be a reasonable explanation of what has happened. Because attributions are self-constructed, they may or may not reflect the true state of affairs. For instance, a student may blame a low test grade on a tricky test or unfair teacher when the cause was really the student's own lack of effort or ineffective learning strategies.

In general, learners tend to attribute their successes to internal causes (e.g., high ability, hard work) and their failures to external causes (e.g., luck, other people's actions) (Mezulis, Abramson, Hyde, & Hankin, 2004; Rhodewalt & Vohs, 2005). By patting themselves on the back for things they do well and putting the blame elsewhere for poor performance, they can maintain their sense of self-worth. But when learners *consistently* fail at tasks—especially when they see their peers succeeding at the same tasks—they're apt to put the blame on a stable and uncontrollable internal factor: their own low ability (Covington, 1987; Y. Hong, Chiu, & Dweck, 1995; Schunk, 1990; Weiner, 1984).

## HOW ATTRIBUTIONS INFLUENCE EMOTION, COGNITION, AND BEHAVIOR

Attributions influence a number of factors that either directly or indirectly affect learners' future performance. First, attributions influence learners' *emotional reactions to success and failure.* Learners are apt to feel proud about their successes and guilty and ashamed about their failures only if they attribute these outcomes to internal causes—for instance, to things they themselves have done. Unpleasant as guilt and shame might feel, such emotions often spur learners to address their shortcomings. If, instead, learners think someone else was to blame for an undesirable outcome, they're

---

[2]This dimension is sometimes referred to as *locus of control*; however, as you can see in the discussion here, *locus* and *control* are two distinct dimensions (Weiner, 1986, 2000)

apt to be angry—an emotion that's unlikely to lead to productive follow-up behaviors (Hareli & Weiner, 2002; Pekrun, 2006).

Second, attributions have an impact on *expectations for future success and failure.* When learners attribute their successes and failures to stable factors—perhaps to innate ability levels—they expect their future performance to be similar to their current performance. In contrast, when they attribute successes and failures to *un*stable factors—for instance, to effort or luck—their current success rate has little influence on future expectations. The most optimistic learners—those with the highest expectations for future success—are the ones who attribute their successes to stable, dependable (and usually internal) factors, such as innate ability and an enduring work ethic, and attribute their failures to unstable factors, such as lack of effort or inappropriate strategies (Dweck, 2000; S. J. Lopez, Rose, Robinson, Marques, & Pais-Ribeiro, 2009; McClure et al., 2011; Pomerantz & Saxon, 2001).

Third, attributions affect *effort and persistence.* Learners who believe their failures result from their own lack of effort (a controllable cause) are apt to try harder and persist in the face of difficulty. Learners who, instead, attribute failure to a lack of innate ability (an uncontrollable cause) give up easily and sometimes can't even perform tasks they've previously done successfully (Dweck, 2000; Feather, 1982; McClure et al., 2011; Weiner, 1984).

Finally, attributions influence *learning strategies and classroom performance.* Learners who expect to succeed in the classroom and believe that academic success is a result of their own actions are more likely to apply effective learning and self-regulation strategies, especially when they're *taught* these strategies. In contrast, learners who expect failure and believe that their academic performance is largely out of their hands often reject effective learning strategies in favor of rote-learning approaches (Mangels, 2004; D. J. Palmer & Goetz, 1988; Zimmerman, 1998). Given all of these effects, it shouldn't surprise you to learn that students with internal, controllable attributions for classroom success are more likely to achieve at high levels and graduate from high school (L. E. Davis, Ajzen, Saunders, & Williams, 2002; Dweck, Mangels, & Good, 2004; McClure et al., 2011; Pintrich, 2003).

Let's consider how some of the factors just discussed play out in the opening case study. Michael initially attributes his failure in algebra to both his own low ability and his teacher's poor instruction—attributions that probably evoke both shame and anger. Furthermore, because the perceived causes of his failure are both stable and out of his control, he expects future failure no matter what he does and therefore has little reason to exert much effort. As Michael acquires new study skills and gains a better understanding of algebra concepts and procedures, he achieves greater success and realizes that his success is the direct result of his own hard work. His new internal and controllable attributions lead him to use effective strategies and be a more self-regulating learner:

> Now I do things in math step by step and listen to each step. . . . I used to just listen and not even take notes. I always told myself I would remember but I always seemed to forget. Now I take notes and I study at home every day except Friday, even if I don't have homework. Now I study so that I know that I have it. I don't just hope I'll remember.[3]

Students are usually happy when they succeed at classroom tasks, but they also feel proud and satisfied if they attribute their successes to internal causes.

## DEVELOPMENTAL TRENDS IN ATTRIBUTIONS

Young children become increasingly able to distinguish among the various possible causes of their successes and failures: effort, ability, luck, task difficulty, and so on (Dweck & Elliott, 1983; Eccles et al., 1998; Nicholls, 1990). One distinction they increasingly get a handle on is that between effort and ability. In the early elementary school grades, children think of effort and ability as

---

[3]Extract from "Cycles of Learning: Demonstrating the Interplay between Motivation, Self-Regulation, and Cognition" by Valerie G. Tucker and Lynley H. Anderman, paper presented at the annual meeting of the American Educational Research Association, April 1999, pp. 5–6. Copyright © 1999 by Valerie G. Tucker and Lynley H. Anderman. Reprinted with permission of the authors.

positively correlated: People who try harder are more competent. Thus they tend to attribute their successes to hard work and are usually optimistic about their chances for future success so long as they try hard. Sometime around age 9, they begin to understand that effort and ability often compensate for each other and that people with less ability may need to exert greater effort. Many begin to attribute their successes and failures to an inherited ability—for instance, intelligence—which they perceive to be fairly stable and beyond their control. If they're usually successful at school tasks, they have high self-efficacy for the tasks, but if they often fail, their self-efficacy is likely to plummet (Dweck, 1986; Eccles [Parsons] et al., 1983; Schunk, 1990). Table 11.3 summarizes developmental trends in attributions and other aspects of motivation.

The degree to which intelligence is the result of environment (and thus able to improve with instruction and practice) or heredity (and thus stable and uncontrollable) is a matter of some controversy among psychologists. Even children and adolescents have differing opinions on the matter (Dweck, 2000; Dweck & Molden, 2005). Those with an incremental view believe that intelligence can improve with effort and practice. In contrast, those with an entity view believe that intelligence is a distinct ability that is built-in and relatively permanent, as Sarah reveals in her explanation of her difficulties in mathematics:

> My dad is very good at math, and my brother, I, and my mom aren't good at math at all, we inherited the "not good at math gene" from my mom and I am good in English but I am not good in math. (K. E. Ryan, Ryan, Arbuthnot, & Samuels, 2007, p. 5)

Students with an incremental view of intelligence and specific academic abilities are likely to adopt mastery goals in the classroom, to work hard at their studies, and to earn increasingly high grades. In contrast, students with an entity view adopt performance goals, quickly lose interest in a topic that doesn't come easily to them, self-handicap in the face of failure, and earn lower grades over time (Blackwell, Trzesniewski, & Dweck, 2007; J. A. Chen & Pajares, 2010; Dweck & Leggett, 1988; Dweck & Molden, 2005).

Learners who have frequently succeeded when they've tried hard are likely to credit success to internal factors such as effort or high ability. Those who have usually failed despite their best efforts are apt to attribute success to something beyond their control—perhaps to an ability they don't possess or to such external factors as luck or a teacher's arbitrary judgment. Yet factors in learners' current environment also influence their attributions. When a classroom task appears to be complex and exceptionally challenging—and especially if classmates are struggling with it as well—failure can easily be attributed to task difficulty rather than to internal causes. But if peers are performing a task with ease, learners are likely to attribute their own failures to low ability (Schunk, 1990; Weiner, 1984). Another important factor is the attributions that adults communicate, as we'll discover shortly.

## MASTERY ORIENTATION VERSUS LEARNED HELPLESSNESS

As children grow older, they gradually develop predictable patterns of attributions and expectations for their future performance. Consider these two students, keeping in mind that *their actual ability level is the same:*

- Jared is an enthusiastic, energetic learner. He works hard at school activities and takes obvious pleasure in doing well. He likes challenge, especially the brainteaser problems his teacher assigns as extra-credit work each day. He can't always solve the problems, but he takes failure in stride and is eager for more problems the following day.

- Jerry is an anxious, fidgety student who doesn't have much confidence in his ability to accomplish school tasks successfully. In fact, he often underestimates what he can do: Even when he has succeeded, he doubts that he can do it again. He prefers filling out drill-and-practice worksheets that help him practice skills he's already mastered, rather than attempting new tasks and problems. As for those daily brainteasers Jared likes so much, Jerry sometimes takes a stab at them but gives up quickly if the answer isn't obvious.

Over time, some learners, like Jared, develop an "I can do it" attitude known as a mastery orientation—a general sense of optimism that they can master new tasks and succeed in a variety of endeavors. Other learners, like Jerry, develop an "I can't do it" attitude known as learned helplessness—a general sense of futility about their chances for future success. You might think

---

*Chapter 5 presents psychologists' varying perspectives on the origins of intelligence.*

*Portray intelligence and domain-specific abilities as characteristics that can change with effort and persistence.*

**incremental view of intelligence** Belief that intelligence can improve with effort and practice.

**entity view of intelligence** Belief that intelligence is a distinct ability that is relatively permanent and unchangeable.

**mastery orientation** General, fairly pervasive belief that one is capable of accomplishing challenging tasks.

**learned helplessness** General, fairly pervasive belief that one is incapable of accomplishing tasks and has little or no control of the environment.

# DEVELOPMENTAL TRENDS

## TABLE 11.3 • Motivation at Different Grade Levels

| GRADE LEVEL | AGE-TYPICAL CHARACTERISTICS | EXAMPLE | SUGGESTED STRATEGIES |
|---|---|---|---|
|   K–2 | • Focus more on acquiring competence than on self-evaluating it<br>• Rapidly changing interests for many students; more stable interests for others<br>• Pursuit of interesting and enjoyable activities regardless of expectancy for success<br>• Tendency to attribute success to hard work and practice, leading to optimism about what can be accomplished | Six-year-old Alex loves learning about lizards. He often draws lizards during his free time, and when he goes to the school library, he invariably looks for books about lizards and other reptiles. One day, with his teacher's permission, he brings his pet iguana to class and explains the things he must do to keep it healthy. | • Engage students' interest in classroom topics through hands-on, playlike activities.<br>• Entice students into reading, writing, and other basic skills through high-interest books and subject matter (e.g., animals, superheroes, princes and princesses).<br>• Show students how they're improving over time; point out how their effort and practice are contributing to their improvement. |
|  3–5 | • Increasing tendency to self-evaluate competence, in part by observing how one's own performance compares to that of peers<br>• Emergence of fairly stable personal interests<br>• Increasing focus on performance goals<br>• Increasing belief in innate ability as a significant and uncontrollable factor affecting learning and achievement<br>• Increasing awareness of the kinds of attributions that will elicit positive reactions from others (e.g., "I didn't feel well during the test"); decrease in verbalized attributions that peers might interpret as boastful and arrogant | During a gymnastics unit in physical education, 9-year-old Marta watches her classmates as they perform forward and backward rolls, handstands, and cartwheels. She willingly executes the rolls, but when she has trouble getting her legs up for a handstand, she quickly gives up, saying, "I can't do handstands and cartwheels—not like Jessie and Sharonda can." | • Allow students to pursue personal interests in independent reading and writing tasks.<br>• Encourage students to judge their performance based on their own improvement, rather than on how it compares with that of peers.<br>• Demonstrate your own fascination and enthusiasm about classroom topics; communicate reasons why many topics are worth learning about for their own sake.<br>• Identify strengths in every student; provide sufficient support to enable students to gain proficiency in areas of weakness. |
|  6–8 | • Decline in general sense of competence (relative to peers) in many academic domains<br>• Increasing tendency to self-handicap as a way of maintaining self-worth during difficult tasks<br>• Increasing interest in activities that are stereotypically "gender-appropriate"<br>• Increasing tendency to value activities associated with long-term goals and high expectancies for success<br>• For many students, decline in perceived value of many content domains (e.g., English, math, music, sports)<br>• Increasing focus on social goals (e.g., interacting with peers, making a good impression) | Thirteen-year-old Regina has always liked math. But now that she's in an advanced eighth-grade math class, she's starting to worry that her peers might think she's a "math geek." She diligently does her math homework each night and earns high grades on assignments and quizzes, but she rarely raises her hand in class to ask or answer questions. And when her friends ask her about the class, she rolls her eyes and says that she's in the class only because "Dad made me take it." | • Promote interest in classroom topics by presenting puzzling phenomena and building on students' personal interests.<br>• Focus students' attention on their improvement; minimize opportunities for them to compare their performance to that of classmates.<br>• Relate classroom subject matter to students' long-term goals (e.g., through authentic activities).<br>• Provide opportunities for social interaction as students study and learn (e.g., through role-playing activities, class debates, cooperative learning projects). |
|   9–12 | • Increasing integration of certain interests and values into one's overall sense of self<br>• For most students, prevalence of performance goals (e.g., getting good grades) rather than mastery goals<br>• Increase in cheating as a means of accomplishing performance goals<br>• Increasing focus on postgraduation goals (e.g., college, careers); for some students, insufficient self-regulation strategies to achieve these goals | Sixteen-year-old Randall wants to become a pediatric oncologist—as he puts it, "a cancer doctor who can help kids with leukemia, like my sister had." He knows he needs good grades in order to get into a prestigious college and then medical school, yet he has trouble saying no when his friends ask him to go to a basketball game the night before an important biology test. And when he gets home after the game, he spends an hour on Facebook instead of studying. | • Provide opportunities to address interests and values through out-of-class projects and extracurricular activities (e.g., community service work).<br>• Make it possible for students to attain good grades through reasonable effort and effective strategies; minimize competitive grading practices, such as grading on a curve.<br>• Discourage cheating (e.g., by giving individualized assignments and monitoring behavior during in-class assessments), and impose appropriate consequences when cheating occurs.<br>• Teach self-regulation strategies that can help students reach their long-term goals. |

*Sources:* J. M. Alexander et al., 2008; Archambault et al., 2010; Blumenfeld et al., 2006; Bong, 2009; Brophy, 2008; Cizek, 2003; Corpus et al., 2009; Dijkstra, Kuyper, van der Werf, Buunk, & van der Zee, 2008; Dotterer, McHale, & Crouter, 2009; Eccles et al., 1998; Hidi, Renninger, & Krapp, 2004; Jacobs, Davis-Kean, Bleeker, Eccles, & Malanchuk, 2005; Jacobs et al., 2002; Juvonen, 2000; LaFontana & Cillessen, 2010; Lepper et al., 2005; Nolen, 2007; Patrick et al., 2002; Shute, 2008; Urdan, 2004; Wigfield, 1994; Wigfield, Byrnes, & Eccles, 2006; Wigfield et al., 1991; B. L. Wilson & Corbett, 2001; Wolters, 2003; Youniss & Yates, 1999.

of this distinction, which really reflects a continuum rather than an either–or dichotomy, as a difference between *optimists* and *pessimists* (Boman, Furlong, Shochet, Lilles, & Jones, 2009; C. Peterson, 1990, 2006; Seligman, 1991).

Even when learners initially have equal ability levels, those with a mastery orientation behave in ways that lead to higher achievement over the long run. In particular, they set ambitious goals, seek challenging situations, and persist in the face of failure. Learners with learned helplessness behave very differently. Because they underestimate their ability, they set goals they can easily accomplish, avoid the challenges likely to maximize their learning and cognitive growth, and respond to failure in counterproductive ways (e.g., giving up quickly) that almost guarantee future failure (Dweck, 2000; Graham, 1989; S. J. Lopez et al., 2009; C. Peterson, 2006; Seligman, 1991).

By age 5 or 6, some children begin to show a consistent tendency either to persist at a task and express confidence that they can master it, on the one hand, or to abandon a task quickly and say they don't have the ability to do it, on the other (Burhans & Dweck, 1995; Ziegert, Kistner, Castro, & Robertson, 2001). However, children younger than 8 rarely exhibit extreme forms of learned helplessness, perhaps because they still believe that success is due largely to their own efforts (Eccles et al., 1998; Lockhart, Chang, & Story, 2002; S. G. Paris & Cunningham, 1996). By early adolescence a general sense of helplessness becomes more common. Some middle schoolers believe they can't control the things that happen to them—for instance, they're apt to have an entity view of intelligence—and are at a loss for strategies about how to avert future failures (Dweck, 2000; S. G. Paris & Cunningham, 1996; C. Peterson, Maier, & Seligman, 1993). In the opening case study, Michael's initial pessimism about his chances of future success in his algebra class suggests some degree of learned helplessness, at least about mathematics.

Strategies we've previously identified for enhancing self-efficacy and a sense of competence (e.g., promoting mastery on challenging tasks) should promote a mastery orientation as well. In addition, students should know that they have a variety of resources—their teacher, their peers, instructional software, volunteer tutors, and so on—to which they can turn in times of difficulty. In general, students must have sufficient academic support to believe "I can do this if I really want to."

When working with students who have learned helplessness, be consistent and persistent in your efforts to help them succeed.

## TEACHER ATTRIBUTIONS AND EXPECTATIONS

Many of students' day-to-day classroom behaviors lend themselves to a variety of interpretations. What teachers conclude from these behaviors—including the attributions they make about students' successes and failures—depends on how they've previously sized up different students' motivation levels, abilities, and so on (M.-L. Chang & Davis, 2009; Turner, Warzon, & Christensen, 2011). For example, imagine that a student, Linda, fails to finish an assignment on time. Her teacher, Mr. Smith, might conclude that Linda (1) didn't try very hard, (2) used her time poorly, or (3) wasn't capable of doing the task. The conclusion he draws will depend on his prior beliefs about Linda—for instance, whether he thinks she (1) is lazy and unmotivated, (2) is both motivated and capable of doing the work but hasn't yet acquired effective self-regulation skills, or (3) has little innate capacity for learning (reflecting an entity view of intelligence).

Teachers' attributions for students' current behaviors affect their expectations for students' future performance. Their expectations, in turn, affect future attributions (Weiner, 2000). And their attributions and expectations both affect the teaching strategies they use with particular students. For example, if Mr. Smith thinks Linda is "unmotivated," he might use some sort of incentive—perhaps offering free time later in the day—to entice her into completing assignments on time. If, instead, he thinks Linda lacks self-regulation skills, he might strive to teach her such skills. But if he thinks Linda has insufficient intelligence to master classroom topics, he may do very little to support her learning.

Teachers typically draw conclusions about their students early in the school year, forming opinions about each one's strengths, weaknesses, and potential for academic success. In many cases teachers size up their students fairly accurately: They know which ones need help with reading skills, which ones have short attention spans, and so on, and then adapt instruction and assistance accordingly (Goldenberg, 1992; T. L. Good & Brophy, 1994; T. L. Good & Nichols, 2001). Yet even the best teachers can make errors in their judgments. For example, teachers often underestimate the abilities of students who come from certain minority groups or from low-income families (Ready & Wright, 2011; Rubie-Davies, Hattie, & Hamilton, 2006; Sirin & Ryce, 2010; van den Bergh, Denessen, Hornstra, Voeten, & Holland, 2010).

Furthermore, many teachers have an entity view of intelligence: They believe that students' achievement typically depends on relatively enduring, uncontrollable ability levels (Dweck & Molden, 2005; Oakes & Guiton, 1995; C. Reyna, 2000). Thus they form fairly stable expectations for students' performance, which in turn lead them to treat different students differently. When teachers have high expectations for students, they present more challenging tasks and topics, interact with students more frequently, and give more positive and specific feedback. In contrast, when teachers have low expectations for certain students, they present easy tasks, offer few opportunities for speaking in class, and provide only limited feedback (Babad, 1993; T. L. Good & Brophy, 1994; Graham, 1990; R. Rosenthal, 1994, 2002).

Teachers' attributions for students' performance often reveal themselves in the things they say to students (Dweck & Molden, 2005; Weiner, 2000). Consider the following interpretations of a student's success:

- "You did it! You're so smart!"
- "Your hard work has really paid off, hasn't it?"
- "It's clear that you really know how to study."
- "Terrific! This is certainly your lucky day!"

And now consider these interpretations of a student's failure:

- "Maybe this just isn't something you're good at. Perhaps we should try a different activity."
- "Why don't you practice a little more and then try again?"
- "Let's come up with some strategies that might work better for you."
- "Maybe you're just having a bad day."

All of these comments are presumably intended to make a student feel good. But notice the different attributions they imply—in some cases, stable and uncontrollable abilities (being naturally smart or incapable); in other cases, controllable and therefore changeable behaviors (hard work, lack of practice, effective or ineffective study strategies); and in still other cases, external, uncontrollable causes (a lucky break, a bad day).

Teachers communicate their attributions for students' successes and failures in more subtle ways as well—for example, through the emotions they convey (M.-L. Chang & Davis, 2009; C. Reyna & Weiner, 2001; Weiner, 2005). They're often sympathetic and forgiving when children fail for uncontrollable reasons (illness, lack of ability, etc.) but frequently get angry when children fail simply because they didn't try very hard. As an example, let's return once more to the opening case study, in which Michael is initially doing poorly in his eighth-grade algebra class. Imagine that you are Michael's teacher. Imagine, too, that you believe Michael has low ability: He just doesn't have a "gift" for math. When you see him consistently getting Ds and Fs on assignments and quizzes, you might reasonably conclude that his poor performance is beyond his control, leading you to communicate pity and sympathy in your interactions with him. But now imagine, instead, that you believe Michael has *high* math ability: He definitely has what it takes to do well in your class. When you see his poor marks on assignments and quizzes, you naturally assume he isn't trying very hard. In your eyes Michael has complete control over the amount of effort he exerts; thus, you might express anger or annoyance when he doesn't do well. With such an attribution, some teachers might even punish him for his poor performance (C. Reyna & Weiner, 2001).

## HOW TEACHER ATTRIBUTIONS AND EXPECTATIONS AFFECT STUDENTS' ACHIEVEMENT

Most students readily pick up on their teachers' subtle messages about their own and others' abilities (R. Butler, 1994; T. L. Good & Nichols, 2001; R. S. Weinstein, 2002). When teachers repeatedly give them low-ability messages, they may begin to see themselves as their teachers do and to behave accordingly (Marachi, Friedel, & Midgley, 2001; Murdock, 1999; van den Bergh et al., 2010). In such cases, teachers' attributions and expectations can lead to a self-fulfilling prophecy: What teachers expect students to achieve becomes what students actually *do* achieve.

A classic study by Rosenthal and Jacobson (1968) provides an example. Near the end of the school year, researchers administered something they called the "Harvard Test of Inflected Acquisition" to elementary school students in a low-income neighborhood. Just before school

Continually ask yourself whether you are giving inequitable treatment to students for whom you have low expectations. Also reflect on your beliefs about students' intelligence: Are you taking an incremental view that gives you optimism about future progress?

Students are more optimistic about their classroom success when they attribute their achievement to factors within their control. Observe a teacher communicate controllable attributions in "Author's Chair."

**self-fulfilling prophecy** Situation in which expectations for an outcome either directly or indirectly lead to the expected result.

resumed the following fall, the researchers gave teachers the names of students who, according to the test results, would probably show dramatic achievement gains during the school year. In fact, the researchers had chosen these academic "spurters" at random—essentially pulling their names out of a hat. Despite the researchers' bogus predictions, the chosen children made greater achievement gains during the school year than their nonchosen classmates, and teachers rated these children in more favorable terms (e.g., as being more intellectually curious). The results were especially dramatic for children in grades 1 and 2.

Certainly teacher expectations don't always lead to self-fulfilling prophecies. In some cases teachers follow up on their initially low assessments of students' abilities by offering the instruction and assistance that students need to improve, and students *do* improve. In other cases students may develop an "I'll show *you*" attitude that spurs them on to greater effort and achievement than a teacher anticipated. In still other cases assertive parents step in and offer evidence that their children are more capable than a teacher initially thought (Dweck & Molden, 2005; Goldenberg, 1992; T. L. Good & Nichols, 2001).

Yet many research studies have revealed that teachers' expectations—whether for individual students or for an entire class of students—*do* have an effect on students' achievement levels (Hattie, 2009; R. Rosenthal, 2002). On average, girls, students from low-income families, and students from ethnic minority groups are more susceptible to teacher expectations than are boys from European American backgrounds. Teacher expectations also appear to have a greater influence in the early elementary school years (grades 1 and 2), the first year of secondary school and, more generally, the first few weeks of school—in other words, at times when students are entering new and unfamiliar school environments (de Boer, Bosker, & van der Werf, 2010; Hinnant, O'Brien, & Ghazarian, 2009; Jussim, Eccles, & Madon, 1996; Kuklinski & Weinstein, 2001).

As teachers, we're most likely to motivate students to achieve at high levels when we attribute their successes and failures to things over which either they or we have control and when, as a result, we have realistically optimistic expectations for their performance. The Into the Classroom feature "Forming Productive Attributions and Expectations for Student Performance" presents several research-based strategies. However, we must be careful when we attribute either success or failure to students' *effort*. There are at least two occasions when effort attributions can backfire. To see what I mean, try the next exercise.

Be especially careful not to form unwarranted expectations for students at transition points in their academic careers.

### EXPERIENCING FIRSTHAND
### CARBERRY AND SEVILLE #2

1. Imagine that Professor Carberry wants you to learn to spell the word *psychoceramics* correctly. He gives you 10 minutes of intensive training in spelling the word and then praises you profusely for spelling it correctly. In which of the following ways would you be most likely to respond?
   a. You're delighted that he approves of your performance.
   b. You proudly show him that you've also learned how to spell *sociocosmetology*.
   c. You wonder, "Hey, is this all he thinks I can do?"

2. Now imagine that you drop by Professor Seville's office to find out why you did so poorly on her sociocosmetology exam. She smiles warmly and suggests that you simply try harder next time. But you tried as hard as you could the *first* time. Which one of the following conclusions would you be most likely to draw?
   a. You need to try even harder next time.
   b. You need to exert the same amount of effort the next time and keep your fingers crossed that you'll make some lucky guesses.
   c. Perhaps you just weren't meant to be a sociocosmetologist.

Chances are good that you answered *c* to both questions. Let's first consider the situation in which Carberry spent 10 minutes teaching you how to spell *psychoceramics*. When students succeed at a very easy task and are then praised for their effort, they may get the unintended message that their teacher doesn't have much confidence in their ability (Graham, 1991; Schunk & Pajares, 2004). Attributing students' successes to effort is apt to be beneficial only when students have, in fact, exerted a great deal of effort.

## Into the Classroom

### Forming Productive Attributions and Expectations for Student Performance

🍎 **Remember that teachers can definitely make a difference.**

The teachers at a historically low-achieving middle school in a poor, inner-city neighborhood meet once a month to learn about teaching strategies that are especially effective with children from low-income families. They experiment with various strategies in their own classrooms and share especially effective strategies at their group meetings.

🍎 **Look for strengths in every student.**

A 9-year-old girl who lives in a homeless shelter seems to have learned little about punctuation and capitalization, and her spelling is more typical of a first grader than a fourth grader. Nonetheless, the stories she writes often have unusual plot twists and creative endings. Her teacher suspects that her frequent moves from one school to another have left big gaps in her knowledge of written language and so finds a parent volunteer who can work with her on her writing several times a week.

🍎 **Consider multiple possible explanations for students' low achievement and classroom misbehavior.**

Several seventh-grade teachers are sharing their experiences with a student who, at age 8, suffered a traumatic brain injury when he fell off a kitchen counter and landed on his head. His art and music teachers describe him as very disruptive in class and believe that he intentionally misbehaves in order to draw attention to himself. In contrast, his math and science teachers have found that he can easily stay on task—and can often achieve at average to above-average levels—so long as they provide reasonable structure for assignments and classroom behavior. They also realize that some children with brain injuries have trouble inhibiting inappropriate behaviors through no fault of their own.

🍎 **Communicate optimism about what students can accomplish.**

In September a high school teacher tells his class, "Next spring I will ask you to write a 15-page research paper. Fifteen pages may seem like a lot now, but in the next few months we'll work on the various skills you'll need to research and write your paper. By April, 15 pages won't seem like a big deal at all!"

🍎 **Objectively assess students' progress, and be open to evidence that contradicts your initial assessments of students' abilities.**

A kindergarten teacher initially has low expectations for the daughter of migrant workers, a girl named Lupita who has previously had little access to books, toys, and other educational resources. When a video camera captures Lupita's strong leadership ability and skill in assembling puzzles, the teacher realizes that she has considerable potential and works hard to help her acquire the math and literacy skills she'll need to be successful in first grade.

🍎 **Attribute students' successes to a combination of high ability and controllable factors such as effort and learning strategies.**

In a unit on basketball, a middle school physical education teacher tells students, "From what I've seen so far, you all have the capability to play a good game of basketball. And it appears that many of you have been regularly practicing after school."

🍎 **Attribute students' successes to effort only when they have actually exerted considerable effort.**

A teacher observes that his students have completed a particular assignment more quickly and easily than he expected. He briefly acknowledges their success and then moves on to a more challenging task.

🍎 **Attribute students' failures to factors that are controllable and easily remedied.**

A high school student seeks his teacher's advice about how he might improve his performance in her class. "I know you can do better than you have been, Frank," she replies. "I wonder if part of the problem might be that with your part-time job and all of your extracurricular activities, you just don't have enough time to study. Let's sit down before school tomorrow and look at what and how much you're doing to prepare for class."

🍎 **When students fail despite obvious effort, attribute their failures to a lack of effective strategies and help them acquire such strategies.**

A student in an advanced science class is having difficulty with the teacher's challenging weekly quizzes. The student works diligently on her science every night and attends the after-school help sessions her teacher offers, but to no avail. The teacher observes that the student is trying to learn the material by rote—an ineffective strategy for answering the higher-level questions typically presented on the quizzes—and teaches her strategies that promote more meaningful learning.

🍎 **Explicitly teach students to form productive attributions for their successes and failures.**

A boy with a learning disability has particular trouble with mathematics. As his special education teacher works with him on developing his math problem-solving skills, she urges him to make self-talk statements that attribute failures to temporary setbacks he can overcome with more effort and different strategies—for example, "I mustn't give up. I need to use a different approach and see if that one might work better."

*Sources:* Brophy, 2006; Carrasco, 1981 (Lupita example); Curtis, 1992; Dweck, 2000, 2009; J. W. Fowler & Peterson, 1981; Hattie, 2009; Hawley, 2005 (brain injury example); J. A. Langer, 2000; Pressley, Borkowski, & Schneider, 1987; Robertson, 2000; Roeser, Marachi, & Gehlbach, 2002; Skaalvik & Skaalvik, 2008; R. S. Weinstein, Madison, & Kuklinski, 1995.

Now consider the second scenario, in which Seville encouraged you to try harder even though you'd previously studied very hard indeed. When students fail at a task on which they've expended a great deal of effort and are then told that they didn't try hard enough, they're likely to conclude that they simply don't have the ability to perform the task successfully (Curtis & Graham, 1991; Robertson, 2000; Stipek, 1996). In such circumstances it's usually better to attribute their failure to ineffective strategies. Students can and do acquire more effective learning and study strategies over time, especially when they're specifically trained to use these strategies. By teaching effective strategies, we not only promote students' academic success but we also foster

Chapter 7 offers suggestions for teaching learning and study strategies.

the belief that they can *control* their success (Miranda, Villaescusa, & Vidal-Abarca, 1997; C. E. Weinstein, Hagen, & Meyer, 1991).

# DIVERSITY IN COGNITIVE AND SOCIOCULTURAL FACTORS AFFECTING MOTIVATION

In the preceding sections we've already seen individual differences in personal interests, values, achievement goals, and general attributional style. Here our focus will be on diversity in students of various cultural and ethnic backgrounds, genders, and income levels, as well as in students with special educational needs.

## CULTURAL AND ETHNIC DIFFERENCES

Most cultural and ethnic groups place high value on getting a good education (P. J. Cook & Ludwig, 2008; Fuligni & Hardway, 2004; Phalet, Andriessen, & Lens, 2004; Spera, 2005). But researchers have observed differences in more specific values related to school learning. For example, many Asian cultures (e.g., in China, Japan, and Russia) emphasize learning for learning's sake: With knowledge come personal growth, better understanding of the world, and greater potential to contribute to society. Important for these cultures, too, are hard work and persistence in academic studies, even when the content isn't intrinsically enjoyable (Hufton et al., 2002; J. Li, 2006; Morelli & Rothbaum, 2007). Students from European American backgrounds are less likely to be diligent when classroom topics have little intrinsic appeal, but they often find value in academic subject matter that piques their curiosity and in assignments that require creativity, independent thinking, or critical analysis (Hess & Azuma, 1991; Kuhn & Park, 2005; Nisbett, 2009).

Learners from diverse cultural backgrounds may also define academic success differently and, as a result, may set different achievement goals. For example, on average, Asian American students aim for higher grades than do students from other ethnic groups, in part to win their parents' approval and in part to bring honor to their families (Nisbett, 2009; Steinberg, 1996). Even so, Asian American students—and African American students as well—tend to focus more on mastery goals (i.e., truly understanding what they're studying) than European American students do (Freeman, Gutman, & Midgley, 2002; Qian & Pan, 2002; Shim & Ryan, 2006). And students brought up in cultures that value group achievement over individual achievement (e.g., many Asian, Native American, Mexican American, and Pacific Islander cultures) tend to focus their mastery goals not on how much they alone can improve but instead on how much they *and their peers* can improve—or in some instances on how much their individual actions can contribute to the betterment of the larger social group or society (C.-Y. Chiu & Hong, 2005; Kağitçibaşi, 2007; J. Li, 2005, 2006).

Learners' cultural and ethnic backgrounds influence their attributions as well. For instance, students from families with traditional Asian cultural beliefs are more likely than students from mainstream Western culture to attribute classroom success and failure to unstable factors—effort in the case of academic achievement, and temporary situational factors in the case of appropriate or inappropriate behaviors (J. Li & Fischer, 2004; Lillard, 1997; Weiner, 2004). Also, some studies have found a greater tendency for African American students to develop a sense of learned helplessness about their ability to achieve academic success. To some extent, racial prejudice may contribute to their learned helplessness: Students may begin to believe that because of the color of their skin, they have little chance of success no matter what they do (G. H. Brody et al., 2006; Graham, 1989; van Laar, 2000).

## GENDER DIFFERENCES

In general, girls are more concerned than boys are about doing well in school: They work harder on assignments, earn higher grades, and more often graduate from high school (H. M. Marks, 2000; Marsh, Martin, & Cheng, 2008; McCall, 1994; J. P. Robinson & Lubienski, 2011). But some students perceive certain domains (e.g., writing, music) to be "for girls" and other domains (e.g., math, science) to be "for boys," dampening their interest and self-efficacy in seemingly opposite-gender content areas and thereby limiting their career options (Eccles, 2005; Jacobs et al., 2002; Leaper & Friedman, 2007; Weisgram, Bigler, & Liben, 2010). Students' long-term life goals come into the picture as well: Girls are more likely than boys to consider how their career choices might mesh with their desires to work with people (rather than objects) and to raise a family (Diekman, Brown, Johnston, & Clark, 2010; Eccles, 2009).

Another commonly observed gender difference is the tendency for girls (especially high-achieving girls) to be more discouraged by failure experiences than boys are (Dweck, 1986, 2000). We can explain this difference, at least in part, by looking at gender differences in attributions. Some research results indicate that boys tend to attribute their successes to a fairly stable ability and their failures to a lack of effort, thus revealing an "I know I can do this" attitude. Girls show the reverse pattern: They attribute their successes to effort and their failures to lack of ability, believing "I don't know whether I can keep on doing it because I'm not very good at this type of thing." Such differences are most often observed in stereotypically male domains (e.g., math, sports) and can appear even when boys' and girls' previous levels of achievement in the domains have been equivalent (Leaper & Friedman, 2007; McClure et al., 2011; Stipek, 1984; Vermeer, Boekaerts, & Seegers, 2000).

As we work to encourage high levels of motivation in all our students, we may want to focus our efforts in somewhat different directions for males and females. For boys, who have less concern about doing well in school, we may need to stress the importance of academic achievement for their long-term life goals and make a particular effort to pique their interest in classroom activities. For girls, we may have to go the extra mile to convince them that their classroom successes are the result not only of their efforts but also of their natural abilities—a stable and dependable internal attribution—and that they have "what it takes" to be successful in traditionally male domains.

> Help boys discover the relevance of their classroom learning and performance to their long-term goals. Encourage girls to consider a wide range of career options and enhance their self-efficacy for success in traditionally male domains.

## SOCIOECONOMIC DIFFERENCES

Many students from low-income backgrounds want to do well in school (Payne, 2005; Shernoff, Schneider, & Csikszentmihalyi, 2001; B. L. Wilson & Corbett, 2001). However, teachers' attitudes, instructional practices, and relationships with students have a significant influence on whether these students choose to pursue academic success; this is especially true for students at high risk for academic failure (L. W. Anderson & Pellicer, 1998; Kumar et al., 2002; Maehr & Anderman, 1993; Murdock, 1999). Students from low-income families are apt to flourish in schools in which teachers have high expectations for achievement, engage students in high-interest activities and subject matter, emphasize mastery goals over performance goals, and make students feel that they're valued members of the classroom community (Hom & Battistich, 1995; Juvonen, 2006; Osterman, 2000; Patrick, Ryan, & Kaplan, 2007).

It's equally important that we increase the perceived value of school activities by making them relevant to students' personal lives and needs (P. A. Alexander et al., 1994; Knapp, Turnbull, & Shields, 1990; Wlodkowski & Ginsberg, 1995). All too often, students at schools in low-income neighborhoods encounter instruction that focuses on basic skills and rote learning and thus is unlikely to entice even the most motivated students (B. E. Becker & Luthar, 2002; Pianta & Hamre, 2009). The following interview with middle school students in an inner-city Philadelphia school illustrates the problem:

> Help students acquire the skills

> Remember that meaningful, personally relevant classroom tasks are especially important for motivating students from lower-income backgrounds.

*Adult:* How often do you write in English class?

*Student:* Every day.

*Adult:* What kinds of things are you writing?

*Student:* We copy notes from the board and we do dictionary work. We also answer questions from our workbook.

*Adult:* Do you ever write your own stories?

*Student:* No.[4]

Such instruction is not only unengaging but also unlikely to prepare students for the demands of a challenging high school or college curriculum (Ogbu, 2003; Suskind, 1998).

It's essential that we help students acquire the skills and strategies they'll need to achieve their long-term goals for higher education and rewarding careers: complex thinking skills, self-regulation strategies, and so on. In addition, if students have had little direct contact with college life or high-income professions, we must promote a realistic understanding of what college

[4]From *Listening to Urban Kids: School, Reform and the Teachers They Want* by Bruce L. Wilson and Dick Corbett, p. 52. Copyright © 2001 by the State University of New York Press, State University of New York. Reprinted with permission. All rights reserved.

achievement and professional success involve. When speaking with a group of middle school boys who hoped to go to college, one researcher encountered considerable naiveté about college life:

> I asked them what they thought college was like. The response was nearly unanimous—it was all about partying—drinking, smoking weed, and hanging out. Never did it come up that they would attend classes or do homework. College meant partying, and that was why they wanted to go. (K. M. Williams, 2001a, p. 106)

Such misconceptions are perhaps not surprising if we consider how college life is often portrayed in television and films. For adolescent viewers, college parties certainly yield more interesting plot lines than going to class and studying at the library.

### ACCOMMODATING STUDENTS WITH SPECIAL NEEDS

Students with special educational needs are typically among those who show the greatest diversity in motivation. For example, students with learning disabilities or general intellectual disabilities may be easily discouraged by challenging tasks; some may even show signs of learned helplessness if their efforts consistently meet with failure (Jacobsen, Lowery, & DuCette, 1986; Mercer & Pullen, 2005; Seligman, 1975). In contrast, students who are gifted may become easily bored or annoyed if classroom activities *don't* challenge their abilities (Bleske-Rechek, Lubinski, & Benbow, 2004; Winner, 2000b). Table 11.4 presents these and other motivational characteristics in students with special needs.

### A TARGETS MNEMONIC FOR REMEMBERING MOTIVATIONAL STRATEGIES

Many strategies for enhancing students' motivation in the classroom can be summed up in seven words or phrases: task, autonomy, recognition, grouping, evaluation, time, and social support (L. H. Anderman & Anderman, 2009; J. L. Epstein, 1989; Maehr & Anderman, 1993). This multifaceted TARGETS approach to motivation is presented in Table 11.5. If you look closely at the entries in the table, you'll find that they reflect many of the concepts we've addressed in the preceding sections. And especially if you look at Column 2, you'll be convinced, as I am, that teachers clearly *can* make a difference—in fact, a very sizable one—not only in promoting students' learning but in enhancing their motivation as well.

## Affect and Its Effects

A close partner of motivation is **affect**: the emotions and general moods that a learner brings to bear on a task. Virtually any form of affect has both psychological elements (subjective feelings) and physiological elements (changes in heart rate, perspiration, muscular tension, etc.). Some forms of affect—such as happiness, excitement, and pride—feel both psychologically and physiologically pleasant. Other forms—such as fear, anger, and shame—feel both psychologically and physiologically aversive.

Affect has its basis in the brain, of course; the Applying Brain Research feature "Understanding How and Why Emotions Influence Learning" provides more details. Furthermore, each form of affect probably has a specific function (Izard, 2007; Minsky, 2006; Tamir, 2009). For example, when we face a dangerous situation, our fearful reaction includes an increased heart rate and muscular tension that spur us to take action, typically a response involving either *fight* or *flight*. In contrast, when we find ourselves enjoying the company of others, we're apt to smile, laugh, and in other ways nurture interpersonal relationships.

### HOW AFFECT AND MOTIVATION ARE INTERRELATED

Without doubt, people's automatic emotional reactions to certain events—for instance, a quick, fearful retreat from someone who is wielding a gun or knife—are designed to keep them alive. But affect also plays a significant role in the more planful, goal-directed aspects of human motivation. As a general rule, people act in ways they think will help them feel happy and comfortable rather than sad, confused, or angry, although they may occasionally work themselves into an angry frenzy as a way of helping them achieve certain outcomes (Mellers & McGraw, 2001; Tamir, 2009; J. L. Tsai, 2007).

---

Communicate that academic success requires hard work not only in the secondary grades but in college as well.

Chapter 5 identifies specific categories of special needs that fall within the five general categories listed in Table 11.4.

Students who don't believe they can achieve academic success are more likely to misbehave in class. Explore some strategies you might use in the simulation "Helping All Students Believe They Can Achieve."

**affect** Feelings, emotions, and moods that a learner brings to bear on a task.

# STUDENTS IN INCLUSIVE SETTINGS

**TABLE 11.4 • Enhancing Motivation in Students with Special Educational Needs**

| CATEGORY | CHARACTERISTICS YOU MIGHT OBSERVE | SUGGESTED STRATEGIES |
|---|---|---|
| Students with specific cognitive or academic difficulties | • Less intrinsic motivation to succeed at academic tasks, due in part to a low sense of self-efficacy and competence<br>• Reluctance to ask questions or seek assistance, especially in the secondary grades<br>• Little or no persistence when confronting difficult tasks<br>• Tendency to attribute poor achievement to low ability rather than to more controllable factors; learned helplessness regarding some classroom tasks | • Use extrinsic reinforcers to encourage effort and achievement; gradually phase out reinforcers as students show signs of intrinsic motivation.<br>• Establish short-term goals for achievement that students perceive as being challenging yet accomplishable.<br>• Offer assistance when you think students may really need it, but refrain from offering help when you know students are capable of succeeding on their own.<br>• Teach effective learning strategies and encourage students to attribute their successes to such strategies. |
| Students with social or behavioral problems | • Desire to succeed in the classroom, despite behaviors that seemingly indicate a lack of motivation<br>• Tendency to interpret praise as an attempt at control (for students who exhibit defiance or oppositional behavior)<br>• Stronger desire for power over classmates than for establishing friendships (for some students with emotional and behavioral disorders)<br>• Little or no apparent interest in social interaction (for some students with autism spectrum disorders)<br>• Perception of classroom tasks as having little relevance to personal needs and goals<br>• Tendency to attribute negative consequences to uncontrollable factors (things "just happen") | • Provide the guidance and support students need to succeed at classroom tasks.<br>• When students are concerned about control issues, use subtle reinforcers (e.g., leave notes commending productive behaviors) rather than more obvious and seemingly controlling ones.<br>• Offer some choices about activities and reinforcers in order to increase a sense of self-determination.<br>• Help students discover the benefits of equitable and prosocial interactions with peers.<br>• Relate the curriculum to students' specific needs and interests.<br>• Teach behaviors that lead to desired consequences; stress cause-and-effect relationships between actions and outcomes. |
| Students with general delays in cognitive and social functioning | • On average, less intrinsic motivation than nondisabled age-mates; occasional curiosity about certain topics<br>• Responsiveness to extrinsic motivators<br>• Tendency to give up easily in the face of difficulty<br>• Limited or no ability to conceptualize long-term goals<br>• Tendency to attribute poor achievement to low ability or to external sources rather than to more controllable factors; in some situations, a sense of learned helplessness | • Use extrinsic reinforcers to encourage productive behaviors; gradually phase out reinforcers as students show signs of intrinsic motivation.<br>• Reinforce persistence as well as success.<br>• Set specific, short-term (proximal) goals for performance; ask students to set some of their own goals as well.<br>• Help students see the relationship between their own actions and resulting consequences. |
| Students with physical or sensory challenges | • Low sense of self-determination about the course of their lives<br>• Fewer opportunities to satisfy the need for relatedness, especially with peers | • Teach self-regulating behaviors and independence skills.<br>• Identify classmates who can serve as "study buddies" to help students with assigned tasks or provide companionship at lunch and recess.<br>• Collaborate with parents to promote interaction with classmates outside school. |
| Students with advanced cognitive development | • High self-efficacy and sense of competence<br>• Eagerness for challenges; boredom when classroom tasks don't challenge their abilities<br>• Persistence in the face of failure (although some may give up easily if they aren't accustomed to failure)<br>• Possible self-handicapping if there is a strong desire to affiliate with low-achieving peers<br>• Social isolation (for some students who are exceptionally gifted)<br>• Variety of interests, sometimes pursued with a passion<br>• Higher than average goal-directedness<br>• Internal, optimistic attributions for classroom achievement<br>• Tendency to adopt an entity view of intelligence; can lead to learned helplessness if failure is encountered after an early string of successes (especially for girls) | • Provide opportunities for students to pursue complex tasks and activities over an extended period.<br>• Give assignments that students find stimulating and challenging.<br>• Keep students' exceptional achievements confidential if their friends don't value high achievement.<br>• Provide opportunities to pursue individual interests, perhaps with other students who have similar interests or perhaps in an apprenticeship with an outside mentor.<br>• Encourage students to set high goals without expecting perfection. |

*Sources:* Beirne-Smith, Patton, & Kim, 2006; Brophy, 2004; B. Clark, 1997; Covington, 1992; Dai, 2010; G. Dawson & Bernier, 2007; Dunlap et al., 1994; Dweck, 2000; Foster-Johnson, Ferro, & Dunlap, 1994; S. Goldstein & Rider, 2006; T. L. Good & Brophy, 1994; D. A. Greenspan, Solomon, & Gardner, 2004; Heward, 2009; Jacobsen et al., 1986; Knowlton, 1995; Mendaglio, 2010; Mercer & Pullen, 2005; Patrick, 1997; Patton, Blackbourn, & Fad, 1996; Piirto, 1999; S. Powell & Nelson, 1997; Prout, 2009; Robertson, 2000; G. F. Schultz & Switzky, 1990; Shavinina & Ferrari, 2004; Turnbull, Turnbull, & Wehmeyer, 2010; Ulke-Kurcuoglu & Kircaali-Iftar, 2010; Wehmeyer et al., 2007; Winner, 1997, 2000a, 2000b; Wong, 1991.

## PRINCIPLES/ASSUMPTIONS

### TABLE 11.5 • Seven "TARGETS" Principles of Motivation

| PRINCIPLE | EDUCATIONAL IMPLICATIONS | EXAMPLE |
|---|---|---|
| Classroom **tasks** affect motivation. | • Present new topics through tasks that students find interesting and engaging.<br>• Encourage meaningful rather than rote learning.<br>• Relate activities to students' lives and goals.<br>• Provide sufficient support to enable students to be successful. | • Ask students to conduct a scientific investigation about an issue that concerns them. |
| The amount of **autonomy** students have affects motivation, especially intrinsic motivation. | • Give students some choice about what and how they learn.<br>• Teach self-regulation strategies.<br>• Solicit students' opinions about classroom practices and policies.<br>• Have students take leadership roles in some activities. | • Let students choose among several ways of accomplishing an instructional goal, being sure that each choice offers sufficient scaffolding to make success likely. |
| The amount and nature of the **recognition** students receive affect motivation. | • Acknowledge not only academic successes but also personal and social successes.<br>• Commend students for improvement as well as for mastery.<br>• Provide concrete reinforcers for achievement only when students are not intrinsically motivated to learn.<br>• Show students how their own efforts and strategies are directly responsible for their successes. | • Commend students for a successful community service project. |
| The **grouping** procedures in the classroom affect motivation. | • Provide frequent opportunities for students to interact (e.g., cooperative learning activities, peer tutoring).<br>• Plan small-group activities in which all students can make significant contributions.<br>• Teach the social skills that students need to interact effectively with peers. | • Have students work in small groups to tackle a challenging issue or problem for which there are two or more legitimate solutions. |
| The forms of **evaluation** in the classroom affect motivation. | • Make evaluation criteria clear; specify them in advance.<br>• Minimize or eliminate competition for grades (e.g., don't grade on a curve).<br>• Give specific feedback about what students are doing well.<br>• Give concrete suggestions about how students can improve.<br>• Teach students how to evaluate their own work. | • Give students concrete criteria with which they can evaluate the quality of their own writing. |
| How teachers schedule **time** affects motivation. | • Give students enough time to achieve mastery of important topics and skills.<br>• Let students' interests dictate some activities.<br>• Include variety in the school day (e.g., intersperse high-energy activities among more sedentary ones).<br>• Include opportunities for independent learning in the school day. | • After explaining a new concept, engage students in a hands-on activity that lets them see the concept in action. |
| The amount of **social support** students believe they have in the classroom affects motivation. | • Create an atmosphere of caring, respect, and support among all class members.<br>• Convey affection and respect for every student, along with a genuine eagerness to help every student succeed.<br>• Create situations in which all students feel comfortable participating actively in classroom activities (including students who are excessively shy, students who have limited academic skills, students who have physical disabilities, etc.). | When working with students who seem chronically disengaged from lessons, identify their specific areas of strength and provide opportunities for them to showcase their expertise in the classroom. |

*Sources:* L. H. Anderman & Anderman, 2009; L. H. Anderman, Andrzejewski, & Allen, 2011; L. H. Anderman, Patrick, Hruda, & Linnenbrink, 2002; J. L. Epstein, 1989; Maehr & Anderman, 1993; Patrick et al., 1997.

**self-conscious emotion** Affective state based on self-evaluations regarding the extent to which one's actions meet society's standards for appropriate and desirable behavior; examples are pride, guilt, and shame.

Some emotions, known as self-conscious emotions, are closely tied to people's self-evaluations and thus affect their sense of self-worth (M. Lewis & Sullivan, 2005; Pekrun, 2006). When people evaluate their own actions and accomplishments as being consistent with their culture's standards for appropriate and desirable behavior, they're apt to feel pride. When, in contrast, they see themselves as failing to live up to those standards—for instance, when they thoughtlessly cause harm to someone else—they're apt to feel guilt and shame.

Affect and motivation are interrelated in other ways as well. For instance, intrinsic motivation is closely connected with pleasure and enjoyment. Learners tackle challenging tasks more willingly and effectively when they enjoy what they're doing, and their successful efforts often bring on feelings of excitement and pride (Linnenbrink & Pintrich, 2004; Pekrun, Goetz, Titz, &

## Applying Brain Research

### Understanding Why and How Emotions Influence Learning

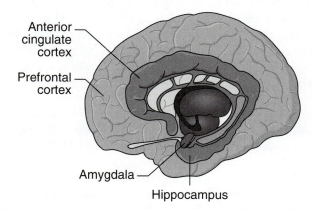

Anterior cingulate cortex

Prefrontal cortex

Amygdala

Hippocampus

A key brain structure in affect is the *amygdala,* an almond-shaped member of the limbic system, which lies in the middle of the brain. We humans have two amygdalae, one each in our left and right hemispheres. The amygdala is especially active in unpleasant feelings (e.g., fear, stress, anger, and depression) and in automatic emotional reactions (e.g., impulsive aggression).

The amygdala has many interconnections with brain structures that underlie and support learning and cognition, including the hippocampus, anterior cingulate cortex, and prefrontal cortex. For one thing, the amygdala alerts us to stimuli in our environment that might in some way threaten our survival. In addition, it enables us to associate particular emotions with particular stimuli or memories. As a result, affective reactions are often closely intertwined with human thinking and learning (Adolphs & Damasio, 2001; Kuhbandner, Spitzer, & Pekrun, 2011; Phelps & Sharot, 2008; M. I. Posner & Rothbart, 2007).

A good deal of emotion-based learning takes the form of *implicit knowledge*—knowledge over which we have little or no conscious awareness and control. For example, such out-of-awareness knowledge might lead us to feel anxious in certain situations without knowing *why* we feel anxious, and it can sometimes lead us to make decisions that are neither rational nor productive (Damasio, 1994; Marcus, 2008; Minsky, 2006; Sapolsky, 2005).

With the close interconnections between emotion and cognition in mind, I offer two general recommendations:

🍏 **Remember that, for better or for worse, learning often involves acquiring emotions as well as knowledge and skills.** Students' feelings are integral parts of what they "know" about various topics and events (Bower & Forgas, 2001; Clore, Gasper, & Garvin, 2001; Minsky, 2006). Sometimes this knowledge is beneficial, but at other times it can work against students' best interests. For example, we would certainly like students to know that reading a good book can be a source of pleasure, but it's not helpful for them to "know" that mathematics is apt to evoke only frustration and anxiety.

🍏 **Create conditions that foster arousal and attention without generating undue stress.** Early in the chapter I suggested that we human beings may have a basic need for arousal—a basic need for either physical or cognitive stimulation—but that we also like our arousal to be at a certain optimal level that feels good. Arousal has an emotional element as well, and at very high levels it can feel quite unpleasant. High, stressful arousal levels increase activity in the amygdala in ways that interfere with the functioning of more "rational" structures such as the hippocampus and prefrontal cortex. Furthermore, lengthy periods of high stress—as might be true for someone who lives in chronically dangerous conditions—can cause permanent damage to the prefrontal cortex (Nisbett, 2009; Sapolsky, 2005).

In the classroom, piquing students' interest and engagement in classroom topics and activities can effectively capitalize on the "good" side of arousal. In contrast, creating constant stress about doing well—and continually reminding students of the negative ramifications of *not* doing well—will adversely affect students' learning, development, and general well-being, quite possibly for the long term.

---

Perry, 2002; Shernoff & Csikszentmihalyi, 2009). Learners are especially likely to feel excited about their successes if they didn't expect to be successful, but they'll also experience more intense negative emotions about their failures—and often about the activity in question—if they didn't expect to fail (Bower & Forgas, 2001; Shepperd & McNulty, 2002). Their specific reactions will depend on how they *interpret* the outcomes of events—in particular, whether they hold themselves, other people, environmental circumstances, or something else responsible for what has happened (recall the earlier discussion of *attributions*).

Another emotion we mustn't overlook is boredom—a generally unpleasant feeling that results from a lack of stimulation and arousal (Pekrun et al., 2010). Recall the earlier discussion of *need for arousal*: Human beings feel more comfortable when they have some degree of either physical or cognitive stimulation. Boredom-inducing activities can take a variety of forms: They might be either too easy or too difficult for learners' current ability levels, or they might involve repetitive, monotonous tasks that seemingly have little relevance to learners' lives. Learners who are bored in their current environment will either seek to escape it or else create their own stimulation—perhaps in the form of passing notes across the aisle or checking their cell phones for recent text messages. In classroom settings, then, students who are bored with the topic at hand are unlikely to pay much attention to or benefit from instructional activities (Daschmann, Nett, Wimmer, Goetz, & Stupnisky, 2010; Nett, Goetz, & Hall, 2011; Pekrun et al., 2010).

In general, how learners feel depends on whether their needs are being met and their goals are being accomplished. Listen to 10-year-old Daniel, 13-year-old Crystal, and 15-year-old Greg in "Emotions."

**boredom** Unpleasant affective state that results from lack of stimulation and arousal.

## HOW AFFECT IS RELATED TO LEARNING AND COGNITION

As the Applying Brain Research feature reveals, brain structures that underlie affect and those that support cognition are closely interconnected. It's not surprising, then, that learners' affective reactions are often inextricably intertwined with their thinking and learning (Damasio, 1994; D. K. Meyer & Turner, 2002). For example, while learning how to perform a task, students simultaneously learn whether or not they like doing it (Zajonc, 1980). And students who feel frustrated and anxious when they struggle to master new material (as Michael initially does in the opening case study) are apt to acquire a dislike for the topic (Carver & Scheier, 1990; Goetz, Frenzel, Hall, & Pekrun, 2008; Stodolsky, Salk, & Glaessner, 1991). Sixteen-year-old Megan expressed her feelings about mastery and nonmastery this way:

> When I haven't learned something I tend to say that I hate it, because I don't understand it. When I am excited and can have a discussion about something is when I know that I fully understand and have studied enough on that topic. (Student quote courtesy of Brian Zottoli)

Get students emotionally involved with classroom subject matter.

Creating cognitive dissonance is often an effective strategy for promoting conceptual change. Watch "Properties of Air."

Learners can also associate specific topics and pieces of information with certain emotions—a phenomenon known as **hot cognition**. On average, learners are more likely to pay attention to, think actively about, and remember emotionally charged information (Bower, 1994; Heuer & Reisberg, 1992; Zeelenberg, Wagenmakers, & Rotteveel, 2006). Sometimes the nature of a topic itself evokes hot cognition, perhaps because it invokes feelings of sympathy for people in dire straits or a sense of outrage about blatant violations of some people's basic human rights. Information that conflicts with what learners currently know or believe can also evoke hot cognition. In particular, such information can cause learners considerable mental discomfort, something that Piaget called *disequilibrium* but many contemporary theorists call **cognitive dissonance**. This dissonance typically leads learners to try to resolve the inconsistency in some way, perhaps undergoing conceptual change or perhaps ignoring or discrediting the new information (Buehl & Alexander, 2001; Harmon-Jones, 2001; Zohar & Aharon-Kraversky, 2005).

How effectively learners think about and make sense of new information also depends on their overall affective state—their general *mood*—while they're studying. They're most likely to engage in meaningful learning and think creatively about a topic if they're in an emotionally positive frame of mind. If, instead, they feel generally sad, frustrated, or bored, they're apt to process new information in superficial, inflexible ways—for instance, through mindless rehearsal (Efklides, 2011; Fredrickson, 2009; Pekrun, 2006; R. E. Snow, Corno, & Jackson, 1996).

One critical way to promote positive affect in the classroom, of course, is to address students' basic needs (e.g., for competence, relatedness, etc.). Researchers have suggested several additional ways in which we might increase positive affect:

- Occasionally incorporate gamelike features into classroom tasks and activities (e.g., crossword puzzles for practicing new spelling words, a television game-show format for a history class review).
- Adjust task difficulty to a level that students believe they can handle.
- Have students ask themselves questions that help them focus on the positive aspects of classroom activities and school in general (e.g., "What excites me about ____?" "What did I enjoy about ___?"). (Brophy, 2004; Pekrun, 2006; Townsend, 2008)

One form of affect—anxiety—can have either positive or negative effects on learning and cognition, depending on the circumstances. Because so many students experience anxiety at school, and because instructional practices and the classroom environment can contribute significantly to students' anxiety levels, we'll look at this particular form of affect more closely.

## ANXIETY IN THE CLASSROOM

Imagine that, as a college student enrolled in Professor Carberry's advanced psychoceramics course, you must give a half-hour presentation about psychoceramic califractions today. You've read several books and numerous articles on your topic and undoubtedly know more about psychoceramic califractions than any of your classmates. Furthermore, you've meticulously prepared note cards to which you can refer during your presentation. As you sit in class waiting for your turn to speak, you should be feeling calm and confident. But instead you're a nervous wreck: Your

**hot cognition**  Learning or cognitive processing that is emotionally charged.

**cognitive dissonance**  Feeling of mental discomfort caused by new information that conflicts with current knowledge or beliefs.

heart is pounding wildly, your palms are sweaty, and your stomach is in a knot. When you are finally called to the front of the room, you have trouble remembering what you planned to say and can't read your note cards because your hands are shaking so much. It's not as if you *want* to be nervous about speaking in front of your class, and you can't think of a single reason that you *should* be nervous. You're an expert on your topic, you're not having a bad-hair day, and your peers aren't likely to snicker or throw rotten tomatoes if you make a mistake. So what's the big deal?

You're a victim of anxiety: You have a feeling of uneasiness and apprehension about an event because you're not sure what its outcome will be. Anxiety has both cognitive and affective aspects (R. Carter, Williams, & Silverman, 2008; E. Hong, O'Neil, & Feldon, 2005; Tryon, 1980). Its cognitive aspect involves *worry*—troubling thoughts and beliefs about whether a situation can be effectively dealt with. Its affective aspect involves *emotionality*, which includes both physiological changes (e.g., muscular tension, a rapid heartbeat, increased perspiration) and such behavioral responses as restlessness and pacing. Anxiety is similar to fear, in the sense that both involve high levels of arousal. But the two emotions are different in one important respect: Although we're usually afraid of something in particular (e.g., a roaring lion or intense thunderstorm), we usually don't know exactly why we're anxious (Lazarus, 1991).

Almost everyone is anxious at one time or another. Many students become anxious just before a test they know will be difficult, and most get nervous before speaking to a large group. Such temporary feelings of anxiety are instances of state anxiety. However, some students are anxious much of the time, even when the situation isn't especially dangerous or threatening. For example, some students get excessively nervous even before very easy exams, and others may be so anxious about mathematics that they can't concentrate on even the simplest math assignment. A learner who shows a pattern of responding with anxiety even in nonthreatening situations has trait anxiety, a chronic condition that often hampers performance.

## HOW ANXIETY AFFECTS LEARNING AND PERFORMANCE

Imagine, for a moment, that you aren't anxious at all—not even the teeniest bit—about your grade in Carberry's psychoceramics class. Will you study for his tests? Will you turn in his assignments? If you have no anxiety whatsoever, you might not even buy the textbook or go to class, and you probably won't get a very good grade in the course.

A small amount of anxiety often improves performance: It's facilitating anxiety. A little anxiety spurs learners into action—for instance, making them go to class, complete assignments, and study for exams (see Figure 11.7). In contrast, a great deal of anxiety usually interferes with effective performance: It's debilitating anxiety. Excessive anxiety distracts learners and interferes with their attention to the task at hand.

At what point does anxiety stop facilitating and begin to debilitate performance? Very easy tasks—those that learners can do almost without thinking (e.g., running)—are typically facilitated by a high level of anxiety. But more difficult tasks—those that require considerable thought and mental effort—are best performed with only a small or moderate level of anxiety (Landers, 2007; Sapolsky, 2005; Yerkes & Dodson, 1908). A high level of anxiety in a complex situation can interfere with several aspects of cognition critical for successful learning and performance:

- Paying attention to what needs to be learned
- Processing information effectively (e.g., elaborating on or organizing it)
- Retrieving and using previously learned information and skills (Eysenck, 1992; K. L. Fletcher & Cassady, 2010; Hagtvet & Johnsen, 1992; Sarason, 1980)

Anxiety is especially likely to interfere with such cognitive processes when a task places heavy demands on either working memory or long-term memory—for instance, when a task involves problem solving or creativity. In such situations learners may be so preoccupied with the possibility of doing poorly that they can't keep their minds on what they need to accomplish (Ashcraft, 2002; Beilock, 2008; K. L. Fletcher & Cassady, 2010; Turner, Thorpe, & Meyer, 1998; Zeidner & Matthews, 2005).

**anxiety** Feeling of uneasiness and apprehension concerning a situation with an uncertain outcome.

**state anxiety** Temporary feeling of anxiety elicited by a threatening situation.

**trait anxiety** General pattern of responding with anxiety even in nonthreatening situations.

**facilitating anxiety** Level of anxiety (usually relatively low) that enhances performance.

**debilitating anxiety** Anxiety of sufficient intensity that it interferes with performance.

**FIGURE 11.7** **This writing sample by 14-year-old Loretta illustrates how anxiety can sometimes improve learning and achievement.**

A Stressful Situation
Once I had a science test that the teacher told us about two days ahead of time. Of course I hadn't thought to read the chapter yet so I had to read it and study. I got nervous and started throwing a fit. I was saying that I couldn't do it over and over again.
Finally I took a deep breath and study as. much as I could. The next day I took the test and I got something like a 96. I was so surprised, and relieved.

When asking students to perform difficult tasks, encourage them to do their best, but don't make them unnecessarily anxious about their performance.

Classical conditioning is described in Chapter 9.

## SOURCES OF ANXIETY

Learners sometimes develop feelings of anxiety about particular situations through the process of classical conditioning. They're also more likely to experience anxiety, especially debilitating anxiety, when they face a **threat**, a situation in which they believe they have little or no chance of succeeding. In contrast, learners can experience *facilitating* anxiety when they face a **challenge**—when they believe they can probably succeed with reasonable effort. Given learners' varying ability levels, tasks that promote facilitating anxiety for some of them can promote debilitating anxiety for others (E. M. Anderman & Dawson, 2011; Combs, Richards, & Richards, 1976; Csikszentmihalyi & Nakamura, 1989; Deci & Ryan, 1992).

Children and adolescents are apt to have some degree of anxiety—possibly facilitating, possibly debilitating—in many of the following circumstances:

- *A situation in which physical safety is at risk*—for example, being regularly exposed to violence at school or in the neighborhood
- *A situation in which self-worth is threatened*—for example, hearing unflattering remarks about one's race or gender
- *Concern about physical appearance*—for example, feeling too fat or too thin, or reaching puberty either earlier or later than peers
- *A new situation*—for example, moving from one school to another midway through the school year
- *Judgment or evaluation by others*—for example, receiving a low grade from a teacher or about being disliked or excluded by peers
- *Frustrating subject matter*—for example, having a history of difficulty with one or more content domains (as is true for many students with learning disabilities)
- *Technology*—for example, not knowing how to use the hardware or software required for assigned classroom tasks
- *Excessive classroom demands*—for example, being expected to learn a great deal of material in a very short time
- *Classroom tests*—for example, facing a high-stakes test that affects one's chances for promotion or graduation
- *Concern about the future*—for example, not knowing how to make a living after high school graduation (Benner & Graham, 2009; Cassady, 2004, 2010a; Chabrán, 2003; Covington, 1992; DuBois, Burk-Braxton, Swenson, Tevendale, & Hardesty, 2002; N. J. King & Ollendick, 1989; Martinez & Huberty, 2010; G. Matthews, Zeidner, & Roberts, 2006; Phelan, Yu, & Davidson, 1994; Stipek, 1993; Walton & Cohen, 2007; K. M. Williams, 2001a; Zeidner & Matthews, 2005)

Learners' particular concerns change somewhat as they grow older. Table 11.6 describes developmental trends in anxiety, as well as in affect more generally, across childhood and adolescence. For many children, one highly anxiety-arousing period is the transition from elementary school to a secondary school format—usually at the beginning of middle school or junior high but in some cases at the beginning of high school. We look at this issue next.

## A MULTIPLE WHAMMY: MAKING THE TRANSITION TO A SECONDARY SCHOOL FORMAT

Elementary school classrooms are often warm, nurturing places in which teachers get to know 20 or 30 students very well. Students in elementary classrooms also get to know *one another* quite well: They often work together on academic tasks and may even see themselves as members of a classroom "family." But somewhere around fifth to seventh grade, many students move from elementary school to a middle school or junior high school. As they do so, they simultaneously encounter numerous changes in the nature of their schooling:

- The school is larger and has more students.
- Students have several teachers, and each teacher has many students. Thus teacher–student relationships are more superficial and less personal than in elementary school, and teachers have less awareness of how well individual students are understanding and mastering classroom subject matter.

**threat** Situation in which a learner believes there is little or no chance of success.

**challenge** Situation in which a learner believes that success is possible with sufficient effort.

# DEVELOPMENTAL TRENDS

## TABLE 11.6 • Affect at Different Grade Levels

| GRADE LEVEL | AGE-TYPICAL CHARACTERISTICS | EXAMPLE | SUGGESTED STRATEGIES |
|---|---|---|---|
| K–2 | • Possible culture shock and intense anxiety upon beginning school, especially if students have had little or no formal preschool experience<br>• Possible separation anxiety when parents first leave the classroom (especially in the first few days of kindergarten)<br>• Reduced anxiety when teachers and other adults are warm and supportive<br>• Only limited control of overt emotional behaviors (e.g., may cry easily if distressed or act impulsively if frustrated) | Although Jeff has attended preschool since age 2, he's quite nervous about going to kindergarten. On his first day at the "big kids' school," he's reluctant to say good-bye to his mother. When Mom finally tells him she has to leave, he bursts into tears—a reaction that some of his classmates will taunt him about for several years. | • Ask parents about routines followed at home; when appropriate, incorporate these routines into classroom procedures.<br>• If possible, provide an opportunity for students to meet you a few days or weeks before school begins.<br>• Be warm, caring, and supportive with all students (but check school policies about hugs and other forms of physical affection).<br>• Address inappropriate behaviors gently but firmly. |
| 3–5 | • Increasing control of overt emotional behaviors<br>• Emergence of math anxiety for some students, especially if they receive little or no assistance with math tasks<br>• Tendency for close friends (especially girls) to talk about and ruminate on negative emotional events; continues into adolescence<br>• Possible stress as a result of others' racist and sexist behaviors (e.g., racial slurs, unkind remarks about emerging sexual characteristics); continues into adolescence | For 9-year-old Tina, basic arithmetic procedures with whole numbers are easy to understand. But she can make no sense of the new procedures she's learning for fractions—how to find common denominators, divide one fraction by another, and so on—and becomes increasingly frustrated when her attempts to solve fraction problems yield incorrect answers. Her aversion to math soon leads her to avoid the subject whenever possible, both in and outside of school. | • Ensure that students master basic concepts and procedures before proceeding to more complex material that depends on those concepts (especially important in teaching math, a subject area in which advanced knowledge and skills build on more basic ones).<br>• Monitor students' behaviors for signs of serious anxiety or depression; talk with students privately if they seem overly anxious or upset, and consult with the school counselor if necessary.<br>• Insist on respect for all class members' characteristics, feelings, and backgrounds; don't tolerate racist or sexist remarks or actions. |
| 6–8 | • General decline in positive, upbeat emotions; extreme mood swings, partly as a result of hormonal changes accompanying puberty<br>• Increased anxiety and potential depression accompanying the transition to middle school or junior high school<br>• Decrease in enjoyment of school (especially for boys)<br>• Increasing anxiety about peer relationships and social acceptance | At the beginning of seventh grade, 12-year-old Jeannie moves from a small, close-knit elementary school to a large junior high school. At her new school she knows only a few students in each class, and her teachers present themselves as cold, no-nonsense disciplinarians. Jeannie struggles in her efforts to make new friends and feels awkward when she must occasionally sit by herself in the cafeteria. Before long, she regularly complains of stomachaches so that she can stay home from school. | • Expect mood swings, but monitor students' behavior for signs of long-term depression.<br>• Make a personal connection with every student; express confidence that students can succeed with effort, and offer support that can facilitate success.<br>• Design activities that capture students' interest in the subject matter; relate topics to students' personal lives and goals.<br>• Provide opportunities for students to form supportive friendships with classmates (e.g., assign cooperative group projects). |
| 9–12 | • Continuing emotional volatility (especially in grades 9 and 10)<br>• Increasing ability to reflect on and control extreme emotional reactions, due in part to ongoing brain maturation<br>• Considerable anxiety about school if transition to a secondary school format has been delayed until high school<br>• Susceptibility to serious depression in the face of significant stress<br>• Increasing prevalence of debilitating anxiety regarding tests, especially high-stakes tests<br>• Feelings of uncertainty about life after graduation | In a text message to a classmate, 15-year-old Jonathan reveals his crush on a popular cheerleader. The classmate thinks the message is amusing ("I can't believe that loser thinks he has a chance with the head cheerleader!") and forwards it to more than 50 members of the sophomore class. Jonathan is at a loss about how to cope with his humiliation and contemplates suicide as the only solution to the problem. (*Teachers should* **immediately** *report any suspicions of planned suicides to school personnel who can effectively intervene.*) | • Be especially supportive if students have just made the transition from an elementary school format (e.g., show personal interest in students' well-being, teach effective study skills).<br>• Take seriously any signs that a student may be considering suicide (e.g., overt or veiled threats, such as "I won't be around much longer"; actions that indicate "putting one's affairs in order," such as giving away prized possessions).<br>• Give frequent classroom assessments so that no single test score is a "fatal" one; help students prepare for high-stakes tests.<br>• Present multiple options for postgraduation career paths. |

*Sources:* Arnett, 1999; Ashcraft, 2002; Benes, 2007; Benner & Graham, 2009; Chabrán, 2003; DuBois et al., 2002; Eccles & Midgley, 1989; Elkind, 1981; Gentry, Gable, & Rizza, 2002; K. T. Hill & Sarason, 1966; Hine & Fraser, 2002; Kerns & Lieberman, 1993; Kuhl & Kraska, 1989; Lapsley, 1993; Larson & Brown, 2007; Larson, Moneta, Richards, & Wilson, 2002; D. K. Meyer & Turner, 2006; Midgley, Middleton, Gheen, & Kumar, 2002; Roderick & Camburn, 1999; A. J. Rose, 2002; Rudolph, Lambert, Clark, & Kurlakowsky, 2001; Seiffge-Krenke, Aunola, & Nurmi, 2009; R. E. Snow et al., 1996; Spear, 2000; R. M. Thomas, 2005; Tomback, Williams, & Wentzel, 2005; Wiles & Bondi, 2001.

Students entering the middle school grades face new challenges—more stringent evaluation criteria, less individualized instruction, greater competition in classes and sports, and so on—while also undergoing the unsettling physiological changes of puberty.

- There is more whole-class instruction, with less individualized instruction that takes into account each student's academic needs.

- Classes are less socially cohesive. Students may not know their classmates very well and thus may be reluctant to ask peers for assistance.

- Students have fewer opportunities to make choices about the topics they pursue and the tasks they complete. At the same time, they have more independence and responsibility regarding their learning. For example, they may have relatively unstructured assignments to be accomplished over a two- or three-week period, and they must take the initiative to seek help when they're struggling.

- Teachers place greater emphasis on demonstrating (rather than acquiring) competence, reflecting a shift from mastery goals to performance goals. Thus mistakes are more costly for students.

- Standards for assigning grades are more rigorous, so students may earn lower grades than they did in elementary school. Grades are often assigned on a comparative and competitive basis, with only the highest-achieving students getting As and Bs.

- High-stakes tests—tests that affect promotion to the next grade level—become increasingly common. (E. M. Anderman & Mueller, 2010; H. A. Davis, 2003; Dijkstra et al., 2008; Eccles & Midgley, 1989; Hine & Fraser, 2002; Midgley, Middleton, Gheen, & Kumar, 2002; Wentzel & Wigfield, 1998; Wigfield et al., 2006)

Furthermore, previously formed friendships can be disrupted as students move to new (and perhaps differing) schools (Pellegrini & Long, 2004; Wentzel, 1999). And of course, students are also dealing with the physiological changes that accompany puberty and adolescence.

This multiple whammy of changes often leads to decreased confidence, a lower sense of self-worth, less intrinsic motivation, and considerable anxiety. Focus on peer relationships increases, and academic achievement drops. Some students become quite depressed or emotionally disengaged from the school environment, increasing the odds that they eventually drop out of school (E. M. Anderman & Mueller, 2010; G. L. Cohen & Garcia, 2008; Danner, 2011; Eccles & Midgley, 1989; Gentry et al., 2002; Urdan & Maehr, 1995).

If students remain in a small elementary school environment in early adolescence, rather than moving to a larger middle or junior high school, their emotions and motivation are more likely to remain healthy and productive (Midgley et al., 2002; Rudolph, Lambert, Clark, & Kurkakowsky, 2001). By the time they reach ninth grade, however, they almost inevitably make the transition to a secondary school format, where they experience many of the changes that their peers elsewhere experienced a few grades earlier (Benner & Graham, 2009; Hine & Fraser, 2002; Midgley et al., 2002; Tomback et al., 2005).

Students who make a smooth transition to secondary school are more likely to be successful there and, as a result, are more likely to graduate from high school. As teachers, the particular school environment we create for adolescents can make a world of difference for their personal, social, and academic well-being (E. M. Anderman & Mueller, 2010; M.-T. Wang & Holcombe, 2010). The Into the Classroom feature "Easing the Transition to Middle and Secondary School" suggests several strategies for teachers in the middle school and high school grades.

## KEEPING STUDENTS' ANXIETY AT A FACILITATIVE LEVEL

Even when students aren't making a significant transition from one educational setting to another, they may have many reasons to be anxious at school. We can address their concerns about social matters—for instance, their worries about peer relationships—by teaching social skills and planning activities that foster frequent and productive student interactions. And we can address their concerns about an uncertain future by teaching skills that will be marketable in the adult world and providing assistance with college applications.

Chapter 3 offers specific recommendations for promoting productive interactions with peers.

But perhaps most importantly, we must take steps to ensure that students don't become overly anxious about classroom tasks and subject matter. Because anxiety is—like all emotions—largely beyond students' immediate control, simply telling them to calm down is unlikely to be effective. The key is to prevent rather than "cure" debilitating anxiety. Following are several strategies that should keep students' anxiety at a facilitative level:

- Communicate clear, concrete, and realistic expectations for performance.

- Match instruction to students' cognitive levels and capabilities (e.g., use concrete materials to teach math to students not yet capable of abstract thought).

## Into the Classroom

### Easing the Transition to Middle and Secondary School

🍏 **Provide a means through which every student can feel part of a small, close-knit group.**

During the first week of school, a ninth-grade math teacher forms 3- to 4-member *base groups* who provide support and assistance for one another throughout the school year. At the beginning or end of every class period, the teacher gives group members five minutes to help one another with questions and concerns about daily lessons and homework assignments.

🍏 **Find time to meet one-on-one with every student.**

Early in the school year, while students are working on a variety of cooperative learning activities, a middle school social studies teacher schedules individual appointments with each of his students. In these meetings he searches for interests that he and his students share and encourages the students to seek him out whenever they need help with academic or personal problems. Throughout the semester he continues to touch base with individual students (often during lunch or before or after school) to see how they're doing.

🍏 **Teach students the skills they need to be successful independent learners.**

After discovering that few of her students know how to take effective class notes, a high school science teacher distributes a daily notes "skeleton" that guides them through the note-taking process. The skeleton includes headings such as "Topic of the Lesson," "Definitions," "Important Ideas," and "Examples." As students' class notes improve over the course of the school year, the teacher gradually reduces the amount of structure she provides.

🍏 **Assign grades based on mastery, not on comparisons with peers, and provide reasonable opportunities for improvement.**

A junior high school language arts teacher requires students to submit two drafts of every essay and short story he assigns; he gives students the option of submitting additional drafts as well. He judges each composition on several criteria, including quality of ideas, organization and cohesiveness, word usage, grammar, and spelling. He explains and illustrates each of these criteria and gives ample feedback on every draft that students turn in.

---

🍏 When students have a high level of trait anxiety, provide considerable structure to guide their activities.

🍏 Provide supplementary sources of support for learning challenging topics and skills until mastery is attained (e.g., provide additional practice, individual tutoring, or a structure for taking notes).

🍏 Teach strategies that can help students improve their overall learning and performance (e.g., effective study skills and self-regulation strategies).

🍏 Assess students' performance independently of how well their classmates are doing, and encourage students to assess their own performance in a similar manner.

🍏 Provide feedback about specific behaviors rather than global evaluations of performance.

🍏 Allow students to correct errors so that no single mistake is ever a "fatal" one. (E. M. Anderman & Dawson, 2011; Brophy, 1986; K. L. Fletcher & Cassady, 2010; Hattie & Timperley, 2007; Huberty, 2008; Jain & Dowson, 2009; Pekrun, 2006; Shute, 2008; Stipek, 1993; Tryon, 1980; Zeidner, 1998)

Chapter 14 offers specific strategies for keeping students' anxiety at reasonable levels during tests and other classroom assessments.

## DIVERSITY IN AFFECT

Some people seem to be consistently more emotionally upbeat than others—an individual difference variable that's probably rooted in biology to some degree (Costa & McCrae, 1992; C. Peterson, 2006). In addition, researchers have observed some consistent differences in affect in students of different cultural and ethnic backgrounds, genders, and socioeconomic levels.

### CULTURAL AND ETHNIC DIFFERENCES

On average, cultural groups differ in the degree to which they show their feelings in their behaviors and facial expressions. For example, whereas Americans and Mexicans are often quite expressive, people from East Asian cultures tend to be more reserved and may be reluctant to confide in other people in times of sadness or distress (Camras, Chen, Bakeman, Norris, & Cain, 2006; P. M. Cole & Tan, 2007; H. S. Kim, Sherman, & Taylor, 2008). Cultures probably differ most in the extent to which they tolerate overt expressions of anger. Mainstream Western culture encourages children to act and speak up if someone infringes on their rights and needs, and expressing anger in a nonviolent way is considered quite acceptable. In many Southeast Asian cultures,

Keep in mind that some students may have been socialized to hide their emotions.

however, any expression of anger is viewed as potentially undermining adults' authority or disrupting social harmony (Adam, Shirako, & Maddux, 2010; Mesquita & Leu, 2007; J. L. Tsai, 2007). Children brought up in some Buddhist communities are encouraged to not even *feel* anger (P. M. Cole, Bruschi, & Tamang, 2002; P. M. Cole, Tamang, & Shrestha, 2006). For example, if unfairly embarrassed or accused, a child who has grown up in the Tamang culture of Nepal might respond, "Tilda bomo khaba?" ("Why be angry?"), because the event has already occurred and being angry about it serves no purpose (P. M. Cole et al., 2002, p. 992).

Even seemingly "positive" emotions aren't always viewed favorably. Some cultures that place a high priority on social harmony discourage children from feeling pride about personal accomplishments, because such an emotion focuses attention on an individual rather than on the overall group (Eid & Diener, 2001). And for some cultural groups, joy and happiness can sometimes be too much of a good thing. For example, many Chinese and Japanese advocate striving for contentment and serenity—relatively calm emotions—rather than joy (Kagan, 2010; Mesquita & Leu, 2007; J. L. Tsai, 2007).

Be especially sensitive to sources of anxiety for particular cultural and racial groups and for recent immigrants.

Finally, learners from various cultural backgrounds may have somewhat different sources of anxiety. For instance, some children and adolescents from Asian American families may feel so much family pressure to perform well in school that they experience debilitating test anxiety (Pang, 1995). Students who are clearly in the racial or ethnic minority at their school—for example, African American students at a predominantly European American school, or vice versa—may be especially anxious about whether their majority-group classmates will accept them without prejudice (G. L. Cohen & Garcia, 2008). And recent immigrants are often anxious about a variety of things in their new country: how to behave, how to interpret other people's behaviors, how to make friends, and, more generally, how to make sense of the strange new culture in which they now find themselves (P. M. Cole & Tan, 2007; Dien, 1998; Igoa, 1995).

Anxiety may be at the root of a phenomenon known as **stereotype threat**, which can lead students from stereotypically low-achieving groups to perform more poorly on classroom assessments than they otherwise would simply because they're aware that their group traditionally *does* do poorly (J. Aronson & Steele, 2005; K. E. Ryan & Ryan, 2005; J. L. Smith, 2004). When students are aware of the unflattering stereotype—and especially when they know that the task they're performing reflects their ability in an important domain—their heart rate and other physiological correlates of anxiety go up and their performance goes down (McKown & Weinstein, 2003; Osborne & Simmons, 2002; Walton & Spencer, 2009). We're more likely to see the negative effects of stereotype threat when students interpret their performance as an evaluation of their general competence and self-worth (P. G. Davies & Spencer, 2005; Huguet & Régner, 2007; McKown & Weinstein, 2003). Furthermore, stereotype threat is more likely to arise when students have an entity view of ability—a belief that ability is relatively fixed and permanent—rather than an incremental view (Dweck et al., 2004; C. Good, Aronson, & Inzlicht, 2003; Osborne, Tillman, & Holland, 2010).

## GENDER DIFFERENCES

Seek professional assistance with anger management training if a student frequently lashes out in anger.

In general, girls express their emotions more openly than boys do. However, girls sometimes hide angry feelings in order to preserve social harmony, whereas boys are often quite willing to show their anger (Eisenberg, Martin, & Fabes, 1996; Lippa, 2002; Sadker & Sadker, 1994). Girls are also more anxious about their classroom performance, which may partly explain their greater diligence in schoolwork (Marsh et al., 2008; Pomerantz, Altermatt, & Saxon, 2002). For instance, girls are more prone to test anxiety than boys are; some become victims of stereotype threat, earning lower scores than they should on tests in stereotypically "male" domains such as math (Ben-Zeev et al., 2005; E. Hong et al., 2005; Huguet & Régner, 2007). But girls and boys alike can experience considerable stress at school, especially in adolescence—perhaps about academic struggles, broken friendships, or romantic relationships—and they don't always have productive strategies for coping with their disappointments (Frydenberg & Lewis, 2000; Seiffge-Krenke et al., 2009). Clearly, then, students of both genders may sometimes need extra social and emotional support.

Be especially supportive when a student experiences extreme stress at school or elsewhere.

**stereotype threat** Awareness of a negative stereotype about one's own group and accompanying uneasiness that low performance will confirm the stereotype; leads (often unintentionally) to lower-quality performance.

## SOCIOECONOMIC DIFFERENCES

As a result of their impoverished and unpredictable life circumstances—uncertainty about future meals and housing, frequent incidents of neighborhood violence, and so on—students from low-income families are, on average, more prone to anxiety and depression than their higher-income classmates (Ashiabi & O'Neal, 2008; G. W. Evans, Gonnella, Marcynyszyn, Gentile, &

Salpekar, 2005; Morales & Guerra, 2006). Furthermore, students in low-income school districts are especially at risk for making a rough transition from an elementary to a secondary school format (Ogbu, 2003; Roderick & Camburn, 1999). Accordingly, students from low socioeconomic backgrounds are apt to have a greater-than-average need for our emotional and social support, and they are the ones who are most likely to benefit from a consistently warm and nurturing classroom environment (B. E. Becker & Luthar, 2002; Masten, 2001; Milner, 2006).

 Be especially attentive to the emotional needs of children from low-income families.

In bringing our discussion of motivation and affect to a close, I must emphasize once again an important point: We teachers can—and *should*—make a significant difference in the lives of children and adolescents. Through the academic and social skills we teach them, the general classroom atmosphere we create for them, and the individualized instructional and emotional support we give them, we can greatly enhance their ability to be both productive and happy in the outside world.

# 11  What Have You Learned?

We now return to the chapter's learning outcomes and identify some key points related to each one.

■ **11.1: Draw on diverse theoretical perspectives to describe the multifaceted nature of motivation.** Motivation energizes, directs, and sustains behavior; for instance, it focuses learners' attention on certain goals, influences what and how learners cognitively process information, and determines the specific consequences that are likely to be reinforcing. *Extrinsic motivation* is based on factors external to learners and unrelated to the task at hand, whereas *intrinsic motivation* arises from conditions within learners themselves or from factors inherent in the task. For the most part, intrinsic motivation leads to more effective learning, both in the short term and over the long haul.

Psychologists have approached the topic of motivation from many angles. *Trait theorists* propose that motivation can sometimes involve relatively enduring personality characteristics. Other theorists focus on internal factors that drive much of what learners do—perhaps a general need for self-actualization *(humanism)*, more task-specific expectations and self-efficacy *(social cognitive theory)*, or attributions regarding cause-and-effect relationships in a learner's personal life *(cognitive theories)*. Still other theorists focus on environmental conditions impacting motivation—perhaps response–consequence contingencies in a learner's immediate surroundings *(behaviorism)* or general values, norms, and support systems within a learner's broader social and cultural environments *(contextual theories)*.

**Evaluate** and **apply** your knowledge related to this learning outcome in MyEducationLab™.

■ **11.2: Describe several basic needs that seem to drive much of human behavior, and identify numerous strategies for helping students address these needs at school.** In addition to basic needs for physical survival (e.g., food and water), human beings appear to have several needs related to their psychological well-being. One is the need for *arousal*—a need for a certain level of physical and cognitive stimulation. People also have a need for *competence* and *self-worth*—a need to believe that they can deal effectively with their surroundings and are,

overall, good, capable individuals. Third, people have a need for *self-determination*—a need to believe that they have some autonomy and control regarding the course of their lives. And finally, people seem to have a need for *relatedness*—a need to feel loved, respected, and socially connected to others. One early theorist, Abraham Maslow, proposed that people have several basic needs—physiological needs and needs for safety, love and belonging, and esteem—that are prioritized as a hierarchy; once these needs are met, Maslow suggested, people work hard to enhance their knowledge and abilities and reach their full potential. As teachers, we're most likely to foster students' intrinsic motivation to master academic subject matter when we also address their basic needs—for example, by conducting stimulating and peer-interactive activities, giving them age-appropriate autonomy in their work, and scaffolding their efforts in challenging tasks.

**Evaluate** and **apply** your knowledge related to this learning outcome in MyEducationLab™.

■ **11.3: Explain how learners' cognitive processes and sociocultural environments can have significant impacts on their motivation, and apply your knowledge of these factors to classroom practice.** Many forms of motivation have both cognitive and sociocultural elements. For example, learners' *interests* in certain topics—whether temporarily induced situational interests or longer-term personal ones—can emerge from learners' own intellectual curiosity, from unusual or puzzling events, or from a general environment in which inquiry and creativity are encouraged. Learners should also find *value* in certain activities and have an *expectancy* that they can be successful in those activities. Learners' values are especially impacted by their sociocultural environment: When conditions are right—when the environment is warm and responsive, with an age-appropriate balance between autonomy and guidance—learners gradually internalize some of the values of people around them.

Learners typically have a number of *goals,* including achievement goals (perhaps to master particular topics and skills or perhaps to demonstrate competence in a particular area), work-avoidance goals, social goals, and long-term life goals. Sometimes learners can accomplish multiple goals simultaneously, but in other cases they can't; for instance, learners can address both their achievement goals and their social goals by forming a study group for a challenging high school course, but it's quite difficult to master a topic while also avoiding hard work. As teachers, we should encourage mastery goals as much as possible—for example, by insisting on genuine understanding of classroom material and by communicating that learning involves exerting effort and making mistakes—but we must also help students achieve other goals important for their well-being, such as certain performance goals, social goals, and career goals.

Learners' self-constructed explanations of why various things happen to them—their *attributions*—influence their learning and performance as well. As students move through the grade levels, many of them increasingly attribute their successes and failures to a relatively fixed, uncontrollable ability; those students who, in contrast, believe they can improve their performance with hard work and more effective strategies achieve at higher levels over the long run. We teachers can foster more optimistic and productive attributions, in part, by conveying the message—not only through our words but also through our actions—that students can, indeed, have considerable control over their destinies.

Evaluate and apply your knowledge related to this learning outcome in MyEducationLab™.

■ **11.4: Describe how various forms of affect are intertwined with motivation, learning, and cognition, and explain how you might promote productive affective states in students.** The emotions and general moods that learners bring to bear on a task—collectively known as *affect*—are closely intertwined with motivation; for example, how learners feel depends on whether their needs are being met. Affect is closely connected with learning and cognition as well; for example, learners typically learn and remember more when they're emotionally as well as cognitively involved in classroom topics.

One particular form of affect—anxiety—has particular implications for classroom learning. A small amount of anxiety often facilitates learning and performance, but a great deal of anxiety typically impedes them, especially when difficult tasks are involved. In most circumstances, we should strive to keep students' anxiety at a low to moderate level—for example, by clearly communicating expectations for achievement and by ensuring that students have a good chance of being successful with reasonable effort.

Evaluate and apply your knowledge related to this learning outcome in MyEducationLab™.

## Practice for Your Licensure Exam

### When "Perfect" Isn't Good Enough

Mrs. Gaskill's second graders are just beginning to learn how to write the letters of the alphabet in cursive. Every day Mrs. Gaskill introduces a new cursive letter and shows her students how to write it correctly. She also shows them some common errors in writing the letter—for instance, claiming that she's going to make the "perfect f" but then making it much too short and crossing the lines in the wrong place—and the children delight in finding her mistakes. After the class explores the shape of a letter, Mrs. Gaskill asks her students to practice the letter, first by writing it in the air using large arm movements and then by writing it numerous times on lined paper.

Meanwhile, Mrs. Gaskill has decided to compare the effects of two kinds of praise on the children's performance. She has placed a small colored sticker on each child's desk to indicate membership in one of two groups. When children in Group 1 write a letter with good form, she gives them a happy-face token, says "Great!" or "Perfect!" and either smiles at them or gives them a pat on the back. When children in Group 2 write a letter with good form at least once, she gives them a happy-face token and says something like "You sure are working hard," "You can write beautifully in cursive," or "You are a natural at this." When children in either group fail to meet her standards for cursive writing, she gives them whatever corrective feedback they need.

Thus, the only way in which Mrs. Gaskill treats the two groups differently is in what she says to them when they do well,

either giving them fairly cryptic feedback (for Group 1) or telling them that they are trying hard or have high ability (for Group 2). Despite such a minor difference, Mrs. Gaskill finds that the children in Group 2 say they enjoy cursive writing more, and they use it more frequently in their spelling tests and other writing tasks. Curiously, too, the children in Group 1 often seem disappointed when they receive their seemingly positive feedback. For instance, on one occasion a girl who writes beautifully but has the misfortune of being in Group 1 asks, "Am *I* a natural at this?" Although the girl consistently gets a grade of "+" for her cursive writing, she never writes in cursive voluntarily throughout the three-week period in which Mrs. Gaskill conducts her experiment. (Study described by Gaskill, 2001)

1. **Multiple-choice question:**

   Which one of the following observations best supports the conclusion that the children in Group 2 have greater *intrinsic* motivation than the children in Group 1?

   a. The children in Group 2 get more detailed feedback.

   b. The children in Group 2 seem happier when Mrs. Gaskill reinforces them.

   c. The children in Group 1 seem disappointed about the feedback they get.

   d. The children in Group 2 use cursive writing more frequently in other assignments.

**2. Constructed-response question:**

Explain why the praise given to Group 2 might be more motivating than the praise given to Group 1. Base your explanation on contemporary principles and theories of motivation.

**3. Constructed-response question:**

Might the feedback given to Group 1 ("e.g., Great!" "Perfect") be more effective if Mrs. Gaskill used it for all, rather than just some, of her students? Explain your reasoning.

---

**PRAXIS**  Go to Appendix C, "Matching Book and MyEducationLab™ to the Praxis Principles of Learning and Teaching Tests," to discover sections of this chapter that may be especially applicable to the Praxis tests.

---

# 12 Instructional Strategies

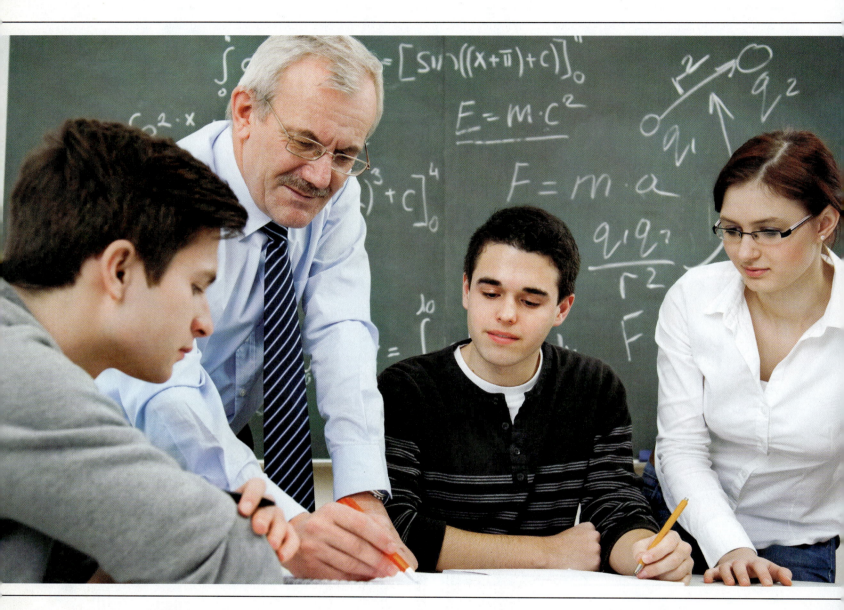

## LEARNING OUTCOMES

**12.1:** Identify eight general principles that can guide your planning and instructional strategies.

**12.2:** Describe important elements of planning for instruction, and explain how planning and instruction are closely intertwined.

**12.3:** Explain how you can effectively promote students' learning through teacher-directed instructional strategies.

**12.4:** Explain how you can also promote students' learning through more learner-directed strategies.

**12.5:** Choose appropriate instructional strategies for varying instructional goals and different kinds of students.

# CASE STUDY: OREGON TRAIL

Michele Minichiello's fifth-grade class is studying the westward migration of European American settlers during the middle 1800s. Today's lesson is about one well-traveled route: the Oregon Trail.[1]

"The covered wagons were about 4 feet by 10 feet," Ms. Minichiello tells her class. She has two students use masking tape to mark a 4-by-10-foot rectangle on the classroom carpet. "How much room would that give you for your family and supplies?" The students agree that people would have to be quite choosy about what they brought with them on the trip west.

"Let's brainstorm some of the things the settlers might have packed," Ms. Minichiello says. The students volunteer many possibilities—food, water, blankets, rifles, medicine, spare wagon parts—and Ms. Minichiello writes them on the dry-erase board. She asks the class to be more specific about the items on the board (e.g., What kinds of food? How much of each kind?) and then passes out reading materials that list the supplies a typical family would pack for the journey. As the students read and discuss the materials in small cooperative groups, Ms. Minichiello circulates among them to show old photographs of how the inside of a covered wagon looked when occupied by a family and its possessions.

When the students have finished their reading, Ms. Minichiello directs their attention to their own supply list on the board and asks them to compare it to the list of typical supplies presented in the reading materials. The students notice many discrepancies:

> **Lacy:** We need much more flour.
> **Janie:** [Referring to an item listed in the reading materials] I don't think they should bring 100 pounds of coffee.
> **Curt:** [Also referring to the reading materials] I don't think they need 50 pounds of lard.
> **Ms. M:** What were some of the things the pioneers had to be prepared for?

After the class discusses possible reasons for the various items the settlers packed, Ms. Minichiello asks students to put themselves in the settlers' shoes.

> **Ms. M:** If *you* were taking such a trip now—if you were moving far away from where you live now—what things would you bring with you?
> **Misha:** Computer.
> **Lou:** Cell phone.
> **Dana:** Refrigerator.
> **Cerise:** My dog.
> **Ms. M:** Imagine that your family isn't doing well, and so you decide to travel to a distant planet. It's very expensive to travel there. You can take only *one* item, so pick the one item you would take. Assume there will be food and a place to sleep. Take five minutes to pick one item, and explain why you'd take it.

Ms. Minichiello distributes index cards on which the students can write their responses. After a few minutes she asks, "Who found it hard to pick just one item?"

---

[1] I observed Michele's lesson when I was supervising her teaching internship, and she gave me permission to describe it here. The students' names are pseudonyms.

**evidence-based practice** Instructional method or other classroom strategy that research has consistently shown to bring about significant gains in students' development and/or academic achievement.

**backward design** Approach to instructional planning in which a teacher first determines the desired end result (i.e., what knowledge and skills students should acquire), then identifies appropriate assessments, and finally determines appropriate instructional strategies.

Almost all of the students raise their hands. "What I wanted you to realize is that if you had been a child back then, it would have been really hard to leave most of your things behind."

• What specific instructional strategies does Ms. Minichiello use to engage and motivate her students? What strategies is she using to help them learn and remember the content of the lesson?

To engage and motivate her students, Ms. Minichiello arouses situational interest through a physical activity (students mark a "wagon" on the carpet), creates cognitive dissonance (the list in the reading materials doesn't entirely match the one the class has generated), poses a challenging question ("You can only take *one* item . . . ."), and makes the lesson a very social, interactive one. Furthermore, she promotes learning and understanding by encouraging visual imagery and elaboration—for instance, by making the subject matter concrete and vivid (through the masking-tape wagon and old photographs), having the class consider needs and hazards that would call for certain supplies ("What were some of the things that pioneers had to be prepared for?"), and asking students to relate the settlers' situation to a hypothetical one they themselves might face.

Effective instruction requires knowledge and use of **evidence-based practices**—those methods and strategies that research has consistently shown to be effective in helping students learn and achieve. It also requires considerable *planning:* We must decide in advance both what needs to be accomplished and how best to accomplish it, and we must continue to revise our plans (mentally, at least) as a lesson or instructional unit proceeds. Not only are planning and instruction closely connected but they're also intertwined with two other critical aspects of classroom practice: creating a productive environment for learning and assessing students' performance. Furthermore, planning, instruction, the classroom environment, and assessment practices both influence and are influenced by students' characteristics and behaviors (see Figure 12.1). As we make our day-to-day decisions in the classroom, we must *always* take into account what we know about each of our students.

# General Principles That Can Guide Instruction

Historically many theorists and practitioners have looked for—and in some cases believe that they have found—the single best way to teach children and adolescents. In reality, *there is no single best approach to instruction.* Instead, effective teachers adhere to several general principles as they plan and carry out instruction:

  • *Effective teachers begin their instructional planning by determining what they ultimately want students to know and be able to do.* An increasingly popular approach is a **backward design**, in which teachers proceed through this sequence (Wiggins & McTighe, 2005):

  1. Identify the desired end results in terms of knowledge and skills that students should attain.

  2. Determine acceptable evidence—in the form of performance on various classroom assessment tasks—to verify that students have achieved those results.

  3. Plan learning experiences and instructional activities that enable students to demonstrate—through their performance on the assessment tasks—attainment of the desired results.

With such an approach, we essentially *begin at the end* and then choose assessment tasks and instructional strategies that are specifically related to that end (see Figure 12.2.). For example, if the objective for a unit on addition is *rapid retrieval* of number facts, we might create a timed quiz to assess students' ability to recall the facts quickly and easily, and we might employ gamelike computer software to enhance students' automaticity for the facts. But if our objective is *application* of number facts, we may instead want to focus our assessment methods and instructional strategies on word problems or, better still, on activities involving real objects and hands-on measurements.

• *Effective teachers use a variety of instructional strategies, often within a single lesson.* The lesson in the opening case study includes a physical activity, two teacher-led class discussions, printed materials, and a small-group cooperative learning task. This combination of instructional strategies engages students' interest and attention and helps students understand what the pioneers' westward migration involved. Much of the lesson reflects teacher-directed instruction, in which a teacher calls most of the shots, choosing which topics will be addressed, closely guiding students' activities, and so on. However, one of Ms. Minichiello's strategies—having students study reading materials in small cooperative groups—reflects learner-directed instruction, in which students have considerable control regarding what and how they learn. Some educators use the terms *teacher-centered* versus *learner-centered* in reference to this distinction, but as Figure 12.1 illustrates, virtually all instructional strategies should focus (center) on learners—what learners currently know and don't know, what their needs and motives are, how instruction can best support effective cognitive processes and meaningful learning, and so on.[2]

Regardless of the specific terminology we use, we must remember that the distinction being made here really reflects a *continuum* rather than an either-or situation, because instructional strategies can vary considerably in the degree to which teachers and students control the course of events. The relative amounts of teacher and student control can change even within a single lesson. For example, although Ms. Minichiello poses specific questions for students to answer—a teacher-directed strategy—the questions are sufficiently open-ended that students' responses influence the nature of subsequent discussions.

• *Effective teachers promote productive cognitive processing of classroom subject matter.* Instruction can be effective only to the extent that it captures students' attention, fosters meaningful learning and appropriate conceptual change, and encourages problem solving, critical thinking, and other complex cognitive processes. It must also keep students' cognitive load at a manageable level: At any particular moment, information and cognitive processing demands mustn't exceed students' limited working memory capacities (R. E. Mayer, 2011a; Sweller, 2010).

To see this principle in action, try the following exercise.

Choose instructional strategies and assessment methods that reflect desired end results of instruction.

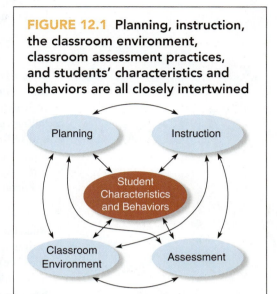

**FIGURE 12.1** Planning, instruction, the classroom environment, classroom assessment practices, and students' characteristics and behaviors are all closely intertwined

**FIGURE 12.2** In a backward-design approach to instructional planning, a teacher mentally travels "backward" in time

START HERE

#1 – Identify desired end results of instruction.

#2 – Identify assessment tasks that genuinely reflect attainment of the desired results.

#3 – Plan instruction that will enable students to complete the assessment tasks successfully.

## EXPERIENCING FIRSTHAND
### FINDING PEDAGOGY IN ONE OF YOUR TEXTBOOKS

1. Look at two or three chapters in this book or another textbook that you've recently read. Identify places where the author has done specific things to help you learn and remember the material more effectively. What specific strategies did the author use to facilitate your cognitive processing?

2. In those same chapters, can you find places where you had trouble making sense of the ideas presented? If so, what might the author have done differently in those instances?

**teacher-directed instruction**
Approach to instruction in which the teacher is largely in control of the content and course of the lesson.

**learner-directed instruction**
Approach to instruction in which students have considerable control regarding the issues they address and the ways they address them.

[2] The American Psychological Association has identified 14 *Learner-Centered Psychological Principles* that encompass many fundamental principles of human learning, motivation, and development. You can find these principles by going to APA's website (www.apa.org) and typing "learner-centered principles" in the search box.

If you've chosen one or more chapters that I, Jeanne Ormrod, have written, I'm hoping that the Experiencing Firsthand exercises have helped you relate new topics to your own knowledge and experiences. I'm hoping, too, that the case studies and student work samples have made abstract ideas more concrete and easy to understand. Perhaps some of the tables and graphics have helped you organize concepts and principles. But if you've found certain parts of a chapter confusing or hard to understand, I encourage you to let me know.[3]

• *Effective teachers focus on knowledge and skills that are most likely to enhance students' long-term success both in and outside of school.* For example, rather than asking students to memorize trivial facts, effective teachers emphasize general themes, principles, and skills—sometimes known as *big ideas*—that are applicable to many topics and contexts (Brophy, Alleman, & Knighton, 2009; Wiggins & McTighe, 2005). Rather than simply chastising students for failing to complete homework assignments, effective teachers foster metacognitive strategies and self-regulation skills essential for self-guided, independent learning. And rather than filling the entire school day with traditional drill-and-practice exercises, effective teachers often assign authentic activities—activities that in some way resemble those that students are likely to encounter in the outside world.

• *Effective teachers provide some structure and scaffolding for activities and assignments.* Even when lessons are largely learner directed, students typically need structure and guidance, especially with new and challenging tasks (e.g., Wise & O'Neill, 2009). The concept of *scaffolding* is useful here: We can provide a great deal of structure for tasks early in the school year, gradually removing it as students become better able to structure tasks for themselves. For example, when students first engage in cooperative learning activities, we might break down each group task into several subtasks, giving clear directions about how each subtask should be carried out and assigning every group member a particular role to serve in the group. As the school year progresses and students become more adept at working cooperatively with their classmates, we can gradually become less directive about how small-group tasks are accomplished.

• *Effective teachers capitalize on technological innovations to enhance students' learning and performance.* Interactive whiteboards, basic computer tools (e.g., word processing programs, electronic spreadsheets), topic-specific instructional software, educational websites—all of these innovations can potentially help students better understand and apply classroom subject matter. Yet, as is true for more traditional, "low-tech" instructional methods, such innovations can be effective only to the extent that they facilitate productive cognitive processes and provide sufficient scaffolding to foster students' success at new tasks and skills. Furthermore, they tend to have a greater impact when they're used in conjunction with—rather than as replacements for—more traditional methods involving face-to-face teacher–student interaction (Azevedo & Witherspoon, 2009; R. E. Clark, Yates, Early, & Moulton, 2009; Tamin, Bernard, Brokhovski, Abrami, & Schmid, 2011).

• *Effective teachers take student diversity into account when planning and carrying out instruction.* Our choice of instructional strategies must, of course, be appropriate for students' current ability levels and existing knowledge about a topic. We must take temperamental and motivational characteristics into consideration as well. For example, some children and adolescents have trouble sitting still and concentrating during lengthy lectures, and many students of all ages find hands-on activities more motivating and engaging than abstract textbook readings. And, of course, students with special educational needs often require accommodations tailored to their unique abilities and disabilities. Ideally, instruction is individually tailored for *all* students—a practice called differentiated instruction.

• *Effective teachers regularly assess and provide feedback about students' progress.* Assessment isn't something we do only at the end of instruction. It's also something we must do *throughout* instruction—a process known as formative assessment. Regularly determining students' ongoing understandings and skill levels—what they understand and misunderstand, what they can and can-

authentic activity  Classroom activity similar to an activity that students are apt to encounter in the outside world.

differentiated instruction  Practice of individualizing instructional methods—and possibly also individualizing specific content and instructional goals—to align with each student's existing knowledge, skills, and needs.

formative assessment  Assessment conducted before or during instruction to facilitate instructional planning and enhance students' learning.

---

[3]I'm always eager to get readers' suggestions for improvement. You can reach me at jormrod@alumni.brown.edu.

not do—enables us to modify our instructional strategies in ways that maximize students' learning. It also enables us to provide the constructive feedback students may need to capitalize on their strengths, work on their weak spots, and, in general, be optimistic that they can ultimately achieve at high levels (Hattie & Gan, 2011; Narciss, 2008).

# Planning for Instruction

Good teachers engage in considerable advance planning: They identify the knowledge and skills they want students to acquire, determine an appropriate sequence in which to teach the knowledge and skills, and develop classroom lessons and activities that will keep students motivated and on task and will maximize learning. Ideally teachers also coordinate their plans with colleagues—for example, identifying common goals toward which they'll all strive or developing interdisciplinary units that involve two or more classes and subject areas. And they regularly share their plans and goals with their students.

## IDENTIFYING THE GOALS OF INSTRUCTION

An essential step in planning instruction is to identify the specific things students should accomplish during a lesson or unit, as well as the things they should accomplish over the course of a semester or school year. Educators use a variety of terms for such end results, including *goals, objectives, proficiencies, targets, benchmarks,* and *outcomes.* For example, each chapter in this book begins with *learning outcomes* that have guided my writing and can help readers anticipate and organize the chapter's various topics. In my discussion here, however, I'll typically use the term instructional goals when referring to desired general, long-term outcomes of instruction. I'll use the term instructional objectives when referring to more specific outcomes of a particular lesson or unit.

Consistent with the concept of *backward design,* identifying instructional goals and objectives should be the very first step in the instructional planning process. Our instructional strategies *must* be dictated by our short- and long-term goals for students' learning.[4] Students, too, benefit from knowing our goals and objectives. When they know what we hope they'll accomplish, they can make more informed decisions about how to focus their efforts and allocate their study time, and they can more effectively monitor their comprehension as they read and study (Gronlund & Brookhart, 2009; McAshan, 1979). For example, if we tell students that we expect them to apply mathematics concepts and procedures to practical, real-world situations, they'll probably think about and study math quite differently than if we tell them—or in some way imply—that they should rote-memorize definitions and formulas (a learning strategy I certainly don't recommend!).

## ALIGNING INSTRUCTIONAL GOALS WITH NATIONAL, INTERNATIONAL, AND STATE STANDARDS

People have varying opinions about the kinds of things students should learn in elementary and secondary school classrooms. For example, you may have heard people advocating for increasing students' knowledge of basic facts—a perspective sometimes called *back to the basics* or *cultural literacy* (e.g., Hirsch, 1996). Certainly some factual knowledge is essential for students' long-term academic and professional success. But equally important are the complex cognitive processes (e.g., problem solving, critical thinking) and general *habits of mind* (e.g., scientific reasoning, drawing inferences from historical documents) that are central to various academic disciplines (P. A. Alexander, 1997; Bransford et al., 2009; Brophy, 2008; R. K. Sawyer, 2006).

One source of guidance comes from content-area standards identified by national and international discipline-specific professional groups (e.g., National Council of Teachers of English, National Council for Geographic Education). Such standards are typically in the form of general statements regarding the knowledge and skills that students should acquire at various grade levels, as well as the characteristics that their accomplishments should reflect. Also, in the United States, state departments of education—as well as some local school districts—have

---

[4]Jay McTighe has posted helpful templates for a backward-design approach to instructional planning at jaymctighe.com

**instructional goal**  Desired long-term outcome of instruction.

**instructional objective**  Desired outcome of a lesson or unit

**standards**  General statements regarding the knowledge and skills that students should gain and the characteristics that their accomplishments should reflect.

MyEducationLab™

Find both national- and state-level standards for various content domains in MyEducationLab™.

**Common Core State Standards**
Set of standards that most U.S. states have adopted to guide instruction and assessment in English-language arts and mathematics (see www.corestandards.org).

established comprehensive lists of standards in reading, writing, math, science, and social studies and sometimes in such domains as art, music, foreign languages, and physical education. In addition, most states in the U.S. have jointly adopted a set of Common Core State Standards in mathematics and English language arts; you can find these on the Internet at www.corestandards.org. Table 12.1 presents examples of reading skills identified in the Common Core State Standards for English Language Arts, along with instructional strategies potentially useful in helping students acquire those skills.

Existing standards for particular content domains are certainly useful in helping us focus instruction on important educational goals (e.g., McDonald, Robles-Piña, & Polnick, 2011).

# DEVELOPMENTAL TRENDS

**TABLE 12.1 • Examples of How You Might Align Instructional Strategies with Common Core State Standards at Different Grade Levels**

| GRADE LEVEL | EXAMPLES OF COMMON CORE STANDARDS FOR ENGLISH LANGUAGE ARTS | EXAMPLES OF INSTRUCTIONAL STRATEGIES THAT ADDRESS THESE STANDARDS |
|---|---|---|
| Grade 2 | Ask and answer such questions as *who, what, where, when, why,* and *how* to demonstrate understanding of key details in a text. (RL.2.1)[a] | During "settling down" time immediately after lunch each day, read a chapter of a high-interest children's novel, stopping frequently to ask questions that require students to go beyond the text itself (e.g., ask students to speculate about what a character might be feeling). |
| Grade 2 | Recount stories, including fables and folktales from diverse cultures, and determine their central message, lesson, or moral. (RL.2.2) | Have several students create props for and act out a story they have recently read, with other class members serving as the audience. Follow up with a class discussion of important lessons that one or more story characters might have learned from events or challenges that they faced. |
| Grade 4 | Refer to details and examples in a text when explaining what the text says explicitly and when drawing inferences from the text. (RL.4.1). | As a reading group discusses Carl Hiaasen's *Hoot,* ask students to speculate about how the plot might progress and to identify clues in the text that support their predictions. |
| Grade 4 | Explain events, procedures, ideas, or concepts in a historical, scientific, or technical text, including what happened and why, based on specific information in the text. (RI.4.3) | When students are reading a chapter in their history textbook, ask *why* questions that encourage cause-and-effect connections (e.g., "Why did Columbus's crew want to sail back to Europe after several weeks on the open sea?"). |
| Grade 7 | Analyze the structure an author uses to organize a text, including how the major sections contribute to the whole and to the development of the ideas. (RI.7.5) | Before students read a chapter in their science textbook, have them use its headings and subheadings to (1) create a general outline of the chapter and (2) generate questions they hope to answer as they read the chapter. Then, for homework, ask them to read and take notes on the chapter, using the outline and self-questions as guides for note taking. |
| Grade 7 | Trace and evaluate the argument and specific claims in a text, assessing whether the reasoning is sound and the evidence is relevant and sufficient to support the claims. (RI.7.8) | Give students an advertisement for a self-improvement product (e.g., a diet pill or exercise equipment); have them work in small cooperative learning groups to (1) identify the advertiser's motives and (2) evaluate the quality of evidence for the product's effectiveness. |
| Grades 11–12 | Analyze and evaluate the effectiveness of the structure an author uses in his or her position or argument, including whether the structure makes points clear, convincing, and engaging. (RI.11–12.5) | Describe common techniques in persuasive writing, and have students identify the various persuasive techniques used in newspaper editorials. |
| Grades 11–12 | Determine an author's point of view or purpose in a text in which the rhetoric is particularly effective, analyzing how style and content contribute to the power, persuasiveness or beauty of the text. (RI.11–12.6) | Ask students to identify the unstated assumptions underlying two news magazines' depictions of the same event (e.g., an assumption that one group is good or right and another is bad or wrong). |

[a]The letters "RL" indicate standards related to reading literature; the letters "RI" indicate standards related to reading informational text. The number or numbers before the period indicate the grade level; the number after the period indicates the particular standard for that grade level. For example, the first entry shown here, identified as "RL.2.1," is the first standard for grade 2 for reading literature.

*Source:* Excerpts from *Common Core State Standards.* Copyright © 2010 by National Governors Association for Best Practices and Council of Chief State School Officers. Reprinted with permission. All rights reserved.

However, such standards have several limitations to keep in mind. First, many are based on topics and skills that are *typically taught* at various grade levels, rather than on developmental research concerning what students can reasonably accomplish at different ages (T. M. McDevitt & Ormrod, 2013; vanSledright & Limón, 2006). Second, some sets of standards are so lengthy that they might lead us to provide only fragmented, superficial coverage of topics, rather than follow the *less-is-more* principle so important for conceptual understanding (M. C. Linn, 2008; Schmidt, 2008). But perhaps most importantly, these standards largely overlook goals that lie *outside* particular content areas—productive learning strategies, self-regulation techniques, effective reading and critical analysis of Internet postings, good social skills, and so on.

## WRITING USEFUL GOALS AND OBJECTIVES

Given the limitations of existing content-area standards, we can't rely on them exclusively: We must also develop some of our own goals and objectives. Ideally we should identify goals and objectives that provide concrete guidance as we plan instructional activities and assessment procedures. The Into the Classroom feature "Identifying Appropriate Goals and Objectives" offers suggestions for writing useful ones.

An especially important suggestion in the Into the Classroom feature is to *include goals and objectives with varying levels of complexity and sophistication.* One tool that can help us keep a broad view of what students should learn and be able to do is a 2001 revision of **Bloom's taxonomy**, a list of six general cognitive processes that vary in complexity:

1. *Remember:* Recognizing or recalling information learned at an earlier time and stored in long-term memory
2. *Understand:* Constructing meaning from instructional materials and messages (e.g., drawing inferences, identifying new examples, summarizing)
3. *Apply:* Using knowledge in a familiar or new situation
4. *Analyze:* Breaking information into its constituent parts and perhaps also identifying interrelationships among the parts
5. *Evaluate:* Making judgments about information using certain criteria or standards
6. *Create:* Putting together knowledge, procedures, or both to form a coherent, structured, and possibly original whole (L. W. Anderson et al., 2001)[5]

Another helpful taxonomy can be found in *Understanding by Design* (Wiggins & McTighe, 2005), a popular resource for guiding teachers through the backward-design process. This taxonomy identifies six forms ("facets") that students' understanding of a topic might take:

1. *Explanation:* Integrating various bits of information into meaningful wholes (e.g., knowing the *hows* and *whys* of various facts and principles), and using this knowledge to support opinions
2. *Interpretation:* Identifying the underlying meanings of events, data, documents, and works of art and literature
3. *Application:* Using acquired knowledge in new situations and diverse contexts
4. *Perspective:* Critically and insightfully analyzing information, and identifying underlying assumptions and implications
5. *Empathy:* Looking at a situation or issue from another person's vantage point, perhaps based on the person's feelings or general worldview
6. *Self-knowledge:* Identifying gaps in one's own understandings, as well as personal prejudices that might bias one's views and interpretations

Neither of the preceding taxonomies are exhaustive lists of what students should be able to do while learning classroom subject matter; for example, they don't include psychomotor skills. Nor do the particular sequences of items necessarily reflect a progression from simpler to more complex processes (L. Anderson et al., 2001; Iran-Nejad & Stewart, 2010; Marzano & Kendall, 2007). Even so, the taxonomies can certainly remind us that there's much more to school learning

Chapter 6 explains the *less-is-more* principle.

Find three classic taxonomies (including Bloom's original taxonomy) in the supplementary reading "Using Taxonomies to Formulate Instructional Goals and Objectives."

These items might remind you of concepts described elsewhere in the book: conceptual understanding (Item 1; see Chapter 6), critical thinking (Items 2 and 4; see Chapter 7), transfer (Item 3; see Chapter 7), perspective taking (Item 5; see Chapter 3), and metacognition (Item 6; see Chapter 7).

---

[5]Bloom's original taxonomy uses nouns rather than verbs: *knowledge, comprehension, application, analysis, synthesis, evaluation.* In the revision shown here, *create* replaces and subsumes *synthesis,* and *evaluate* moves from sixth to fifth place.

**Bloom's taxonomy**   Taxonomy of six cognitive processes, varying in complexity, that lessons might be designed to foster.

## Into the Classroom

### Identifying Appropriate Goals and Objectives

🍏 **Consult state, national, and international standards, but don't rely on them exclusively.**
In identifying instructional goals for the year, a middle school science teacher considers both the state science standards and the standards developed by the National Academy of Sciences. In addition, he identifies specific goals related to two issues directly affecting many students in his inner-city school district: air pollution and poor nutrition.

🍏 **Be realistic about what can be accomplished in a given time frame; allow time to pursue important topics in depth.**
Rather than expect students to remember a lot of discrete facts in social studies, a second-grade teacher identifies several "Big Ideas" students should master during the school year—for instance, the ideas that (1) all people have certain needs and desires that affect their behaviors and (2) different cultural groups may strive to satisfy those needs and desires in different ways.

🍏 **Identify both short-term objectives and long-term goals.**
A fourth-grade teacher wants students to learn how to spell 10 new words each week. She also wants them to write a coherent and grammatically correct short story by the end of the school year.

🍏 **In addition to goals related to specific topics and content areas, identify goals related to students' general long-term academic success.**
A middle school teacher knows that early adolescence is an important time for developing the learning and study strategies students will need in high school and college. Throughout the school year, he continually introduces new strategies for learning and remembering classroom subject matter—for example, effective ways to organize class notes, mnemonic techniques for remembering important facts, and self-questions to answer while reading a textbook chapter.

🍏 **Include goals and objectives with varying levels of complexity and sophistication.**
A high school physics teacher wants students not only to understand basic kinds of machines (e.g., levers, wedges) but also to recognize examples in their own lives and to use the machines to solve real-world problems.

🍏 **Consider physical, social, motivational, and affective outcomes as well as cognitive outcomes.**
A physical education teacher wants his students to know the basic rules of basketball and to dribble and pass the ball appropriately.

He also wants them to acquire a love of basketball, effective ways of working cooperatively with teammates, and a general desire to stay physically fit.

🍏 **Describe goals and objectives not in terms of what the teacher will do during a lesson but in terms of what *students* should be able to do at the *end* of instruction—and, ideally, also in ways that point to appropriate assessment tasks.**
A Spanish teacher knows that students often confuse the verbs *estar* and *ser* because both are translated into English as "to be." She identifies this objective for her students: "Students will correctly conjugate *estar* and *ser* in the present tense and use each one in appropriate contexts." She assesses students' ability to use the two verbs correctly through both paper–pencil quizzes and in-class conversations.

🍏 **When writing short-term objectives, identify specific behaviors that will reflect accomplishment of the objectives.**
In a unit on the food pyramid, a health teacher identifies this objective for students: "Students will create menus for a breakfast, lunch, and dinner that, in combination, include all elements of the pyramid in appropriate proportions."

🍏 **When writing long-term goals that involve complex topics or skills, list a few abstract outcomes and give examples of specific behaviors that reflect each one.**
Faculty members at a middle school identify this instructional goal for all students at their school: "Students will demonstrate effective listening skills, for example by taking thorough and accurate notes, answering teacher questions correctly, and seeking clarification when they don't understand."

🍏 **Provide opportunities for students to identify goals and objectives of their own.**
A high school art teacher asks students to choose a particular medium they'd each like to focus on during the semester (e.g., pastels, oils, clay) and to identify at least three skills they want to improve while working with the chosen medium. She helps students develop concrete goals toward which they'll work and specific criteria they can use to evaluate their progress.

*Sources:* Brophy, 2008; Brophy et al., 2009; N. S. Cole, 1990; Gronlund & Brookhart, 2009; M. D. Miller, Linn, & Gronlund, 2009; Pellegrino, Chudowsky, & Glaser, 2001; Popham, 1995; Wiggins & McTighe, 2005.

and academic achievement than remembering discrete facts. More detailed, comprehensive taxonomies—which are too complex to present here—can provide additional guidance (e.g., see Marzano & Kendall, 2007).

## CONDUCTING A TASK ANALYSIS

In addition to identifying goals and objectives for instruction, we need to determine how best to break down complex topics and skills into manageable chunks. Consider these four teachers:

- Ms. Begay, a third-grade teacher, plans to teach her students how to solve arithmetic word problems. She also wants to help them learn more effectively from reading materials.

- Mr. Marino, a middle school physical education teacher, wants his students to develop enough proficiency in basketball to feel comfortable playing either on organized basketball teams or in pick-up games in their neighborhoods.

- Mr. Wu, a junior high school music teacher, hopes to teach his new trumpet students how to play "Seventy-Six Trombones" in time for the New Year's Day parade.

- Ms. Flores, a high school social studies teacher, is going to introduce her students to the intricacies of the federal judicial system.

**task analysis** Process of identifying the specific behaviors, knowledge, or cognitive processes necessary to master a particular topic or skill.

All four teachers want to teach complex topics or skills. Accordingly, each of them should conduct a task analysis, identifying the essential behavioral or cognitive aspects of mastering a particular topic or skill. The task analyses can then guide the teachers in selection of appropriate methods and sequences in which to teach the subject matter.

Figure 12.3 illustrates three general approaches to task analysis (Jonassen, Hannum, & Tessmer, 1989; also see R. E. Clark, Feldon, van Merriënboer, Yates, & Early, 2008):

- *Behavioral analysis.* One way of analyzing a complex task is to identify the specific behaviors required to perform it (much as a behaviorist might do). For example, Mr. Marino can identify the specific physical movements involved in dribbling, passing, and shooting a basketball. Similarly, Mr. Wu can identify the behaviors students must master in order to play a trumpet, such as how to correctly hold the instrument and how to blow into the mouthpiece.

Identify the specific behaviors required to perform a task.

- *Subject matter analysis.* Another approach is to break down the subject matter into the specific topics, concepts, and principles that it includes. For example, Ms. Flores can identify various aspects of the judicial system (concepts such as *innocent until proven guilty* and *reasonable doubt,* the roles that judges and juries play, etc.) and their interrelationships. And Mr. Wu can identify the basic elements of written music that his trumpet students must be able to interpret, such as the treble and bass clefs and whole, half, and quarter notes. Subject matter analysis is especially important when the subject matter being taught includes many interrelated concepts and ideas that students should learn meaningfully and with conceptual understanding.

Break down the subject matter in terms of specific topics, ideas, concepts, and so on.

- *Information processing analysis.* A third approach is to specify the cognitive processes involved in a task. To illustrate, Ms. Begay can identify the mental processes involved in successfully solving a word problem—for instance, correct encoding of the problem (e.g., determining whether it requires addition, subtraction, etc.) and rapid retrieval of basic number facts. She can also identify specific cognitive strategies useful in reading comprehension, such as finding main ideas, elaborating, and summarizing.

Break down a task in terms of the specific cognitive processes it requires.

To get an idea of what a task analysis involves, try the next exercise.

**FIGURE 12.3  Three ways of analyzing a task**

| BEHAVIORAL ANALYSIS | SUBJECT MATTER ANALYSIS | INFORMATION PROCESSING ANALYSIS |
|---|---|---|
| Playing basketball | Reading music | Solving a word problem |
| • Dribbling<br>• Passing<br>• Shooting<br>• Rebounding<br>• etc... | • Treble & bass clefs<br>• Measures<br>• Whole, half, & quarter notes<br>• Sharps & flats<br>• etc... | • Defining the problem<br>• Identifying appropriate operations<br>• Retrieving relevant number facts<br>• Applying operations<br>• etc... |

## EXPERIENCING FIRSTHAND
### PEANUT BUTTER SANDWICH

Conduct a task analysis for the process of making a peanut butter sandwich, as follows:

1. Decide whether your approach should be a behavioral analysis, a subject matter analysis, or an information processing analysis.
2. Using the approach you've selected, break the sandwich-making task into a number of small, teachable steps.
3. (Optional) If you're hungry and have the necessary materials close at hand, make an actual sandwich following the steps you've identified. Did your initial analysis omit any important steps?

Chances are good that you chose a behavioral analysis, because making a peanut butter sandwich is largely a behavioral rather than a mental task. For example, you must know how to unscrew the lid of a peanut butter jar, get an appropriate amount of peanut butter on your knife, and spread the peanut butter gently enough that you don't tear the bread.

Conducting task analyses for complex skills and topics has at least two advantages (Desberg & Taylor, 1986; Jonassen et al., 1989; Stokes, Luiselli, & Reed, 2010). First, when we identify a task's specific components—whether behaviors, concepts and ideas, or cognitive processes—we gain a better sense of what things students need to learn and the order in which to most effectively learn them. Second, a task analysis helps us choose appropriate instructional strategies. For example, if one necessary component of solving arithmetic word problems is rapid retrieval of math facts from long-term memory, repeated practice of the facts may be critical for developing automaticity. If another aspect of such problem solving is identifying the relevant procedure to apply (addition, subtraction, etc.), we must promote a true understanding of math concepts and principles, perhaps by using concrete manipulatives or authentic activities.

Sometimes a task analysis will lead us to conclude that we can most effectively teach a complex task by initially teaching some or all of its components separately. For instance, Mr. Wu may first ask his beginning trumpet students to practice blowing into the mouthpiece correctly without worrying about the specific notes they produce. On other occasions, however, it may be more appropriate to teach the desired knowledge and behaviors entirely within the context of the overall task; by doing so, we make the subject matter more meaningful for students. For example, Ms. Begay should almost certainly teach her students the processes involved in learning effectively from reading materials—elaborating, summarizing, and so on—primarily within the context of authentic reading tasks.

## DEVELOPING A LESSON PLAN

After identifying goals for instruction and perhaps also conducting a task analysis, effective teachers develop one or more lesson plans to guide them during instruction. A lesson plan typically includes the following:

- The goal(s) or objective(s) of the lesson
- Instructional materials (e.g., textbooks, handouts, software programs) and equipment required
- Specific instructional strategies and the sequence in which they'll be used
- Assessment method(s) planned

Any lesson plan should, of course, take into account the students who will be learning—their developmental levels, prior knowledge, cultural backgrounds, and so on.

As a beginning teacher, you'll probably want to develop fairly detailed lesson plans that describe how you're going to help your students learn the subject matter in question (Calderhead, 1996; Sternberg & Horvath, 1995). For instance, when I began teaching middle school geography—and also when I began teaching college psychology—I spent many hours each week writing down the information, examples, questions, and student activities I wanted to use during the following week. But as you gain experience teaching certain topics, you'll learn which strategies

---

MyEducationLab™

Use the Lesson Plan Builder to guide you as you create lesson plans appropriate for your age-group and subject matter.

**lesson plan** Predetermined guide for a lesson that identifies instructional goals or objectives, necessary materials, instructional strategies, and one or more assessment methods.

work effectively and which do not, and you may use some of the effective ones frequently enough that you can retrieve them quickly and easily from long-term memory. Consequently, as time goes on, you'll find that planning lessons becomes far less time consuming and that you can do a lot of your planning mentally rather than on paper.

In planning lessons, we teachers have many resources at our disposal, including experienced teachers' lesson plans in books and on the Internet. For example, the following websites offer lesson plans and related materials concerning a wide range of topics:

- Smithsonian Institution (www.smithsonianeducation.org)
- Educator's Reference Desk (www.eduref.org)
- Discovery Education (school.discoveryeducation.com)

In taking advantage of such resources, however, we must always keep in mind that *lessons should be closely tied to instructional goals and objectives.*

Generally speaking, a lesson plan is a guide rather than a recipe: It can and should be adjusted as events unfold. For example, during the course of a lesson, we may find that we need to back up and teach material we'd mistakenly assumed students had already mastered. And if students express considerable curiosity or have intriguing insights about a particular topic, we might want to capitalize on this unique opportunity—this teachable moment—and spend more time exploring the topic than originally planned.

As we proceed through the school year, our long-range plans may also change to some degree. For instance, we may find that our initial task analyses of certain topics are overly simplistic, or we may discover that our initial expectations for students' achievement are either unrealistically high or unnecessarily low. Both short-term and long-term lesson planning, then, must continue to be a work in progress.

## CREATING A CLASS WEBSITE TO SHARE GOALS AND FACILITATE COMMUNICATION THROUGHOUT THE SCHOOL YEAR

A traditional practice at the secondary and college levels is to give students a printed syllabus that lists course topics, instructional goals, homework assignments, due dates, and scheduled assessments. But increasingly teachers at all levels are sharing such information—and much more—on class-specific Internet websites within their school's overall website. In the K–12 grades, students' parents typically have access to these websites as well.

Figure 12.4 shows the opening screen for a website my son Jeff created for his sixth-grade humanities (IT) class at Prem Tinsulanonda International School in Thailand. Notice that the course resources include two documents—a course outline and assessment criteria—that students can download. Scrolling farther down in the website, students learn about instructional goals for the class, get detailed information about various units and assignments, and find many more downloadable documents. Students can also interact in a class-specific electronic *chat room,* and they upload their completed assignments to the website. Jeff created the site using software called Moodle (moodle.org); similar software is available through Sakai (sakaiproject.org).

Class websites provide one easy way for us to communicate regularly with students and their parents. They can't be the *only* way, however. Not all students and parents have easy access to computers and the Internet at home. And some individuals—parents especially—may simply not have the technology skills they need to access and navigate through an Internet website. Accordingly, we should also provide hard copies of assignments we want students to do as homework and information we want parents to know.

**teachable moment** Situation or event (often unplanned) in which students might be especially predisposed to acquire particular knowledge or skills.

**expository instruction** Approach to instruction in which information is presented in essentially the same form in which students are expected to learn it.

In your first few months of teaching, create fairly detailed lesson plans to guide you, but be flexible when circumstances call for adjustments.

**FIGURE 12.4** Opening screen of a website for a sixth-grade humanities class

*Source:* Screenshot courtesy of Jeffrey Ormrod. Copyright © by Jeffrey Ormrod. Reprinted with permission of the author.

## Teacher-Directed Instructional Strategies

Teacher-directed instruction can include a variety of strategies. Much of it involves expository instruction, in which information is presented (i.e., *exposed*) in essentially the same form in which students are expected to learn it. Ms. Minichiello's lesson about the Oregon Trail has several

**lower-level question** Question that requires students to retrieve and recite what they have learned in essentially the same way they learned it.

elements of expository instruction: She presents the dimensions of a typical covered wagon, distributes reading materials about how the settlers packed for the long trip west, and shows photographs of pioneer families and their temporary covered-wagon homes.

Yet as we'll see in upcoming sections, teachers can direct students' learning in other ways as well—for instance, by asking questions that get students thinking in particular ways or by assigning tasks that require students to practice and apply new skills.

## PRESENTING NEW MATERIAL THROUGH TRADITIONAL EXPOSITORY METHODS: LECTURES AND TEXTBOOKS

Some theorists have criticized lectures and textbooks for putting students in a physically passive role (e.g., B. F. Skinner, 1968). But cognitive psychologists argue that students are often *mentally* active during such seemingly passive activities as listening and reading (Ausubel, Novak, & Hanesian, 1978; R. E. Mayer, 2011a; Weinert & Helmke, 1995). The degree to which students learn from expository instruction depends on the particular cognitive processes they engage in—the extent to which they pay attention, focus on meaningful rather than rote learning, self-monitor their comprehension, and so on.

Unfortunately, lectures and textbooks don't always present information in ways that promote learning. For instance, you can probably think of high school or college instructors whose lectures were dry, disorganized, confusing, or in some other way unmotivating and noninformative. And analyses of school textbooks in such diverse disciplines as history, geography, and science have found the focus of many texts to be on teaching specific facts, with little attention to helping students learn the facts in a meaningful way (I. L. Beck & McKeown, 1994, 2001; Brophy et al., 2009; M. C. Linn & Eylon, 2011).

The Into the Classroom feature "Using Expository Instruction Effectively" suggests several research-based strategies for promoting productive cognitive processes through explanations, lectures, and other expository approaches. Expository instruction has a distinct advantage: It enables us to present information quickly and efficiently. By itself, however, it doesn't allow us to assess students' progress in learning the subject matter. Whenever possible, then, we should use it in combination with other instructional strategies—perhaps asking questions and having students apply what they're studying in in-class and homework assignments.

## ASKING QUESTIONS AND GIVING FEEDBACK

Some teacher questions are **lower-level questions** that ask students to retrieve information in their existing knowledge base. Such questions have several benefits:

Ask lower-level questions to check for basic understanding and recall.

- They give us a good idea of students' current understandings and misconceptions about a topic.
- They help keep students' attention on the lesson in progress.
- They help us assess whether students are learning class material successfully or, instead, are confused about particular points. (Even very experienced teachers sometimes overestimate what students are actually learning during expository instruction.)
- They give students the opportunity to monitor their *own* comprehension—to determine whether they understand the information being presented or, instead, should ask for help or clarification.
- When students are asked questions about material they've studied at an earlier time, they must review that material, which should promote greater recall later on. (Airasian, 1994; Brophy, 2006; F. W. Connolly & Eisenberg, 1990; P. W. Fox & LeCount, 1991; Wixson, 1984)

Following is an example of how one eighth-grade teacher promoted review of a lesson on ancient Egypt by asking questions:

Teacher questions can simultaneously foster both learning and motivation. For example, watch "Properties of Air" and "Scarlet Letter."

> *Teacher:* The Egyptians believed the body had to be preserved. What did they do to preserve the body in the earliest times?
>
> *Student:* They dried them and stuffed them.
>
> *Teacher:* I am talking about from the earliest times. What did they do? Carey.
>
> *Carey:* They buried them in the hot sands.

## Into the Classroom

### Using Expository Instruction Effectively

🍏 **Use an advance organizer—a verbal or graphic introduction that lays out the general organizational framework of upcoming material—to help students make meaningful connections among the things they learn.**

A high school biology teacher introduces a unit on vertebrates by saying, "Vertebrates all have backbones. We'll be talking about five phyla of vertebrates—mammals, birds, reptiles, amphibians, and fish—that differ from one another in several ways, including whether their members are warm-blooded or cold-blooded; whether they have hair, scales, or feathers; and whether they lay eggs or bear live young."

🍏 **Make ongoing connections between new information and things students already know, perhaps by drawing analogies between abstract ideas and students' everyday experiences.**

A middle school geography teacher draws an analogy between how a glacier grows and how pancake batter behaves as it's poured into a frying pan: "As more and more substance is added to the middle, the edges spread farther and farther out."

🍏 **Informally assess students' existing understandings of the topic to determine whether they have misconceptions that require conceptual change.**

When beginning a unit on the solar system, a fourth-grade teacher asks her students, "What do we mean when we say that the sun *sets*? Does the sun really go down at the end of the day?" Several students respond that the sun does indeed go down and then travels to the other side of the world. The teacher isn't surprised (as this is a common misconception) but works hard to show students that the earth's rotation gives the appearance of the sun moving around it, when actually the opposite is true: The earth revolves around the sun.

🍏 **Present new ideas in a logical, organized manner that enables students to make appropriate interconnections among them.**

While describing the contributions of different vitamins and minerals to people's health and well-being, a ninth-grade health teacher writes each nutrient and its benefits in a two-column table on the whiteboard.

🍏 **Give students numerous signals about the things that are most important for them to learn and remember.**

A high school government teacher begins a unit about the U.S. government system by writing the phrase "Checks and Balances" on the board and underlining it with big, bold strokes. "This is a key principle that guided delegates to the Constitutional Convention as they wrote the Constitution. We're going to look at how each of the three branches of government—executive, legislative, and judicial—places limits on the power of the other two branches. Be sure to include at least four examples of checks and balances in your class notes for today." Later in the class session, the teacher assigns a textbook chapter for homework and distributes a list of questions that students should be able to answer after they've finished reading the chapter.

🍏 **Use visual aids to help students encode material visually as well as verbally.**

In a lesson on the Oregon Trail, a fifth-grade teacher shows photographs of wagon trains and typical covered wagons to help students get a sense of how arduous the westward migration was for many pioneer families.

🍏 **Pace your presentation slowly enough to give students adequate time to think about and meaningfully process the information.**

To demonstrate how to make a pinch pot from a ball of clay, an elementary school art teacher proceeds through the steps slowly and deliberately, explaining what he's doing every step of the way: "First I roll the clay into a nice round ball—as round as I can make it, with no cracks or rough edges. . . . Okay, see how I've done that? Now I hold the ball in both hands and gently push my thumbs into the middle, slowly pushing them farther and farther in, but being sure that I don't push them out the other side of the ball. . . . And then I gradually push the sides of the ball outward, continually turning the ball so that I make the sides of my pot an even thickness all the way around."

🍏 **At the end of a lecture or reading assignment, summarize key points as a way of helping students organize the material and identify its main ideas.**

A high school English teacher sums up a lesson on the poems of Emily Dickinson by describing the characteristics that make Dickinson's poetry so unique and powerful.

*Sources:* Bulgren, Deshler, Schumaker, & Lenz, 2000; Carney & Levin, 2002; Corkill, 1992; Dansereau, 1995; Donnelly & McDaniel, 1993; Edmonds et al., 2009; E. L. Ferguson & Hegarty, 1995; Hansen & Pearson, 1983; J. Hartley & Trueman, 1982; Krajcik, 1991; Ku, Chan, Wu, & Chen, 2008; J. R. Levin & Mayer, 1993; M. C. Linn, Songer, & Eylon, 1996; Lorch, Lorch, & Inman, 1993; R. E. Mayer, 1989, 2010a; R. E. Mayer & Gallini, 1990; M. A. McDaniel & Einstein, 1989; Morra, Gobbo, Marini, & Sheese, 2008; Newby, Ertmer, & Stepich, 1994; Pittman & Beth-Halachmy, 1997; R. E. Reynolds & Shirey, 1988; Sadoski & Paivio, 2001; Scevak, Moore, & Kirby, 1993; M. Y. Small, Lovett, & Scher, 1993; Tennyson & Cocchiarella, 1986; Verdi & Kulhavy, 2002; Wade, 1992; P. T. Wilson & Anderson, 1986; Winn, 1991; Wittwer & Renkl, 2008; Zook, 1991; Zook & Di Vesta, 1991.

*Teacher:* Right. They buried them in the hot sands. The sand was very dry, and the body was naturally preserved for many years. It would deteriorate more slowly, at least compared with here. What did they do later on after this time?

*Student:* They started taking out the vital organs.

*Teacher:* Right. What did they call the vital organs then?

*Norm:* Everything but the heart and brain.

*Teacher:* Right, the organs in the visceral cavity. The intestines, liver, and so on which were the easiest parts to get at.

*Teacher:* Question?

*Student:* How far away from the Nile River was the burial of most kings? (Aulls, 1998, p. 62)

**advance organizer** Introduction to a lesson that provides an overall organizational scheme for the lesson.

**higher-level question** Question that requires students to use previously learned information in a new way—that is, to engage in complex cognitive processes.

At the end of the dialogue, a *student* asks a question, one that requests additional information. The student is apparently trying to elaborate on the material, perhaps speculating that only land a fair distance from the Nile would be dry enough to preserve bodies for a lengthy period. We can encourage such elaboration, as well as more complex cognitive processes, by asking higher-level questions—those that require students to expand on the information they've learned (Brophy, 2006; Minstrell & Stimpson, 1996; Redfield & Rousseau, 1981). For instance, a higher-level question might ask students to think of their own examples of a concept, use a newly learned principle to solve a problem, or speculate about possible explanations for a cause–and–effect relationship. As an illustration, when a science class is studying the nature of air pressure at different altitudes, a teacher might describe the following scenario in Rocky Mountain National Park, which has altitudes ranging from 1½ to more than 2 miles above sea level:

Ask higher-level questions to encourage elaboration and complex cognitive processes such as problem solving and critical thinking.

> A group of Girl Scouts went hiking in Rocky Mountain National Park. They noticed that it was harder to breathe when hiking in the mountains than when hiking in [hometown]. During the hike, one girl opened a tube of suntan lotion that she bought in [hometown]. When she opened it, a small squirt of air and lotion shot out.

> - Why did the girls have a hard time breathing?
> - Why did the air and lotion squirt out of the tube? (Pugh, Schmidt, & Russell, 2010, p. 9)

Often we can simultaneously pose questions to *all* of our students. For example, we might ask a multiple-choice question and have students "vote" on various answers by raising their hands, holding up premade response cards, or using hand-held electronic clickers that send signals to the class computer (Lambert, Cartledge, Heward, & Lo, 2006; R. E. Mayer et al., 2009; Munro & Stephenson, 2009). However, we must give students adequate time to think about our questions and retrieve information relevant to possible answers. We must remember, too, that students from some cultural and ethnic backgrounds may intentionally allow several seconds to elapse before responding as a way of being courteous and showing respect for the speaker (Castagno & Brayboy, 2008; M. B. Rowe, 1987; Tharp, 1989).

The importance of such *wait time* is discussed in more detail in Chapters 4 and 6.

Unless we specifically want to have students deliberate about particular issues over a lengthy period, we should, of course, give them feedback about their responses to our questions. Furthermore, we must help students save face when an initial response is incorrect, perhaps by gently nudging them toward a better one. For example, in an elementary school lesson on the food pyramid, a student incorrectly answered that orange juice was a member of the "milk" group, and his teacher nudged him in the right direction with these hints:

A Creating a Productive Classroom Environment box in Chapter 9 offers additional strategies for giving feedback.

> Everything in the milk group comes from a cow. What does orange juice come from? . . . Orange juice comes from oranges. If it comes from oranges, which group is oranges? . . . Is it fruit or bread? (Brophy et al., 2009, p. 225)

## PROVIDING PRACTICE THROUGH IN-CLASS ASSIGNMENTS

Prioritize assignments based on their relevance to important instructional goals.

When we choose or create assignments for students, our number-one criterion must be to help students accomplish important instructional goals. Some goals may be at the *remember* or *understand* level in Bloom's taxonomy—for example, correctly conjugating the French verb *être* ("to be") or showing knowledge of current events around the globe. Other goals will be higher-level ones—for example, writing a well-organized persuasive essay or applying scientific principles to everyday phenomena and problems.

Especially when higher-level goals are involved, we should assign tasks that help students learn classroom material in a meaningful, integrated manner. Often we'll want to assign authentic activities, perhaps within the context of small cooperative groups in which students can share ideas, ask one another questions, and offer explanations of their thinking. Because authentic activities are typically less structured and more complex than traditional classroom tasks, they're apt to require a good deal of teacher scaffolding (Hmelo-Silver, 2006; Mergendoller, Markham, Ravitz, & Larmer, 2006; van Merriënboer, Kirschner, & Kester, 2003).

It usually isn't a good idea to fill the entire curriculum with authentic tasks, however. For one thing, students can often master basic skills more effectively when they practice them in relative isolation from more complex activities (J. R. Anderson, Reder, & Simon, 1996). For example, when learning to play the violin, students need to master their fingering before they join an orchestra, and when learning to play softball, students need to practice hitting, throwing, and catching the ball before they can have an enjoyable game. In addition, some authentic tasks are too expensive and time consuming to warrant regular use in the classroom (Bereiter & Scardamalia, 2006; M. M. Griffin & Griffin, 1994). It's probably most important that assignments encourage effective cognitive processing (e.g., organization, elaboration) and that students understand the relevance of what they're learning for larger tasks they'll face down the road (J. R. Anderson et al., 1996; Bransford et al., 2006).

Regardless of whether assignments are authentic or more traditional ones, we're most likely to facilitate students' learning and achievement when we:

🍏 Clearly define each task and its purpose.

🍏 Stimulate interest and cognitive engagement in the task.

🍏 Begin at an appropriate difficulty level—ideally by assigning tasks that challenge students to "stretch" their existing knowledge and skills; accommodate diversity in students' abilities and needs. (Vygotsky's concept of *zone of proximal development* is helpful here.)

🍏 Increase difficulty and complexity—or perhaps gradually decrease scaffolding—as students gain proficiency.

🍏 Frequently monitor students' progress and give feedback that promotes further growth.

🍏 Assess students' work in ways that reward high quality but also allow for experimentation and risk taking.

🍏 Encourage students to reflect on and evaluate their own work. (Brophy et al., 2009; W. Doyle, 1983; Dymond, Renzaglia, & Chun, 2007; Edelson & Reiser, 2006)

When assigning tasks for students to complete at school, we might occasionally ask them to use various *computer tools,* as illustrated in the following examples:

- Word processing programs can enhance the quality of students' essays and short stories (e.g., see Figure 12.5).

- Database programs can help students organize information about trees or planets.

- Spreadsheets can enable students to predict changes in weather patterns or declines in endangered species populations.

- Concept mapping and brainstorming software can help students generate and organize ideas as they study for a test or write a research paper.

- Music editors let students create musical compositions and experiment with different notes, keys, instrumental sounds, and time signatures.

- With geographic mapping software (known as *geographic information systems software,* or *GIS*), students can map data on pollutants or environmental wetlands. (Egbert, 2009; Guinee, 2003; P. F. Merrill et al., 1996; Sitko, 1998)

We must keep in mind, however, that such tools are most likely to be effective when students have already acquired some automaticity in keyboarding and other basic computer skills. Have students use computer tools to complete tasks in various content domains.

## GIVING HOMEWORK

Students can accomplish only so much during class time, and homework provides a means through which we can extend the school day. On some occasions we may want to use homework to give students extra practice with familiar information and procedures (perhaps as a way of promoting review and automaticity) or to introduce them to new but simple material (H. Cooper, 1989). In other situations we might give homework assignments that ask students to apply classroom material to their outside lives. For example, in a unit on lifestyle patterns, we might ask second graders to compare their own homes with homes of earlier time periods (e.g., caves, log

**FIGURE 12.5** Darren, a fifth grader who struggles with reading and writing, wrote this very cohesive paragraph with the help of a word processing program. A spell checker enabled him to spell most, but not all, of the words correctly. (He meant to use *very* and *sight*, not *vary* and *site*.)

> When I was young it was almost impossible to read. One of my teachers told me I could learn to read if I worked hard. Learning to read was like climbing Mount Rushmore. It took a very long time but I finally got it. My Mom said she was vary proud. Reading was hard for me. It took five years for me to learn to read. Every day I would go to the learning center to learn my 400 site words. It was hard for me to learn these words but I did it. Reading is one of the most important things I have learned so far in my life.

🍏 Assign homework to enhance automaticity of basic knowledge and skills, encourage review, introduce students to new but relatively simple material, or help students make connections between classroom subject matter and the outside world.

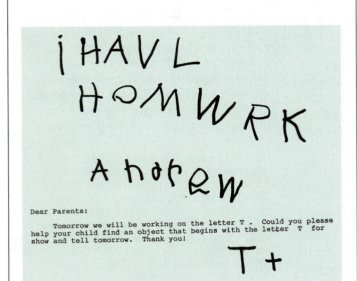

Dear Parents:

Tomorrow we will be working on the letter T . Could you please help your child find an object that begins with the letter T for show and tell tomorrow. Thank you!

T+

Young children don't always have the self-regulation skills they need to complete homework on their own. Six-year-old Andrew and his teacher jointly constructed the homework reminder shown here.

Remember that some students have few resources at home to help them complete homework assignments.

See Chapter 11 for a discussion of self-determination as an important factor in motivation.

Giving extra homework as punishment for misbehavior communicates the message that schoolwork is unpleasant (see Chapter 9).

**direct instruction** Approach to instruction that uses a variety of techniques (e.g., explanations, questions, guided and independent practice) in a fairly structured manner to promote learning of fundamental knowledge and skills.

cabins) and to identify modern conveniences that make their lives easier and more comfortable (Alleman & Brophy, 1998). On still other occasions we might encourage students to bring items or ideas from home (e.g., small biological specimens from the neighborhood, information about family ancestry) and use them as the basis for in-class activities (Alleman et al., 2010; Corno, 1996). When we ask students to make connections between classroom material and the outside world through homework assignments, we're potentially promoting transfer.

Doing homework appears to have a greater effect on achievement in the middle school and high school grades than in the elementary grades (H. Cooper, Robinson, & Patall, 2006). Although homework in the elementary grades may not enhance achievement very much, it can help students develop some of the study strategies and self-regulation skills they'll need in later years (H. Cooper & Valentine, 2001; Zimmerman, 1998). Without doubt, the *quality* of homework assignments—for instance, whether they encourage rote memorization, on the one hand, or meaningful learning and elaboration, on the other—makes an appreciable difference both in what and how much students learn and in what kinds of learning and self-regulating strategies they develop (Dettmers, Trautwein, Lüktke, Kunter, & Baumert, 2010; Trautwein, Lüdtke, Kastens, & Köller, 2006).

For many students, doing homework isn't an intrinsically enjoyable activity. These students are more likely to do homework because they want to please their teacher or stay out of trouble than because they want to master a topic (Trautwein & Lüdtke, 2007; J. M. T. Walker, 2001; Xu, 2008). Yet even when students are intrinsically motivated to complete homework, not all of them have the self-regulation skills they need to stay on task at home (Bembenutty & Karabenick, 2004; Eilam, 2001; Fries, Dietz, & Schmid, 2008). Furthermore, some students may have few resources (e.g., reference books, computers, etc.) and little or no family support to enable them to complete certain kinds of assignments (H. Cooper, 1989; Garbe & Guy, 2006; Hoover-Dempsey et al., 2001). With these issues in mind, I offer the following guidelines:

- Use assignments primarily for instructional and diagnostic purposes; minimize the degree to which homework is used to assess learning and determine final class grades.
- Make homework sufficiently intriguing and challenging that students *want* to complete it; for example, give it an authentic, real-world quality, but don't make it so difficult that it leaves students confused and frustrated.
- Provide the information and structure students need to complete assignments with little or no assistance from others.
- Give a mixture of required and voluntary assignments. (Voluntary ones should help to give students a sense of personal control and self-determination, enhancing their intrinsic motivation.)
- Discuss homework assignments in class the following day or as soon after that as possible.
- When students have poor self-regulation skills or limited resources at home, establish supervised after-school homework programs. (Alleman et al., 2010; Belfiore & Hornyak, 1998; H. Cooper, 1989; Cosden, Morrison, Albanese, & Macias, 2001; Dettmers et al., 2011; Garbe & Guy, 2006; Patall, Cooper, & Wynn, 2010; Trautwein et al., 2006; Trautwein, Niggli, Schnyder, & Lüdtke, 2009)

We should remember, too, that homework is appropriate only to help students achieve important educational goals—*never* to punish students for misbehavior.

## CONDUCTING DIRECT INSTRUCTION

**Direct instruction** incorporates all of the preceding strategies—expository instruction, asking questions, providing feedback, and giving in-class assignments and homework—to keep students continually and actively engaged in learning and applying classroom subject matter. To some extent, direct instruction is based on behaviorist ideas: It requires learners to make frequent responses and provides immediate reinforcement of correct responses through teacher feedback. But it also capitalizes on principles from cognitive psychology, including the importance of attention and long-term memory storage processes in learning, the limited capacity of working memory, and the value of learning basic skills to automaticity (Rosenshine & Stevens, 1986).

Various experts describe and implement direct instruction somewhat differently. But in general, this approach involves small and carefully sequenced steps, fast pacing, and a great deal of teacher–student interaction. Each lesson typically involves most or all of the following components (Rosenshine, 2009; Rosenshine & Stevens, 1986):

1. *Review of previously learned material.* The teacher reviews relevant content from previous lessons, checks homework assignments involving that content, and reteaches any information or skills that students haven't yet mastered.

2. *Statement of the current lesson's objectives.* The teacher describes one or more concepts or skills that students should master in the lesson.

3. *Presentation of new material in small, logically sequenced steps.* The teacher presents a small amount of information or a specific skill, perhaps through a verbal explanation, modeling, and one or more examples. The teacher may also provide an advance organizer, ask questions, or in other ways scaffold students' efforts to process and remember the material.

4. *Guided student practice and assessment after each step.* Students have numerous opportunities to practice what they're learning, perhaps by answering questions, solving problems, or performing modeled procedures. The teacher gives hints during students' early responses, provides immediate feedback about their performance, makes suggestions about how to improve, and provides additional instruction as needed. After students have completed guided practice, the teacher checks to be sure they've mastered the information or skill in question, perhaps by having them summarize what they've learned or answer a series of follow-up questions.

5. *Independent practice.* Once students have demonstrated some degree of competence, they engage in further practice either independently or in small cooperative groups. By doing so, they work toward achieving automaticity for the material in question.

6. *Frequent follow-up reviews.* Over the course of the school year, the teacher provides opportunities for students to review previously learned material, perhaps through homework assignments, writing tasks, or quizzes.

> Explicitly teach basic skills, giving lots of scaffolded practice and frequent feedback. As students gain competence, provide less-structured practice activities.

The teacher moves back and forth among these steps as necessary to ensure that all students are truly comprehending the subject matter.

Direct instruction is most suitable for teaching information and skills that are well defined and best taught in a step-by-step sequence (Rosenshine & Stevens, 1986; Spiro & DeSchryver, 2009). Because of the high degree of teacher–student interaction, it's often implemented more easily with small groups or in one-on-one tutoring sessions. Especially in such circumstances, it can lead to substantial gains in achievement (Rittle-Johnson, 2006; Watkins, 1997; Weinert & Helmke, 1995). Using direct instruction *exclusively* may be too much of a good thing, however, particularly if we don't vary instructional methods to maintain students' interest and engagement—for instance, if we just present one drill-and-practice worksheet after another (Mac Iver, Reuman, & Main, 1995; Wasley, Hampel, & Clark, 1997).

## PROMOTING MASTERY

Imagine that a class of 27 students, listed in Figure 12.6, is beginning a unit on fractions. The class progresses through several lessons as follows:

*Lesson 1:* The class studies the basic idea that a fraction represents a part of a whole: The denominator indicates the number of pieces into which the whole has been divided, and the numerator indicates how many of those pieces are present. By the end of the lesson, 23 children understand what a fraction is. But Sarah, LaShaun, Jason K., and Jason M. are either partly or totally confused.

*Lesson 2:* The class studies the process of reducing fractions to lowest terms (e.g., $^{12}/_{20}$ can be reduced to $^{3}/_{5}$). By the end of the lesson, 20 children understand this process.

**FIGURE 12.6** How the sequential and hierarchical nature of knowledge about fractions can affect students' learning

| Students | Lesson 1: Concept of Fraction | Lesson 2: Reducing to Lowest Terms (Builds on Lesson 1) | Lesson 3: Adding Fractions with Same Denominators (Builds on Lesson 1) | Lesson 4: Adding Fractions & Reducing to Lowest Terms (Builds on Lessons 2 & 3) |
|---|---|---|---|---|
| Sarah | ---> | ---> | ---> | ---> |
| LaShaun | ---> | ---> | ---> | ---> |
| Jason K. | ---> | ---> | ---> | ---> |
| Jason M. | ---> | ---> | ---> | ---> |
| Alison | → | ---> | → | ---> |
| Reggie | → | ---> | → | ---> |
| Jason S. | → | ---> | → | ---> |
| Matt | → | → | ---> | ---> |
| Charlie | → | → | ---> | ---> |
| Maria F. | → | → | ---> | ---> |
| Maria W. | → | → | ---> | ---> |
| Muhammed | → | → | → | ---> |
| Aretha | → | → | → | ---> |
| Karen | → | → | → | ---> |
| Kevin | → | → | → | → |
| Nori | → | → | → | → |
| Marcy | → | → | → | → |
| Janelle | → | → | → | → |
| Joyce | → | → | → | → |
| Ming Tang | → | → | → | → |
| Georgette | → | → | → | → |
| LaVeda | → | → | → | → |
| Mark | → | → | → | → |
| Seth | → | → | → | → |
| Joanne | → | → | → | → |
| Rita | → | → | → | → |
| Shauna | → | → | → | → |

To promote mastery, break the subject matter into small, logically sequenced units, assess students' mastery of each one, and provide additional instruction and practice as needed.

But Alison, Reggie, and Jason S. haven't mastered the idea that they need to divide both the numerator and denominator by the same number. Sarah, LaShaun, and the other two Jasons still don't understand what fractions *are* and therefore have trouble with this lesson as well.

*Lesson 3:* The class studies the process of adding two fractions that have equal denominators (e.g., $^1/_{20} + {}^{11}/_{20} = {}^{12}/_{20}$). By the end of the lesson, 19 children can add fractions with the same denominator. But Matt, Charlie, Maria F., and Maria W. keep adding the denominators together as well as the numerators (e.g., figuring that $^1/_{20} + {}^{11}/_{20} = {}^{12}/_{40}$). And Sarah, LaShaun, Jason K., and Jason M. still don't know what fractions actually are.

*Lesson 4:* The class combines the processes of adding fractions and reducing fractions to lowest terms. They must first add two fractions together and then, if necessary, reduce the sum to its lowest terms (e.g., after adding $^1/_{20} + {}^{11}/_{20}$, they must reduce the sum of $^{12}/_{20}$ to $^3/_5$). Here we lose Muhammed, Aretha, and Karen because they keep forgetting to reduce the sum to its lowest terms. And of course, we've already lost Sarah, LaShaun, Alison, Reggie, Matt, Charlie, the two Marias, and the three Jasons on prerequisite skills. *We now have 13 of our original 27 students understanding what they're doing—less than half the class* (see the rightmost column of Figure 12.6).

**Mastery learning**—a variation of direct instruction in which students must demonstrate competence in one topic before proceeding to the next—minimizes the likelihood of leaving some students behind as we proceed to increasingly challenging material (e.g., Bloom, 1981; Guskey, 1985, 2010; Zimmerman & Didenedetto, 2008). This approach is based on three assumptions:

- Almost every student can learn a particular topic to mastery.
- Some students need more time to master a topic than others.
- Some students need more assistance than others.

As you can see, mastery learning represents a very optimistic approach to instruction: It assumes that most children *can* learn school subject matter if given sufficient time and instruction to do so.[6]

In general, mastery learning includes the following components:

1. *Small, discrete units.* The subject matter is broken up into numerous lessons, with each lesson covering a small amount of material and aimed at accomplishing only a very small number of instructional objectives.
2. *A logical sequence.* Units are sequenced so that basic, foundational concepts and procedures are studied before more complex ones.
3. *Demonstration of mastery at the end of each unit.* Students move to a new unit only after they show mastery of the preceding one (e.g., by taking a quiz). Mastery is defined in specific, concrete terms (e.g., answering at least 90% of quiz items correctly).
4. *Additional activities for students needing extra help or practice to attain mastery.* Support and resources are tailored to individual needs and might include alternative approaches to instruction, different materials, specially tailored assignments, study groups, or individual tutoring.

Students engaged in mastery learning often proceed through units at their own speed; hence different students may be studying different units at any given time. But it's also possible for an entire class to proceed through a sequence at the same rate: Students who master a unit more quickly than their classmates can pursue various enrichment activities, or they can serve as tutors for those still working on the unit (Block, 1980; Guskey, 1985).

The various elements of mastery learning are consistent with several theoretical perspectives. Behaviorists tell us that complex behaviors are often acquired more easily through *shaping,*

**mastery learning** Approach to instruction in which students learn one topic thoroughly before moving to a subsequent one.

---

[6]Don't confuse mastery *learning* with mastery *goals.* Here we're talking about an instructional strategy. In contrast, mastery goals are an aspect of motivation: They reflect students' focus on gaining competence in the subject matter rather than on, say, simply getting a good grade.

whereby a simple response is reinforced until it occurs frequently (i.e., until it's mastered), then a slightly more difficult response is reinforced, and so on. Cognitive psychologists point out that information and skills that need to be retrieved rapidly or used in complex problem-solving situations must be practiced sufficiently to ensure automaticity. And as social cognitive theorists have noted, the ability to perform a particular task successfully and easily is likely to enhance students' sense of self-efficacy for performing similar tasks.

Researchers have found mastery learning to have several advantages over nonmastery approaches. In particular, students tend to have a better attitude toward the subject matter, learn more, and perform at higher levels on classroom assessments. The benefits are especially striking for low-ability students (Guskey, 2010; Hattie, 2009; C. C. Kulik, Kulik, & Bangert-Drowns, 1990; Shuell, 1996). Mastery learning is most appropriate when the subject matter is hierarchical in nature—that is, when certain concepts and skills provide the foundation for future learning. If instructional goals deal with such basics as word recognition, rules of grammar, arithmetic, or key scientific concepts, instruction designed to promote mastery learning may be in order. However, the very notion of mastery may be irrelevant to some long-term instructional goals. For example, skills related to critical thinking, scientific reasoning, and creative writing may continue to improve throughout childhood and adolescence without ever being completely mastered.

## USING INSTRUCTIONAL WEBSITES

Internet search engines such as Google, Bing, and Yahoo! enable students and teachers to find instructional websites on virtually any topic. Many of these websites take the form of **hypermedia**, collections of both visual and auditory material related to a particular topic (text, diagrams, photographs, spoken messages, videos, etc.).

A good general informational resource is Wikipedia (www.wikipedia.org), an ever-expanding online encyclopedia to which virtually anyone can contribute about a limitless number of topics. Also, many government offices, public institutions, and private associations have websites that provide information, mini-lessons, and links to other relevant websites. Following are just a few of the innumerable possibilities:

U.S. Geological Survey: www.usgs.gov

U.S. Census Bureau: www.census.gov

National Aeronautic and Space Administration: www.nasa.gov

National Museum of Natural History: www.mnh.si.edu

The Knowledge Loom: www.knowledgeloom.org

Discovery Channel: school.discovery.com

Web-based Scientific Inquiry Environment (WISE): wise.berkeley.edu

One especially noteworthy website is Khan Academy (www.khanacademy.org), which offers a large and growing collection of instructional videos on a wide variety of topics in math, science, history, civics, economics, and art. For example, the screenshot shown in Figure 12.7 is from a series of engaging animated videos called "Genetics 101," in which students learn about genes, deoxyribonucleic acid (DNA), X and Y chromosomes, and related topics.

Keep in mind, however, that students don't always have the self-regulation skills and technological literacy they need to learn effectively as they explore the many resources the Internet offers (Azevedo & Witherspoon, 2009; Warschauer, 2011; Winters, Greene, & Costich, 2008). Furthermore, the Internet doesn't have a good quality-control mechanism to ensure that information is accurate, especially when posted by individuals rather than by government agencies or professional organizations. (For example, entries in Wikipedia, although generally accurate, occasionally include inaccuracies added by nonexperts, and some individuals may intentionally "rewrite" history or science to advance a particular personal or political agenda.) An additional concern is that some students may venture into unproductive domains, perhaps finding research papers

**hypermedia** Interlinked collection of computer-based, multimedia instructional materials (e.g., text, pictures, sound, animations) that students can examine in a sequence of their own choosing.

**FIGURE 12.7** In Khan Academy's animated video "Genetics 101 Part 1: What are genes?," students learn about the basic nature of genes and DNA. *Note:* All Khan Academy content is available for free at www.khanacademy.org.

they can pass off as their own (this is plagiarism), stumbling upon sites that preach racist attitudes or offer pornographic images, or sharing personal information with people who might jeopardize their well-being (Nixon, 2005; Schofield, 2006).

Clearly, then, students often need considerable scaffolding as they study a particular topic online, and their journeys into cyberspace should be closely monitored. Even in the secondary grades, students are apt to need considerable guidance about how to distinguish between helpful and unhelpful websites, sift through mountains of information in search of tidbits most relevant to their own purposes, critically evaluate the quality of the information they're finding, and synthesize what they discover into a cohesive, meaningful whole (Afflerbach & Cho, 2010; Egbert, 2009; Leu, O'Byrne, Zawilinski, McVerry, & Everett-Cacopardo, 2009).

One helpful strategy is to post links to suitable Internet sites on a class website. We might also give students explicit instructional objectives they need to accomplish as they conduct Internet searches—for instance, by giving them specific questions to which they need to find answers (Niederhauser, 2008). Also, many school computer systems now include a *remote desktop* feature that can help us both scaffold and monitor students' use of the Internet. With this feature, we can share our own computer screen with students and demonstrate how to use a search engine, explore various websites, and so on. The feature also allows us to view every student's computer screen from afar. If a particular student goes astray, we can lock the student's screen and send an appropriate message.

## USING TECHNOLOGY TO INDIVIDUALIZE INSTRUCTION

The Internet provides limitless ways in which we can individualize instruction to match students' ability levels, interests, and needs. For instance, students can pursue personal interests through in-depth Internet searches, and many high schools now give credit for online courses offered by universities or accredited agencies. Also, many instructional software programs—sometimes known as computer-based instruction—are specifically designed to take individual differences into account. Historically, such programs were based largely on behaviorist principles of active responding, shaping, and reinforcement: Students progressed through a series of lockstep computer frames that presented small amounts of new information, asked for responses to questions, and then provided feedback. More contemporary programs typically reflect cognitivist principles as well as those of behaviorism: They capture and hold students' attention with engaging tasks and graphics, encourage meaningful learning, and present diverse examples and practice exercises that promote such complex cognitive processes as problem solving, critical thinking, and scientific reasoning. Students tend to remain physically and cognitively engaged with such programs, in large part because they must continually respond to questions and problems.

Some instructional software programs provide drill and practice of basic knowledge and skills (e.g., math facts, typing, fundamentals of music), helping students develop automaticity in these areas. Others, known as intelligent tutoring systems, skillfully guide students through complex subject matter and can anticipate and address a wide variety of misconceptions and learning difficulties (e.g., Koedinger & Corbett, 2006; VanLehn, 2011; Woolf, 2009). Still others teach and scaffold complex study strategies, metacognitive skills, and self-regulation (Azevedo & Witherspoon, 2009; Graesser, McNamara, & VanLehn, 2005; Koedinger, Aleven, Roll, & Baker, 2009; Quintana, Zhang, & Krajcik, 2005; Wade-Stein & Kintsch, 2004).

Well-designed programs are often quite effective in helping students learn academic subject matter (H. S. Kim & Kamil, 2004; Slavin & Lake, 2008; Tamin et al., 2011). They can also be highly motivating, piquing situational interest, and giving students the independence and frequent successes that can enhance their feelings of self-determination and competence (Blumenfeld, Kempler, & Krajcik, 2006; Snir, Smith, & Raz, 2003; Swan, Mitrani, Guerrero, Cheung, & Schoener, 1990).

A downside of computer-based instruction is that, although it may sometimes include online student discussions, it gives students few opportunities for face-to-face social interaction and thus may do little to address students' need for relatedness (A. Collins & Halverson, 2009; Winn, 2002). Yet it offers several advantages that we often don't have with other approaches. For one thing, computer-based instructional programs can seamlessly include animations, video clips, and spoken messages—components that aren't possible with traditional printed materials. Second, a computer can record and maintain ongoing data for every student, including such

---

Chapter 8 offers suggestions for promoting students' technological literacy skills.

Scaffold students' early research on the Internet, and monitor their explorations to ensure that they don't venture into inappropriate websites and subject matter.

Figure 7.6 in Chapter 7 presents an example of an intelligent tutoring system—AnimalWatch—that teaches both math and science skills in an authentic context.

**computer-based instruction (CBI)** Academic instruction provided by means of specially designed computer software.

**intelligent tutoring system** Computer software program that provides individually tailored instruction and practice, plus ongoing guidance and feedback, related to a particular topic and set of skills.

information as how far each of them has progressed in a program, how quickly they respond to questions, and how often they're right and wrong. With such data we can monitor each student's progress and identify students who appear to be struggling with the material. Finally, a computer can be used to provide instruction when flesh-and-blood teachers aren't available—for instance, in distance learning, in which learners receive much or all of their technology-based instruction at a location far away from that of their instructor.

To the extent that instructional websites and software programs give students control over the information they get and the order in which they get it, they're really midway along the teacher-directed–learner-directed continuum. We now turn to strategies that are even more learner-directed in nature.

## Learner-Directed Instructional Strategies

By definition, learner-directed instruction places control of learning activities largely in students' hands. Yet for all but the most self-regulating of students, learner-directed instruction requires *some* teacher control and guidance, as we'll see in the upcoming sections.

### STIMULATING AND GUIDING CLASS DISCUSSIONS

When students exchange ideas in whole-class or small-group discussions, they must elaborate on and organize their thoughts, may discover gaps and inconsistencies in their understandings, and may encounter explanations that are more accurate and useful than their own (e.g., D. W. Johnson & Johnson, 2009b; Sinatra & Mason, 2008; C. L. Smith, 2007). Class discussions can be fruitful in virtually any academic discipline. For example, in language arts, students might discuss various interpretations of classic works of literature, addressing questions with no easy answers and possibly finding parallels to their own lives (Applebee, Langer, Nystrand, & Gamoran, 2003; Eeds & Wells, 1989; L. M. McGee, 1992). In science classes, discussions of various and conflicting explanations of observed phenomena can enhance scientific reasoning skills, promote conceptual change, and help students understand that science is a dynamic and continually evolving set of concepts and principles, rather than just a collection of discrete facts (P. Bell & Linn, 2002; K. Hogan, Nastasi, & Pressley, 2000; M. C. Linn, 2008). And in mathematics, discussions that focus on alternative approaches to solving the same problem can promote more complete understandings, more creative problem solutions, and greater transfer to new situations and problems (M. M. Chiu, 2008; Cobb et al., 1991; Webb et al., 2008).

Although students typically do most of the talking in class discussions, teachers play critical roles, as illustrated in the following guidelines.

🍏 *Focus on topics that lend themselves to multiple perspectives, explanations, or approaches.* Such topics appear to have several benefits: Students are more likely to express their opinions, seek out new information that resolves seemingly contradictory data, reevaluate their positions on issues, and develop a meaningful and well-integrated understanding of the subject matter (Applebee et al., 2003; Jadallah et al., 2011; Sinatra & Mason, 2008; C. L. Smith, 2007).

🍏 *Make sure students have enough prior knowledge about a topic to discuss it intelligently.* This knowledge might come either from previous class sessions or from students' personal experience. Often it comes from studying a particular topic in depth (Bruning, Schraw, & Ronning, 1995; Onosko, 1996).

🍏 *Create a classroom atmosphere conducive to open debate and the constructive evaluation of ideas.* Students are more likely to share their ideas and opinions if their teacher is supportive of multiple viewpoints and if disagreeing with classmates is socially acceptable (A.-M. Clark et al., 2003; Hadjioannou, 2007; Walshaw & Anthony, 2008). The following strategies can promote such an atmosphere:

  🍏 Communicate that understanding a topic at the end of a discussion is more important than having a correct answer at the beginning of it.

  🍏 Communicate that asking questions reflects curiosity, that differing perspectives on a controversial topic are both inevitable and healthy, and that changing one's opinion on a topic is a sign of thoughtful reflection.

distance learning Technology-based instruction in which students are at a location physically separate from that of their instructor.

Learners' beliefs about the nature of science is an example of an *epistemic belief* (see Chapter 7).

- Encourage students to explain and justify their reasoning and to try to understand one another's explanations.
- Suggest that students build on one another's ideas whenever possible.
- Encourage students to be open in their agreement or disagreement with classmates—that is, to agree to disagree.
- Stress that, although it's acceptable to critique ideas, it *isn't* acceptable to criticize people.
- When students' perspectives reflect misconceptions or errors in reasoning, gently guide them toward more productive understandings.
- Depersonalize challenges to a student's line of reasoning by framing questions in a third-person voice—for example, "What if someone were to respond to your claim by saying . . . ?"
- Occasionally ask students to defend a position that is the opposite of what they actually believe.
- Require students to develop compromise solutions that take into account opposing perspectives. (Cobb & Yackel, 1996; Hadjioannou, 2007; Hatano & Inagaki, 1993, 2003; Herrenkohl & Guerra, 1998; K. Hogan et al., 2000; D. W. Johnson & Johnson, 2009b; Lampert, Rittenhouse, & Crumbaugh, 1996; Nussbaum, 2008; Staples, 2007; Walshaw & Anthony, 2008; Webb et al., 2008)

When students become comfortable with disagreeing in a congenial way, they often find the interactions highly motivating (Certo, 2011; A.-M. Clark et al., 2003; Hadjioannou, 2007). One fourth grader, whose class regularly had small-group discussions about literature, put it this way:

> I like it when we get to argue, because I have a big mouth sometimes, and I like to talk out in class, and I get really tired of holding my hand up in the air. Besides, we only get to talk to each other when we go outside at recess, and this gives us a chance to argue in a nice way. (A.-M. Clark et al., 2003, p. 194)

Small-group and whole-class discussions can be effectively combined into a single lesson. For example, watch *"Scarlet Letter."*

- *Create a class discussion board or chat room that enables students to converse about a topic or issue both in and out of school.* Such electronic mechanisms can be integral parts of a class website and—if students have Internet access at home—can easily extend the school day. Students should understand, however, that the rules for in-class discussions apply to electronic discussions as well. For example, students must accept that varying perspectives are both welcome and to be expected, and although they can certainly critique their classmates' ideas, they must do so respectfully and without ridicule (Bellanca & Stirling, 2011).

- *Use small-group discussions as a way of encouraging all students to participate.* Students gain more from a class discussion when they actively participate in it (Lotan, 2006; P. K. Murphy, Wilkinson, Soter, Hennessey, & Alexander, 2009; A. M. O'Donnell, 1999). And they're more likely to speak openly when their audience is a handful of classmates rather than the class as a whole—a difference especially noticeable for girls and for students with disabilities (A.-M. Clark et al., 2003; Théberge, 1994). On some occasions, then, we may want to have students first discuss an issue in small groups—thereby allowing them to test and possibly gain support for their ideas in a relatively private context—before bringing them together for a whole-class discussion (Minstrell & Stimpson, 1996; Onosko, 1996).

- *Provide a structure to guide the discussion.* Discussions are more productive when they have some sort of structure. For example, we might do the following:

  - Set a particular goal toward which students should work.
  - Assign different roles to different class members (e.g., some might evaluate the quality of evidence presented, others might evaluate the validity of conclusions, etc.).
  - Before conducting an experiment, ask students to make and defend predictions about what will happen; later, ask them to explain what actually happened and why. (I. L. Beck & McKeown, 2001; Calfee, Dunlap, & Wat, 1994; Hatano & Inagaki, 1991; Herrenkohl & Guerra, 1998; Nolen, 2011; Palincsar & Herrenkohl, 1999; C. L. Smith, 2007; B. Y. White & Frederiksen, 1998)

At the same time, we must recognize that the most effective group discussions are often those in which students have some control over the direction of discourse—perhaps asking their own questions, initiating new issues related to the topic, or taking a creative but risky approach or viewpoint (Aulls, 1998; M. M. Chiu, 2008; K. Hogan et al., 2000). Learner-directed discussions are also more likely to encourage effective group interaction skills (R. C. Anderson et al., 2001). For example, when elementary school students meet in small, self-directed groups to discuss children's literature, they can develop and model such skills as expressing agreement ("I agree with Kordell because . . ."), disagreeing tactfully ("Yeah, but they could see the fox sneak in"), justifying an opinion ("I think it shouldn't be allowed, because if he got to be king, who knows what he would do to the kingdom"), and seeking everyone's participation ("Ssshhh! Be quiet! Let Zeke talk!") (R. C. Anderson et al., 2001, pp. 16, 25; Certo, 2011; A.-M. Clark et al., 2003).

Ultimately, the amount of structure we impose must depend on how much scaffolding students need to have a productive discussion. For instance, we may want to be more directive with a small discussion group that seems to be unfocused and floundering than with one in which students are effectively articulating, critiquing, and building on one another's ideas (K. Hogan et al., 2000).

🍏 *Provide closure at the end of the discussion.* Even when the topic of discussion has no single right answer, a class discussion should have some form of closure that helps students tie various ideas together. For example, when I conduct discussions about controversial topics in my own classes, I spend a few minutes at the end of class summarizing important ideas that students have identified. Another, more learner-directed approach is to have students themselves summarize the key issues; their thoughts might be written on an interactive whiteboard and then uploaded to the class website.

## CONDUCTING RECIPROCAL TEACHING SESSIONS

Student discussions not only encourage students to think about and process classroom subject matter more thoroughly but can also promote more effective metacognitive strategies during reading and listening activities (A. L. Brown & Reeve, 1987; P. K. Murphy, Wilkinson, & Soter, 2011; Nussbaum, 2008). One form of discussion, reciprocal teaching, is especially effective in this regard. It focuses on promoting four metacognitive strategies:

- *Summarizing:* Identifying the gist and main ideas of a reading passage.
- *Questioning:* Asking oneself questions to make sure one understands a reading passage—that is, engaging in comprehension monitoring.
- *Clarifying:* Taking active steps to make sense of confusing or ambiguous parts of a passage, perhaps by rereading or making logical inferences.
- *Predicting:* Anticipating what is likely to come next based on cues in the text (e.g., headings) and ideas that have already been presented. (A. L. Brown & Palincsar, 1987; Palincsar & Brown, 1984, 1989; Palincsar & Herrenkohl, 1999)

In a typical reciprocal teaching session, a teacher and several students meet in a group to read a piece of text, occasionally stopping to discuss what they're reading. Initially the teacher leads the discussion, asking questions about the text to promote summarizing, questioning, clarifying, and predicting. But gradually the role of "teacher" is turned over to different students, who then take charge of the discussion and ask one another the kinds of questions their teacher has modeled. Eventually students can read and discuss a text almost independently of their teacher: They work together to construct meaning and check one another for comprehension and possible misunderstandings, and they become increasingly flexible in how they apply their newly acquired strategies (A. L. Brown & Palincsar, 1987; Palincsar & Herrenkohl, 1999).

In most instances of reciprocal teaching, students take turns reading sections of the text being discussed. Sometimes, however, the teacher reads the text, especially when working with novice readers. As an illustration, let's look at a reciprocal teaching session in which six first graders and their teacher are discussing a text about snowshoe rabbits. The teacher has just read a description of a mother rabbit giving birth to and caring for several babies. In the discussion that follows, a student named Kam takes the role of "teacher." As you read the dialogue, look for

🍏 When reading a story or textbook with students, ask questions that promote summarizing, questioning, clarifying, and predicting. Gradually turn the role of teacher over to students.

**reciprocal teaching** Approach to fostering reading and listening comprehension skills in which students take turns asking teacherlike questions of classmates.

examples of summarizing, questioning, clarifying, and predicting—there's at least one instance of each.

*Kam:* When was the babies born?

*Teacher:* That's a good question to ask. Call on someone to answer that question.

*Kam:* Robby? Milly?

*Milly:* Summer.

*Teacher:* What would happen if the babies were born in the winter? Let's think.

[Several children make a number of responses, including "The baby would be very cold," "They would need food," "They don't have no fur when they are just born."]

*Kam:* I have another question. How does she get the babies safe?

*Kris:* She hides them.

*Kam:* That's right, but something else. . . .

*Teacher:* There is something very unusual about how she hides them that surprised me. I didn't know this.

*Travis:* They are all in a different place.

*Teacher:* Why do you think she does this?

*Milly:* Probably because I heard another story, and when they're babies they usually eat each other or fight with each other.

*Teacher:* That could be! And what about when that lynx comes?

[Several children comment that that would be the end of all the babies.]

*Travis:* If I was the mother, I would hide mine, I would keep them all together.

*Kris:* If the babies are hidden and the mom wants to go and look at them, how can she remember where they are?

*Teacher:* Good question. Because she does have to find them again. Why? What does she bring them?

*Milly:* She needs to bring food. She probably leaves a twig or something.

*Teacher:* Do you think she puts out a twig like we mark a trail?

[Several children disagree and suggest that she uses her sense of smell. One child, recalling that the snowshoe rabbit is not all white in the winter, suggests that the mother might be able to tell her babies apart by their coloring.]

*Teacher:* So we agree that the mother rabbit uses her senses to find her babies after she hides them. Kam, can you summarize for us now?

*Kam:* The babies are born in the summer. . . .

*Teacher:* The mother . . .

*Kam:* The mother hides the babies in different places.

*Teacher:* And she visits them . . .

*Kam:* To bring them food.

*Travis:* She keeps them safe.

*Teacher:* Any predictions?

*Milly:* What she teaches her babies . . . like how to hop.

*Kris:* They know how to hop already.

*Teacher:* Well, let's read and see. (Used courtesy of A. Palincsar)[7]

Reciprocal teaching provides a mechanism through which both the teacher and the students can model effective reading and learning strategies; hence this approach has an element of social cognitive theory. But when we consider that we're encouraging effective cognitive processes by first

---

[7]Excerpt by Annmarie Palincsar. Copyright © by Annemarie Palincsar. Reprinted with permission of the author.

having students practice them aloud in group sessions, we realize that Vygotsky's theory of cognitive development is also at work here: Students should eventually *internalize* processes they first use in their discussions with others. Furthermore, the structured nature of a reciprocal teaching session scaffolds students' efforts to make sense of what they read and hear. For example, in the preceding dialogue the teacher models elaborative questions and connections to prior knowledge (e.g., "What would happen if the babies were born in the winter?") and provides general guidance and occasional hints about how students should cognitively process the text ("Kam, can you summarize for us now?"). Also notice in the dialogue how students support one another in their efforts to make sense of what they are learning (e.g., Kam says, "That's right, but something else").

Reciprocal teaching promotes more effective reading and listening comprehension skills in students at all grade levels, and in English language learners as well as native English speakers (Alfassi, 2004; Johnson-Glenberg, 2000; K. D. McGee, Knight, & Boudah, 2001; Palincsar & Brown, 1989; Rosenshine & Meister, 1994; Slater, 2004). In an early study of reciprocal teaching (Palincsar & Brown, 1984), six seventh graders with a history of poor reading comprehension participated in 20 reciprocal teaching sessions, each lasting about 30 minutes. Despite this relatively short intervention, students showed remarkable improvement in their reading comprehension skills. Furthermore, they generalized their new reading strategies to other classes, sometimes surpassing the achievement of their classmates (A. L. Brown & Palincsar, 1987; Palincsar & Brown, 1984).

We shouldn't think of reciprocal teaching as something that only reading teachers use. It's also been successfully used in science classes (where teachers have adapted it for whole-class discussions of passages in science textbooks) and math classes (where teachers have adapted it to help students make sense of complex word problems) (A. L. Brown & Palincsar, 1987; van Garderen, 2004). Furthermore, reciprocal teaching sessions can be conducted online as well as in the classroom (Reinking & Leu, 2008). Effectively using reciprocal teaching may take some practice, however. It may also require a concerted effort to make sure that students do, in fact, generate and model higher-level questions as well as lower-level ones (e.g., Hacker & Tenent, 2002).

## CONDUCTING DISCOVERY AND INQUIRY ACTIVITIES

When student discussions revolve around assigned reading materials (as is true for the preceding reciprocal teaching session about snowshoe rabbits), they obviously have an element of expository instruction. In **discovery learning**, however, students derive information for *themselves*—perhaps by randomly exploring and manipulating objects or perhaps by performing systematic experiments. Hands-on discovery experiences can often convey ideas that language alone can't fully communicate. For example, in the excerpt from a lab report shown in Figure 12.8, 10-year-old Berlinda describes what she has learned about anatomy from a small-group dissection of several pig organs. Notice how her focus is largely on how the various organs *felt* when she touched them.

In his early theory of cognitive development, Jean Piaget suggested that effective discovery learning should be largely a child-initiated and child-directed effort. However, researchers are finding that in classroom settings, students typically benefit more from carefully planned and structured activities that help them construct appropriate interpretations (Alfieri, Brooks, Aldrich, & Tenenbaum, 2011; M. C. Brown, McNeil, & Glenberg, 2009; Hardy, Jonen, Möller, & Stern, 2006; R. E. Mayer, 2004).

A variation of discovery learning, **inquiry learning**, typically has the goal of helping students acquire more effective *reasoning processes* either instead of or in addition to acquiring new information. For example, to help students learn to separate and control variables in scientific investigations, we might have them design and conduct experiments related to, say, factors affecting how fast a pendulum swings or how far a ball travels after rolling down an incline. And we might foster critical thinking skills in history by having students read historical documents with the mind-set that they are reading *interpretations* rather than facts and therefore must look for evidence that either supports or disconfirms those interpretations. Such activities can often promote more advanced reasoning skills, especially when combined with appropriate instruction and scaffolding (Kuhn, 2007; Levstik, 2011; Lorch et al., 2010; Monte-Sano, 2008).

**discovery learning** Approach to instruction in which students construct their own knowledge about a topic through firsthand interaction with an aspect of their environment.

**inquiry learning** Approach to instruction in which students apply complex reasoning skills in their examination and interpretation of new phenomena and data sources.

Chapter 2 describes Piaget's theory of development.

**FIGURE 12.8** Ten-year-old Berlinda's report about her group's dissection of several pig organs

Our table was given an esophogus with felt wet and smooth. The main blood vessel which felt hard, almost as though someone had stuck a toothpick inside of it. The tracea which felt felt wet and it slitely textured. The heart which, well you couldn't tell. Two lungs which felt a little pit. Like silly pudy.

## Into the Classroom

### Using Discovery and Inquiry Learning Activities Effectively

🍎 **Identify a concept or principle about which students can learn something significant through interaction with their physical or social environment.**

A fifth-grade teacher realizes that rather than tell students how to calculate the area of a triangle, he can help them discover the procedure for themselves by applying what they've previously learned about the area of a rectangle.

🍎 **Make sure students have the necessary prior knowledge to discover new ideas and principles.**

A high school physics class studies basic principles of velocity, acceleration, and force. In a follow-up lab activity, students place metal balls of various weights and sizes at the top of an inclined plane and observe each ball's progress as it rolls down the slope. A computer attached to the plane enables the students to measure the rate of acceleration for each ball, thereby also enabling them to determine whether either weight or size influences acceleration. From the data, the students can draw conclusions about the effects of gravity.

🍎 **Explicitly teach relevant reasoning processes, such as separation and control of variables in science or critical analysis of historical documents in history.**

A high school history teacher gives students copies of 12 political cartoons that appeared in U.S. newspapers at various times during the Vietnam War. He first reminds students about previous lessons regarding the personal biases that underlie many human-created historical documents. He then explains the symbolic nature of political cartoons and common symbols used in them. Finally, he asks students to work in small cooperative groups to identify pro-war or anti-war messages in the cartoons, as well as possible trends in the cartoonists' opinions over time.

🍎 **Show puzzling results to arouse curiosity.**

A science teacher shows her class two glasses of water. In one glass an egg floats at the water's surface; in the other glass an egg rests on the bottom. The students give a simple and logical explanation

for the difference: One egg has more air inside and so must be lighter. But then the teacher switches the eggs into opposite glasses. The egg that the students believe to be heavier now floats, and the supposedly lighter egg sinks to the bottom. The students are quite surprised and demand to know how this has happened. (Ordinarily, because water is less dense than an egg, an egg placed in it will quickly sink. But in this situation, one glass contains salt water, a mixture denser than an egg and thus capable of keeping it afloat.)

🍎 **Simplify and structure the experience sufficiently that students can proceed logically toward discoveries you want them to make.**

To demonstrate the effects of prejudice, a middle school social studies teacher creates a situation in which some students experience the prejudice of classmates because of an arbitrarily chosen physical characteristic: an inability to roll their tongues. After 15 minutes—long enough for students to feel the sting of prejudice but not so long as to damage peer relationships—the teacher stops the activity and asks students to share their reactions to the experience.

🍎 **Have students record their findings.**

Students in a biology class collect data from a local stream and use hand-held wireless computer-networking devices to send their findings to a central class computer. Once back in the classroom, the students consolidate and graph the data and look for general patterns and trends.

🍎 **Help students relate their findings to concepts and principles in the academic discipline they are studying.**

After students in a social studies class have collected data on average incomes and voting patterns in different counties within their state, their teacher asks, "How can we interpret these data, given what we've learned about the relative wealth of members of the two major political parties?"

*Sources:* Bruner, 1966; de Jong & van Joolingen, 1998; N. Frederiksen, 1984a; Hardy, Jonen, Möller, & Stern, 2006; P. Kirschner, Sweller, & Clark, 2006; Klahr, 2009; Leach & Scott, 2008; M. C. Linn & Eylon, 2011; Minstrell & Stimpson, 1996; Monte-Sano, 2008; Moreno, 2006; E. L. Palmer, 1965 (egg example); Pea & Maldonado, 2006 (stream example); Schwartz & Martin, 2004; B. Y. White & Frederiksen, 1998, 2005.

Effective hands-on discovery activities often need considerable teacher scaffolding. For example, watch "Water Wheels Activity: Teacher Scaffolding."

Discovery and inquiry activities need not be limited to materials we have in the classroom, of course. With access to the Internet, our options are virtually unlimited. For example, my middle school geography students and I once used the U.S. Geological Survey website (www.usgs.gov) to track the path of a hurricane as it made its way through the Caribbean and up the Atlantic Coast. Similarly, data available from the U.S. Census Bureau (www.census.gov) can enable students to explore issues related to population growth and poverty. And data from the Centers for Disease Control and Prevention (www.cdc.gov) can enable students to delve into issues related to cancer, air pollution, and other health-threatening conditions.

At the same time, we must note several potential problems with discovery learning and inquiry learning activities. First, students don't always have sufficient reasoning and metacognitive skills to effectively direct their explorations and monitor their findings (de Jong, 2011; Plass, Kalyuga, & Leutner, 2010; B. White, Frederiksen, & Collins, 2009). Second, students may be overwhelmed by the many facets and subfacets of what they're observing—so much so that they can't adequately think about and sort through all the data available to them (Moreno

& Park, 2010). Third, students may construct incorrect understandings from their discovery and inquiry activities; for instance, they may misinterpret or distort the evidence they gather in an experiment, possibly finding support for existing misconceptions (de Jong & van Joolingen, 1998; Karpov, 2003). Finally, such activities often take considerably more time than expository instruction, and teachers may feel torn between providing hands-on experiences, on the one hand, and covering all topics in the school-mandated curriculum, on the other (Klahr, 2009; M. C. Linn, 2008). In my own experience students typically remember what they learn in hands-on activities so much more effectively than what they learn through expository instruction alone that the extra time I occasionally devote to these activities is time well spent—another instance of the *less-is-more* principle.

The Into the Classroom feature "Using Discovery and Inquiry Learning Activities Effectively" offers several suggestions for maximizing the advantages and minimizing potential shortcomings of these approaches.

Mistakenly finding evidence that supports existing misconceptions is a phenomenon known as *confirmation bias* (see Chapter 6 and Chapter 8).

## USING COMPUTER SIMULATIONS AND GAMES

Effective discovery and inquiry learning sessions don't necessarily have to involve actual physical objects; they can instead involve experimentation in computer-based simulations. For example, children can learn a great deal about fractions with virtual "manipulatives" on a computer screen, and adolescents can systematically test various hypotheses that affect earthquakes or avalanches in a computer-simulated world. A particular advantage of technology-based simulations is that they can be designed in ways that keep students' cognitive load within reasonable bounds and appropriately scaffold students' efforts (de Jong, 2011; Kuhn & Pease, 2010; Sarama & Clements, 2009).

Use well-designed computer simulations when actual hands-on activities are impractical or impossible.

Some computer simulations promote complex cognitive processes within seemingly authentic contexts—in some cases in the form of videogames that students play alone or with peers. Following are examples:

- *Civilization.* Learners begin "living" several thousand years ago and, over many centuries, build an increasingly complex society. In an effort to survive and thrive, they must make decisions about food, natural resources, government, emerging technologies, and interactions with other social and cultural groups (www.civilization.com).

- *StockTrak.* Learners "invest" in various stocks in the stock market and track profits and losses in their virtual "portfolios" over time (www.stocktrak.com).

- *Science Court.* In a courtlike setting, learners confront common misconceptions about science, examine evidence, and make predictions (www.tomsnyder.com). Figure 12.9 shows a scene from a courtroom "trial" on the nature of living things.

Computer-based simulations are often both motivating and challenging—thereby keeping students on task for extended periods—and can significantly enhance students' reasoning and problem-solving skills (Barab, Gresalfi, & Ingram-Goble, 2010; de Jong, 2011; Kuhn & Pease, 2008; Squire, 2011; Zohar & Aharon-Kraversky, 2005).

A few Internet-based computer simulations involve many students—and sometimes many schools—working together on common problems. For example, in an Internet-based simulation called GlobalEd (www.globaled.uconn.edu), middle school social studies classes become representatives for particular countries (e.g., one class might be France, another might be Nigeria), with different members of a class tackling different global issues (e.g., international conflicts, human rights, environmental issues). Students study their countries and issues and then electronically communicate with representatives from other "countries" (i.e., students in other schools) to share perspectives and negotiate treaties. Not only does the simulation enhance students' understanding of global issues, but it also enhances their perspective-taking ability and interest in social studies as a discipline (Gehlbach et al., 2008). In another, globally distributed simulation, Quest Atlantis (questatlantis.org), students take on various roles (e.g., scientist, accountant, writer) to tackle complex worldwide problems (e.g., erosion, diminishing fish populations) and make decisions that have significant virtual "effects" on long-term outcomes (Barab et al., 2010).

**FIGURE 12.9** In the instructional software program *Science Court*, students explore a variety of science topics in a simulated courtroom environment. The screen shown here is a scene from "Living Things."

*Source:* Screenshot from "Living Things," *Science Court,* by Tom Snyder Productions. Copyright © by Scholastic Inc. Reprinted by permission.

**cooperative learning** Approach to instruction in which students work with a small group of peers to achieve a common goal and help one another learn.

**base group** Cooperative learning group in which students work together for an entire semester or school year to provide mutual support for one another's learning.

## CONDUCTING COOPERATIVE LEARNING ACTIVITIES

In your many years as a student, you've undoubtedly had a variety of incentives to do well in your classes. In the next exercise you'll consider three possibilities.

### ■■ EXPERIENCING FIRSTHAND
### PURPLE SATIN

Imagine yourself as a student in each of the three classrooms described here. How would you behave in each situation?

1. Mr. Alexander tells your class, "Let's find out which students can learn the most in this week's unit on the human digestive system. The three students getting the highest scores on Friday's quiz will get free tickets to the Purple Satin concert on Saturday." Purple Satin is a popular musical group. You'd give your eyeteeth to hear them perform, but the concert has been sold out for months.

2. Ms. Bernstein introduces her lesson this way: "I'm hoping that all of you will master the basics of human digestion this week. If you get a score of at least 90% on Friday's quiz, I'll give you a free ticket to the Purple Satin concert."

3. Mr. Camacho begins the same lesson like this: "Beginning today, you'll be working in groups of three to study the human digestive system. On Friday I'll give you a quiz to see how much you've learned. If all three members of your group score at least 90% on the quiz, your group will get free tickets to the Purple Satin concert."

In which class(es) are you likely to work hard to get free tickets to Purple Satin? How might you work *differently* in the three situations?

The first class (Mr. Alexander's) is obviously a very competitive one: Only the three best students are getting tickets to the concert. Will you try to earn one of those tickets? It all depends on what you think your chances are of being a top scorer on Friday's quiz. If you've been doing well on quizzes all year, you'll undoubtedly study harder than ever during this week's unit. If, instead, you've been doing poorly in class despite your best efforts, you probably won't work for something you're unlikely to get. But in either case, will you help your fellow students learn about the digestive system? Not if you want to go to the concert yourself!

In Ms. Bernstein's class there's no competition for concert tickets. As long as you get a score of 90% or higher on the quiz, you'll get a ticket. But will you help your classmates understand what the pancreas does or learn the difference between the large and small intestines? Maybe—*if* you have the time and are feeling charitable.

Now consider Mr. Camacho's class. Whether or not you get a concert ticket depends on how well you *and two other students* score on Friday's quiz. Are you going to help those two students learn about salivation and digestive enzymes? And can you expect them, in turn, to help you understand where the liver fits into the whole system? Absolutely!

In cooperative learning,[8] students work in small groups to achieve a common goal. Unlike an individualistic classroom such as Ms. Bernstein's (where one student's success is unrelated to peers' achievement) or a competitive classroom such as Mr. Alexander's (where one student's success depends partly on the *failure* of others), students in a cooperative learning environment such as Mr. Camacho's work together to achieve joint successes. On some occasions cooperative groups are formed on a short-term basis to accomplish specific tasks—perhaps to study new material, solve a problem, or complete an assigned project. In other instances groups are formed to work toward long-term classroom goals. For example, base groups are cooperative groups that work together for an entire semester or school year, clarifying assignments for one another, helping one another with class notes, and giving one another a general sense of support and belonging in the classroom (D. W. Johnson & Johnson, 1991).

Create cooperative base groups in which students can get support from two or three classmates throughout the school year.

---

[8]Some theorists distinguish between *cooperative* learning and *collaborative* learning, with different theorists drawing the dividing line somewhat differently. I am using *cooperative learning* broadly to include collaborative approaches to learning.

When students engage in cooperative learning, they reap the many benefits of student dialogue, including greater comprehension and integration of the subject matter, exposure to new strategies, and increased perspective taking. Furthermore, when students help one another learn, they provide scaffolding for one another's efforts and thus tend to have higher self-efficacy for accomplishing challenging tasks. And, of course, cooperative learning activities can provide valuable experience with the collaboration and negotiation skills that the adult world so often requires (Good, McCaslin, & Reys, 1992; D. W. Johnson & Johnson, 2009a; A. M. O'Donnell & O'Kelly, 1994; Webb & Palincsar, 1996; J. R. White & McVeigh, 2010).

When designed and structured appropriately, cooperative learning activities can promote high achievement in students of all ability levels, including many who have historically been at risk for academic failure (Ginsburg-Block, Rohrbeck, & Fantuzzo, 2006; Lou et al., 1996; Slavin & Lake, 2008). Cooperative activities are especially suitable for complex, challenging tasks and problems in which group members can share the cognitive load and model effective learning and problem-solving strategies for one another (Blumenfeld et al., 1996; A. King, 1999; F. Kirschner, Paas, & Kirschner, 2009). An additional, nonacademic benefit is that students are more likely to believe that their classmates like them, and friendships across racial and ethnic groups and between students with and without disabilities are apt to form (Lou et al., 1996; Pfeifer, Brown, & Juvonen, 2007; Slavin, Hurley, & Chamberlain, 2003).

Cooperative learning activities have several potential pitfalls, however. Some students may be more interested in meeting social and performance goals (e.g., creating a good impression, getting the right answer quickly) than they are in mastering the material; consequently, their willingness to assist others or ask for help may be compromised (Levy, Kaplan, & Patrick, 2000; Moje & Shepardson, 1998; Wentzel, 2009). Furthermore, students who do most of the work and most of the talking are likely to learn more than other group members (Gayford, 1992; Lotan, 2006; Webb, 1989). In addition, students may occasionally agree to use an incorrect strategy or method that a particular group member has suggested, or they may share misconceptions about a topic they're studying (Good et al., 1992; Stacey, 1992). And in some cases students simply don't have the skills to help one another learn (D. M. Hogan & Tudge, 1999; Webb & Mastergeorge, 2003). Clearly, then, we must keep a close eye on group discussions, providing structure and guidance as necessary to promote maximal learning and achievement.

Following are several strategies that tend to enhance the effectiveness of cooperative learning groups.

🍎 *Form groups based on knowledge about which students are likely to work effectively with one another.* Cooperative groups are typically comprised of two to six members; groups of three to four students are especially effective (Hatano & Inagaki, 1991; Lou et al., 1996). In most cases we teachers should form the groups, identifying student combinations that will be productive (D. W. Johnson & Johnson, 1991; Lotan, 2006). Some advocates of cooperative learning suggest that groups be heterogeneous, with each group including high achievers and low achievers, boys and girls, and children of various ethnic backgrounds. Others disagree, arguing that too much heterogeneity makes students' differing ability levels obvious and discourages low-ability students from actively participating (Lotan, 2006; Moje & Shepardson, 1998; A. M. O'Donnell & O'Kelly, 1994; Webb, Nemer, & Zuniga, 2002).

Research regarding the effects of heterogeneous cooperative groups has yielded mixed results. Some studies indicate that heterogeneous groups benefit both high-achieving students (who can sharpen their knowledge by explaining it to peers) and low-achieving students (who benefit from hearing such explanations) (Lou et al., 1996; R. J. Stevens & Slavin, 1995; Webb, Nemer, Chizhik, & Sugrue, 1998; Webb & Palincsar, 1996). However, other studies indicate that high-achieving students *don't* always gain from working with low-achieving classmates and can occasionally even lose ground (D. M. Hogan & Tudge, 1999; Lou et al., 1996; Webb et al., 2002). Ideally cooperative group activities require a sufficiently wide range of talents and skills that every group member has something unique and useful to contribute to the group's overall success (E. G. Cohen, 1994; Esmonde, 2009; Lotan, 2006).

🍏 Create cooperative activities that require multiple talents and skills, enabling all group members to contribute meaningfully to their group's success.

🍎 *Give group members one or more common goals toward which to work.* Effective cooperative learning activities have clear, concrete goals regarding what each group should accomplish (Crook, 1995; Slavin et al., 2003). For example, when my daughter Tina was enrolled in a high school Spanish class, the goal of one cooperative activity was to write and videotape an episode of

**FIGURE 12.10**  To be effective, cooperative learning groups should work toward common goals. Here eighth-grade history teacher Mark Nichols identifies several things students need to accomplish as they prepare their group presentations about colonial America.

Group Responsibilities:

Groups will be established with 3-4 students.

Each group will be responsible for reading and thoroughly understanding their assigned sub-chapter.

Each group will prepare an outline of the chapter which will be typed in final draft format. Copies will be made for each student in class.

Each group will create an artistic example of their material and a board game to be played at the end of the presentations.

The day before your group presentation you are to instruct the class to read your sub-chapter and prepare a homework assignment for the class.

A presentation of the material will be made to the class, which will include going over the homework assignment, the outline, and explanation of your creative display of the sub-chapter information. Class members are required to question the presenting group on their material.

An open-notes test will be given at the end of this unit in order to ensure understanding of the material.

---

a television soap opera spoken entirely in Spanish. The students knew that these *telenovelas* would eventually be shown at an "Academy Awards" banquet for the students and parents, and "Oscars" would be presented for best picture, best screenplay, and so on. (Tina won for best actress, no surprise to me given her frequent displays of emotional drama at home.) Another example, used in an eighth-grade social studies class, is presented in Figure 12.10.

🍎 *Provide clear guidelines about how to behave.* Cooperative learning is more successful when students act respectfully and prosocially toward one another (Blumenfeld et al., 1996; Slavin, 2011; Windschitl, 2002). Following are possible guidelines to give them:

- Give everyone an equal chance to participate.
- Back up your ideas with logic or evidence.
- Listen to others politely and attentively; ask questions when you don't understand.
- Encourage others, and offer assistance as needed.
- Address differences of opinion in respectful and constructive ways.
- Change your mind when others present persuasive arguments and evidence.
- Whenever possible, identify compromises that pull together differing perspectives.
- Make sure everyone eventually understands the material. (E. G. Cohen, 1994; M. Deutsch, 1993; Gillies & Ashman, 1998; Lotan, 2006; Lou et al., 1996; A. M. O'Donnell & O'Kelly, 1994; Webb & Farivar, 1999)

🍎 *Structure tasks so that group members must depend on one another for success.* Students must believe that it's to their advantage to cooperate and help other group members learn (Ginsburg-Block et al., 2006; D. W. Johnson & Johnson, 2009a; Lou et al., 1996). In some situations each student might have a unique and essential function within the group, perhaps serving as group leader, critic, bookkeeper, peacekeeper, summarizer, or the like (Esmonde, 2009; D. W. Johnson & Johnson, 1991; Lotan, 2006). In other situations the jigsaw technique is useful: New information is divided equally among all group members, and each student must teach his or her portion to the others (E. Aronson & Patnoe, 1997).

When students are novices at cooperative learning, it's often helpful to give them a set of steps—a script to follow, if you will—that guides their interaction (Gillies, 2003; A. M. O'Donnell, 1999, 2006; Webb & Palincsar, 1996). In one approach, known as scripted cooperation, students work together in pairs to read and study expository text. One member of the pair might act as *recaller*, summarizing the contents of a textbook passage, while the other student acts as *listener*, correcting any errors and recalling additional important information. The two students switch roles for the

**jigsaw technique**  Instructional technique in which materials are divided among members of a cooperative group, with different students being responsible for learning different content and teaching it to other group members.

**scripted cooperation**  Technique in which cooperative learning groups follow a specified set of steps, or script, that guides members' verbal interactions.

subsequent passage. Such an approach can help students improve learning strategies such as elaboration, summarizing, and comprehension monitoring (Dansereau, 1988; A. M. O'Donnell, 1999).

🍎 *Serve primarily as a monitor and resource.* During any cooperative learning activity, we must monitor both the content and the behaviors of group interactions (D. W. Johnson & Johnson, 1991; Meloth & Deering, 1999). For example, we might consider issues such as these:

- Are students all actively working toward a common goal?

- Are their ideas and strategies productive ones?

- Are they asking one another questions when they don't understand?

- Are they behaving in mutually respectful ways?

We must also take corrective actions when necessary. For instance, if students seem to be buying into peers' misconceptions about a topic, a gentle intervention may steer a discussion in a more fruitful direction—for instance, "Lydia thinks such-and-such; do the rest of you agree with that?" And if students make hurtful remarks to peers, a reminder about the rules for behavior—and in some cases a request for an apology—may be in order.

We may occasionally need to offer assistance if group members are unable to provide information or insights that are critical for accomplishing the group's goal. Too much intervention can be counterproductive, however: Students tend to talk less with one another when their teacher joins the group (E. G. Cohen, 1994).

🍎 *Make students individually accountable for their achievement, but also reinforce them for group success.* Students are more likely to learn assigned subject matter during cooperative learning activities when they know they'll have to demonstrate individual mastery or accomplishment of the group's goal—for example, by answering questions in class, taking a quiz, or making a unique and easily identifiable contribution to an overall group product. Such an approach minimizes the likelihood that some students will do most or all of the work while others contribute little or nothing (Finn, Pannozzo, & Achilles, 2003; Ginsburg-Block et al., 2006; D. W. Johnson & Johnson, 2009a).

In addition to holding students accountable for their own learning and achievement, we might also reinforce group members for the success of the group as a whole—a *group contingency* in action (Lou et al., 1996; Slavin, 2011). Such group rewards often promote higher achievement overall, perhaps because students have a vested interest in one another's performance and thus make a concerted effort to help fellow group members understand the subject matter (R. J. Stevens & Slavin, 1995). One commonly used approach is to give students a quiz over material they've studied in cooperative learning groups and award one or two bonus points if all group members perform at or above a certain level.

🍎 *At the end of an activity, have groups evaluate their effectiveness.* After cooperative groups have accomplished their goals, we should have them look analytically and critically (perhaps with our assistance) at the ways in which they've functioned effectively and the ways in which they need to improve (E. G. Cohen, 1994; M. Deutsch, 1993; D. W. Johnson & Johnson, 2009a). We might ask groups to consider some of the same issues we kept in mind as we monitored the activity—for instance, whether all members participated actively and respectfully and whether they asked one another questions when they didn't understand. In Figure 12.11, 12-year-old Amaryth reflects on her group's effectiveness in a collaborative task. Notice her concerns: "not really focused," "not lisening [listening] to each other," "yelling a lot." As you can see, members of her group still have much to learn about how to work well together.

Cooperative learning activities are more effective when students have guidelines for behavior and when students are rewarded for both individual and group success. For example, watch "Cooperative Learning."

See Chapter 9 for a discussion of group contingencies.

**FIGURE 12.11** In an entry in her class journal, 12-year-old Amaryth reflects on the effectiveness of a cooperative learning group. (She misspells *group* as "gobe.")

Obsevations from gobe

* laghing not really focused
* silly ideas
* eraser passing
* not really lising
* lots of diffrent ideas
* leaders = Heha / Marte (no really lealrs
* lots of brian storming
* Marce frust ated (yelling tomad)(bossy, dimanding, not lisening to any body
* trying to invold other people but not workng  ] elsey
* (Not lisening to each other
* yelling to each other
* neded nots of help fom observers
* yelling alot

**peer tutoring** Approach to instruction in which one student provides instruction to help another student master a classroom topic.

## STRUCTURING PEER TUTORING SESSIONS

In peer tutoring, students who have mastered a topic teach those who haven't. Peer tutoring sometimes occurs spontaneously in cooperative learning activities, but we can also use it as an instructional strategy in its own right. On some occasions we might have students within a single class tutor one another. At other times we might have older students teach younger ones—perhaps fourth or fifth graders teaching students in kindergarten or first grade. And the high school I attended many years ago had a schoolwide tutoring program coordinated by the school's chapter of the National Honor Society.

Peer tutoring can lead to considerable gains in academic achievement (Ginsburg-Block et al., 2006; Graesser, D'Mello, & Cade, 2011; D. R. Robinson, Schofield, & Steers-Wentzell, 2005; Roscoe & Chi, 2007). One possible reason for its effectiveness is that it gives students many opportunities to make the active responses that, from a behaviorist perspective, are so essential to learning. It also provides a context in which struggling students can ask questions when they don't understand something and get regular feedback about their performance (Graesser & Person, 1994; J. R. Sullivan & Conoley, 2004).

Typically peer tutoring benefits tutors as well as those being tutored (Graesser et al., 2011; Inglis & Biemiller, 1997; D. R. Robinson et al., 2005). Students are more intrinsically motivated to learn something if they know they'll have to teach it to someone else, and they're apt to engage in considerable elaboration as they study and explain it (Benware & Deci, 1984; A. M. O'Donnell, 2006; Roscoe & Chi, 2007). Furthermore, in the process of directing and guiding other students' learning and problem solving, tutors may, in a Vygotskian fashion, internalize these processes and thus become better able to direct and guide their *own* learning and problem solving. In other words, peer tutoring can foster greater self-regulation in the tutors (Biemiller, Shany, Inglis, & Meichenbaum, 1998).

Peer tutoring has nonacademic benefits as well. Cooperation and other social skills improve, behavior problems diminish, and friendships form among students of different ethnic groups and between students with and without disabilities (Cushing & Kennedy, 1997; DuPaul, Ervin, Hook, & McGoey, 1998; Greenwood, Carta, & Hall, 1988; D. R. Robinson et al., 2005).

Following are several research-based recommendations for enhancing the effectiveness of peer tutoring.

🍎 *Make sure that tutors have mastered the material they are teaching and that they use sound instructional techniques.* In most cases, good tutors have a solid understanding of the subject matter they're teaching and can provide explanations that focus on meaningful (rather than rote) learning. Good tutors also use teaching strategies that are likely to promote learning—for instance, asking questions, providing appropriate scaffolding, and giving regular feedback (L. S. Fuchs et al., 1996; Lepper, Aspinwall, Mumme, & Chabay, 1990; Roscoe & Chi, 2007).

Especially in the elementary grades, explicit training in tutoring skills can be helpful. For example, student tutors might be shown how to establish a good relationship with the students they're tutoring, how to break a task into simple steps, and how and when to give feedback (Fueyo & Bushell, 1998; Graesser et al., 2011; Inglis & Biemiller, 1997; D. R. Robinson et al., 2005).

🍎 *Provide a structure for students' interactions.* Providing a structure for tutoring sessions can often help students facilitate their classmates' learning (Fantuzzo, King, & Heller, 1992; L. S. Fuchs et al., 1996; Mathes, Torgesen, & Allor, 2001; Spörer & Brunstein, 2009). As an example, in one study (D. Fuchs, Fuchs, Mathes, & Simmons, 1997), 20 second- through sixth-grade classes participated in a program called Peer-Assisted Learning Strategies (PALS), designed to foster more effective reading comprehension skills. In each class, students were ranked by reading ability, and the ranked list was divided into two parts. The first-ranked student in the top half of the list was paired with the first-ranked student in the bottom half of the list, the second student in the top half was paired with the second student in the bottom half, and so on. Through this procedure, students who were paired together had moderate but not extreme differences in reading level. Each pair read material at the level of the weaker reader and engaged in the following activities:

- *Partner reading with retell.* The stronger reader read aloud for five minutes, then the weaker reader read the same passage of text. Reading something that had previously been read presumably enabled the weaker reader to read the material easily. After the double reading, the weaker reader described the material just read.

- *Paragraph summary.* The students both read a passage one paragraph at a time. Then, with help from the stronger reader, the weaker reader tried to identify the subject and main idea of the paragraph.

- *Prediction relay.* Both students read a page of text, and then, with help from the stronger reader, the weaker reader summarized the text and also made a prediction about what the next page would say. The pair then read the following page, and the weaker reader confirmed or disconfirmed the prediction, summarized the new page, made a new prediction, and so on.

This procedure enabled students in the PALS program to make significantly more progress in reading than students who had traditional reading instruction, even though the amount of class time devoted to reading was similar for both groups. The researchers speculated that the PALS students performed better because they had more frequent opportunities to make verbal responses to what they were reading, received more feedback about their performance, and, in general, were more often encouraged to use effective reading strategies.

At the middle and secondary school levels, we can incorporate a tutoring component into paired study sessions by teaching students the kinds of questions they might ask one another as they jointly study science, social studies, and other academic disciplines. In one approach (A. King, 1997, 1999), students are given question "starters" to help them formulate higher-level questions (e.g., "What is the difference between ___ and ___?" "What do you think would happen to ___ if ___ happened?") (A. King, 1997, p. 230). In the following dialogue, two seventh graders use question starters as they work together to learn more about muscles, a topic that neither of them has previously known much about:

*Jon:* How does the muscular system work, Kyle?

*Kyle:* Well . . . it retracts and contracts when you move.

*Jon:* Can you tell me more? . . . Um, why are muscles important, Kyle?

*Kyle:* They are important because if we didn't have them we couldn't move around.

*Jon:* But . . . how do muscles work? Explain it more.

*Kyle:* Um, muscles have tendons. Some muscles are called skeletal muscles. They are in the muscles that—like—in your arms—that have tendons that hold your muscles to your bones—to make them move and go back and forth. So you can walk and stuff.

*Jon:* Good. All right! How are the skeletal muscles and the cardiac muscles the same? . . .

*Kyle:* Well, they're both a muscle. And they're both pretty strong. And they hold things. I don't really think they have much in common.

*Jon:* Okay. Why don't you think they have much in common?

*Kyle:* Because the smooth muscle is—I mean the skeletal muscle is voluntary and the cardiac muscle is involuntary. Okay, I'll ask now. What do you think would happen if we didn't have smooth muscles?

*Jon:* We would have to be chewing harder. And so it would take a long time to digest food. We would have to think about digesting because the smooth muscles—like the intestines and stomach—are *in*voluntary. . . .

*Kyle:* Yeah, well—um—but, do you think it would *hurt* you if you didn't have smooth muscles?

*Jon:* Well, yeah—because you wouldn't have muscles to push the food along—in the stomach and intestines—you'd get plugged up! Maybe you'd hafta drink liquid—just liquid stuff. Yuk. (A. King, Staffieri, & Adelgais, 1998, p. 141)

Notice how the boys ask each other questions that encourage elaboration and metacognitive self-reflection (e.g., "Why don't you think they have much in common?" "Do you think it would hurt you if you didn't have smooth muscles?"). Through such structured interactions, students at the same grade and ability levels can provide valuable scaffolding for one another's learning efforts (A. King, 1998).

🍏 *Be careful that your use of higher-achieving students to tutor lower-achieving students is not excessive or exploitative.* As we've seen, tutors often gain just as much from tutoring sessions as the students they're tutoring. Nevertheless, we mustn't assume that high-achieving students will always learn from a tutoring session. Instead, we should regularly monitor the effects of peer tutoring sessions to make sure that all students are reaping benefits.

🍏 *Give all students opportunities to tutor other individuals.* This is often easier said than done, as a few students may show consistently lower achievement than most of their peers. One effective approach is to ask low-achieving students to tutor classmates with disabilities (Cushing & Kennedy, 1997; DuPaul et al., 1998; D. Fuchs et al., 1997). Another possibility is to teach low-achieving students specific tasks or procedures they can share with their higher-achieving, but in this case uninformed, classmates (E. G. Cohen, Lockheed, & Lohman, 1976; Webb & Palincsar, 1996). Still another is to have students teach basic skills to younger children (Inglis & Biemiller, 1997). In fact, students with significant social or behavioral problems (e.g., autism spectrum disorders, emotional and behavioral disorders) can make significant gains in both academic and social skills when they have opportunities to tutor children several years younger than they are (J. R. Sullivan & Conoley, 2004).

## CONDUCTING TECHNOLOGY-BASED COLLABORATIVE LEARNING ACTIVITIES

Effective cooperative and collaborative activities don't necessarily have to be face to face. Software created at the University of Toronto provides an example of how technology can enhance student interaction and collaborative learning. The software, called Knowledge Forum (www.knowledge forum.com), provides a multimedia database that enables students to jointly construct a body of shared knowledge about a particular topic (e.g., optics, aerodynamics, the American Civil War). In this electronic environment, students post their work in the forms of reports, problem solutions, diagrams, flowcharts, short stories, and the like. Their classmates respond regularly, perhaps by giving feedback, building on ideas, offering alternative perspectives, or synthesizing what's been learned; sometimes a subject matter expert gets involved in the conversation as well. The electronic nature of interactions gives students the time they may need to reflect on one another's ideas and may be especially welcoming for students who are shy or for other reasons feel uncomfortable communicating with peers more publicly. In essence, the software provides the foundation for a computer-based *community of learners* in which most students feel comfortable and psychologically "safe" (Hewitt & Scardamalia, 1996, 1998; Lamon, Chan, Scardamalia, Burtis, & Brett, 1993; Scardamalia & Bereiter, 2006).

 Chapter 8 describes communities of learners in more detail.

Research regarding the use of Knowledge Forum has generally been quite favorable (Bereiter & Scardamalia, 2006; Lamon et al., 1993; Scardamalia & Bereiter, 2006; Zhang, Scardamalia, Reeve, & Messina, 2009). Students are concerned about truly understanding classroom subject matter rather than simply "getting things done." They actively try to relate new material to what they already know—that is, they adopt mastery goals rather than performance goals—and they show greater ability to remember, synthesize, and apply classroom subject matter. In addition, the ongoing student discussions can foster more sophisticated epistemic beliefs about the subject matter in question. For example, in an anthropology unit "Prehistory of the New World" conducted in a combined fifth- and sixth-grade classroom, students worked in groups of three or four to study particular topics and then shared their findings through their computer database (Hewitt, Brett, Scardamalia, Frecker, & Webb, 1995). One group, which studied various theories about how human beings first migrated from Asia to the Americas, reported the following:

> **What We Have Learned:** We know that we have learned lots on this project, but the more that we learn the more we get confused about which is fact and which is fiction. The problem within this problem is that there isn't any real proof to say when they came or how. The theory that is most believed is the Bering Strait theory in which people from Asia walked over a land bridge. Another theory is they kayaked the distance between the two continents. We have also unfortunately found racist theories done by people who hate people unlike their own saying that the people of the New World are these people because of human sacrifices and only this race of people would do that.

We have made are [our] own theories using information we found and trying to make sense of it. We have heard some people say they come from outer space but this theory is pretty much out of the question. I don't think the Native peoples or the Inuit would like to hear that theory either. How they came isn't easily answered for some of the theories but it does make since [sense] with the Bering Strait theory. (Hewitt et al., 1995, p. 7)

Notice the sophisticated epistemic beliefs that the group's summary reveals: The students recognize that as a discipline, anthropology isn't just a set of facts but also encompasses varying perspectives that may or may not be correct. Furthermore, the students acknowledge that different theories may have greater or lesser usefulness in explaining the evidence anthropologists have gathered.

Another option for technology-based collaborative learning is the GLOBE Program (www.globe.gov), through which student groups around the world collaborate on inquiry-based projects related to environmental and earth sciences. Students in participating schools and classrooms collect and analyze data about various environmental topics (e.g., climate change, watershed dynamics), write reports, and share their findings with students and professional scientists elsewhere.

As the Internet becomes increasingly accessible to learners worldwide, then, not only do we have limitless sources of information on which to draw, but we also have limitless mechanisms for communicating and collaborating with other people in faraway settings about issues of common interest. Multinational student–student collaborations are an excellent way to get young learners thinking and acting as *global* citizens as well as citizens of a particular community and country.

This Knowledge Forum software allows students to exchange and interconnect ideas not only with their classmates but also with peers and adults at other institutions.

*Source:* Screenshot from Knowledge Forum. Copyright © by Institute of Knowledge Innovation and Technology and Learning in Motion. Used with permission. For more information, see www.knowledgeforum.com.

# Taking Instructional Goals and Student Diversity into Account

Let's return to the first of the general principles presented at the beginning of the chapter: *Effective teachers begin their instructional planning by determining what they ultimately want students to know and be able to do.* Table 12.2 presents several general instructional goals we might have, along with potentially useful instructional strategies for accomplishing each one. Notice that many of the strategies we've examined in this chapter appear two or more times in the table, reflecting the multiple purposes for which they might flexibly be used.

To some degree, the instructional strategies we choose must also take into account students' ages and developmental levels. For example, strategies that involve a lot of active responding and frequent feedback (e.g., direct instruction, mastery learning) may be especially appropriate for younger students (Brophy et al., 2009; Rosenshine & Stevens, 1986). Lectures (which are often somewhat abstract) and complex homework assignments tend to be more effective with older students (Ausubel et al., 1978; H. Cooper et al., 2006).

The knowledge and skills that students bring to a topic must be a consideration as well (Gustafsson & Undheim, 1996; Kintsch, 2009; Rosenshine & Stevens, 1986). Structured, teacher-directed approaches are probably most appropriate when students know little or nothing about the topic. But when students have mastered basic knowledge and skills—and especially when they're self-regulating learners—they should begin to direct some of their own learning, perhaps in hypermedia, small-group discussions, or technology-based collaborative activities.

In general, however, *all* students should have experience with a wide variety of instructional methods. For example, although some students may need a considerable amount of direct instruction to learn and practice basic skills, authentic activities—perhaps within the context of small cooperative groups—can give them a greater appreciation for the relevance and meaningfulness

When choosing instructional strategies, take into account students' developmental levels, background knowledge, and self-regulation skills.

# COMPARE/CONTRAST

## TABLE 12.2 • Choosing an Instructional Strategy

| WHEN YOUR GOAL IS TO HELP STUDENTS . . . | CONSIDER USING . . . |
|---|---|
| Master and review basic skills | • Direct instruction<br>• Mastery learning<br>• Instructional websites<br>• Intelligent tutoring systems<br>• Cooperative learning<br>• Peer tutoring |
| Gain firsthand, concrete experience with a particular topic | • Discovery and inquiry learning<br>• Computer simulations |
| Gain a general, relatively abstract body of knowledge about a topic | • Lectures<br>• Textbooks and other assigned readings<br>• Instructional websites<br>• Computer-based instruction (some programs) |
| Connect school subject matter to real-world contexts and problems | • Authentic activities<br>• Appropriately designed and scaffolded homework assignments<br>• Inquiry learning<br>• Computer simulations<br>• Technology-based collaborative learning |
| Acquire advanced understandings about a topic and/or develop complex cognitive processes (e.g., problem solving, critical thinking, scientific reasoning) | • Higher-level teacher questions<br>• Authentic activities<br>• Computer-based instruction (some programs)<br>• Class discussions<br>• Inquiry learning<br>• Computer simulations (some programs)<br>• Cooperative learning<br>• Technology-based collaborative learning |
| Acquire increased metacognitive awareness and more effective reading comprehension and self-regulation strategies | • Age-appropriate homework assignments that foster independent study habits<br>• Computer-based instruction (some programs)<br>• Reciprocal teaching<br>• Cooperative learning<br>• Peer tutoring (which can enhance tutors' self-regulation skills) |
| Acquire computer literacy skills | • Regular use of a class website<br>• Instructional websites<br>• Computer-based instruction<br>• Computer simulations<br>• Technology-based collaborative learning |
| Acquire effective strategies for interacting and working with others | • Class discussions<br>• Reciprocal teaching<br>• Small-group inquiry learning<br>• Multiplayer computer simulations and games<br>• Cooperative learning<br>• Peer tutoring<br>• Technology-based collaborative learning |

of classroom subject matter. Furthermore, too much time in structured, teacher-directed activities can minimize opportunities to choose what and how to study and learn and, as a result, can prevent students from developing the sense of self-determination so important for intrinsic motivation (Battistich, Solomon, Kim, Watson, & Schaps, 1995; Reeve, 2009).

## CONSIDERING GROUP DIFFERENCES

Students' cultural and ethnic backgrounds may occasionally have implications for our choice of instructional strategies. For instance, students from cultures that place a high premium on interpersonal cooperation (e.g., many Hispanic and Native American communities) are apt to achieve at higher levels in classrooms with many interactive and collaborative activities (Castagno & Brayboy, 2008; García, 1994, 1995; Webb & Palincsar, 1996). In contrast, recent immigrants from some Asian countries may be more accustomed to teacher-directed instruction than to learner-directed classroom activities, and students who have only limited proficiency in English may be reluctant to speak up in class discussions (Igoa, 1995; Walshaw & Anthony, 2008). When working with English language learners, technology can often come to our assistance, perhaps in the form of bilingual software for teaching basic skills, English-language tutorials, and word processing programs with spell checkers and grammar checkers (Egbert, 2009; P. F. Merrill et al., 1996).

Identify teaching strategies that are compatible with students' cultural backgrounds.

We must take gender differences into account as well. For example, videogames that engage students in simulated real-world problems can often captivate boys who aren't otherwise motivated to master academic skills (Carr-Chellman, 2012). Meanwhile, although many boys thrive on competition, girls tend to do better when instructional activities are interactive and cooperative. However, girls can be intimidated by whole-class discussions; they're more likely to participate when discussions and activities take place in small groups (Théberge, 1994). Because boys sometimes take charge of small-group activities, we may occasionally want to form all-female groups. By doing so, we're likely to increase girls' participation in group activities and to encourage them to take leadership roles (Fennema, 1987; MacLean, Sasse, Keating, Stewart, & Miller, 1995; Slavin et al., 2003).

Use cooperative approaches to enhance the achievement of females and students from certain ethnic minority groups.

Our choice of instructional strategies may be especially critical when we work in schools in low-income, inner-city neighborhoods. Students in such schools often get a lot of drill-and-practice work in basic skills—work that's hardly conducive to fostering excitement about academic subject matter (R. Ferguson, 1998; Pianta & Hamre, 2009; Portes, 1996). Mastering basic skills is essential, to be sure, but we can frequently incorporate them into authentic activities and computer-based simulations and games in which students apply what they're learning to personal interests and real-world contexts (Eccles, 2007; Lee-Pearce, Plowman, & Touchstone, 1998; Squire, 2011). For example, in a curriculum called Kids Voting USA, students in kindergarten through grade 12 have age-appropriate lessons about voting, political parties, and political issues, and they relate what they learn to local election campaigns (M. McDevitt & Chaffee, 1998; also see kidsvotingusa.org). Depending on the grade level, they might conduct their own mock elections, analyze candidates' attacks on opponents, or give speeches about particular propositions on a ballot. Students who participate in the program are more likely to attend regularly to media reports about an election, initiate discussions about the election with friends and family members, and be knowledgeable about candidates and election results. In fact, their knowledge and excitement about politics is contagious, because even their *parents* begin to pay more attention to the news, talk more frequently about politics, and acquire more knowledge about candidates and political issues.

Interactive and collaborative strategies are particularly valuable when our instructional goals include promoting social development as well as academic achievement. As we've seen, such interactive approaches as cooperative learning and peer tutoring encourage friendly relationships across ethnic groups. Furthermore, collaborative activities—especially when they require multiple skills and abilities—can foster an appreciation for the various talents that students with diverse backgrounds can contribute (E. G. Cohen, 1994; E. G. Cohen & Lotan, 1995).

## ACCOMMODATING STUDENTS WITH SPECIAL NEEDS

We must often modify our instructional goals and strategies for students who have exceptional cognitive abilities or disabilities—an example of the *differentiated instruction* mentioned early in the chapter. For example, to ensure that all students are working on tasks appropriate for their current skill levels (i.e., tasks within each student's zone of proximal development), we may need to identify more basic goals for some students (e.g., those with intellectual disabilities) and more challenging goals for others (e.g., those who are gifted). In addition, different instructional strategies may be more or less useful for students with different kinds of special needs. For instance, strictly expository instruction (e.g., a lecture or textbook chapter) can provide a quick and efficient means of presenting new ideas to students who process information quickly and abstractly but might be incomprehensible and overwhelming to students with low cognitive ability. Similarly, inquiry learning and discussion-based approaches are often effective in enhancing the academic achievement of students with high ability but may be detrimental to the achievement of lower-ability students who haven't yet mastered basic concepts and skills (Corno & Snow, 1986; Lorch et al., 2010). In contrast, mastery learning and direct instruction have been shown to be effective with students who have learning difficulties but might prevent rapid learners from progressing at a rate commensurate with their potential (Arlin, 1984; Rosenshine & Stevens, 1986; J. A. Stein & Krishnan, 2007). Table 12.3 identifies some characteristics of students with special needs that might influence instructional decision making.

Include your instructional strategies in the individualized education programs (IEPs) you develop for students with special needs.

Chapter 5 identifies specific categories of special needs that fall within the five general categories listed in Table 12.3.

# STUDENTS IN INCLUSIVE SETTINGS

**TABLE 12.3 • Identifying Appropriate Instructional Goals and Strategies for Students with Special Educational Needs**

| CATEGORY | CHARACTERISTICS YOU MIGHT OBSERVE | SUGGESTED STRATEGIES |
|---|---|---|
| **Students with specific cognitive or academic difficulties** | • Uneven patterns of achievement<br>• Difficulty with complex cognitive tasks in some content domains<br>• Difficulty processing or remembering information presented in particular modalities<br>• Poor listening skills, reading skills, or both<br>• Greater-than-average difficulty in completing homework | • Tailor goals to individual students' strengths and weaknesses.<br>• Identify the specific cognitive skills involved in a complex task; consider teaching each skill separately.<br>• Use direct instruction, mastery learning, computer-based instruction, cooperative learning, and peer tutoring to help students master basic knowledge and skills.<br>• Provide information through multiple modalities (e.g., videotapes, audiotapes, graphic materials); also provide advance organizers and study guides.<br>• Have students use computer tools (e.g., grammar and spell checkers) to compensate for areas of weakness.<br>• Assign homework that provides additional practice in basic skills; provide extra scaffolding (e.g., solicit parents' help, explicitly teach effective study habits).<br>• Use reciprocal teaching to promote listening and reading comprehension. |
| **Students with social or behavioral problems** | • Frequent off-task behaviors<br>• Inability to work independently for extended periods<br>• Poor social skills | • Use small-group direct instruction and peer tutoring as ways of providing one-on-one attention.<br>• Keep unsupervised seatwork assignments to a minimum.<br>• Use cooperative learning to foster social skills and friendships.<br>• Give explicit guidelines about how to behave during interactive learning activities; closely monitor students' behavior in small groups.<br>• As appropriate, use strategies listed above for students with specific cognitive or academic difficulties. |
| **Students with general delays in cognitive and social functioning** | • Difficulty with complex tasks<br>• Difficulty thinking abstractly<br>• Need for a great deal of repetition and practice of basic information and skills<br>• Difficulty transferring information and skills to new situations | • Identify realistic goals related to both academic and social development.<br>• Break complex behaviors into simpler responses that students can easily learn.<br>• Present information in a concrete form (e.g., through hands-on experiences).<br>• Provide extended practice in basic skills.<br>• Embed skills within simple authentic tasks to promote transfer to the real world.<br>• Use peer tutoring to promote friendships with nondisabled classmates; also identify skills these students can teach to classmates or younger students. |

*(continued)*

| TABLE 12.3 • Continued | | |
|---|---|---|
| **CATEGORY** | **CHARACTERISTICS YOU MIGHT OBSERVE** | **SUGGESTED STRATEGIES** |
| Students with physical or sensory challenges | • Average intelligence in most instances<br>• Tendency to tire easily (for some)<br>• Limited motor skills (for some)<br>• Difficulty with speech (for some) | • Aim for instructional goals similar to those for nondisabled students unless there is a compelling reason to do otherwise.<br>• Allow frequent breaks from strenuous or intensive activities.<br>• Use instructional software (with any needed mechanical adaptations) to individualize instruction.<br>• When students have trouble speaking, provide assistive technology that enables them to participate actively in group activities. |
| Students with advanced cognitive development | • Rapid learning<br>• Greater frequency of responses at higher levels of Bloom's taxonomy (e.g., analysis, evaluation)<br>• Greater ability to think abstractly; earlier appearance of abstract thinking<br>• Greater conceptual understanding of classroom material<br>• Ability to learn independently | • Identify goals and objectives that challenge students and encourage them to develop to their full potential.<br>• Use expository instruction (e.g., lectures) as a way of transmitting abstract information about particular topics quickly and efficiently.<br>• Provide opportunities to pursue topics in greater depth (e.g., through assigned readings, the Internet, or homogeneous cooperative learning groups).<br>• Teach strategies that enable students to learn on their own (e.g., teach the scientific method, library skills, effective use of Internet websites).<br>• Ask predominantly higher-level questions.<br>• Introduce students to safe Internet outlets where they can communicate with others who have similar interests and abilities.<br>• Use advanced students as peer tutors only if both tutors and learners will benefit. |

*Sources:* Strategies based on suggestions from T. Bryan, Burstein, & Bryan, 2001; Carnine, 1989; Connor, 2006; DuNann & Weber, 1976; Egbert, 2009; Fiedler, Lange, & Winebrenner, 1993; Fletcher, Lyon, Fuchs, & Barnes, 2007; Greenwood et al., 1988; Heward, 2009; C. C. Kulik et al., 1990; Mercer & Pullen, 2005; P. F. Merrill et al., 1996; Morgan & Jenson, 1988; Piirto, 1999; A. Robinson, 1991; Ruef, Higgins, Glaeser, & Patnode, 1998; Schiffman, Tobin, & Buchanan, 1984; Spicker, 1992; R. J. Stevens & Slavin, 1995; J. R. Sullivan & Conoley, 2004; Tarver, 1992; Turnbull, Turnbull, & Wehmeyer, 2010; J. W. Wood & Rosbe, 1985.

## 12  What Have You Learned?

As a way of summarizing key ideas in the chapter, we now return to the chapter's learning outcomes.

■ **12.1: Identify eight general principles that can guide your planning and instructional strategies.** As teachers, we must choose our strategies on the basis of our instructional goals and objectives, the specific topics we're teaching, and the unique characteristics of our students. More specifically, we should:

■ Begin our planning with what we ultimately want students to achieve and then choose instructional strategies accordingly.

■ Flexibly combine multiple strategies into each lesson or unit.

■ Promote meaningful learning and other beneficial cognitive processes.

■ Focus on knowledge and skills most important for students' long-term success.

■ Provide structure and scaffolding appropriate for students' ability levels.

■ Capitalize on technological innovations that can enhance students' performance.

■ Take individual and group differences into account in instructional decision making.

■ Regularly assess students' progress in order to both modify lesson plans and provide constructive feedback.

Evaluate and apply your knowledge related to this learning outcome in MyEducationLab™.

■ **12.2: Describe important elements of planning for instruction, and explain how planning and instruction are closely intertwined.** Effective teachers engage in considerable advance planning, and they continually evaluate and modify their plans as the school year progresses. They identify the general instructional goals and more specific instructional objectives they would like students to accomplish. They conduct task analyses to break complex tasks into smaller and simpler components, and they develop lesson plans that spell out the instructional activities and assessments they'll use each day. And with the increasing availability of computer technology and the Internet in today's world, many teachers now create class-specific websites that enable them to communicate effectively with students and parents.

Evaluate and apply your knowledge related to this learning outcome in MyEducationLab™.

■ **12.3: Explain how you can effectively promote students' learning through teacher-directed instructional strategies.** In teacher-directed instruction, a teacher is largely in control of the content and course of a lesson. Teacher-directed strategies take multiple forms, but to some extent they all involve *expository* instruction; that is, they present (expose) information in essentially the same form that students are expected to learn it. Lectures, textbooks, and other predominantly expository approaches are most effective when we apply basic principles of cognitive psychology—for example, when we show students how new material relates to their prior knowledge and help them encode ideas in multiple ways. Many teacher-directed strategies include ongoing teacher–student interactions. For example, we can encourage students to elaborate on what they've learned through the questions we ask and the feedback we give, and we can provide practice and encourage complex cognitive processes (e.g., transfer and problem solving) through in-class assignments and homework. We can also combine multiple teacher-directed strategies into direct instruction and/or mastery learning sessions. Internet websites and computer-based instruction—which often fall midway along the teacher-directed–learner-directed continuum—provide additional options for teaching a variety of academic topics and skills.

**Evaluate** and **apply** your knowledge related to this learning outcome in MyEducationLab™.

■ **12.4: Explain how you can also promote students' learning through more learner-directed strategies.** Learner-directed instruction is instruction in which students have considerable control regarding the issues they address and the ways they address them. Like teacher-directed instruction, it can take a variety of forms. For example, class discussions and technology-based collaborative learning provide arenas in which students can encounter multiple perspectives on complex or controversial topics and

build on one another's ideas. Reciprocal teaching encourages more sophisticated metacognition and study skills by modeling and providing practice in effective reading strategies. Structured discovery learning and inquiry learning activities provide opportunities for students to self-construct new knowledge or develop advanced reasoning skills through in-depth observations and/or data analyses. Well-designed computer simulations and games can immerse students in virtual environments in which they apply classroom subject matter to real-worldlike problems. Cooperative learning activities encourage students to work collaboratively on challenging tasks and to mutually support one another's efforts to learn and achieve. And peer tutoring sessions can help both the tutor and the student being tutored gain better understandings of classroom subject matter.

**Evaluate** and **apply** your knowledge related to this learning outcome in MyEducationLab™.

■ **12.5: Choose appropriate instructional strategies for varying instructional goals and different kinds of students.** Different instructional goals and objectives often require somewhat different instructional strategies. For instance, whereas expository methods may be quite useful in teaching basic knowledge and skills, learner-directed approaches tend to be better for promoting complex cognitive processes such as problem solving and critical thinking. Students' unique characteristics, abilities, and circumstances are important considerations as well. For example, cooperative instructional strategies may be especially effective with students whose cultural backgrounds encourage cooperation rather than competition, and authentic activities and computer simulations can be quite motivating for students from low-income backgrounds.

**Evaluate** and **apply** your knowledge related to this learning outcome in MyEducationLab™.

---

## Practice for Your Licensure Exam

## Cooperative Learning Project

One Monday morning Ms. Mihara begins the unit "Customs in Other Lands" in her fourth-grade class. She asks students to choose two or three students with whom they would like to work to study a particular country. After the students have assembled into six small groups, she assigns each group a country: Australia, Colombia, Ireland, Greece, Japan, or South Africa. She tells the students, "Today we'll go to the school library, where your group can find information on the customs of your country and check out materials you think will be useful. Every day over the next two weeks you'll have time to work with your group. A week from Friday, each group will give an oral report to the class."

During the next few class sessions, Ms. Mihara runs into many more problems than she anticipated. She realizes that the high achievers have gotten together to form two of the groups,

and many socially oriented, "popular" students have flocked to two others. The remaining two groups are comprised of whichever students were left over. Some groups get to work immediately on their task, others spend their group time joking and sharing gossip, and still others are neither academically nor socially productive.

As the unit progresses, Ms. Mihara hears more and more complaints from students about their task: "Janet and I are doing all the work; Karen and Mary Kay aren't helping at all," "Eugene thinks he can boss the rest of us around because we're studying Ireland and he's Irish," "We're spending all this time but just can't seem to get anywhere!" And the group reports at the end of the unit differ markedly in quality: Some are carefully planned and informative, whereas others are disorganized and have little substance.

"So much for this cooperative learning stuff," Ms. Mihara mumbles to herself. "If I want students to learn something, I'll just have to teach it to them myself."

1. **Constructed-response question:**

   Describe two things you might do to improve Ms. Mihara's cooperative learning activity. Base your improvements on research findings related to cooperative learning or on contemporary principles and theories of learning, development, or motivation.

2. **Multiple-choice question:**

   Ms. Mihara never identifies an instructional objective for her unit "Customs in Other Lands." Which one of the following objectives reflects commonly accepted guidelines about how instructional objectives should be formulated?

   a. The teacher should expose students to many differences in behaviors and beliefs that exist in diverse cultures (e.g., eating habits, ceremonial practices, religious beliefs, moral values).

   b. The teacher should use a variety of instructional practices, including (but not limited to) lectures, direct instruction, textbook readings, and cooperative learning activities.

   c. Students should study a variety of cultural behaviors and beliefs, including those of countries in diverse parts of the world.

   d. Students should demonstrate knowledge of diverse cultural practices—for example, by describing three distinct ways in which another culture is different from their own.

---

**PRAXIS** Go to Appendix C, "Matching Book and MyEducationLab™ to the Praxis Principles of Learning and Teaching Tests," to discover sections of this chapter that may be especially applicable to the Praxis tests.

---

# 13 Creating a Productive Learning Environment

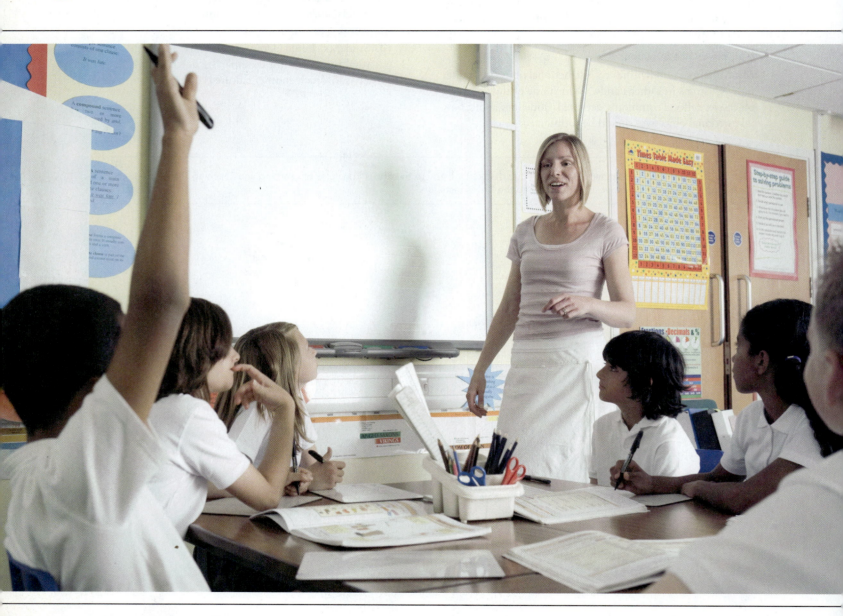

## LEARNING OUTCOMES

**13.1:** Describe numerous strategies for creating a classroom environment conducive to academic achievement and students' personal well-being.

**13.2:** Explain how you can coordinate your efforts with colleagues, community agencies, and parents to maximize students' academic and personal development.

**13.3:** Identify six general approaches to dealing with student misbehaviors and the circumstances and cultural contexts in which each approach might be appropriate.

**13.4:** Describe a three-level approach that can effectively reduce aggression and violence in the overall school community, as well as additional strategies you might use to address gang-related hostilities.

## CASE STUDY: A CONTAGIOUS SITUATION

After receiving a teaching certificate in May, Ms. Cornell has accepted a position as a fifth-grade teacher. She has spent the summer identifying instructional goals for the year and planning lessons that should help students achieve those goals. Today, on the first day of school, she has jumped headlong into the curriculum she planned. But three problems quickly present themselves—in the forms of Eli, Jake, and Vanessa.

These three students seem determined to disrupt the class at every possible opportunity. They move around the room without permission, intentionally annoying others as they walk to the pencil sharpener or wastebasket. They talk out of turn, often in disrespectful ways to their teacher and peers. They rarely complete assignments, preferring instead to engage in horseplay or practical jokes. They seem especially prone to misbehavior during downtimes in the daily schedule—for example, at the beginning and end of the school day, before and after recess and lunch, and whenever Ms. Cornell is preoccupied with other students.

Ms. Cornell continues to follow her daily lesson plans, ignoring her problem students and hoping they'll eventually shape up. Yet the disruptive behavior continues, with the three of them delighting in one another's antics. Furthermore, the misbehavior begins to spread to other students. By the middle of October, Ms. Cornell's classroom is out of control, and the few students who are still interested in learning something are having a hard time doing so.

- In what ways has Ms. Cornell planned in advance for her classroom? In what ways has she *not* planned?

---

As a first-year teacher, Ms. Cornell is well prepared in some respects but not at all prepared in others. She has carefully identified her instructional goals and planned relevant lessons. But she has neglected to think about how she might keep students on task or how she might adjust her lessons based on how students are progressing. And she hasn't considered how she might nip behavior problems in the bud, before they begin to interfere with instruction and learning. In the absence of such planning, no curriculum can be effective—not even one grounded firmly in contemporary theories of learning, development, and motivation.

Learning always takes place within particular contexts—for instance, within particular physical settings, social groups, and cultures. In academic learning, one important context is, of course, the classroom. Skillful teachers not only choose instructional strategies that foster effective learning and thinking but also create a classroom environment that keeps students busily engaged in productive learning activities. They certainly deal with the inappropriate behaviors that occur, but their emphasis is on *preventing* such behaviors. As we explore classroom management strategies in this chapter, our focus, too, will be on prevention. We'll frequently return to the opening case study and consider how Ms. Cornell might have gotten the school year off to a better start.

# Creating a Setting Conducive to Learning

In general, **classroom management** involves creating and maintaining a classroom environment conducive to students' learning and achievement. Students definitely learn more in some classrooms than in others. Consider these four classes as examples:

- Mr. Aragon's class is calm and orderly. Students are working independently at their seats, and all of them appear to be concentrating on individually tailored tasks. Occasionally students approach Mr. Aragon to seek clarification of an assignment or to get feedback about a task they've completed, and he quietly confers with them.

**classroom management**
Establishment and maintenance of a classroom environment that's conducive to learning and achievement.

Chapter 3 discusses the benefits of authoritative parenting from a developmental perspective.

- Mr. Boitano's class is chaotic and noisy. A few students are doing their schoolwork, but most are engaged in nonacademic activities. One girl is painting her nails, a boy nearby is picking chewing gum off the underside of his desk, three students are exchanging gossip, and several others are attacking one another with paperclips and rubber bands.

- Mr. Cavalini's class is as noisy as Mr. Boitano's. But rather than exchanging gossip or waging battle, students are debating—often loudly and passionately—the pros and cons of nuclear energy. After 20 minutes of heated discussion, Mr. Cavalini stops the conversation, lists students' various arguments on the board, and then explains why there's no simple "correct" resolution of the issue.

- Mr. Durocher believes that students learn most effectively when rules for their behavior are clearly spelled out, so he has 53 rules that cover almost every conceivable occasion: "Always use a ballpoint pen with blue or black ink," "Don't submit assignments on torn-out pages from spiral notebooks," "Don't ask questions unrelated to the lesson," and so on. He punishes each infraction severely enough that students follow the rules to the letter. As a result, his students are a quiet and obedient bunch, but their achievement levels remain discouragingly low.

Two of these classrooms are quiet and orderly; the other two are active and noisy. But as you can see, the activity and noise levels are poor indicators of how much students are learning. Students are learning in Mr. Aragon's quiet class and in Mr. Cavalini's noisier one. Neither the students in Mr. Boitano's loud, chaotic battlefield nor those in Mr. Durocher's peaceful dictatorship seem to be learning much at all. A well-managed classroom is one in which students are consistently engaged in productive learning activities and in which students' behaviors rarely interfere with the achievement of instructional goals (Brophy, 2006; W. Doyle, 1990; Emmer & Evertson, 1981). It *isn't* one in which students' every move is closely controlled.

Creating and maintaining an environment in which students are continually engaged in productive activities can be a challenging task. We must tend to the unique needs of many different students, must sometimes coordinate several activities at once, and must often make quick decisions about how to respond to unanticipated events. Furthermore, we must vary our classroom management techniques considerably depending on the particular instructional strategies in progress; for instance, direct instruction, hands-on activities, and cooperative learning all require somewhat different management techniques. It isn't surprising, then, that many beginning teachers mention classroom management as their number-one concern (Evertson & Weinstein, 2006; V. Jones, 1996; Veenman, 1984).

A good general model of effective classroom management is *authoritative parenting*. Authoritative parents tend to do the following:

- Provide a generally loving and supportive environment.
- Hold high expectations and standards for children's behavior.
- Explain why some behaviors are acceptable and others are not.
- Consistently enforce reasonable rules for behavior.
- Include children in decision making.
- Provide age-appropriate opportunities for independence.

As we explore classroom management strategies in this chapter, we'll often see one or more of these characteristics at work.

I've organized my discussion of preventive classroom management strategies around eight general strategies:

- Create a physical arrangement that helps to focus students' attention on classroom lessons and academic subject matter.
- Establish and maintain good working relationships with students.

- 🍏 Create a psychological climate in which students feel emotionally safe and are intrinsically motivated to learn.
- 🍏 Set reasonable limits for behavior.
- 🍏 Plan activities that keep students on task and productive.
- 🍏 Regularly monitor what students are doing.
- 🍏 Modify instructional strategies when necessary.
- 🍏 Take developmental differences and student diversity into account in making classroom management decisions.

In the upcoming sections we'll identify specific ways to implement each of these strategies.

## ARRANGING THE CLASSROOM

Good management begins well before the first day of class. As we arrange desks and chairs, decide where to put instructional materials and equipment, and think about where each student will sit, we should consider the effects that various arrangements are likely to have on students' behavior. The following strategies are especially helpful.

🍏 *Arrange furniture in ways that encourage student interaction when it's appropriate and discourage it when it's counterproductive.* When I was a child, student desks and chairs were bolted to the floor in tidy rows—an arrangement that was compatible only with a traditional lecture format. Fortunately the great majority of classrooms now have movable furniture, giving us considerable flexibility in how we might arrange and occasionally rearrange things. Several clusters of desks and chairs facing one another are useful for small-group work, whereas traditional rows are often more effective in keeping students on task during individual assignments (K. Carter & Doyle, 2006). However, we should be sensitive to cultural differences here: Students who are accustomed to cooperating regularly with peers (e.g., students from many Native American communities) might find an everyone-faces-the-teacher arrangement strange and unnerving (Lipka, 1994).

Ideally the classroom's furniture and physical layout should enable a variety of instructional strategies, including not only whole-group lectures and computer-based presentations but also small-group work, independent assignments, and hands-on, physical activities. A classroom should also be well organized and visually appealing, but without presenting unnecessary distractions.

🍏 *Minimize possible distractions.* Certainly we want to make our classrooms visually appealing and enticing—for example, by putting colorful messages and posters on walls and bulletin boards—but we shouldn't bombard students with so much visual stimulation that they have trouble concentrating on their schoolwork. We should also arrange our classrooms in ways that minimize the likelihood of off-task behaviors—for instance, by establishing traffic patterns that allow students to move around the room without disturbing one another and by seating overly chatty friends on opposite sides of the room. And we should keep intriguing materials out of sight and reach until we need them (Emmer & Evertson, 2009; Hanley, Tiger, Ingvarsson, & Cammilleri, 2009; Sabers, Cushing, & Berliner, 1991).

🍏 *Arrange the classroom so that it's easy to interact with students.* Our arrangement of desks, tables, and chairs should make it easy for us to converse with virtually any student as necessary. It's often beneficial to place chronically misbehaving or uninvolved students close at hand: Students seated near us are more likely to pay attention, interact with us, and become actively involved in classroom activities (G. A. Davis & Thomas, 1989; Strother, 1991; Woolfolk & Brooks, 1985).

 Place chronically misbehaving or uninvolved students close at hand.

🍏 *Identify locations that allow easy monitoring of students' behavior.* As we proceed through various lessons and activities—even when working with a single individual or small group—we should regularly be able to see *all* students (Emmer & Evertson, 2009; Gettinger & Kohler, 2006). By occasionally surveying the classroom for possible signs of confusion, frustration, or boredom, we can more easily detect minor student difficulties and misbehaviors before they develop into serious problems.

🍏 *Make appropriate changes for classwide use of technology.* If students are individually using laptops or computer tablets—something that's happening more frequently as schools increasingly invest in technology—we should arrange furniture *and* position ourselves in ways that enable us to monitor the contents of each student's computer screen. My son Jeff (a middle school teacher) arranges his students in rows to work on their laptops. He displays the contents of his own computer screen on a whiteboard at the front of the room but uses a wireless keyboard and mouse while standing at the back of the room, where he can simultaneously see all of his students' screens.

## ESTABLISHING AND MAINTAINING PRODUCTIVE TEACHER–STUDENT RELATIONSHIPS

Research consistently indicates that the quality of teacher–student relationships is one of the most important factors—perhaps *the* most important factor—affecting students' emotional well-being, motivation, and learning during the school day. When students have positive, supportive relationships with teachers, they have more intrinsic motivation to learn, engage in more self-regulated learning, behave more appropriately in class, and achieve at higher levels (J. N. Hughes, Luo, Kwok, & Loyd, 2008; Marzano, 2003; Patrick, Ryan, & Kaplan, 2007; Pianta, Belsky, Vandergrift, Houts, & Morrison, 2008; Roorda, Koomen, Spilt, & Oort, 2011).

Without a doubt, high-quality teacher–student relationships help students satisfy their *need for relatedness*—their need to feel socially connected with others. Although some students may misbehave as a way of gaining our attention (this might be true for Eli, Jake, and Vanessa in the opening case study), in my own experiences as a parent, teacher, and school psychologist, I've never met a child or adolescent who, deep down, didn't want to have positive, productive relationships with school faculty members.

The following strategies must be central in our efforts to have productive working relationships with students.

🍏 *Regularly communicate caring and respect for students as individuals.* To some degree we can communicate affection and respect through the many little things we do each day (Allday, Bush, Ticknor, & Walker, 2011; Allday & Pakurar, 2007; Certo, Cauley, & Chafin, 2003). For example, we can give students a smile and warm greeting at the beginning of the day. We can compliment them when they get a flattering haircut, excel in an extracurricular activity, or receive recognition in the local newspaper. We can be good listeners when they come to school angry or upset. And we should certainly learn every student's name within the first few days of school. One high school student described caring teachers this way:

> You might see them in the hallway and they ask how you're doing, how was your last report card, is there anything you need. Or, maybe one day you're looking a little upset. They'll pull you to the side and ask you what's wrong, is there anything I can do. (Certo, Cauley, & Chafin, 2002, p. 15)

Such caring gestures can be especially important for students who have few, if any, supportive relationships at home (Juvonen, 2006; E. O'Connor, Dearing, & Collins, 2011; E. O'Connor & McCartney, 2007).

🍏 *Remember that caring and respect involve much more than just showing affection.* Some beginning teachers erroneously think that good teaching involves little more than showing that they really like their students—in other words, being "warm and fuzzy" (L. H. Anderman, Patrick, Hruda, & Linnenbrink, 2002, p. 274; Goldstein & Lake, 2000; Patrick & Pintrich, 2001). In fact, to show students that we *truly* care about and respect them, we must take steps such as these:

- Be well prepared for class, and in other ways demonstrate a love of teaching and an eagerness to take teaching responsibilities seriously.
- Communicate high yet realistic expectations for performance, and provide the support students need to meet those expectations.
- Include students in decision making and evaluation of their work.
- Acknowledge that students can occasionally have an "off" day. (Certo et al., 2003; M.-L. Chang & Davis, 2009; H. A. Davis, 2003; H. A. Davis, Schutz, & Chambless, 2001; Patrick, Kaplan, & Ryan, 2011; Wentzel, Battle, Russell, & Looney, 2010)

Another important strategy is to establish means through which students can communicate privately with us. One option, especially for older students, is email, perhaps through a class website or other online mechanism that prevents students from wandering into potentially inappropriate Internet sites (e.g., see Gaggle at www.gaggle.net). A low-tech alternative is a "What's Up?" form

A need for relatedness may be one of human beings' most basic psychological needs (see Chapter 11).

Establish mechanisms through which you can communicate regularly and privately with every student.

**FIGURE 13.1** Two-way *dialogue journals* provide one effective means of maintaining one-on-one communication with all students. In these excerpts from 6-year-old Matt's journal, Matt and his first-grade teacher discover common outside interests.

I am a couch potato. ara you?

> Sometimes I am! I like to curl up under an afghan and read until way past my bedtime. What else do you like to do?

I love soccer. I am grit at golf.

> I see you playing soccer all the time at recess. And I saw you at Woodridge fields last fall. You really are good! Do you play any other sports?

I play bas ball sam tim. Do you play ini sprts?

> I love to play basketball. I used to be on a team in high school. I am a good skier too. And I like to swim and dive.

I lak skiein spshal don hilscein. Are you god at sceih?

> I am a very good skier. I like to go fast. Do you think you could keep up with me? We used to have our own ski lift in our back yard!

I can go fastr than you.

> I guess we will just have to have a race sometime! Where do you usually go skiing? Besides, you said you are a couch potato. I am sure that I can beat a couch potato! Cinchy!

on which students might occasionally write and submit information about especially noteworthy or challenging events in their personal lives (A. K. Smith, 2009). A third possibility is the use of two-way *dialogue journals,* in which individual students and their teacher both write one or more times each week. Figure 13.1 shows several entries in 6-year-old Matt's journal; each entry is followed by a response (indented) from his first-grade teacher. Notice that Matt feels comfortable enough with his teacher to engage in playful one-upmanship ("I can go fastr then you"). Although his writing skills are far from perfect—for instance, he writes *especially downhill skiing* as "spshal don hilscein"—they're certainly adequate to communicate his thoughts. Notice, too, that his teacher doesn't correct his misspellings. Her primary purposes are to encourage him to write and to open the lines of communication; giving negative feedback about spelling here might interfere with both of these goals.

🍎 *Work hard to improve relationships that have gotten off to a bad start.* Occasionally students may come to us with an apparent chip on the shoulder, distrusting us from the start because of previous hurtful relationships with parents, teachers, or other adults (H. A. Davis, 2003; Hyman et al., 2006; Pianta, 1999). At other times we may get relationships off to a bad beginning through our own actions—perhaps because we've incorrectly attributed low achievement to lack of effort rather than lack of skill or perhaps because we've accused a temperamentally high-energy child of being intentionally disobedient (M.-L. Chang & Davis, 2009; B. K. Keogh, 2003; Silverberg, 2003). Occasionally, too, students might misinterpret something we say or do. For example, the first day that 8-year-old Darcy attended third grade at a new school, she accidentally got egg in her hair. Her teacher, Mrs. Whaley, took her to the nurse's office to have the egg washed out. As revealed in the journal entries in Figure 13.2, Darcy initially misinterpreted Mrs. Whaley's comment about the situation. Not until five days later did she gain a more accurate understanding of what Mrs. Whaley had said.

**FIGURE 13.2** As her journal entries show, 8-year-old Darcy initially interpreted her teacher's casual remark to the school nurse in a way very different from the teacher's intended meaning. Fortunately, the teacher corrected the misunderstanding a few days later.

October 22
I went to a new school today. My teacher's name is Mrs. Whaley. I accidentally cracked an egg on my head. Mrs. Whaley told the nurse that I was a showoff and a nuisance. I got really sad and wanted to run away from school, but I didn't leave.

. . .

October 27
We presented our book reports today. I was the last one to present my book report. Whenever I did my book report, they laughed at me, but the teacher said they were laughing with me. I asked the teacher why she had called me a nuisance the first day. And she said, "Darcy, I didn't call you a nuisance. I was saying to Mrs. Larson that it was a nuisance to try to wash egg out of your hair." I was so happy. I decided to like Mrs. Whaley again.

Good teacher–student relationships are one essential element of an effective classroom climate. Explore strategies in the simulation "Developing Positive Teacher–Student Relationships with All Students."

Unfortunately, students who have the poorest relationships with their teachers are often the ones most in need of good ones (Juvonen, 2006; Stipek & Miles, 2008; Wentzel, Donlan, Morrison, Russell, & Baker, 2009). Thus, regardless of the causes of nonproductive relationships, we must work hard to turn them into productive ones. The first step, of course, is to *identify* nonproductive relationships, recognizing signs such as these:

- We have hostile feelings (e.g., dislike, anger) toward a student.
- We rarely interact with a student.
- Our messages to a student usually involve criticism or faultfinding.
- We have a sense of learned helplessness about our ability to work effectively with a student. (Houts, Caspi, Pianta, Arseneault, & Moffitt, 2010; Pianta, 1999; Sutherland & Morgan, 2003)

Once we've identified troublesome relationships, several strategies can help us repair them:

- Meet one on one with a student to talk openly about the problem and possible ways to fix it (more on this point later in the chapter).
- Think actively—perhaps in a brainstorming session with one or more colleagues—about alternative hypotheses that might explain a student's behavior and about potential solutions that varying hypotheses suggest.
- Spend time with a student in a relaxed, noninstructional context—perhaps a mutually enjoyable recreational activity—that can allow more positive feelings to emerge. (M.-L. Chang & Davis, 2009; Pianta, 1999, 2006; Silverberg, 2003; Sutton & Wheatley, 2003)

## CREATING AN EFFECTIVE PSYCHOLOGICAL CLIMATE

Caring and supportive teacher–student relationships are important contributors to the overall classroom climate—the general psychological environment that permeates classroom interactions. Ultimately we want a classroom in which students feel safe and secure, make learning a high priority, and are willing to take the risks and make the mistakes so critical for maximal cognitive growth (Brand, Felner, Shim, Seitsinger, & Duman, 2003; Hamre & Pianta, 2005; Hattie & Gan, 2011). Such an environment minimizes discipline problems and seems to be especially important for students at risk for academic failure and dropping out of school (Freiberg & Lapointe, 2006; V. E. Lee & Burkam, 2003; Pianta, 1999). Following are several critical strategies.

- *Establish a goal-oriented, businesslike, yet nonthreatening atmosphere.* We and our students must all recognize that we're in school to get certain things accomplished (G. A. Davis & Thomas, 1989). Effective classroom activities and tasks are typically interesting and engaging—occasionally even exhilarating—rather than tedious and boring. However, entertainment and excitement shouldn't be goals in and of themselves. Rather, they're means to a more important goal: mastering academic subject matter.

Despite our emphasis on business, the classroom atmosphere should never be uncomfortable or threatening, because students who are excessively anxious are unlikely to give us their best (Cassady, 2010a; Sapolsky, 2005). Strategies such as these enable us to be businesslike without being threatening:

Chapter 11 discusses the potential adverse effects of anxiety.

- Hold students accountable for achieving instructional objectives but without placing them under continual surveillance.
- Point out students' errors and misconceptions within the context of messages that highlight their strengths (e.g., inquisitiveness, critical thinking skills) and ongoing progress.
- Admonish students for misbehavior without holding grudges against them from one day to the next. (K. L. Fletcher & Cassady, 2010; Narciss, 2008; C. R. Rogers, 1983; Spaulding, 1992)

**classroom climate** Overall psychological atmosphere of the classroom.

🍎 *Communicate and demonstrate that school tasks and academic subject matter have value.* As teachers, we give students messages about the value of school subject matter by both what we say and what we do (Brophy, 2008; W. Doyle, 1983). For example, if we ask students to spend hours each day engaged in what seems like meaningless busy work and if we assess learning primarily through tests that encourage rote memorization, we're indirectly telling students that classroom tasks are merely things that need to be "gotten over with" (E. H. Hiebert & Raphael, 1996; Stodolsky, Salk, & Glaessner, 1991). Furthermore, if we continually focus students' attention on performance goals—what their grades are, how their work compares to that of others, and so on—we may increase their anxiety about academic achievement and indirectly increase the frequency of disruptive behavior (Kumar, Gheen, & Kaplan, 2002; Marachi, Friedel, & Midgley, 2001; Patrick et al., 2011). If, instead, we continually communicate that learning classroom subject matter can help students make better sense of the outside world, if we assess learning in ways that require meaningful learning, and if we focus on how well each student is improving over time, we show students that mastering the subject matter can potentially enhance the quality of students' lives.

🍎 *Give students some control over classroom activities.* To make sure students accomplish important instructional goals, we must direct the course of classroom activities to some degree. Nevertheless, we can give students control over some aspects of classroom life—for example, through strategies such as these:

- 🍎 Give advance notice of upcoming activities and assignments, enabling students to plan ahead.

- 🍎 Create a regular routine for completing assignments, enabling students to do them with only minimal guidance.

- 🍎 Allow students to set their own deadlines for some assignments, enabling them to establish a manageable schedule.

- 🍎 Occasionally let students choose how to accomplish certain instructional goals and objectives, enabling them to set some of their own priorities. (Patall, Cooper, & Wynn, 2010; Spaulding, 1992)

Through such strategies, we promote the sense of self-determination so important for intrinsic motivation, along with the development of self-regulation skills so essential for students' long-term academic success.

🍎 *Promote a general sense of community and belongingness.* An increasingly popular instructional strategy is to create a *community of learners,* a classroom in which one or more teachers and their students collaborate to build a body of knowledge about a topic and help one another learn about it. Ultimately we also want to create a general sense of community in the classroom—a sense that we and our students have shared goals, are mutually respectful and supportive of one another's efforts, and believe that everyone makes an important contribution to classroom learning (Clani, Middleton, Summers, & Sheldon, 2010; Hom & Battistich, 1995; D. Kim, Solomon, & Roberts, 1995; Osterman, 2000). Creating a sense of community engenders feelings of belongingness: Students see themselves as important and valued members of the classroom (E. M. Anderman, 2002; J. Ellis, Fitzsimmons, & Small-McGinley, 2010).

When students share a sense of community, they're more likely to exhibit prosocial behavior, stay on task, be enthusiastic about classroom activities, and achieve at high levels. Furthermore, a sense of classroom community is associated with lower rates of emotional distress, disruptive classroom behavior, truancy, and dropping out (Hom & Battistich, 1995; Juvonen, 2006; Osterman, 2000; Patrick et al., 2007). And consistent experiences with caring and equitable classroom communities help students internalize attitudes essential for a successful democratic society, including a commitment to fairness and justice for everyone (C. A. Flanagan, Cumsille, Gill, & Gallay, 2007).

Perhaps the most important characteristic of a sense of classroom community is that students always treat one another with kindness and respect. Even when students must take issue with something that one of their classmates has said or done, they can do so tactfully and respectfully (e.g., see Figure 13.3). When classmates *aren't* kind and respectful—for example,

**sense of community** Shared belief that teacher and students have common goals, are mutually respectful and supportive, and all make important contributions to classroom learning.

**belongingness** General sense that one is an important and valued member of the classroom.

Chapter 11 discusses the importance of giving students a sense of self-determination.

You can learn more about communities of learners in Chapter 8.

 Create a sense of shared goals, interpersonal respect, and mutual support.

**FIGURE 13.3** Especially in the elementary grades, many students benefit from visual reminders about how to interact with classmates, as illustrated in these two posters displayed in a second-grade classroom.

<u>Words to use</u>

I don't like it when _____.

Can you not do _____?

Can you please stop _____?

I need a break and then I'll come back to talk about it.

<u>Working with a Partner</u>

Be polite.

Help each other.

Share.

Listen to your partner.

Be a good sport.

Take turns.

Take about problems.

Speak respectfully.

Posters courtesy of Christina Fox.

when they ridicule or bully certain other class members—their victims are apt to withdraw either physically or mentally from classroom activities (Swearer, Espelage, Vaillancourt, & Hymel, 2010).

As teachers, we must make it very clear. that remarks or behaviors that deride or denigrate other class members are *totally unacceptable* both inside and outside the classroom. The Creating a Productive Classroom Environment feature "Creating and Enhancing a Sense of Classroom Community" offers several strategies that can enhance students' sense that they're important and valued members of the classroom.

> Refuse to tolerate statements or behaviors that show lack of concern or respect for other class members.

## SETTING LIMITS

In the opening case study, Ms. Cornell failed to provide guidelines for how students should behave—something she should have done the first week of school. Students must know that certain behaviors simply won't be tolerated, especially those that cause physical or psychological harm, damage school property, or interfere with others' learning and performance. And over the long run, setting reasonable limits on classroom behavior helps students become productive members of adult society. In other words, imposing limits on students' behavior is one important way in which schools help *socialize* children to work effectively in their cultural group.

> See Chapter 3 for a discussion of socialization as an important factor in children's development.

As we set limits, however, we must remember that students are more likely to be intrinsically motivated to master classroom subject matter if we preserve their sense of autonomy and self-determination. With this caution in mind, I offer the following recommendations.

*Establish a few rules and procedures at the beginning of the year.* Effective classroom managers establish and communicate certain rules and procedures right from the start. For example, they identify acceptable and unacceptable behaviors and describe the consequences of noncompliance. They develop consistent procedures and routines for such things as completing seatwork, asking for help, and turning in assignments. They have procedures in place for nonroutine events such as school assemblies, field trips, and fire drills. And in today's high-tech world, many teachers forbid cell phone use during class time, perhaps by having a box in which students deposit their phones at the beginning of class. Taking time to clarify rules and procedures seems to be especially important in the early elementary grades, when students may not be very familiar with how things are typically done at school (K. Carter & Doyle, 2006; W. Doyle, 1990; Gettinger & Kohler, 2006; K. L. Lane, Menzies, Bruhn, & Crnobori, 2011).

## Creating a Productive Classroom Environment

### Creating and Enhancing a Sense of Classroom Community

🍎 **Consistently communicate the message that *all* students deserve the respect of their classmates and are important members of the classroom community.**
A middle school language arts class has three students with reading disabilities that are obvious in much of the students' oral and written work in class. The teacher doesn't publicly identify the students with disabilities, because doing so would violate their right to confidentiality about their conditions. However, she frequently communicates the message that students at any grade level vary widely in their literacy skills—usually through no fault of their own—and continually stresses that it's the class's responsibility to help *everyone* improve their literacy skills.

🍎 **Create mechanisms through which students can all help to make the class run smoothly and efficiently.**
A kindergarten teacher creates several "helper" roles (e.g., distributing art supplies, feeding the class goldfish) that he assigns to different students on a rotating basis.

🍎 **Emphasize such prosocial values as sharing and cooperation, and provide opportunities for students to help one another.**
As students work on in-class assignments each day, a seventh-grade math teacher often asks, "Who has a problem that someone else might be able to help you solve?"

🍎 **Make frequent use of interactive and collaborative teaching strategies.**
In assigning students to cooperative learning groups, a high school social studies teacher usually puts a student with poor social skills (e.g., a student with Asperger syndrome) in a group with two or three more socially proficient students. Before the groups begin their work, the teacher reminds students of the class's rules for cooperative group work, such as "Listen to others politely and attentively" and "Address differences of opinion in respectful and constructive ways."

🍎 **Solicit students' ideas and opinions, and incorporate them into class discussions and activities.**
A first-grade teacher regularly has students vote on the storybook she should read during "settling-down" time after lunch each day.

She first reads the book that gets the most votes, but she assures students who voted differently that she'll read their choices later in the week, saying, "It's important that everyone has a say in what we read."

🍎 **Use competition only to create an occasional sense of playfulness in the class and only when all students have an equal chance of winning.**
A high school Spanish teacher assigns a long-term cooperative group project in which students write and videotape Spanish soap operas (*telenovelas*). A few weeks later the teacher holds an "Academy Awards Banquet"—a potluck dinner for the students and their families. At the banquet the teacher shows all the videos and awards a variety of "Oscars." Although she gives only one group an Oscar for best telenovela, she gives every student an Oscar for some aspect of his or her performance.

🍎 **Encourage students to be on the lookout for classmates on the periphery of ongoing activities—perhaps students with disabilities— and to ask these children to join in.**
Teachers at an elementary school all adhere to and enforce the same *no-exclusion* policy on the playground: Any student who wants to be involved in a play activity *can* be involved.

🍎 **Work on social skills with students whose interpersonal behaviors may victimize or alienate others.**
A third grader often behaves aggressively toward classmates who have something she wants. For example, when waiting for her turn at the class computer, she may yell "*I* need to use it now!" or, instead, shove its current user out of the chair. In a private conference, her teacher points out the importance of patience and turn taking and suggests several ways she might politely make her needs known (e.g., "When might you be finished with the computer? Can I use it after you're done?") The teacher also has the student practice the strategies in various role-playing scenarios.

*Sources:* C. Ames, 1984; M.-L. Chang & Davis, 2009; Evertson & Emmer, 2009; Hamovitch, 2007; D. Kim, Solomon, & Roberts, 1995; Lickona, 1991; Osterman, 2000; A. M. Ryan & Patrick, 2001; Sapon-Shevin, Dobbelaere, Corrigan, Goodman, & Mastin, 1998 (playground example); Stipek, 1996; Turnbull, Pereira, & Blue-Banning, 2000; M.-T. Wang & Holcombe, 2010; Wentzel et al., 2010.

---

Ideally students should understand that rules and procedures aren't based on our personal whims but are, instead, designed to help the class run smoothly and efficiently. One way of promoting such understanding is to include students in decision making about the rules and procedures by which the class will operate. For example, we might solicit students' suggestions for making sure that unnecessary distractions are kept to a minimum and that everyone has a chance to speak during class discussions. By incorporating students' ideas and listening to their concerns about the limits we set, we help them understand the reasons for—and also enhance their sense of ownership of—those limits (Evertson & Emmer, 2009; Fuller, 2001; M. Watson, 2008).

Keep in mind that rules and procedures are easier to remember—and therefore easier to follow—if they're relatively simple and few in number (W. Doyle, 1986a; Emmer & Gerwels, 2006; K. L. Lane et al., 2011). Effective classroom managers tend to stress only the most important rules and procedures at the beginning of the school year and introduce additional rules and procedures as needed later on. You should also keep in mind that, although some order and

**FIGURE 13.4** We are more likely to motivate students to follow classroom rules and procedures if we communicate those rules and procedures as information *without* conveying a desire to impose a lot of control.

| We might say this (as information) . . . | Rather than this (as control) |
| --- | --- |
| "You'll finish your independent assignments sooner if you get right to work." | "Please be quiet and do your own work." |
| "As we practice for our fire drill, it's important to line up quickly and quietly so that we can hear the instructions we're given and will know what to do." | "When the fire alarm sounds, line up quickly and quietly, and then wait for further instructions." |
| "This assignment can help you develop the writing skills you'll need after you graduate. It's unfair to other authors to copy their work word for word, so we'll practice putting ideas into our own words and giving credit to authors whose ideas we borrow. Passing off another's writing as your own can lead to suspension in college or a lawsuit in the business world." | "Cheating and plagiarism are not acceptable in this classroom." |

predictability are essential for student productivity, *too much* order can make a classroom a routine, boring place—one without any element of fun and spontaneity. We don't necessarily need rules and procedures for everything!

🍏 *Present rules and procedures in an informational rather than controlling manner.* We're more likely to maintain students' sense of self-determination if we present rules and procedures as items of information rather than as forms of control (Deci, 1992; Koestner, Ryan, Bernieri, & Holt, 1984; Reeve, 2009). Figure 13.4 presents several examples of rules and procedures presented in an informational manner. Each of these statements includes the reasons for imposing certain guidelines—a strategy that's likely to increase students' compliance. The following scenario provides a simple illustration of how giving a reason can make a noticeable difference:

> Gerard has little tolerance for frustration. Whenever he asks Ms. Donnelly for assistance, he wants it *now*. If she can't immediately help him, he screams, "You're no good!" or "You don't care!" and shoves other students' desks as he angrily walks back to his seat.
>
> At one point during the school year, the class has a unit on interpersonal skills. One lesson addresses *timing*—the most appropriate and effective time to ask for someone's assistance. A week later, Gerard approaches Ms. Donnelly for help with a math problem. She is working with another student but briefly turns to Gerard and says, "Timing." She expects the usual screaming, but instead he responds, "Hey, Ms. D., I get it! I can ask you at another time!" He returns to his seat with a smile. (Based on Sullivan-DeCarlo, DeFalco, & Roberts, 1998, p. 81)

🍏 *Periodically review the usefulness of existing rules and procedures.* As the school year progresses, we may discover that some rules and procedures need revision. For example, we may find that rules about when students can move around the room are overly restrictive or that procedures for turning in homework don't accommodate students who must leave class early for doctors' appointments or certain extracurricular events.

Regularly scheduled class meetings provide one mechanism through which we and our students can periodically review classroom rules and procedures (D. E. Campbell, 1996; Glasser, 1969; Striepling-Goldstein, 2004). Consider this scenario as an example:

> Every Friday afternoon Ms. Ayotte's students move their chairs into a circle for their weekly class meeting. First on the agenda is a review of the past week's successes, including both

When it's necessary to change classroom rules and procedures, include students in the decision making.

academic achievements and socially productive events. Next, the group identifies problems that have emerged during the week and brainstorms possible ways to avert such problems in the future. Finally, the students consider whether existing class rules and procedures are serving their purpose, and, if not, the group either modifies existing rules and procedures or establishes new ones. During the first few meetings, Ms. Ayotte leads the discussions, but once students have become familiar and comfortable with the process, she relinquishes control of the meetings to one or another of her students on a rotating basis.

By providing frequent opportunities for students to review classroom policies, we find another way of giving them a sense of ownership about the policies. Furthermore, more advanced moral reasoning may gradually emerge, perhaps as a result of occasional moral dilemmas with which students must wrestle (Milner, 2006; Nucci, 2006, 2009; Power, Higgins, & Kohlberg, 1989).

You can learn more about the nature and benefits of moral dilemmas in Chapter 3.

🍎 *Acknowledge students' feelings about requirements.* There will undoubtedly be times when we must ask students to do things they would prefer not to do. Rather than pretend that students are eager to do what we've asked of them, we're better advised to acknowledge their displeasure and lack of motivation. For example, we might tell students that we know how difficult it can be to sit quietly during a lengthy school assembly or to spend an entire evening on a particular assignment. At the same time we can explain that the behaviors we're requesting of them can help them achieve their own long-term goals. By acknowledging students' feelings about tasks they'd rather not do but also pointing out the benefits, we increase the likelihood that students will willingly comply (Jang, Reeve, & Deci, 2010; Reeve, 2009).

🍎 *Enforce rules consistently and equitably.* Classroom rules are likely to be effective only if they're consistently enforced. For example, in the opening case study Ms. Cornell imposes no consequences when her three troublesome students misbehave. Not only do their antics continue, but other students follow suit, realizing that "anything goes" in Ms. Cornell's classroom. As social cognitive theorists have pointed out, imposing no adverse consequence for inappropriate behavior—especially when that consequence has been spelled out in advance—can actually be a form of *reinforcement* for the misbehavior (Bandura, 1986).

Chapter 10 describes social cognitive theory's perspectives on reinforcement and punishment.

Consistency in enforcing classroom rules should apply not only across occasions but also across *students*. As teachers, we may often like some students more than others (e.g., we're apt to prefer high achievers), but we must keep our preferences to ourselves. Students can be quite resentful of teachers who grant special favors to and overlook rule infractions of a few favorite students (Babad, 1995; Babad, Avni-Babad, & Rosenthal, 2003; J. Baker, 1999). And students who are unfairly accused or punished are, of course, even more resentful, as one high school student explains:

> Because like if you had a past record or whatever like in middle school if you got in trouble like at all, they would think that you're a slight trouble maker and if you got in trouble again, they would always . . . if you were anywhere that something bad happened or something against the rules or whatever, they pick you first because they think that you have a past. So they wouldn't like pick the kids that had never done anything. (Certo et al., 2002, p. 25)

Classroom rules are more likely to be effective when students are involved in creating and evaluating them. Explore effective strategies in the simulation "Creating Classroom Behavioral Expectations."

Thus, consistency and equitable treatment for all students—or the lack thereof—is apt to have a significant effect on teacher–student relationships and overall classroom climate (Babad et al., 2003; Peter & Dalbert, 2010; Wentzel et al., 2010).

## PLANNING ACTIVITIES THAT KEEP STUDENTS ON TASK

As effective teachers plan their lessons, they think not only about how to facilitate students' learning and productive cognitive processes but also how to keep students consistently on task. Certainly a key strategy is to motivate students to *want* to master classroom subject matter, but experienced educators have offered several other suggestions as well:

🍎 *Make sure students are always productively engaged in worthwhile activities.* Virtually all human beings have a basic *need for arousal*—a need for some degree of physical or cognitive

Chapter 11 describes the need for arousal in more depth.

stimulation. At school, children and adolescents should find their stimulation in ongoing tasks and activities. If, instead, they have a lot of free time on their hands, they'll generate stimulation of their own, sometimes in the form of misbehaviors.

Effective classroom managers make sure that there's little unscheduled time in which nothing's going on. Following are several strategies for keeping students productively engaged:

- Have something specific for students to do each day, even on the first day of class.
- Have materials organized and equipment set up before class.
- Plan activities that ensure *all* students' involvement and participation.
- Maintain a brisk pace throughout each lesson, but without moving so quickly that students can't keep up.
- Ensure that students' comments are relevant and helpful but not excessively long winded. For example, take chronic time-monopolizers aside for a private discussion about giving classmates a chance to speak.
- Spend only short periods of class time assisting individual students unless other students are capable of working independently in the meantime.
- Ensure that students who finish an assigned task quickly have something else to do (e.g., reading a book or writing in a class journal). (W. Doyle, 1986a; Emmer & Evertson, 2009; Emmer & Gerwels, 2006; Gettinger, 1988; K. L. Lane et al., 2011; Munn, Johnstone, & Chalmers, 1990)

♦ *Choose tasks at an appropriate difficulty level for students' knowledge and skills.* Students are more likely to work diligently at their classwork when they have activities and assignments appropriate for their current knowledge and skills (Mac Iver, Reuman, & Main, 1995; J. W. Moore & Edwards, 2003; S. L. Robinson & Griesemer, 2006). They're apt to misbehave when they're asked to do things that they perceive—either accurately or not—to be exceptionally difficult. Hence classroom misbehaviors are more often observed with students who have a history of struggling in their schoolwork (W. Doyle, 1986a; Miles & Stipek, 2006). In the opening case study, Eli, Jake, and Vanessa may very well have such a history of failure.

Avoiding overly difficult tasks *doesn't* mean that we should plan activities so easy that students aren't challenged and learn nothing new. One strategy is to *begin* the school year with relatively easy tasks that students can readily complete. Such tasks enable students to practice normal classroom routines and procedures and gain a sense that they can succeed in and enjoy classroom activities. Once we've established a supportive classroom climate and made students comfortable with our procedures, we can gradually introduce more difficult and challenging assignments (W. Doyle, 1990; Emmer & Evertson, 2009).

♦ *Provide some structure for activities and assignments.* As an example of how important structure can be, try the following exercise.

> Begin the school year with easy and familiar tasks, introducing more difficult ones after a supportive classroom climate has been firmly established.

### EXPERIENCING FIRSTHAND
### POP QUIZ

Complete these two tasks either on paper or on your computer:

**Task A:** Using single words or short phrases, list six characteristics of an effective teacher.

**Task B:** Explain the general effects of school attendance on children's lives.

Don't read further until you've either (1) completed each task or (2) spent at least five minutes on it.

Once you've tackled the two tasks, answer each of the following questions:

1. For which task did you have a better understanding of what you were being asked to do?
2. During which task did your mind more frequently wander to irrelevant topics?
3. During which task did you engage in more off-task behaviors—perhaps looking around the room, doodling, or getting out of your seat?

I'm guessing that you found the first task relatively straightforward, whereas the second wasn't at all clear-cut. Did the ambiguity of Task B lead to more irrelevant thoughts and off-task behaviors? Off-task behavior occurs more frequently when activities are so loosely structured that students don't have a clear sense of what they're supposed to do.

Effective teachers tend to give assignments with some degree of structure—not only sufficient scaffolding to support learning but also clear guidance about how to proceed, especially during the first few weeks of the school year (W. Doyle, 1990; Evertson & Emmer, 1982; Gettinger & Kohler, 2006). However, we need to strike a happy medium here: We don't want to structure tasks to the point that they require only basic skills and never allow students to make decisions. In addition to keeping students on task, we also want them to have a sense of self-determination, practice self-regulation skills, and develop and use complex cognitive processes—for example, to think analytically, critically, and creatively (W. Doyle, 1986a; J. D. Nichols, 2004; Weinert & Helmke, 1995).

🍎 *Plan for transition times in the school day.* In the opening case study, Eli, Jake, and Vanessa often misbehave at the beginning and end of the school day, as well as before and after recess and lunch. Misbehaviors occur most frequently during transition times—as students end one activity and begin a second or as they move from one classroom to another. Effective classroom managers take steps to ensure that transitions proceed quickly and without a loss of momentum (W. Doyle, 1984; Gettinger & Kohler, 2006). For example, they establish procedures for moving from one activity to the next, and they ensure that there's little slack time in which students have nothing to do. And especially in the secondary grades, when students change classes every hour or so, effective classroom managers typically have a task for students to complete as soon as they enter the classroom. Consider these examples:

- An elementary school teacher has students follow the same procedure each day as lunchtime approaches: (1) Place completed assignments in the teacher's "In" basket, (2) put away supplies, (3) get out any home-packed lunches, and (4) line up quietly by the door.

- A middle school math teacher has students copy the night's homework assignment as soon as they come into class.

- As students first enter the classroom, a middle school social studies teacher always hands them a short "Do It Now" assignment. For example, on one occasion he hands out a map of U.S. states and state capitals and instructs students to identify place names that might have Native American names and those that probably have European roots—a task that leads to a class discussion on the origins of place names.

- Before each class period begins, a ninth-grade creative writing teacher writes a topic or question on the board (e.g., "My biggest pet peeve"). Students know that when they come to class, they should immediately begin to write on the topic or question of the day.

- A high school physical education teacher has students begin each class session with five minutes of stretching exercises.

Although very different in nature, all of these strategies share the common goal of keeping students focused on productive behaviors.

Some students may have considerable trouble moving from one activity to another, especially if they're deeply engaged in what they're doing. Accordingly, it's often helpful to give students advance warning that a transition is coming, describe for them what the subsequent activity will be, and remind them of the usual procedures for switching from one task to another (K. Carter & Doyle, 2006; Emmer & Gerwels, 2006).

## MONITORING WHAT STUDENTS ARE DOING

Effective teachers communicate something called **withitness**: They know—and their students *know* that they know—what students are doing at all times. These teachers regularly scan the classroom and make frequent eye contact with individual students. They know what misbehaviors are occurring *when* those misbehaviors occur, and they know who the perpetrators are. When we demonstrate withitness, especially at the beginning of the school year, students are more likely to stay on task and display appropriate classroom behavior. Not surprisingly, they're also more likely to achieve at high levels (Gettinger & Kohler, 2006; T. Hogan, Rabinowitz, & Craven, 2003; Kounin, 1970).

**withitness** Classroom management strategy in which a teacher gives the impression of knowing what all students are doing at all times.

Effective teachers help students make smooth transitions from one activity to another. Examine possible strategies in the simulation "Effectively Handling Transitions."

🍎 Continually monitor what students are doing, and let students know that *you* know what's going on in your classroom.

## MODIFYING INSTRUCTIONAL STRATEGIES

As should now be clear, principles of effective classroom management go hand in hand with principles of learning and motivation. When students are learning and achieving successfully and when they clearly want to pursue the class's instructional goals, they're apt to be busily engaged in productive activities for most of the school day. In contrast, when students have trouble understanding classroom subject matter or little interest in learning it, they're likely to exhibit the nonproductive or counterproductive classroom behaviors that result from frustration or boredom (W. Doyle, 1990; Pekrun, Goetz, Daniels, Stupnisky, & Perry, 2010).

When students misbehave, beginning teachers often think about what the students are doing wrong. In contrast, experienced teachers are more apt to think about what *they themselves* could do differently to keep students on task, and they modify their plans accordingly (Emmer & Stough, 2001; Sabers et al., 1991; H. L. Swanson, O'Connor, & Cooney, 1990). Thus, when behavior problems arise, we should think as the experts do, considering questions such as these:

- How can I change my instructional strategies to stimulate students' interest?
- Are instructional materials so difficult or unstructured that students are getting frustrated? Alternatively, are they so easy or lock-step that students are bored?
- What are students really concerned about? For example, are they more concerned about interacting with peers than in gaining new knowledge and skills? How can I address students' motives and goals while simultaneously helping them achieve classroom objectives?

Answering such questions enables us to focus our efforts on our ultimate goal: helping students *learn.*

Occasionally students are justifiably preoccupied by current events on the local or national scene—perhaps a tragic car accident involving classmates or a contentious political event—to the point that they can't focus on classroom subject matter. In such circumstances we may want to abandon our lesson plans altogether, at least for a short time.

## TAKING DEVELOPMENTAL DIFFERENCES INTO ACCOUNT

To some degree our students' age levels must influence our classroom management decisions. Many children in the early elementary grades haven't had enough experience with formal education to know all the unspoken rules that govern classroom interactions: Students should remain silent when a teacher or other adult is talking, only the student who is called on should answer a question, and so on (Mehan, 1979; R. K. Payne, 2005). In addition, children just beginning kindergarten or first grade may find their new school environment to be unsettling and anxiety arousing, as do many adolescents making the transition to middle school or high school. And children's social skills—which affect their ability to interact effectively with others—continue to develop with age. Table 13.1 presents these and other developmental considerations, along with recommendations for accommodating them in classroom practices.

## TAKING INDIVIDUAL AND GROUP DIFFERENCES INTO ACCOUNT

Earlier I mentioned the importance of consistency and equity in enforcing classroom rules. But when it comes to preventing off-task behaviors and supporting more productive ones, optimal strategies may differ considerably from one student to another. For example, during independent seatwork assignments, some students may work quite well with classmates close by, whereas others may be easily distracted unless they can work in a quiet spot, perhaps near their teacher's desk. And during small-group work, some groups may function effectively on their own, whereas others may need considerable guidance and supervision.

One important individual difference factor affecting classroom behavior is *temperament:* the extent to which a student is naturally inclined to be energetic, irritable, impulsive, and so on. To be truly effective classroom managers, we must realize that students' vastly different classroom behaviors may be due, in part, to biological predispositions that aren't entirely within their control. Such a realization should influence our beliefs about why students are acting as they are— that is, it should influence our *attributions*—and these beliefs will, in turn, affect our willingness to adapt classroom strategies to foster productive classroom behavior (W. Johnson, McGue, & Iacono, 2005; B. K. Keogh, 2003; A. Miller, 2006; Rothbart, 2011).

Consider whether instructional strategies or classroom assignments might be partly to blame for off-task behaviors.

Take developmental differences into account in planning your classroom management strategies.

Chapter 11 describes the many reasons that students so often find the transition to middle school or high school unsettling.

See Chapter 3 for more information about individual differences in temperament.

# DEVELOPMENTAL TRENDS

## TABLE 13.1 • Effective Classroom Management at Different Grade Levels

| GRADE LEVEL | AGE-TYPICAL CHARACTERISTICS | EXAMPLE | SUGGESTED STRATEGIES |
|---|---|---|---|
|  K–2 | • Anxiety about being in school, especially in the first few weeks and especially for students without preschool experience<br>• Lack of familiarity with unspoken rules about appropriate classroom behavior<br>• Short attention span and high level of distractibility<br>• Little self-regulation<br>• Desire for teacher affection and approval<br>• Considerable individual differences in social skills | Immediately after lunch on the first day of school, a first-grade teacher gathers students at the front of the room for a storybook reading. Before she begins to read, she explains the importance of sitting quietly so that everyone can hear the story, and when students occasionally behave in ways that might distract others, she gently reminds them of appropriate classroom behaviors. | • Invite students and their parents to visit the classroom before the school year begins.<br>• Especially during the first few weeks of school, place high priority on forming a warm, supportive relationship with every student.<br>• Be explicit about acceptable classroom behavior; correct inappropriate behaviors gently but consistently.<br>• Keep assigned tasks relatively short and focused.<br>• Create a gathering place (e.g., a carpet) where students can sit close at hand for whole-class discussions.<br>• Give students frequent opportunities to release pent-up energy.<br>• Create areas where students can work independently on tasks of their choosing (e.g., a reading center where students can listen to storybooks on tape). |
|  3–5 | • Continuing desire for teacher approval, but with increasing concern about peer approval as well.<br>• Greater attentiveness to teachers who are emotionally expressive (e.g., teachers who often smile and show obvious concern in times of distress)<br>• Increasing self-regulation skills<br>• Gradually improving ability to reflect on one's own and others' thoughts and motives (i.e., increasing social cognition)<br>• Increasing disengagement from school if students are consistently encountering academic or social failure | Nine-year-old Bailey is often disruptive and socially inappropriate in class—so much so that her classmates avoid her as much as possible. On several occasions her teacher takes her aside and respectfully requests more productive behavior. For example, on one occasion the teacher says, "Bailey, I'm very happy to have you in my class. But it would really help me—and I think it would help you, too—if you could raise your hand before you answer a question. That way, other kids also have a chance to answer questions." | • Use two-way journals to communicate regularly with students about academic and personal issues.<br>• In both words and actions, frequently show students that you're concerned about their academic progress and emotional well-being.<br>• Provide increasing opportunities for independent work, but with enough structure to guide students' efforts.<br>• In times of disagreement or conflict among classmates, ask students to reflect on one another's thoughts and feelings.<br>• Make an extra effort to establish close, supportive relationships with students who appear to be academically and socially disengaged. |
| 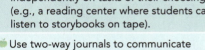 6–8 | • Considerable anxiety about the transition to middle school, often due to more distant and less supportive relationships with teachers<br>• Decrease in intrinsic motivation to learn academic subject matter<br>• Increasing tendency to challenge traditional school norms for behavior—for instance, norms regarding clothing and hairstyle (for some students)<br>• Increase in cheating behaviors; cheating less common if students think teachers respect them and are committed to helping them learn<br>• Heightened concern about ability to fit in and be accepted by peers<br>• Increase in bullying behaviors | The son of a neglectful mother, 14-year-old D.J. has frequently moved from one relative's home to another. He's now spending a second year in seventh grade, where he's extremely disruptive and disrespectful. When he calls a classmate a "fag," his teacher takes him aside and says, "I won't tolerate that offensive word. But I know you're going through a lot at home, and I really want you to be successful here at school. How can I help?" D.J. admits he has gay friends who wouldn't like the word he just used, and his teacher's obvious concern for his well-being leads to better behavior in class. Furthermore, D.J. starts asking the teacher for help on assignments. | • Find occasions to interact with students outside of class (e.g., attend sports events, chaperone school dances).<br>• Plan lessons that are engaging and relevant to students' lives and needs.<br>• Prohibit modes of dress that may threaten students' safety and well-being (e.g., gang insignia, racist T-shirts, sexually revealing attire), but otherwise give students some freedom of expression in what they wear.<br>• Provide sufficient academic support that students have no reason to cheat; nevertheless, be on the lookout for possible cheating.<br>• Don't tolerate bullying and other forms of aggression; address their underlying causes.<br>• Reach out to students who seem socially unconnected (e.g., invite them to join you for lunch in your classroom). |

*(continued)*

| GRADE LEVEL | AGE-TYPICAL CHARACTERISTICS | EXAMPLE | SUGGESTED STRATEGIES |
|---|---|---|---|
| 9–12 | • Anxiety about the transition to high school, especially if the seventh and eighth grades were part of elementary school<br>• Social and romantic relationships often a source of distraction<br>• Considerable self-regulation ability in some but not all students<br>• High incidence of cheating, in part because many peers communicate that it's acceptable<br>• Disdain for classmates who work too hard for teacher approval (i.e., "brown-nosers")<br>• Tendency for some adolescents to think that misbehavior will gain peers' admiration<br>• Increase in violent behaviors, especially at schools in low-income neighborhoods | When a high school teacher sees 16-year-old Jerrod standing alone at a school dance, he approaches the boy to express empathy. "I remember my first school dance," the teacher tells him. "Boy, did I feel awkward! I was too shy to ask a girl to dance, and I was so afraid of making a fool of myself. What do you think we might do to make these events less intimidating?" Jerrod smiles and admits that he feels the same way his teacher once did, and they brainstorm ideas for helping students feel more comfortable at future dances. | • Remember that even in the high school grades, students achieve at higher levels when they have close, supportive relationships with teachers.<br>• Regularly plan activities that involve social interaction; if possible, move desks and chairs to allow students to interact more easily.<br>• When students have few self-regulation skills, provide guidance and support to help them stay on task.<br>• Describe what cheating is and why it's unacceptable.<br>• Communicate approval privately rather than publicly.<br>• Proactively address violence (see the section "Addressing Aggression and Violence at School" later in the chapter). |

*Sources:* Some characteristics and recommendations based on Blanton & Burkley, 2008; Blugental, Lyon, Lin, McGrath, & Bimbela, 1999; K. Carter & Doyle, 2006; Castagno & Brayboy, 2008; Cizek, 2003; Emmer & Gerwels, 2006; Espinoza & Juvonen, 2011; Fingerhut & Christoffel, 2002; Hamre & Pianta, 2005; J. N. Hughes, Luo, Kwok, & Loyd, 2008; Ladd, Herald-Brown, & Reiser, 2008; Mehan, 1979; Murdock, Hale, & Weber, 2001; E. O'Connor & McCartney, 2007; Pellegrini, 2002; many other ideas derived from discussions in earlier chapters.

## CULTURAL AND ETHNIC DIFFERENCES

Remember that some students from diverse backgrounds may need explicit guidance about how they should behave at school.

Students who've grown up in diverse cultural and ethnic groups aren't always familiar with the unspoken standards for behavior in Western schools (Igoa, 1995; Tyler et al., 2008). Furthermore, some students may be unfamiliar with questions and hints that only indirectly tell them how they should behave—for instance, "Sally, would you like to sit down?" Such students are apt to be better behaved (and also less confused) if we're more explicit in our requests—for instance, "Sally, please sit down and focus on your schoolwork" (Adger, Wolfram, & Christian, 2007; Woolfolk Hoy & Weinstein, 2006, p. 186).

But perhaps most important for students from diverse backgrounds is a warm, supportive classroom atmosphere (Castagno & Brayboy, 2008; García, 1995; Meehan, Hughes, & Cavell, 2003). For example, African American students in one eighth-grade social studies class explained why they liked their teacher so much:

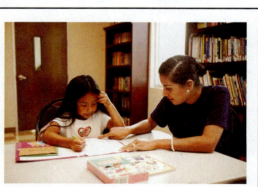

A warm, supportive classroom climate may be especially important for students from diverse ethnic backgrounds.

"She lets us express our opinions!"

"She looks us in the eye when she talks to us!"

"She smiles at us!"

"She speaks to us when she sees us in the hall or in the cafeteria!" (Ladson-Billings, 1994a, p. 68)

Simple gestures such as these go a long way toward establishing the kinds of teacher–student relationships that lead to a productive learning environment. It's also essential that we create a sense of community in the classroom—a sense that we and our students share common goals and are mutually supportive of everyone's reaching those goals. This sense of community is consistent with the cooperative spirit evident in many Hispanic, Native American, and African American groups. It can also be reassuring to students who perceive themselves to be different in an obvious way and thus might have exceptional concerns about not fitting in with their peer group (G. L. Cohen & Garcia, 2008; Ladson-Billings, 1994a; Tyler et al., 2008).

## GENDER DIFFERENCES

On average, girls form more affectionate and productive relationships with teachers than boys do (Pianta, 2006; Tutwiler, 2007; Wentzel et al., 2010). A variety of reasons may underlie some boys' nonproductive relationships with teachers. Boys are more prone to physical aggression than girls, and they're more likely than girls to be oppositional and defiant when asked to engage in tasks they'd rather not do. And in general, boys are temperamentally more active and have less self-control, to the point that they may have trouble sitting still for lengthy periods (W. O. Eaton & Enns, 1986; Rothbart, 2011). Notice what happened to one fourth grader (now a successful college professor) when his teacher took his temperament into consideration:

> One day when I was especially restless . . . I could see Miss Rickenbrood circling to the back of the room. . . . After a few minutes she leaned over and whispered in my ear, "Tom, would you like to go outside and run?"
>
> I was stunned. To go outside and run? On my own? When it wasn't recess? What could have possessed this woman to ignore all school rules and allow me to run? I said yes and quietly went to put on my coat. As I recall, I didn't actually run in the playground (people would be watching from inside the building), but stood outside in the doorway, in the cold, marveling at my freedom. I returned to class after about ten minutes, settled for the rest of the day. (Newkirk, 2002, pp. 25–26)

### SOCIOECONOMIC DIFFERENCES

Having teachers' affection, respect, and support is even more important for students who face exceptional hardships at home—poverty, violent neighborhoods, homelessness, and so on. Some of these students may be prone to anger and disrespectful classroom behavior, undoubtedly as a result of their difficult circumstances outside of school (R. K. Payne, 2005). Yet when students from economically impoverished backgrounds have one or more caring, trustworthy adults in their lives—and when they regularly come to a classroom that's warm, predictable, and dependable—they often have a strong sense of self-worth and self-determination. Hence they're better equipped to succeed both at school and in the outside world. In other words, they're more likely to be *resilient*—to rise above their adverse circumstances (B. E. Becker & Luthar, 2002; Masten, 2001; D. A. O'Donnell, Schwab-Stone, & Muyeed, 2002; Polakow, 2007).

### ACCOMMODATING STUDENTS WITH SPECIAL NEEDS

Most students with special needs can more easily adapt to a general education setting when the classroom is orderly and well structured. Even more so than their nondisabled peers, students with disabilities benefit from classrooms in which procedures for performing certain tasks are specified, expectations for student behavior are clear, and misbehaviors are treated consistently (Heward, 2009; Pfiffner, Barkley, & DuPaul, 2006; Scruggs & Mastropieri, 1994). Although some students with disabilities may need considerable guidance and support in order to behave appropriately, unless there are extenuating circumstances, these students must incur the same consequences as everyone else when their behaviors are out of line. Table 13.2 offers many suggestions for accommodating students with special needs.

# Expanding the Sense of Community Beyond the Classroom

Students' learning and development depend not only on what happens inside a particular classroom but also on what happens in other parts of the school building, in the neighborhood and community, and at home. To be most effective, then, we should coordinate our efforts with other influential individuals in students' lives—with other school faculty members, with professionals at community agencies, and especially with students' parents or other primary caregivers. Ideally we should think of such joint efforts as *partnerships* in which everyone is working together to promote students' long-term development and learning.

## WORKING WITH OTHER FACULTY MEMBERS

It's important that all school faculty members communicate consistent messages and expectations using strategies such as these:

- Identify common goals regarding what students should learn and achieve.
- Work together to identify and overcome obstacles to students' achievement.

Make a special effort to establish good relationships with emotionally distant or chronically misbehaving students.

When students face exceptional challenges at home, make an extra effort to create an affectionate, supportive, predictable, and safe environment at school.

You can learn more about resilience in the discussion of *students at risk* in Chapter 4.

Chapter 5 identifies specific categories of special needs that fall within the five general categories listed in Table 13.2.

## STUDENTS IN INCLUSIVE SETTINGS

**TABLE 13.2 • Maintaining a Productive Classroom Environment for Students with Special Educational Needs**

| CATEGORY | CHARACTERISTICS YOU MIGHT OBSERVE | SUGGESTED STRATEGIES |
|---|---|---|
| Students with specific cognitive or academic difficulties | • Difficulty staying on task<br>• Misbehaviors such as hyperactivity, impulsiveness, disruptiveness, and inattentiveness (in some students)<br>• Poor time management skills and/or a disorganized approach to accomplishing tasks (in some students) | • Closely monitor students during independent assignments.<br>• Make sure students understand their assignments; if appropriate, give extra time to complete them.<br>• Make expectations for behavior clear, and enforce classroom rules consistently.<br>• Reinforce (e.g., praise) desired behaviors immediately; be specific about the behaviors you are reinforcing.<br>• For hyperactive students, plan short activities that help them settle down after periods of physical activity (e.g., after recess, lunch, or physical education).<br>• For impulsive students, teach self-regulation skills (e.g., verbal self-reminders about appropriate behavior).<br>• Teach strategies for organizing time and work (e.g., tape a schedule of daily activities to students' desks, provide folders that students can use to carry assignments to and from home). |
| Students with social or behavioral problems | • Frequent overt misbehaviors, such as acting out, aggression, noncompliance, destructiveness, or stealing (in some students)<br>• Difficulty inhibiting impulses<br>• Misbehaviors triggered by changes in the environment or daily routine or by sensory overstimulation (for some students with autism spectrum disorders)<br>• Difficulty interacting effectively with peers<br>• Difficulty staying on task<br>• Tendency to engage in power struggles with teachers (for some students) | • Specify in precise terms what behaviors are acceptable and unacceptable in the classroom; establish and enforce rules for behavior.<br>• Maintain a predictable schedule; warn students ahead of time about changes in the routine.<br>• Use self-regulation techniques and behaviorist approaches to promote productive classroom behaviors.<br>• Explicitly teach social skills.<br>• Closely monitor students during independent assignments.<br>• Give students a sense of self-determination about some aspects of classroom life; minimize use of coercive techniques.<br>• Make an extra effort to show students that you care about them as individuals. |
| Students with general delays in cognitive and social functioning | • Occasional disruptive classroom behavior (for some students)<br>• Dependence on others for guidance about how to behave<br>• More appropriate classroom behavior when expectations are clear | • Establish clear, concrete rules for classroom behavior.<br>• As necessary, remind students about appropriate behavior; keep directions simple.<br>• Use structured behaviorist approaches to promote desired behaviors.<br>• Give explicit feedback about what students are and are not doing appropriately. |
| Students with physical or sensory challenges | • Social isolation from classmates (for some students)<br>• Difficulty accomplishing tasks as quickly as other students<br>• Difficulty understanding directions and other spoken messages about desired behaviors (for students with hearing loss) | • Establish a strong sense of community within the classroom.<br>• When appropriate, give extra time to complete assignments.<br>• Keep unnecessary noise to a minimum if one or more students have hearing loss. |
| Students with advanced cognitive development | • Off-task behavior in some students, often due to boredom during easy assignments and activities | • Assign tasks appropriate to students' cognitive abilities. |

*Sources:* Barkley, 2006; Beirne-Smith, Patton, & Kim, 2006; Buchoff, 1990; M.-L. Chang & Davis, 2009; B. Clark, 1997; Dai, 2010; Dempster & Corkill, 1999; S. C. Diamond, 1991; D. A. Granger, Whalen, Henker, & Cantwell, 1996; N. Gregg, 2009; Heward, 2009; Koegel, Koegel, & Dunlap, 1996; Mendaglio, 2010; Mercer & Pullen, 2005; Morgan & Jenson, 1988; Patton, Blackbourn, & Fad, 1996; Pellegrini & Horvat, 1995; Turnbull, Turnbull, & Wehmeyer, 2010; Winner, 1997.

• Establish a common set of standards for students' behavior, along with systematic, school-wide procedures for encouraging productive and respectful behaviors.

• Make a group commitment to promote equality and multicultural sensitivity throughout the school community. (Battistich, Solomon, Watson, & Schaps, 1997; K. L. Lane, Kalberg, & Menzies, 2009; J. Lee & Shute, 2010; Levine & Lezotte, 1995; T. J. Lewis, Newcomer, Trussell, & Richter, 2006)

One increasingly popular approach is schoolwide positive behavior support, in which school faculty members jointly and explicitly define, teach, and reinforce appropriate behaviors and provide varying levels of support tailored to students' needs (e.g., Ihlo & Nantais, 2010; Osher, Bear, Sprague, & Doyle, 2010; J. S. Warren et al., 2006).

Ideally, too, in addition to creating a sense of community within our individual classrooms, we should create an overall sense of school community—a shared belief that all teachers and students within a school are working together to help everyone learn and succeed (Battistich, Solomon, Kim, Watson, & Schaps, 1995, Battistich et al., 1997; M. Watson & Battistich, 2006). When a school has a genuine sense of school community, students regularly get two very important messages: (1) All faculty members are working together to help students become informed and productive citizens; and (2) students can and should *help one another*. A sense of school community involves close student–student relationships not only within individual classrooms but also across classrooms and grade levels. Cross-class peer tutoring, participation in extracurricular activities, student involvement in school decision making, frequent use of school mascots and other traditional school symbols—all of these help to create a sense that students are members of a mutually supportive school "family" (Juvonen, 2006; Nucci, 2009; D. R. Robinson, Schofield, & Steers-Wentzell, 2005).

When teachers and students share an overall sense of school community, students have more positive attitudes toward school, are more motivated to achieve at high levels, exhibit more prosocial behavior, and interact more often with peers from diverse backgrounds. Furthermore, teachers have higher expectations for students' achievement and a greater sense of self-efficacy about their teaching effectiveness (Battistich et al., 1995, 1997; J. A. Langer, 2000). In fact, when teachers work together, they have higher *collective self-efficacy*—a belief that by working as a team, they can definitely have an impact on students' and achievement—and this collective self-confidence is correlated with students' academic performance (Goddard, Hoy, & Woolfolk Hoy, 2000; Hoy, Tarter, & Woolfolk Hoy, 2006; J. Lee & Shute, 2010). Such a team spirit has an additional advantage for beginning teachers: It provides the support structure (scaffolding) they may need, especially when working with students who are at risk for school failure. New teachers report greater confidence in their ability to help students learn and achieve when they collaborate regularly with their colleagues (Chester & Beaudin, 1996).

## WORKING WITH THE COMMUNITY AT LARGE

Students almost always have regular contact with other institutions besides school—possibly youth groups, community organizations, social services, churches, hospitals, mental health clinics, and local judicial systems. And some students live in cultural environments very different from our own. As teachers, we enhance our effectiveness if we understand the environments in which our students live and if we think of ourselves as integral members of a larger community that promotes children's and adolescents' long-term development. For example, we must educate ourselves about students' cultural backgrounds, perhaps by taking course work and getting involved in local community events (Castagno & Brayboy, 2008; McIntyre, 2010). We must also keep in contact with other people and institutions that play major roles in students' lives, coordinating our efforts whenever possible (J. L. Epstein, 1996; Kincheloe, 2009).

## WORKING WITH PARENTS

Above all, we must work cooperatively with students' parents and other primary caregivers. Productive parent–teacher relationships may be especially important when working with students from diverse cultural backgrounds, and they're *essential* when working with students who have physical, cognitive, or behavioral disabilities (Hidalgo, Siu, Bright, Swap, & Epstein, 1995; J. N. Hughes & Kwok, 2007; J. Lee & Shute, 2010; Reschly & Christenson, 2009).

We must keep in mind that families come in a variety of forms and that students' primary caregivers aren't always their parents. For example, in some ethnic minority communities, grandmothers take primary responsibility for raising children (Dantas & Manyak, 2010;

Chapter 9 describes schoolwide positive behavior support in more detail.

 Collaborate with colleagues to create an overall sense of school community.

Collective self-efficacy is a key concept in social cognitive theory (see Chapter 10).

 Work cooperatively with other agencies that play key roles in students' lives.

**schoolwide positive behavior support** Systematic use of behaviorist principles to encourage and reinforce productive behaviors in all students; typically involves multiple layers of support in order to accommodate the varying needs and behavior patterns of different students.

**sense of school community** Shared belief that all faculty and students within a school are working together to help everyone learn and succeed.

Remember that some students' primary caregivers are people other than their parents.

Remember that communication with parents should be a two-way street, with information traveling in both directions.

Consider including students in parent–teacher conferences.

Regularly communicate with parents in written form.

Stack & Burton, 1993). To keep my discussion simple, I use the term *parents* in upcoming paragraphs, but I am, in fact, referring to all primary caregivers.

## COMMUNICATING WITH PARENTS

We should open lines of communication with parents as soon as classes begin—perhaps even before that—and stay in regular contact with them throughout the school year. We should inform them of their children's accomplishments and keep them apprised of any behaviors that are consistently interfering with learning and achievement. Regular communication also provides a means through which parents can give *us* information, which might yield new ideas about how we might most effectively work with their children. In addition, regular communication enables us to coordinate our classroom strategies with those that parents use at home. Following are several common mechanisms for enhancing school–family communication.

**Parent–teacher conferences.**   In most school districts, formal parent–teacher conferences are scheduled one or more times a year. We may often want to include students in conferences—essentially making them parent–teacher–student conferences—and in some instances we might even ask students to *lead* the conferences. By holding student-led conferences, we increase the likelihood that parents will come to the conferences, we encourage students to reflect on their own academic progress, and we give students practice in communication and leadership skills. Furthermore, teachers, students, and parents alike are apt to leave such meetings with a shared understanding of the progress that has been made and of subsequent steps that need to be taken. Figure 13.5 offers suggestions for conducting effective conferences.

**Written communication.**   Written communication can take a variety of forms. It can be a general welcome letter sent to students and parents before the school year begins. It can be a weekly checklist that documents a student's progress. It can be a quick, informal note acknowledging a significant accomplishment. Or it can be a newsletter that describes class activities, expectations for homework, and so on. All of these mechanisms have two things in common: They let parents know what's happening at school and convey a genuine desire to stay in touch with families.

---

**FIGURE 13.5 Suggestions for conducting effective parent–teacher conferences**

**Suggestions for Any Parent–Teacher Conference**

- Schedule the conference at a time that accommodates parents' jobs and other obligations.

- Accommodate cultural differences. For example, invite extended family members who play key roles in caregiving, and include a trusted individual who can translate for non-native-English speakers.

- Prepare ahead of time. For example, review what you know about the student (e.g., academic progress, classroom behavior), organize your thoughts, create an agenda for the meeting, and have examples of the student's work on hand.

- Create a warm, nonjudgmental atmosphere. For example, express appreciation that the parents have come and encourage them to offer their thoughts and perspectives. Remember that your objective is to work cooperatively and constructively with parents to create the best educational program possible for their child.

- Describe your general goals and expectations for students.

- Avoid educational jargon with which parents may be unfamiliar; describe the student's performance in ways a noneducator can understand.

- Actively seek information. For example, ask parents to describe their child's strong points and favorite activities.

- Jointly explore possible ways in which you and parents might support one another's efforts to promote the student's development.

- End on a positive note—perhaps with a review of the student's many strengths and the progress he or she has made.

- Follow through with anything you have said you will do.

**Additional Suggestions for a Student-Led Conference:**

- Meet with the student ahead of time to agree on appropriate work samples to share.

- Model and role-play effective conferences in class, and give students time to practice with their classmates.

- Schedule a backup audience (e.g., a former teacher or trusted friend) who can sit in if the student's parents don't attend.

- Offer additional time in which you can meet without the student if the parents so desire.

- Talk with the student afterward about what went well and how the two of you might improve the next conference.

*Sources:* Carini & Himley, 2010; C. Davis & Yang, 2005; M. D. Miller, Linn, & Gronlund, 2009; Polloway & Patton, 1993; Reschly & Christenson, 2009; Salend & Taylor, 1993; Stiggins & Chappuis, 2012.

A parent letter written by second-grade teacher Ann Reilly provides an illustration (see Figure 13.6). The letter was written on September 14, 2001, three days after terrorist attacks on the World Trade Center and Pentagon and during a week when students were taking a district-wide standardized test. The letter communicates a great deal of information: what topics the class is studying, how parents will get results of the standardized test, and why the class isn't talking much about the terrorist attacks. It communicates attitudes as well; for instance, Ms. Reilly is eager to keep the lines of communication with parents open, is approachable (she signs the letter "Ann"), and cares about how well her students are doing (e.g., "I don't like telling them that they are on their own" during classroom assessments). She also suggests several simple ways in which parents might contribute to the class: helping with spelling assessments, donating tissues, and providing instructions for making baby wipes. Because she teaches in a school district in which most parents have Internet access either at home or at work, she has given parents her e-mail address. Suggesting the use of e-mail would be less appropriate in communities where many families can't afford computers or parents have limited knowledge of English.

**Class websites.**    Many teachers now create class websites on which they post instructional goals, assignments, and so on. Typically such websites are available to parents as well as students, but, as is true for e-mail messages, they're most appropriate for parents who regularly use computers and the Internet.

> See Chapter 12 for more information about constructing class websites.

**Telephone conversations.**    In the elementary grades, telephone calls are a useful way of introducing oneself at the start of the school year and following up on conferences that parents have missed (C. Davis & Yang, 2005; Striepling-Goldstein, 2004). And at all grade levels, telephone calls are often appropriate when something unusual has happened—for instance, when a student has either made a noteworthy step forward or, instead, has recently shown an unexpected decline in performance. Likewise, parents should feel free to call *us*. Because many parents are at work during the school day, it's often helpful to accept and encourage calls at home during the early evening hours.

> Make a quick telephone call to inform parents of exciting new accomplishments or potential areas of concern.

**Parent discussion groups.**    In some instances we may want to assemble a group of parents to discuss issues of mutual interest—perhaps specific topics that might be included in the class

---

**FIGURE 13.6**  **An example of a teacher's letter to parents**

9/14/01

Dear Parents,

I have been lucky so far and have not had to go back for jury duty. I have two more weeks to go [in terms of possibly being summoned for duty] and hope I will continue to be in the classroom.

We have been trying to keep the routine pretty regular, despite one or two testing sessions per day. The children have been pretty focused, although it is difficult when they are unfamiliar with the format and look to us for help. I don't like telling them that they are on their own. We are done, thank goodness. I believe you will receive results in the mail.

Homework and spelling will resume next week. I could also use my regular volunteers to help get through the spelling assessments. The times you have been coming are still fine. Call or e-mail me if you need the available times for helping.

We finished our unit on germs and sanitation, although we did not get into any discussions about Anthrax. It seems that you are keeping the children protected at home from details of the scary news, as we are at school. We kept our discussions to common illnesses that they are aware of and how they can avoid them with proper sanitation.

A few classrooms are doing activities to raise money for many of the children involved in the tragedy. Sarah [the teacher intern] and I decided not to work with our children on a fundraiser because we don't want to get into anxiety-producing discussions. It is hard to help young children understand that they are safe where they are and that it is unlikely that they will be involved in such things.

Next week, we will be starting a Nutrition Unit and beginning to read some Halloween stories. We will continue working to become automatic with math facts, along with our regular routine of phonics lessons, DOL [daily oral language], reading, writing, spelling, etc.

We are running out of Kleenex and could use some donations. We would also like some boxes of baby wipes to use in cleaning hands and desks when there is not time for the entire class to wash. Someone mentioned to me that there is a homemade recipe for baby wipes out there somewhere. Is there a parent who knows and would be willing to share?

Have a great weekend.

*Ann*

*Source:* Text of "Dear Parents" letter dated September 14, 2001, by Ann L. Reilly. Copyright © 2001 by Anne L. Reilly. Reprinted with permission.

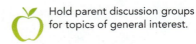
Hold parent discussion groups for topics of general interest.

curriculum or effective strategies that parents can use to promote their children's academic, personal, and social development (J. L. Epstein, 1996; Fosnot, 1996; Rudman, 1993). Also, some teachers have successfully used parent *coffee nights,* during which they explain a new instructional strategy, or *author teas,* during which students read poetry and short stories they have written.

## GETTING PARENTS INVOLVED IN SCHOOL ACTIVITIES

Ultimately the best means of communicating and collaborating with parents is to get them actively involved in school life and in children's learning, and perhaps get other family members involved as well. Students whose parents are involved in school activities have better attendance records, higher achievement, and more positive attitudes toward school. Although the reasons for the correlations aren't entirely clear, they appear to be due partly to the fact that parents who actively participate in school activities can more effectively coordinate their efforts at home with teachers' efforts in the classroom (N. E. Hill & Craft, 2003; N. E. Hill & Taylor, 2004; Mattingly, Prislin, McKenzie, Rodrigues, & Kayzar, 2002; Spera, 2005).

Parental involvement in school activities can take a variety of forms. For instance, we might:

- Invite parents to an open house or musical performance in the evening.
- Request parents' help with a weekend fund-raiser.
- Seek volunteers to help with field trips, special projects, or individual tutoring during the school day.
- Use parents and other community members as resources to provide a multicultural perspective of the local community. (C. Davis & Yang, 2005; McCarty & Watahomigie, 1998; McIntyre, 2010; Minami & Ovando, 1995)

Most parents are apt to become involved in such activities only when they have a specific invitation to do so and when they know that school personnel genuinely want them to be involved (C. L. Green, Walker, Hoover-Dempsey, & Sandler, 2007; Serpell, Baker, & Sonnenschein, 2005). Some parents—especially those from certain minority groups or low-income families—may not take a general, open-ended invitation seriously. A personal invitation can often make all the difference, as one mother explained:

> The thing of it is, had someone not walked up to me and asked me specifically, I would not hold out my hand and say, "I'll do it." . . . You get parents here all the time, black parents that are willing, but maybe a little on the shy side and wouldn't say I really want to serve on this subject. You may send me the form, I may never fill the form out. Or I'll think about it and not send it back. But you know if that principal, that teacher, my son's math teacher called and asked if I would . . . (A. A. Carr, 1997, p. 2)

Extend personal invitations to school events.

Parents can also be invaluable in helping children with homework. Even parents who have few academic skills themselves can provide worthwhile support—for instance, by communicating the importance of doing well, providing a quiet place to study, and making television viewing contingent on homework completion. The more parents do such things, the higher their children's achievement is likely to be. Furthermore, many parents are open to teacher suggestions about how they might best be of assistance (N. E. Hill, Castellino, et al., 2004; S. Hong & Ho, 2005; J. Lee & Shute, 2010; J.-S. Lee & Bowen, 2006; Patall, Cooper, & Robinson, 2008; J. M. T. Walker & Hoover-Dempsey, 2006).

Offer suggestions about things parents might do to help their children with homework.

## ENCOURAGING RELUCTANT PARENTS

Despite our best efforts, a few parents may remain uninvolved in their children's education; for example, they may never attend scheduled parent–teacher conferences. But before we jump too quickly to the conclusion that these parents are also *uninterested* in their children's education, we must recognize several possible reasons that parents might be reluctant to make contact with us. Some may have an exhausting work schedule or lack adequate child care. Others may know little English, have difficulty finding their way through the school system, or believe it's inappropriate to bother teachers with their concerns. Still others may have had such bad experiences when they themselves were students that they feel uncomfortable in a school building. And a few parents may be victims of mental illness or substance abuse, limiting their ability to support their children financially, academically, or otherwise (Bornstein & Cote, 2010; Carbrera, Shannon, West, & Brooks-Gunn, 2006; Cazden, 2001; Dantas & Manyak, 2010; J.-S. Lee & Bowen, 2006; Ogbu, 2003).

Experienced educators have offered numerous suggestions for getting reluctant parents more involved in their children's schooling:

Identify alternative sources of academic support when a student's family is unable to provide it.

- Make an extra effort to gain parents' trust and confidence—for instance, by demonstrating that their contributions are both helpful and appreciated.
- Encourage parents to be assertive when they have questions or concerns.
- Invite other important family members (e.g., grandparents, aunts, uncles) to participate in school activities, especially if a student's cultural group places high value on extended families.
- Offer suggestions about learning activities parents can easily do with their children at home.
- Find out what parents do exceptionally well (e.g., carpentry, cooking), and ask them to share their talents with students.
- Provide opportunities for parents to volunteer for jobs that don't require them to leave home (e.g., to be someone whom students can call when they're unsure of homework assignments).
- Identify specific individuals (e.g., bilingual parents) who can translate for those who speak little or no English.
- Make home visits *if* such visits are welcomed.
- Offer resources for parents at the school building—for instance, contacts with social and health services, or classes in English, literacy, home repairs, and crafts. (Castagno & Brayboy, 2008; Dantas & Manyak, 2010; C. Davis & Yang, 2005; J. L. Epstein, 1996; Finders & Lewis, 1994; Hidalgo et al., 1995; G. R. López, 2001; Salend & Taylor, 1993; M. G. Sanders, 1996; J. M. T. Walker & Hoover-Dempsey, 2006)

Another potentially effective strategy is to reinforce *parents* as well as students when the students do well at school. One administrator at a school serving many immigrant students put it this way:

> One of the things we do . . . is that we identify those students that had perfect attendance, those students that passed all areas of the [statewide achievement tests] and were successful. We don't honor the student, we honor the parents. We give parents a certificate. Because, we tell them, "Through your efforts, and through your hard work, your child was able to accomplish this." (G. R. López, 2001, p. 273)

Give recognition to parents whose children do well at school.

A few parents may resist all our efforts to get them involved. Especially in such circumstances, we must never penalize students for their parents' actions or inactions. And we must realize that as teachers, *we* are apt to be among the most important academic and emotional resources in these students' lives.

Don't penalize students for things that their parents do or don't do.

## CONSIDERING CULTURAL DIFFERENCES WHEN WORKING WITH PARENTS

As we work with students' parents, we must be aware that people from different cultural and ethnic groups sometimes have radically different ideas about how—and also how *much*—to control their children's behavior. For example, many parents from Asian cultures expect children to obey adult authority figures without question; such parents often think that Western teachers are much too lenient with students (Dien, 1998; Hidalgo et al., 1995; Kağıtçıbaşi, 2007; Tamis-Lemonda & McFadden, 2010). In contrast, parents in some Native American cultures believe that children have a right to make their own decisions; from their perspective, good parenting involves providing gentle suggestions and guidance rather than insisting that children behave in certain ways (Deyhle & LeCompte, 1999). Some cultural and religious groups use ostracism in an effort to keep children in line: The child is ignored—for instance, given the "silent treatment"—for an extended period (K. D. Williams, 2001).

We must realize that the vast majority of parents want what's best for their children and recognize the value of a good education. It's essential, then, that we not leave parents out of the loop

Communicate your confidence in each student's ability to succeed, as well as your commitment to working cooperatively with parents.

when we're concerned about how their children are performing in school. And as we talk with them, we must listen to their attitudes and opinions with an open mind and try to find common ground on which to develop strategies for helping their children thrive in the classroom.

# Dealing with Misbehaviors

Despite our best efforts to create a classroom environment that promotes learning, one or more of our students will occasionally behave in undesirable ways. For purposes of our discussion, we'll define a misbehavior as any action that can potentially disrupt learning and planned classroom activities, puts one or more students' physical safety or psychological well-being in jeopardy, or violates basic moral and ethical standards. Some misbehaviors are relatively minor and have little long-term impact on students' achievement. Such behaviors as talking out of turn, writing brief notes to classmates during a lecture, and submitting homework assignments after their due date—especially if these behaviors occur infrequently—generally fall in this category. Other misbehaviors are far more serious, in that they definitely interfere with the learning or well-being of one or more students. For example, when students scream at their teachers, hit classmates, or habitually refuse to participate in learning activities, then classroom learning—certainly that of the guilty party, and sometimes that of other students as well—can be adversely affected, as can the overall classroom climate.

Typically only a few students are responsible for the great majority of misbehaviors in any single class (W. Doyle, 2006). These students are apt to be among our greatest challenges, and it can be all too tempting to write them off as lost causes. Yet we must work vigorously to turn them in more productive directions: Without active interventions by teachers and other caring adults, students who are consistently disruptive or in other ways off task in the early grades may continue to show behavior problems later on (Dishion, Piehler, & Myers, 2008; Emmer & Gerwels, 2006; Vitaro, Brendgen, Larose, & Tremblay, 2005).

As teachers, we need to plan ahead about how we'll address students' misbehaviors. Although we must certainly be consistent in the consequences we impose for blatant rule infractions (recall our earlier discussion of consistency and equity), a variety of strategies can be useful in reducing counterproductive behaviors over the long run. Here we'll examine six general strategies and their appropriate applications: ignoring a behavior, cueing a student, talking with a student in private, teaching self-regulation skills, conferring with parents, and planning and conducting a systematic intervention.

## IGNORING CERTAIN BEHAVIORS

On some occasions our best course of action is *no* action, at least nothing of a disciplinary nature. For example, consider these situations:

- Dimitra rarely breaks classroom rules. But on one occasion, after you've just instructed students to work quietly and independently at their seats, you see her briefly whisper to the girl beside her. Other students don't seem to notice that she is temporarily disobeying your instructions.
- Herb is careless in chemistry lab and accidentally knocks over a small container of liquid—a harmless one, fortunately. He quickly apologizes and cleans up the mess.

Will these behaviors interfere with Dimitra's or Herb's academic achievement? Are they "contagious" behaviors that will spread to other students, as the horseplay did in Ms. Cornell's class? The answer to both questions is "Probably not."

Whenever we stop an instructional activity to deal with a misbehavior, even for a few seconds, we may disrupt the momentum of the activity and draw students' attention to a misbehaving classmate. Furthermore, by drawing other students' attention to a particular misbehavior, we may unintentionally be reinforcing it.

Ignoring misbehavior is often reasonable in circumstances such as these:

- When the behavior is a rare occurrence and probably won't be repeated
- When the behavior is unlikely to spread to other students
- When the behavior is the result of unusual and temporary conditions (e.g., the last day of school before a holiday, unsettling events in a student's personal life)

misbehavior  Action that disrupts learning and planned classroom activities, puts students' physical safety or psychological well-being in jeopardy, or violates basic moral standards.

- When the behavior is typical for the age-group (e.g., kindergartners becoming restless after sitting for an extended time, sixth-grade boys and girls resisting holding one another's hands during dance instruction)
- When the behavior's natural consequence is unpleasant enough to deter a student from repeating it
- When the behavior isn't interfering with classroom learning (G. A. Davis & Thomas, 1989; W. Doyle, 1986a, 2006; Dreikurs & Cassel, 1972; Munn et al., 1990; Silberman & Wheelan, 1980; Wynne, 1990)

Dimitra's behavior—briefly whispering to a classmate during independent seatwork—is unlikely to spread to her classmates (they don't see her do it) and probably isn't an instance of cheating (it occurs before she begins working on the assignment). Herb's behavior—knocking over a container of liquid in chemistry lab—has in and of itself resulted in an unpleasant consequence: He must clean up the mess. In both situations, then, ignoring the misbehavior is probably the best thing to do.

## CUEING STUDENTS

In some situations off-task behaviors, although not serious in nature, *do* interfere with classroom learning and must be discouraged. Consider these situations as examples:

- As you're explaining a difficult concept, Marjorie is busily writing. At first you think she's taking notes, but then you see her pass the paper across the aisle to Kang. A few minutes later you see Kang pass the same sheet back to Marjorie. It appears that the two students are exchanging personal notes when they should be attending to the lesson.
- You've separated your class into small groups for a cooperative learning activity. One group is frequently off task and probably won't complete the assignment if the students don't get down to business soon.

Effective classroom managers handle such minor behavior problems as unobtrusively as possible: They don't stop the lesson, distract other students, or call unnecessary attention to the inappropriate behavior. In many cases they use cueing: They give a brief signal—perhaps a stern look or a simple verbal directive—to communicate that the misbehavior has been noticed and should cease. Ideally such cues focus students' attention on what *should* be done rather than on what *isn't* being done (Evertson & Emmer, 2009; K. L. Lane et al., 2011). For instance, instead of chastising students for being overly noisy during a cooperative group activity, a teacher might say, "As you exchange ideas, remember to use your *indoor voices* so that you don't distract other groups."

## DISCUSSING PROBLEMS PRIVATELY WITH STUDENTS

Sometimes brief cues are insufficient to change a student's misbehavior. Consider these situations:

- Alonzo is almost always a few minutes late to your third-period algebra class. When he finally arrives, he takes several more minutes to pull his textbook and other class materials out of his backpack. You've often reminded him about the importance of coming to class on time, yet his tardiness continues.
- Trudy rarely completes assignments; in fact, she often doesn't even *begin* them. On many previous occasions you've gently tried to get her on task, but usually without success. Today, when you look Trudy in the eye and ask her point blank to get to work, she defiantly responds, "I'm not going to do it. You can't make me!"

In such situations, talking privately with the student is the next logical step. The discussion should be *private* for several reasons. First, as noted earlier, calling peers' attention to a problem behavior may actually reinforce the behavior rather than discourage it. Or, instead, the attention of classmates may cause a student to feel excessively embarrassed or humiliated—feelings that can make the student overanxious about coming to school in the future. Finally, when we spend too much class time dealing with a single misbehaving student, other students are apt to get off task as well (W. Doyle, 2006; Emmer & Gerwels, 2006; Scott & Bushell, 1974).

 Private conversations give us an opportunity to explain why certain behaviors are unacceptable and must stop. They also give students a chance to explain why they behave as they do. For

**cueing** Use of a verbal or nonverbal signal to indicate that a certain behavior is desired or that a certain behavior should stop.

Ignore minor infractions that are unlikely to be repeated or to spread to other students.

Gently cue students about desired behaviors.

Speak privately with students about chronic behavior problems.

Mild interventions are often effective in reducing unproductive classroom behaviors. Examine several strategies in the simulation "Responding to Student Disruptions."

example, Alonzo might explain his chronic tardiness by revealing that he has diabetes and must check his blood sugar level between his second- and third-period classes. He can perform the procedure himself but would prefer to do it in the privacy of the school nurse's office. Meanwhile, Trudy might describe her long-standing frustration with subject matter and assignments she perceives as being impossible to make sense of. A boy with a reading disability once voiced such frustration in an interview with a researcher:

> They [teachers] used to hand us all our homework on Mondays. One day my teacher handed me a stack about an inch thick and as I was walking out of class there was a big trash can right there and I'd, in front of everybody including the teacher, just drop it in the trash can and walk out. I did this because I couldn't read what she gave me. It was kind of a point that I wanted to get the teacher to realize. That while I'm doing it, inside it kind of like hurt because I really wanted to do it but I couldn't and just so it didn't look like I was goin' soft or anything like that I'd walk over to the trash and throw it in. (Zambo & Brem, 2004, p. 6)

Students' explanations often provide clues about how best to deal with their behavior over the long run. For example, given his diabetes, Alonzo's continued tardiness to class might be inevitable. Perhaps we could reassign him to a seat by the door, enabling him to join class unobtrusively when he arrives, and we might ask the student next to him to quietly fill him in on the lesson in progress. Trudy's frustration with her schoolwork suggests that she needs additional scaffolding to help her succeed. It also hints at a possible undiagnosed learning disability that might warrant a referral to the school psychologist or other diagnostician.

Students won't always provide explanations that lead to such logical solutions, however. For example, it may be that Alonzo is late to class simply because he wants to spend more time in the hall with friends. Or perhaps Trudy says she doesn't want to do her assignments because, she says, "I'm sick and tired of other people always telling me what to do." In such circumstances it's essential that we not get into a power struggle with the student—a situation in which one person wins by dominating the other in some way. Several strategies can minimize the likelihood of a power struggle:

- Speak in a calm, matter-of-fact manner, describing the problem as you see it. ("You haven't turned in a single assignment in the past three weeks. You and I would both like for you to do well in my class, but that can't happen unless we *both* work to make it happen.")
- Present the problem as one involving unproductive behavior, *not* a personality flaw. ("You've come to class late almost every day this month.")
- Listen empathetically to what the student has to say, being openly accepting of his or her feelings and opinions. ("I get the impression that you don't enjoy my class very much; I'd really like to hear your concerns.")
- Summarize what you think the student has told you, and seek clarification if necessary. ("It sounds as if you'd rather not let your classmates know how much trouble you're having with your schoolwork. Is that the problem, or is it something else?")
- Give **I-messages**; that is, describe the effects of the problem behavior, including your personal reactions to it, in a calm, relatively nonaccusatory manner. ("When you come to class late each day, I worry that you're getting further and further behind, and sometimes I feel hurt that you don't seem to value your time in my classroom.")
- Give the student a choice from among two or more acceptable options. ("Would you rather try to work quietly at your group's table, or would it be easier if you sat somewhere by yourself to complete your work?")
- Especially when working with an adolescent, try to identify a solution that allows the student to maintain credibility in the eyes of peers. ("I suspect you might be worrying that your friends will think less of you if you comply with my request. What might we do to address this problem?") (Colvin, Ainge, & Nelson, 1997; Emmer & Evertson, 2009; Henley, 2010; Keller & Tapasak, 2004; K. Lane, Falk, & Wehby, 2006)

**I-message** Statement that communicates the adverse effects of a student's misbehavior, including one's own reactions to it, in a calm, relatively nonaccusatory manner; its intent is to convey information, not to lay blame.

Ultimately we must communicate (1) our interest in the student's long-term school achievement, (2) our concern that the misbehavior is interfering with that achievement, and (3) our commitment to working cooperatively with the student to alleviate the problem.

## TEACHING SELF-REGULATION SKILLS

Sometimes students simply need guidance in how they might better control their own behaviors. Consider these examples:

- Bradley's performance on assigned tasks is usually rather poor. You know he's capable of better work because he occasionally submits assignments of very high quality. The root of Bradley's problem seems to be that he's off task most of the time—perhaps sketching pictures of sports cars, mindlessly fiddling with objects he's found on the floor, or daydreaming. Bradley would really like to improve his academic performance but doesn't seem to know how to do it.

- Georgia often talks without permission—for instance, blurting out answers to questions, interrupting classmates who are speaking, and initiating off-task conversations at inopportune times. On several occasions you've spoken with Georgia about the problem, and she always vows to exercise more self-control in the future. Her behavior improves for a day or so, but after that her mouth is off and running once again.

Bradley's off-task behavior interferes with his own learning, and Georgia's excessive chattiness interferes with the learning of her peers. Cueing and private discussions haven't led to any improvement. But both Bradley and Georgia have something going for them: They *want* to change their behavior.

When students express concern about their problem behaviors, teaching self-regulation skills can be helpful. One valuable skill is *self-monitoring,* especially when students need a reality check about the severity of a problem. For example, Bradley may think he's on task far more often than he really is; thus we might give him a timer set to beep every five minutes and ask him to write down whether he's been on task each time he hears a beep. Similarly, Georgia may not realize how frequently she prevents her classmates from speaking; thus we might ask her to make a check mark on a tally sheet every time she talks without permission.

If self-monitoring alone doesn't do the trick, *self-instructions* might help Georgia gain some self-restraint in class discussions:

1. *Button* my lips (by holding them tightly together).
2. *Raise* my hand.
3. *Wait* until I'm called on.

In addition, both students might use *self-imposed contingencies* to give themselves a motivational boost. For example, Bradley might award himself a point for each 15-minute period he's been on task. Georgia might give herself 5 points at the beginning of each school day and then subtract a point each time she speaks out of turn. By accumulating a certain number of points, the two students could earn opportunities to engage in favorite activities.

Self-regulation strategies have several advantages. They help us avoid power struggles with students about who's in charge. They increase students' sense of self-determination and thus also increase their intrinsic motivation to learn and achieve in the classroom. Furthermore, self-regulation techniques benefit students over the long run, promoting productive behaviors that are likely to continue after students have moved on from a particular classroom or school. And when we teach students to monitor and modify their own behavior, rather than depend on us to do it for them, we become free to do other things—for example, to teach!

Encourage self-regulation by teaching such strategies as self-monitoring, self-instructions, and self-imposed contingencies.

The discussion of social cognitive theory in Chapter 10 offers additional strategies for fostering self-regulation skills.

## CONFERRING WITH PARENTS

We may sometimes need to consult with students' parents or other primary caregivers about a serious or chronic behavior problem. Consider these situations:

- You give your students short homework assignments almost every night. Carolyn has turned in only about one-third of them. You're pretty sure she's capable of doing the work, and you know from previous parent–teacher conferences that her parents give her the time and support she needs to get assignments done. You've spoken with Carolyn several times about the problem, but she shrugs you off as if she doesn't really care whether she does well in your class.

- Students have often found things missing from their desks or personal storage bins shortly after Roger has been in the vicinity. A few students have told you that they've seen Roger take things that belong to others, and many of the missing objects have later turned up in Roger's possession. When you confront him about your suspicion that he's been stealing from classmates, he adamantly denies it. He says he has no idea how Cami's gloves or Marvin's baseball trading cards ended up in his desk.

Conferring with parents is especially important when students' behavior problems show a pattern over time and have serious implications for students' long-term academic or social success. In some cases a simple telephone call may be sufficient. For example, Carolyn's parents may be unaware that she hasn't been doing her homework (she's been telling them she doesn't have any) and may be able to take the steps necessary to ensure that it gets done. In other cases a school conference may be necessary. For example, you may want to discuss Roger's suspected thefts with both Roger and his parent(s) together—something you can do more effectively when you all sit face to face in the same room.

Some ways of talking with parents are far more effective than others. Put yourself in a parent's shoes in the following exercise.

*Confer with parents about chronic problems that have serious implications for students' long-term success.*

### EXPERIENCING FIRSTHAND
### PUTTING YOURSELF IN A PARENT'S SHOES

Imagine you're the parent of a seventh grader named Tommy. As you and Tommy are eating dinner one evening, you get a telephone call.

> *You:* Hello?
>
> *Ms. J.:* This is Ms. Johnson, Tommy's teacher. May I talk with you for a few minutes?
>
> *You:* Of course. What can I do for you?
>
> *Ms. J.:* Well, I'm afraid I've been having some trouble with your son, and I thought you should know about it.
>
> *You:* Really? What's the problem?
>
> *Ms. J.:* Tommy hardly ever gets to class on time. When he does arrive, he spends most of his time talking with friends rather than paying attention to what I'm saying. It seems as if I have to speak to him three or four times every day about his behavior.
>
> *You:* How long has all this been going on?
>
> *Ms. J.:* For several weeks now. And the problem's getting worse rather than better. I'd really appreciate it if you'd talk with Tommy about the situation.
>
> *You:* Thank you for letting me know about this, Ms. Johnson.
>
> *Ms. J.:* You're most welcome. Good night.
>
> *You:* Good night, Ms. Johnson.

Take a few minutes to jot down some of the things that, as a parent, you might be thinking after this conversation.

You may have had a variety of thoughts, possibly including these:

- Why isn't Tommy taking his schoolwork more seriously?
- Isn't Tommy doing anything *right?*
- Has Ms. Johnson tried anything besides reprimanding Tommy for his behavior? Or is she laying all of this on *my* shoulders?
- Tommy's a good kid. I should know, because I raised him. For some reason Ms. Johnson doesn't like him and so is finding fault with anything he does.

Only the first of these four reactions is likely to lead to a productive response on your part.

Notice how Ms. Johnson focused strictly on the negative aspects of Tommy's classroom performance. As a result, you (as Tommy's parent) may possibly have felt anger toward your son or guilt about your ineffective parenting skills. Alternatively, if you remained confident about your son's scholastic abilities and your own ability as a parent, you may have begun to wonder about Ms. Johnson's ability to teach and motivate seventh graders. Sadly, too many teachers reach out to parents only to talk about students' weaknesses—never their strengths—as the following interview with Jamal illustrates:

*Adult:* Has your grandpa [Jamal's primary caregiver] come to school?

*Jamal:* Yup, when the teachers call him.

*Adult:* What did they call him for?

*Jamal:* The only time they call him is when I am being bad, the teacher will call him, he will come up here and have a meeting with the teacher.

*Adult:* If you are being good do the teachers call?

*Jamal:* No. (Kumar et al., 2002, p. 164)

Ideally a teacher–parent discussion about problem behaviors is initiated within the context of an ongoing relationship characterized by mutual trust and respect and a shared concern for the student's learning and well-being. For example, a phone call to parents is most likely to yield productive results if we already have a good working relationship with them and are sure that they won't overreact with harsh, excessive punishment. Furthermore, when communicating with parents, our overall messages about their child should be positive and optimistic. For instance, we might describe negative aspects of a student's classroom performance within the context of the many things the student does *well.* (Rather than start out by complaining about Tommy's behavior, Ms. Johnson might have begun by saying that Tommy is a bright, capable young man with many friends and a good sense of humor.) And we must be clear about our commitment to working *together* with parents to help a student succeed in the classroom. The Into the Classroom feature "Talking with Parents About a Student's Misbehaviors" presents several strategies for effectively approaching parents about a challenging behavior problem.

## CONDUCTING PLANNED, SYSTEMATIC INTERVENTIONS

Sometimes problem behaviors are so disruptive and persistent that they require a systematic effort to change them. Consider these situations:

- Tucker finds many reasons to roam about the room—he "has to" sharpen a pencil, "has to" get his homework out of his backpack, "has to" get a drink of water, and so on. As a result, Tucker gets very little work done and often distracts his classmates with his perpetual motion.
- Janet's verbal abusiveness is getting out of hand. She frequently offends you and your other students with sexually explicit language. You've tried praising her on occasions when she's pleasant to others, and she seems to appreciate your doing so, yet her abusive remarks continue.

Imagine that both Tucker and Janet are in your class. You've already spoken with each of them about their unacceptable behavior, yet you've seen no improvement. You've suggested self-regulation techniques, but neither student is interested in changing for the better. You've tried putting them in time-out for their actions, but Janet seems to enjoy the time away from her schoolwork, and Tucker sometimes has a valid reason for getting out of his seat. Although both students' parents are aware of and concerned about their children's classroom behaviors, their efforts at home haven't had an impact. And after all, these are largely *school* problems rather than home problems. So what do you do now?

When simpler, short-term intervention strategies haven't been productive, individually tailored behaviorist approaches can be quite useful, perhaps in the form of *applied behavior analysis* or *positive behavior support.* Such approaches can be especially effective when combined with other strategies, such as fostering perspective-taking, teaching effective social skills, and scaffolding self-regulation. Combining behaviorist principles with other, more cognitively oriented techniques is sometimes called cognitive behavioral therapy (e.g., Forman & Barakat, 2011; Platts & Williamson, 2000).

How might we use behaviorist techniques to improve Tucker's classroom behavior? One approach would be to identify one or more effective reinforcers—given Tucker's constant fidgeting, opportunities for physical activity might be reinforcing—and then gradually shape more sedentary behavior. We might also give Tucker a reasonable allotment of "tickets" he can use to "purchase" permission to get out of his seat during class activities. An alternative strategy might be to conduct a *functional analysis* to determine the particular purpose that out-of-seat behaviors serve for Tucker. Perhaps they allow him to avoid difficult tasks or to release the physical energy his body seems to overproduce. If we discover that Tucker acts out only when he expects challenging assignments, we should provide the instruction and support he needs to accomplish those assignments successfully—for example, by teaching him effective learning strategies. If, instead,

Some students benefit from multiple approaches to changing their behavior. Examine strategies for teaching such skills in the simulation "Developing Behavior Change Plans for Students Who Demonstrate Serious, Persistent Disruptive Behaviors."

Plan a systematic intervention when other, simpler interventions haven't been successful.

See Chapter 9 for more information about behaviorist approaches to intervention, including applied behavior analysis, functional analysis, and positive behavior support.

**cognitive behavioral therapy**
Planned, systematic combination of behaviorist techniques and cognition-based strategies (e.g., modeling, self-regulation techniques) as a means of bringing about desired behaviors.

## Into the Classroom

### Talking with Parents about a Student's Misbehaviors

🍎 **Consult with parents if a collaborative effort might bring about a behavior change.**

At a parent–teacher–student conference, a high school math teacher expresses concern that a student often falls asleep in class. Because the student has a computer and a cable outlet in her room, her father speculates that perhaps she's surfing the Internet when she should be in bed. He looks at his daughter inquisitively, and her guilty facial expression confirms his suspicion. With the teacher's prompting, the father and the student identify an appropriate policy for home computer use—one that includes moving the computer to another room, where its use can be more closely monitored.

🍎 **Begin with a description of the child's many strengths.**

In a phone conversation with a student's mother, a teacher describes several areas in which the student has made considerable progress and then asks for advice about strategies for helping the student stay on task and be more conscientious about completing his work.

🍎 **Describe the problem in terms of inappropriate behaviors, *not* in terms of undesirable personality characteristics.**

When describing a student's poor record of turning in homework assignments, her teacher says, "Carolyn has turned in only one-third of the homework I've assigned this year. Her attendance record is excellent, so I know she's been healthy, and she's certainly capable of doing the work." At no point does the teacher suggest that Carolyn is lazy, unmotivated, or stubborn.

🍎 **Don't place blame; instead, acknowledge that raising children is rarely easy.**

When talking with the mother of a middle school student, a teacher mentions that the student seems to be more interested in talking to friends than in getting her schoolwork done. The mother describes a similar problem at home: "Marnie's always been a much more social girl than I ever was. It's like pulling teeth just getting her off the phone to do her homework, and then we end up having a shouting match that gets us nowhere!" The teacher sympathetically responds, "Students seem to become especially concerned about social matters once they reach adolescence. How about if you, Marnie, and I meet some day after school to talk about the problem? Perhaps by working together the three of us can find a way to solve it."

🍎 **Ask for information, and express your desire to work together to address the problem.**

When a teacher discovers that a student has regularly been taking items from classmates' personal storage bins, she sets up an appointment to meet with the student and his grandmother (the student's primary caregiver). "I like Roger a lot," she says. "He has a great sense of humor, and his smile often lights up my day. I can't understand why he might want to 'borrow' items from other children without asking them first. His actions have cost him several friendships. Do either of you have any ideas about how we might tackle the problem? I'd like to do whatever I can to help Roger repair his reputation with his peers."

🍎 **Agree on a strategy.**

While reviewing a student's academic progress at a parent–teacher conference, an elementary teacher says, "Mark has a tendency to fiddle with things at his desk—for example, twisting paperclips, playing with rubber bands, or making paper airplanes—when he should be getting his work done. As a result, he often doesn't complete his assignments." The student's father replies, "I've noticed the same thing when he works on his homework, but I bring a lot of paperwork home from the office every night and don't have time to constantly hound him to stay on task." The teacher and father talk more about the problem and agree that reinforcement for completed assignments might be helpful. Mark will earn points for high scores that will help him "buy" the new bicycle he's been asking for.

*Sources:* Christenson & Sheridan, 2001; C. Davis & Yang, 2005; Emmer & Evertson, 2009; Evertson & Emmer, 2009; A. Miller, 2006; Woolfolk Hoy, Davis, & Pape, 2006.

---

we find that Tucker's hyperactivity emerges in a wide variety of situations, we might suspect a physiological cause and give him numerous opportunities to release pent-up energy during the school day. Finally, Tucker might benefit from instruction and scaffolding regarding general organizational skills—in particular, assembling necessary supplies (notebooks, sharpened pencils, completed homework, etc.) before lessons begin.

Cognitive behavioral therapy could be helpful for Janet as well. In this case we might suspect that Janet lacks the social skills she needs to interact effectively with others; we might therefore begin by teaching her such skills through modeling, role-playing, and so on. Once Janet has gained some competence in interpersonal skills, we can begin to reinforce her for using them (perhaps with praise, as she has responded well to praise in the past). Meanwhile, we should also punish any relapses into old, abusive behavior patterns (perhaps with a short time-out).

Table 13.3 summarizes the six general strategies we've examined for addressing student misbehaviors, along with the circumstances in which each strategy is likely to be useful.

## TAKING STUDENTS' CULTURAL BACKGROUNDS INTO ACCOUNT

As we determine which behaviors are truly unacceptable in our classrooms, we must remember that some behaviors that our own culture deems inappropriate may be quite appropriate in another culture. In the next exercise, we look at some examples.

# PRINCIPLES/ASSUMPTIONS

## TABLE 13.3 • Strategies for Addressing Inappropriate Classroom Behaviors

| STRATEGY | SITUATIONS IN WHICH IT'S APPROPRIATE | EXAMPLES |
|---|---|---|
| Ignoring the behavior | • The misbehavior is unlikely to be repeated.<br>• The misbehavior is unlikely to spread to other students.<br>• Unusual circumstances have temporarily elicited the misbehavior.<br>• The misbehavior doesn't seriously interfere with learning. | • One student discreetly passes a note to another student just before the end of class.<br>• A student accidentally drops her books, startling other students and temporarily distracting them from their work.<br>• An entire class is hyperactive on the last afternoon before spring break. |
| Cueing the student | • The misbehavior is a minor infraction but definitely interferes with students' learning.<br>• Behavior is likely to improve with a subtle reminder. | • A student forgets to close his notebook at the beginning of a test.<br>• Members of a cooperative learning group are talking so loudly that they distract other groups.<br>• Several students are exchanging jokes during an independent seatwork assignment. |
| Discussing the problem privately with the student | • Cueing has been ineffective in changing the behavior.<br>• If made clear, the reasons for the misbehavior might suggest possible strategies for addressing it. | • A student is frequently late to class.<br>• A student refuses to do certain kinds of assignments.<br>• A student shows a sudden drop in motivation for no apparent reason. |
| Promoting self-regulation | • The student has a strong desire to improve his or her behavior. | • A student doesn't realize how frequently she interrupts her classmates.<br>• A student seeks help in learning to control his anger.<br>• A student acknowledges that his inability to stay on task is adversely affecting the good grades he wants to get. |
| Conferring with parents | • A chronic behavior problem is likely to interfere with long-term academic and/or social success.<br>• The source of the problem may possibly lie outside school walls.<br>• Parents are likely to work collaboratively with school faculty members to bring about a behavior change. | • A student does well in class but rarely turns in required homework assignments.<br>• A student falls asleep in class almost every day.<br>• A student is caught stealing classmates' lunches. |
| Conducting a planned, systematic intervention | • The misbehavior has continued over a period of time and significantly interferes with student learning.<br>• Other, less intensive approaches (e.g., cueing, private conferences) have been ineffective.<br>• The student seems unwilling or unable to use self-regulation techniques. | • A student has unusual difficulty sitting still for age-appropriate time periods.<br>• A student's obscene remarks continue even though her teacher has spoken with her about the behavior on several occasions.<br>• A member of the soccer team displays bursts of anger and aggression that are potentially dangerous to other players. |

## EXPERIENCING FIRSTHAND
### IDENTIFYING MISBEHAVIORS

As you read each scenario below, consider these questions:

• Whether you would classify the behavior as a *misbehavior?*
• What cultural group(s) might find the behavior appropriate?
• How might you deal with the behavior?

The section on cultural and ethnic differences in Chapter 4 can help you with this exercise.

**Scenarios:**

1. A student is frequently late for school, sometimes arriving more than an hour after the school bell has rung.
2. Two students are sharing answers as they take a quiz.
3. Several students are exchanging insults that become increasingly derogatory.

Tardiness (Example 1) interferes with learning because the student loses valuable instructional time; thus, it might reasonably be construed as a misbehavior. However, a student who is chronically tardy may live in a community that doesn't observe strict schedules and timelines—a pattern common in some Hispanic and Native American communities. Furthermore, arrival time may not be entirely within the student's control; for instance, perhaps the student has household responsibilities or transportation issues that make punctuality difficult. A private conversation with the student, perhaps followed up by a conference with family members, might be the most effective way to determine the root of the problem and identify potential solutions.

Sharing answers during a quiz (Example 2) is a misbehavior *if* students have been specifically instructed to do their own work. Because a quiz can help us determine what students have and haven't learned, inaccurate quiz scores affect our instructional planning and thus indirectly affect students' future learning. Although the behavior represents cheating to many people, it may reflect the cooperative spirit and emphasis on group achievement evident in the cultures of many Native American and Mexican American students. An adverse consequence is in order *if* we have previously explained what cheating is in a way that students understand and *if* we have clearly described the situations in which collaboration is and isn't appropriate—in other words, if the students know full well that their behavior violates classroom policy. But if we *haven't* laid such groundwork, we must take the incident as a lesson for ourselves about what we must do to prevent such behavior from occurring again.

Exchanging insults (Example 3) might be psychologically harmful for the students involved and might adversely affect the overall classroom climate. Alternatively, however, it might simply be an instance of *playing the dozens,* a playful verbal interaction involving creative one-upmanship common in some African American communities. How we handle the situation depends on the spirit in which the students seem to view the exchange. Their body language—whether they're smiling or scowling, whether they seem relaxed or tense—will tell us a great deal. If the insults truly signal escalating hostilities, immediate intervention is in order—perhaps separating the students, imposing an appropriate consequence, and following up with a private conference. If, instead, the insults reflect creative verbal play, we may simply need to establish reasonable boundaries (e.g., "indoor" voices should be used, racial or ethnic slurs are unacceptable).

## Addressing Aggression and Violence at School

In recent years the news media have focused considerable attention on violent school crime, and especially on school shootings, leading many people to believe that aggression in our schools is on the rise. In reality, violent aggression involving serious injury or death is relatively rare on school grounds and, has, if anything, been *declining* rather than increasing, at least in the United States. Most aggression at school involves minor physical injury, psychological harm (e.g., sexual or racial harassment), or destruction of property (e.g., vandalization of student lockers) (Borum, Cornell, Modzeleski, & Jimerson, 2010; Kupchik & Bracy, 2009; Mayer & Furlong, 2010; Robers, Zhang, Truman, & Snyder, 2012).

If we consider *only* violent aggression that causes serious injury or death, then school is probably the safest place that young people can be (DeVoe, Peter, Noonan, Snyder, & Baum, 2005; Garbarino, Bradshaw, & Vorrasi, 2002). But if we consider *all* forms of aggression (mild as well as severe), then aggression among children and adolescents occurs more frequently at school than at any other location—especially in areas where adult supervision is minimal (e.g., hallways, restrooms, parking lots) (Astor, Meyer, & Behre, 1999; Casella, 2001b; Finkelhor & Ormrod, 2000). The relative prevalence of aggression at school is almost certainly due to two factors. First, children and adolescents spend a great deal of time at school, more so than in any other place except home. Second, the sheer number of students attending even the smallest of schools makes some interpersonal conflict almost inevitable.

The roots of school aggression and violence are many and diverse. A variety of cognitive factors (e.g., lack of perspective taking, misinterpretation of social cues, poor social problem-solving skills) predispose some students to aggressive behavior (Coie & Dodge, 1998; Dodge et al., 2003; Troop-Gordon & Asher, 2005). Furthermore, some school- or neighborhood-specific cultures endorse the belief that defending one's reputation in the face of personal insults or indignities is a matter of "honor" that calls for aggressive action (R. P. Brown, Osterman, & Barnes, 2009; K. M. Williams, 2001a). Developmental factors come into play as well; for instance, many young children and a few adolescents have poor impulse control, and in early adolescence the unsettling transition to middle school can lead some students to bully weaker age-mates as a way of gaining social status with peers (Espelage, Holt, & Henkel, 2003; National Center for Education Statistics, 2007; Pellegrini, 2002). Finally, aggression is a common reaction to frustration, and some students are repeatedly frustrated in their efforts to be academically and socially successful at school (G. Bender, 2001; Casella, 2001b; Miles & Stipek, 2006).

Inappropriately sharing answers also lowers the *validity* of a quiz score (see Chapter 14 and Chapter 15).

Remember that some behaviors that are unacceptable in your culture may be quite acceptable in a student's culture. When these behaviors interfere with classroom achievement, be patient and understanding as you help the student acquire behaviors consistent with school expectations.

See Chapter 3 for more information about cognitive factors underlying aggression, as well as for recommendations on addressing the causes and emotional consequences of peer bullying.

# A THREE-LEVEL APPROACH

Regardless of the roots of the behavior, we mustn't tolerate *any* form of aggression or violence on school grounds. Students can learn and achieve at optimal levels only if they know they're both physically and psychologically safe at school. And if they *don't* feel safe, they're at increased risk for dropping out before high school graduation (Filax, 2007; Rumberger, 1995). To be truly effective in combating aggression and violence, we must address these challenges on three levels, depicted graphically in Figure 13.7 (Dwyer & Osher, 2000; Hyman et al., 2006; Ihlo & Nantais, 2010; H. M. Walker et al., 1996).[1]

> Don't tolerate *any* form of aggression at school. For example, be on the lookout for bullying and other forms of psychological intimidation.

## LEVEL I: CREATING A NONVIOLENT SCHOOL ENVIRONMENT

One-shot "antiviolence" campaigns have little lasting effect on school aggression and violence (Burstyn & Stevens, 2001). Instead, creating a peaceful, nonviolent school environment must be a long-term effort that includes numerous strategies:

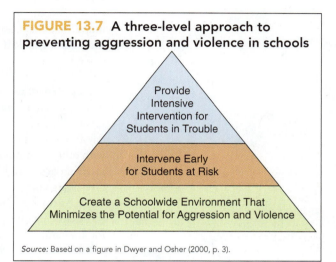

**FIGURE 13.7** **A three-level approach to preventing aggression and violence in schools**

*Source:* Based on a figure in Dwyer and Osher (2000, p. 3).

- Make a schoolwide commitment to supporting *all* students' academic and social success.
- Provide a challenging and engaging curriculum.
- Form caring, trusting faculty–student relationships.
- Insist on genuine and equal respect—among students and faculty alike—for people of diverse backgrounds, races, and ethnic groups.
- Emphasize prosocial behaviors (e.g., sharing, helping, cooperating).
- Establish schoolwide policies and practices that foster appropriate behavior (e.g., give clear guidelines for behavior, consistently apply consequences for infractions, provide instruction in effective social interaction and problem-solving skills).
- Teach specific skills that students can use to intervene when they witness bullying.
- Provide mechanisms through which students can communicate their concerns about aggression and victimization openly and without fear of reprisal.
- Involve students in school decision making.
- Establish close working relationships with community agencies and families.
- Openly discuss safety issues. (Burstyn & Stevens, 2001; Dwyer & Osher, 2000; Learning First Alliance, 2001; Meehan et al., 2003; G. M. Morrison, Furlong, D'Incau, & Morrison, 2004; Pellegrini, 2002; S. W. Ross & Horner, 2009; Syvertsen, Flanagan, & Stout, 2009; J. S. Warren et al., 2006)

Most of these strategies should look familiar, as they've been mentioned frequently throughout this and other chapters of the book. The final strategy on the list—openly discussing safety issues—encompasses a variety of more specific strategies, such as these:

- Explain what bullying is (i.e., that it involves harassing and intimidating peers who can't easily defend themselves) and why it's unacceptable.
- Solicit students' input about potentially unsafe areas that require more faculty supervision (e.g., an infrequently used restroom or back stairwell).
- Convey willingness to hear students' complaints about troublesome classmates. (Such complaints can provide important clues about which students most need assistance and intervention.)
- Most importantly, take active steps to *address* students' safety concerns.

## LEVEL II: INTERVENING EARLY FOR STUDENTS AT RISK

Usually, when educators use the term *students at risk,* they're referring to students who are at risk for academic failure. But students can be at risk for *social* failure as well. For instance, they may have few or no friends, be overtly bullied or rejected by many of their peers, or in other ways find themselves excluded from the social life of the school.

---

[1]For a more in-depth discussion of the three levels, I urge you to read Safeguarding Our Children: An Action Guide by K. Dwyer and D. Osher (2000). You can download a copy from a variety of Internet websites, including www2.ed.gov/admins/lead/safety/actguide/index.html.

Provide individually tailored guidance and support for students who experience consistent social failure at school.

Perhaps 10 to 15% of students need some sort of minor intervention to help them interact effectively with peers, establish good working relationships with teachers, and become bona fide members of the school community (Ihlo & Nantais, 2010; K. L. Lane et al., 2011). Such intervention can't be a one-size-fits-all approach but must instead be tailored to students' particular strengths and needs. For some students, it might require instruction in effective social skills. For other students, it might mean getting them actively involved in school clubs or extracurricular activities. For still others, it may require a well-planned, systematic effort to encourage and reinforce productive behaviors, perhaps through applied behavior analysis or positive behavior support. Regardless of type, interventions are most effective when they occur *early* in the game—before students go too far down the path of antisocial behavior—and when they're developed by a multidisciplinary team of teachers and other professionals who bring various areas of expertise to the planning table (Crone, Horner, & Hawken, 2004; Dwyer & Osher, 2000; Osher et al., 2010).

### LEVEL III: PROVIDING INTENSIVE INTERVENTION FOR STUDENTS IN TROUBLE

For a variety of reasons, minor interventions aren't always sufficient for a small percentage of students who are predisposed to be aggressive and violent. For example, some students have serious mental illnesses that interfere with their ability to think rationally, cope appropriately with everyday frustrations, and control impulses. Typically schools must work closely and collaboratively with other community groups—perhaps mental health clinics, police and probation officers, and social services—to help students at high risk for aggression and violence (Dwyer & Osher, 2000; Greenberg et al., 2003; Hyman et al., 2006).

As teachers, our frequent interactions with students put us in an ideal position to identify those children and adolescents most in need of intensive intervention and get them back on track for academic and social success. As you gain teaching experience, you'll begin to get a good sense of which characteristics are and aren't normal for a particular age-group. You should especially be on the lookout for the early warning signs of violence presented in Figure 13.8.

Although we must be ever vigilant for signals that a student may be planning to cause harm to others, it's essential that we keep several points in mind. First, as mentioned earlier, extreme violence is *very rare* in schools; unreasonable paranoia about potential school violence will prevent us from working effectively with students. Second, the great majority of students who exhibit one or a few of the warning signs listed in Figure 13.8 *won't* become violent (U.S. Secret Service National Threat Assessment Center, 2000). And most importantly, we must *never* use the warning signs as a reason to unfairly accuse, isolate, or punish a student (Dwyer, Osher, & Warger, 1998). These signs provide a means of getting students help if they need it, not of excluding them from the education that all children and adolescents deserve.

Keep the common warning signs of violence in mind. Use them as possible indicators that a student needs significant assistance to gain emotional well-being and social success.

## ADDRESSING GANG-RELATED PROBLEMS

A frequent source of aggression at some schools is gang-related hostilities. Although gangs are more prevalent in low-income, inner-city schools, they're sometimes found in suburban and rural schools as well (Howell & Lynch, 2000; Kodluboy, 2004).

The three-level approach to combating school aggression and violence just described can go a long way toward suppressing violent gang activities, but we'll often need to take additional measures as well. Recommended strategies include these:

- Develop, communicate, and enforce clear-cut policies regarding potential threats to other students' safety.
- Identify the specific nature and scope of gang activity in the student population.
- Forbid clothing, jewelry, and behaviors that signify membership in a particular gang (e.g., bandanas, shoelaces in gang colors, certain hand signs).[2]
- Actively mediate between-gang and within-gang disputes. (Kodluboy, 2004)

A case study at one middle school (Sanchez & Anderson, 1990) illustrates just how effective the last of these strategies—mediation—can be in addressing gang-related aggression. Many students

---

[2]A potential problem with this strategy is that it may violate students' civil liberties. For guidance on how to walk the line between ensuring students' safety and giving them reasonable freedom of expression, see Kodluboy (2004) and Rozalski and Yell (2004).

---

**FIGURE 13.8** **Early warning signs of possible violent behavior**

Experts have identified numerous warning signs that a student may possibly be contemplating violent actions against others. Any one of them alone is unlikely to signal a violent attack, but several of them *in combination* should lead us to consult with school administrators and specially trained professionals.

- *Social withdrawal:* Over time, a student interacts less and less frequently with teachers and with all or most peers.

- *Excessive feelings of isolation, rejection, or persecution:* A student directly or indirectly expresses the belief that he or she is friendless, disliked, or unfairly picked on; such feelings are sometimes the result of long-term physical or psychological bullying by peers.

- *Rapid decline in academic performance:* A student shows a dramatic change in academic performance and seems unconcerned about doing well. Cognitive and physical factors (e.g., learning disabilities, ineffective study strategies, brain injury) have been ruled out as causes of the decline.

- *Poor coping skills:* A student has little ability to deal effectively with frustration, takes the smallest affront personally, and has trouble bouncing back after minor disappointments.

- *Lack of anger control:* A student frequently responds with uncontrolled anger to even the slightest injustice and may misdirect anger at innocent bystanders.

- *Apparent sense of superiority, self-centeredness, and lack of empathy:* A student depicts himself or herself as smarter or in some other way better than peers, is preoccupied with his or her own needs, and has little regard for the needs of others. Underlying such characteristics may be low-esteem and depression.

- *Lengthy grudges:* A student is unforgiving of others' transgressions, even after considerable time has elapsed.

- *Violent themes in drawings and written work:* Violence predominates in a student's artwork, stories, or journal entries, and perhaps certain individuals (e.g., a parent or particular classmate) are regularly targeted in these fantasies. (Keep in mind that *occasional* violence in writing and art isn't unusual, especially for boys.)

- *Intolerance of individual and group differences:* A student shows intense disdain for and prejudice toward people of a certain race, ethnicity, gender, sexual orientation, religion, or disability.

- *History of violence, aggression, and other discipline problems:* A student has a long record of seriously inappropriate behavior extending over several years.

- *Association with violent peers:* A student associates regularly with a gang or other antisocial peer group.

- *Inappropriate role models:* A student speaks with admiration about Satan, Adolf Hitler, Osama bin Laden, or some other malevolent figure.

- *Excessive alcohol or drug use:* A student who abuses alcohol or drugs may have reduced self-control. In some cases substance abuse signals significant mental illness.

- *Inappropriate access to firearms:* A student has easy access to guns and ammunition and may regularly practice using them.

- *Threats of violence:* A student has openly expressed an intent to harm someone else, perhaps in explicit terms or perhaps through ambiguous references to "something spectacular" happening at school on a particular day. ***This warning sign requires immediate action.***

*Sources:* Dwyer et al., 1998; O'Toole, 2000; U.S. Secret Service National Threat Assessment Center, 2000; M. W. Watson, Andreas, Fischer, & Smith, 2005.

---

belonged to one of several gangs that seemed to "rule the school." Fights among rival gangs were common, and nongang members were frequent victims of harassment. Dress codes, counseling, and suspensions of chronic trouble makers had little impact on students' behavior. In desperation, two school counselors suggested that the school implement a mediation program, beginning with three large gangs that were responsible for most of the trouble. Interpersonal problems involving two or more gangs would be brought to a mediation team, comprised of five school faculty members and three representatives from each of the three gangs. Team members had to abide by certain rules:

1. Really try to solve the problem.
2. No name-calling or put-downs.
3. No interrupting.
4. Be as honest as possible.
5. No weapons or acts of intimidation.
6. All sessions to be confidential until an agreement is reached or mediation is called off.[3]

To lay the groundwork for productive discussions, faculty members of the mediation team met separately with each of the three gangs to establish feelings of rapport and trust, explain how the mediation process would work, and gain students' cooperation with the plan.

In the first mediation session, common grievances were aired. Students agreed that they didn't like being insulted or intimidated, that they worried about their physical safety, and that they all wanted one another's respect. In several additional meetings during the next two weeks, the team reached agreement that a number of behaviors would be unacceptable at school: There

---

[3]List of rules from "Gang Mediation: A Process That Works" by Flora M. Sanchez and M. L. Anderson, From *Principal*, 1990, Volume 69(5), p. 54. Copyright © 2009 by National Association of Elementary School Principals. Reprinted with permission. All rights reserved.

would be no put-downs, name calling, hateful stares, threats, shoving, or gang graffiti. After the final meeting, each gang was separately called into the conference room. Its representatives on the mediation team explained the agreement, and other members of the gang were asked to sign it. Despite some skepticism, most members of all three gangs signed it.

A month later, it was clear that the process had been successful. Members of rival gangs nodded pleasantly to one another or gave one another a high-five sign as they passed in the hall. Gang members no longer felt compelled to hang out in groups for safety's sake. Members of two of the gangs were seen playing soccer together one afternoon. And there had been no gang-related fights all month.

As should be apparent from our discussion in this chapter, helping growing children and adolescents develop into successful, productive adults can occasionally be quite a challenge. But in my own experience, discovering that you actually *can* make a difference in students' lives— including the lives of some who are at risk for academic or social failure—is one of the most rewarding aspects of being a teacher.

# 13 What Have You Learned?

We now return to the chapter's learning outcomes to review some of the chapter's key ideas.

■ **13.1: Describe numerous strategies for creating a classroom environment conducive to academic achievement and students' personal well-being.** Good teachers create a setting in which students are regularly engaged in planned tasks and activities and in which few student behaviors interfere with those tasks and activities. The physical arrangement of the classroom makes a difference, but more important is a psychological environment—*classroom climate*—in which students feel safe and secure, make learning a high priority, and are willing to take risks and make mistakes. Central to such a climate are (1) teacher–student relationships that communicate genuine caring and concern for every student and (2) an overall sense of community in the classroom—a sense that teachers and students have shared goals, are mutually respectful and supportive of one another's efforts, and believe that everyone makes an important contribution to classroom learning. Creating a warm, supportive atmosphere and a sense of classroom community may be especially important for students in minority cultural groups, students from lower socioeconomic backgrounds, and students with disabilities. At the same time, we teachers must take charge to some extent, establishing rules and planning age-appropriate activities to ensure that students are continually working toward instructional goals and objectives.

Evaluate and apply your knowledge related to this learning outcome in MyEducationLab™.

■ **13.2: Explain how you can coordinate your efforts with colleagues, community agencies, and parents to maximize students' academic and personal development.** As teachers, we'll be most effective when we work cooperatively with other faculty members, other institutions, and parents to promote students' learning, development, and achievement. It's especially important to keep in regular contact with parents, sharing information in both directions about the progress students are making and coordinating efforts at school with those on the home front. We can keep the lines of

communication open through a variety of mechanisms—for instance, through parent–teacher conferences, newsletters, class websites, and family activities at school. We may need to make an extra effort to establish productive working relationships with those parents who, on the surface, seem reluctant to become involved in their children's education.

Evaluate and apply your knowledge related to this learning outcome in MyEducationLab™.

■ **13.3: Identify six general approaches to dealing with student misbehaviors and the circumstances and cultural contexts in which each approach might be appropriate.** Despite our best efforts, students sometimes engage in behaviors that disrupt classroom learning, put one or more students' physical safety or psychological well-being in jeopardy, or violate basic moral and ethical standards. Some minor misbehaviors are best ignored, including those that probably won't be repeated, those that are unlikely to be imitated by other students, and those that occur only temporarily and within the context of unusual circumstances. Other minor infractions can be dealt with simply and quickly by cueing students or talking privately with them about our concerns. More serious and chronic behavior problems may require instruction in self-regulation skills, consultation with parents, or intensive, multifaceted interventions. Regardless of the approach we take in dealing with students' misbehaviors, we must take into account the fact that some of those behaviors may be the product of a particular cultural upbringing or the result of a specific disability.

Evaluate and apply your knowledge related to this learning outcome in MyEducationLab™.

■ **13.4: Describe a three-level approach that can effectively reduce aggression and violence in the overall school community, as well as additional strategies you might use to address gang-related hostilities.** Although violent crime in schools in on the decline, milder forms of aggression (e.g., minor physical injuries, psychological harm, destruction of property) continue to be common in and around school buildings. Some experts recommend a three-level approach in combating aggression and violence in schools. First, we must collaboratively create a school-wide environment that makes aggression and violence unlikely—for instance, by establishing trusting teacher–student relationships, fostering a sense of caring and respect among students from diverse backgrounds, and providing mechanisms through which students can communicate their concerns without fear of reprisal. Second, we must intervene early for students who appear to be at risk for academic or social failure, providing them with the cognitive and social skills they need to be successful at school. And third, we must seek

intensive intervention for a small number of students who are prone to violence, have a disabling mental illness, or in some other way are seriously troubled. If well-organized gangs have a significant presence in our schools, we may need to take additional measures as well—for instance, by engaging gang members in discussions about their grievances and potential strategies for addressing their differences.

**Evaluate** and **apply** your knowledge related to this learning outcome in **MyEducationLab™**.

## Practice for Your Licensure Exam

### The Good Buddy

Mr. Schulak has wanted to be a teacher for as long as he can remember. In his many volunteer activities over the years—coaching a girls' basketball team, assisting with a Boy Scout troop, teaching Sunday school—he has discovered how much he enjoys working with children. Children obviously enjoy working with him as well: Many occasionally call or stop by his home to shoot baskets, talk over old times, or just say hello. Some of them even call him by his first name.

Now that Mr. Schulak has completed his college degree and obtained his teaching certificate, he has accepted a teaching position at his hometown's junior high school. He's delighted to find that he already knows many of his students, and he spends the first few days of class renewing his friendships with them. But by the end of the week, he realizes that his classes have accomplished little of an academic nature.

The next Monday Mr. Schulak vows to get down to business. He begins each of his six class sessions by describing his instructional goals for the weeks to come and then introduces the first lesson. Unfortunately, many of his students are resistant to settling down and getting to work. They want to move from one seat to another, talk with friends, toss wadded-up paper "basketballs" across the room, and do anything *except* the academic tasks Mr. Schulak has in mind. In his second week as a new teacher, Mr. Schulak has already lost control of his classes.

1. **Constructed-response question:**

   Mr. Schulak is having considerable difficulty bringing his classes to order.

   **A.** Identify two critical things that Mr. Schulak has *not* done to get the school year off to a good start.

   **B.** Describe two strategies that Mr. Schulak might now use to remedy the situation.

2. **Multiple-choice question:**

   Mr. Schulak is undoubtedly aware that good teachers show that they care about and respect their students. Which one of the following statements describes the kind of teacher–student relationship that is most likely to foster students' learning and achievement?

   a. The teacher communicates optimism about students' potential for success and offers the support necessary for that success.

   b. The teacher spends a lot of time engaging in recreational activities with students after school and on weekends.

   c. The teacher focuses almost exclusively on what students do well and ignores or downplays what students do poorly.

   d. The teacher listens patiently to students' concerns but reminds them that he or she alone will ultimately decide what transpires in the classroom.

### PRAXIS

Go to Appendix C, "Matching Book and **MyEducationLab™** to the Praxis Principles of Learning and Teaching Tests," to discover sections of this chapter that may be especially applicable to the Praxis tests.

# 14 Classroom Assessment Strategies

## LEARNING OUTCOMES

**14.1:** Describe the various forms that classroom assessment can take and the various purposes it can serve for teachers and students.

**14.2:** Explain how you might enhance students' learning through formative assessments and other classroom assessment practices.

**14.3:** Define and apply four important RSVP characteristics of good assessments: reliability, standardization, validity, and practicality.

**14.4:** Explain how you might conduct informal assessments, paper–pencil assessments, and performance assessments to assess students' learning and achievement.

**14.5:** Describe individual and group differences that have implications for classroom assessment practices.

## CASE STUDY: THE MATH TEST

Ms. Ford is teaching a middle school math class to students with low achievement levels. She has just returned a set of graded test papers, and the following discussion with her students ensues:

*Ms. Ford:* When I corrected these papers, I was really, really shocked at some of the scores. And I think you will be too. I thought there were some that were so-so, and there were some that were devastating, in my opinion.

*Student:* [Noise increasing.] Can we take them over?

*Ms. Ford:* I am going to give them back to you. This is what I would like you to do: Every single math problem that you got wrong, for homework tonight and tomorrow, it is your responsibility to correct these problems and turn them in. In fact, I will say this, I want this sheet back to me by Wednesday at least. All our math problems that we got wrong I want returned to me with the correct answer.

*Student:* Did anybody get 100?

*Ms. Ford:* No.

*Student:* Nobody got 100? [Groans]

*Ms. Ford:* OK, boys and girls, shhh. I would say, on this test in particular, boys and girls, if you received a grade below 75 you definitely have to work on it. I do expect this quiz to be returned with Mom or Dad's signature on it. I want Mom and Dad to be aware of how we're doing.

*Student:* No!

*Student:* Do we have to show our parents? Is it a requirement to pass the class?

*Ms. Ford:* If you do not return it with a signature, I will call home. (J. C. Turner, Meyer, et al., 1998, pp. 740–741)

- What information have the test results actually given Ms. Ford? What inferences does Ms. Ford make based on this information?
- What underlying messages does Ms. Ford communicate about the poor test scores? How might these messages affect students' motivation and the classroom climate?

---

The only thing Ms. Ford knows for sure is that her students have performed poorly on the test. From this fact she infers that they haven't mastered the knowledge and skills the test was designed to assess—an inference that's appropriate *only* if the test is a good measure of what the students have actually learned. When she tells them they must "work on it" and correct wrong answers as a homework assignment, she's putting the blame for their poor scores entirely on their shoulders. Furthermore, with her insistence that students get parents' signatures on the graded tests, she's focusing their attention on performance goals rather than mastery goals—demonstrating competence rather than actually *acquiring* it—and potentially raising students' anxiety to debilitating levels.

Classroom assessment practices are intertwined with virtually every other aspect of classroom functioning. They affect (1) our future planning and instruction (e.g., what we teach and how we teach it); (2) students' motivation and affect (e.g., what specific achievement goals they adopt and whether they feel confident or anxious); and (3) the overall classroom climate (e.g., whether it feels psychologically safe or threatening). Only when we consider the very integral roles that assessment plays in the classroom can we truly harness its benefits to help students accomplish important instructional goals. It's essential, then, that we give considerable thought to how we assess students' learning and achievement, both informally through daily observations of their behavior and more formally through preplanned assignments and tests.

How Ms. Ford tries to communicate students' test scores to parents is yet another issue, as you'll discover in Chapter 15.

Look once again at Figure 12.1, which graphically shows how assessment practices are intertwined with planning, instruction, classroom management, and student characteristics.

**assessment** Process of observing a
sample of a student's behavior and
drawing inferences about the student's
knowledge and abilities.

**formative assessment** Assessment
conducted before or during instruction
to facilitate instructional planning and
enhance students' learning.

**summative assessment** Assessment
conducted after instruction to assess
students' final achievement.

# The Many Forms and Purposes of Assessment

We begin our discussion of assessment with a definition:

> **Assessment** is a process of observing a sample of a student's behavior and drawing inferences about the student's knowledge and abilities.

Several parts of this definition are important to note. First, assessment involves an observation of *behavior.* As behaviorists have pointed out, it's impossible to look inside students' heads and see what knowledge lurks there; we can see only how students perform in particular situations. Second, an assessment typically involves just a *sample* of behavior; we certainly can't observe and keep track of every single thing that every single student does during the school day. Finally, assessment involves drawing *inferences* from observed behaviors to make judgments about students' overall classroom achievement—a tricky business at best. It's critical, then, that we select behaviors that can provide reasonably accurate estimates of what students know and can do.

Notice that the definition doesn't include anything about decision making. By themselves, educational assessments are merely *tools* that can help people make decisions about students and sometimes about teachers, instructional programs, and schools as well. When people use these tools for the wrong purposes, or when they interpret assessment results in ways the results were never meant to be interpreted, it's the *people*—not the assessment instruments—that are to blame.

Classroom assessments vary in six key ways, which are summarized in Figure 14.1. Let's look more closely at each distinction.

**Formative Versus Summative Assessment**   A **formative assessment** involves determining what students know and can do *before or during instruction.* Ongoing formative assessments can help us determine what students already know and believe about a topic (e.g., see Figure 14.2), whether they need further practice on a particular skill, and so on, and we can develop or revise our lesson plans accordingly. In contrast, **summative assessment** involves conducting an assessment *after instruction* to make final determinations about what students have achieved. Summative assessments are used to determine whether students have mastered the content of a lesson or unit, what final grades we should assign, which students are eligible for more advanced classes, and the like.

**Informal Versus Formal Assessment**   An **informal assessment** involves a spontaneous, unplanned observation of something a student says or does. For example, when Mitchell asks "How come people in Australia don't fall into space?" he reveals a misconception about gravity. And when Jaffa continually squints at the chalkboard, we might wonder if she needs an appointment with an eye doctor. In contrast, a **formal assessment** is planned in advance and used for a specific purpose—perhaps to determine what students have learned from a geography unit or whether they can apply the Pythagorean theorem to real-world geometry problems. Formal assessment is *formal* in several respects: A particular time is set aside for it, students can prepare for it ahead of time, and it's intended to yield information about particular instructional goals or content area standards.

**Paper–Pencil Versus Performance Assessment**   As teachers, we may sometimes choose **paper–pencil assessment**, in which we present questions or problems that students must address on paper. But we may also find it helpful to use **performance assessment**, in which students physically demonstrate their abilities—for example, by giving an oral presentation in a language arts class, singing in a concert, or taking prescribed safety precautions in a chemistry lab.

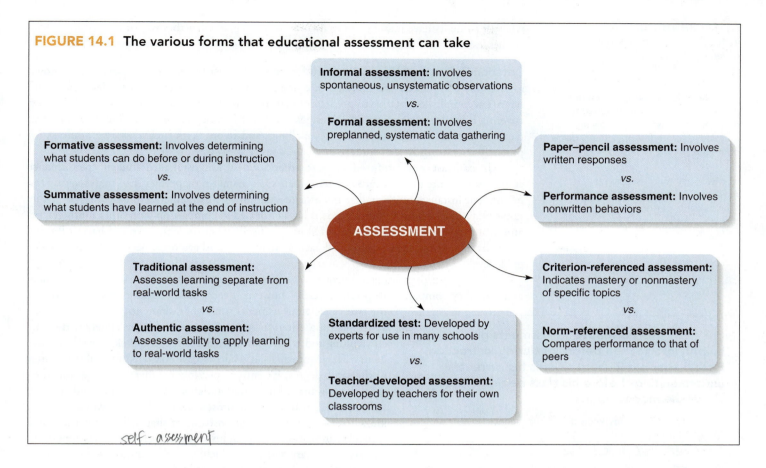

**FIGURE 14.1** The various forms that educational assessment can take

self-assessment

**Traditional Versus Authentic Assessment** Historically, most educational assessments have focused on measuring knowledge and skills in relative isolation from real-world tasks. Spelling quizzes, mathematics word problems, and physical fitness tests are examples of such traditional assessment. Yet ultimately students must be able to transfer their knowledge and skills to complex situations outside the classroom. The notion of authentic assessment—measuring students' knowledge and skills in a real-life (i.e., *authentic*) context—has gained considerable popularity in recent years. Keep in mind, however, that the distinction between traditional and authentic assessment really represents a *continuum* rather than an either–or situation: Assessment tasks can resemble real-world situations to varying degrees.

Some authentic assessment tasks involve paper and pencil. For example, we might ask students to write a letter to a friend or develop a school newspaper. But in many cases authentic assessment is based on nonwritten performance and closely integrated with instruction. For instance, we might ask students to bake a cake, converse in a foreign language, or successfully maneuver a car into a parallel parking space. Often teachers ask students to create *portfolios* that present a collection of authentic artifacts they've created—perhaps short stories, newspaper editorials, audiotapes of oral or musical performances, or videotapes of dramatic performances.[1]

**Standardized Tests Versus Teacher-Developed Assessments** Sometimes classroom assessments involve tests developed by test construction experts and published for use in many different schools and classrooms. Such tests, commonly called standardized tests, can be quite helpful in assessing students' general achievement and ability levels. But when we want to assess students' learning and achievement related to specific instructional objectives—for example,

**informal assessment** Assessment that results from a teacher's spontaneous, day-to-day observations of how a student performs in class.

**formal assessment** Preplanned, systematic attempt to ascertain what students know and can do.

**paper–pencil assessment** Assessment in which students provide written responses to written items.

**performance assessment** Assessment in which students demonstrate their knowledge and skills in a nonwritten fashion.

**traditional assessment** Assessment that focuses on measuring basic knowledge and skills in relative isolation from activities typical of the outside world.

**authentic assessment** Assessment of students' knowledge and skills in a context similar to one that might be found in the outside world.

**standardized test** Test developed by test construction experts and published for use in many different schools and classrooms.

---

[1]Educators aren't in complete agreement in their use of the terms *performance assessment* and *authentic assessment*; many treat them as synonyms. However, I find it useful to consider separately whether an assessment involves physical *performance* (rather than paper and pencil) and whether it involves a complex, real-world (*authentic*) task. Thus I am *not* using the two terms interchangeably.

**teacher-developed assessment instrument** Assessment tool developed by an individual teacher for use in a specific classroom.

**criterion-referenced assessment** Assessment instrument designed to determine what students know and can do relative to predetermined standards or criteria.

**norm-referenced assessment** Assessment instrument that indicates how students perform relative to a peer group.

whether students have mastered long division or can apply what they've just learned in a social studies lesson—we'll usually want to construct our own teacher-developed assessments.

**Criterion-Referenced Versus Norm-Referenced Assessments** Some assessments, known as criterion-referenced assessments, are designed to tell us exactly what students have and haven't accomplished relative to predetermined standards or criteria. A simple example is a test covering a fourth-grade class's 20 spelling words for the week: A score of 20 indicates a perfect paper, a score of 15 indicates 15 correct spellings, and so on. With such a test, we would know precisely which words each student does and doesn't know how to spell.

In contrast, norm-referenced assessments reveal how well each student's performance compares with the performance of peers—perhaps classmates or perhaps age-mates across the nation. For instance, ninth graders might take a nationwide mathematics test yielding percentile ranks that indicate how well each student has performed in comparison with other ninth graders around the country. Such scores don't tell us specifically what students have and haven't learned in math; instead they tell us how well each student stacks up against others at the same age or grade level.

Strictly speaking, any assessment has the potential to tell us *both* what students have learned and how they compare with peers. In reality, however, experienced educators tend to construct the two types of assessments somewhat differently. Ideally questions and tasks on a criterion-referenced assessment are closely tied to the curriculum and to the particular knowledge and skills we hope students have acquired. If all students have mastered the subject matter to the same degree, it's entirely possible for them all to get the same score. If we want to know how students *differ* from one another—and we'll soon identify some circumstances in which we would want to know that—we must have an instrument that will yield considerable variability in scores. In such an instrument, we're apt to have questions and tasks that vary widely in difficulty level, including some that only a few students can respond to correctly.

**FIGURE 14.2** Formative assessments give us helpful information before or during instruction. Here 8-year-old Richard reveals his current understandings before his class begins a lesson about the moon.

What I already know about the moon:
Solar ~~LUNAR~~ eclipse; Sun, Earth and sun are all in a line.
It is big.
Gravitational pull effects tides.
It has craters, People have ben on it.
It looks like a face.
It can be blue and yellow.

With the various kinds of assessments in mind, we now consider how we might use educational assessments for five interrelated purposes.

## GUIDING INSTRUCTIONAL DECISION MAKING

Obviously formative assessments can guide instructional decision making: They can help us determine a suitable point at which to begin instruction and give us ongoing information about the appropriateness of instructional goals and the effectiveness of instructional strategies. For instance, if we find that almost all students are completing assignments quickly and easily, we might set our goals a bit higher. Or if we discover that many students are struggling with important material we've presented only through verbal explanations, we might consider trying a different instructional approach—perhaps a more concrete, hands-on one.

Chapter 12 presents more details about backward design.

Yet summative assessments, too, should guide our decision making to some degree. For example, in an approach to instructional planning known as *backward design,* teachers begin with what they ultimately want students to achieve—defining it in terms of both desired instructional goals and suitable classroom assessments—and plan instruction accordingly. Furthermore, any general summative assessments (e.g., annual districtwide or statewide tests of basic skills) will—for better or for worse—influence the topics and skills on which we focus in our teaching.

## DETERMINING WHAT STUDENTS HAVE LEARNED FROM INSTRUCTION

In most cases we'll need to use planned, formal assessments—rather than more casual, informal ones—to determine whether students have achieved instructional goals or met certain content area standards. Formal assessments of achievement are important in any mastery-learning approach to instruction, and they're essential for assigning final grades. School counselors and administrators, too, may use assessments of students' achievement levels to make placement decisions, such as which students are most likely to do well in advanced classes, which ones might need additional course work in basic skills, and so on.

## EVALUATING THE QUALITY OF INSTRUCTION

Final measures of student achievement are also useful in evaluating how effective instruction has been. When most students perform poorly after an instructional unit—as Ms. Ford's students did in the opening case study—we must consider not only what students might have done differently but also what we, as teachers, might have done differently. For example, perhaps we moved too quickly through material or provided insufficient opportunities for students to practice critical skills. In any event, consistently low assessment results should tell us that some modification of instruction is in order.

## DIAGNOSING LEARNING AND PERFORMANCE PROBLEMS

Why is Louis having trouble learning to read? Why does Gretel misbehave every time we assign a challenging task? We ask such questions when we suspect that certain students might learn differently from their classmates and may possibly require special educational services. A variety of standardized tests have been designed specifically to identify the unique academic and personal needs that some students have. Most of these tests require explicit training in their use and thus are often administered and interpreted by specialists (school psychologists, counselors, speech and language pathologists, etc.). As a general rule, the tests tend to be norm-referenced rather than criterion-referenced in order to identify students who are well above or well below their age-group with respect to certain abilities or characteristics.

Yet teacher-developed assessments can provide considerable diagnostic information as well, especially when they reveal consistent error patterns and areas of difficulty (e.g., see Figure 14.3). In other words, teacher-developed assessments can—and ideally *should*—give us information we can use to help students improve.

Increasingly teachers are using short, formative assessments to determine whether certain students might have exceptional instructional needs. In this approach, known as **response to intervention (RTI)**, a teacher regularly assesses students' progress, keeping a lookout for students who have unusual difficulty acquiring certain basic skills (e.g., in reading or math) despite both whole-class instruction and follow-up small-group work. The RTI approach has gained particular popularity as a means of identifying students who have learning disabilities, but it's potentially useful for other students as well (T. A. Glover & Vaughn, 2010; J. J. Hoover, 2009; Mellard & Johnson, 2008).

**response to intervention (RTI)**
Approach to diagnosing a cognitive impairment in which students are identified for in-depth assessment after failing to master certain basic skills despite both whole-class and remedial small-group instruction that research has shown to be effective for most students; can also be useful with nondisabled but chronically low-achieving students.

Use the results of classroom assessments not only to assess what students have learned but also to reflect on the effectiveness of your instructional strategies.

See Chapter 5 for more information about response to intervention as a diagnostic tool.

---

**FIGURE 14.3** In these and other work samples, 7-year-old Casey shows consistent difficulty in making connections between the sounds he hears and the sounds he represents in his writing—a difficulty that in his case reflects a learning disability known as *dyslexia*.

Classroom assessments should be closely aligned with important instructional goals—*not* measures of trivial, isolated facts.

# PROMOTING LEARNING

Whenever we conduct formative assessments to help us develop or modify lesson plans, we're obviously using assessment to facilitate students' learning. But summative assessment can influence learning as well, and in several ways:

• *Assessments can motivate students to study and learn.* On average, students study class material more, review it more regularly, and learn it better when they know they'll be tested on it or in some other way held accountable for it, rather than when they're simply told to learn it (Dempster, 1991; N. Frederiksen, 1984b; Rohrer & Pashler, 2010). Yet *how* students are assessed is as important as *whether* they're assessed. Assessments are especially effective as motivators when they're criterion-referenced, are closely aligned with instructional goals and objectives, and challenge students to do their best (Mac Iver, Reuman, & Main, 1995; Maehr & Anderman, 1993; L. H. Meyer, Weir, McClure, & Walkey, 2008). Students' self-efficacy and attributions affect their perceptions of the challenge, of course: Students must believe that success on an assigned task is possible if they exert reasonable effort and use appropriate strategies.

Although regular classroom assessments can be highly motivating, they are, in and of themselves, usually *extrinsic* motivators. Thus they may direct students' attention to performance goals and undermine any intrinsic motivation to learn, especially if students perceive them to be primarily an evaluation of their performance rather than a mechanism for helping them master useful topics and skills (Danner, 2008; Grolnick & Ryan, 1987; S. G. Paris & Turner, 1994).

With the potentially motivating effects of classroom assessments in mind, let's return to the opening case study. With her focus on students' test scores and parents' approval or disapproval, Ms. Ford is fostering performance goals and extrinsic motivation. Furthermore, notice how controlling, even threatening, some of her statements are: "It is your responsibility to correct these problems and turn them in. . . . All our math problems that we got wrong I want returned to me with the correct answer. . . . If you do not return it with a [parent's] signature, I will call home." Such comments are likely to undermine students' sense of self-determination and will hardly endear students to mathematics as a content domain.

🍎 Construct assessment instruments that reflect how you want students to think about and cognitively process information as they study.

• *Assessments can influence students' cognitive processes as they study.* Different kinds of assessment tasks can lead students to study and learn quite differently (N. Frederiksen, 1984b; Lundeberg & Fox, 1991; L. Shepard, Hammerness, Darling-Hammond, & Rust, 2005). For instance, students will typically spend more time studying the things they think will be addressed on an assessment than the things they think the assessment won't cover. Furthermore, their expectations about the kinds of tasks they'll need to perform and the questions they'll need to answer will influence whether they memorize isolated facts, on the one hand, or construct a meaningful, integrated body of information, on the other.

As an example, look at the sixth-grade test about rocks shown in Figure 14.4. Part A (identifying rocks shown at the front of the room) might be assessing either basic knowledge or application (transfer) to new situations, depending on whether the students have seen those particular rock specimens before. The rest of the test clearly focuses on memorized facts and is likely to encourage students to engage in rote learning as they study for future tests. For instance, consider the last item: "Every rock has a _____." Students can answer this item correctly *only* if they've learned the material verbatim: The missing word here is "story."

Epistemic beliefs are described in Chapter 7.

Classroom assessments can also influence students' views about the nature of various academic disciplines; that is, they can influence students' *epistemic beliefs.* For example, if we give quizzes that assess knowledge of specific facts, students are apt to conclude that a discipline is just

**FIGURE 14.4** Much of this sixth-grade geology test focuses on knowledge of specific facts and may encourage students to memorize, rather than understand, information about rocks.

A. Write whether each of the rocks shown at the front of the room is a sedimentary, igneous, or metamorphic rock.
   1. _____
   2. _____
   3. _____

B. The following are various stages of the rock cycle. Number them from 1 to 9 to indicate the order in which they occur.
   ____ Heat and pressure
   ____ Crystallization and cooling
   ____ Igneous rock forms
   ____ Magma
   ____ Weathering and erosion into sediments
   ____ Melting
   ____ Sedimentary rock forms
   ____ Pressure and cementing
   ____ Metamorphic rock forms

C. Write the letter for the correct definition of each rock group.
   1. ____ Igneous          a. Formed when particles of eroded rock are deposited together and become cemented.
   2. ____ Sedimentary      b. Produced by extreme pressures or high temperatures below the earth's surface.
   3. ____ Metamorphic      c. Formed by the cooling of molten rock material from within the earth.

D. Fill in the blank in each sentence.
   1. The process of breaking down rock by the action of water, ice, plants, animals, and chemical changes is called _____ .
   2. All rocks are made of _____ .
   3. The hardness of rocks can be determined by a _____ .
   4. Continued weathering of rock will eventually produce _____ .
   5. Every rock has a _____ .

[The test continues with several additional fill-in-the-blank and short-answer items.]

that: a collection of undisputed facts. If, instead, we ask students to take a position on a controversial issue and justify their position with evidence and logic, they get a very different message: that the discipline involves an integrated set of understandings that must be supported with reasoning and are subject to change over time.

• *Assessments can serve as learning experiences in and of themselves.* In general, the very process of completing an assessment on classroom material helps students review the material and learn it better. Assessment tasks are especially valuable if they ask students to elaborate on or apply the material in a new way (Fall, Webb, & Chudowsky, 2000; Foos & Fisher, 1988; Rohrer & Pashler, 2010).

Think about how assessment tasks might encourage new learning.

• *Assessments can provide valuable feedback about learning progress.* Simply knowing one's final score on a test or assignment isn't terribly helpful. To facilitate students' learning and achievement—and also to enhance students' self-efficacy for mastering school subject matter—assessment feedback must include specific information about where students have succeeded, where they've had difficulty, and how they might improve (Andrade & Cizek, 2010; Hattie & Gan, 2011; Pintrich & Schunk, 2002).

In general, then, sound assessment practices are closely tied to instruction: They reflect instructional goals and content area standards, guide instructional strategies, and provide a means

Remember that to some degree, assessment *is* instruction: It tells students what things are most important to learn and facilitates their achievement.

Make assessment criteria explicit, perhaps in the form of a rubric that identifies key components of desired performance.

of tracking students' progress through the curriculum. In a very real sense, assessment *is* instruction: It gives students clear messages about what things are most important for them to accomplish and how best to accomplish them.

# Enhancing Learning through Formative Assessments and Other Assessment Practices

Certainly formative assessments—those that occur before or during instruction rather than after it—have the greatest potential to enhance students' learning and achievement (Andrade & Cizek, 2010; Black & Wiliam, 1998). Yet as we've just seen in the preceding section, certain practices associated with summative assessment can have a significant positive impact as well.

Perhaps the most critical strategy for enhancing students' learning and achievement through classroom assessments—formative and summative assessments alike—is to make assessment criteria explicit for students. One widely recommended technique is to create and distribute a concrete scoring guide, or rubric, that identifies key characteristics and components of desired performance. Rubrics take a variety of forms—some quite simple, others more complex. Some simple rubrics consist of a list of characteristics that should be evident in students' work. For example, Figure 14.5 shows a rubric that one fourth-grade teacher has used for scoring students' performance on mathematics word problems. Notice that the rubric includes both objectively scorable criteria (e.g., the correct answer) and more qualitative, subjectively scorable criteria (e.g., neatness of work, explanation of the problem solution).

More detailed, complex rubrics often take the form of a two-dimensional matrix that includes specific guidelines about how two or more distinct aspects of students' performance should be evaluated. Such rubrics are particularly valuable in assessing complex topics and skills. For example, in a unit on ancient civilizations, one ninth-grade social studies teacher had cooperative groups create tourist guidebooks depicting one of several locations (e.g., for ancient Egypt, China, or Central America). His rubric for grading the guidebooks is shown in Figure 14.6. Notice how the rubric describes general qualities of three possible levels of performance ("Proficient,"

**rubric**  List of characteristics and components that a student's performance on an assessment should ideally have; used to guide scoring.

**FIGURE 14.5**  In this rubric for scoring solutions to mathematics word problems in a fourth-grade class, both teacher and student evaluate various aspects of the student's performance.

| Elements | Possible Points | Points Earned Self | Teacher |
|---|---|---|---|
| 1. You highlighted the question(s) to solve. | 2 | ___ | ___ |
| 2. You picked an appropriate strategy. | 2 | ___ | ___ |
| 3. Work is neat and organized. | 2 | ___ | ___ |
| 4. Calculations are accurate. | 2 | ___ | ___ |
| 5. Question(s) answered. | 2 | ___ | ___ |
| 6. You have explained in words how you solved the problem. | 5 | ___ | ___ |
| Total | ___ | ___ | ___ |

---

**FIGURE 14.6** Rubric for evaluating guidebooks in a ninth-grade social studies unit on ancient civilizations

| | Proficient | Adequate | Poor |
|---|---|---|---|
| Elements of Civilization | The guidebook shows a clear understanding of what a civilization is and how the group's particular civilization developed with respect to each of the factors characterizing a civilization. | The guidebook shows some understanding of what a civilization is. Each of the civilization factors is discussed at least briefly. | The guidebook shows little or no understanding of what a civilization is. Many factors are missing. |
| Evidence | The guidebook reflects class notes, class handouts, homework, and a variety of outside sources to achieve a comprehensive overview of the civilization. | The guidebook reflects class notes, class handouts, and homework to achieve a mostly complete overview of the civilization. | The guidebook does not reflect class notes, homework, or any outside sources. |
| Visuals | Visuals have been well chosen and relate to the elements of civilization being discussed. There is a thorough analysis of each image and how it relates to the topic and culture. | Visuals relate to the elements of civilization being discussed. | Irrelevant or no visuals have been included in the guide book. |

*Source:* Figure by Jeffrey Ormrod. Copyright © by Jeffrey Ormrod. Reprinted with permission of the author.

---

"Adequate," and "Poor") to three different components of the guidebooks ("Elements of Civilization," "Evidence," and "Visuals").

Rubrics have three benefits. First, they give students clear targets toward which to shoot. Second, they enable us teachers to evaluate students' performance consistently and with reasonable objectivity (more about this point in the upcoming discussion of *reliability*). And third, they provide a means through which we can give students detailed feedback about the strengths and limitations of their performance—feedback that ideally can help them improve.

Using scoring rubrics certainly isn't the only way of enhancing students' learning through classroom assessment practices. Other key strategies are these:

- Describe the instructional goals and objectives being assessed in clear, understandable language.
- Assess students' progress frequently rather than infrequently.
- When giving an assessment, communicate a desire to enhance understanding and promote mastery, rather than to pass judgment.
- Help students detect important (yet possibly subtle) differences between genuine mastery and more superficial knowledge.
- Engage students in constructive discussions of one another's work, with a focus on ideas for improvement.
- Give students opportunities to revise their work based on feedback they've received. (Andrade & Cizek, 2010; Black & Wiliam, 1998; Chappuis, 2009; Hattie & Gan, 2011; McDaniel, Agarwal, Huelser, McDermott, & Roediger, 2011; Rohrer & Pashler, 2010)

Such strategies may be especially important when working with students who are at risk for academic failure (G. B. Hughes, 2010).

Still another formative assessment strategy is **dynamic assessment**, in which a teacher assesses students' ability to learn something new, typically in a one-on-one situation that includes instruction, assistance, or some other form of scaffolding (e.g., Feuerstein, Feuerstein, & Falik, 2010; Lidz & Gindis, 2003; L. A. Shepard, 2000; H. L. Swanson & Lussier, 2001). Such an approach reflects Vygotsky's *zone of proximal development* and can give us an idea of what students might be able to accomplish with appropriate structure and guidance. Dynamic assessment can provide a wealth of qualitative information about

**dynamic assessment** Systematic examination of how easily and in what ways a student can acquire new knowledge or skills, usually within the context of instruction or scaffolding.

children's abilities, cognitive strategies, and approaches to learning. For example, it can give us insights into the following:

- Students' readiness for instruction in particular topics and skills
- Students' motivational and affective patterns (e.g., self-efficacy, achievement goals, attributions, anxiety)
- Students' work habits (e.g., impulsiveness, persistence, reactions to frustration and failure)
- Potential obstacles to students' learning (e.g., distractibility, poor reading comprehension skills, lack of effective self-monitoring and self-evaluation skills) (Feuerstein et al., 2010; L. S. Fuchs, Compton, et al., 2008; Hamers & Ruijssenaars, 1997; Haywood & Lidz, 2007; Tzuriel, 2000)

See Chapter 2 for additional information about Vygotsky's zone of proximal development and dynamic assessment.

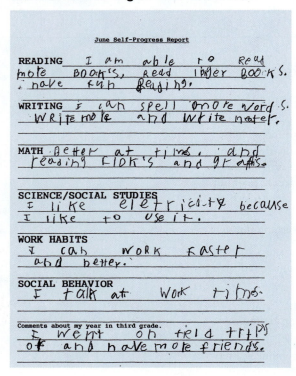

**FIGURE 14.7** At the end of third grade, 9-year-old Philip reviewed the work he had completed over the course of the year and identified his strengths and weaknesses.

## INCLUDING STUDENTS IN THE ASSESSMENT PROCESS

As noted earlier, classroom assessments are typically extrinsic motivators that provide only externally imposed reasons for learning school subject matter. Yet students learn more effectively when they're *intrinsically* motivated, and they're more likely to be intrinsically motivated if they have some sense of autonomy and self-determination about classroom activities. Furthermore, if students are to become self-regulating learners, they must acquire skills in self-monitoring and self-evaluation. For such reasons, we should think of assessment as something we do *with* students rather than *to* them (Andrade, 2010; S. G. Paris & Ayres, 1994; Reeve, Deci, & Ryan, 2004; L. Shepard et al., 2005; Vye et al., 1998).

Students become more skillful in self-assessment as they grow older (van Kraayenoord & Paris, 1997), but even students in the elementary grades have some ability to evaluate their own performance (e.g., see Figure 14.7). Here are several strategies for including students in the assessment process and helping them develop important self-monitoring and self-evaluation skills:

- Solicit students' ideas about assessment criteria and rubric design.
- Provide examples of good and not-so-good products, and ask students to compare them on the basis of several criteria.
- Have students compare self-ratings of their performance with teacher ratings (e.g., notice the "Self" and "Teacher" columns in Figure 14.5).
- Ask students to write practice questions similar to those they might see on an upcoming paper–pencil test.
- Have students keep ongoing records of their performance and chart their progress over time.
- Have students reflect on their work in daily or weekly journal entries, where they can keep track of knowledge and skills they have and haven't mastered, as well as learning strategies that have and haven't been effective.
- Have students compile a portfolio of their work, including self-reflective explanations of what the items in the portfolio reveal about their learning and achievement.
- Ask students to lead parent–teacher conferences. (Andrade, 2010; A. L. Brown & Campione, 1996; Chappuis, 2009; McMillan, 2010; S. G. Paris & Ayres, 1994; L. A. Shepard, 2000; Stiggins & Chappuis, 2012)

It's important, too, that we encourage productive attributions; for instance, students should genuinely believe that they can overcome their existing shortcomings with reasonable effort and good strategies (Andrade, 2010). And we should ask students to develop a follow-up action plan—to explicitly address the question *What do I need to do now?* based on their assessment results. Such an action plan might include identifying answers to more specific questions such as these:

- What specific things do I need to do to improve?
- What resources and assistance do I need to help me improve?
- How will I know when I have reached my goal? (based on Chappuis, 2009)

# Important Qualities of Good Assessments

As a student, have you ever been assessed in a way you thought was unfair? If so, *why* was it unfair?

1. Did the teacher evaluate students' responses inconsistently?
2. Were some students assessed under more favorable conditions than others?
3. Was the assessment a poor measure of what you had learned?
4. Was the assessment so time consuming that after a while you no longer cared how well you performed?

In light of your experiences, what characteristics seem to be essential for good classroom assessment instruments and practices?

The four numbered questions just posed reflect, respectively, four *RSVP* characteristics of good classroom assessments: reliability, standardization, validity, and practicality. Such characteristics are important considerations for any assessment activity, but they're especially important when we're using summative assessments to make potentially life-changing decisions—for instance, decisions about final class grades, placements in advanced classes, and appropriate services for students with disabilities.

## RELIABILITY

The reliability of an assessment instrument or procedure is the extent to which it yields consistent information about the knowledge, skills, or characteristics being assessed. To get a sense of what reliability involves, try the following exercise.

### EXPERIENCING FIRSTHAND
### FOWL PLAY

Consider this sequence of events in the life of biology teacher Ms. Fowler:

- *Monday.* After completing a lesson on bone structures of birds and dinosaurs, Ms. Fowler asks students to write an essay explaining why many scientists believe that birds are descended from dinosaurs. After school she tosses the essays on the back seat of her cluttered car.
- *Tuesday.* Ms. Fowler looks high and low for the essays both at home and in her classroom, but she can't find them anywhere.
- *Wednesday.* Because Ms. Fowler wants to use the students' essays to determine what they've learned, she asks the class to write the same essay a second time.
- *Thursday.* Ms. Fowler finally discovers Monday's essays on the back seat of her car.
- *Friday.* Ms. Fowler grades both sets of essays. She's surprised to find little consistency between them: Students who wrote the best essays on Monday didn't necessarily do well on Wednesday, and some of Monday's poorest performers did quite well on Wednesday.

Which results should Ms. Fowler use, Monday's or Wednesday's? Why?

When we assess students' learning and achievement, we must be confident that our assessment results will be essentially the same regardless of whether we give the assessment on Monday or Wednesday, whether the weather is sunny or rainy, or whether we evaluate students' responses while we're in a good mood or a foul frame of mind. Ms. Fowler's assessment instrument has poor reliability, because the results it yields are completely different from one day to another. So which day's results should she use? I've asked you a trick question: There's no way of knowing which set is more accurate.

Any single assessment instrument will rarely yield *exactly* the same results for the same student on two different occasions, even if the knowledge or ability being assessed remains the same. Many temporary conditions unrelated to the knowledge or ability being measured are apt to affect students' performance and almost inevitably lead to some fluctuation in assessment results. For instance, the inconsistencies in Ms. Fowler's two sets of student essays might have been due to temporary factors such as these:

- *Day-to-day changes in students*—for example, changes in health, motivation, mood, and energy level

    A 24-hour flu was making the rounds in Ms. Fowler's classroom.

**reliability** Extent to which an assessment yields consistent information about the knowledge, skills, or characteristics being assessed.

- *Variations in the physical environment*—for example, variations in room temperature, noise level, and outside distractions

  On Monday students who sat by the window in Ms. Fowler's class enjoyed peace and quiet, but on Wednesday they wrote their essays while noisy construction machinery was tearing up the pavement outside.

- *Variations in administration of the assessment*—for example, variations in instructions, timing, and the teacher's responses to students' questions

  On Monday a few students wrote the essay after school because they had attended a dress rehearsal for the school play during class time. Ms. Fowler explained the task more clearly to them than she had during class, and she gave them as much time as they needed to finish. On Wednesday a different group of students had to write the essay after school because of an across-town band concert during class time. Ms. Fowler explained the task very hurriedly and collected the essays before students had finished.

- *Characteristics of the assessment instrument*—for example, the length, clarity, and difficulty of tasks (e.g., ambiguous and very difficult tasks increase students' tendency to guess randomly)

  The essay topic—"Explain why many scientists believe that birds are descended from dinosaurs"—was an ambiguous one that students interpreted differently from one day to the next.

- *Subjectivity in scoring*—for example, judgments made on the basis of vague, imprecise criteria

  Ms. Fowler graded both sets of essays while watching *Chainsaw Murders at Central High* on television Friday night. She gave higher scores during kissing scenes, lower scores during stalking scenes.

All the factors just listed lead to a certain amount of *error* in students' test scores and other assessment results. Rarely are assessment results dead-on measures of what students have learned and can do. Psychologists distinguish among different kinds of reliability, which take different error factors into account. *Test–retest reliability* is the extent to which an assessment instrument yields similar results over a short time interval. *Scorer reliability* is the extent to which two or more independent evaluators of students' performance agree in their judgments. *Internal consistency reliability* is the extent to which different parts of a single instrument all measure the same characteristic.

Whenever we draw conclusions about students' learning and achievement, we must be confident that the information on which we're basing our conclusions isn't overly distorted by temporary, irrelevant factors. Several strategies can increase the likelihood that an assessment yields reliable results:

- Include a variety of tasks, and look for consistency in students' performance on different tasks.
- Define each task clearly enough that students know exactly what they're being asked to do.
- Use a rubric that identifies specific, concrete criteria with which to evaluate students' performance.
- Try not to let expectations for students' performance influence judgments of *actual* performance.
- Avoid assessing students' achievement when they're unlikely to give their best performance—for example, when they're ill.
- Administer the assessment in similar ways as well as under similar conditions for all students.

The last recommendation suggests that assessment procedures also be *standardized,* especially when—for whatever reason—students need to be compared to one another. We turn to this RSVP characteristic now.

Appendix B explains how we can determine each of these reliabilities. It also explains how we can estimate the amount of error that a particular assessment result might have.

## STANDARDIZATION

The term **standardization** refers to the extent to which an assessment involves similar content and format and is administered and scored in the same way for everyone. Especially in norm-referenced summative assessments, students should all get the same instructions, perform identical or similar tasks, have the same time limits, and work under the same constraints. Furthermore, all students' responses should be scored using the same criteria. For example, unless there are extenuating circumstances, we shouldn't use tougher standards for one student than for another.

At the beginning of the chapter, I mentioned that many tests constructed and published by testing experts are called *standardized* tests. This label indicates that such tests have explicit procedures for administration and scoring that are consistently applied wherever the tests are used. Yet standardization is important in teacher-developed assessments as well: It reduces the amount of error in assessment results, especially error due to variation in test administration or subjectivity in scoring. The more an assessment is standardized for all students, then, the higher its reliability. Equity is an additional consideration: Under most circumstances, it's only fair to ask all students to be evaluated under similar conditions. We find an obvious exception to this guideline in the assessment of students with special educational needs; we'll consider appropriate accommodations for these students near the end of the chapter.

## VALIDITY

Earlier you learned about *reliability*. The following exercise can help you determine how well you understand what reliability involves.

### ■ EXPERIENCING FIRSTHAND
### FTOI

I've developed a new test called the FTOI: the Fathead Test of Intelligence. It consists of only a tape measure and a *table of norms* that shows how children and adults of various ages typically perform on the test. Administration of the FTOI is quick and easy. You simply measure a person's head circumference just above the eyebrows (firmly but not too tightly) and compare your measure against the average head circumference for the person's age-group. People with large heads (comparatively speaking) get high IQ scores. People with smaller heads get low scores.

Does the FTOI have high reliability? Answer the question before you read further.

---

No matter how often you measure a person's head circumference, you're going to get a similar score: Fatheads will continue to be fatheads, and pinheads will always be pinheads. So the answer to my question is *yes:* The FTOI has high reliability because it yields consistent results. If you answered *no,* you were probably thinking that the FTOI isn't a very good measure of intelligence. But that's a problem with the instrument's *validity,* not with its reliability.

The **validity** of an assessment instrument is the extent to which it measures what it's intended to measure and allows us to draw appropriate inferences about the characteristic or ability in question. Does the FTOI measure intelligence? Are scores on a standardized, multiple-choice achievement test a good indication of whether students have mastered basic skills in reading and writing? Does students' performance at a school concert reflect what they've achieved in their instrumental music class? When our assessments don't do these things well—when they're poor measures of students' knowledge and abilities—we have a validity problem.

As noted earlier, numerous irrelevant factors are apt to influence how well students perform in assessment situations. Some of these—students' health, classroom distractions, inconsistencies in scoring, and so on—are temporary conditions that lead to fluctuation in assessment results from one time to the next and thereby lower reliability. But other irrelevant factors—perhaps reading ability or chronic test anxiety—are more stable, and thus their effects on assessment results will be relatively constant. For example, if Joe has poor reading skills, he may get consistently low scores on paper–pencil, multiple-choice achievement tests regardless of how much he has actually achieved in science, math, or social studies. When assessment results continue to be affected by the same irrelevant variables, the *validity* of the results is in doubt.

**standardization** Extent to which an assessment involves similar content and format and is administered and scored similarly for everyone.

**validity** Extent to which an assessment actually measures what it is intended to measure and allows appropriate inferences about the characteristic or ability in question.

**content validity** Extent to which an assessment includes a representative sample of tasks within the content domain being assessed.

**curriculum-based measurement (CBM)** Use of frequent assessments to track students' progress in acquiring basic skills; assessments are typically quite short (e.g., one to four minutes) and each focus on a specific skill.

Align classroom assessment instruments and procedures both with relevant content area standards and with your own specific goals, objectives, and curriculum.

The entries in the first three columns of Table 14.1 previously appeared in Table 12.1 in Chapter 12.

Psychologists distinguish among different kinds of validity, which are important in different situations. Three kinds of particular interest to educators and other practitioners are content validity, predictive validity, and construct validity.

## CONTENT VALIDITY

Classroom teachers should typically be most concerned with content validity—the extent to which assessment questions and tasks are a representative sample of the overall body of knowledge and skills being assessed. Assessments with high content validity are, like effective instruction, closely aligned with instructional goals and any relevant content area standards. Different instructional goals and standards require different assessment strategies. In some situations—for example, when the desired outcome is the simple recall of facts—we might ask students to respond to a series of multiple-choice or short-answer questions on a paper–pencil quiz. In other situations—for example, when the goal is to critique a work of literature or to use principles of physics to explain everyday phenomena—essay tasks that require students to follow a logical line of reasoning might be appropriate. And for some skills—for example, reading aloud, cooking a hard-boiled egg, executing a front dismount from the parallel bars—only performance assessment can give us reasonable content validity. In the end, we'll probably find that we can best assess students' achievement with a combination of paper–pencil and performance assessments.

As an illustration of how we might align classroom assessments with standards, goals and objectives, and instruction. Table 14.1 presents examples of key reading skills identified in the Common Core State Standards for English Language Arts, along with relevant instructional lessons and tasks (Column 3) and assessment strategies (Column 4). Some of the entries in Column 4 can potentially serve as *formal summative assessment* tasks. But notice that the entries to their immediate left (in Column 3) also require students to do, say, or write something—thus providing opportunities for *informal assessment* or *formative assessment* of students' current knowledge and ongoing progress.

## DEVELOPMENTAL TRENDS

| GRADE LEVEL | EXAMPLES OF COMMON CORE STANDARDS FOR ENGLISH LANGUAGE ARTS | EXAMPLES OF INSTRUCTIONAL STRATEGIES THAT ADDRESS THESE STANDARDS *AND* PROVIDE A MEANS OF INFORMALLY ASSESSING STUDENTS' PROGRESS | EXAMPLES OF ASSESSMENTS THAT ALIGN WITH THE STANDARDS AND WITH CLASSROOM INSTRUCTION |
|---|---|---|---|
| | Ask and answer such questions as *who, what, where, when, why,* and *how* to demonstrate understanding of key details in a text. (RL.2.1)[a] | • During "settling down" time immediately after lunch each day, read a chapter of a high-interest children's novel, stopping frequently to ask questions that require students to go beyond the text itself (e.g., ask students to speculate about what a character might be feeling). | • Meet with students in small groups and ask each group member to describe a story in his or her own words. Follow up with questions such as "What happened next?" and "Why did [a character] do that?" to determine the extent to which each student has understood important elements of the story. |
| Grade 2 | Recount stories, including fables and folktales from diverse cultures, and determine their central message, lesson, or moral. (RL.2.2) | • Have several students create props for and act out a story they have recently read, with other class members serving as the audience. Follow up with a class discussion of important lessons that one or more story characters might have learned from events or challenges that they faced. | • Give a reading group several age-appropriate Middle Eastern or Chinese folktales to read, and then ask the students, "What advice do you think this story is giving us?" Be sure that every group member answers the question, and communicate that there isn't necessarily a single right answer. |

**TABLE 14.1** • Examples of How You Might Align Classroom Assessments with Common Core Standards and Instruction at Different Grade Levels

*(continued)*

## TABLE 14.1 • (Continued)

| | Standard | Classroom Learning Activity | Classroom Assessment |
|---|---|---|---|
| | Refer to details and examples in a text when explaining what the text says explicitly and when drawing inferences from the text. (RL.4.1) | As a reading group discusses Carl Hiaasen's *Hoot*, ask students to speculate about how the plot might progress and to identify clues in the text that support their predictions. | After students have read the first few chapters of Natalie Babbitt's *Tuck Everlasting* (in which the Tuck family has drunk from a well that gives everlasting life), ask them to write an essay speculating on problems the Tucks' immortality might create for them. Later, after they learn that Mae Tuck has killed someone, ask them to speculate about the implications of her arrest and to back up their predictions with clues in the text. |
| **Grade 4**  | Explain events, procedures, ideas, or concepts in a historical, scientific, or technical text, including what happened and why, based on specific information in the text. (RI.4.3) | When students are reading a chapter in their history textbook, ask *why* questions that encourage cause-and-effect connections (e.g., "Why did Columbus's crew want to sail back to Europe after several weeks on the open sea?"). | Ask students to create concept maps that show interrelationships (including cause–and–effect) among various events during a particular period in history. |
| | Analyze the structure an author uses to organize a text, including how the major sections contribute to the whole and to the development of the ideas. (RI.7.5) | Before students read a chapter in their science textbook, have them use its headings and subheadings to (1) create a general outline of the chapter and (2) generate questions they hope to answer as they read the chapter. Then, for homework, ask them to read and take notes on the chapter, using the outline and self-questions as guides for note taking. | Ask students to write a two-page summary of a chapter in their science book, using chapter headings and subheadings to organize their discussion. |
| **Grade 7**  | Trace and evaluate the argument and specific claims in a text, assessing whether the reasoning is sound and the evidence is relevant and sufficient to support the claims. (RI.7.8) | Give students an advertisement for a self-improvement product (e.g., a diet pill or exercise equipment); have them work in small cooperative learning groups to (1) identify the advertiser's motives and (2) evaluate the quality of evidence for the product's effectiveness. | Have students examine an Internet website that promotes an allegedly health-promoting product. Ask them to identify, either orally or in writing, possible flaws in the evidence and logic the website uses to convince people to purchase the product. |
| | Analyze and evaluate the effectiveness of the structure an author uses in his or her position or argument, including whether the structure makes points clear, convincing, and engaging. (RI.11–12.5) | Describe common techniques in persuasive writing, and have students identify the various persuasive techniques used in newspaper editorials. | Ask students to (1) identify three specific persuasive techniques used in the U.S. Declaration of Independence and (2) explain their particular purposes and probable effectiveness in the American colonies in 1776. |
| **Grades 11–12**  | Determine an author's point of view or purpose in a text in which the rhetoric is particularly effective, analyzing how style and content contribute to the power, persuasiveness or beauty of the text. (RI.11–12.6) | Ask students to identify the unstated assumptions underlying two news magazines' depictions of the same event (e.g., an assumption that one group is good or right and another is bad or wrong). | Give students a magazine article describing a recent event in the national or international news. Ask them to underline five sentences that reveal the author's cultural and/or political biases and to describe those biases in a two-page essay. |

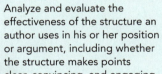

aThe letters "RL" indicate standards related to reading literature; the letters "RI" indicate standards related to reading informational text. The number or numbers before the period indicate the grade level; the number after the period indicates the particular standard for that grade level. For example, the first entry shown here, identified as "RL.2.1," is the first standard for grade 2 for reading literature.

*Source:* Excerpts from *Common Core State Standards.* Copyright © 2010 by National Governors Association Center for Best Practices and Council of Chief State School Officers. Reprinted with permission. All rights reserved.

One strategy for ensuring content validity in formative assessments is **curriculum-based measurement (CBM),** which is especially useful both in basic skills instruction and in a response-to-intervention approach to identifying learning disabilities and other persistent learning problems. In this approach teachers regularly administer assessments that each focus on a single, specific skill in the curriculum (e.g., word recognition in reading, addition of 2-digit numbers)

**table of specifications** Two-way grid indicating the topics to be covered in an assessment and the things students should be able to do with those topics.

To enhance the content validity of a summative assessment, develop a table of specifications that can guide your selection of topics and tasks.

Bloom's taxonomy is described in Chapter 12.

as a means of tracking individual students' progress. Each assessment is typically quite short (perhaps only 1 to 4 minutes in length) and yet can help teachers identify students who may need additional instruction in a certain skill in order to move forward. In recent years computer software programs have made CBM increasingly easy and powerful, as we'll discover in our discussion of digital technologies later in the chapter.

High content validity is, of course, also important whenever we're using an assessment instrument for summative assessment purposes—that is, to determine what knowledge and skills students have ultimately acquired from instruction. When a summative assessment addresses multiple topics, concepts, and skills, we can't necessarily include each and every one of them in the assessment. But taken as a whole, the things we ask students to do in the assessment should comprise a *representative* sample of the content domain we're assessing. The most widely recommended strategy is to construct a blueprint that identifies the specific things we want to assess and the proportion of questions or tasks that should address each one. This blueprint frequently takes the form of a table of specifications: a two-way grid that indicates both what topics should be covered and what students should be able to *do* with each topic. Each cell of the grid indicates the relative importance of each topic–behavior combination, perhaps as a particular number or percentage of tasks to be included in the overall assessment. Figure 14.8 shows two examples. The table on the left, constructed for a 30-item paper–pencil quiz on addition, assigns different weights (i.e., different numbers of test items) to different topic–behavior combinations, with some combinations intentionally not being assessed at all. The table on the right, constructed for a high school physics unit on classical mechanics, instead uses percentages to identify the relative weights assigned to different topic–behavior combinations; the three behaviors it includes are based loosely on the first three processes in Bloom's taxonomy (*remember, understand, apply*). Both tables in Figure 14.8 intentionally place greater emphasis on some topic–behavior combinations than on others, but in other situations equal weightings across the board may be quite appropriate.

Content validity is important not only for teacher-developed assessments but also for any published achievement tests being used to assess students' abilities and academic progress. Because these tests have already been constructed, we can follow the steps for ensuring content validity in reverse order. By looking at the items on the test, we can identify the topics covered and the behaviors required (e.g., recalling information, applying procedures, solving

**FIGURE 14.8  Two examples of a table of specifications**

| Topics | Computation using number line | Rapid recall of sum | Regrouping ("carrying") | Estimation | Application to word problems |
|---|---|---|---|---|---|
| Single digits | 2 | 6 | | | 4 |
| Multiples of 10 and 100 | 2 | | | | 2 |
| Two-digit numbers | | | 2 | 2 | 3 |
| Three-digit numbers | | | 2 | 2 | 3 |

| Topics | Recall of facts | Understanding of concepts | Application to new situations | Total for each topic |
|---|---|---|---|---|
| Statics: properties of objects at rest | 5% | 10% | 10% | 25% |
| Kinematics: properties of objects in motion | 10% | 10% | 10% | 30% |
| Dynamics: properties of objects under the influence of force | 10% | 10% | 25% | 45% |

problems). Once again, we can construct a table of specifications, indicating the number of test items that fall in each cell (sometimes the publisher provides such a table). We can then decide whether the specifications match our curriculum closely enough that the test has content validity for our particular situation—that is, whether the test reflects what we actually do in our classrooms.

## PREDICTIVE VALIDITY

Shantel is thinking about a career in mathematics. But even though she's doing well in her eighth-grade math class, she worries that she'll eventually have trouble with advanced courses in trigonometry and calculus. To get an idea of her chances for future math success, Shantel takes the Mathematics Aptitude Test (MAT) that her school counselor makes available to her. Shantel does quite well on the MAT, bolstering her confidence that she can succeed in a mathematics career. But does the MAT actually measure a student's potential for success as a mathematician? This is a question of predictive validity—the extent to which an assessment instrument accurately predicts future performance in some arena.

Publishers of standardized, norm-referenced ability tests often determine, mathematically, the accuracy with which test scores predict later success in certain domains. Keep in mind, however, that a test has no *single* predictive validity. Its validity in a given situation depends on the specific behavior being predicted, the age-group being tested (e.g., many tests have greater predictive validity for older students than for younger ones), and the amount of time between the test and the predicted performance.

See Appendix B for details about how predictive validity is calculated.

## CONSTRUCT VALIDITY

In psychology, a *construct* is a hypothesized internal trait that can't be directly observed but must instead be inferred from consistencies we see in people's behavior. *Motivation, self-efficacy,* and *intelligence* are all constructs; we can't actually *see* any of these things but must instead draw conclusions about them from what students do and don't do. For example, we might use our observations of students' on-task and off-task behaviors to make inferences about their self-efficacy for various classroom topics and skills. Similarly, we might use tasks that ask students to reason abstractly to make inferences about their intelligence.

By construct validity, then, we mean the extent to which an assessment instrument actually measures an abstract, unobservable characteristic. Construct validity is of most concern when we're trying to draw general conclusions about students' traits and abilities—perhaps when we're trying to identify certain disabling conditions that may require specialized instruction and support systems. The problem with the Fathead Test of Intelligence (FTOI) described earlier is one of poor construct validity: Despite its high reliability, the scores it yields have little—probably nothing—to do with intelligence.

How do we determine whether a test or other assessment instrument measures something we can't actually *see?* Assessment experts have developed a variety of strategies for doing so. For example, they might determine how well assessment results correlate with other measures of the same trait (e.g., do scores on one intelligence test correlate with scores on other IQ tests?). They might also find out whether older students perform better than younger students on instruments measuring traits that presumably increase with age (e.g., do 12-year-olds correctly answer more items on an intelligence test than 6-year-olds?). Or they might compare the performance of two groups known to be different with respect to the trait in question (e.g., do nondisabled 12-year-olds perform better on an intelligence test than 12-year-olds with intellectual disabilities?). When data from a variety of sources are consistent with what we would expect if the instrument is a good measure of the characteristic in question, we conclude that it probably does have construct validity.

One principle applies to all three forms of validity: *Virtually any assessment tool is more valid for some purposes than for others.* A math achievement test may be a valid measure of how well students can solve arithmetic word problems but a terrible measure of how well they can apply arithmetic to real-life situations. And a paper–pencil quiz on the rules of tennis may accurately assess students' knowledge of how many games are in a set, what *deuce* means, and so on, but it probably won't tell us much about how well students can actually play the game.

**predictive validity** Extent to which the results of an assessment predict future performance in a particular domain.

**construct validity** Extent to which an assessment accurately measures an unobservable educational or psychological characteristic.

# COMPARE/CONTRAST

## TABLE 14.2 • RSVP Characteristics of Good Assessment

| CHARACTERISTIC | DEFINITION | RELEVANT QUESTIONS TO CONSIDER | COMMENTS |
|---|---|---|---|
| Reliability | The extent to which an assessment instrument or procedure yields consistent results for each student | • How much are students' scores affected by temporary conditions unrelated to the characteristic being measured (*test–retest reliability*)?<br>• Do different people score students' performance similarly (*scorer reliability*, also known as *interrater reliability*)?<br>• Do different parts of a single assessment instrument lead to similar conclusions about a student's achievement (*internal consistency reliability*)? | Reliability is a necessary condition for validity and is especially important in summative assessments. It's less critical in short formative assessments that are used simply to guide instruction over the short term (e.g., those use in curriculum-based measurement). |
| Standardization | The extent to which assessment instruments and procedures are similar for all students | • Are all students assessed on identical or similar content?<br>• Are all students asked to perform the same types of tasks?<br>• Is everyone given the same instructions?<br>• Do all students have the same time limit?<br>• Is everyone's performance evaluated using the same criteria? | Standardization is essential for legitimate and equitable comparisons among students (e.g., in norm-referenced tests). It's less important when assessments are used to guide and individualize instruction. Also, appropriate accommodations must be made for students with disabilities. |
| Validity | The extent to which an assessment instrument or procedure measures what it is intended to measure and enables appropriate inferences to be made | • Does the assessment tap into a representative sample of the content domain being assessed (*content validity*)?<br>• Do students' scores predict their later success in a domain (*predictive validity*)?<br>• Does the instrument measure a particular psychological or educational characteristic (*construct validity*)? | Validity must be the most central concern in all classroom assessments. Assessment results are meaningless unless they're closely aligned with instructional goals and the academic curriculum. |
| Practicality | The extent to which an assessment instrument or procedure is easy and inexpensive to use | • How much class time does the assessment take to administer?<br>• How quickly and easily can students' responses be scored?<br>• Is special training required to administer or score the assessment?<br>• Does the assessment require specialized materials that must be purchased? | Especially when using summative assessments to make potentially life-altering decisions, practicality should be a consideration only to the extent that validity isn't seriously jeopardized. Brief formative assessments (e.g., in CBM) should be highly practical so that they don't consume much instructional time. |

## PRACTICALITY

The final RSVP characteristic is practicality—the extent to which assessment instruments and procedures are easy to use.[2] Practicality encompasses issues such as these:

- How much time will it take to develop the questions and/or tasks to be administered?
- Can the assessment be administered to many students at once, or is one-on-one administration required?
- Are expensive materials involved?
- How much time will the assessment take away from instructional activities?
- How quickly and easily can students' performance be evaluated?

There's often a trade-off between practicality and characteristics such as validity and reliability. For example, a true–false test on tennis would be easier to construct and administer, but a performance assessment in which students actually demonstrate their tennis skills—even though it would take more time and energy—would undoubtedly be a more valid measure of how well students have mastered the game.

The four RSVP characteristics of good assessments are summarized in Table 14.2. Of these, *validity is the most important:* We must use assessment techniques that validly assess students'

**practicality** Extent to which an assessment instrument or procedure is inexpensive and easy to use and takes only a small amount of time to administer and score.

---

[2]Many psychologists use the term *usability*, but I think *practicality* better communicates this idea.

achievement of instructional goals and objectives. Yet we should keep in mind that *reliability is a necessary condition for validity*, especially when summative assessments are involved. Reliability doesn't guarantee validity, however, as the earlier FTOI exercise illustrated. Standardization is most relevant to summative assessments, particularly norm-referenced ones in which each student's performance is evaluated in comparison with peers. Furthermore, standardization can enhance the reliability of assessment results and hence can indirectly enhance their validity. Practicality should be a consideration only when validity isn't lost in the process.

# Assessing Learning and Performance Both Informally and Formally

Effective teachers regularly draw inferences both from their ongoing, spontaneous observations of students' behaviors and from students' performance on preplanned paper–pencil and performance tasks. And many teachers are now capitalizing on the assistance that computer technology can offer in assessing and monitoring students' progress. We examine each of these strategies now.

## INFORMALLY OBSERVING STUDENTS' BEHAVIORS

From our daily observations of students' classroom behaviors, we can discover a great deal about what students have and haven't learned, enabling us to make reasonable decisions about how future instruction should proceed. For example, we can:

- Ask questions during a lesson (see the Into the Classroom feature "Asking Questions to Assess Learning and Achievement Informally").
- Listen to what and how much students contribute to whole-class and small-group discussions; make note of the kinds of questions they ask.
- Have students write daily or weekly entries in personal journals.
- Observe how well students perform physical tasks.
- Identify the kinds of activities in which students engage voluntarily.
- Watch for body language that may reflect students' feelings about particular classroom tasks.
- Observe students' interactions with peers in class, at lunch, and on the playground.
- Look at the relative frequency of on-task and off-task behaviors; look for patterns in *when* students are off task.

## Into the Classroom

### Asking Questions to Assess Learning and Achievement Informally

- **Direct questions to the entire class, not just to a few students who seem eager to respond.**
  The girls in a high school science class rarely volunteer when their teacher asks questions. Although the teacher often calls on students who raise their hands, he occasionally calls on those who don't, and he makes sure that he calls on *every* student at least once a week.

- **When a question has only a few possible answers, have students vote on the particular answers they think are correct.**
  When beginning a lesson on dividing one fraction by another, a middle school math teacher writes this problem on the chalkboard:

  $$\tfrac{3}{4} \div \tfrac{1}{2} = ?$$

  She asks, "Before we talk about how we solve this problem, how many of you think the answer will be less than 1? How many think it will be greater than 1? How many think it will be exactly 1?" She tallies the number of hands that go up after each question and then says, "Hmmm, most of you think the answer will be less than 1. Let's look at how we solve a problem like this. Then each of you will know whether you were right or wrong."

- **Ask follow-up questions to probe students' reasoning.**
  In a geography lesson on Canada, a fourth-grade teacher points to the St. Lawrence River on a map and asks, "Which way does the water flow, toward the ocean or away from it?" One student shouts out, "Away from it." "Why do you think so?" the teacher asks. The student's explanation reveals a common misconception: that rivers can flow only from north to south, never vice versa.

**FIGURE 14.9** This page from 6-year-old Meghan's kindergarten portfolio shows her teacher's assessment of her work habits and social skills.

### Group Participation and Work Habits

☺ **Demonstrates attentiveness as a listener through body language or facial expressions-** Meghan is still developing this skill. Sometimes it is difficult for her to listen when she is sitting near her friends.

☺ **Follows directions.**

☺ **Enters ongoing discussion on the subject.** -Sometimes needs to be encouraged to share her ideas.

☺ **Makes relevant contributions to ongoing activities.**

☺ **Completes assigned activities.** -Meghan is very responsible about her assignments.

☺ **Shows courtesy in conversations and discussions by waiting for turn to speak.**

Meghan enjoys lunch with her friends.

🍏 Don't take any single observation of a student's behavior too seriously; instead, look for patterns over time.

🍏 Keep a written record of what students say and do, especially if final assessments will depend heavily on in-class observations.

Informal assessment has several advantages. First and foremost, it offers continuing feedback about the effectiveness of the day's instructional tasks and activities. Second, it's easily adjusted at a moment's notice; for example, when students reveal misconceptions about a topic, we can ask follow-up questions that probe their beliefs and reasoning processes. Third, informal assessment provides information that may either support or call into question the data we obtain from more formal assessments such as paper–pencil tests and quizzes; for instance, it might provide more optimistic assessments of English language learners. Finally, ongoing observations of students' behaviors provide clues about social, emotional, and motivational factors affecting students' classroom performance and may often be the only practical means through which we can assess such goals as "Shows courtesy" and "Enjoys reading." In the portfolio excerpt shown in Figure 14.9, a kindergarten teacher describes 6-year-old Meghan's progress in work habits and social skills—areas that the teacher can probably assess only through informal observation.

## RSVP CHARACTERISTICS OF INFORMAL ASSESSMENTS

When we get information about students' characteristics and achievements through informal means, we must be aware of the strengths and limitations of this approach with respect to reliability, standardization, validity, and practicality.

**Reliability**   Most informal assessments are quite short, and such snippets of students' behavior aren't always reliable indicators of their overall accomplishments and dispositions. Perhaps we happen to ask Manuel the *only* question to which he doesn't know the answer. Perhaps we happen to notice Naomi being off task during the *only* time she's off task. Perhaps we misinterpret something Jacquie says after school. When we use informal assessment to draw conclusions about what students know and can do, we should base our conclusions on many observations over a long period. And given the fact that our long-term memories can never be totally accurate, dependable records of our observations, we should keep ongoing, written records of what we see and hear (M. D. Miller, Linn, & Gronlund, 2009; Stiggins & Chappuis, 2012).

**Standardization**   Informal assessments can rarely, if ever, be standardized; for example, we're apt to ask different questions of different students, and we'll probably observe each student's behavior in different contexts. Hence such assessments definitely *don't* give us the same information for each student. In most cases, then, we can't make legitimate comparisons among students merely on the basis of a few casual observations.

**Validity**   Even when students' behavior is consistent over time, it won't always give us accurate data about what students know and can do. For example, Tom may intentionally answer questions incorrectly so that he doesn't come across as a know-it-all, and Margot may be reluctant to say anything because of a chronic stuttering problem. In general, when we use in-class questions to assess students' learning, we must keep in mind that some students—especially females and students from certain ethnic minority groups—will be less likely to respond than others (Castagno & Brayboy, 2008; Rogoff, 2003; Wentzel, 2009).

Our personal biases and expectations also come into play in informal assessments (Carbonneau & Selig, 2011; Ritts, Patterson, & Tubbs, 1992; J. P. Robinson & Lubienski, 2011). As cognitive psychologists have revealed, we human beings typically impose meanings on what we see and hear based on things we already know or believe to be true.

For instance, we're apt to expect academic or social competence from students we like or admire and thus perceive their actions in an overly positive light—a phenomenon known as the **halo effect**. In much the same way, we might expect inappropriate behavior from students with a history of misbehavior, and our observations might be biased accordingly—a phenomenon aptly called the **horns effect**.

In addition, teachers' expectations for students are sometimes influenced by students' ethnic backgrounds or socioeconomic status, and such expectations may unfairly bias judgments of students' performance (Ready & Wright, 2011; van den Bergh, Denessen, Hornstra, Voeten, & Holland, 2010). In one experimental study (Darley & Gross, 1983), college students were told that they were participating in a study on teacher assessment methods and then shown a videotape of a fourth grader named Hannah. Two versions of the videotape gave differing impressions about Hannah's socioeconomic status: Her clothing, the kind of playground on which she played, and information about her parents' occupations indirectly conveyed to some students that she was from a high socioeconomic background and to others that she was from a low socioeconomic background. All students watched Hannah taking an oral achievement test (on which she performed at grade level) and were asked to rate her on several characteristics. Students who had been led to believe that Hannah came from a wealthy family rated her ability well above grade level, whereas students believing that she came from a poor family evaluated her as being below grade level. The two groups of students also rated Hannah's work habits, motivation, social skills, and general maturity differently.

Teachers tend to evaluate well-behaved students as achieving at higher levels than badly behaved students, even when the students' actual academic achievement levels are the same.

**Practicality**    The greatest strength of informal assessment is its practicality. It involves little or none of our time either before or after the fact, except when we keep written records of our observations. It's also quite flexible: We can adjust our assessment procedures on the spot as circumstances change.

Despite the practicality of informal assessment, we've just noted serious problems regarding its reliability, standardization, and validity. Hence we should treat any conclusions we draw only as *hypotheses* that we must either confirm or disconfirm through other means. In the end, we must rely more heavily on preplanned, formal assessment techniques to determine whether our students have achieved instructional goals and met content area standards.

Ask yourself whether your existing beliefs and expectations might be biasing your interpretations of students' performance.

Treat the conclusions you draw from informal assessment as hypotheses that need confirmation through more formal means.

## USING PAPER–PENCIL ASSESSMENTS

When we need to conduct a formal assessment, paper–pencil assessment is typically easier and faster—and thus has greater practicality—than performance assessment. Questions that require brief responses—for instance, multiple-choice and short-answer questions—are often suitable for assessing students' knowledge of single, isolated facts. Paper–pencil tasks that require extended responses—for instance, essay questions and geometry proofs—lend themselves more easily to assessment of complex cognitive processes, such as logical reasoning, critical thinking, and problem solving. However, item type alone doesn't tell us whether we're assessing simple or complex thinking skills. For example, it's quite possible (and also quite common) for an essay question to ask students only to retrieve and explain things they've previously been taught, and some teachers are quite creative in writing multiple-choice questions that require students to apply classroom subject matter to new situations.

One important distinction to consider regarding various paper–pencil item formats is whether they involve recognition or recall. A **recognition task** (e.g., a multiple-choice, true–false, or matching question) asks students to identify a correct answer within the context of incorrect statements or irrelevant information. In contrast, a **recall task** (e.g., a short-answer question, word problem, or essay task) requires students to generate the correct answer themselves. When a recall task requires

**halo effect**    Phenomenon in which people are more likely to perceive positive behaviors in someone they like or admire.

**horns effect**    Phenomenon in which people are more likely to perceive negative behaviors in someone for whom they have little affection or respect.

**recognition task**    Assessment task in which one must identify correct information among incorrect statements or irrelevant information.

**recall task**    Assessment task in which one must retrieve information from long-term memory with only minimal retrieval cues.

Use recognition tasks to assess students' ability to identify facts, especially when the content domain is large. Use recall tasks when it's important to assess students' ability to retrieve information on their own and use it in new ways.

a lengthy response—and especially when it also involves elaborating on, analyzing, synthesizing, or applying information in new ways—it's sometimes called a **constructed-response task**.

Recognition items have two major advantages. First, we can often include a relatively large number of questions and tasks in a single assessment, enabling us to get a representative sample of a broad content domain and hence potentially increasing content validity. In addition, we can score students' responses quickly and consistently, thus addressing our need for practicality and reliability. However, recognition tasks tend to overestimate achievement: Students can sometimes guess correctly when they don't know the material very well.

When our instructional goal involves retrieving knowledge and skills *without* the benefit of seeing the correct answer within the context of distracting information, and especially when we want to examine students' reasoning processes—for instance, their ability to justify a particular point of view on a controversial topic—recall tasks generally have greater validity than recognition tasks. Also, students tend to study classroom material more thoroughly when they're preparing for recall rather than recognition test questions, and they remember the material better (D'Ydewalle, Swerts, & De Corte, 1983; Roediger & Karpicke, 2006; Rohrer & Pashler, 2010; G. Warren, 1979). But because students may require considerable time to respond to each recall item, we'll be able to present fewer items in a single assessment session (adversely affecting reliability) and will tap a more limited sample of the content domain (potentially affecting content validity). In addition, we'll typically take longer to score such items (a practicality issue) and will make more errors in scoring them (another reliability issue).

## CONSTRUCTING A PAPER–PENCIL ASSESSMENT

Most recognition assessment items take one of three basic forms:

- An *alternative-response item* is one for which there are only two or three possible answers (e.g., *true* versus *false, fact* versus *opinion*). The answer choices are the same for all items in a series.

- A *multiple-choice item* consists of a question or incomplete statement (the *stem*) followed by one correct answer and several incorrect alternatives *(distractors)*.

- A *matching item* presents two columns of information; students must match each item in the first column with an appropriate item in the second.

Of these three formats, most assessment experts recommend multiple-choice items. Multiple-choice items have two advantages relative to other recognition items. First, the number of items students can answer correctly simply by guessing is relatively low, especially in comparison with alternative-response items. (For example, when multiple-choice items have five possible answers, students can get only about 20% of them correct through guessing alone.) Second, other things being equal, the multiple-choice format lends itself most readily to measuring complex thinking skills.

Think creatively about paper–pencil tasks that might require students to synthesize, apply, or critically analyze things they have learned.

Recall items range widely in format and are essentially limited only by our imaginations. Some are quite simple and straightforward—for instance, "How much is two plus two?" and "What's the capital of France?" Others may call for considerable thought. For example, we might give students a problem that requires them to manipulate or synthesize data and develop a solution. Alternatively, we might give students new material (e.g., a table, graph, map, or section of text) and ask them to analyze and draw conclusions from it. Figure 14.10 presents an example.

With RSVP characteristics of good assessments in mind, I offer the following general recommendations for constructing paper–pencil assessments.

 *Combine multiple formats in a single assessment.* Often we'll want to assess students' ability to synthesize, evaluate, or in other ways elaborate on the things they've learned, and we can usually do this more easily with constructed-response tasks. Yet assessments consisting of only one or two lengthy constructed-response items don't always provide a representative sample of the topics and skills being assessed, and any errors in scoring a single item can seriously impact students' overall scores. A workable compromise is to combine both quick-response recognition and recall items—which allow broad sampling—and lengthier, constructed-response recall items—which better enable us to examine students' reasoning skills—in a single paper–pencil assessment. Also, we must keep in mind that paper–pencil assessments don't need to be entirely verbal in nature; they can also include visual materials, as the example in Figure 14.10 does.

🍎 *When assessing basic knowledge, rephrase ideas presented in class or reading materials.* If we want to encourage meaningful rather than rote learning as students prepare for a formal assessment, we must—I repeat, we *must*—create items for which word-for-word memorization is counterproductive. Consider, for example, a middle school language arts teacher who uses short multiple-choice quizzes to assess students' understanding of each week's new vocabulary words. The items never include the exact definitions students have been given. As an illustration, students have been given this definition for *manacle*: "Device used to restrain a person's hands or wrists." But the item on the quiz is this one:

Which one of the following words or phrases is closest in meaning to the word *manacle?*

a. Insane

b. Handcuffs

c. Out of control

d. Saltwater creature that clings to hard surfaces

(*The correct answer is* b.)

🍎 *Use new examples to encourage further learning and transfer.* When we present situations or problems that students have already studied, students may respond correctly simply because they've memorized the answers. We can truly assess transfer only when we ask students to apply what they've learned to a novel context. With a little thought and creativity, we can even assess transfer and other complex cognitive processes with recognition items, as this multiple-choice question for a science unit on simple machines does:

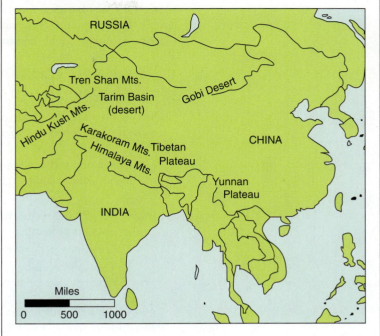

**FIGURE 14.10** Example of an assessment item that requires students to analyze and draw conclusions from new material.

Using the map shown here, explain why early people living in Russia, China, and India developed distinctly different languages and cultures.

An inventor has just designed a new device for cutting paper. Which one of the following simple machines is this device most likely to include?

a. A lever

b. A movable pulley

c. An inclined plane

d. A wedge

(*The correct answer is* d.)

🍎 *Define tasks clearly and unambiguously.* Regardless of whether students know how to correctly respond to assessment tasks, they should at least understand what we're asking them to do. The next exercise can show you what I mean.

## EXPERIENCING FIRSTHAND
## ASSESSING YOUR KNOWLEDGE OF ASSESSMENT

Your educational psychology instructor gives you a test that includes these questions:

1. List four qualities of a good classroom assessment.

2. Summarize the purposes of classroom assessment.

Take a few minutes to think about how you might answer each question. Jot down your thoughts about what you would include in your responses.

Was your answer to Question 1 as simple as "reliability, standardization, validity, and practicality"? Did you think you needed to explain each of the RSVP characteristics? Did you identify legitimate qualities of "goodness" other than the four RSVP characteristics? And what about Question 2? What purposes did you focus on, and how long do you think your actual summary might be? Words such as *list, qualities,* and *summarize* are hard to interpret and can be misleading.

Defining tasks clearly and unambiguously also means staying away from confusing language, including double negatives. Here's another short exercise to illustrate the point.

### EXPERIENCING FIRSTHAND
### ASSESSING YOUR KNOWLEDGE OF GIFTEDNESS

Drawing on what you've learned either in your college classes or from your everyday experiences, choose the best answer in this multiple-choice question.

Which one of the following is *not* a characteristic of most children who have exceptionally high academic ability in comparison with peers?

a. They are not as old as their classmates.
b. They are physically uncoordinated.
c. They don't feel uncomfortable in social situations.
d. They don't perform poorly on standardized achievement tests.

Confused? It's difficult to sort through all the *not* and *un-* language to determine which three statements are true and which one is false. Having negatives such as *not, don't,* and *un-* in two places at once amounts to a double negative, which many people of all ages have trouble interpreting correctly. The answer is *b:* Contrary to a popular stereotype, students who have high academic ability are, on average, just as coordinated as their nongifted peers.

🍎 *Provide guidance and structure for students' responses.* To some degree, we should do this by clearly defining the assessment task. For example, to assess students' knowledge of eighteenth-century American history, rather than ask them only to "List three causes of the American Revolution," we might instead ask them to do this:

Identify three policies or events during the 1760s and/or 1770s that contributed to the outbreak of the American Revolution. For each one, explain in three to five sentences how it increased tension between England and the American colonies.

Alternatively, to assess students' ability to separate and control variables, we might ask them to do this:

A student wants to demonstrate the effect of temperature on the rate of dissolving. Describe a demonstration that could be performed. Be sure to include:
• the materials to be used to perform the demonstration,
• the hypothesis, and
• the steps to follow during the demonstration
Materials: _____

_____

Hypothesis: _____

_____

Steps: _____

_____

Such clarity and structure are especially important when a great deal of information is potentially relevant to a constructed-response task. Otherwise, students' responses might go in so many different directions that scoring them consistently and reliably is virtually impossible.

Students also need guidance about how to respond to recognition items. At a minimum, we should provide information about the following:

- *Time limits*—for example, how long students should spend on each item and whether they have a fixed time in which to complete the overall assessment
- *Nature of desired responses*—for example, whether students should choose a single best answer for each multiple-choice question or instead mark all correct alternatives
- *Method of recording responses*—for example, whether students should mark their answers on the assessment instrument itself or on a separate answer sheet
- *Acceptability of guessing*—for example, whether students should guess if they're not sure of an answer or, instead, will be penalized for wrong answers

Examine the pros and cons of correcting for guessing in "Correcting for Guessing in Paper–Pencil Assessments."

🍎 *Minimize the likelihood that students can guess correctly when they don't know the answer.* Assessment tasks have content validity only to the extent that they can help us accurately determine whether students have mastered the knowledge and skills being assessed. Poorly written assessment items sometimes provide logical clues that enable even uninformed students to answer correctly. The following exercise provides examples.

## EXPERIENCING FIRSTHAND
## CALIFRACTIONS

Imagine that you're enrolled in Professor Carberry's psychoceramics course. Early in the semester, before you've had a chance to read the assigned chapter, Professor Carberry gives a surprise quiz on califractions. Below are the first three quiz items; there's only one correct answer for each one:

1. Because they are furstier than other califractions, califors are most often used to
   a. reassignment of matherugs
   b. disbobble a fwing
   c. mangelation
   d. in the burfews
2. Calendation is a process of
   a. combining two califors
   b. adding two califors together
   c. joining two califors
   d. taking two califors apart
3. The furstiest califraction is the
   a. califor
   b. calderost
   c. calinga
   d. calidater

You could possibly answer all three questions without knowing anything about califractions. Because Item 1 says "califors are most often used to . . . ," the answer must begin with a verb and so must be Alternative *b* (Alternatives *a* and *c* begin with nouns—"reassign*ment*" and "mangela-*tion*"—and *d* begins with a preposition). Item 2 includes three similar-meaning alternatives *(a, b, c);* because the item can have only one right answer, the correct choice must be *d.* And the answer to Item 3 must be *a* because Item 1 has already told you that califors are furstier than other califractions.

In constructing multiple-choice items and other recognition tasks, we should take care that all alternatives are equally logical choices in two respects: (1) They're grammatically parallel to one another and consistent with the stem and (2) only one of them is legitimately correct. Hence many experts recommend that we *not* use "all of the above" as an option in a multiple-choice question: If this is the correct answer (and it often is), the other alternatives must be correct as well, and students who've been told to choose the "correct" answer might reasonably be confused.

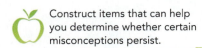

Construct items that can help you determine whether certain misconceptions persist.

A better strategy is to use one or more common misconceptions as distractors, as the following item about the causes of the seasons does:

What is the *main* reason that it's colder in winter than in summer?

a. Because the earth is in the part of its orbit farthest away from the sun

b. Because wind is more likely to come from the north than from the south

c. Because the sun's rays hit our part of the earth at more of an angle

d. Because the snow on the ground reflects rather than absorbs the sun's heat

(*The correct answer is* c. *Alternative* a *is a common misconception.*)

Another strategy for minimizing correct guesses—one that's especially useful in constructed-response tasks—is to include information that's irrelevant to the answer. For example, at some point in your schooling you almost certainly learned how to calculate the area of a parallelogram. If you did, can you quickly calculate the area of the parallelogram shown here?

If you can recall the formula (Area = Base × Height), you should easily arrive at the answer (8 × 4, or 32 square cm). But if you've forgotten the procedure, you might be led astray by some of the information the figure provides. An additional advantage of including extraneous information is that it often enhances the real-life nature of an assessment task. The outside world typically presents a lot of information that has little or nothing to do with the task at hand, and students must ultimately be able to determine what information they actually need.

Reduce the likelihood of a correct guess—and also enhance the real-world nature of a task—by including irrelevant information.

🍎 *Consider giving students access to reference materials.* In some cases we may want students to have only one resource—long-term memory—as they complete an assessment activity. But in other cases it may be appropriate to let them use reference materials as they work—perhaps a dictionary, map, magazine article, or class notes. An assessment task in which reference materials are allowed is especially appropriate when our objective is for students to locate, analyze, or apply information rather than memorize it.

🍎 *Place shorter and easier items before more challenging ones.* Some students approach paper–pencil assessments strategically, answering quick and easy items first, regardless of the order in which the items are sequenced. But other students tend to address items in the order they appear, sometimes spending so much time on one item (e.g., a lengthy essay) that they leave little time to tackle other, shorter ones. By beginning an assessment with short, relatively easy items, we can both (1) keep students' anxiety at a facilitative, productive level and (2) ensure that they demonstrate some of what they've learned before they get bogged down in especially challenging tasks.

🍎 *Identify scoring criteria in advance.* We should identify correct responses—or at least the components of a good response—at the same time we develop our assessment tasks. To the extent that students' responses will require some professional judgment on our part, we might develop one or more rubrics to guide our scoring. We should also develop policies about what to do when students give partially correct answers, respond correctly but include additional *in*correct information, or write responses with numerous grammatical and spelling errors (more about the last of these issues shortly).

## ADMINISTERING A PAPER–PENCIL ASSESSMENT

The validity of a classroom assessment instrument depends not only on how we've constructed the instrument but also on how we administer it. Following are three general strategies that should increase the validity of our results when we administer a paper–pencil assessment.

🍎 *Provide a quiet and comfortable environment.* Students are more likely to perform at their best when they have adequate lighting, reasonable work space, and minimal distractions. Such comfort factors may be especially important for students who are easily distracted, unaccustomed to formal assessments, or uninterested in exerting much effort—for instance, students who are at risk for academic failure and dropping out of school (Popham, 2006; Shriner & Spicuzza, 1995).

🍏 *Encourage students to ask questions when tasks aren't clear.* Despite our best intentions, we may sometimes present assessment tasks that are ambiguous or misleading. Thus we should encourage students to seek clarification whenever they're uncertain about what we're asking them to do. Without such encouragement, some students—including many from ethnic minority groups—may be reluctant to ask questions during formal assessments (L. R. Cheng, 1987; C. A. Grant & Gomez, 2001; J. Li & Fischer, 2004).

🍏 *Take reasonable steps to discourage cheating.* For a variety of reasons, the prevalence of cheating increases as students get older. Some students may be more interested in doing well on an assessment than in actually learning the subject matter; for them, performance goals predominate over mastery goals. Others may believe that teachers' or parents' expectations for their performance are unattainably high and that success is possible only if they *do* cheat. In addition, students may perceive certain assessments— especially paper–pencil tests—to be poorly constructed, arbitrarily graded, or in some other way a poor reflection of what they've learned. Often, too, peers may communicate through words or actions that cheating is quite acceptable (L. H. Anderman, Freeman, & Mueller, 2007; Cizek, 2003; Danner, 2008; E. D. Evans & Craig, 1990; Lenski, Husemann, Trautwein, & Lüdtke, 2010; Murdock, Miller, & Kohlhardt, 2004).

When students cheat, their assessment scores don't accurately reflect what they know and can do—hence, the scores have little or no validity. Furthermore, cheating can be habit forming if students discover that it enables them to get good grades with minimal effort (Cizek, 2003). The best approach is prevention—making sure students don't cheat in the first place—through strategies such as these:

### In the Weeks or Days Before the Assessment

🍏 Focus students' attention on mastery goals rather than performance goals.

🍏 Make success without cheating a realistic possibility.

🍏 Construct assessment instruments with obvious validity for important instructional goals.

🍏 Create two or more instruments that are equivalent in form and content but have different answers (e.g., arrange the same set of multiple-choice questions in two different orders).

🍏 Explain exactly what cheating is and why it's unacceptable.

🍏 Describe the consequence that will be imposed for cheating.

### During the Assessment

🍏 Have teacher-assigned seats during any assessments that require individual (rather than group) work.

🍏 Seat students as far away from one another as possible.

🍏 Insist that cell phones and other electronic devices be turned off and checked in at the classroom door.

🍏 Remain attentive to what students are doing throughout the assessment session, but without hovering over particular students.

If, despite reasonable precautions, cheating occurs, we must administer whatever consequence we've previously described. This consequence should be severe enough to discourage a student from cheating again yet not so severe that the student's motivation and chances for academic success are affected over the long run. Having the student honestly redo the task is, of course, an appropriate consequence; we might also ask the student to write a paper about the moral implications and negative repercussions of academic dishonesty (K. O'Connor, 2011). In general, we must remember that students' final grades should ultimately reflect *what they have learned*. For this reason, many assessment experts recommend that the consequence for cheating *not* be a failing final grade if a student has, in other assessments, demonstrated mastery of the subject matter (K. O'Connor, 2011; Stiggins & Chappuis, 2012).

Identify an appropriate consequence for cheating, one severe enough to discourage cheating yet not so severe that it undermines students' motivation and long-term success. Alert students to this consequence and administer it consistently when cheating occurs.

## SCORING STUDENTS' RESPONSES TO A PAPER–PENCIL ASSESSMENT

As we evaluate students' performance on an assessment task, we must continue to be concerned about the four RSVP characteristics. Also, we must keep in mind that our most important goal isn't to evaluate students but rather to *help students learn.* Each of the following strategies is valuable in achieving one or both of these ends.

🍏 *Strive for objectivity.* Some assessment tasks have clear right and wrong answers, but others—for example, students' essays and lab reports—can require teacher judgments regarding quality. Whenever scoring involves considerable decision making, a scoring rubric can help us be reasonably objective in our evaluations. Occasionally a rubric might simply be a checklist that identifies the components of a good response, as the rubric in Figure 14.5 does. But for especially complex, multifaceted responses, we may instead want to use one or more rating scales that help us evaluate the quality of responses along one or more continua. To be maximally useful, a rating scale includes concrete descriptions of various points along the scale, as the rubric in Figure 14.6 does, and perhaps also examples of student work that illustrate each point on the scale.

🍏 *To the extent possible, score grammar and spelling separately from the content of students' responses unless specifically assessing writing skills.* This recommendation is especially important when assessing students with limited writing skills, such as English language learners and students with disabilities (Hamp-Lyons, 1992; Scarcella, 1990; Valdés, Bunch, Snow, & Lee, 2005).

🍏 *Before beginning to score, skim a few students' responses, looking for unanticipated responses and revising the criteria if necessary.* As a general rule, we should use the criteria we've previously told students we'll use. Occasionally, however, we may need to adjust one or more criteria—or perhaps add or subtract one or two criteria—to accommodate unexpected responses and enhance our ability to score all responses consistently, fairly, and reliably. Any adjustments should be made *before* we begin scoring, rather than midway through scoring a stack of papers.

🍏 *Score item by item rather than paper by paper.* When scoring involves subjective decision making, we can score students' responses more reliably if we score them item by item—scoring all responses to the first question, then all responses to the second question, and so on.

🍏 *Try not to let prior expectations for students' performance influence judgments of their actual performance.* The halo and horns effects described earlier can come into play in formal assessments as well as informal ones. The more variable and complex students' responses are on a paper–pencil assessment, the greater the difficulty we'll have in scoring responses objectively and reliably. Strategies such as shuffling papers after grading one question and using small self-stick notes to cover up students' names can help us prevent our expectations from inappropriately influencing our judgments.

🍏 *Accompany any overall scores with detailed feedback.* As we score students' responses, we must remember that all of our assessments—including our summative ones—can and should enhance students' *future* achievement. Accordingly, we should provide detailed comments that tell students what they've done well, where their weaknesses lie, and how they can improve. When students get only a single score or grade on an assessment, without an accompanying explanation of *why* they were evaluated as they were, they're likely to attribute the evaluation to something beyond their control—perhaps to their own innate ability or *in*ability, or perhaps to highly subjective and arbitrary teacher judgments—and to work toward performance goals rather than mastery goals (E. M. Anderman & Dawson, 2011; Stupnisky, Stewart, Daniels, & Perry, 2011).

## RSVP CHARACTERISTICS OF PAPER–PENCIL ASSESSMENTS

How do paper–pencil assessments measure up in terms of the four RSVP characteristics? Let's consider each characteristic in turn.

**Reliability**   When paper–pencil assessment tasks have definite right and wrong answers, we can usually evaluate students' responses with a high degree of consistency. In contrast, when we must make subjective judgments about the relative rightness or wrongness of students' responses, reliability inevitably goes down a bit.

**Standardization**   As a general rule, paper–pencil instruments are easily standardized. We can give all students similar tasks and instructions, provide similar time limits and environmental conditions, and score everyone's responses in essentially the same way. At the same time, we must balance the need for standardization against other considerations. For example, we may need to tailor assessment tasks to the particular abilities and disabilities of students with special needs. And when assessing students' writing skills, we might sometimes let students choose a writing topic, perhaps as a way of increasing their sense of self-determination. We shouldn't go overboard in allowing student choices on summative assessments, however. For example, if we're giving two or three constructed-response questions, we'll typically want to have all students answer *all* those questions, rather than having them choose and respond to only one. If we give students choices in the questions they answer, they can avoid topics they haven't studied very well, and we might unintentionally score responses to one question more stringently than we score responses to another.

Standardize paper–pencil assessments as much as possible, but make appropriate accommodations for students with disabilities.

**Validity**　　When we ask questions that require only short, simple responses, we can sample students' knowledge about many topics within a short period of time. In this sense, then, such questions can give us greater content validity. Yet such items won't always reflect our instructional goals. To assess students' ability to apply what they've learned to new situations and complex real-world problems, we may need to be satisfied with a few tasks requiring lengthy responses, even if those tasks provide a somewhat limited sample of the content domain.

**Practicality**　　Paper–pencil assessment is typically more practical than performance assessment; for example, we can assess all students at the same time, and in many cases we can score students' responses in a short time. Thus paper–pencil assessment should be our method of choice *if* it can yield a valid measure of what students know and can do. But when paper–pencil tasks aren't a good reflection of what students have learned, we may need to sacrifice practicality to gain the greater validity that a performance assessment provides.

Choose paper–pencil assessment over performance assessment *if* a paper–pencil instrument can yield a valid measure of students' achievement.

## USING PERFORMANCE ASSESSMENTS

A wide variety of performance tasks can be used to assess students' mastery of classroom subject matter. Here are just a few of the many possibilities:

- Playing a musical instrument
- Conversing in a foreign language
- Engaging in a debate about social issues
- Fixing a malfunctioning machine
- Performing a workplace routine
- Role-playing a job interview
- Presenting research findings to a group of teachers, peers, and community members

Performance assessment lends itself especially well to the assessment of complex achievements, such as those that involve simultaneous use of multiple skills. It can also be quite helpful in assessing such complex cognitive processes as problem solving, creativity, and critical thinking. Furthermore, performance tasks are often more meaningful, thought provoking, and authentic—and thus often more motivating—than paper–pencil tasks (Darling-Hammond, Ancess, & Falk, 1995; DiMartino & Castaneda, 2007; R. L. Johnson et al., 2009; Khattri & Sweet, 1996; S. G. Paris & Paris, 2001).

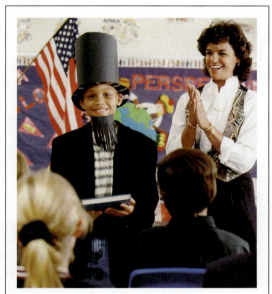

Some skills, such as public speaking, can be assessed only with performance tasks.

### CHOOSING APPROPRIATE PERFORMANCE TASKS

Our selection of appropriate performance assessment tasks must, of course, be closely aligned with our instructional goals and objectives. We must also consider whether a particular task will enable us to make reasonable generalizations about what our students know and can do in the content domain in question. Following are three distinctions that can help us zero in on the most appropriate tasks for our purposes.

**Products versus Processes**　　Some performance assessments focus on tangible *products* that students create—perhaps a pen-and-ink drawing, scientific invention, or poster display. Others instead focus on the specific *processes and behaviors* that students exhibit—perhaps giving an oral

> **FIGURE 14.11** Example of a group-based performance assessment task in a high school geography class
>
> 1. Select one of the neighborhoods marked on the city map.
>
> 2. Identify its current features by doing an inventory of its buildings, businesses, housing, and public facilities. Also, identify current transportation patterns and traffic flow. From the information made available, identify any special problems this neighborhood has, such as dilapidated housing, traffic congestion, or a high crime rate.
>
> 3. As a group, consider various plans for changing and improving your neighborhood.
>
> *Source:* "Authentic Assessment in Social Studies: Standards and Examples" by Fred M. Newmann, from *Handbook of Classroom Assessment: Learning, Achievement, and Adjustment*, edited by Gary D. Phye. Academic Press, 1997, p. 369.

Piaget's assessment strategy, known as the *clinical method,* is described more fully in Chapter 2.

presentation, demonstrating a forward roll, or playing an instrumental solo. Sometimes we might be interested in students' *thinking* processes. For example, if we want to determine whether students have acquired certain logical thinking abilities (e.g., conservation, separation and control of variables), we might present tasks similar to those Jean Piaget used and, through a series of probing questions, ask students to explain their reasoning. And we can often learn a great deal about how students conceptualize and reason about scientific phenomena when we ask them to manipulate physical objects (e.g., chemicals in a chemistry lab, electrical circuit boards in a physics class), make predictions about what will happen under varying circumstances, and explain their results (Baxter, Elder, & Glaser, 1996; diSessa, 2007; Magnusson, Boyle, & Templin, 1994; Quellmalz & Hoskyn, 1997).

**Individual versus Group Performance**   Many performance tasks require *individual* students to complete them with little or no assistance. Other tasks are sufficiently complex that they're best accomplished by a *group* of students. For instance, we might assess high school students' mastery of a unit on urban geography by using a field-based cooperative group project like the one shown in Figure 14.11. Such a task requires students to collect data systematically, use the data to draw conclusions and make predictions, and, in general, think as an urban planner would think (Newmann, 1997).

One challenge in using group tasks for assessment purposes is determining how to evaluate each student's contribution. Often teachers consider individual students' behaviors and achievements—for instance, what and how much a student contributes to the group effort and how much the student has learned by the end of the project—in addition to or instead of the entire group's accomplishments (Lester, Lambdin, & Preston, 1997; Stiggins & Chappuis, 2012).

**Restricted versus Extended Performance**   Some performance tasks are quite short; that is, they involve *restricted performance.* For instance, we might ask each student in a beginning instrumental music class to play the C-major scale in brief, one-on-one sessions with us. Or we might ask students in a chemistry class to demonstrate mastery of basic safety procedures before beginning their lab experiments.

We assess *extended performance* when we want to determine what students are capable of doing over several days or weeks. Extended performance tasks might provide opportunities for students to collect data, engage in collaborative problem solving, and edit and revise their work. Many extended performance tasks embody authentic assessment: They closely resemble the situations and problems that students might eventually encounter in the outside world. Because extended performance tasks take a great deal of time, we should use them primarily for assessing achievement related to our most important and central instructional goals (Alleman & Brophy, 1997; Lester et al., 1997; Wiggins & McTigue, 2007).

## PLANNING AND ADMINISTERING A PERFORMANCE ASSESSMENT

Three guidelines presented earlier for paper–pencil assessments are equally relevant to performance assessment:

🍎 Define tasks clearly and unambiguously.

🍎 Identify scoring criteria in advance.

🍎 Encourage students to ask questions when tasks aren't clear.

Three additional guidelines pertain primarily to performance assessments:

🍎 *Consider incorporating the assessment into normal instructional activities.* We can sometimes make more efficient use of class time if we combine instruction and assessment into a single activity (Baxter et al., 1996; Boschee & Baron, 1993). For example, in a unit on bar graphs, a first-grade teacher gave each of her students a two-dimensional grid with the months of the year written in the leftmost column. She instructed students to write their own name in a box beside their birthday month and then to circulate around the room to get each classmate's signature in a box in the appropriate row. Ideally, this procedure would yield a horizontal bar graph depicting the number of children born in each month. The completed graph shown in Figure 14.12 reveals that some but not all students understood the nature of simple bar graphs. Many students (e.g., Cam, Allison, Spencer) wrote their names inside a single box on the grid. However, a few students (e.g., Kristen, Jesse, Kristah) used two boxes to write their names, perhaps because they (1) hadn't mastered the idea that one person equals one box or (2) couldn't write small enough to fit their name inside a box and didn't know how to solve this problem. Also, one student (Meg, with a March birthday) hadn't yet learned that she must always write words, including her name, in a left-to-right direction.

When we incorporate performance assessments into instructional activities, we must keep in mind that we won't be able to completely standardize conditions for all students, and we won't necessarily see students' best work. Furthermore, although it's quite appropriate to give students assistance or feedback during instruction, it may be *in*appropriate to do so during a summative assessment of what they've achieved. In some situations, then, we may want to conduct an assessment separately from instructional activities, announce it in advance, and give students guidance beforehand about how they can maximize their performance.

🍎 *Provide some structure to guide students' efforts, but not so much structure that it reduces the authenticity of the task.* Especially if we're conducting a summative assessment, we should probably structure performance assessments to some degree. For example, we can provide detailed directions about what students should accomplish, what materials and equipment they can use, and how much time they have to get the job done (Gronlund & Waugh, 2009; E. H. Hiebert, Valencia, & Afflerbach, 1994). Such structure helps to standardize the assessment and thus enables us to evaluate students' performance more reliably. A *lot* of structure can decrease the validity of a performance task, however. Imposing a great deal of structure is particularly problematic when we intend performance tasks to be authentic ones that resemble real-world situations—which often *don't* have much structure.

🍎 *Plan classroom management strategies for the assessment activity.* As we conduct a performance assessment, we should put into practice two important principles of classroom management: Effective teachers are continually aware of what their students are doing (the notion of *withitness*), and they make sure that students are always productively engaged. When we can assess students' performance only individually or in small groups, we must make sure that other students are actively involved in a learning activity (L. M. Carey, 1994). For example, in an English class, when one student is giving an oral presentation, we might have the other students jot down notes about the topic being presented—facts they find interesting, ideas they disagree with, or questions they wonder about. Or in a unit on soccer, when a few students are demonstrating their ability to dribble and pass the ball as they run down the field, we might have other students work in pairs to practice their footwork.

## SCORING STUDENTS' RESPONSES IN A PERFORMANCE ASSESSMENT

Occasionally responses to performance assessment tasks are objectively scorable; for instance, we can easily time students' performance in a 100-meter dash and count students' errors on a typing test. But more often we'll find ourselves making subjective decisions as we assess students'

**FIGURE 14.12** In this "Birthday Graph" exercise, first-grade teacher Susan O'Byrne gained information about students' writing and graphing skills.

🍎 When using a performance assessment for summative assessment, keep the assessment separate from instruction.

Chapter 13 presents these and other guidelines for effective classroom management.

**analytic scoring** Scoring a student's performance on an assessment by evaluating various aspects of it separately.

**holistic scoring** Summarizing a student's performance on an assessment with a single score.

performance. There are no clear-cut right or wrong responses when students give oral reports, create clay sculptures, or engage in heated debates on controversial issues. Consequently, if we aren't careful, our judgments may be unduly influenced by our expectations for each student (L. M. Carey, 1994; Gronlund & Waugh, 2009).

Especially for summative assessments, we should carefully consider the criteria to use in judging students' responses and develop a rubric that identifies these criteria. A rubric can guide us during the assessment process and later serve as a written record of what we've observed. The following strategies can help us design and use scoring rubrics effectively when we conduct performance assessments.

🍎 *When using several criteria to evaluate students' performance, describe each criterion in concrete terms, and develop a checklist or rating scale to guide scoring.* Some performance tasks lend themselves well to checklists, whereas others are more effectively evaluated with rating scales; Figure 14.13 provides illustrations. Both approaches enhance the reliability of scoring and have instructional benefits as well: They identify specific areas of difficulty and thereby give students feedback about how performance can be improved.

🍎 *Decide whether analytic or holistic scoring better serves your purpose(s) in conducting the assessment.* When we need detailed information about students' performance, we may want to use analytic scoring, in which we evaluate various aspects of the performance separately, perhaps with a checklist or several rating scales. In contrast, when we need to summarize students' performance in a single score, we should probably use holistic scoring, in which we consider all relevant criteria but make a single judgment; for instance, we might have a single rating scale of "1" to "5" or "Poor" to "Proficient" that describes typical overall performance at various points along the scale. Analytic scoring tends to be more useful in conducting formative assessments and promoting students' learning, whereas holistic scoring is often used in final, summative assessments.

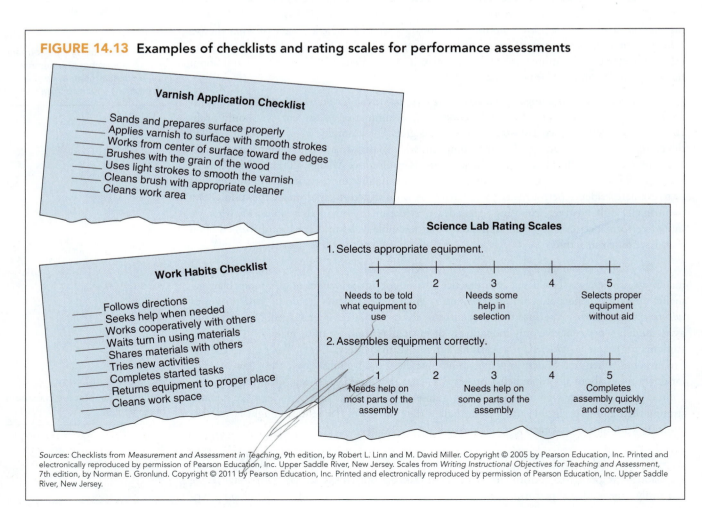

**FIGURE 14.13** Examples of checklists and rating scales for performance assessments

**Varnish Application Checklist**

_____ Sands and prepares surface properly
_____ Applies varnish to surface with smooth strokes
_____ Works from center of surface toward the edges
_____ Brushes with the grain of the wood
_____ Uses light strokes to smooth the varnish
_____ Cleans brush with appropriate cleaner
_____ Cleans work area

**Work Habits Checklist**

_____ Follows directions
_____ Seeks help when needed
_____ Works cooperatively with others
_____ Waits turn in using materials
_____ Shares materials with others
_____ Tries new activities
_____ Completes started tasks
_____ Returns equipment to proper place
_____ Cleans work space

**Science Lab Rating Scales**

1. Selects appropriate equipment.

| 1 | 2 | 3 | 4 | 5 |

1 — Needs to be told what equipment to use
3 — Needs some help in selection
5 — Selects proper equipment without aid

2. Assembles equipment correctly.

| 1 | 2 | 3 | 4 | 5 |

1 — Needs help on most parts of the assembly
3 — Needs help on some parts of the assembly
5 — Completes assembly quickly and correctly

*Sources:* Checklists from *Measurement and Assessment in Teaching,* 9th edition, by Robert L. Linn and M. David Miller. Copyright © 2005 by Pearson Education, Inc. Printed and electronically reproduced by permission of Pearson Education, Inc. Upper Saddle River, New Jersey. Scales from *Writing Instructional Objectives for Teaching and Assessment,* 7th edition, by Norman E. Gronlund. Copyright © 2011 by Pearson Education, Inc. Printed and electronically reproduced by permission of Pearson Education, Inc. Upper Saddle River, New Jersey.

🍎 *Limit scoring criteria to the most important aspects of the desired response.* Scoring criteria should focus on aspects of the performance that are critical indicators of proficiency and most relevant to instructional goals and objectives (M. D. Miller et al., 2009; Wiggins, 1992). The criteria should also be relatively few in number (perhaps five or six) so that we can keep track of them as we observe each student's performance (Airasian, 1994; Gronlund & Waugh, 2009; Popham, 1995). Remember the limited capacity of working memory: Human beings—including teachers!—can think about only so many things at a single time.

🍎 *Make note of any significant aspects of a student's performance that the rubric doesn't address.* Whenever we break down performance on a complex task into discrete behaviors, we can lose valuable information in the process (Delandshere & Petrosky, 1998). Thus, when we use rubrics to assist us in scoring performance, we may occasionally want to jot down other noteworthy characteristics of students' performance. This aspect of our scoring process will be neither standardized nor reliable, of course, but it can sometimes be useful in identifying students' unique strengths and needs and can therefore assist us in future instructional planning.

## RSVP CHARACTERISTICS OF PERFORMANCE ASSESSMENTS

Compared with traditional paper–pencil assessment, many performance assessment techniques are relative newcomers on the educational scene, and educators continue to wrestle with concerns related to reliability, standardization, validity, and practicality.

**Reliability**   Researchers have reported varying degrees of reliability in performance assessments. Assessment results are often inconsistent over time, and different teachers may rate the same performance differently (Crehan, 2001; P. J. Hay, 2008; Haywood & Lidz, 2007; R. L. Johnson et al., 2009).

There are probably several reasons for the low reliability of many performance assessments. First, students don't always behave consistently; even in a task as simple as shooting a basketball, a student is likely to make a basket on some occasions but not on others. Second, we sometimes need to evaluate various aspects of complex behaviors rather quickly; things may happen so fast that we miss important parts of a student's performance. Finally, one form of reliability—*internal consistency* (see Table 14.2)—is largely irrelevant when we're assessing complex, multifaceted behaviors (L. M. Carey, 1994; Parkes, 2001; Wiley & Haertel, 1996).

Given these limitations, a single performance assessment may very well *not* be a reliable indicator of what students have achieved. Accordingly, we should ask students to demonstrate behaviors related to important instructional goals on more than one occasion. And when an important summative assessment is involved, we should ideally have more than one rater evaluate each student's performance (R. L. Johnson et al., 2009; M. D. Miller et al., 2009).

**Standardization**   Some performance assessments are easily standardized, but others are not. If we want to assess students' keyboarding speed and accuracy, we can easily make instructions, tasks, and time limits the same for everyone. In contrast, if we want to assess artistic creativity, we may want to let students choose the materials they use and the particular products they create. In such nonstandardized situations, it's especially important to use multiple assessments and look for consistency in students' performance across several occasions.

🍎 Remember that a single performance assessment may not be a standardized or reliable indicator of what students have achieved.

**Validity**   As previously noted, performance assessment tasks can sometimes provide more valid indicators of what students have accomplished relative to instructional goals. However, students' responses to a *single* performance assessment task often are *not* a good indication of their overall achievement. Content validity is the issue here: If we have time for students to perform only one or two complex tasks, we may not get a representative sample of what they've learned and can do. In addition, any biases that affect our judgment (e.g., beliefs about particular students' abilities) can distort our assessments of students' performance—the halo and horns effects at work once again. To ensure that our conclusions are reasonably valid, then, we'll typically want to administer several different performance tasks, perhaps on two or more different occasions (S. Klassen, 2006; R. L. Linn, 1994; Messick, 1994a; Parkes, 2001; Stiggins & Chappuis, 2012).

🍎 Remember that a single performance task may not provide a sufficiently representative sample of the content domain.

**testwiseness** Test-taking know-how that enhances test performance.

Think about how you might use a combination of paper–pencil and performance tasks to assess what students know and can do.

**Practicality** Unfortunately, performance assessments are often less practical than more traditional paper–pencil assessments. Administering an assessment can be quite time-consuming, especially when we must observe students one at a time or when they must perform relatively complex (perhaps authentic) tasks. In addition, we may need considerable equipment to conduct the assessment—perhaps enough for every student to have a personal set. Clearly, then, we must carefully consider whether the benefits of a performance assessment outweigh its impracticality. Ultimately the best strategy overall may be to use *both* paper–pencil and performance assessments when drawing conclusions about students' achievement.

Table 14.3 presents a summary of our RSVP analyses of informal assessment, formal paper–pencil assessment, and formal performance assessment.

## ADDITIONAL CONSIDERATIONS IN FORMAL ASSESSMENT

In our discussion of formal assessment so far, our focus has been on the design, administration, and scoring of particular paper–pencil and performance tasks. We now step back and look at more general issues related to formal assessment.

### TEACHING TESTWISENESS

If you did well on the califractions quiz earlier in the chapter, you have some degree of **testwiseness**: You use test-taking strategies that enhance your test performance. Testwiseness includes strategies such as these:

- *Pinning down the task(s) to be performed*—for example, carefully reading the directions and every question
- *Using time efficiently*—for example, allocating enough time for each task and saving difficult items for last

## COMPARE/CONTRAST

**TABLE 14.3 • Evaluating RSVP Characteristics of Different Kinds of Summative Assessment**

| KIND OF ASSESSMENT | RELIABILITY | STANDARDIZATION | VALIDITY | PRACTICALITY |
|---|---|---|---|---|
| Informal assessment | A single, brief assessment is not a reliable indicator of achievement. We must look for consistency in a student's performance across time and in different contexts. | Informal observations are rarely, if ever, standardized. Thus, we should not compare one student to another on the basis of informal assessment alone. | Students' public behaviors in the classroom aren't always valid indicators of their achievement (e.g., some students may try to hide high achievement from their peers). | Informal assessment is definitely practical: It's flexible and can occur spontaneously during instruction. |
| Formal paper–pencil assessment | Objectively scorable items are highly reliable. We can enhance the reliability of subjectively scorable items by specifying scoring criteria in concrete terms. | In most instances, paper–pencil instruments are easily standardized for all students. Giving students choices (e.g., regarding topics to write about or questions to answer) may increase motivation but reduces standardization. | Numerous questions requiring short, simple responses can provide a more representative sample of the content domain. But tasks requiring lengthy responses may sometimes more closely match instructional goals. | Paper–pencil assessment is usually practical: All students can be assessed at once, and no special materials are required. |
| Formal performance assessment | Performance assessment tasks are often difficult to score reliably. We can enhance reliability by specifying scoring criteria in concrete terms (e.g., with a rubric). | Some performance assessment tasks are easily standardized, but many are not. | Performance tasks may sometimes be more consistent with instructional goals than paper–pencil tasks are. However, a single performance task may not provide a representative sample of the content domain; several tasks may be necessary to ensure adequate content validity. | Performance assessment is typically less practical than other approaches: It may involve special materials, and it can take a fair amount of class time, especially if students must be assessed one at a time. |

- *Deductive reasoning*—for example, eliminating two alternatives that say the same thing and using information from one question to answer another
- *Avoiding sloppy errors*—for example, checking answers a second time and erasing stray pencil marks on a computer-scored answer sheet
- *Guessing*—for example, eliminating obviously wrong alternatives and then guessing one of the others, or guessing randomly if time runs out and there's no penalty for guessing (Hong, Sas, & Sas, 2006; Millman, Bishop, & Ebel, 1965; Petersen, Sudweeks, & Baird, 1990; L. Shepard et al., 2005)

Certain aspects of testwiseness, such as guessing strategically and erasing stray pencil marks, are applicable primarily to paper–pencil recognition items (e.g., multiple-choice, true–false). But others, such as clarifying assigned tasks and managing time carefully, can make a difference in virtually any kind of formal classroom assessment.

As teachers, we must remember that many students—especially younger ones and those whose prior schooling has been in a different culture—may need explicit instruction in common item formats and useful test-taking strategies. At the same time, we should keep in mind that testwiseness typically has only a small impact on students' assessment scores. Furthermore, test-taking skills and student achievement are positively correlated: Students with many test-taking strategies tend to be higher achievers than students with few strategies. In other words, very few students get low test scores *only* because they're poor test takers. In most cases, then, we can best serve students by teaching them the knowledge and skills a given assessment is designed to measure, rather than spending an inordinate amount of time teaching them how to take tests (J. R. Frederiksen & Collins, 1989; Geiger, 1997; Scruggs & Lifson, 1985; L. Shepard et al., 2005).

## KEEPING TEST ANXIETY IN CHECK

A small amount of anxiety about tests and other important assessments can enhance performance. But some students become extremely anxious in assessment situations—they have test anxiety—to the point that their scores significantly underestimate what they've learned. Such students appear to be concerned primarily about the *evaluative* aspect of assessments, worrying that someone will find them to be "stupid" or in other ways inadequate. Test anxiety interferes not only with retrieval and performance at the time of an assessment but also with encoding and storage when learners are preparing for the assessment. Thus, highly test-anxious students don't just *test* poorly; they also *learn* poorly (Cassady, 2010b; Cassady & Johnson, 2002; Hagtvet & Johnsen, 1992; Lang & Lang, 2010; I. G. Sarason, 1980).

Excessive, debilitating test anxiety is especially common in students from ethnic minority groups and in students with disabilities (R. Carter, Williams, & Silverman, 2008; Putwain, 2007; Whitaker Sena, Lowe, & Lee, 2007). On average, students with the highest test anxiety are those who've performed poorly in school in the past. One important strategy for helping students overcome excessive test anxiety, then, is to help them acquire the skills they need to master course material in the first place (e.g., good study strategies and self-regulation skills). In addition, we must present classroom assessments in ways that motivate students to do their best without succumbing to debilitating anxiety levels. One middle school student, Jamaal, explained how his math teacher helped to keep his anxiety about assessments in check:

> Ms. Wheeler doesn't call it a test. She says, "It's a quiz, it's a worksheet, it's whatever you want it to be. Just make sure you do your best. It's a puzzle, it's a game. Just do your best." And [on] most tests she doesn't even put the word "Test" on it, or she doesn't tell us it's a test. It takes the pressure off so you can think about what you're doing more. (Usher, 2009, p. 303)

Table 14.4 presents some *dos* and *don'ts* for keeping students' test anxiety at productive levels.

Teach test-taking strategies, but not at the expense of shortchanging instruction in the knowledge and skills being assessed.

*Speed Tests!*
*Speed Tests make everyone a nervous reck before I pasted Speed Test I I would barle eat and had troble sleeping. Now, this very day I find out I pasted Speed Test II and maybe I pasted Speed Test III! Oh God please, oh please let me passe Speed Test III. Effen if I never passi Speed Test 15 teen I want you to know I tried my hardest.*

In this reflection on "Speed Tests"—those in which many questions must be answered in a very short time—8-year-old Connie describes how overwhelming test anxiety can be.

Minimize debilitating test anxiety by helping students master academic subject matter.

**test anxiety** Excessive anxiety about a particular test or about assessment in general.

# COMPARE/CONTRAST

## TABLE 14.4 • Keeping Students' Anxiety at a Facilitative Level During Classroom Assessments

| WHAT TO DO | WHAT *NOT* TO DO |
|---|---|
| Point out the value of the assessment as a feedback mechanism to improve learning. | Stress the fact that students' competence is being evaluated. |
| Administer a practice assessment or pretest that gives students an idea of what the final assessment instrument will be like. | Keep the nature of the assessment a secret until the day it is administered. |
| Encourage students to do their best but not necessarily to expect perfection; for instance, say, "We're here to learn, and you can't do that without making mistakes." | Remind students that failing will have dire consequences. |
| Provide or allow the use of memory aids (e.g., a list of formulas or a single note card containing key facts) when instructional goals don't require students to commit information to memory. | Insist that students commit even trivial facts to memory. |
| Eliminate time limits unless speed is an important part of the skill being measured. | Give more questions or tasks than students can possibly respond to in the time allotted. |
| Continually survey the room, and be available to answer students' questions. | Hover over students, watching them closely as they complete the assessment. |
| Use unannounced assessments (i.e., pop quizzes) only for formative evaluation (e.g., to determine an appropriate starting point for instruction). | Give occasional pop quizzes to motivate students to study regularly and to punish those who *don't*. |
| Use the results of several assessments to make decisions (e.g., to assign grades). | Evaluate students on the basis of a single assessment. |

*Sources:* Brophy, 1986, 2004 ("We're here to learn . . ." suggestion on p. 274); Cassady, 2010b; Cizek, 2003; Gaudry & Bradshaw, 1971; K. T. Hill, 1984; K. T. Hill & Wigfield, 1984; Sieber, Kameya, & Paulson, 1970; Spaulding, 1992; Stipek, 1993.

## ENCOURAGING RISK TAKING

Only when students feel free to take risks and make mistakes will they tackle the challenging tasks that can maximize their learning and cognitive development. We encourage risk taking—and lower students' anxiety levels as well—when our assessment strategies give students some leeway to be wrong without penalty (Clifford, 1990; McMillan, 2010). Certainly no single assessment should ever be "sudden death" for a student who earns a low score. Following are three recommended strategies for encouraging risk taking during classroom assessments.

🍎 *Assess students' achievement frequently rather than infrequently.* Regular assessments are, of course, a key means by which we and our students can track students' progress and address areas of weakness needing attention. But frequent assessments—rather than infrequent ones—have several additional benefits. First, students are less likely to experience debilitating anxiety if they complete a number of assessments that each contribute only a small amount to their final grade. Second, frequent assessments motivate students—especially those with lower achievement levels—to study regularly. Third, when students no longer feel pressure to perform well on every quiz and assignment, they're less likely to cheat in order to get good grades. Finally and most importantly, students who are assessed frequently achieve at higher levels than students who are assessed infrequently (Crooks, 1988; E. D. Evans & Craig, 1990; J. A. Glover, 1989; McDaniel et al., 2011; Roediger & Karpicke, 2006; Rohrer & Pashler, 2010; Sax, 2010).

🍎 *Provide opportunities to correct errors.* Especially when an assessment includes most or all the content domain in question, students may learn as much—possibly even more— by correcting the errors they've made on an assessment task. For example, in an approach known as *mastery reform,* some mathematics teachers have students correct their errors as follows:

1. *Identification of the error.* Students describe in a short paragraph exactly what they don't yet know how to do.
2. *Statement of the process.* Using words rather than mathematical symbols, students explain the steps involved in the procedure they're trying to master.

3. *Practice.* Students demonstrate their mastery of the procedure with three new problems similar to the problem(s) they previously solved incorrectly.

4. *Statement of mastery.* Students state in a sentence or two that they've now mastered the procedure.

By completing these steps, students can replace a grade on a previous assessment with the new, higher one. One high school math teacher has told me that this approach has a more general, long-term benefit as well: Many of his students eventually incorporate the four steps into their regular, internalized learning strategies.

🍎 *When appropriate, allow students to retake assessments.* Some students will invariably need more time than others to master a topic and may therefore need to be assessed on the same material more than once. In addition, students are less likely to have debilitating test anxiety if they know they can have another try if they need one. Retakes are obviously quite appropriate for most formative assessments, but they have certain disadvantages for summative assessments. When students know they can retake a summative assessment if they get a low score the first time, they may prepare less well than they would otherwise. Furthermore, if they're allowed to retake the *same* assessment a second time, they may work on the specific things the assessment covers without studying equally important but nonassessed material. (Remember, most assessment tasks can be only a small sample of the content in question.)

If we truly want students to master course material but also to take risks in their learning and classroom performance, we may want to make retakes a regular practice. To encourage students to take the first assessment seriously and to discourage them from focusing only on the content of specific test items as they study for the retake, we might construct two assessment instruments for the same content domain, using one as the initial assessment and the other for retakes (this is what I've typically done in my undergraduate classes). If this strategy is too time consuming to be practical, we might allow students to redo the same assessment a second time and average the two scores earned.

## EVALUATING AN ASSESSMENT AFTER THE FACT: ITEM ANALYSIS

Not only must we assess students' learning and achievement but we must also *assess our assessments.* In the process of scoring students' performance on an assessment, we may discover that some items or tasks simply don't provide the information we had hoped they would. For example, it may become obvious that one item isn't measuring the knowledge or skill we had in mind (a validity problem) and that another is hard to score consistently (a reliability problem that indirectly affects validity as well).

We can't always predict which items are going to be good ones and which are not. For this reason, assessment experts frequently recommend conducting an **item analysis** after an assessment has been administered and scored. Such an analysis typically involves an examination of both the difficulty level and the discriminative power of each item.

🍎 Conduct an item analysis as one source of evidence for the validity and reliability of an assessment instrument.

**Item Difficulty**  The **item difficulty** *(p)* of an assessment item is simply the proportion of students who have responded correctly relative to the total number of students who took the assessment:

$$p = \frac{\text{Number of students getting the item correct}}{\text{Number of students taking the assessment}}$$

This formula yields a number between 0.0 and 1.0. A high *p* value indicates that the item was relatively easy for students; for example, a *p* of .85 means that 85% of the students answered it correctly. A low *p* value indicates that the item was difficult; for example, a *p* of .10 means that only 10% gave a correct response.

On a norm-referenced assessment, *p* values tell us which items have a difficulty level that's best for comparing the performance of individual students. In this situation, ideal *p* values are somewhere between .30 and .70, indicating that the items are difficult enough that some but not all students get them wrong. When, instead, almost all students answer an item in the same

**item analysis** Follow-up analysis of patterns in students' responses to various items in an assessment.

**item difficulty** *(p)* Index reflecting the proportion of students getting a particular assessment item correct.

**item discrimination** *(D)* Index reflecting the relative proportion of high-scoring versus low-scoring students getting a particular assessment item correct.

way—either correctly (a very high $p$) or incorrectly (a very low $p$)—we get little or no information about how students differ from one another.

In contrast, there's no optimal item difficulty for a criterion-referenced assessment. In this case, $p$ values help us determine how effectively students are accomplishing instructional goals and objectives. If most students have responded to an item correctly and we can rule out guessing and other factors that may have contributed to the high success rate, we can conclude that students have mastered the knowledge or skill the item represents. A low $p$ value tells us either that students haven't learned what we're assessing or that the item doesn't accurately reflect what students *have* learned.

**Item Discrimination**   Imagine that you're scoring a 30-item multiple-choice test you've just given your class. You notice that the best students—those who've done well on most of the test—have answered Question 12 incorrectly. You also notice that several students who got very low test scores got Question 12 correct. This doesn't make sense: You'd expect the students who do well on any one item to be the same ones who perform well on the test overall. When the "wrong" students are getting an item correct—that is, when the item inaccurately identifies informed versus uninformed students—we have a problem with item discrimination.

To determine item discrimination *(D)*, we use the approach just described. That is, we identify two groups of students, those who've gotten the highest overall scores and those who've gotten the lowest overall scores, putting about 20 to 30% of the total number of students in each group. We then compare the proportions of students in the two groups getting each item correct using this formula:

$$D = \frac{\text{Number of high-scoring students getting item correct}}{\text{Total number of high-scoring students}} - \frac{\text{Number of low-scoring students getting item correct}}{\text{Total number of low-scoring students}}$$

The $D$ formula yields a number ranging from $-1.0$ to $+1.0$. Positive $D$ values tell us that more high-scoring students than low-scoring students have done well on an item; in other words, the item discriminates between knowledgeable and unknowledgeable students, which is exactly what we want. In contrast, negative $D$ values reflect circumstances similar to the situation with our hypothetical Question 12: Low-scoring students answered the item correctly, but high-scoring students didn't. A negative $D$ is often a sign that something's wrong with the item; perhaps it misleads knowledgeable students to choose what was intended to be an incorrect response, or perhaps we've marked an incorrect answer on the answer key.

Let's return to an assumption we made in the Question 12 situation: The students who do well on any single item should be the same ones who perform well overall. Here we're talking about *internal consistency reliability,* the extent to which different parts of an assessment instrument all measure more or less the same thing. However, when the items or tasks on an assessment instrument are all designed to measure very *different* things—as is often true for performance assessments—$D$ values are less helpful in evaluating an item's effectiveness.

Follow up on negative $D$ values; for example, disregard performance on items that high-achieving students have consistently responded to incorrectly and then recalculate students' overall scores.

Many teachers save good assessment items for use on future occasions, perhaps putting them in an appropriately labeled document or folder on their computer. As teachers accumulate items over the years, they eventually have a large enough collection that they don't have to use any one item very often.

Save good test questions and assessment tasks for use in future years; take precautions to prevent students from getting unauthorized access to them.

## USING DIGITAL TECHNOLOGIES IN CLASSROOM ASSESSMENTS

Thanks to recent advances in both hardware and software, technology now makes ongoing assessments of students' progress and achievement increasingly easy and effective. Following are several helpful technology-based resources and strategies to keep in mind.

**Online Resources for Formative Assessment**    Extensive online resources are currently available to facilitate administration and interpretation of formative assessments, especially for key skills in literacy, math, and science. Following are several noteworthy examples:

- AIMSweb (www.aimsweb.com)
- DIBELS (Dynamic Indicators of Basic Early Literacy Skills; dibels.uoregon.edu)
- mCLASS (www.wirelessgeneration.com/assessment/mclass)
- Accelerated Reader (www.renlearn.com/ar)
- Diagnoser (depts.washington.edu/huntlab/diagnoser or www.diagnoser.com)

Such resources provide many short formative assessments that can help us regularly monitor students' progress with respect to important instructional goals and standards and individualize instruction accordingly. Some of them provide means through which we can immediately enter students' responses onto a handheld digital device, such as a tablet computer or personal digital assistant (PDA); others present short assessments that students themselves complete on a laptop or desktop computer. The programs keep track of students' performance over time and, at our request, can quickly generate reports and graphs regarding both individual students and an entire class. Thus they're especially useful in two strategies mentioned earlier in the chapter: response to intervention and curriculum-based measurement.

**Templates and Management Systems for Teacher-Developed Assessments**
Certainly we can use word processing software to create paper–pencil assessments. But some online resources and software programs now enable us to create electronic alternatives to paper and pencil—alternatives that the programs will also score for us. An example is Quia (www. quia.com/web), where we can create tests and quizzes using a variety of traditional paper–pencil item formats (e.g., multiple-choice, true–false, short-answer) and, if we like, include graphics or audio messages in one or more items. Students take an assessment on the computer and get immediate feedback once they've completed it; the website also records students' scores in a class database for us. In using resources such as Quia, we must of course, remember that they're limited largely to assessment tasks with clear-cut right and wrong responses, and they may not be suitable for students who have limited computer skills or for some other reason find computers intimidating.

**Electronic Essay Graders**    A handful of software programs can quickly evaluate certain qualities of students' written work; examples are Latent Semantic Analysis (LSA) (lsa.colorado. edu) and T. A. Toolbar (tatoolbar.com). Such programs provide quick analyses of students' electronically written essays, short stories, and other compositions—whether students have used plausible word combinations, appropriate grammatical structures, and the like. Most word processing software programs also provide this service to some degree through grammar checkers. Certainly we shouldn't let these programs replace us in evaluating students' written work; ultimately only *we* can reasonably evaluate the accuracy, organization, and logic of what students have written. However, when students use the programs for formative assessment purposes, they gain substantive feedback that can help them improve the quality of their writing (Russell, 2010).

**Strategies for Facilitating Self-Assessment and Peer Feedback**    The electronic essay graders just described are probably most useful as *self*-assessment tools. Other digital technologies can also enhance students' self-assessment abilities. For example, class websites provide a good mechanism through which students can voluntarily upload early drafts of their work in order to get their peers' constructive feedback and suggestions. And consider the possible ways in which we might use a video camera or a laptop computer with a built-in video recorder. For instance, we might videotape a student's execution of a complex behavior and have the student apply certain criteria in self-evaluating the performance (Stokes, Luiselli, Reed, & Fleming, 2010). And at one middle school, students designed and built small models of wooden bridges, then videotaped their bridges as they placed a brick on top; analyzing the videos frame by frame, they could detect possible flaws in their bridge design (Warschauer, 2011).

Consider how you might use technology to help students assess themselves and give their classmates constructive feedback.

# Taking Student Diversity into Account in Classroom Assessments

As we've seen, standardization of assessment instruments and procedures is important for fairness, reliability, and (indirectly) validity in our assessment results. Yet standardization has a downside: It limits our ability to accommodate students' diverse backgrounds and needs, capitalize on their individual strengths, and help them compensate for areas of weakness.

Standardization in classroom assessment practices is essential if, for some reason, we need to compare a student's performance to that of others. But in many other situations—for example, when we're trying to ascertain an appropriate starting point for instruction or specific weaknesses that each student needs to address—standardization is less critical. In some instances, in fact, we may find that the best way of assessing one student's learning is a relatively *ineffective* way of assessing another's.

## ACCOMMODATING GROUP DIFFERENCES

Let's remind ourselves of a few commonly observed differences, also remembering that these are only *average* differences:

- Boys tend to talk more in class than girls do.
- Girls tend to work harder on classroom assignments than boys do.
- Many students who have grown up in mainstream Western culture place high value on individual achievement, but those from some other cultures are more accustomed to working as a group than to working alone.
- Many students brought up in mainstream Western culture are accustomed to showing others what they know and can do, but students from some cultural backgrounds are accustomed to practicing skills in private until they've achieved mastery.
- English language learners need considerable time—perhaps five to seven years—to master the levels of English vocabulary and syntax necessary to fully understand and learn from English-based instruction.
- Some students from low-income families lack adequate nutrition and health care to perform their best at school.
- Students at risk for academic failure may perceive academic subject matter to have little relevance to their own lives.

All these factors may, of course, affect students' ability to learn and achieve in the classroom. But they may also affect how students perform on our informal and formal assessments *independently* of their learning and achievement. This is just one of the many reasons that we should consider multiple assessments—as well as several different kinds of assessments—to assign grades and make other important decisions (e.g., Haywood & Lidz, 2007; Spinelli, 2008; Sternberg, 2005). In addition, we should scrutinize our assessment tasks to be sure that they don't unfairly put some students at a disadvantage because of diversity in their life experiences—a disadvantage known as *cultural bias*. Ultimately our assessment practices must be fair and equitable for students of all groups and backgrounds.

## ACCOMMODATING STUDENTS WITH SPECIAL NEEDS

In the United States, the Individuals with Disabilities Education Act (IDEA) mandates that schools make appropriate accommodations for students with physical, mental, social, or emotional disabilities. This mandate applies not only to instruction but to assessment practices as well. Consequently, we may sometimes have to disregard our concern about standardization so that we can gain more *valid* assessments of what students with certain disabilities know and can do. For example, we may have to develop student-specific summative assessments for students whose individualized education programs (IEPs) identify instructional goals different from those of their peers. Suggestions for additional accommodations for students with special needs are presented in Table 14.5.

You can find more information about these differences in Chapter 2 and Chapter 4.

Use assessment tasks that are sufficiently diverse in nature to give all students have numerous opportunities to show what they have learned.

Chapter 15 provides more information about cultural bias.

Chapter 5 provides details about IDEA; it also identifies specific categories of special needs that fall within the five general categories listed in Table 14.5.

# STUDENTS IN INCLUSIVE SETTINGS

**TABLE 14.5 • Using Classroom Assessments with Students Who Have Special Educational Needs**

| CATEGORY | CHARACTERISTICS YOU MIGHT OBSERVE | SUGGESTED STRATEGIES |
|---|---|---|
| Students with specific cognitive or academic difficulties | • Poor listening, reading, and/or writing skills<br>• Inconsistent performance due to off-task behaviors (for some students with learning disabilities or ADHD)<br>• Difficulty processing specific kinds of information<br>• Higher than average test anxiety | • Make paper–pencil instruments easy to read and respond to; for instance, let students use word processing software to self-check written essays, space test items far apart, and have students respond to multiple-choice items directly on their test papers rather than on separate answer sheets.<br>• If appropriate for the disability, provide extra time for students to complete assessment tasks and/or minimize reliance on literacy skills (e.g., read aloud paper–pencil test items and have students respond orally).<br>• When students have a limited attention span, break lengthy assignments into several shorter tasks.<br>• Let students take tests in a quiet place (e.g., the school's resource room)<br>• Provide extra scaffolding to guide students' efforts; give explicit directions about what students are expected to do.<br>• Be sure students are motivated to do their best but not overly anxious.<br>• Score responses separately for content and quality of writing.<br>• Look at students' errors for clues about specific cognitive processing difficulties.<br>• Use informal assessments to confirm or disconfirm the results of formal assessments. |
| Students with social or behavioral problems | • Inconsistent performance on classroom assessments due to off-task behaviors or lack of motivation (for some students) | • Make modifications in assessment procedures as necessary (see the strategies just presented for students with specific cognitive or academic difficulties).<br>• Use informal assessments (e.g., observations of behavior) to confirm or disconfirm the results of formal assessments. |
| Students with general delays in cognitive and social functioning | • Slow learning and cognitive processing<br>• Limited, if any, reading skills<br>• Poor listening skills | • Be very explicit and concrete about what you're asking students to do.<br>• Tailor any written assessment items to students' reading levels.<br>• Use performance assessments that require little reading or writing.<br>• Allow considerable time for students to complete assigned tasks. |
| Students with physical or sensory challenges | • Mobility problems (for some students with physical challenges)<br>• Tendency to tire easily (for some students with physical challenges)<br>• Less developed language abilities (for some students with hearing loss) | • Use written rather than oral assessments (for students with hearing loss).<br>• Minimize reliance on visual materials (for students with visual impairments).<br>• Use appropriate technology to facilitate students' performance.<br>• Provide extra time for students to complete assessments.<br>• Limit assessments to short time periods, and give frequent breaks.<br>• Use simple language if students have language difficulties. |
| Students with advanced cognitive development | • Greater ability to perform exceptionally complex tasks<br>• Unusual, sometimes creative responses to assessment tasks<br>• Tendency to hide giftedness to avoid possible ridicule by peers (in some students) | • Use performance assessments to assess complex activities.<br>• Establish scoring criteria that allow for unusual and creative responses.<br>• Provide opportunities for students to demonstrate their achievements privately, especially if they're concerned that peers might disapprove of their exceptional ability level. |

Sources: Barkley, 2006; Beirne-Smith, Patton, & Kim, 2006; D. Y. Ford & Harris, 1992; N. Gregg, 2009; R. L. Johnson et al., 2009; B. J. Lovett, 2010; Mercer & Pullen, 2005; D. P. Morgan & Jenson, 1988; Piirto, 1999; Sireci, Scarpati, & Li, 2005; Stein & Krishnan, 2007; Turnbull, Turnbull, & Wehmeyer, 2010; Whitaker Sena et al., 2007.

# 14 What Have You Learned?

Ongoing assessment of students' progress is—and *must* be—a critical part of our role as teachers. We now return to the chapter's learning outcomes as a way of revisiting key ideas about classroom assessment.

■ **14.1: Describe the various forms that classroom assessment can take and the various purposes it can serve for teachers and students.** In general, *assessment* is a process of observing a sample of students' behavior and drawing inferences about their knowledge and abilities. It can take any number of forms: It might be formative or summative, informal or formal, paper–pencil or performance based, traditional or authentic, criterion-referenced or norm-referenced. Occasionally it takes the form of a standardized test, but far more often it consists of a teacher-development instrument or procedure. Classroom assessments serve a variety of interrelated purposes—perhaps to guide instructional decision making, determine students' achievement levels at the end of instruction, evaluate the quality of instruction, diagnose learning and performance problems, or promote students' short- and long-term learning and development. Regardless of our primary purpose in assessing students' knowledge and skills, we must remember that the nature of our assessment instruments will give students messages about what their learning priorities should be and how they should think about and study classroom subject matter. Not only is assessment closely interconnected with instruction, but in a very real sense it *is* instruction.

Evaluate and apply your knowledge related to this learning outcome in MyEducationLab™.

■ **14.2: Explain how you might enhance students' learning through formative assessments and other classroom assessment practices.** Formative assessments are those that occur before or during instruction in order to (1) guide instructional decision making and (2) facilitate students' progress toward instructional goals. To be useful, formative assessments must closely reflect the subject matter to be mastered—that is, they should have content validity—and yield information about what students currently can and can't do. One key strategy is to construct a rubric that identifies the characteristics and components of desired performance; such a rubric provides clear targets toward which to shoot. To most effectively promote students' learning and achievement over the long run, we should regularly include students in the assessment process—for example, by soliciting their ideas about evaluation criteria and by having them constructively critique their own and others' work.

Evaluate and apply your knowledge related to this learning outcome in MyEducationLab™.

■ **14.3: Define and apply four important RSVP characteristics of good assessments: reliability, standardization, validity, and practicality.** As we identify our classroom assessment tasks and procedures, we should keep four characteristics in mind, especially when conducting summative assessments. First, a good assessment is *reliable,* yielding consistent results regardless of the circumstances in which we administer and score it. Second, it is *standardized,* in the sense that it has similar content and

is administered and scored in a similar manner for everyone (excepting students who have certain extenuating circumstances). Third, it is *valid,* in that it's an accurate reflection of the knowledge or skills we're trying to assess. And fourth, it is *practical,* staying within reasonable costs and time constraints. No matter how well planned and executed, however, any single assessment almost invariably has limitations with respect to one or more of these characteristics. According, we must think of our classroom assessments as useful tools—but *imperfect* tools at best—that can guide us in our classroom decision making.

Evaluate and apply your knowledge related to this learning outcome in MyEducationLab™.

■ **14.4: Explain how you might conduct informal assessments, paper–pencil assessments, and performance assessments to assess students' learning and achievement.** We can sometimes assess achievement informally, perhaps by simply observing what students do and say in ongoing school activities. Informal assessment is flexible and requires little or no advance planning, but unfortunately it doesn't give us a representative sample of what students have learned, and our judgments will inevitably be biased by our existing beliefs about various students.

Whenever we must draw firm conclusions about what students have and haven't achieved—for example, when we assign final grades—we should base our conclusions largely on formal assessments that are reasonably valid and reliable. Especially important in this context is *content validity*: Our assessment tasks should provide a representative sample of what students have accomplished relative to instructional goals and objectives.

Paper–pencil assessment tasks take a variety of forms; for instance, they might be multiple-choice questions, word problems, or essays. Different formats are suitable for assessing different instructional goals, and each format has advantages and disadvantages. Performance assessment tasks are often more appropriate for assessing complex achievements that require the integration of many skills, and accomplishment of some instructional goals can be assessed *only* through direct observation of what students can physically do. Paper–pencil tasks and performance tasks alike yield more valid and reliable results when students have a clear understanding of what they're supposed to do and when we evaluate students' responses as objectively as possible.

Several additional strategies can, in one way or another, impact the quality of classroom assessments. First, we must be sure that students have some test-taking know-how, or test-wiseness; for instance, they should have some sense of how to manage their time in any formal assessment task. Second, we should keep students' anxiety at productive, facilitative levels—for example, by emphasizing that learning is an ongoing process and inevitably involves making mistakes along the way. Third, our assessment practices must allow leeway for students to take the risks so essential for the pursuit of challenging topics and activities. Finally, after we've developed and used a particular assessment, an item analysis can help us determine whether the assessment results are reasonably representative of what students have learned.

Many recent technological innovations can support and enhance our assessment of students' ongoing academic learning and achievement levels. Some online resources offer brief, formative measures of key literacy, math, and science skills. Some software programs and websites provide templates and scoring systems that make the use of electronic paper–pencil-like quizzes easier and more expedient; other programs and websites enable students to self-evaluate certain qualities of their written work. And video cameras provide a means through which we and our students can more closely examine students' progress toward mastering complex physical skills.

Evaluate and apply your knowledge related to this learning outcome in MyEducationLab™.

■ **14.5: Describe individual and group differences that have implications for classroom assessment practices.** Although

standardization of assessment instruments and procedures is important for fairness and reliability, it has a downside: It limits our ability to accommodate students' diverse characteristics, backgrounds, and abilities. Standardization is essential when we need to compare students' performances to one another in a norm-referenced manner. It's less important when we're trying to ascertain appropriate starting points for instruction or specific student weaknesses that need to be addressed, and it can sometimes be counterproductive when we're working with students who have disabilities.

Of the four RSVP characteristics, validity is the most critical one, and we can typically get a better handle on what students know and can do when we flexibly and open-mindedly assess their knowledge and skills in multiple ways.

Evaluate and apply your knowledge related to this learning outcome in MyEducationLab™.

# Practice for Your Licensure Exam

## Pick and Choose

Knowing that frequent paper–pencil quizzes will encourage students to study and review class material regularly, Mr. Bloskas tells his middle school science students that they will have a quiz every Friday. As a first-year teacher, he has had little experience developing test questions; thus, he decides to use the questions in the test-item manual that accompanies the class textbook. The night before the first quiz, Mr. Bloskas selects 30 multiple-choice and true–false items from the manual, making sure they cover the specific topics he has addressed in class.

Mr. Bloskas's students complain that the questions are "picky." As he looks carefully at his quiz, he realizes they are right: The quiz measures nothing more than memorization of trivial details. So when he prepares the second quiz, Mr. Bloskas casts the test-item manual aside and writes two essay questions that ask students to apply principles they have studied to new, real-life situations.

The following Friday, students complain even more loudly about the second quiz: "This is too hard!" "We never studied this stuff!" "I liked the first quiz better!" Later, as Mr. Bloskas scores the essays, he's appalled to discover how poorly his students have performed. "Back to the publisher's picky test items," he tells himself.

1. **Constructed-response question:**

    When identifying classroom assessment tasks, teachers must be sure that the tasks have validity, especially *content validity*.

    a. Compare the content validity of Mr. Bloskas's two quizzes.

    b. Describe an approach Mr. Bloskas might use to create quizzes that have reasonable content validity for his classes.

2. **Multiple-choice question:**

    The alternatives below present four possible explanations for the students' negative reactions to the second quiz. Drawing on contemporary theories of learning and motivation, choose the most likely explanation.

    a. Multiple-choice and true–false items are more likely than essay questions to enhance students' sense of self-determination.

    b. Learners are most likely to behave and study in ways that they expect will lead to reinforcement.

    c. Multiple-choice and true–false items are apt to foster mastery goals, whereas essay questions are more likely to foster performance goals.

    d. Multiple-choice and true–false items assess information in working memory, whereas essay questions are more apt to assess information in long-term memory.

---

**PRAXIS** Go to Appendix C, "Matching Book and MyEducationLab™ to the Praxis Principles of Learning and Teaching Tests," to discover sections of this chapter that may be especially applicable to the Praxis tests.

# 15 Summarizing Students' Achievement and Abilities

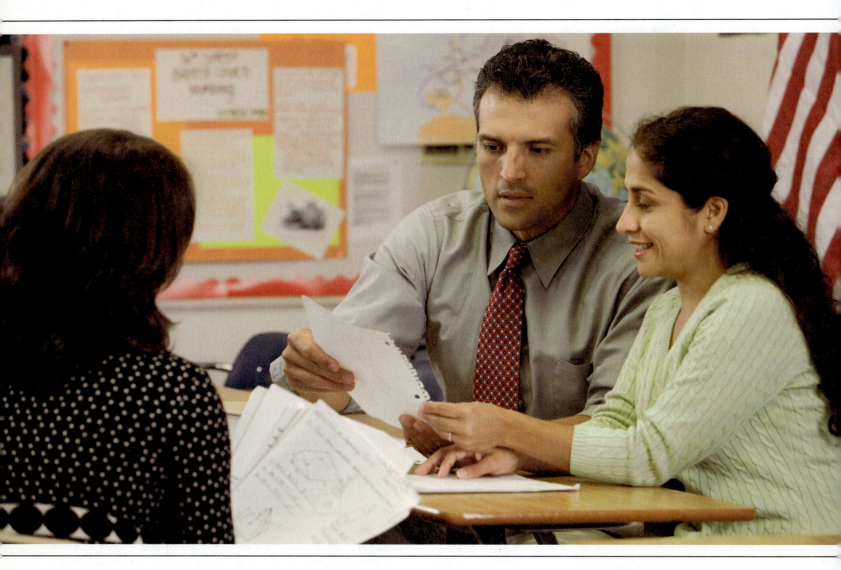

## LEARNING OUTCOMES

**15.1:** Describe the nature, advantages, and disadvantages of three types of test scores: raw scores, criterion-referenced scores, and norm-referenced scores.

**15.2:** Identify important guidelines to follow in summarizing students' achievement with final grades and portfolios.

**15.3:** Describe four general kinds of standardized tests, and explain how you might appropriately use and interpret these tests.

**15.4:** Explain how high-stakes testing and accountability practices can affect instruction and classroom

learning, and suggest several strategies for maximizing the benefits of these practices.

**15.5:** Explain how you might accommodate cultural and linguistic diversity and special educational needs in your efforts to summarize students' achievement.

**15.6:** Distinguish between the circumstances in which you should and should *not* reveal students' assessment results, and explain how you can effectively communicate these results to students and parents.

## CASE STUDY: B IN HISTORY

Twelve-year-old Ellie is the top student in Ms. Davidson's sixth-grade class. She is bright, motivated, and conscientious about completing her classwork, and she has consistently earned straight As on report cards in previous years.

At the end of the school day one Friday, Ms. Davidson tells her class, "As you all know, our first-quarter grading period ended last week. Today I have your report cards for you to take home to your parents. I'm especially proud of one student who always puts forth her best effort, and her grades are almost perfect." She smiles at Ellie with obvious affection and hands her a report card. "Here you are. Just one B, Ellie, in history. I'm sure you'll be able to bring it up to an A next quarter."

Despite the praise, Ellie is devastated. The B has blindsided her; she had no idea it was coming. Embarrassed beyond words, she successfully fights back tears but looks down at her desk while Ms. Davidson distributes the other report cards. When the final school bell rings, Ellie quickly gathers her backpack and heads out the door, forgoing the usual after-school good-byes to her friends.

- Ellie's parents are unlikely to be concerned about her single B; they're more worried about Ellie's younger brother, a second grader who still can't read and probably has an undiagnosed learning disability. Why, then, might Ellie be so upset? Suggest at least two possible explanations.
- Was it appropriate for Ms. Davidson to announce Ellie's grades to the class? Why or why not?

---

Although Ellie undoubtedly knows that she has made occasional errors on history assessments, she apparently hasn't been aware of how those errors might add up to a B rather than an A. And with her past straight-A record, she has set an extremely high standard for herself. Only perfection is good enough—an unrealistic standard held by perhaps 25% of high-achieving sixth graders (Parker, 1997). In addition, Ms. Davidson has announced Ellie's imperfection to the entire class. As a young adolescent, Ellie isn't sure which is worse: that her peers know she has earned the highest grades in the class or that they know she's *not* perfect in history. Not only does Ms. Davidson's announcement make Ellie extremely uncomfortable, but it also violates Ellie's right to confidentiality. In fact, as we'll discover later in the chapter, making a student's grades public, as Ms. Davidson does, is illegal, at least in the United States.

As teachers, we must eventually determine what students have accomplished during an academic term or school year. As we do so, we must keep the four RSVP characteristics of good assessment in mind. In particular, any overall indicator of achievement should be *reliable*, reflecting a consistent pattern of achievement rather than a rare, chance occurrence. It should also be *standardized*: Except for extenuating circumstances (e.g., for some students with disabilities), the same assessment criteria should apply to everyone. In addition, any summary of achievement should be *valid*; that is, it should accurately reflect what students have learned and achieved. Finally, it must be *practical* in terms of the time and effort it requires.

Our first order of business in this chapter will be to consider how we might summarize students' performance on a single assessment instrument. After that, we'll consider ways to summarize students' achievement on a broader scale.

# Summarizing the Results of a Single Assessment

On some occasions we might find it appropriate to describe in detailed written form how a student has performed on a particular assessment. But such an approach for every student and every assessment would be extremely time consuming—a significant practicality issue. More often,

**raw score**  Assessment score based solely on the number or point value of correctly answered items.

**criterion-referenced score**  Assessment score that specifically indicates what a student knows or can do.

**norm-referenced score**  Assessment score that indicates how a student's performance compares with the performance of others.

**norms**  In assessment, data regarding the typical performance of various groups of students on a standardized test or other norm-referenced measure of a particular characteristic or ability.

**grade-equivalent score**  Test score matching a particular student's performance with the average performance of students at a certain grade level.

**age-equivalent score**  Test score matching a particular student's performance with the average performance of students of a certain age.

then, we'll need to have some easy way of summarizing students' performance on individual assessments, perhaps using numbers or letter grades. To simplify our discussion, we'll focus largely on numbers, which we'll call *scores*. The scores on individual assessments, whether teacher-developed instruments or standardized tests, typically take one of three forms: raw scores, criterion-referenced scores, and norm-referenced scores.

## RAW SCORES

A raw score is a score based solely on the number or percentage of points earned or items answered correctly. For example, a student who correctly answers 15 items on a 20-item multiple-choice test might get a score of 75%. A student who gets 3 points, 5 points, and 8 points on two essay questions and one performance task, respectively, might get an overall score of 16. Raw scores are easy to calculate, and they appear to be easy to understand. But in fact, we sometimes have trouble knowing what raw scores really mean. Are scores of 75% and 16 good scores or bad ones? Without knowing what kinds of tasks an assessment includes, we have no easy way of interpreting a raw score.

## CRITERION-REFERENCED SCORES

As you might guess, criterion-referenced scores and norm-referenced scores are used, respectively, with criterion-referenced and norm-referenced assessments. More specifically, a criterion-referenced score indicates what students have achieved in relation to specific instructional objectives or content area standards. Some criterion-referenced scores are either–or scores indicating that a student has mastered or not mastered a skill, met or not met an objective, or passed or failed a unit. Figure 15.1 illustrates this approach in a beginning swimming class. Other criterion-referenced scores indicate various levels of competence or achievement. For example, Figure 15.2 presents a rubric that provides one-to-five rating scales for six possible criteria for grading students' written work. Depending on the purpose of the assessment, a teacher might use all of them—perhaps weighing some more heavily than others—or just one or two of them—perhaps using only "Ideas and Content" and "Organization" for essays in a history class assessment.

## NORM-REFERENCED SCORES

A norm-referenced score is derived by comparing a student's performance on an assessment with the performance of others—perhaps that of classmates or perhaps that of students in a nationwide *norm group*. The scores for the comparison group comprise the norms for the assessment. A norm-referenced score tells us little about what a student specifically knows and can do; instead, it tells us whether a student's performance is typical or unusual for his or her age or grade level.

Many published standardized tests yield norm-referenced scores. In some cases the scores are derived by comparing a student's performance with that of students at a variety of grade or age levels; such comparisons give us grade- or age-equivalent scores. In other cases the scores are based on comparisons only with students of the *same* age or grade; these comparisons give us either percentile scores or standard scores.

### GRADE-EQUIVALENT AND AGE-EQUIVALENT SCORES

Imagine that Shawn takes a standardized test, the Reading Achievement Test (RAT). He gets 46 of the 60 test items correct; thus 46 is his raw score. We turn to the norms reported in the test manual and find the average raw scores for students at different grade and age levels, shown in Figure 15.3. Shawn's raw score of 46 is the same as the average score of eleventh graders in the norm group, so he has a grade-equivalent score of 11. His score is also halfway between the average score of 16-year-old and 17-year-old students, so he has an age-equivalent score of about 16 ¹/₂. Shawn is 13 years old and in the eighth grade and so has obviously done well on the RAT.

In general, grade- and age-equivalent scores are determined by matching a student's raw score to that of a particular grade or age level in the norm group. A student who performs as well as the average second grader on a reading test will get a grade-equivalent score of 2, regardless of the student's actual grade level. A student who earns the same raw score as the average 10-year-old on a physical fitness test will get an age-equivalent score of 10, regardless of whether that student is 5, 10, or 15 years old.

Grade- and age-equivalent scores are frequently used because they seem so simple and straightforward. But they have a serious drawback: They give us no idea of the typical *range* of performance for students at a particular grade or age level. For example, a raw score of 34 on the RAT gives us a grade-equivalent score of 8, but obviously not all eighth graders will get raw scores of exactly 34. It's possible (and in fact quite likely) that many eighth graders will get raw scores several points above or below 34—yielding grade-equivalent scores of 9 or 7, perhaps even 10 or higher, or 6 or lower. Yet grade-equivalent scores are often used inappropriately as a standard for performance: Parents, school personnel, government officials, and the public at large may believe that *all* students should perform at grade level on an achievement test. Given that students' abilities vary considerably in most classrooms, this goal is virtually impossible to meet.

**FIGURE 15.1 Example of a criterion-referenced checklist rubric in a beginning swimming class**

**Springside Parks and Recreation Department Beginner Swimmer Class**

Students must demonstrate proficiency in each of the following:

- ☐ Jump into chest-deep water
- ☐ Hold breath under water for 8 seconds
- ☐ Float in prone position for 10 seconds
- ☐ Glide in prone position with flutter kick
- ☐ Float on back for 10 seconds
- ☐ Glide on back with flutter kick
- ☐ Demonstrate crawl stroke and rhythmic breathing while standing in chest-deep water
- ☐ Show knowledge of basic water safety rules

**FIGURE 15.2 Example of a criterion-referenced rating-scale rubric for summarizing the quality of high school students' writing samples**

| Score | Ideas and Content | Organization | Voice | Word Choice | Sentence Fluency | Conventions |
|---|---|---|---|---|---|---|
| 5 | • Clear, focused topic.<br>• Relevant and accurate supporting details. | • Clear intro and body and satisfying conclusion.<br>• Thoughtful transitions clearly show how ideas are connected.<br>• Sequencing is logical and effective. | • Tone furthers purpose and appeals to audience.<br>• Appropriately individual and expressive. | • Words are specific and accurate.<br>• Language and phrasing is natural, effective, and appropriate. | • Sentence construction produces natural flow and rhythm. | • Grammar and usage are correct and contribute to clarity and style. |
| 3 | • Broad topic.<br>• Support is generalized or insufficient. | • Recognizable beginning, middle, and end.<br>• Transitions often work well; sometimes connections between ideas are fuzzy.<br>• Sequencing is functional. | • Tone is appropriate for purpose and audience.<br>• Not fully engaged or involved. | • Words are adequate and support the meaning.<br>• Language is general but functional. | • Sentences are constructed correctly. | • Grammar and usage mistakes do not impede meaning. |
| 1 | • Unclear topic.<br>• Lacking or irrelevant support. | • No apparent organization.<br>• Lack of transitions.<br>• Sequencing is illogical. | • Not concerned with audience or fails to match purpose.<br>• Indifferent or inappropriate. | • Improper word choice/usage makes writing difficult to understand.<br>• Language is vague or redundant. | • Sentences are choppy, incomplete, or unnatural. | • Grammar and usage mistakes distract the reader or impede meaning. |

*Source:* From *Breaking Ranks II: Strategies for Leading High School Reform.* Copyright © by the National Association of Secondary School Principals (NASSP), p. 103. Reprinted with permission. For more information on NASSP products and services to promote excellence in middle level and high school leadership, visit www.nassp.org.

**FIGURE 15.3** Hypothetical norm-group data for the Reading Achievement Test (RAT)

| Norms for Grade Levels | | Norms for Age Levels | |
|---|---|---|---|
| Grade | Average Raw Score | Age | Average Raw Score |
| 5 | 19 | 10 | 18 |
| 6 | 25 | 11 | 24 |
| 7 | 30 | 12 | 28 |
| 8 | 34 | 13 | 33 |
| 9 | 39 | 14 | 37 |
| 10 | 43 | 15 | 41 |
| 11 | 46 | 16 | 44 |
| 12 | 50 | 17 | 48 |

## PERCENTILE RANKS

A percentile rank (sometimes simply called a percentile) is the percentage of people at the *same* age or grade level getting a raw score less than or equal to the student's raw score. To illustrate, let's once again consider Shawn's performance on the RAT. Because Shawn is in the eighth grade, we would turn to the eighth-grade norms in the RAT test manual. If we discover that a raw score of 46 is at the 98th percentile for eighth graders, we know that Shawn has done as well as or better than 98% of eighth graders in the norm group. Similarly, a student getting a percentile rank of 25 has performed better than 25% of the norm group, and a student getting a score at the 60th percentile has done better than 60%. It's important to note that a percentile ranks refers to a percentage of *people*, not to the percentage of correct items—a misconception that teacher education students sometimes have.

Percentile ranks are relatively easy to understand and therefore used frequently in reporting test results. But they have a major weakness: They distort actual differences among students. For example, consider the RAT percentile ranks of these four boys:

| Student | Percentile Rank |
|---|---|
| Ernest | 45 |
| Frank | 55 |
| Giorgio | 89 |
| Wayne | 99 |

In *actual achievement*—at least as measured by the RAT—Ernest and Frank are probably very similar to one another even though their percentile ranks are 10 points apart. However, a 10-point difference at the upper end of the scale probably reflects a substantial difference in achievement: Giorgio's percentile rank of 89 tells us that he knows quite a bit, but Wayne's percentile rank of 99 tells us that he knows an exceptional amount.

In general, percentiles tend to *over*estimate differences in the middle range of the characteristic being measured: Scores a few points apart reflect similar achievement or ability. Meanwhile, percentiles *under*estimate differences at the upper and lower extremes: Scores only a few points apart often reflect significant differences in achievement or ability. We can avoid these problems with percentiles by using standard scores.

## STANDARD SCORES

The school nurse measures the heights of the 25 students in Ms. Oppenheimer's third-grade class; these heights are listed on the left side of Figure 15.4. The nurse then creates a graph of the children's heights, shown on the right side of Figure 15.4. Notice that the graph is high in the middle and low at both ends. This shape tells us that most of Ms. Oppenheimer's students are more or less average in height, with only a handful of students being very short (e.g., Pat, Amy, Wil) and just a few others being very tall (e.g., Hal, Roy, Jan).

Many educational and psychological characteristics—including many academic abilities—seem to show roughly the same pattern we see for height: Most people are close to average, with fewer and fewer people being counted as we move farther from the average. This theoretical pattern of educational and psychological characteristics, known as the normal distribution (or normal curve), is shown to the right. Standard scores are based on the normal distribution: Many students have scores in the middle range, and only a few have very high or very low scores.

Before we examine standard scores more closely, we need to understand two numbers used to derive these

**percentile rank (percentile)** Test score indicating the percentage of peers in the norm group getting a raw score less than or equal to a particular student's raw score.

**normal distribution (normal curve)** Theoretical pattern of educational and psychological characteristics in which most individuals score in the middle range and only a few score at either extreme.

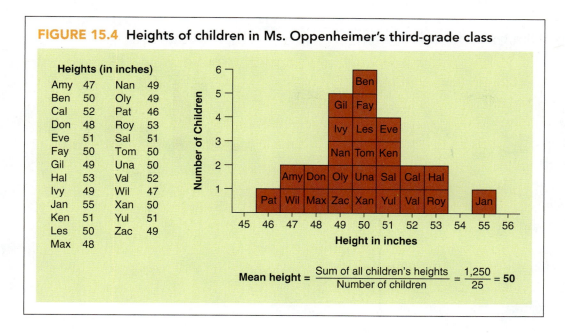

**FIGURE 15.4** Heights of children in Ms. Oppenheimer's third-grade class

**Heights (in inches)**

| Amy | 47 | Nan | 49 |
|-----|----|----|----|
| Ben | 50 | Oly | 49 |
| Cal | 52 | Pat | 46 |
| Don | 48 | Roy | 53 |
| Eve | 51 | Sal | 51 |
| Fay | 50 | Tom | 50 |
| Gil | 49 | Una | 50 |
| Hal | 53 | Val | 52 |
| Ivy | 49 | Wil | 47 |
| Jan | 55 | Xan | 50 |
| Ken | 51 | Yul | 51 |
| Les | 50 | Zac | 49 |
| Max | 48 |     |    |

$$\text{Mean height} = \frac{\text{Sum of all children's heights}}{\text{Number of children}} = \frac{1,250}{25} = 50$$

scores: the mean and the standard deviation. The mean (M) is the *average* of a set of scores: We add all the scores together and divide by the total number of scores (or people) in the set. For example, if we add the heights of all 25 students in Ms. Oppenheimer's class and divide the sum by 25, we get a mean height of 50 inches (see the calculation at the bottom of Figure 15.4).

The standard deviation (SD) indicates the *variability* of a set of scores. A small number tells us that, generally speaking, the scores are close together, and a large number tells us that they're spread far apart. For example, third graders tend to be more similar in height than eighth-grade children; some eighth graders are less than five feet tall, whereas others may be almost six feet tall. The standard deviation for the heights of third-grade children is therefore smaller than the standard deviation for the heights of eighth graders. The formula for calculating a standard deviation is fairly complex; fortunately, we don't need to know the formula in order to understand the role that a standard deviation plays in standard scores.

The mean and standard deviation can be used to divide the normal distribution into several parts, as shown in Figure 15.5. The vertical line in the middle of the curve shows the mean; for a normal distribution, it's both the midpoint and the highest point of the curve. The thinner lines to either side reflect the standard deviation: We count out 1 standard deviation higher and lower than the mean and mark those two spots with vertical lines, and then we count another standard deviation to either side and draw two more lines. When we divide a normal distribution in this way, the percentages of students getting scores in each part are always the same. Approximately two-thirds (68%) get scores within 1 standard deviation of the mean (34% in each direction). As we go farther away from the mean, we find fewer and fewer students, with 28% being between 1 and 2 standard deviations away (14% on each side) and only about 4% being more than 2 standard deviations away (2% at each end).

Now that we better understand the normal distribution and two statistics that describe it, let's return to standard scores. A standard score reflects a person's position in the normal distribution: It tells us how far the person's performance is from the mean in terms of standard deviation units. Unfortunately, not all standard scores use the same scale: Scores used for various tests have different means and standard deviations. Five commonly used standard scores, depicted graphically in Figure 15.6, are the following:

**FIGURE 15.5** A normal distribution divided by the mean and the standard deviation

Learn how to calculate a standard deviation in "Calculating Standard Deviations."

**mean (M)** Mathematical average of a set of scores.

**standard deviation (SD)** Statistic indicating the amount of variability characterizing a set of scores.

**standard score** Test score indicating how far a student's performance is from the mean in terms of standard deviation units.

**FIGURE 15.6** Distributions of five types of standard scores

Figure 5.1 in Chapter 5 shows the distribution of IQ scores broken up by lines that each reflect *one-third* of a standard deviation (5 points). The lines for 85 and 115 are 1 standard deviation from the mean of 100. The lines for 70 and 130 are 2 SDs from the mean.

**IQ score** Score on an intelligence test, determined by comparing a person's performance on the test with that of others in the same age-group; for most tests, it's a standard score with a mean of 100 and a standard deviation of 15.

**ETS score** Standard score with a mean of 500 and a standard deviation of 100.

**stanine** Standard score with a mean of 5 and a standard deviation of 2; always reported as a whole number between 1 and 9.

**NCE score** Standard score with a mean of 50 and a standard deviation of 21.06; an NCE score of 1 equals a percentile rank of 1, and an NCE score of 99 equals a percentile rank of 99.

**z-score** Standard score with a mean of 0 and a standard deviation of 1.

**confidence interval** Range around an assessment score reflecting the amount of error that is likely to be affecting the score's accuracy.

- **IQ scores** are frequently used to report students' performance on intelligence tests. They have a *mean of 100* and, for most tests, a *standard deviation of 15*.

- **ETS scores** are used on tests published by the Educational Testing Service, such as the SAT Reasoning Test and the Graduate Record Examinations (GREs). They have a *mean of 500* and a *standard deviation of 100*. However, no scores fall below 200 or above 800.

- **Stanines** (short for *standard nines*) are often used in reporting standardized achievement test results. They have a *mean of 5* and a *standard deviation of 2*. Because they're always reported as whole numbers, each score reflects a *range* of test performance, indicated by the shaded and nonshaded portions of the upper-right-hand curve in Figure 15.6.

- **NCE scores** (short for *normal-curve-equivalent scores*) are increasingly being used in reporting standardized achievement test results. They have a *mean of 50* and a *standard deviation of 21.06*. However, it isn't possible to get a score of zero or below, nor is it possible to get a score of 100 or above.

- **z-scores** are the standard scores that statisticians most often use. They have a *mean of 0* and a *standard deviation of 1*.

The odd standard deviation for NCE scores (21.06) requires an explanation. It turns out that with this particular standard deviation, an NCE score of 1 is equivalent to a percentile score of 1 and, likewise, an NCE score of 99 is equivalent to a percentile score of 99. And, of course, an NCE score of 50 (being the mean and midpoint of the curve) is also a percentile score of 50. Thus NCE scores have the same general range as percentile ranks.

Typically the publishers of standardized achievement tests report students' test results using two or more types of scores. For example, Figure 15.7 presents a computer printout that lists both stanine scores and percentile ranks for 12-year-old Ingrid in several content domains. The printout is admittedly a very dated one—as we'll see later, contemporary computer-generated reports tend to be much more complex—but its simplicity can better help you see how such scores might be represented. Ingrid's scores reveal average to below-average achievement in spelling and math computation, average to above-average achievement in math concepts, and well-above-average achievement in reading comprehension, science, and social studies. The "national percentile bands" (shown as rows of Xs within some of the green lines)—more commonly called **confidence intervals** or *confidence bands*—reflect the amount of error (due to imperfect reliability) that's likely to be affecting Ingrid's percentile scores.

**FIGURE 15.7** Computer printout revealing 12-year-old Ingrid's scores on standardized achievement tests in several content domains

| | | | NATIONAL PERCENTILE BANDS | | | |
| --- | --- | --- | --- | --- | --- | --- |
| | | | WELL BELOW AVERAGE | BELOW AVERAGE : AVERAGE : ABOVE AVERAGE | WELL ABOVE AVERAGE | |
| | STANINE | PERCENTILE | 1      5      10      20 | 30   40   50   60   70   80 | 90      95      99 | |
| READING COMPREHENSION | 8 | 92 | | | XXXXXXXXXXXXX | |
| SPELLING | 4 | 39 | | XXXXXXXXXXX | | |
| MATH COMPUTATION | 4 | 37 | | XXXXXXXXXX | | |
| MATH CONCEPTS | 5 | 57 | | XXXXXXXXXXX | | |
| SCIENCE | 8 | 90 | | | XXXXXXXXXXXXXX | |
| SOCIAL STUDIES | 7 | 84 | | | XXXXXXXX | |
| | | | 1      5      10      20 | 30   40   50   60   70   80 | 90      95      99 | |

Notice how the numbers at the bottom of the computer printout (1, 5, 10, 20, etc.) are unevenly spaced. Remember a point made earlier about percentile ranks: They overestimate differences near the mean and underestimate differences at the extremes. The uneven spacing is the test publisher's way of showing this fact: It squishes the middle percentile scores closer together and spreads high and low percentile scores farther apart. In this way, the publisher tries to give students and parents an idea about where students' test scores fall in a normal distribution.

Table 15.1 provides a summary of raw scores, criterion-referenced scores, and norm-referenced scores.

*You can learn more about confidence intervals in Appendix B.*

## USING CRITERION-REFERENCED VERSUS NORM-REFERENCED SCORES IN THE CLASSROOM

In most instances criterion-referenced scores communicate what we and our students most need to know: whether instructional goals and content area standards are being achieved. Criterion-referenced scores focus attention on mastery goals and, by showing improvement over time, should enhance students' self-efficacy for learning classroom subject matter. When criterion-referenced

*Use criterion-referenced scores to indicate mastery of specific instructional goals and objectives.*

## COMPARE/CONTRAST

**TABLE 15.1 • Scores Used to Summarize the Results of a Single Assessment**

| TYPE OF SCORE | METHOD OF DETERMINING SCORE | USES | POTENTIAL DRAWBACKS |
| --- | --- | --- | --- |
| Raw score | Counting the number (or calculating a percentage) of correct responses or points earned | Often used in teacher-developed assessment instruments | Scores may be difficult to interpret without knowledge of how performance relates either to a specific criterion or to a norm group. |
| Criterion-referenced score | Comparing performance to one or more criteria or standards for success | Useful when determining whether specific instructional objectives or standards have been achieved | Concrete criteria for assessing mastery of complex skills are sometimes difficult to identify. |
| Grade- or age- equivalent score (norm-referenced) | Equating a student's performance to the average performance of students at a particular grade or age level | Useful when explaining norm-referenced test performance to people who are unfamiliar with standard scores | Scores are frequently misinterpreted (especially by parents), may be inappropriately used as a standard that all students must meet, and are often inapplicable when achievement is being assessed in adolescence or adulthood. |
| Percentile rank (norm-referenced) | Determining the percentage of students at the same age or grade level who obtained the same score or lower scores | Useful when explaining norm-referenced test performance to people who are unfamiliar with standard scores | Scores overestimate differences near the mean and underestimate differences at the extremes. |
| Standard score (norm-referenced) | Determining how far the performance is from the mean (for the age or grade level) in terms of standard deviation units | More accurate in characterizing students' ability differences than grade-equivalent scores, age-equivalent scores, or percentile ranks | Scores are not easily understood by people who don't have some basic knowledge of statistics. |

scores are hard to determine—perhaps because an assessment simultaneously addresses many instructional goals and objectives (something I don't generally recommend)—raw scores are usually the second-best choice for teacher-developed assessments. But we must remember an important point about raw scores: They don't tell us much about what students have and haven't learned.

Norm-referenced scores—in everyday lingo, *grading on the curve*—may occasionally be appropriate if we truly need to know how students have performed relative to one another. For example, we might find these scores helpful when designating first chairs in an instrumental music class (best violinist, best trombone player, etc.) or when choosing the best entries for a regional science fair. We may also need to resort to a norm-referenced approach when assessing complex skills (e.g., writing poetry, demonstrating advanced athletic skills, or critically analyzing scientific research studies) that we can't really describe as "mastered" or "not mastered."

We probably *shouldn't* use norm-referenced scores for teacher-developed assessments on a regular basis, however. Such scores create a competitive situation, because students do well only if their performance surpasses that of their classmates. Thus norm-referenced scores focus students' attention primarily on performance goals rather than on mastery goals and may possibly encourage students to cheat on assessment tasks. Furthermore, the competitive atmosphere that norm-referenced scores create is likely to undermine students' general *sense of community* as a class (E. M. Anderman, Griesinger, & Westerfield, 1998; Brophy, 2004; M.-T. Wang & Holcombe, 2010).

> Use norm-referenced scores only when you truly need to compare various students' performances.

> Chapter 13 describes the many benefits of having a sense of community in the classroom.

# Determining Final Class Grades

Especially in the upper elementary and secondary school years, most schools use letter or number grades to summarize students' overall achievement in various content domains. Such grades have several limitations. First, different teachers use varying criteria to assign grades; for instance, some are more lenient than others, and some stress rote memorization whereas others stress complex cognitive skills. Second, different students may be working to accomplish different instructional goals, especially in classes that include children of diverse backgrounds and needs. Third, typical grading practices promote performance goals rather than mastery goals and may encourage students to go for the "easy A" instead of taking risks. Finally, students under pressure to achieve high grades may resort to cheating (e.g., plagiarizing someone else's work) in order to attain those grades (Cizek, 2003; K. O'Connor, 2011; Pulfrey, Buchs, & Butera, 2011; L. Shepard, Hammerness, Darling-Hammond, & Rust, 2005; S. Thomas & Oldfather, 1997).

Despite their drawbacks, final class grades continue to be the most common method of summarizing students' classroom achievement. The following recommendations can enhance the validity and usefulness of these grades.

  🍎 *Take the job of grading seriously.* Consider these scenarios:
  - A high school math teacher makes numerous errors in calculating students' final grades. As a result, some of his students get lower grades than they've earned.
  - A middle school Spanish teacher asks her teenage son to calculate her students' final grades. Some columns in her gradebook are only for scores on retests, so students who didn't need to retake tests have blanks in these columns. The son treats all blank spaces as zeros and thus gives grades of D or F to some of the highest achievers.

A math teacher who makes mathematical errors? A Spanish teacher who relies on a teenager to determine final grades? Preposterous? No, both scenarios are true stories. Students' final class grades are often the *only* data that appear in their school records, so we must take the time and make the effort to ensure that they're accurate.

Many computer software programs provide electronic gradebooks that can help us with record keeping and grading; most online resources that support class websites (e.g., moodle.org) also include gradebooks. In addition to helping us keep track of a sizable body of assessment information, electronic gradebooks make it easy to keep students continually informed about their performance and progress. We can't use these gradebooks mindlessly, however. For example, if we make errors when entering information or don't take into account the idiosyncrasies of our record-keeping system, we might as well have the Spanish teacher's son calculate our grades for us!

🍏 *Base grades on achievement.* Tempting as it might be to reward well-behaved, cooperative students with good grades and to punish chronic misbehavers with Ds or Fs, grades should ultimately reflect how much students have *learned*. Awarding good grades simply for good behavior may mislead students and their parents to believe that students are making better progress than they really are. And awarding low grades as punishment for disruptive behavior leads students to conclude, perhaps with good reason, that their teacher's grading system is arbitrary and meaningless (Brookhart, 2004; Cizek, 2003; K. O'Connor, 2011; L. Shepard et al., 2005).

🍏 *Base grades on hard data.* Our informal judgments of students' current achievement levels will be imperfect assessments at best, and they can easily be influenced by other things we know about students—for example, how often they misbehave in class and what their past achievement levels have been (Carbonneau & Selig, 2011; Hoge & Coladarci, 1989; J. P. Robinson & Lubienski, 2011). For this reason and also for the sake of our students—who learn more and achieve at higher levels when we tell them what we expect in concrete terms—we should base grades on objective information derived from formal assessments, *not* on subjective impressions of what students appear to know.

🍏 *Use many assessments to determine grades, but don't count everything.* Using multiple assessments to determine final grades can help us compensate for the imperfect reliability and validity of any single assessment task. At the same time, we probably don't want to consider *everything* students do, in part because we want them to feel comfortable taking risks and making mistakes. Thus we may not want to include students' early efforts at new tasks, which are likely to involve considerable trial and error. And, course, many assessments are more appropriately used for formative assessment purposes—to help students learn—than for summative assessment (Frisbie & Waltman, 1992; Nitko & Brookhart, 2011; L. Shepard et al., 2005).

🍏 *Assign criterion-referenced grades unless there is a compelling reason to do otherwise.* Many experts recommend that final grades reflect mastery of classroom subject matter and instructional goals—in other words, that final grades be criterion-referenced. Criterion-referenced grades are especially appropriate during the elementary years: Much of the elementary curriculum consists of basic skills that are either mastered or not mastered, and there's little need to use grades as a basis for comparing students to one another.

The issue becomes more complicated at the secondary level: Students' grades are sometimes used to choose college applicants, award scholarships, and make other comparative decisions. Historically, then, some secondary school teachers have used norm-referenced grades—for instance, giving As to the top 10% of each class, Bs to the next 20%, Cs to the middle 40%, and so on. My personal recommendation is that high school grades be criterion-referenced to the extent that such is possible. The most critical decisions for which grades are used—decisions about promotion and graduation—should be based on students' mastery or nonmastery of the school curriculum, not on their standing relative to others. Furthermore, because different classes of students often differ in ability level, a strictly norm-referenced approach might assign a C grade to a student's performance in one class (e.g., Honors Math), whereas the same performance might warrant an A in another class (e.g., General Math). (Under such circumstances a student striving for a high grade point average would be foolish to enroll in the honors section.) Finally, only a very few students (i.e., the highest achievers) find a norm-referenced grading system motivating; most students quickly resign themselves to achieving at an average level at best (Ames, 1984; Graham & Golen, 1991; Shih & Alexander, 2000; Stipek, 1996).[1]

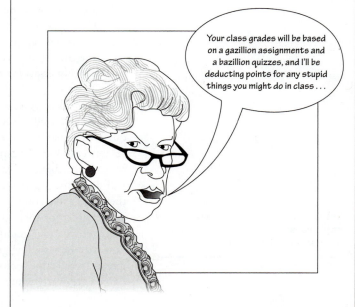

*Your class grades will be based on a gazillion assignments and a bazillion quizzes, and I'll be deducting points for any stupid things you might do in class . . .*

Although overall class grades should be based on multiple sources of data, not everything needs to be graded. Furthermore, students must feel confident that they have some leeway to take risks and make errors.

---

[1]Over the past several decades, teachers have gradually moved from norm-referenced grading (i.e., grading on the curve) to criterion-referenced grading. This focus on mastery of instructional goals and objectives, rather than on comparing students with one another, accounts in part for the increasing grade point averages (i.e., "grade inflation") about which some public figures complain.

When setting up a criterion-referenced grading system, we should determine as concretely as possible what we want each grade to communicate. For example, if we're assigning traditional letter grades, we might use criteria such as the following:

| Grade | Criteria |
|---|---|
| A | The student has a firm command of both basic and advanced knowledge and skills in the content domain. He or she is well prepared for future learning tasks. |
| B | The student has mastered all basic knowledge and skills. Mastery at a more advanced level is evident in some but not all areas. In most respects he or she is ready for future learning tasks. |
| C | The student has mastered basic knowledge and skills but has difficulty with more advanced aspects of the subject matter. He or she lacks a few prerequisites critical for future learning tasks. |
| D | The student has mastered some but not all of the basics in the content domain. He or she lacks many prerequisites for future learning tasks. |
| F | The student shows little or no mastery of instructional objectives and cannot demonstrate the most elementary knowledge and skills. He or she lacks most of the prerequisites essential for success in future learning tasks. (Based on criteria described by Frisbie & Waltman, 1992) |

Only when final grades reflect criteria such as these can they legitimately be used for instructional decision making.

🍏 *Identify a reasonable grading system and stick to it.* Consider this situation:

At the beginning of the school year, Ms. Giroux announces that final class grades will be based entirely on students' quiz scores. But after a few weeks she realizes that if she relies *only* on quiz scores, most students will get a D or F for the semester. To help students boost their grades, she asks them to turn in all their previous homework assignments, which can contribute up to 20 percentage points toward final grades. The students protest loudly and angrily: Thinking there was no reason to keep completed assignments, many students have already discarded them.

If most students are getting Ds and Fs, something's definitely wrong. Perhaps Ms. Giroux's instructional methods aren't as effective as other approaches might be. Perhaps she's moving so quickly through the curriculum that students never have time to master a topic. Perhaps her quizzes reflect unrealistic expectations about what students should be able to do.

As teachers, we can't always anticipate how best to teach a new topic or how well students will perform on particular assessments. Nevertheless, if we want to give students a sense that they have some control over their grades—that is, if we want them to have internal, controllable attributions for their classroom performance—we must tell them early in the school year or semester what our grading criteria will be. In addition, by providing concrete information about how we'll be assigning grades, we avoid unpleasant surprises when students actually receive their grades (recall Ellie's sense of devastation in the opening case study). If we find that our initial criteria are overly stringent, we may need to lighten up in some way, perhaps by adjusting cutoffs or allowing retakes of critical assessments. But we must never change our criteria in midstream in a way that unfairly penalizes some students or imposes additional, unanticipated requirements.

🍏 *Accompany grades with qualitative information about students' performance.* Whether final grades take the form of letters or numbers, final grades are, at best, only general indicators of some *quantity* of what students have learned. Thus it's often helpful to accompany grades with *qualitative* information—for instance, information about students' particular academic strengths, work habits, attitudes, social skills, and unique contributions to the classroom community (e.g., see Figure 15.8). Students and parents alike often find such qualitative feedback just as informative as final class grades—sometimes even more informative. The feedback should be fairly explicit, however; comments such as "A pleasure to have in class" communicate little (Brookhart, 2004, p. 183).

See Chapter 11 for a discussion of how students' attributions influence their motivation and learning.

Explore various grading systems you might use in "Combining Assessment Results to Determine Final Grades."

# CONSIDERING—OR NOT CONSIDERING—OTHER FACTORS IN GRADING

Some educators suggest that students be graded at least partly on the basis of how much they improve, how hard they try, how much extra work they do, or whether they've turned assignments in late (if at all). Assessment experts have weighed in on each of these issues.

**Considering Improvement**    Most motivation theorists stress the importance of focusing students' attention more on their own improvement than on how their performance compares with that of peers. But assessment experts have made two good arguments against basing final grades solely on students' improvement over the course of a semester or school year. First, students who already show accomplishment of some of the year's instructional goals will have less room for improvement than their classmates. Second, when we use improvement as a criterion, students trying to "beat the system" may quickly realize that they can achieve high grades simply by performing as poorly as possible when the school year begins (Airasian, 1994; M. D. Miller, Linn, & Gronlund, 2009; Sax, 2010).

How do we balance what motivation theorists recommend on the one hand with what assessment experts recommend on the other? Following are several possible strategies:

- Assign greater weight to assessments conducted at the end of the semester or school year, after *all* students have had a reasonable opportunity to achieve instructional goals.
- Give students a chance to correct their errors and, in doing so, to demonstrate mastery.
- Administer retakes of assessments, perhaps using items or tasks different from those presented the first time.
- Reinforce improvement in other ways—for instance, with free time or special privileges. (Lester, Lambdin, & Preston, 1997; K. O'Connor, 2011; L. Shepard et al., 2005)

**Considering Effort**    Most assessment experts urge us *not* to base final grades on the amount of effort students appear to exert in their studies. For one thing, students who begin the year already performing at a high level are penalized because they may not have to work as hard as their less knowledgeable classmates. Furthermore, student effort is something we can evaluate only subjectively and imprecisely at best (Brookhart, 2004; K. O'Connor, 2011; L. Shepard et al., 2005).

An alternative is to have students work for individualized instructional goals appropriate for their existing ability levels. Such an approach is workable *if,* when we report students' final grades, we also report the instructional goals on which the grades are based. In fact, this approach is widely used for students with special educational needs, whose goals are described in their individualized education programs (IEPs).

Obviously we enhance students' motivation when we explicitly acknowledge their effort. Some school systems have multidimensional grading systems that allow teachers to assign separate grades to the various aspects of students' classroom performance. Such mechanisms as brief written notes to parents, parent–teacher conferences, and letters of recommendation to colleges provide additional means by which we can describe the multifaceted nature of students' classroom performance.

**Giving Extra Credit**    As a college professor I've occasionally had students appear at my office door, asking—sometimes begging—for an opportunity to improve their grades at the last minute by completing extra-credit projects. My response is invariably *no* for a very good reason: My course grades are based on the extent to which students achieve instructional goals for the course, as determined by their performance on assessments that are the same or equivalent (therefore standardized and fair) for all students. Extra-credit projects assigned to only one or two students (typically those achieving at a low level) are insufficient to demonstrate mastery of the subject matter and aren't standardized for the entire class.

**FIGURE 15.8 Examples of qualitative feedback one second-grade teacher gave her students at the end of the school year**

- To Amanda: You are a good friend to everyone in the class. You look out for people's feelings and work hard to make others feel good.

- To Andrea: You have a beautiful singing voice and are a very animated performer. You show self-confidence in all that you do.

- To Angus: You are always willing to lend a hand to teachers and peers alike. You have practical advice and reasonable solutions to many questions and situations that arise.

- To Charlotte: You are a very thoughtful worker. You always give 100% on everything you do. Your positive attitude and great work ethic are a wonderful addition to the class.

- To Colin: I love your sense of humor. You make me laugh with your great riddles and jokes. The humor in your stories is very creative and keeps your audience wanting to know more about the story.

Most assessment experts recommend that we NOT base grades solely on students' improvement. Observe a strategy for reinforcing improvement separately from achievement in "Cooperative Learning."

  Evaluate students' effort separately from their achievement.

Be sure that any extra-credit assignments relate to instructional goals and are available to all students.

Extra-credit work is occasionally appropriate *provided that* (1) the work relates to instructional goals and (2) all students have the same opportunity to complete it (Padilla-Walker, 2006; L. Shepard et al., 2005). It *isn't* appropriate when its only purpose is to help a failing student earn a passing grade.

**Addressing Lateness and Missing Work**    Certainly we want students to learn to be punctual in submitting assignments, in part because it will be difficult to complete all of their work at the last minute—and they're apt to learn less when they finally do it—and in part because a habit of meeting deadlines will be important for their success in the adult workplace. Nevertheless, students may occasionally have justifiable reasons for a late submission—perhaps an unexpected crisis at home or unanticipated confusion about what an assignment requires.

A few students may consistently *not* turn in assignments, especially ones they've been asked to do outside of class. Some of these students may believe these assignments are pointless and irrelevant to their lives and needs. Others may be reluctant to admit that they don't have the basic knowledge and skills they need to complete the assignments. Still others may have poor self-regulation skills; for example, they may be easily enticed into nonacademic activities once they leave the school building.

With such issues in mind, experts recommend that we *not* take off points for late submissions or grade missing assignments as *zeroes* that enter into our final grade calculations. Remember, final grades should reflect *actual achievement* related to instructional goals and objectives. Strategies such as the following can be more productive:

- Explain why punctuality is important for students' long-term success.
- Solicit students' input about reasonable deadlines for assignments.
- Give students the extra guidance and support they might need to complete assignments in a timely manner.
- If the school grading system allows it, record a student's grade as "Incomplete" and describe the work the student must do in order to get a passing grade.
- Base *all* students' final grades on only a subset of summative assessment results; this final strategy works only if the subset can validly and reliably reflect all instructional goals. (Brookhart, 2004; Nitko & Brookhart, 2011; K. O'Connor, 2011)

## INCLUDING STUDENTS IN THE GRADING PROCESS

Let's return to the opening case study, in which Ellie is blindsided by her B in history. Although Ellie has been informed of her scores on various assessments during the grading period, she apparently hasn't been aware of how those scores would be combined into an overall grade. Ms. Davidson has presumably been tracking Ellie's progress over time, but Ellie herself hasn't been doing so.

In previous chapters we've repeatedly seen the benefits of self-assessment for self-regulation and motivation. In the end, however, we teachers must be the ones to determine students' final grades, as most students are likely to give themselves grades based on what they would *prefer* rather than what they've objectively *earned* (e.g., see Figure 15.9). Yet final grades shouldn't seemingly come out of the blue. Students must know, in advance and in concrete terms, our criteria for assigning grades, and we must frequently update students about their progress toward earning good ones. Under these conditions students *do* have a say in their grades—by working hard to master classroom subject matter.

**FIGURE 15.9**  In her rationale for getting an A for the term, 15-year-old Lexee focuses on effort, punctuality, and class participation rather than on achievement.

I think that I deserve an A+ for this term. I tried my best just some of the grammer things were hard for me so I got a few lower grades. oops! I'll list the other two reasons.
- I got everything in on time.
- I tried to participate as much as possible in class.

# Using Portfolios

portfolio  Collection of a student's work compiled systematically over a lengthy time period.

Whenever we boil down students' achievement into single letter or number grades, we lose valuable information about students' specific strengths and weaknesses, inclinations and disinclinations, and so on. In contrast, portfolios—collections of work systematically collected over a lengthy time period—can capture the complex, multifaceted nature of students' accomplishments and interests. Portfolios might include writing samples, student-constructed objects (e.g., sculptures, inventions), photographs, audiotapes, video recordings, technology-based creations (e.g., PowerPoint presentations, student-authored videogames), or any combination of these. For example, in the excerpt from a kindergarten portfolio shown in Figure 15.10, 6-year-old Meghan and her teacher used photographs to reveal Meghan's emerging math skills.

Traditionally most portfolios have been actual physical entities that include various examples of students' work. But such a collection can sometimes be cumbersome and hard to transport from one place to another. An alternative gaining increasing popularity is an electronic portfolio (sometimes simply called an *e-folio*) in which portfolio contents—writing samples, audiovisual materials, photographs of creations, and so on—are stored and presented via portable electronic storage devices (e.g., CDs, DVDs, or flash drives).

The items included in a portfolio are often called *artifacts*. Students typically decide for themselves which artifacts to include, perhaps with the guidance of a teacher or other mentor. This decision-making process can give students a sense of ownership of their portfolios, enhance their sense of self-determination, and bolster their intrinsic motivation to gain new knowledge and skills.

In addition to specific artifacts, most school portfolios include student reflections that (1) identify the purpose(s) and goals of the portfolio, (2) describe each artifact and the reason(s) it was included, and (3) summarize what the collection of artifacts reveals about the student's achievement. For example, in Figure 15.11, 14-year-old Kurt describes and evaluates the writing samples he has included in a portfolio for his eighth-grade language arts class (his portfolio includes two or more drafts of each piece of writing). Student reflections encourages them to look at and judge their own work in ways that teachers typically do, thereby promoting the self-monitoring and self-evaluation skills so essential for self-regulated learning (Arter & Spandel, 1992; R. S. Johnson, Mims-Cox, & Doyle-Nichols, 2006; Vucko & Hadwin, 2004).

**FIGURE 15.10** In a kindergarten portfolio, Meghan and her teacher included two digital photographs to illustrate Meghan's developing math skills.

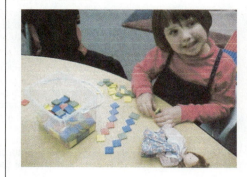

Meghan makes arrangements of six in math.

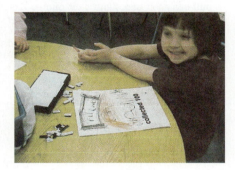

Meghan displays her collection of 100.

## TYPES AND PURPOSES OF PORTFOLIOS

Portfolios take a variety of forms. Following are four types commonly used in school settings:

- *Working portfolio*—Shows competencies up to the present time; is dynamic in content, with new artifacts that show greater proficiency gradually replacing older, less skillful ones.
- *Developmental portfolio*—Includes several artifacts related to a particular set of skills; shows how a student has improved over time.
- *Course portfolio*—Includes assignments and reflections for a single course; typically also includes a summarizing reflection in which the student identifies his or her general accomplishments in the course.
- *Best-work portfolio*—Includes artifacts intended to showcase the student's particular achievements and unique talents. (R. S. Johnson et al., 2006; Spandel, 1997)

These categories aren't necessarily mutually exclusive. For example, a course portfolio might have a developmental component, showing how a student has improved in, say, persuasive writing skills over the school year. And a best-work portfolio may be a work-in-progress for quite some time, thereby having the dynamic nature of a working portfolio.

Some portfolios are most appropriate for formative assessment, whereas others are appropriate for summative assessment. Developmental portfolios can show whether students are making reasonable progress toward long-term instructional goals; as such, they're often best used for formative assessment. Best-work portfolios are better suited for summative assessment; for example, they might be used to communicate students' final accomplishments to parents, school administrators, college admissions officers, or potential employers.

**electronic portfolio (e-folio)**
Portfolio compiled and available for inspection on a CD, DVD, flash drive, or other electronic storage mechanism.

**FIGURE 15.11**  In this self-reflection 14-year-old Kurt explains why he has chosen certain pieces to include in his eighth-grade language arts portfolio.

SELF-EVALUATION

The three pieces of writing in my portfolio that best represent who I am are: 1) "Author Ben Hoff," which is a story in the language of Ben Hoff; 2) "Quotes from The Tao of Pooh"; and 3) "Discrimination."

What "Author Ben Hoff" shows about me as a learner or a writer is that I am able to analyze and absorb the types and styles of an author and then transfer what I learn onto paper in a good final understandable piece of writing. This piece has good description, a good plot line, gets the point across, has a basic setting, and is understandable. I did not change too much of this piece from one draft to the next except punctuation, grammar and spelling. I did, however, add a quote from The Tao of Pooh.

"Quotes from The Tao of Pooh" shows that I am able to pull out good and significant quotes from a book, understand them, and put them into my own words. Then I can make them understandable to other people. This piece gets the point across well and is easy to understand. I really only corrected spelling and punctuation from one draft to the next.

"Discrimination" shows me that I am learning more about discrimination and how it might feel (even though I have never experienced really bad discrimination). I found I can get my ideas across through realistic writing. This piece has good description and was well written for the assignment. Besides correcting some punctuation and spelling, I changed some wording to make the story a little more clear.

For all three pieces, the mechanics of my writing tend to be fairly poor on my first draft, but that is because I am writing as thoughts come into my mind rather than focusing on details of grammar. Then my final drafts get better as I get comments and can turn my attention to details of writing.

The four most important things that I'm able to do as a writer are to: 1) get thoughts pulled into a story; 2) have that story understandable and the reader get something from it; 3) have the reader remember it was a good piece of writing; and 4) like the piece myself.

## BENEFITS AND LIMITATIONS OF PORTFOLIOS

Portfolios have several benefits, some of which we've already identified:

- They capture the wide-ranging, complex nature of students' achievement, with a particular emphasis on complex thinking skills.
- They can show growth over time—something that a single assessment at a single time can't do.
- They can demonstrate students' performance in real-world, authentic activities (e.g., science experiments, service-learning projects).
- They provide practice in self-monitoring and self-evaluation, thereby enhancing students' self-regulation skills.
- They give students a sense of accomplishment and self-efficacy about areas that have been mastered, while possibly also alerting students to areas needing improvement.
- They provide a mechanism through which teachers can easily intertwine assessment with instruction: Students often include products that their teachers have assigned primarily for instructional purposes.
- Because the focus of portfolios is on complex skills, teachers are more likely to *teach* those skills. (Banta, 2003; Darling-Hammond, Ancess, & Falk, 1995; DiMartino & Castaneda, 2007; R. S. Johnson et al., 2006; Koretz, Stecher, Klein, & McCaffrey, 1994; Paulson, Paulson, & Meyer, 1991; Spandel, 1997)

Student portfolios provide an effective means through which students can track their progress. Listen to 8-year-old Keenan in "Portfolio."

RSVP characteristics are often a source of concern with portfolios, however, especially if they're used to evaluate—rather than simply communicate—students' learning and achievement (Arter & Spandel, 1992; R. S. Johnson et al., 2006; Haertel & Linn, 1996; Koretz et al., 1994). When portfolios must be scored in a holistic manner, the scoring is often unreliable, with different teachers rating them differently. In addition, there's an obvious standardization problem: Because portfolios typically contain student-selected products, different students are evaluated on the basis of different bodies of information. Validity may or may not be a problem: Some portfolios may include enough work samples to adequately represent what students have accomplished relative to instructional goals, but others may be unrepresentative. And because portfolios are apt to take a great deal of teacher time, they're less practical than other methods of summarizing achievement. All of this isn't to say that we should shy away from using portfolios. But when we ask students to compile them, we should be sure that the potential benefits outweigh the disadvantages. And we must interpret them cautiously if we use them as summative reflections of what students have accomplished.

Keep in mind the limitations of portfolios with respect to the RSVP characteristics.

## HELPING STUDENTS CONSTRUCT PORTFOLIOS

Creating a portfolio is typically a lengthy process that stretches out over several weeks or months; some best-work portfolios evolve over several years. So that students aren't overwhelmed by such a complex undertaking, it's often helpful to break the portfolio-construction process into a series of steps, scaffolding students' efforts at each step:

Break the construction of portfolios into a sequence of several manageable steps.

1. *Planning:* Decide on the purpose(s) the portfolio will serve—for instance, which instructional goals and/or content area standards it will address and whether it will be used primarily for formative or summative assessment; identify a preliminary plan of attack for creating the portfolio.
2. *Collection:* Save artifacts that demonstrate progress toward or achievement of particular goals and standards.
3. *Selection:* Review the saved artifacts, and choose those that best reflect achievement of the specified goals and standards.
4. *Reflection:* Write explanations and self-evaluations of each artifact; describe how the artifacts show current competencies and growth over time; relate achievements to previously identified goals and standards.
5. *Projection:* Identify new goals toward which to strive.
6. *Presentation:* Share the portfolio with an appropriate audience (e.g., classmates, parents, college admissions officers). (Six steps based on R. S. Johnson et al., 2006)

The Into the Classroom feature "Summarizing Students' Achievements with Portfolios" offers and illustrates several suggestions for scaffolding students' efforts in creating portfolios.

# Standardized Tests

A standardized test is one developed by test construction experts and published for use in many different schools and classrooms. Standardized tests are *standardized* in several ways: All students receive the same instructions, have the same time limits, respond to the same (or very similar) questions or tasks, and have their responses evaluated relative to the same criteria. These tests come with manuals that include the instructions to give students, the time limits to impose, and explicit scoring criteria to use. If the tests are norm-referenced—and many of them are—their manuals also provide norms for various age or grade levels. Also, the manuals often provide information about test reliability for various populations and age-groups, as well as information from which we can draw inferences about test validity for our own purpose and situation.

## TYPES OF STANDARDIZED TESTS

School districts use four kinds of standardized tests fairly frequently: tests of achievement, general scholastic aptitude and intelligence, specific aptitudes and abilities, and school readiness.[2]

### ACHIEVEMENT TESTS

Standardized achievement tests are designed to assess how much students have learned from what they've specifically been taught. The test items are intended to reflect the curriculum common to most schools; for example, a history test will focus on national or world history rather than the history of a particular state or province. Typically these tests yield norm-referenced scores, although some tests are now being constructed to yield criterion-referenced scores tied to particular national or state standards. The overall test scores reflect achievement in a broad sense:

standardized test   Test developed by test construction experts and published for use in many different schools and classrooms.

[2]You can find examples of popular standardized tests at the websites for CTB and McGraw-Hill (www.ctb.com), Pearson (www.pearsonassessments.com), and Riverside Publishing (www.riverpub.com).

## Into the Classroom

### Summarizing Students' Achievements with Portfolios

🍏 **Identify in advance the specific purpose(s) for which a portfolio will be used.**

A third-grade teacher and her students agree to create portfolios that will show parents and other family members how much their writing skills improve over the school year. Throughout the year students save their fiction and nonfiction, and eventually they choose pieces that best demonstrate mastery of some writing skills and progress on other skills. The children proudly present their portfolios at parent–teacher–student conferences at the end of the year.

🍏 **Align portfolio contents with important instructional goals and/or content area standards.**

At a high school in Ohio, twelfth graders complete graduation portfolios with three components, each of which reflects one or more of the school's instructional goals for all graduates:

- A *lifelong-learning skills* section shows mastery of a student's key skills in writing, math, science, and at least one other content domain.
- A *democratic citizenship* section provides specific examples of how a student has been actively engaged in issues related to the local community or larger society (e.g., by contributing to a public service activity).
- A *career-readiness* section contains a résumé, letters of recommendation from teachers or other adults, and other documents that show preparedness for postsecondary education or the workplace.

🍏 **Ask students to select the contents of their portfolios; provide the scaffolding they need to make wise choices.**

A fifth-grade teacher meets one-on-one with each of his students to help them choose artifacts that best reflect their achievements for the year. To give the students an idea of the kinds of things they might include, he shows them several portfolios that students have created in previous years. He shares only those portfolios that previous students and parents have given him permission to use in this way.

🍏 **Identify specific criteria that should guide students' selections; possibly include students in the criteria identification process.**

A middle school geography teacher leads his class in a discussion of criteria that students might use to identify artifacts for a course portfolio. After reviewing the instructional goals for the course, the class agrees that each portfolio should include at least one artifact demonstrating each of the following:

- Map interpretation skills
- Map construction skills
- Understanding of interrelationships between physical environments and socioeconomic practices
- Knowledge of cultural differences within the nation
- Recognition that all cultures have many positive qualities

🍏 **Have students include reflections on the products they include.**

At the beginning of the school year, a ninth-grade journalism teacher tells students that they will be creating portfolios that show progress in journalistic writing during the semester. She asks them to save all of their drafts—"Even simple notes and sketchy outlines," she says. Later in the semester, as students begin to compile their portfolios, she asks them to look at their various drafts of each piece and to describe how the progression from one draft to the next shows their gradual mastery of journalistic skills. She occasionally assigns these reflections as homework so that students spread the portfolio construction task over a four-week period and therefore don't leave everything until the last minute.

🍏 **Give students a general organizational scheme to follow.**

When a high school requires students to complete portfolios as one of their graduation requirements, students get considerable guidance from their homeroom teachers. These teachers also provide a handout describing the elements each portfolio should include: title page, table of contents, introduction to the portfolio's contents and criteria guiding artifact selection, distinct sections for each content domain included, and final reflection summarizing achievements.

🍏 **Determine whether a physical format or electronic format is more suitable for the circumstances.**

At a high school that places particular emphasis on visual and performing arts, students create electronic portfolios that showcase their talents in art, drama, dance, and/or instrumental music. They digitally photograph, videotape, or audiotape their projects and performances, and they create word processing documents that describe and evaluate each one. They then divide their electronic documents into several logical categories, each of which they put in a separate electronic folder on a flash drive, DVD, or CD.

🍏 **When using portfolios for final summative assessments, develop a rubric for scoring it.**

At a high school in New York City, a key instructional goal is for students to acquire certain dispositions and thinking processes—which the school collectively calls *habits of mind*—in their academic work. One of these habits of mind is the use of credible, convincing evidence to support statements and positions. The school develops a four-point rating scale to evaluate students' work on this criterion. A score of 4 is given to work that reflects "Generalizations and ideas supported by specific relevant and accurate information, which is developed in appropriate depth." At the other end of the scale, a score of 1 is given to work that reflects "Mostly general statements; little specific evidence relating to the topic."

*Sources:* Darling-Hammond et al., 1995, p. 39 (New York City high school example); DiMartino & Castaneda, 2007, pp. 40–41 (Ohio high school example); R. L. Johnson, Penny, & Gordon, 2009; R. S. Johnson et al., 2006; Paulson et al., 1991; Popham, 1995; Spandel, 1997.

They tell us how much a student has learned in general about, say, mathematics or language mechanics—and perhaps whether the student has mastered certain basic skill areas—but won't give us information related to specific instructional objectives (e.g., multiplying fractions or using commas appropriately).

Standardized achievement tests are useful in two primary ways. First, they tell us how well our own students' achievement compares with that of students elsewhere—information that may indirectly tell us something about the effectiveness of our instruction. Second, they help us track students' general progress over time and alert us to potential trouble spots. For example, imagine that Lucas gets average test scores year after year but then suddenly performs well below average in the ninth grade, even though the test and norm group are the same as in previous years. At this point we would want to ascertain whether the low performance is a temporary fluke—perhaps Lucas was sick on the test day—or, instead, due to more enduring factors that require attention.

Most standardized achievement tests are highly reliable; that is, they lead to fairly consistent results for individual students, especially for students in the upper elementary and secondary grades. However, our main concern whenever we assess achievement is *content validity*, which we need to determine for *our own situation.* We can determine the content validity of a standardized achievement test by comparing a table of specifications—one provided in the test manual or one we construct ourselves by analyzing the test items—to our own curriculum. A test has high content validity only if the topics and thinking skills emphasized in test items match our curriculum, instructional goals, and content area standards.

## GENERAL SCHOLASTIC APTITUDE AND INTELLIGENCE TESTS

Whereas achievement tests are designed to assess what students have specifically learned from what they've been taught, scholastic aptitude tests are designed to assess a general *capacity* to learn. Traditionally many of these tests have been called *intelligence tests.* However, some experts are beginning to shy away from the latter term, in part because psychologists don't agree about what intelligence *is* and in part because many people mistakenly believe that IQ scores reflect inherited ability almost exclusively. Other commonly used terms are *general aptitude test, school ability test,* and *cognitive ability test.*

Regardless of what we call them, tests that fall into this category are used mainly for prediction—that is, to estimate how well students are likely to learn and perform in future academic situations. Typically these tests are designed to assess how much students have learned and deduced from their general, everyday experiences. For example, they may assess understanding of vocabulary words that most students are likely to have encountered at one time or another. They may include analogy items intended to assess how well students can recognize similarities among well-known relationships. They may ask students to analyze pictures or manipulate concrete objects. And most of them include measures of general knowledge and tasks that require deductive reasoning and problem solving.

Like standardized achievement tests, scholastic aptitude tests tend to be quite reliable, especially for older students. Of greater concern, however, is their *predictive validity*—the accuracy with which they can help us estimate students' future achievement levels. Their predictive validity for future academic success varies considerably depending on the situation and population at hand, but in general you should think of these tests as providing only rough estimates of how students are likely to perform in school in the next two or three years; they're even *less* accurate in predicting students' academic and professional success over the long run. Keep in mind, too, that many factors not measured by these tests—for instance, motivation, self-regulation skills, and the quality of instruction—also influence students' learning and classroom performance (Dai, 2010; Duckworth & Seligman, 2005; Kuhn, 2001a; Perkins, Tishman, Ritchhart, Donis, & Andrade, 2000).

## SPECIFIC APTITUDE AND ABILITY TESTS

General scholastic aptitude tests are useful when we want to predict overall academic performance. But when we're interested in how well students are apt to perform in a particular content domain (e.g., math, music, or auto mechanics), specific aptitude tests are more useful. Some aptitude tests are designed to predict future performance in just one content domain. Others, called *multiple aptitude batteries,* yield subscores for a variety of domains simultaneously.

Specific aptitude tests are sometimes used to identify students who are most likely to benefit from certain domain-specific instructional programs (e.g., advanced math or science classes). They may also be used for counseling students about future educational plans and career choices. But two caveats are important to keep in mind when using these tests for such purposes. First, their predictive validity in academic contexts tends to be lower than that for general scholastic aptitude tests—that is, they yield only very rough estimates of students' future academic

---

Use standardized achievement tests to track students' general progress in a content domain and to evaluate the effectiveness of your instructional program relative to other programs across the country.

Determine the content validity of a standardized achievement test for your own curriculum, instructional goals, and content area standards.

You can learn more about intelligence tests and IQ scores in Chapter 5.

**scholastic aptitude test** Test designed to assess a general capacity to learn and used to predict future academic achievement.

**specific aptitude test** Test designed to predict future ability to succeed in a particular content domain.

**school readiness test** Test designed to assess cognitive skills important for success in a typical kindergarten or first-grade curriculum.

performance in the domain in question. Second, they're based on the assumption that the ability being measured is a fairly stable one—an assumption that may or may not be accurate. Rather than trying to identify students with high aptitudes for particular subject areas, then, some educators argue that we should focus more on *developing* abilities in *all* students (Boykin, 1994; P. D. Nichols & Mittelholtz, 1997; Sternberg, 2002). Accordingly, specific aptitude tests now appear less frequently in wide-scale school testing programs than they once did.

### SCHOOL READINESS TESTS

A school readiness test is designed to determine whether children have acquired knowledge and skills essential for success in kindergarten or first grade—for instance, knowledge of colors, shapes, letters, and numbers. When used in combination with other information, school readiness tests can be helpful if we're looking for significant developmental delays that require immediate attention (Bracken & Walker, 1997; Lidz, 1991). On their own, however, they have limited predictive validity: The scores they yield typically correlate only moderately with children's academic performance even a year or so later (Duncan et al., 2007; La Paro & Pianta, 2000; C. E. Sanders, 1997; Stipek, 2002).

Use the results of school readiness tests more for instructional planning than for making decisions about which children are ready to begin school.

School readiness tests can often give us an idea of where to begin instruction with particular children. But as a general rule, we should *not* use them to identify children who should postpone formal schooling. By age 5 almost all children are probably ready for some form of structured educational program. Rather than focus on determining which children might have trouble in a particular educational curriculum and environment, we better serve children when we determine how to adapt the curriculum and environment to fit each child's developmental progress and particular needs (Farran, 2001; Lidz, 1991; Stipek, 2002).

Table 15.2 summarizes the four categories of standardized tests just described.

## INDIVIDUAL VERSUS GROUP ADMINISTRATION OF STANDARDIZED TESTS

Some standardized tests are administered one on one. Such tests enable the examiner to observe a student's attention span, motivation, and other factors that may affect academic performance. For this reason, individually administered tests are typically used when identifying cognitive disabilities and other special educational needs.

## COMPARE/CONTRAST

### TABLE 15.2 • Commonly Used Standardized Tests

| KIND OF TEST | PURPOSE | RECOMMENDATIONS |
|---|---|---|
| Achievement tests | To assess how much students have learned from what they have been specifically taught | • Use these tests primarily for assessing broad areas of achievement rather than specific knowledge and skills. |
| Scholastic aptitude and intelligence tests | To assess students' general capability to learn; to predict their general academic success over the short run | • Use test scores as rough predictors of performance in the near future, *not* as predictors of learning potential over the long run.<br>• Use tests designed for one-on-one administration if a student's verbal skills are limited or if exceptional giftedness or a significant disability is suspected. |
| Specific aptitude and ability tests | To predict how easily students are likely to learn in a specific content domain | • Use test scores as rough predictors of performance in the near future, *not* as predictors of learning potential over the long run.<br>• Because predictive validities for many of these tests are low, use test scores only in combination with other information about students. |
| School readiness tests | To determine whether young children have the prerequisite skills to be successful in a typical kindergarten or first-grade curriculum | • Use test results only in combination with other information about children.<br>• Use test results primarily for instructional planning, *not* for deciding whether students are ready to begin formal schooling. |

When circumstances call for giving *all* students a standardized test, testing them as a group is usually the only practical approach. Fortunately, computer technology comes to our assistance here. Since the middle of the twentieth century, computers have often been used to score standardized tests and generate reports about each student's performance. Now, in the twenty-first century, computer-based standardized testing can provide several options that are either impractical or impossible with paper–pencil tests:

- It allows adaptive testing, which adjusts the difficulty level of items as students proceed through a test and can thereby zero in on students' specific strengths and weaknesses fairly quickly.

- It can include animations, simulations, videos, and audiotaped messages—all of which can expand the kinds of knowledge and skills that test items assess.

- It enables assessment of how students approach specific problems and how quickly they accomplish specific tasks.

- It allows the possibility of assessing students' abilities under varying levels of support (e.g., by providing one or more hints as needed to guide students' reasoning).

- It can provide on-the-spot scoring and analyses of students' performance.

Computer-based standardized tests tend to have reliability and validity levels similar to those of traditional paper–pencil tests. Their use should, of course, be limited to students who are familiar and comfortable with computers and have adequate keyboarding skills.

## GUIDELINES FOR CHOOSING AND USING STANDARDIZED TESTS

As teachers, we'll sometimes have input into the selection of standardized tests for our districts, and we'll often be involved in administering them. Following are guidelines for choosing and using a standardized test appropriately:

🍎 *Choose a test with high validity for your particular purpose and high reliability for students similar to your own.* I've described four categories of standardized tests as if they're four distinctly different entities, but in fact the differences among them aren't always clear-cut. To some extent, all of these tests assess what a student has already learned, and all of them can be used to predict future performance. Our best bet is to choose the test that has the greatest validity for our particular purpose, regardless of what the test might be called. Of course, we also want a test that has been shown to be highly reliable with a population similar to ours.

🍎 *Make sure the test's norm group is relevant to your own population.* Scrutinize the test manual's description of the norm group used for the test, with questions like these in mind:

- Does the norm group include students of both genders and students of the same ages, educational levels, and cultural backgrounds as those of your own students?

- Is it a representative sample of the population at large or in some other way appropriate for any comparisons you plan to make?

- Have the normative data been collected recently enough that they reflect how students typically perform in the current year?

When we determine norm-referenced test scores by comparing students with an *in*appropriate norm group, the scores are meaningless. For example, I recall a situation in which teacher education students at a major state university were required to take basic skills tests in language and math. Because the tests had been normed on a high school population, the university students' performance was compared to that of high school seniors—a practice that made no sense whatsoever.

🍎 *Take students' ages and developmental levels into account.* A variety of irrelevant factors—motivation, mood, energy level, and so on—affect students' performance on tests and other assessments. When factors such as these are relatively stable characteristics, they affect test validity. When they're temporary and variable from day to day (perhaps even hour to hour), they affect test reliability and thus also indirectly affect validity. Such sources of error in students' test scores and other assessment results are especially common in young children, who may have limited language skills, short attention spans, little motivation to do their best, and low tolerance for

**adaptive testing** Computer-based assessment in which students' performance on early items determines which items are presented subsequently.

frustration. Furthermore, young children's erratic behaviors may make it difficult to maintain standardized testing conditions (Bracken & Walker, 1997; Messick, 1983; Wodtke, Harper, & Schommer, 1989).

In adolescence other variables can affect the validity of standardized test scores. For example, especially in high school, some students become quite cynical about the validity and usefulness of standardized paper–pencil tests. Thus they may read test items superficially, if at all, and a few may complete answer sheets simply by following a certain pattern (e.g., alternating between A and B) or filling in bubbles to make pictures or designs (S. G. Paris, Lawton, Turner, & Roth, 1991). Table 15.3 describes these and other developmental differences affecting students' performance on standardized tests.

🍏 *Make sure students are adequately prepared to take the test.* In most instances we'll want to prepare students ahead of time for a standardized test. For example, we can do the following:

- 🍏 Explain the general nature of the test and the tasks it involves (e.g., if applicable, mention that students aren't expected to know all of the answers and that many students won't have enough time to respond to every item).

- 🍏 Encourage students to do their best, but without describing the test as a life-or-death matter.

- 🍏 Give students practice with the test's format and item types (e.g., demonstrate how to fill in electronically scored answer sheets).

- 🍏 Give suggestions about effective test-taking strategies; in other words, foster *testwiseness*. But don't overdo it; remember that your time is best spent helping students master the content domain being assessed.

- 🍏 Encourage students to get a full night's sleep and eat a good breakfast before taking the test.

🍏 *When administering the test, follow the directions closely, and report any unusual circumstances.* Once a test session begins, we should follow the test administration procedures to the letter, distributing test booklets as directed, asking students to complete any practice items provided, keeping time faithfully, and responding to questions in the prescribed manner. If we don't replicate the conditions under which the norm group has taken a test, any norm-referenced scores derived from the test will be meaningless. When unanticipated events significantly alter the test environment (e.g., when electrical power unexpectedly goes out), they jeopardize the validity of the test results and must be reported. We should also make note of any students who are behaving in ways unlikely to lead to maximum performance—appearing exceptionally nervous, staring out the window for long periods, marking answers haphazardly, and so on (M. D. Miller et al., 2009).

## INTERPRETING STANDARDIZED TEST SCORES

Thanks to increasingly sophisticated software programs, computer-generated reports of students' performance on standardized tests can be quite detailed and complex. Figure 15.12 presents a hypothetical example for a student we'll call "Sarah," who took both the Stanford Achievement Test and the Otis-Lennon School Ability Test in second grade. As you can see in the purple-and-white-striped section of the form, the Stanford Achievement Test yields scores related to students' overall achievement in a variety of content domains and subdomains. The Otis-Lennon is designed to assess students' general cognitive abilities with respect to both *verbal* tasks (those that depend heavily on language skills) and *nonverbal* tasks (those that involve numbers, pictures, or graphical configurations).

At first glance, the report can be quite daunting, but let's make sense of some of the data presented in the purple-and-white section. The "Number Correct" columns are, of course, Sarah's raw scores on the overall tests and various subtests within them. The PR-S scores are really two separate scores: The first two digits indicate a percentile rank and the digit after the hyphen is a stanine score. The Stanford yields percentiles and stanines based on a national norm group of second graders; the Otis-Lennon yields two sets of percentiles and stanines, one set derived from the second-grade norms (the "Natl Grade PR-S") and the other derived from students in the norm group who are the same age as Sarah (the "Age PR-S"). I've previously explained the

See Chapter 14 for more information on testwiseness.

# DEVELOPMENTAL TRENDS

## TABLE 15.3 • Characteristics Affecting Standardized Test Performance at Different Grade Levels

| GRADE LEVEL | AGE-TYPICAL CHARACTERISTICS | EXAMPLE | SUGGESTED STRATEGIES |
|---|---|---|---|
| K–2 | • Short attention span; significant individual differences in ability to stay focused on test items<br>• Little intrinsic motivation to perform well on tests<br>• Inconsistency in test performance from one occasion to another | One Saturday morning each spring, an elementary school conducts a "Kindergarten Roundup" at which it collects information about children who will be enrolling in kindergarten in the fall. Escorted by a parent, each child goes to various booths in the gym, where teachers conduct various short assessments of basic knowledge and emerging literacy skills. Some children willingly comply with the teachers' instructions, but others are bouncy and have trouble staying on task. | • Don't use school readiness tests to determine which children are "ready" for elementary school; instead, plan early school experiences that can prepare students for future academic learning.<br>• Leave assessment for diagnostic purposes (e.g., to identify students with special needs) in the hands of trained professionals who have experience in assessing young children.<br>• Don't make long-term predictions about achievement on the basis of standardized test scores.<br>• Use multiple measures when important decisions about students' education must be made. |
| 3–5 | • Unquestioning acceptance of standardized tests as valid measures of ability or achievement<br>• Increasing ability to stay focused on a paper–pencil assessment instrument<br>• Increasing facility with computer-scored answer sheets<br>• Considerable variability in knowledge and use of effective test-taking strategies | Students in a fourth-grade class work quietly and diligently on a statewide achievement test. Most of them address the questions in the order they appear in the test booklet, and some students spend so much time on especially difficult items that they must leave many questions still unanswered when the allotted time is up. | • Stress the value of standardized tests for tracking students' progress and identifying areas in which students may need extra instruction and support.<br>• Give students plenty of practice using computer-scored answer sheets.<br>• Explicitly teach basic test-taking strategies (e.g., skipping difficult test items and returning to them later if time allows). |
| 6–8 | • Increase in debilitating test anxiety (for some students)<br>• Continuing variability in testwiseness<br>• Emerging skepticism about the value of standardized tests (for some students) | When a junior high school homeroom teacher announces an upcoming national achievement test, a few low-achieving students argue that it will be a "complete waste of time" and insist that they won't take it seriously. | • Explain that standardized tests provide only a rough idea of what students know and can do; reassure students that test results won't be the only things affecting instructional decision making.<br>• Encourage students to do their best on a test; assure them that test results will be used not to judge them but rather to help them learn more effectively.<br>• Provide some practice in test-taking skills, but remember that students' performance depends more on their knowledge and abilities in content domains than on their general test-taking ability. |
| 9–12 | • Increasing cynicism about the validity and usefulness of standardized tests (especially common in low-achieving students)<br>• Decreasing motivation to perform well on standardized tests; in some instances may reflect self-handicapping as a way of justifying poor performance | After a high school teacher has passed out test booklets, read the instructions, and started her stopwatch, one student puts down his pencil, slouches back in his chair, and looks absentmindedly out the window. A few minutes later, he grabs his pencil and fills in bubbles on his answer sheet to spell his name: "JESSE." | • Acknowledge that standardized tests aren't perfect, but explain that they *can* help teachers and administrators assess school effectiveness and plan future instruction.<br>• Be alert for signs that a student may intentionally subvert an assessment or has already done so; speak privately with the student about his or her concerns and offer your support to enhance test performance. |

*Sources:* Bracken & Walker, 1997; S. M. Carver, 2006; Dempster & Corkill, 1999; R. L. Johnson et al., 2009; Lidz, 1991; Messick, 1983; S. G. Paris et al., 1991; Petersen, Sudweeks, & Baird, 1990; Sarason, 1980; Scruggs & Lifson, 1985; Stipek, 2002.

**FIGURE 15.12** Hypothetical report for a second grader's performance on the Stanford Achievement Tests and Otis-Lennon School Ability Test

**STANFORD** ACHIEVEMENT TEST SERIES, TENTH EDITION
KNOWLEDGE · POWER · EXCELLENCE

with Otis-Lennon School Ability Test®, Eighth Edition

### About This Student's Performance:

Afirst recently took the *Stanford Achievement Test*, Tenth Edition (Stanford 10). This test is one measure of this child's achievement. This report compares this child's performance to students in the same grade across the nation. Percentile Bands show ranges within which this child's true scores likely fall. For example, a student whose Percentile Band spans the 70th percentile performed as well as or better than 70% of students nationally in that subject.

The chart below shows this child's performance in each subject area tested.

### Lexile measure = 430L

Information on the use of Lexiles can be found at www.PearsonLexile.com. Lexiles used with permission.

## Student Report | AFIRST N ALASTNAME

**National Comparison**   AGE: 8 Yrs 07 Mos

TEACHER: VVVVVVVVVV
SCHOOL: NEWTOWN ELEMENTARY
DISTRICT: NEWTOWN
GRADE: 02
TEST DATE: 04/03

| Subtests and Totals | Number Possible | Number Correct | Scaled Score | National PR-S | National NCE | AAC Range |
|---|---|---|---|---|---|---|
| Total Reading | 100 | 70 | 587 | 26-4 | 36.5 | MIDDLE |
| Word Study Skills | 30 | 23 | 617 | 40-5 | 44.7 | MIDDLE |
| Reading Vocabulary | 30 | 24 | 579 | 30-4 | 39.0 | MIDDLE |
| Reading Comprehension | 40 | 23 | 576 | 20-3 | 32.3 | HIGH |
| Total Mathematics | 74 | 62 | 604 | 66-6 | 58.7 | HIGH |
| Mathematics Problem Solving | 44 | 35 | 602 | 63-6 | 57.0 | HIGH |
| Mathematics Procedures | 30 | 27 | 611 | 66-6 | 58.7 | HIGH |
| Language | 48 | 41 | 609 | 52-5 | 51.1 | HIGH |
| Spelling | 36 | 34 | 621 | 67-6 | 59.3 | HIGH |
| Environment | 40 | 31 | 611 | 55-5 | 52.6 | MIDDLE |
| Listening | 40 | 18 | 563 | 10-2 | 23.0 | LOW |
| Basic Battery | 298 | 225 | NA | 42-5 | 45.6 | MIDDLE |
| Complete Battery | 338 | 256 | NA | 43-5 | 46.4 | MIDDLE |

National Grade Percentile Bands: 1 — 10 — 30 — 50 — 70 — 90 — 99

| Otis-Lennon School Ability Test® | Number Possible | Number Correct | SAI | Age PR-S | Scaled Score | Natl Grade PR-S |
|---|---|---|---|---|---|---|
| Total | 60 | 36 | 93 | 33-4 | 565 | 35-4 |
| Verbal | 30 | 19 | 97 | 43-5 | 566 | 48-5 |
| Nonverbal | 30 | 17 | 89 | 25-4 | 563 | 25-4 |

National Grade Percentile Bands: 1 — 10 — 30 — 50 — 70 — 90 — 99

| Clusters | NP | NA | NC | Below Avg | Avg | Above Avg |
|---|---|---|---|---|---|---|
| **Word Study Skills** | | | | | | |
| C Structural Analysis | 30 | | 23 | | H✓ | |
| C Phonetic Analysis-Consonants | 12 | 12 | 12 | | ✓ | |
| C Phonetic Analysis-Vowels | 9 | 9 | 5 | | ✓ | |
| **Reading Vocabulary** | | | | | | |
| C Synonyms | 30 | 30 | 24 | | ✓ | |
| C Multiple Meaning Words | 18 | 18 | 17 | | ✓ | |
| C Context Clues | 6 | 6 | 3 | | ✓ | |
| **Reading Comprehension** | | | | | | |
| P Literary | 40 | 40 | 23 | | ✓ | |
| P Informational | 14 | 14 | 7 | ✓ | | |
| P Functional | 13 | 13 | 8 | ✓ | | |
| P Initial Understanding | 13 | 13 | 8 | ✓ | | |
| P Interpretation | 18 | 18 | 11 | ✓ | | |
| P Critical Analysis & Strategies | 14 | 14 | 5 | | ✓ | |
| **Mathematics Problem Solving** | | | | | | |
| C Number Sense & Operations | 44 | 44 | 35 | | ✓ | |
| C Patterns/Relationships/Algebra | 4 | 4 | 4 | | ✓ | |
| C Data, Statistics & Probability | 6 | 6 | 5 | | ✓ | |
| C Geometry & Measurement | 10 | 10 | 6 | | ✓ | |
| P Communication & Representation | 6 | 6 | 6 | | ✓ | |
| P Estimation | 3 | 3 | 1 | | ✓ | |
| P Mathematical Connections | 22 | 22 | 18 | | ✓ | |
| P Reasoning & Problem Solving | 13 | 13 | 10 | | ✓ | |
| **Mathematics Procedures** | | | | | | |
| C Number Facts | 30 | 30 | 27 | | ✓ | |
| C Computation w/Whole Numbers | 13 | 13 | 11 | | ✓ | |
| P Computation in Context | 17 | 17 | 16 | | ✓ | |

| Clusters | NP | NA | NC | Below Avg | Avg | Above Avg |
|---|---|---|---|---|---|---|
| **Mathematics Procedures (cont.)** | | | | | | |
| P Computation/Symbolic Notation | 22 | 22 | 19 | | ✓ | |
| **Language** | | | | | | |
| C Capitalization | 48 | 48 | 41 | | ✓ | |
| C Usage | 8 | 8 | 7 | | ✓ | |
| C Punctuation | 8 | 8 | 8 | | H✓ | |
| C Sentence Structure | 7 | 7 | 7 | | ✓ | |
| C Prewriting | 5 | 5 | 4 | | ✓ | |
| C Content and Organization | 12 | 12 | 9 | | ✓ | |
| **Spelling** | | | | | | |
| C Sight Words | 36 | 36 | 34 | | ✓ | |
| C Phonetic Principles | 6 | 6 | 6 | | ✓ | |
| C Structural Principles | 24 | 24 | 23 | | ✓ | |
| **Environment** | | | | | | |
| C History | 40 | 40 | 31 | | ✓ | |
| C Geography | 6 | 6 | 5 | | ✓ | |
| C Political Science | 5 | 5 | 3 | ✓ | | |
| C Economics | 5 | 5 | 5 | | ✓ | |
| C Life | 7 | 7 | 4 | ✓ | | |
| C Earth | 4 | 4 | 3 | | ✓ | |
| C Physical | 6 | 6 | 4 | | ✓ | |
| P Science Process Skills | 3 | 3 | 3 | | H✓ | |
| **Listening** | | | | | | |
| C Vocabulary | 40 | 40 | 18 | ✓ | | |
| C Comprehension | 30 | 30 | 13 | | ✓ | |
| P Initial Understanding | 15 | 15 | 7 | | ✓ | |
| P Interpretation | 15 | 15 | 6 | | ✓ | |
| P Literary | 14 | 14 | 8 | | ✓ | |

| Clusters (cont.) | NP | NA | NC | Below Avg | Avg | Above Avg |
|---|---|---|---|---|---|---|
| **Listening (cont.)** | | | | | | |
| C Informational | 8 | 8 | 1 | ✓ | | |
| C Functional | 8 | 8 | 4 | ✓ | | |

STANFORD LEVEL/FORM: PRIMARY 2/A
2007 NORMS: Spring National

OLSAT LEVEL/FORM: C/5
2002 NORMS: Spring National

C= Content Cluster   P= Process Cluster

nature of NCE scores, and the SAI scores on the Otis-Lennon are based on the IQ-score scale I also described earlier ("SAI" refers to "School Ability Index"). We haven't specifically talked about scaled scores or what an AAC range might be, and I don't want to overwhelm my readers with too much information—in common instant messaging lingo, "TMI"—so I'm putting explanations of these columns in a footnote for readers who might be curious.[3]

Notice the "National Grade Percentile Bands" in the upper right part of the figure. These are *confidence intervals* intended to reflect the amount of error (and imperfect reliability) affecting Sarah's percentile scores. As is true in the simpler printout in Figure 15.7, the graph squishes middle-range percentile ranks close together and spreads the high and low percentiles farther apart as a way of reflecting the scores' underlying normal distribution.

Despite the many numbers that standardized tests can yield, we must remember that students' scores on these tests are, at best, only *imprecise estimates* of what students generally know and can do, and they may have little or no validity for some students. We must be *extremely cautious*—and occasionally downright skeptical—in our interpretation of students' standardized test results, and we mustn't place too much stock in the *exact* scores that the tests yield. Following are three additional guidelines to keep in mind when interpreting and using standardized test scores:

🍎 *Have a clear and justifiable rationale for establishing any cutoffs for acceptable performance.* If we want to use test results to make *either–or* decisions—for instance, whether a student should move to a more advanced math class, be exempt from a basic writing skills course, and so on—we must have a clear rationale for the cutoff scores we use. The process can be relatively easy for criterion-referenced scores, provided that they truly reflect mastery and nonmastery of the subject matter. It's far more difficult for norm-referenced scores: At what point does a student's performance become acceptable? At the 20th percentile? At a stanine of 6? Without more information about the knowledge and skills the scores represent, there's no easy way for determining a cutoff for acceptable scores.

🍎 *Compare two standardized test scores only when the scores have been derived from the same or equivalent norm group(s).* Because different standardized tests almost always have different norm groups, we can't really compare students' performance on one test with their performance on another. For example, if Susan takes the Basic Skills Test (BST), we can compare her score on the BST Reading subtest with her score on the BST Math subtest because in both cases her performance has been compared to the same large group of students. But we can't compare Susan's BST scores with her scores on a *different* standardized achievement test (e.g., the Reading Achievement Test that Shawn took) because the students in the two tests' norm groups may have, on average, been different in some way.

🍎 *Never use a single test score to make important decisions.* No test—no matter how carefully constructed and widely used—has perfect reliability and validity. Every test is fallible, and students may do poorly on a test for a variety of reasons. Thus, we should never—and I do mean *never*—use a single assessment instrument or a single test score to make important decisions about individual students. Similarly, we should never use single test scores to make important decisions about large groups of students or about the teachers who teach them.

## High-Stakes Testing and Accountability

In recent years a great deal of emphasis has been placed on students' performance on standardized achievement tests—entirely *too* much emphasis, in my opinion. Many policy makers, business leaders, and other public figures have lamented students' low achievement test scores and called for a major overhaul of our educational system.[4]

🍏 Remember that despite the apparent precision of standardized test scores, these scores are, at best, only imprecise estimates of students' abilities, and for some students the scores may be way off target.

Appendix B offers additional insights on comparing test scores.

---

[3]The "Scaled Scores" are statistical adjustments that reflect the difficulty level of a particular form of each test; they allow comparisons among students who've taken different forms of the tests, with some forms almost inevitably being slightly more difficult than others. "AAC Range" refers to "Ability-Achievement Comparison"; entries in this column indicate how Sarah's various achievement test scores compare with the Otis-Lennon's estimates of her general cognitive ability. For example, Sarah is "High" in her Math achievement scores, indicating that she has done better than have most students with Otis-Lennon scores similar to hers.

[4]In the United States, you may occasionally see or hear people cite a pessimistic report titled *A Nation at Risk*, published in 1983 by the National Commission on Excellence in Education.

Some students do seem to progress through several grade levels without acquiring basic skills in reading, writing, and math; a few graduate from high school without such skills. To address these problems, many states and school districts now use students' performance on tests or other assessments as a basis for promoting students to the next grade level or awarding high school diplomas. Typically educators begin by identifying certain instructional goals or standards that students' final achievement should reflect. They then assess students' performance levels at the end of instruction, and only those students whose performance meets the predetermined goals and standards move forward. You might see such labels as *minimum competency testing* and *outcomes-based education* used for this approach.

Whenever we use a single assessment instrument to make major decisions about students, we're using a high-stakes test. Because high-stakes tests are typically used to make judgments about *mastery* of school subject matter, they require criterion-referenced rather than norm-referenced scores. For example, a high-stakes test might yield a score such as "In progress," "Proficient," or "Advanced" with respect to a student's knowledge and skills in a particular subject area.

Students' scores on high-stakes tests are sometimes used to make important decisions not only about the students themselves but also about their teachers and schools (e.g., decisions about salaries and school funding). In such circumstances—that is, when teachers, administrators, and other school personnel are mandated to accept responsibility for students' performance on high-stakes assessments—we're talking about accountability.

## THE U.S. NO CHILD LEFT BEHIND ACT

In the United States the No Child Left Behind Act of 2001—sometimes known simply as NCLB—mandates both high-stakes testing and accountability in all public elementary and secondary schools. It also mandates that states establish

challenging academic content standards in academic subjects that—
  I. specify what children are expected to know and be able to do;
 II. contain coherent and rigorous content; and
III. encourage the teaching of advanced skills (P.L. 107-110, Sec. 1111)

School districts must annually assess students in grades 3 through 8 and at least once during grades 10 through 12 to determine whether students are making *adequate yearly progress* in meeting state-determined standards in reading, math, and science. The nature of this progress is defined by the state (and thus differs from state to state), but assessment results must clearly show that all students—including those from diverse racial and socioeconomic groups—are making significant gains in knowledge and skills. (Students with diagnosed cognitive disabilities may be given alternative assessments, but these students must show improvement commensurate with their ability levels.) Schools that demonstrate progress receive rewards, such as teacher bonuses and increased funding. Schools that don't demonstrate progress are subject to sanctions and corrective actions (e.g., bad publicity, administrative restructuring, dismissal of staff members), and their students have the option of attending a better public school at the school district's expense. The U.S. Department of Education's website provides more details (www.ed.gov/nclb).

The No Child Left Behind Act has been highly controversial and in many respects hasn't brought about the changes it was intended to generate (Forte, 2010; Mintrop & Sunderman, 2009). As this book goes to press in 2012, many U.S. states have gotten waivers from certain parts of the legislation. Waivers don't get states off the hook; rather, states must develop and implement their own comprehensive plans for improving instruction and significantly increasing students' achievement levels, especially for historically low-performing minority groups.

Systematic efforts to monitor schools' instructional effectiveness and students' academic progress are certainly well intentioned. Ideally they can help schools determine whether instructional methods need revision and whether teachers need retooling. They can also help teachers identify students who aren't acquiring the basic skills necessary for successful participation in the adult world. And the focus on improving *all* students' achievement levels is long overdue. However, the current emphasis on boosting students' test scores is fraught with difficulties in implementation, and solutions to these difficulties are only slowly emerging.

**high-stakes testing**  Practice of using students' performance on a single assessment to make major decisions about students, school personnel, or overall school quality.

**accountability**  An obligation of teachers and other school personnel to accept responsibility for students' performance on high-stakes assessments; often mandated by policy makers calling for school reform.

**No Child Left Behind Act (NCLB)**  U.S. legislation passed in 2001 that mandates regular assessments of basic skills to determine whether students are making adequate yearly progress relative to state-determined standards in reading, math, and science.

## PROBLEMS WITH HIGH-STAKES TESTING

Experts have identified several problems with the use of high-stakes tests to make decisions about students, teachers, and schools:

🍏 *The tests don't always reflect important instructional goals.* High-stakes achievement tests don't always have good content validity for the contexts in which they're used. Even if well constructed, they may reflect only a small portion of a school's curriculum and instructional goals. For instance, the emphasis in NCLB and in some state-level and district-level assessments is primarily on achievement in certain content domains (e.g., NCLB focuses on reading, math, and science), with little regard for achievement in other areas. Furthermore, the preponderance of multiple-choice and other objectively scorable items on many standardized tests limits the extent to which these tests assess complex cognitive skills and performance on authentic, real-world tasks (E. L. Baker, 2007; Hursh, 2007; Leu, O'Byrne, Zawilinski, McVerry, & Everett-Cacopardo, 2009; Mintrop & Sunderman, 2009; Siskin, 2003a; R. M. Thomas, 2005).

🍏 *Teachers spend a great deal of time teaching to the tests.* When teachers are held accountable for their students' performance on a particular test, many of them understandably devote many class hours to the topics and skills the test assesses, and students may focus their studying accordingly. The result is often that students perform at higher levels on a high-stakes test *without* improving their achievement and abilities more generally. If a test truly measures the things that are most important for students to learn—including problem solving, critical thinking, and other complex thinking skills—then focusing on those things is quite appropriate. But if the test primarily assesses only rote knowledge and simple skills, it can undermine the achievement gains we *really* want to see (Amrein & Berliner, 2002; W. Au, 2007; Hursh, 2007; Jacob, 2003; R. M. Ryan & Brown, 2005; L. Shepard et al., 2005).

Sometimes, too, high-stakes tests are based on lengthy lists of prescribed competencies or standards—far too many for most students to master in a single school year. Thus teachers may try to cover many topics rapidly, without giving students sufficient time and instruction to master any of them. As one ninth-grade math teacher put it when her class was facing a statewide math competency exam, "Mastery probably isn't possible at this point, but I should at least *present* what students need to know. Maybe this will help a few of them with some of the test items." Such superficial coverage is common when maximizing students' scores on high-stakes tests must be at the top of teachers' priority lists (W. Au, 2007; La Guardia, 2009; R. M. Thomas, 2005; Valli & Buese, 2007).

🍏 *Teachers and schools may focus much of their attention on helping some students while shortchanging others.* The focus of NCLB and many state- and district-level assessment policies is on maximizing the number of students who meet certain minimal criteria for acceptable performance. Within such a context, the key to doing well as a school is to push as many low-achieving students as possible over the minimal cutoff for success. In the process, students who fall way below the cutoff and students who are already well above it may be given short shrift; for instance, schools may devote little instructional time or resources to students who are most in need of them (Balfanz, Legters, West, & Weber, 2007; A. D. Ho, 2008; Porter & Polikoff, 2007).

🍏 *School personnel have disincentives to follow standardized testing procedures and to assess the achievement of chronically low performers.* In a high-stakes situation, teachers and administrators sometimes conclude that *dis*honesty is the best policy. Imagine that, as a teacher or school administrator, you want to maximize your school's average test scores. Might you give students more than the allotted time to finish the test? Might you provide hints about correct answers or possibly even *give* students correct answers? Might you find reasons to exempt certain students from taking the test—perhaps finding a place for them in a special education program or retaining them at a grade level where they won't be assessed? Such practices occur when teachers and administrators are under pressure to raise a school's average test scores (Hursh, 2007; Mintrop & Sunderman, 2009; R. M. Ryan & Brown, 2005; R. M. Thomas, 2005).

A few years after NCLB was instituted, I spoke with a high school principal in a small rural school district in northern New England. Although he certainly saw benefits to regularly assessing students' progress in basic skills, he revealed that one group of minority students at his school

Teach to the test *if* it reflects important instructional goals.

You can learn more about this math teacher's dilemma in the opening case study in Chapter 7.

By their very nature, high-stakes paper–pencil tests neglect some important skills, such as public speaking and technological know-how.

had *not* shown the NCLB-mandated yearly progress during the preceding school year. "We have very few minority students at our school and only five students in that particular group," he told me. "As a result of difficult family circumstances, one of those five—a 16-year-old—lives on his own and comes to school only about 40% of the time. His performance on the annual assessment pulled the average scores for his group way down. If we truly wanted our test results to look good for the group, we should just have let him drop out—something he was inclined to do anyway. Instead, we did everything we could to keep him in school." The school's decision was certainly in the student's best interest, but it was a costly one in terms of the achievement results it reported for the school year.

🍏 *Different criteria lead to different conclusions about which students and schools are performing at high levels.* When we base school funding, salary increases, and other incentives on students' test performance, what specific criterion do we use? A predetermined, absolute level of achievement? Improvement over time? Superior performance relative to other school districts? There's no easy answer to this question. Yet depending on which criterion we use, we'll reach different conclusions as to which students and schools are and are not performing well. Compounding the problem is the fact that students in lower-income communities achieve at lower levels, on average, than those in higher-income communities, even when both groups have excellent teachers and instructional programs (Hursh, 2007; R. L. Linn, 2000; Mintrop & Sunderman, 2009; R. M. Thomas, 2005).

🍏 *Too much emphasis is placed on punishing low-performing schools; not enough is placed on helping schools improve.* Many advocates of school reform think that a quick, easy "fix" to students' low achievement levels is simply to reward schools whose students do well and to punish schools whose students do poorly. This strategy is unlikely to be effective, especially if some of the factors affecting students' academic performance (health, family support, peer group norms, etc.) are beyond teachers' and administrators' control. In fact, there's *no* convincing evidence that simply holding school personnel accountable for students' performance on high-stakes assessments—without also providing sufficient support to make change possible—has a significant positive influence on teachers' instructional strategies or on students' learning and achievement. Furthermore, the threat of harsh consequences for insufficient improvements in test scores can adversely affect teachers' morale and lead some teachers, including some very good ones, to leave teaching altogether (A. B. Brown & Clift, 2010; Finnigan & Gross, 2007; Forte, 2010; Stringfield & Yakimowski-Srebnick, 2005).

🍏 *Students' motivation affects their performance on the tests, and consistently low test performance can, in turn, affect their motivation.* For a variety of reasons—perhaps because of low self-efficacy or external, uncontrollable attributions for academic achievement—some students have little motivation to do well on high-stakes tests, and others become so anxious that they *can't* do as well as they should (Chabrán, 2003; Siskin, 2003b). Furthermore, when students get consistently low test scores—and especially when their scores pose obstacles to promotion and graduation—they may see little point in staying in school. Thus the use of high-stakes tests for high school graduation doesn't necessarily increase students' achievement levels. Instead, it can increase school dropout rates, especially for students from certain ethnic minority groups and students from low-income neighborhoods (Amrein & Berliner, 2002; Holme, Richards, Jimerson, & Cohen, 2010; Kumar, Gheen, & Kaplan, 2002, R. M. Ryan & Brown, 2005).

## PRODUCTIVE STEPS FORWARD IN HIGH-STAKES TESTING

Public concern about students' achievement levels isn't going away any time soon, nor should it. Many students *are* achieving at low levels, especially those in low-income school districts, those in certain minority groups, and those with special educational needs. Hence I offer several potential solutions that, in combination, may help to alleviate the problems just identified.

🍏 *Identify and assess those things most important for students to know and do.* If we're going to make important decisions about students, teachers, and schools based on assessment results, we must be sure we're assessing aspects of achievement most critical for students' long-term success both in school and in the adult world. For instance, students should not only acquire basic skills in literacy and math but also gain a solid understanding of how their government works, what social factors affect the welfare and behaviors of their fellow human beings, and how they can productively use their leisure time and contribute to the general betterment of society (R. M. Thomas, 2005). I don't pretend that assessing such things is easy, but it's essential if we're going to rely on assessment results to determine whether schools are truly meeting students' long-term needs.

🍏 *Advocate for a focus on academic improvement rather than on age-group averages.* Instead of maximizing the number of students who demonstrate minimally acceptable levels of achievement, we should assess the degree to which every student *makes progress* during the school year. This may not be the best approach to assigning final grades (recall my earlier concerns about basing grades on improvement) but it's a reasonable approach to evaluating teachers and schools. You may sometimes see the term value-added assessment used in reference to progress-based evaluation of teachers and schools (e.g., E. M. Anderman, Anderman, Yough, & Gimbert, 2010; Ballou, Sanders, & Wright, 2004).

🍏 *Educate the public about what standardized tests can and cannot do for us.* What I've recently seen and heard in the media leads me to think that many public figures and policy makers overestimate how much standardized achievement tests can tell us: They assume that such instruments are highly accurate, comprehensive measures of what students know and can do. True, these tests are usually developed by experts in test construction, but no test is completely reliable, and its validity will vary considerably depending on the context in which it's being used. It behooves all of us—whether we're teachers, school administrators, parents, or simply members of the general public—to learn about the limitations of standardized tests and educate our fellow citizens accordingly.

🍏 *Consider alternatives to traditional standardized tests.* Especially when a test will be administered to many students at once, it's apt to consist largely of machine-scorable item formats such as multiple-choice. Well-constructed multiple-choice tests certainly have the capacity to assess complex cognitive skills, but they inevitably limit how effectively we can assess certain skill areas, such as in writing and computer technology. Thus some experts argue that we should use authentic assessments either instead of or in addition to more traditional paper–pencil tests (e.g., E. L. Baker, 2007; DiMartino, 2007; L. Shepard et al., 2005). We should be aware, however, that states and school districts that have used authentic, performance assessments on a large scale have encountered difficulties with reliability and validity. As a society, then, we must tread cautiously as we move in this direction.

🍏 *Advocate for the use of multiple measures in any high-stakes decisions.* No matter what kind of assessment techniques we use, no single technique is likely to give us a comprehensive picture of what students have learned and achieved. Even if a single assessment could give us such a picture, perfect reliability is an elusive goal: Students' test results are inevitably subject to temporary swings in motivation, attention, mood, health, and other factors. To base life-altering decisions about students on a single test score is unconscionable.

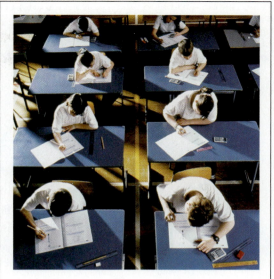

As teachers, we must help educate the public about the limitations of standardized tests, especially those that are used in making important decisions about students and instructional programs.

## Taking Student Diversity into Account

Whenever students take standardized tests, their performance can be affected by factors that aren't necessarily related to the characteristics the tests are intended to assess. If two students have *learned equally* yet *perform differently* on an assessment, the information obtained from the assessment has bias and questionable validity. We have a biased assessment whenever either the specific contents of items or the general behaviors and skills required to do well give some students an unfair advantage over others.

**value-added assessment** Approach to evaluating teacher and school effectiveness based on students' progress rather than on absolute achievement levels.

**bias (in assessment)** Factor in an assessment instrument or procedure that consistently and differentially influences students' performance for reasons unrelated to the characteristic being measured; reduces the validity of assessment results.

**cultural bias** Extent to which assessment tasks either offend or unfairly penalize some students because of their ethnicity, gender, or socioeconomic status.

## CULTURAL BIAS IN TEST CONTENT

An assessment instrument has **cultural bias** if any of its items either offend or unfairly penalize some students on the basis of their ethnicity, gender, or socioeconomic status (e.g., Buck, Kostin, & Morgan, 2002; Popham, 1995). To get a sense of this phenomenon, try the following exercise.

### ◼ EXPERIENCING FIRSTHAND
### HOW PRODUCTIVE WILL YOU BE?

Imagine that you're taking a test designed to estimate your general ability to make productive contributions to the society in which you live. Here are the first three questions on the test:

1. When you enter a hogan, in which direction should you move around the fire?
2. Why is turquoise often attached to a baby's cradleboard?
3. If you need black wool for weaving a rug, which one of the following alternatives would give you the blackest color?
   a. Dye the wool with a mixture of sumac, ochre, and piñon gum.
   b. Dye the wool with a mixture of indigo, lichen, and mesquite.
   c. Use the undyed wool of specially bred black sheep.

Try to answer these questions before you read further.

Did you have trouble answering some or all of the questions? All three were written from the perspective of a particular culture—that of the Navajos in the 1960s. Unless you've had considerable exposure to this culture, you would probably perform poorly. The three answers are (1) clockwise, (2) to ward off evil, and (3) Alternative *a*—"Dye the wool with a mixture of sumac, ochre, and piñon gum" (Gilpin, 1968).

Is the test culturally biased? That depends. If the test is designed to assess your ability to succeed in a Navajo community, the questions might be quite appropriate. But if it's designed to assess your ability to accomplish tasks for which knowledge of Navajo culture is totally irrelevant, the questions have cultural bias.

Two points about cultural bias are important to note. First, the term includes biases related to *gender* and *socioeconomic status* as well as to culture and ethnicity. For example, consider the following hypothetical assessment items, one for a mathematics achievement test and the other for a test of writing skills:

1. As a member of his high school baseball team this year, Mark has hit the ball 17 times in the 36 times he's been at bat. Of those hits, only 12 got him safely to base; the other 5 were either fly balls or sacrifice bunts that resulted in outs. And in three of Mark's at-bats, poor pitches enabled Mark to walk to first base. Based on this information, calculate Mark's batting average for the year so far.
2. Would you rather swim in an ocean, a lake, or a swimming pool? Write a two-page essay defending your choice.

Question 1 assumes a fair amount of knowledge about baseball—knowledge that some students, especially boys, are more likely to have than other students. Question 2 would obviously be difficult for students who haven't swum in all three situations and would be even more difficult for those who have never swum at all; students from low-income, inner-city families might easily fall into one of these two categories.

A second important point is that an assessment instrument is culturally biased if it *offends* a particular group. For example, imagine a test item that implies that girls are more intelligent than boys, and imagine another item that portrays people of a certain country in an unflattering light. Such questions have cultural bias because some students are likely to be offended by the items and thus may be distracted from doing their best. These students might also take the stereotypes to heart, which would adversely affect their sense of self.

An assessment instrument isn't necessarily biased simply because one group gets higher scores on it than another group. It's biased only if the groups' scores are different when the characteristic we're trying to measure *isn't* different for the groups or if the instrument has higher predictive validity for one group than for another. Yes, we may sometimes see group differences in students' scores on particular assessment instruments, but these differences often reflect inequities in students' previous experiences that will affect their future educational performance. For example, if, on average, high school boys are more likely than girls to earn extremely high scores on standardized math tests, the difference may be partly due to the fact that—again, on average—parents more actively encourage boys than girls to learn math (Bleeker & Jacobs, 2004; Halpern et al., 2007; Valla & Ceci, 2011). Similarly, if students from low-income families have had few opportunities to venture beyond their immediate neighborhoods (fewer trips to science museums, less educational travel to other states or countries, etc.), their more limited exposure to diverse environments is likely to impact both their test performance *and* their classroom achievement.

Most publishers of large-scale standardized tests employ individuals who represent numerous minority groups and who actively screen test items for possible sources of cultural bias. Furthermore, most scholastic aptitude tests show similar predictive validity for various ethnic and cultural groups, provided that the members of those groups are native English speakers (R. T. Brown, Reynolds, & Whitaker, 1999; Sattler, 2001; Zwick & Sklar, 2005). Nevertheless, any standardized test should be carefully scrutinized for any items that might be offensive to either gender or to any cultural group, as well as for items that might be more difficult for one group than another for reasons unrelated to the characteristic being measured. And, of course, we should continually be on the lookout for any unintentional cultural bias in the classroom assessment instruments that we ourselves construct.

## CULTURAL AND ETHNIC DIFFERENCES

Even when test content isn't culturally biased, traditional group-administered standardized tests—the paper–pencil variety that involve time limits and electronically scored answer sheets—put students from some cultural and ethnic backgrounds at a disadvantage. For example, timed tests that require answering many questions very quickly can be troublesome for Native American students whose communities have socialized them to carefully think and reflect before responding to questions (Tyler et al., 2008). And children from some cultural backgrounds may have little prior experience with questions to which the adult already knows the answer (Adger, Wolfram, & Christian, 2007; Heath, 1989; Rogoff, 2003). In addition, debilitating test anxiety is more common among students from cultural and ethnic minority groups (R. Carter, Williams, & Silverman, 2008; G. E. García & Pearson, 1994; Putwain, 2007). One possible contributor to this anxiety is a phenomenon known as stereotype threat, in which students from stereotypically low-achieving groups perform more poorly on classroom assessments than they otherwise would simply because they're aware that their group traditionally *does* do poorly (J. Aronson & Steele, 2005; Osborne, Tillman, & Holland, 2010; J. L. Smith, 2004; Walton & Spencer, 2009).

For such reasons, less traditional assessment methods—perhaps dynamic assessment or portfolios—can often provide a more optimistic picture of minority-group students' achievements and abilities (Feuerstein, Feuerstein, & Falik, 2010; Haywood & Lidz, 2007; R. S. Johnson et al., 2006). When circumstances *require* traditional paper–pencil tests, students should have plenty of advance practice in taking them. And to ease students' anxiety, we should encourage them to think of the tests as only rough measures of abilities that will almost certainly improve with future schooling and effort (e.g., C. Good, Aronson, & Inzlicht, 2003).

## LANGUAGE DIFFERENCES AND ENGLISH LANGUAGE LEARNERS

In the earlier section on cultural bias I stated that most scholastic aptitude tests show similar predictive validity for various groups *provided that the members of those groups are native English speakers.* Without question, students' experience and facility with English affects

**stereotype threat** Awareness of a negative stereotype about one's own group and accompanying uneasiness that low performance will confirm the stereotype; leads (often unintentionally) to lower-quality performance.

Scrutinize assessment instruments carefully for tasks that some students might find offensive or might have difficulty answering solely because of their ethnic background, gender, or socioeconomic status.

See Chapter 11 for a more detailed explanation of stereotype threat.

See Chapter 14 for a description of dynamic assessment.

When students' backgrounds put them at a disadvantage in traditional standardized tests, assess their achievements and abilities in other ways. If a standardized paper–pencil test is mandated, give students practice in taking that kind of test, and encourage them to think of the ability being measured as something that will improve with time and practice.

When students have limited proficiency in English, minimize the use of written or spoken English to assess knowledge and skills that are not primarily linguistic in nature.

their performance on English-based assessments of achievement and ability (Kieffer, Lesaux, Rivera, & Francis, 2009; Solórzano, 2008). Poor reading and writing skills are likely to interfere with success on paper–pencil tests, and poor speaking skills can adversely affect students' ability to perform well on oral exams. For example, students whose native language is Spanish perform better on math tests that are given in Spanish rather than English (J. P. Robinson, 2010). For immigrant students in particular, "any test in English is a test *of* English" (E. E. Garcia, 2005).

A particular concern is the use of high-stakes tests with English language learners. When children have learned a language other than English at home, it typically takes them considerable time—perhaps five to seven years—to gain sufficient proficiency in English to perform at their best in English-speaking classrooms (Cummins, 1981, 2000, 2008; Padilla, 2006). Yet many school districts require these students to take high-stakes tests in English when they have only a superficial understanding of the language. Clearly such a practice leads to significant underestimations of English language learners' academic achievement—in other words, the test scores may have poor content validity for these students (Carhill, Suárez-Orozco, & Páez, 2008; Forte, 2010; Solórzano, 2008).

Following are examples of practices we should advocate for English language learners, especially in high-stakes situations:

- Translate a test into a student's native language.
- Let students use a dictionary or other appropriate reference tool.
- Administer a test one on one, perhaps eliminating time limits, presenting questions orally, and allowing students to respond in their native language.
- Use alternative assessment methods (e.g., dynamic assessment, portfolios) to document achievement.
- Exclude students' test scores when computing averages that reflect the overall achievement of a school or a particular subgroup within the school. (Haywood & Lidz, 2007; R. S. Johnson et al., 2006; Kieffer et al., 2009; Solórzano, 2008; W. E. Wright, 2006)

## ACCOMMODATING STUDENTS WITH SPECIAL NEEDS

We must keep students' unique needs and disabilities in mind whenever we want to assess their abilities and summarize their achievements. For example, if instructional goals for a student with a learning disability are different from those for nondisabled classmates, our grading criteria should be altered accordingly, perhaps to be in line with the student's IEP. However, letter grades alone communicate very little information about what students have specifically learned and achieved; if we change the criteria for a particular student, the grades may communicate even *less* information. Portfolios—perhaps including teacher checklists, photographs, audiotapes, and videotapes, as well as students' written work—can be quite helpful for conveying the progress and achievements of students with a variety of disabilities and special needs (Mastropieri & Scruggs, 2007; Venn, 2000).

We may also have to modify standardized testing procedures to accommodate students with special educational needs. In the United States the Individuals with Disabilities Education Act (IDEA) mandates appropriate accommodations for students' disabilities. Such accommodations might involve one or more of the following:

- For a student with limited proficiency in English, administer assessments in his or her native language.
- Modify the presentation format of the assessment (e.g., using Braille or American Sign Language to present test items and other assessment tasks).
- Modify the response format (e.g., dictating answers, allowing use of a word processor).
- Modify the timing (e.g., giving extra time or frequent breaks).
- Modify the assessment setting (e.g., having a student take a standardized paper–pencil test alone in a quiet room).

- Administer only part of an assessment.
- Use instruments different from those given to nondisabled classmates, to be more compatible with students' ability levels and needs. (American Educational Research Association, American Psychological Association, & National Council on Measurement in Education, 1999)

We can often use students' IEPs for guidance about appropriate accommodations for each student. Table 15.4 offers additional suggestions for using standardized tests with students who have special needs.

When we modify educational assessment instruments for students with special needs, we must recognize that there's a trade-off between two of our RSVP characteristics. On the one hand, we're violating the idea that an assessment should be standardized with respect to content, administration, and scoring criteria. On the other hand, if we fail to accommodate the disabilities that some students have, we'll get results that have little validity. There's no magic formula for determining the right balance between standardization and validity for students with special needs. As teachers, we must use our best professional judgment—and perhaps also seek the advice of specialists—in each situation.

We must keep in mind, too, that modifying assessment instruments or procedures for a standardized test may render the test's norms irrelevant; hence any norm-referenced scores we derive may be uninterpretable. When our purpose is to *identify* students' learning and performance difficulties, standardized testing procedures and norm-referenced scores are often quite appropriate. But when we're concerned about how to modify instructional methods and materials to *address* those difficulties, criterion-referenced scores and a close inspection of students' responses to particular tasks and items may be more helpful.

> Chapter 5 identifies specific categories of special needs that fall within the five general categories listed in Table 15.4.

> Keep in mind that published peer-group norms for a standardized test may no longer be applicable when the test is modified in a significant way.

# Confidentiality and Communication about Assessment Results

Students' test scores, class grades, and other assessment results should be confidential, as the following exercise can show you.

### EXPERIENCING FIRSTHAND
### HOW WOULD YOU FEEL?

How would you feel if one of your instructors did the following?

- Returned test papers in the order of students' test scores, so that those with highest scores were handed out first, and you received yours *last*.
- Told your other instructors how poorly you had done on the test, so that they could be on the lookout for other stupid things you might do.
- Looked through your school records and discovered that you scored 87 on an IQ test you took last year and that a schoolwide personality test you unknowingly also took has revealed some unusual sexual fantasies.

You'd probably be outraged if your instructor did *any* of these things.

But exactly *how* confidential should students' assessment results be? When should people know the results of students' assessments, and who should know them? In the United States we get legal guidance on these questions from the **Family Educational Rights and Privacy Act (FERPA)**, passed by the U.S. Congress in 1974. This legislation limits normal school testing practices primarily to the assessment of achievement and scholastic aptitude—two things that are clearly within the school's domain. Furthermore, it restricts access to students' assessment results to the few individuals who really need to know them: the students

> **Family Educational Rights and Privacy Act (FERPA)** U.S. legislation passed in 1974 that gives students and parents access to school records and limits other people's access to those records.

## STUDENTS IN INCLUSIVE SETTINGS

**TABLE 15.4 • Using Standardized Tests with Students Who Have Special Educational Needs**

| CATEGORY | CHARACTERISTICS YOU MIGHT OBSERVE | SUGGESTED STRATEGIES |
|---|---|---|
| Students with specific cognitive or academic difficulties | • Poor listening, reading, and/or writing skills (for some students)<br>• Tendency for test scores to underestimate overall achievement levels (if students have poor reading skills)<br>• Inconsistent performance due to off-task behaviors (e.g., hyperactivity, inattentiveness), affecting reliability and validity of scores (for some students with learning disabilities or ADHD)<br>• Higher-than-average test anxiety | • Modify test administration procedures to accommodate disabilities identified in students' IEPs (e.g., when administering a districtwide essay test, allow students with writing disabilities to use a word processor and spell checker).<br>• Have students take tests in a room with minimal distractions.<br>• Make sure students understand what they're being asked to do.<br>• Be sure students are motivated to do their best but not overly anxious.<br>• Use classroom assessments (both formal and informal) to confirm or disconfirm results of standardized test results.<br>• Record and report all modifications of standardized procedures. |
| Students with social or behavioral problems | • Inconsistent performance due to off-task behaviors or lack of motivation, affecting reliability and validity of scores (for some students) | • Modify test administration procedures to accommodate disabilities identified in students' IEPs (e.g., when students are easily distracted, administer tests individually in a quiet room).<br>• Convince students that doing their best can in some way enhance their long-term well-being.<br>• Use classroom assessments (both formal and informal) to confirm or disconfirm results of standardized test results.<br>• Record and report all modifications of standardized procedures. |
| Students with general delays in cognitive and social functioning | • Slow learning and cognitive processing<br>• Limited or no reading skills<br>• Poor listening skills | • Choose assessments appropriate for students' cognitive abilities and reading and writing skills.<br>• Minimize the use of assessments that are administered to an entire class at once; rely more on those that are administered one on one.<br>• Make sure students understand what they're being asked to do. |
| Students with physical or sensory challenges | • Mobility problems (for some students with physical challenges)<br>• Tendency to tire easily (for some students with physical challenges)<br>• Less developed language skills, affecting reading and writing ability (for some students with hearing loss) | • Obtain modified test materials for students with visual impairments (e.g., large-print or Braille test booklets).<br>• Modify test administration procedures to accommodate students' unique needs (e.g., have a sign language interpreter give directions to students with hearing loss, or have students with limited muscle control dictate their answers).<br>• If reading and writing skills are impaired, read test items to students.<br>• Break lengthy assessments into segments that can be administered on separate occasions.<br>• Schedule tests at times when students feel rested and alert.<br>• Record and report all modifications of standardized procedures.<br>• Don't compare a student's performance to that of the norm group if significant modifications have been made. |
| Students with advanced cognitive development | • Greater interest and engagement in challenging tests<br>• Tendency in some students to hide giftedness to avoid possible ridicule by peers<br>• In some instances, ability levels beyond the scope of typical tests for the grade level | • Keep assessment results confidential.<br>• When students consistently earn perfect or near-perfect scores (e.g., percentile ranks of 99), request individualized testing that can more accurately assess their very high ability levels.<br>• Use dynamic assessments as an alternative to traditional ability tests to identify giftedness in students from diverse cultural or linguistic backgrounds. |

*Sources:* Barkley, 2006; Beirne-Smith, Patton, & Kim, 2006; D. Y. Ford & Harris, 1992; A. W. Gottfried, Fleming, & Gottfried, 1994; N. Gregg, 2009; Haywood & Lidz, 2007; Mastropieri & Scruggs, 2007; Mercer & Pullen, 2005; M. S. Meyer, 2000; B. N. Phillips, Pitcher, Worsham, & Miller, 1980; Piirto, 1999; Pitoniak & Royer, 2001; J. A. Stein & Krishnan, 2007; Turnbull, Turnbull, & Wehmeyer, 2010; Venn, 2000; Whitaker Sena, Lowe, & Lee, 2007.

who earn them, their parents, and school personnel directly involved with students' education and well-being. Assessment results can be shared with other individuals (e.g., a family doctor or a psychologist in private practice) *only* if the student (if at least 18 years old) or a parent gives written permission. Following are three implications of this legislative mandate for our classroom practices:

- We *cannot* ask students to reveal their political affiliation, sexual attitudes, illegal behaviors, potentially embarrassing psychological problems, or family income. (An exception: Questions about income to determine eligibility for financial assistance are allowed.)

- We *cannot* post test scores in ways that allow students to learn one another's scores. (For example, we can't post scores in alphabetical order or according to birthdays or social security numbers.)

- We *cannot* distribute papers in any way that allows students to observe one another's scores. (For example, we can't let students search through a stack of scored papers to find their own.)

Many educators initially interpreted FERPA as forbidding teachers to have students grade one another's test papers. In 2002, however, the U.S. Supreme Court ruled that this practice doesn't violate FERPA because the test scores obtained aren't yet a part of students' permanent school records.[5] Nevertheless, although students can certainly give one another feedback on tasks used for formative assessment purposes, I strongly urge you *not* to have students swap and grade quizzes or other assessments that yield obvious high and low scores.

Keeping students' assessment results confidential makes educational as well as legal sense. Low scores can be a source of shame and embarrassment—and are even more so if classmates know about them—and thus can increase students' anxiety levels about future assessments. Students with high scores can also suffer from having the results made public: At many schools it isn't cool to be smart, and high achievers may perform at lower levels to avoid risking peer rejection. And, of course, publicizing students' assessment results focuses students' attention on performance goals—how they appear to others—rather than on mastering the subject matter.

In the opening case study, the teacher announces Ellie's grades to the entire class. The teacher's remarks violate FERPA, which applies to final grades as well as to individual assessments. Furthermore, making Ellie's grades public isn't in Ellie's best interest. Rather than motivate her to work harder (she's already highly motivated), it distresses her to the point that she no longer feels comfortable in the classroom.

An additional provision of FERPA is that parents and students (if at least 18 years old) have the right to review test scores and other school records. And school personnel must present and interpret this information in a way that parents and students can understand.

## COMMUNICATING ASSESSMENT RESULTS TO STUDENTS AND PARENTS

Consider what happens when students in Ms. Ford's middle school math class learn that many of them have done poorly on a recent quiz:

> *Ms. Ford:* If you received a grade below 75 you definitely have to work on it. I do expect this quiz to be returned with Mom or Dad's signature on it. I want Mom and Dad to be aware of how we're doing.
>
> *Student:* No!
>
> *Student:* Do we have to show our parents? Is it a requirement to pass the class?
>
> *Ms. Ford:* If you do not return it with a signature, I will call home. (J. C. Turner, Meyer, et al., 1998, p. 741)

Ms. Ford wants parents to know that their children aren't doing well in her class, but her approach has three drawbacks. First, many students may find it easier to forge an adultlike signature than

**Keep students' assessment results confidential; for example, don't post assessment results in ways that allow students to discover how their classmates have performed.**

You can see more of this class discussion in the opening case study in Chapter 14.

---

[5] *Owasso Independent School District v. Falvo*, 534 U.S. 426.

to deliver bad news to a parent. Second, parents who do see their children's test papers won't have much information to help them interpret the results. (Are the low scores due to little effort? Poor study strategies? Poor instruction?) And third, Ms. Ford focuses entirely on the problem—low achievement—without offering suggestions for *solving* it.

As teachers, we must think of ourselves as working in cooperation with students and parents for something that everyone wants: students' academic success. Our primary goal in communicating classroom assessment results is to share information that will help achieve that end—something Ms. Ford neglects to do. Furthermore, because many students have done poorly on the test, Ms. Ford should consider whether something *she* has done—or not done—might account for the low scores. For instance, perhaps she allocated insufficient class time to certain concepts and skills, used ineffective strategies in teaching them, or constructed an exceptionally difficult test.

When we need to report standardized test results, we face a different challenge: How do we explain the results to students and parents who know very little about such tests and the kinds of scores they yield? Following are several guidelines that experts offered many years ago (Durost, 1961; Ricks, 1959) but are still relevant today:

🍎 *Make sure you understand the results yourself.* When conveying information about standardized test results, we need to know something about a test's reliability and validity for the situation in which we've used it. We also need to know the general nature of the test scores—for example, whether they're criterion-referenced or norm-referenced and, if norm-referenced, how to interpret them.

🍎 *Remember that in many cases it is sufficient to describe the test and students' performance in broad, general terms.* To illustrate, we might describe an achievement test as a general measure of how much a student has learned in science compared to what other students around the country have learned, or we might describe a scholastic aptitude test as something that provides a rough idea of how well a student is likely to do in a particular instructional program. It's sometimes possible to describe a student's performance without mentioning test scores at all. For example, we might say, "Your daughter scores like students who do well in college math courses" or "Your son had more-than-average difficulty on the spelling subtest; this is an area in which he may need extra help in the next few years." However, if parents want to know their child's specific test scores, in the United States FERPA requires that we reveal them and help parents understand what they mean.

🍎 *When reporting specific test scores, emphasize scores that are least likely to be misinterpreted.* Many parents mistakenly believe that a child's grade-equivalent score reflects the grade level the child should actually be in; consequently they may argue for advanced placement of high-achieving children or feel distressed that low-achieving children are in over their heads. And many parents interpret scores labeled as "IQs" as reflecting a permanent, unchangeable ability rather than a rough estimate of a child's present cognitive functioning (recall that the printout in Figure 15.12 uses the label "SAI" for Otis-Lennon scores based on the IQ scale). By reporting other kinds of scores—perhaps percentile ranks, stanines, or NCEs—we're less likely to have parents jumping to such erroneous conclusions. Many parents are familiar with percentile ranks, and many others can easily grasp the notion of a percentile if it's explained to them. But because percentile ranks misrepresent actual differences among students (i.e., by overestimating actual ability differences in the middle range and underestimating differences at the extremes), we may also want to provide stanine scores or NCEs. Although most parents are unfamiliar with standard scores in general, we can help them understand these two particular scores using a concrete graphic, such as the one presented in Figure 15.13.

Also, when test results include confidence intervals, such as those depicted in the computer printouts previously shown in Figures 15.7 and 15.12, it's helpful to explain them to parents. By reporting confidence intervals along with specific test scores, we communicate an important point about classroom assessment: Any test score has some error associated with it.

You can learn more about fostering teacher–parent partnerships in Chapter 13.

**FIGURE 15.13  A graphic for helping parents understand stanines and NCE scores**

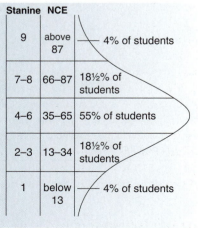

| Stanine | NCE | |
|---|---|---|
| 9 | above 87 | 4% of students |
| 7–8 | 66–87 | 18½% of students |
| 4–6 | 35–65 | 55% of students |
| 2–3 | 13–34 | 18½% of students |
| 1 | below 13 | 4% of students |

Whenever we assess students' achievement and abilities, we must remember that our primary purpose is to *help students learn and achieve more effectively*. When students perform well on classroom assessments and standardized tests, we have cause for celebration, because we know that our instructional strategies are working as they should. But when students perform poorly, our primary concern—and that of students and parents as well—should be how to improve the situation. You can see more of this class discussion in the opening case study in Chapter 14.

# 15    What Have You Learned?

Not only are the RSVP characteristics important for individual assessments, but they're also important—in fact, they're even *more* important—for summaries of students' general achievement and ability levels. Indicators of overall achievement should be reliable (reflecting a consistent pattern over time), standardized for all students (except in extenuating circumstances, such as when students have certain disabilities), valid (reflecting actual achievement and abilities), and practical (taking only a reasonable amount of a teacher's time and effort). What's ultimately *most* important is that assessment results are sufficiently accurate and dependable that they can effectively guide decision making in classrooms and schools.

With these points in mind, we now return to the chapter's learning outcomes and review some of the chapter's key ideas.

■ **15.1: Describe the nature, advantages, and disadvantages of three types of test scores: raw scores, criterion-referenced scores, and norm-referenced scores.** Assessment scores take a number of forms, with different scores having distinctly different meanings. *Raw scores,* based on the number or percentage of items answered correctly or the number of points accumulated, have only limited utility unless they can be compared to a criterion for performance or to the performance of a norm group. *Criterion-referenced scores* tell us specifically what students know and can do. *Norm-referenced scores*—age and grade equivalents, percentile ranks, and standard scores—enable us to compare our own students' performance to the performance of others. Because age and grade equivalents are often misinterpreted and percentile ranks distort actual ability differences among students, standard scores are preferable whenever we need to compare students to their peers.

*Evaluate* and *apply* your knowledge related to this learning outcome in MyEducationLab™.

■ **15.2: Identify important guidelines to follow in summarizing students' achievement with final grades and portfolios.** Most teachers eventually need to boil down the results of classroom assessments into general indicators of what students have learned. The most common procedure, of course, is to assign final grades that summarize what students have achieved over the course of the term or school year. Typically final grades should reflect actual achievement (rather than effort or some other subjective quality) and be based on hard data.

The problem with grades, of course, is that they communicate very little about what a student specifically has learned and can do. An alternative to grades—a *portfolio*—provides a means for representing the multifaceted, complex nature of students' accomplishments. When used to summarize students' achievement, portfolio contents should be closely tied to important instructional goals and standards, and students should have teacher guidance in choosing artifacts to include.

*Evaluate* and *apply* your knowledge related to this learning outcome in MyEducationLab™.

■ **15.3: Describe four different kinds of standardized tests, and explain how you might appropriately use and interpret such tests.** A wide variety of standardized tests are available for use in classrooms, including tests of achievement, general scholastic aptitude, specific aptitudes and abilities, and school readiness. As teachers, we must make sure that any standardized test we use meets the RSVP characteristics for our own situation and, if norm-referenced, has appropriate norms to which our students can be compared. Furthermore, we must take developmental factors into account when interpreting the results of standardized tests; for instance, young children's limited language skills and short attention spans make it more difficult to get valid assessments of their abilities, and some adolescents may be so cynical about the value of standardized tests that they put little thought or effort into their responses.

*Evaluate* and *apply* your knowledge related to this learning outcome in MyEducationLab™.

■ **15.4: Explain how high-stakes testing and accountability practices can affect instruction and classroom learning, and suggest several strategies for maximizing the benefits of these practices.** Increasingly standardized achievement tests are being used to make important decisions about students and to hold school personnel accountable for students' achievement levels. For example, in the United States the No Child Left Behind Act of 2001 mandates ongoing assessments of students' achievement in reading, math, and science; sanctions and corrective actions can be imposed on schools that don't show regular progress in these areas. Many experts believe that such *high-stakes testing* and *accountability* create as many problems as they solve, but these practices are here to stay, at least for the short run. Thus, educators must become vocal advocates for reasonable, valid approaches to assessing students' overall progress and achievement, with an emphasis on enhancing instruction and learning rather than on punishing low-achieving students and schools.

*Evaluate* and *apply* your knowledge related to this learning outcome in MyEducationLab™.

■ **15.5: Explain how you might accommodate cultural and linguistic diversity and special educational needs in your efforts to summarize students' achievement.** Students' test scores and other assessment results are affected by a variety of factors (motivation, energy level, misinterpretation of assessment tasks, etc.) that impact reliability and validity. Furthermore, limited proficiency with the English language can interfere with some students' performance, as can cultural bias in the questions or tasks presented. Whenever we suspect that such factors may be affecting students' performance, we should interpret assessment results cautiously and look for other information that might either confirm or disconfirm those results. Furthermore, we should make reasonable accommodations for students' disabilities when administering tests to assess their achievement and abilities; such accommodations will increase the likelihood that the assessments yield useful information.

*Evaluate* and *apply* your knowledge related to this learning outcome in MyEducationLab™.

■ **15.6: Distinguish between the circumstances in which you should and should not reveal students' assessment results, and explain how you can effectively communicate these results to students and parents.** For both legal and pedagogical reasons, we must keep students' assessment results confidential, communicating assessment scores and other information only to the students themselves, to their parents, and to school personnel directly involved in the students' education and well-being. We must also describe assessment results in ways that students and parents can understand—for instance, by using graphics that illustrate the nature of various norm-referenced scores—and we must remember that the ultimate purpose of any assessment is to *help students learn and achieve more effectively.*

*Evaluate* and *apply* your knowledge related to this learning outcome in MyEducationLab™.

## Practice for Your Licensure Exam

### Can Johnny Read?

Ms. Beaudry is serving on a committee to study reading curricula in her school district. As part of her work with the committee, she plans to administer a standardized reading achievement test to determine whether her sixth graders have mastered the reading skills she has been trying to teach them this year. She's been given the opportunity to select the test from three instruments approved for purchase in her district. She scrutinizes the test manuals carefully and eliminates one test when she sees that it has poor test-retest reliability. She looks closely at tables of specifications for the other two tests and eventually selects the Comprehensive Reading Test (CRT) as the most reliable and valid measure for her own class.

Ms. Beaudry gives the test to her class, following the prescribed administration procedures closely. Because the test consists entirely of multiple-choice items, she is able to score the results quickly and easily that night. She computes each student's raw score and then turns to the norms in the test manual to obtain stanine scores. Her students' stanines range from 3 to 8. "Hmmm, what now?" she asks herself. "After all of this, I still don't know if my students have learned what I've been trying to teach them."

1. **Constructed-response question:**

   Ms. Beaudry chooses the wrong test for her purpose. What specifically does she do wrong?

2. **Multiple-choice question:**

   Ms. Beaudry uses tables of specifications to determine the validity of two of the tests for her own situation. Which one of the following statements best describes a typical table of specifications?

   a. It describes the ideal curriculum for a particular content domain and grade level.

   b. It provides specific, item-by-item scoring criteria that enable objective, reliable scoring.

   c. It indicates the topics covered by an assessment and the things that students should be able to do related to each topic.

   d. It presents the average performance of students at various grade and age levels, thereby enabling conversion of a raw score to one or more norm-referenced scores.

---

**PRAXIS**  Go to AppendixC , "Matching Book and MyEducationLab™ to the Praxis Principles of Learning and Teaching Tests," to discover sections of this chapter that may be especially applicable to the Praxis tests.

# Appendix A

## Describing Associations with Correlation Coefficients

- Do students with high self-esteem perform better in school than students with low self-esteem?
- As students move through the grade levels, do they become more intrinsically motivated to learn classroom subject matter or, instead, less intrinsically motivated to learn it?
- When students are given two different tests of general cognitive ability in the same week, how similar are their scores on the two tests likely to be?
- Are intellectually gifted students more emotionally well adjusted than their classmates of average intelligence?

Each of these questions asks about an association between two variables—whether it be an association between self-esteem and school achievement, between grade level and intrinsic motivation, between two tests of general cognitive ability, or between giftedness and emotional adjustment. The nature of such associations is sometimes summarized by a statistic known as a correlation coefficient.

A correlation coefficient is a number between −1 and +1; most correlation coefficients are decimals (either positive or negative) somewhere between these two extremes. A correlation coefficient for two variables tells us about both the direction and the strength of the association between the variables.

**Direction.** The direction of the association is indicated by the *sign* of the coefficient—in other words, by whether the number is positive or negative. A positive number indicates a *positive correlation:* As one variable increases, the other variable also increases. For example, there's a positive correlation between self-esteem and school achievement: Students with higher self-esteem achieve at higher levels (e.g., Marsh, Gerlach, Trautwein, Lüdtke, & Brettschneider, 2007). In contrast, a negative number indicates a *negative correlation:* As one variable increases, the other variable decreases instead. For example, there's a negative correlation between grade level and intrinsic motivation: On average, students in the upper grades (e.g., in junior high) have less intrinsic motivation to master classroom subject matter than younger students do (e.g., Gottfried, Fleming, & Gottfried, 2001). Figure A.1 graphically depicts the two correlations just described.

**Strength.** The strength of the association is indicated by the *size* of the coefficient. A number close to either +1 or −1 (e.g., +.89 or −.76) indicates a *strong* correlation: The two variables are closely related, so knowing the level of one variable allows us to predict the level of the other variable with considerable accuracy. For example, we often find a strong correlation between two tests of general cognitive ability given within a short time period: Students tend to get similar scores on both tests, especially if the tests cover similar kinds of content (e.g., McGrew, Flanagan, Zeith, & Vanderwood, 1997). In contrast, a number close to 0 (e.g., +.15 or −.22) indicates a *weak* correlation: Knowing the level of one variable allows us to predict the level of the other variable but without much accuracy. For example, there's a weak association between intellectual giftedness and emotional adjustment: In general, students with higher measured intelligence levels (IQ scores) show better emotional well-being than students with lower scores (e.g., Janos & Robinson, 1985), but many students are exceptions to this general rule. Correlations in the middle range (e.g., those in the .40s and .50s, either positive or negative) indicate a *moderate* correlation.

As teachers, we'll often encounter correlation coefficients in research articles in our professional books and journals. For instance, we might read that students' visual–spatial thinking ability is positively correlated with their success in a math class or that there's a negative correlation between class size and students' achievement test scores. Whenever we see such evidence of correlation, we must remember one very important point: *Correlation does not necessarily indicate*

**correlation coefficient** Statistic that indicates the strength and direction of an association between two variables.

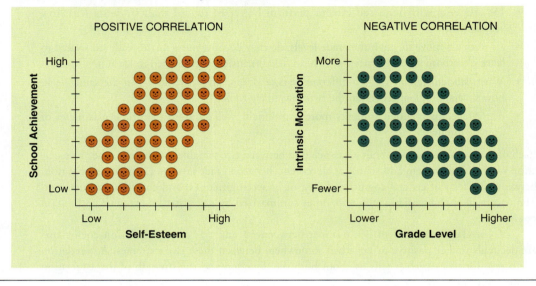

**FIGURE A.1** Each face in these two graphs represents one student in a group of 50 students. The location of the face tells the extent to which a student is high or low on the two characteristics indicated. There is a *positive correlation* between self-esteem and school achievement: Students with higher self-esteem tend to achieve at higher levels. There is a *negative correlation* between grade level and intrinsic motivation: Students in higher grades tend to have less intrinsic motivation to learn school subject matter than students in lower grades.

Experimental studies are described in Chapter 1.

*causation.* For example, we can't say that visual–spatial thinking ability specifically *leads to* greater mathematical ability, nor can we say that a large class size specifically *interferes with* classroom achievement. Each of these italicized phrases implies a causal relationship that doesn't necessarily exist. Only carefully designed experimental studies enable us to draw conclusions about the extent to which one thing causes or influences another.

Many calculators are now programmed to compute correlation coefficients. You can also find websites that enable you to calculate correlations and other simple statistics (e.g., www .easycalculation.com). Computing a correlation coefficient by hand is complicated but certainly possible. If you're interested in learning more, you can find the formula through an Internet search or in most introductory statistics textbooks.

# Appendix B

## Determining Reliability and Predictive Validity

If you've read Appendix A, you've already learned something about correlation coefficients—statistics that indicate the strength and direction of an association between two variables. A correlation coefficient is always a number between −1 and +1. A coefficient close to either +1 or −1 (e.g., +.89 or −.76) indicates a strong correlation, whereas a number close to 0 (e.g., +.15 or −.22) indicates a weak correlation. A *positive* coefficient (i.e., one preceded by either a plus sign or no sign at all) indicates a positive relationship: As one variable increases, the other variable also increases. A negative coefficient (i.e., one preceded by a minus sign) indicates a negative relationship: As one variable increases, the other variable *decreases*.

Psychologists sometimes use correlation coefficients to determine the reliability and predictive validity of an assessment instrument.

### Determining Reliability

The reliability of a test or other assessment instrument is the extent to which it yields consistent information about the knowledge, skills, or characteristics we're trying to assess. To mathematically calculate the reliability of an assessment instrument, we begin by getting two scores on the same instrument for the same group of students. We can get these two sets of scores in at least three different ways, with each approach giving us a somewhat different angle on the instrument's reliability. If we use the same instrument to assess students on two different occasions, we get information about test–retest reliability: the extent to which the instrument yields similar results over a short time interval. If we ask two or more people to judge students' performance (e.g., to grade the same set of essays or rate the same gymnastic performance), we get information about scorer reliability: the extent to which different people agree in their judgments of students' performance. If we compute two or more subscores for different items on the same instrument and look at how similar those subscores are, we get information about internal consistency reliability: the extent to which different parts of the instrument all assess the same characteristic.

Once we have two sets of scores for a single group of students, we can determine how similar the two sets are by computing a correlation coefficient; in this case it's more frequently called a *reliability coefficient*. A reliability coefficient typically ranges from 0 to +1.[1] A number close to +1 indicates high reliability: The two sets of test scores are very similar. Although a perfect reliability coefficient of 1.00 is rare, many objectively scorable standardized achievement and ability tests have reliabilities of .90 or above, reflecting a high degree of consistency in the scores they yield. As reliability coefficients decrease, they indicate more error in the assessment results—error due to temporary, and in most cases irrelevant, factors. Publishers of standardized achievement and ability tests typically calculate and report reliability coefficients for the various scores and subscores the tests yield.

#### ESTIMATING ERROR IN ASSESSMENT RESULTS

A reliability coefficient tells us, in general, the degree to which temporary errors contribute to fluctuations in students' assessment results. But how much error is apt to be present in a *single* score? In other words, how close is a particular student's score to what it really should be? A number known as the standard error of measurement (SEM) allows us to estimate how close or far off the score might be. The standard error of measurement is calculated from the reliability coefficient; you can find details by searching "calculating standard error of measurement" through a

The "Fowl Play" exercise in Chapter 14 is an example of poor test–retest reliability.

**correlation coefficient** Statistic that indicates the strength and direction of an association between two variables.

**reliability** Extent to which an assessment yields consistent information about the knowledge, skills, or characteristics being assessed.

**test–retest reliability** Extent to which a particular assessment instrument yields similar results over a short time interval.

**scorer reliability** Extent to which different people agree in their judgments of students' performance on an assessment; sometimes called *interrater reliability*.

**internal consistency reliability** Extent to which different parts of an assessment instrument all assess the same characteristic.

**standard error of measurement (SEM)** Statistic estimating the amount of error in a test score or other assessment result.

---

[1]A negative coefficient is possible but would be obtained only when an *inverse* relationship between the two sets of scores exists—that is, when students who get the highest scores one time get the lowest scores the other time, and vice versa. Such an outcome is highly unlikely when calculating reliability.

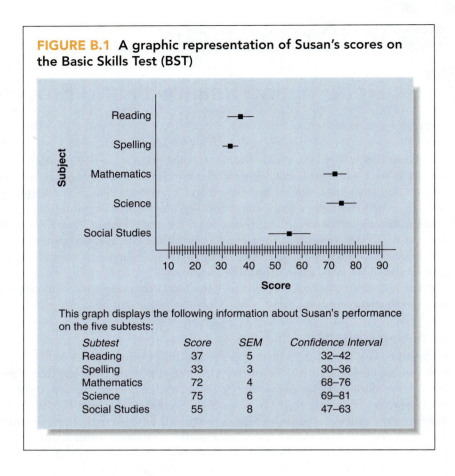

**FIGURE B.1** A graphic representation of Susan's scores on the Basic Skills Test (BST)

This graph displays the following information about Susan's performance on the five subtests:

| Subtest | Score | SEM | Confidence Interval |
|---|---|---|---|
| Reading | 37 | 5 | 32–42 |
| Spelling | 33 | 3 | 30–36 |
| Mathematics | 72 | 4 | 68–76 |
| Science | 75 | 6 | 69–81 |
| Social Studies | 55 | 8 | 47–63 |

search engine such as Google or Yahoo! (Be careful *not* to click on sites that address standard error of the *mean,* which is a statistic used for an entirely different purpose.)

Let's look at a concrete example. Imagine that Susan takes an academic achievement test known as the Basic Skills Test (BST). Imagine, too, that with her current level of reading ability, Susan should ideally get a score of 40 on the BST Reading subtest. Susan's ideal score of 40 is her **true score**: This is what she would theoretically get if we could measure her reading achievement with complete accuracy. But Susan misinterprets a few test items, answering them incorrectly when in fact she knows the correct answers, so she actually gets a score of only 37. Because we can't see inside Susan's head, we have no way of determining what her true score is; we know only that she's earned a 37 on the test. To estimate the amount of error in her score, we consult the BST test manual and learn that the standard error of measurement for the Reading subtest is, let's say, 5 points. We can then guess that Susan's true score probably lies somewhere within a range that's one SEM to either side of her test score: 37±5, or between 32 and 42.[2]

Because almost any assessment score includes a certain amount of error, assessment results are sometimes reported not as specific scores, but as a range, or **confidence interval**. (The term *confidence band* is sometimes used instead, especially in computer-generated test reports for students and parents.) A confidence interval extends 1 SEM to either side of the actual test score. By reporting confidence intervals along with specific test scores, we communicate an important point about the tests we give: Any test score has some error associated with it. Figure B.1 shows how we might report Susan's scores on the Reading and other subtests of the BST. Notice that the confidence intervals for the different subtests are different lengths, because each subtest has a different standard error of measurement.

**true score** Hypothetical score a student would obtain if an assessment measured a characteristic or ability with complete accuracy.

**confidence interval** Range around an assessment score reflecting the amount of error that is likely to be affecting the score's accuracy.

[2]Technically speaking, the simple add–and–subtract approach I describe here applies only to standard scores; it's a tad more complicated for other norm-referenced scores, such as percentile ranks and grade- and age-equivalents. But for most of my readers, details might be TMI—too much information—in an introductory discussion of assessment such as this one.

When we use a single standard error of measurement (SEM) to determine the confidence interval, there's a 68 percent chance that the student's true score lies within that interval. If we instead use two SEMs to determine the interval (for Susan's reading score, such an interval would be 27 to 47), we can be 95 percent confident that the true score lies within it.[3]

If two or more test scores come from the same test battery—and thus involve the same norm group—we can use the 68 percent confidence intervals for the scores to make meaningful comparisons. Overlapping confidence intervals for any two subtests indicate that the student has performed equally well in the two areas. But if the intervals show no overlap, we can reasonably conclude that the student has done appreciably better in one area than the other. Using this approach with Susan's BST scores, we can conclude that Susan has performed best on the math and science subtests, less well on the social studies subtest, and least well on the reading and spelling subtests. We would *not* say that she has done better in science than in math or that she has done better in reading than in spelling, because the confidence intervals overlap for those two pairs of scores.

## DETERMINING PREDICTIVE VALIDITY

The predictive validity of an assessment instrument (you may also see the term *criterion validity*) is the extent to which the instrument accurately predicts future performance in some domain. Publishers of standardized, norm-referenced ability tests often determine the accuracy with which test scores predict later success in certain content areas. To do so, they first give a test to a group of people; a few months or years later, they measure the same group's success or competence in the behavior being predicted (i.e., the criterion behavior). They then calculate the correlation coefficient between the test scores and the criterion behavior. As is true for a reliability coefficient, this *validity coefficient* is typically a number between 0 and +1, with higher numbers indicating greater predictive validity. Tests with relatively high predictive validity for a particular behavior (e.g., validity coefficients in the .60s and .70s are usually considered high) predict that behavior fairly well. Those with lower predictive validity (e.g., coefficients in the .30s and .40s) yield less accurate predictions.

Any test's predictive validity can vary considerably depending on the specific criterion being predicted; for example, many scholastic aptitude tests more accurately predict academic performance in the near future (e.g., within the next two or three years) than in the distant future. Predictive validity also depends somewhat on the age-group in question; for instance, validity coefficients tend to be higher for students in the upper elementary and secondary grades than they are for young children. Typical validity coefficients for general scholastic aptitude tests (including intelligence tests) range between .40 and .70. Those for specific aptitude tests often fall below .50.

**predictive validity** Extent to which the results of an assessment predict future performance in a particular domain; sometimes called *criterion validity.*

---

[3]If you have some knowledge of descriptive statistics, it may help you to know that the SEM is the standard deviation for the hypothetical distribution of all possible scores that a student with a particular true score might get.

# Appendix C

## Matching Book and MyEducationLab™ Content to the Praxis® *Principles of Learning and Teaching* Tests

In the United States, state teacher licensing requirements in many states include passing Praxis tests published by Educational Testing Service (ETS). Among the Praxis tests are four Principles of Learning and Teaching (PLT) tests, one each for teachers seeking licensure for early childhood and for grades K–6, 5–9, and 7–12. This text, *Educational Psychology: Developing Learners* addresses most of the topics covered in the PLT tests. The left column of Table C.1 presents the topics covered on the tests, as identified in *The Praxis Series: Official Guide* (Educational Testing Service, 2008, pp. 348–364). The middle column of the table indicates chapters and sections in *Educational Psychology: Developing Learners* that are relevant to these topics. The right column suggests relevant exercises and readings in MyEducationLab™.

*The Praxis Series*™ Assessments* involve reading and analyzing case studies. For this reason, the case studies and "Practice for Your Licensure Exam" exercises presented in *Educational Psychology: Developing Learners* may be especially helpful as you prepare for these tests. The opening case study in each chapter is addressed in several places throughout the chapter. The "Practice for Your Licensure Exam" exercise presents a second case study and poses questions that encourage you to apply the chapter content. You will find additional case study material in some of the resources in MyEducationLab™.

You may also want to obtain your own copy of *The Praxis Series: Official Guide*. It provides practice case studies and offers suggestions for analyzing them and responding to test questions. You can purchase a copy through various online vendors, including the following:

- Educational Testing Service
  www.ets.org/store.html
- McGraw-Hill
  www.mhprofessional.com
- Amazon
  www.amazon.com
- Barnes and Noble
  www.barnesandnoble.com

At some of these websites, you may need to type "Praxis Official Guide" in the "Search" box.

* *The Praxis Series, Professional Assessments for Beginning Teachers* is a registered trademark of Educational Testing Service (ETS). Praxis materials are reprinted by permission of ETS. Permission to reprint does not constitute review or endorsement by Educational Testing Service of this publication.

## TABLE C.1 • Matching Book and MyEducationLab™ Content to the PRAXIS™ Principles of Learning and Teaching Tests

| TOPICS IN THE PRAXIS PRINCIPLES OF LEARNING AND TEACHING (PLT) TESTS | LOCATION OF TOPICS IN ORMROD'S *EDUCATIONAL PSYCHOLOGY* (8TH ED.) | LOCATION OF TOPICS AND PRACTICE OPPORTUNITIES IN MyEducationLab™ |
|---|---|---|
| **I. Students as Learners** | | |
| **A. Student Development and the Learning Process** | | |
| ► Theoretical foundations about how learning occurs: how students construct knowledge, acquire skills, and develop habits of mind | **Chapter 2:** "The Multiple Layers of Environmental Influence: Bronfenbrenner's Theory" (pp. 21–22); "Piaget's Theory of Cognitive Development" (pp. 25–36); "Vygotsky's Theory of Cognitive Development" (pp. 36–45) **Chapters 6–10:** Entire chapters (pp. 154–331) | |
| ► Examples of important theorists: | **Chapter 10:** Entire chapter (pp. 298–331); especially see "Basic Assumptions of Social Cognitive Theory" (pp. 299–301) | |
| • Albert Bandura | | |
| • Jerome Bruner | See Bruner citations in the Name Index. | |
| • John Dewey | | |
| • Jean Piaget | **Chapter 2:** "Piaget's Theory of Cognitive Development" (pp. 25–36); "Contrasting Piaget's and Vygotsky's Theories" (pp. 44–45); **Practice for Your Licensure Exam: "Stones Lesson"** (pp. 52–53) | **Assignments and Activities: Understanding Research** exercise "Class Inclusion" in topic "Cognitive and Linguistic Development" |
| • Lev Vygotsky | **Chapter 2:** "Vygotsky's Theory of Cognitive Development" (pp. 36–45); **Practice for Your Licensure Exam: "Stones Lesson"** (pp. 52–53) | **Building Teaching Skills and Dispositions** exercise "Using Cognitive Tools" in topic "Cognitive and Linguistic Development" |
| • Howard Gardner | **Chapter 5:** "Gardner's Multiple Intelligences" (pp. 121–122) | |
| • Abraham Maslow | **Chapter 11:** "A Possible Hierarchy of Needs: Maslow's Theory" (pp. 344–345) | |
| • B. F. Skinner | **Chapter 9: Case Study: "The Attention Getter"** (p. 265); "Learning from Consequences: Instrumental Conditioning" (pp. 270–280); "Shaping New Behaviors" (pp. 284–285) | **Supplementary Reading** "Schedules of Reinforcement" in Book-Specific Resources for Chapter 9 **Supplementary Reading** "Programmed Instruction and Computer-Assisted Instruction" in Book-Specific Resources for Chapter 12 |
| ► Important terms that relate to learning theory: • Constructivism | **Chapter 2:** "Piaget's Basic Assumptions" (pp. 26–28); "Social Construction of Meaning" (pp. 41–42) **Chapter 6: Case Study: "The New World"** (pp. 155); "Basic Assumptions of Cognitive Psychology" (pp. 156–159); "How Declarative Knowledge Is Learned" (pp. 169–173); "When Knowledge Construction Goes Awry: Addressing Learners' Misconceptions" (pp. 179–183); **Practice for Your Licensure Exam: "Vision Unit"** (p. 193) **Chapter 8:** "Basic Assumptions of Contextual Theories" (pp. 228–230) | **Building Teaching Skills and Dispositions** exercise "Knowledge Construction and Conceptual Change" in topic "Knowledge Construction" **Assignments and Activities: Understanding Research** exercise "Knowledge Construction in History" in topic "Knowledge Construction" |
| • Metacognition | **Chapter 7: Case Study: "Taking Over"** (p. 195); "Metacognition and Learning Strategies" (pp. 196–205); "Metacognition in Problem Solving" (pp. 214–215); **Practice for Your Licensure Exam: "Interview with Charlie"** (p. 225) **Chapter 8:** "Academic Content Domains as Contexts" (pp. 242–261); **Chapter 12:** "Conducting Reciprocal Teaching Sessions" (pp. 403–405) | **Building Teaching Skills and Dispositions** exercise "Encouraging Self-Regulation" in topic "Social Cognitive Perspectives" **Assignments and Activities: Understanding Research** exercise "Self-Discipline and Academic Achievement" in topic "Student Diversity" **Assignments and Activities: Understanding Research** exercise "Teaching Reading Comprehension Strategies" in topic "Memory and Cognitive Processes" **Assignments and Activities: Understanding Research** exercise "High School Students' Study Strategies" in topic "Memory and Cognitive Processes" |
| • Readiness | **Chapter 2:** "Role of the Brain in Learning and Development" (pp. 22–25) **Chapter 15:** "School Readiness Tests" (p. 522) | **Assignments and Activities: Understanding Research** exercise "Usefulness of School Readiness Tests" in topic "Assessment" |

*(continued)*

**TABLE C.1 • (Continued)**

| TOPICS IN THE PRAXIS PRINCIPLES OF LEARNING AND TEACHING (PLT) TESTS | LOCATION OF TOPICS IN ORMROD'S *EDUCATIONAL PSYCHOLOGY* (8TH ED.) | LOCATION OF TOPICS AND PRACTICE OPPORTUNITIES IN MyEducationLab™ |
|---|---|---|
| **I. Students as Learners-continued** | | |
| **A. Student Development and the Learning Process-continued** | | |
| • Schemata | **Chapter 2:** "Piaget's Basic Assumptions" (pp. 26–28) **Chapter 6:** "How Knowledge Can Be Organized" (pp. 166–169) | |
| • Transfer | **Chapter 7:** "Transfer" (pp. 206–209) | |
| • Scaffolding | **Chapter 2:** "Scaffolding" (pp. 42–43) **Chapter 8:** "Promoting Reading and Writing Development" (pp. 248–249); "Technological Literacy" (pp. 250–251) **Chapter 13:** "Planning Activities That Keep Students on Task" (pp. 433–435) | |
| • Bloom's taxonomy | **Chapter 12:** "Identifying the Goals of Instruction" (pp. 385–388) | **Supplementary Reading** "Using Taxonomies to Formulate Instructional Goals and Objectives" in Book-Specific Resources for Chapter 12 |
| • Zone of proximal development | **Chapter 2:** "Vygotsky's Basic Assumptions" (pp. 37–40) | **Building Teaching Skills and Dispositions** exercise "Using Cognitive Tools" in topic "Cognitive and Linguistic Development" |
| • Intrinsic and extrinsic motivation | **Chapter 9:** "Positive Reinforcement" (pp. 272–275); "Strengths and Potential Limitations of Behaviorist Approaches" (pp. 293, 295) **Chapter 11: Case Study: "Passing Algebra"** (p. 333); "Extrinsic versus Intrinsic Motivation" (p. 336); "Basic Human Needs" (pp. 337–345); "Interests" (pp. 345–347); "Expectancies and Values" (pp. 347–349); "Achievement Goals" (pp. 349–352); **Practice for Your Licensure Exam: "When 'Perfect' Isn't Good Enough"** (pp. 378–379) | **Building Teaching Skills and Dispositions** exercise "Promoting Interest" in topic "Motivation and Affect" **Assignments and Activities: Understanding Research** exercise "Self-Discipline & Academic Achievement" in topic "Student Diversity" |
| ▶ Human development in the physical, social, emotional, moral, and cognitive domains: | **Chapters 2–3**: Entire chapters (pp. 18–89) **Chapters 4, 6–15:** Developmental Trends tables (pp. 107, 174, 197, 246, 276, 316, 359, 386, 437–438, 475, 425) **Chapter 4:** "Origins of Gender Differences" (pp. 106, 108) **Chapter 5:** "Developmental Views of Intelligence" (p. 123); "Nature and Nurture in the Development of Intelligence" (pp. 125–126) **Chapter 6:** "Developmental Trends in Storage Processes for Declarative Information" (p. 173) **Chapter 8: Practice for Your Licensure Exam: "The Birth of a Nation"** (p. 263) **Chapter 9:** "Classical Conditioning of Involuntary Emotional Responses" (pp. 268–269) **Chapter 10:** "Factors in the Development of Self-Efficacy" (pp. 311–313); "Applying Brain Research: Understanding and Accommodating Individual Differences in Self-Regulation" (p. 324) **Chapter 11:** "Developmental Trends in Achievement Goals" (pp. 350–351); "Developmental Trends in Attributions" (pp. 357–358); "Applying Brain Research: Understanding How and Why Emotions Influence Learning" (p. 369) **Chapter 13:** "Taking Developmental Differences into Account" (p. 436) **Chapter 15:** "Guidelines for Choosing and Using Standardized Tests" (pp. 523–524) | **Assignments and Activities: Understanding Research** exercise "Class Inclusion" in topic "Cognitive and Linguistic Development" **Supplementary Reading** "Physical Development Across Childhood and Adolescence" in Book-Specific Resources for Chapter 2 |
| • The theoretical contributions of important theorists such as Erik Erikson, Lawrence Kohlberg, Carol Gilligan, Jean Piaget, Abraham | **Chapter 2:** "The Multiple Layers of Environmental Influence: Bronfenbrenner's Theory" (pp. 21–22); "Piaget's Theory of Cognitive Development" (pp. 25–36); "Vygotsky's Theory of Cognitive Development" (pp. 36–45) | **Building Teaching Skills and Dispositions** exercise "Using Cognitive Tools" in topic "Cognitive and Linguistic Development" |

## TABLE C.1 • (Continued)

| TOPICS IN THE PRAXIS PRINCIPLES OF LEARNING AND TEACHING (PLT) TESTS | LOCATION OF TOPICS IN ORMROD'S *EDUCATIONAL PSYCHOLOGY* (8TH ED.) | LOCATION OF TOPICS AND PRACTICE OPPORTUNITIES IN MyEducationLab™ |
|---|---|---|
| **I. Students as Learners-continued** | | |
| **A. Student Development and the Learning Process-continued** | | |
| Maslow, Albert Bandura, and Lev Vygotsky | **Chapter 3:** Figure 3.1 ("Erikson's eight stages of psychosocial development," p. 62); "Developmental Trends in Morality and Prosocial Behavior" (pp. 79–87); "Diversity in Moral and Prosocial Development" (pp. 84–85) **Chapter 10:** Entire chapter (pp. 298–331) **Chapter 11:** "A Possible Hierarchy of Needs: Maslow's Theory" (pp. 344–345) | **Assignments and Activities: Understanding Research** exercise "Self-Efficacy and Achievement" in topic "Social Cognitive Perspectives" **Supplementary Reading** "Ecological Systems Perspectives of Child Development" in Book-Specific Resources for Chapter 2 |
| • The major progressions in each developmental domain and the ranges of individual variation within each domain | **Chapter 2:** "Piaget's Stages of Cognitive Development" (pp. 29–32); "Contemporary Extensions and Applications of Piaget's Theory" (pp. 34–36); "Language Development" (pp. 45–51) **Chapter 3:** "Developmental Changes in Sense of Self" (pp. 62–65); "Development of Peer Relationships and Interpersonal Understanding" (pp. 67–78); "Developmental Trends in Morality and Prosocial Behavior" (pp. 79–83) **Chapters 2–4, 6–15:** Developmental Trends tables (pp. 46–47, 66, 107, 174, 197, 246, 276, 316, 359, 386, 437–438, 475 425) | **Building Teaching Skills and Dispositions** exercise "Encouraging Self-Regulation" in topic "Social Cognitive Perspectives" **Assignments and Activities: Understanding Research** exercise "Class Inclusion" in topic "Cognitive and Linguistic Development" **Supplementary Reading** "Physical Development Across Childhood and Adolescence" in Book-Specific Resources for Chapter 2 |
| • The impact of students' physical, social, emotional, moral, and cognitive development on their learning and how to address these factors when making instructional decisions | **Chapters 2–3:** See apple icons throughout **Chapter 2:** Case Study: "Apple Tarts" (p. 19); **Practice for Your Licensure Exam: "Stones Lesson"** (pp. 52–53) **Chapter 3:** Case Study: "Hidden Treasure" (p. 55); **Practice for Your Licensure Exam: "The Scarlet Letter"** (pp. 88–89) **Chapter 5:** "Emotional and Behavioral Disorders" (pp. 140–142); "Intellectual Disabilities" (pp. 144–145) **Chapter 9:** "Classical Conditioning of Involuntary Emotional Responses" (pp. 268–269) | **Building Teaching Skills and Dispositions** exercise "Using Cognitive Tools" in topic "Cognitive and Linguistic Development" **Assignments and Activities: Understanding Research** exercise "Supporting Children at Risk" in topic "Student Diversity" **Assignments and Activities: Understanding Research** exercise "Need for Approval and Emotional Well-Being" in topic "Motivation and Affect" **Assignments and Activities: Understanding Research** exercise "Usefulness of School Readiness Tests" in topic "Assessment" |
| • How development in one domain, such as physical, may affect performance in another domain, such as social | **Chapter 2:** "Role of the Brain in Learning and Development" (pp. 22–25) **Chapter 3:** "Temperament" (p. 56); "Developmental Changes in Sense of Self" (pp. 62–65); "Applying Brain Research: Understanding and Addressing Adolescent Risk Taking" (p. 64); "Social Cognition" (pp. 71–73); "Factors Influencing Moral and Prosocial Development" (pp. 83–84) **Chapter 4:** "Characteristics of Students at Risk" (pp. 113–114) **Chapter 6:** "Applying Brain Research: Enhancing Students' Brain Functioning" (p. 165) **Chapter 10:** "Applying Brain Research: Understanding and Accommodating Individual Differences in Self-Regulation" (p. 324) **Chapter 11:** "Applying Brain Research: Understanding How and Why Emotions Influence Learning" (p. 369) | **Building Teaching Skills and Dispositions** exercise "Perspective Taking & Social Skills" in topic "Personal, Social, & Moral Development" **Supplementary Reading** "Physical Development Across Childhood and Adolescence" in Book-Specific Resources for Chapter 2 |
| **B. Students as Diverse Learners** | | |
| ▶ Differences in the ways students learn and perform: | **Chapter 2:** Diversity sections (pp. 33–34, 40, 47–48); "Second-Language Learning and English Language Learners" (pp. 48–50) **Chapter 3:** "Personality Development" (pp. 55–60); "Diversity" sections (pp. 65–67, 76, 84–85) **Chapters 4–5:** Entire chapters (pp. 90–153) **Chapter 6:** "Diversity in Cognitive Processes" (pp. 189–191) | |

*(continued)*

**TABLE C.1 • (Continued)**

| TOPICS IN THE PRAXIS PRINCIPLES OF LEARNING AND TEACHING (PLT) TESTS | LOCATION OF TOPICS IN ORMROD'S *EDUCATIONAL PSYCHOLOGY* (8TH ED.) | LOCATION OF TOPICS AND PRACTICE OPPORTUNITIES IN MyEducationLab™ |
|---|---|---|
| **I. Students as Learners-continued** | | |
| **B. Students as Diverse Learners-continued** | | |
| | **Chapter 7:** "Diversity in Creativity, Critical Thinking, and Other Complex Cognitive Processes" (pp. 222–223) **Chapter 8:** "Schemas, Scripts, and Worldviews as Aspects of Culture" (pp. 234–236) **Chapter 9:** "Diversity in Student Behaviors and Reactions to Consequences" (pp. 292–293) **Chapter 10:** "Diversity in Self-Regulation" (pp. 323–325) **Chapter 11:** "Universality and Diversity in Basic Needs" (pp. 343–344); "Diversity in Cognitive and Sociocultural Factors Affecting Motivation" (pp. 364–366); "Diversity in Affect" (pp. 375–377) **Chapter 12:** "Taking Instructional Goals and Student Diversity into Account" (pp. 415–419) **Chapter 13:** "Taking Individual and Group Differences into Account" (p. 436); "Taking Students' Cultural Backgrounds into Account" (pp. 452–454) **Chapter 14:** "Taking Student Diversity into Account in Classroom Assessments" (pp. 500–501) **Chapter 15:** "Taking Student Diversity into Account" (pp. 531–536) | |
| ▶ Differences in the ways students learn and perform: | **Chapter 2:** Diversity sections (pp. 33–34, 40, 47–48); "Second-Language Learning and English Language Learners" (pp. 48–50) **Chapter 3:** "Personality Development" (pp. 55–60); "Diversity" sections (pp. 65–67, 76, 84–85) **Chapters 4–5:** Entire chapters (pp. 90–153) **Chapter 6:** "Diversity in Cognitive Processes" (pp. 189–191) **Chapter 7:** "Diversity in Creativity, Critical Thinking, and Other Complex Cognitive Processes" (pp. 222–223) **Chapter 8:** "Schemas, Scripts, and Worldviews as Aspects of Culture" (pp. 234–236) **Chapter 9:** "Diversity in Student Behaviors and Reactions to Consequences" (pp. 292–293) **Chapter 10:** "Diversity in Self-Regulation" (pp. 323–325) **Chapter 11:** "Universality and Diversity in Basic Needs" (pp. 343–344); "Diversity in Cognitive and Sociocultural Factors Affecting Motivation" (pp. 364–366); "Diversity in Affect" (pp. 375–377) **Chapter 12:** "Taking Instructional Goals and Student Diversity into Account" (pp. 415–419) **Chapter 13:** "Taking Individual and Group Differences into Account" (p. 436); "Taking Students' Cultural Backgrounds into Account" (pp. 452–454) **Chapter 14:** "Taking Student Diversity into Account in Classroom Assessments" (pp. 500–501) **Chapter 15:** "Taking Student Diversity into Account" (pp. 531–536) | |
| • Learning styles | **Chapter 5:** "Cognitive Styles and Dispositions" (pp. 128–130) **Chapter 6:** "Diversity in Cognitive Processes" (pp. 189–191) | **Assignments and Activities: Understanding Research** exercise "Self-Discipline & Academic Achievement" in topic "Student Diversity" |
| • Multiple intelligences | **Chapter 5:** "Gardner's Multiple Intelligences" (pp. 121–123) | |

## TABLE C.1 • (Continued)

| TOPICS IN THE PRAXIS PRINCIPLES OF LEARNING AND TEACHING (PLT) TESTS | LOCATION OF TOPICS IN ORMROD'S *EDUCATIONAL PSYCHOLOGY* (8TH ED.) | LOCATION OF TOPICS AND PRACTICE OPPORTUNITIES IN MyEducationLab™ |
|---|---|---|
| **I. Students as Learners-continued** | | |
| **B. Students as Diverse Learners-continued** | | |
| • Performance modes<br> • Concrete operational thinkers<br> • Visual and aural learners | **Chapter 2:** Table 2.1 ("Piaget's Four State of Cognitive" (pp. 30–31); "Concrete Operations Stage" (pp. 30–31)<br>**Chapter 5:** "Learning Disabilities" (pp. 135–137)<br>**Chapter 6:** "Visual Imagery" (pp. 171–173)<br>**Chapter 7: Practice for Your Licensure Exam: "Interview with Charlie"** (pp. 225) | **Assignments and Activities: Understanding Research** exercise "Teaching Reading Comprehension Strategies" in topic "Memory and Cognitive Processes" |
| • Gender differences | **Chapter 3:** "Gender Differences" sections (pp. 65, 76, 84)<br>**Chapter 4:** "Gender Differences" (pp. 103–109); **Practice for Your Licensure Exam: "The Active and the Passive"** (pp. 116–117)<br>**Chapter 10: Case Study: "Parlez-Vous Français?"** (p. 299)<br>**Chapter 11:** "Gender Differences" sections (pp. 364–365, 376)<br>**Chapter 12:** "Considering Group Differences" (p. 417)<br>**Chapter 13:** "Gender Differences" (pp. 438–439)<br>**Chapter 15:** "Cultural Bias in Test Content" (pp. 532–533) | |
| • Cultural expectations and styles | **Chapter 2:** "Considering Diversity from the Perspective of Vygotsky's Theory" (pp. 33–34)<br>**Chapter 3: Case Study: "Hidden Treasure"** (p. 55); "Family Dynamics" (pp. 56–58); "Cultural Expectations and Socialization" (pp. 58); "Cultural and Ethnic Differences" sections (pp. 65, 67, 76, 85)<br>**Chapter 4: Case Study: "Why Jack Wasn't in School"** (p. 91); "Cultural and Ethnic Differences" (pp. 92–103); **Practice for Your Licensure Exam: "The Active and the Passive"** (pp. 116–117)<br>**Chapter 5:** "Cultural and Ethnic Diversity in Intelligence" (pp. 126–127)<br>**Chapter 6:** "Diversity in Cognitive Processes" (pp. 189–191)<br>**Chapter 7:** "Diversity in Creativity, Critical Thinking, and Other Complex Cognitive Processes" (pp. 222–223)<br>**Chapter 8: Case Study: "It's All in How You Look at Things"** (p. 227); "Cultures as Contexts" (pp. 234–237)<br>**Chapter 9:** "Diversity in Student Behaviors and Reactions to Consequences" (pp. 292–293)<br>**Chapter 10:** "Diversity in Self-Regulation" (pp. 323–325)<br>**Chapter 11:** "Universality and Diversity in Basic Needs" (pp. 343–344); "Diversity in Cognitive and Sociocultural Factors Affecting Motivation" (pp. 364–366); "Diversity in Affect" (pp. 375–379)<br>**Chapter 12:** "Considering Group Differences" (p. 417)<br>**Chapter 13:** "Taking Students' Cultural Backgrounds into Account" (pp. 452–454)<br>**Chapter 14:** "Teaching Testwiseness" (pp. 494–495); "Accommodating Group Differences" (p. 500)<br>**Chapter 15:** "Cultural Bias in Test Content" (pp. 532–533); "Cultural and Ethnic Differences" (p. 533) | **Building Teaching Skills and Dispositions** exercise "Accommodating Cultural Differences" in topic "Student Diversity"<br>**Assignments and Activities: Understanding Research** exercise "Navigating Adolescence" in topic "Personal, Social, & Moral Development" |

(continued)

## TABLE C.1 • (Continued)

| TOPICS IN THE PRAXIS PRINCIPLES OF LEARNING AND TEACHING (PLT) TESTS | LOCATION OF TOPICS IN ORMROD'S *EDUCATIONAL PSYCHOLOGY* (8TH ED.) | LOCATION OF TOPICS AND PRACTICE OPPORTUNITIES IN MyEducationLab™ |
|---|---|---|
| **I. Students as Learners-continued** | | |
| **B. Students as Diverse Learners-continued** | | |
| ▶ Areas of exceptionality in student learning: | **Chapter 5:** Entire chapter (pp. 118–153); see especially **Case Study: "Tim"** (p. 119) and **Practice for Your Licensure Exam: "Quiet Amy"** (p. 153) **Chapters 6–15:** Students in Inclusive Settings tables (pp. 191, 205, 261, 294, 326, 367, 418, 440, 501, 536) **Chapters 6–15:** "Special Needs" sections (pp. 190–191, 204–205, 223, 260–261, 293–294, 325–326, 366–367, 417–419, 439–440, 500–501, 534–536) | **Assignments and Activities: Understanding Research** exercise "Conducting a Functional Analysis" in topic "Behaviorist Perspectives" **Assignments and Activities: Understanding Research** exercise "Identifying Reinforcers Through Functional Analysis" in topic "Classroom Management" |
| • Visual and perceptual differences | **Chapter 5:** Figure 5.3 ("Examples of cognitive processing deficiencies in students with learning disabilities," p. 135); "Autism Spectrum Disorders" (pp. 142–143) | |
| • Special physical or sensory challenges | **Chapter 5:** "Students with Physical or Sensory Challenges" (pp. 146–149) | |
| • Learning disabilities | **Chapter 5:** "Learning Disabilities" (pp. 135–137) | |
| • Attention deficit disorder (ADD); Attention deficit-hyperactivity disorder (ADHD) | **Chapter 5: Case Study: "Tim"** (p. 119); "Attention-Deficit Hyperactivity Disorder (ADHD)" (pp. 137–138) | |
| • Functional mental retardation | **Chapter 5:** "Intellectual Disabilities" (pp. 144–145) | **Supplementary Reading** "Adaptive Behaviors and Intellectual Disabilities" in Book-Specific Resources for Chapter 5 |
| • Behavioral disorders | **Chapter 5:** "Emotional and Behavioral Disorders" (pp. 140–142) | **Simulation** exercise "Developing Behavior Change Plans" in topic "Classroom Management" **Assignments and Activities: Understanding Research** exercise "Identifying Reinforcers Through Functional Analysis" in topic "Classroom Management" |
| • Developmental delays | **Chapter 5:** "Students with General Delays in Cognitive and Social Functioning" (pp. 144–145) | |
| ▶ Legislation and institutional responsibilities relating to exceptional students: | | |
| • Americans with Disabilities Act (ADA) | | |
| • Individuals with Disabilities Education Act (IDEA) | **Chapter 5:** "Public Law 94-142: Individuals with Disabilities Education Act (IDEA)" (pp. 131–132) | |
| • Inclusion, mainstreaming, and "least restrictive environment" | **Chapter 5:** "Educating Students with Special Needs in General Education Classrooms" (pp. 130–134) **Chapters 6–15:** Students in Inclusive Settings tables (pp. 191, 223, 261, 294, 326, 367, 418–419, 501, 536) | |
| • IEP (individual education plan), including what, by law, must be included in each IEP | **Chapter 5:** Figure 5.2 ("Components of an individualized education program," p. 131) **Chapter 12:** "Accommodating Students with Special Needs" (pp. 417–419) **Chapter 14:** "Accommodating Students with Special Needs" (pp. 500) **Chapter 15:** "Considering Effort" (p. 515); "Accommodating Students with Special Needs" (pp. 534–536) | |
| • Section 504 of the Rehabilitation Act | **Chapter 5:** "Identifying Students' Special Needs: Response to Intervention and People-First Language" (p.133) | |

**TABLE C.1 • (Continued)**

| TOPICS IN THE PRAXIS PRINCIPLES OF LEARNING AND TEACHING (PLT) TESTS | LOCATION OF TOPICS IN ORMROD'S *EDUCATIONAL PSYCHOLOGY* (8TH ED.) | LOCATION OF TOPICS AND PRACTICE OPPORTUNITIES IN MyEducationLab™ |
|---|---|---|
| **I. Students as Learners-continued** | | |
| **B. Students as Diverse Learners-continued** | | |
| • Due process | **Chapter 5:** "Public Law 94-142: Individuals with Disabilities Education Act (IDEA)" (pp. 131–132) | |
| • Family involvement | **Chapter 5:** "Public Law 94-142: Individuals with Disabilities Education Act (IDEA)" (pp. 131–132); "General Recommendations for Working with Students Who Have Special Needs" (pp. 151–152) **Chapter 13:** "Working with Parents" (pp. 441–446) | |
| ▶ Approaches for accommodating various learning styles, intelligences, or exceptionalities, including: | **Chapter 5:** Entire chapter (pp. 118–153) **Chapter 6:** "Diversity in Cognitive Processes" (pp. 189–191) **Chapters 6–15:** Students in Inclusive Settings tables (pp. 191, 22, 261, 294, 326, 367, 418–419, 501, 536) | |
| • Differentiated instruction | **Chapter 12:** "General Principles that Can Guide Instruction" (pp. 382–385); "Accommodating Students with Special Needs" (pp. 417–419) | |
| • Alternative assessments | **Chapter 14:** "The Many Forms and Purposes of Assessment" (pp. 462–468); "Enhancing Learning through Formative Assessments and Other Assessment Practices" (pp. 468–470); "Using Performance Assessments" (pp. 489–494) **Chapter 15:** "Using Portfolios" (pp. 516–519) | |
| • Testing modifications | **Chapter 14:** Table 14.5 (p. 501) **Chapter 15:** "Accommodating Students with Special Needs" (pp. 534–535); Table 15.4 (p. 536) | |
| ▶ The process of second-language acquisition and strategies to support the learning of students for whom English is not a first language | **Chapter 2:** "Second-Language Learning and English Language Learners" (pp. 48–51) **Chapter 12:** "Considering Group Differences" (p. 417) **Chapter 14:** "Informally Observing Students' Behaviors" (pp. 479–481); "Accommodating Group Differences" (p. 500) **Chapter 15:** "Language Differences and English Language Learners" (pp. 533–534) | |
| ▶ How students' learning is influenced by individual experiences, talents, and prior learning, as well as language, culture, family, and community values, including: | **Chapter 2:** "The Multiple Layers of Environmental Influence: Bronfenbrenner's Theory" (pp. 21–22) **Chapter 5:** "Cognitive Styles and Dispositions" (pp. 128–130) **Chapter 6:** "Roles of Prior Knowledge and Working Memory in Long-Term Memory Storage" (pp. 175–176); "Diversity in Cognitive Processes" (pp. 189–191) | **Assignments and Activities: Understanding Research** exercise "Knowledge Construction in History" in topic "Knowledge Construction" **Supplementary Reading** "Ecological Systems Perspectives of Child Development" in Book-Specific Resources for Chapter 2 |
| • Multicultural backgrounds | **Chapter 3: Case Study: "Hidden Treasure"** (p. 55); "Cultural Expectations and Socialization" (p. 58); Creating a Productive Classroom Environment box "Encouraging Positive Interactions among Diverse Individuals and Groups" (p. 77) **Chapter 4: Case Study: "Why Jack Wasn't in School"** (p. 91); "Cultural and Ethnic Differences" (pp. 92–103) **Chapter 5:** "Cultural and Ethnic Diversity in Intelligence" (pp. 126–127) **Chapter 8: Case Study: "It's All in How You Look at Things"** (p. 227); "Cultures as Contexts (pp. 234–237) **Chapter 12:** "Considering Group Differences" (p. 417) | **Building Teaching Skills and Dispositions** exercise "Accommodating Cultural Differences" in topic "Student Diversity" **Assignments and Activities: Understanding Research** exercise "Navigating Adolescence" in topic "Personal, Social, & Moral Development" |

*(continued)*

**TABLE C.1 • (Continued)**

| TOPICS IN THE PRAXIS PRINCIPLES OF LEARNING AND TEACHING (PLT) TESTS | LOCATION OF TOPICS IN ORMROD'S *EDUCATIONAL PSYCHOLOGY* (8TH ED.) | LOCATION OF TOPICS AND PRACTICE OPPORTUNITIES IN MyEducationLab™ |
|---|---|---|
| **I. Students as Learners-continued** | | |
| **B. Students as Diverse Learners-continued** | | |
| • Age-appropriate knowledge and behavior | **Chapter 2:** "Piaget's Stages of Cognitive Development" (pp. 29–32); "Language Development" (pp. 45–51) **Chapter 3:** "Developmental Changes in Sense of Self" (pp. 60–67); "Perspective Taking" (pp. 71–73); "Developmental Trends in Morality and Prosocial Behavior" (pp. 79–83) **Chapters 4–15:** Developmental Trends tables (pp. 107, 174, 197, 246, 276, 316, 359, 386, 437–438, 474–475, 525) | |
| • The student culture at the school | **Chapter 3:** "Roles of Peers in Children's Development" (pp. 67–68); "Characteristics of Peer Relationships" (pp. 68–70); "Technology and Peer Relationships" (p. 75) **Chapter 4:** "Navigating Different Cultures at Home and at School" (pp. 93–94) **Chapter 13:** "Addressing Aggression and Violence at School" (pp. 454–458) | **Simulation** exercise "Dealing with Situations Where Students Are Being Bullied/Harassed" in topic "Classroom Management" **Assignments and Activities: Understanding Research** exercise "Navigating Adolescence" in topic "Personal, Social, & Moral Development" **Assignments and Activities: Understanding Research** exercise "Cheating in High School Students" in topic "Assessment" |
| • Family backgrounds | **Chapter 3:** "Family Dynamics" (pp. 56–58) **Chapter 4:** "Socioeconomic Differences" (pp. 109–113) | **Assignments and Activities: Understanding Research** exercise "Supporting Children at Risk" in topic "Student Diversity" |
| • Linguistic patterns and differences | **Chapter 2:** "Language Development" (pp. 45–51)" **Chapter 5:** "Speech and Communication Disorders" (pp. 138–139) **Chapter 8: Practice for Your Licensure Exam: "The Birth of a Nation"** (pp. 263) | |
| • Cognitive patterns and differences | **Chapter 5:** "Cognitive Styles and Dispositions" (pp. 128–130) **Chapter 6:** "Diversity in Cognitive Processes" (pp. 189–191) **Chapter 7: Practice for Your Licensure Exam: "Interview with Charlie"** (p. 225) | **Assignments and Activities: Understanding Research** exercise "Self-Discipline & Academic Achievement" in topic "Student Diversity" **Assignments and Activities: Understanding Research** exercise "High School Students' Study Strategies" in topic "Memory and Cognitive Processes" |
| • Social and emotional issues | **Chapter 3:** "Personality Development" (pp. 56–60); "Development of a Sense of Self" (pp. 60–67); "Social Cognition" (pp. 71–73); "Aggression" (pp. 73–75); "Factors Influencing Moral and Prosocial Development" (pp. 83–84) **Chapter 5:** "Emotional and Behavioral Disorders" (pp. 140–144); "Autism Spectrum Disorders" (pp. 142–143) **Chapter 9:** "Classical Conditioning of Involuntary Emotional Responses" (pp. 268–269) **Chapter 10:** "Emotion Regulation" (p. 317) **Chapter 11:** "Affect and Its Effects" (pp. 366–317) **Chapter 14:** "Keeping Test Anxiety in Check" (pp. 495–496) | **Assignments and Activities: Understanding Research** exercise "Navigating Adolescence" in topic "Personal, Social, & Moral Development" **Assignments and Activities: Understanding Research** exercise "Need for Approval and Emotional Well-Being" in topic "Motivation and Affect" |
| **C. Student Motivation and the Learning Environment** | | |
| ▶ Theoretical foundations about human motivation and behavior: | **Chapter 11** Entire chapter (pp. 332–379) | |
| • Abraham Maslow | **Chapter 11:** "A Possible Hierarchy of Needs: Maslow's Theory" (pp. 344–345) | |
| • Albert Bandura | **Chapter 10:** Entire chapter (pp. 298–331) | |

## TABLE C.1 • (Continued)

| TOPICS IN THE PRAXIS PRINCIPLES OF LEARNING AND TEACHING (PLT) TESTS | LOCATION OF TOPICS IN ORMROD'S *EDUCATIONAL PSYCHOLOGY* (8TH ED.) | LOCATION OF TOPICS AND PRACTICE OPPORTUNITIES IN MyEducationLab™ |
|---|---|---|
| **I. Students as Learners-continued** | | |
| **C. Student Motivation and the Learning Environment-continued** | | |
| • B. F. Skinner | **Chapter 9: Case Study: "The Attention Getter"** (p. 265); "Learning from Consequences: Instrumental Conditioning" (pp. 270–280); "Shaping New Behaviors" (pp. 284–285) | **Supplementary Reading** "Schedules of Reinforcement" in Book-Specific Resources for Chapter 9 **Supplementary Reading** "Programmed Instruction and Computer-Assisted Instruction" in Book-Specific Resources for Chapter 12 |
| ► Important terms that relate to motivation and behavior: | | |
| • Hierarchy of needs | **Chapter 11:** "A Possible Hierarchy of Needs: Maslow's Theory" (pp. 344–345) | |
| • Correlational and causal relationships | **Chapter 11: Case Study: "Passing Algebra"** (pp. 333); "Attributions" (pp. 355–360) | |
| • Intrinsic motivation | **Chapter 9:** "Strengths and Potential Limitations of Behavioral Approaches" (pp. 293–295) **Chapter 11:** "Extrinsic Versus Intrinsic Motivation" (pp. 336); "Basic Human Needs" (pp. 337–345); "Interests" (pp. 345–347); "Expectancies and Values" (pp. 347–349); "Achievement Goals" (pp. 349–342); | **Building Teaching Skills and Dispositions** exercises "Addressing Students' Basic Needs" and "Promoting Interest" in topic "Motivation and Affect" **Assignments and Activities: Understanding Research** exercise "Self-Discipline & Academic Achievement" in topic "Student Diversity" |
| • Extrinsic motivation | **Chapter 9:** "Learning from Consequences: Instrumental Conditioning" (pp. 270–280) **Chapter 11:** "Extrinsic Versus Intrinsic Motivation" (p. 336); "Achievement Goals" (pp. 349–342) **Chapter 14:** "Promoting Learning" (pp. 466–468) | |
| • Learned helplessness | **Chapter 11:** "Mastery Orientation Versus Learned Helplessness" (pp. 358–360) | |
| • Self-efficacy | **Chapter 3:** "Development of a Sense of Self" (pp. 60–67) **Chapter 10: Case Study: "Parlez-Vous Français?"** (p. 299); "Self-Efficacy" (pp. 308–314) | **Assignments and Activities: Understanding Research** exercise "Self-Efficacy and Achievement" in topic "Social Cognitive Perspectives" |
| • Operant conditioning | **Chapter 9:** "Learning from Consequences: Instrumental Conditioning" (pp. 270–280) | |
| • Reinforcement | **Chapter 9: Case Study: "The Attention Getter"** (pp. 270–280); "The Various Forms That Reinforcement Can Take" (pp. 271–277); "Using Reinforcement Effectively" (pp. 280–284); "Reinforcing Incompatible Behaviors" (pp. 287–288) **Chapter 10:** "The Social Cognitive View of Reinforcement and Punishment" (pp. 301–304); **Practice for Your Licensure Exam: "Teacher's Lament"** (pp. 330–331) **Chapter 13:** "Conducting Planned, Systematic Interventions" (p. 452) | **Assignments and Activities: Understanding Research** exercise "Conducting a Functional Analysis" in topic "Behaviorist Perspectives" |
| • Positive reinforcement | **Chapter 9:** "Positive Reinforcement" (pp. 272–275) | **Assignments and Activities: Understanding Research** exercise "Identifying Reinforcers Through Functional Analysis" in topic "Classroom Management" |
| • Negative reinforcement | **Chapter 9:** "Negative Reinforcement" (pp. 275) | **Assignments and Activities: Understanding Research** exercise "Identifying Reinforcers Through Functional Analysis" in topic "Classroom Management" |
| • Shaping successive approximations | **Chapter 9:** "Shaping New Behaviors" (pp. 284–285) | **Supplementary Reading** "Programmed Instruction and Computer-Assisted Instruction" in Book-Specific Resources for Chapter 12 |

*(continued)*

**TABLE C.1 • (Continued)**

| TOPICS IN THE PRAXIS PRINCIPLES OF LEARNING AND TEACHING (PLT) TESTS | LOCATION OF TOPICS IN ORMROD'S *EDUCATIONAL PSYCHOLOGY* (8TH ED.) | LOCATION OF TOPICS AND PRACTICE OPPORTUNITIES IN MyEducationLab™ |
|---|---|---|
| **I. Students as Learners-continued** | | |
| **C. Student Motivation and the Learning Environment-continued** | | |
| • Prevention | **Chapter 9:** "Functional Analysis and Positive Behavior Support" (pp. 290–292)<br>**Chapter 13:** "Creating a Setting Conducive to Learning" (pp. 423–439); "Addressing Aggression and Violence at School" (pp. 454–458) | |
| • Extinction | **Chapter 9:** "Creating Conditions for Extinction" (p. 287); **Practice for Your Licensure Exam: "Hostile Helen"** (pp. 296–297)<br>**Chapter 13:** "Ignoring Certain Behaviors" (pp. 446–447) | |
| • Punishment | **Chapter 9:** "The Various Forms That Punishment Can Take" (pp. 277–280); "Using Punishment When Necessary" (pp. 288–289)<br>**Chapter 10:** "The Social Cognitive View of Reinforcement and Punishment" (pp. 301–304); **Practice for Your Licensure Exam: "Teacher's Lament"** (pp. 330–331) | |
| • Continuous reinforcement | **Chapter 9:** "Using Reinforcement Effectively" (pp. 280–284) | |
| • Intermittent reinforcement | **Chapter 9:** "Using Reinforcement Effectively" (pp. 280–284) | **Supplementary Reading** "Schedules of Reinforcement" in Book-Specific Resources for Chapter 9 |
| ▶ How knowledge of human motivation and behavior should influence strategies for organizing and supporting individual and group work in the classroom | **Chapter 11:** Entire chapter (pp. 333–379) | **Building Teaching Skills and Dispositions** exercise "Applying Behaviorist Principles" in topic "Behaviorist Perspectives "<br>**Building Teaching Skills and Dispositions** exercise "Addressing Students' Basic Needs" in topic "Motivation and Affect"<br>**Assignments and Activities: Understanding Research** exercise "Combining Achievement Goals" in topic "Motivation and Affect" |
| ▶ Factors and situations that are likely to promote or diminish students' motivation to learn; how to help students become self-motivated | **Chapter 9:** "Strengths and Potential Limitations of Behavioral Approaches" (pp. 293–295)<br>**Chapter 10:** "Self-Regulated Learning" (pp. 320–321); "Diversity in Self-Regulation" (pp. 323–325)<br>**Chapter 11:** Entire chapter  (pp. 333–379)<br>**Chapter 13:** "Teaching Self-Regulation Skills" (p. 449) | **Building Teaching Skills and Dispositions** exercise "Promoting Interest" in topic "Motivation and Affect"<br>**Simulation** exercise "Helping All Students Believe They Can Achieve" in topic "Classroom Management"<br>**Assignments and Activities: Understanding Research** exercise  "Navigating Adolescence" in topic "Personal, Social, & Moral Development"<br>**Assignments and Activities: Understanding Research** exercises  "Need for Approval and Emotional Well-Being" and "Combining Achievement Goals" in topic "Motivation and Affect"<br>**Assignments and Activities: Understanding Research** exercise  "Cheating in High School Students" in topic "Assessment" |
| ▶ Principles of effective classroom management and strategies to promote positive relationships, cooperation, and purposeful learning, including: | **Chapters 3, 5, 9, 13:** "Creating a Productive Classroom Environment" boxes (pp. 59, 77, 144, 274, 282, 431)<br>**Chapter 3:** "Social Cognition" (pp. 71–73); "Aggression" (pp. 73–75); "Promoting Healthy Peer Relationships" (pp. 76–78) "Encouraging Moral and Prosocial and Development in the Classroom" (pp. 85–87) | **Building Teaching Skills and Dispositions** exercise "Applying Behaviorist Principles" in topic "Behaviorist Perspectives "<br>**Building Teaching Skills and Dispositions** exercise "Maintaining On-Task Behavior" in topic "Classroom Management" |

**TABLE C.1 • (Continued)**

| TOPICS IN THE PRAXIS PRINCIPLES OF LEARNING AND TEACHING (PLT) TESTS | LOCATION OF TOPICS IN ORMROD'S *EDUCATIONAL PSYCHOLOGY* (8TH ED.) | LOCATION OF TOPICS AND PRACTICE OPPORTUNITIES IN MyEducationLab™ |
|---|---|---|
| **I. Students as Learners-continued** | | |
| **C. Student Motivation and the Learning Environment-continued** | | |
| | **Chapter 8:** "Creating a Community of Learners" (pp. 232–234) **Chapter 11:** "Relatedness" (pp. 342–343) **Chapter 13:** "Establishing and Maintaining Productive Teacher–Student Relationships" (pp. 426–428); "Creating an Effective Psychological Climate" (pp. 428–430); "Addressing Aggression and Violence at School" (pp. 454–458) | **Simulation** exercise "Developing Positive Teacher-Student Relationships with All Students" in topic "Classroom Management" **Simulation** exercise "Helping All Students Believe They Can Achieve" in topic "Classroom Management" **Assignments and Activities: Understanding Research** exercise "Supporting Children at Risk" in topic "Student Diversity" |
| • Establishing daily procedures and routines | **Chapter 13:** "Setting Limits" (pp. 430–433); **Practice for Your Licensure Exam: "The Good Buddy"** (p. 459) | |
| • Establishing classroom rules | **Chapter 10:** "The Social Cognitive View of Reinforcement and Punishment" (pp. 301–304) **Chapter 13:** "Setting Limits" (pp. 430–433) | **Simulation** exercise "Creating Classroom Behavioral Expectations" in topic "Classroom Management" |
| • Using natural and logical consequences | **Chapter 9:** "Logical Consequences" (p. 278) | |
| • Providing positive guidance | **Chapter 3:** "Promoting Healthy Peer Relationships" (pp. 76–78) **Chapter 9:** "Shaping New Behaviors" (pp. 284–285); "Cueing Inappropriate Behaviors" (p. 287); "Reinforcing Incompatible Behaviors" (p. 287); "Functional Analysis and Positive Behavior Support" (pp. 290–292) **Chapter 13:** "A Three-Level Approach" (pp. 455–456) | **Simulation** exercise "Developing Behavior Change Plans" in topic "Classroom Management" |
| • Modeling conflict resolution, problem solving, and anger management | **Chapter 10:** "Self-Regulated Problem Solving" (pp. 322–323) **Chapter 13:** "Addressing Aggression and Violence at School" (pp. 454–458) | |
| • Giving timely feedback | **Chapter 9:** Creating a Productive Classroom Environment box "Using Feedback to Improve Learning and Behavior" (p. 274); "Cueing Inappropriate Behaviors" (p. 287) **Chapter 11:** "Fostering Productive Achievement Goals" (p. 352); **Practice for Your Licensure Exam: "When 'Perfect' Isn't Good Enough"** (pp. 378–379) **Chapter 12:** Asking Questions and Giving Feedback (pp. 392–394) **Chapter 13:** "Cueing Students" (p. 447); "Discussing Problems Privately with Students" (pp. 447–448) **Chapter 14:** "Enhancing Learning through Formative Assessments and Other Assessment Practices" (pp. 468–470) | |
| • Maintaining accurate records | **Chapter 14:** "RSVP Characteristics of Informal Assessment" (pp. 480–481) **Chapter 15:** "Determining Final Class Grades" (pp. 512–516) | |
| • Communicating with parents and caregivers | **Chapter 13:** "Working with Parents" (pp. 441–446); "Conferring with Parents" (pp. 449–452) | |
| • Using objective behavior descriptions | **Chapter 9:** "Using Reinforcement Effectively" (pp. 280–284); "Addressing Especially Difficult Classroom Behaviors" (pp. 290–292) | |
| • Responding to student misbehavior | **Chapter 9:** "Strategies for Discouraging Undesirable Behaviors" (pp. 287–289); "Addressing Especially Difficult Classroom Behaviors" (pp. 290–292) | **Simulation** exercise "Dealing with Situations Where Students Are Being Bullied/Harassed" in topic "Classroom Management" |

*(continued)*

## TABLE C.1 • (Continued)

| TOPICS IN THE PRAXIS PRINCIPLES OF LEARNING AND TEACHING (PLT) TESTS | LOCATION OF TOPICS IN ORMROD'S *EDUCATIONAL PSYCHOLOGY* (8TH ED.) | LOCATION OF TOPICS AND PRACTICE OPPORTUNITIES IN MyEducationLab™ |
|---|---|---|
| **I. Students as Learners-continued** | | |
| **C. Student Motivation and the Learning Environment-continued** | | |
| | **Chapter 13:** "Dealing with Misbehaviors" (pp. 446–454); "Addressing Aggression and Violence at School" (pp. 454–458) | **Simulation** exercise "Responding to Student Disruptions" in topic "Classroom Management" |
| • Arranging of classroom space | **Chapter 13:** "Arranging the Classroom" (pp. 425–426) | |
| • Pacing and structuring the lesson | **Chapter 5:** "Intellectual Disabilities" (pp. 144–145) **Chapter 6:** "Wait Time" (pp. 187) **Chapter 12:** "Conducting a Task Analysis" (pp. 388–390); Into the Classroom box "Using Expository Instruction Effectively" (p. 393) **Chapter 13:** "Planning Activities That Keep Students on Task" (pp. 433–435) | |
| **II. Instruction and Assessment** | | |
| **A. Instructional Strategies** | | |
| ▶ The major cognitive processes associated with student learning, including: | **Chapters 6–7:** Entire chapters (pp. 154–193, 194–225) **Chapter 8:** "Academic Content Domains as Contexts" (pp. 242–261) | |
| • Critical thinking | **Chapter 5:** "Cognitive Styles and Dispositions" (pp. 128–130) **Chapter 7:** "Critical Thinking" (pp. 194–225) **Chapter 8:** "Technological Literacy" (pp. 250–251) | **Assignments and Activities: Understanding Research** exercise "Self-Efficacy and Achievement" in topic "Social Cognitive Perspectives" |
| • Creative thinking | **Chapter 7:** "Creativity" (pp. 216–219) | |
| • Higher-order thinking | **Chapter 7:** Entire chapter (pp. 194–225) **Chapter 8:** "Academic Content Domains as Contexts" (pp. 242–261) **Chapter 12:** "Identifying the Goals of Instruction" (pp. 385–388) | |
| • Inductive and deductive thinking | **Chapter 2:** "Piaget's Stages of Cognitive Development" (pp. 39–32) **Chapter 7:** "Critical Thinking" (pp. 219–222) | |
| • Problem-structuring and problem-solving | **Chapter 7: Case Study: "Taking Over"** (pp. 195); "Problem Solving" (pp. 210–216) **Chapter 8:** "Mathematics" (pp. 251–253) | **Building Teaching Skills and Dispositions** exercise "Teaching Problem Solving Skills" in topic "Memory and Cognitive Processes" |
| • Invention | **Chapter 7:** "Creativity" (pp. 216–219) | |
| • Memorization and recall | **Chapter 6:** "Long-Term Memory Storage" (pp. 166–179); "Long-Term Memory Retrieval" (pp. 183–189) **Chapter 7: Practice for Your Licensure Exam: "Interview with Charlie"** (p. 225) | **Building Teaching Skills and Dispositions** exercise "Facilitating Long-Term Memory Storage Processes" in topic "Memory and Cognitive Processes" |
| • Social reasoning | **Chapter 3:** "Social Cognition" (pp. 71–73); "Aggression" (pp. 73–75); "Developmental Trends in Morality and Prosocial Behavior" (pp. 79–83); "Gender Differences" (p. 84); **Practice for Your Licensure Exam: *The Scarlet Letter*** (pp. 88–89) | **Building Teaching Skills and Dispositions** exercise "Fostering Perspective Taking and Social Skills" in topic "Personal, Social, & Moral Development" |
| • Representation of ideas | **Chapter 6:** "The Nature of Long-Term Memory" (pp. 164); "How Knowledge Can Be Organized" (pp. 166–169); "How Declarative Knowledge Is Learned" (pp. 169–173) | **Building Teaching Skills and Dispositions** exercise "Knowledge Construction & Conceptual Change" in topic "Knowledge Construction" **Assignments and Activities: Understanding Research** exercise "Knowledge Construction in History" in topic "Knowledge Construction" |
| ▶ Major categories of instructional strategies, including: | **Chapter 12:** "Teacher-Directed Instructional Strategies" (pp. 391–401); "Learner-Directed Instructional Strategies" (pp. 401–415); "Taking Instructional Goals and Student Diversity into Account" (pp. 415–419) | |

## TABLE C.1 • (Continued)

| TOPICS IN THE PRAXIS PRINCIPLES OF LEARNING AND TEACHING (PLT) TESTS | LOCATION OF TOPICS IN ORMROD'S *EDUCATIONAL PSYCHOLOGY* (8TH ED.) | LOCATION OF TOPICS AND PRACTICE OPPORTUNITIES IN MyEducationLab™ |
|---|---|---|
| **II. Instruction and Assessment-continued** | | |
| **A. Instructional Strategies-continued** | | |
| • Cooperative learning | **Chapter 12:** "Conducting Cooperative Learning Activities" (pp. 408–411); **Practice for Your Licensure Exam: "Cooperative Learning Project"** (pp. 420–421) | |
| • Direct instruction | **Chapter 12:** "Conducting Direct Instruction" (pp. 396–397); "Promoting Mastery" (pp. 397–399) | |
| • Discovery learning | **Chapter 12:** "Conducting Discovery and Inquiry Activities" (pp. 405–407) | |
| • Whole-group discussion | **Chapter 8:** "Interactions with Peers" (pp. 231–232) **Chapter 12:** "Stimulating and Guiding Class Discussions" (pp. 401–403) | |
| • Independent study | **Chapter 5:** "Giftedness" (pp. 149–150; (see especially subsection "Adapting Instruction," p. 150) **Chapter 8:** "Technology in Learning and Instruction" (pp. 240–242) **Chapter 12:** "Giving Homework" (pp. 395–396); "Using Instructional Websites" (pp. 399–400); "Using Technology to Individualize Instruction" (pp. 400–401) | **Supplementary Reading** "Programmed Instruction and Computer-Assisted Instruction" in Book-Specific Resources for Chapter 12 |
| • Interdisciplinary instruction | **Chapter 6:** "Multiple Connections with Existing Knowledge and a Variety of Contexts" (p. 184) **Chapter 7:** "Factors Affecting Transfer" (pp. 000–000) | |
| • Concept mapping | **Chapter 6:** "Organization" (p. 171) | |
| • Inquiry method | **Chapter 8:** "Promoting Learning in Science" (pp. 255–256) **Chapter 12:** "Conducting Discovery and Inquiry Activities" (pp. 405–407); "Using Computer Simulations and Games" (p. 407) | |
| • Questioning | **Chapter 4:** "Responding to Questions" (pp. 96–97) **Chapter 7:** "Fostering Creativity" (pp. 217–219) **Chapter 12:** "Asking Questions and Giving Feedback" (pp. 392–394) | |
| • Play | **Chapter 2:** "Vygotsky's Basic Assumptions" (pp. 37–40) **Chapter 12:** "Using Computer Simulations and Games" (p. 407) | |
| • Learning centers | | |
| • Small group work | **Chapter 2: Case Study: "Apple Tarts"** (p. 19) **Chapter 12:** "Conducting Cooperative Learning Activities" (pp. 408–411); "Structuring Peer Tutoring Sessions" (pp. 412–414) | **Assignments and Activities: Understanding Research** exercise "Teaching Reading Comprehension Strategies" in topic "Memory and Cognitive Processes" |
| • Revisiting | **Chapter 6:** "Regular Practice" (pp. 185–186) | |
| • Reflection | **Chapter 10:** "Self-Evaluation" (pp. 318–319) **Chapter 14:** "Including Students in the Assessment Process" (p. 470) | |
| • Project approach | **Chapter 8:** "Authentic Activities" (pp. 238–239) **Chapter 12:** "Providing Practice through In-Class Assignments" (pp. 394–395); "Conducting Cooperative Learning Activities" (pp. 408–411); **Practice for Your Licensure Exam: "Cooperative Learning Project"** (pp. 420–421) | |
| ▶ Principles, techniques, and methods associated with various instructional strategies, including: | **Chapter 12:** Entire chapter (pp. 380–421) | **Building Teaching Skills and Dispositions** exercise "Identifying Effective Instructional Strategies" in topic "Planning and Instruction" |

*(continued)*

**TABLE C.1 • (Continued)**

| TOPICS IN THE PRAXIS PRINCIPLES OF LEARNING AND TEACHING (PLT) TESTS | LOCATION OF TOPICS IN ORMROD'S *EDUCATIONAL PSYCHOLOGY* (8TH ED.) | LOCATION OF TOPICS AND PRACTICE OPPORTUNITIES IN MyEducationLab™ |
|---|---|---|
| **II. Instruction and Assessment-continued** | | |
| **A. Instructional Strategies-continued** | | |
| • Direct instruction: | **Chapter 12:** "Conducting Direct Instruction" (pp. 396–397) | **Building Teaching Skills and Dispositions** exercise "Facilitating Long-Term Memory Storage Processes" in topic "Memory and Cognitive Processes" |
| • Madeline Hunter's "Effective Teaching Model" | | |
| • David Ausubel's "Advance Organizers" | **Chapter 12:** Into the Classroom box "Using Expository Instruction Effectively" (p. 393) | |
| • Mastery learning | **Chapter 12:** "Promoting Mastery" (pp. 397–399) | |
| • Demonstrations | **Chapter 8:** "Promoting Learning in Science" (pp. 255–256) **Chapter 10:** Into the Classroom box "Promoting Learning Through Modeling" (p. 309) | |
| • Mnemonics | **Chapter 6:** "Using Mnemonics in the Absence of Relevant Prior Knowledge" (pp. 177–179) | |
| • Note taking | **Chapter 7:** "Overt Strategies" (pp. 198–199) | |
| • Outlining | **Chapter 7:** "Accommodating Students with Special Needs" (pp. 204–205) | |
| • Use of visual aids | **Chapter 5:** "Visual Impairments" (pp. 146–147); "Hearing Loss" (pp. 147–148) **Chapter 6:** "Visual Imagery" (pp. 171–173) **Chapter 12:** Into the Classroom box "Using Expository Instruction Effectively" (p. 393) | |
| • Student-centered models: | **Chapter 12:** Learner-Directed Instructional Strategies (pp. 401–415) | |
| • Inquiry model | **Chapter 12:** "Conducting Discovery and Inquiry Activities" (pp. 405–407) | |
| • Discovery learning | **Chapter 12:** "Conducting Discovery and Inquiry Activities" (pp. 405–407) | |
| • Cooperative learning (pair-share, jigsaw, STAD, teams, games, tournaments) | **Chapter 12:** "Conducting Cooperative Learning Activities" (pp. 408–411) | |
| • Collaborative learning | **Chapter 8:** "Creating a Community of Learners" (pp. 232–234) **Chapter 12:** "Structuring Peer Tutoring Sessions" (pp. 412–414); "Conducting Technology-Based Collaborative Learning Activities" (pp. 414–415) | **Assignments and Activities: Understanding Research** exercise "Effects of Ability Level" in topic "Planning and Instruction" |
| • Concept models (concept development, concept attainment, concept mapping) | **Chapter 6:** "How Knowledge Can Be Organized" (pp. 166–169); "Organization" (p. 171) | **Building Teaching Skills and Dispositions** exercise "Knowledge Construction & Conceptual Change" in topic "Knowledge Construction" |
| • Discussion models | **Chapter 2: Case Study: "Apple Tarts"** (p. 19) **Chapter 8:** "Creating a Community of Learners" (pp. 232–234) **Chapter 12:** "Stimulating and Guiding Class Discussions" (pp. 401–403) | **Assignments and Activities: Understanding Research** exercise "Teaching Reading Comprehension Strategies" in topic "Memory and Cognitive Processes" |
| • Laboratories | **Chapter 8:** "Promoting Learning in Science" (pp. 255–256) **Chapter 12:** "Conducting Discovery and Inquiry Activities" (pp. 405–407) | |
| • Project-based learning | **Chapter 8:** "Authentic Activities" (pp. 238–239) **Chapter 12:** "Conducting Cooperative Learning Activities" (pp. 408–411); **Practice for Your Licensure Exam: "Cooperative Learning Project"** (pp. 420–421) | |

## TABLE C.1 • (Continued)

| TOPICS IN THE PRAXIS PRINCIPLES OF LEARNING AND TEACHING (PLT) TESTS | LOCATION OF TOPICS IN ORMROD'S *EDUCATIONAL PSYCHOLOGY* (8TH ED.) | LOCATION OF TOPICS AND PRACTICE OPPORTUNITIES IN MyEducationLab™ |
|---|---|---|
| **II. Instruction and Assessment-continued** | | |
| **A. Instructional Strategies-continued** | | |
| Simulations | **Chapter 12:** "Using Computer Simulations and Games" (p. 407) | |
| ▶ Methods for enhancing student learning through the use of a variety of resources and materials: | | |
| • Computers, Internet resources, Web pages, e-mail | **Chapter 5:** "Students with Physical or Sensory Challenges" (146–149; see especially subsection "General Recommendations" pp. 148–149) **Chapter 7:** "Using Computer Technology to Teach Problem Solving Skills" (pp. 215–216) **Chapter 8:** "Technological Innovations" (pp. 239–242) **Chapter 12:** "Creating a Class Website to Share Goals and Facilitate Communication throughout the School Year" (pp. 391–392); "Providing Practice through In-Class Assignments" (pp. 394–395); "Using Instructional Websites" (pp. 399–400); "Using Technology to Individualize Instruction" (pp. 400–401); "Using Computer Simulations and Games" (p. 407); "Conducting Technology-Based Collaborative Learning Activities" (pp. 414–425) **Chapter 14:** "Using Digital Technologies in Classroom Assessments" (pp. 498–499) | |
| • Audiovisual technologies such as videotapes and compact discs | **Chapter 8:** "Technology in Learning and Instruction" (pp. 240–242) **Chapter 10:** "Self-Monitoring" (p. 318) | |
| • Local experts | **Chapter 5:** "Giftedness" (pp. 149–150; see especially subsection "Adapting Instruction", p. 150) **Chapter 8:** "Interactions with More Advanced Individuals" (pp. 230–231) | |
| • Primary documents and artifacts | **Chapter 8:** "Promoting Learning in Social Studies" (pp. 258–259) | |
| • Field trips | **Chapter 4:** "Fostering Resilience" (pp. 112–113) **Chapter 5:** "Students with Physical or Sensory Challenges" (pp. 146–149; see especially subsection "General Recommendations", pp. 148–149) | |
| • Libraries | **Chapter 8:** "Technological Literacy" (pp. 250–251) | |
| • Service learning | **Chapter 3:** "Encouraging Moral and Prosocial Development in the Classroom" (pp. 85–87) **Chapter 8:** "Authentic Activities" (pp. 238–239) | |
| **B. Planning instruction** | | |
| ▶ Techniques for planning instruction to meet curriculum goals, including the incorporation of learning theory, subject matter, curriculum development, and student development: | **Chapter 12:** "General Principles That Can Guide Instruction"; (pp. 382–385); "Planning for Instruction" (pp. 385–391) **Chapter 13: Case Study: "A Contagious Situation"** (p. 423) | |
| • National and state learning standards | **Chapter 7: Case Study: "Taking Over"** (p. 195) **Chapter 12:** "Aligning Instructional Goals with National, International, and State Standards" (pp. 385–386) **Chapter 14:** Table 14.1 (pp. 471–475) **Chapter 15:** "High-Stakes Testing and Accountability" (pp. 527–531) | |

*(continued)*

## TABLE C.1 • (Continued)

| TOPICS IN THE PRAXIS PRINCIPLES OF LEARNING AND TEACHING (PLT) TESTS | LOCATION OF TOPICS IN ORMROD'S *EDUCATIONAL PSYCHOLOGY* (8TH ED.) | LOCATION OF TOPICS AND PRACTICE OPPORTUNITIES IN MyEducationLab™ |
|---|---|---|
| **II. Instruction and Assessment-continued** | | |
| **B. Planning instruction-continued** | | |
| • State and local curriculum frameworks | **Chapter 12:** "Aligning Instructional Goals with National, International, and State Standards" (pp. 385–386) **Chapter 15:** "High-Stakes Testing and Accountability" (pp. 527–531) | |
| • State and local curriculum guides | | |
| • Scope and sequence in specific disciplines | **Chapter 8:** "Academic Content Domains as Contexts" (pp. 242–261) **Chapter 12:** "Conducting a Task Analysis" (pp. 388–390) | |
| • Units and lessons—rationale for selecting content topics | **Chapter 12:** "Developing a Lesson Plan" (pp. 390–391) | **Lesson Plan Builder** |
| • Behavioral objectives: affective, cognitive, psychomotor | **Chapter 12:** Into the Classroom box "Identifying Appropriate Goals and Objectives" (p. 388) | **Supplementary Reading** "Using Taxonomies to Formulate Instructional Goals and Objectives" in Book-Specific Resources for Chapter 12 |
| • Learner objectives and outcomes | **Chapter 11:** "Achievement Goals" (pp. 349–352) **Chapter 12:** Into the Classroom box "Identifying Appropriate Goals and Objectives" (p. 388) | |
| • Emergent curriculum | | |
| • Antibias curriculum | **Chapter 4:** "Creating a Culturally Inclusive Classroom Environment" (pp. 99–103) | |
| • Themes/projects | **Chapter 6:** "Encouraging a Meaningful Learning Set and Conceptual Understanding" (p. 177) **Chapter 12:** "General Principles That Can Guide Instruction" (pp. 382–385) | |
| • Curriculum webbing | | |
| ▶ Techniques for creating effective bridges between curriculum goals and students' experiences: | **Chapter 12:** "General Principles That Can Guide Instruction" (pp. 382–385); "Planning for Instruction" (pp. 385–391) | |
| • Modeling | **Chapter 10:** "Modeling" (pp. 304–308) | |
| • Guided practice | **Chapter 2:** "Scaffolding" (pp. 42–43); "Guided Participation in Adult Activities" (p. 43); "Apprenticeships" (pp. 43–44) **Chapter 8:** "Communities of Practice as Aspects of Culture" (pp. 236–237) | |
| • Independent practice, including homework | **Chapter 10:** "Self-Regulated Learning" (pp. 320–322) **Chapter 12:** "Giving Homework" (pp. 395–396) | |
| • Transitions | **Chapter 13:** "Planning Activities That Keep Students on Task" (pp. 433–435) | **Simulation** exercise "Effectively Handling Transitions" in topic "Classroom Management" |
| • Activating students' prior knowledge | **Chapter 6:** "Roles of Prior Knowledge and Working Memory in Long-Term Memory Storage" (pp. 175–176) **Chapter 12:** Into the Classroom box "Using Expository Instruction Effectively" (p. 393) | **Assignments and Activities: Understanding Research** exercise "Knowledge Construction in History" in topic "Knowledge Construction" |
| • Anticipating preconceptions | **Chapter 6:** "When Knowledge Construction Goes Awry: Addressing Learners' Misconceptions" (pp. 179–183); **Practice for Your Licensure Exam: "Vision Unit"** (p. 193) **Chapter 12:** "Asking Questions and Giving Feedback" (pp. 392–394) | **Building Teaching Skills and Dispositions** exercise "Knowledge Construction & Conceptual Change" in topic "Knowledge Construction" **Assignments and Activities: Understanding Research** exercise "Knowledge Construction in History" in topic "Knowledge Construction" |
| • Encouraging exploration and problem-solving | **Chapter 2:** "Piaget's Basic Assumptions" (pp. 26–28); "Contrasting Piaget's and Vygotsky's Theories" (pp. 44–45) | **Building Teaching Skills and Dispositions** exercise "Teaching Problem Solving Skills" in topic "Memory and Cognitive Processes" |

## TABLE C.1 • (Continued)

| TOPICS IN THE PRAXIS PRINCIPLES OF LEARNING AND TEACHING (PLT) TESTS | LOCATION OF TOPICS IN ORMROD'S *EDUCATIONAL PSYCHOLOGY* (8TH ED.) | LOCATION OF TOPICS AND PRACTICE OPPORTUNITIES IN MyEducationLab™ |
|---|---|---|
| **II. Instruction and Assessment-continued** | | |
| **B. Planning instruction-continued** | | |
| • Building new skills on those previously acquired | **Chapter 7:** "Problem Solving" (pp. 210–216) <br> **Chapter 12:** "Conducting Discovery and Inquiry Activities" (pp. 405–407) <br> **Chapter 6:** "How Procedural Knowledge Is Learned" (pp. 173–175) <br> **Chapter 9:** "Shaping New Behaviors" (pp. 284–285) <br> **Chapter 12:** "Promoting Mastery" (pp. 397–399) | |
| • Predicting | **Chapter 8:** "Promoting Learning in Science" (pp. 255–256) | |
| **C. Assessment Strategies** | | |
| ▶ Measurement theory and assessment-related issues: | **Chapters 14–15:** Entire chapters (pp. 460–503, 504–541) | |
| • Types of assessments | **Chapter 14:** "The Many Forms and Purposes of Assessment" (pp. 462–468) | **Building Teaching Skills and Dispositions** exercise "Assessing Students' Written Work" in topic "Assessment" |
| • Standardized tests, norm-referenced or criterion-referenced | **Chapter 14:** "The Many Forms and Purposes of Assessment" (pp. 462–468) <br> **Chapter 15:** "Standardized Tests" (pp. 519–527); "High-Stakes Testing and Accountability" (pp. 527–531) | **Assignments and Activities: Understanding Research** exercise "Usefulness of School Readiness Tests" in topic "Assessment" |
| • Achievement tests | **Chapter 14:** "Assessing Learning and Performance Both Informally and Formally" (pp. 479–499) <br> **Chapter 15:** "Achievement Tests" (pp. 519–521); **Practice for Your Licensure Exam: "Can Johnny Read?"** (pp. 540–541) | |
| • Aptitude tests | **Chapter 5:** "Measuring Intelligence" (pp. 124–125); "Being Smart about Intelligence and IQ Scores" (pp. 127–128) <br> **Chapter 15:** "General Scholastic Aptitude and Intelligence Tests" (p. 521); "Specific Aptitude and Ability Tests" (pp. 521–522) | |
| • Structured observations | **Chapter 14:** "Using Performance Assessments" (pp. 489–494) | |
| • Anecdotal notes | **Chapter 14:** "Informally Observing Students' Behaviors" (pp. 479–481) | |
| • Assessments of prior knowledge | **Chapter 12:** Asking Questions and Giving Feedback" (pp. 392–394); Into the Classroom box "Using Expository Instruction Effectively" (p. 393) | |
| • Student response during a lesson | **Chapter 14:** "Informally Observing Students' Behaviors" (pp. 479–481) | |
| • Portfolios | **Chapter 15:** "Using Portfolios" (pp. 516–520) | **Building Teaching Skills and Dispositions** exercise "Encouraging Self-Regulation" in topic "Social Cognitive Perspectives" |
| • Essays written to prompts | **Chapter 14:** "Using Paper–Pencil Assessments" (pp. 481–489) | |
| • Journals | **Chapter 13:** "Establishing and Maintaining Productive Teacher–Student Relationships" (pp. 426–428) <br> **Chapter 14:** "Including Students in the Assessment Process" (p. 470) | |
| • Self-evaluations | **Chapter 10:** "Self-Evaluation" (pp. 318–319) <br> **Chapter 14:** "Including Students in the Assessment Process" (p. 470) <br> **Chapter 15:** "Including Students in the Grading Process" (p. 516); "Using Portfolios" (pp. 516–519) | **Building Teaching Skills and Dispositions** exercise "Encouraging Self-Regulation" in topic "Social Cognitive Perspectives" |

*(continued)*

## TABLE C.1 • (Continued)

| TOPICS IN THE PRAXIS PRINCIPLES OF LEARNING AND TEACHING (PLT) TESTS | LOCATION OF TOPICS IN ORMROD'S *EDUCATIONAL PSYCHOLOGY* (8TH ED.) | LOCATION OF TOPICS AND PRACTICE OPPORTUNITIES IN MyEducationLab™ |
|---|---|---|
| **II. Instruction and Assessment-continued** | | |
| **C. Assessment Strategies-continued** | | |
| • Performance assessments | **Chapter 14:** "Using Performance Assessments" (pp. 489–494) | |
| • Characteristics of assessments: | **Chapter 14: Practice for Your Licensure Exam: "Pick and Choose"** (p. 503) **Chapter 15: Practice for Your Licensure Exam: "Can Johnny Read?"** (pp. 540–541) | **Building Teaching Skills and Dispositions** exercise "Assessing Students' Written Work" in topic "Assessment" |
| • Validity | **Chapter 14:** "Validity" (pp. 473–477); "RSVP Characteristics of Informal Assessments" (pp. 480–481); "RSVP Characteristics of Paper–Pencil Assessments" (pp. 488–489); "RSVP Characteristics of Performance Assessments" (pp. 493–494) **Chapter 15:** "Using Portfolios" (pp. 516–519); "Guidelines for Choosing and Using Standardized Tests" (pp. 523–524) | **Assignments and Activities: Understanding Research** exercise "Usefulness of School Readiness Tests" in topic "Assessment" |
| • Reliability | **Chapter 14:** "Reliability" (pp. 471–472); "RSVP Characteristics of Informal Assessments" (pp. 480–481); "RSVP Characteristics of Paper–Pencil Assessments" (pp. 488–489); "RSVP Characteristics of Performance Assessments" (pp. 493–494) **Chapter 15:** "Using Portfolios" (pp. 516–519) | |
| • Norm-referenced | **Chapter 14:** "Criterion-Referenced Versus Norm-Referenced Assessments" (p. 464) **Chapter 15:** "Norm-Referenced Scores" (pp. 506–511); "Using Criterion-Referenced Versus Norm-Referenced Scores in the Classroom" (pp. 511–512); "Interpreting Standardized Test Scores" (pp. 524, 526–527) | |
| • Criterion-referenced | **Chapter 14:** "Criterion-Referenced Versus Norm-Referenced Assessments" (p. 464) **Chapter 15:** "Criterion-Referenced Scores" (p. 506); "Using Criterion-Referenced Versus Norm-Referenced Scores in the Classroom" (pp. 511–512); "Interpreting Standardized Test Scores" (pp. 524, 526–527) | |
| • Mean, median, mode | **Chapter 15:** "Standard Scores" (pp. 508–511) | |
| • Sampling strategy | **Chapter 14:** "Content Validity" (pp. 474–477) | |
| • Scoring assessments: | **Chapter 14:** "Enhancing Learning through Formative Assessments and Other Assessment Practices" (pp. 468–470); "Reliability" (pp. 471–472); "Scoring Students' Responses to a Paper–Pencil Assessment" (pp. 487–488); "Scoring Students' Responses in a Performance Assessment" (pp. 491–493) | |
| • Analytical scoring | **Chapter 14:** "Scoring Students' Responses in a Performance Assessment" (pp. 491–493) | |
| • Holistic scoring | **Chapter 14:** "Scoring Students' Responses in a Performance Assessment" (pp. 491–493) | |
| • Rubrics | **Chapter 14:** "Enhancing Learning through Formative Assessments and Other Assessment Practices" (pp. 468–470); "Scoring Students' Responses to a Paper–Pencil Assessment" (pp. 487–488); "Scoring Students' Responses in a Performance Assessment" (pp. 491–493) | |
| • Reporting assessment results | **Chapter 15:** "Summarizing the Results of a Single Assessment" (pp. 505–512); "Communicating Assessment Results to Students and Parents" (pp. 537–539) **Appendix B:** "Estimating Error in Assessment Results" (pp. B-1–B-2) | **Supplementary Reading** "Correcting for Guessing in Paper–Pencil Assessments" in Book-Specific Resources for Chapter 14 **Supplementary Reading** "Calculating Standard Deviations" in Book-Specific Resources for Chapter 15 |

**TABLE C.1 • (Continued)**

| TOPICS IN THE PRAXIS PRINCIPLES OF LEARNING AND TEACHING (PLT) TESTS | LOCATION OF TOPICS IN ORMROD'S *EDUCATIONAL PSYCHOLOGY* (8TH ED.) | LOCATION OF TOPICS AND PRACTICE OPPORTUNITIES IN MyEducationLab™ |
|---|---|---|
| **II. Instruction and Assessment-continued** | | |
| **C. Assessment Strategies-continued** | | |
| • Percentile rank | **Chapter 15:** "Percentile Ranks" (p. 508) | |
| • Stanines | **Chapter 15:** "Standard Scores" (pp. 508–511) | |
| • Mastery levels | **Chapter 15:** "Criterion-Referenced Scores" (p. 506) | |
| • Raw score | **Chapter 15:** "Raw Scores" (p. 506) | |
| • Scaled score | **Chapter 15:** "Interpreting Standardized Test Scores" (see footnote, p. 527) | |
| • Grade equivalent score | **Chapter 15:** "Grade-Equivalent and Age-Equivalent Scores" (pp. 506–507) | |
| • Standard deviation | **Chapter 15:** "Standard Scores" (pp. 508–511) | |
| • Standard error of measurement | **Appendix B:** "Estimating Error in Assessment Results" (pp. B-1–B-2) | |
| • Use of assessments | **Chapter 14:** "The Many Forms and Purposes of Assessment" (pp. 462–468) | |
| • Formative evaluation | **Chapter 1: Case Study: The 'No D' Policy"** (p. 3) **Chapter 14:** "Enhancing Learning through Formative Assessments and Other Assessment Practices" (pp. 468–470) | **Building Teaching Skills and Dispositions** exercise "Assessing Students' Written Work" in topic "Assessment" |
| • Summative evaluation | **Chapter 14:** "Assessing Learning and Performance Both Informally and Formally" (pp. 479–499) **Chapter 15:** "Determining Final Class Grades" (pp. 512–516); "Achievement Tests" (pp. 519–521); "High-Stakes Testing and Accountability" (pp. 527–531) | **Supplementary Reading** "Combining Assessment Results to Determine Final Grades" in Book-Specific Resources for Chapter 15 |
| • Diagnostic evaluation | **Chapter 8: Practice for Your Licensure Exam: "The Birth of a Nation"** (p. 263) **Chapter 14:** "Diagnosing Learning and Performance Problems" (p. 465); "Enhancing Learning through Formative Assessments and Other Assessment Practices" (pp. 468–470) | |
| • Understanding measurement theory and assessment-related issues | **Chapter 14:** "Important Qualities of Good Assessments" (pp. 471–479); "Additional Considerations in Formal Assessment" (pp. 494–498) **Chapter 15:** "Considering—Or Not Considering—Other Factors in Grading" (pp. 515–516); "High-Stakes Testing and Accountability" (p. 527); "Cultural Bias in Test Content" (pp. 532–533) | **Assignments and Activities: Understanding Research** exercise "Cheating in High School Students" in topic "Assessment" |
| • Interpreting and communicating results of assessments | **Chapter 15:** "Confidentiality and Communication about Assessment Results" (pp. 535–539) | |
| **III. Communication Techniques** | | |
| ▶ Basic, effective verbal and nonverbal communication techniques | **Chapter 1: Case Study: The 'No D' Policy"** (p. 3) **Chapter 11:** "Enhancing Students' Sense of Self-Determination" (p. 339); "Teacher Attributions and Expectations" (pp. 360–364); **Practice for Your Licensure Exam: "When 'Perfect' Isn't Good Enough"** (pp. 378–379) **Chapter 12:** "Creating a Class Website to Share Goals and Facilitate Communication throughout the School Year" (p. 391) **Chapter 13:** "Establishing and Maintaining Productive Teacher–Student Relationships" (pp. 426–428); "Creating an Effective Psychological Climate" (pp. 428–430); "Setting Limits" (pp. 430–433); "Working with Parents" (pp. 441–446); "Discussing Problems Privately with Students" (pp. 447–448) | **Simulation** exercise "Developing Positive Teacher Student-Relationships with All Students" in topic "Classroom Management" |

*(continued)*

## TABLE C.1 • (Continued)

| TOPICS IN THE PRAXIS PRINCIPLES OF LEARNING AND TEACHING (PLT) TESTS | LOCATION OF TOPICS IN ORMROD'S *EDUCATIONAL PSYCHOLOGY* (8TH ED.) | LOCATION OF TOPICS AND PRACTICE OPPORTUNITIES IN MyEducationLab™ |
|---|---|---|
| **III. Communication Techniques-continued** | | |
| | **Chapter 14: Case Study: "The Math Test"** (p. 461)<br>**Chapter 15:** "Communicating Assessment Results to Students and Parents" (pp. 537–539) | |
| ▶ Effect of cultural and gender differences on communications in the classroom | **Chapter 4:** "Examples of Cultural and Ethnic Diversity" (p. 94); "Research Findings Regarding Gender Differences" (pp. 103–106; see especially subsections "Interpersonal Behaviors and Relationships" pp. 105–106 and "Classroom Behaviors" p. 106) | |
| ▶ Types of questions that can stimulate discussion in different ways for particular purposes: | **Chapter 12:** "Asking Questions and Giving Feedback" (pp. 392–394) | |
| • Probing for learner understanding | **Chapter 6:** "Elaboration" (pp. 170–171); "Promoting Conceptual Change" (pp. 181–183) | |
| • Helping students articulate their ideas and thinking processes | **Chapter 6:** "Wait Time" (p. 187); "Promoting Conceptual Change" (pp. 181–183) | |
| • Promoting risk-taking and problem-solving | **Chapter 7:** "Problem Solving" (pp. 210–216); "Fostering Creativity" (pp. 217–219)<br>**Chapter 13:** "Creating an Effective Psychological Climate" (pp. 428–430) | |
| • Facilitating factual recall | **Chapter 6:** "Factors Affecting Retrieval" (pp. 184–187) | **Assignments and Activities: Understanding Research** exercise "Knowledge Construction in History" in topic "Knowledge Construction" |
| • Encouraging convergent and divergent thinking | **Chapter 7:** "Creativity" (pp. 216–219) | |
| • Stimulating curiosity | **Chapter 2:** "Piaget's Basic Assumptions" (pp. 26–28); **Practice for Your Licensure Exam: "Stones Lesson"** (pp. 52–53)<br>**Chapter 11:** "Promoting Interest in Classroom Subject Matter" (pp. 346–347)<br>**Chapter 12:** "Conducting Discovery and Inquiry Activities" (pp. 405–407); "Using Computer Simulations and Games" (p. 407) | |
| • Helping students to question | **Chapter 7:** "Regularly Monitoring Learning" (p. 200); "Critical Thinking" (pp. 219–222) | |
| • Promoting a caring community | **Chapter 8:** "Creating a Community of Learners" (pp. 232–234)<br>**Chapter 11:** "Relatedness" (pp. 342–343)<br>**Chapter 13:** "Creating an Effective Psychological Climate" (pp. 428–430); "Working with Other Faculty Members" (pp. 439–441) | |
| **IV. Profession and Community** | | |
| **A. The Reflective Practitioner** | | |
| ▶ Types of resources available for professional development and learning: | | |
| • Professional literature | **Chapter 1:** "Developing as a Teacher" (pp. 13–14) | |
| • Colleagues | **Chapter 13:** "Working with Other Faculty Members" (pp. 439–441) | |
| • Professional associations | **Chapter 1:** "Developing as a Teacher" (pp. 13–14) | |

## TABLE C.1 • (Continued)

| TOPICS IN THE PRAXIS PRINCIPLES OF LEARNING AND TEACHING (PLT) TESTS | LOCATION OF TOPICS IN ORMROD'S *EDUCATIONAL PSYCHOLOGY* (8TH ED.) | LOCATION OF TOPICS AND PRACTICE OPPORTUNITIES IN MyEducationLab™ |
|---|---|---|
| **IV. Profession and Community-continued** | | |
| **A. The Reflective Practitioner-continued** | | |
| • Professional development activities | **Chapter 1:** "Developing as a Teacher" (pp. 13–14) | |
| ▶ Ability to read, understand, and apply articles and books about current research, views, ideas, and debates regarding best teaching practices | **Chapter 1: Case Study: "The 'No D' Policy"** (p. 3); "Teaching as Evidence-Based Practice" (pp. 4–6); "Understanding and Interpreting Research Findings" (pp. 6–11); "From Research to Practice: The Importance of Theories" (p. 11); **Practice for Your Licensure Exam: "New Software"** (pp. 16–17) **Appendix A:** "Describing Associations with Correlation Coefficients" (pp. A–1–A-2) | All **Assignments and Activities: Understanding Research** exercises in various topic areas |
| ▶ Why personal reflection on teaching practices is critical, and approaches that can be used to reflect and evaluate: | **Chapter 1: Case Study: "The 'No D' Policy"** (p. 3); "Conducting Action Research" (pp. 12–13); "Developing as a Teacher" (pp. 13–14) **Chapter 3: Case Study: "Hidden Treasure"** (p. 55) **Chapter 4:** "Creating a Culturally Inclusive Classroom Environment" (pp. 99–103) **Chapter 11:** "Teacher Attributions and Expectations" (pp. 360–364) | |
| • Code of ethics | | |
| • Advocacy for learners | **Chapter 4:** "Supporting Students at Risk" (pp. 114–115) | |
| **B. The Larger Community** | | |
| ▶ The role of the school as a resource to the larger community: | **Chapter 13:** "Working with the Community at Large" (p. 441); "Getting Parents Involved in School Activities" (p. 444) | |
| • Teacher as a resource | **Chapter 13:** "Communicating with Parents" (pp. 442–444) | |
| ▶ Factors in the students' environment outside of school (family circumstances, community environments, health and economic conditions) that may influence students' life and learning | **Chapter 2:** "The Multiple Layers of Environmental Influence: Bronfenbrenner's Theory" (pp. 21–22) **Chapter 3:** "Family Dynamics" (pp. 56–58) **Chapter 4: Case Study: "Why Jack Wasn't in School"** (p. 91); "Navigating Different Cultures at Home and at School" (pp. 93–94); "Family Relationships and Expectations" (p. 98); "Socioeconomic Differences" (pp. 109–113); "Students at Risk" (pp. 113–115) **Chapter 5:** "Nature and Nurture in the Development of Intelligence" (pp. 125–126) **Chapter 8:** "Basic Assumptions of Contextual Theories" (pp. 228–230); "Cultures as Contexts" (pp. 234–237) | **Supplementary Reading** "Ecological Systems Perspectives of Child Development" in Book-Specific Resources for Chapter 2 |
| ▶ Basic strategies for developing and utilizing active partnerships among teachers, parents/guardians, and leaders in the community to support the educational process: | **Chapter 5:** "General Recommendations for Working with Students Who Have Special Needs" (pp. 151–152) **Chapter 13:** "Expanding the Sense of Community Beyond the Classroom" (pp. 439–446); "Addressing Aggression and Violence at School" (pp. 454–458) | |
| • Shared ownership | | |
| • Shared decision making | **Chapter 5:** "Public Law 94-142: Individuals with Disabilities Education Act (IDEA)" (pp. 131–132) | |
| • Respectful/reciprocal communication | **Chapter 13:** "Working with Parents" (pp. 441–446) | |

*(continued)*

## TABLE C.1 • (Continued)

| TOPICS IN THE PRAXIS PRINCIPLES OF LEARNING AND TEACHING (PLT) TESTS | LOCATION OF TOPICS IN ORMROD'S *EDUCATIONAL PSYCHOLOGY* (8TH ED.) | LOCATION OF TOPICS AND PRACTICE OPPORTUNITIES IN MyEducationLab™ |
|---|---|---|
| **IV. Profession and Community-continued** | | |
| **B. The Larger Community-continued** | | |
| ▶ Major laws related to students' rights and teacher responsibilities: | | |
| • Equal education | | |
| • Appropriate education for students with special needs | **Chapter 5:** "Public Law 94-142: Individuals with Disabilities Education Act (IDEA)" (pp. 131–132) | |
| • Confidentiality and privacy | **Chapter 15: Case Study: "B in History"** (p. 505); "Confidentiality and Communication about Assessment Results" (pp. 535–539) | |
| • Appropriate treatment of students | | |
| • Reporting in situations related to possible child abuse | **Chapter 3:** "Child Maltreatment" (p. 58) | |

# Glossary

**accommodation.** Process of dealing with a new object or event by either modifying an existing scheme or forming a new one.

**accountability.** An obligation of teachers and other school personnel to accept responsibility for students' performance on high-stakes assessments; often mandated by policy makers calling for school reform.

**acculturation.** Gradual process of adopting the values and customs of a new culture.

**action research.** Research conducted by teachers and other school personnel to address issues and problems in their own schools or classrooms.

**activation.** Degree to which something in memory is being actively attended to and mentally processed.

**actual developmental level.** Upper limit of tasks that a learner can successfully perform independently.

**adaptive behavior.** Behavior related to daily living skills or appropriate conduct in social situations; used as a criterion for identifying students with intellectual disabilities.

**adaptive testing.** Computer-based assessment in which students' performance on early items determines which items are presented subsequently.

**advance organizer.** Introduction to a lesson that provides an overall organizational scheme for the lesson.

**affect.** Feelings, emotions, and moods that a learner brings to bear on a task.

**African American English.** Dialect of some African American communities that includes some pronunciations, idioms, and grammatical constructions different from those of Standard English.

**age-equivalent score.** Test score matching a particular student's performance with the average performance of students of a certain age.

**aggressive behavior.** Action intentionally taken to hurt another either physically or psychologically.

**algorithm.** Prescribed sequence of steps that guarantees a correct problem solution.

**analytic scoring.** Scoring a student's performance on an assessment by evaluating various aspects of it separately.

**antecedent response.** Response that influences the probability that a certain other response will follow.

**antecedent stimulus.** Stimulus that influences the probability that a particular response will follow.

**anxiety.** Feeling of uneasiness and apprehension concerning a situation with an uncertain outcome.

**applied behavior analysis (ABA).** Systematic application of behaviorist principles in educational and therapeutic settings.

**apprenticeship.** Mentorship in which a novice works intensively with an expert to learn how to perform complex new skills.

**appropriation.** Process of internalizing but also adapting the cognitive tools of one's culture for one's own use.

**Asperger syndrome.** Mild form of an autism spectrum disorder in which students have normal intelligence and language skills but show significant deficits in social cognition and social skills.

**assessment.** Process of observing a sample of a student's behavior and drawing inferences about the student's knowledge and abilities.

**assimilation.** Process of dealing with an object or event in a way that is consistent with an existing scheme.

**assistive technology.** Any electronic or nonelectronic device that can enhance certain abilities or performance areas for students with disabilities.

**astrocyte.** Star-shaped brain cell hypothesized to be involved in learning and memory; has chemically mediated connections with many other astrocytes and with neurons.

**attachment.** Strong, affectionate bond formed between a child and a caregiver.

**attention.** Focusing of mental processing on particular stimuli.

**attention-deficit hyperactivity disorder (ADHD).** Disorder marked by inattention, hyperactivity, impulsive behavior, or some combination of these characteristics.

**attribution.** Self-constructed causal explanation for a personally experienced or observed event, such as one's own or another person's success or failure.

**authentic activity.** Classroom activity similar to an activity that students are apt to encounter in the outside world.

**authentic assessment.** Assessment of students' knowledge and skills in a context similar to one that might be found in the outside world.

**authoritarian parenting.** Parenting style characterized by rigid rules and expectations for behavior that children are asked to obey without question.

**authoritative parenting.** Parenting style characterized by emotional warmth, high standards for behavior, explanation and consistent enforcement of rules, and inclusion of children in decision making.

**autism spectrum disorders.** Disorders marked by impaired social cognition, social skills, and social interaction, presumably due to a brain abnormality; extreme forms often associated with significant cognitive and linguistic delays and highly unusual behaviors.

**automaticity.** Ability to respond quickly and efficiently while mentally processing or physically performing a task.

**backward design.** Approach to instructional planning in which a teacher first determines the desired end result (i.e., what knowledge and skills students should acquire), then identifies appropriate assessments, and finally determines appropriate instructional strategies.

**base group.** Cooperative learning group in which students work together for an entire semester or school year to provide mutual support for one another's learning.

**baseline.** Frequency of a response before it is intentionally and systematically reinforced.

**basic interpersonal communication skills.** (BICS) Proficiency in English sufficient for day-to-day conversation with English speakers but *not* sufficient for academic success in an English-only curriculum.

**behavioral momentum.** Increased tendency for a learner to make a particular response immediately after making similar responses.

**behaviorism.** Theoretical perspective in which learning and behavior are described and explained in terms of stimulus–response relationships.

**belongingness.** General sense that one is an important and valued member of the classroom.

**bias (in assessment).** Factor in an assessment instrument or procedure that consistently and differentially influences students' performance for reasons unrelated to the characteristic being measured; reduces the validity of assessment results.

**bilingual education.** Second-language instruction in which students are instructed in academic subject areas in their native language while simultaneously being taught to speak and write in the second language.

**Bloom's taxonomy.** Taxonomy of six cognitive processes, varying in complexity, that lessons might be designed to foster.

**boredom.** Unpleasant affective state that results from lack of stimulation and arousal.

**bully.** Person who frequently threatens, harasses, or causes injury to particular peers.

**central executive.** Component of the human memory system that oversees the flow of information throughout the system.

**challenge.** Situation in which a learner believes that success is possible with sufficient effort.

**child maltreatment.** Consistent neglect or abuse of a child that jeopardizes the child's physical and psychological well-being.

**class inclusion.** Recognition that an object simultaneously belongs to a particular category and to one of its subcategories.

**classical conditioning.** Form of learning in which a new, involuntary response is acquired as a result of two stimuli being presented close together in time.

**classroom climate.** Overall psychological atmosphere of the classroom.

**classroom management.** Establishment and maintenance of a classroom environment that's conducive to learning and achievement.

**clinical method.** Procedure in which an adult presents a task or problem and asks a child a series of questions about it, tailoring later questions to the child's responses to previous ones.

**clique.** Moderately stable friendship group of perhaps three to ten members.

**cognitive academic language proficiency.** (CALP) Mastery of English vocabulary and syntax sufficient for English language learners to achieve academic success in an English-only curriculum.

**cognitive apprenticeship.** Mentorship in which a teacher and a student work together on a challenging task and the teacher provides guidance in how to think about the task.

**cognitive behavioral therapy.** Planned, systematic combination of behaviorist techniques and cognition-based strategies (e.g., modeling, self-regulation techniques) as a means of bringing about desired behaviors.

**cognitive development.** Development of increasingly sophisticated thinking, reasoning, and language with age.

**cognitive dissonance.** Feeling of mental discomfort caused by new information that conflicts with current knowledge or beliefs.

**cognitive load.** Cognitive burden that a particular learning activity places on working memory at any one time; includes both the amount of information students must simultaneously think about and the specific cognitive processes students must engage in to understand what they're studying.

**cognitive modeling.** Demonstrating how to think about as well as how to do a task.

**cognitive process.** Particular way of thinking about and mentally responding to a certain event or piece of information.

**cognitive psychology.** General theoretical perspective that focuses on the mental processes underlying learning and behavior.

**cognitive style.** Characteristic way in which a learner tends to think about a task and process new information; typically comes into play automatically rather than by choice.

**cognitive tool.** Concept, symbol, strategy, procedure, or other culturally constructed mechanism that helps people think about and respond to situations more effectively.

**collective self-efficacy.** People's beliefs about their ability to be successful when they work together on a task.

**Common Core State Standards.** Set of standards that most U.S. states have adopted to guide instruction and assessment in English-language arts and mathematics (see www.corestandards.org).

**community of learners.** Class in which teachers and students actively and collaboratively work to create a body of knowledge and help one another learn.

**community of practice.** Group of people who share common interests and goals and regularly interact and coordinate their efforts in pursuit of those interests and goals.

**complex cognitive process.** Cognitive process that involves going well beyond information specifically learned (e.g., by analyzing, applying, or evaluating it).

**comprehension monitoring.** Process of checking oneself to verify understanding and memory of newly acquired information.

**computer-based instruction (CBI).** Academic instruction provided by means of specially designed computer software.

**concept.** Mental grouping of objects or events that have something in common.

**concept map.** Diagram of concepts and their interrelationships; used to enhance the learning and memory of a topic.

**conceptual change.** Significant revision of an existing theory or belief system, enabling new and discrepant information to be better understood and explained.

**conceptual understanding.** Meaningfully learned and well-integrated knowledge about a topic, including many logical connections among specific concepts and ideas.

**concrete operations stage.** Piaget's third stage of cognitive development, in which adultlike logic appears but is limited to concrete reality.

**conditional knowledge.** Knowledge concerning appropriate ways to respond (physically or mentally) under various circumstances.

**conditioned response (CR).** Response that begins to be elicited by a particular (conditioned) stimulus through classical conditioning.

**conditioned stimulus (CS).** Stimulus that begins to elicit a particular response through classical conditioning.

**conditioning.** Term commonly used by behaviorists for *learning*; typically involves specific environmental events leading to the acquisition of specific responses.

**confidence interval.** Range around an assessment score reflecting the amount of error that is likely to be affecting the score's accuracy.

**confirmation bias.** Tendency to seek information that confirms rather than discredits current beliefs.

**conservation.** Recognition that if nothing is added or taken away, amount stays the same regardless of alterations in shape or arrangement.

**consolidation.** Neurological process in which newly acquired knowledge is firmed up in the brain; often takes several hours, sometimes even longer.

**construct validity.** Extent to which an assessment accurately measures an unobservable educational or psychological characteristic.

**constructed-response task.** Recall assessment task that requires a lengthy response; typically also requires elaboration, analysis, synthesis, and/or application of learned information.

**construction.** Mental process in which a learner takes many separate pieces of information and uses them to build an overall understanding or interpretation.

**constructivism.** Theoretical perspective proposing that learners actively construct (rather than passively absorb) knowledge from their experiences.

**content validity.** Extent to which an assessment includes a representative sample of tasks within the content domain being assessed.

**contextual theory.** Theory of learning that focuses on how people's general physical, social, and/or cultural surroundings support their learning, development, and behavior.

**contiguity.** Occurrence of two or more events (e.g., two stimuli, or a stimulus and a response) at approximately the same time.

**contingency.** Situation in which one event happens only after another event has already occurred; one event is *contingent* on the other's occurrence.

**contingency contract.** Formal agreement between a teacher and a student that identifies behaviors the student will exhibit and the reinforcers that will follow.

**continuous reinforcement.** Reinforcement of a response every time it occurs.

**control group.** Group of people in a research study who are given either no intervention or a *placebo* treatment that is unlikely to have an effect on the dependent variable.

**controversial student.** Student whom some peers strongly like and other peers strongly dislike.

**conventional morality.** Uncritical acceptance of society's conventions regarding right and wrong.

**conventional transgression.** Action that violates a culture's general expectations regarding socially appropriate behavior.

**convergent thinking.** Process of pulling together several pieces of information to draw a conclusion or solve a problem.

**cooperative learning.** Approach to instruction in which students work with a small group of peers to achieve a common goal and help one another learn.

**coping model.** Model who initially struggles with a task but successfully overcomes obstacles.

**co-regulated learning.** Process through which an adult and child share responsibility for directing various aspects of the child's learning; alternatively, collaborative process in which one or more learners jointly support and monitor one another's learning progress.

**correlation.** Extent to which two variables are associated, such that when one variable increases, the other either increases or decreases somewhat predictably.

**correlation coefficient.** Statistic that indicates the strength and direction of an association between two variables.

**correlational study.** Research study that explores possible associations among two or more variables.

**cortex.** Upper part of the brain; site of complex, conscious thinking processes.

**covert strategy.** Learning strategy that is strictly mental (rather than behavioral) in nature and thus cannot be directly observed by others.

**creativity.** New and original behavior that yields a productive and culturally appropriate result.

**criterion-referenced assessment.** Assessment instrument designed to determine what students know and can do relative to predetermined standards or criteria.

**criterion-referenced score.** Assessment score that specifically indicates what a student knows or can do.

**critical thinking.** Process of evaluating the accuracy, credibility, and worth of information and lines of reasoning.

**crowd.** Large, loose-knit social group that shares certain common interests and behaviors.

**crystallized intelligence.** Knowledge and skills accumulated from prior experience, schooling, and culture.

**cueing.** Use of a verbal or nonverbal signal to indicate that a certain behavior is desired or that a certain behavior should stop.

**cultural bias.** Extent to which assessment tasks either offend or unfairly penalize some students because of their ethnicity, gender, or socioeconomic status.

**cultural mismatch.** Situation in which a child's home culture and the school culture hold conflicting expectations for behavior.

**culturally responsive teaching.** Use of instructional strategies that build on students' existing knowledge and skills and are consistent with their culturally preferred ways of learning and behaving.

**culture.** Behaviors and belief systems of a long-standing social group.

**culture of transfer.** Learning environment in which applying school subject matter to new situations, cross-disciplinary contexts, and real-world problems is both the expectation and the norm.

**culture shock.** Sense of confusion when a student encounters a new environment with behavioral expectations very different from those previously learned.

**curriculum-based measurement (CBM).** Use of frequent assessments to track students' progress in acquiring basic skills; assessments are typically quite short (e.g., one to four minutes) and each focus on a specific skill.

**cyberbullying.** Engaging in psychological aggression via wireless technologies or the Internet.

**debilitating anxiety.** Anxiety of sufficient intensity that it interferes with performance.

**decay.** Gradual weakening of information stored in long-term memory, especially if the information is used infrequently or not at all.

**declarative knowledge.** Knowledge concerning the nature of how things are, were, or will be.

**delay of gratification.** Ability to forego small, immediate reinforcers in order to obtain larger ones later on.

**descriptive study.** Research study that enables researchers to draw conclusions about the current state of affairs regarding an issue but not about correlation or cause–and–effect relationships.

**developmental milestone.** Appearance of a new, more advanced behavior that indicates significant progress in a child's development.

**dialect.** Form of a language that has certain unique pronunciations, idioms, and grammatical structures and is characteristic of a particular region or ethnic group.

**differentiated instruction.** Practice of individualizing instructional methods—and possibly also individualizing specific content and instructional goals—to align with each student's existing knowledge, skills, and needs.

**direct instruction.** Approach to instruction that uses a variety of techniques (e.g., explanations, questions, guided and independent practice) in a fairly structured manner to promote learning of fundamental knowledge and skills.

**discovery learning.** Approach to instruction in which students construct their own knowledge about a topic through firsthand interaction with an aspect of their environment.

**discrimination.** Phenomenon in which a student learns that a response is reinforced in the presence of one stimulus but not in the presence of another, similar stimulus.

**disequilibrium.** State of being unable to address new events with existing schemes; typically accompanied by some mental discomfort.

**disposition.** General inclination and desire to approach and think about learning and problem-solving tasks in a particular way; typically has a motivational component in addition to cognitive components.

**distance learning.** Technology-based instruction in which students are at a location physically separate from that of their instructor.

**distributed cognition and intelligence.** Enhancement of thinking through the use of physical objects and technology, concepts and symbols of one's culture, and/or social collaboration and support.

**distributed knowledge.** Possession of different areas of expertise by various members of a social group, such that group members must rely on one another to maximize their personal and collective performance and success.

**divergent thinking.** Process of mentally moving in a variety of directions from a single idea.

**doing-just-enough goal.** Desire to get reasonable school grades through the easiest possible routes—routes that may or may not involve actually learning classroom material.

**dynamic assessment.** Systematic examination of how easily and in what ways a student can acquire new knowledge or skills, usually within the context of instruction or scaffolding.

**dyslexia.** Inability to master basic reading skills in a developmentally typical time frame despite normal reading instruction; often has biological roots.

**educational psychology.** Academic discipline that (1) systematically studies the nature of learning, child development, motivation, and related topics and (2) applies its research findings to the identification and development of effective classroom practices.

**effortful control.** Ability to inhibit dominant responses in favor of other, less dominant ones that might be more productive; an aspect of temperament that is influenced by biology and brain maturation.

**elaboration.** Cognitive process in which learners embellish on new information based on what they already know.

**e-learning.** Instruction and learning that occur largely or entirely within the context of digital technologies.

**electronic portfolio (e-folio).** Portfolio compiled and available for inspection on a CD, DVD, flash drive, or other electronic storage mechanism.

**emergent literacy.** Knowledge and skills that lay a foundation for reading and writing; typically develops from early experiences with written language.

**emotion regulation.** Process of keeping in check or intentionally altering feelings that might lead to counterproductive behavior.

**emotional and behavioral disorders.** Emotional states and behavior patterns that consistently and significantly disrupt academic learning and performance.

**empathy.** Experience of sharing the same feelings as someone in unfortunate circumstances.

**encoding.** Changing the format of new information as it is being stored in memory.

**English language learner (ELL).** School-age child who is not fully fluent in English because of limited exposure to English prior to enrollment in an English-speaking school.

**entity view of intelligence.** Belief that intelligence is a distinct ability that is relatively permanent and unchangeable.

**epistemic belief.** Belief about the nature of knowledge or knowledge acquisition.

**equilibration.** Movement from equilibrium to disequilibrium and back to equilibrium, a process that promotes development of more complex thought and understandings.

**equilibrium.** State of being able to address new events with existing schemes.

**ethnic group.** People who have common historical roots, values, beliefs, and behaviors and who share a sense of interdependence.

**ethnic identity.** Awareness of one's membership in a particular ethnic or cultural group, and willingness to adopt behaviors characteristic of the group.

**ETS score.** Standard score with a mean of 500 and a standard deviation of 100.

**evidence-based practice.** Instructional method or other classroom strategy that research has consistently shown to bring about significant gains in students' development and/or academic achievement.

**expectancy.** Belief about the likelihood of success in an activity, given present ability levels and external circumstances that may either help or hinder performance.

**experimental study.** Research study that involves both (1) the manipulation of one variable to determine its possible effect on another variable and (2) control of additional variables that might potentially have an impact on the outcome; allows conclusions about cause–and–effect relationships.

**explicit knowledge.** Knowledge that a person is consciously aware of and can verbally describe.

**expository instruction.** Approach to instruction in which information is presented in essentially the same form in which students are expected to learn it.

**externalizing behavior.** Symptom of an emotional or behavioral disorder that has a direct effect on other people (e.g., aggression, lack of self-control).

**extinction.** Gradual disappearance of an acquired response. In classical conditioning, results from repeated presentation of a conditioned stimulus in the absence of the unconditioned stimulus; in instrumental conditioning, results from repeated lack of reinforcement.

**extrinsic motivation.** Motivation resulting from factors external to the individual and unrelated to the task being performed.

**extrinsic reinforcer.** Reinforcer that comes from the outside environment, rather than from within the learner.

**facilitating anxiety.** Level of anxiety (usually relatively low) that enhances performance.

**Family Educational Rights and Privacy Act (FERPA).** U.S. legislation passed in 1974 that gives students and parents access to school records and limits other people's access to those records.

**flow.** Intense form of intrinsic motivation, involving complete absorption in and concentration on a challenging activity.

**fluid intelligence.** Ability to acquire knowledge quickly and adapt effectively to new situations.

**formal assessment.** Preplanned, systematic attempt to ascertain what students know and can do.

**formal discipline.** View of transfer suggesting that the study of rigorous subject matter enhances one's ability to learn other, unrelated things.

**formal operational egocentrism.** Inability of adolescents in Piaget's formal operations stage to separate their own abstract logic from the perspectives of others and from practical considerations.

**formal operations stage.** Piaget's fourth and final stage of cognitive development, in which logical reasoning processes are applied to abstract ideas as well as to concrete objects.

**formative assessment.** Assessment conducted before or during instruction to facilitate instructional planning and enhance students' learning.

**functional analysis.** Examination of inappropriate behavior and its antecedents and consequences to determine one or more purposes (functions) that the behavior might serve for the learner.

*g.* Theoretical general factor in intelligence that influences one's ability to learn and perform in a wide variety of contexts.

**gang.** Cohesive social group characterized by initiation rites, distinctive colors and symbols, territorial orientation, and feuds with rival groups.

**gender schema.** Self-constructed, organized body of beliefs about characteristics and behaviors of males or females.

**general transfer.** Instance of transfer in which the original learning task and the transfer task are different in content.

**generalization.** Phenomenon in which a person learns a response to a particular stimulus and then makes the same response to a similar stimulus. In classical conditioning, involves making a conditioned response to a stimulus similar to a conditioned stimulus; in instrumental conditioning, involves making a voluntary response to a stimulus that is similar to one previously associated with a response–reinforcement contingency.

**giftedness.** Unusually high ability or aptitude in one or more areas, to such a degree that students require special educational services to help them meet their full potential.

**glial cell.** Cell in the brain that supports neurons or general brain functioning.

**goodness of fit.** Situation in which classroom conditions and expectations are compatible with students' temperaments and personality characteristics.

**grade-equivalent score.** Test score matching a particular student's performance with the average performance of students at a certain grade level.

**group contingency.** Situation in which everyone in a group must make a particular response before reinforcement occurs.

**group differences.** Consistently observed differences (on average) among diverse groups of students (e.g., students of different genders or ethnic backgrounds).

**guided participation.** A child's performance of a real-world adult activity, facilitated by developmentally appropriate adult support.

**guilt.** Feeling of discomfort about having caused someone else pain or distress.

**halo effect.** Phenomenon in which people are more likely to perceive positive behaviors in someone they like or admire.

**hearing loss.** Malfunction of the ears or associated nerves that interferes with perception of sounds within the frequency range of normal human speech.

**heuristic.** General strategy that facilitates problem solving but doesn't always yield a solution.

**higher-level question.** Question that requires students to use previously learned information in a new way—that is, to engage in complex cognitive processes.

**high-stakes testing.** Practice of using students' performance on a single assessment to make major decisions about students, school personnel, or overall school quality.

**holistic scoring.** Summarizing a student's performance on an assessment with a single score.

**horns effect.** Phenomenon in which people are more likely to perceive negative behaviors in someone for whom they have little affection or respect.

**hostile attributional bias.** Tendency to interpret others' behaviors as reflecting hostile or aggressive intentions.

**hot cognition.** Learning or cognitive processing that is emotionally charged.

**hypermedia.** Interlinked collection of computer-based, multimedia instructional materials (e.g., text, pictures, sound, animations) that students can examine in a sequence of their own choosing.

**identity.** Self-constructed definition of who one is and what things are important to accomplish in life.

**ill-defined problem.** Problem in which the desired goal is unclear, some information needed to solve the problem is missing, and/or several possible solutions to the problem exist.

**illusion of knowing.** Thinking that one knows something that one actually does *not* know.

**imaginary audience.** Belief that one is the center of attention in any social situation.

**I-message.** Statement that communicates the adverse effects of a student's misbehavior, including one's own reactions to it, in a calm, relatively nonaccusatory manner; its intent is to convey information, not to lay blame.

**immersion.** Second-language instruction in which students hear and speak that language almost exclusively in the classroom.

**implicit knowledge.** Knowledge that a person cannot consciously recall or explain but that nevertheless affects the person's thinking or behavior.

**incentive.** Hoped-for, but not guaranteed, future consequence of behavior.

**inclusion.** Practice of educating all students, including those with severe and multiple disabilities, in neighborhood schools and general education classrooms.

**incompatible behaviors.** Two or more behaviors that cannot be performed simultaneously.

**incremental view of intelligence.** Belief that intelligence can improve with effort and practice.

**individual constructivism.** Theoretical perspective that focuses on how people, as individuals, construct meaning from their experiences.

**individual differences.** Diversity in abilities and characteristics (intelligence, personality, etc.) among students at a particular age and within a particular gender or cultural group.

**individualized education program (IEP).** Written description of an appropriate instructional program for a student with special needs.

**Individuals with Disabilities Education Act (IDEA).** U.S. federal legislation granting educational rights from birth until age 21 for people with cognitive, emotional, or physical disabilities.

**induction.** Explanation of why a certain behavior is unacceptable, often with a focus on the pain or distress that someone has caused another.

**informal assessment.** Assessment that results from a teacher's spontaneous, day-to-day observations of how a student performs in class.

**information literacy.** Knowledge and skills that help a learner find, use, evaluate, organize, and present information about a particular topic.

**information processing theory.** Theoretical perspective that focuses on the specific ways in which learners mentally think about, or process, new information and events.

**inner speech.** Process of talking to and guiding oneself mentally rather than aloud.

**inquiry learning.** Approach to instruction in which students apply complex reasoning skills in their examination and interpretation of new phenomena and data sources.

**in-school suspension.** Consequence for misbehavior in which a student is placed in a quiet, boring room within the school building, typically to do schoolwork under close adult supervision.

**instructional goal.** Desired long-term outcome of instruction.

**instructional objective.** Desired outcome of a lesson or unit.

**instrumental conditioning.** Learning process in which a response either increases or decreases as a result of being followed by either reinforcement or punishment, respectively.

**intellectual disability.** Disability characterized by significantly below-average general intelligence and deficits in adaptive behavior, both of which first appear in infancy or childhood; also known as *mental retardation*.

**intelligence.** Ability to apply prior knowledge and experiences flexibly to accomplish challenging new tasks.

**intelligence test.** General measure of current level of cognitive functioning; often used to predict academic achievement in the short run.

**intelligent tutoring system.** Computer software program that provides individually tailored instruction and practice, plus ongoing guidance and feedback, related to a particular topic and set of skills.

**interest.** Perception that an activity is intriguing and enticing; typically accompanied by both cognitive engagement and positive affect.

**interference.** Phenomenon whereby something stored in long-term memory inhibits one's ability to remember something else correctly.

**intermittent reinforcement.** Reinforcement of a response only occasionally, with some occurrences of the response *not* being reinforced.

**internal consistency reliability.** Extent to which different parts of an assessment instrument all assess the same characteristic.

**internalization.** Process through which a learner gradually incorporates socially based activities into his or her internal cognitive processes.

**internalized motivation.** Adoption of other people's priorities and values as one's own.

**internalizing behavior.** Symptom of an emotional or behavioral disorder that adversely affects the student with the disorder but has little or no direct effect on other people (e.g., depression, social withdrawal).

**intrinsic motivation.** Motivation resulting from internal personal characteristics or inherent in the task being performed.

**intrinsic reinforcer.** Reinforcer that is provided by the learner or inherent in the task being performed.

**IQ score.** Score on an intelligence test, determined by comparing a person's performance on the test with that of others in the same age-group; for most tests, it's a standard score with a mean of 100 and a standard deviation of 15.

**IRE cycle.** Adult–child interaction marked by adult initiation (usually involving a question), child response, and adult evaluation.

**item analysis.** Follow-up analysis of patterns in students' responses to various items in an assessment.

**item difficulty (p).** Index reflecting the proportion of students getting a particular assessment item correct.

**item discrimination (D).** Index reflecting the relative proportion of high-scoring versus low-scoring students getting a particular assessment item correct.

**jigsaw technique.** Instructional technique in which materials are divided among members of a cooperative group, with different students being responsible for learning different content and teaching it to other group members.

**keyword method.** Mnemonic technique in which an association is made between two ideas by forming a visual image of one or more concrete objects (*keywords*) that either sound similar to or symbolically represent those ideas.

**knowledge base.** One's existing knowledge about specific topics and the world in general.

**knowledge telling.** Writing ideas in whatever order they come to mind, with little regard for communicating the ideas effectively.

**knowledge transforming.** Writing about ideas in a manner that intentionally helps the reader comprehend them.

**learned helplessness.** General, fairly pervasive belief that one is incapable of accomplishing tasks and has little or no control of the environment.

**learner-directed instruction.** Approach to instruction in which students have considerable control regarding the issues they address and the ways they address them.

**learning.** Long-term change in mental representations or associations as a result of experience.

**learning disabilities.** Deficiencies in one or more specific cognitive processes but not in overall cognitive functioning.

**learning strategy.** One or more cognitive processes used intentionally for a particular learning task.

**least restrictive environment.** Most typical and standard educational environment that can reasonably meet the needs of a student with a disability.

**legitimate peripheral participation.** Initially participating at the fringe of a community of practice as a way of gaining knowledge and skills related to the group's typical ways of doing things.

**lesson plan.** Predetermined guide for a lesson that identifies instructional goals or objectives, necessary materials, instructional strategies, and one or more assessment methods.

**level of potential development.** Upper limit of tasks that a learner can successfully perform with the assistance of a more competent individual.

**logical consequence.** Unpleasant consequence that follows naturally or logically from a student's misbehavior.

**long-term memory.** Component of memory that holds knowledge and skills for a relatively long time.

**lower-level question.** Question that requires students to retrieve and recite what they have learned in essentially the same way they learned it.

**maintenance rehearsal.** Rapid repetition of a small amount of information to keep it fresh in working memory.

**mastery goal.** Desire to acquire new knowledge or master new skills.

**mastery learning.** Approach to instruction in which students learn one topic thoroughly before moving to a subsequent one.

**mastery orientation.** General, fairly pervasive belief that one is capable of accomplishing challenging tasks.

**maturation.** Occurrence of genetically controlled physical advancements as a child develops.

**mean (M).** Mathematical average of a set of scores.

**meaningful learning.** Cognitive process in which learners relate new information to things they already know.

**meaningful learning set.** Attitude that one can make sense of the information one is studying.

**mediated learning experience.** Discussion between an adult and a child in which the adult helps the child make sense of an event they are mutually experiencing.

**memory.** Ability to mentally save something that has been previously learned; also, the mental "location" where such information is saved.

**mental set.** Inclination to encode a problem in a way that excludes potential solutions.

**metacognition.** Knowledge and beliefs about the nature of human cognitive processes (including one's own), as well as conscious attempts to engage in behaviors and thought processes that increase learning and memory.

**metalinguistic awareness.** Ability to think consciously about the nature and functions of language.

**mirror neuron.** Neuron in the brain that fires either when a person is performing a particular behavior or when the person sees someone else perform the behavior.

**misbehavior.** Action that disrupts learning and planned classroom activities, puts students' physical safety or psychological well-being in jeopardy, or violates basic moral standards.

**misconception.** Belief that is inconsistent with commonly accepted and well-validated explanations of phenomena or events.

**mixed-methods study.** Research study that includes elements of both quantitative and qualitative research.

**mnemonic.** Memory aid or trick designed to help students learn and remember one or more specific pieces of information.

**model.** In science, physical or symbolic representation of a phenomenon that depicts its key components and important interrelationships. In social cognitive theory, real or fictional individual who demonstrates a behavior that learners might emulate; alternatively, a set of instructions for successfully executing the behavior.

**modeling.** Demonstrating a behavior for another person *or* observing and imitating another person's behavior.

**moral dilemma.** Situation in which two or more people's rights or needs may be at odds and the morally correct action is not clear-cut.

**moral transgression.** Action that causes harm or infringes on the needs or rights of others.

**morality.** One's general standards about right and wrong behavior.

**motivation.** Inner state that energizes, directs, and sustains behavior.

**multicultural education.** Instruction that integrates throughout the curriculum the perspectives and experiences of numerous cultural groups.

**myelination.** Growth of a fatty sheath (myelin) around the axons of neurons, enabling faster transmission of electrical impulses.

**NCE score.** Standard score with a mean of 50 and a standard deviation of 21.06; an NCE score of 1 equals a percentile rank of 1, and an NCE score of 99 equals a percentile rank of 99.

**need for arousal.** Ongoing need for either physical or cognitive stimulation.

**need for competence.** Basic need to believe that one can deal effectively with one's overall environment.

**need for relatedness.** Basic need to feel socially connected to others and to secure others' love and respect.

**need for self-determination.** Basic need to believe that one has some autonomy and control regarding the course of one's life.

**negative reinforcement.** Consequence that brings about the increase of a behavior through the removal (rather than the presentation) of a stimulus.

**negative transfer.** Phenomenon in which something learned at one time interferes with learning or performance at a later time.

**neglected student.** Student about whom most peers have no strong feelings, either positive or negative.

**neo-Piagetian theory.** Theoretical perspective that combines elements of Piaget's theory with more contemporary research and theories and suggests that development in specific content domains is often stagelike in nature.

**neuron.** Cell in the brain or another part of the nervous system that transmits information to other cells.

**neuropsychology.** Study of how various brain structures and functions are related to human learning and behavior.

**neurotransmitter.** Chemical substance through which one neuron sends a message to another.

**neutral stimulus.** Stimulus that does not elicit any particular response.

**No Child Left Behind Act (NCLB).** U.S. legislation passed in 2001 that mandates regular assessments of basic skills to determine whether students are making adequate yearly progress relative to state-determined standards in reading, math, and science.

**normal distribution (normal curve).** Theoretical pattern of educational and psychological characteristics in which most individuals score in the middle range and only a few score at either extreme.

**norm-referenced assessment.** Assessment instrument that indicates how students perform relative to a peer group.

**norm-referenced score.** Assessment score that indicates how a student's performance compares with the performance of others.

**norms.** In assessment, data regarding the typical performance of various groups of students on a standardized test or other norm-referenced measure of a particular characteristic or ability.

**operant conditioning.** Learning process in which a response increases as a result of being followed by reinforcement; is one form of *instrumental conditioning*.

**organization.** Cognitive process in which learners make connections among various pieces of information they need to learn (e.g., by forming categories, identifying hierarchies, determining cause–and–effect relationships).

**outcome expectation.** Prediction regarding the consequence that a particular behavior is likely to yield.

**overt strategy.** Learning strategy that is at least partially evident in a learner's behavior (e.g., taking notes during a lecture).

**paper–pencil assessment.** Assessment in which students provide written responses to written items.

**pedagogical content knowledge.** Knowledge about effective methods of teaching a specific topic or content area.

**peer mediation.** Approach to conflict resolution in which a student (serving as a *mediator*) asks peers in conflict to express their differing viewpoints and then work together to devise a reasonable resolution.

**peer pressure.** Phenomenon whereby age-mates encourage some behaviors and discourage others.

**peer tutoring.** Approach to instruction in which one student provides instruction to help another student master a classroom topic.

**people-first language.** Language usage in which a student's disability is identified *after* the student is named.

**percentile rank (percentile).** Test score indicating the percentage of peers in the norm group getting a raw score less than or equal to a particular student's raw score.

**performance assessment.** Assessment in which students demonstrate their knowledge and skills in a nonwritten fashion.

**performance goal.** Desire to demonstrate high ability and make a good impression.

**performance-approach goal.** Desire to look good and receive favorable judgments from others.

**performance-avoidance goal.** Desire not to look bad or receive unfavorable judgments from others.

**personal development.** Development, with age, of distinctive behavioral styles and increasingly complex self-understandings.

**personal fable.** Belief that one is completely unlike anyone else and so cannot be understood by others.

**personal interest.** Long-term, relatively stable interest in a particular topic or activity.

**personal space.** Personally or culturally preferred distance between people during social interaction.

**personality.** Characteristic ways in which an individual behaves and thinks in a wide range of circumstances.

**perspective taking.** Ability to look at a situation from someone else's viewpoint.

**phonological awareness.** Ability to hear the distinct sounds of which spoken words are comprised.

**physical aggression.** Action that can potentially cause bodily injury.

**physical and health impairment.** General physical or medical condition that interferes so significantly with school performance that special accommodations are required.

**plasticity.** Ability to reorganize in order to adapt to changing circumstances; term often used in describing the human brain.

**popular student.** Student whom many peers like and perceive to be kind and trustworthy.

**portfolio.** Collection of a student's work compiled systematically over a lengthy time period.

**positive behavior support.** Variation of traditional applied behavior analysis that involves identifying the purposes of undesirable behaviors and encouraging alternative behaviors that more appropriately accomplish those purposes.

**positive reinforcement.** Consequence that brings about the increase of a behavior through the presentation (rather than the removal) of a stimulus.

**positive transfer.** Phenomenon in which something learned at one time facilitates learning or performance at a later time.

**positive-practice overcorrection.** Consequence of a poorly performed response in which a learner must repeat the response correctly and appropriately, perhaps in an exaggerated manner.

**postconventional morality.** Thinking in accordance with self-constructed, abstract principles regarding right and wrong.

**practicality.** Extent to which an assessment instrument or procedure is inexpensive and easy to use and takes only a small amount of time to administer and score.

**preconventional morality.** Lack of internalized standards about right and wrong; decision making based primarily on what seems best for oneself.

**predictive validity.** Extent to which the results of an assessment predict future performance in a particular domain; sometimes called *criterion validity*.

**Premack principle.** Phenomenon in which learners do less-preferred activities in order to engage in more-preferred activities.

**preoperational egocentrism.** Inability of children in Piaget's preoperational stage to view situations from another person's perspective.

**preoperational stage.** Piaget's second stage of cognitive development, in which children can think about objects and events beyond their immediate view but do not yet reason in logical, adultlike ways.

**presentation punishment.** Punishment involving presentation of a new stimulus, presumably one a learner finds unpleasant.

**primary reinforcer.** Consequence that satisfies a biologically built-in need.

**prior knowledge activation.** Process of reminding learners of what they already know relative to a new topic.

**proactive aggression.** Deliberate aggression against another as a means of obtaining a desired goal.

**problem solving.** Using existing knowledge and skills to address an unanswered question or troubling situation.

**problem-based learning.** Classroom activity in which students acquire new knowledge and skills while working on a complex problem similar to one that might exist in the outside world.

**procedural knowledge.** Knowledge concerning how to do something (e.g., a skill).

**project-based learning.** Classroom activity in which students acquire new knowledge and skills while working on a complex, multifaceted project that yields a concrete end product.

**prosocial behavior.** Behavior directed toward promoting the well-being of people other than oneself.

**proximal goal.** Concrete goal that can be accomplished within a short time period; may be a stepping stone toward a long-term goal.

**psychological aggression.** Action intended to cause mental anguish or reduce self-esteem.

**psychological punishment.** Consequence that seriously threatens self-esteem and general psychological well-being.

**punishment.** Consequence (stimulus) that decreases the frequency of the response it follows.

**qualitative research.** Research yielding information that cannot easily be reduced to numbers; typically involves an in-depth examination of a complex phenomenon.

**quantitative research.** Research yielding information that is inherently numerical in nature or can easily be reduced to numbers.

**quasi-experimental study.** Research study that involves the manipulation of one variable to determine its possible effect on another variable, but without total control of additional variables that might have an impact on the outcome.

**raw score.** Assessment score based solely on the number or point value of correctly answered items.

**reactive aggression.** Aggressive response to frustration or provocation.

**recall task.** Assessment task in which one must retrieve information from long-term memory with only minimal retrieval cues.

**reciprocal causation.** Interdependence of environmental, behavioral, and personal variables in influencing learning and development.

**reciprocal teaching.** Approach to fostering reading and listening comprehension skills in which students take turns asking teacher-like questions of classmates.

**recognition task.** Assessment task in which one must identify correct information among incorrect statements or irrelevant information.

**reconstruction error.** Construction of a logical but incorrect "memory" by combining information retrieved from one's long-term memory with one's general knowledge and beliefs about the world.

**recursive thinking.** Thinking about what other people may be thinking about oneself, possibly through multiple iterations.

**reflective teaching.** Regular, ongoing examination and critique of one's assumptions and instructional strategies, and revision of them as necessary to enhance students' learning and development.

**rehearsal.** Cognitive process in which information is repeated over and over within a short timeframe (typically a few minutes or less) as a possible way of learning and remembering it.

**reinforcer.** Consequence (stimulus) of a response that increases the frequency of the response it follows; the act of following a response with a reinforcer is known as **reinforcement**.

**rejected student.** Student whom many peers identify as being an undesirable social partner.

**relational aggression.** Action that can adversely affect interpersonal relationships; a form of psychological aggression.

**reliability.** Extent to which an assessment yields consistent information about the knowledge, skills, or characteristics being assessed.

**removal punishment.** Punishment involving removal of an existing stimulus, presumably one a learner doesn't want to lose.

**resilient self-efficacy.** Belief that one can perform a task successfully even after experiencing setbacks.

**resilient student.** Student who succeeds in school and in life despite exceptional hardships at home.

**response (R).** Specific behavior that an individual exhibits.

**response cost.** Loss either of a previously earned reinforcer or of an opportunity to obtain reinforcement.

**response to intervention (RTI).** Approach to diagnosing a cognitive impairment in which students are identified for in-depth assessment after failing to master certain basic skills despite both whole-class and remedial small-group instruction that research has shown to be effective for most students; can also be useful with nondisabled but chronically low-achieving students.

**retrieval.** Process of finding information previously stored in memory.

**retrieval cue.** Stimulus that provides guidance about where to "look" for a piece of information in long-term memory.

**rote learning.** Learning information in a relatively uninterpreted form, without making sense of it or attaching much meaning to it.

**rubric.** List of characteristics and components that a student's performance on an assessment should ideally have; used to guide scoring.

**scaffolding.** Support mechanism that helps a learner successfully perform a challenging task (i.e., a task within the learner's zone of proximal development).

**schema.** Tightly organized set of facts about a specific topic.

**scheme.** Organized group of similar actions or thoughts that are used repeatedly in response to the environment.

**scholastic aptitude test.** Test designed to assess a general capacity to learn and used to predict future academic achievement.

**school readiness test.** Test designed to assess cognitive skills important for success in a typical kindergarten or first-grade curriculum.

**schoolwide positive behavior support.** Systematic use of behaviorist principles to encourage and reinforce productive behaviors in all students; typically involves multiple layers of support in order to accommodate the varying needs and behavior patterns of different students.

**scorer reliability.** Extent to which different people agree in their judgments of students' performance on an assessment; sometimes called *interrater reliability*.

**script.** Schema that involves a predictable sequence of events related to a common activity.

**scripted cooperation.** Technique in which cooperative learning groups follow a specified set of steps, or script, that guides members' verbal interactions.

**secondary reinforcer.** Consequence that becomes reinforcing over time through its association with another reinforcer.

**self-conscious emotion.** Affective state based on self-evaluations regarding the extent to which one's actions meet society's standards for appropriate and desirable behavior; examples are pride, guilt, and shame.

**self-efficacy.** Belief that one is capable of executing certain behaviors or reaching certain goals.

**self-evaluation.** Process of judging one's own performance or behavior.

**self-explanation.** Process of occasionally stopping to verbalize to oneself (and hence to better understand) material being read or studied.

**self-fulfilling prophecy.** Situation in which expectations for an outcome either directly or indirectly lead to the expected result.

**self-handicapping.** Behavior that undermines one's own success as a way of protecting self-worth during potentially difficult tasks.

**self-imposed contingency.** Self-reinforcement or self-punishment that follows a behavior.

**self-instructions.** Instructions that one gives oneself while performing a complex behavior.

**self-monitoring.** Process of observing and recording one's own behavior.

**self-questioning.** Process of asking oneself questions as a way of checking understanding of a topic.

**self-regulated behavior.** Self-chosen and self-directed behavior that leads to the fulfillment of personally constructed standards and goals.

**self-regulated learning.** Regulation of one's own cognitive processes and studying behaviors in order to learn successfully.

**self-regulated problem solving.** Use of self-directed strategies to address complex problems.

**self-regulation.** Process of setting goals for oneself and engaging in behaviors and cognitive processes that lead to goal attainment.

**self-socialization.** Tendency to integrate personal observations and others' input into self-constructed standards for behavior and to choose actions consistent with those standards.

**self-talk.** Process of talking to oneself as a way of guiding oneself through a task.

**self-worth.** General belief about the extent to which one is a good, capable individual.

**sense of community.** Shared belief that teacher and students have common goals, are mutually respectful and supportive, and all make important contributions to classroom learning.

**sense of school community.** Shared belief that all faculty and students within a school are working together to help everyone learn and succeed.

**sense of self.** Perceptions, beliefs, judgments, and feelings about oneself as a person; includes *self-concept* and *self-esteem*.

**sensitive period.** Age range during which a certain aspect of a child's development is especially susceptible to environmental conditions (you may sometimes see the term *critical period*).

**sensorimotor stage.** Piaget's first stage of cognitive development, in which schemes are based largely on behaviors and perceptions.

**sensory register.** Component of memory that holds incoming information in an unanalyzed form for a very brief period of time (two or three seconds at most, depending on the modality).

**service learning.** Activity that promotes learning and development through contributing to the betterment of other people and the outside community.

**setting event.** Complex environmental condition that is likely to evoke certain voluntary behaviors.

**severe and multiple disabilities.** Combination of two or more disabilities that, taken together, require significant classroom adaptations and highly specialized educational services.

**shame.** Feeling of embarrassment or humiliation after failing to meet certain standards for moral behavior.

**shaping.** Process of reinforcing successively closer and closer approximations to a desired terminal behavior.

**situated learning and cognition.** Knowledge, behaviors, and thinking skills acquired and used primarily within certain contexts, with limited or no retrieval and use in other contexts.

**situated motivation.** Phenomenon in which aspects of the immediate environment enhance motivation to learn particular things or behave in particular ways.

**situational interest.** Interest evoked temporarily by something in the environment.

**social cognition.** Process of thinking about how other people are likely to think, act, and react.

**social cognitive theory.** Theoretical perspective that focuses on how people learn by observing others and how they eventually assume control over their own behavior.

**social constructivism.** Theoretical perspective that focuses on people's collective efforts to impose meaning on the world.

**social development.** Development, with age, of increasingly sophisticated understandings of other people and of society as a whole, as well as increasingly effective interpersonal skills and more internalized standards for behavior.

**social information processing.** Mental processes involved in making sense of and responding to social events.

**socialization.** Process of molding a child's behavior and beliefs to be appropriate for his or her cultural group.

**society.** Very large, enduring social group that has fairly explicit social and economic structures and collective institutions and activities.

**sociocognitive conflict.** Situation in which one encounters and has to wrestle with ideas and viewpoints inconsistent with one's own.

**sociocultural theory.** Theoretical perspective emphasizing the importance of society and culture in promoting learning and development.

**socioeconomic status (SES).** One's general social and economic standing in society; encompasses family income, occupation, and educational level.

**specific aptitude test.** Test designed to predict future ability to succeed in a particular content domain.

**specific language impairment.** Disability characterized by abnormalities in the production or comprehension of spoken language, to the point that special educational services are required.

**specific transfer.** Instance of transfer in which the original learning task and the transfer task overlap in content.

**speech and communication disorders.** Impairments in spoken language or language comprehension that significantly interfere with classroom performance.

**standard deviation (SD).** Statistic indicating the amount of variability characterizing a set of scores.

**Standard English.** Form of English generally considered acceptable at school, as reflected in textbooks and grammar instruction.

**standard error of measurement (SEM).** Statistic estimating the amount of error in a test score or other assessment result.

**standard score.** Test score indicating how far a student's performance is from the mean in terms of standard deviation units.

**standardization.** Extent to which an assessment involves similar content and format and is administered and scored similarly for everyone.

**standardized test.** Test developed by test construction experts and published for use in many different schools and classrooms.

**standards.** General statements regarding the knowledge and skills that students should gain and the characteristics that their accomplishments should reflect.

**stanine.** Standard score with a mean of 5 and a standard deviation of 2; always reported as a whole number between 1 and 9.

**state anxiety.** Temporary feeling of anxiety elicited by a threatening situation.

**stereotype.** Rigid, simplistic, and erroneous view of a particular group of people.

**stereotype threat.** Awareness of a negative stereotype about one's own group and accompanying uneasiness that low performance will confirm the stereotype; leads (often unintentionally) to lower-quality performance.

**stimulus (S).** Specific object or event that influences an individual's learning or behavior.

**storage.** Process of putting new information into memory.

**student at risk.** Student with a high probability of failing to acquire minimal academic skills necessary for success in the adult world.

**students with special needs.** Students different enough from their peers that they require specially adapted instructional materials and practices to maximize their learning and achievement.

**subculture.** Group that resists the ways of the dominant culture and adopts its own norms for behavior.

**subtractive bilingualism.** Phenomenon in which immersion in a new-language environment leads to deficits in a child's native language.

**summative assessment.** Assessment conducted after instruction to assess students' final achievement.

**superimposed meaningful structure.** Familiar shape, word, sentence, poem, or story imposed on information to facilitate recall.

**sympathy.** Feeling of sorrow for another person's distress, accompanied by concern for the person's well-being.

**synapse.** Junction between two neurons that allows transmission of messages from one to the other.

**synaptic pruning.** Universal process in brain development in which many previously formed synapses wither away.

**synaptogenesis.** Universal process in early brain development in which many new synapses form spontaneously.

**table of specifications.** Two-way grid indicating the topics to be covered in an assessment and the things students should be able to do with those topics.

**task analysis.** Process of identifying the specific behaviors, knowledge, or cognitive processes necessary to master a particular topic or skill.

**teachable moment.** Situation or event (often unplanned) in which students might be especially predisposed to acquire particular knowledge or skills.

**teacher-developed assessment instrument.** Assessment tool developed by an individual teacher for use in a specific classroom.

**teacher-directed instruction.** Approach to instruction in which the teacher is largely in control of the content and course of the lesson.

**temperament.** Genetic predisposition to respond in particular ways to one's physical and social environments.

**terminal behavior.** Form and frequency of a desired response that a teacher hopes to foster through reinforcement.

**test anxiety.** Excessive anxiety about a particular test or about assessment in general.

**test–retest reliability.** Extent to which a particular assessment instrument yields similar results over a short time interval.

**testwiseness.** Test-taking know-how that enhances test performance.

**theory.** Integrated set of concepts and principles developed to explain a particular phenomenon.

**theory of mind.** Self-constructed understanding of one's own and other people's mental and psychological states (thoughts, feelings, etc.).

**threat.** Situation in which a learner believes there is little or no chance of success.

**time on task.** Amount of time that students are both physically and cognitively engaged in a learning activity.

**time-out.** Consequence for misbehavior in which a learner is placed in a dull, boring situation with no opportunity for reinforcement or social interaction.

**token economy.** Technique in which desired behaviors are reinforced by small, insignificant items (tokens) that learners can use to "purchase" a variety of other, more desirable reinforcers.

**traditional assessment.** Assessment that focuses on measuring basic knowledge and skills in relative isolation from activities typical of the outside world.

**trait anxiety.** General pattern of responding with anxiety even in nonthreatening situations.

**transfer.** Phenomenon in which something a person has learned at one time affects how the person learns or performs in a later situation.

**treatment group.** Group of people in a research study who are given a particular experimental intervention (e.g., a particular method of instruction).

**true score.** Hypothetical score a student would obtain if an assessment measured a characteristic or ability with complete accuracy.

**unconditioned response (UCR).** Response that is elicited by a particular (unconditioned) stimulus without prior learning.

**unconditioned stimulus (UCS).** Stimulus that elicits a particular response without prior learning.

**universals.** Similar patterns in how children change and progress over time regardless of their specific environment.

**validity.** Extent to which an assessment actually measures what it is intended to measure and allows appropriate inferences about the characteristic or ability in question.

**value.** Belief regarding the extent to which an activity has direct or indirect benefits.

**value-added assessment.** Approach to evaluating teacher and school effectiveness based on students' progress rather than on absolute achievement levels.

**verbal mediator.** Word or phrase that forms a logical connection, or cognitive "bridge," between two pieces of information.

**vicarious punishment.** Phenomenon in which a response decreases in frequency when another person is observed being punished for that response.

**vicarious reinforcement.** Phenomenon in which a response increases in frequency when another person is observed being reinforced for that response.

**visual imagery.** Process of forming a mental picture of an object or idea.

**visual impairment.** Malfunction of the eyes or optic nerves that prevents normal vision even with corrective lenses.

**visual–spatial ability.** Ability to imagine and mentally manipulate two- and three-dimensional figures.

**wait time.** Length of time a teacher pauses, either after asking a question or hearing a student's comment, before saying something.

**well-defined problem.** Problem in which the goal is clearly stated, all the information needed to solve the problem is present, and only one correct answer exists.

**withitness.** Classroom management strategy in which a teacher gives the impression of knowing what all students are doing at all times.

**work-avoidance goal.** Desire either to avoid classroom tasks or to complete them with minimal effort, often because of low self-efficacy for the tasks.

**working memory.** Component of memory that holds and actively thinks about and processes a limited amount of information for a short time.

**worldview.** General, culturally based set of assumptions about reality that influence understandings of a wide variety of phenomena.

**zone of proximal development (ZPD).** Range of tasks that a learner can perform with the help and guidance of others but cannot yet perform independently.

**z-score.** Standard score with a mean of 0 and a standard deviation of 1.

# References

## CHAPTER 1

Anderson, J. R. (2005). *Cognitive psychology and its implications* (6th ed.). New York: Worth.

Barab, S. A., Gresalfi, M., & Ingram-Goble, A. (2010). Transformational play: Using games to position person, content, and context. *Educational Researcher, 39,* 525–536.

Baumert, J., Kunter, M., Blum, W., Brunner, M., Voss, T., Jordan, A., et al. (2010). Teachers' mathematical knowledge, cognitive activation in the classroom, and student progress. *American Educational Research Journal, 47,* 133–180.

Berliner, D. C. (2001). Learning about and learning from expert teachers. *International Journal of Educational Research, 35,* 463–483.

Borko, H., & Putnam, R. T. (1996). Learning to teach. In D. C. Berliner & R. C. Calfee (Eds.), *Handbook of educational psychology* (pp. 673–708). New York: Macmillan.

Bransford, J., Darling-Hammond, L., & LePage, P. (2005). Introduction. In L. Darling-Hammond & J. Bransford (Eds.), *Preparing teachers for a changing world: What teachers should learn and be able to do* (pp. 1–39). San Francisco: Jossey-Bass/Wiley.

Bransford, J., Derry, S., Berliner, D., & Hammerness, K. (with Beckett, K. L.) (2005). Theories of learning and their roles in teaching. In L. Darling-Hammond & J. Bransford (Eds.), *Preparing teachers for a changing world: What teachers should learn and be able to do* (pp. 40–87). San Francisco: Jossey-Bass/Wiley.

Brayboy, B. M. J., & Searle, K. A. (2007). Thanksgiving and serial killers: Representations of American Indians in schools. In S. Books (Ed.), *Invisible children in the society and its schools* (3rd ed., pp. 173–192). Mahwah, NJ: Erlbaum.

Bressler, S. L. (2002). Understanding cognition through large-scale cortical networks. *Current Directions in Psychological Science, 11,* 58–61.

Brouwer, N., & Korthagen, F. (2005). Can teacher education make a difference? *American Educational Research Journal, 42,* 153–224.

Cassady, J. C. (2010b). Test anxiety: Contemporary theories and implications for learning. In J. C. Cassady (Ed.), *Anxiety in schools: The causes, consequences, and solutions for academic anxieties* (pp. 7–26). New York: Peter Lang.

Castagno, A. E., & Brayboy, B. M. J. (2008). Culturally responsive schooling for Indigenous youth: A review of the literature. *Review of Educational Research, 78,* 941–993.

Clotfelter, C. T., Ladd, H. F., & Vigdor, J. (2007). Who teaches whom? Race and the distribution of novice teachers. *Economics of Education Review, 24,* 377–392.

Cochran, K. F., & Jones, L. L. (1998). The subject matter knowledge of preservice science teachers.

In B. J. Fraser & K. G. Tobin (Eds.), *International handbook of science education* (Pt. II, pp. 707–718). Dordrecht, Netherlands: Kluwer.

Cochran-Smith, M., & Lytle, S. (1993). *Inside out: Teacher research and knowledge.* New York: Teachers College Press.

Craig, D. V. (2009). *Action research essentials.* San Francisco: Jossey-Bass.

Darling-Hammond, L. (2006). *Powerful teacher education: Lessons from exemplary programs.* San Francisco: Jossey-Bass.

Desimone, L. M. (2009). Improving impact studies of teachers' professional development: Toward better conceptualizations and measures. *Educational Researcher, 38,* 181–199.

Feldon, D. F. (2007). Cognitive load and classroom teaching: The double-edged sword of automaticity. *Educational Psychologist, 42,* 123–137.

Frederiksen, N. (1984b). The real test bias: Influences of testing on teaching and learning. *American Psychologist, 39,* 193–202.

Gage, N. L. (1991). The obviousness of social and educational research results. *Educational Researcher, 20*(1), 10–16.

Gee, J. P. (2010). Looking where the light is bad: Video games and the future of assessment. *Edge, 6,* 3–19.

Graesser, A. C., & Bower, G. H. (Eds.). (1990). *Inferences and text comprehension. The psychology of learning and motivation: Advances in research and theory* (Vol. 25). Orlando: Academic Press.

Gregoire, M. (2003). Is it a challenge or a threat? A dual-process model of teachers' cognition and appraisal processes during conceptual change. *Educational Psychology Review, 15,* 147–179.

Haier, R. J. (2001). PET studies of learning and individual differences. In J. L. McClelland & R. S. Siegler (Eds.), *Mechanisms of cognitive development: Behavioral and neural perspectives* (pp. 123–145). Mahwah, NJ: Erlbaum.

Hammerness, K., Darling-Hammond, L., & Bransford, J. (with Berliner, D., Cochran-Smith, M., McDonald, M., & Zeichner, K.). (2005). How teachers learn and develop. In L. Darling-Hammond & J. Bransford (Eds.), *Preparing teachers for a changing world: What teachers should learn and be able to do* (pp. 358–389). San Francisco: Jossey-Bass/Wiley.

Hattie, J. A. C. (2009). *Visible learning: A synthesis of over 800 meta-analyses relating to achievement.* London: Routledge.

Heck, A., Collins, J., & Peterson, L. (2001). Decreasing children's risk taking on the playground. *Journal of Applied Behavior Analysis, 34,* 349–352.

Hemmings, A. B. (2004). *Coming of age in U.S. high schools: Economic, kinship, religious, and political crosscurrents.* Mahwah, NJ: Erlbaum.

Henry, G. T., Bastian, K. C., & Fortner, C. K. (2011). Stayers and leavers: Early-career teacher effectiveness and attrition. *Educational Researcher, 40,* 271–280.

Hill, H. C., Blunk, M. L., Charalambous, C. Y., Lewis, J. M., Phelps, G. C., Sleep, L., et al. (2008). Mathematical knowledge for teaching and the mathematical quality of instruction: An exploratory study. *Cognition and Instruction, 26,* 430–511.

Hogan, T., Rabinowitz, M., & Craven, J. A., III. (2003). Representation in teaching: Inferences from research of expert and novice teachers. *Educational Psychologist, 38,* 235–247.

Johnson, A. P. (2012). *A short guide to action research* (4th ed.). Upper Saddle River, NJ: Pearson.

Johnson, B. (2001). Toward a new classification of nonexperimental quantitative research. *Educational Researcher, 30*(2), 3–13.

Kagan, J., & Snidman, N. (2007). Temperament and biology. In D. Coch, K. W. Fischer, & G. Dawson (Eds.), *Human behavior, learning, and the developing brain: Typical development* (pp. 219–246). New York: Guilford.

Keogh, B. K. (2003). *Temperament in the classroom.* Baltimore: Brookes.

Konstantopoulos, S., & Chung, V. (2011). The persistence of teacher effects in elementary grades. *American Educational Research Journal, 48,* 361–386.

Krauss, S., Brunner, M., Kunter, M., Baumert, J., Blum, W., Neubrand, M., et al. (2008). Pedagogical content knowledge and content knowledge of secondary mathematics teachers. *Journal of Educational Psychology, 100,* 716–725.

Ladson-Billings, G. (1995b). Toward a theory of culturally relevant pedagogy. *American Educational Research Journal, 32,* 465–491.

Langer, J. A. (2000). Excellence in English in middle and high school: How teachers' professional lives support student achievement. *American Educational Research Journal, 37,* 397–439.

Larrivee, B. (2006). The convergence of reflective practice and effective classroom management. In C. M. Evertson & C. S. Weinstein (Eds.), *Handbook of classroom management: Research, practice, and contemporary issues* (pp. 983–1001). Mahwah, NJ: Erlbaum.

Lennon, R., Ormrod, J. E., Burger, S., & Warren, E. (1990, October). *Belief systems of teacher education majors and their possible influences on future classroom performance.* Paper presented at the Northern Rocky Mountain Educational Research Association, Greeley, CO.

Luna, B., & Sweeney, J. A. (2004). The emergence of collaborative brain function: fMRI studies of the development of response inhibition. *Annals of the New York Academy of Sciences, 1021,* 296–309.

Lundeberg, M. A., & Fox, P. W. (1991). Do laboratory findings on test expectancy generalize to classroom outcomes? *Review of Educational Research, 61,* 94–106.

McDonald, B. O., Robles-Piña, R., & Polnick, B. (2011, April). *A comparison of urban middle school mathematics teachers with high student gain scores and low student gain scores.* Paper presented at the annual meeting of the American Educational Research Association, New Orleans, LA.

McIntyre, E. (2010). Issues in funds of knowledge teaching and research: Key concepts from a study of Appalachian families and schooling. In M. L. Dantas & P. C. Manyak (Eds.), *Home–school connections in a multicultural society: Learning from and with culturally and linguistically diverse families* (pp. 201–217). New York: Routledge.

Mills, G. E. (2011). *Action research: A guide for the teacher researcher* (4th ed.). Upper Saddle River, NJ: Pearson.

Moje, E. B., & Hinchman, K. (2004). Culturally reponsive practices for youth literacy learning. In T. L. Jetton & J. A. Dole (Eds.), *Adolescent literacy research and practice* (pp. 321–350). New York: Guilford.

Ogbu, J. U. (2003). *Black American students in an affluent suburb: A study of academic disengagement.* Mahwah, NJ: Erlbaum.

Perry, N. E., Turner, J. C., & Meyer, D. K. (2006). Classrooms as contexts for motivating learning. In P. A. Alexander & P. H. Winne (Eds.), *Handbook of educational psychology* (2nd ed., pp. 327–348). Mahwah, NJ: Erlbaum.

Posner, M. I., & Rothbart, M. K. (2007). *Educating the human brain.* Washington, DC: American Psychological Association.

Raudenbush, S. W. (2009). The *Brown* legacy and the O'Connor challenge: Transforming schools in the images of children's potential. *Educational Researcher, 38,* 169–180.

Richardson, V. (2003). Preservice teachers' beliefs. In J. Raths & A. C. McAninch (Eds.), *Teacher beliefs and classroom performance: The impact of teacher education* (pp. 1–22). Greenwich, CT: Information Age.

Roderick, M., & Camburn, E. (1999). Risk and recovery from course failure in the early years of high school. *American Educational Research Journal, 36,* 303–343.

Rothbart, M. K. (2011). *Becoming who we are: Temperament and personality in development.* New York: Guilford.

Shipman, S., & Shipman, V. C. (1985). Cognitive styles: Some conceptual, methodological, and applied issues. In E. W. Gordon (Ed.), *Review of research in education* (Vol. 12, pp. 229–291). Washington, DC: American Educational Research Association.

Shulman, L. S. (1986). Those who understand: Knowledge growth in teaching. *Educational Researcher, 15*(2), 4–14.

Skaalvik, E. M., & Skaalvik, S. (2008). Teacher self-efficacy: Conceptual analysis and relations with teacher burnout and perceived school context. In H. W. Marsh, R. G. Craven, & D. M. McInerney (Eds.), *Self-processes, learning,* *and enabling human potential* (pp. 223–247). Charlotte, NC: Information Age.

Smith, A. K. (2009). *The art of possibility: Creating more successful learners.* Malibu, CA: Center for Collaborative Action Research, Pepperdine University. Retrieved from http://cadres .pepperdine.edu/ccar/projects.school.html

Steinberg, L. (2009). Should the science of adolescent brain development inform public policy? *American Psychologist, 64,* 739–750.

Stone, N. J. (2000). Exploring the relationship between calibration and self-regulated learning. *Educational Psychology Review, 12,* 437–475.

Thiede, K. W., Griffin, T. D., Wiley, J., & Redford, J. S. (2009). Metacognitive monitoring during and after reading. In D. J. Hacker, J. Dunlosky, & A. C. Graesser (Eds.), *Handbook of metacognition in education* (pp. 85–106). New York: Routledge.

Tschannen-Moran, M., Woolfolk Hoy, A., & Hoy, W. K. (1998). Teacher efficacy: Its meaning and measure. *Review of Educational Research, 68,* 202–248.

Tyler, K. M., Uqdah, A. L., Dillihunt, M. L., Beatty-Hazelbaker, R., Connor, T., Gadson, N., et al. (2008). Cultural discontinuity: Toward a quantitative investigation of a major hypothesis in education. *Educational Researcher, 37,* 280–297.

## CHAPTER 2

Adesope, O. O., Lavin, T., Thompson, T., & Ungerleider, C. (2010). A systematic review and meta-analysis of the cognitive correlates of bilingualism. *Review of Educational Research, 80,* 207–245.

Adger, C. T., Wolfram, W., & Christian, D. (2007). *Dialects in schools and communities* (2nd ed.). New York: Routledge.

Aitchison, J. (1996). *The seeds of speech: Language origin and evolution.* Cambridge, England: Cambridge University Press.

Andriessen, J. (2006). Arguing to learn. In R. K. Sawyer (Ed.), *The Cambridge handbook of the learning sciences* (pp. 443–459). Cambridge, England: Cambridge University Press.

Artman, L., & Cahan, S. (1993). Schooling and the development of transitive inference. *Developmental Psychology, 29,* 753–759.

Ash, D. (2002). Negotiations of thematic conversations about biology. In G. Leinhardt, K. Crowley, & K. Knutson (Eds.), *Learning conversations in museums* (pp. 357–400). Mahwah, NJ: Erlbaum.

Bebko, J. M., Burke, L., Craven, J., & Sarlo, N. (1992). The importance of motor activity in sensorimotor development: A perspective from children with physical handicaps. *Human Development, 35*(4), 226–240.

Beck, S. R., Robinson, E. J., Carroll, D. J., & Apperly, I. A. (2006). Children's thinking about counterfactuals and future hypotheticals as possibilities. *Child Development, 77,* 413–426.

Belsky, J., Bakermans-Kranenburg, M. J., & van IJzendoorn, M. H. (2007). For better *and* for worse: Differential susceptibility to environmental influences. *Current Directions in Psychological Science, 16,* 300–304.

Benton, S. L. (1997). Psychological foundations of elementary writing instruction. In G. D. Phye (Ed.), *Handbook of academic learning: Construction of knowledge* (pp. 235–264). San Diego, CA: Academic Press.

Berk, L. E. (1994). Why children talk to themselves. *Scientific American, 271,* 78–83.

Bialystok, E. (1994). Representation and ways of knowing: Three issues in second language acquisition. In N. C. Ellis (Ed.), *Implicit and explicit learning of languages* (pp. 549–569). London: Academic Press.

Bialystok, E. (2001). *Bilingualism in development: Language, literacy, and cognition.* Cambridge, England: Cambridge University Press.

Bialystok, E., Craik, F. I. M., Green, D. W., & Gollan, T. H. (2009). Bilingual minds. *Psychological Science in the Public Interest, 10,* 89–129.

Bishop, D. V. M. (2006). What causes specific language impairment in children? *Current Directions in Psychological Science, 15,* 217–221.

Bishop, D. V. M., McDonald, D., Bird, S., & Hayiou-Thomas, M. E. (2009). Children who read words accurately despite language impairment: Who are they and how do they do it? *Child Development, 80,* 593–605.

Bivens, J. A., & Berk, L. E. (1990). A longitudinal study of the development of elementary school children's private speech. *Merrill-Palmer Quarterly, 36,* 443–463.

Bjorklund, D. F. (1997). In search of a metatheory for cognitive development (or, Piaget is dead and I don't feel so good myself). *Child Development, 68,* 144–148.

Bortfeld, H., & Whitehurst, G. J. (2001). Sensitive periods in first language acquisition. In D. B. Bailey, Jr., J. T. Bruer, F. J. Symons, & J. W. Lichtman (Eds.), *Critical thinking about critical periods* (pp. 173–192). Baltimore: Brookes.

Brainerd, C. J. (2003). Jean Piaget, learning research, and American education. In B. J. Zimmerman & D. H. Schunk (Eds.), *Educational psychology: A century of contributions* (pp. 251–287). Mahwah, NJ: Erlbaum.

Bressler, S. L. (2002). Understanding cognition through large-scale cortical networks. *Current Directions in Psychological Science, 11,* 58–61.

Bronfenbrenner, U. (1989). Ecological systems theory. In R. Vasta (Ed.), *Annals of child development* (Vol. 6, pp. 187–251). Greenwich, CT: JAI Press.

Bronfenbrenner, U. (2005). *Making human beings human: Bioecological perspectives on human development.* Thousand Oaks, CA: Sage.

Bronfenbrenner, U., & Morris, P. A. (1998). The ecology of developmental processes. In W. Damon (Series Ed.) & R. M. Lerner (Vol. Ed.), *Handbook of child psychology: Vol. 1. Theoretical models of human development* (5th ed., pp. 993–1028). New York: Wiley.

Brown, J. S., Collins, A., & Duguid, P. (1989). Situated cognition and the culture of learning. *Educational Researcher, 18*(1), 32–42.

Brown, M. C., McNeil, N. M., & Glenberg, A. M. (2009). Using concreteness in education: Real problems, potential solutions. *Child Development Perspectives, 3,* 160–164.

Brown, R. D., & Bjorklund, D. F. (1998). The biologizing of cognition, development, and education: Approach with cautious enthusiasm. *Educational Psychology Review, 10,* 355–373.

Bruer, J. T. (1999). *The myth of the first three years: A new understanding of early brain development and lifelong learning.* New York: Free Press.

Bruer, J. T., & Greenough, W. T. (2001). The subtle science of how experience affects the brain. In D. B. Bailey, Jr., J. T. Bruer, F. J. Symons, & J. W. Lichtman (Eds.), *Critical thinking about critical periods* (pp. 209–232). Baltimore: Brookes.

Byrnes, J. P. (1996). *Cognitive development and learning in instructional contexts.* Boston: Allyn & Bacon.

Byrnes, J. P. (2001). *Minds, brains, and learning: Understanding the psychological and educational relevance of neuroscientific research.* New York: Guilford.

Byrnes, J. P. (2007). Some ways in which neuroscientific research can be relevant to education. In D. Coch, K. W. Fischer, & G. Dawson (Eds.), *Human behavior, learning, and the developing brain: Typical development* (pp. 30–49). New York: Guilford.

Byrnes, J. P., & Fox, N. A. (1998). The educational relevance of research in cognitive neuroscience. *Educational Psychology Review, 10,* 297–342.

Cairns, H. S. (1996). *The acquisition of language* (2nd ed.). Austin, TX: Pro-Ed.

Capelli, C. A., Nakagawa, N., & Madden, C. M. (1990). How children understand sarcasm: The role of context and intonation. *Child Development, 61,* 1824–1841.

Carey, S. (1978). The child as word learner. In M. Halle, J. Bresnan, & G. A. Miller (Eds.), *Linguistic theory and psychological reality* (pp. 264–293). Cambridge, MA: MIT Press.

Carey, S. (1985). *Conceptual change in childhood.* Cambridge, MA: MIT Press.

Carhill, A., Suárez-Orozco, C., & Páez, M. (2008). Explaining English language proficiency among adolescent immigrant students. *American Educational Research Journal, 45,* 1045–1079.

Case, R. (1985). *Intellectual development: Birth to adulthood.* Orlando, FL: Academic Press.

Case, R., & Mueller, M. P. (2001). Differentiation, integration, and covariance mapping as fundamental processes in cognitive and neurological growth. In J. L. McClelland & R. S. Siegler (Eds.), *Mechanisms of cognitive development: Behavioral and neural perspectives* (pp. 185–219). Mahwah, NJ: Erlbaum.

Case, R., & Okamoto, Y., in collaboration with Griffin, S., McKeough, A., Bleiker, C., Henderson, B., & Stephenson, K. M. (1996). The role of central conceptual structures in the development of children's thought. *Monographs of the Society for Research in Child Development, 61*(1, Serial No. 246).

Chapman, M. (1988). *Constructive evolution: Origins and development of Piaget's thought.* Cambridge, England: Cambridge University Press.

Chen, X., Anderson, R. C., Li, W., Hao, M., Wu, X., & Shu, H. (2004). Phonological awareness of bilingual and monolingual Chinese children. *Journal of Educational Psychology, 96,* 142–151.

Chinn, C. A., Anderson, R. C., & Waggoner, M. A. (2001). Patterns of discourse in two kinds of literature discussion. *Reading Research Quarterly, 36,* 378–411.

Chomsky, N. (1972). *Language and mind* (enlarged ed.). San Diego, CA: Harcourt Brace Jovanovich.

Chomsky, N. (2006). *Language and mind* (3rd ed.). Cambridge, England: Cambridge University Press.

Cole, M. (1990). Cognitive development and formal schooling: The evidence from cross-cultural research. In L. C. Moll (Ed.), *Vygotsky and education* (pp. 89–110). New York: Cambridge University Press.

Cole, M. (2006). Culture and cognitive development in phylogenetic, historical and ontogenetic perspective. In W. Damon & R. M. Lerner (Series Eds.), D. Kuhn, & R. Siegler (Vol. Eds.), *Handbook of child psychology: Vol. 2. Cognition, perception, and language* (6th ed., pp. 636–683). New York: Wiley.

Collier, V. P. (1992). The Canadian bilingual immersion debate: A synthesis of research findings. *Studies in Second Language Acquisition, 14,* 87–97.

Collins, A. (2006). Cognitive apprenticeship. In R. K. Sawyer (Ed.), *The Cambridge handbook of the learning sciences* (pp. 47–60). Cambridge, England: Cambridge University Press.

Collins, A., Brown, J. S., & Newman, S. E. (1989). Cognitive apprenticeship: Teaching the crafts of reading, writing, and mathematics. In L. B. Resnick (Ed.), *Knowing, learning, and instruction: Essays in honor of Robert Glaser* (pp. 453–494). Mahwah, NJ: Erlbaum.

Comeau, L., Cormier, P., Grandmaison, É., & Lacroix, D. (1999). A longitudinal study of phonological processing skills in children learning to read in a second language. *Journal of Educational Psychology, 91,* 29–43.

Coplan, R. J., & Arbeau, K. A. (2009). Peer interactions and play in early childhood. In K. H. Rubin, W. M. Bukowski, & B. Laursen (Eds.), *Handbook of peer interactions, relationships, and groups* (pp. 143–161). New York: Guilford.

Corriveau, K., Pasquini, E., & Goswami, U. (2007). Basic auditory processing skills and specific language impairment: A new look at an old hypothesis. *Journal of Speech, Language, and Hearing Research, 50,* 647–666.

Cromer, R. F. (1987). Language growth with experience without feedback. *Journal of Psycholinguistic Research, 16,* 223–231.

Cummins, J. (1981). Age on arrival and immigrant second language learning in Canada: A reassessment. *Applied Linguistics, 2,* 132–149.

Cummins, J. (1984). *Bilingualism and special education: Issues in assessment and pedagogy.* Clevedon, England: Multilingual Matters.

Cummins, J. (2000). *Language, power, and pedagogy: Bilingual children in the crossfire.* Clevedon, England: Multlingual Matters.

Cummins, J. (2008). BICS and CALP: Empirical and theoretical status of the distinction. In B. Street & N. H. Hornberger (Eds.), *Encyclopedia of language and education* (2nd ed., Vol. 2, pp. 71–83). New York: Springer.

Curtiss, S. (1977). *Genie: A psycholinguistic study of a modern-day "wild child."* New York: Academic Press.

DeCasper, A. J., & Fifer, W. P. (1980). Of human bonding: Newborns prefer their mothers' voices. *Science, 208,* 1174–1176.

De Corte, E., Greer, B., & Verschaffel, L. (1996). Mathematics teaching and learning. In D. C. Berliner & R. C. Calfee (Eds.), *Handbook of educational psychology* (pp. 491–549). New York: Macmillan.

Dennen, V. P., & Burner, K. J. (2008). The cognitive apprenticeship model in educational practice. In J. M. Spector, M. D. Merrill, J. van Merriënboer, & M. P. Driscoll (Eds.), *Handbook of research on educational communications and technology* (3rd ed., pp. 425–439). New York: Erlbaum.

Diamond, A., Barnett, W. S., Thomas, J., & Munro, S. (2007). Preschool program improves cognitive control. *Science, 318,* 1387–1338.

Diaz, R. M. (1983). Thought and two languages: The impact of bilingualism on cognitive development. In E. W. Gordon (Ed.), *Review of research in education* (Vol. 10. pp. 23–54). Washington, DC: American Educational Research Association.

diSessa, A. A. (2006). A history of conceptual change research. In R. K. Sawyer (Ed.), *The Cambridge handbook of the learning sciences* (pp. 265–281). Cambridge, England: Cambridge University Press.

diSessa, A. A. (2007). An interactional analysis of clinical interviewing. *Cognition and Instruction, 25,* 523–565.

Doyle, A. (1982). Friends, acquaintances, and strangers: The influence of familiarity and ethnolinguistic backgrounds on social interaction. In K. Rubin & H. Ross (Eds.), *Peer relationships and social skills in childhood* (pp. 229–252). New York: Springer-Verlag.

Duff, P. A. (2001). Language, literacy, content, and (pop) culture: Challenges for ESL students in mainstream courses. *Canadian Modern Language Review, 58*(1), 103–132.

Egbert, J. (2009). *Supporting learning with technology: Essentials of classroom practice.* Upper Saddle River, NJ: Pearson/Merrill Prentice-Hall.

Elliott, D. J. (1995). *Music matters: A new philosophy of music education.* New York: Oxford University Press.

Empson, S. B. (1999). Equal sharing and shared meaning: The development of fraction concepts in a first-grade classroom. *Cognition and Instruction, 17,* 283–342.

Espinosa, L. (2007). English-language learners as they enter school. In R. Pianta, M. Cox, & K. Snow (Eds.), *School readiness and the transition to kindergarten in the era of accountability* (pp. 175–196). Baltimore: Brookes.

Espinosa, L. M. (2008, January). *Challenging common myths about young English language learners.* (FCD Policy Brief No. 8). New York: Foundation for Child Development.

Fahrmeier, E. D. (1978). The development of concrete operations among the Hausa. *Journal of Cross-Cultural Psychology, 9,* 23–44.

Ferretti, R. P., MacArthur, C. A., & Dowdy, N. S. (2000). The effects of an elaborated goal on the persuasive writing of students with learning disabilities and their normally achieving peers. *Journal of Educational Psychology, 92,* 694–702.

Feuerstein, R, Feuerstein, R. S., & Falik, L. H. (2010). *Beyond smarter: Mediated learning and the brain's capacity for change.* New York: Teachers College Press.

Fischer, K. W., & Bidell, T. R. (2006). Dynamic development of action, thought, and emotion. In R. M. Lerner (Ed.), *Handbook of child psychology. Vol. 1: Theoretical models of human development* (6th ed., pp. 319–399). New York: Wiley.

Fischer, K. W., & Daley, S. G. (2007). Connecting cognitive science and neuroscience to education: Potentials and pitfalls in inferring executive processes. In L. Meltzer (Ed.), *Executive function in education: From theory to practice* (pp. 55–72). New York: Guilford.

Fischer, K. W., & Immordino-Yang, M. H. (2002). Cognitive development and education: From dynamic general structure to specific learning and teaching. In E. Lagemann (Ed.), *Traditions of scholarship in education* (pp. 1–55). Chicago: Spencer Foundation.

Flavell, J. H. (1994). Cognitive development: Past, present, and future. In R. D. Parke, P. A. Ornstein, J. J. Rieser, & C. Zahn-Waxler (Eds.), *A century of developmental psychology* (pp. 569–587). Washington, DC: American Psychological Association.

Flavell, J. H., Miller, P. H., & Miller, S. A. (2002). *Cognitive development* (4th ed.). Upper Saddle River, NJ: Prentice-Hall.

Flieller, A. (1999). Comparison of the development of formal thought in adolescent cohorts aged 10 to 15 years (1967–1996 and 1972–1993). *Developmental Psychology, 35,* 1048–1058.

Fujimura, N. (2001). Facilitating children's proportional reasoning: A model of reasoning processes and effects of intervention on strategy change. *Journal of Educational Psychology, 93,* 589–603.

García, E. (1995). Educating Mexican American students: Past treatment and recent developments in theory, research, policy, and practice. In J. A. Banks & C. A. M. Banks (Eds.), *Handbook of research on multicultural education* (pp. 372–387). New York: Macmillan.

Garcia, E., & Jensen, B. (2009). Early educational opportunities for children of Hispanic origins. *Social Policy Report, 23*(2), 3–19.

García, E. (1995). Educating Mexican American students: Past treatment and recent developments in theory, research, policy, and practice. In J. A. Banks & C. A. M. Banks (Eds.), *Handbook of research on multicultural education* (pp. 372–387). New York: Macmillan.

Gauvain, M. (2001). *The social context of cognitive development.* New York: Guilford.

Geary, D. C. (1998). What is the function of mind and brain? *Educational Psychology Review, 10,* 377–387.

Geary, D. C. (2008). An evolutionarily informed education science. *Educational Psychologist, 43,* 179–195.

Genesee, F. (1985). Second language learning through immersion: A review of U.S. programs. *Review of Educational Research, 55,* 541–561.

Gentner, D., & Namy, L. L. (2006). Analogical processes in language learning. *Current Directions in Psychological Science, 15,* 297–301.

Gershkoff-Stowe, L., & Thelen, E. (2004). U-shaped changes in behavior: A dynamic systems perspective. *Journal of Cognition and Development, 1*(5), 11–36.

Girotto, V., & Light, P. (1993). The pragmatic bases of children's reasoning. In P. Light & G. Butterworth (Eds.), *Context and cognition: Ways of learning and knowing* (pp. 134–156). Mahwah, NJ: Erlbaum.

Gonsalves, B. D., & Cohen, N. J. (2010). Brain imaging, cognitive processes, and brain Goodman, C. S., & Tessier-Lavigne, M. (1997). Molecular mechanisms of axon guidance and target recognition. In W. M. Cowan, T. M. Jessell, & S. L. Zipursky (Eds.), *Molecular and cellular approaches to neural development* (pp. 108–137). New York: Oxford University Press.

Goodman, C. S., & Tessier-Lavigne, M. (1997). Molecular mechanisms of axon guidance and target recognition. In W. M. Cowan, T. M. Jessell, & S. L. Zipursky (Eds.), *Molecular and cellular approaches to neural development* (pp. 108–137). New York: Oxford University Press.

Gopnik, M. (Ed.). (1997). *The inheritance and innateness of grammars.* New York: Oxford University Press.

Goswami, U., & Pauen, S. (2005). The effects of a "family" analogy on class inclusion reasoning by young children. *Swiss Journal of Psychology, 64*(2), 115–124.

Grant, C. A., & Gomez, M. L. (2001). *Campus and classroom: Making schooling multicultural* (2nd ed.). Upper Saddle River, NJ: Merrill/Prentice-Hall.

Haenan, J. (1996). Piotr Gal'perin's criticism and extension of Lev Vygotsky's work. *Journal of Russian and East European Psychology, 34*(2), 54–60.

Halford, G. S., & Andrews, G. (2006). Reasoning and problem solving. In W. Damon & R. M. Lerner (Series Eds.), D. Kuhn, & R. Siegler (Vol. Eds.), *Handbook of child psychology: Vol. 2. Cognition, perception, and language* (6th ed., pp. 557–608). New York: Wiley.

Hardy, I., Jonen, A., Möller, K., & Stern, E. (2006). Effects of instructional support within constructivist learning environments for elementary school students' understanding of "floating and sinking." *Journal of Educational Psychology, 98,* 307–326.

Harris, K. R., Graham, S., & Mason, L. H. (2006). Improving the writing, knowledge, and motivation of struggling young writers: Effects of self-regulated strategy development with and without peer support. *American Educational Research Journal, 43,* 295–340.

Harris, K. R., Santangelo, T., & Graham, S. (2010). Metacognition and strategies instruction in writing. In H. S. Waters & W. Schneider (Eds.), *Metacognition, strategy use, and instruction* (pp. 226–256). New York: Guilford.

Haxby, J. V., Gobbini, M. I., Furey, M. L., Ishai, A., Schouten, J. L., & Pietrini, P. (2001). Distributed and overlapping representations of faces and objects in ventral temporal cortex. *Science, 293,* 2425–2430.

Herrell, A., & Jordan, M. (2004). *Fifty strategies for teaching English language learners* (2nd ed.). Upper Saddle River, NJ: Merrill/Prentice-Hall.

Hiebert, J., Carpenter, T. P., Fennema, E., Fuson, K. C., Wearne, D., Murray, H., et al. (1997). *Making sense: Teaching and learning mathematics with understanding.* Portsmouth, NH: Heinemann.

Hmelo-Silver, C. E. (2006). Design principles for scaffolding technology-based inquiry. In A. M. O'Donnell, C. E. Hmelo-SIlver, & G. Erkens (Eds.), *Collaborative learning, reasoning, and technology* (pp. 147–170). Mahwah, NJ: Erlbaum.

Hoff, E. (2003). The specificity of environmental influence: Socioeconomic status affects early vocabulary development via maternal speech. *Child Development, 74,* 1368–1378.

Hoff-Ginsberg, E. (1997). *Language development.* Pacific Grove, CA: Brooks/Cole.

Hutt, S. J., Tyler, S., Hutt, C., & Christopherson, H. (1989). *Play, exploration, and learning: A natural history of the pre-school.* London: Routledge.

Huttenlocher, P. R., & Dabholkar, A. S. (1997). Regional differences in synaptogenesis in human cerebral cortex. *Journal of Comparative Neurology, 387,* 167–178.

Hyde, K. L., Lerch, J., Norton, A., Forgeard, M., Winner, E., Evans, A. C., et al. (2009). Musical training shapes structural brain development. *Journal of Neuroscience, 29,* 3019–3025.

Igoa, C. (1995). *The inner world of the immigrant child.* Mahwah, NJ: Erlbaum.

Igoa, C. (2007). Immigrant children: Art as a second language. In S. Books (Ed.), *Invisible children in the society and its schools* (3rd ed., pp. 117–140). Mahwah, NJ: Erlbaum.

Inhelder, B., & Piaget, J. (1958). *The growth of logical thinking from childhood to adolescence* (A. Parsons & S. Milgram, Trans.). New York: Basic Books.

Janzen, J. (2008). Teaching English language learners in the content areas. *Review of Educational Research, 78,* 1010–1038.

Johnson, D. W., & Johnson, R. T. (2009b). Energizing learning: The instructional power of conflict. *Educational Researcher, 38,* 37–51.

Jusczyk, P. W. (1995). Language acquisition: Speech sounds and phonological development. In J. L. Miller & P. D. Eimas (Eds.), *Handbook of perception and cognition: Vol. 11. Speech, language, and communication* (pp. 261–301). Orlando, FL: Academic Press.

Karmiloff-Smith, A. (1979). Language development after five. In P. Fletcher & M. Garman (Eds.), *Language acquisition: Studies in first language development.* Cambridge, England: Cambridge University Press.

Karmiloff-Smith, A. (1993). Innate constraints and developmental change. In P. Bloom (Ed.), *Language acquisition: Core readings.* Cambridge, MA: MIT Press.

Kieffer, M. J. (2008). Catching up or falling behind? Initial English proficiency, concentrated poverty, and the reading growth of language minority learners in the United States. *Journal of Educational Psychology, 100,* 851–868.

Kitayama, S., & Cohen, D. (Eds.) (2007). *Handbook of cultural psychology.* New York: Guilford.

Klaczynski, P. A. (2001). Analytic and heuristic processing influences on adolescent reasoning and decision-making. *Child Development, 72,* 844–861.

Klahr, D. (2001). Time matters in cognitive development. In J. L. McClelland & R. S. Siegler (Eds.), *Mechanisms of cognitive development: Behavioral and neural perspectives* (pp. 291–301). Mahwah, NJ: Erlbaum.

Kolb, B., Gibb, R., & Robinson, T. E. (2003). Brain plasticity and behavior. *Current Directions in Psychological Science, 12,* 1–5.

Krashen, S. D. (1996). *Under attack: The case against bilingual education.* Culver City, CA: Language Education Associates.

Kuhl, P. K. (2004). Early language acquisition: Cracking the speech code. *Nature Reviews Neuroscience, 5,* 831–843.

Kuhl, P. K., Conboy, B. T., Padden, D., Nelson, T., & Pruitt, J. (2005). Early speech perception and later language development: Implications for the "critical period." *Language Learning and Development, 1,* 237–264.

Kuhn, D. (2006). Do cognitive changes accompany developments in the adolescent brain? *Perspectives on Psychological Science, 1,* 59–67.

Kuhn, D., & Franklin, S. (2006). The second decade: What develops (and how)? In W. Damon & R. M. Lerner (Series Eds.), D. Kuhn, & R. Siegler (Vol. Eds.), *Handbook of child psychology: Vol. 2. Cognition, perception, and language* (6th ed., pp. 953–993). New York: Wiley.

Kuhn, D., & Pease, M. (2008). What needs to develop in the development of inquiry skills? *Cognition and Instruction, 26,* 512–599.

Lajoie, S. P., & Derry, S. J. (Eds.). (1993). *Computers as cognitive tools.* Mahwah, NJ: Erlbaum.

Lampert, M., Rittenhouse, P., & Crumbaugh, C. (1996). Agreeing to disagree: Developing sociable mathematical discourse. In D. R. Olson & N. Torrance (Eds.), *The handbook of education and human development: New models of learning, teaching,and schooling* (pp. 731–764). Cambridge, MA: Blackwell.

Lautrey, J. (1993). Structure and variability: A plea for a pluralistic approach to cognitive development. In R. Case & W. Edelstein (Eds.), *The new structuralism in cognitive development: Theory and research on individual pathways* (pp. 101–114). Basel, Switzerland: Karger.

Lave, J., & Wenger, E. (1991). *Situated learning: Legitimate peripheral participation.* Cambridge, England: Cambridge University Press.

Lee, C. D. (2005). Intervention research based on current views of cognition and learning. In J. E. King (Ed.), *Black education: A transformative research and action agenda for the new century* (pp. 45–71). Washington, DC: American Educational Research Association.

Lee, C. D. (2010). Soaring above the clouds, delving the ocean's depths: Understanding the ecologies of human learning and the challenge for education science. *Educational Researcher, 39,* 643–655.

Lee, S. (1985). Children's acquisition of conditional logic structure: Teachable? *Contemporary Educational Psychology, 10,* 14–27.

Lenroot, R. K., & Giedd, J. N. (2007). The structural development of the human brain as measured longitudinally with magnetic resonance imaging. In D. Coch, K. W. Fischer, & G. Dawson (Eds.), *Human behavior, learning, and the developing brain: Typical development* (pp. 50–73). New York: Guilford.

Liben, L. S., & Downs, R. M. (1989). Understanding maps as symbols: The development of map concepts in children. In H. W. Reese (Ed.), *Advances in Child Development and behavior* (Vol. 22, pp. 145–201). San Diego, CA: Harcourt Brace Jovanovich.

Liben, L. S., & Myers, L. J. (2007). Developmental changes in children's understanding of maps: What, when, and how? In J. M. Plumert & J. P. Spencer (Eds.), *The emerging spatial mind* (pp. 193–218). New York: Oxford University Press.

Lichtman, J. W. (2001). Developmental neurobiology overview: Synapses, circuits, and plasticity. In D. B. Bailey, Jr., J. T. Bruer, F. J. Symons, & J. W. Lichtman (Eds.), *Critical thinking about critical periods* (pp. 27–42). Baltimore: Brookes.

Linn, M. C. (2008). Teaching for conceptual change: Distinguish or extinguish ideas. In S. Vosniadou (Ed.), *International handbook on conceptual change* (pp. 694–722). New York: Routledge.

Linn, M. C., Clement, C., Pulos, S., & Sullivan, P. (1989). Scientific reasoning during adolescence: The influence of instruction in science knowledge and reasoning strategies. *Journal of Research in Science Teaching, 26,* 171–187.

Locke, J. L. (1993). *The child's path to spoken language.* Cambridge, MA: Harvard University Press.

Lodewyk, K. R., & Winne, P. H. (2005). Relations among the structure of learning tasks, achievement, and changes in self-efficacy in secondary students. *Journal of Educational Psychology, 97,* 3–12.

Lorch, R. F., Jr., Lorch, E. P., Calderhead, W. J., Dunlap, E. E., Hodell, E. C., & Freer, B. D. (2010). Learning the control of variables strategy in higher and lower achieving classrooms: Contributions of explicit instruction and experimentation. *Journal of Educational Psychology, 102,* 90–101.

Lovell, K. (1979). Intellectual growth and the school curriculum. In F. B. Murray (Ed.), *The impact of Piagetian theory: On education, philosophy, psychiatry, and psychology.* Baltimore: University Park Press.

Maratsos, M. (1998). Some problems in grammatical acquisition. In W. Damon (Series Ed.), D. Kuhn, & R. S. Siegler (Vol. Eds.), *Handbook of child psychology: Vol. 2. Cognition, perception, and language* (5th ed., pp. 421–466). New York: Wiley.

Mareschal, D., Johnson, M. H., Sirois, S., Spratling, M. W., Thomas, M. S. C., & Westermann, G. (2007). *Neuroconstructivism: Vol. 1. How the brain constructs cognition.* Oxford, England: Oxford University Press.

Marsh, H. W., Hau, K.-T., & Kong, C.-K. (2002). Multilevel causal ordering of academic self-concept and achievement: Influence of language of instruction (English compared with Chinese)

for Hong Kong students. *American Educational Research Journal, 39,* 727–763.

Mayer, R. E. (2004). Should there be a three-strikes rule against pure discovery learning? *American Psychologist, 59,* 14–19.

Maynard, A. E., & Greenfield, P. M. (2003). Implicit cognitive development in cultural tools and children: Lessons from Maya Mexico. *Cognitive Development, 18,* 489–510.

McBrien, J. L. (2005b). Educational needs and barriers for refugee students in the United States: A review of the literature. *Review of Educational Research, 75,* 329–364.

McCarty, T. L., & Watahomigie, L. J. (1998). Language and literacy in American Indian and Alaska Native communities. In B. Pérez (Ed.), *Sociocultural contexts of language and literacy* (pp. 69–98). Mahwah, NJ: Erlbaum.

McClelland, J. L. (2001). Failures to learn and their remediation: A Hebbian account. In J. L. McClelland & R. S. Siegler (Eds.), *Mechanisms of cognitive development: Behavioral and neural perspectives* (pp. 97–121). Mahwah, NJ: Erlbaum.

McClelland, J. L., Fiez, J. A., & McCandliss, B. D. (2002). Teaching the /r/–/l/ discrimination to Japanese adults: Behavioral and neural aspects. *Physiology and Behavior, 77,* 657–662.

McDevitt, T. M., & Ford, M. E. (1987). Processes in young children's communicative functioning and development. In M. E. Ford & D. H. Ford (Eds.), *Humans as self-constructing living systems: Putting the framework to work* (pp. 145–175). Mahwah, NJ: Erlbaum.

McDevitt, T. M., Spivey, N., Sheehan, E. P., Lennon, R., & Story, R. (1990). Children's beliefs about listening: Is it enough to be still and quiet? *Child Development, 61,* 713–721.

McGivern, R. F., Andersen, J., Byrd, D., Mutter, K. L., & Reilly, J. (2002). Cognitive efficiency on a match to sample task decreases at the onset of puberty in children. *Brain and Cognition, 50*(1), 73–89.

McNeil, N. M., & Uttal, D. H. (2009). Rethinking the use of concrete materials in learning: Perspectives from development and education. *Child Development Perspectives, 3,* 137–139.

Mechelli, A., Crinion, J. T., Noppeney, U., O'Doherty, J., Ashburner, J., Frackowiak, R., et al. (2004). Structural plasticity in the bilingual brain. *Nature, 431,* 757.

Merrill, P. F., Hammons, K., Vincent, B. R., Reynolds, P. L., Christensen, L., & Tolman, M. N. (1996). *Computers in education* (3rd ed.). Boston: Allyn & Bacon.

Merzenich, M. M. (2001). Cortical plasticity contributing to child development. In J. L. McClelland & R. S. Siegler (Eds.), *Mechanisms of cognitive development: Behavioral and neural perspectives* (pp. 67–95). Mahwah, NJ: Erlbaum.

Metz, K. E. (1995). Reassessment of developmental constraints on children's science instruction. *Review of Educational Research, 65,* 93–127.

Miller, G. A. (2010). Mistreating psychology in the decades of the brain. *Perspectives on Psychological Science, 5,* 716–743.

Miller, J. G. (1997). A cultural-psychology perspective on intelligence. In R. J. Sternberg

& E. L. Grigorenko (Eds.), *Intelligence, heredity, and environment* (pp. 269–302). Cambridge, England: Cambridge University Press.

Moran, S., & John-Steiner, V. (2003). Creativity in the making: Vygotsky's contemporary contribution to the dialectic of development and creativity. In R. K. Sawyer, V. John-Steiner, S. Moran, R. J. Sternberg, D. H. Feldman, J. Nakamura, & M. Csikszentmihalyi, *Creativity and development* (pp. 61–90). Oxford, England: Oxford University Press.

Morra, S., Gobbo, C., Marini, Z., & Sheese, R. (2008). *Cognitive development: Neo-Piagetian perspectives.* New York: Erlbaum.

Murphy, P. K., Wilkinson, I. A. G., & Soter, A. O. (2011). Instruction based on discussion. In R. E. Mayer & P. A. Alexander (Eds.), *Handbook of research on learning and instruction* (pp. 382–407). New York: Routledge.

Nelson, C. A., III, Thomas, K. M., & de Haan, M. (2006). Neural bases of cognitive development. In D. Kuhn, R. Siegler (Vol. Eds.), W. Damon, & R. M. Lerner (Series Eds.), *Handbook of child psychology. Vol. 2: Cognition, perception, and language* (6th ed., pp. 3–57). New York: Wiley.

Nelson, K. (1996). *Language in cognitive development: The emergence of the mediated mind.* Cambridge, England: Cambridge University Press.

Nettles, S. M., Caughy, M. O., & O'Campo, P. J. (2008). School adjustment in the early grades: Toward an integrated model of neighborhood, parental, and child processes. *Review of Educational Research, 78,* 3–32.

Newport, E. L. (1990). Maturational constraints on language learning. *Cognitive Science, 14,* 11–28.

Nieto, S. (1995). *Affirming diversity* (2nd ed.). White Plains, NY: Longman.

Nippold, M. A. (1988). The literate lexicon. In M. A. Nippold (Ed.), *Later language development: Ages nine through nineteen* (pp. 29–48). Boston: Little, Brown.

Norenzayan, A., Choi, I., & Peng, K. (2007). Perception and cognition. In S. Kitayama & D. Cohen (Eds.), *Handbook of cultural psychology* (pp. 569–594). New York: Guilford.

Nuemi, J.-W. (2008). Self and socialization: How do young people navigate through adolescence? In H. W. Marsh, R. G. Craven, & D. M. McInerney (Eds.), *Self-processes, learning, and enabling human potential* (pp. 305–327). Charlotte, NC: Information Age.

O'Boyle, M. W., & Gill, H. S. (1998). On the relevance of research findings in cognitive neuroscience to educational practice. *Educational Psychology Review, 10,* 397–409.

O'Grady, W. (1997). *Syntactic development.* Chicago: University of Chicago.

Ornstein, R. (1997). *The right mind: Making sense of the hemispheres.* San Diego, CA: Harcourt Brace.

Ortony, A., Turner, T. J., & Larson-Shapiro, N. (1985). Cultural and instructional influences on figurative comprehension by inner city children. *Research in the Teaching of English, 19*(1), 25–36.

Owens, R. E., Jr. (2008). *Language development* (7th ed.). Boston: Allyn & Bacon.

Padilla, A. M. (2006). Second language learning: Issues in research and teaching. In P. A. Alexander & P. H. Winne (Eds.), *Handbook of educational psychology* (2nd ed., pp. 571–591). Mahwah, NJ: Erlbaum.

Paus, T., Zijdenbos, A., Worsley, K., Collins, D. L., Blumenthal, J., Giedd, J. N., et al. (1999). Structural maturation of neural pathways in children and adolescents: In vivo study. *Science, 283,* 1908–1911.

Pellegrini, A. D. (2009). Research and policy on children's play. *Child Development Perspectives, 3,* 131–136.

Pelucchi, B., Hay, J. F., & Saffran, J. R. (2009). Statistical learning in a natural language by 8-month-old infants. *Child Development, 80,* 674–685.

Pérez, B. (1998). *Sociocultural contexts of language and literacy.* Mahwah, NJ: Erlbaum.

Perkins, D. N. (1992). *Smart schools: From training memories to educating minds.* New York: Free Press/Macmillan.

Piaget, J. (1929). *The child's conception of the world.* New York: Harcourt, Brace.

Piaget, J. (1952a). *The child's conception of number* (C. Gattegno & F. M. Hodgson, Trans.). London: Routledge & Kegan Paul.

Piaget, J. (1952b). *The origins of intelligence in children* (M. Cook, Trans.). New York: Norton.

Piaget, J. (1959). *The language and thought of the child* (3rd ed.; M. Gabain, Trans.). London: Routledge & Kegan Paul.

Piaget, J. (1970). Piaget's theory. In P. H. Mussen (Ed.), *Carmichael's manual of psychology* (pp. 703–732). New York: Wiley.

Piaget, J. (1971). The theory of stages in cognitive development. In D. R. Green (Ed.), *Measurement and Piaget* (pp. 1–11). New York: McGraw-Hill.

Piaget, J. (1980). *Adaptation and intelligence: Organic selection and phenocopy* (S. Eames, Trans.). Chicago: University of Chicago Press.

Pinker, S. (2007). *The stuff of thought: Language as a window into human nature.* New York: Viking.

Premack, D. (2004). Is language the key to human intelligence? *Science, 303,* 318–320.

Price-Williams, D. R., Gordon, W., & Ramirez, M. (1969). Skill and conservation: A study of pottery-making children. *Developmental Psychology, 1,* 769.

Pulos, S., & Linn, M. C. (1981). Generality of the controlling variables scheme in early adolescence. *Journal of Early Adolescence, 1,* 26–37.

Radziszewska, B., & Rogoff, B. (1988). Influence of adult and peer collaborators on children's planning skills. *Developmental Psychology, 24,* 840–848.

Raikes, H., Pan, B. A., Luze, G., Tamis-LeMonda, C. S., Brooks-Gunn, J., Constantine, J., et al. (2006). Mother-child bookreading in low-income families: Correlates and outcomes during the first three years of life. *Child Development, 77,* 924–953.

Rayner, K., Foorman, B. R., Perfetti, C. A., Pesetsky, D., & Seidenberg, M. S. (2001). How psychological science informs the teaching of reading. *Psychological Science in the Public Interest, 2,* 31–74.

Reich, P. A. (1986). *Language development.* Upper Saddle River, NJ: Prentice-Hall.

Risley, T. R., & Hart, B. (2006). Promoting early language development. In N. F. Watt, C. Ayoub, R. H. Bradley, J. E. Puma, & W. A. LeBoeuf (Eds.), *The crisis in young mental health: Critical issues and effective programs: Vol. 4. Early intervention programs and policies* (pp. 83–88). Westport, CT: Praeger.

Rogoff, B. (1990). *Apprenticeship in thinking: Cognitive development in social context.* New York: Oxford University Press.

Rogoff, B. (1991). Social interaction as apprenticeship in thinking: Guidance and participation in spatial planning. In L. B. Resnick, J. M. Levine, & S. D. Teasley (Eds.), *Perspectives on socially shared cognition* (pp. 349–364). Washington, DC: American Psychological Association.

Rogoff, B. (2003). *The cultural nature of human development.* Oxford, England: Oxford University Press.

Rogoff, B., Moore, L., Najafi, B., Dexter, A., Correa-Chávez, M., & Solís, J. (2007). Children's development of cultural repertoires through participation in everyday routines and practices. In J. E. Grusec & P. D. Hastings (Eds.), *Handbook of socialization: Theory and research* (pp. 490–515). New York: Guilford.

Rosenshine, B., & Meister, C. (1992). The use of scaffolds for teaching higher-level cognitive strategies. *Educational Leadership, 49*(7), 26–33.

Rosser, R. (1994). *Cognitive development: Psychological and biological perspectives.* Boston: Allyn & Bacon.

Ruffman, T., Perner, J., Olson, D. R., & Doherty, M. (1993). Reflecting on scientific thinking: Children's understanding of the hypothesis-evidence relation. *Child Development, 64,* 1617–1636.

Saffran, J. R. (2003). Statistical language learning: Mechanisms and constraints. *Current Directions in Psychological Science, 12,* 110–114.

Sarama, J., & Clements, D. H. (2009). "Concrete" computer manipulatives in mathematics education. *Child Development Perspectives, 3,* 145–150.

Scardamalia, M., & Bereiter, C. (1985). Fostering the development of self-regulation in children's knowledge processing. In S. F. Chipman, J. W. Segal, & R. Glaser (Eds.), *Thinking and learning skills: Vol. 2. Research and open questions* (pp. 65–80). Mahwah, NJ: Erlbaum.

Scarr, S., & McCartney, K. (1983). How people make their own environments: A theory of genotype environment effects. *Child Development, 54,* 424–435.

Schauble, L. (1990). Belief revision in children: The role of prior knowledge and strategies for generating evidence. *Journal of Experimental Child Psychology, 49,* 31–57.

Schimmoeller, M. A. (1998, April). *Influence of private speech on the writing behaviors of young children: Four case studies.* Paper presented at the annual meeting of the American

Educational Research Association, San Diego, CA.

Schliemann, A. D., & Carraher, D. W. (1993). Proportional reasoning in and out of school. In P. Light & G. Butterworth (Eds.), *Context and cognition: Ways of learning and knowing* (pp. 47–73). Mahwah, NJ: Erlbaum.

Shen, H., Sabaliauskas, N., Sherpa, A., Fenton, A. A., Stelzer, A., Aoki, C., et al. (2010). A critical role for α4βδ GABA$_A$ receptors in shaping learning deficits at puberty in mice. *Science, 327*(5972), 1515–1518.

Sherman, J., & Bisanz, J. (2009). Equivalence in symbolic and nonsymbolic contexts: Benefits of solving problems with manipulatives. *Journal of Educational Psychology, 101,* 88–100.

Shweder, R. A., Goodnow, J., Hatano, G., Levine, R. A., Marcus, H., & Miller, P. (1998). The cultural psychology of development: One mind, many mentalities. In W. Damon (Editor-in-Chief) & R. M. Lerner (Vol. Ed.), *Handbook of child psychology: Vol. 1. Theoretical models of human development* (5th ed., pp. 865–937). New York: Wiley.

Siegel, D. J. (2012). *The developing mind: How relationships and the brain interact to shape who we are* (2nd ed.). New York: Guilford.

Siegler, R. S., & Alibali, M. W. (2005). *Children's thinking* (4th ed.). Upper Saddle River, NJ: Prentice-Hall.

Siegler, R. S., & Chen, Z. (2008). Differentiation and integration: Guiding principles for analyzing cognitive change. *Developmental Science, 11,* 433–448.

Siegler, R. S., & Lin, X. (2010). Self-explanations promote children's learning. In H. S. Waters & W. Schneider (Eds.), *Metacognition, strategy use, and instruction* (pp. 85–112.). New York: Guilford.

Silveri, M. M., Rohan, M. L., Pimentel, P. J., Gruber, S. A., Rosso, I. M., & Yurgelun-Todd, D. A. (2006). Sex differences in the relationship between white matter microstructure and impulsivity in adolescents. *Magnetic Resonance Imaging, 24,* 833–841.

Slavin, R. E., & Cheung, A. (2005). A synthesis of research on language of reading instruction for English language learners. *Review of Educational Research, 75,* 247–284.

Smith, C. L. (2007). Bootstrapping processes in the development of students' commonsense matter theories: Using analogical mappings, thought experiments, and learning to measure to promote conceptual restructuring. *Cognition and Instruction, 25,* 337–398.

Smith, H. L. (1998). Literacy and instruction in African American communities: Shall we overcome? In B. Pérez (Ed.), *Sociocultural contexts of language and literacy* (pp. 189–222). Mahwah, NJ: Erlbaum.

Smitherman, G. (2007). The power of the rap: The Black idiom and the new Black poetry. In H. S. Alim & J. Baugh (Eds.), *Talkin Black talk: Language, education, and social change* (pp. 77–91). New York: Teachers College Press.

Solórzano, R. W. (2008). High stakes testing: Issues, implications, and remedies for English language learners. *Educational Researcher, 78,* 260–329.

Spear, L. P. (2007). Brain development and adolescent behavior. In D. Coch, K. W. Fischer, & G. Dawson (Eds.), *Human behavior, learning, and the developing brain: Typical development* (pp. 362–396). New York: Guilford.

Spelke, E. S. (2003). What makes humans smart? In D. Gentner & S. Goldin-Meadow (Eds.), *Advances in the investigation of language and thought* (pp. 277–311). Cambridge, MA: MIT Press.

Spencer, J. P., Blumberg, M. S., McMurray, B., Robinson, S. R., Samuelson, L. K., & Tomblin, J. B. (2009). Short arms and talking eggs: Why we should no longer abide the nativist–empiricist debate. *Child Development Perspectives, 3,* 79–87.

Spinath, F. M., Price, T. S., Dale, P. S., & Plomin, R. (2004). The genetic and environmental origins of language disability and ability. *Child Development, 75,* 445–454.

Stanovich, K. E. (2000). *Progress in understanding reading: Scientific foundations and new frontiers.* New York: Guilford.

Steinberg, L. (2009). Should the science of adolescent brain development inform public policy? *American Psychologist, 64,* 739–750.

Stevens, G. (2004). Using census data to test critical-period hypothesis for second-language acquisition. *Psychological Science, 15,* 215–216.

Strozer, J. R. (1994). *Language acquisition after puberty.* Washington, DC: Georgetown University Press.

Tamburrini, J. (1982). Some educational implications of Piaget's theory. In S. Modgil & C. Modgil (Eds.), *Jean Piaget: Consensus and controversy* (pp. 309–325). New York: Praeger.

Tanner, J. M., & Inhelder, B. (Eds.) (1960). *Discussions of child development: A consideration of the biological, psychological, and cultural approaches to the understanding of human development and behavior: Vol. 4. The proceedings of the fourth meeting of the World Health Organization Study Group on the Psychobiological Development of the Child, Geneva, 1956.* New York: International Universities Press.

Tatum, B. D. (1997). *"Why are all the black kids sitting together in the cafeteria?" and other conversations about race.* New York: Basic Books.

Thelen, E., & Smith, L. B. (1998). Dynamic systems theories. In W. Damon (Series Ed.) & R. M. Lerner (Vol. Ed.), *Handbook of child psychology: Vol. 1. Theoretical models of human development* (5th ed., pp. 563–634). New York: Wiley.

Thomas, M. S. C., & Johnson, M. H. (2008). New advances in understanding sensitive periods in brain development. *Current Directions in Psychological Science, 17,* 1–5.

Thompson, R. A., & Nelson, C. A. (2001). Developmental science and the media: Early brain development. *American Psychologist, 56,* 5–15.

Tong, F., Lara-Alecio, R., Irby, B., Mathes, P., & Kwok, O.-M. (2008). Accelerating early academic oral English development in transitional bilingual and structured English immersion programs. *American Educational Research Journal, 45,* 1011–1044.

Torres-Guzmán, M. E. (1998). Language, culture, and literacy in Puerto Rican communities. In B. Pérez (Ed.), *Sociocultural contexts of language and literacy* (pp. 99–122). Mahwah, NJ: Erlbaum.

Tourniaire, F., & Pulos, S. (1985). Proportional reasoning: A review of the literature. *Educational Studies in Mathematics, 16,* 181–204.

Trout, J. D. (2003). Biological specializations for speech: What can the animals tell us? *Current Directions in Psychological Science, 12,* 155–159.

Tse, L. (2001). *Why don't they learn English: Separating fact from fallacy in the U.S. language debate.* New York: Teachers College Press.

Tyler, K. M., Uqdah, A. L., Dillihunt, M. L., Beatty-Hazelbaker, R., Connor, T., Gadson, N., et al. (2008). Cultural discontinuity: Toward a quantitative investigation of a major hypothesis in education. *Educational Researcher, 37,* 280–297.

U.S. Department of Education. (1993). *National excellence: A case for developing America's talent.* Washington, DC: Office of Educational Research and Improvement.

Valdés, G., Bunch, G., Snow, C., & Lee, C. (with Matos, L.) (2005). Enhancing the development of students' language(s). In L. Darling-Hammond & J. Bransford (Eds.), *Preparing teachers for a changing world: What teachers should learn and be able to do* (pp. 126–168). San Francisco: Jossey-Bass/Wiley.

Van Dooren, W., De Bock, D., Hessels, A., Janssens, D., & Verschaffel, L. (2005). Not everything is proportional: Effects of age and problem type on propensities for overgeneralization. *Cognition and Instruction, 23,* 57–86.

Varma, S., McCandliss, B. D., & Schwartz, D. L. (2008). Scientific and pragmatic challenges for bridging education and neuroscience. *Educational Researcher, 37*(3), 140–152.

Vygotsky, L. S. (1978). *Mind in society: The development of higher psychological processes.* Cambridge, MA: Harvard University Press.

Vygotsky, L. S. (1986). *Thought and language* (rev. ed; A. Kozulin, Ed. and Trans.). Cambridge, MA: MIT Press. (Original work published 1934)

Vygotsky, L. S. (1987). *The collected works of L. S. Vygotsky* (Vol. 3; R. W. Rieber & A. S. Carton, Eds.). New York: Plenum Press.

Vygotsky, L. S. (1997). *Educational psychology* (R. Silverman, Trans.). Boca Raton, FL: St. Lucie Press.

Walker, E. F. (2002). Adolescent neurodevelopment and psychopathology. *Current Directions in Psychological Science, 11,* 24–28.

Walshaw, M., & Anthony, G. (2008). The teacher's role in classroom discourse: A review of recent research into mathematics classrooms. *Review of Educational Research, 78,* 516–551.

Winsler, A., Díaz, R. M., Espinosa, L., & Rodriguez, J. L. (1999). When learning a second language does not mean losing the first: Bilingual language development in low-income, Spanish-speaking children attending bilingual preschool. *Child Development, 70,* 349–362.

Winsler, A., & Naglieri, J. (2003). Overt and covert verbal problem-solving strategies: Developmental trends in use, awareness, and relations with task performance in children aged 5 to 17. *Child Development, 74,* 659–678.

Wong, B. Y. L., Hoskyn, M., Jai, D., Ellis, P., & Watson, K. (2008). The comparative efficacy of two approaches to teaching sixth graders opinion essay writing. *Contemporary Educational Psychology, 33,* 757–784.

Wood, D., Bruner, J. S., & Ross, G. (1976). The role of tutoring in problem-solving. *Journal of Child Psychology and Psychiatry, 17,* 89–100.

Wright, S. C., Taylor, D. M., & Macarthur, J. (2000). Subtractive bilingualism and the survival of the Inuit language: Heritage- versus second-language education. *Journal of Educational Psychology, 92,* 63–84.

Yaden, D. B., Jr., & Templeton, S. (Eds.). (1986). *Metalinguistic awareness and beginning literacy: Conceptualizing what it means to read and write.* Portsmouth, NH: Heinemann.

## CHAPTER 3

Adalbjarnardottir, S., & Selman, R. L. (1997). "I feel I have received a new vision": An analysis of teachers' professional development as they work with students on interpersonal issues. *Teaching and Teacher Education, 13,* 409–428.

Ainsworth, M. D. S., Blehar, M. C., Waters, E., & Wall, S. (1978). *Patterns of attachment.* Hillsdale, NJ: Erlbaum.

Alemán, A. M. M., & Vartman, K. L. (2009). *Online social networking on campus: Understanding what matters in student culture.* New York: Routledge.

Alessandri, S. M., & Lewis, M. (1993). Parental evaluation and its relation to shame and pride in young children. *Sex Roles, 29,* 335–343.

Allen, J. P., & Antonishak, J. (2008). Adolescent peer influences: Beyond the dark side. In M. J. Prinstein & K. A. Dodge (Eds.), *Understanding peer influence in children and adolescents* (pp. 141–160). New York: Guilford.

Allen, J. P., Porter, M., McFarland, C., McElhaney, K. B., & Marsh, P. (2007). The relation of attachment security to adolescents' paternal and peer relationships, depression, and externalizing behavior. *Child Development, 78,* 1222–1239.

Allen, L., & Aber, J. L. (2006). The development of ethnic identity during adolescence. *Developmental Psychology, 42,* 1–10.

Altschul, I., Oyserman, D., & Bybee, D. (2006). Racial-ethnic identity in mid-adolescence: Content and change as predictors of academic achievement. *Child Development, 77,* 1155–1169.

Anderman, L. H., Freeman, T. M., & Mueller, C. E. (2007). The "social" side of social context: Interpersonal affiliative dimensions of students' experiences and academic dishonesty. In E. M. Anderman & T. B. Murdock (Eds.), *The psychology of academic cheating* (pp. 203–228). San Diego, CA: Elsevier.

Anderson, C. A., Berkowitz, L., Donnerstein, E., Huesmann, L. R., Johnson, J. D., Linz, D., et al. (2003). The influence of media violence on youth. *Psychological Science in the Public Interest, 4,* 81–110.

Asher, S. R., & McDonald, K. A. (2009). The behavioral basis of acceptance, rejection, and perceived popularity. In K. H. Rubin, W. M. Bukowski, & B. Laursen (Eds.), *Handbook of peer interactions, relationships, and groups* (pp. 232–248). New York: Guilford.

Asher, S. R., & Renshaw, P. D. (1981). Children without friends: Social knowledge and social skill training. In S. R. Asher & J. M. Gottman (Eds.), *The development of children's friendships* (pp. 273–296). New York: Cambridge University Press.

Aunola, K., & Nurmi, J.-E. (2005). The role of parenting style in children's problem behavior. *Child Development, 76,* 1144–1159.

Bakermans-Kranenburg, M. J., van IJzendoorn, M. H., Pijlman, F. T. A., Mesman, J., & Juffer, F. (2008). Experimental evidence for differential susceptibility: Dopamine D4 receptor polymorphism (DRD4 VNTR) moderates intervention effects on toddlers' externalizing behavior in a randomized control trial. *Developmental Psychology, 44,* 293–300.

Bandura, A. (2008). Toward an agentic theory of the self. In H. W. Marsh, R. G. Craven, & D. M. McInerney (Eds.), *Self-processes, learning, and enabling human potential* (pp. 15–49). Charlotte, NC: Information Age.

Banks, J. A., & Banks, C. A. M. (Eds.). (1995). *Handbook of research on multicultural education.* New York: Macmillan.

Barber, B. K., Stolz, H. E., & Olsen, J. A. (2005). Parental support, psychological control, and behavioral control: Assessing relevance across time, culture, and method. *Monographs of the Society for Research in Child Development, 70* (4; Serial No. 282).

Basinger, K. S., Gibbs, J. C., & Fuller, D. (1995). Context and the measurement of moral judgment. *International Journal of Behavioral Development, 18,* 537–556.

Bates, J. E., & Pettit, G. S. (2007). Temperament, parenting, and socialization. In J. E. Grusec & P. D. Hastings (Eds.), *Handbook of socialization: Theory and research* (pp. 153–177). New York: Guilford.

Batson, C. D. (1991). *The altruism question: Toward a social-psychological answer.* Hillsdale, NJ: Erlbaum.

Batson, C. D., & Thompson, E. R. (2001). Why don't moral people act morally? Motivational considerations. *Current Directions in Psychological Science, 10,* 54–57.

Baumeister, R. F., Campbell, J. D., Krueger, J. I., & Vohs, K. D. (2003). Does high self-esteem cause better performance, interpersonal success, happiness, or healthier lifestyles? *Psychological Science in the Public Interest, 4,* 1–44.

Baumeister, R. F., Smart, L., & Boden, J. M. (1996). Relation of threatened egotism to violence and aggression: The dark side of high self-esteem. *Psychological Review, 103,* 5–33.

Baumrind, D. (1989). Rearing competent children. In W. Damon (Ed.), *Child development today and tomorrow* (pp. 349–378). San Francisco: Jossey-Bass.

Baumrind, D. (1991). Parenting styles and adolescent development. In R. Lerner, A. C. Petersen, & J. Brooks-Gunn (Eds.), *The encyclopedia of adolescence* (pp. 746–758). New York: Garland.

Belfiore, P. J., & Hornyak, R. S. (1998). Operant theory and application to self-monitoring in adolescents. In D. H. Schunk & B. J. Zimmerman (Eds.), *Self-regulated learning: From teaching to self-reflective practice* (pp. 184–202). New York: Guilford.

Bellmore, A. (2011). Peer rejection and unpopularity: Associations with GPAs across the transition to middle school. *Journal of Educational Psychology, 103,* 282–295.

Belsky, J., & Pluess, M. (2009). The nature (and nurture?) of plasticity in early human development. *Perspectives on Psychological Science, 4,* 345–351.

Benenson, J. F., Maiese, R., Dolenszky, E., Dolensky, N., Sinclair, N., & Simpson, A. (2002). Group size regulates self-assertive versus self-deprecating responses to interpersonal competition. *Child Development, 73,* 1818–1829.

Bergin, D. A., & Cooks, H. C. (2008). High school students of color talk about accusations of "acting White." In J. U. Ogbu (Ed.), *Minority status, oppositional culture, and schooling* (pp. 145–166). New York: Routledge.

Berndt, T. J. (1992). Friendship and friends' influence in adolescence. *Current Directions in Psychological Science, 1,* 156–159.

Berndt, T. J., Laychak, A. E., & Park, K. (1990). Friends' influence on adolescents' academic achievement motivation: An experimental study. *Journal of Educational Psychology, 82,* 664–670.

Berzonsky, M. D., & Kuk, L. S. (2000). Identity status, identity processing style, and the transition to university. *Journal of Adolescent Research, 15,* 81–98.

Bierman, K. L., Miller, C. L., & Stabb, S. D. (1987). Improving the social behavior and peer acceptance of rejected boys: Effect of social skill training with instructions and prohibitions. *Journal of Consulting and Clinical Psychology, 55,* 194–200.

Bierman, K. L., & Powers, C. J. (2009). Social skills training to improve peer relations. In K. H. Rubin, W. M. Bukowski, & B. Laursen (Eds.), *Handbook of peer interactions, relationships, and groups* (pp. 603–621). New York: Guilford.

Bjorklund, D. F., & Green, B. L. (1992). The adaptive nature of cognitive immaturity. *American Psychologist, 47,* 46–54.

Blanton, H., & Burkley, M. (2008). Deviance regulation theory: Applications to adolescent social influence. In M. J. Prinstein & K. A. Dodge (Eds.), *Understanding peer influence in children and adolescents* (pp. 94–121). New York: Guilford.

Blasi, A. (1980). Bridging moral cognition and moral action: A critical review of the literature. *Psychological Bulletin, 88,* 593–637.

Blasi, A. (1995). Moral understanding and the moral personality: The process of moral integration. In W. M. Kurtines & J. L. Gewirtz (Eds.), *Moral development: An introduction* (pp. 229–253). Boston: Allyn & Bacon.

Bong, M., & Skaalvik, E. M. (2003). Academic self-concept and self-efficacy: How different are they really? *Educational Psychology Review, 15,* 1–40.

Boom, J., Brugman, D., & van der Heijden, P. G. M. (2001). Hierarchical structure of moral stages assessed by a sorting task. *Child Development, 72,* 535–548.

Bosacki, S. L. (2000). Theory of mind and self-concept in preadolescents: Links with gender and language. *Journal of Educational Psychology, 92,* 709–717.

Bouchey, H. A., & Harter, S. (2005). Reflected appraisals, academic self-perceptions, and math/science performance during early adolescence. *Journal of Educational Psychology, 97,* 673–686.

Bracken, B. (2009). Positive self-concepts. In R. Gilman, E. S. Huebner, & M. J. Furlong (Eds.), *Handbook of positive psychology in schools* (pp. 89–106). New York: Routledge.

Bradley, R. H. (2010). The HOME environment. In M. H. Bornstein (Ed.), *Handbook of cultural developmental science* (pp. 505–530). New York: Psychology Press.

Brendgen, M., Boivin, M., Vitaro, F., Bukowski, W. M., Dionne, G., Tremblay, R. E., et al. (2008). Linkages between children's and their friends' social and physical aggression: Evidence for a gene-environment interaction? *Child Development, 79,* 13–29.

Brody, G. H., & Shaffer, D. R. (1982). Contributions of parents and peers to children's moral socialization. *Developmental Review, 2,* 31–75.

Brophy, J., Alleman, J., & Knighton, B. (2009). *Inside the social studies classroom.* New York: Routledge.

Brown, B. B. (1990). Peer groups. In S. Feldman & G. Elliott (Eds.), *At the threshold: The developing adolescent* (pp. 171–196). Cambridge, MA: Harvard University Press.

Brown, B. B. (1999). "You're going out with *who?*" Peer group influences on adolescent romantic relationships. In W. Furman, B. B. Brown, & C. Feiring (Eds.), *The development of romantic relationships in adolescence* (pp. 291–329). Cambridge, England: Cambridge University Press.

Brown, B. B. (2011). Popularity in peer group perspective: The role of status in adolescent peer systems. In A. H. N. Cillessen, D. Schwartz, & L. Mayeux (Eds.), *Popularity in the peer system* (pp. 165–192). New York: Guilford.

Brown, B. B., Bakken, J. P., Ameringer, S. W., & Mahon, S. D. (2008). A comprehensive conceptualization of the peer influence process in adolescence. In M. J. Prinstein & K. A. Dodge (Eds.), *Understanding peer influence in children and adolescents* (pp. 17–44). New York: Guilford.

Brown, B. B., Eicher, S. A., & Petrie, S. (1986). The importance of peer group ("crowd") affiliation in adolescence. *Journal of Adolescence, 9,* 73–96.

Brown, L. M., Tappan, M. B., & Gilligan, C. (1995). Listening to different voices. In W. M. Kurtines & J. L. Gewirtz (Eds.), *Moral development: An introduction* (pp. 311–335). Boston: Allyn & Bacon.

Brown, R. P., Osterman, L. L., & Barnes, C. D. (2009). School violence and the culture of honor. *Psychological Science, 20,* 1400–1405.

Bryan, T. (1991). Social problems and learning disabilities. In B. Y. L. Wong (Ed.), *Learning about learning disabilities* (pp. 195–229). San Diego, CA: Academic Press.

Bukowski, W. M., Brendgen, M., & Vitaro, F. (2007). Peers and socialization: Effects on externalizing and internalizing problems. In J. E. Grusec & P. D. Hastings (Eds.), *Handbook of socialization: Theory and research* (pp. 355–381). New York: Guilford.

Bukowski, W. M., Motzoi, C., & Meyer, F. (2009). Friendship as process, function, and outcome. In K. H. Rubin, W. M. Bukowski, & B. Laursen (Eds.), *Handbook of peer interactions, relationships, and groups* (pp. 217–231). New York: Guilford.

Bukowski, W. M., Velasquez, A. M., & Brendgen, M. (2008). Variation in patterns of peer influence: Considerations of self and other. In M. J. Prinstein & K. A. Dodge (Eds.), *Understanding peer influence in children and adolescents* (pp. 125–140). New York: Guilford.

Burgess, K. B., Wojslawowicz, J. C., Rubin, K. H., Rose-Krasnor, L., & Booth-LaForce, C. (2006). Social information processing and coping strategies of shy/withdrawn and aggressive children: Does friendship matter? *Child Development, 77,* 371–383.

Buston, K., & Hart, G. (2001). Heterosexism and homophobia in Scottish school education: Exploring the nature of the problem. *Journal of Adolescence, 24*(1), 95–110.

Butler, R. (2008). Evaluating competence and maintaining self-worth between early and middle childhood: Blissful ignorance or the construction of knowledge and strategies in context? In H. W. Marsh, R. G. Craven, & D. M. McInerney (Eds.), *Self-processes, learning, and enabling human potential* (pp. 193–222). Charlotte, NC: Information Age.

Byrne, B. M. (2002). Validating the measurement and structure of self-concept: Snapshots of past, present, and future research. *American Psychologist, 57,* 897–909.

Caldwell, M. S., Rudolph, K. D., Troop-Gordon, W., & Kim, D. (2004). Reciprocal influences among relational self-views, social disengagement, and peer stress during early adolescence. *Child Development, 75,* 1140–1154.

Caprara, G. V., Barbaranelli, C., Pastorelli, C., Bandura, A., & Zimbardo, P. G. (2000). Prosocial foundations of children's academic achievement. *Psychological Science, 11,* 302–306.

Caprara, G. V., Dodge, K. A., Pastorelli, C., & Zelli, A. (2007). How marginal deviations sometimes grow into serious aggression. *Child Development Perspectives, 1,* 33–39.

Card, N. A., Stucky, B. D., Sawalani, G. M., & Little T. D. (2008). Direct and indirect aggression during childhood and adolescence: A meta-analytic review of gender differences, intercorrelations, and relations to maladjustment. *Child Development, 79,* 1185–1229.

Carrasco, R. L. (1981). Expanded awareness of student performance: A case study in applied ethnographic monitoring in a bilingual classroom. In H. T. Trueba, G. P. Guthrie, & K. H. Au (Eds.), *Culture and the bilingual classroom: Studies in classroom ethnography* (pp. 153–177). Rowley, MA: Newbury House.

Carter, K., & Doyle, W. (2006). Classroom management in early childhood and elementary classrooms. In C. M. Evertson & C. S. Weinstein (Eds.), *Handbook of classroom management: Research, practice, and contemporary issues* (pp. 373–406). Mahwah, NJ: Erlbaum.

Caspi, A. (1998). Personality development across the life course. In W. Damon (Series Ed.) & N. Eisenberg (Vol. Ed.), *Handbook of child psychology: Vol. 3. Social, emotional, and personality development* (5th ed., pp. 311–388). New York: Wiley.

Caspi, A., & Silva, P. A. (1995). Temperamental qualities at age three predict personality traits in young adulthood: Longitudinal evidence from a birth cohort. *Child Development, 66,* 486–498.

Certo, J. (2011). Social skills and leadership abilities among children in small group literature discussions. *Journal of Research in Childhood Education, 25*(1), 62–81.

Certo, J. L., Cauley, K. M., & Chafin, C. (2003). Students' perspectives on their high school experience. *Adolescence, 38,* 705–724.

Chang, L. (2003) Variable effects of children's aggression, social withdrawal, and prosocial leadership as functions of teacher beliefs and behaviors. *Child Development, 74,* 535–548.

Chang, L., Liu, H., Wen, Z., Fung, K. Y., Wang, Y, & Xu, Y. (2004). Mediating teacher liking and moderating authoritative teaching on Chinese adolescents' perceptions of antisocial and prosocial behaviors. *Journal of Educational Psychology, 96,* 369–380.

Chapman, J. W., Tunmer, W. E., & Prochnow, J. E. (2000). Early reading-related skills and performance, reading self-concept, and the development of academic self-concept: A longitudinal study. *Journal of Educational Psychology, 92,* 703–708.

Chen, W.-B., & Gregory, A. (2008, March). *Parental involvement in schooling: What types work for low-achieving adolescents and what does this mean for schools?* Paper presented at the annual meeting of the American Educational Research Association, New York.

Chen, X., Chung, J., & Hsiao, C. (2009). Peer interactions and relationships from a cross-cultural perspective. In K. H. Rubin, W. M. Bukowski, & B. Laursen (Eds.), *Handbook of peer interactions, relationships, and groups* (pp. 432–451). New York: Guilford.

Chen, X., & Wang, L. (2010). China. In M. H. Bornstein (Ed.), *Handbook of cultural developmental science* (pp. 429–444). New York: Psychology Press.

Christensen, S. L. (2004). Families with aggressive children and adolescents. In J. C. Conoley & A. P. Goldstein (Eds.), *School violence intervention* (2nd ed., pp. 359–399). New York: Guilford.

Cillessen, A. H. N., & Rose, A. J. (2005). Understanding popularity in the peer system. *Current Directions in Psychological Science, 14,* 102–105.

Cillessen, A. H. N., Schwartz, D., & Mayeux, L. (Eds.). (2011). *Popularity in the peer system.* New York: Guilford.

Cleveland, M. J., Gibbons, F. X., Gerrard, M., Pomery, E. A., & Brody, G. H. (2005). The impact of parenting on risk cognitions and risk behavior: A study of mediation and moderation in a panel of African American adolescents. *Child Development, 76,* 900–916.

Cohen, G. L., & Garcia, J. (2008). Identity, belonging, and achievement: A model, interventions, implications. *Current Directions in Psychological Science, 17,* 365–369.

Coie, J. D., & Cillessen, A. H. N. (1993). Peer rejection: Origins and effects on children's development. *Current Directions in Psychological Science, 2,* 89–92.

Coie, J. D., & Dodge, K. A. (1998). Aggression and antisocial behavior. In W. Damon (Series Ed.) & N. Eisenberg (Vol. Ed.), *Handbook of child psychology: Vol. 3. Social, emotional, and personality development* (5th ed., pp. 779–862). New York: Wiley.

Colby, A., & Kohlberg, L. (1984). Invariant sequence and internal consistency in moral judgment stages. In W. M. Kurtines & J. L. Gewirtz (Eds.), *Morality, moral behavior, and moral development* (pp. 41–51). New York: Wiley.

Colby, A., Kohlberg, L., Gibbs, J., & Lieberman, M. (1983). A longitudinal study of moral judgment. *Monographs of the Society for Research in Child Development, 48*(1–2, Serial No. 200).

Cole, D. A., Maxwell, S. E., Martin, J. M., Peeke, L. G., Seroczynski, A. D., Tram, J. M., et al. (2001). The development of multiple domains of child and adolescent self-concept: A cohort sequential longitudinal design. *Child Development, 72,* 1723–1746.

Cole, P. M., & Tan, P. Z. (2007). Emotion socialization from a cultural perspective. In J. E. Grusec & P. D. Hastings (Eds.), *Handbook of socialization: Theory and research* (pp. 516–542). New York: Guilford.

Collins, W. A., Maccoby, E. E., Steinberg, L., Hetherington, E. M., & Bornstein, M. H. (2000). Contemporary research on parenting: The case for nature and nurture. *American Psychologist, 55,* 218–232.

Connolly, J., & Goldberg, A. (1999). Romantic relationships in adolescence: The role of friends and peers in their emergence and development. In W. Furman, B. B. Brown, & C. Feiring (Eds.), *The development of romantic relationships in adolescence* (pp. 266–290). Cambridge, England: Cambridge University Press.

Connor, D. J., & Baglieri, S. (2009). Tipping the scales: Disabilities studies ask "How much diversity can you take?" In S. R. Steinberg (Ed.), *Diversity and multiculturalism: A reader* (pp. 341–361). New York: Peter Lang.

Cook, P. J., & Ludwig, J. (2008). The burden of "acting White": Do Black adolescents disparage academic achievement? In J. U. Ogbu (Ed.), *Minority status, oppositional culture, and schooling* (pp. 275–297). New York: Routledge.

Coplan, R. J., & Arbeau, K. A. (2009). Peer interactions and play in early childhood. In

K. H. Rubin, W. M. Bukowski, & B. Laursen (Eds.), *Handbook of peer interactions, relationships, and groups* (pp. 143–161). New York: Guilford.

Correa-Chávez, M., Rogoff, B., & Mejía Arauz, R. (2005). Cultural patterns in attending to two events at once. *Child Development, 76,* 664–678.

Crain, W. (2005). *Theories of development: Concepts and applications* (5th ed.). Upper Saddle River, NJ: Prentice Hall/Pearson.

Creasey, G. L., Jarvis, P. A., & Berk, L. E. (1998). Play and social competence. In O. N. Saracho & B. Spodek (Eds.), *Multiple perspectives on play in early childhood education* (pp. 116–143). Albany: State University of New York Press.

Crick, N. R., & Dodge, K. A. (1996). Social information-processing mechanisms in reactive and proactive aggression. *Child Development, 67,* 993–1002.

Crick, N. R., Grotpeter, J. K., & Bigbee, M. A. (2002). Relationally and physically aggressive children's intent attributions and feelings of distress for relational and instrumental peer provocation. *Child Development, 73,* 1134–1142.

Crick, N. R., Murray-Close, D., Marks, P. E. L., & Mohajeri-Nelson, N. (2009). Aggression and peer relationships in school-age children: Relational and physical aggression in group and dyadic contexts. In K. H. Rubin, W. M. Bukowski, & B. Laursen (Eds.), *Handbook of peer interactions, relationships, and groups* (pp. 287–302). New York: Guilford.

Crocker, J., & Knight, K. M. (2005). Contingencies of self-worth. *Current Directions in Psychological Science, 14,* 200–203.

Crockett, L., Losoff, M., & Peterson, A. C. (1984). Perceptions of the peer group and friendship in early adolescence. *Journal of Early Adolescence, 4,* 155–181.

Crosnoe, R. (2011). *Fitting in, standing out: Navigating the social challenge of high school to get an education.* Cambridge, England: Cambridge University Press.

Cross, W. E., Jr., Strauss, L., & Fhagen-Smith, P. (1999). African American identity development across the life span: Educational implications. In R. H. Sheets & E. R. Hollins (Eds.), *Racial and ethnic identity in school practices: Aspects of human development* (pp. 29–47). Mahwah, NJ: Erlbaum.

Crosson-Tower, C. (2010). *Understanding child abuse and neglect* (8th ed.). Boston: Allyn & Bacon.

Cunningham, C. E., & Cunningham, L. J. (2006). Student-mediated conflict resolution programs. In R. A. Barkley, *Attention-deficit hyperactivity disorder: A handbook for diagnosis and treatment* (3rd ed., pp. 590–607). New York: Guilford.

Damon, W. (1988). *The moral child: Nurturing children's natural moral growth.* New York: Free Press.

Damon, W., & Hart, D. (1988). *Self-understanding from childhood and adolescence.* New York: Cambridge University Press.

Davila, J. (2008). Depressive symptoms and adolescent romance: Theory, research, and implications. *Child Development Perspectives, 2*(1), 26–31.

Davis-Kean, P. E., Huesmann, R., Jager, J., Collins, W. A., Bates, J. E., & Lansford, J. E. (2008). Changes in the relation of self-efficacy beliefs and behaviors across development. *Child Development, 79,* 1257–1269.

Davis-Kean, P. E., & Sandler, H. M. (2001). A meta-analysis of measures of self-esteem for young children: A framework for future measures. *Child Development, 72,* 887–906.

Davison, M. (2011, April). *Are you standing in my shoes? How affective and cognitive teaching sequences influence historical empathy.* Paper presented at the annual meeting of the American Educational Research Association, New Orleans, LA.

Dawson, G., & Bernier, R. (2007). Development of social brain circuitry in autism. In D. Coch, G. Dawson, & K. W. Fischer (Eds.), *Human behavior, learning, and the developing brain: Atypical development* (pp. 28–55). New York: Guilford.

DeRidder, L. M. (1993). Teenage pregnancy: Etiology and educational interventions. *Educational Psychology Review, 5,* 87–107.

Deutsch, M. (1993). Educating for a peaceful world. *American Psychologist, 48,* 510–517.

DeVries, R., & Zan, B. (1996). A constructivist perspective on the role of the sociomoral atmosphere in promoting children's development. In C. T. Fosnot (Ed.), *Constructivism: Theory, perspectives, and practice* (pp. 103–119). New York: Teachers College Press.

DeYoung, C. G., Hirsh, J. B., Shane, M. S., Papademetris, X., Rajeevan, N., & Gray, J. R. (2010). Testing predictions from personality neuroscience: Brain structure and the Big Five. *Psychological Science, 21,* 820–828.

Dijkstra, P., Kuyper, H., van der Werf, G., Buunk, A. P., & van der Zee, Y. G. (2008). Social comparison in the classroom: A review. *Review of Educational Research, 78,* 828–879.

Dilg, M. (2010). *Our worlds in our words: Exploring race, class, gender, and sexual orientation in multicultural classrooms.* New York: Teachers College Press.

Dishion, T. J., Piehler, T. F., & Myers, M. W. (2008). Dynamics and ecology of adolescent peer influence. In M. J. Prinstein & K. A. Dodge (Eds.), *Understanding peer influence in children and adolescents* (pp. 72–93). New York: Guilford.

Dodge, K. A., Lansford, J. E., Burks, V.·S., Bates, J. E., Pettit, G. S., Fontaine, R., et al. (2003). Peer rejection and social information-processing factors in the development of aggressive behavior problems in children. *Child Development, 74,* 374–393.

Dodge, K. A., Malone, P. S., Lansford, J. E., Miller, S., Pettit, G. S., & Bates, J. E. (2009). A dynamic cascade model of the development of substance-use onset. *Monographs of the Society for Research in Child Development, 74*(3, Serial No. 294), 1–119.

Doll, B., Song, S., & Siemers, E. (2004). Classroom ecologies that support or discourage bullying. In D. L. Espelage & S. M. Swearer (Eds.), *Bullying in American schools: A social-ecological perspective on prevention and intervention* (pp. 161–183). Mahwah, NJ: Erlbaum.

Donaldson, S. K., & Westerman, M. A. (1986). Development of children's understanding of ambivalence and causal theories of emotion. *Developmental Psychology, 22,* 655–662.

Dowson, M., & McInerney, D. M. (2001). Psychological parameters of students' social and work avoidance goals: A qualitative investigation. *Journal of Educational Psychology, 93,* 35–42.

DuBois, D. L., Burk-Braxton, C., Swenson, L. P., Tevendale, H. D., & Hardesty, J. L. (2002). Race and gender influences on adjustment in early adolescence: Investigation of an integrative model. *Child Development, 73,* 1573–1592.

Dubow, E. F., Huesmann, L. R., & Greenwood, D. (2007). Media and youth socialization: Underlying processes and moderators of effects. In J. E. Grusec & P. D. Hastings (Eds.), *Handbook of socialization: Theory and research* (pp. 404–430). New York: Guilford.

Dunning, D., Heath, C., & Suls, J. M. (2004). Flawed self-assessment: Implications for health, education, and the workplace. *Psychological Science in the Public Interest, 5,* 69–106.

Dweck, C. S. (2000). *Self-theories: Their role in motivation, personality, and development.* Philadelphia: Psychology Press.

Eccles, J. S. (2007). Families, schools, and developing achievement-related motivations and engagement. In J. E. Grusec & P. D. Hastings (Eds.), *Handbook of socialization: Theory and research* (pp. 665–691). New York: Guilford.

Eccles, J. (2009). Who am I and what am I going to do with my life? Personal and collective identities as motivators of action. *Educational Psychologist, 44,* 78–89.

Eckert, P. (1989). *Jocks and burnouts: Social categories and identity in the high school.* New York: Teachers College Press.

Eisenberg, N. (1982). The development of reasoning regarding prosocial behavior. In N. Eisenberg (Ed.), *The development of prosocial behavior* (pp. 219–249). San Diego, CA: Academic Press.

Eisenberg, N. (1995). Prosocial development: A multifaceted model. In W. M. Kurtines & J. L. Gewirtz (Eds.), *Moral development: An introduction* (pp. 401–429). Boston: Allyn & Bacon.

Eisenberg, N., Carlo, G., Murphy, B., & Van Court, N. (1995). Prosocial development in late adolescence: A longitudinal study. *Child Development, 66,* 1179–1197.

Eisenberg, N., & Fabes, R. A. (1998). Prosocial development. In W. Damon (Series Ed.) & N. Eisenberg (Vol. Ed.), *Handbook of child psychology: Vol. 3. Social, emotional, and personality development* (5th ed., pp. 701–778). New York: Wiley.

Eisenberg, N., Lennon, R., & Pasternack, J. F. (1986). Altruistic values and moral judgment. In N. Eisenberg (Ed.), *Altruistic emotion, cognition, and behavior.* Mahwah, NJ: Erlbaum.

Eisenberg, N., Martin, C. L., & Fabes, R. A. (1996). Gender development and gender effects. In D. C. Berliner & R. C. Calfee (Eds.), *Handbook*

*of educational psychology* (pp. 358–396). New York: Macmillan.

Eisenberg, N., Spinrad, T. L., & Sadovsky, A. (2006). Empathy-related responding in children. In M. Killen & J. Smetana (Eds.), *Handbook of moral development* (pp. 517–549). Mahwah, NJ: Erlbaum.

Eisenberg, N., Zhou, Q., & Koller, S. (2001). Brazilian adolescents' prosocial moral judgment and behavior: Relations to sympathy, perspective taking, gender-role orientation, and demographic characteristics. *Child Development, 72,* 518–534.

Elkind, D. (1981). *Children and adolescents: Interpretive essays on Jean Piaget* (3rd ed.). New York: Oxford University Press.

Ellenwood, S., & Ryan, K. (1991). Literature and morality: An experimental curriculum. In W. M. Kurtines & J. L. Gewirtz (Eds.), *Moral behavior and development: Vol. 3. Application.* Mahwah, NJ: Erlbaum.

Ellis, W. E., & Zarbatany, L. (2007). Peer group status as a moderator of group influence on children's deviant, aggressive, and prosocial behavior. *Child Development, 78,* 1240–1254.

Ellison, N. B., Steinfield, C., & Lampe, C. (2007). The benefits of *Facebook* "friends": Social capital and college students' use of online social network sites. *Journal of Computer-Mediated Communication, 12,* 1143–1168.

Epstein, J. S. (1998). Introduction: Generation X, youth culture, and identity. In J. S. Epstein (Ed.), *Youth culture: Identity in a postmodern world* (pp. 1–23). Malden, MA: Blackwell.

Erikson, E. H. (1963). *Childhood and society* (2nd ed.). New York: Norton.

Erikson, E. H. (1972). Eight ages of man. In C. S. Lavatelli & F. Stendler (Eds.), *Readings in child behavior and child development.* San Diego, CA: Harcourt Brace Jovanovich.

Erwin, P. (1993). *Friendship and peer relations in children.* Chichester, England: Wiley.

Espelage, D. L., Aragon, S. R., Birkett, M., & Koenig, B. W. (2008). Homophobic teasing, psychological outcomes, and sexual orientation among high school students: What influence do parents and schools have? *School Psychology Review, 37,* 202–216.

Espelage, D. L., & Swearer, S. W. (Eds.). (2004). *Bullying in American schools: A social-ecological perspective on prevention and intervention.* Mahwah, NJ: Erlbaum.

Farver, J. A. M., & Branstetter, W. H. (1994). Preschoolers' prosocial responses to their peers' distress. *Developmental Psychology, 30,* 334–341.

Feddes, A. R., Noack, P., & Rutland, A. (2009). Direct and extended friendship effects on minority and majority children's interethnic attitudes: A longitudinal study. *Child Development, 80,* 377–390.

Feldman, A. F., & Matjasko, J. L. (2005). The role of school-based extracurricular activities in adolescent development: A comprehensive review and future directions. *Review of Educational Research, 75,* 159–210.

Figner, B., & Weber, E. U. (2011). Who takes risks when and why? Determinants of risk taking.

*Current Directions in Psychological Science, 20,* 211–216.

Flanagan, C. A., & Faison, N. (2001). Youth civic development: Implications of research for social policy and programs. *Social Policy Report of the Society for Research in Child Development, 15*(1), 1–14.

Flanagan, C. A., & Tucker, C. J. (1999). Adolescents' explanations for political issues: Concordance with their views of self and society. *Developmental Psychology, 35,* 1198–1209.

Flavell, J. H. (2000). Development of children's knowledge about the mental world. *International Journal of Behavioral Development, 24*(1), 15–23.

Flavell, J. H., & Miller, P. H. (1998). Social cognition. In W. Damon (Series Ed.), D. Kuhn, & R. S. Siegler (Vol. Eds.), *Handbook of child psychology: Vol. 2. Cognition, perception, and language* (5th ed., pp. 851–898). New York: Wiley.

Flavell, J. H., Miller, P. H., & Miller, S. A. (2002). *Cognitive development* (4th ed.). Upper Saddle River, NJ: Prentice-Hall.

Fontaine, R. G., Yang, C., Dodge, K. A., Bates, J. E., & Pettit, G. S. (2008). Testing an individual systems model of response evaluation and decision (RED) and antisocial behavior across adolescence. *Child Development, 79,* 462–475.

Fox, N. A., Henderson, H. A., Rubin, K. H., Calkins, S. D., & Schmidt, L. A. (2001). Continuity and discontinuity of behavioral inhibition and exuberance: Psychophysical and behavioral influences across the first four years of life. *Child Development, 72,* 1–21.

Freedman, S. G. (1990). *Small victories: The real world of a teacher, her students, and their high school.* New York: Harper & Row.

The Freedom Writers (with Gruwell, E.). (1999). *The Freedom Writers diary: How a teacher and 150 teens used writing to change themselves and the world around them.* New York: Broadway Books.

Frey, K. S., Hirschstein, M. K., Edstrom, L. V., & Snell, J. L. (2009). Observed reductions in school bullying, nonbullying aggression, and destructive bystander behavior: A longitudinal evaluation. *Journal of Educational Psychology, 101,* 466–481.

Furman, W., Brown, B. B., & Feiring, C. (Eds.). (1999). *The development of romantic relationships in adolescence.* Cambridge, England: Cambridge University Press.

Furman, W., & Collins, W. A. (2009). Adolescent romantic relationships and experiences. In K. H. Rubin, W. M. Bukowski, & B. Laursen (Eds.), *Handbook of peer interactions, relationships, and groups* (pp. 341–360). New York: Guilford.

Furman, W., & Simon, V. A. (2008). Homophily in adolescent romantic relationships. In M. J. Prinstein & K. A. Dodge (Eds.), *Understanding peer influence in children and adolescents* (pp. 203–224). New York: Guilford.

Galambos, N. L., Barker, E. T., & Almeida, D. M. (2003). Parents *do* matter: Trajectories of change in externalizing and internalizing problems in early adolescence. *Child Development, 74,* 578–594.

Gallese, V., Gernsbacher, M. A., Heyes, C., Hickok, G., & Iacoboni, M. (2011). Mirror neuron forum. *Perspectives on Psychological Science, 6,* 369–407.

Gardiner, H. W., & Kosmitzki, C. (2008). *Lives across cultures: Cross-cultural human development* (4th ed.). Boston: Allyn & Bacon.

Gavin, L. A., & Fuhrman, W. (1989). Age differences in adolescents' perceptions of their peer groups. *Developmental Psychology, 25,* 827–834.

Gazelle, H., & Ladd, G. W. (2003). Anxious solitude and peer exclusion: A diathesis-stress model of internalizing trajectories in childhood. *Child Development, 74,* 257–278.

Gehlbach, H., Brinkworth, M. E., & Harris, A. D. (2011, April). *The promise of social perspective taking to facilitate teacher-student relationships.* Paper presented at the annual meeting of the American Educational Research Association, New Orleans, LA.

Gehlbach, H., Brown, S. W., Ioannou, A., Boyer, M. A., Hudson, N., Niv-Solomon, A., et al. (2008). Increasing interest in social studies: Social perspective taking and self-efficacy in stimulating stimulations. *Contemporary Educational Psychology, 33,* 894–914.

Gentile, D. A., Anderson, C. A., Yukawa, S., Ihori, N., Saleem, M., Ming, L. K., et al. (2009). The effects of prosocial video games on prosocial behaviors: International evidence from correlational, longitudinal, and experimental studies. *Personality and Social Psychology Bulletin, 35,* 1395–1409.

Gest, S. D., Domitrovich, C. E., & Welsh, J. A. (2005). Peer academic reputation in elementary school: Associations with changes in self-concept and academic skills. *Journal of Educational Psychology, 97,* 337–346.

Gianotti, L. R. R., Knoch, D., Faber, P. L., Lehmann, D., Pascual-Marqui, R. D., Diezi, C., et al. (2009). Tonic activity level in the right prefrontal cortex predicts individuals' risk taking. *Psychological Science, 20,* 33–38.

Gibbs, J. C. (1995). The cognitive developmental perspective. In W. M. Kurtines & J. L. Gewirtz (Eds.), *Moral development: An introduction* (pp. 27–48). Boston: Allyn & Bacon.

Gilligan, C. F. (1982). *In a different voice.* Cambridge, MA: Harvard University Press.

Gilligan, C. F. (1985, March). Keynote address. Conference on Women and Moral Theory, Stony Brook, NY.

Gilligan, C. F. (1987). Moral orientation and moral development. In E. F. Kittay & D. T. Meyers (Eds.), *Women and moral theory* (pp. 19–33). Totowa, NJ: Rowman & Littlefield.

Gilligan, C., & Attanucci, J. (1988). Two moral orientations: Gender differences and similarities. *Merrill-Palmer Quarterly, 34,* 223–237.

Gnepp, J. (1989). Children's use of personal information to understand other people's feelings. In C. Saarni & P. L. Harris (Eds.), *Children's understanding of emotion* (pp. 151–180). Cambridge, England: Cambridge University Press.

Goodnow, J. J. (1992). *Parental belief systems: The psychological consequences for children.* Mahwah, NJ: Erlbaum.

Goodwin, M. H. (2006). *The hidden life of girls: Games of stance, status, and exclusion.* Malden, MA: Blackwell.

Gopnik, A., & Meltzoff, A. N. (1997). *Words, thoughts, and theories.* Cambridge, MA: MIT Press.

Gottman, J. M. (1986). The world of coordinated play: Same- and cross-sex friendship in young children. In J. M. Gottman & J. G. Parker (Eds.), *Conversations of friends: Speculations on affective development* (pp. 139–191). Cambridge, England: Cambridge University Press.

Gray, M. R., & Steinberg, L. (1999). Unpacking authoritative parenting: Reassessing a multidimensional concept. *Journal of Marriage and the Family, 61,* 574–587.

Greene, J. D., Sommerville, R. B., Nystrom, L. E., Darley, J. M., & Cohen, J. D. (2001). An fMRI investigation of emotional engagement in moral judgment. *Science, 293*(5537), 2105–2108.

Greenhow, C., Robelia, B., & Hughes, J. E. (2009). Web 2.0 and classroom research: What path should we take now? *Educational Researcher, 38,* 246–259.

Greeno, J. G. (2006). Learning in activity. In R. K. Sawyer (Ed.), *The Cambridge handbook of the learning sciences* (pp. 79–96). Cambridge, England: Cambridge University Press.

Greenspan, S., & Granfield, J. M. (1992). Reconsidering the construct of mental retardation: Implications of a model of social competence. *American Journal of Mental Retardation, 96,* 442–453.

Greitemeyer, T. (2011). Effects of prosocial media on social behavior: When and why does media exposure affect helping and aggression? *Current Directions in Psychological Science, 20,* 251–255.

Grimes, N. (2002). *Bronx masquerade.* New York: Penguin.

Gross, E. F., Juvonen, J., & Gable, S. L. (2002). Internet use and well-being in adolescence. *Journal of Social Issues, 58,* 75–90.

Guay, F., Boivin, M., & Hodges, E. V. E. (1999). Social comparison processes and academic achievement: The dependence of the development of self-evaluations on friends' performance. *Journal of Educational Psychology, 91,* 564–568.

Guerra, N. G., Huesmann, L. R., & Spindler, A. (2003). Community violence exposure, social cognition, and aggression among urban elementary school children. *Child Development, 74,* 1561–1576.

Guerra, N. G., & Slaby, R. G. (1990). Cognitive mediators of aggression in adolescent offenders: 2. Intervention. *Developmental Psychology, 26,* 269–277.

Gummerum, M., Keller, M., Takezawa, M., & Mata, J. (2008). To give or not to give: Children's and adolescents' sharing and moral negotiations in economic decision situations. *Child Development, 79,* 562–576.

Guthrie, P. (2001). "Catching sense" and the meaning of belonging on a South Carolina sea island. In S. S. Walker (Ed.), *African roots/American cultures: Africa in the creation of the Americas* (pp. 275–283). Lanham, MD: Rowman & Littlefield.

Gutiérrez, K. D., & Rogoff, B. (2003). Cultural ways of learning: Individual traits or repertoires of practice. *Educational Researcher, 32*(5), 19–25.

Hale-Benson, J. E. (1986). *Black children: Their roots, culture, and learning styles.* Baltimore: Johns Hopkins University Press.

Halgunseth, L. C., Ispa, J. M., & Rudy, D. (2006). Parental control in Latino families: An integrated review of the literature. *Child Development, 77,* 1282–1297.

Hamlin, J. K., & Wynn, K. (2011). Young infants prefer prosocial to antisocial others. *Cognitive Development, 26,* 30–39.

Hamovitch, B. (2007). Hoping for the best: "Inclusion" and stigmatization in a middle school. In S. Books (Ed.), *Invisible children in the society and its schools* (3rd ed., pp. 263–281). Mahwah, NJ: Erlbaum.

Hampson, S. E. (2008). Mechanisms by which childhood personality traits influence adult well-being. *Current Directions in Psychological Science, 17,* 264–268.

Hanish, L. D., Kochenderfer-Ladd, B., Fabes, R. A., Martin, C. L., & Denning, D. (2004). Bullying among young children: The influence of peers and teachers. In D. L. Espelage & S. M. Swearer (Eds.), *Bullying in American schools: A social-ecological perspective on prevention and intervention* (pp. 141–159). Mahwah, NJ: Erlbaum.

Harris, J. R. (1998). *The nurture assumption: Why children turn out the way they do.* New York: Free Press.

Harris, M. J., & Rosenthal, R. (1985). Mediation of interpersonal expectancy effects: 31 meta-analyses. *Psychological Bulletin, 97,* 363–386.

Harris, P. L. (2006). Social cognition. In W. Damon & R. M. Lerner (Series Eds.), D. Kuhn, & R. Siegler (Vol. Eds.), *Handbook of child psychology: Vol. 2. Cognition, perception, and language* (6th ed., pp. 811–858). New York: Wiley.

Hart, D. (1988). The adolescent self-concept in social context. In D. K. Lapsley & F. C. Power (Eds.), *Self, ego, and identity: Integrative approaches* (pp. 71–90). New York: Springer-Verlag.

Hart, D., Atkins, R., & Fegley, S. (2003). Personality and development in childhood: A person-centered approach. *Monographs of the Society for Research in Child Development, 68*(1, Serial No. 272).

Hart, D., & Fegley, S. (1995). Prosocial behavior and caring in adolescence: Relations to self-understanding and social judgment. *Child Development, 66,* 1346–1359.

Harter, S. (1983). Children's understanding of multiple emotions: A cognitive-developmental approach. In W. F. Overton (Ed.), *The relationship between social and cognitive development* (pp. 147–194). Mahwah, NJ: Erlbaum.

Harter, S. (1999). *The construction of the self: A developmental perspective.* New York: Guilford.

Harter, S., & Whitesell, N. R. (1989). Developmental changes in children's understanding of single, multiple, and blended emotion concepts. In C. Saarni & P. Harris (Eds.), *Children's understanding of emotion* (pp. 81–116). Cambridge, England: Cambridge University Press.

Harter, S., Whitesell, N. R., & Junkin, L. J. (1998). Similarities and differences in domain-specific and global self-evaluations of learning-disabled, behaviorally disordered, and normally achieving adolescents. *American Educational Research Journal, 35,* 653–680.

Harwood, R. L., Miller, J. G., & Irizarry, N. L. (1995). *Culture and attachment: Perceptions of the child in context.* New York: Guilford.

Hastings, P. D., Utendale, W. T., & Sullivan, C. (2007). The socialization of prosocial development. In J. E. Grusec & P. D. Hastings (Eds.), *Handbook of socialization: Theory and research* (pp. 638–664). New York: Guilford.

Hattie, J. A. C. (2009). *Visible learning: A synthesis of over 800 meta-analyses relating to achievement.* London: Routledge.

Hearold, S. (1986). A synthesis of 1,043 effects of television on social behavior. In G. Comstock (Ed.), *Public communication and behavior* (Vol. 1, pp. 65–133). New York: Academic Press.

Helwig, C. C., & Jasiobedzka, U. (2001). The relation between law and morality: Children's reasoning about socially beneficial and unjust laws. *Child Development, 72,* 1382–1393.

Helwig, C. C., Zelazo, P. D., & Wilson, M. (2001). Children's judgments of psychological harm in normal and noncanonical situations. *Child Development, 72,* 66–81.

Hemmings, A. B. (2004). *Coming of age in U.S. high schools: Economic, kinship, religious, and political crosscurrents.* Mahwah, NJ: Erlbaum.

Herbert, J., & Stipek, D. (2005). The emergence of gender differences in children's perceptions of their academic competence. *Journal of Applied Developmental Psychology, 26,* 276–295.

Hewitt, J., & Scardamalia, M. (1998). Design principles for distributed knowledge building processes. *Educational Psychology Review, 10,* 75–96.

Higgins, A. (1995). Educating for justice and community: Lawrence Kohlberg's vision of moral education. In W. M. Kurtines & J. L. Gewirtz (Eds.), *Moral development: An introduction* (pp. 49–81). Boston: Allyn & Bacon.

Hill, P. L., & Roberts, B. W. (2010). Propositions for the study of moral personality development. *Current Directions in Psychological Science, 19,* 380–383.

Hitlin, S., Brown, J. S., & Elder, G. H., Jr. (2006). Racial self-categorization in adolescence: Multiracial development and social pathways. *Child Development, 77,* 1298–1308.

Hobson, P. (2004). *The cradle of thought: Exploring the origins of thinking.* Oxford, England: Oxford University Press.

Hodson, G. (2011). Do ideologically intolerant people benefit from intergroup contact? *Current Directions in Psychological Science, 20,* 154–159.

Hoffman, M. L. (1975). Altruistic behavior and the parent-child relationship. *Journal of Personality and Social Psychology, 31,* 937–943.

Hoffman, M. L. (2000). *Empathy and moral development: Implications for caring and justice.* New York: Cambridge University Press.

Hoglund, W. L. G. (2007). School functioning in early adolescence: Gender-linked responses to peer victimization. *Journal of Educational Psychology, 99,* 683–699.

Hong, Y.-Y., Wan, C., No, S., & Chiu, C.-Y. (2007). Multicultural identities. In S. Kitayama & D. Cohen (Eds.), *Handbook of cultural psychology* (pp. 323–345). New York: Guilford.

Honz, K., Kiewra, K. A., & Yang, Y.-S. (2010). Cheating perceptions and prevalence across academic settings. *Mid-Western Educational Researcher, 23,* 10–17.

Horne, A. M., Orpinas, P., Newman-Carlson, D., & Bartolomucci, C. L. (2004). Elementary school Bully Busters Program: Understanding why children bully and what to do about it. In D. L. Espelage & S. M. Swearer (Eds.), *Bullying in American schools: A social-ecological perspective on prevention and intervention* (pp. 297–325). Mahwah, NJ: Erlbaum.

Hudley, C., & Graham, S. (1993). An attributional intervention to reduce peer-directed aggression among African American boys. *Child Development, 64,* 124–138.

Huesmann, L. R., Moise-Titus, J., Podolski, C., & Eron, L. (2003). Longitudinal relations between children's exposure to TV violence and their aggressive and violent behavior in young adulthood: 1977–1992. *Developmental Psychology, 39,* 201–221.

Huntsinger, C. S., & Jose, P. E. (2006). A longitudinal investigation of personality and social adjustment among Chinese American and European American adolescents. *Child Development, 77,* 1309–1324.

Igoa, C. (2007). Immigrant children: Art as a second language. In S. Books (Ed.), *Invisible children in the society and its schools* (3rd ed., pp. 117–140). Mahwah, NJ: Erlbaum.

Izard, C., Fine, S., Schultz, D., Mostow, A., Ackerman, B., & Youngstrom, E. (2001). Emotion knowledge as a predictor of social behavior and academic competence in children at risk. *Psychological Science, 12,* 18–23.

Jacobs, J. E., & Klaczynski, P. A. (2002). The development of judgment and decision making during childhood and adolescence. *Current Directions in Psychological Science, 11,* 145–149.

Joët, G., Usher, E., & Bressoux, P. (2011). Sources of self-efficacy: An investigation of elementary school students in France. *Journal of Educational Psychology, 103,* 649–663.

Johnson, D. W., & Johnson, R. T. (1996). Conflict resolution and peer mediation programs in elementary and secondary schools: A review of the research. *Review of Educational Research, 66,* 459–506.

Johnson, D. W., & Johnson, R. T. (2006). Conflict resolution, peer mediation, and peacemaking. In C. M. Evertson & C. S. Weinstein (Eds.), *Handbook of classroom management: Research, practice, and contemporary issues* (pp. 803–832). Mahwah, NJ: Erlbaum.

Jordan, J. V. (2006). Relational resilience in girls. In S. Goldstein & R. B. Brooks (Eds.), *Handbook of resilience in children* (pp. 79–90). New York: Springer.

Joseph, J. E., Liu, X., Jiang, Y., Lynam, D., & Kelly, T. H. (2009). Neural correlates of emotional reactivity in sensation seeking. *Psychological Science, 20,* 215–223.

Joshi, M. S., & MacLean, M. (1994). Indian and English children's understanding of the distinction between real and apparent emotion. *Child Development, 65,* 1372–1384.

Josselson, R. (1988). The embedded self: I and Thou revisited. In D. K. Lapsley & F. C. Power (Eds.), *Self, ego, and identity: Integrative approaches* (pp. 91–106). New York: Springer-Verlag.

Joussemet, M., Vitaro, F., Barker, E. D., Côté, S., Nagin, D. S., Zoccolillo, M., et al. (2008). Controlling parenting and physical aggression during elementary school. *Child Development, 79,* 411–425.

Juvonen, J. (2006). Sense of belonging, social bonds, and school functioning. In P. A. Alexander & P. H. Winne (Eds.), *Handbook of educational psychology* (2nd ed., pp. 655–674). Mahwah, NJ: Erlbaum.

Juvonen, J., & Cadigan, R. J. (2002). Social determinants of public behavior of middle school youth: Perceived peer norms and need to be accepted. In F. Pajares & T. Urdan (Eds.), *Adolescence and education, Vol. 2: Academic motivation of adolescents* (pp. 277–297). Greenwich, CT: Information Age.

Juvonen, J., & Galván, A. (2008). Peer influence in involuntary social groups. In M. J. Prinstein & K. A. Dodge (Eds.), *Understanding peer influence in children and adolescents* (pp. 225–244). New York: Guilford.

Juvonen, J., & Weiner, B. (1993). An attributional analysis of students' interactions: The social consequences of perceived responsibility. *Educational Psychology Review, 5,* 325–345.

Kağıtçıbaşi, Ç. (2007). *Family, self, and human development across cultures: Theory and applications* (2nd ed.). Mahwah, NJ: Erlbaum.

Kahne, J. E., & Sporte, S. E. (2008). Developing citizens: The impact of civic learning opportunities on students' commitment to civic participation. *American Educational Research Journal, 45,* 738–766.

Kaplan, A., & Flum, H. (2009). Motivation and identity: The relations of action and development in educational contexts—An introduction to the special issue. *Educational Psychologist, 44,* 73–77.

Keogh, B. K. (2003). *Temperament in the classroom.* Baltimore: Brookes.

Killen, M., & Smetana, J. (2008). Moral judgment and moral neuroscience: Intersections, definitions, and issues. *Child Development Perspectives, 2*(1), 1–6.

Kim, J., & Cicchetti, D. (2006). Longitudinal trajectories of self-system processes and depressive symptoms among maltreated and nonmaltreated children. *Child Development, 77,* 624–639.

Kindermann, T. A. (2007). Effects of naturally existing peer groups on changes in academic engagement in a cohort of sixth graders. *Child Development, 78,* 1186–1203.

Kindermann, T. A., McCollam, T., & Gibson, E. (1996). Peer networks and students' classroom engagement during childhood and adolescence.

In J. Juvonen & K. Wentzel (Eds.), *Social motivation: Understanding children's school adjustment* (pp. 279–312). Cambridge, England: Cambridge University Press.

Kochanska, G., Aksan, N., Knaack, A., & Rhines, H. M. (2004). Maternal parenting and children's conscience: Early security as moderator. *Child Development, 75,* 1229–1242.

Kochanska, G., Gross, J. N., Lin, M.-H., & Nichols, K. E. (2002). Guilt in young children: Development, determinants, and relations with a broader system of standards. *Child Development, 73,* 461–482.

Kochanska, G., Tjebkes, T. L., & Forman, D. R. (1998). Children's emerging regulation of conduct: Restraint, compliance, and internalization from infancy to the second year. *Child Development, 69,* 1378–1389.

Kodluboy, D. W. (2004). Gang-oriented interventions. In J. C. Conoley & A. P. Goldstein (Eds.), *School violence intervention* (2nd ed., pp. 194–232). New York: Guilford.

Kohlberg, L. (1976). Moral stages and moralization: The cognitive-developmental approach. In T. Lickona (Ed.), *Moral development and behavior: Theory, research, and social issues* (pp. 219–240). New York: Holt, Rinehart & Winston.

Kohlberg, L. (1984). *The psychology of moral development: The nature and validity of moral stages.* San Francisco: Harper & Row.

Kohlberg, L. (1986). A current statement on some theoretical issues. In S. Modgil & C. Modgil (Eds.), *Lawrence Kohlberg: Consensus and controversy* (pp. 485–546). Philadelphia: Falmer.

Kohlberg, L., & Kramer, R. (1969). Continuities and discontinuities in childhood and adult moral development. *Human Development, 12,* 93–120.

Köller, O., Zeinz, H., & Trautwein, U. (2008). Class-average achievement, marks, and academic self-concept in German primary schools. In H. W. Marsh, R. G. Craven, & D. M. McInerney (Eds.), *Self-processes, learning, and enabling human potential* (pp. 331–352). Charlotte, NC: Information Age.

Kowalski, R. M., & Limber, S. P. (2007). Electronic bullying among middle school students. *Journal of Adolescent Health, 41,* S22–S30.

Krebs, D. L. (2008). Morality: An evolutionary account. *Perspectives on Psychological Science, 3,* 149–172.

Krebs, D. L., & Van Hesteren, F. (1994). The development of altruism: Toward an integrative model. *Developmental Review, 14,* 103–158.

Kurtines, W. M., Berman, S. L., Ittel, A., & Williamson, S. (1995). Moral development: A co-constructivist perspective. In W. M. Kurtines & J. L. Gewirtz (Eds.), *Moral development: An introduction* (pp. 337–376). Boston: Allyn & Bacon.

Ladd, G. W., Herald-Brown, S. L., & Reiser, M. (2008). Does chronic classroom peer rejection predict the development of children's classroom participation during the grade school years? *Child Development, 79,* 1001–1015.

Ladd, G. W., & Troop-Gordon, W. (2003). The role of chronic peer difficulties in the development of children's psychological adjustment problems. *Child Development, 74,* 1344–1367.

LaFontana, K. M., & Cillessen, A. H. N. (2010). Developmental changes in the priority of perceived status in childhood and adolescence. *Social Development, 19,* 130–147.

Lamborn, S. D., Mounts, N. S., Steinberg, L., & Dornbusch, S. M. (1991). Patterns of competence and adjustment among adolescents from authoritative, authoritarian, indulgent, and neglectful families. *Child Development, 62,* 1049–1065.

Lapsley, D. K. (1993). Toward an integrated theory of adolescent ego development: The "new look" at adolescent egocentrism. *American Journal of Orthopsychiatry, 63,* 562–571.

Larson, R. W., & Brown, J. R. (2007). Emotional development in adolescence: What can be learned from a high school theater program? *Child Development, 78,* 1083–1099.

Larson, R. W., Clore, G. L., & Wood, G. A. (1999). The emotions of romantic relationships: Do they wreak havoc on adolescents? In W. Furman, B. B. Brown, & C. Feiring (Eds.), *The development of romantic relationships in adolescence* (pp. 19–49). Cambridge, England: Cambridge University Press.

Laupa, M., & Turiel, E. (1995). Social domain theory. In W. M. Kurtines & J. L. Gewirtz (Eds.), *Moral development: An introduction.* Boston: Allyn & Bacon.

Laursen, B., Bukowski, W. M., Aunola, K., & Nurmi, J.-E. (2007). Friendship moderates prospective associations between social isolation and adjustment problems in young children. *Child Development, 78,* 1395–1404.

Leary, M. R. (1999). Making sense of self-esteem. *Current Directions in Psychological Science, 8,* 32–35.

Leffert, J. S., Siperstein, G. N., & Millikan, E. (2000). Understanding social adaptation in children with mental retardation: A social-cognitive perspective. *Exceptional Children, 66,* 530–545.

Lenski, A., Husemann, N., Trautwein, U., & Lüdtke, O. (2010, April–May). *Academic cheating: A multidimensional point of view.* Paper presented at the annual meeting of the American Educational Research Association, Denver.

Levitt, M. J., Guacci-Franco, N., & Levitt, J. L. (1993). Convoys of social support in childhood and early adolescence: Structure and function. *Developmental Psychology, 29,* 811–818.

Lewis, M., & Sullivan, M. W. (2005). The development of self-conscious emotions. In A. J. Elliot & C. S. Dweck (Eds.), *Handbook of competence and motivation* (pp. 185–201). New York: Guilford.

Li, Y., Anderson, R. C., Nguyen-Jahiel, K., Dong, T., Archodidou, A., Kim, I.-H., et al. (2007). Emergent leadership in children's discussion groups. *Cognition and Instruction, 25,* 75–111.

Lind, G. (1994, April). *Why do juvenile delinquents gain little from moral discussion programs?* Paper presented at the annual meeting of the American Educational Research Association, New Orleans, LA.

Lippa, R. A. (2002). *Gender, nature, and nurture.* Mahwah, NJ: Erlbaum.

Liu, D., Sabbagh, M. A., Gehring, W. J., & Wellman, H. M. (2009). Neural correlates of children's theory of mind development. *Child Development, 80,* 318–326.

Lockhart, K. L., Chang, B., & Story, T. (2002). Young children's beliefs about the stability of traits: Protective optimism? *Child Development, 73,* 1408–1430.

Maccoby, E. E. (2002). Gender and group process: A developmental perspective. *Current Directions in Psychological Science, 11,* 54–58.

Mac Iver, D. J., Reuman, D. A., & Main, S. R. (1995). Social structuring of the school: Studying what is, illuminating what could be. In J. T. Spence, J. M. Darley, & D. J. Foss (Eds.), *Annual review of psychology* (Vol. 46, pp. 375–400). Palo Alto, CA: Annual Review.

Mahoney, J. L., Cairns, B. D., & Farmer, T. W. (2003). Promoting interpersonal competence and educational success through extracurricular activity participation. *Journal of Educational Psychology, 95,* 409–418.

Maikovich, A. K., Jaffee, S. R., Odgers, C. L., & Gallop, R. (2008). Effects of family violence on psychopathology symptoms in children previously exposed to maltreatment. *Child Development, 79,* 1498–1512.

Malti, T., Gummerum, M., Keller, M., & Buchman, M. (2009). Children's moral motivation, sympathy, and prosocial behavior. *Child Development, 80,* 442–460.

Manning, M. L., & Baruth, L. G. (2009). *Multicultural education of children and adolescents* (5th ed.). Boston: Allyn & Bacon/ Pearson.

Marcia, J. E. (1980). Identity in adolescence. In J. Adelson (Ed.), *Handbook of adolescent psychology* (pp. 159–187). New York: Wiley.

Marcia, J. E. (1988). Common processes underlying ego identity, cognitive/moral development, and individuation. In D. K. Lapsley & F. C. Power (Eds.), *Self, ego, and identity: Integrative approaches* (pp. 211–225). New York: Springer-Verlag.

Marcia, J. E. (1991). Identity and self-development. In R. M. Lerner, A. C. Petersen, & J. Brooks-Gunn (Eds.), *Encyclopedia of adolescence* (Vol. 1, pp. 529–533). New York: Garland.

Marcus, R. F. (1980). Empathy and popularity of preschool children. *Child Study Journal, 10,* 133–145.

Margolin, G., & Gordis, E. B. (2004). Children's exposure to violence in the family and community. *Current Directions in Psychological Science, 13,* 152–155.

Markus, H. R., & Kitayama, S. (1991). Culture and the self: Implications for cognition, emotion, and motivation. *Psychological Review, 98,* 224–253.

Marsh, H. W., & Craven, R. (1997). Academic self-concept: Beyond the dustbowl. In G. D. Phye (Ed.), *Handbook of classroom assessment: Learning, achievement, and adjustment* (pp. 131–198). San Diego, CA: Academic Press.

Marsh, H. W., Gerlach, E., Trautwein, U., Lüdtke, O., & Brettschneider, W.-D. (2007). Longitudinal study of preadolescent sport self-concept and performance reciprocal effects and causal ordering. *Child Development, 78,* 1640–1656.

Marsh, H. W., & O'Mara, A. J. (2008). Self-concept is as multidisciplinary as it is multidimensional: A review of theory, measurement, and practice in self-concept research. In H. W. Marsh, R. G. Craven, & D. M. McInerney (Eds.), *Self-processes, learning, and enabling human potential* (pp. 87–115). Charlotte, NC: Information Age.

Martin, A. J., & Dowson, M. (2009). Interpersonal relationships, motivation, engagement, and achievement: Yields for theory, current issues, and educational practice. *Review of Educational Research, 79,* 327–365.

Martinez, R. S., & Huberty, T. J. (2010). Anxiety in students with learning difficulties and learning disabilities. In J. C. Cassady (Ed.), *Anxiety in schools: The causes, consequences, and solutions for academic anxieties* (pp. 137–152). New York: Peter Lang.

Matthews, G., Zeidner, M., & Roberts, R. D. (2006). Models of personality and affect for education: A review and synthesis. In P. A. Alexander & P. H. Winne (Eds.), *Handbook of educational psychology* (2nd ed., pp. 163–186). Mahwah, NJ: Erlbaum.

Maughan, A., & Cicchetti, D. (2002). Impact of child maltreatment and interadult violence on children's emotion regulation abilities and socioemotional adjustment. *Child Development, 73,* 1525–1542.

Mayer, J. D., Salovey, P., & Caruso, D. R. (2008). What is emotional intelligence and what does it predict? In P. C. Kyllonen, R. D. Roberts, & L. Stankov (Eds.), *Extending intelligence: Enhancement and new constructs* (pp. 319–348). New York: Erlbaum/Taylor & Francis.

Mayer, M. J., & Furlong, M. J. (2010). How safe are our schools? *Educational Researcher, 39,* 16–26.

Mayeux, L., Houser, J. J., & Dyches, K. D. (2011). Social acceptance and popularity: Two distinct forms of peer status. In A. H. N. Cillessen, D. Schwartz, & L. Mayeux (Eds.), *Popularity in the peer system* (pp. 79–102). New York: Guilford.

McDevitt, T. M., & Ormrod, J. E. (2007). *Child development and education* (3rd ed.). Upper Saddle River, NJ: Merrill/Prentice Hall.

McElhaney, K. B., Antonishak, J., & Allen, J. P. (2008). "They like me, they like me not": Popularity and adolescents' perceptions of acceptance predicting social functioning over time. *Child Development, 79,* 720–731.

McInerney, D. M., Marsh, H. W., & Craven, R. (2008). Self-processes, learning, and enabling human potential. In H. W. Marsh, R. G. Craven, & D. M. McInerney (Eds.), *Self-processes, learning, and enabling human potential* (pp. 3–11). Charlotte, NC: Information Age.

McLoyd, V. C. (1998). Socioeconomic disadvantage and child development. *American Psychologist, 53,* 185–204.

McMillan, J. H., Singh, J., & Simonetta, L. G. (1994). The tyranny of self-oriented self-esteem. *Educational Horizons, 72*(3), 141–145.

Mendoza-Denton, R., & Mischel, W. (2007). Integrating system approaches to culture and personality: The cultural cognitive-affective processing system. In S. Kitayama & D. Cohen (Eds.), *Handbook of cultural psychology* (pp. 175–195). New York: Guilford.

Menon, M., Tobin, D. D., Corby, B. C., Menon, M., Hodges, E. V. E., & Perry, D. G. (2007). The developmental costs of high self-esteem for antisocial children. *Child Development, 78,* 1627–1639.

Meyer, E. J. (2009). Creating schools that value sexual diversity. In S. R. Steinberg (Ed.), *Diversity and multiculturalism: A reader* (pp. 173–192). New York: Peter Lang.

Meyers, D. T. (1987). The socialized individual and individual autonomy: An intersection between philosophy and psychology. In E. F. Kittay and D. T. Meyers (Eds.), *Women and moral theory* (pp. 139–153). Totowa, NJ: Rowman & Littlefield.

Mikulincer, M., & Shaver, P. R. (2005). Attachment security, compassion, and altruism. *Current Directions in Psychological Science, 14,* 34–38.

Miller, B. C., & Benson, B. (1999). Romantic and sexual relationship development during adolescence. In W. Furman, B. B. Brown, & C. Feiring (Eds.), *The development of romantic relationships in adolescence* (pp. 99–121). Cambridge, England: Cambridge University Press.

Miller, D. T., & Prentice, D. A. (1994). The self and the collective. *Personality and Social Psychology Bulletin, 20,* 451–453.

Miller, J. G. (2007). Cultural psychology of moral development. In S. Kitayama & D. Cohen (Eds.), *Handbook of cultural psychology* (pp. 477–499). New York: Guilford.

Miller, P. A., Eisenberg, N., Fabes, R. A., & Shell, R. (1996). Relations of moral reasoning and vicarious emotion to young children's prosocial behavior toward peers and adults. *Developmental Psychology, 32,* 210–219.

Moll, J., de Oliveira-Souza, R., Garrido, G. J., Bramati, I. E., Caparelli-Daquer, E. M., Paiva, M. L., et al. (2007). The self as a moral agent: Linking the neural bases of social agency and moral sensitivity. *Social Neuroscience, 2,* 336–352.

Moore, S., & Rosenthal, D. (2006). *Sexuality in adolescence: Current trends.* London: Routledge.

Morelli, G. A., & Rothbaum, F. (2007). Situating the child in context: Attachment relationships and self-regulation in different cultures. In S. Kitayama & D. Cohen (Eds.), *Handbook of cultural psychology* (pp. 500–527). New York: Guilford.

Narváez, D., & Rest, J. (1995). The four components of acting morally. In W. M. Kurtines & J. L. Gewirtz (Eds.), *Moral development: An introduction* (pp. 385–400). Boston: Allyn & Bacon.

Nasir, N. S., McLaughlin, M. W., & Jones, A. (2009). What does it mean to be African American? Constructions of race and academic identity in an urban public high school. *American Educational Research Journal, 46,* 73–114.

Neel, R. S., Jenkins, Z. N., & Meadows, N. (1990). Social problem-solving behaviors and aggression in young children: A descriptive observational study. *Behavioral Disorders, 16,* 39–51.

Nell, V. (2002). Why young men drive dangerously: Implications for injury prevention. *Current Directions in Psychological Science, 11,* 75–79.

Newcomb, A. F., & Bagwell, C. L. (1995). Children's friendship relations: A meta-analysis review. *Psychological Bulletin, 117,* 306–347.

Newman, R. S. (2008). Adaptive and nonadaptive help seeking with peer harassment: An integrative perspective of coping and self-regulation. *Educational Psychologist, 43,* 1–15.

Nucci, L. P. (2001). *Education in the moral domain.* Cambridge, England: Cambridge University Press.

Nucci, L. P. (2006). Classroom management for moral and social development. In C. M. Evertson & C. S. Weinstein (Eds.), *Handbook of classroom management: Research, practice, and contemporary issues* (pp. 711–731). Mahwah, NJ: Erlbaum.

Nucci, L. (2009). *Nice is not enough: Facilitating moral development.* Upper Saddle River, NJ: Merrill/Pearson.

Nucci, L. P., & Nucci, M. S. (1982). Children's social interactions in the context of moral and conventional transgressions. *Child Development, 53,* 403–412.

Nucci, L. P., & Weber, E. K. (1995). Social interactions in the home and the development of young children's conceptions of the personal. *Child Development, 66,* 1438–1452.

Nuemi, J.-W. (2008). Self and socialization: How do young people navigate through adolescence? In H. W. Marsh, R. G. Craven, & D. M. McInerney (Eds.), *Self-processes, learning, and enabling human potential* (pp. 305–327). Charlotte, NC: Information Age.

Nunner-Winkler, G. (1984). Two moralities? A critical discussion of an ethic of care and responsibility versus an ethic of rights and justice. In W. M. Kurtines & J. L. Gewirtz (Eds.), *Morality, moral behavior, and moral development* (pp. 348–361). New York: Wiley.

O'Connor, M. C., & Paunonen, S. V. (2007). Big Five personality predictors of post-secondary academic performance. *Personality and Individual Differences, 43,* 971–990.

Ogbu, J. U. (2008a). Collective identity and the burden of "acting White" in Black history, community, and education. In J. U. Ogbu (Ed.), *Minority status, oppositional culture, and schooling* (pp. 29–63). New York: Routledge.

Ogbu, J. U. (2008b). Multiple sources of peer pressures among African American students. In J. U. Ogbu (Ed.), *Minority status, oppositional culture, and schooling* (pp. 89–111). New York: Routledge.

O'Mara, A. J., Marsh, H. W., Craven, R. G., & Debus, R. L. (2006). Do self-concept interventions make a difference? A synergistic blend of construct validation and meta-analysis. *Educational Psychologist, 41,* 181–206.

Oppenheimer, L. (1986). Development of recursive thinking: Procedural variations. *International Journal of Behavioral Development, 9,* 401–411.

Orenstein, P. (1994). *Schoolgirls: Young women, self-esteem, and the confidence gap.* New York: Doubleday.

Oskamp, S. (Ed.). (2000). *Reducing prejudice and discrimination.* Mahwah, NJ: Erlbaum.

Paciello, M., Fida, R., Tramontano, C., Lupinetti, C., & Caprara, G. V. (2008). Stability and change of moral disengagement and its impact on aggression and violence in late adolescence. *Child Development, 79*, 1288–1309.

Paget, K. F., Kritt, D., & Bergemann, L. (1984). Understanding strategic interactions in television commercials: A developmental study. *Journal of Applied Developmental Psychology, 5*, 145–161.

Pajares, F. (2009). Toward a positive psychology of academic motivation: The role of self-efficacy beliefs. In R. Gilman, E. S. Huebner, & M. J. Furlong (Eds.), *Handbook of positive psychology in schools* (pp. 149–160). New York: Routledge.

Parada, R. H., Craven, R. G., & Marsh, H. W. (2008). The Beyond Bullying Secondary Program: An innovative program empowering teachers to counteract bullying in schools. In H. W. Marsh, R. G. Craven, & D. M. McInerney (Eds.), *Self-processes, learning, and enabling human potential* (pp. 373–395). Charlotte, NC: Information Age.

Park, N., & Peterson, C. (2009). Strengths of character in schools. In R. Gilman, E. S. Huebner, & M. J. Furlong (Eds.), *Handbook of positive psychology in schools* (pp. 65–76). New York: Routledge.

Parks, C. P. (1995). Gang behavior in the schools: Reality or myth? *Educational Psychology Review, 7*, 41–68.

Patrick, H., Anderman, L. H., & Ryan, A. M. (2002). Social motivation and the classroom social environment. In C. Midgley (Ed.), *Goals, goal structures, and patterns of adaptive learning* (pp. 85–108). Mahwah, NJ: Erlbaum.

Pearce, M. J., Jones, S. M, Schwab-Stone, M. E., & Ruchkin, V. (2003). The protective effects of religiousness and parent involvement on the development of conduct problems among youth exposed to violence. *Child Development, 74*, 1682–1696.

Pedersen, S., Vitaro, F., Barker, E. D., & Borge, A. I. H. (2007). The timing of middle-childhood peer rejection and friendship: Linking early behavior to early-adolescent adjustment. *Child Development, 78*, 1037–1051.

Pellegrini, A. D. (2002). Bullying, victimization, and sexual harassment during the transition to middle school. *Educational Psychologist, 37*, 151–163.

Pellegrini, A. D. (2011). "In the eye of the beholder": Sex bias in observations and ratings of children's aggression. *Educational Researcher, 40*, 281–286.

Pellegrini, A. D., & Archer, J. (2005). Sex differences in competitive and aggressive behavior. In B. J. Ellis & D. F. Bjorklund (Eds.), *Origins of the social mind: Evolutionary psychology and child development* (pp. 219–244). New York: Guilford.

Pellegrini, A. D., & Bartini, M. (2000). A longitudinal study of bullying, victimization, and peer affiliation during the transition from primary school to middle school. *American Educational Research Journal, 37*, 699–725.

Pellegrini, A. D., Bartini, M., & Brooks, F. (1999). School bullies, victims, and aggressive victims: Factors relating to group affiliation and victimization in early adolescence. *Journal of Educational Psychology, 91*, 216–224.

Pellegrini, A. D., & Bohn, C. M. (2005). The role of recess in children's cognitive performance and school adjustment. *Educational Researcher, 34*(1), 13–19.

Pellegrini, A. D., Roseth, C. J., Van Ryzin, M. J., & Solberg, D. W. (2011). Popularity as a form of social dominance: An evolutionary perspective. In A. H. N. Cillessen, D. Schwartz, & L. Mayeux (Eds.), *Popularity in the peer system* (pp. 123–139). New York: Guilford.

Perner, J., & Wimmer, H. (1985). "John *thinks* that Mary *thinks* that . . ." Attribution of second-order beliefs by 5- to 10-year-old children. *Journal of Experimental Child Psychology, 39*, 437–471.

Petersen, R. D. (2004). *Understanding contemporary gangs in America: An interdisciplinary approach.* Upper Saddle River, NJ: Prentice-Hall.

Pettit, G. S. (2004). Violent children in developmental perspective: Risk and protective factors and the mechanisms through which they (may) operate. *Current Directions in Psychological Science, 13*, 194–197.

Pfeifer, J. H., Brown, C. S., & Juvonen, J. (2007). Teaching tolerance in schools: Lessons learned since *Brown* v. *Board of Education* about the development and reduction of children's prejudice. *Social Policy Report, 21*(2), 3–13, 16–17, 20–23. Ann Arbor, MI: Society for Research in Child Development.

Phinney, J. (1990). Ethnic identity in adolescents and adults: Review of research. *Psychological Bulletin, 108*, 499–514.

Poulin, F., & Boivin, M. (1999). Proactive and reactive aggression and boys' friendship quality in mainstream classrooms. *Journal of Emotional and Behavioral Disorders, 7*, 168–177.

Powell, G. J. (1983). *The psychosocial development of minority children.* New York: Brunner/Mazel.

Power, F. C., Higgins, A., & Kohlberg, L. (1989). *Lawrence Kohlberg's approach to moral education.* New York: Columbia University Press.

Powers, S. I., Hauser, S. T., & Kilner, L. A. (1989). Adolescent mental health. *American Psychologist, 44*, 200–208.

Prinstein, M. J., & Dodge, K. A. (Eds.). (2008). *Understanding peer influence in children and adolescents.* New York: Guilford.

Raine, A. (2008). From genes to brain to antisocial behavior. *Current Directions in Psychological Science, 17*, 323–328.

Reimer, J., Paolitto, D. P., & Hersh, R. H. (1983). *Promoting moral growth: From Piaget to Kohlberg* (2nd ed.). White Plains, NY: Longman.

Rest, J., Narvaez, D., Bebeau, M., & Thoma, S. (1999). A neo-Kohlbergian approach: The DIT and schema theory. *Educational Psychology Review, 11*, 291–324.

Reyna, V. F., & Farley, F. (2006). Risk and rationality in adolescent decision making: Implications for theory, practice, and public policy. *Psychological Science in the Public Interest, 7*(1), 1–44.

Rivers, I., Chesney, T., & Coyne, I. (2011). Cyberbullying. In C. P. Monks & I. Coyne (Eds.), *Bullying in different contexts* (pp. 211–230). Cambridge, England: Cambridge University Press.

Rivers, I., Poteat, V. P., Noret, N., & Ashurst, N. (2009). Observing bullying at school: The mental health implications of witness status. *School Psychology Quarterly, 24*(4), 211–223.

Rizzolatti, G., & Sinigaglia, C. (2008). *Mirrors in the brain—How our minds share actions and emotions* (F. Anderson, Trans.). Oxford, England: Oxford University Press.

Robins, R. W., & Trzesniewski, K. H. (2005). Self-esteem development across the lifespan. *Current Directions in Psychological Science, 14,* 158–162.

Robinson, J. P., & Espelage, D. L. (2011). Inequities in educational and psychological outcomes between LGBTQ and straight students in middle and high school. *Educational Researcher, 40*, 315–330.

Rogoff, B. (2003). *The cultural nature of human development.* Oxford, England: Oxford University Press.

Rose, A. J. (2002). Co-rumination in the friendship of girls and boys. *Child Development, 73*, 1830–1843.

Ross, M., & Wang, Q. (2010). Why we remember and what we remember: Culture and autobiographical memory. *Perspectives on Psychological Science, 5*, 401–409.

Ross, S. W, & Horner, R. H. (2009). Bully prevention in positive behavior support. *Journal of Applied Behavior Analysis, 42*, 747–759.

Rothbart, M. K. (2011). *Becoming who we are: Temperament and personality in development.* New York: Guilford.

Rothbaum, F., & Trommsdorff, G. (2007). Do roots and wings complement or oppose one another? The socialization of relatedness and autonomy in cultural context. In J. E. Grusec & P. D. Hastings (Eds.), *Handbook of socialization: Theory and research* (pp. 461–489). New York: Guilford.

Rubin, K. H., Cheah, C., & Menzer, M. M. (2010). Peers. In M. H. Bornstein (Ed.), *Handbook of cultural developmental science* (pp. 223–237). New York: Psychology Press.

Rudolph, K. D., Caldwell, M. S., & Conley, C. S. (2005). Need for approval and children's well-being. *Child Development, 76*, 309–323.

Ruffman, T., Slade, L., & Crowe, E. (2002). The relation between children's and mothers' mental state language and theory-of-mind understanding. *Child Development, 73*, 734–751.

Rushton, J. P. (1980). *Altruism, socialization, and society.* Upper Saddle River, NJ: Prentice-Hall.

Russell, S. T., Ryan, C., Toomey, R. B., Diaz, R. M., & Sanchez, J. (2011). Lesbian, gay, bisexual, and transgender adolescent school victimization: Implications for young adult health and adjustment. *Journal of School Health, 81*(5), 223–230.

Ryan, A. M. (2000). Peer groups as a context for the socialization of adolescents' motivation, engagement, and achievement in school. *Educational Psychologist, 35*, 101–111.

Ryan, A. M. (2001). The peer group as a context for the development of young adolescent motivation and achievement. *Child Development, 72*, 1135–1150.

Ryan, R. M., & Kuczkowski, R. (1994). The imaginary audience, self-consciousness, and public individuation in adolescence. *Journal of Personality, 62,* 219–237.

Saarni, C., Campos, J. J., Camras, L. A., & Witherington, D. (2006). Emotional development: Action, communication, and understanding. In W. Damon & R. M. Lerner (Eds. in Chief) & N. Eisenberg (Vol. Ed.), *Handbook of child psychology, Vol. 3. Social, emotional, and personality development* (6th ed., pp. 226–299). Hoboken, NJ: Wiley.

Salmivalli, C., & Peets, K. (2009). Bullies, victims, and bully–victim relationships in middle childhood and early adolescence. In K. H. Rubin, W. M. Bukowski, & B. Laursen (Eds.), *Handbook of peer interactions, relationships, and groups* (pp. 322–340). New York: Guilford.

Saudino, K. J., & Plomin, R. (2007). Why are hyperactivity and academic achievement related? *Child Development, 78,* 972–986.

Savin-Williams, R. C. (2008). Then and now: Recruitment, definition, diversity, and positive attributes of same-sex populations. *Developmental Psychology, 44,* 135–138.

Schlaefli, A., Rest, J. R., & Thoma, S. J. (1985). Does moral education improve moral judgment? A meta-analysis of intervention studies using the defining issues test. *Review of Educational Research, 55,* 319–352.

Schofield, J. W. (1995). Improving intergroup relations among students. In J. A. Banks & C. A. M. Banks (Eds.), *Handbook of research on multicultural education* (pp. 635–646). New York: Macmillan.

Schult, C. A. (2002). Children's understanding of the distinction between intentions and desires. *Child Development, 73,* 1727–1747.

Schultz, K., Buck, P., & Niesz, T. (2000). Democratizing conversations: Racialized talk in a post-desegregated middle school. *American Educational Research Journal, 37,* 33–65.

Schunk, D. H., & Pajares, F. (2004). Self-efficacy in education revisited: Empirical and applied evidence. In D. M. McInerney & S. Van Etten (Eds.), *Big theories revisited* (pp. 115–138). Greenwich, CT: Information Age.

Schwartz, D., Dodge, K. A., Coie, J. D., Hubbard, J. A., Cillessen, A. H., Lemerise, E. A., et al. (1998). Social-cognitive and behavioral correlates of aggression and victimization in boys' play groups. *Journal of Abnormal Child Psychology, 26,* 431–440.

Schwartz, D., & Gorman, A. H. (2011). The high price of high status: Popularity as a mechanism of risk. In A. H. N. Cillessen, D. Schwartz, & L. Mayeux (Eds.), *Popularity in the peer system* (pp. 245–270). New York: Guilford.

Schwartz, D., Gorman, A. H., Nakamoto, J., & Toblin, R. L. (2005). Victimization in the peer group and children's academic functioning. *Journal of Educational Psychology, 97,* 425–435.

Seaton, M., Marsh, H. W., & Craven, R. G. (2010). Big-fish-little-pond effect: Generalizability and moderation—Two sides of the same coin. *American Educational Research Journal, 47,* 390–433.

Seaton, E. K., Scottham, K. M., & Sellers, R. M. (2006). The status model of racial identity development in African American adolescents: Evidence of structure, trajectories, and well-being. *Child Development, 77,* 1416–1426.

Selman, R. L. (1980). *The growth of interpersonal understanding.* San Diego, CA: Academic Press.

Shariff, S. (2008). *Cyber-bullying: Issues and solutions for the school, the classroom and the home.* London: Routledge.

Sheets, R. H. (1999). Human development and ethnic identity. In R. H. Sheets & E. R. Hollins (Eds.), *Racial and ethnic identity in school practices: Aspects of human development* (pp. 91–101). Mahwah, NJ: Erlbaum.

Shrum, W., & Cheek, N. H. (1987). Social structure during the school years: Onset of the degrouping process. *American Sociological Review, 52,* 218–223.

Shulman, S., Elicker, J., & Sroufe, L. A. (1994). Stages of friendship growth in preadolescence as related to attachment history. *Journal of Social and Personal Relationships, 11,* 341–361.

Simons, R. L., Whitbeck, L. B., Conger, R. D., & Conger, K. J. (1991). Parenting factors, social skills, and value commitments as precursors to school failure, involvement with deviant peers, and delinquent behavior. *Journal of Youth and Adolescence, 20,* 645–664.

Singer, D. G., & Singer, J. L. (1994). *Barney & Friends as education and entertainment: Phase 3. A national study: Can preschoolers learn through exposure to Barney & Friends?* New Haven, CT: Yale University Family Television Research and Consultation Center.

Sleeter, C. E., & Grant, C. A. (1999). *Making choices for multicultural education: Five approaches to race, class, and gender* (3rd ed.). Upper Saddle River, NJ: Merrill/Prentice Hall.

Smetana, J. G. (1981). Preschool children's conceptions of moral and social rules. *Child Development, 52,* 1333–1336.

Smetana, J. G. (2005). Adolescent–parent conflict: Resistance and subversion as developmental process. In L. Nucci (Ed.), *Conflict, contradiction, and contrarian elements in moral development and education* (pp. 69–91). Mahwah, NJ: Erlbaum.

Smetana, J. G. (2006). Social cognitive domain theory: Consistencies and variations in children's moral and social judgments. In M. Killen & J. Smetana (Eds.), *Handbook of moral development* (pp. 119–154). Mahwah, NJ: Erlbaum.

Smetana, J. G., & Braeges, J. L. (1990). The development of toddlers' moral and conventional judgments. *Merrill-Palmer Quarterly, 36,* 329–346.

Smith, E. R., & Semin, G. R. (2007). Situated social cognition. *Current Directions in Psychological Science, 16,* 132–135.

Smokowski, P., Buchanan, R. L., & Bacalleo, M. L. (2009). Acculturation and adjustment in Latino adolescents: How cultural risk factors and assets influence multiple domains of adolescent mental health. *Journal of Primary Prevention, 30,* 371–393.

Snarey, J. (1995). In a communitarian voice: The sociological expansion of Kohlbergian theory, research, and practice. In W. M. Kurtines & J. L. Gewirtz (Eds.), *Moral development: An introduction* (pp. 109–134). Boston: Allyn & Bacon.

Snyder, J., Schrepferman, L., McEachern, A., Barner, S., Johnson, K., & Provines, J. (2008). Peer deviancy training and peer coercion: Dual processes associated with early-onset conduct problems. *Child Development, 79,* 252–268.

Somerville, L. H., Jones, R. M., & Casey, B. J. (2010). A time of change: Behavioral and neural correlates of adolescent sensitivity to appetitive and aversive environmental cues. *Brain and Cognition, 72,* 124–133.

Spear, L. P. (2007). Brain development and adolescent behavior. In D. Coch, K. W. Fischer, & G. Dawson (Eds.), *Human behavior, learning, and the developing brain: Typical development* (pp. 362–396). New York: Guilford.

Spencer, M. B., Noll, E., Stoltzfus, J., & Harpalani, V. (2001). Identity and school adjustment: Revisiting the "acting White" phenomenon. *Educational Psychologist, 36,* 21–30.

Spinrad, T. L., & Eisenberg, N. (2009). Empathy, prosocial behavior, and positive development in schools. In R. Gilman, E. S. Huebner, & M. J. Furlong (Eds.), *Handbook of positive psychology in schools* (pp. 119–129). New York: Routledge.

Sroufe, L. A., Carlson, E., & Shulman, S. (1993). Individuals in relationships: Development from infancy through adolescence. In D. C. Funder, R. D. Parke, C. Tomlinson-Keasey, & K. Widaman (Eds.), *Studying lives through time: Personality and development* (pp. 315–342). Washington, DC: American Psychological Association.

Steinberg, L. (1996). *Beyond the classroom: Why school reform has failed and what parents need to do.* New York: Touchstone.

Steinberg, L. (2007). Risk taking in adolescence. *Current Directions in Psychological Science, 16,* 55–59.

Steinberg, L. (2009). Should the science of adolescent brain development inform public policy? *American Psychologist, 64,* 739–750.

Steinberg, L., Cauffman, E., Woolard, J., Graham, S., & Banich, M. (2009). Are adolescents less mature than adults? *American Psychologist, 64,* 583–594.

Stewart, L., & Pascual-Leone, J. (1992). Mental capacity constraints and the development of moral reasoning. *Journal of Experimental Child Psychology, 54,* 251–287.

Stice, E. (2003). Puberty and body image. In C. Hayward (Ed.), *Gender differences at puberty* (pp. 61–76). Cambridge, England: Cambridge University Press.

Stice, E., & Barrera, M., Jr. (1995). A longitudinal examination of the reciprocal relations between perceived parenting and adolescents' substance use and externalizing behaviors. *Developmental Psychology, 31,* 322–334.

Strelau, J. (2008). *Temperament as a regulator of behavior: After fifty years of research.* Clinton Corners, NY: Werner.

Sullivan, J. R., & Conoley, J. C. (2004). Academic and instructional interventions with aggressive students. In J. C. Conoley & A. P. Goldstein

(Eds.), *School violence intervention* (2nd ed., pp. 235–255). New York: Guilford.

Suttles, G. D. (1970). Friendship as a social institution. In G. J. McCall, M. McCall, N. K. Denzin, G. D. Scuttles, & S. Kurth (Eds.), *Social relationships* (pp. 95–135). Chicago: Aldine de Gruyter.

Swearer, S. M., Espelage, D. L., Vaillancourt, T., & Hymel, S. (2010). What can be done about school bullying? Linking research to educational practice. *Educational Researcher, 39,* 38–47.

Tager-Flusberg, H. (2007). Evaluating the theory-of-mind hypothesis of autism. *Current Directions in Psychological Science, 16,* 311–315.

Tatum, B. D. (1997). *"Why are all the black kids sitting together in the cafeteria?" and other conversations about race.* New York: Basic Books.

Themann, K. S., & Goldstein, H. (2001). Social stories, written text cues, and video feedback: Effects on social communication of children with autism. *Journal of Applied Behavior Analysis, 34,* 425–446.

Thomas, A., & Chess, S. (1977). *Temperament and development.* New York: Brunner/Mazel.

Thompson, M., & Grace, C. O. (with Cohen, L. J.) (2001). *Best friends, worst enemies: Understanding the social lives of children.* New York: Ballantine.

Thompson, R. A., & Wyatt, J. M. (1999). Current research on child maltreatment: Implications for educators. *Educational Psychology Review, 11,* 173–201.

Thorkildsen, T. A., Golant, C. J., & Cambray-Engstrom, E. (2008). Essential solidarities for understanding Latino adolescents' moral and academic engagement. In C. Hudley & A. E. Gottfried (Eds.), *Academic motivation and the culture of school in childhood and adolescence* (pp. 73–98). New York: Oxford University Press.

Tisak, M. (1993). Preschool children's judgments of moral and personal events involving physical harm and property damage. *Merrill-Palmer Quarterly, 39,* 375–390.

Trautwein, U., Gerlach, E., & Lüdtke, O. (2008). Athletic classmates, physical self-concept, and free-time physical activity: A longitudinal study of frame of reference effects. *Journal of Educational Psychology, 100,* 988–1001.

Triandis, H. C. (1995). *Individualism and collectivism.* Boulder, CO: Westview.

Troop-Gordon, W., & Asher, S. R. (2005). Modification in children's goals when encountering obstacles in conflict resolution. *Child Development, 76,* 568–582.

Tsethlikai, M., & Greenhoot, A. F. (2006). The influence of another's perspective on children's recall of previously misconstrued events. *Developmental Psychology, 42,* 732–745.

Tsethlikai, M., Guthrie-Fulbright, Y., & Loera, S. (2007, March). *Social perspective coordination ability and children's recall of mutual conflict.* Paper presented at the biennial meeting of the Society for Research in Child Development, Boston.

Turiel, E. (1983). *The development of social knowledge: Morality and convention.* Cambridge, England: Cambridge University Press.

Turiel, E. (1998). The development of morality. In W. Damon (Series Ed.) & N. Eisenberg (Vol. Ed.), *Handbook of child psychology: Vol. 3. Social, emotional, and personality development* (5th ed., pp. 863–932). New York: Wiley.

Turiel, E. (2002). *The culture of morality: Social development, context, and conflict.* Cambridge, England: Cambridge University Press.

Turnbull, A. P., Pereira, L., & Blue-Banning, M. (2000). Teachers as friendship facilitators. *Teaching Exceptional Children, 32*(5), 66–70.

Urdan, T. C., & Maehr, M. L. (1995). Beyond a two-goal theory of motivation and achievement: A case for social goals. *Review of Educational Research, 65,* 213–243.

Valentine, J. C., DuBois, D. L., & Cooper, H. (2004). The relation between self-beliefs and academic achievement: A meta-analytic review. *Educational Psychologist, 39,* 111–133.

Valiente, C., Lemery-Chalfant, K., & Swanson, J. (2010). Prediction of kindergartners' academic achievement from their effortful control and emotionality: Evidence for direct and moderated relations. *Journal of Educational Psychology, 102,* 550–560.

Valkenburg, P. M., & Peter, J. (2009). Social consequences of the Internet for adolescents: A decade of research. *Current Directions in Psychological Science, 18,* 1–5.

van Goozen, S. H. M., Fairchild, G., & Harold, G. T. (2008). The role of neurobiological deficits in childhood antisocial behavior. *Current Directions in Psychological Science, 17,* 224–228.

Vaughn, S. (1991). Social skills enhancement in students with learning disabilities. In B. Y. L. Wong (Ed.), *Learning about learning disabilities* (pp. 407–440). San Diego, CA: Academic Press.

Vitaro, F., Gendreau, P. L., Tremblay, R. E., & Oligny, P. (1998). Reactive and proactive aggression differentially predict later conduct problems. *Journal of Child Psychology and Psychiatry and Allied Disciplines, 39,* 377–385.

Wainryb, C., Brehl, B. A., & Matwin, S. (2005). Being hurt and hurting others: Children's narrative accounts and moral judgments of their own interpersonal conflicts. *Monographs of the Society for Research in Child Development, 70*(3; Serial No. 281).

Walker, E. N. (2006). Urban high school students' academic communities and their effects on mathematics success. *American Educational Research Journal, 43,* 43–73.

Walker, J. M. T., & Hoover-Dempsey, K. V. (2006). Why research on parental involvement is important to classroom management. In C. M. Evertson & C. S. Weinstein (Eds.), *Handbook of classroom management: Research, practice, and contemporary issues* (pp. 665–684). Mahwah, NJ: Erlbaum.

Walker, L. J. (1991). Sex differences in moral reasoning. In W. M. Kurtines & J. L. Gewirtz (Eds.), *Handbook of moral behavior and development: Vol. 2. Research* (pp. 333–364). Mahwah, NJ: Erlbaum.

Walker, L. J. (1995). Sexism in Kohlberg's moral psychology? In W. M. Kurtines & J. L. Gewirtz (Eds.), *Moral development: An introduction* (pp. 83–107). Boston: Allyn & Bacon.

Ward, C., Bochner, S., & Furnham, A. (2001). *The psychology of culture shock* (2nd ed.). London: Routledge.

Waterhouse, L. (2006). Multiple intelligences, the Mozart effect, and emotional intelligence: A critical review. *Educational Psychologist, 41,* 207–225.

Watkins, D. E., & Wentzel, K. R. (2008). Training boys with ADHD to work collaboratively: Social and learning outcomes. *Contemporary Educational Psychology, 33,* 625–646.

Watson, M. (2008). Developmental discipline and moral education. In L. Nucci & D. Narvaez (Eds.), *Handbook of moral and character education* (pp. 175–203). New York: Routledge.

Watson, M. W., Andreas, J. B., Fischer, K. W., & Smith, K. (2005). Patterns of risk factors leading to victimization and aggression in children and adolescents. In K. A. Kendall-Tackett & S. M. Giacomoni (Eds.), *Child Victimization: Maltreatment, bullying and dating violence, prevention and intervention* (pp. 12.1–12.23). Kingston, NJ: Civic Research Institute.

Way, N. (1998). *Everyday courage: The lives and stories of urban teenagers.* New York: New York University Press.

Webb, N. M., & Farivar, S. (1994). Promoting helping behavior in cooperative small groups in middle school mathematics. *American Educational Research Journal, 31,* 369–395.

Webb, N. M., & Palincsar, A. S. (1996). Group processes in the classroom. In D. C. Berliner & R. C. Calfee (Eds.), *Handbook of educational psychology* (pp. 841–873). New York: Macmillan.

Wellman, H. M., Cross, D., & Watson, J. (2001). Meta-analysis of theory-of-mind development: The truth about false belief. *Child Development, 72,* 655–684.

Wellman, H. M., & Gelman, S. A. (1998). Knowledge acquisition in foundational domains. In W. Damon (Series Ed.), D. Kuhn, & R. S. Siegler (Vol. Eds.), *Handbook of child psychology: Vol. 2. Cognition, perception, and language* (5th ed., pp. 523–573). New York: Wiley.

Wellman, H. M., Phillips, A. T., & Rodriguez, T. (2000). Young children's understanding of perception, desire, and emotion. *Child Development, 71,* 895–912.

Wentzel, K. R. (1999). Social-motivational processes and interpersonal relationships: Implications for understanding motivation at school. *Journal of Educational Psychology, 91,* 76–97.

Wentzel, K. R. (2009). Peers and academic functioning at school. In K. H. Rubin, W. M. Bukowski, & B. Laursen (Eds.), *Handbook of peer interactions, relationships, and groups* (pp. 531–547). New York: Guilford.

Wentzel, K. R., Filisetti, L., & Looney, L. (2007). Adolescent prosocial behavior: The role of self-processes and contextual cues. *Child Development, 78,* 895–910.

Wentzel, K. R., & Looney, L. (2007). Socialization in school settings. In J. E. Grusec & P. D. Hastings (Eds.), *Handbook of socialization: Theory and research* (pp. 382–403). New York: Guilford.

White, R., & Cunningham, A. M. (1991). *Ryan White: My own story.* New York: Signet.

Whitesell, N. R., Mitchell, C. M., Kaufman, C. E., Spicer, P., & the Voices of Indian Teens Project Team (2006). Developmental trajectories of personal and collective self-concept among American Indian adolescents. *Child Development, 77,* 1487–1503.

Wigfield, A., Eccles, J. S., & Pintrich, P. R. (1996). Development between the ages of 11 and 25. In D. C. Berliner & R. C. Calfee (Eds.), *Handbook of educational psychology* (pp. 148–185). New York: Macmillan.

Willard, N. E. (2007). *Cyberbullying and cyberthreats: Responding to the challenge of online social aggression, threats, and distress.* Champaign, IL: Research Press.

Wimmer, H., & Perner, J. (1983). Beliefs about beliefs: Representation and constraining function of wrong beliefs in young children's understanding of deception. *Cognition, 13,* 103–128.

Witmer, S. (1996). Making peace, the Navajo way. *Tribal College Journal, 8,* 24–27.

Wittmer, D. S., & Honig, A. S. (1994). Encouraging positive social development in young children. *Young Children, 49*(5), 4–12.

Woolfe, T., Want, S. C., & Siegal, M. (2002). Signposts to development: Theory of mind in deaf children. *Child Development, 73,* 768–778.

Yates, M., & Youniss, J. (1996). A developmental perspective on community service in adolescence. *Social Development, 5,* 85–111.

Yau, J., & Smetana, J. G. (2003). Conceptions of moral, social-conventional, and personal events among Chinese preschoolers in Hong Kong. *Child Development, 74,* 647–658.

Yeung, R. S., & Leadbeater, B. J. (2007, March). *Peer victimization and emotional and behavioral problems in adolescence: The moderating effect of adult emotional support.* Paper presented at the biennial meeting of the Society for Research in Child Development, Boston.

Yip, T., & Fuligni, A. J. (2002). Daily variation in ethnic identity, ethnic behaviors, and psychological well-being among American adolescents of Chinese descent. *Child Development, 73,* 1557–1572.

Young, L., & Saxe, R. (2009). Innocent intentions: A correlation between forgiveness for accidental harm and neural activity. *Neuropsychologia, 47,* 2065–2072.

Youniss, J., & Yates, M. (1999). Youth service and moral-civic identity: A case for everyday morality. *Educational Psychology Review, 11,* 361–376.

Yuker, H. E. (Ed.). (1988). *Attitudes toward persons with disabilities.* New York: Springer.

Yun, C., Farran, D. C., Lipsey, M. W., & Bilbrey, C. (2010, April–May). *Academic self-concept and achievement in young children.* Poster presented at the annual meeting of the American Educational Research Association, Denver.

Zahn-Waxler, C., Radke-Yarrow, M., Wagner, E., & Chapman, M. (1992). Development of concern for others. *Developmental Psychology, 28,* 126–136.

Zahn-Waxler, C., & Robinson, J. (1995). Empathy and guilt: Early origins of feelings of responsibility. In J. P. Tangney & K. W. Fischer (Eds.), *Self-conscious emotions: The psychology of shame, guilt, embarrassment, and pride* (pp. 143–173). New York: Guilford.

Zeidner, M., Roberts, R. D., & Matthews, G. (2002). Can emotional intelligence be schooled? A critical review. *Educational Psychologist, 37,* 215–231.

Zelli, A., Dodge, K. A., Lochman, J. E., & Laird, R. D. (1999). The distinction between beliefs legitimizing aggression and deviant processing of social cues: Testing measurement validity and the hypothesis that biased processing mediates the effects of beliefs on aggression. *Journal of Personality and Social Psychology, 77,* 150–166.

Zimmerman, B. J., & Moylan, A. R. (2009). Self-regulation: Where metacognition and motivation intersect. In D. J. Hacker, J. Dunlosky, & A. C. Graesser (Eds.), *Handbook of metacognition in education* (pp. 299–315). New York: Routledge.

## CHAPTER 4

Adger, C. T., Wolfram, W., & Christian, D. (2007). *Dialects in schools and communities* (2nd ed.). New York: Routledge.

Aikens, N. L., & Barbarin, O. (2008). Socioeconomic differences in reading trajectories: The contribution of family, neighborhood, and school contexts. *Journal of Educational Psychology, 100,* 235–251.

Alexander, K. L., Entwisle, D. R., & Dauber, S. L. (1995). *On the success of failure.* New York: Cambridge University Press.

Alim, H. S., & Baugh, J. (Eds.). (2007). *Talkin Black talk: Language, education, and social change.* New York: Teachers College Press.

Allen, J. P., & Antonishak, J. (2008). Adolescent peer influences: Beyond the dark side. In M. J. Prinstein & K. A. Dodge (Eds.), *Understanding peer influence in children and adolescents* (pp. 141–160). New York: Guilford.

Allison, K. W. (1998). Stress and oppressed social category membership. In J. Swim & C. Stangor (Eds.), *Prejudice: The target's perspective* (pp. 149–170). San Diego, CA: Academic Press.

Altermatt, E. R., Jovanovic, J., & Perry, M. (1998). Bias or responsivity? Sex and achievement-level effects on teachers' classroom questioning practices. *Journal of Educational Psychology, 90,* 516–527.

Anderson, L. W., & Pellicer, L. O. (1998). Toward an understanding of unusually successful programs for economically disadvantaged students. *Journal of Education for Students Placed at Risk, 3,* 237–263.

Aronson, J., & Steele, C. M. (2005). Stereotypes and the fragility of academic competence, motivation, and self-concept. In A. J. Elliot & C. S. Dweck (Eds.), *Handbook of competence and motivation* (pp. 436–456). New York: Guilford.

Ashiabi, G. S., & O'Neal, K. K. (2008). A framework for understanding the association between food insecurity and children's developmental outcomes. *Child Development Perspectives, 2,* 71–77.

Atran, S., Medin, D. L., & Ross, N. O. (2005). The cultural mind: Environmental decision making and cultural modeling within and across populations. *Psychological Review, 112,* 744–776.

Attie, I., Brooks-Gunn, J., & Petersen, A. (1990). A developmental perspective on eating disorders and eating problems. In M. Lewis & S. M. Miller (Eds.), *Handbook of developmental psychopathology* (pp. 409–420). New York: Plenum.

Au, K. H. (1980). Participation structures in a reading lesson with Hawaiian children: Analysis of a culturally appropriate instructional event. *Anthropology and Education Quarterly, 11,* 91–115.

Auyeung, B., Baron-Cohen, S., Ashwin, E., Knickmeyer, R., Taylor, K., Hackett, G., et al. (2009). Fetal testosterone predicts sexually differentiated childhood behavior in girls and in boys. *Psychological Science, 20,* 144–148.

Bandura, A., Barbaranelli, C., Caprara, G. V., & Pastorelli, C. (2001). Self-efficacy beliefs as shapers of children's aspirations and career trajectories. *Child Development, 72,* 187–206.

Banks, J. A., & Banks, C. A. M. (Eds.). (1995). *Handbook of research on multicultural education.* New York: Macmillan.

Banks, J., Cochran-Smith, M., Moll, L., Richert, A., Zeichner, K., LePage, P., et al. (with McDonald, M.) (2005). Teaching diverse learners. In L. Darling-Hammond & J. Bransford (Eds.), *Preparing teachers for a changing world: What teachers should learn and be able to do* (pp. 232–274). San Francisco: Jossey-Bass/Wiley.

Barbarin, O., Mercado, M., & Jigjidsuren, D. (2010). Development for tolerance and respect for diversity in the context of immigration. In E. L. Grigorenko & R. Takanishi (Eds.), *Immigration, diversity, and education* (pp. 276–288). New York: Routledge.

Battin-Pearson, S., Newcomb, M. D., Abbott, R. D., Hill, K. G., Catalano, R. F., & Hawkins, J. D. (2000). Predictors of early high school dropout: A test of five theories. *Journal of Educational Psychology, 92,* 568–582.

Becker, B. E., & Luthar, S. S. (2002). Social-emotional factors affecting achievement outcomes among disadvantaged students: Closing the achievement gap. *Educational Psychologist, 37,* 197–214.

Belfiore, P. J., & Hornyak, R. S. (1998). Operant theory and application to self-monitoring in adolescents. In D. H. Schunk & B. J. Zimmerman (Eds.), *Self-regulated learning: From teaching to self-reflective practice* (pp. 184–202). New York: Guilford.

Bem, S. L. (1981). Gender schema theory: A cognitive account of sex typing. *Psychological Review, 88,* 354–364.

Bem, S. L. (1983). Gender schema theory and its implications for child development: Raising gender-aschematic children in a gender-schematic society. *Signs: Journal of Women in Culture and Society, 8,* 598–616.

Bem, S. L. (1984). Androgyny and gender schema theory: A conceptual and empirical integration. In T. B. Sonderegger (Ed.), *Nebraska Symposium on Motivation* (Vol. 32, pp. 179–226). Lincoln: University of Nebraska Press.

Benenson, J. F., & Christakos, A. (2003). The greater fragility of females' versus males' closest same-sex friendships. *Child Development, 74,* 1123–1129.

Benenson, J. F., Maiese, R., Dolenszky, E., Dolensky, N., Sinclair, N., & Simpson, A. (2002). Group size regulates self-assertive versus self-deprecating responses to interpersonal competition. *Child Development, 73,* 1818–1829.

Berliner, D. C. (2005, April). *Ignoring the forest, blaming the trees: Our impoverished view of educational reform.* Paper presented at the annual meeting of the American Educational Research Association, Montreal.

Bigler, R. S., & Liben, L. S. (2007). Developmental intergroup theory: Explaining and reducing children's social stereotyping and prejudice. *Current Directions in Psychological Science, 16,* 162–166.

Binns, K., Steinberg, A., Amorosi, S., & Cuevas, A. M. (1997). *The Metropolitan Life survey of the American teacher 1997: Examining gender issues in public schools.* New York: Louis Harris and Associates.

Bleeker, M. M., & Jacobs, J. E. (2004). Achievement in math and science: Do mothers' beliefs matter 12 years later? *Journal of Educational Psychology, 96,* 97–109.

Boling, C. J., & Evans, W. H. (2008). Reading success in the secondary classroom. *Preventing School Failure, 52*(2), 59–66.

Bornholt, L. J., Goodnow, J. J., & Cooney, G. H. (1994). Influences of gender stereotypes on adolescents' perceptions of their own achievement. *American Educational Research Journal, 31,* 675–692.

Bosacki, S. L. (2000). Theory of mind and self-concept in preadolescents: Links with gender and language. *Journal of Educational Psychology, 92,* 709–717.

Boutte, G. S., & McCormick, C. B. (1992). Authentic multicultural activities: Avoiding pseudomulticulturalism. *Childhood Education, 68,* 140–144.

Branch, C. (1999). Race and human development. In R. H. Sheets & E. R. Hollins (Eds.), *Racial and ethnic identity in school practices: Aspects of human development* (pp. 7–28). Mahwah, NJ: Erlbaum.

Brayboy, B. M. J., & Searle, K. A. (2007). Thanksgiving and serial killers: Representations of American Indians in schools. In S. Books (Ed.), *Invisible children in the society and its schools* (3rd ed., pp. 173–192). Mahwah, NJ: Erlbaum.

Brody, G. H., Chen, Y.-F., Murry, V. M., Ge, X., Simons, R. L., Gibbons, F. X., et al. (2006). Perceived discrimination and the adjustment of African American youths: A five-year longitudinal analysis with contextual moderation effects. *Child Development, 77,* 1170–1189.

Brooks-Gunn, J. (2003). Do you believe in magic? What we can expect from early childhood intervention programs. *Social Policy Report of the Society for Research in Child Development, 17*(1), 3–14.

Brooks-Gunn, J., Linver, M. R., & Fauth, R. C. (2005). Children's competence and socioeconomic status in the family and neighborhood. In A. J. Elliot & C. S. Dweck (Eds.), *Handbook of competence and motivation* (pp. 414–435). New York: Guilford.

Brophy, J., Alleman, J., & Knighton, B. (2009). *Inside the social studies classroom.* New York: Routledge.

Bussey, K., & Bandura, A. (1992). Self-regulatory mechanisms governing gender development. *Child Development, 63,* 1236–1250.

Byrnes, J. P. (2003). Factors predictive of mathematics achievement in White, Black, and Hispanic 12th graders. *Journal of Educational Psychology, 95,* 316–326.

Cameron, L., Rutland, A., Brown, R., & Douch, R. (2006). Changing children's intergroup attitudes toward refugees: Testing different models of extended contact. *Child Development, 77,* 1208–1219.

Card, N. A., Stucky, B. D., Sawalani, G. M., & Little T. D. (2008). Direct and indirect aggression during childhood and adolescence: A meta-analytic review of gender differences, intercorrelations, and relations to maladjustment. *Child Development, 79,* 1185–1229.

Casey, B. M., Andrews, N., Schindler, H., Kersh, J. E., Samper, A., & Copley, J. (2008). The development of spatial skills through interventions involving block building activities. *Cognition and Instruction, 26,* 269–309.

Castagno, A. E., & Brayboy, B. M. J. (2008). Culturally responsive schooling for Indigenous youth: A review of the literature. *Review of Educational Research, 78,* 941–993.

Cazden, C. B. (2001). *Classroom discourse: The language of teaching and learning* (2nd ed.). Portsmouth, NH: Heinemann.

Chapman, C., Laird, J., & KewalRamani, A. (2010). *Trends in high school dropout and completion rates in the United States: 1972–2008.* Washington, DC: National Center for Education Statistics, U.S. Department of Education.

Chen, X., Chung, J., & Hsiao, C. (2009). Peer interactions and relationships from a cross-cultural perspective. In K. H. Rubin, W. M. Bukowski, & B. Laursen (Eds.), *Handbook of peer interactions, relationships, and groups* (pp. 432–451). New York: Guilford.

Chisholm, J. S. (1996). Learning "respect for everything": Navajo images of development. In C. P. Hwant, M. E. Lamb, & I. E. Sigel (Eds.), *Images of childhood* (pp. 167–183). Mahwah, NJ: Erlbaum.

Christenson, S. L., & Thurlow, M. L. (2004). School dropouts: Prevention, considerations, interventions, and challenges. *Current Directions in Psychological Science, 13,* 36–39.

Clark, R. M. (1983). *Family life and school achievement: Why poor black children succeed or fail.* Chicago: University of Chicago Press.

Coe, J., Salamon, L., & Molnar, J. (1991). *Homeless children and youth.* New Brunswick, NJ: Transaction.

Cohen, A. B. (2009). Many forms of culture. *American Psychologist, 64,* 194–204.

Cole, D. A., Martin, J. M., Peeke, L. A., Seroczynski, A. D., & Fier, J. (1999). Children's over- and underestimation of academic competence: A longitudinal study of gender differences, depression, and anxiety. *Child Development, 70,* 459–473.

Cole, P. M., Tamang, B. L., & Shrestha, S. (2006). Cultural variations in the socialization of young children's anger and shame. *Child Development, 77,* 1237–1251.

Cook, T. D., Herman, M. R., Phillips, M., & Settersten, R. A., Jr. (2002). Some ways in which neighborhoods, nuclear families, friendship groups, and schools jointly affect changes in early adolescent development. *Child Development, 73,* 1283–1309.

Correa-Chávez, M., Rogoff, B., & Mejía Arauz, R. (2005). Cultural patterns in attending to two events at once. *Child Development, 76,* 664–678.

Cosden, M., Morrison, G., Albanese, A. L., & Macias, S. (2001). When homework is not home work: After-school programs for homework assistance. *Educational Psychologist, 36,* 211–221.

Crago, M. B., Annahatak, B., & Ningiuruvik, L. (1993). Changing patterns of language socialization in Inuit homes. *Anthropology and Education Quarterly, 24,* 205–223.

Crick, N. R., Grotpeter, J. K., & Bigbee, M. A. (2002). Relationally and physically aggressive children's intent attributions and feelings of distress for relational and instrumental peer provocation. *Child Development, 73,* 1134–1142.

Croninger, R. G., & Valli, L. (2009). "Where is the action?" Challenges to studying the teaching of reading in elementary classrooms. *Educational Researcher, 38,* 100–108.

Crosnoe, R., & Cooper, C. E. (2010). Economically disadvantaged children's transitions into elementary school: Linking family processes, school contexts, and educational policy. *American Educational Research Journal, 47,* 258–291.

Cross, W. E., Jr., Strauss, L., & Fhagen-Smith, P. (1999). African American identity development across the life span: Educational implications. In R. H. Sheets & E. R. Hollins (Eds.), *Racial and ethnic identity in school practices: Aspects of human development* (pp. 29–47). Mahwah, NJ: Erlbaum.

Crouter, A. C., Whiteman, S. D., McHale, S. M., & Osgood, D. W. (2007). Development of gender attitude traditionality across middle childhood and adolescence. *Child Development, 78,* 911–926.

D'Amato, R. C., Chittooran, M. M., & Whitten, J. D. (1992). Neuropsychological consequences of malnutrition. In D. I. Templer, L. C. Hartlage, & W. G. Cannon (Eds.), *Preventable brain damage: Brain vulnerability and brain health* (pp. 193–213). New York: Springer.

Davenport, E. C., Jr., Davison, M. L., Kuang, H., Ding, S., Kim, S., & Kwak, N. (1998). High school mathematics course-taking by gender and ethnicity. *American Educational Research Journal, 35,* 497–514.

Davila, J. (2008). Depressive symptoms and adolescent romance: Theory, research, and implications. *Child Development Perspectives, 2*(1), 26–31.

Deaux, K. (1984). From individual differences to social categories: Analysis of a decade's research on gender. *American Psychologist, 39,* 105–116.

de Boer, H., Bosker, R. J.,& van der Werf, M. P. C. (2010). Sustainability of teacher expectation bias effects on long-term student performance. *Journal of Educational Psychology, 102,* 168–179.

DeBose, C. E. (2007). The Ebonics phenomenon, language planning, and the hegemony of Standard English. In H. S. Alim & J. Baugh (Eds.), *Talkin Black talk: Language, education, and social change* (pp. 30–42). New York: Teachers College Press.

Delgado-Gaitan, C. (1994). Socializing young children in Mexican-American families: An intergenerational perspective. In P. M. Greenfield & R. R. Cocking (Eds.), *Cross-cultural roots of minority child development* (pp. 55–86). Mahwah, NJ: Erlbaum.

Deyhle, D. (2008). Navajo youth and Anglo racism: Cultural integrity and resistance. In J. U. Ogbu (Ed.), *Minority status, oppositional culture, and schooling* (pp. 433–480). New York: Routledge.

Deyhle, D., & LeCompte, M. (1999). Cultural differences in child development: Navajo adolescents in middle schools. In R. H. Sheets & E. R. Hollins (Eds.), *Racial and ethnic identity in school practices: Aspects of human development* (pp. 123–139). Mahwah, NJ: Erlbaum.

Deyhle, D., & Margonis, F. (1995). Navajo mothers and daughters: Schools, jobs, and the family. *Anthropology and Education Quarterly, 26,* 135–167.

Diekman, A. B., Brown, E. R., Johnston, A. M., & Clark, E. K. (2010). Seeking congruity between goals and roles: A new look at why women opt out of science, technology, engineering, and mathematics careers. *Psychological Science, 21,* 1051–1057.

Dovidio, J. F., & Gaertner, S. L. (1999). Reducing prejudice: Combating intergroup biases. *Current Directions in Psychological Science, 8,* 101–105.

Duncan, G. J., & Magnuson, K. A. (2005). Can family socioeconomic resources account for racial and ethnic test score gaps? *The Future of Children, 15*(1), 35–54.

Dweck, C. S. (2000). *Self-theories: Their role in motivation, personality, and development.* Philadelphia: Psychology Press.

Eaton, W. O., & Enns, L. R. (1986). Sex differences in human motor activity level. *Psychological Bulletin, 100,* 19–28.

Eccles, J. S. (2005). Subjective task value and the Eccles et al. model of achievement-related choices. In A. J. Elliot & C. S. Dweck (Eds.), *Handbook of competence and motivation* (pp. 105–121). New York: Guilford.

Eccles, J. S. (2007). Families, schools, and developing achievement-related motivations and engagement. In J. E. Grusec & P. D. Hastings (Eds.), *Handbook of socialization: Theory and research* (pp. 665–691). New York: Guilford.

Eccles, J. (2009). Who am I and what am I going to do with my life? Personal and collective identities as motivators of action. *Educational Psychologist, 44,* 78–89.

Edwards, P. A., & Turner, J. D. (2010). Do you hear what I hear? Using the parent story approach to listen and learn from African American parents. In M. L. Dantas & P. C. Manyak (Eds.), *Home–school connections in a multicultural society: Learning from and with culturally and linguistically diverse families* (pp. 137–155). New York: Routledge.

Eisenberg, N., Martin, C. L., & Fabes, R. A. (1996). Gender development and gender effects. In D. C. Berliner & R. C. Calfee (Eds.), *Handbook of educational psychology* (pp. 358–396). New York: Macmillan.

Eriks-Brophy, A., & Crago, M. B. (1994). Transforming classroom discourse: An Inuit example. *Language and Education, 8*(3), 105–122.

Evans, G. W. (2004). The environment of childhood poverty. *American Psychologist, 59,* 77–92.

Evans, G. W., Gonnella, C., Marcynyszyn, L. A., Gentile, L., & Salpekar, N. (2005). The role of chaos in poverty and children's socioemotional adjustment. *Psychological Science, 16,* 560–565.

Evans, G. W., & Schamberg, M. A. (2009). Childhood poverty, chronic stress, and adult working memory. *Proceedings of the National Academy of Sciences of the United States of America, 106,* 6545–6549.

Evans-Winters, V., & Ivie, C. (2009). Lost in the shuffle: Re-calling a critical pedagogy for urban girls. In S. R. Steinberg (Ed.), *Diversity and multiculturalism: A reader* (pp. 411–421). New York: Peter Lang.

Fabes, R. A., Martin, C. L., & Hanish, L. D. (2003). Young children's play qualities in same-, other-, and mixed-sex peer groups. *Child Development, 74,* 921–932.

Fairchild, H. H., & Edwards-Evans, S. (1990). African American dialects and schooling: A review. In A. M. Padilla, H. H. Fairchild, & C. M. Valadez (Eds.), *Bilingual education: Issues and strategies* (pp. 75–85). Newbury Park, CA: Sage.

Farkas, G. (2008). Quantitative studies of oppositional culture: Arguments and evidence. In J. U. Ogbu (Ed.), *Minority status, oppositional culture, and schooling* (pp. 312–347). New York: Routledge.

Farrell, E. (1990). *Hanging in and dropping out: Voices of at-risk high school students.* New York: Teachers College Press.

Feng, J., Spence, I., & Pratt, J. (2007). Playing an action video game reduces gender differences in spatial cognition. *Psychological Science, 18,* 850–855.

Fennema, E. (1987). Sex-related differences in education: Myths, realities, and interventions. In V. Richardson-Koehler (Ed.), *Educators' handbook: A research perspective* (pp. 329–347). White Plains, NY: Longman.

Finn, J. D. (1989). Withdrawing from school. *Review of Educational Research, 59,* 117–142.

Ford, M. E. (1996). Motivational opportunities and obstacles associated with social responsibility and caring behavior in school contexts. In J. Juvonen & K. R. Wentzel (Eds.), *Social motivation: Understanding children's school adjustment* (pp. 126–153). Cambridge, England: Cambridge University Press.

Fredricks, J. A., Blumenfeld, P. C., & Paris, A. H. (2004). School engagement: Potential of the concept, state of the evidence. *Review of Educational Research, 74,* 59–109.

The Freedom Writers (with Gruwell, E.). (1999). *The Freedom Writers diary: How a teacher and 150 teens used writing to change themselves and the world around them.* New York: Broadway Books.

French, D. C., Jansen, E. A., & Pidada, S. (2002). United States and Indonesian children's and adolescents' reports of relational aggression by disliked peers. *Child Development, 73,* 1143–1150.

Frost, J. L., Shin, D., & Jacobs, P. J. (1998). Physical environments and children's play. In O. N. Saracho & B. Spodek (Eds.), *Multiple perspectives on play in early childhood education* (pp. 255–294). Albany: State University of New York Press.

Fuchs, L. S., Fuchs, D., Craddock, C., Hollenbeck, K. N., Hamlett, C. L., & Schatschneider, C. (2008). Effects of small-group tutoring with and without validated classroom instruction on at-risk, students' math problem solving: Are two tiers of prevention better than one? *Journal of Educational Psychology, 100,* 491–509.

Fuligni, A. J. (1998). The adjustment of children from immigrant families. *Current Directions in Psychological Science, 7,* 99–103.

Furnham, A., & Mak, T. (1999). Sex-role stereotyping in television commercials: A review and comparison of fourteen studies done on five continents over 25 years. *Sex Roles, 41,* 413–437.

Gallagher, A. M., & Kaufman, J. C. (Eds.). (2005). *Gender differences in mathematics: An integrative psychological approach.* Cambridge, England: Cambridge University Press.

García, E. E. (1994). *Understanding and meeting the challenge of student cultural diversity.* Boston: Houghton Mifflin.

Garibaldi, A. M. (1992). Educating and motivating African American males to succeed. *Journal of Negro Education, 61*(1), 4–11.

Garnier, H. E., Stein, J. A., & Jacobs, J. K. (1997). The process of dropping out of high school: A 19-year perspective. *American Educational Research Journal, 34,* 395–419.

Gay, G. (2006). Connections between classroom management and culturally responsive teaching. In C. M. Evertson & C. S. Weinstein (Eds.), *Handbook of classroom management: Research, practice, and contemporary issues* (pp. 343–370). Mahwah, NJ: Erlbaum.

Gay, G. (2010). *Culturally responsive teaching: Theory, research, and practice* (2nd ed.). New York: Teachers College Press.

Gerard, J. M., & Buehler, C. (2004). Cumulative environmental risk and youth maladjustment: The role of youth attributes. *Child Development, 75,* 1832–1849.

Gilliland, H. (1988). Discovering and emphasizing the positive aspects of the culture. In H. Gilliland & J. Reyhner (Eds.), *Teaching the Native American.* Dubuque, IA: Kendall/Hunt.

Godley, A., & Escher, A. (2011, April). *Bidialectical African-American students' views on code-switching in and out of school*. Paper presented at the annual meeting of the American Educational Research Association, New Orleans, LA.

Goldenberg, C. (2001). Making schools work for low-income families in the 21st century. In S. B. Neuman & D. K. Dickinson (Eds.), *Handbook of early literacy research* (pp. 211–231). New York: Guilford.

Goldstein, S., & Brooks, R. B. (2006). Why study resilience? In. S. Goldstein & R. B. Brooks (Eds.), *Handbook of resilience in children* (pp. 3–15). New York: Springer.

Gollnick, D. M., & Chinn, P. C. (2009). *Multicultural education in a pluralistic society* (8th ed.). Upper Saddle River, NJ: Merrill/Pearson.

Goodnow, J. J. (2010). Culture. In M. H. Bornstein (Ed.), *Handbook of cultural developmental science* (pp. 3–19). New York: Psychology Press.

Grant, C. A., & Gomez, M. L. (2001). *Campus and classroom: Making schooling multicultural* (2nd ed.). Upper Saddle River, NJ: Merrill/Prentice Hall.

Greenfield, P. M., Trumbull, E., Keller, H., Rothstein-Fisch, C., Suzuki, L. K., & Quiroz, B. (2006). Cultural conceptions of learning and development. In P. A. Alexander & P. H. Winne (Eds.), *Handbook of educational psychology* (2nd ed., pp. 675–692). Mahwah, NJ: Erlbaum.

Greenhow, C., Robelia, B., & Hughes, J. E. (2009). Web 2.0 and classroom research: What path should we take now? *Educational Researcher, 38,* 246–259.

Griffin, S. A., Case, R., & Capodilupo, A. (1995). Teaching for understanding: The importance of the central conceptual structures in the elementary mathematics curriculum. In A. McKeough, J. Lupart, & A. Marini (Eds.), *Teaching for transfer: Fostering generalization in learning* (pp. 123–151). Mahwah, NJ: Erlbaum.

Grissmer, D. W., Williamson, S., Kirby, S. N., & Berends, M. (1998). Exploring the rapid rise in Black achievement scores in the United States (1970–1990). In U. Neisser (Ed.), *The rising curve: Long-term gains in IQ and related measures* (pp. 251–285). Washington, DC: American Psychological Association.

Gruman, D. H., Harachi, T. W., Abbott, R. D., Catalano, R. F., & Fleming, C. B. (2008). Longitudinal effects of student mobility on three dimensions of elementary school engagement. *Child Development, 79,* 1833–1852.

Grusec, J. E., & Hastings, P. D. (Eds.). (2007). *Handbook of socialization: Theory and research.* New York: Guilford.

Gutiérrez, K. D., & Rogoff, B. (2003). Cultural ways of learning: Individual traits or repertoires of practice. *Educational Researcher, 32*(5), 19–25.

Halpern, D. F. (2004). A cognitive-process taxonomy for sex differences in cognitive abilities. *Current Directions in Psychological Science, 13,* 135–139.

Halpern, D. F. (2006). Assessing gender gaps in learning and academic achievement. In P. A. Alexander & P. H. Winne (Eds.), *Handbook of educational psychology* (2nd ed., pp. 635–653). Mahwah, NJ: Erlbaum.

Halpern, D. F., Benbow, C. P., Geary, D. C., Gur, R. C., Hyde, J. S., & Gernsbacher, M. A. (2007). The science of sex differences in science and mathematics. *Psychological Science in the Public Interest, 8*(1), 1–51.

Halpern, D. F., & LaMay, M. L. (2000). The smarter sex: A critical review of sex differences in intelligence. *Educational Psychology Review, 12,* 229–246.

Hamre, B. K., & Pianta, R. C. (2005). Can instructional and emotional support in the first-grade classroom make a difference for children at risk of school failure? *Child Development, 76,* 949–967.

Hankin, B. L., Mermelstein, R., & Roesch, L. (2007). Sex differences in adolescent depression: Stress exposure and reactivity models. *Child Development, 78,* 279–295.

Hardré, P. L., & Reeve, J. (2003). A motivational model of rural students' intentions to persist in, versus drop out of, high school. *Journal of Educational Psychology, 95,* 347–356.

Hardy, M. S. (2002). Behavior-oriented approaches to reducing youth gun violence. *The Future of Children, 12*(2), 101–117.

Harris, J. R. (1995). Where is the child's environment? A group socialization theory of development. *Psychological Review, 102,* 458–489.

Harter, S. (1999). *The construction of the self: A developmental perspective.* New York: Guilford.

Hattie, J. A. C. (2009). *Visible learning: A synthesis of over 800 meta-analyses relating to achievement.* London: Routledge.

Hawkins, F. P. L. (1997). *Journey with children: The autobiography of a teacher.* Niwot: University Press of Colorado.

Hayward, C. (Ed.). (2003). *Gender differences at puberty.* Cambridge, England: Cambridge University Press.

Heath, S. B. (1982). Questioning at home and at school: A comparative study. In G. Spindler (Ed.), *The ethnography of schooling: Educational anthropology in action* (pp. 102–131). New York: Holt, Rinehart & Winston.

Heath, S. B. (1989). Oral and literate traditions among black Americans living in poverty. *American Psychologist, 44,* 367–373.

Herbert, J., & Stipek, D. (2005). The emergence of gender differences in children's perceptions of their academic competence. *Journal of Applied Developmental Psychology, 26,* 276–295.

Herman, M. (2004). Forced to choose: Some determinants of racial identification in multiracial adolescents. *Child Development, 75,* 730–748.

Hernandez, D. J., Denton, N. A., & Macartney, S. E. (2008). Children in immigrant families: Looking to America's future. *Social Policy Report, 22*(3) (Society for Research in Child Development).

Hill, N. E., Bush, K. R., & Roosa, M. W. (2003). Parenting and family socialization strategies and children's mental health: Low-income Mexican-American and Euro-American mothers and children. *Child Development, 74,* 189–204.

Hines, M., Golombok, S., Rust, J., Johnston, K. J., Golding, J., & the Avon Longitudinal Study of Parents and Children Study Team. (2002). Testosterone during pregnancy and gender role behavior of preschool children: A longitudinal, population study. *Child Development, 73,* 1678–1687.

Hong, Y., Morris, M. W., Chiu, C., & Benet-Martínez, V. (2000). Multicultural minds: A dynamic constructivist approach to culture and cognition. *American Psychologist, 55,* 709–720.

Hubbs-Tait, L., Nation, J. R., Krebs, N. F., & Bellinger, D. C. (2005). Neurotoxicants, micronutrients, and social environments: Individual and combined effects on children's development. *Psychological Science in the Public Interest, 6,* 57–121.

Hughes, J. M., Bigler, R. S., & Levy, S. R. (2007). Consequences of learning about historical racism among European American and African American children. *Child Development, 78,* 1689–1705.

Huguet, P., & Régner, I. (2007). Stereotype threat among schoolgirls in quasi-ordinary classroom circumstances. *Journal of Educational Psychology, 99,* 545–560.

Hulit, L. M., & Howard, M. R. (2006). *Born to talk* (4th ed.). Boston: Allyn & Bacon.

Hursh, D. (2007). Assessing No Child Left Behind and the rise of neoliberal education policies. *American Educational Research Journal, 44,* 493–518.

Hyde, J. S. (2005). The gender similarities hypothesis. *American Psychologist, 60,* 581–592.

Hyde, J. S. (2007). New directions in the study of gender similarities and differences. *Current Directions in Psychological Science, 16,* 259–263.

Hyde, J. S., & Durik, A. M. (2005). Gender, competence, and motivation. In A. J. Elliot & C. S. Dweck (Eds.), *Handbook of competence and motivation* (pp. 375–391). New York: Guilford.

Hyde, J. S., Lindberg, S. M., Linn, M. C., Ellis, A. B., & Williams, C. C. (2008). Gender similarities characterize math performance. *Science, 321*(5888), 494–495.

Hymel, S., Comfort, C., Schonert-Reichl, K., & McDougall, P. (1996). Academic failure and school dropout: The influence of peers. In J. Juvonen & K. R. Wentzel (Eds.), *Social motivation: Understanding children's school adjustment* (pp. 313–345). Cambridge, England: Cambridge University Press.

Igoa, C. (1995). *The inner world of the immigrant child.* Mahwah, NJ: Erlbaum.

Inglehart, M., Brown, D. R., & Vida, M. (1994). Competition, achievement, and gender: A stress theoretical analysis. In P. R. Pintrich, D. R. Brown, & C. E. Weinstein (Eds.), *Student motivation, cognition, and learning: Essays in honor of Wilbert J. McKeachie* (pp. 311–329). Mahwah, NJ: Erlbaum.

Irving, M. A., & Hudley, C. (2008). Oppositional identity and academic achievement among African American males. In J. U. Ogbu (Ed.), *Minority status, oppositional culture, and schooling* (pp. 374–394). New York: Routledge.

Ivory, J. D. (2006). Still a man's game: Gender representation in online reviews of video games. *Mass Communication and Society, 9*(1), 103–114.

Janosz, M., Le Blanc, M., Boulerice, B., & Tremblay, R. E. (2000). Predicting different types of school dropouts: A typological approach with two longitudinal samples. *Journal of Educational Psychology, 92,* 171–190.

Jenlink, C. L. (1994, April). *Music: A lifeline for the self-esteem of at-risk students.* Paper presented at the annual meeting of the American Educational Research Association, New Orleans, LA.

Jiang, B. (2010). English language learners: Understanding their needs. In G. S. Goodman (Ed.), *Educational psychology reader: The art and science of how people learn* (pp. 179–194). New York: Peter Lang.

Jimerson, S., Egeland, B., & Teo, A. (1999). A longitudinal study of achievement trajectories: Factors associated with change. *Journal of Educational Psychology, 91,* 116–126.

Jones, S. M., & Dindia, K. (2004). A meta-analytic perspective on sex equity in the classroom. *Review of Educational Research, 74,* 443–471.

Jovanovic, J., & King, S. S. (1998). Boys and girls in the performance-based science classroom: Who's doing the performing? *American Educational Research Journal, 35,* 477–496.

Jozefowicz, D. M., Arbreton, A. J., Eccles, J. S., Barber, B. L., & Colarossi, L. (1994, April). *Seventh grade student, parent, and teacher factors associated with later school dropout or movement into alternative educational settings.* Paper presented at the annual meeting of the American Educational Research Association, New Orleans, LA.

Kağitçibaşi, Ç. (2007). *Family, self, and human development across cultures: Theory and applications* (2nd ed.). Mahwah, NJ: Erlbaum.

Kahne, J. E., & Sporte, S. E. (2008). Developing citizens: The impact of civic learning opportunities on students' commitment to civic participation. *American Educational Research Journal, 45,* 738–766.

Keil, F. C., & Newman, G. E. (2008). Two tales of conceptual change: What changes and what remains the same. In S. Vosniadou (Ed.), *International handbook on conceptual change* (pp. 83–101). New York: Routledge.

Kelly, A., & Smail, B. (1986). Sex stereotypes and attitudes to science among eleven-year-old children. *British Journal of Educational Psychology, 56,* 158–168.

Killen, M. (2007). Children's social and moral reasoning about exclusion. *Current Directions in Psychological Science, 16,* 32–36.

Kim, J. (2011). Is it bigger than hip-hop? Examining the problems and potential of hip-hop in the curriculum. In V. Kinloch (Ed.), *Urban literacies: Critical perspectives on language, learning, and community* (pp. 160–176). New York: Teachers College Press.

Kincheloe, J. L. (2009). No short cuts in urban education: Metropedagogy and diversity. In S. R. Steinberg (Ed.), *Diversity and multiculturalism: A reader* (pp. 379–409). New York: Peter Lang.

Kitayama, S., Duffy, S., & Uchida, Y. (2007). Self as cultural mode of being. In S. Kitayama & D. Cohen (Eds.), *Handbook of cultural psychology* (pp. 136–174). New York: Guilford.

Koeppel, J., & Mulrooney, M. (1992). The Sister Schools Program: A way for children to learn about cultural diversity—When there isn't any in their school. *Young Children, 48*(1), 44–47.

Koger, S. M., Schettler, T., & Weiss, B. (2005). Environmental toxins and developmental disabilities: A challenge for psychologists. *American Psychologist, 60,* 243–255.

Koltko-Rivera, M. E. (2004). The psychology of worldviews. *Review of General Psychology, 8,* 3–58.

Kraus, M. W., Piff, P. K., & Keltner, D. (2011). Social class as culture: The convergence of resources and rank in the social realm. *Current Directions in Psychological Science, 20,* 246–250.

Ladson-Billings, G. (1994a). *The dreamkeepers: Successful teachers of African American children.* San Francisco: Jossey-Bass.

Ladson-Billings, G. (1995a). But that's just good teaching! The case for culturally relevant pedagogy. *Theory into Practice, 34,* 159–165.

LaFromboise, T., Coleman, H. L. K., & Gerton, J. (1993). Psychological impact of biculturalism: Evidence and theory. *Psychological Bulletin, 114,* 395–412.

Laird, J., Kienzl, G., DeBell, M., & Chapman, C. (2007). *Dropout rates in the United States: 2005* (Compendium Report, National Center for Education Statistics 2007–059). Washington: NCES.

Lareau, A. (2003). *Unequal childhoods: Class, race, and family life.* Berkeley: University of California Press.

Leaper, C., & Friedman, C. K. (2007). The socialization of gender. In J. E. Grusec & P. D. Hastings (Eds.), *Handbook of socialization: Theory and research* (pp. 561–587). New York: Guilford.

Lee, J.-S., & Bowen, N. K. (2006). Parent involvement, cultural capital, and the achievement gap among elementary school children. *American Educational Research Journal, 43,* 193–218.

Lee, O. (1999). Science knowledge, world views, and information sources in social and cultural contexts: Making sense after a natural disaster. *American Educational Research Journal, 36,* 187–219.

Lee, V. E., & Burkam, D. T. (2003). Dropping out of high school: The role of school organization and structure. *American Educational Research Journal, 40,* 353–393.

Leventhal, T., & Brooks-Gunn, J. (2000). The neighborhoods they live in: The effects of neighborhood residence upon child and adolescent outcomes. *Psychological Bulletin, 126,* 309–337.

Li, J. (2005). Mind or virtue: Western and Chinese beliefs about learning. *Current Directions in Psychological Science, 14,* 190–194.

Li, J., & Fischer, K. W. (2004). Thought and affect in American and Chinese learners' beliefs about learning. In D. Y. Dai & R. J. Sternberg (Eds.), *Motivation, emotion, and cognition: Integrative*

perspectives on intellectual functioning and development (pp. 385–418). Mahwah, NJ: Erlbaum.

Liben, L. S., & Bigler, R. S. (2002). The developmental course of gender differentiation: Conceptualizing, measuring, and evaluating constructs and pathways. *Monographs of the Society for Research in Child Development, 67*(2, Serial No. 269).

Lipka, J., with Mohatt, G. V., & the Ciulistet Group. (1998). *Transforming the culture of schools: Yup'ik Eskimo examples.* Mahwah, NJ: Erlbaum.

Lipka, J., Yanez, E., Andrew-Ihrke, D., & Adam, S. (2009). A two-way process for developing effective culturally based math: Examples from math in a cultural context. In B. Greer, S. Mukhopadhyay, A. B. Powell, & S. Nelson-Barber (Eds.), *Culturally responsive mathematics education* (pp. 257–280). New York: Routledge.

Lipman, P. (1995). "Bringing out the best in them": The contribution of culturally relevant teachers to educational reform. *Theory into Practice, 34,* 202–208.

Lippa, R. A. (2002). *Gender, nature, and nurture.* Mahwah, NJ: Erlbaum.

Liss, M. B. (1983). Learning gender-related skills through play. In M. B. Liss (Ed.), *Social and cognitive skills: Sex roles and children's play* (pp. 147–166). San Diego, CA: Academic Press.

Lomawaima, K. T. (1995). Educating Native Americans. In J. A. Banks & C. A. M. Banks (Eds.), *Handbook of research on multicultural education* (pp. 451–467). New York: Macmillan.

Lopez, A. M. (2003). Mixed-race school-age children: A summary of census 2000 data. *Educational Researcher, 32*(6), 25–37.

Losh, S. C. (2003). On the application of social cognition and social location to creating causal explanatory structures. *Educational Research Quarterly, 26*(3), 17–33.

Lucas, K., & Sherry, J. L. (2004). Sex differences in video game play: A communication-based explanation. *Communication Research, 31,* 499–523.

Lundeberg, M., & Mohan, L. (2009). Context matters: Gender and cross-cultural differences in confidence. In D. J. Hacker, J. Dunlosky, & A. C. Graesser (Eds.), *Handbook of metacognition in education* (pp. 221–239). New York: Routledge.

Luthar, S. S. (2006). Over-scheduling versus other stressors: Challenges of high socioeconomic status families. *Social Policy Report, 20*(4), 16–17. Ann Arbor, MI: Society for Research in Child Development.

Luthar, S. S., & Latendresse, S. J. (2005). Children of the affluent: Challenges to well-being. *Current Directions in Psychological Science, 14,* 49–53.

Lytton, H., & Romney, D. M. (1991). Parents' differential socialization of boys and girls: A meta-analysis. *Psychological Bulletin, 109,* 267–296.

Maccoby, E. E. (2002). Gender and group process: A developmental perspective. *Current Directions in Psychological Science, 11,* 54–58.

MacLean, D. J., Sasse, D. K., Keating, D. P., Stewart, B. E., & Miller, F. K. (1995, April). *All-girls' mathematics and science instruction in early adolescence: Longitudinal effects.* Paper presented at the annual meeting of the American Educational Research Association, San Francisco.

Manning, M. L., & Baruth, L. G. (2009). *Multicultural education of children and adolescents* (5th ed.). Boston: Allyn & Bacon/Pearson.

Marks, H. M. (2000). Student engagement in instructional activity: Patterns in the elementary, middle, and high school years. *American Educational Research Journal, 37,* 153–184.

Markus, H. R., & Hamedani, M. G. (2007). Sociocultural psychology: The dynamic interdependence among self systems and social systems. In S. Kitayama & D. Cohen (Eds.), *Handbook of cultural psychology* (pp. 3–39). New York: Guilford.

Marsh, H. W., Martin, A. J., & Cheng, J. H. S. (2008). A multilevel perspective on gender in classroom motivation and climate: Potential benefits of male teachers for boys? *Journal of Educational Psychology, 100,* 78–95.

Martin, C. L., & Ruble, D. (2004). Children's search for gender cues: Cognitive perspectives on gender development. *Current Directions in Psychological Science, 13,* 67–70.

Masten, A. S. (2001). Ordinary magic: Resilience processes in development. *American Psychologist, 56,* 227–238.

Masten, A. S., & Coatsworth, J. D. (1998). The development of competence in favorable and unfavorable environments. *American Psychologist, 53,* 205–220.

Mathews, J. (1988). *Escalante: The best teacher in America.* New York: Henry Holt.

Matthews, J. S., Ponitz, C. C., & Morrison, F. J. (2009). *Journal of Educational Psychology, 101,* 689–704.

Matute-Bianchi, M. E. (2008). Situational ethnicity and patterns of school performance among immigrant and nonimmigrant Mexican-descent students. In J. U. Ogbu (Ed.), *Minority status, oppositional culture, and schooling* (pp. 398–432). New York: Routledge.

McBrien, J. L. (2005a). *Discrimination and academic motivation in adolescent refugee girls.* Unpublished doctoral dissertation, Emory University, Atlanta, GA.

McCall, R. B. (1994). Academic underachievers. *Current Directions in Psychological Science, 3,* 15–19.

McCall, R. B., & Plemons, B. W. (2001). The concept of critical periods and their implications for early childhood services. In D. B. Bailey, Jr., J. T. Bruer, F. J. Symons, & J. W. Lichtman (Eds.), *Critical thinking about critical periods* (pp. 267–287). Baltimore: Brookes.

McCarthy, A., Lee, K., Itakura, S., & Muir, D. W. (2006). Cultural display rules drive eye gaze during thinking. *Journal of Cultural Psychology, 37,* 717–722.

McDevitt, T. M., & Ormrod, J. E. (2013). *Child development and education* (5th ed.). Upper Saddle River, NJ: Merrill/Prentice-Hall.

McGlothlin, H., & Killen, M. (2006). Intergroup attitudes of European American children attending ethnically homogeneous schools. *Child Development, 77,* 1375–1386.

McIntyre, E. (2010). Issues in funds of knowledge teaching and research: Key concepts from a study of Appalachian families and schooling. In M. L. Dantas & P. C. Manyak (Eds.), *Home–school connections in a multicultural society: Learning from and with culturally and linguistically diverse families* (pp. 201–217). New York: Routledge.

McLoyd, V. C. (1998). Socioeconomic disadvantage and child development. *American Psychologist, 53,* 185–204.

McMillan, J. H., & Reed, D. F. (1994). At-risk students and resiliency: Factors contributing to academic success. *Clearing House, 67*(3), 137–140.

Medin, D. L. (2005, August). *Role of culture and expertise in cognition.* Invited address presented at the annual meeting of the American Psychological Association, Washington, DC.

Mehan, H. (1979). *Social organization in the classroom.* Cambridge, MA: Harvard University Press.

Mejía-Arauz, R., Rogoff, B., Dexter, A., & Najafi, B. (2007). Cultural variation in children's social organization. *Child Development, 78,* 1001–1014.

Miller, L. S. (1995). *An American imperative: Accelerating minority educational advancement.* New Haven, CT: Yale University Press.

Miller, M. K., & Summers, A. (2007). Gender differences in video game characters' roles, appearances, and attire as portrayed in video game magazines. *Sex Roles, 57,* 733–742.

Miller, P. M. (2011). A critical analysis of the research on student homelessness. *Review of Educational Research, 81,* 308–337.

Miller, S. M. (2003). How literature discussion shapes thinking: ZPDs for teaching/learning habits of the heart and mind. In A. Kozulin, B. Gindis, V. S. Ageyev, & S. M. Miller (Eds.), *Vygotsky's educational theory in cultural context* (pp. 289–316). Cambridge, England: Cambridge University Press.

Milner, H. R. (2006). Classroom management in urban classrooms. In C. M. Evertson & C. S. Weinstein (Eds.), *Handbook of classroom management: Research, practice, and contemporary issues* (pp. 491–522). Mahwah, NJ: Erlbaum.

Mohan, E. (2009). Putting multiethnic students on the radar: A case for greater consideration of our multiethnic students. In S. R. Steinberg (Ed.), *Diversity and multiculturalism: A reader* (pp. 132–141). New York: Peter Lang.

Mohatt, G., & Erickson, F. (1981). Cultural differences in teaching styles in an Odawa school: A sociolinguistic approach. In H. T. Trueba, G. P. Guthrie, & K. H. Au (Eds.), *Culture and the bilingual classroom: Studies in classroom ethnography* (pp. 105–119). Rowley, MA: Newbury House.

Moje, E. B., & Hinchman, K. (2004). Culturally responsive practices for youth literacy learning. In T. L. Jetton & J. A. Dole (Eds.), *Adolescent literacy research and practice* (pp. 321–350). New York: Guilford.

Monzó, L. D. (2010). Fostering academic identities among Latino immigrant students: Contextualizing parents' roles. In M. L. Dantas & P. C. Manyak (Eds.), *Home–school connections in a multicultural society: Learning from and with culturally and linguistically diverse families* (pp. 112–130). New York: Routledge.

Moore, S., & Rosenthal, D. (2006). *Sexuality in adolescence: Current trends.* London: Routledge.

Morales, J. R., & Guerra, N. G. (2006). Effects of multiple context and cumulative stress on urban children's adjustment in elementary school. *Child Development, 77,* 907–923.

Morelli, G. A., & Rothbaum, F. (2007). Situating the child in context: Attachment relationships and self-regulation in different cultures. In S. Kitayama & D. Cohen (Eds.), *Handbook of cultural psychology* (pp. 500–527). New York: Guilford.

Mosborg, S. (2002). Speaking of history: How adolescents use their knowledge of history in reading the daily news. *Cognition and Instruction, 20,* 323–358.

Murdock, T. B. (2000). Incorporating economic context into educational psychology: Methodological and conceptual challenges. *Educational Psychologist, 35,* 113–124.

National Research Council. (2004). *Engaging schools: Fostering high school students' motivation to learn.* Washington, DC: National Academies Press.

National Science Foundation. (2007). *Women, minorities, and persons with disabilities in science and engineering: 2007.* Arlington, VA: Author. Retrieved July 12, 2007, from www.nsf.gov/statistics/wmpd.

NCSS Task Force on Ethnic Studies Curriculum Guidelines. (1992). Curriculum guidelines for multicultural education. *Social Education, 56,* 274–294.

Nelson-Barber, S., & Estrin, E. T. (1995). Bringing Native American perspectives to mathematics and science teaching. *Theory into Practice, 34,* 174–185.

Nesdale, D., Maass, A., Durkin, K., & Griffiths, J. (2005). Group norms, threat, and children's racial prejudice. *Child Development, 76,* 652–663.

Nettles, S. M., Caughy, M. O., & O'Campo, P. J. (2008). School adjustment in the early grades: Toward an integrated model of neighborhood, parental, and child processes. *Review of Educational Research, 78,* 3–32.

Newkirk, T. (2002). *Misreading masculinity: Boys, literacy, and popular culture.* Portsmouth, NH: Heinemann.

Newmann, F. M. (1981). Reducing student alienation in high schools: Implications of theory. *Harvard Educational Review, 51,* 546–564.

Noble, K. G., Tottenham, N., & Casey, B. J. (2005). Neuroscience perspectives on disparities in school readiness and cognitive achievement. *The Future of Children, 15*(1), 71–89.

Norenzayan, A., Choi, I., & Peng, K. (2007). Perception and cognition. In S. Kitayama & D. Cohen (Eds.), *Handbook of cultural psychology* (pp. 569–594). New York: Guilford.

Nosek, B. A., & Smyth, F. L. (2011). Implicit social cognitions predict sex difference in math engagement and achievement. *American Educational Research Journal, 48*, 1125–1156.

Nuttall, R. L., Casey, M. B., & Pezaris, E. (2005). Spatial ability as mediator of gender differences on mathematics tests. In A. M. Gallagher & J. C. Kaufman (Eds.), *Gender differences in mathematics: An integrative psychological approach* (pp. 121–142). Cambridge, England: Cambridge University Press.

Ochs, E. (1982). Talking to children in western Samoa. *Language and Society, 11*, 77–104.

O'Donnell, D. A., Schwab-Stone, M. E., & Muyeed, A. Z. (2002). Multidimensional resilience in urban children exposed to community violence. *Child Development, 73*, 1265–1282.

Ogbu, J. U. (1999). Beyond language: Ebonics, proper English, and identity in a Black-American speech community. *American Educational Research Journal, 36*, 147–184.

Ogbu, J. U. (2003). *Black American students in an affluent suburb: A study of academic disengagement.* Mahwah, NJ: Erlbaum.

Oskamp, S. (Ed.). (2000). *Reducing prejudice and discrimination.* Mahwah, NJ: Erlbaum.

Owens, R. E., Jr. (1995). *Language disorders: A functional approach to assessment and intervention* (2nd ed.). Boston: Allyn & Bacon.

Padilla, A. M. (1994). Bicultural development: A theoretical and empirical examination. In R. G. Malgady & O. Rodriguez (Eds.), *Theoretical and conceptual issues in Hispanic mental health* (pp. 20–51). Malabar, FL: Krieger.

Pajares, F. (2005). Gender differences in mathematics self-efficacy beliefs. In A. M. Gallagher & J. C. Kaufman (Eds.), *Gender differences in mathematics: An integrative psychological approach* (pp. 294–315). Cambridge, England: Cambridge University Press.

Paris, D., & Kirkland, D. E. (2011). "The consciousness of the verbal artist": Understanding vernacular literacies in digital and embodied spaces. In V. Kinloch (Ed.), *Urban literacies: Critical perspectives on language, learning, and community* (pp. 177–194). New York: Teachers College Press.

Parke, R. D., Coltrane, S., Duffy, S., Buriel, R., Dennis, J., Powers, J., et al. (2004). Economic stress, parenting, and child adjustment in Mexican American and European American families. *Child Development, 75*, 1632–1656.

Pawlas, G. E. (1994). Homeless students at the school door. *Educational Leadership, 51*(8), 79–82.

Payne, R. K. (2005). *A framework for understanding poverty* (4th rev. ed.). Highlands, TX: aha! Process.

Pearce, R. R. (2006). Effects of cultural and social structural factors on the achievement of White and Chinese American students at school transition points. *American Educational Research Journal, 43*, 75–101.

Pedersen, E., Faucher, T. A., & Eaton, W. W. (1978). A new perspective on the effects of first-grade teachers on children's subsequent adult status. *Harvard Educational Review, 48*(1), 1–31.

Pellegrini, A. D. (2011). "In the eye of the beholder": Sex bias in observations and ratings of children's aggression. *Educational Researcher, 40*, 281–286.

Pellegrini, A. D., & Archer, J. (2005). Sex differences in competitive and aggressive behavior. In B. J. Ellis & D. F. Bjorklund (Eds.), *Origins of the social mind: Evolutionary psychology and child development* (pp. 219–244). New York: Guilford.

Pellegrini, A. D., Kato, K., Blatchford, P., & Baines, E. (2002). A short-term longitudinal study of children's playground games across the first year of school: Implications for social competence and adjustment to school. *American Educational Research Journal, 39*, 991–1015.

Pfeifer, J. H., Brown, C. S., & Juvonen, J. (2007). Teaching tolerance in schools: Lessons learned since *Brown* v. *Board of Education* about the development and reduction of children's prejudice. *Social Policy Report, 21*(2), 3–13, 16–17, 20–23. Ann Arbor, MI: Society for Research in Child Development.

Phalet, K., Andriessen, I., & Lens, W. (2004). How future goals enhance motivation and learning in multicultural classrooms. *Educational Psychology Review, 16*, 59–89.

Phelan, P., Yu, H. C., & Davidson, A. L. (1994). Navigating the psychosocial pressures of adolescence: The voices and experiences of high school youth. *American Educational Research Journal, 31*, 415–447.

Phillips, G., McNaughton, S., & MacDonald, S. (2004). Managing the mismatch: Enhancing early literacy progress for children with diverse language and cultural identities in mainstream urban schools in New Zealand. *Journal of Educational Psychology, 96*, 309–323.

Pianta, R. C. (1999). *Enhancing relationships between children and teachers.* Washington, DC: American Psychological Association.

Pianta, R. C., & Hamre, B. K. (2009). Conceptualization, measurement, and improvement of classroom processes: Standardized observation can leverage capacity. *Educational Researcher, 38*, 109–119.

Pipher, M. (1994). *Reviving Ophelia: Saving the selves of adolescent girls.* New York: Putnam.

Pitner, R. O., Astor, R. A., Benbenishty, R., Haj-Yahia, M. M., & Zeira, A. (2003). The effects of group stereotypes on adolescents' reasoning about peer retribution. *Child Development, 74*, 413–425.

Polakow, V. (2007). In the shadows of the ownership society: Homeless children and their families. In S. Books (Ed.), *Invisible children in the society and its schools* (3rd ed., pp. 39–62). Mahwah, NJ: Erlbaum.

Pollack, W. S. (2006). Sustaining and reframing vulnerability and connection: Creating genuine resilience in boys and young males. In S. Goldstein & R. B. Brooks (Eds.), *Handbook of resilience in children* (pp. 65–77). New York: Springer.

Ponitz, C. C., Rimm-Kaufman, S. E., Brock, L. L., & Nathanson, L. (2009). Early adjustment, gender differences, and classroom organizational climate in first grade. *Elementary School Journal, 110*, 142–162.

Portes, P. R. (1996). Ethnicity and culture in educational psychology. In D. C. Berliner & R. C. Calfee (Eds.), *Handbook of educational psychology* (pp. 331–357). New York: Macmillan.

Quinn, P. C., & Liben, L. S. (2008). A sex difference in mental rotation in young infants. *Psychological Science, 19*, 1067–1070.

Raikes, H., Pan, B. A., Luze, G., Tamis-LeMonda, C. S., Brooks-Gunn, J., Constantine, J., et al. (2006). Mother-child bookreading in low-income families: Correlates and outcomes during the first three years of life. *Child Development, 77*, 924–953.

Ramey, C. T., & Ramey, S. L. (1998). Early intervention and early experience. *American Psychologist, 53*, 109–120.

Raudenbush, S. W. (2009). The *Brown* legacy and the O'Connor challenge: Transforming schools in the images of children's potential. *Educational Researcher, 38*, 169–180.

Reis, S. M., McCoach, D. B., Little, C. A., Muller, L. M., & Kaniskan, R. B. (2011). The effects of differentiated instruction and enrichment pedagogy on reading achievement in five elementary schools. *American Educational Research Journal, 48*, 462–501.

Reschly, A. L., & Christenson, S. L. (2009). Parents as essential partners for fostering students' learning outcomes. In R. Gilman, E. S. Huebner, & M. J. Furlong (Eds.), *Handbook of positive psychology in schools* (pp. 257–272). New York: Routledge.

Reynolds, R. E., Taylor, M. A., Steffensen, M. S., Shirey, L. L., & Anderson, R. C. (1982). Cultural schemata and reading comprehension. *Reading Research Quarterly, 17*, 353–366.

Rhodes, M., & Gelman, S. A. (2008). Categories influence predictions about individual consistency. *Child Development, 79*, 1270–1287.

Robinson, J. P., & Lubienski, S. T. (2011). The development of gender achievement gaps in mathematics and reading during elementary and middle school: Examining direct cognitive assessments and teacher ratings. *American Educational Research Journal, 48*, 268–302.

Rogoff, B. (2003). *The cultural nature of human development.* Oxford, England: Oxford University Press.

Rogoff, B. (2007, March). Cultural perspectives help us see developmental processes. In M. Gauvain & R. L. Munroe (Chairs), *Contributions of socio-historical theory and cross-cultural research to the study of child development.* Symposium conducted at the biennial meeting of the Society for Research in Child Development, Boston.

Rose, A. J., & Smith, R. L. (2009). Sex differences in peer relationships. In K. H. Rubin, W. M. Bukowski, & B. Laursen (Eds.), *Handbook of peer interactions, relationships, and groups* (pp. 379–393). New York: Guilford.

Rothbart, M. K. (2011). *Becoming who we are: Temperament and personality in development.* New York: Guilford.

Rubie-Davies, C., Hattie, J., & Hamilton, R. (2006). Expecting the best for students: Teacher expectations and academic outcomes. *British Journal of Educational Psychology, 76*, 429–444.

Ruble, D. N., Martin, C. L., & Berenbaum, S. A. (2006). Gender development. In W. Damon & R. M. Lerner (Series Eds.) & N. Eisenberg (Vol. Ed.), *Handbook of child psychology: Vol. 3. Social, emotional, and personality development* (6th ed., pp. 858–932). Hoboken, NJ: Wiley.

Rudolph, K. D., Caldwell, M. S., & Conley, C. S. (2005). Need for approval and children's well-being. *Child Development, 76,* 309–323.

Rumberger, R. W. (1995). Dropping out of middle school: A multilevel analysis of students and schools. *American Educational Research Journal, 32,* 583–625.

Ryan, R. M., & Kuczkowski, R. (1994). The imaginary audience, self-consciousness, and public individuation in adolescence. *Journal of Personality, 62,* 219–237.

Sadker, M. P., & Sadker, D. (1994). *Failing at fairness: How our schools cheat girls.* New York: Touchstone.

Sam, D. L., & Berry, J. W. (2010). Acculturation: When individuals and groups of different cultural backgrounds meet. *Perspectives on Psychological Science, 5,* 472–481.

Sanders, M. G. (1996). Action teams in action: Interviews and observations in three schools in the Baltimore School—Family—Community Partnership Program. *Journal of Education for Students Placed at Risk, 1,* 249–262.

Schoon, I. (2006). *Risk and resilience: Adaptations in changing times.* Cambridge, England: Cambridge University Press.

Schultz, K., Buck, P., & Niesz, T. (2000). Democratizing conversations: Racialized talk in a post-desegregated middle school. *American Educational Research Journal, 37,* 33–65.

Seiffge-Krenke, I., Aunola, K., & Nurmi, J.-E. (2009). Changes in stress perception and coping during adolescence: The role of situational and personal factors. *Child Development, 80,* 259–279.

Sidel, R. (1996). *Keeping women and children last: America's war on the poor.* New York: Penguin.

Siegler, R. S. (2009). Improving the numerical understanding of children from low-income families. *Child Development Perspectives, 3,* 118–124.

Sigman, M., & Whaley, S. E. (1998). The role of nutrition in the development of intelligence. In U. Neisser (Ed.), *The rising curve: Long-term gains in IQ and related measures* (pp. 155–182). Washington, DC: American Psychological Association.

Sirin, S. R. (2005). Socioeconomic status and academic achievement: A meta-analytic review of research. *Review of Educational Research, 75,* 417–453.

Sirin, S. R., & Ryce, P. (2010). Cultural incongruence between teachers and families: Implications for immigrant students. In E. L. Grigorenko & R. Takanishi (Eds.), *Immigration, diversity, and education* (pp. 151–169). New York: Routledge.

Sleeter, C. E., & Grant, C. A. (1999). *Making choices for multicultural education: Five approaches to race, class, and gender* (3rd ed.). Upper Saddle River, NJ: Merrill/Prentice Hall.

Slonim, M. B. (1991). *Children, culture, ethnicity: Evaluating and understanding the impact.* New York: Garland.

Smitherman, G. (1994). "The blacker the berry the sweeter the juice": African American student writers. In A. H. Dyson & C. Genishi (Eds.), *The need for story: Cultural diversity in classroom and community* (pp. 80–101). Urbana, IL: National Council of Teachers of English.

Smitherman, G. (1998). Black English/Ebonics: What it be like? In T. Perry & L. Delpit (Eds.), *The real Ebonics debate: Power, language, and the education of African-American children* (pp. 29–37). Boston: Beacon Press.

Spears, A. K. (2007). Improvisation, semantic license, and augmentation. In H. S. Alim & J. Baugh (Eds.), *Talkin Black talk: Language, education, and social change* (pp. 100–111). New York: Teachers College Press.

Spelke, E. S. (2005). Sex differences in intrinsic aptitude for mathematics and science? A critical review. *American Psychologist, 60,* 950–958.

Spera, C. (2005). A review of the relationship among parenting practices, parenting styles, and adolescent school achievement. *Educational Psychology Review, 17,* 125–146.

Stack, C. B., & Burton, L. M. (1993). Kinscripts. *Journal of Comparative Family Studies, 24,* 157–170.

Steinberg, L., Blinde, P. L., & Chan, K. S. (1984). Dropping out among language minority youth. *Review of Educational Research, 54,* 113–132.

Suh, S., Suh, J., & Houston, I. (2007). Predictors of categorical at-risk high school dropouts. *Journal of Counseling & Development, 85,* 196–203.

Suina, J. H., & Smolkin, L. B. (1994). From natal culture to school culture to dominant society culture: Supporting transitions for Pueblo Indian students. In P. M. Greenfield & R. R. Cocking (Eds.), *Cross-cultural roots of minority child development* (pp. 115–130). Mahwah, NJ: Erlbaum.

Tate, W. F. (1995). Returning to the root: A culturally relevant approach to mathematics pedagogy. *Theory into Practice, 34,* 166–173.

Tatum, B. D. (1997). *"Why are all the black kids sitting together in the cafeteria?" and other conversations about race.* New York: Basic Books.

Tharp, R. G. (1989). Psychocultural variables and constants: Effects on teaching and learning in schools. *American Psychologist, 44,* 349–359.

Théberge, C. L. (1994, April). *Small-group vs. whole-class discussion: Gaining the floor in science lessons.* Paper presented at the annual meeting of the American Educational Research Association, New Orleans, LA.

Theobald, P., & Herley, W. (2009). Rurality, locality, and the diversity question. In S. R. Steinberg (Ed.), *Diversity and multiculturalism: A reader* (pp. 423–434). New York: Peter Lang.

Thomas, J. R., & French, K. E. (1985). Gender differences across age in motor performance: A meta-analysis. *Psychological Bulletin, 98,* 260–282.

Thompson, T. L., & Zerbinos, E. (1995). Gender roles in animated cartoons: Has the picture changed in 20 years? *Sex Roles, 32,* 651–673.

Torrance, E. P. (1995). Insights about creativity: Questioned, rejected, ridiculed, ignored. *Educational Psychology Review, 7,* 313–322.

Trawick-Smith, J. (2003). *Early childhood development: A multicultural perspective* (3rd ed.). Upper Saddle River, NJ: Merrill/Prentice Hall.

Tyler, K. M., Uqdah, A. L., Dillihunt, M. L., Beatty-Hazelbaker, R., Connor, T., Gadson, N., et al. (2008). Cultural discontinuity: Toward a quantitative investigation of a major hypothesis in education. *Educational Researcher, 37,* 280–297.

Ulichny, P. (1996). Cultures in conflict. *Anthropology and Education Quarterly, 27,* 331–364.

U.S. Census Bureau (2010). *Income, poverty, and health insurance coverage in the United States: 2010.* Washington, DC: U.S. Author.

Valkenburg, P. M., & Peter, J. (2009). Social consequences of the Internet for adolescents: A decade of research. *Current Directions in Psychological Science, 18,* 1–5.

Valla, J. M., & Ceci, S. J. (2011). Can sex differences in science be tied to the long reach of prenatal hormones? Brain organization theory, digit ratio (2D/4D), and sex differences in preferences and cognition. *Perspectives in Psycholopical Science, 6,* 134–146.

van den Bergh, L., Denessen, E., Hornstra, L., Voeten, M., & Holland, R. W. (2010). The implicit prejudiced attitudes of teachers: Relations to teacher expectations and the ethnic achievement gap. *American Educational Research Journal, 47,* 497–527.

Vang, C. (2010). The psycho-social dimensions of multicultural education. In G. S. Goodman (Ed.), *Educational psychology reader: The art and science of how people learn* (pp. 195–208). New York: Peter Lang.

Varelas, M., & Pappas, C. C. (2006). Intertextuality in read-alouds of integrated science-literacy units in urban primary classrooms: Opportunities for the development of thought and language. *Cognition and Instruction, 24,* 211–259.

Volet, S. (1999). Learning across cultures: Appropriateness of knowledge transfer. *International Journal of Educational Research, 31,* 625–643.

Vuoksimaa, E., Kaprio, J., Kremen, W. S., Hokkanen, L., Viken, R. J., Tuulio-Henriksson, A., et al. (2010). *Psychological Science, 21,* 1069–1071.

Walton, G. M., & Spencer, S. J. (2009). Latent ability: Grades and test scores systematically underestimate intellectual ability of negatively stereotyped students. *Psychological Science, 20,* 1132–1139.

Ward, C., Bochner, S., & Furnham, A. (2001). *The psychology of culture shock* (2nd ed.). London: Routledge.

Weatherford, J. (1988). *Indian givers: How the Indians of the Americas transformed the world.* New York: Crown.

Weichold, K., Silbereisen, R. K., & Schmitt-Rodermund, E. (2003). Short-term and long-term consequences of early versus late physical maturation in adolescents. In C. Hayward (Ed.),

*Gender differences at puberty* (pp. 241–276). Cambridge, England: Cambridge University Press.

Weis, R., & Cerankosky, B. C. (2010). Effects of video-game ownership on young boys' academic and behavioral functioning: A randomized, controlled study. *Psychological Science, 21,* 463–470.

Weisgram, E. S., Bigler, R. S., & Liben, L. S. (2010). Gender, values, and occupational interests among children, adolescents, and adults. *Child Development, 81,* 778–796.

Wentzel, K. R. (2009). Peers and academic functioning at school. In K. H. Rubin, W. M. Bukowski, & B. Laursen (Eds.), *Handbook of peer interactions, relationships, and groups* (pp. 531–547). New York: Guilford.

Wentzel, K. R., Battle, A., Russell, S. L., & Looney, L. B. (2010). Social supports from teachers and peers as predictors of academic and social motivation. *Contemporary Educational Psychology, 35,* 193–202.

Werner, E. E. (1995). Resilience in development. *Current Directions in Psychological Science, 4,* 81–85.

Werner, E. E. (2006). What can we learn about resilience from large-scale longitudinal studies? In. S. Goldstein & R. B. Brooks (Eds.), *Handbook of resilience in children* (pp. 91–105). New York: Springer.

Werner, E. E., & Smith, R. S. (2001). *Journeys from childhood to midlife: Risk, resilience, and recovery.* Ithaca, NY: Cornell University Press.

Wigfield, A., Byrnes, J. P., & Eccles, J. S. (2006). Development during early and middle adolescence. In P. A. Alexander & P. H. Winne (Eds.), *Handbook of educational psychology* (2nd ed., pp. 87–113). Mahwah, NJ: Erlbaum.

Wigfield, A., Eccles, J. S., & Pintrich, P. R. (1996). Development between the ages of 11 and 25. In D. C. Berliner & R. C. Calfee (Eds.), *Handbook of educational psychology* (pp. 148–185). New York: Macmillan.

Williams, K. M. (2001a). "Frontin' it": Schooling, violence, and relationships in the 'hood. In J. N. Burstyn, G. Bender, R. Casella, H. W. Gordon, D. P. Guerra, K. V. Luschen, R. Stevens, & K. M. Williams, *Preventing violence in schools: A challenge to American democracy* (pp. 95–108). Mahwah, NJ: Erlbaum.

Wright, M. O., & Masten, A. S. (2006). Resilience processes in development: Fostering positive adaptation in the context of adversity. In. S. Goldstein & R. B. Brooks (Eds.), *Handbook of resilience in children* (pp. 17–37). New York: Springer.

Yu, S. L., Elder, A. D., & Urdan, T. C. (1995, April). *Motivation and cognitive strategies in students with a "good student" or "poor student" self-schema.* Paper presented at the annual meeting of the American Educational Research Association, San Francisco.

Zambo, D., & Brozo, W. G. (2009). *Bright beginnings for boys: Engaging young boys in active literacy.* Newark, DE: International Reading Association.

## CHAPTER 5

Accardo, P. J. (Ed.). (2008). *Capute and Accardo's neurodevelopmental disabilities in infancy and childhood: Vol. II: The spectrum of developmental disabilities* (3rd ed.). Baltimore: Brookes.

Ackerman, P. L., & Lohman, D. F. (2006). Individual differences in cognitive functions. In P. A. Alexander & P. H. Winne (Eds.), *Handbook of educational psychology* (2nd ed., pp. 139–161). Mahwah, NJ: Erlbaum.

Algozzine, B., Browder, D., Karvonen, M., Test, D. W., & Wood, W. M. (2001). Effects of interventions to promote self-determination for individuals with disabilities. *Review of Educational Research, 71,* 219–277.

Ambrose, D., Allen, J., & Huntley, S. B. (1994). Mentorship of the highly creative. *Roeper Review, 17,* 131–133.

American Psychiatric Association. (2000). *Diagnostic and statistical manual of mental disorders* (4th ed.). Washington, DC: Author.

Angold, A., Worthman, C., & Costello, E. J. (2003). Puberty and depression. In C. Hayward (Ed.), *Gender differences at puberty* (pp. 137–164). Cambridge, England: Cambridge University Press.

Barkley, R. A. (2006). *Attention-deficit hyperactivity disorder: A handbook for diagnosis and treatment* (3rd ed.). New York: Guilford.

Barkley, R. A. (2010). School interventions. In G. S. Goodman (Ed.), *Educational psychology reader: The art and science of how people learn* (pp. 66–74). New York: Peter Lang.

Bassett, D. S., Jackson, L., Ferrell, K. A., Luckner, J., Hagerty, P. J., Bunsen, T. D., & MacIsaac, D. (1996). Multiple perspectives on inclusive education: Reflections of a university faculty. *Teacher Education and Special Education, 19,* 355–386.

Beckett, C., Maughan, B., Rutter, M., Castle, J., Colvert, E., Groothues, C., et al. (2006). Do the effects of early severe deprivation on cognition persist into early adolescence? Findings from the English and Romanian adoptees study. *Child Development, 77,* 696–711.

Beirne-Smith, M., Patton, J. R., & Kim, S. H. (2006). *Mental retardation: An introduction to intellectual disabilities* (7th ed.). Upper Saddle River, NJ: Merrill/Prentice Hall.

Bergeron, R., & Floyd, R. G. (2006). Broad cognitive abilities of children with mental retardation: An analysis of group and individual profiles. *American Journal of Mental Retardation, 111,* 417–432.

Beukelman, D. R., & Mirenda, P. A. (2005). *Augmentative and alternative communication: Supporting children and adults with complex communication needs* (3rd ed.). Baltimore: Brookes.

Bishop, D. V. M. (2006). What causes specific language impairment in children? *Current Directions in Psychological Science, 15,* 217–221.

Bornstein, M. H., Hahn, C.-S., Bell, C., Haynes, O. M., Slater, A., Golding, J., et al. (2006). Stability in cognition across early childhood: A developmental cascade. *Psychological Science, 17,* 151–158.

Bouchard, T. J., Jr. (1997). IQ similarity in twins reared apart: Findings and responses to critics. In R. J. Sternberg & E. L. Grigorenko (Eds.), *Intelligence, heredity, and environment* (pp. 126–160). Cambridge, England: Cambridge University Press.

Bracken, B. (2009). Positive self-concepts. In R. Gilman, E. S. Huebner, & M. J. Furlong (Eds.), *Handbook of positive psychology in schools* (pp. 89–106). New York: Routledge.

Bracken, B. A., McCallum, R. S., & Shaughnessy, M. F. (1999). An interview with Bruce A. Bracken and R. Steve McCallum, authors of the Universal Nonverbal Intelligence Test (UNIT). *North American Journal of Psychology, 1,* 277–288.

Braden, J. P. (1992). Intellectual assessment of deaf and hard-of-hearing people: A quantitative and qualitative research synthesis. *School Psychology Review, 21,* 82–94.

Bressler, S. L. (2002). Understanding cognition through large-scale cortical networks. *Current Directions in Psychological Science, 11,* 58–61.

Brody, N. (1992). *Intelligence* (2nd ed.). San Diego, CA: Academic Press.

Brody, N. (1997). Intelligence, schooling, and society. *American Psychologist, 52,* 1046–1050.

Brody, N. (1999). What is intelligence? *International Review of Psychiatry, 11,* 19–25.

Brooks-Gunn, J., Klebanov, P. K., & Duncan, G. J. (1996). Ethnic differences in children's intelligence test scores: Role of economic deprivation, home environment, and maternal characteristics. *Child Development, 67,* 396–408.

Buchoff, T. (1990). Attention deficit disorder: Help for the classroom teacher. *Childhood Education, 67,* 86–90.

Byrnes, J. P. (2003). Factors predictive of mathematics achievement in White, Black, and Hispanic 12th graders. *Journal of Educational Psychology, 95,* 316–326.

Cacioppo, J. T., Petty, R. E., Feinstein, J. A., & Jarvis, W. B. G. (1996). Dispositional differences in cognitive motivation: The life and times of individuals varying in need for cognition. *Psychological Bulletin, 119,* 197–253.

Campbell, F. A., & Burchinal, M. R. (2008). Early childhood interventions: The Abecedarian Project. In P. C. Kyllonen, R. D. Roberts, & L. Stankov (Eds.), *Extending intelligence: Enhancement and new constructs* (pp. 61–84). New York: Erlbaum/Taylor & Francis.

Campbell, L., Campbell, B., & Dickinson, D. (1998). *Teaching and learning through multiple intelligences* (2nd ed.). Boston: Allyn & Bacon.

Candler-Lotven, A., Tallent-Runnels, M. K., Olivárez, A., & Hildreth, B. (1994, April). *A comparison of learning and study strategies of gifted, average-ability, and learning-disabled ninth-grade students.* Paper presented at the annual meeting of the American Educational Research Association, New Orleans, LA.

Capron, C., & Duyme, M. (1989). Assessment of effects of socio-economic status on IQ in a full cross-fostering study. *Nature, 340,* 552–554.

Carlin, M. T., Soraci, S. A., Strawbridge, C. P., Dennis, N., Loiselle, R., & Checile, N. A. (2003). Detection of changes in naturalistic scenes: Comparison of individuals with and without mental retardation. *Journal of Mental Retardation, 108,* 181–193.

Carroll, J. B. (1993). *Human cognitive abilities: A survey of factor-analytic studies.* New York: Cambridge University Press.

Carroll, J. B. (2003). The higher stratum structure of cognitive abilities: Current evidence supports *g* and about ten broad factors. In H. Nyborg (Ed.), *The scientific study of general intelligence* (pp. 5–21). New York: Pergamon.

Casey, B. J. (2001). Disruption of inhibitory control in developmental disorders: A mechanistic model of implicated frontostriatal circuitry. In J. L. McClelland & R. S. Siegler (Eds.), *Mechanisms of cognitive development: Behavioral and neural perspectives* (pp. 327–349). Mahwah, NJ: Erlbaum.

Cassidy, S. (2004). Learning styles: An overview of theories, models, and measures. *Educational Psychology, 24,* 419–444.

Cattell, R. B. (1963). Theory of fluid and crystallized intelligence: A critical experiment. *Journal of Educational Psychology, 54,* 1–22.

Cattell, R. B. (1987). *Intelligence: Its structure, growth, and action.* Amsterdam: North-Holland.

Ceci, S. J. (2003). Cast in six ponds and you'll reel in something: Looking back on 25 years of research. *American Psychologist, 58,* 855–864.

Chall, J. S. (1996). *Stages of reading development* (2nd ed.). Fort Worth, TX: Harcourt Brace.

Chan, J. M., & O'Reilly, M. F. (2008). A Social Stories™ intervention package for students with autism in inclusive classroom settings. *Journal of Applied Behavior Analysis, 41,* 405–409.

Chang, M.-L., & Davis, H. A. (2009). Understanding the role of teacher appraisals in shaping the dynamics of their relationships with students: Deconstructing teachers' judgments of disruptive behavior/students. In P. Schutz & M. Zembylas (Eds.), *Advances in teacher emotion research: The impact of teachers' lives* (pp. 95–125). New York: Springer.

Cherkassky, V. L., Kana, R. K., Keller, T. A., & Just, M. A. (2006). Functional connectivity in a baseline resting-state network in autism. *NeuroReport, 17,* 1687–1690.

Clarke, S., Dunlap, G., Foster-Johnson, L., Childs, K. E., Wilson, D., White, R., et al. (1995). Improving the conduct of students with behavioral disorders by incorporating student interests into curricular areas. *Behavioral Disorders, 20,* 221–237.

Cohen, I. L. (2007). A neural network model of autism: Implications for theory and treatment. In D. Mareschal, S. Sirois, G. Westermann, & M. H. Johnson (Eds.), *Neuroconstructivism: Vol. 2. Perspectives and prospects* (pp. 231–264). Oxford, England: Oxford University Press.

Cole, C. M., Waldron, N., & Majd, M. (2004). Academic progress of students across inclusive and traditional settings. *Mental Retardation, 42,* 136–144.

Cornell, D. G., Pelton, G. M., Bassin, L. E., Landrum, M., Ramsay, S. G., Cooley, M. R., et al. (1990). Self-concept and peer status among gifted program youth. *Journal of Educational Psychology, 82,* 456–463.

Corno, L., Cronbach, L. J., Kupermintz, H., Lohman, D. F., Mandinach, E. B., Porteu, A. W., et al. (2002). *Remaking the concept of aptitude:*

*Extending the legacy of Richard E. Snow.* Mahwah, NJ: Erlbaum.

Cornoldi, C. (2010). Metacognition, intelligence, and academic performance. In H. S. Waters & W. Schneider (Eds.), *Metacognition, strategy use, and instruction* (pp. 257–277). New York: Guilford.

Coyle, T. R., Pillow, D. R., Snyder, A. C., & Kochunov, P. (2011). Processing speed mediates the development of general intelligence (*g*) in adolescence. *Psychological Science, 22,* 1265–1269.

Crago, M. B. (1988). *Cultural context in the communicative interaction of young Inuit children.* Unpublished doctoral dissertation, McGill University.

Curry, L. (1990). A critique of the research on learning styles. *Educational Leadership, 47*(2), 50–56.

Cutting, L. E., Eason, S. H., Young, K. M., & Alberstadt, A. L. (2009). Reading comprehension: Cognition and neuroimaging. In K. Pugh & P. McCardle (Eds.), *How children learn to read: Current issues and new directions in the integration of cognition, neurobiology and genetics of reading and dyslexia research and practice* (pp. 195–213). New York: Psychology Press.

Dai, D. Y. (2002, April). *Effects of need for cognition and reader beliefs on the comprehension of narrative text.* Paper presented at the annual meeting of the American Educational Research Association, New Orleans.

Dai, D. Y. (2010). *The nature and nurture of giftedness: A new framework for understanding gifted education.* New York: Teachers College Press.

Dai, D. Y., & Sternberg, R. J. (2004). Beyond cognitivism: Toward an integrated understanding of intellectual functioning and development. In D. Y. Dai & R. J. Sternberg (Eds.), *Motivation, emotion, and cognition: Integrative perspectives on intellectual functioning and development* (pp. 3–38). Mahwah, NJ: Erlbaum.

Dalrymple, N. J. (1995). Environmental supports to develop flexibility and independence. In K. A. Quill (Ed.), *Teaching children with autism: Strategies to enhance communication and socialization* (pp. 243–264). New York: Delmar.

D'Amato, R. C., Chittooran, M. M., & Whitten, J. D. (1992). Neuropsychological consequences of malnutrition. In D. I. Templer, L. C. Hartlage, & W. G. Cannon (Eds.), *Preventable brain damage: Brain vulnerability and brain health* (pp. 193–213). New York: Springer.

Davies, P. T., & Woitach, M. J. (2008). Children's emotional security in the interparental relationship. *Current Directions in Psychological Science, 17,* 269–274.

Davis, O. S. P., Haworth, C. M. A., & Plomin, R. (2009). Dramatic increase in heritability of cognitive development from early to middle childhood: An 8-year longitudinal study of 8,700 pairs of twins. *Psychological Science, 20,* 1301–1308.

Dawson, M., Soulières, I., Gernsbacher, M. A., & Mottron, L. (2007). The level and nature of

autistic intelligence. *Psychological Science, 18,* 657–662.

DeBacker, T. K., & Crowson, H. M. (2008). Measuring need for closure in classroom learners. *Contemporary Educational Psychology, 33,* 711–732.

DeBacker, T. K., & Crowson, H. M. (2009). The influence of need for closure on learning and teaching. *Educational Psychology Review, 21,* 303–323.

deBettencourt, L. U. (2002). Understanding the differences between IDEA and Section 504, *Teaching Exceptional Children, 34*(3), 16–23.

de Jong, T. (2011). Instruction based on computer simulations. In R. E. Mayer & P. A. Alexander (Eds.), *Handbook of research on learning and instruction* (pp. 446–466). New York: Routledge.

Deshler, D. D., Schumaker, J. B., Lenz, B. K., Bulgren, J. A., Hock, M. F., Knight, J., et al. (2001). Ensuring content-area learning by secondary students with learning disabilities. *Learning Disabilities Research and Practice, 16,* 96–108.

Diamond, S. C. (1991). What to do when you can't do anything: Working with disturbed adolescents. *Clearing House, 64,* 232–234.

Dickens, W. T., & Flynn, J. R. (2006). Black Americans reduce the racial IQ gap: Evidence from standardization samples. *Psychological Science, 17,* 913–920.

Dirks, J. (1982). The effect of a commercial game on children's Block Design scores on the WISC-R test. *Intelligence, 6,* 109–123.

Dodge, K. A. (2009). Mechanisms of gene–environment interaction effects in the development of conduct disorder. *Perspectives on Psychological Science, 4,* 408–414.

Duckworth, A. L., & Seligman, M. E. P. (2005). Self-discipline outdoes IQ in predicting academic performance of adolescents. *Psychological Science, 16,* 939–944.

DuPaul, G. J., Ervin, R. A., Hook, C. L., & McGoey, K. E. (1998). Peer tutoring for children with attention deficit hyperactivity disorder: Effects on classroom behavior and academic performance. *Journal of Applied Behavior Analysis, 31,* 579–592.

Dyson, A. (2008). Disproportionality in special needs education in England. *Journal of Special Education, 42*(1), 36–46.

Ericsson, K. A. (2003). The acquisition of expert performance as problem solving. In J. E. Davidson & R. J. Sternberg (Eds.), *The psychology of problem solving* (pp. 31–83). Cambridge, England: Cambridge University Press.

Espelage, D. L., Mebane, S. E., & Adams, R. S. (2004). Empathy, caring, and bullying: Toward an understanding of complex associations. In D. L. Espelage & S. M. Swearer (Eds.), *Bullying in American schools: A social-ecological perspective on prevention and intervention* (pp. 37–61). Mahwah, NJ: Erlbaum.

Estell, D. B., Jones, M. H., Pearl, R., Van Acker, R., Farmer, T. W., & Rodkin, P. C. (2008). Peer groups, popularity, and social preference: Trajectories of social functioning among students with and without learning disabilities. *Journal of Learning Disabilities, 41,* 5–14.

Evans, J. J., Floyd, R. G., McGrew, K. S., & Leforgee, M. H. (2001). The relations between measures of Cattell-Horn-Carroll (CHC) cognitive abilities and reading achievement during childhood and adolescence. *School Psychology Review, 31,* 246–262.

Evertson, C. M., & Weinstein, C. S. (Eds.). (2006). *Handbook of classroom management: Research, practice, and contemporary issues.* Mahwah, NJ: Erlbaum.

Faranoe, S. V., Perlis, R. H., Doyle, A. E., Smoller, J., Goralnick, J., Holmgren, M., et al. (2005). Molecular genetics of attention-deficit/hyperactivity disorder. *Biological Psychiatry, 57,* 1313–1323.

Ferrell, K. A. (1996). Your child's development. In M. C. Holbrook (Ed.), *Children with visual impairments: A parent's guide* (pp. 73–96). Bethesda, MD: Woodbine House.

Fessler, M. A., Rosenberg, M. S., & Rosenberg, L. A. (1991). Concomitant learning disabilities and learning problems among students with behavioral/emotional disorders. *Behavioral Disorders, 16,* 97–106.

Feuerstein, R, Feuerstein, R. S., & Falik, L. H. (2010). *Beyond smarter: Mediated learning and the brain's capacity for change.* New York: Teachers College Press.

Fey, M. E., Catts, H., & Larrivee, L. (1995). Preparing preschoolers for the academic and social challenges of school. In M. E. Fey, J. Windsor, & S. F. Warren (Eds.), *Language intervention: Preschool through elementary years* (pp. 3–37). Baltimore: Brookes.

Fidler, D. J., Hepburn, S. L., Mankin, G., & Rogers, S. J. (2005). Praxis skills in young children with Down syndrome, other developmental disabilities, and typically developing children. *American Journal on Occupational Therapy, 59,* 129–138.

Flanagan, D. P., & Ortiz, S. O. (2001). *Essentials of cross-battery assessment.* New York: Wiley.

Fletcher, J. M., Lyon, G. R., Fuchs, L. S., & Barnes, M. A. (2007). *Learning disabilities: From identification to intervention.* New York: Guilford.

Fletcher, J. M., & Vaughn, S. (2009). Response to intervention: Preventing and remediating academic difficulties. *Child Development Perspectives, 3,* 30–37.

Florence, B., Gentaz, E., Pascale, C., & Sprenger-Charolles, L. (2004). The visuo-haptic and haptic exploration of letters increases the kindergarten-children's understanding of the alphabetic principle. *Cognitive Development, 19,* 433–449.

Flum, H., & Kaplan, A. (2006). Exploratory orientation as an educational goal. *Educational Psychologist, 41,* 99–110.

Flynn, J. R. (2007). *What is intelligence? Beyond the Flynn effect.* New York: Cambridge University Press.

Ford, D. Y., Moore, J. L., III, & Whiting, G. W. (2006). Eliminating deficit orientations: Creating classrooms and curricula for gifted students from diverse cultural backgrounds. In M. G. Constantine & D. W. Sue (Eds.), *Addressing racism: Facilitating cultural competence in mental health and educational settings* (pp. 173–193). New York: Wiley.

Fuchs, L. S., Compton, D. L., Fuchs, D., Paulsen, K., Bryant, J. D., & Hamlett, C. L. (2005). The prevention, identification, and cognitive determinants of math difficulty. *Journal of Educational Psychology, 97,* 493–513.

Fuchs, L. S., & Fuchs, D. (2009). On the importance of a unified model of responsiveness to intervention. *Child Development Perspectives, 3,* 41–43.

Funder, D. C. (1991). Global traits: A neo-Allportian approach to personality. *Psychological Science, 2,* 31–39.

Gallese, V., Gernsbacher, M. A., Heyes, C., Hickok, G., & Iacoboni, M. (2011). Mirror neuron forum. *Perspectives on Psychological Science, 6,* 369–407.

Gardner, H. (1983). *Frames of mind: The theory of multiple intelligences.* New York: Basic Books.

Gardner, H. (1998, April). *Where to draw the line: The perils of new paradigms.* Paper presented at the annual meeting of the American Educational Research Association, San Diego, CA.

Gardner, H. (1999). *Intelligence reframed: Multiple intelligences for the 21st century.* New York: Basic Books.

Gardner, H. (2000a). A case against spiritual intelligence. *International Journal of the Psychology of Religion, 10*(1), 27–34.

Gardner, H. (2000b). *The disciplined mind: Beyond facts and standardized tests, the K–12 education that every child deserves.* New York: Penguin.

Gardner, H. (2003, April). *Multiple intelligences after twenty years.* Paper presented at the annual meeting of the American Educational Research Association, Chicago.

Gardner, H., & Hatch, T. (1990). Multiple intelligences go to school: Educational implications of the theory of multiple intelligences. *Educational Researcher, 18*(8), 4–10.

Gathercole, S. E., Lamont, E., & Alloway, T. P. (2006). Working memory in the classroom. In S. Pickering (Ed.), *Working memory and education* (pp. 219–240). New York: Academic Press.

Gatzke-Kopp, L. M., & Beauchaine, T. P. (2007). Central nervous system substrates of impulsivity: Implications for the development of attention-deficit/hyperactivity disorder and conduct disorder. In D. Coch, G. Dawson, & K. W. Fischer (Eds.), *Human behavior, learning, and the developing brain: Atypical development* (pp. 239–263). New York: Guilford.

Gay, G. (2006). Connections between classroom management and culturally responsive teaching. In C. M. Evertson & C. S. Weinstein (Eds.), *Handbook of classroom management: Research, practice, and contemporary issues* (pp. 343–370). Mahwah, NJ: Erlbaum.

Gearheart, B. R., Weishahn, M. W., & Gearheart, C. J. (1992). *The exceptional child in the regular classroom* (5th ed.). Upper Saddle River, NJ: Merrill/Prentice Hall.

Gernsbacher, M. A., Stevenson, J. L., Khandakar, S., & Goldsmith, H. H. (2008). Why does joint attention look atypical in autism? *Child Development Perspectives, 2*(1), 38–45.

Gladwell, M. (2006, May). Behavior in the blink of an eye. Presentation at the annual meeting of the Association for Psychological Science, New York.

Glaser, D. (2000). Child abuse and neglect and the brain: A review. *Journal of Child Psychology and Psychiatry and Allied Disciplines, 41,* 97–116.

Goldstein, S., & Rider, R. (2006). Resilience and the disruptive disorders of childhood. In S. Goldstein & R. B. Brooks (Eds.), *Handbook of resilience in children* (pp. 203–222). New York: Springer.

Goldston, D. B., Molock, S. D., Whitbeck, L. B., Murakami, J. L., Zayas, L. H., & Nagayama Hall, G. C. (2008). Cultural considerations in adolescent suicide prevention and psychosocial treatment. *American Psychologist, 63,* 14–31.

Gonsalves, B. D., & Cohen, N. J. (2010). Brain imaging, cognitive processes, and brain networks. *Perspectives on Psychological Science, 5,* 744–752.

Goswami, U. (2007). Typical reading development and developmental dyslexia across languages. In D. Coch, G. Dawson, & K. W. Fischer (Eds.), *Human behavior, learning, and the developing brain: Atypical development* (pp. 145–167). New York: Guilford.

Graham, S. (2009). Giftedness in adolescence: African American gifted youth and their challenges from a motivational perspective. In F. D. Horowitz, R. F. Subotnik, & D. J. Matthews (Eds.), *The development of giftedness and talent across the life span* (pp. 109–129). Washington, DC: American Psychological Association.

Grandin, T. (1995). *Thinking in pictures and other reports of my life with autism.* New York: Random House.

Grandin, T., & Johnson, C. (2005). *Animals in translation: Using the mysteries of autism to decode animal behavior.* New York: Simon & Schuster.

Greenfield, P. M. (1998). The cultural evolution of IQ. In U. Neisser (Ed.), *The rising curve: Long-term gains in IQ and related measures* (pp. 81–123). Washington, DC: American Psychological Association.

Greenfield, P. M., Trumbull, E., Keller, H., Rothstein-Fisch, C., Suzuki, L. K., & Quiroz, B. (2006). Cultural conceptions of learning and development. In P. A. Alexander & P. H. Winne (Eds.), *Handbook of educational psychology* (2nd ed., pp. 675–692). Mahwah, NJ: Erlbaum.

Gregg, N. (2009). *Adolescents and adults with learning disabilities and ADHD: Assessment and accommodation.* New York: Guilford.

Gresalfi, M. S. (2009). Taking up opportunities to learn: Constructing dispositions in mathematics classrooms. *Journal of the Learning Sciences, 18,* 327–369.

Grinberg, D., & McLean-Heywood, D. (1999). *Perceptions of behavioural competence in depressed and non-depressed children with behavioural difficulties.* Paper presented at the annual meeting of the American Educational Research Association, Montreal, Canada.

Griswold, K. S., & Pessar, L. F. (2000). Management of bipolar disorder. *American Family Physician, 62,* 1343–1356.

Gustafsson, J., & Undheim, J. O. (1996). Individual differences in cognitive functions. In D. C. Berliner & R. C. Calfee (Eds.), *Handbook of educational psychology* (pp. 186–242). New York: Macmillan.

Haier, R. J. (2003). Positron emission tomography studies of intelligence: From psychometrics to neurobiology. In H. Nyborg (Ed.), *The scientific study of general intelligence* (pp. 41–52). New York: Pergamon.

Hallahan, D. P., Kauffman, J. M., & Pullen, P. C. (2009). *Exceptional learners: An introduction to special education* (11th ed.). Boston: Allyn & Bacon.

Hallenbeck, M. J. (1996). The cognitive strategy in writing: Welcome relief for adolescents with learning disabilities. *Learning Disabilities Research and Practice, 11,* 107–119.

Hallowell, E. (1996). *When you worry about the child you love.* New York: Simon & Schuster.

Halpern, D. F. (1998). Teaching critical thinking for transfer across domains. *American Psychologist, 53,* 449–455.

Halpern, D. F. (2008). Is intelligence critical thinking? Why we need a new definition of intelligence. In P. C. Kyllonen, R. D. Roberts, & L. Stankov (Eds.), *Extending intelligence: Enhancement and new constructs* (pp. 349–370). New York: Erlbaum/Taylor & Francis.

Halvorsen, A. T., & Sailor, W. (1990). Integration of students with severe and profound disabilities: A review of research. In R. Gaylord-Ross (Ed.), *Issues and research in special education* (Vol. 1, pp. 110–172). New York: Teachers College Press.

Hamovitch, B. (2007). Hoping for the best: "Inclusion" and stigmatization in a middle school. In S. Books (Ed.), *Invisible children in the society and its schools* (3rd ed., pp. 263–281). Mahwah, NJ: Erlbaum.

Harris, C. R. (1991). Identifying and serving the gifted new immigrant. *Teaching Exceptional Children, 23*(4), 26–30.

Harris, M. (1992). *Language experience and early language development: From input to uptake.* Hove, England: Erlbaum.

Harris, P. L. (2006). Social cognition. In W. Damon & R. M. Lerner (Series Eds.), D. Kuhn, & R. Siegler (Vol. Eds.), *Handbook of child psychology: Vol. 2. Cognition, perception, and language* (6th ed., pp. 811–858). New York: Wiley.

Hart, E. L., Lahey, B. B., Loeber, R., Applegate, B., & Frick, P. J. (1995). Developmental changes in attention-deficit hyperactivity disorder in boys: A four-year longitudinal study. *Journal of Abnormal Child Psychology, 23,* 729–750.

Harter, S. (1999). *The construction of the self: A developmental perspective.* New York: Guilford.

Hathaway, W. L., Dooling-Litfin, J. K., & Edwards, G. (2006). Integrating the results of an evaluation: Ten clinical cases. In R. A. Barkley, *Attention-deficit hyperactivity disorder: A handbook for diagnosis and treatment* (3rd ed., pp. 410–412). New York: Guilford.

Hattie, J. A. C. (2009). *Visible learning: A synthesis of over 800 meta-analyses relating to achievement.* London: Routledge.

Haxby, J. V., Gobbini, M. I., Furey, M. L., Ishai, A., Schouten, J. L., & Pietrini, P. (2001). Distributed and overlapping representations of faces and objects in ventral temporal cortex. *Science, 293,* 2425–2430.

Hayward, C. (Ed.). (2003). *Gender differences at puberty.* Cambridge, England: Cambridge University Press.

Haywood, H. C., & Lidz, C. S. (2007). *Dynamic assessment in practice: Clinical and educational applications.* Cambridge, England: Cambridge University Press.

Heath, S. B. (1989). Oral and literate traditions among black Americans living in poverty. *American Psychologist, 44,* 367–373.

Heward, W. L. (2009). *Exceptional children: An introduction to special education* (9th ed.). Upper Saddle River, NJ: Merrill/Pearson Education.

Hobson, P. (2004). *The cradle of thought: Exploring the origins of thinking.* Oxford, England: Oxford University Press.

Horn, J. L. (2008). Spearman, *g,* expertise, and the nature of human cognitive capability. In P. C. Kyllonen, R. D. Roberts, & L. Stankov (Eds.), *Extending intelligence: Enhancement and new constructs* (pp. 185–230). New York: Erlbaum/Taylor & Francis.

Hughes, F. P. (1998). Play in special populations. In O. N. Saracho & B. Spodek (Eds.), *Multiple perspectives on play in early childhood education* (pp. 171–193). Albany: State University of New York Press.

Hunt, E. (2008). Improving intelligence: What's the difference from education? In P. C. Kyllonen, R. D. Roberts, & L. Stankov (Eds.), *Extending intelligence: Enhancement and new constructs* (pp. 15–35). New York: Erlbaum/Taylor & Francis.

Hunt, P., & Goetz, L. (1997). Research on inclusive educational programs, practices, and outcomes for students with severe disabilities. *Journal of Special Education, 31,* 3–29.

Hutchins, E. (1995). *Cognition in the wild.* Cambridge, MA: MIT Press.

Jacoby, R., & Glauberman, N. (Eds.). (1995). *The bell curve debate: History, documents, opinions.* New York: Random House.

Johnson, W. (2010). Understanding the genetics of intelligence: Can height help? Can corn oil? *Current Perspectives in Psychological Science, 19,* 177–182.

Jung, R. E., & Haier, R. J. (2007). The parieto-frontal integration theory (P-FIT) of intelligence: Converging neuroimaging evidence. *Behavioral and Brain Sciences, 30,* 135–154.

Kağitçibaşi, Ç. (2007). *Family, self, and human development across cultures: Theory and applications* (2nd ed.). Mahwah, NJ: Erlbaum.

Kana, R. K., Keller, T. A., Minshew, N. J., & Just, M. A. (2007). Inhibitory control in high-functioning autism: Decreased activation and underconnectivity in inhibition networks. *Biological Psychiatry, 62,* 198–206.

Kang, M. J., Hsu, M., Krajbich, I. M., Loewenstein, G., McClure, S. M., Wang, J. T.-Y., et al. (2009). The wick in the candle of learning: Epistemic curiosity activates reward circuitry and enhances memory. *Psychological Science, 20,* 963–973.

Kardash, C. A. M., & Scholes, R. J. (1996). Effects of preexisting beliefs, epistemological beliefs, and need for cognition on interpretation of controversial issues. *Journal of Educational Psychology, 88,* 260–271.

Keogh, B. K. (2003). *Temperament in the classroom.* Baltimore: Brookes.

Kern, L., Dunlap, G., Childs, K. E., & Clark, S. (1994). Use of a classwide self-management program to improve the behavior of students with emotional and behavioral disorders. *Education and Treatment of Children, 17,* 445–458.

Kerns, L. L., & Lieberman, A. B. (1993). *Helping your depressed child.* Rocklin, CA: Prima.

King, P. M., & Kitchener, K. S. (2002). The reflective judgment model: Twenty years of research on epistemic cognition. In B. K. Hofer & P. R. Pintrich (Eds.), *Personal epistemology: The psychology of beliefs about knowledge and knowing* (pp. 37–61). Mahwah, NJ: Erlbaum.

Klingberg, A. K., Keonig, J. I., & Bilbe, G. (2002). Training of working memory in children with ADHD. *Journal of Clinical and Experimental Neuropsychology, 24,* 781–791.

Kornhaber, M., Fierros, E., & Veenema, S. (2004). *Multiple intelligences: Best ideas from research and practice.* Boston: Allyn & Bacon.

Kovas, Y., & Plomin, R. (2007). Learning abilities and disabilities: Generalist genes, specialist environments. *Current Directions in Psychological Science, 16,* 284–288.

Krätzig, G. P., & Arbuthnott, K. D. (2006). Perceptual learning style and learning proficiency: A test of the hypothesis. *Journal of Educational Psychology, 98,* 238–246.

Kuhn, D. (2001a). How do people know? *Psychological Science, 12,* 1–8.

Kuhn, D. (2001b). Why development does (and does not) occur: Evidence from the domain of inductive reasoning. In J. L. McClelland & R. S. Siegler (Eds.), *Mechanisms of cognitive development: Behavioral and neural perspectives* (pp. 221–249). Mahwah, NJ: Erlbaum.

Kuhn, D. (2006). Do cognitive changes accompany developments in the adolescent brain? *Perspectives on Psychological Science, 1,* 59–67.

Kuhn, D., & Franklin, S. (2006). The second decade: What develops (and how)? In W. Damon & R. M. Lerner (Series Eds.), D. Kuhn, & R. Siegler (Vol. Eds.), *Handbook of child psychology: Vol. 2. Cognition, perception, and language* (6th ed., pp. 953–993). New York: Wiley.

Kulik, J. A., & Kulik, C. C. (1997). Ability grouping. In N. Colangelo & G. Davis (Eds.), *Handbook of gifted education* (2nd ed., pp. 230–242). Boston: Allyn & Bacon.

LaBlance, G. R., Steckol, K. F., & Smith, V. L. (1994). Stuttering: The role of the classroom teacher. *Teaching Exceptional Children, 26*(2), 10–12.

Laboratory of Comparative Human Cognition. (1982). Culture and intelligence. In R. J. Sternberg (Ed.), *Handbook of human intelligence* (pp. 462–719). Cambridge, England: Cambridge University Press.

Lane, K., Falk, K., & Wehby, J. (2006). Classroom management in special education classrooms and resource rooms. In C. M. Evertson & C. S. Weinstein (Eds.), *Handbook of classroom management: Research, practice, and contemporary issues* (pp. 439–460). Mahwah, NJ: Erlbaum.

Leiter, J., & Johnsen, M. C. (1997). Child maltreatment and school performance declines: An event-history analysis. *American Educational Research Journal, 34*, 563–589.

Li, J. (2004). High abilities and excellence: A cultural perspective. In L. V. Shavinina & M. Ferrari (Eds.), *Beyond knowledge: Extracognitive aspects of developing high ability* (pp. 187–208). Mahwah, NJ: Erlbaum.

Li, J., & Fischer, K. W. (2004). Thought and affect in American and Chinese learners' beliefs about learning. In D. Y. Dai & R. J. Sternberg (Eds.), *Motivation, emotion, and cognition: Integrative perspectives on intellectual functioning and development* (pp. 385–418). Mahwah, NJ: Erlbaum.

Linn, M. C., Clement, C., Pulos, S., & Sullivan, P. (1989). Scientific reasoning during adolescence: The influence of instruction in science knowledge and reasoning strategies. *Journal of Research in Science Teaching, 26*, 171–187.

Locke, J. L. (1993). *The child's path to spoken language*. Cambridge, MA: Harvard University Press.

Lord, C. E. (2010). Autism: From research to practice. *American Psychologist, 65*, 815–826.

Luckasson, R., Borthwick-Duffy, S., Buntinx, W. H. E., Coulter, D. L., Craig, E. M., Reeve, A., et al. (Eds.). (2002). *Mental retardation: Definition, classification, and systems of supports* (10th ed.). Washington, DC: American Association on Mental Retardation.

Lupart, J. L. (1995). Exceptional learners and teaching for transfer. In A. McKeough, J. Lupart, & A. Marini (Eds.), *Teaching for transfer: Fostering generalization in learning* (pp. 215–228). Mahwah, NJ: Erlbaum.

MacMaster, K., Donovan, L. A., & MacIntyre, P. D. (2002). The effects of being diagnosed with a learning disability on children's self-esteem. *Child Study Journal, 32*, 101–108.

Madden, N. A., & Slavin, R. E. (1983). Mainstreaming students with mild handicaps: Academic and social outcomes. *Review of Educational Research, 53*, 519–569.

Maker, C. J., & Schiever, S. W. (Eds.). (1989). *Critical issues in gifted education: Vol. 2. Defensible programs for cultural and ethnic minorities*. Austin, TX: Pro-Ed.

Mason, L. (2003). Personal epistemologies and intentional conceptual change. In G. M. Sinatra & P. R. Pintrich (Eds.), *Intentional conceptual change* (pp. 199–236). Mahwah, NJ: Erlbaum.

Mastropieri, M. A., & Scruggs, T. E. (1992). Science for students with disabilities. *Review of Educational Research, 62*, 377–411.

Mastropieri, M. A., & Scruggs, T. E. (2007). *The inclusive classroom: Strategies for effective instruction* (3rd ed.). Upper Saddle River, NJ: Merrill/Prentice Hall.

Matthews D. J. (2009). Developmental transitions in giftedness and talent: Childhood into adolescence. In F. D. Horowitz, R. F. Subotnik, & D. J. Matthews (Eds.), *The development of giftedness and talent across the life span* (pp. 89–107). Washington, DC: American Psychological Association.

Matthews, G., Zeidner, M., & Roberts, R. D. (2006). Models of personality and affect for education: A review and synthesis. In P. A. Alexander & P. H. Winne (Eds.), *Handbook of educational psychology* (2nd ed., pp. 163–186). Mahwah, NJ: Erlbaum.

Maughan, A., & Cicchetti, D. (2002). Impact of child maltreatment and interadult violence on children's emotion regulation abilities and socioemotional adjustment. *Child Development, 73*, 1525–1542.

Mayer, R. E. (2011b). Instruction based on visualizations. In R. E. Mayer & P. A. Alexander (Eds.), *Handbook of research on learning and instruction* (pp. 427–445). New York: Routledge.

Mayer, R. E., & Massa, L. J. (2003). Three facets of visual and verbal learners: Cognitive ability, cognitive style, and learning preference. *Journal of Educational Psychology, 95*, 833–846.

McGinn, P. V., Viernstein, M. C., & Hogan, R. (1980). Fostering the intellectual development of verbally gifted adolescents. *Journal of Educational Psychology, 72*, 494–498.

McGlynn, S. M. (1998). Impaired awareness of deficits in a psychiatric context: Implications for rehabilitation. In D. J. Hacker, J. Dunlosky, & A. C. Graesser (Eds.), *Metacognition in educational theory and practice* (pp. 221–248). Mahwah, NJ: Erlbaum.

McGrew, K. S., Flanagan, D. P., Zeith, T. Z., & Vanderwood, M. (1997). Beyond g: The impact of Gf–Gc specific cognitive abilities research on the future use and interpretation of intelligence tests in the schools. *School Psychology Review, 26*, 189–210.

McLoyd, V. C. (1998). Socioeconomic disadvantage and child development. *American Psychologist, 53*, 185–204.

Mehan, H. (1979). *Social organization in the classroom*. Cambridge, MA: Harvard University Press.

Mellard, D. F., & Johnson, E. (2008). *RTI: A practitioner's guide to implementing response to intervention*. Thousand Oaks, CA: Corwin.

Meltzer, L. (Ed.). (2007). *Executive function in education: From theory to practice*. New York: Guilford.

Meltzer, L., & Krishnan, K. (2007). Executive function difficulties and learning disabilities: Understandings and misunderstandings. In L. Meltzer (Ed.), *Executive function in education: From theory to practice* (pp. 77–105). New York: Guilford.

Mendaglio, S. (2010). Anxiety in gifted students. In J. C. Cassady (Ed.), *Anxiety in schools: The causes, consequences, and solutions for academic anxieties* (pp. 153–173). New York: Peter Lang.

Messick, S. (1994b). The matter of style: Manifestations of personality in cognition, learning, and testing. *Educational Psychologist, 29*, 121–136.

Miller, L. K. (2005). What the savant syndrome can tell us about the nature and nurture of talent. *Journal for the Education of the Gifted, 28*, 361–373.

Minami, M., & McCabe, A. (1996). Compressed collections of experiences: Some Asian American traditions. In A. McCabe (Ed.), *Chameleon readers: Some problems cultural differences in narrative structure pose for multicultural literacy programs* (pp. 72–97). New York: McGraw-Hill.

Moon, S. M., Feldhusen, J. F., & Dillon, D. R. (1994). Long-term effects of an enrichment program based on the Purdue Three-Stage Model. *Gifted Child Quarterly, 38*, 38–48.

Moreno, R. (2006). Learning in high-tech and multimedia environments. *Current Directions in Psychological Science, 15*, 63–67.

Murphy, P. K., & Mason, L. (2006). Changing knowledge and beliefs. In P. A. Alexander & P. H. Winne (Eds.), *Handbook of educational psychology* (2nd ed., pp. 305–324). Mahwah, NJ: Erlbaum.

Myles, B. S., & Simpson, R. L. (2001). Understanding the hidden curriculum: An essential social skill for children and youth with Asperger syndrome. *Intervention in School and Clinic, 36*, 279–286.

Neisser, U. (Ed.). (1998). *The rising curve: Long-term gains in IQ and related measures*. Washington, DC: American Psychological Association.

Neisser, U., Boodoo, G., Bouchard, T. J., Boykin, A. W., Brody, N., Ceci, S. J., et al. (1996). Intelligence: Knowns and unknowns. *American Psychologist, 51*, 77–101.

Nichols, P. D., & Mittelholtz, D. J. (1997). Constructing the concept of aptitude: Implications for the assessment of analogical reasoning. In G. D. Phye (Ed.), *Handbook of academic learning: Construction of knowledge* (pp. 128–147). San Diego, CA: Academic Press.

Nieto, S., & Bode, P. (2008). *Affirming diversity: The sociopolitical context of multicultural education* (5th ed.). Boston: Allyn & Bacon.

Nigg, J. T. (2010). Attention-deficit/hyperactivity disorder: Endophenotypes, structure, and etiological pathways. *Current Directions in Psychological Science, 19*, 24–29.

Nikopoulos, C. K., & Keenan, M. (2004). Effects of video modeling on social initiations by children with autism. *Journal of Applied Behavior Analysis, 37*, 93–96.

Nisbett, R. E. (2009). *Intelligence and how to get it*. New York: Norton.

Norenzayan, A., Choi, I., & Peng, K. (2007). Perception and cognition. In S. Kitayama & D. Cohen (Eds.), *Handbook of cultural psychology* (pp. 569–594). New York: Guilford.

Ormrod, J. E., & McGuire, D. J. (2007). *Case studies: Applying educational psychology* (2nd ed.). Upper Saddle River, NJ: Merrill/Prentice-Hall.

Ozonoff, S., & Schetter, P. L. (2007). Executive dysfunction in autism spectrum disorders: From research to practice. In L. Meltzer (Ed.), *Executive function in education: From theory to practice* (pp. 133–160). New York: Guilford.

Palincsar, A. S., & Herrenkohl, L. R. (1999). Designing collaborative contexts: Lessons from three research programs. In A. M. O'Donnell & A. King (Eds.), *Cognitive perspectives on peer learning* (pp. 151–177). Mahwah, NJ: Erlbaum.

Park, D. C., & Huang, C.-M. (2010). Culture wires the brain: A cognitive neuroscience perspective. *Perspectives on Psychological Science, 5,* 391–400.

Parker, W. D. (1997). An empirical typology of perfectionism in academically talented children. *American Educational Research Journal, 34,* 545–562.

Patton, J. R., Blackbourn, J. M., & Fad, K. S. (1996). *Exceptional individuals in focus* (6th ed.). Upper Saddle River, NJ: Merrill/Prentice-Hall.

Pea, R. D. (1993). Practices of distributed intelligence and designs for education. In G. Salomon (Ed.), *Distributed cognitions: Psychological and educational considerations* (pp. 47–87). Cambridge, England: Cambridge University Press.

Pellegrini, A. D., & Bohn, C. M. (2005). The role of recess in children's cognitive performance and school adjustment. *Educational Researcher, 34*(1), 13–19.

Pellegrini, A. D., & Horvat, M. (1995). A developmental contextualist critique of attention deficit hyperactivity disorder. *Educational Researcher, 24*(1), 13–19.

Pelphrey, K. A., & Carter, E. J. (2007). Brain mechanisms underlying social perception deficits in autism. In D. Coch, G. Dawson, & K. W. Fischer (Eds.), *Human behavior, learning, and the developing brain: Atypical development* (pp. 56–86). New York: Guilford.

Perkins, D. N. (1992). *Smart schools: From training memories to educating minds.* New York: Free Press/Macmillan.

Perkins, D. N. (1995). *Outsmarting IQ: The emerging science of learnable intelligence.* New York: Free Press.

Perkins, D. N., & Ritchhart, R. (2004). When is good thinking? In D. Y. Dai & R. J. Sternberg (Eds.), *Motivation, emotion, and cognition: Integrative perspectives on intellectual functioning and development* (pp. 351–384). Mahwah, NJ: Erlbaum.

Perkins, D. N., Tishman, S., Ritchhart, R., Donis, K., & Andrade, A. (2000). Intelligence in the wild: A dispositional view of intellectual traits. *Educational Psychology Review, 12,* 269–293.

Peterson, C. C. (2002). Drawing insight from pictures: The development of concepts of false drawing and false belief in children with deafness, normal hearing, and autism. *Child Development, 73,* 1442–1459.

Pfiffner, L. J., Barkley, R. A., & DuPaul, G. J. (2006). Treatment of ADHD in school settings. In R. A. Barkley, *Attention-deficit hyperactivity disorder: A handbook for diagnosis and treatment* (3rd ed., pp. 547–589). New York: Guilford.

Phelps, L., McGrew, K. S., Knopik, S. N., & Ford, L. (2005). The general (*g*), broad, and narrow CHC stratum characteristics of the WJ III and WISC-III tests: A confirmatory cross-battery investigation. *School Psychology Quarterly, 20,* 66–88.

Piirto, J. (1999). *Talented children and adults: Their development and education* (2nd ed.). Upper Saddle River, NJ: Merrill/Prentice Hall.

Posner, M. I., & Rothbart, M. K. (2007). *Educating the human brain.* Washington, DC: American Psychological Association.

Price, G. R., Holloway, I., Räsänen, P., Vesterinen, M., & Ansari, D. (2007). Impaired parietal magnitude processing in developmental dyscalculia. *Current Biology, 17*(24), 1042–1043.

Proctor, B. E., Floyd, R. G., & Shaver, R. B. (2005). Cattell-Horn-Carroll broad cognitive ability profiles of low math achievers. *Psychology in the Schools, 42*(1), 1–12.

Prout, H. T. (2009). Positive psychology and students with intellectual disabilities. In R. Gilman, E. S. Huebner, & M. J. Furlong (Eds.), *Handbook of positive psychology in schools* (pp. 371–381). New York: Routledge.

Pugh, K., & McCardle, P. (Eds.) (2009). *How children learn to read: Current issues and new directions in the integration of cognition, neurobiology and genetics of reading and dyslexia research and practice.* New York: Psychology Press.

Purdie, N., Hattie, J., & Carroll, A. (2002). A review of the research on interventions for attention deficit hyperactivity disorder: What works best? *Review of Educational Research, 72,* 61–99.

Quill, K. A. (1995). Visually cued instruction for children with autism and pervasive developmental disorders. *Focus on Autistic Behavior, 10*(3), 10–20.

Raine, A. (2008). From genes to brain to antisocial behavior. *Current Directions in Psychological Science, 17,* 323–328.

Raine, A., Reynolds, C., & Venables, P. H. (2002). Stimulation seeking and intelligence: A prospective longitudinal study. *Journal of Personality and Social Psychology, 82,* 663–674.

Ramey, C. T. (1992). High-risk children and IQ: Altering intergenerational patterns. *Intelligence, 16,* 239–256.

Ratey, J. J. (2001). *A user's guide to the brain: Perception, attention, and the four theaters of the brain.* New York: Vintage.

Rhodes, B. (2008). Challenges and opportunities for intelligence augmentation. In P. C. Kyllonen, R. D. Roberts, & L. Stankov (Eds.), *Extending intelligence: Enhancement and new constructs* (pp. 395–405). New York: Erlbaum/Taylor & Francis.

Ricciuti, H. N. (1993). Nutrition and mental development. *Current Directions in Psychological Science, 2,* 43–46.

Rice, M., Hadley, P. A., & Alexander, A. L. (1993). Social biases toward children with speech and language impairments: A correlative causal model of language limitations. *Applied Psycholinguistics, 14,* 445–471.

Richards, C. M., Symons, D. K., Greene, C. A., & Szuszkiewicz, T. A. (1995). The bidirectional relationship between achievement and externalizing behavior disorders. *Journal of Learning Disabilities, 28,* 8–17.

Rogoff, B. (2003). *The cultural nature of human development.* Oxford, England: Oxford University Press.

Rowe, D. C., Jacobson, K. C., & Van den Oord, E. J. C. G. (1999). Genetic and environmental influences on Vocabulary IQ: Parental education level as moderator. *Child Development, 70,* 1151–1162.

Rowe, M. B. (1978). *Teaching science as continuous inquiry.* New York: McGraw-Hill.

Rueda, M. R., Rothbart, M. K., McCandliss, B. D., Saccomanno, L., & Posner, M. I. (2005). Training, maturation, and genetic influences on the development of executive attention. *Proceedings of the National Academy of Sciences, USA, 102,* 14931–14936.

Rutter, M. L. (1997). Nature-nurture integration: The example of antisocial behavior. *American Psychologist, 52,* 390–398.

Salomon, G. (1993). No distribution without individuals' cognition: A dynamic interactional view. In G. Salomon (Ed.), *Distributed cognitions: Psychological and educational considerations* (pp. 111–138). Cambridge, England: Cambridge University Press.

Sampson, M. B., Szabo, S., Falk-Ross, F., Foote, M. M., & Linder, P. E. (Eds.). (2007). *Multiple literacies in the 21st century: The twenty-eighth yearbook of the College Reading Association.* Logan, UT: College Reading Association.

Sattler, J. M. (2001). *Assessment of children: Cognitive applications* (4th ed.). San Diego, CA: Author.

Scarr, S., & McCartney, K. (1983). How people make their own environments: A theory of genotype environment effects. *Child Development, 54,* 424–435.

Schick, B., de Villiers, P., de Villiers, J., & Hoffmeister, R. (2007). Language and theory of mind: A study of deaf children. *Child Development, 78,* 376–396.

Schirmer, B. R. (1994). *Language and literacy development in children who are deaf.* Boston: Allyn & Bacon.

Schrandt, J. A., Townsend, D. B., & Poulson, C. L. (2009). Teaching empathy skills to children with autism. *Journal of Applied Behavior Analysis, 42,* 17–32.

Scruggs, T. E., & Mastropieri, M. A. (1994). Successful mainstreaming in elementary science classes: A qualitative study of three reputational cases. *American Educational Research Journal, 31,* 785–811.

Seeley, K. (1989). Facilitators for the gifted. In J. Feldhusen, J. VanTassel-Baska, & K. Seeley, *Excellence in educating the gifted* (pp. 279–298). Denver, CO: Love.

Shavinina, L. V., & Ferrari, M. (2004). Extracognitive facets of developing high ability: Introduction to some important issues. In L. V. Shavinina & M. Ferrari (Eds.), *Beyond knowledge: Extracognitive aspects of developing high ability* (pp. 3–13). Mahwah, NJ: Erlbaum.

Shaw, P., Greenstein, D., Lerch, J., Clasen, L., Lenroot, R., Gogtay, N., et al. (2006, March 30). Intellectual ability and cortical development in children and adolescents. *Nature, 440,* 676–679.

Siegler, R. S., & Alibali, M. W. (2005). *Children's thinking* (4th ed.). Upper Saddle River, NJ: Prentice Hall.

Simonton, D. K. (2001). Talent development as a multidimensional, multiplicative, and dynamic process. *Current Directions in Psychological Science, 10,* 39–42.

Skowronek, J. S., Leichtman, M. D., & Pillemer, D. B. (2008). Long-term episodic memory in children with attention-deficit/hyperactivity disorder. *Learning Disabilities Research and Practice, 23*(1), 25–35.

Slavin, R. E. (1987). Ability grouping and student achievement in elementary schools: A best-evidence synthesis. *Review of Educational Research, 57,* 293–336.

Slavin, R. E. (2011). Instruction based on cooperative learning. In R. E. Mayer & P. A. Alexander (Eds.), *Handbook of research on learning and instruction* (pp. 344–360). New York: Routledge.

Snider, V. E. (1990). What we know about learning styles from research in special education. *Educational Leadership, 48*(2), 53.

Snyder, J., Schrepferman, L., McEachern, A., Barner, S., Johnson, K., & Provines, J. (2008). Peer deviancy training and peer coercion: Dual processes associated with early-onset conduct problems. *Child Development, 79,* 252–268.

Soodak, L. C., & McCarthy, M. R. (2006). Classroom management in inclusive settings. In C. M. Evertson & C. S. Weinstein (Eds.), *Handbook of classroom management: Research, practice, and contemporary issues* (pp. 461–489). Mahwah, NJ: Erlbaum.

Southerland, S. A., & Sinatra, G. M. (2003). Learning about biological evolution: A special case of intentional conceptual change. In G. M. Sinatra & P. R. Pintrich (Eds.), *Intentional conceptual change* (pp. 317–345). Mahwah, NJ: Erlbaum.

Spearman, C. (1904). General intelligence, objectively determined and measured. *American Journal of Psychology, 15,* 201–293.

Spearman, C. (1927). *The abilities of man: Their nature and measurement.* New York: Macmillan.

Spinath, F. M., Price, T. S., Dale, P. S., & Plomin, R. (2004). The genetic and environmental origins of language disability and ability. *Child Development, 75,* 445–454.

Stainback, S., & Stainback, W. (1992). Schools as inclusive communities. In W. Stainback & S. Stainback (Eds.), *Controversial issues confronting special education: Divergent perspectives* (pp. 29–43). Boston: Allyn & Bacon.

Stanley, J. C. (1980). On educating the gifted. *Educational Researcher, 9*(3), 8–12.

Stanovich, K. E. (1999). *Who is rational? Studies of individual differences in reasoning.* Mahwah, NJ: Erlbaum.

Stanovich, K. (2009). *What intelligence tests miss: The psychology of rational thought.* New Haven, CT: Yale University Press.

Staub, D. (1998). *Delicate threads: Friendships between children with and without special needs in inclusive settings.* Bethesda, MD: Woodbine House.

Stein, J. A., & Krishnan, K. (2007). Nonverbal learning disabilities and executive function: The challenges of effective assessment and teaching. In L. Meltzer (Ed.), *Executive function in education: From theory to practice* (pp. 106–132). New York: Guilford.

Steiner, H. H., & Carr, M. (2003). Cognitive development in gifted children: Toward a more precise understanding of emerging differences in intelligence. *Educational Psychology Review, 15,* 215–246.

Sternberg, R. J. (1985). *Beyond IQ: A triarchic theory of human intelligence.* Cambridge, England: Cambridge University Press.

Sternberg, R. J. (1997). The concept of intelligence and its role in lifelong learning and success. *American Psychologist, 52,* 1030–1037.

Sternberg, R. J. (1998). Teaching triarchically improves school achievement. *Journal of Educational Psychology, 90,* 374–384.

Sternberg, R. J. (2002). Raising the achievement of all students: Teaching for successful intelligence. *Educational Psychology Review, 14,* 383–393.

Sternberg, R. J. (2003). *Wisdom, intelligence, and creativity synthesized.* Cambridge, England: Cambridge University Press.

Sternberg, R. J. (2004). Culture and intelligence. *American Psychologist, 59,* 325–338.

Sternberg, R. J. (2005). Intelligence, competence, and expertise. In A. J. Elliot & C. S. Dweck (Eds.), *Handbook of competence and motivation* (pp. 15–30). New York: Guilford.

Sternberg, R. J. (2007). Intelligence and culture. In S. Kitayama & D. Cohen (Eds.), *Handbook of cultural psychology* (pp. 547–568). New York: Guilford.

Sternberg, R. J., & Detterman, D. K. (Eds.). (1986). *What is intelligence? Contemporary views on its nature and definition.* Norwood, NJ: Ablex.

Sternberg, R. J., Forsythe, G. B., Hedlund, J., Horvath, J. A., Wagner, R. K., Williams, W. M., et al. (2000). *Practical intelligence in everyday life.* Cambridge, England: Cambridge University Press.

Sternberg, R. J., Grigorenko, E. L., & Kidd, K. K. (2005). Intelligence, race, and genetics. *American Psychologist, 60,* 46–59.

Subotnik, R. F., Olszewski-Kubilus, P., & Worrell, F. C. (2011). Rethinking giftedness and gifted education: A proposed direction forward base on psychological science. *Psychological Science in the Public Interest, 12,* 3–54.

Sullivan, A. L. (2008, March). *Examining the local context of English language learner representation in special education.* Poster presented at the annual meeting of the American Educational Research Association, New York.

Sullivan, R. C. (1994). Autism: Definitions past and present. *Journal of Vocational Rehabilitation, 4,* 4–9.

Swanson, H. L. (2008). Working memory and intelligence in children: What develops? *Journal of Educational Psychology, 100,* 581–602.

Swanson, H. L., Hoskyn, M., & Lee, C. (1999). *Interventions for students with learning disabilities: A meta-analysis of treatment outcomes.* New York: Guilford.

Tager-Flusberg, H. (2007). Evaluating the theory-of-mind hypothesis of autism. *Current Directions in Psychological Science, 16,* 311–315.

Tager-Flusberg, H., & Skwerer, D. P. (2007). Williams syndrome: A model developmental syndrome for exploring brain-behavior relationships. In D. Coch, G. Dawson, & K. W. Fischer (Eds.), *Human behavior, learning, and the developing brain: Atypical development* (pp. 87–116). New York: Guilford.

Terry, A. W. (2008). Student voices, global echoes: Service-learning and the gifted. *Roeper Review, 30,* 45–51.

Theimann, K. S., & Goldstein, H. (2004). Effects of peer training and written text cueing on social communication of school-age children with pervasive developmental disorder. *Journal of Speech, Language, and Hearing Research, 47,* 126–144.

Tompkins, G. E., & McGee, L. M. (1986). Visually impaired and sighted children's emerging concepts about written language. In D. B. Yaden, Jr., & S. Templeton (Eds.), *Metalinguistic awareness and beginning literacy: Conceptualizing what it means to read and write* (pp. 259–275). Portsmouth, NH: Heinemann.

Torrance, E. P. (1989). A reaction to "Gifted black students: Curriculum and teaching strategies." In C. J. Maker & S. W. Schiever (Eds.), *Critical issues in gifted education: Vol. 2. Defensible programs for cultural and ethnic minorities* (pp. 270–274). Austin, TX: Pro-Ed.

Treffert, D. A., & Wallace, G. L. (2002). Islands of genius. *Scientific American, 286*(6), 76–85.

Turkheimer, E., Haley, A., Waldron, M., D'Onofrio, B., & Gottesman, I. I. (2003). Socioeconomic status modifies heritability of IQ in young children. *Psychological Science, 14,* 623–628.

Turnbull, A. P., Pereira, L., & Blue-Banning, M. (2000). Teachers as friendship facilitators. *Teaching Exceptional Children, 32*(5), 66–70.

Turnbull, A. P., Turnbull, R., & Wehmeyer, M. L. (2010). *Exceptional lives: Special education in today's schools* (6th ed.). Upper Saddle River, NJ: Merrill.

Turner, J. C., Meyer, D. K., Cox, K. E., Logan, C., DiCintio, M., & Thomas, C. T. (1998). Creating contexts for involvement in mathematics. *Journal of Educational Psychology, 90,* 730–745.

Tuttle, D. W., & Tuttle, N. R. (1996). *Self-esteem and adjusting with blindness: The process of responding to life's demands* (2nd ed.). Springfield, IL: Charles C Thomas.

Udall, A. J. (1989). Curriculum for gifted Hispanic students. In C. J. Maker & S. W. Schiever (Eds.), *Critical issues in gifted education: Vol. 2. Defensible programs for cultural and ethnic minorities* (pp. 41–56). Austin, TX: Pro-Ed.

U.S. Department of Education. (2006). *26th annual report to Congress on the implementation of the Individuals with Disabilities Education Act, 2004.* Washington, DC: Author.

U.S. Department of Education, National Center for Education Statistics. (2010). *Digest of Education Statistics: 2010.* Retrieved from http://nces.ed.gov/programs/digest/2010menu_tables.asp

U.S. Department of Education, Office of Special Education and Rehabilitative Services. (2000). *A guide to the individualized education program.* Washington, DC: Author.

van IJzendoorn, M. H., & Juffer, F. (2005). Adoption is a successful natural intervention enhancing adopted children's IQ and school performance. *Current Directions in Psychological Science, 14,* 326–330.

vanSledright, B., & Limón, M. (2006). Learning and teaching social studies: A review of cognitive research in history and geography. In P. A. Alexander & P. H. Winne (Eds.), *Handbook of educational psychology* (2nd ed., pp. 545–570). Mahwah, NJ: Erlbaum.

VanTassel-Baska, J. L. (Ed.). (2008). *Alternative assessments with gifted and talented students.* Waco, TX: Prufrock.

Varnum, M. E. W., Grossmann, I., Kitayama, S., & Nisbett, R. E. (2010). The origin of cultural differences in cognition: The social orientation hypothesis. *Current Directions in Psychological Science, 19,* 9–13.

Waber, D. P. (2010). *Rethinking learning disabilities:Understanding children who struggle in school.* New York: Guilford.

Wanzek, J., & Vaughn, S. (2007). Research-based implications from extensive early reading interventions. *School Psychology Review, 36,* 541–561.

Waterhouse, L. (2006). Multiple intelligences, the Mozart effect, and emotional intelligence: A critical review. *Educational Psychologist, 41,* 207–225.

Webber, J., & Plotts, C. A. (2008). *Emotional and behavioral disorders: Theory and practice* (5th ed.). Boston: Allyn & Bacon.

Wehmeyer, M. L., Agran, M., Hughes, C., Martin, J., Mithaug, D. E., & Palmer, S. (2007). *Promoting self-determination in students with intellectual and developmental disabilities.* New York: Guilford.

West, R. F., Toplak, M. E., & Stanovich, K. E. (2008). Heuristics and biases as measures of critical thinking: Associations with cognitive ability and thinking dispositions. *Journal of Educational Psychology, 100,* 930–941.

Westefeld, J. S., Bell, A., Bermingham, C., Button, C., Shaw, K., Skow, C., et al. (2010). Suicide among preadolescents: A call to action. *Journal of Loss and Trauma, 15,* 381–407.

White, R., & Cunningham, A. M. (1991). *Ryan White: My own story.* New York: Signet.

Wilder, A. A., & Williams, J. P. (2001). Students with severe learning disabilities can learn higher order comprehension skills. *Journal of Educational Psychology, 93,* 268–278.

Wiles, J., & Bondi, J. (2001). *The new American middle school: Educating preadolescents in an era of change.* Upper Saddle River, NJ: Merrill/Prentice Hall.

Williams, D. (1996). *Autism: An inside-outside approach.* London: Jessica Kingsley.

Winner, E. (1996). The rage to master: The decisive role of talent in the visual arts. In K. A. Ericsson (Ed.), *The road to excellence: The acquisition of expert performance in the arts and sciences, sports, and games* (pp. 271–302). Mahwah, NJ: Erlbaum.

Winner, E. (2000a). Giftedness: Current theory and research. *Current Directions in Psychological Science, 9,* 153–156.

Winner, E. (2000b). The origins and ends of giftedness. *American Psychologist, 55,* 159–169.

Wood, J. W. (1998). *Adapting instruction to accommodate students in inclusive settings* (3rd ed.). Upper Saddle River, NJ: Merrill/Prentice Hall.

Wood, J. W., & Rosbe, M. (1985). Adapting the classroom lecture for the mainstreamed student in the secondary schools. *Clearing House, 58,* 354–358.

Yeo, R. A., Gangestad, S. W., & Thoma, R. J. (2007). Developmental instability and individual variation in brain development: Implications for the origin of neurodevelopmental disorders. *Current Directions in Psychological Science, 16,* 245–249.

Zhang, L.-F., & Sternberg, R. J. (2006). *The nature of intellectual styles.* Mahwah, NJ: Erlbaum.

Zigler, E. F., & Finn-Stevenson, M. (1992). Applied developmental psychology. In M. H. Bornstein & M. E. Lamb (Eds.), *Developmental psychology: An advanced textbook* (pp. 555–598). Mahwah, NJ: Erlbaum.

## CHAPTER 6

Alexander, P. A., & Judy, J. E. (1988). The interaction of domain-specific and strategic knowledge in academic performance. *Review of Educational Research, 58,* 375–404.

Alexander, P. A., Kulikowich, J. M., & Schulze, S. K. (1994). How subject-matter knowledge affects recall and interest. *American Educational Research Journal, 31,* 313–337.

Alexander, P. A., Schallert, D. L., & Reynolds, R. E. (2009). What is learning anyway? A topographic perspective considered. *Educational Psychologist, 44,* 176–192.

Allen, B. A., & Boykin, A. W. (1991). The influence of contextual factors on Afro-American and Euro-American children's performance: Effects of movement opportunity and music. *International Journal of Psychology, 26,* 373–387.

Alloway, T. P., Gathercole, S. E., Kirkwood, H., & Elliott, J. (2009). The cognitive and behavioral characteristics of children with low working memory. *Child Development, 80,* 606–621.

Altmann, E. M., & Gray, W. D. (2002). Forgetting to remember: The functional relationship of decay and interference. *Psychological Science, 13,* 27–33.

Anderson, J. R. (1983). *The architecture of cognition.* Cambridge, MA: Harvard University Press.

Anderson, J. R. (2005). *Cognitive psychology and its implications* (6th ed.). New York: Worth.

Anderson, J. R., Reder, L. M., & Simon, H. A. (1996). Situated learning and education. *Educational Researcher, 25*(4), 5–11.

Anderson, M. C., Ochsner, K. N., Kuhl, B., Cooper, J., Robertson, E., Gabrieli, S. W., Glover, G. H., & Gabrieli, J. D. E. (2004). Neural systems underlying the suppression of unwanted memories. *Science, 303,* 232–235.

Anderson, R. C., Reynolds, R. E., Schallert, D. L., & Goetz, E. T. (1977). Frameworks for comprehending discourse. *American Educational Research Journal, 14,* 367–381.

Aron, A. R. (2008). Progress in executive-function research: From tasks to functions to regions to networks. *Current Directions in Psychological Science, 17,* 124–129.

Atkinson, R. C., & Shiffrin, R. M. (1968). Human memory: A proposed system and its control processes. In K. W. Spence & J. T. Spence (Eds.), *The psychology of learning and motivation: Advances in research and theory* (Vol. 2, pp. 89–195). San Diego, CA: Academic Press.

Atkinson, R. K., Levin, J. R., Kiewra, K. A., Meyers, T., Kim, S., Atkinson, L. A., Renandya, W. A., & Hwang, Y. (1999). Matrix and mnemonic text-processing adjuncts: Comparing and combining their components. *Journal of Educational Psychology, 91,* 342–357.

Atran, S., Medin, D. L., & Ross, N. O. (2005). The cultural mind: Environmental decision making and cultural modeling within and across populations. *Psychological Review, 112,* 744–776.

Ausubel, D. P., Novak, J. D., & Hanesian, H. (1978). *Educational psychology: A cognitive view* (2nd ed.). New York: Holt, Rinehart & Winston.

Baddeley, A. D. (2001). Is working memory still working? *American Psychologist, 56,* 851–864.

Baer, J., & Garrett, T. (2010). Teaching for creativity in an era of content standards and accountability. In R. A. Beghetto & J. C. Kaufman (Eds.), *Nurturing creativity in the classroom* (pp. 6–23). New York: Cambridge University Press.

Bangert-Drowns, R. L., Hurley, M. M., & Wilkinson, B. (2004). The effects of school-based writing-to-learn interventions on academic achievement: A meta-analysis. *Review of Educational Research, 74,* 29–58.

Banich, M. T. (2009). Executive function: The search for an integrated account. *Current Directions in Psychological Science, 18,* 89–94.

Banks, J. A. (1991). Multicultural literacy and curriculum reform. *Educational Horizons, 69*(3), 135–140.

Barkley, R. A. (2006). *Attention-deficit hyperactivity disorder: A handbook for diagnosis and treatment* (3rd ed.). New York: Guilford.

Barron, E., Riby, L. M., Greer, J., & Smallwood, J. (2011). Absorbed in thought: The effect of mind wandering on the processing of relevant and irrelevant events. *Psychologial Science, 22,* 596–601.

Barsalou, L. W., Simmons, W. K., Barbey, A., & Wilson, C. D. (2003). Grounding conceptual knowledge in modality-specific systems. *Trends in Cognitive Sciences, 7,* 84–91.

Barton, A. C., Tan, E., & Rivet, A. (2008). Creating hybrid spaces for engaging school science among urban middle school girls. *American Educational Research Journal, 45,* 68–103.

Bauer, P. J. (2002). Long-term recall memory: Behavioral and neuro-developmental changes in the first 2 years of life. *Current Directions in Psychological Science, 11,* 137–141.

Bauer, P. J., DeBoer, T., & Lukowski, A. F. (2007). In the language of multiple memory systems: Defining and describing developments in long-term declarative memory. In L. M. Oakes & P. J. Bauer (Eds.), *Short- and long-term memory in infancy and early childhood: Taking the first steps toward remembering* (pp. 240–270). New York: Oxford University Press.

Behrmann, M. (2000). The mind's eye mapped onto the brain's matter. *Current Directions in Psychological Science, 9,* 50–54.

Beilock, S. L., & Carr, T. H. (2004). From novice to expert performance: Memory, attention, and the control of complex sensorimotor skills. In A. M. Williams & N. J. Hodges (Eds.), *Skill acquisition in sport: Research, theory, and practice* (pp. 309–327). London: Routledge.

Beirne-Smith, M., Patton, J. R., & Kim, S. H. (2006). *Mental retardation: An introduction to intellectual disabilities* (7th ed.). Upper Saddle River, NJ: Merrill/Prentice-Hall.

Bellezza, F. S. (1986). Mental cues and verbal reports in learning. In G. H. Bower (Ed.), *The psychology of learning and motivation: Advances in research and theory* (Vol. 20, pp. 237–273). San Diego, CA: Academic Press.

Ben-Yehudah, G., & Fiez, J. A. (2007). Development of verbal working memory. In D. Coch, K. W. Fischer, & G. Dawson (Eds.), *Human behavior, learning, and the developing brain: Typical development* (pp. 301–328). New York: Guilford.

Best, R. M., Dockrell, J. E., & Braisby, N. (2006). Lexical acquisition in elementary science classes. *Journal of Educational Psychology, 98,* 824–838.

Bjorklund, D. F., & Coyle, T. R. (1995). Utilization deficiencies in the development of memory strategies. In F. E. Weinert & W. Schneider (Eds.), *Research on memory development: State of the art and future directions* (pp. 161–180). Mahwah, NJ: Erlbaum.

Bjorklund, D. F., & Jacobs, J. W. (1985). Associative and categorical processes in children's memory: The role of automaticity in the development of organization in free recall. *Journal of Experimental Child Psychology, 39,* 599–617.

Bjorklund, D. F., Muir-Broaddus, J. E., & Schneider, W. (1990). The role of knowledge in the development of strategies. In D. F. Bjorklund (Ed.), *Children's strategies: Contemporary views of cognitive development* (pp. 93–128). Mahwah, NJ: Erlbaum.

Bjorklund, D. F., Schneider, W., Cassel, W. S., & Ashley, E. (1994). Training and extension of a memory strategy: Evidence for utilization deficiencies in high- and low-IQ children. *Child Development, 65,* 951–965.

Bower, G. H. (1994). Some relations between emotions and memory. In P. Ekman & R. J. Davidson (Eds.), *The nature of emotion: Fundamental questions* (pp. 303–305). New York: Oxford University Press.

Bower, G. H., Black, J. B., & Turner, T. J. (1979). Scripts in memory for text. *Cognitive Psychology, 11,* 177–220.

Bower, G. H., & Forgas, J. P. (2001). Mood and social memory. In J. P. Forgas (Ed.), *Handbook of affect and social cognition* (pp. 95–120). Mahwah, NJ: Erlbaum.

Bower, G. H., Karlin, M. B., & Dueck, A. (1975). Comprehension and memory for pictures. *Memory and Cognition, 3,* 216–220.

Brainerd, C. J., & Reyna, V. F. (2005). *The science of false memory.* Oxford, England: Oxford University Press.

Bransford, J. D., & Franks, J. J. (1971). The abstraction of linguistic ideas. *Cognitive Psychology, 2,* 331–350.

Brewer, W. F. (2008). Naive theories of observational astronomy: Review, analysis, and theoretical implications. In S. Vosniadou (Ed.), *International handbook of research on conceptual change* (pp. 155–204). New York: Routledge.

Brophy, J. E. (2004). *Motivating students to learn* (2nd ed.). Mahwah, NJ: Erlbaum.

Brophy, J., Alleman, J., & Knighton, B. (2009). *Inside the social studies classroom.* New York: Routledge.

Brown, J. S., Collins, A., & Duguid, P. (1989). Situated cognition and the culture of learning. *Educational Researcher, 18*(1), 32–42.

Bulgren, J. A., Schumaker, J. B., & Deshler, D. D. (1994). The effects of a recall enhancement routine on the test performance of secondary students with and without learning disabilities. *Learning Disabilities Research and Practice, 9,* 2–11.

Byrnes, J. P. (2001). *Minds, brains, and learning: Understanding the psychological and educational relevance of neuroscientific research.* New York: Guilford.

Carlson, R., Chandler, P., & Sweller, J. (2003). Learning and understanding science instructional material. *Journal of Educational Psychology, 95,* 629–640.

Carlson, S. M., & Moses, L. J. (2001). Individual differences in inhibitory control and children's theory of mind. *Child Development, 72,* 1032–1053.

Carmichael, C. A., & Hayes, B. K. (2001). Prior knowledge and exemplar encoding in children's concept acquisition. *Child Development, 72,* 1071–1090.

Castagno, A. E., & Brayboy, B. M. J. (2008). Culturally responsive schooling for Indigenous youth: A review of the literature. *Review of Educational Research, 78,* 941–993.

Castelli, D. M., Hillman, C. H., Buck, S. M., & Erwin, H. E. (2007). Physical fitness and academic achievement in third- and fifth-grade students. *Journal of Sport & Exercise Psychology, 29,* 239–252.

Cattani, A., Clibbens, J., & Perfect, T. J. (2007). Visual memory for shapes in deaf signers and nonsigners and in hearing signers and nonsigners: Atypical lateralization and enhancement. *Neuropsychology, 21,* 114–121.

Charness, N., Tuffiash, M., & Jastrzembski, T. (2004). Motivation, emotion, and expert skill acquisition. In D. Y. Dai & R. J. Sternberg (Eds.), *Motivation, emotion, and cognition: Integrative perspectives on intellectual functioning and development* (pp. 299–319). Mahwah, NJ: Erlbaum.

Cherry, E. C. (1953). Some experiments on the recognition of speech, with one and with two ears. *Journal of the Acoustical Society of America, 25,* 975–979.

Chi, M. T. H. (1978). Knowledge structures and memory development. In R. S. Siegler (Ed.), *Children's thinking: What develops?* (pp. 73–96). Mahwah, NJ: Erlbaum.

Chi, M. T. H. (2008). Three types of conceptual change: Belief revision, mental model transformation, and categorical shift. In S. Vosniadou (Ed.), *International handbook on conceptual change* (pp. 61–82). New York: Routledge.

Chinn, C. A., & Malhotra, B. A. (2002). Children's responses to anomalous scientific data: How is conceptual change impeded? *Journal of Educational Psychology, 94,* 327–343.

Chinn, C. A., & Samarapungavan, A. (2009). Conceptual change—Multiple routes, multiple mechanisms: A commentary on Ohlsson (2009). *Educational Psychologist, 44,* 48–57.

Clark, B. (1997). *Growing up gifted* (5th ed.). Upper Saddle River, NJ: Merrill/Prentice-Hall.

Clark, D. B. (2006). Longitudinal conceptual change in students' understanding of thermal equilibrium: An examination of the process of conceptual restructuring. *Cognition and Instruction, 24,* 467–563.

Clark, J. M., & Paivio, A. (1991). Dual coding theory and education. *Educational Psychology Review, 3,* 149–210.

Cohen, G. D. (2005). *The mature mind: The positive power of the aging brain.* New York: Basic Books.

Cohen, I. L. (2007). A neural network model of autism: Implications for theory and treatment. In D. Mareschal, S. Sirois, G. Westermann, & M. H. Johnson (Eds.), *Neuroconstructivism: Vol. 2. Perspectives and prospects* (pp. 231–264). Oxford, England: Oxford University Press.

Coltheart, M., Lea, C. D., & Thompson, K. (1974). In defense of iconic memory. *Quarterly Journal of Experimental Psychology, 26,* 633–641.

Cook, R. G., & Smith, J. D. (2006). Stages of abstraction and exemplar memorization in pigeon category learning. *Psychological Science, 17,* 1059–1067.

Correa-Chávez, M., Rogoff, B., & Mejía Arauz, R. (2005). Cultural patterns in attending to two events at once. *Child Development, 76,* 664–678.

Courchesne, E., Townsend, J., Akshoomoff, N. A., Saitoh, O., Yeung-Courchesne, R., Lincoln, A. J., James, H. E., Haas, R. H., Schreibman, L., & Lau, L. (1994). Impairment of shifting attention in autistic and cerebellar patients. *Behavioral Neuroscience, 108,* 848–865.

Cowan, N. (1995). *Attention and memory: An integrated framework.* New York: Oxford University Press.

Cowan, N. (2007). What infants can tell us about working memory development. In L. M. Oakes & P. J. Bauer (Eds.), *Short- and long-term memory in infancy and early childhood: Taking the first steps toward remembering* (pp. 126–150). New York: Oxford University Press.

Cowan, N. (2010). The magical mystery four: How is working memory capacity limited, and why? *Current Directions in Psychological Science, 19,* 51–57.

Cowan, N., Saults, J. S., & Morey, C. C. (2006). Development of working memory for verbal-spatial associations. *Journal of Memory and Language, 55,* 274–289.

Coyle, T. R., Pillow, D. R., Snyder, A. C., & Kochunov, P. (2011). Processing speed mediates the development of general intelligence (*g*) in adolescence. *Psychological Science, 22,* 1265–1269.

Craik, F. I. M. (2006). Distinctiveness and memory: Comments and a point of view. In R. R. Hunt & J. B. Worthen, J. B. (Eds.) *Distinctiveness and memory* (pp. 425–442). Oxford, England: Oxford University Press.

Craik, F. I. M., & Watkins, M. J. (1973). The role of rehearsal in short-term memory. *Journal* of Verbal Learning and Verbal Behavior, 12, 598–607.

Crooks, T. J. (1988). The impact of classroom evaluation practices on students. *Review of Educational Research, 58,* 438–481.

Dahan, D. (2010). The time course of interpretation in speech comprehension. *Current Directions in Psychological Science, 19,* 121–126.

Danthiir, V., Roberts, R. D., Schulze, R., & Wilhelm, O. (2005). Mental speed: On frameworks, paradigms, and a platform for the future. In O. Wilhelm & R. W. Engle (Eds.), *Handbook of understanding and measuring intelligence* (pp. 27–46). Thousand Oaks, CA: Sage.

Das, J. P., Naglieri, J. A., & Kirby, J. R. (1994). *Assessment of cognitive processes.* Boston: Allyn & Bacon.

De Corte, E., Greer, B., & Verschaffel, L. (1996). Mathematics teaching and learning. In D. C. Berliner & R. C. Calfee (Eds.), *Handbook of educational psychology* (pp. 491–549). New York: Macmillan.

De La Paz, S., & McCutchen, D. (2011). Learning to write. In R. E. Mayer & P. A. Alexander (Eds.), *Handbook of research on learning and instruction* (pp. 32–54). New York: Routledge.

De Lisi, R., & Golbeck, S. L. (1999). Implications of Piagetian theory for peer learning. In A. M. O'Donnell & A. King (Eds.), *Cognitive perspectives on peer learning* (pp. 3–37). Mahwah, NJ: Erlbaum.

DeLoache, J. S., & Todd, C. M. (1988). Young children's use of spatial categorization as a mnemonic strategy. *Journal of Experimental Child Psychology, 46,* 1–20.

Delval, J. (1994). Stages in the child's construction of social knowledge. In M. Carretero & J. F. Voss (Eds.), *Cognitive and instructional processes in history and the social sciences* (pp. 77–102). Mahwah, NJ: Erlbaum.

Demetriou, A., Christou, C., Spanoudis, G., & Platsidou, M. (2002). The development of mental processing: Efficiency, working memory, and thinking. *Monographs of the Society for Research in Child Development, 67*(1, Serial No. 268).

Dempster, F. N. (1985). Proactive interference in sentence recall: Topic-similarity effects and individual differences. *Memory and Cognition, 13,* 81–89.

Dempster, F. N. (1991). Synthesis of research on reviews and tests. *Educational Leadership, 48*(7), 71–76.

Dempster, F. N., & Corkill, A. J. (1999). Interference and inhibition in cognition and behavior: Unifying themes for educational psychology. *Educational Psychology Review, 11,* 1–88.

Dinges, D. F., & Rogers, N. L. (2008). The future of human intelligence: Enhancing cognitive capability in a 24/7 world. In P. C. Kyllonen, R. D. Roberts, & L. Stankov (Eds.), *Extending intelligence: Enhancement and new constructs* (pp. 407–430). New York: Erlbaum/Taylor & Francis.

diSessa, A. A. (1996). What do "just plain folk" know about physics? In D. R. Olson & N. Torrance (Eds.), *The handbook of education and human development: New models of learning, teaching, and schooling* (pp. 709–730). Cambridge, MA: Blackwell.

diSessa, A. A. (2006). A history of conceptual change research. In R. K. Sawyer (Ed.), *The Cambridge handbook of the learning sciences* (pp. 265–281). Cambridge, England: Cambridge University Press.

Di Vesta, F. J., & Gray, S. G. (1972). Listening and notetaking. *Journal of Educational Psychology, 63,* 8–14.

Driver, R., Asoko, H., Leach, J., Mortimer, E., & Scott, P. (1994). Constructing scientific knowledge in the classroom. *Educational Researcher, 23*(7), 5–12.

Eaton, J. F., Anderson, C. W., & Smith, E. L. (1984). Students' misconceptions interfere with science learning: Case studies of fifth-grade students. *Elementary School Journal, 84,* 365–379.

Edens, K. M., & Potter, E. F. (2001). Promoting conceptual understanding through pictorial representation. *Studies in Art Education, 42,* 214–233.

Engle, R. W. (2002). Working memory capacity as executive attention. *Current Directions in Psychological Science, 11,* 19–23.

Ennis, C. D., & Chen, A. (2011). Learning motor skill in physical education. In R. E. Mayer & P. A. Alexander (Eds.), *Handbook of research on learning and instruction* (pp. 148–165). New York: Routledge.

Erdelyi, M. H. (2010). The ups and downs of memory. *American Psychologist, 65,* 623–633.

Ericsson, K. A. (1996). *The road to excellence: The acquisition of expert performance in the arts and science, sports, and games.* Mahwah, NJ: Erlbaum.

Ericsson, K. A. (2003). The acquisition of expert performance as problem solving. In J. E. Davidson & R. J. Sternberg (Eds.), *The psychology of problem solving* (pp. 31–83). Cambridge, England: Cambridge University Press.

Evans, G. W., & Schamberg, M. A. (2009). Childhood poverty, chronic stress, and adult working memory. *Proceedings of the National Academy of Sciences of the United States of America, 106,* 6545–6549.

Feltz, D. L., Landers, D. M., & Becker, B. J. (1988). A revised meta-analysis of the mental practice literature on motor skill performance. In D. Druckman & J. A. Swets (Eds.), *Enhancing human performance: Issues, theories, and techniques* (pp. 1–65). Washington, DC: National Research Council.

Féry, Y.-A., & Morizot, P. (2000). Kinesthetic and visual image in modeling closed motor skills: The example of the tennis serve. *Perceptual and Motor Skills, 90,* 707–722.

Flavell, J. H. (2000). Development of children's knowledge about the mental world. *International Journal of Behavioral Development, 24*(1), 15–23.

Flavell, J. H., Miller, P. H., & Miller, S. A. (2002). *Cognitive development* (4th ed.). Upper Saddle River, NJ: Prentice Hall.

Fletcher, J. M., Lyon, G. R., Fuchs, L. S., & Barnes, M. A. (2007). *Learning disabilities: From identification to intervention.* New York: Guilford.

Fox, E. (2009). The role of reader characteristics in processing and learning from informational text. *Review of Educational Research, 79,* 197–261.

Frederiksen, N. (1984b). The real test bias: Influences of testing on teaching and learning. *American Psychologist, 39,* 193–202.

Gagné, R. M. (1985). *The conditions of learning and theory of instruction* (4th ed.). New York: Holt, Rinehart & Winston.

Gardner, H., Torff, B., & Hatch, T. (1996). The age of innocence reconsidered: Preserving the best of the progressive traditions in psychology and education. In D. R. Olson & N. Torrance (Eds.), *The handbook of education and human development: New models of learning, teaching, and schooling* (pp. 28–55). Cambridge, MA: Blackwell.

Gaskins, I. W., & Pressley, M. (2007). Teaching metacognitive strategies that address executive function processes within a schoolwide curriculum. In L. Meltzer (Ed.), *Executive function in education: From theory to practice* (pp. 261–286). New York: Guilford.

Gathercole, S. E., & Hitch, G. J. (1993). Developmental changes in short-term memory: A revised working memory perspective. In A. F. Collins, S. E. Gathercole, M. A. Conway, & P. E. Morris (Eds.), *Theories of memory* (pp. 189–209). Hove, England: Erlbaum.

Gathercole, S. E., Lamont, E., & Alloway, T. P. (2006). Working memory in the classroom. In S. Pickering (Ed.), *Working memory and education* (p. 219–240). New York: Academic Press.

Geary, D. C. (2005). Folk knowledge and academic learning. In B. J. Ellis & D. F. Bjorklund (Eds.), *Origins of the social mind: Evolutionary psychology and child development* (pp. 493–519). New York: Guilford.

Geary, D. C., Hoard, M. K., Byrd-Craven, J., Nugent, L., & Numtee, C. (2007). Cognitive mechanisms underlying achievement deficits in children with mathematical learning disability. *Child Development, 78,* 1343–1359.

Gelman, S. A. (2003). *The essential child: Origins of essentialism in everyday thought.* New York: Oxford University Press.

Gelman, S. A., & Kalish, C. W. (2006). Conceptual development. In W. Damon & R. M. Lerner (Series Eds.), D. Kuhn, & R. Siegler (Vol. Eds.), *Handbook of child psychology: Vol. 2. Cognition, perception, and language* (6th ed., pp. 687–733). New York: Wiley.

Giaconia, R. M. (1988). Teacher questioning and wait-time (Doctoral dissertation, Stanford University, 1988). *Dissertation Abstracts International, 49,* 462A.

Gilliland, H. (1988). Discovering and emphasizing the positive aspects of the culture. In H. Gilliland & J. Reyhner (Eds.), *Teaching the Native American.* Dubuque, IA: Kendall/Hunt.

Glanzer, M., & Nolan, S. D. (1986). Memory mechanisms in text comprehension. In G. H. Bower (Ed.), *The psychology of learning and motivation: Advances in research and theory* (Vol. 20, pp. 275–317). San Diego, CA: Academic Press.

Glynn, S. M., Yeany, R. H., & Britton, B. K. (Eds.). (1991). *The psychology of learning science.* Mahwah, NJ: Erlbaum.

Gonsalves, B. D., & Cohen, N. J. (2010). Brain imaging, cognitive processes, and brain networks. *Perspectives on Psychological Science, 5,* 744–752.

Gould, E., Beylin, A., Tanapat, P., Reeves, A., & Shors, T. J. (1999). Learning enhances adult neurogenesis in the hippocampal formation. *Nature Neuroscience, 2,* 260–265.

Grandin, T., & Johnson, C. (2005). *Animals in translation: Using the mysteries of autism to decode animal behavior.* New York: Simon & Schuster.

Gregg, N. (2009). *Adolescents and adults with learning disabilities and ADHD: Assessment and accommodation.* New York: Guilford.

Greif, M. L., Kemler Nelson, D. G., Keil, F. C., & Gutierrez, F. (2006). What do children want to know about animals and artifacts? Domain-specific requests for information. *Psychological Science, 17,* 455–459.

Hacker, D. J., Dunlosky, J., & Graesser, A. C. (2009a). A growing sense of "agency." In D. J. Hacker, J. Dunlosky, & A. C. Graesser (Eds.), *Handbook of metacognition in education* (pp. 1–4). New York: Routledge.

Halford, G. S. (1989). Cognitive processing capacity and learning ability: An integration of two areas. *Learning and Individual Differences, 1,* 125–153.

Halpern, D. F. (2006). Assessing gender gaps in learning and academic achievement. In P. A. Alexander & P. H. Winne (Eds.), *Handbook of educational psychology* (2nd ed., pp. 635–653). Mahwah, NJ: Erlbaum.

Halpern, D. F., & LaMay, M. L. (2000). The smarter sex: A critical review of sex differences in intelligence. *Educational Psychology Review, 12,* 229–246.

Haskell, R. E. (2001). *Transfer of learning: Cognition, instruction, and reasoning.* San Diego, CA: Academic Press.

Hatano, G., & Inagaki, K. (1993). Desituating cognition through the construction of conceptual knowledge. In P. Light & G. Butterworth (Eds.), *Context and cognition: Ways of learning and knowing* (pp. 115–133). Mahwah, NJ: Erlbaum.

Hatano, G., & Inagaki, K. (2003). When is conceptual change intended? A cognitive-sociocultural view. In G. M. Sinatra & P. R. Pintrich (Eds.), *Intentional conceptual change* (pp. 407–427). Mahwah, NJ: Erlbaum.

Hattie, J. A. C. (2009). *Visible learning: A synthesis of over 800 meta-analyses relating to achievement.* London: Routledge.

Hattie, J., & Timperley, H. (2007). The power of feedback. *Review of Educational Research, 77,* 81–112.

Healey, M. K., Campbell, K. L., Hasher, L., & Ossher, L. (2010). Direct evidence for the role of inhibition in resolving interference in memory. *Psychological Science, 21,* 1464–1470.

Heatherton, T. F., Macrae, C. N., & Kelley, W. M. (2004). What the social brain sciences can tell us about the self. *Current Directions in Psychological Science, 13,* 190–193.

Hecht, S. A., Close, L., & Santisi, M. (2003). Sources of individual differences in fraction skills. *Journal of Experimental Child Psychology, 86,* 277–302.

Hecht, S. A., & Vagi, K. J. (2010). Sources of group and individual differences in emerging fraction skills. *Journal of Educational Psychology, 102,* 843–859.

Heuer, F., & Reisberg, D. (1992). Emotion, arousal, and memory for detail. In S. Christianson (Ed.), *Handbook of emotion and memory* (pp. 151–180). Hillsdale, NJ: Erlbaum.

Heward, W. L. (2009). *Exceptional children: An introduction to special education* (9th ed.). Upper Saddle River, NJ: Merrill/Pearson Education.

Horn, J. L. (2008). Spearman, g, expertise, and the nature of human cognitive capability. In P. C. Kyllonen, R. D. Roberts, & L. Stankov (Eds.), *Extending intelligence: Enhancement and new constructs* (pp. 185–230). New York: Erlbaum/Taylor & Francis.

Huey, E. D., Krueger, F., & Grafman, J. (2006). Representations in the human prefrontal cortex. *Current Directions in Psychological Science, 15,* 167–171.

Hunt, R. R., & Worthen, J. B. (Eds.). (2006). *Distinctiveness and memory.* Oxford, England: Oxford University Press.

Hynd, C. (1998a). Conceptual change in a high school physics class. In B. Guzzetti & C. Hynd (Eds.), *Perspectives on conceptual change: Multiple ways to understand knowing and learning in a complex world* (pp. 27–36). Mahwah, NJ: Erlbaum.

Hynd, C. (1998b). Observing learning from different perspectives: What does it mean for Barry and his understanding of gravity? In B. Guzzetti & C. Hynd (Eds.), *Perspectives on conceptual change: Multiple ways to understand knowing and learning in a complex world* (pp. 235–244). Mahwah, NJ: Erlbaum.

Hynd, C. (2003). Conceptual change in response to persuasive messages. In G. M. Sinatra & P. R. Pintrich (Eds.), *Intentional conceptual change* (pp. 291–315). Mahwah, NJ: Erlbaum.

Igoa, C. (2007). Immigrant children: Art as a second language. In S. Books (Ed.), *Invisible children in the society and its schools* (3rd ed., pp. 117–140). Mahwah, NJ: Erlbaum.

Inagaki, K., & Hatano, G. (2006). Young children's conception of the biological world. *Current Directions in Psychological Science, 15,* 177–181.

Jegede, O. J., & Olajide, J. O. (1995). Wait-time, classroom discourse, and the influence of sociocultural factors in science teaching. *Science Education, 79,* 233–249.

Johnson, J., Im-Bolter, N., & Pascual-Leone, J. (2003). Development of mental attention in gifted and mainstream children: The role of mental capacity, inhibition, and speed of processing. *Child Development, 74,* 1594–1614.

Johnson-Glenberg, M. C. (2000). Training reading comprehension in adequate decoders/poor comprehenders: Verbal versus visual strategies. *Journal of Educational Psychology, 92,* 772–782.

Jones, M. S., Levin, M. E., Levin, J. R., & Beitzel, B. D. (2000). Can vocabulary-learning strategies and

pair-learning formats be profitably combined? *Journal of Educational Psychology, 92,* 256–262.

Kahl, B., & Woloshyn, V. E. (1994). Using elaborative interrogation to facilitate acquisition of factual information in cooperative learning settings: One good strategy deserves another. *Applied Cognitive Psychology, 8,* 465–478.

Kail, R. V. (1990). *The development of memory in children* (3rd ed.). New York: Freeman.

Kail, R. V. (2007). Longitudinal evidence that increases in processing speed and working memory enhance children's reasoning. *Psychological Science, 18,* 312–313.

Kalyuga, S. (2010). Schema acquisition and sources of cognitive load. In J. L. Plass, R. Moreno, & R. Brünken (Eds.), *Cognitive Load Theory* (pp. 48–64). Cambridge, England: Cambridge University Press.

Keil, F. C. (1986). The acquisition of natural kind and artifact terms. In W. Demopolous & A. Marras (Eds.), *Language learning and concept acquisition* (pp. 133–153). Norwood, NJ: Ablex.

Keil, F. C. (1987). Conceptual development and category structure. In U. Neisser (Ed.), *Concepts and conceptual development: Ecological and intellectual factors in categorization* (pp. 175–200). Cambridge, England: Cambridge University Press.

Keil, F. C. (1989). *Concepts, kinds, and cognitive development.* Cambridge, MA: MIT Press.

Keil, F. C., & Newman, G. E. (2008). Two tales of conceptual change: What changes and what remains the same. In S. Vosniadou (Ed.), *International handbook on conceptual change* (pp. 83–101). New York: Routledge.

Kelemen, D. (1999). Why are rocks pointy? Children's preference for teleological explanations of the natural world. *Developmental Psychology, 35,* 1440–1452.

Kelemen, D. (2004). Are children "intuitive theists"?: Reasoning about purpose and design in nature. *Psychological Science, 15,* 295–301.

Kesebir, S., & Oishi, S. (2010). A spontaneous self-reference effect in memory: Why some birthdays are harder to remember than others. *Psychological Science, 21,* 1525–1531.

Kiewra, K. A. (1989). A review of note-taking: The encoding-storage paradigm and beyond. *Educational Psychology Review, 1,* 147–172.

Kiewra, K. A., DuBois, N. F., Christian, D., & McShane, A. (1988). Providing study notes: Comparison of three types of notes for review. *Journal of Educational Psychology, 80,* 595–597.

King, A. (1992). Comparison of self-questioning, summarizing, and notetaking-review as strategies for learning from lectures. *American Educational Research Journal, 29,* 303–323.

King, A. (1994). Guiding knowledge construction in the classroom: Effects of teaching children how to question and how to explain. *American Educational Research Journal, 31,* 338–368.

King, A. (1999). Discourse patterns for mediating peer learning. In A. M. O'Donnell & A. King (Eds.), *Cognitive perspectives on peer learning* (pp. 87–115). Mahwah, NJ: Erlbaum.

Kintsch, W. (2009). Learning and constructivism. In S. Tobias & T. M. Duffy (Eds.), *Constructivist* instruction: Success or failure? (pp. 223–241). New York: Routledge.

Kirby, M., Maggi, S., & D'Angiulli, A. (2011). School start times and the sleep–wake cycle of adolescents: A review of critical evaluation of available evidence. Educational Researcher, 40, 56–61.

Kitsantas, A., Zimmerman, B. J., & Cleary, T. (2000). The role of observation and emulation in the development of athletic self-regulation. Journal of Educational Psychology, 92, 811–817.

Koob, A. (2009). The root of thought. Upper Saddle River, NJ: Pearson.

Kosslyn, S. M. (1985). Mental imagery ability. In R. J. Sternberg (Ed.), Human abilities: An information-processing approach (pp. 151–172). New York: Freeman.

Kosslyn, S. M., Margolis, J. A., Barrett, A. M., Goldknopf, E. J., & Daly, P. F. (1990). Age differences in imagery ability. Child Development, 61, 995–1010.

Ku, Y.-M., Chan, W.-C., Wu, Y.-C., & Chen, Y.-H. (2008, March). Improving children's comprehension of science text: Effects of adjunct questions and notetaking. Paper presented at the annual meeting of the American Educational Research Association, New York.

Kuhn, D. (2006). Do cognitive changes accompany developments in the adolescent brain? Perspectives on Psychological Science, 1, 59–67.

Kunzinger, E. L., III. (1985). A short-term longitudinal study of memorial development during early grade school. Developmental Psychology, 21, 642–646.

LaBar, K. S., & Phelps, E. A. (1998). Arousal-mediated memory consolidation: Role of the medial temporal lobe in humans. Psychological Science, 9, 490–493.

Lave, J., & Wenger, E. (1991). Situated learning: Legitimate peripheral participation. Cambridge, England: Cambridge University Press.

Lee, V. R. (2010, April–May). Misconstruals or more? The interactions of orbit diagrams and explanations of the seasons. Paper presented at the annual meeting of the American Educational Research Association, Denver.

Lehmann, M., & Hasselhorn, M. (2007). Variable memory strategy use in children's adaptive intratask learning behavior: Developmental changes and working memory influences in free recall. Child Development, 78, 1068–1082.

Leichtman, M. D., & Ceci, S. J. (1995). The effects of stereotypes and suggestions on preschoolers' reports. Developmental Psychology, 31, 568–578.

Leuner, B., Mendolia-Loffredo, S., Kozorovitskiy, Y., Samburg, D., Gould, E., & Shors, T. J. (2004). Learning enhances the survival of new neurons beyond the time when the hippocampus is required for memory. Journal of Neuroscience, 24, 7477–7481.

Levstik, L. S. (2011). Learning history. In R. E. Mayer & P. A. Alexander (Eds.), Handbook of research on learning and instruction (pp. 208–126). New York: Routledge.

Lien, M.-C., Ruthruff, E., & Johnston, J. C. (2006). Attentional limitations in doing two tasks at once: The search for exceptions. Current Directions in Psychological Science, 15, 89–93.

Linn, M. C. (2008). Teaching for conceptual change: Distinguish or extinguish ideas. In S. Vosniadou (Ed.), International handbook on conceptual change (pp. 694–722). New York: Routledge.

Linn, M. C., & Eylon, B.-S. (2011). Science learning and instruction: Taking advantage of technology to promote knowledge integration. New York: Routledge.

Linnenbrink, E. A., & Pintrich, P. R. (2003). Achievement goals and intentional conceptual change. In G. M. Sinatra & P. R. Pintrich (Eds.), Intentional conceptual change (pp. 347–374). Mahwah, NJ: Erlbaum.

Loftus, E. F., & Loftus, G. R. (1980). On the permanence of stored information in the human brain. American Psychologist, 35, 409–420.

Logie, R. H. (2011). The functional organization and capacity limits of working memory. Current Directions in Psychological Science, 20, 240–245.

Lucariello, J., Kyratzis, A., & Nelson, K. (1992). Taxonomic knowledge: What kind and when? Child Development, 63, 978–998.

Luna, B., Garver, K. E., Urban, T. A., Lazar, N. A., & Sweeney, J. A. (2004). Maturation of cognitive processes from late childhood to adulthood. Child Development, 75, 1357–1372.

Lustig, C., Konkel, A., & Jacoby, L. L. (2004). Which route to recovery? Controlled retrieval and accessibility bias in retroactive interference. Psychological Science, 15, 729–735.

Lyon, G. R., & Krasnegor, N. A. (Eds.). (1996). Attention, memory, and executive function. Baltimore: Brookes.

Machiels-Bongaerts, M., Schmidt, H. G., & Boshuizen, H. P. (1993). Effects of mobilizing prior knowledge on information processing: Studies of free recall and allocation of study time. British Journal of Psychology, 84, 481–498.

Mac Iver, D. J., Reuman, D. A., & Main, S. R. (1995). Social structuring of the school: Studying what is, illuminating what could be. In J. T. Spence, J. M. Darley, & D. J. Foss (Eds.), Annual review of psychology (Vol. 46, pp. 375–400). Palo Alto, CA: Annual Review.

Mandler, G. (2011). From association to organization. Current Directions in Psychological Science, 20, 232–235.

Mandler, J. M. (2007). On the origins of the conceptual system. American Psychologist, 62, 741–751.

Marcus, G. (2008). Kluge: The haphazard construction of the human mind. Boston: Houghton Mifflin.

Marley, S. C., Szabo, Z., Levin, J. R., & Glenberg, A. M. (2008, March). Activity, observed activity, and children's recall of orally presented narrative passages. Paper presented at the annual meeting of the American Educational Research Association, New York.

Martínez, P., Bannan-Ritland, B., Kitsantas, A., & Baek, J. Y. (2008, March). The impact of an integrated science reading intervention on elementary children's misconceptions regarding slow geomorphological changes caused by water. Paper presented at the annual meeting of the American Educational Research Association, New York.

Mason, L. (2003). Personal epistemologies and intentional conceptual change. In G. M. Sinatra & P. R. Pintrich (Eds.), Intentional conceptual change (pp. 199–236). Mahwah, NJ: Erlbaum.

Masters, J., Russell, M. K., Humez, A., Driscoll, M. J., Wing, R. E., & Nikula, J. (2010, April–May). The impact of collaborative, scaffolded learning in K–12 schools: A meta-analysis. Paper presented at the annual meeting of the American Educational Research Association, Denver.

Mather, M., & Sutherland, M. R. (2011). Arousal-biased competition in perception and memory. Perspectives on Psychological Science, 6, 114–133.

Mayer, R. E. (1996). Learning strategies for making sense out of expository text: The SOI model for guiding three cognitive processes in knowledge construction. Educational Psychology Review, 8, 357–371.

Mayer, R. E. (2011b). Instruction based on visualizations. In R. E. Mayer & P. A. Alexander (Eds.), Handbook of research on learning and instruction (pp. 427–445). New York: Routledge.

McCrudden, M. T., & Schraw, G. (2007). Relevance and goal-focusing in text processing. Educational Psychology Review, 19, 113–139.

McDaniel, M. A., & Einstein, G. O. (1989). Material-appropriate processing: A contextualist approach to reading and studying strategies. Educational Psychology Review, 1, 113–145.

Medin, D. L. (2005, August). Role of culture and expertise in cognition. Invited address presented at the annual meeting of the American Psychological Association, Washington, DC.

Meltzer, L. (Ed.) (2007). Executive function in education: From theory to practice. New York: Guilford.

Mercer, C. D., & Pullen, P. C. (2005). Students with learning disabilities (6th ed.). Upper Saddle River, NJ: Merrill/Prentice-Hall.

Merzenich, M. M. (2001). Cortical plasticity contributing to child development. In J. L. McClelland & R. S. Siegler (Eds.), Mechanisms of cognitive development: Behavioral and neural perspectives (pp. 67–95). Mahwah, NJ: Erlbaum.

Middleton, M. J., & Midgley, C. (2002). Beyond motivation: Middle school students' perceptions of press for understanding in math. Contemporary Educational Psychology, 27, 373–391.

Miller, G. A. (1956). The magical number seven, plus or minus two: Some limits on our capacity for processing information. Psychological Review, 63, 81–97.

Minsky, M. (2006). The emotion machine: Commonsense thinking, artificial intelligence, and the future of the human mind. New York: Simon & Schuster.

Minstrell, J., & Stimpson, V. (1996). A classroom environment for learning: Guiding students' reconstruction of understanding and reasoning. In L. Schauble & R. Glaser (Eds.), Innovations in learning: New environments for education (pp. 175–202). Mahwah, NJ: Erlbaum.

Mooney, C. M. (1957). Age in the development of closure ability in children. Canadian Journal of Psychology, 11, 219–226.

Moran, S., & Gardner, H. (2006). Extraordinary achievements: A developmental and systems analysis. In W. Damon & R. M. Lerner (Series Eds.), D. Kuhn, & R. Siegler (Vol. Eds.), *Handbook of child psychology: Vol. 2. Cognition, perception, and language* (6th ed., pp. 905–949). New York: Wiley.

Moreno, R. (2006). Learning in high-tech and multimedia environments. *Current Directions in Psychological Science, 15,* 63–67.

Morris, C. D., Bransford, J. D., & Franks, J. J. (1977). Levels of processing versus transfer appropriate processing. *Journal of Verbal Learning and Verbal Behavior, 16,* 519–533.

Mosborg, S. (2002). Speaking of history: How adolescents use their knowledge of history in reading the daily news. *Cognition and Instruction, 20,* 323–358.

Murphy, P. K. (2007). The eye of the beholder: The interplay of social and cognitive components in change. *Educational Psychologist, 42,* 41–53.

Murphy, P. K., & Alexander, P. A. (2004). Persuasion as a dynamic, multidimensional process: An investigation of individual and intraindividual differences. *American Educational Research Journal, 41,* 337–363.

Murphy, P. K., & Alexander, P. A. (2008). Examining the influence of knowledge, beliefs, and motivation in conceptual change. In S. Vosniadou (Ed.), *Handbook of research on conceptual change* (pp. 583–616). New York: Taylor & Francis.

Murphy, P. K., & Mason, L. (2006). Changing knowledge and beliefs. In P. A. Alexander & P. H. Winne (Eds.), *Handbook of educational psychology* (2nd ed., pp. 305–324). Mahwah, NJ: Erlbaum.

Nee, D. E., Berman, M. G., Moore, K. S., & Jonides, J. (2008). Neuroscientific evidence about the distinction between short- and long-term memory. *Current Directions in Psychological Science, 17,* 102–106.

Neisser, U. (1967). *Cognitive psychology.* New York: Appleton-Century-Crofts.

Nelson, C. A., III, Thomas, K. M., & de Haan, M. (2006). Neural bases of cognitive development. In D. Kuhn, R. Siegler (Vol. Eds.), W. Damon, & R. M. Lerner (Series Eds.), *Handbook of child psychology. Vol. 2: Cognition, perception, and language* (6th ed., pp. 3–57). New York: Wiley.

Nelson-Barber, S., & Estrin, E. T. (1995). Bringing Native American perspectives to mathematics and science teaching. *Theory into Practice, 34,* 174–185.

Nesbit, J. C., & Adesope, O. O. (2006). Learning with concept and knowledge maps: A meta-analysis. *Review of Educational Research, 76,* 413–448.

Newman, L. S. (1990). Intentional and unintentional memory in young children: Remembering vs. playing. *Journal of Experimental Child Psychology, 50,* 243–258.

Noble, K. G., McCandliss, B. D., & Farah, M. J. (2007). Socioeconomic gradients predict individual differences in neurocognitive abilities. *Developmental Science, 10,* 464–460.

Novak, J. D. (1998). *Learning, creating, and using knowledge: Concept maps as facilitative tools in schools and corporations.* Mahwah, NJ: Erlbaum.

Oakes, L. M., & Rakison, D. H. (2003). Issues in the early development of concepts and categories: An introduction. In D. H. Rakison & L. M. Oakes (Eds.), *Early category and concept development: Making sense of the blooming, buzzing confusion* (pp. 3–23). Oxford, England: Oxford University Press.

Oberheim, N. A., Takano, T., Han, X., He, W., Lin, J. H. C., Wang, F., et al. (2009). Uniquely hominid features of adult human astrocytes. *Journal of Neuroscience, 29,* 3276–3287.

Ohlsson, S. (2009). Resubsumption: A possible mechanism for conceptual change and belief revision. *Educational Psychologist, 44,* 20–40.

Ormrod, J. E. (2012). *Human learning* (6th ed.). Upper Saddle River, NJ: Merrill/Prentice-Hall.

Ornstein, P. A., Grammer, J. K., & Coffman, J. L. (2010). Teachers' "mnemonic style" and the development of skilled memory. In H. S. Waters & W. Schneider (Eds.), *Metacognition, strategy use, and instruction* (pp. 23–53). New York: Guilford.

Öztekin, I., Davachi, L., & McElree, B. (2010). Are representations in working memory distinct from representations in long-term memory? Neural evidence in support of a single store. *Psychological Science, 21,* 1123–1133.

Pashler, H., Rohrer, D., Cepeda, N. J., & Carpenter, S. K. (2007). Enhancing learning and retarding forgetting: Choices and consequences. *Psychonomic Bulletin & Review, 14,* 187–193.

Paxton, R. J. (1999). A deafening silence: History textbooks and the students who read them. *Review of Educational Research, 69,* 315–339.

Payne, J. D., & Kensinger, E. A. (2010). Sleep's role in the consolidation of emotional episodic memories. *Current Directions in Psychological Science, 19,* 290–295.

Pellegrini, A. D., & Bjorklund, D. F. (1997). The role of recess in children's cognitive performance. *Educational Psychologist, 32,* 35–40.

Perkins, D. N., & Ritchhart, R. (2004). When is good thinking? In D. Y. Dai & R. J. Sternberg (Eds.), *Motivation, emotion, and cognition: Integrative perspectives on intellectual functioning and development* (pp. 351–384). Mahwah, NJ: Erlbaum.

Perry, R. P. (1985). Instructor expressiveness: Implications for improving teaching. In J. G. Donald & A. M. Sullivan (Eds.), *Using research to improve teaching* (pp. 35–49). San Francisco: Jossey-Bass.

Peterson, L. R., & Peterson, M. J. (1959). Short-term retention of individual items. *Journal of Experimental Psychology, 58,* 193–198.

Pezdek, K., & Banks, W. P. (Eds.). (1996). *The recovered memory/false memory debate.* San Diego: Academic Press.

Phelps, E. A., & Sharot, T. (2008). How (and why) emotion enhances the subjective sense of recollection. *Current Directions in Psychological Science, 17,* 147–152.

Phye, G. D. (1997). Classroom assessment: A multidimensional perspective. In G. D. Phye (Ed.), *Handbook of classroom assessment: Learning, achievement, and adjustment* (pp. 33–51). San Diego, CA: Academic Press.

Piirto, J. (1999). *Talented children and adults: Their development and education* (2nd ed.). Upper Saddle River, NJ: Merrill/Prentice-Hall.

Pine, K. J., & Messer, D. J. (2000). The effect of explaining another's actions on children's implicit theories of balance. *Cognition and Instruction, 18,* 35–51.

Pintrich, P. R., Marx, R. W., & Boyle, R. A. (1993). Beyond cold conceptual change: The role of motivational beliefs and classroom contextual factors in the process of conceptual change. *Review of Educational Research, 63,* 167–199.

Plass, J. L., Moreno, R., & Brünken, R. (Eds.). (2010). *Cognitive Load Theory.* Cambridge, England: Cambridge University Press.

Plumert, J. M. (1994). Flexibility in children's use of spatial and categorical organizational strategies in recall. *Developmental Psychology, 30,* 738–747.

Porat, D. A. (2004). *It's not written here, but this is what happened:* Students' cultural comprehension of textbook narratives on the Israeli-Arab conflict. *American Educational Research Journal, 41,* 963–996.

Posner, G. J., Strike, K. A., Hewson, P. W., & Gertzog, W. A. (1982). Accommodation of a scientific conception: Toward a theory of conceptual change. *Science Education, 66,* 211–227.

Posner, M. I., & Rothbart, M. K. (2007). *Educating the human brain.* Washington, DC: American Psychological Association.

Pressley, M. (1982). Elaboration and memory development. *Child Development, 53,* 296–309.

Pressley, M., & Hilden, K. (2006). Cognitive strategies: Production deficiencies and successful strategy instruction everywhere. In W. Damon & R. M. Lerner (Series Eds.), D. Kuhn, & R. Siegler (Vol. Eds.), *Handbook of child psychology: Vol. 2. Cognition, perception, and language* (6th ed., pp. 511–556). New York: Wiley.

Pressley, M., Levin, J. R., & Delaney, H. D. (1982). The mnemonic keyword method. *Review of Educational Research, 52,* 61–91.

Pritchard, R. (1990). The effects of cultural schemata on reading processing strategies. *Reading Research Quarterly, 25,* 273–295.

Proctor, R. W., & Dutta, A. (1995). *Skill acquisition and human performance.* Thousand Oaks, CA: Sage.

Purdie, N., & Hattie, J. (1996). Cultural differences in the use of strategies for self-regulated learning. *American Educational Research Journal, 33,* 845–871.

Putnam, R. T. (1992). Thinking and authority in elementary-school mathematics tasks. In J. Brophy (Ed.), *Advances in research on teaching: Vol. 3. Planning and managing learning tasks and activities* (pp. 161–189). Greenwich, CT: JAI.

Quinn, P. C. (2002). Category representation in young infants. *Current Directions in Psychological Science, 11,* 66–70.

Rabinowitz, M., & Glaser, R. (1985). Cognitive structure and process in highly competent performance. In F. D. Horowitz & M. O'Brien (Eds.), *The gifted and the talented:*

*Developmental perspectives* (pp. 75–97). Washington, DC: American Psychological Association.

Rasch, B., & Born, J. (2008). Reactivation and consolidation of memory during sleep. *Current Directions in Psychological Science, 17,* 188–192.

Reiner, M., Slotta, J. D., Chi, M. T. H., & Resnick, L. B. (2000). Naive physics reasoning: A commitment to substance-based conceptions. *Cognition and Instruction, 18,* 1–34.

Reisberg, D., & Heuer, F. (1992). Remembering the details of emotional events. In E. Winograd & U. Neisser (Eds.), *Affect and accuracy in recall: Studies of "flashbulb" memories* (pp. 162–190). Cambridge, England: Cambridge University Press.

Resnick, L. B. (1989). Developing mathematical knowledge. *American Psychologist, 44,* 162–169.

Rittle-Johnson, B. (2006). Promoting transfer: Effects of self-explanation and direct instruction. *Child Development, 77,* 1–15.

Robbins, P., & Aydede, M. (Eds.).(2009). *The Cambridge handbook of situated cognition.* Cambridge, England: Cambridge University Press.

Robinson, D. H., & Kiewra, K. A. (1995). Visual argument: Graphic organizers are superior to outlines in improving learning from text. *Journal of Educational Psychology, 87,* 455–467.

Roediger, H. L., III, & McDermott, K. B. (2000). Tricks of memory. *Current Directions in Psychological Science, 9,* 123–127.

Rogers, T. B., Kuiper, N. A., & Kirker, W. S. (1977). Self-reference and the encoding of personal information. *Journal of Personality and Social Psychology, 35,* 677–688.

Rogoff, B. (2001). *Everyday cognition: Its development in social context.* New York: Replica Books.

Rogoff, B. (2003). *The cultural nature of human development.* Oxford, England: Oxford University Press.

Rogoff, B., Moore, L., Najafi, B., Dexter, A., Correa-Chávez, M., & Solís, J. (2007). Children's development of cultural repertoires through participation in everyday routines and practices. In J. E. Grusec & P. D. Hastings (Eds.), *Handbook of socialization: Theory and research* (pp. 490–515). New York: Guilford.

Rohrer, D., & Pashler, H. (2010). Recent research on human learning challenges conventional instructional strategies. *Educational Researcher, 39,* 406–412.

Rosch, E. H. (1977). Human categorization. In N. Warren (Ed.), *Advances in cross-cultural psychology* (Vol. 1, pp. 1–72). San Diego, CA: Academic Press.

Roscoe, R. D., & Chi, M. T. H. (2007). Understanding tutor learning: Knowledge-building and knowledge-telling in peer tutors' explanations and questions. *Review of Educational Research, 77,* 534–574.

Rosenshine, B., Meister, C., & Chapman, S. (1996). Teaching students to generate questions: A review of the intervention studies. *Review of Educational Research, 66,* 181–221.

Ross, B. H., & Spalding, T. L. (1994). Concepts and categories. In R. J. Sternberg (Ed.), *Handbook of*

*perception and cognition* (Vol. 12, pp. 119–148). New York: Academic Press.

Roth, K. J. (1990). Developing meaningful conceptual understanding in science. In B. F. Jones & L. Idol (Eds.), *Dimensions of thinking and cognitive instruction* (pp. 139–175). Mahwah, NJ: Erlbaum.

Roth, K. J. (2002). Talking to understand science. In J. Brophy (Ed.), *Social constructivist teaching: Affordances and constraints* (pp. 197–262). New York: Elsevier.

Roth, K. J., & Anderson, C. (1988). Promoting conceptual change learning from science textbooks. In P. Ramsden (Ed.), *Improving learning: New perspectives* (pp. 109–141). London: Kogan Page.

Rowe, M. B. (1974). Wait-time and rewards as instructional variables, their influence on language, logic, and fate control: Part one—Wait time. *Journal of Research in Science Teaching, 11,* 81–94.

Rowe, M. B. (1987). Wait-time: Slowing down may be a way of speeding up. *American Educator, 11,* 38–43, 47.

Ruchkin, D. S., Grafman, J., Cameron, K., & Berndt, R. S. (2003). Working memory retention systems: A state of activated long-term memory. *Behavioral and Brain Sciences, 26,* 709–728.

Rumelhart, D. E., & Ortony, A. (1977). The representation of knowledge in memory. In R. C. Anderson, R. J. Spiro, & W. E. Montague (Eds.), *Schooling and the acquisition of knowledge* (pp. 99–136). Mahwah, NJ: Erlbaum.

Sadoski, M., & Paivio, A. (2001). *Imagery and text: A dual coding theory of reading and writing.* Mahwah, NJ: Erlbaum.

Sapolsky, R. M. (1999). Glucocorticoids, stress, and their adverse neurological effects: Relevance to aging. *Experimental Gerontology, 34,* 721–732.

Schacter, D. L. (1999). The seven sins of memory: Insights from psychology and neuroscience. *American Psychologist, 54,* 182–203.

Schneider, W. (1993). Domain-specific knowledge and memory performance in children. *Educational Psychology Review, 5,* 257–273.

Schneider, W., & Pressley, M. (1989). *Memory development between 2 and 20.* New York: Springer-Verlag.

Schraw, G. (2006). Knowledge: Structures and processes. In P. A. Alexander & P. H. Winne (Eds.), *Handbook of educational psychology* (2nd ed., pp. 245–263). Mahwah, NJ: Erlbaum.

Schunk, D. H. (1998). Teaching elementary students to self-regulate practice of mathematical skills with modeling. In D. H. Schunk & B. J. Zimmerman (Eds.), *Self-regulated learning: From teaching to self-reflective practice* (pp. 137–159). New York: Guilford.

Schwamborn, A., Mayer, R. E., Thillmann, H., Leopold, C., & Leutner, D. (2010). Drawing as a generative activity and drawing as a prognostic activity. *Journal of Educational Psychology, 102,* 872–879.

Schwartz, D. L., & Heiser, J. (2006). Spatial representations and imagery in learning. In R. K. Sawyer (Ed.), *The Cambridge handbook of the learning sciences* (pp. 283–298). Cambridge, England: Cambridge University Press.

Shanahan, T. (2004). Overcoming the dominance of communication: Writing to think and to learn. In T. L. Jetton & J. A. Dole (Eds.), *Adolescent literacy research and practice* (pp. 59–74). New York: Guilford.

Shepard, L., Hammerness, K., Darling-Hammond, L., & Rust, F. (with Snowden, J. B., Gordon, E., Gutierrez, C., & Pacheco, A.) (2005). Assessment. In L. Darling-Hammond & J. Bransford (Eds.), *Preparing teachers for a changing world: What teachers should learn and be able to do* (pp. 275–326). San Francisco: Jossey-Bass/Wiley.

Sherman, D. K., & Cohen, G. L. (2002). Accepting threatening information: Self-affirmation and the reduction of defensive biases. *Current Directions in Psychological Science, 11,* 119–123.

Shute, V. J. (2008). Focus on formative feedback. *Review of Educational Research, 78,* 153–189.

Siegel, D. J. (2012). *The developing mind: How relationships and the brain interact to shape who we are* (2nd ed.). New York: Guilford.

Siegler, R. S., & Alibali, M. W. (2005). *Children's thinking* (4th ed.). Upper Saddle River, NJ: Prentice-Hall.

Sinatra, G. M., & Mason, L. (2008). Beyond knowledge: Learner characteristics influencing conceptual change. In S. Vosniadou (Ed.), *International handbook on conceptual change* (pp. 560–582). New York: Routledge.

Sinatra, G. M., & Pintrich, P. R. (Eds.). (2003). *Intentional conceptual change.* Mahwah, NJ: Erlbaum.

Sizer, T. R. (1992). *Horace's school: Redesigning the American high school.* Boston: Houghton Mifflin.

Sizer, T. R. (2004). *Horace's compromise: The dilemma of the American high school.* Boston: Houghton Mifflin.

Skowronek, J. S., Leichtman, M. D., & Pillemer, D. B. (2008). Long-term episodic memory in children with attention-deficit/hyperactivity disorder. *Learning Disabilities Research and Practice, 23*(1), 25–35.

Smith, C. L. (2007). Bootstrapping processes in the development of students' commonsense matter theories: Using analogical mappings, thought experiments, and learning to measure to promote conceptual restructuring. *Cognition and Instruction, 25,* 337–398.

Smith, C. L., Maclin, D., Grosslight, L., & Davis, H. (1997). Teaching for understanding: A study of students' preinstruction theories of matter and a comparison of the effectiveness of two approaches to teaching about matter and density. *Cognition and Instruction, 15,* 317–393.

Sneider, C., & Pulos, S. (1983). Children's cosmographies: Understanding the earth's shape and gravity. *Science Education, 67,* 205–221.

SooHoo, S., Takemoto, K. Y., & McCullagh, P. (2004). A comparison of modeling and imagery on the performance of a motor skill. *Journal of Sport Behavior, 27,* 349–366.

Spires, H. A., & Donley, J. (1998). Prior knowledge activation: Inducing engagement with informational texts. *Journal of Educational Psychology, 90,* 249–260.

Squire, L. R., & Alvarez, P. (1998). Retrograde amnesia and memory consolidation: A neurobiological perspective. In L. R. Squire & S. M. Kosslyn (Eds.), *Findings and current opinion in cognitive neuroscience* (pp. 75–84). Cambridge, MA: MIT Press.

Stanovich, K. E. (2000). *Progress in understanding reading: Scientific foundations and new frontiers.* New York: Guilford.

Stepans, J. (1991). Developmental patterns in students' understanding of physics concepts. In S. M. Glynn, R. H. Yeany, & B. K. Britton (Eds.), *The psychology of learning science* (pp. 89–115). Mahwah, NJ: Erlbaum.

Strike, K. A., & Posner, G. J. (1992). A revisionist theory of conceptual change. In R. A. Duschl & R. J. Hamilton (Eds.), *Philosophy of science, cognitive psychology, and educational theory and practice* (pp. 147–176). New York: State University of New York Press.

Swanson, H. L., Cooney, J. B., & O'Shaughnessy, T. E. (1998). Learning disabilities and memory. In B. Y. L. Wong (Ed.), *Learning about learning disabilities* (2nd ed., pp. 107–162). San Diego, CA: Academic Press.

Sweller, J. (1988). Cognitive load during problem solving: Effects on learning. *Cognitive Science, 12,* 257–285.

Sweller, J. (2008). Human cognitive architecture. In J. M. Spector, M. D. Merrill, J. van Merriënboer, & M. P. Driscoll (Eds.), *Handbook of research on educational communications and technology* (3rd ed., pp. 369–381). New York: Erlbaum.

Sweller, J. (2010). Cognitive Load Theory: Recent theoretical advances. In J. L. Plass, R. Moreno, & R. Brünken (Eds.), *Cognitive Load Theory* (pp. 29–47). Cambridge, England: Cambridge University Press.

Talmi, D., Grady, C. L., Goshen-Gottstein, Y., & Moscovitch, M. (2005). Neuroimaging the serial position curve: A test of single-store versus dual-store models. *Psychological Science, 16,* 716–723.

Tennyson, R. D., & Cocchiarella, M. J. (1986). An empirically based instructional design theory for teaching concepts. *Review of Educational Research, 56,* 40–71.

Tharp, R. G. (1989). Psychocultural variables and constants: Effects on teaching and learning in schools. *American Psychologist, 44,* 349–359.

Thompson, H., & Carr, M. (1995, April). *Brief metacognitive intervention and interest as predictors of memory for text.* Paper presented at the annual meeting of the American Educational Research Association, San Francisco.

Tirosh, D., & Graeber, A. O. (1990). Evoking cognitive conflict to explore preservice teachers' thinking about division. *Journal for Research in Mathematics Education, 21,* 98–108.

Tobin, K. (1987). The role of wait time in higher cognitive level learning. *Review of Educational Research, 57,* 69–95.

Tomporowski, P. D., Davis, C. L., Miller, P. H., & Naglieri, J. A. (2008). Exercise and children's intelligence, cognition, and academic achievement. *Educational Psychology Review, 20,* 111–131.

Torney-Purta, J. (1994). Dimensions of adolescents' reasoning about political and historical issues: Ontological switches, developmental processes, and situated learning. In M. Carretero & J. F. Voss (Eds.), *Cognitive and instructional processes in history and the social sciences* (pp. 103–122). Mahwah, NJ: Erlbaum.

Trachtenberg, J. T., Chen, B. E., Knott, G. W., Feng, G., Sanes, J. R., Welker, E., et al. (2002). Long-term *in vivo* imaging of experience-dependent synaptic plasticity in adult cortex. *Nature, 420,* 788–794.

Tulving, E. (1983). *Elements of episodic memory.* Oxford, England: Oxford University Press.

Tulving, E., & Thomson, D. M. (1973). Encoding specificity and retrieval processes in episodic memory. *Psychological Review, 80,* 352–373.

Turnbull, A. P., Turnbull, R., & Wehmeyer, M. L. (2010). *Exceptional lives: Special education in today's schools* (6th ed.). Upper Saddle River, NJ: Merrill.

Tyler, K. M., Uqdah, A. L., Dillihunt, M. L., Beatty-Hazelbaker, R., Connor, T., Gadson, N., et al. (2008). Cultural discontinuity: Toward a quantitative investigation of a major hypothesis in education. *Educational Researcher, 37,* 280–297.

van Merriënboer, J. J. G., & Kester, L. (2008). Whole-task models in education. In J. M. Spector, M. D. Merrill, J. van Merriënboer, & M. P. Driscoll (Eds.), *Handbook of research on educational communications and technology* (3rd ed., pp. 441–456). New York: Erlbaum.

Van Meter, P., & Garner, J. (2005). The promise and practice of learner-generated drawing: Literature review and synthesis. *Educational Psychology Review, 17,* 285–325.

VanSledright, B., & Brophy, J. (1992). Storytelling, imagination, and fanciful elaboration in children's historical reconstructions. *American Educational Research Journal, 29,* 837–859.

Verdi, M. P., Kulhavy, R. W., Stock, W. A., Rittschof, K. A., & Johnson, J. T. (1996). Text learning using scientific diagrams: Implications for classroom use. *Contemporary Educational Psychology, 21,* 487–499.

Verkhratsky, A., & Butt, A. (2007). *Glial neurobiology.* Chichester, England: Wiley.

Vosniadou, S. (Ed.). (2008). *International handbook of research on conceptual change.* New York: Routledge.

Vosniadou, S., & Brewer, W. F. (1987). Theories of knowledge restructuring in development. *Review of Educational Research, 57,* 51–67.

Vosniadou, S., Vamvakoussi, X., & Skopeliti, I. (2008). The framework theory approach to the problem of conceptual change. In S. Vosniadou (Ed.), *International handbook on conceptual change* (pp. 3–34). New York: Routledge.

Wagner, R. K. (1996). From simple structure to complex function: Major trends in the development of theories, models, and measurements of memory. In G. R. Lyon & N. A. Krasnegor (Eds.), *Attention, memory, and executive function* (pp. 139–156). Baltimore: Brookes.

Wang, Q., & Ross, M. (2007). Culture and memory. In S. Kitayama & D. Cohen (Eds.), *Handbook of cultural psychology* (pp. 645–667). New York: Guilford.

Waters, H. S. (1982). Memory development in adolescence: Relationships between metamemory, strategy use, and performance. *Journal of Experimental Child Psychology, 33,* 183–195.

Weiss, M. R., & Klint, K. A. (1987). "Show and tell" in the gymnasium: An investigation of developmental differences in modeling and verbal rehearsal of motor skills. *Research Quarterly for Exercise and Sport, 58,* 234–241.

Wellman, H. M., & Gelman, S. A. (1998). Knowledge acquisition in foundational domains. In W. Damon (Series Ed.), D. Kuhn, & R. S. Siegler (Vol. Eds.), *Handbook of child psychology: Vol. 2. Cognition, perception, and language* (5th ed., pp. 523–573). New York: Wiley.

White, J. J., & Rumsey, S. (1994). Teaching for understanding in a third-grade geography lesson. In J. Brophy (Ed.), *Advances in research on teaching: Vol. 4. Case studies of teaching and learning in social studies* (pp. 33–69). Greenwich, CT: JAI.

Willingham, D. B. (1999). The neural basis of motor-skill learning. *Current Directions in Psychological Science, 8,* 178–182.

Wilson, P. T., & Anderson, R. C. (1986). What they don't know will hurt them: The role of prior knowledge in comprehension. In J. Orasanu (Ed.), *Reading comprehension: From research to practice* (pp. 31–48). Mahwah, NJ: Erlbaum.

Winer, G. A., & Cottrell, J. E. (1996). Does anything leave the eye when we see? Extramission beliefs of children and adults. *Current Directions in Psychological Science, 5,* 137–142.

Winer, G. A., Cottrell, J. E., Gregg, V., Fournier, J. S., & Bica, L. A. (2002). Fundamentally misunderstanding visual perception: Adults' belief in visual emissions. *American Psychologist, 57,* 417–424.

Wingfield, A., & Byrnes, D. L. (1981). *The psychology of human memory.* San Diego, CA: Academic Press.

Winn, W. (1991). Learning from maps and diagrams. *Educational Psychology Review, 3,* 211–247.

Wiser, M., & Smith, C. L. (2008). Learning and teaching about matter in grades K–8: When should the atomic–molecular theory be introduced? In S. Vosniadou (Ed.), *International handbook on conceptual change* (pp. 205–231). New York: Routledge.

Wittrock, M. C. (1974). Learning as a generative process. *Educational Psychologist, 11,* 87–95.

Wixted, J. T. (2005). A theory about why we forget what we once knew. *Current Directions in Psychological Science, 14,* 6–9.

Wood, E., Willoughby, T., Bolger, A., & Younger, J. (1993). Effectiveness of elaboration strategies for grade school children as a function of academic achievement. *Journal of Experimental Child Psychology, 56,* 240–253.

Wood, E., Willoughby, T., McDermott, C., Motz, M., Kaspar, V., & Ducharme, M. J. (1999). Developmental differences in study behavior. *Journal of Educational Psychology, 91,* 527–536.

Zeelenberg, R., Wagenmakers, E.-J., & Rotteveel, M. (2006). The impact of emotion on perception: Bias or enhanced processing? *Psychological Science, 17,* 287–291.

Zhang, W., & Luck, S. J. (2009). Sudden death and gradual decay in visual working memory. *Psychological Science, 20,* 423–428.

Zimmerman, B. J., & Kitsantas, A. (1999). Acquiring writing revision skill: Shifting from process to outcome self-regulatory goals. *Journal of Educational Psychology, 91,* 241–250.

## CHAPTER 7

Abrami, P. C., Bernard, R. M., Borokhovski, E., Wade, A., Surkes, M. A., Tamim, R., et al. (2008). Instructional interventions affecting critical thinking skills and dispositions: A stage 1 meta-analysis. *Review of Educational Research, 78,* 1102–1134.

Afflerbach, P., & Cho, B.-Y. (2010). Determining and describing reading strategies: Internet and traditional forms of reading. In H. S. Waters & W. Schneider (Eds.), *Metacognition, strategy use, and instruction* (pp. 201–225). New York: Guilford.

Alexander, P. A., Graham, S., & Harris, K. R. (1998). A perspective on strategy research: Progress and prospects. *Educational Psychology Review, 10,* 129–154.

Alexander, P. A., & Judy, J. E. (1988). The interaction of domain-specific and strategic knowledge in academic performance. *Review of Educational Research, 58,* 375–404.

Amabile, T. M. (1996). *Creativity in context: Update to the social psychology of creativity.* Boulder, CO: Westview.

Amabile, T. M., & Hennessey, B. A. (1992). The motivation for creativity in children. In A. K. Boggiano & T. S. Pittman (Eds.), *Achievement and motivation: A social-developmental perspective* (pp. 54–74). Cambridge, England: Cambridge University Press.

Amsterlaw, J. (2006). Children's beliefs about everyday reasoning. *Child Development, 77,* 443–464.

Anderson, J. R., Greeno, J. G., Reder, L. M., & Simon, H. A. (2000). Perspectives on learning, thinking, and activity. *Educational Researcher, 29*(4), 11–13.

Andre, T., & Windschitl, M. (2003). Interest, epistemological belief, and intentional conceptual change. In G. M. Sinatra & P. R. Pintrich (Eds.), *Intentional conceptual change* (pp. 173–197). Mahwah, NJ: Erlbaum.

Anzai, Y. (1991). Learning and use of representations for physics expertise. In K. A. Ericsson & J. Smith (Eds.), *Toward a general theory of expertise: Prospects and limits* (pp. 64–92). Cambridge, England: Cambridge University Press.

Astington, J. W., & Pelletier, J. (1996). The language of mind: Its role in teaching and learning. In D. R. Olson & N. Torrance (Eds.), *The handbook of education and human development: New models of learning, teaching, and schooling* (pp. 593–620). Cambridge, MA: Blackwell.

Azevedo, R., & Witherspoon, A. M. (2009). Self-regulated learning with hypermedia. In D. J.

Hacker, J. Dunlosky, & A. C. Graesser (Eds.), *Handbook of metacognition in education* (pp. 319–339). New York: Routledge.

Baer, J., & Garrett, T. (2010). Teaching for creativity in an era of content standards and accountability. In R. A. Beghetto & J. C. Kaufman (Eds.), *Nurturing creativity in the classroom* (pp. 6–23). New York: Cambridge University Press.

Baker, L., & Brown, A. L. (1984). Metacognitive skills of reading. In D. Pearson (Ed.), *Handbook of reading research* (pp. 353–394). White Plains, NY: Longman.

Bangert-Drowns, R. L., Hurley, M. M., & Wilkinson, B. (2004). The effects of school-based writing-to-learn interventions on academic achievement: A meta-analysis. *Review of Educational Research, 74,* 29–58.

Barnett, J. E. (2001, April). *Study strategies and preparing for exams: A survey of middle and high school students.* Paper presented at the annual meeting of the American Educational Research Association, Seattle, WA.

Barnett, J. E., Di Vesta, F. J., & Rogozinski, J. T. (1981). What is learned in note taking? *Journal of Educational Psychology, 73,* 181–192.

Barnett, S. M., & Ceci, S. J. (2002). When and where do we apply what we learn? A taxonomy of far transfer. *Psychological Bulletin, 128,* 612–637.

Barron, B. (2000). Problem solving in video-based microworlds: Collaborative and individual outcomes of high-achieving sixth-grade students. *Journal of Educational Psychology, 92,* 391–398.

Bassok, M. (2003). Analogical transfer in problem solving. In J. E. Davidson & R. J. Sternberg (Eds.), *The psychology of problem solving* (pp. 343–369). Cambridge, England: Cambridge University Press.

Beal, C. R., Arroyo, I., Cohen, P. R., & Woolf, B. P. (2010). Evaluation of AnimalWatch: An intelligent tutoring system for arithmetic and fractions. *Journal of Interactive Online Learning, 9,* 64–77.

Beghetto, R. A., & Kaufman, J. C. (2010). Broadening conceptions of creativity in the classroom. In R. A. Beghetto & J. C. Kaufman (Eds.), *Nurturing creativity in the classroom* (pp. 191–205). New York: Cambridge University Press.

Beirne-Smith, M., Patton, J. R., & Kim, S. H. (2006). *Mental retardation: An introduction to intellectual disabilities* (7th ed.). Upper Saddle River, NJ: Merrill/Prentice-Hall.

Bendixen, L. D., & Feucht, F. C. (Eds.). (2010). *Personal epistemology in the classroom: Theory, research, and implications for practice.* Cambridge, England: Cambridge University Press.

Bereiter, C. (1995). A dispositional view of transfer. In A. McKeough, J. Lupart, & A. Marini (Eds.), *Teaching for transfer: Fostering generalization in learning* (pp. 21–34). Mahwah, NJ: Erlbaum.

Bermejo, V. (1996). Cardinality development and counting. *Developmental Psychology, 32,* 263–268.

Berthold, K., & Renkl, A. (2009). Instructional aids to support a conceptual understanding of

multiple representations. *Journal of Educational Psychology, 101,* 70–87.

Beyer, B. K. (1985). Critical thinking: What is it? *Social Education, 49,* 270–276.

Bonney, C. R., & Sternberg, R. J. (2011). Learning to think critically. In R. E. Mayer & P. A. Alexander (Eds.), *Handbook of research on learning and instruction* (pp. 166–196). New York: Routledge.

Bransford, J. D., & Schwartz, D. L. (1999). Rethinking transfer: A simple proposal with multiple implications. *Review of Research in Education* (Vol. 24, pp. 61–100). Washington, DC: American Educational Research Association.

Brenner, M. E., Mayer, R. E., Moseley, B., Brar, T., Durán, R., Reed, B. S., et al. (1997). Learning by understanding: The role of multiple representations in learning algebra. *American Educational Research Journal, 34,* 663–689.

Brooks, L. W., & Dansereau, D. F. (1987). Transfer of information: An instructional perspective. In S. M. Cormier & J. D. Hagman (Eds.), *Transfer of learning: Contemporary research and applications* (pp. 121–150). San Diego, CA: Academic Press.

Brown, A. L., Campione, J., & Day, J. (1981). Learning to learn: On training students to learn from texts. *Educational Researcher, 10*(2), 14–21.

Brownell, M. T., Mellard, D. F., & Deshler, D. D. (1993). Differences in the learning and transfer performance between students with learning disabilities and other low-achieving students on problem-solving tasks. *Learning Disabilities Quarterly, 16,* 138–156.

Buehl, M. M., & Alexander, P. A. (2006). Examining the dual nature of epistemological beliefs. *International Journal of Educational Research, 45,* 28–42.

Bulgren, J. A., Marquis, J. G., Lenz, B. K., Deshler, D. D., & Schumaker, J. B. (2011). The effectiveness of a question-exploration routine for enhancing the content learning of secondary students. *Journal of Educational Psychology, 103,* 578–593.

Butler, D. L., & Winne, P. H. (1995). Feedback and self-regulated learning: A theoretical synthesis. *Review of Educational Research, 65,* 245–281.

Campione, J. C., Brown, A. L., & Bryant, N. R. (1985). Individual differences in learning and memory. In R. J. Sternberg (Ed.), *Human abilities: An information-processing approach* (pp. 103–126). New York: Freeman.

Carr, M. (2010). The importance of metacognition for conceptual change and strategy use in mathematics. In H. S. Waters & W. Schneider (Eds.), *Metacognition, strategy use, and instruction* (pp. 176–197). New York: Guilford.

Carr, M., & Biddlecomb, B. (1998). Metacognition in mathematics from a constructivist perspective. In D. J. Hacker, J. Dunlosky, & A. C. Graesser (Eds.), *Metacognition in educational theory and practice* (pp. 69–91). Mahwah, NJ: Erlbaum.

Center for Media Literacy (n.d.). CML's five key questions. In *Five key questions that can change the world: Deconstruction.* Retrieved January 27,

2009, from http://www.medialit.org/reading_room/article661.html.

Chandler, M. J., Hallett, D., & Sokol, B. W. (2002). Competing claims about competing knowledge claims. In B. K. Hofer & P. R. Pintrich (Eds.), *Personal epistemology: The psychology of beliefs about knowledge and knowing* (pp. 145–168). Mahwah, NJ: Erlbaum.

Chen, Z. (1999). Schema induction in children's analogical problem solving. *Journal of Educational Psychology, 91,* 703–715.

Chinn, C. A., Anderson, R. C., & Waggoner, M. A. (2001). Patterns of discourse in two kinds of literature discussion. *Reading Research Quarterly, 36,* 378–411.

Clark, B. (1997). *Growing up gifted* (5th ed.). Upper Saddle River, NJ: Merrill/Prentice-Hall.

Clark, R. E., & Blake, S. B. (1997). Designing training for novel problem-solving transfer. In R. D. Tennyson, F. Schott, N. M. Seel, & S. Dijkstra (Eds.), *Instructional design: International perspectives. Vol. 1: Theory, research, and models* (pp. 183–214). Mahwah, NJ: Erlbaum.

Cognition and Technology Group at Vanderbilt. (1990). Anchored instruction and its relationship to situated cognition. *Educational Researcher, 19*(6), 2–10.

Cognition and Technology Group at Vanderbilt. (1996). Looking at technology in context: A framework for understanding technology and education research. In D. C. Berliner & R. C. Calfee (Eds.), *Handbook of educational psychology* (pp. 807–840). New York: Macmillan.

Collins, A., Brown, J. S., & Newman, S. E. (1989). Cognitive apprenticeship: Teaching the crafts of reading, writing, and mathematics. In L. B. Resnick (Ed.), *Knowing, learning, and instruction: Essays in honor of Robert Glaser* (pp. 453–494). Mahwah, NJ: Erlbaum.

Cornoldi, C. (2010). Metacognition, intelligence, and academic performance. In H. S. Waters & W. Schneider (Eds.), *Metacognition, strategy use, and instruction* (pp. 257–277). New York: Guilford.

Cox, B. D. (1997). The rediscovery of the active learner in adaptive contexts: A developmental-historical analysis of transfer of training. *Educational Psychologist, 32,* 41–55.

Crowley, K., & Siegler, R. S. (1999). Explanation and generalization in young children's strategy learning. *Child Development, 70,* 304–316.

Csikszentmihalyi, M. (1996). *Creativity: Flow and the psychology of discovery and invention.* New York: HarperCollins.

Dahlin, B., & Watkins, D. (2000). The role of repetition in the processes of memorizing and understanding: A comparison of the views of Western and Chinese secondary students in Hong Kong. *British Journal of Educational Psychology, 70,* 65–84.

Dai, D. Y. (2010). *The nature and nurture of giftedness: A new framework for understanding gifted education.* New York: Teachers College Press.

Davidson, J. E., & Sternberg, R. J. (1998). Smart problem solving: How metacognition helps. In D. J. Hacker, J. Dunlosky, & A. C. Graesser (Eds.), *Metacognition in educational theory and practice* (pp. 47–68). Mahwah, NJ: Erlbaum.

Davidson, J. E., & Sternberg, R. J. (Eds.). (2003). *The psychology of problem solving.* Cambridge, England: Cambridge University Press.

De Corte, E. (2003). Transfer as the productive use of acquired knowledge, skills, and motivations. *Current Directions in Psychological Science, 12,* 142–146.

De Corte, E., Op't Eynde, P., Depaepe, F., & Verschaffel, L. (2010). The reflexive relation between students' mathematics-related beliefs and the mathematics classroom culture. In L. D. Bendixen & F. C. Feucht (Eds.), *Personal epistemology in the classroom: Theory, research, and implications for practice* (pp. 292–327). Cambridge, England: Cambridge University Press.

Dee-Lucas, D., & Larkin, J. H. (1991). Equations in scientific proofs: Effects on comprehension. *American Educational Research Journal, 28,* 661–682.

De La Paz, S., & Felton, M. K. (2010). Reading and writing from multiple source documents in history: Effects of strategy instruction with low to average high school writers. *Contemporary Educational Psychology, 35,* 174–192.

Derry, S. J., Levin, J. R., Osana, H. P., & Jones, M. S. (1998). Developing middle school students' statistical reasoning abilities through simulation gaming. In S. P. Lajoie (Ed.), *Reflections on statistics: Learning, teaching, and assessment in grades K–12* (pp. 175–195). Mahwah, NJ: Erlbaum.

Di Vesta, F. J., & Peverly, S. T. (1984). The effects of encoding variability, processing activity and rule example sequences on the transfer of conceptual rules. *Journal of Educational Psychology, 76,* 108–119.

Dole, J. A., Duffy, G. G., Roehler, L. R., & Pearson, P. D. (1991). Moving from the old to the new: Research on reading comprehension instruction. *Review of Educational Research, 61,* 239–264.

Dominowski, R. L. (1998). Verbalization and problem solving. In D. J. Hacker, J. Dunlosky, & A. C. Graesser (Eds.), *Metacognition in educational theory and practice* (pp. 25–45). Mahwah, NJ: Erlbaum.

Duncker, K. (1945). On problem solving. *Psychological Monographs, 58*(Whole No. 270).

Dunning, D., Heath, C., & Suls, J. M. (2004). Flawed self-assessment: Implications for health, education, and the workplace. *Psychological Science in the Public Interest, 5,* 69–106.

DuPaul, G. J., & Eckert, T. L. (1994). The effects of social skills curricula: Now you see them, now you don't. *School Psychology Quarterly, 9,* 113–132.

Edmonds, M. S., Vaughn, S., Wexler, J., Reutebuch, C., Cable, A., Tackett, K. K., et al. (2009). A synthesis of reading interventions and effects of reading comprehension outcomes for older struggling students. *Review of Educational Research, 79,* 262–300.

Eigsti, I.-M., Zayas, V., Mischel, W., Shoda, Y., Ayduk, O., Dadlani, M. B., et al. (2006). Predicting cognitive control from preschool to late adolescence and young adulthood. *Psychological Science, 17,* 478–484.

Elder, A. D. (2002). Characterizing fifth grade students' epistemological beliefs in science. In B. K. Hofer & P. R. Pintrich (Eds.), *Personal epistemology: The psychology of beliefs about knowledge and knowing* (pp. 347–363). Mahwah, NJ: Erlbaum.

Ellis, E. S., & Friend, P. (1991). Adolescents with learning disabilities. In B. Y. L. Wong (Ed.), *Learning about learning disabilities* (pp. 505–561). San Diego, CA: Academic Press.

Ellis, N. R. (Ed.). (1979). *Handbook of mental deficiency: Psychological theory and research.* Mahwah, NJ: Erlbaum.

Emmer, E. T. (1994, April). *Teacher emotions and classroom management.* Paper presented at the annual meeting of the American Educational Research Association, New Orleans, LA.

Engle, R. A. (2006). Framing interactions to foster generative learning: A situative explanation of transfer in a community of learners. *Journal of the Learning Sciences, 15,* 451–498.

Ennis, R. H. (1996). *Critical thinking.* Upper Saddle River, NJ: Prentice-Hall.

Esquivel, G. B. (1995). Teacher behaviors that foster creativity. *Educational Psychology Review, 7,* 185–202.

Fairweather, E., & Cramond, B. (2010). Infusing creative and critical thinking into the curriculum together. In R. A. Beghetto & J. C. Kaufman (Eds.), *Nurturing creativity in the classroom* (pp. 113–141). New York: Cambridge University Press.

Feldhusen, J. F., & Treffinger, D. J. (1980). *Creative thinking and problem solving in gifted education.* Dubuque, IA: Kendall/Hunt.

Flavell, J. H., Friedrichs, A. G., & Hoyt, J. D. (1970). Developmental changes in memorization processes. *Cognitive Psychology, 1,* 324–340.

Flavell, J. H., Miller, P. H., & Miller, S. A. (2002). *Cognitive development* (4th ed.). Upper Saddle River, NJ: Prentice Hall.

Fonseca, B. A., & Chi, M. T. H. (2011). Instruction based on self-explanation. In R. E. Mayer & P. A. Alexander (Eds.), *Handbook of research on learning and instruction* (pp. 296–321). New York: Routledge.

Frederiksen, N. (1984a). Implications of cognitive theory for instruction in problem-solving. *Review of Educational Research, 54,* 363–407.

Fuchs, L. S., Fuchs, D., Prentice, K., Burch, M., Hamlett, C. L., Owen, R., et al. (2003). Explicitly teaching for transfer: Effects on third-grade students' mathematical problem solving. *Journal of Educational Psychology, 95,* 295–305.

Gijbels, D., Dochy, F., Van den Bossche, P., & Segers, M. (2005). Effects of problem-based learning: A meta-analysis from the angle of assessment. *Review of Educational Research, 75,* 27–61.

Ginsburg, H. P., Cannon, J., Eisenband, J., & Pappas, S. (2006). Mathematical thinking and learning. In K. McCartney & D. Phillips (Eds.), *Blackwell handbook of early childhood development* (pp. 208–229). Malden, MA: Blackwell.

Glover, J. A., Ronning, R. R., & Reynolds, C. R. (Eds.). (1989). *Handbook of creativity.* New York: Plenum.

Goldstein, S., & Rider, R. (2006). Resilience and the disruptive disorders of childhood. In S. Goldstein & R. B. Brooks (Eds.), *Handbook of resilience in children* (pp. 203–222). New York: Springer.

Graham, S., & Harris, K. R. (1996). Addressing problems in attention, memory, and executive functioning. In G. R. Lyon & N. A. Krasnegor (Eds.), *Attention, memory, and executive function* (pp. 349–365). Baltimore: Brookes.

Grant, H., & Dweck, C. (2001). Cross-cultural response to failure: Considering outcome attributions with different goals. In F. Salili & C. Chiu (Eds.), *Student motivation: The culture and context of learning* (pp. 203–219). Dordrecht, The Netherlands: Kluwer Academic.

Gray, W. D., & Orasanu, J. M. (1987). Transfer of cognitive skills. In S. M. Cormier & J. D. Hagman (Eds.), *Transfer of learning: Contemporary research and applications* (pp. 184–215). San Diego, CA: Academic Press.

Gregg, N. (2009). *Adolescents and adults with learning disabilities and ADHD: Assessment and accommodation.* New York: Guilford.

Gresalfi, M. S., & Lester, F. (2009). What's worth knowing in mathematics? In S. Tobias & T. M. Duffy (Eds.), *Constructivist instruction: Success or failure?* (pp. 264–290). New York: Routledge.

Grodzinsky, G. M., & Diamond, R. (1992). Frontal lobe functioning in boys with attention-deficit hyperactivity disorder. *Developmental Neuropsychology, 8,* 427–445.

Hacker, D. J. (1998). Self-regulated comprehension during normal reading. In D. J. Hacker, J. Dunlosky, & A. C. Graesser (Eds.), *Metacognition in educational theory and practice* (pp. 165–191). Mahwah, NJ: Erlbaum.

Hacker, D. J., Bol, L., Horgan, D. D., & Rakow, E. A. (2000). Test prediction and performance in a classroom context. *Journal of Educational Psychology, 92,* 160–170.

Hacker, D. J., Dunlosky, J., & Graesser, A. C. (Eds.). (2009b). *Handbook of metacognition in education.* New York: Routledge.

Haller, E. P., Child, D. A., & Walberg, H. J. (1988). Can comprehension be taught? A quantitative synthesis of "metacognitive" studies. *Educational Researcher, 17*(9), 5–8.

Halpern, D. F. (1997). *Critical thinking across the curriculum: A brief edition of thought and knowledge.* Mahwah, NJ: Erlbaum.

Halpern, D. F. (1998). Teaching critical thinking for transfer across domains. *American Psychologist, 53,* 449–455.

Halpern, D. F. (2008). Is intelligence critical thinking? Why we need a new definition of intelligence. In P. C. Kyllonen, R. D. Roberts, & L. Stankov (Eds.), *Extending intelligence: Enhancement and new constructs* (pp. 349–370). New York: Erlbaum/Taylor & Francis.

Hamman, D., Berthelot, J., Saia, J., & Crowley, E. (2000). Teachers' coaching of learning and its relation to students' strategic learning. *Journal of Educational Psychology, 92,* 342–348.

Harris, K. R. (1982). Cognitive-behavior modification: Application with exceptional students. *Focus on Exceptional Children, 15,* 1–16.

Harris, R. J. (1977). Comprehension of pragmatic implications in advertising. *Journal of Applied Psychology, 62,* 603–608.

Haskell, R. E. (2001). *Transfer of learning: Cognition, instruction, and reasoning.* San Diego, CA: Academic Press.

Hatano, G., & Inagaki, K. (2003). When is conceptual change intended? A cognitive-sociocultural view. In G. M. Sinatra & P. R. Pintrich (Eds.), *Intentional conceptual change* (pp. 407–427). Mahwah, NJ: Erlbaum.

Hatano, G., & Oura, Y. (2003). Commentary: Reconceptualizing school learning using insight from expertise research. *Educational Researcher, 32*(8), 26–29.

Hattie, J. A. C. (2009). *Visible learning: A synthesis of over 800 meta-analyses relating to achievement.* London: Routledge.

Hattie, J., Biggs, J., & Purdie, N. (1996). Effects of learning skills interventions on student learning: A meta-analysis. *Review of Educational Research, 66,* 99–136.

Hennessey, B. A. (2010). Intrinsic motivation and creativity in the classroom: Have we come full circle? In R. A. Beghetto & J. C. Kaufman (Eds.), *Nurturing creativity in the classroom* (pp. 329–361). New York: Cambridge University Press.

Hennessey, B. A., & Amabile, T. M. (1987). *Creativity and learning.* Washington, DC: National Education Association.

Heward, W. L. (2009). *Exceptional children: An introduction to special education* (9th ed.). Upper Saddle River, NJ: Merrill/Pearson Education.

Hewitt, J., Brett, C., Scardamalia, M., Frecker, K., & Webb, J. (1995, April). Supporting knowledge building through the synthesis of CSILE, FCL, & Jasper. In M. Lamon (Chair), *Schools for thought: Transforming classrooms into learning communities.* Symposium conducted at the annual meeting of the American Educational Research Association, San Francisco.

Heyman, G. D. (2008). Children's critical thinking when learning from others. *Current Directions in Psychological Science, 17,* 344–347.

Hidi, S., & Anderson, V. (1986). Producing written summaries: Task demands, cognitive operations, and implications for instruction. *Review of Educational Research, 86,* 473–493.

Hmelo-Silver, C. E. (2004). Problem-based learning: What and how do students learn? *Educational Psychology Review, 16,* 235–266.

Hmelo-Silver, C. E., Duncan, R. G., & Chinn, C. A. (2007). Scaffolding and achievement in problem-based and inquiry learning: A response to Kirschner, Sweller, and Clark (2006). *Educational Psychologist, 42,* 99–107.

Ho, D. Y. F. (1994). Cognitive socialization in Confucian heritage cultures. In P. M. Greenfield & R. R. Cocking (Eds.), *Cross-cultural roots of minority child development* (pp. 285–313). Mahwah, NJ: Erlbaum.

Hofer, B. K., & Pintrich, P. R. (1997). The development of epistemological theories: Beliefs about knowledge and knowing and their relation to learning. *Review of Educational Research, 67,* 88–140.

Hofer, B. K., & Pintrich, P. R. (Eds.). (2002). *Personal epistemology: The psychology of beliefs about knowledge and knowing.* Mahwah, NJ: Erlbaum.

Houtz, J. C. (1990). Environments that support creative thinking. In C. Hedley, J. Houtz, & A. Baratta (Eds.), *Cognition, curriculum, and literacy* (pp. 61–76). Norwood, NJ: Ablex.

Hung, W., Jonassen, D. H., & Liu, R. (2008). Problem-based learning. In J. M. Spector, M. D. Merrill, J. van Merriënboer, & M. P. Driscoll (Eds.), *Handbook of research on educational communications and technology* (3rd ed., pp. 485–506). New York: Erlbaum.

James, W. (1890). *The principles of psychology.* New York: Holt.

Johanning, D. I., D'Agostino, J. V., Steele, D. F., & Shumow, L. (1999, April). *Student writing, post-writing group collaboration, and learning in pre-algebra.* Paper presented at the annual meeting of the American Educational Research Association, Montreal, Canada.

Kağitçibaşi, Ç. (2007). *Family, self, and human development across cultures: Theory and applications* (2nd ed.). Mahwah, NJ: Erlbaum.

Kahl, B., & Woloshyn, V. E. (1994). Using elaborative interrogation to facilitate acquisition of factual information in cooperative learning settings: One good strategy deserves another. *Applied Cognitive Psychology, 8,* 465–478.

Kalyuga, S. (2010). Schema acquisition and sources of cognitive load. In J. L. Plass, R. Moreno, & R. Brünken (Eds.), *Cognitive Load Theory* (pp. 48–64). Cambridge, England: Cambridge University Press.

Kardash, C. A. M., & Amlund, J. T. (1991). Self-reported learning strategies and learning from expository text. *Contemporary Educational Psychology, 16,* 117–138.

Kardash, C. A. M., & Howell, K. L. (2000). Effects of epistemological beliefs and topic-specific beliefs on undergraduates' cognitive and strategic processing of dual-positional text. *Journal of Educational Psychology, 92,* 524–535.

Kardash, C. A. M., & Scholes, R. J. (1996). Effects of preexisting beliefs, epistemological beliefs, and need for cognition on interpretation of controversial issues. *Journal of Educational Psychology, 88,* 260–271.

Kaufman, J. C., & Beghetto, R. A. (2009). Creativity in the schools: A rapidly developing area of positive psychology. In R. Gilman, E. S. Huebner, & M. J. Furlong (Eds.), *Handbook of positive psychology in schools* (pp. 175–188). New York: Routledge.

Kiewra, K. A. (1985). Investigating notetaking and review: A depth of processing alternative. *Educational Psychologist, 20,* 23–32.

Kiewra, K. A. (1989). A review of note-taking: The encoding-storage paradigm and beyond. *Educational Psychology Review, 1,* 147–172.

Kiewra, K. A., Benton, S. L., & Lewis, L. B. (1987). Qualitative aspects of notetaking and their relationship with information-processing ability and academic achievement. *Journal of Instructional Psychology, 14*(3), 110–117.

King, A. (1992). Comparison of self-questioning, summarizing, and notetaking-review as strategies for learning from lectures. *American Educational Research Journal, 29,* 303–323.

King, A. (1999). Discourse patterns for mediating peer learning. In A. M. O'Donnell & A. King (Eds.), *Cognitive perspectives on peer learning* (pp. 87–115). Mahwah, NJ: Erlbaum.

King, A., Staffieri, A., & Adelgais, A. (1998). Mutual peer tutoring: Effects of structuring tutorial interaction to scaffold peer learning. *Journal of Educational Psychology, 90,* 134–152.

King, P. M., & Kitchener, K. S. (2002). The reflective judgment model: Twenty years of research on epistemic cognition. In B. K. Hofer & P. R. Pintrich (Eds.), *Personal epistemology: The psychology of beliefs about knowledge and knowing* (pp. 37–61). Mahwah, NJ: Erlbaum.

Kinnebrew, J. S., & Biswas, G. (2011). Modeling and measuring self-regulated learning in teachable agent environments. *Journal of e-Learning and Knowledge Society, 7*(2), 19–35.

Kirschner, P. A., Sweller, J., & Clark, R. E. (2006). Why minimal guidance during instruction does not work: An analysis of the failure of constructivist, discovery, problem-based, experiential, and inquiry-based teaching. *Educational Psychologist, 41,* 75–86.

Kirsh, D. (2009). Problem solving and situated cognition. In P. Robbins & M. Aydede (Eds.), *The Cambridge handbook of situated cognition* (pp. 264–306). Cambridge, England: Cambridge University Press.

Klein, P. D. (1999). Reopening inquiry into cognitive processes in writing-to-learn. *Educational Psychology Review, 11,* 203–270.

Kramarski, B., & Mevarech, Z. R. (2003). Enhancing mathematical reasoning in the classroom: The effects of cooperative learning and metacognitive training. *American Educational Research Journal, 40,* 281–310.

Ku, Y.-M., Chan, W.-C., Wu, Y.-C., & Chen, Y.-H. (2008, March). *Improving children's comprehension of science text: Effects of adjunct questions and notetaking.* Paper presented at the annual meeting of the American Educational Research Association, New York.

Kucan, L., & Beck, I. L. (1997). Thinking aloud and reading comprehension research: Inquiry, instruction, and social interaction. *Review of Educational Research, 67,* 271–299.

Kuhn, D. (2001a). How do people know? *Psychological Science, 12,* 1–8.

Kuhn, D. (2009). The importance of learning about knowing: Creating a foundation for development of intellectual values. *Child Development Perspectives, 3,* 112–117.

Kuhn, D., Daniels, S., & Krishnan, A. (2003, April). *Epistemology and intellectual values as core metacognitive constructs.* Paper presented at the annual meeting of the American Educational Research Association, Chicago.

Kuhn, D., & Dean, D., Jr. (2005). Is developing scientific thinking all about learning to control variables? *Psychological Science, 16,* 866–870.

Kuhn, D., & Franklin, S. (2006). The second decade: What develops (and how)? In W. Damon & R. M. Lerner (Series Eds.), D. Kuhn, & R. Siegler (Vol. Eds.), *Handbook of child psychology: Vol. 2.*

*Cognition, perception, and language* (6th ed., pp. 953–993). New York: Wiley.

Kuhn, D., Garcia-Mila, M., Zohar, A., & Andersen, C. (1995). Strategies of knowledge acquisition. *Monographs of the Society for Research in Child Development, 60* (Whole No. 245).

Kuhn, D., & Park, S.-H. (2005). Epistemological understanding and the development of intellectual values. *International Journal of Educational Research, 43,* 111–124.

Kuhn, D., & Pease, M. (2008). What needs to develop in the development of inquiry skills? *Cognition and Instruction, 26,* 512–599.

Kuhn, D., & Weinstock, M. (2002). What is epistemological thinking and why does it matter? In B. K. Hofer & P. R. Pintrich (Eds.), *Personal epistemology: The psychology of beliefs about knowledge and knowing* (pp. 121–144). Mahwah, NJ: Erlbaum.

Langer, E. J. (2000). Mindful learning. *Current Directions in Psychological Science, 9,* 220–223.

Lee, J., & Shute, V. J. (2010). Personal and social-contextual factors in K–12 academic performance: An integrative perspective on student learning. *Educational Psychologist, 45,* 185–202.

Lee, K., Ng, E. L., & Ng, S. F. (2009). The contributions of working memory and executive function to problem representation and solution generation in algebraic word problems. *Journal of Educational Psychology, 101,* 373–387.

Leung, A. K., Maddux, W. W., Galinsky, A. D., & Chiu, C. (2008). Multicultural experience enhances creativity: The when and how. *American Psychologist, 63,* 169–181.

Levstik, L. S. (2011). Learning history. In R. E. Mayer & P. A. Alexander (Eds.), *Handbook of research on learning and instruction* (pp. 208–126). New York: Routledge.

Li, J. (2005). Mind or virtue: Western and Chinese beliefs about learning. *Current Directions in Psychological Science, 14,* 190–194.

Li, J., & Fischer, K. W. (2004). Thought and affect in American and Chinese learners' beliefs about learning. In D. Y. Dai & R. J. Sternberg (Eds.), *Motivation, emotion, and cognition: Integrative perspectives on intellectual functioning and development* (pp. 385–418). Mahwah, NJ: Erlbaum.

Linn, M. C. (2008). Teaching for conceptual change: Distinguish or extinguish ideas. In S. Vosniadou (Ed.), *International handbook on conceptual change* (pp. 694–722). New York: Routledge.

Linn, M. C., Clement, C., Pulos, S., & Sullivan, P. (1989). Scientific reasoning during adolescence: The influence of instruction in science knowledge and reasoning strategies. *Journal of Research in Science Teaching, 26,* 171–187.

Lodico, M. G., Ghatala, E. S., Levin, J. R., Pressley, M., & Bell, J. A. (1983). The effects of strategy monitoring training on children's selection of effective memory strategies. *Journal of Experimental Child Psychology, 35,* 273–277.

Loranger, A. L. (1994). The study strategies of successful and unsuccessful high school students. *Journal of Reading Behavior, 26,* 347–360.

Losh, S. C. (2003). On the application of social cognition and social location to creating causal

explanatory structures. *Educational Research Quarterly, 26*(3), 17–33.

Lovett, S. B., & Flavell, J. H. (1990). Understanding and remembering: Children's knowledge about the differential effects of strategy and task variables on comprehension and memorization. *Child Development, 61,* 1842–1858.

Lubart, T. I., & Mouchiroud, C. (2003). Creativity: A source of difficulty in problem solving. In J. E. Davidson & R. J. Sternberg (Eds.), *The psychology of problem solving* (pp. 127–148). Cambridge, England: Cambridge University Press.

Luchins, A. S. (1942). Mechanization in problem solving: The effect of Einstellung. *Psychological Monographs, 54* (Whole No. 248).

MacDonald, S., Uesiliana, K., & Hayne, H. (2000). Cross-cultural and gender differences in childhood amnesia. *Memory, 8,* 365–376.

Maker, C. J. (1993). Creativity, intelligence, and problem solving: A definition and design for cross-cultural research and measurement related to giftedness. *Gifted Education International, 9*(2), 68–77.

Marcus, G. (2008). *Kluge: The haphazard construction of the human mind.* Boston: Houghton Mifflin.

Martínez, P., Bannan-Ritland, B., Kitsantas, A., & Baek, J. Y. (2008, March). *The impact of an integrated science reading intervention on elementary children's misconceptions regarding slow geomorphological changes caused by water.* Paper presented at the annual meeting of the American Educational Research Association, New York.

Mason, L. (2010). Beliefs about knowledge and revision of knowledge: On the importance of epistemic beliefs for intentional conceptual change in elementary and middle school students. In L. D. Bendixen & F. C. Feucht (Eds.), *Personal epistemology in the classroom: Theory, research, and implications for practice* (pp. 258–291). Cambridge, England: Cambridge University Press.

Mason, L., Gava, M., & Boldrin, A. (2008). On warm conceptual change: The interplay of text, epistemological beliefs, and topic interest. *Journal of Educational Psychology, 100,* 291–309.

Mastropieri, M. A., & Scruggs, T. E. (2007). *The inclusive classroom: Strategies for effective instruction* (3rd ed.). Upper Saddle River, NJ: Merrill/Prentice-Hall.

Mayer, R. E. (1985). Implications of cognitive psychology for instruction in mathematical problem solving. In E. A. Silver (Ed.), *Teaching and learning mathematical problem solving: Multiple research perspectives* (pp. 123–138). Mahwah, NJ: Erlbaum.

Mayer, R. E. (1992). *Thinking, problem solving, cognition* (2nd ed.). New York: Freeman.

Mayer, R. E. (2010b). Merlin C. Wittrock's enduring contributions to the science of learning. *Educational Psychologist, 45,* 46–50.

Mayer, R. E., & Wittrock, M. C. (1996). Problem-solving transfer. In D. C. Berliner & R. C. Calfee (Eds.), *Handbook of educational psychology* (pp. 47–62). New York: Macmillan.

Mayer, R. E., & Wittrock, M. C. (2006). Problem solving. In P. A. Alexander & P. H. Winne

(Eds.), *Handbook of educational psychology* (2nd ed., pp. 287–303). Mahwah, NJ: Erlbaum.

Mayfield, K. H., & Chase, P. N. (2002). The effects of cumulative practice on mathematics problem solving. *Journal of Applied Behavior Analysis, 35,* 105–123.

McCrudden, M. T., & Schraw, G. (2007). Relevance and goal-focusing in text processing. *Educational Psychology Review, 19,* 113–139.

McGlynn, S. M. (1998). Impaired awareness of deficits in a psychiatric context: Implications for rehabilitation. In D. J. Hacker, J. Dunlosky, & A. C. Graesser (Eds.), *Metacognition in educational theory and practice* (pp. 221–248). Mahwah, NJ: Erlbaum.

McGovern, M. L., Davis, A., & Ogbu, J. U. (2008). The Minority Achievement Committee: Students leading students to greater success in school. In J. U. Ogbu (Ed.), *Minority status, oppositional culture, and schooling* (pp. 560–573). New York: Routledge.

McKeown, M. G., & Beck, I. L. (2009). The role of metacognition in understanding and supporting reading comprehension. In D. J. Hacker, J. Dunlosky, & A. C. Graesser (Eds.), *Handbook of metacognition in education* (pp. 7–25). New York: Routledge.

McNamara, D. S., & Magliano, J. P. (2009). Self-explanation and metacognition: The dynamics of reading. In D. J. Hacker, J. Dunlosky, & A. C. Graesser (Eds.), *Handbook of metacognition in education* (pp. 60–81). New York: Routledge.

Meichenbaum, D. (1977). *Cognitive-behavior modification: An integrative approach.* New York: Plenum.

Meltzer, L. (Ed.). (2007). *Executive function in education: From theory to practice.* New York: Guilford.

Meltzer, L., Pollica, L. S., & Barzillai, M. (2007). Executive function in the classroom: Embedding strategy instruction into daily teaching practices. In L. Meltzer (Ed.), *Executive function in education: From theory to practice* (pp. 165–193). New York: Guilford.

Mendaglio, S. (2010). Anxiety in gifted students. In J. C. Cassady (Ed.), *Anxiety in schools: The causes, consequences, and solutions for academic anxieties* (pp. 153–173). New York: Peter Lang.

Mercer, C. D., & Pullen, P. C. (2005). *Students with learning disabilities* (6th ed.). Upper Saddle River, NJ: Merrill/Prentice-Hall.

Metzger, M. J., Flanagin, A. J., & Zwarun, L. (2003). College student Web use, perceptions of information credibility, and verification behavior. *Computers and Education, 41,* 271–290.

Minsky, M. (2006). *The emotion machine: Commonsense thinking, artificial intelligence, and the future of the human mind.* New York: Simon & Schuster.

Monte-Sano, C. (2008). Qualities of historical writing instruction: A comparative case study of two teachers' practices. *American Educational Research Journal, 45,* 1045–1079.

Moon, J. (2008). *Critical thinking: An exploration of theory and practice.* London: Routledge.

Moreno, R., & Park, B. (2010). Cognitive Load Theory: Historical development and relation to other theories. In J. L. Plass, R. Moreno, & R. Brünken (Eds.), *Cognitive Load Theory* (pp. 9–28). Cambridge, England: Cambridge University Press.

Muis, K. R. (2007). The role of epistemic beliefs in self-regulated learning. *Educational Psychologist, 42,* 173–190.

Muis, K. R., Bendixen, L. D., & Haerle, F. C. (2006). Domain-generality and domain-specificity in personal epistemology research: Philosophical and empirical reflections in the development of a theoretical framework. *Educational Psychology Review, 18,* 3–54.

Ni, Y., & Zhou, Y.-D. (2005). Teaching and learning fraction and rational numbers: The origins and implications of whole number bias. *Educational Psychologist, 40,* 27–52.

Nokes, J. D., & Dole, J. A. (2004). Helping adolescent readers through explicit strategy instruction. In T. L. Jetton & J. A. Dole (Eds.), *Adolescent literacy research and practice* (pp. 162–182). New York: Guilford.

Nolen, S. B. (1996). Why study? How reasons for learning influence strategy selection. *Educational Psychology Review, 8,* 335–355.

Nussbaum, E. M. (2008). Collaborative discourse, argumentation, and learning: Preface and literature review. *Contemporary Educational Psychology, 33,* 345–359.

Nussbaum, E. M., & Edwards, O. V. (2011). Critical questions and argument strategems: A framework for enhancing and analyzing students' reasoning practices. *Journal of the Learning Sciences, 20,* 443–488.

Ornstein, P. A., Grammer, J. K., & Coffman, J. L. (2010). Teachers' "mnemonic style" and the development of skilled memory. In H. S. Waters & W. Schneider (Eds.), *Metacognition, strategy use, and instruction* (pp. 23–53). New York: Guilford.

O'Sullivan, J. T., & Joy, R. M. (1994). If at first you don't succeed: Children's metacognition about reading problems. *Contemporary Educational Psychology, 19,* 118–127.

Palmer, D. J., & Goetz, E. T. (1988). Selection and use of study strategies: The role of the studier's beliefs about self and strategies. In C. E. Weinstein, E. T. Goetz, & P. A. Alexander (Eds.), *Learning and study strategies: Issues in assessment, instruction, and evaluation* (pp. 41–61). San Diego: Academic Press.

Paris, S. G., & Paris, A. H. (2001). Classroom applications of research on self-regulated learning. *Educational Psychologist, 36,* 89–101.

Paris, S. G., & Winograd, P. (1990). How metacognition can promote academic learning and instruction. In B. F. Jones & L. Idol (Eds.), *Dimensions of thinking and cognitive instruction* (pp. 15–52). Mahwah, NJ: Erlbaum.

Paxton, R. J. (1999). A deafening silence: History textbooks and the students who read them. *Review of Educational Research, 69,* 315–339.

Pea, R. D. (1987). Socializing the knowledge transfer problem. *International Journal of Educational Research, 11,* 639–663.

Perkins, D. N. (1990). The nature and nurture of creativity. In B. F. Jones & L. Idol (Eds.), *Dimensions of thinking and cognitive instruction* (pp. 415–441). Mahwah, NJ: Erlbaum.

Perkins, D. N. (1992). *Smart schools: From training memories to educating minds.* New York: Free Press/Macmillan.

Perkins, D. N. (1995). *Outsmarting IQ: The emerging science of learnable intelligence.* New York: Free Press.

Perkins, D. N., & Salomon, G. (1989). Are cognitive skills context-bound? *Educational Researcher, 18*(1), 16–25.

Perkins, D. N., & Simmons, R. (1988). Patterns of misunderstanding: An integrative model for science, math, and programming. *Review of Educational Research, 58,* 303–326.

Perkins, D. N., Tishman, S., Ritchhart, R., Donis, K., & Andrade, A. (2000). Intelligence in the wild: A dispositional view of intellectual traits. *Educational Psychology Review, 12,* 269–293.

Perry, M. (1991). Learning and transfer: Instructional conditions and conceptual change. *Cognitive Development, 6,* 449–468.

Piirto, J. (1999). *Talented children and adults: Their development and education* (2nd ed.). Upper Saddle River, NJ: Merrill/Prentice-Hall.

Pillow, B. H. (2002). Children's and adults' evaluation of the certainty of deductive inferences, inductive inferences, and guesses. *Child Development, 73,* 779–792.

Polya, G. (1957). *How to solve it.* Garden City, NY: Doubleday.

Posner, M. I., & Rothbart, M. K. (2007). *Educating the human brain.* Washington, DC: American Psychological Association.

Prawat, R. S. (1989). Promoting access to knowledge, strategy, and disposition in students: A research synthesis. *Review of Educational Research, 59,* 1–41.

Pressley, M., with McCormick, C. B. (1995). *Advanced educational psychology for educators, researchers, and policymakers.* New York: HarperCollins.

Pressley, M., Borkowski, J. G., & Schneider, W. (1987). Cognitive strategies: Good strategy users coordinate metacognition and knowledge. In R. Vasta & G. Whitehurst (Eds.), *Annals of child development* (Vol. 5, pp. 80–129). New York: JAI.

Pressley, M., Harris, K. R., & Marks, M. B. (1992). But good strategy instructors are constructivists! *Educational Psychology Review, 4,* 3–31.

Pressley, M., & Hilden, K. (2006). Cognitive strategies: Production deficiencies and successful strategy instruction everywhere. In W. Damon & R. M. Lerner (Series Eds.), D. Kuhn, & R. Siegler (Vol. Eds.), *Handbook of child psychology: Vol. 2. Cognition, perception, and language* (6th ed., pp. 511–556). New York: Wiley.

Pressley, M., Yokoi, L., van Meter, P., Van Etten, S., & Freebern, G. (1997). Some of the reasons why preparing for exams is so hard: What can be done to make it easier? *Educational Psychology Review, 9,* 1–38.

Pugh, K. J., & Bergin, D. A. (2005). The effect of schooling on students' out-of-school experience. *Educational Researcher, 34*(9), 15–23.

Pugh, K. J., & Bergin, D. A. (2006). Motivational influences on transfer. *Educational Psychologist, 41,* 147–160.

Pulos, S., & Linn, M. C. (1981). Generality of the controlling variables scheme in early adolescence. *Journal of Early Adolescence, 1,* 26–37.

Purdie, N., & Hattie, J. (1996). Cultural differences in the use of strategies for self-regulated learning. *American Educational Research Journal, 33,* 845–71.

Qian, G., & Pan, J. (2002). A comparison of epistemological beliefs and learning from science text between American and Chinese high school students. In B. K. Hofer & P. R. Pintrich (Eds.), *Personal epistemology: The psychology of beliefs about knowledge and knowing* (pp. 365–385). Mahwah, NJ: Erlbaum.

Renkl, A. (2011). Instruction based on examples. In R. E. Mayer & P. A. Alexander (Eds.), *Handbook of research on learning and instruction* (pp. 272–295). New York: Routledge.

Renkl, A., Mandl, H., & Gruber, H. (1996). Inert knowledge: Analyses and remedies. *Educational Psychologist, 31,* 115–121.

Reynolds, R. E., & Shirey, L. L. (1988). The role of attention in studying and learning. In C. E. Weinstein, E. T. Goetz, & P. A. Alexander (Eds.), *Learning and study strategies: Issues in assessment, instruction, and evaluation* (pp. 77–100). San Diego, CA: Academic Press.

Ripple, R. E. (1989). Ordinary creativity. *Contemporary Educational Psychology, 14,* 189–202.

Rittle-Johnson, B. (2006). Promoting transfer: Effects of self-explanation and direct instruction. *Child Development, 77,* 1–15.

Rittle-Johnson, B., & Star, J. R. (2009). Compared with what? The effects of different comparisons on conceptual knowledge and procedural flexibility for equation solving. *Journal of Educational Psychology, 101,* 529–544.

Roditi, B. N., & Steinberg, J. (2007). The strategy math classroom: Executive function processes and mathematics learning. In L. Meltzer (Ed.), *Executive function in education: From theory to practice* (pp. 237–260). New York: Guilford.

Rogoff, B., Moore, L., Najafi, B., Dexter, A., Correa-Chávez, M., & Solís, J. (2007). Children's development of cultural repertoires through participation in everyday routines and practices. In J. E. Grusec & P. D. Hastings (Eds.), *Handbook of socialization: Theory and research* (pp. 490–515). New York: Guilford.

Rohrer, D., & Pashler, H. (2010). Recent research on human learning challenges conventional instructional strategies. *Educational Researcher, 39,* 406–412.

Rosenshine, B., Meister, C., & Chapman, S. (1996). Teaching students to generate questions: A review of the intervention studies. *Review of Educational Research, 66,* 181–221.

Rule, D. C., & Bendixen, L. D. (2010). The integrative model of personal epistemology development: Theoretical underpinnings and implications for education. In L. D. Bendixen & F. C. Feucht (Eds.), *Personal epistemology in the classroom: Theory, research, and implications for practice* (pp. 94–123). Cambridge, England: Cambridge University Press.

Runco, M. A. (2004). Creativity as an extracognitive phenomenon. In L. V. Shavinina & M. Ferrari (Eds.), *Beyond knowledge: Extracognitive aspects of developing high ability* (pp. 17–25). Mahwah, NJ: Erlbaum.

Runco, M. A., & Chand, I. (1995). Cognition and creativity. *Educational Psychology Review, 7,* 243–267.

Russ, S. W. (1993). *Affect and creativity: The role of affect and play in the creative process.* Mahwah, NJ: Erlbaum.

Saljo, R., & Wyndhamn, J. (1992). Solving everyday problems in the formal setting: An empirical study of the school as context for thought. In S. Chaiklin & J. Lave (Eds.), *Understanding practice* (pp. 327–342). New York: Cambridge University Press.

Sawyer, R. K. (2003). Emergence in creativity and development. In R. K. Sawyer, V. John-Steiner, S. Moran, R. J. Sternberg, D. H. Feldman, J. Nakamura, & M. Csikszentmihalyi, *Creativity and development* (pp. 12–60). Oxford, England: Oxford University Press.

Schmidt, R. A., & Bjork, R. A. (1992). New conceptualizations of practice: Common principles in three paradigms suggest new concepts for training. *Psychological Science, 3,* 207–217.

Schneider, W. (2010). Metacognition and memory development in childhood and adolescence. In H. S. Waters & W. Schneider (Eds.), *Metacognition, strategy use, and instruction* (pp. 54–81). New York: Guilford.

Schommer, M. (1990). Effects of beliefs about the nature of knowledge on comprehension. *Journal of Educational Psychology, 82,* 498–504.

Schommer, M. (1994a). An emerging conceptualization of epistemological beliefs and their role in learning. In R. Garner & P. A. Alexander (Eds.), *Beliefs about text and instruction with text* (pp. 25–40). Mahwah, NJ: Erlbaum.

Schommer, M. (1994b). Synthesizing epistemological belief research: Tentative understandings and provocative confusions. *Educational Psychology Review, 6,* 293–319.

Schommer, M. (1997). The development of epistemological beliefs among secondary students: A longitudinal study. *Journal of Educational Psychology, 89,* 37–40.

Schommer, M., Calvert, C., Gariglietti, G., & Bajaj, A. (1997). The development of epistemological beliefs among secondary students: A longitudinal study. *Journal of Educational Psychology, 89,* 37–40.

Schommer-Aikins, M. (2002). An evolving theoretical framework for an epistemological belief system. In B. K. Hofer & P. R. Pintrich (Eds.), *Personal epistemology: The psychology of beliefs about knowledge and knowing* (pp. 103–118). Mahwah, NJ: Erlbaum.

Schommer-Aikins, M., & Easter, M. (2008). Epistemological beliefs' contributions to study strategies of Asian Americans and European Americans. *Journal of Educational Psychology, 100,* 920–929.

Schraw, G., Wade, S. E., & Kardash, C. A. M. (1993). Interactive effects of text-based and task-based importance on learning from text. *Journal of Educational Psychology, 85,* 652–661.

Schwamborn, A., Mayer, R. E., Thillmann, H., Leopold, C., & Leutner, D. (2010). Drawing as a generative activity and drawing as a prognostic activity. *Journal of Educational Psychology, 102,* 872–879.

Schwartz, D. L., Bransford, J. D., & Sears, D. (2005). Efficiency and innovation in transfer. In J. P. Mestre (Ed.), *Transfer of learning from a modern multidisciplinary perspective* (pp. 1–51). Greenwich, CT: Information Age.

Schwartz, D. L., Lindgren, R., & Lewis, S. (2009). Constructivism in an age of non-constructivist assessments. In S. Tobias & T. M. Duffy (Eds.), *Constructivist instruction: Success or failure?* (pp. 34–61). New York: Routledge.

Scruggs, T. E., & Mastropieri, M. A. (1992). Classroom applications of mnemonic instruction: Acquisition, maintenance, and generalization. *Exceptional Children, 58,* 219–229.

Shanahan, T. (2004). Overcoming the dominance of communication: Writing to think and to learn. In T. L. Jetton & J. A. Dole (Eds.), *Adolescent literacy research and practice* (pp. 59–74). New York: Guilford.

Sherman, J., & Bisanz, J. (2009). Equivalence in symbolic and nonsymbolic contexts: Benefits of solving problems with manipulatives. *Journal of Educational Psychology, 101,* 88–100.

Short, E. J., Schatschneider, C. W., & Friebert, S. E. (1993). Relationship between memory and metamemory performance: A comparison of specific and general strategy knowledge. *Journal of Educational Psychology, 85,* 412–423.

Siegler, R. S. (2002). Microgenetic studies of self-explanations. In N. Granott & J. Parziale (Eds.), *Microdevelopment: Transition processes in development and learning* (pp. 31–58). New York: Cambridge University Press.

Siegler, R. S., & Jenkins, E. (1989). *How children discover new strategies.* Hillsdale, NJ: Erlbaum.

Simonton, D. K. (2000). Creativity: Cognitive, personal, developmental, and social aspects. *American Psychologist, 55,* 151–158.

Simonton, D. K. (2004). Exceptional creativity and chance: Creative thought as a stochastic combinatorial process. In L. V. Shavinina & M. Ferrari (Eds.), *Beyond knowledge: Extracognitive aspects of developing high ability* (pp. 39–72). Mahwah, NJ: Erlbaum.

Sinatra, G. M., & Pintrich, P. R. (Eds.). (2003). *Intentional conceptual change.* Mahwah, NJ: Erlbaum.

Slife, B. R., Weiss, J., & Bell, T. (1985). Separability of metacognition and cognition: Problem solving in learning disabled and regular students. *Journal of Educational Psychology, 77,* 437–445.

Son, L. K., & Schwartz, B. L. (2002). The relation between metacognitive monitoring and control. In T. J. Perfect & B. L. Schwartz (Eds.), *Applied metacognition* (pp. 15–38). Cambridge, England: Cambridge University Press.

Spörer, N., & Brunstein, J. C. (2009). Fostering the reading comprehension of secondary school students through peer-assisted learning: Effects on strategy knowledge, strategy use, and task performance. *Contemporary Educational Psychology, 34,* 289–297.

Stahl, S. A., & Shanahan, C. (2004). Learning to think like a historian: Disciplinary knowledge through critical analysis of multiple documents. In T. L. Jetton & J. A. Dole (Eds.), *Adolescent literacy research and practice* (pp. 94–115). New York: Guilford.

Stanley, J. C. (1980). On educating the gifted. *Educational Researcher, 9*(3), 8–12.

Starr, E. J., & Lovett, S. B. (2000). The ability to distinguish between comprehension and memory: Failing to succeed. *Journal of Educational Psychology, 92,* 761–771.

Sternberg, R. J. (2010). Teaching for creativity. In R. A. Beghetto & J. C. Kaufman (Eds.), *Nurturing creativity in the classroom* (pp. 394–414). New York: Cambridge University Press.

Sternberg, R. J., & Frensch, P. A. (1993). Mechanisms of transfer. In D. K. Detterman & R. J. Sternberg (Eds.), *Transfer on trial: Intelligence, cognition, and instruction* (pp. 25–38). Norwood, NJ: Ablex.

Stone, N. J. (2000). Exploring the relationship between calibration and self-regulated learning. *Educational Psychology Review, 12,* 437–475.

Sun-Alperin, M. K., & Wang, M. (2008). Spanish-speaking children's spelling errors with English vowel sounds that are represented by different graphemes in English and Spanish words. *Contemporary Educational Psychology, 33,* 932–948.

Swanson, H. L. (1993). An information processing analysis of learning disabled children's problem solving. *American Educational Research Journal, 30,* 861–893.

Swanson, H. L., Jerman, O., & Zheng, X. (2008). Growth in working memory and mathematical problem solving in children at risk and not at risk for serious math difficulties. *Journal of Educational Psychology, 100,* 343–379.

Sweller, J. (1994). Cognitive load theory, learning difficulty, and instructional design. *Learning and Instruction, 4,* 295–312.

Sweller, J. (2009a). Cognitive bases of human creativity. *Educational Psychology Review, 21,* 11–19.

Thomas, J. W. (1993a). Expectations and effort: Course demands, students' study practices, and academic achievement. In T. M. Tomlinson (Ed.), *Motivating students to learn: Overcoming barriers to high achievement* (pp. 139–176). Berkeley, CA: McCutchan.

Thomas, J. W. (1993b). Promoting independent learning in the middle grades: The role of instructional support practices. *Elementary School Journal, 93,* 575–591.

Thorndike, E. L. (1924). Mental discipline in high school studies. *Journal of Educational Psychology, 15,* 1–22, 83–98.

Tirosh, D., & Graeber, A. O. (1990). Evoking cognitive conflict to explore preservice teachers' thinking about division. *Journal for Research in Mathematics Education, 21,* 98–108.

Torrance, E. P. (1970). *Encouraging creativity in the classroom.* Dubuque, IA: Wm. C. Brown.

Torrance, E. P. (1989). A reaction to "Gifted black students: Curriculum and teaching strategies." In C. J. Maker & S. W. Schiever (Eds.), *Critical issues in gifted education: Vol. 2. Defensible programs for cultural and ethnic minorities* (pp. 270–274). Austin, TX: Pro-Ed.

Turnbull, A. P., Turnbull, R., & Wehmeyer, M. L. (2010). *Exceptional lives: Special education in today's schools* (6th ed.). Upper Saddle River, NJ: Merrill.

Turner, J. C. (1995). The influence of classroom contexts on young children's motivation for literacy. *Reading Research Quarterly, 30,* 410–441.

Turner, J. C., Meyer, D. K., Cox, K. E., Logan, C., DiCintio, M., & Thomas, C. T. (1998). Creating contexts for involvement in mathematics. *Journal of Educational Psychology, 90,* 730–745.

Tyler, K. M., Uqdah, A. L., Dillihunt, M. L., Beatty-Hazelbaker, R., Connor, T., Gadson, N., et al. (2008). Cultural discontinuity: Toward a quantitative investigation of a major hypothesis in education. *Educational Researcher, 37,* 280–297.

Van Meter, P., Yokoi, L., & Pressley, M. (1994). College students' theory of notetaking derived from their perceptions of notetaking. *Journal of Educational Psychology, 86,* 323–338.

vanSledright, B., & Limón, M. (2006). Learning and teaching social studies: A review of cognitive research in history and geography. In P. A. Alexander & P. H. Winne (Eds.), *Handbook of educational psychology* (2nd ed., pp. 545–570). Mahwah, NJ: Erlbaum.

Vaughn, S., Klingner, J. K., Swanson, E. A., Boardman, A. G., Roberts, G., Mohammed, S. S., et al. (2011). Efficacy of collaborative strategic reading with middle school students. *American Educational Research Journal, 48,* 938–964.

Veenman, M. V. J. (2011). Learning to self-monitor and self-regulate. In R. E. Mayer & P. A. Alexander (Eds.), *Handbook of research on learning and instruction* (pp. 197–218). New York: Routledge.

Volet, S. (1999). Learning across cultures: Appropriateness of knowledge transfer. *International Journal of Educational Research, 31,* 625–643.

Voss, J. F. (1987). Learning and transfer in subject-matter learning: A problem-solving model. *International Journal of Educational Research, 11,* 607–622.

Vye, N. J., Schwartz, D. L., Bransford, J. D., Barron, B. J., Zech, L., & The Cognition and Technology Group at Vanderbilt. (1998). SMART environments that support monitoring, reflection, and revision. In D. J. Hacker, J. Dunlosky, & A. C. Graesser (Eds.), *Metacognition in educational theory and practice* (pp. 305–346). Mahwah, NJ: Erlbaum.

Vygotsky, L. S. (1978). *Mind in society: The development of higher psychological processes.* Cambridge, MA: Harvard University Press.

Waber, D. P. (2010). *Rethinking learning disabilities: Understanding children who struggle in school.* New York: Guilford.

Wade-Stein, D., & Kintsch, E. (2004). Summary Street: Interactive computer support for writing. *Cognition and Instruction, 22,* 333–362.

Wagner, J. F. (2010). A transfer-in-pieces consideration of the perception of structure in the transfer of learning. *Journal of the Learning Sciences, 19,* 443–479.

Walkington, C., Sherman, M., & Petrosino, A. (2010, April–May). *"Playing the game" of story problems: Situated cognition in algebra problem-solving.* Paper presented at the annual meeting of the American Educational Research Association, Denver.

Wang, Q., & Ross, M. (2007). Culture and memory. In S. Kitayama & D. Cohen (Eds.), *Handbook of cultural psychology* (pp. 645–667). New York: Guilford.

Waters, H. S., & Kunnmann, T. W. (2010). Metacognition and strategy discovery in early childhood. In H. S. Waters & W. Schneider (Eds.), *Metacognition, strategy use, and instruction* (pp. 3–22). New York: Guilford.

Weinstein, C. E., Goetz, E. T., & Alexander, P. A. (Eds.). (1988). *Learning and study strategies: Issues in assessment, instruction, and evaluation.* San Diego, CA: Academic Press.

Weinstein, C. E., & Hume, L. M. (1998). *Study strategies for lifelong learning.* Washington, DC: American Psychological Association.

Weisberg, R. W. (1993). *Creativity: Beyond the myth of genius.* New York: Freeman.

Weissberg, R. P. (1985). Designing effective social problem-solving programs for the classroom. In B. H. Schneider, K. H. Rubin, & J. E. Ledingham (Eds.), *Children's peer relations: Issues in assessment and intervention* (pp. 225–242). New York: Springer-Verlag.

Wellman, H. M. (1985). The child's theory of mind: The development of conceptions of cognition. In S. R. Yussen (Ed.), *The growth of reflection in children* (pp. 169–206). San Diego, CA: Academic Press.

Wellman, H. M. (1990). *The child's theory of mind.* Cambridge, MA: MIT Press.

Wentzel, K. R. (2009). Peers and academic functioning at school. In K. H. Rubin, W. M. Bukowski, & B. Laursen (Eds.), *Handbook of peer interactions, relationships, and groups* (pp. 531–547). New York: Guilford.

Wentzel, K. R., & Watkins, D. E. (2011). Instruction based on peer interactions. In R. E. Mayer & P. A. Alexander (Eds.), *Handbook of research on learning and instruction* (pp. 322–343). New York: Routledge.

Williams, J. P., Stafford, K. B., Lauer, K. D., Hall, K. M., & Pollini, S. (2009). Embedding reading comprehension training in content-area instruction. *Journal of Educational Psychology, 101,* 1–20.

Wong, B. Y. L. (1985). Self-questioning instructional research: A review. *Review of Educational Research, 55,* 227–268.

Wong, B. Y. L. (Ed.). (1991). *Learning about learning disabilities.* San Diego, CA: Academic Press.

Wood, E., Willoughby, T., McDermott, C., Motz, M., Kaspar, V., & Ducharme, M. J. (1999). Developmental differences in study behavior. *Journal of Educational Psychology, 91,* 527–536.

Yang, F.-Y., & Tsai, C.-Ch. (2010). An epistemic framework for scientific reasoning in informal contexts. In L. D. Bendixen & F. C. Feucht (Eds.), *Personal epistemology in the classroom: Theory, research, and implications for practice* (pp. 124–162). Cambridge, England: Cambridge University Press.

Zhong, C.-B., Dijksterhuis, A., & Galinsky, A. D. (2008). The merits of unconscious thought in creativity. *Psychological Science, 19,* 912–918.

Zimmerman, B. J., & Moylan, A. R. (2009). Self-regulation: Where metacognition and motivation intersect. In D. J. Hacker, J. Dunlosky, & A. C. Graesser (Eds.), *Handbook of metacognition in education* (pp. 299–315). New York: Routledge.

## CHAPTER 8

Afflerbach, P., & Cho, B.-Y. (2010). Determining and describing reading strategies: Internet and traditional forms of reading. In H. S. Waters & W. Schneider (Eds.), *Metacognition, strategy use, and instruction* (pp. 201–225). New York: Guilford.

Afflerbach, P, VanSledright, B., & Dromsky, A. (2003, April). *Reading and thinking like historians: Investigating a 4th grade performance assessment.* Paper presented at the annual meeting of the American Educational Research Association, Chicago.

Alfassi, M. (2004). Reading to learn: Effects of combined strategy instruction on high school students. *Journal of Educational Research, 97,* 171–184.

Alibali, M. W., Spencer, R. C., Knox, L., & Kita, S. (2011). Spontaneous gestures influence strategy choices in problem solving. *Psychological Science, 22,* 1138–1144.

Anderson, L. W., & Pellicer, L. O. (1998). Toward an understanding of unusually successful programs for economically disadvantaged students. *Journal of Education for Students Placed at Risk, 3,* 237–263.

Andriessen, J. (2006). Arguing to learn. In R. K. Sawyer (Ed.), *The Cambridge handbook of the learning sciences* (pp. 443–459). Cambridge, England: Cambridge University Press.

Anthony, J. L., & Francis, D. J. (2005). Development of phonological awareness. *Current Directions in Psychological Science, 14,* 255–259.

Atran, S., Medin, D. L., & Ross, N. O. (2005). The cultural mind: Environmental decision making and cultural modeling within and across populations. *Psychological Review, 112,* 744–776.

Banks, J. A. (1991). Multicultural literacy and curriculum reform. *Educational Horizons, 69*(3), 135–140.

Barab, S. A., & Dodge, T. (2008). Strategies for designing embodied curriculum. In J. M. Spector, M. D. Merrill, J. van Merriënboer, & M. P. Driscoll (Eds.), *Handbook of research on educational communications and technology* (3rd ed., pp. 97–110). New York: Erlbaum.

Barchfeld, P., Sodian, B., Thoermer, C., & Bullock, M. (2005, April). *The development of experiment generation abilities from primary school to late adolescence.* Poster presented at the biennial meeting of the Society for Research in Child Development, Atlanta, GA.

Barnett, M. (2005, April). *Engaging inner city students in learning through designing remote operated vehicles.* Paper presented at the annual meeting of the American Educational Research Association, Montreal.

Bartlett, F. C. (1932). *Remembering: A study in experimental and social psychology.* Cambridge, England: Cambridge University Press.

Barton, K. C., & Levstik, L. S. (1996). "Back when God was around and everything": Elementary children's understanding of historical time. *American Educational Research Journal, 33,* 419–454.

Bassett, D. S., Jackson, L., Ferrell, K. A., Luckner, J., Hagerty, P. J., Bunsen, T. D., & MacIsaac, D. (1996). Multiple perspectives on inclusive education: Reflections of a university faculty. *Teacher Education and Special Education, 19,* 355–386.

Beck, I. L., McKeown, M. G., Sinatra, G. M., & Loxterman, J. A. (1991). Revising social studies text from a text-processing perspective: Evidence of improved comprehensibility. *Reading Research Quarterly, 26,* 251–276.

Bellanca, J. A., & Stirling, T. (2011). *Classrooms without borders: Using Internet projects to teach communication and collaboration.* New York: Teachers College Press.

Bendixen, L. D., & Rule, D. C. (2004). An integrative approach to personal epistemology: A guiding model. *Educational Psychologist, 39,* 69–80.

Benton, S. L. (1997). Psychological foundations of elementary writing instruction. In G. D. Phye (Ed.), *Handbook of academic learning: Construction of knowledge* (pp. 235–264). San Diego, CA: Academic Press.

Bereiter, C., & Scardamalia, M. (1987). *The psychology of written composition.* Hillsdale, NJ: Erlbaum.

Bereiter, C., & Scardamalia, M. (2006). Education for the Knowledge Age[LG6]: Design-centered models of teaching and instruction. In P. A. Alexander & P. H. Winne (Eds.), *Handbook of educational psychology* (2nd ed., pp. 695–713). Mahwah, NJ: Erlbaum.

Berkin, C., Crocco, M., & Winslow, B. (2009). *Clio in the classroom: A guide to teaching U.S. women's history.* New York: Oxford University Press.

Bermejo, V. (1996). Cardinality development and counting. *Developmental Psychology, 32,* 263–268.

Berninger, V. W., Fuller, F., & Whitaker, D. (1996). A process model of writing development across the life span. *Educational Psychology Review, 8,* 193–218.

Berti, A. E., Toneatti, L., & Rosati, V. (2010). Children's conceptions about the origin of species: A study of Italian children's conceptions with and without instruction. *Journal of the Learning Sciences, 19,* 506–538.

Betjemann, R. S., & Keenan, J. M. (2008). Phonological and semantic priming in children with reading disability. *Child Development, 79,* 1086–1102.

Bielaczyc, K., & Collins, A. (2006). Fostering knowledge-creating communities. In A. M. O'Donnell, C. E. Hmelo-Silver, & G. Erkens (Eds.), *Collaborative learning, reasoning, and technology* (pp. 37–60). Mahwah, NJ: Erlbaum.

Bochenhauer, M. H. (1990, April.) *Connections: Geographic education and the National Geographic Society.* Paper presented at the annual meeting of the American Educational Research Association, Boston.

Boscardin, C. K., Muthén, B., Francis, D. J., & Baker, E. L. (2008). Early identification of reading difficulties using heterogeneous developmental trajectories. *Journal of Educational Psychology, 100,* 192–208.

Botelho, M. J., Cohen, S. L., Leoni, L., Chow, P., & Sastri, P. (2010). Respecting children's cultural and linguistic knowledge. In M. L. Dantas & P. C. Manyak (Eds.), *Home–school connections in a multicultural society: Learning from and with culturally and linguistically diverse families* (pp. 237–256). New York: Routledge.

Boxerman, J. Z. (2009, April). *Students' understanding of erosion.* Paper presented at the annual meeting of the American Educational Research Association, San Diego, CA.

Bråten, I., Britt, M. A., Strømsø, H. I., & Rouet, J.-F. (2011). The role of epistemic beliefs in the comprehension of multiple expository texts: Toward an integrated model. *Educational Psychologist, 46,* 48–70.

Brayboy, B. M. J., & Searle, K. A. (2007). Thanksgiving and serial killers: Representations of American Indians in schools. In S. Books (Ed.), *Invisible children in the society and its schools* (3rd ed., pp. 173–192). Mahwah, NJ: Erlbaum.

Britton, B. K., Stimson, M., Stennett, B., & Gülgöz, S. (1998). Learning from instructional text: Test of an individual differences model. *Journal of Educational Psychology, 90,* 476–491.

Bromme, R., Kienhues, D., & Porsch, T. (2010). Who knows what and who can we believe? Epistemological beliefs are beliefs about knowledge (mostly) to be attained from others. In L. D. Bendixen & F. C. Feucht (Eds.), *Personal epistemology in the classroom: Theory, research, and implications for practice* (pp. 163–193). Cambridge, England: Cambridge University Press.

Bronfenbrenner, U. (2005). *Making human beings human: Bioecological perspectives on human development.* Thousand Oaks, CA: Sage.

Brophy, J. E., & Alleman, J. (1996). *Powerful social studies for elementary students.* Fort Worth, TX: Harcourt, Brace.

Brophy, J., Alleman, J., & Knighton, B. (2009). *Inside the social studies classroom.* New York: Routledge.

Brown, A. L., & Campione, J. C. (1994). Guided discovery in a community of learners. In K. McGilly (Ed.), *Classroom lessons: Integrating cognitive theory and classroom practice* (pp. 229–270). Cambridge, MA: MIT Press.

Brown, A. L., & Campione, J. C. (1996). Psychological theory and the design of innovative learning environments: On procedures, principles, and systems. In

L. Schauble & R. Glaser (Eds.), *Innovations in learning: New environments for education* (pp. 289–325). Mahwah, NJ: Erlbaum.

Brown, D. E., & Clement, J. (1989). Overcoming misconceptions via analogical reasoning: Abstract transfer versus explanatory model construction. *Instructional Science, 18,* 237–262.

Bullock, M., & Ziegler, A. (1999). Scientific reasoning: Developmental and individual differences. In F. E. Weinert & W. Schneider (Eds.), *Individual development from 3 to 12: Findings from the Munich longitudinal study.* New York: Cambridge University Press.

Byrnes, J. P. (1996). *Cognitive development and learning in instructional contexts.* Boston: Allyn & Bacon.

Cain, K., Oakhill, J., & Bryant, P. (2004). Children's reading comprehension ability: Concurrent prediction by working memory, verbal ability, and component skills. *Journal of Educational Psychology, 96,* 31–42.

Campione, J. C., Shapiro, A. M., & Brown, A. L. (1995). Forms of transfer in a community of learners: Flexible learning and understanding. In A. McKeough, J. Lupart, & A. Marini (Eds.), *Teaching for transfer: Fostering generalization in learning* (pp. 35–68). Mahwah, NJ: Erlbaum.

Carr, M. (2010). The importance of metacognition for conceptual change and strategy use in mathematics. In H. S. Waters & W. Schneider (Eds.), *Metacognition, strategy use, and instruction* (pp. 176–197). New York: Guilford.

Carr, M., & Biddlecomb, B. (1998). Metacognition in mathematics from a constructivist perspective. In D. J. Hacker, J. Dunlosky, & A. C. Graesser (Eds.), *Metacognition in educational theory and practice* (pp. 69–91). Mahwah, NJ: Erlbaum.

Case, R., & Okamoto, Y., in collaboration with Griffin, S., McKeough, A., Bleiker, C., Henderson, B., & Stephenson, K. M. (1996). The role of central conceptual structures in the development of children's thought. *Monographs of the Society for Research in Child Development, 61*(1, Serial No. 246).

Certo, J. (2011). Social skills and leadership abilities among children in small group literature discussions. *Journal of Research in Childhood Education, 25*(1), 62–81.

Chall, J. S. (1996). *Stages of reading development* (2nd ed.). Fort Worth, TX: Harcourt Brace.

Chambliss, M. J. (1998, April). *Children as thinkers composing scientific explanations.* Paper presented at the annual meeting of the American Educational Research Association, San Diego, CA.

Chinn, C. A. (2006). Learning to argue. In A. M. O'Donnell, C. E. Hmelo-Silver, & G. Erkens (Eds.), *Collaborative learning, reasoning, and technology* (pp. 355–383). Mahwah, NJ: Erlbaum.

Christenson, S. L., & Thurlow, M. L. (2004). School dropouts: Prevention, considerations, interventions, and challenges. *Current Directions in Psychological Science, 13,* 36–39.

Clark, D. B. (2006). Longitudinal conceptual change in students' understanding of thermal equilibrium: An examination of the process of conceptual restructuring. *Cognition and Instruction, 24,* 467–563.

Clark, R. E., Yates, K., Early, S., & Moulton, K. (2009). An analysis of the failure of electronic media and discovery-based learning: Evidence for the performance benefits of guided training methods. In K. H. Silber & R. Foshay (Eds.), *Handbook of training and improving workplace performance: Vol. 1. Instructional design and training delivery* (pp. 263–297). New York: Wiley.

Clarke, B., Gersten, R., & Newman-Gonchar, R. (2010). RTI in mathematics: Beginnings of a knowledge base. In T. A. Glover & S. Vaughn (Eds.), *The promise of response to intervention: Evaluating current science and practice* (pp. 187–203). New York: Guilford.

Clarke, L. K. (1988). Invented versus traditional spelling in first graders' writings: Effects on learning to spell and read. *Research in the Teaching of English, 22,* 281–309.

Clement, J. (1982). Algebra word problem solutions: Thought processes underlying a common misconception. *Journal for Research in Mathematics Education, 13,* 16–30.

Clement, J. (2008). The role of explanatory models in teaching for conceptual change. In S. Vosniadou (Ed.), *International handbook on conceptual change* (pp. 417–452). New York: Routledge.

Cognition and Technology Group at Vanderbilt. (1993). Anchored instruction and situated cognition revisited. *Educational Technology, 33*(3), 52–70.

Cole, M., & Hatano, G. (2007). Cultural-historical activity theory: Integrating phylogeny, cultural history, and ontogenesis in cultural psychology. In S. Kitayama & D. Cohen (Eds.), *Handbook of cultural psychology* (pp. 109–135). New York: Guilford.

Collins, A. (2006). Cognitive apprenticeship. In R. K. Sawyer (Ed.), *The Cambridge handbook of the learning sciences* (pp. 47–60). Cambridge, England: Cambridge University Press.

Collins, A., Hawkins, J., & Carver, S. M. (1991). A cognitive apprenticeship for disadvantaged students. In B. Means, C. Chelemer, & M. S. Knapp (Eds.), *Teaching advanced skills to at-risk students* (pp. 216–243). San Francisco: Jossey-Bass.

Cromley, J. G., & Azevedo, R. (2007). Testing and refining the direct and inferential mediation model of reading comprehension. *Journal of Educational Psychology, 99,* 311–325.

Cummins, J. (2007). Pedagogies for the poor? Realigning reading instruction for low-income students with scientifically based reading research. *Educational Researcher, 36,* 564–572.

Curtis, M. E. (2004). Adolescents who struggle with word identification: Research and practice. In T. L. Jetton & J. A. Dole (Eds.), *Adolescent literacy research and practice* (pp. 119–134). New York: Guilford.

Davis, J. H. (2008). *Why our schools need the arts.* New York: Teachers College Press.

Davison, M. (2011, April). *Are you standing in my shoes? How affective and cognitive teaching sequences influence historical empathy.* Paper presented at the annual meeting of the American Educational Research Association, New Orleans, LA.

De Corte, E., Greer, B., & Verschaffel, L. (1996). Mathematics teaching and learning. In D. C. Berliner & R. C. Calfee (Eds.), *Handbook of educational psychology* (pp. 491–549). New York: Macmillan.

De Corte, E., Op't Eynde, P., Depaepe, F., & Verschaffel, L. (2010). The reflexive relation between students' mathematics-related beliefs and the mathematics classroom culture. In L. D. Bendixen & F. C. Feucht (Eds.), *Personal epistemology in the classroom: Theory, research, and implications for practice* (pp. 292–327). Cambridge, England: Cambridge University Press.

De La Paz, S. (2005). Effects of historical reasoning instruction and writing strategy mastery in culturally and academically diverse middle school classrooms. *Journal of Educational Psychology, 97,* 139–156.

De La Paz, S., & McCutchen, D. (2011). Learning to write. In R. E. Mayer & P. A. Alexander (Eds.), *Handbook of research on learning and instruction* (pp. 32–54). New York: Routledge.

Dehaene, S. (2007). A few steps toward a science of mental life. *Mind, Brain, and Education, 1*(1), 28–47.

Dennen, V. P., & Burner, K. J. (2008). The cognitive apprenticeship model in educational practice. In J. M. Spector, M. D. Merrill, J. van Merriënboer, & M. P. Driscoll (Eds.), *Handbook of research on educational communications and technology* (3rd ed., pp. 425–439). New York: Erlbaum.

Driver, R. (1995). Constructivist approaches to science teaching. In L. P. Steffe & J. Gale (Eds.), *Constructivism in education.* Hillsdale, NJ: Erlbaum.

Eberbach, C., & Crowley, K. (2009). From everyday to scientific observation: How children learn to observe the biologist's world. *Review of Educational Research, 79,* 39–68.

Edelson, D. C., & Reiser, B. J. (2006). Making authentic practices accessible to learners. In R. K. Sawyer (Ed.), *The Cambridge handbook of the learning sciences* (pp. 335–354). Cambridge, England: Cambridge University Press.

Edwards, A. R., Esmonde, I., & Wagner, J. F. (2011). Learning mathematics. In R. E. Mayer & P. A. Alexander (Eds.), *Handbook of research on learning and instruction* (pp. 55–77). New York: Routledge.

Egbert, J. (2009). *Supporting learning with technology: Essentials of classroom practice.* Upper Saddle River, NJ: Pearson/Merrill Prentice-Hall.

Ehri, L. C. (1998). Word reading by sight and by analogy in beginning readers. In C. Hulme & R. M. Joshi (Eds.), *Reading and spelling: Development and disorders* (pp. 87–111). Mahwah, NJ: Erlbaum.

Ehri, L. C., Dreyer, L. G., Flugman, B., & Gross, A. (2007). Reading Rescue: An effective tutoring intervention model for language-minority students who are struggling readers in first grade. *American Educational Research Journal, 44,* 414–448.

Ehri, L. C., Nunes, S. R., Stahl, S. A., & Willows, D. M. (2001). Systematic phonics instruction helps students learn to read: Evidence from the National Reading Panel's meta-analysis. *Review of Educational Research, 71,* 393–447.

Elbro, C., & Petersen, D. K. (2004). Long-term effects of phoneme awareness and letter sound training: An intervention study with children at risk for dyslexia. *Journal of Educational Psychology, 96,* 660–670.

Engle, R. A. (2006). Framing interactions to foster generative learning: A situative explanation of transfer in a community of learners. *Journal of the Learning Sciences, 15,* 451–498.

Engle, R. A., & Conant, F. R. (2002). Guiding principles for fostering productive disciplinary engagement: Explaining an emergent argument in a community of learners classroom. *Cognition and Instruction, 20,* 399–483.

Enyedy, N. (2005). Inventing mapping: Creating cultural forms to solve collective problems. *Cognition and Instruction, 23,* 427–466.

Epstein, T. (2000). Adolescents' perspectives on racial diversity in U.S. history: Case studies from an urban classroom. *American Educational Research Journal, 37,* 185–214.

Epstein, T., & Shiller, J. (2009). Race, gender, and the teaching and learning of national history. In W. Parker (Ed.), *Social studies today: Research and practice* (pp. 95–104). New York: Routledge.

Evans, E. M. (2008). Conceptual change and evolutionary biology: A developmental analysis. In S. Vosniadou (Ed.), *International handbook on conceptual change* (pp. 263–294). New York: Routledge.

Feinberg, M., & Willer, R. (2011). Apocalypse soon? Dire messages reduce belief in global warming by contradicting just-world beliefs. *Psychological Science, 22,* 34–38.

Felton, R. H. (1998). The development of reading skills in poor readers: Educational implications. In C. Hulme & R. M. Joshi (Eds.), *Reading and spelling: Development and disorders* (pp. 219–233). Mahwah, NJ: Erlbaum.

Ferretti, R. P., Lewis, W. E., & Andrews-Weckerly, S. (2009). Do goals affect the structure of students' argumentative writing strategies? *Journal of Educational Psychology, 101,* 577–589.

Ferretti, R. P., MacArthur, C. A., & Dowdy, N. S. (2000). The effects of an elaborated goal on the persuasive writing of students with learning disabilities and their normally achieving peers. *Journal of Educational Psychology, 92,* 694–702.

Fitzgerald, J. (1992). Variant views about good thinking during composing: Focus on revision. In M. Pressley, K. R. Harris, & J. T. Guthrie (Eds.), *Promoting academic competence and literacy in school* (337–358). San Diego, CA: Academic Press.

Forbes, M. L., Ormrod, J. E., Bernardi, J. D., Taylor, S. L., & Jackson, D. L. (1999, April). *Children's conceptions of space, as reflected in maps of their hometown.* Paper presented at the annual meeting of the American Educational Research Association, Montreal, Canada.

Fox, E., & Alexander, P. A. (2011). Learning to read. In R. E. Mayer & P. A. Alexander (Eds.), *Handbook of research on learning and instruction* (pp. 7–31). New York: Routledge.

Fuchs, D., Fuchs, L. S., Mathes, P. G., & Simmons, D. C. (1997). Peer-assisted learning strategies: Making classrooms more responsive to diversity. *American Educational Research Journal, 34,* 174–206.

Fuchs, L. S., Fuchs, D., Craddock, C., Hollenbeck, K. N., Hamlett, C. L., & Schatschneider, C. (2008). Effects of small-group tutoring with and without validated classroom instruction on at-risk, students' math problem solving: Are two tiers of prevention better than one? *Journal of Educational Psychology, 100,* 491–509.

Fuchs, L. S., Fuchs, D., Prentice, K., Burch, M., Hamlett, C. L., Owen, R., et al. (2003). Explicitly teaching for transfer: Effects on third-grade students' mathematical problem solving. *Journal of Educational Psychology, 95,* 295–305.

Furnham, A. (2003). Belief in a just world: Research progress over the past decade. *Personality and Individual Differences, 34,* 795–817.

Gallistel, C. R., & Gelman, R. (1992). Preverbal and verbal counting and computation. *Cognition, 44,* 43–74.

Garner, R. (1998). Epilogue: Choosing to learn or not-learn in school. *Educational Psychology Review, 10,* 227–237.

Gaskins, I. W., Satlow, E., & Pressley, M. (2007). Executive control of reading comprehension in the elementary school. In L. Meltzer (Ed.), *Executive function in education: From theory to practice* (pp. 194–215). New York: Guilford.

Gauvain, M., & Munroe, R. L. (2009). Contributions of societal modernity to cognitive development: A comparison of four cultures. *Child Development, 80,* 1628–1642.

Geary, D. C. (2006). Development of mathematical understanding. In W. Damon & R. M. Lerner (Series Eds.), D. Kuhn, & R. Siegler (Vol. Eds.), *Handbook of child psychology: Vol. 1. Cognition, perception, and language* (6th ed., pp. 777–810). New York: Wiley.

Gijbels, D., Dochy, F., Van den Bossche, P., & Segers, M. (2005). Effects of problem-based learning: A meta-analysis from the angle of assessment. *Review of Educational Research, 75,* 27–61.

Gil, L., Bråten, I., Vidal-Abarca, E., & Strømsø, H. I. (2010). Summary versus argument tasks when working with multiple documents: Which is better for whom? *Contemporary Educational Psychology, 35,* 157–173.

Ginsburg, H. P., Cannon, J., Eisenband, J., & Pappas, S. (2006). Mathematical thinking and learning. In K. McCartney & D. Phillips (Eds.), *Blackwell handbook of early childhood development* (pp. 208–229). Malden, MA: Blackwell.

Goldberg, R. F., & Thompson-Schill, S. L. (2009). Developmental "roots" in mature biological knowledge. *Psychological Science, 20,* 480–487.

Goldin-Meadow, S., & Beilock, S. L. (2010). Action's influence on thought: The case of gesture. *Perspectives on Psychological Science, 5,* 664–674.

Goswami, U. (2007). Typical reading development and developmental dyslexia across languages. In D. Coch, G. Dawson, & K. W. Fischer (Eds.), *Human behavior, learning, and the developing brain: Atypical development* (pp. 145–167). New York: Guilford.

Graesser, A. C., McNamara, D. S., & VanLehn, K. (2005). Scaffolding deep comprehension strategies through Point&Query, AutoTutor, and iSTART. *Educational Psychologist, 40,* 225–234.

Graham, S. (2006). Writing. In P. A. Alexander & P. H. Winne (Eds.), *Handbook of educational psychology* (2nd ed., pp. 457–478). Mahwah, NJ: Erlbaum.

Graham, S., Harris, K. R., & Olinghouse, N. (2007). Addressing executive function problems in writing: An example from the self-regulated strategy development model. In L. Meltzer (Ed.), *Executive function in education: From theory to practice* (pp. 216–236). New York: Guilford.

Graham, S., & Perin, D. (2007). A meta-analysis of writing instruction for adolescent students. *Journal of Educational Psychology, 99,* 445–476.

Greeno, J. G., Collins, A. M., & Resnick, L. B. (1996). Cognition and learning. In D. C. Berliner & R. C. Calfee (Eds.), *Handbook of educational psychology* (pp. 15–46). New York: Macmillan.

Gregg, M., & Leinhardt, G. (1994a, April). *Constructing geography.* Paper presented at the annual meeting of the American Educational Research Association, New Orleans, LA.

Gregg, M., & Leinhardt, G. (1994b). Mapping out geography: An example of epistemology and education. *Review of Educational Research, 64,* 311–361.

Gregg, N. (2009). *Adolescents and adults with learning disabilities and ADHD: Assessment and accommodation.* New York: Guilford.

Griffin, S., & Case, R. (1996). Evaluating the breadth and depth of training effects when central conceptual structures are taught. In R. Case & Y. Okamoto (Eds.), The role of central structures in the development of children's thought. *Monographs of the Society for Research in Child Development, 61,* Serial No. 246, Nos. 1–2.

Gustafson, B. J., Mahaffy, P., Martin, B., & Gentilini, S. (2011, April). *Elementary children learning about the nature of models and the behaviour of small, unseen particles.* Paper presented at the annual meeting of the American Educational Research Association, New Orleans, LA.

Guthrie, J. T., Wigfield, A., Barbosa, P., Perencevich, K. C., Taboada, A., Davis, M. H., et al. (2004). Increasing reading comprehension and engagement through concept-oriented reading instruction. *Journal of Educational Psychology, 96,* 403–423.

Hacker, D. J., & Bol, L. (2004). Metacognitive theory: Considering the social-cognitive influences. In D. M. McNerney & S. Van Etten (Eds.), *Big theories revisited* (pp. 275–297). Greenwich, CT: Information Age.

Hacker, D. J., Dunlosky, J., & Graesser, A. C. (Eds.). (2009b). *Handbook of metacognition in education.* New York: Routledge.

Hacker, D. J., Keener, M. C., & Kircher, J. C. (2009). Writing is applied metacognition. In D. J. Hacker, J. Dunlosky, & A. C. Graesser (Eds.), *Handbook of metacognition in education* (pp. 154–172). New York: Routledge.

Halford, G. S., & Andrews, G. (2006). Reasoning and problem solving. In W. Damon & R. M. Lerner (Series Eds.), D. Kuhn, & R. Siegler (Vol. Eds.), *Handbook of child psychology: Vol. 2. Cognition, perception, and language* (6th ed., pp. 557–608). New York: Wiley.

Hallenbeck, M. J. (1996). The cognitive strategy in writing: Welcome relief for adolescents with learning disabilities. *Learning Disabilities Research and Practice, 11,* 107–119.

Harris, K. R., Santangelo, T., & Graham, S. (2010). Metacognition and strategies instruction in writing. In H. S. Waters & W. Schneider (Eds.), *Metacognition, strategy use, and instruction* (pp. 226–256). New York: Guilford.

Hartley, K., & Bendixen, L. D. (2001). Educational research in the Internet age: Examining the role of individual characteristics. *Educational Researcher, 30*(9), 22–26.

Hatano, G., & Inagaki, K. (2003). When is conceptual change intended? A cognitive-sociocultural view. In G. M. Sinatra & P. R. Pintrich (Eds.), *Intentional conceptual change* (pp. 407–427). Mahwah, NJ: Erlbaum.

Hecht, S. A., & Vagi, K. J. (2010). Sources of group and individual differences in emerging fraction skills. *Journal of Educational Psychology, 102,* 843–859.

Hemphill, L., & Snow, C. (1996). Language and literacy development: Discontinuities and differences. In D. R. Olson & N. Torrance (Eds.), *The handbook of education and human development: New models of learning, teaching, and schooling* (pp. 170–201). Cambridge, MA: Blackwell.

Herbert, J., & Stipek, D. (2005). The emergence of gender differences in children's perceptions of their academic competence. *Journal of Applied Developmental Psychology, 26,* 276–295.

Hewitt, J., Brett, C., Scardamalia, M., Frecker, K., & Webb, J. (1995, April). Supporting knowledge building through the synthesis of CSILE, FCL, & Jasper. In M. Lamon (Chair), *Schools for thought: Transforming classrooms into learning communities.* Symposium conducted at the annual meeting of the American Educational Research Association, San Francisco.

Hewitt, J., & Scardamalia, M. (1998). Design principles for distributed knowledge building processes. *Educational Psychology Review, 10,* 75–96.

Hickey, D. T. (1997). Motivation and contemporary socio-constructivist instructional perspectives. *Educational Psychologist, 32,* 175–193.

Hiebert, E. H., & Fisher, C. W. (1992). The tasks of school literacy: Trends and issues. In J. Brophy (Ed.), *Advances in research on teaching: Vol. 3. Planning and managing learning tasks and activities* (pp. 191–223). Greenwich, CT: JAI.

Hiebert, E. H., & Raphael, T. E. (1996). Psychological perspectives on literacy and extensions to educational practice. In D. C. Berliner & R. C. Calfee (Eds.), *Handbook of educational psychology* (pp. 550–602). New York: Macmillan.

Hiebert, J., Carpenter, T. P., Fennema, E., Fuson, K., Human, P., Murray, H., et al. (1996). Problem solving as a basis for reform in curriculum

and instruction: The case of mathematics. *Educational Researcher, 25*(4), 12–21.

Hmelo-Silver, C. E. (2004). Problem-based learning: What and how do students learn? *Educational Psychology Review, 16,* 235–266.

Hmelo-Silver, C. E. (2006). Design principles for scaffolding technology-based inquiry. In A. M. O'Donnell, C. E. Hmelo-SIlver, & G. Erkens (Eds.), *Collaborative learning, reasoning, and technology* (pp. 147–170). Mahwah, NJ: Erlbaum.

Hmelo-Silver, C. E., Duncan, R. G., & Chinn, C. A. (2007). Scaffolding and achievement in problem-based and inquiry learning: A response to Kirschner, Sweller, and Clark (2006). *Educational Psychologist, 42,* 99–107.

Hogan, K., Nastasi, B. K., & Pressley, M. (2000). Discourse patterns and collaborative scientific reasoning in peer and teacher-guided discussions. *Cognition and Instruction, 17,* 379–432.

Hughes, J. M., Bigler, R. S., & Levy, S. R. (2007). Consequences of learning about historical racism among European American and African American children. *Child Development, 78,* 1689–1705.

Hulme, C., & Joshi, R. M. (Eds.). (1998). *Reading and spelling: Development and disorders.* Mahwah, NJ: Erlbaum.

Hung, W., Jonassen, D. H., & Liu, R. (2008). Problem-based learning. In J. M. Spector, M. D. Merrill, J. van Merriënboer, & M. P. Driscoll (Eds.), *Handbook of research on educational communications and technology* (3rd ed., pp. 485–506). New York: Erlbaum.

Hynd, C. (1998b). Observing learning from different perspectives: What does it mean for Barry and his understanding of gravity? In B. Guzzetti & C. Hynd (Eds.), *Perspectives on conceptual change: Multiple ways to understand knowing and learning in a complex world* (pp. 235–244). Mahwah, NJ: Erlbaum.

Inglis, A., & Biemiller, A. (1997, March). *Fostering self-direction in mathematics: A cross-age tutoring program that enhances math problem solving.* Paper presented at the annual meeting of the American Educational Research Association, Chicago.

Ito, M., Baumer, S., Bittanti, M., Boyd, D., Cody, R., Herr-Stephenson, B., et al. (2009). *Hanging out, messing around, geeking out: Living and learning with new media.* Cambridge, MA: MIT Press.

Jacoby, K. (2008). *Shadows at dawn: A borderlands massacre and the violence of history.* New York: Penguin.

Janzen, J. (2008). Teaching English language learners in the content areas. *Review of Educational Research, 78,* 1010–1038.

Jetton, T. L., & Dole, J. A. (Eds.). (2004). *Adolescent literacy research and practice.* New York: Guilford.

Johnson, D. W., & Johnson, R. T. (2009b). Energizing learning: The instructional power of conflict. *Educational Researcher, 38,* 37–51.

Juel, C. (1998). What kind of one-on-one tutoring helps a poor reader? In C. Hulme & R. M. Joshi (Eds.), *Reading and spelling: Development and disorders* (pp. 449–471). Mahwah, NJ: Erlbaum.

Katzir, T., & Paré-Blagoev, J. (2006). Applying cognitive neuroscience research to education: The case of literacy. *Educational Psychologist, 41,* 53–74.

Keil, F. C., & Newman, G. E. (2008). Two tales of conceptual change: What changes and what remains the same. In S. Vosniadou (Ed.), *International handbook on conceptual change* (pp. 83–101). New York: Routledge.

Kellogg, R. T. (1994). *The psychology of writing.* New York: Oxford University Press.

Kester, L., Paas, F., & van Merriënboer, J. J. G. (2010). Instructional control of cognitive load in the design of complex learning environments. In J. L. Plass, R. Moreno, & R. Brünken (Eds.), *Cognitive Load Theory* (pp. 109–130). Cambridge, England: Cambridge University Press.

Kincheloe, J. L. (2009). No short cuts in urban education: Metropedagogy and diversity. In S. R. Steinberg (Ed.), *Diversity and multiculturalism: A reader* (pp. 379–409). New York: Peter Lang.

King, A. (1999). Discourse patterns for mediating peer learning. In A. M. O'Donnell & A. King (Eds.), *Cognitive perspectives on peer learning* (pp. 87–115). Mahwah, NJ: Erlbaum.

Kintsch, W. (2009). Learning and constructivism. In S. Tobias & T. M. Duffy (Eds.), *Constructivist instruction: Success or failure?* (pp. 223–241). New York: Routledge.

Kirsh, D. (2009). Problem solving and situated cognition. In P. Robbins & M. Aydede (Eds.), *The Cambridge handbook of situated cognition* (pp. 264–306). Cambridge, England: Cambridge University Press.

Kitayama, S. (2002). Culture and basic psychological processes—Toward a system view of culture: Comment on Oyserman et al. (2002). *Psychological Bulletin, 128,* 89–96.

Klauda, S. L., & Guthrie, J. T. (2008). Relationships of three components of reading fluency to reading comprehension. *Journal of Educational Psychology, 100,* 310–321.

Klingner, J. K., & Vaughn, S. (2004). Strategies for struggling second-language readers. In T. L. Jetton & J. A. Dole (Eds.), *Adolescent literacy research and practice* (pp. 183–209). New York: Guilford.

Knapp, N. F. (1995, April). *Tom and Joshua: Two at-risk readers at home and at school.* Paper presented at the annual meeting of the American Educational Research Association, San Francisco.

Koltko-Rivera, M. E. (2004). The psychology of worldviews. *Review of General Psychology, 8,* 3–58.

Kornhaber, M., Fierros, E., & Veenema, S. (2004). *Multiple intelligences: Best ideas from research and practice.* Boston: Allyn & Bacon.

Krajcik, J. S., & Blumenfeld, P. C. (2006). Project-based learning. In R. K. Sawyer (Ed.), *The Cambridge handbook of the learning sciences* (pp. 317–333). Cambridge, England: Cambridge University Press.

Kuhn, D. (2009). The importance of learning about knowing: Creating a foundation for development of intellectual values. *Child Development Perspectives, 3,* 112–117.

Kuhn, D., & Crowell, A. (2011). Dialogic argumentation as a vehicle for developing young adolescents' thinking. *Psychological Science, 22,* 545–552.

Kuhn, D., & Dean, D., Jr. (2005). Is developing scientific thinking all about learning to control variables? *Psychological Science, 16,* 866–870.

Kuhn, D., & Franklin, S. (2006). The second decade: What develops (and how)? In W. Damon & R. M. Lerner (Series Eds.), D. Kuhn, & R. Siegler (Vol. Eds.), *Handbook of child psychology: Vol. 2. Cognition, perception, and language* (6th ed., pp. 953–993). New York: Wiley.

Kuhn, D., & Pearsall, S. (2000). Developmental origins of scientific thinking. *Journal of Cognition and Development, 1,* 113–129.

Ladson-Billings, G. (1995b). Toward a theory of culturally relevant pedagogy. *American Educational Research Journal, 32,* 465–491.

Lampert, M., Rittenhouse, P., & Crumbaugh, C. (1996). Agreeing to disagree: Developing sociable mathematical discourse. In D. R. Olson & N. Torrance (Eds.), *The handbook of education and human development: New models of learning, teaching, and schooling* (pp. 731–764). Cambridge, MA: Blackwell.

Langer, J. A. (2011). *Envisioning knowledge: Building literacy in the academic disciplines.* New York: Teachers College Press.

Larkin, S. (2008, March). *The development of metacognition within the context of learning to write.* Paper presented at the annual meeting of the American Educational Research Association, New York.

Lave, J. (1991). Situating learning in communities of practice. In L. B. Resnick, J. M. Levine, & S. D. Teasley (Eds.), *Perspectives on socially shared cognition* (pp. 63–82). Washington, DC: American Psychological Association.

Lave, J., & Wenger, E. (1991). *Situated learning: Legitimate peripheral participation.* Cambridge, England: Cambridge University Press.

Leaper, C., & Friedman, C. K. (2007). The socialization of gender. In J. E. Grusec & P. D. Hastings (Eds.), *Handbook of socialization: Theory and research* (pp. 561–587). New York: Guilford.

Lee, P., & Ashby, R. (2001). Empathy, perspective taking, and rational understanding. In O. L. Davis, E. A. Yeager, & S. J. Foster (Eds.), *Historical empathy and perspective taking in the social studies* (pp. 21–50). Lanham, MD: Rowman & Littlefield.

Lehrer, R., & Schauble, L. (2006). Cultivating model-based reasoning in science education. In R. K. Sawyer (Ed.), *The Cambridge handbook of the learning sciences* (pp. 371–387). Cambridge, England: Cambridge University Press.

Leinhardt, G., Beck, I. L., & Stainton, C. (Eds.). (1994). *Teaching and learning in history.* Hillsdale, NJ: Erlbaum.

Leon, T. M. (2008, March). *Middle school readers comprehending, analyzing, and evaluating persuasive text.* Paper presented at the annual meeting of the American Educational Research Association, New York.

Leu, D. J., O'Byrne, W. I., Zawilinski, L., McVerry, J. G., & Everett-Cacopardo, H. (2009). Expanding the new literacies conversation. *Educational Researcher, 38,* 264–269.

Levstik, L. S. (2011). Learning history. In R. E. Mayer & P. A. Alexander (Eds.), *Handbook of research on learning and instruction* (pp. 208–126). New York: Routledge.

Li, Y., Anderson, R. C., Nguyen-Jahiel, K., Dong, T., Archodidou, A., Kim, I.-H., et al. (2007). Emergent leadership in children's discussion groups. *Cognition and Instruction, 25,* 75–111.

Liben, L. S., & Downs, R. M. (1989a). Educating with maps: Part I, the place of maps. *Teaching Thinking and Problem Solving, 11*(1), 6–9.

Liben, L. S., & Downs, R. M. (1989b). Understanding maps as symbols: The development of map concepts in children. In H. W. Reese (Ed.), *Advances in child development and behavior* (Vol. 22, pp. 145–201). San Diego, CA: Harcourt Brace Jovanovich.

Liben, L. S., & Myers, L. J. (2007). Developmental changes in children's understanding of maps: What, when, and how? In J. M. Plumert & J. P. Spencer (Eds.), *The emerging spatial mind* (pp. 193–218). New York: Oxford University Press.

Linn, M. C., & Eylon, B.-S. (2011). *Science learning and instruction: Taking advantage of technology to promote knowledge integration.* New York: Routledge.

Linn, M. C., Songer, N. B., & Eylon, B. (1996). Shifts and convergences in science learning and instruction. In D. C. Berliner & R. C. Calfee (Eds.), *Handbook of educational psychology* (pp. 438–490). New York: Macmillan.

Lipson, M. Y. (1983). The influence of religious affiliation on children's memory for text information. *Reading Research Quarterly, 18,* 448–457.

Losh, S. C. (2003). On the application of social cognition and social location to creating causal explanatory structures. *Educational Research Quarterly, 26*(3), 17–33.

MacDonald, S., Uesiliana, K., & Hayne, H. (2000). Cross-cultural and gender differences in childhood amnesia. *Memory, 8,* 365–376.

Manning, F. H., Lawless, K. A., Goldman, S. R., & Braasch, J. L. G. (2011, April). *Evaluating the usefulness of multiple sources with respect to an inquiry question: Middle school students' analysis and ranking of Internet search results.* Paper presented at the annual meeting of the American Educational Research Association, New Orleans, LA.

Marks, H. M. (2000). Student engagement in instructional activity: Patterns in the elementary, middle, and high school years. *American Educational Research Journal, 37,* 153–184.

Martínez, P., Bannan-Ritland, B., Kitsantas, A., & Baek, J. Y. (2008, March). *The impact of an integrated science reading intervention on elementary children's misconceptions regarding slow geomorphological changes caused by water.* Paper presented at the annual meeting of the American Educational Research Association, New York.

Mason, L. (2003). Personal epistemologies and intentional conceptual change. In G. M. Sinatra & P. R. Pintrich (Eds.), *Intentional conceptual change* (pp. 199–236). Mahwah, NJ: Erlbaum.

Mastropieri, M. A., & Scruggs, T. E. (1992). Science for students with disabilities. *Review of Educational Research, 62,* 377–411.

Mastropieri, M. A., & Scruggs, T. E. (2000). *The inclusive classroom: Strategies for effective instruction.* Upper Saddle River, NJ: Merrill/Prentice-Hall.

Mayer, R. E. (1982). Memory for algebra story problems. *Journal of Educational Psychology, 74,* 199–216.

Mayer, R. E. (1999). *The promise of educational psychology: Learning in the content areas.* Upper Saddle River, NJ: Merrill/Prentice Hall.

Mayer, R. E. (2008). Applying the science of learning: Evidence-based principles for the design of multimedia instruction. *American Psychologist, 63,* 760–769.

McCrink, K., & Wynn, K. (2007). Ratio abstraction by 6-month-old infants. *Psychological Science, 18,* 740–745.

McCutchen, D. (1996). A capacity theory of writing: Working memory in composition. *Educational Psychology Review, 8,* 299–325.

McDevitt, M., & Chaffee, S. H. (1998). Second chance political socialization: "Trickle-up" effects of children on parents. In T. J. Johnson, C. E. Hays, & S. P. Hays (Eds.), *Engaging the public: How government and the media can reinvigorate American democracy* (pp. 57–66). Lanhan, MD: Rowman & Littlefield.

McLane, J. B., & McNamee, G. D. (1990). *Early literacy.* Cambridge, MA: Harvard University Press.

Medin, D. L. (2005, August). *Role of culture and expertise in cognition.* Invited address presented at the annual meeting of the American Psychological Association, Washington, DC.

Meltzer, L. (Ed.) (2007). *Executive function in education: From theory to practice.* New York: Guilford.

Mergendoller, J. R., Markham, T., Ravitz, J., & Larmer, J. (2006). Pervasive management of project based learning: Teachers as guides and facilitators. In C. M. Evertson & C. S. Weinstein (Eds.), *Handbook of classroom management: Research, practice, and contemporary issues* (pp. 583–615). Mahwah, NJ: Erlbaum.

Metz, K. E. (2004). Children's understanding of scientific inquiry: Their conceptualizations of uncertainty in investigations of their own design. *Cognition and Instruction, 22,* 219–290.

Metz, K. E. (2011). Disentangling robust developmental constraints from the instructionally mutable: Young children's epistemic reasoning about a study of their own design. *Journal of the Learning Sciences, 20,* 50–110.

Minstrell, J., & Stimpson, V. (1996). A classroom environment for learning: Guiding students' reconstruction of understanding and reasoning. In L. Schauble & R. Glaser (Eds.), *Innovations in learning: New environments for education* (pp. 175–202). Mahwah, NJ: Erlbaum.

Monte-Sano, C. (2008). Qualities of historical writing instruction: A comparative case study of two teachers' practices. *American Educational Research Journal, 45,* 1045–1079.

Morra, S., Gobbo, C., Marini, Z., & Sheese, R. (2008). *Cognitive development: Neo-Piagetian perspectives*. New York: Erlbaum.

Mosborg, S. (2002). Speaking of history: How adolescents use their knowledge of history in reading the daily news. *Cognition and Instruction, 20*, 323–358.

Muis, K. R. (2004). Personal epistemology and mathematics: A critical review and synthesis of research. *Review of Educational Research, 74*, 317–377.

Mullen, M. K., & Yi, S. (1995). The cultural context of talk about the past: Implications for the development of autobiographical memory. *Cognitive Development, 10*, 407–419.

Murphy, P. K., & Mason, L. (2006). Changing knowledge and beliefs. In P. A. Alexander & P. H. Winne (Eds.), *Handbook of educational psychology* (2nd ed., pp. 305–324). Mahwah, NJ: Erlbaum.

Murphy, P. K., Wilkinson, I. A. G., & Soter, A. O. (2011). Instruction based on discussion. In R. E. Mayer & P. A. Alexander (Eds.), *Handbook of research on learning and instruction* (pp. 382–407). New York: Routledge.

Myers, L. J., & Liben, L. S. (2008). The role of intentionality and iconicity in children's developing comprehension and production of cartographic symbols. *Child Development, 79*, 668–684.

Nagy, W., Berninger, V. W., & Abbott, R. D. (2006). Contributions of morphology beyond phonology to literacy outcomes of upper elementary and middle-school students. *Journal of Educational Psychology, 98*, 134–147.

Nagy, W., Berninger, V., Abbott, R., Vaughan, K., & Vermeulen, K. (2003). Relationship of morphology and other language skills to literacy skills in at-risk second-grade readers and at-risk fourth-grade writers. *Journal of Educational Psychology, 95*, 730–742.

National Council for the Social Studies (NCSS). (1994). *Expectations of excellence: Curriculum standards for social studies*. Washington, DC: Author.

National Geographic Education Project. (1994). *Geography for life: National geography standards*. Washington, DC: National Geographic Research and Education, National Geographical Society.

Newmann, F. M., & Wehlage, G. G. (1993). Five standards of authentic instruction. *Educational Leadership, 50*(7), 8–12.

Nokes, J. D., Dole, J. A., & Hacker, D. J. (2007). Teaching high school students to use heuristics while reading historical texts. *Journal of Educational Psychology, 99*, 492–504.

Norton, E. S., Kovelman, I., & Pettito, L.-A. (2007). Are there separate neural systems for spelling? New insights into the role of rules and memory in spelling from functional magnetic resonance imaging. *Mind, Brain, and Behavior, 1*(1), 48–59.

Nussbaum, E. M. (2008). Collaborative discourse, argumentation, and learning: Preface and literature review. *Contemporary Educational Psychology, 33*, 345–359.

Oliver, B. R., Dale, P. S., & Plomin, R. (2005). Predicting literacy at age 7 from preliteracy at age 4: A longitudinal genetic analysis. *Psychological Science, 16*, 861–865.

Olsen, D. G. (1995). "Less" can be "more" in the promotion of thinking. *Social Education, 59*(3), 130–134.

Ormrod, J. E., Jackson, D. L., Kirby, B., Davis, J., & Benson, C. (1999, April). *Cognitive development as reflected in children's conceptions of early American history*. Paper presented at the annual meeting of the American Educational Research Association, Montreal, Canada.

Owens, R. E., Jr. (2008). *Language development* (7th ed.). Boston: Allyn & Bacon.

Page-Voth, V., & Graham, S. (1999). Effects of goal setting and strategy use on the writing performance and self-efficacy of students with writing and learning problems. *Journal of Educational Psychology, 91*, 230–240.

Palincsar, A. S., & Brown, A. L. (1984). Reciprocal teaching of comprehension-fostering and comprehension-monitoring activities. *Cognition and Instruction, 1*, 117–175.

Paris, S. G., & Turner, J. C. (1994). Situated motivation. In P. R. Pintrich, D. R. Brown, & C. E. Weinstein (Eds.), *Student motivation, cognition, and learning: Essays in honor of Wilbert J. McKeachie* (pp. 213–238). Mahwah, NJ: Erlbaum.

Park, D. C., & Huang, C.-M. (2010). Culture wires the brain: A cognitive neuroscience perspective. *Perspectives on Psychological Science, 5*, 391–400.

Patrick, H., Mantzicopoulos, Y., & Samarapungavan, A. (2009). Motivation for learning science in kindergarten: Is there a gender gap and does integrated inquiry and literacy instruction make a difference? *Journal of Research in Science Teaching, 46*, 166–191.

Paxton, R. J. (1999). A deafening silence: History textbooks and the students who read them. *Review of Educational Research, 69*, 315–339.

Pea, R. D. (1993). Practices of distributed intelligence and designs for education. In G. Salomon (Ed.), *Distributed cognitions: Psychological and educational considerations* (pp. 47–87). Cambridge, England: Cambridge University Press.

Pearson, P. D., Hansen, J., & Gordon, C. (1979). The effect of background knowledge on young children's comprehension of explicit and implicit information. *Journal of Reading Behavior, 11*, 201–209.

Piaget, J. (1929). *The child's conception of the world*. New York: Harcourt, Brace.

Pickens, J. (2006, Winter). "Poop study" engages primary students. *Volunteer Monitor* (National Newsletter of Volunteer Watershed Monitoring), *18*(1), 13, 21.

Piirto, J. (1999). *Talented children and adults: Their development and education* (2nd ed.). Upper Saddle River, NJ: Merrill/Prentice-Hall.

Plass, J. L., Kalyuga, S., & Leutner, D. (2010). Individual differences and Cognitive Load Theory. In J. L. Plass, R. Moreno, & R. Brünken (Eds.), *Cognitive Load Theory*

(pp. 65–87). Cambridge, England: Cambridge University Press.

Plumert, J. M., & Spencer, J. P. (Eds.). (2007). *The emerging spatial mind*. Oxford, England: Oxford University Press.

Porat, D. A. (2004). *It's not written here, but this is what happened:* Students' cultural comprehension of textbook narratives on the Israeli-Arab conflict. *American Educational Research Journal, 41*, 963–996

Posner, M. I., & Rothbart, M. K. (2007). *Educating the human brain*. Washington, DC: American Psychological Association.

Pressley, M., & Harris, K. R. (2006). Cognitive strategies instruction: From basic research to classroom instruction. In P. A. Alexander & P. H. Winne (Eds.), *Handbook of educational psychology* (2nd ed., pp. 265–286). Mahwah, NJ: Erlbaum.

Price, G. R., Holloway, I., Räsänen, P., Vesterinen, M., & Ansari, D. (2007). Impaired parietal magnitude processing in developmental dyscalculia. *Current Biology, 17*(24), 1042–1043.

Purcell-Gates, V., McIntyre, E., & Freppon, P. A. (1995). Learning written storybook language in school: A comparison of low-SES children in skills-based and whole language classrooms. *American Educational Research Journal, 32*, 659–685.

Quinlan, T. (2004). Speech recognition technology and students with writing difficulties: Improving fluency. *Journal of Educational Psychology, 96*, 337–346.

Rayner, K., Foorman, B. R., Perfetti, C. A., Pesetsky, D., & Seidenberg, M. S. (2001). How psychological science informs the teaching of reading. *Psychological Science in the Public Interest, 2*, 31–74.

Reis, S. M., McCoach, D. B., Little, C. A., Muller, L. M., & Kaniskan, R. B. (2011). The effects of differentiated instruction and enrichment pedagogy on reading achievement in five elementary schools. *American Educational Research Journal, 48*, 462–501.

Renkl, A., & Atkinson, R. K. (2010). Learning from worked-out examples and problem solving. In J. L. Plass, R. Moreno, & R. Brünken (Eds.), *Cognitive Load Theory* (pp. 91–108). Cambridge, England: Cambridge University Press.

Reynolds, R. E., Taylor, M. A., Steffensen, M. S., Shirey, L. L., & Anderson, R. C. (1982). Cultural schemata and reading comprehension. *Reading Research Quarterly, 17*, 353–366.

Rittle-Johnson, B. (2006). Promoting transfer: Effects of self-explanation and direct instruction. *Child Development, 77*, 1–15.

Rittle-Johnson, B., Siegler, R. S., & Alibali, M. W. (2001). Developing conceptual understanding and procedural skill in mathematics: An iterative process. *Journal of Educational Psychology, 93*, 346–362.

Rittle-Johnson, B., & Star, J. R. (2009). Compared with what? The effects of different comparisons on conceptual knowledge and procedural flexibility for equation solving. *Journal of Educational Psychology, 101*, 529–544.

Rivers, I., Chesney, T., & Coyne, I. (2011). Cyberbullying. In C. P. Monks & I. Coyne (Eds.), *Bullying in different contexts* (pp. 211–230). Cambridge, England: Cambridge University Press.

Roberts, T. A., & Meiring, A. (2006). Teaching phonics in the context of children's literature or spelling: Influences on first-grade reading, spelling, and writing and fifth-grade comprehension. *Journal of Educational Psychology, 98,* 690–713.

Roditi, B. N., & Steinberg, J. (2007). The strategy math classroom: Executive function processes and mathematics learning. In L. Meltzer (Ed.), *Executive function in education: From theory to practice* (pp. 237–260). New York: Guilford.

Rogoff, B. (1990). *Apprenticeship in thinking: Cognitive development in social context.* New York: Oxford University Press.

Rogoff, B. (1994, April). *Developing understanding of the idea of communities of learners.* Paper presented at the annual meeting of the American Educational Research Association, New Orleans, LA.

Rogoff, B. (2003). *The cultural nature of human development.* Oxford, England: Oxford University Press.

Rogoff, B., Matusov, E., & White, C. (1996). Models of teaching and learning: Participation in a community of learners. In D. R. Olson & N. Torrance (Eds.), *The handbook of education and human development: New models of learning, teaching, and schooling* (pp. 388–414). Cambridge, MA: Blackwell.

Rohrer, D., & Pashler, H. (2010). Recent research on human learning challenges conventional instructional strategies. *Educational Researcher, 39,* 406–412.

Rothstein-Fisch, C. & Trumbull, E. (2008). *Managing diverse classrooms: How to build on students' strengths.* Alexandria, VA: Association for Supervision and Curriculum Development.

Sacks, C. H., & Mergendoller, J. R. (1997). The relationship between teachers' theoretical orientation toward reading and student outcomes in kindergarten children with different initial reading abilities. *American Educational Research Journal, 34,* 721–739.

Salend, S. J., & Hofstetter, E. (1996). Adapting a problem-solving approach to teaching mathematics to students with mild disabilities. *Intervention in School and Clinic, 31*(4), 209–217.

Salomon, G. (1993). No distribution without individuals' cognition: A dynamic interactional view. In G. Salomon (Ed.), *Distributed cognitions: Psychological and educational considerations* (pp. 111–138). Cambridge, England: Cambridge University Press.

Sampson, M. B., Szabo, S., Falk-Ross, F., Foote, M. M., & Linder, P. E. (Eds.). (2007). *Multiple literacies in the 21st century: The twenty-eighth yearbook of the College Reading Association.* Logan, UT: College Reading Association.

Sarama, J., & Clements, D. H. (2009). "Concrete" computer manipulatives in mathematics education. *Child Development Perspectives, 3,* 145–150.

Sawyer, R. K., & Greeno, J. G. (2009). Situativity and learning. In P. Robbins & M. Aydede (Eds.), *The Cambridge handbook of situated cognition* (pp. 347–367). Cambridge, England: Cambridge University Press.

Saxe, G. B., & Esmonde, I. (2005). Studying cognition in flux: A historical treatment of *fu* in the shifting structure of Oksapmin mathematics. *Mind, Culture, and Activity, 12,* 171–225.

Scardamalia, M., & Bereiter, C. (1986). Research on written composition. In M. C. Wittrock (Ed.), *Handbook of research on teaching* (3rd ed., pp. 778–803). New York: Macmillan.

Scardamalia, M., & Bereiter, C. (2006). Knowledge building: Theory, pedagogy, and technology. In R. K. Sawyer (Ed.), *The Cambridge handbook of the learning sciences* (pp. 97–115). Cambridge, England: Cambridge University Press.

Schatschneider, C., Fletcher, J. M., Francis, D. J., Carlson, C. D., & Foorman, B. R. (2004). Kindergarten prediction of reading skills: A longitudinal comparative analysis. *Journal of Educational Psychology, 96,* 265–282.

Schauble, L. (1996). The development of scientific reasoning in knowledge-rich contexts. *Developmental Psychology, 32,* 102–119.

Schoenfeld, A. H. (1988). When good teaching leads to bad results: The disasters of "well-taught" mathematics courses. *Educational Psychologist, 23,* 145–166.

Schoenfeld, A. H. (1992). Learning to think mathematically: Problem solving, metacognition, and sense making in mathematics. In D. A. Grouws (Ed.), *Handbook of research on mathematics teaching and learning* (pp. 334–370). New York: Macmillan.

Schwarz, B. B., Neuman, Y., & Biezuner, S. (2000). Two wrongs may make a right . . . if they argue together! *Cognition and Instruction, 18,* 461–494.

Serpell, R., Baker, L., & Sonnenschein, S. (2005). *Becoming literate in the city: The Baltimore Early Childhood Project.* Cambridge, England: Cambridge University Press.

Shanahan, C. (2004). Teaching science through literacy. In T. L. Jetton & J. A. Dole (Eds.), *Adolescent literacy research and practice* (pp. 75–93). New York: Guilford.

Shanahan, T., & Tierney, R. J. (1990). Reading–writing connections: The relations among three perspectives. In J. Zutell & S. McCormick (Eds.), *Literacy theory and research: Analyses from multiple paradigms. Thirty-ninth yearbook of the National Reading Conference* (pp. 13–34). Chicago: National Reading Conference.

Share, D. L. (1995). Phonological recoding and self-teaching: Sine qua non of reading acquisition. *Cognition, 55,* 151–218.

Shaywitz, S. E., Mody, M., & Shaywitz, B. A. (2006). Neural mechanisms in dyslexia. *Current Directions in Psychological Science, 15,* 278–281.

Siegler, R. S. (1989). Mechanisms of cognitive growth. *Annual Review of Psychology, 40,* 353–379.

Siegler, R. S., & Jenkins, E. (1989). *How children discover new strategies.* Hillsdale, NJ: Erlbaum.

Sinatra, G. M., & Pintrich, P. R. (Eds.). (2003). *Intentional conceptual change.* Mahwah, NJ: Erlbaum.

Singer, J., Marx, R. W., Krajcik, J., & Chambers, J. C. (2000). Constructing extended inquiry projects: Curriculum materials for science education reform. *Educational Psychologist, 35,* 165–178.

Sitko, B. M. (1998). Knowing how to write: Metacognition and writing instruction. In D. J. Hacker, J. Dunlosky, & A. C. Graesser (Eds.), *Metacognition in educational theory and practice* (pp. 93–115). Mahwah, NJ: Erlbaum.

Slavin, R. E., Lake, C., Chambers, B., Cheung, A., & Davis, S. (2009). Effective reading programs for the elementary grades: A best-evidence synthesis. *Review of Educational Research, 79,* 1391–1466.

Smith, C. L. (2007). Bootstrapping processes in the development of students' commonsense matter theories: Using analogical mappings, thought experiments, and learning to measure to promote conceptual restructuring. *Cognition and Instruction, 25,* 337–398.

Smith, E. R., & Conrey, F. R. (2009). The social context of cognition. In P. Robbins & M. Aydede (Eds.), *The Cambridge handbook of situated cognition* (pp. 454–466). Cambridge, England: Cambridge University Press.

Snir, J., Smith, C. L., & Raz, G. (2003). Linking phenomena with competing underlying models: A software tool for introducing students to the particulate model of matter. *Science Education, 87,* 794–830.

Snowling, M. J., Gallagher, A., & Frith, U. (2003). Family risk of dyslexia is continuous: Individual differences in the precursors of reading skill. *Child Development, 74,* 358–373.

Southerland, S. A., & Sinatra, G. M. (2003). Learning about biological evolution: A special case of intentional conceptual change. In G. M. Sinatra & P. R. Pintrich (Eds.), *Intentional conceptual change* (pp. 317–345). Mahwah, NJ: Erlbaum.

Spiro, R. J., & DeSchryver, M. (2009). Constructivism: When it's the wrong idea and when it's the only idea. In S. Tobias & T. M. Duffy (Eds.), *Constructivist instruction: Success or failure?* (pp. 106–123). New York: Routledge.

Spivey, N. N. (1997). *The constructivist metaphor: Reading, writing, and the making of meaning.* San Diego, CA: Academic Press.

Spörer, N., & Brunstein, J. C. (2009). Fostering the reading comprehension of secondary school students through peer-assisted learning: Effects on strategy knowledge, strategy use, and task performance. *Contemporary Educational Psychology, 34,* 289–297.

Spunt, R. P., Falk, E. B., & Lieberman, M. D. (2010). Dissociable neural systems support retrieval of *how* and *why* action knowledge. *Psychological Science, 21,* 1593–1598.

Squire, K. (2011). *Video games and learning: Teaching and participatory culture in the digital age.* New York: Teachers College Press.

Stahl, G., Koschmann, T., & Suthers, D. D. (2006). Computer-supported collaborative learning. In R. K. Sawyer (Ed.), *The Cambridge handbook of the learning sciences* (pp. 409–425). Cambridge, England: Cambridge University Press.

Stahl, S. A., & Miller, P. D. (1989). Whole language and language experience approaches for beginning reading: A quantitative research synthesis. *Review of Educational Research, 59,* 87–116.

Stahl, S. A., & Shanahan, C. (2004). Learning to think like a historian: Disciplinary knowledge through critical analysis of multiple documents. In T. L. Jetton & J. A. Dole (Eds.), *Adolescent literacy research and practice* (pp. 94–115). New York: Guilford.

Stanovich, K. E. (2000). *Progress in understanding reading: Scientific foundations and new frontiers.* New York: Guilford.

Steffensen, M. S., Joag-Dev, C., & Anderson, R. C. (1979). A cross-cultural perspective on reading comprehension. *Reading Research Quarterly, 15,* 10–29.

Stuebing, K. K., Barth, A. E., Cirino, P. T., Francis, D. J., & Fletcher, J. M. (2008). A response to recent reanalyses of the National Reading Panel Report: Effects of systematic phonics instruction are practically significant. *Journal of Educational Psychology, 100,* 123–134.

Swanson, H. L. (2006). Cross-sectional and incremental changes in working memory and mathematical problem solving. *Journal of Educational Psychology, 98,* 265–281.

Swanson, H. L., Cooney, J. B., & O'Shaughnessy, T. E. (1998). Learning disabilities and memory. In B. Y. L. Wong (Ed.), *Learning about learning disabilities* (2nd ed., pp. 107–162). San Diego, CA: Academic Press.

Sweller, J., Kirschner, P. A., & Clark, R. E. (2007). Why minimally guided teaching techniques do not work: A reply to commentaries. *Educational Psychologist, 42,* 115–121.

Tate, W. F. (1995). Returning to the root: A culturally relevant approach to mathematics pedagogy. *Theory into Practice, 34,* 166–173.

Thompson, M., & Grace, C. O. (with Cohen, L. J.) (2001). *Best friends, worst enemies: Understanding the social lives of children.* New York: Ballantine.

Tompkins, G. E., & McGee, L. M. (1986). Visually impaired and sighted children's emerging concepts about written language. In D. B. Yaden, Jr., & S. Templeton (Eds.), *Metalinguistic awareness and beginning literacy: Conceptualizing what it means to read and write* (pp. 259–275). Portsmouth, NH: Heinemann.

Tourniaire, F., & Pulos, S. (1985). Proportional reasoning: A review of the literature. *Educational Studies in Mathematics, 16,* 181–204.

Trawick-Smith, J. (2003). *Early childhood development: A multicultural perspective* (3rd ed.). Upper Saddle River, NJ: Merrill/Prentice-Hall.

Turkanis, C. G. (2001). Creating curriculum with children. In B. Rogoff, C. G. Turkanis, & L. Bartlett (Eds.), *Learning together: Children and adults in a school community* (pp. 91–102). New York: Oxford University Press.

Turnbull, A. P., Turnbull, R., & Wehmeyer, M. L. (2010). *Exceptional lives: Special education in today's schools* (6th ed.). Upper Saddle River, NJ: Merrill.

Turner, J. C. (1995). The influence of classroom contexts on young children's motivation for literacy. *Reading Research Quarterly, 30,* 410–441.

Vadasy, P. F., Sanders, E. A., & Peyton, J. A. (2006). Code-oriented instruction for kindergarten students at risk for reading difficulties: A randomized field trial with paraeducator implementers. *Journal of Educational Psychology, 98,* 508–528.

Valkenburg, P. M., & Peter, J. (2009). Social consequences of the Internet for adolescents: A decade of research. *Current Directions in Psychological Science, 18,* 1–5.

van den Broek, P., Lynch, J. S., Naslund, J., Ievers-Landis, C. E., & Verduin, K. (2003). The development of comprehension of main ideas in narratives: Evidence from the selection of titles. *Journal of Educational Psychology, 95,* 707–718.

van Drie, J., van Boxtel, C., & van der Linden, J. (2006). Historical reasoning in a computer-supported collaborative learning environment. In A. M. O'Donnell, C. E. Hmelo-SIlver, & G. Erkens (Eds.), *Collaborative learning, reasoning, and technology* (pp. 265–296). Mahwah, NJ: Erlbaum.

VanLehn, K. (2011). The relative effectiveness of human tutoring, intelligent tutoring systems, and other tutoring systems. *Educational Psychologist, 46,* 197–221.

vanSledright, B., & Limón, M. (2006). Learning and teaching social studies: A review of cognitive research in history and geography. In P. A. Alexander & P. H. Winne (Eds.), *Handbook of educational psychology* (2nd ed., pp. 545–570). Mahwah, NJ: Erlbaum.

Verhallen, M. J. A. J., Bus, A. G., & de Jong, M. T. (2006). The promise of multimedia stories for kindergarten children at risk. *Journal of Educational Psychology, 98,* 410–419.

Vidal-Abarca, E., Martínez, G., & Gilabert, R. (2000). Two procedures to improve instructional text: Effects on memory and learning. *Journal of Educational Psychology, 92,* 1–10.

Vosniadou, S. (Ed.). (2008). *International handbook of research on conceptual change.* New York: Routledge.

Vygotsky, L. S. (1978). *Mind in society: The development of higher psychological processes.* Cambridge, MA: Harvard University Press.

Vygotsky, L. S. (1986). *Thought and language* (rev. ed; A. Kozulin, Ed. and Trans.). Cambridge, MA: MIT Press. (Original work published 1934)

Walshaw, M., & Anthony, G. (2008). The teacher's role in classroom discourse: A review of recent research into mathematics classrooms. *Review of Educational Research, 78,* 516–551.

Wang, Q., & Ross, M. (2007). Culture and memory. In S. Kitayama & D. Cohen (Eds.), *Handbook of cultural psychology* (pp. 645–667). New York: Guilford.

Warschauer, M. (2011). *Learning in the cloud: How (and why) to transform schools with digital media.* New York: Teachers College Press.

Wasley, P. A., Hampel, R. L., & Clark, R. W. (1997). *Kids and school reform.* San Francisco: Jossey-Bass.

Webb, N. M., & Farivar, S. (1994). Promoting helping behavior in cooperative small groups in middle school mathematics. *American Educational Research Journal, 31,* 369–395.

Webb, N. M., & Palincsar, A. S. (1996). Group processes in the classroom. In D. C. Berliner & R. C. Calfee (Eds.), *Handbook of educational psychology* (pp. 841–873). New York: Macmillan.

Wenger, E. (1998). *Communities of practice: Learning, meaning, and identity.* Cambridge, England: Cambridge University Press.

Wentzel, K. R., & Watkins, D. E. (2011). Instruction based on peer interactions. In R. E. Mayer & P. A. Alexander (Eds.), *Handbook of research on learning and instruction* (pp. 322–343). New York: Routledge.

White, B., Frederiksen, J., & Collins, A. (2009). The interplay of scientific inquiry and metacognition: More than a marriage of convenience. In D. J. Hacker, J. Dunlosky, & A. C. Graesser (Eds.), *Handbook of metacognition in education* (pp. 175–205). New York: Routledge.

White, T., & Pea, R. (2011). Distributed by design: On the promises and pitfalls of collaborative learning with multiple representations. *Journal of the Learning Sciences, 20,* 489–547.

Wigfield, A., Byrnes, J. P., & Eccles, J. S. (2006). Development during early and middle adolescence. In P. A. Alexander & P. H. Winne (Eds.), *Handbook of educational psychology* (2nd ed., pp. 87–113). Mahwah, NJ: Erlbaum.

Wiley, J., Goldman, S. R., Graesser, A. C., Sanchez, C. A., Ash, I. K., & Hemmerich, J. A. (2009). Source evaluation, comprehension, and learning in Internet science inquiry tasks. *American Educational Research Journal, 46,* 1060–1106.

Williams, J. P., Stafford, K. B., Lauer, K. D., Hall, K. M., & Pollini, S. (2009). Embedding reading comprehension training in content-area instruction. *Journal of Educational Psychology, 101,* 1–20.

Wilson, A. J., & Dehaene, S. (2007). Number sense and developmental dyscalculia. In D. Coch, G. Dawson, & K. W. Fischer (Eds.), *Human behavior, learning, and the developing brain: Atypical development* (pp. 212–238). New York: Guilford.

Wimmer, H., Landerl, K., & Frith, U. (1999). Learning to read German: Normal and impaired acquisition. In M. Harris & G. Hatano (Eds.), *Learning to read and write: A cross-linguistic perspective* (pp. 34–50). Cambridge, England: Cambridge University Press.

Wirkala, C., & Kuhn, D. (2011). Problem-based learning in K–12 education: Is it effective and how does it achieve its effects? *American Educational Research Journal, 48,* 1157–1186.

Wiser, M., & Smith, C. L. (2008). Learning and teaching about matter in grades K–8: When should the atomic–molecular theory be introduced? In S. Vosniadou (Ed.), *International handbook on conceptual change* (pp. 205–231). New York: Routledge.

Wolfe, M. B. W., & Goldman, S. R. (2005). Relations between adolescents' text processing and reasoning. *Cognition and Instruction, 23,* 467–502.

Wood, D. K., Frank, A. R., & Wacker, D. P. (1998). Teaching multiplication facts to students with learning disabilities. *Journal of Applied Behavior Analysis, 31,* 323–338.

Woolf, B. P. (2009). *Building intelligent interactive tutors: Student-centered strategies for revolutionizing e-learning.* Burlington, MA: Morgan Kaufmann/Elsevier.

Xue, Y., & Meisels, S. J. (2004). Early literacy instruction and learning in kindergarten: Evidence from the early childhood longitudinal study—Kindergarten class of 1998–1999. *American Educational Research Journal, 41,* 191–229.

Yeager, E. A., Foster, S. J., Maley, S. D., Anderson, T., Morris, J. W., III, & Davis, O. L., Jr. (1997, March). *The role of empathy in the development of historical understanding.* Paper presented at the annual meeting of the American Educational Research Association, Chicago.

Zaragoza, J. M., & Fraser, B. J. (2008, March). Learning environments and attitudes among elementary-school students in traditional environmental science and field-study classrooms. Paper presented at the annual meeting of the American Educational Research Association, New York.

Zhang, J., Scardamalia, M., Reeve, R., & Messina, R. (2009). Designs for collective cognitive responsibility in knowledge-building communities. *Journal of the Learning Sciences, 18*(1), 7–44.

Zohar, A., & Aharon-Kraversky, S. (2005). Exploring the effects of cognitive conflict and direct teaching for students of different academic levels. *Journal of Research in Science Teaching, 42,* 829–855.

Zusho, A., & Clayton, K. (2011). Culturalizing achievement goal theory and research. *Educational Psychologist, 46,* 239–260.

## CHAPTER 9

Alberto, P. A., & Troutman, A. C. (2013). *Applied behavior analysis for teachers* (9th ed.). Upper Saddle River, NJ: Merrill/Pearson.

American Psychological Association Zero Tolerance Task Force (2008). Are zero tolerance policies effective in the schools? An evidentiary review and recommendations. *American Psychologist, 63,* 852–862.

Anderman, E. M., & Anderman, L. H. (2010). *Classroom motivation.* Upper Saddle River, NJ: Pearson.

Anderman, E. M., & Mueller, C. E. (2010). Middle school transitions and adolescent development. In J. Meece & J. Eccles (Eds.), *Handbook of research on schools, schooling, and human development* (pp. 198–215). Mahwah, NJ: Erlbaum.

Anderman, L. H., Patrick, H., Hruda, L. Z., & Linnenbrink, E. A. (2002). Observing classroom goal structures to clarify and expand goal theory. In C. Midgley (Ed.), *Goals, goal structures, and patterns of adaptive learning* (pp. 243–278). Mahwah, NJ: Erlbaum.

Appel, J. B., & Peterson, N. J. (1965). Punishment: Effects of shock intensity on response suppression. *Psychological Reports, 16,* 721–730.

Ardoin, S. P., Martens, B. K., & Wolfe, L. A. (1999). Using high-probability instructional sequences with fading to increase student compliance during transitions. *Journal of Applied Behavior Analysis, 32,* 339–351.

Atance, C. M. (2008). Future thinking in young children. *Current Directions in Psychological Science, 17,* 295–298.

Austin, J. L, & Soeda, J. M. (2008). Fixed-time teacher attention to decrease off-task behaviors of typically developing third graders. *Journal of Applied Behavior Analysis, 41,* 279–283.

Azrin, N. H. (1960). Effects of punishment intensity during variable-interval reinforcement. *Journal of the Experimental Analysis of Behavior, 3,* 123–142.

Azrin, N. H., Vinas, V., & Ehle, C. T. (2007). Physical activity as reinforcement for classroom calmness of ADHD children: A preliminary study. *Child and Family Behavior Therapy, 29,* 1–8.

Ballenger, C., (1992). Because you like us: The language of control. *Harvard Educational Review, 62,* 199–208.

Bangert-Drowns, R. L., Kulik, C. C., Kulik, J. A., & Morgan, M. (1991). The instructional effect of feedback in test-like events. *Review of Educational Research, 61,* 213–238.

Barbetta, P. M. (1990). GOALS: A group-oriented adapted levels system for children with behavior disorders. *Academic Therapy, 25,* 645–656.

Barbetta, P. M., Heward, W. L., Bradley, D. M., & Miller, A. D. (1994). Effects of immediate and delayed error correction on the acquisition and maintenance of sight words by students with developmental disabilities. *Journal of Applied Behavior Analysis, 27,* 177–178.

Barrish, H. H., Saunders, M., & Wolf, M. M. (1969). Good behavior game: Effects of individual contingencies for group consequences on disruptive behavior in a classroom. *Journal of Applied Behavior Analysis, 2,* 119–124.

Bay-Hinitz, A. K., Peterson, R. F., & Quilitch, H. R. (1994). Cooperative games: A way to modify aggressive and cooperative behaviors in young children. *Journal of Applied Behavior Analysis, 27,* 435–446.

Beirne-Smith, M.,, Patton, J. R., & Kim, S. H. (2006). *Mental retardation: An introduction to intellectual disabilities* (7th ed.). Upper Saddle River, NJ: Merrill/Prentice Hall.

Belfiore, P. J., Lee, D. L., Vargas, A. U., & Skinner, C. H. (1997). Effects of high-preference single-digit mathematics problem completion on multiple-digit mathematics problem performance. *Journal of Applied Behavior Analysis, 30,* 327–330.

Bembenutty, H., & Karabenick, S. A. (2004). Inherent association between academic delay of gratification, future time perspective, and self-regulated learning. *Educational Psychology Review, 16,* 35–57.

Berg, W. K., Wacker, D. P., Cigrand, K., Merkle, S., Wade J., Henry, K., et al. (2007). Comparing functional analysis and paired-choice assessment results in classroom settings. *Journal of Applied Behavior Analysis, 40,* 545–552.

Binder, L. M., Dixon, M. R., & Ghezzi, P. M. (2000). A procedure to teach self-control to children with attention deficit hyperactivity disorder. *Journal of Applied Behavior Analysis, 33,* 233–237.

Boyanton, D., (2010). Behaviorism and its effect upon learning in the schools. In G. S. Goodman (Ed.), *Educational psychology reader: The art and science of how people learn* (pp. 49–65). New York: Peter Lang.

Brendgen, M., Wanner, G., Vitaro, F., Bukowski, W. M., & Tremblay, R. E. (2007). Verbal abuse by the teacher during childhood and academic, behavioral, and emotional adjustment in young adulthood. *Journal of Educational Psychology, 99,* 26–38.

Brown, W. H., Fox, J. J., & Brady, M. P. (1987). Effects of spatial density on 3- and 4-year-old children's socially directed behavior during freeplay: An investigation of a setting factor. *Education and Treatment of Children, 10,* 247–258.

Buchoff, T., (1990). Attention deficit disorder: Help for the classroom teacher. *Childhood Education, 67,* 86–90.

Burnett, P., (2001). Elementary students' preferences for teacher praise. *Journal of Classroom Interaction, 36,* 16–23.

Butler, D. L., & Winne, P. H. (1995). Feedback and self-regulated learning: A theoretical synthesis. *Review of Educational Research, 65,* 245–281.

Cameron, J., (2001). Negative effects of reward on intrinsic motivation—A limited phenomenon: Comment on Deci, Koestner, and Ryan (2001). *Review of Educational Research, 71,* 29–42.

Cammilleri, A. P., Tiger, J. H., & Hanley, G. P. (2008). Developing stimulus control of young children's requests to teachers: Classwide applications of multiple schedules. *Journal of Applied Behavior Analysis, 41,* 299–303.

Carey, R. G., & Bucher, B., (1983). Positive practice overcorrection: The effects of duration of positive practice on acquisition and response reduction. *Journal of Applied Behavior Analysis, 16,* 101–109.

Christenson, S. L., & Thurlow, M. L. (2004). School dropouts: Prevention, considerations, interventions, and challenges. *Current Directions in Psychological Science, 13,* 36–39.

Cizek, G. J. (2003). *Detecting and preventing classroom cheating: Promoting integrity in assessment.* Thousand Oaks, CA: Corwin.

Conyers, C., Miltenberger, R., Maki, A., Barenz, R., Jurgens, M., Sailer, A., et al. (2004). A comparison of response cost and differential reinforcement of other behavior to reduce disruptive behavior in a preschool classroom. *Journal of Applied Behavior Analysis, 37,* 411–415.

Cooper, H., (1989). Synthesis of research on homework. *Educational Leadership, 47*(3), 85–91.

Cooper, J. O., Heron, T. E., & Heward, W. L. (2007). *Applied behavior analysis* (2nd ed.). Upper Saddle River, NJ: Pearson/Merrill/Prentice-Hall.

Corno, L., (1996). Homework is a complicated thing. *Educational Researcher, 25*(8), 27–30.

Covington, M. V. (1992). *Making the grade: A self-worth perspective on motivation and school reform.* Cambridge, England: Cambridge University Press.

Craft, M. A., Alberg, S. R., & Heward, W. L. (1998). Teaching elementary students with developmental disabilities to recruit teacher attention in a general education classroom: Effects on teacher praise and academic productivity. *Journal of Applied Behavior Analysis, 31*, 399–415.

Crone, D. A., & Horner, R. H. (2003). *Building positive behavior support systems in schools: Functional behavioral assessment.* New York: Guilford.

Cuskelly, M., Zhang, A., & Hayes, A., (2003). A mental age-matched comparison study of delay of gratification in children with Down syndrome. *International Journal of Disability, Development and Education, 50*, 239–251.

Deci, E. L., Koestner, R., & Ryan, R. M. (2001). Extrinsic rewards and intrinsic motivation in education: Reconsidered once again. *Review of Educational Research, 71*, 1–27.

Deci, E. L., & Moller, A. C. (2005). The concept of competence: A starting place for understanding intrinsic motivation and self-determined extrinsic motivation. In A. J. Elliot & C. S. Dweck (Eds.), *Handbook of competence and motivation* (pp. 579–597). New York: Guilford.

Deci, E. L., & Ryan, R. M. (1985). *Intrinsic motivation and self-determination in human behavior.* New York: Plenum.

DeGrandpre, R. J. (2000). A science of meaning: Can behaviorism bring meaning to psychological science? *American Psychologist, 55*, 721–739.

DeVault, G., Krug, C., & Fake, S., (1996, September). Why does Samantha act that way: Positive behavioral support leads to successful inclusion. *Exceptional Parent*, 43–47.

Donaldson, J. M., & Vollmer, T. R. (2011). An evaluation and comparison of time-out procedures with and without release contingencies. *Journal of Applied Behavior Analysis, 44*, 693–705.

Donaldson, J. M., Vollmer, T. R., Krous, T., Downs, S., & Berard, K. P. (2011). An evaluation of the good behavior game in kindergarten classrooms. *Journal of Applied Behavior Analysis, 44*, 605–609.

Doyle, W., (1990). Classroom management techniques. In O. C. Moles (Ed.), *Student discipline strategies: Research and practice* (pp. 113–127). Albany: State University of New York Press.

Dreikurs, R., (1998). *Maintaining sanity in the classroom: Classroom management teehniques* (2nd ed.). Bristol, PA: Hemisphere.

Ebbinghaus, H., (1913). *Memory: A contribution to experimental psychology* (H. A. Ruger & C. E. Bussenius, Trans.) New York: Teachers College, Columbia University. (Original work published 1885)

Elliott, S. N., & Busse, R. T. (1991). Social skills assessment and intervention with children and adolescents. *School Psychology International, 12*, 63–83.

Ellis, E. S., & Friend, P., (1991). Adolescents with learning disabilities. In B. Y. L. Wong (Ed.), *Learning about learning disabilities* (pp. 505–561). San Diego, CA: Academic Press.

Ellis, J., Fitzsimmons, S., & Small-McGinley, J., (2010). Encouraging the discouraged: Students' views for elementary classrooms. In G. S. Goodman (Ed.), *Educational psychology reader: The art and science of how people learn* (pp. 251–272). New York: Peter Lang.

Emmer, E. T. (1987). Classroom management and discipline. In V. Richardson-Koehler (Ed.), *Educators' handbook: A research perspective* (pp. 233–258). White Plains, NY: Longman.

Evertson, C. M., & Weinstein, C. S. (Eds.). (2006). *Handbook of classroom management: Research, practice, and contemporary issues.* Mahwah, NJ: Erlbaum.

Feltz, D. L., Chase, M. A., Moritz, S. E., & Sullivan, P. J. (1999). A conceptual model of coaching efficacy: Preliminary investigation and instrument development. *Journal of Educational Psychology, 91*, 765–776.

Ferster, C. B., & Skinner, B. F. (1957). *Schedules of reinforcement.* Englewood Cliffs, NJ: Prentice-Hall.

Fowler, S. A., & Baer, D. M. (1981). "Do I have to be good all day?" The timing of delayed reinforcement as a factor in generalization. *Journal of Applied Behavior Analysis, 14*, 13–24.

Freeland, J. T., & Noell, G. H. (1999). Maintaining accurate math responses in elementary school students: The effects of delayed intermittent reinforcement and programming common stimuli. *Journal of Applied Behavior Analysis, 32*, 211–215.

Frost, J. L., Shin, D., & Jacobs, P. J. (1998). Physical environments and children's play. In O. N. Saracho & B. Spodek (Eds.), *Multiple perspectives on play in early childhood education* (pp. 255–294). Albany: State University of New York Press.

Fuller, M. L. (2001). Multicultural concerns and classroom management. In C. A. Grant & M. L. Gomez, *Campus and classroom: Making schooling multicultural* (2nd ed., pp. 109–134). Upper Saddle River, NJ: Merrill/Prentice-Hall.

Galton, F., (1880). Statistics of mental imagery. *Mind, 5*, 301–318.

Geckeler, A. S., Libby, M. E., Graff, R. B., & Ahearn, W. H. (2000). Effects of reinforcer choice measured in single-operant and concurrent-schedule procedures. *Journal of Applied Behavior Analysis, 33*, 347–351.

Goldstein, S., & Rider, R., (2006). Resilience and the disruptive disorders of childhood. In. S. Goldstein & R. B. Brooks (Eds.), *Handbook of resilience in children* (pp. 203–222). New York: Springer.

Gootman, M. E. (1998). Effective in-house suspension. *Educational Leadership, 56*(1), 39–41.

Grauvogel-MacAleese, A. N., & Wallace, M. D. (2010). Use of peer-mediated intervention in children with attention deficit hyperactivity disorder. *Journal of Applied Behavior Analysis, 43*, 547–551.

Green, L., Fry, A. F., & Myerson, J., (1994). Discounting of delayed rewards: A life-span comparison. *Psychological Science, 5*, 33–36.

Gregory, A., Skiba, R. J., & Noguera, P. A. (2010). The achievement gap and the discipline gap: Two sides of the same coin? *Educational Researcher, 39*, 59–68.

Hall, R. V., Axelrod, S., Foundopoulos, M., Shellman, J., Campbell, R. A., & Cranston, S. S. (1971). The effective use of punishment to modify behavior in the classroom. *Educational Technology, 11*(4), 24–26.

Haring, N. G., & Liberty, K. A. (1990). Matching strategies with performance in facilitating generalization. *Focus on Exceptional Children, 22*(8), 1–16.

Harlow, H. F., & Zimmerman, R. R. (1959). Affectional responses in the infant monkey. *Science, 130*, 421–432.

Hattie, J., & Gan, M., (2011). Instruction based on feedback. In R. E. Mayer & P. A. Alexander (Eds.), *Handbook of research on learning and instruction* (pp. 249–271). New York: Routledge.

Hattie, J., & Timperley, H., (2007). The power of feedback. *Review of Educational Research, 77*, 81–112.

Heck, A., Collins, J., & Peterson, L., (2001). Decreasing children's risk taking on the playground. *Journal of Applied Behavior Analysis, 34*, 349–352.

Heward, W. L. (2009). *Exceptional children: An introduction to special education* (9th ed.). Upper Saddle River, NJ: Merrill/Pearson Education.

Hidi, S., & Harackiewicz, J. M. (2000). Motivating the academically unmotivated: A critical issue for the 21st century. *Review of Educational Research, 70*, 151–179.

Hine, P., & Fraser, B. J. (2002, April). *Combining qualitative and quantitative methods in a study of Australian students' transition from elementary to high school.* Paper presented at the annual meeting of the American Educational Research Association, New Orleans, LA.

Hobson, P., (2004). *The cradle of thought: Exploring the origins of thinking.* Oxford, England: Oxford University Press.

Hoerger, M. L., & Mace, F. C. (2006). A computerized test of self-control predicts classroom behavior. *Journal of Applied Behavior Analysis, 39*, 147–159.

Hoffman, M. L. (1975). Altruistic behavior and the parent-child relationship. *Journal of Personality and Social Psychology, 31*, 937–943.

Hoffman, M. L. (2000). *Empathy and moral development: Implications for caring and justice.* New York: Cambridge University Press.

Homme, L. E., deBaca, P. C., Devine, J. V., Steinhorst, R., & Rickert, E. J. (1963). Use of the Premack principle in controlling the behavior of nursery school children. *Journal of the Experimental Analysis of Behavior, 6*, 544.

Huff, J. A. (1988). Personalized behavior modification: An in-school suspension program that teaches students how to change. *School Counselor, 35,* 210–214.

Hyman, I., Kay, B., Tabori, A., Weber, M., Mahon, M., & Cohen, I., (2006). Bullying: Theory, research, and interventions. In C. M. Evertson & C. S. Weinstein (Eds.), *Handbook of classroom management: Research, practice, and contemporary issues* (pp. 855–884). Mahwah, NJ: Erlbaum.

Igoa, C., (1995). *The inner world of the immigrant child.* Mahwah, NJ: Erlbaum.

Ihlo, T., & Nantais, M., (2010). Evidence-based interventions within a multi-tier framework for positive behavioral supports. In T. A. Glover & S. Vaughn (Eds.), *The promise of response to intervention: Evaluating current science and practice* (pp. 239–266). New York: Guilford.

James, W., (1890). *The principles of psychology.* New York: Holt.

Jiang, B., (2010). English language learners: Understanding their needs. In G. S. Goodman (Ed.), *Educational psychology reader: The art and science of how people learn* (pp. 179–194). New York: Peter Lang.

Johnson, B. M., Miltenberger, R. G., Knudson, P., Emego-Helm, K., Kelso, P., Jostad, C., et al. (2006). A preliminary evaluation of two behavioral skills training procedures for teaching abduction-prevention skills to schoolchildren. *Journal of Applied Behavior Analysis, 39,* 25–34.

Johnson, D. W., & Johnson, R. T. (1987). *Learning together and alone: Cooperative, competitive, and individualistic learning* (2nd ed.). Englewood Cliffs, NJ: Prentice-Hall.

Jones, M. C. (1924). The elimination of children's fears. *Journal of Experimental Psychology, 7,* 382–390.

Kellam, S. G., Rebok, G. W., Ialongo, N., & Mayer, L. S. (1994). The course and malleability of aggressive behavior from early first grade into middle school: Results of a developmental epidemiology-based preventive trial. *Journal of Child Psychology and Psychiatry and Allied Disciplines, 35,* 259–281.

Kelley, M. L., & Carper, L. B. (1988). Home-based reinforcement procedures. In J. C. Witt, S. N. Elliott, & F. M. Gresham (Eds.), *Handbook of behavior therapy in education* (pp. 419–438). New York: Plenum.

Kitayama, S., Duffy, S., & Uchida, Y., (2007). Self as cultural mode of being. In S. Kitayama & D. Cohen (Eds.), *Handbook of cultural psychology* (pp. 136–174). New York: Guilford.

Krumboltz, J. D., & Krumboltz, H. B. (1972). *Changing children's behavior.* Upper Saddle River, NJ: Prentice-Hall.

Kulik, J. A., & Kulik, C. C. (1988). Timing of feedback and verbal learning. *Review of Educational Research, 58,* 79–97.

Landau, S., & McAninch, C., (1993). Young children with attention deficits. *Young Children, 48*(4), 49–58.

Landrum, T. J., & Kauffman, J. M. (2006). Behavioral approaches to classroom management. In C. M. Evertson & C. S. Weinstein (Eds.), *Handbook of classroom management: Research, practice, and contemporary issues* (pp. 47–71). Mahwah, NJ: Erlbaum.

Lane, K., Falk, K., & Wehby, J., (2006). Classroom management in special education classrooms and resource rooms. In C. M. Evertson & C. S. Weinstein (Eds.), *Handbook of classroom management: Research, practice, and contemporary issues* (pp. 439–460). Mahwah, NJ: Erlbaum.

Lane, K. L., Menzies, H. M., Bruhn, A. L., & Crnobori, M., (2011). *Managing challenging behaviors in schools: Research-based strategies that work.* New York: Guilford.

Lannie, A. L., & Martens, B. K. (2004). Effects of task difficulty and type of contingency on students' allocation of responding to math worksheets. *Journal of Applied Behavior Analysis, 37,* 53–65.

Lejuez, C. W., Schaal, D. W., & O'Donnell, J., (1998). Behavioral pharmacology and the treatment of substance abuse. In J. J. Plaud & G. H. Eifert (Eds.), *From behavior theory to behavior therapy* (pp. 116–135). Boston: Allyn & Bacon.

Lepper, M. R., & Hodell, M., (1989). Intrinsic motivation in the classroom. In C. Ames & R. Ames (Eds.), *Research on motivation in education: Vol. 3. Goals and cognitions* (pp. 73–105). San Diego, CA: Academic Press.

Lerman, D. C., & Iwata, B. A. (1995). Prevalence of the extinction burst and its attenuation during treatment. *Journal of Applied Behavior Analysis, 28,* 93–94.

Lerman, D. C., Kelley, M. E., Vorndran, C. M., Kuhn, S. A. C., & LaRue, R. H., Jr. (2002). Reinforcement magnitude and responding during treatment with differential reinforcement. *Journal of Applied Behavior Analysis, 35,* 29–48.

Lerman, D. C., & Vorndran, C. M. (2002). On the status of knowledge for using punishment: Implications for treating behavior disorders. *Journal of Applied Behavior Analysis, 35,* 431–464.

Lewis, T. J., Newcomer, L. L., Trussell, R., & Richter, M., (2006). Schoolwide positive behavior support: Building systems to develop and maintain appropriate social behavior. In C. M. Evertson & C. S. Weinstein (Eds.), *Handbook of classroom management: Research, practice, and contemporary issues* (pp. 833–854). Mahwah, NJ: Erlbaum.

Lovitt, T. C., Guppy, T. E., & Blattner, J. E. (1969). The use of free-time contingency with fourth graders to increase spelling accuracy. *Behaviour Research and Therapy, 7,* 151–156.

Mace, F. C., Hock, M. L., Lalli, J. S., West, B. J., Belfiore, P., Pinter, E., et al. (1988). Behavioral momentum in the treatment of noncompliance. *Journal of Applied Behavior Analysis, 21,* 123–141.

Martin, S. S., Brady, M. P., & Williams, R. E. (1991). Effects of toys on the social behavior of preschool children in integrated and nonintegrated groups: Investigation of a setting event. *Journal of Early Intervention, 15,* 153–161.

Maxmell, D., Jarrett, O. S., & Dickerson, C., (1998, April). *Are we forgetting the children's needs? Recess through the children's eyes.* Paper presented at the annual meeting of the American Educational Research Association, San Diego, CA.

McCaslin, M., & Good, T. L. (1996). The informal curriculum. In D. C. Berliner & R. C. Calfee (Eds.), *Handbook of educational psychology* (pp. 622–670). New York: Macmillan.

McClowry, S. G. (1998). The science and art of using temperament as the basis for intervention. *School Psychology Review, 27,* 551–563.

McComas, J. J., Thompson, A., & Johnson, L., (2003). The effects of presession attention on problem behavior maintained by different reinforcers. *Journal of Applied Behavior Analysis, 36,* 297–307.

McGill, P., (1999). Establishing operations: Implications for the assessment, treatment, and prevention of problem behavior. *Journal of Applied Behavior Analysis, 32,* 393–418.

McGinnis, M. A., Houchins-Juárez, N., McDaniel, J. L., & Kennedy, C. H. (2010). Abolishing and establishing operation analyses of social attention as positive reinforcement for problem behavior. *Journal of Applied Behavior Analysis, 43,* 119–123.

Mercer, C. D., & Pullen, P. C. (2005). *Students with learning disabilities* (6th ed.). Upper Saddle River, NJ: Merrill/Prentice-Hall.

Meyer, K. A. (1999). Functional analysis and treatment of problem behavior exhibited by elementary school children. *Journal of Applied Behavior Analysis, 32,* 229–232.

Michael, J., (2000). Implications and refinements of the establishing operation concept. *Journal of Applied Behavior Analysis, 33,* 401–410.

Miller, D. L., & Kelley, M. L. (1994). The use of goal setting and contingency contracting for improving children's homework performance. *Journal of Applied Behavior Analysis, 27,* 73–84.

Miller, R. R., & Barnet, R. C. (1993). The role of time in elementary associations. *Current Directions in Psychological Science, 2,* 106–111.

Mineka, S., & Zinbarg, R., (2006). A contemporary learning theory perspective on the etiology of anxiety disorders: It's not what you thought it was. *American Psychologist, 61,* 10–26.

Moles, O. C. (Ed.). (1990). *Student discipline strategies: Research and practice.* Albany: State University of New York Press.

Mueller, M. M., Nkosi, A., & Hine, J. F. (2011). Functional analysis in public schools: A summary of 90 functional analyses. *Journal of Applied Behavior Analysis, 44,* 807–818.

Murphy, E. S., McSweeney, F. K., Smith, R. G., & McComas, J. J. (2003). Dynamic changes in reinforcer effectiveness: Theoretical, methological, and practical implications for applied research. *Journal of Applied Behavior Analysis, 36,* 421–438.

Narciss, S., (2008). Feedback strategies for interactive learning tasks. In J. M. Spector, M. D. Merrill, J., van Merriënboer, & M. P. Driscoll (Eds.), *Handbook of research on educational communications and technology* (3rd ed., pp. 125–143). New York: Erlbaum.

Neef, N. A., Marckel, J., Ferreri, S. J., Bicard, D. F., Endo, S., Aman, M. G., et al. (2005). Behavioral assessment of impulsivity: A comparison of children with and without attention deficit hyperactivity disorder. *Journal of Applied Behavior Analysis, 38,* 23–37.

Nichols, J. D., Ludwin, W. G., & Iadicola, P., (1999). A darker shade of gray: A year-end analysis of discipline and suspension data. *Equity and Excellence in Education, 32*(1), 43–55.

Northup, J., Broussard, C., Jones, K., George, T., Vollmer, T. R., & Herring, M., (1995). The differential effects of teachers and peer attention on the disruptive classroom behavior of three children with a diagnosis of attention deficit hyperactivity disorder. *Journal of Applied Behavior Analysis, 28,* 227–228.

Nucci, L. P. (2001). *Education in the moral domain.* Cambridge, England: Cambridge University Press.

Osher, D., Bear, G. G., Sprague, J. R., & Doyle, W., (2010). How can we improve school discipline? *Educational Researcher, 39,* 48–58.

Parke, R. D. (1974). Rules, roles, and resistance to deviation: Explorations in punishment, discipline, and self-control. In A. Pick (Ed.), *Minnesota Symposia on Child Psychology* (Vol. 8, pp. 111–144). Minneapolis: University of Minnesota Press.

Patton, J. R., Blackbourn, J. M., & Fad, K. S. (1996). *Exceptional individuals in focus* (6th ed.). Upper Saddle River, NJ: Merrill/Prentice-Hall.

Pavlov, I. P. (1927). *Conditioned reflexes* (G. V. Anrep, Trans.). London: Oxford University Press.

Pellegrini, A. D., & Bohn, C. M. (2005). The role of recess in children's cognitive performance and school adjustment. *Educational Researcher, 34*(1), 13–19.

Pellegrini, A. D., Huberty, P. D., & Jones, I., (1995). The effects of recess timing on children's playground and classroom behaviors. *American Educational Research Journal, 32,* 845–864.

Perry, D. G., & Perry, L. C. (1983). Social learning, causal attribution, and moral internalization. In J. Bisanz, G. L. Bisanz, & R. Kail (Eds.), *Learning in children: Progress in cognitive development research* (pp. 105–136). New York: Springer-Verlag.

Pfiffner, L. J., Barkley, R. A., & DuPaul, G. J. (2006). Treatment of ADHD in school settings. In R. A. Barkley, *Attention-deficit hyperactivity disorder: A handbook for diagnosis and treatment* (3rd ed., pp. 547–589). New York: Guilford.

Pfiffner, L. J., & O'Leary, S. G. (1993). School-based psychological treatments. In J. L. Matson (Ed.), *Handbook of hyperactivity in children* (pp. 234–255). Boston: Allyn & Bacon.

Pfiffner, L. J., Rosen, L. A., & O'Leary, S. G. (1985). The efficacy of an all-positive approach to classroom management. *Journal of Applied Behavior Analysis, 18,* 257–261.

Phillips, E. L., Phillips, E. A., Fixsen, D. L., & Wolf, M. M. (1971). Achievement place: Modification of the behaviors of predelinquent boys within a token economy. *Journal of Applied Behavior Analysis, 4,* 45–59.

Piersel, W. C. (1987). Basic skills education. In C. A. Maher & S. G. Forman (Eds.), *A*

*behavioral approach to education of children and youth* (pp. 39–74). Mahwah, NJ: Erlbaum.

Pigott, H. E., Fantuzzo, J. W., & Clement, P. W. (1986). The effects of reciprocal peer tutoring and group contingencies on the academic performance of elementary school children. *Journal of Applied Behavior Analysis, 19,* 93–98.

Piirto, J., (1999). *Talented children and adults: Their development and education* (2nd ed.). Upper Saddle River, NJ: Merrill/Prentice-Hall.

Pintrich, P. R., & Schunk, D. H. (2002). *Motivation in education: Theory, research, and applications* (2nd ed.). Upper Saddle River, NJ: Merrill/Prentice-Hall.

Pipkin, C. S. P., & Vollmer, T. R. (2009). Applied implications of reinforcement history effects. *Journal of Applied Behavior Analysis, 42,* 83–103.

Pipkin, C. S., Vollmer, T. R., & Sloman, K. N. (2010). Effects of treatment integrity failures during differential reinforcement of alternative behavior: A translational model. *Journal of Applied Behavior Analysis, 43,* 47–70.

Powers, M. D., & Crowel, R. L. (1985). The educative effects of positive practice overcorrection: Acquisition, generalization, and maintenance. *School Psychology Review, 14,* 360–372.

Premack, D., (1959). Toward empirical behavior laws: I. Positive reinforcement. *Psychological Review, 66,* 219–233.

Premack, D., (1963). Rate differential reinforcement in monkey manipulation. *Journal of Experimental Analysis of Behavior, 6,* 81–89.

Pressley, M., with McCormick, C. B. (1995). *Advanced educational psychology for educators, researchers, and policymakers.* New York: HarperCollins.

Rachlin, H., (1991). *Introduction to modern behaviorism* (3rd ed.). New York: Freeman.

Reeve, J., (2006). Extrinsic rewards and inner motivation. In C. M. Evertson & C. S. Weinstein (Eds.), *Handbook of classroom management: Research, practice, and contemporary issues* (pp. 645–664.). Mahwah, NJ: Erlbaum.

Rescorla, R. A. (1967). Pavlovian conditioning and its proper control procedures. *Psychological Review, 74,* 71–80.

Rescorla, R. A. (1988). Pavlovian conditioning: It's not what you think it is. *American Psychologist, 43,* 151–160.

Ricciardi, J. N., Luiselli, J. K., & Camare, M., (2006). Shaping approach responses as intervention for specific phobia in a child with autism. *Journal of Applied Behavior Analysis, 39,* 445–448.

Rimm, D. C., & Masters, J. C. (1974). *Behavior therapy: Techniques and empirical findings.* San Diego, CA: Academic Press.

Rispoli, M., O'Reilly, M., Lang, R., Machalicek, W., Davis, T., Lancioni, G., et al. (2011). Effects of motivating operations on problem and academic behavior in classrooms. *Journal of Applied Behavior Analysis, 44,* 187–192.

Robinson, S. L., & Griesemer, S. M. R. (2006). Helping individual students with problem behavior. In C. M. Evertson & C. S. Weinstein (Eds.), *Handbook of classroom management: Research, practice, and contemporary issues* (pp. 787–802). Mahwah, NJ: Erlbaum.

Rodriguez, N. M., Thompson, R. H., & Baynham, T. Y. (2010). Assessment of the relative effects of attention and escape on noncompliance. *Journal of Applied Behavior Analysis, 43,* 143–147.

Rortvedt, A. K., & Miltenberger, R. G. (1994). Analysis of a high-probability instructional sequence and time-out in the treatment of child noncompliance. *Journal of Applied Behavior Analysis, 27,* 327–330.

Rotenberg, K. J., & Mayer, E. V. (1990). Delay of gratification in Native and White children: A cross-cultural comparison. *International Journal of Behavioral Development, 13,* 23–30.

Rothbart, M. K. (2011). *Becoming who we are: Temperament and personality in development.* New York: Guilford.

Ruef, M. B., Higgins, C., Glaeser, B., & Patnode, M., (1998). Positive behavioral support: Strategies for teachers. *Intervention in School and Clinic, 34*(1), 21–32.

Sanders, M. G. (1996). Action teams in action: Interviews and observations in three schools in the Baltimore School–Family–Community Partnership Program. *Journal of Education for Students Placed at Risk, 1,* 249–262.

Schunk, D. H., & Pajares, F., (2005). Competence perceptions and academic functioning. In A. J. Elliot & C. S. Dweck (Eds.), *Handbook of competence and motivation* (pp. 85–104). New York: Guilford.

Shabani, D. B., Katz, R. C., Wilder, D. A., Beauchamp, K., Taylor, C. R., & Fischer, K. J. (2002). Increasing social initiations in children with autism: Effects of a tactile prompt. *Journal of Applied Behavior Analysis, 35,* 79–83.

Shoda, Y., Mischel, W., & Peake, P. K. (1990). Predicting adolescent cognitive and self-regulatory competencies from preschool delay of gratification: Identifying diagnostic conditions. *Developmental Psychology, 26,* 978–986.

Shute, V. J. (2008). Focus on formative feedback. *Review of Educational Research, 78,* 153–189.

Skinner, B. F. (1938). *The behavior of organisms: An experimental analysis.* Englewood Cliffs, NJ: Prentice-Hall.

Skinner, B. F. (1953). *Science and human behavior.* New York: Macmillan.

Skinner, B. F. (1954). The science of learning and the art of teaching. *Harvard Educational Review, 24,* 86–97.

Skinner, B. F. (1968). *The technology of teaching.* New York: Appleton-Century-Crofts.

Skinner, B. F., & Epstein, R., (1982). *Skinner for the classroom.* Champaign, IL: Research Press.

Slavin, R. E. (1983). When does cooperative learning increase student achievement? *Psychological Bulletin, 94,* 429–445.

Sran, S. K., & Borrero, J. C. (2010). Assessing the value of choice in a token system. *Journal of Applied Behavior Analysis, 43,* 553–557.

Steinberg, L., Graham, S., O'Brien, L., Woolard, J., Cauffman, E., & Banich, M., (2009). Age differences in future orientation and delay discounting. *Child Development, 80,* 28–44.

Stokes, J. V., Luiselli, J. K., & Reed, D. D. (2010). A behavioral intervention for teaching tackling skills to high school football athletes. *Journal of Applied Behavior Analysis, 43,* 509–512.

Stokes, J. V., Luiselli, J. K., Reed, D. D., & Fleming, R. K. (2010). Behavioral coaching to improve offensive line pass-blocking skills of high school football athletes. *Journal of Applied Behavior Analysis, 43,* 463–472.

Stokes, T. F., & Baer, D. M. (1977). An implicit technology of generalization. *Journal of Applied Behavior Analysis, 10,* 349–367.

Sullivan, J. S. (1989). Planning, implementing, and maintaining an effective in-school suspension program. *Clearing House, 62,* 409–410.

Taub, J., & Pearrow, M., (2006). Resilience through violence prevention in schools. In. S. Goldstein & R. B. Brooks (Eds.), *Handbook of resilience in children* (pp. 357–371). New York: Springer.

Taylor, J. C., & Romanczyk, R. G. (1994). Generating hypotheses about the function of student problem behavior by observing teacher behavior. *Journal of Applied Behavior Analysis, 27,* 251–265.

Tiger, J. H., Hanley, G. P., & Hernandez, E., (2006). An evaluation of the value of choice with preschool children. *Journal of Applied Behavior Analysis, 39,* 1–16.

Tunstall, P., & Gipps, C., (1996). Teacher feedback to young children in formative assessment: A typology. *British Educational Research Journal, 22,* 389–404.

Turnbull, A. P., Turnbull, R., & Wehmeyer, M. L. (2010). *Exceptional lives: Special education in today's schools* (6th ed.). Upper Saddle River, NJ: Merrill.

Ulke-Kurcuoglu, B., & Kircaali-Iftar, G., (2010). A comparison of the effects of providing activity and material choice to children with autism spectrum disorders. *Journal of Applied Behavior Analysis, 43,* 717–721.

Urdan, T., & Mestas, M., (2006). The goals behind performance goals. *Journal of Educational Psychology, 98,* 354–365.

Van Camp, C. M., Lerman, D. C., Kelley, M. E., Roane, H. S., Contrucci, S. A., & Vorndran, C. M. (2000). Further analysis of idiosyncratic antecedent influences during the assessment and treatment of problem behavior. *Journal of Applied Behavior Analysis, 33,* 207–221.

Van Houten, R., Nau, P., MacKenzie-Keating, S., Sameoto, D., & Colavecchia, B., (1982). An analysis of some variables influencing the effectiveness of reprimands. *Journal of Applied Behavior Analysis, 15,* 65–83.

Vollmer, T. R., & Hackenberg, T. D. (2001). Reinforcement contingencies and social reinforcement: Some reciprocal relations between basic and applied research. *Journal of Applied Behavior Analysis, 34,* 241–253.

Wang, M.,-T., & Holcombe, R., (2010). Adolescents' perceptions of school environment, engagement, and academic achievement in middle school. *American Educational Research Journal, 47,* 633–662.

Warren, J. S., Bohanon-Edmonson, H. M., Turnbull, A. P., Sailor, W., Wickham, D., Griggs, P., et al. (2006). School-wide positive behavior support: Addressing behavior problems that impeded student learning. *Educational Psychology Review, 18,* 187–198.

Watson, J. B., & Rayner, R., (1920). Conditioned emotional reactions. *Journal of Experimental Psychology, 3,* 1–14.

Wheeler, J. J., & Richey, D. D. (2010). *Behavior management: Principles and practices of positive behavioral supports* (2nd ed.). Columbus, OH: Merrill/Pearson.

White, A. G., & Bailey, J. S. (1990). Reducing disruptive behaviors of elementary physical education students with sit and watch. *Journal of Applied Behavior Analysis, 23,* 353–359.

Wolpe, J., & Plaud, J. J. (1997). Pavlov's contributions to behavior therapy: The obvious and the not so obvious. *American Psychologist, 52,* 966–972.

Woolfolk, A. E., & Brooks, D. M. (1985). The influence of teachers' nonverbal behaviors on students' perceptions and performances. *Elementary School Journal, 85,* 513–528.

Zambo, D., & Brem, S. K. (2004). Emotion and cognition in students who struggle to read: New insights and ideas. *Reading Psychology, 25,* 1–16.

## CHAPTER 10

Aikins, J. W., & Litwack, S. D. (2011). Prosocial skills, social competence, and popularity. In A. H. N. Cillessen, D. Schwartz, & L. Mayeux (Eds.), *Popularity in the peer system* (pp. 140–162). New York: Guilford.

Anderson, C. A., Berkowitz, L., Donnerstein, E., Huesmann, L. R., Johnson, J. D., Linz, D., et al. (2003). The influence of media violence on youth. *Psychological Science in the Public Interest, 4,* 81–110.

Anderson, D. R. (2003). The Children's Television Act: A public policy that benefits children. *Applied Developmental Psychology, 24,* 337–340.

Anderson, L. H. (1999). *Speak.* New York: Puffin Books.

Anderson, R. C., Nguyen-Jahiel, K., McNurlen, B., Archodidou, A., Kim, S.-Y., Reznitskaya, A., et al. (2001). The snowball phenomenon: Spread of ways of talking and ways of thinking across groups of children. *Cognition and Instruction, 19,* 1–46.

Arbib, M. (Ed.). (2005). *Action to language via the mirror neuron system.* New York: Cambridge University Press.

Assor, A., & Connell, J. P. (1992). The validity of students' self-reports as measures of performance affecting self-appraisals. In D. H. Schunk & J. L. Meece (Eds.), *Student perceptions in the classroom* (pp. 25–46). Mahwah, NJ: Erlbaum.

Bandura, A. (1965). Influence of models' reinforcement contingencies on the acquisition of imitative responses. *Journal of Personality and Social Psychology, 1,* 589–595.

Bandura, A. (1977). *Social learning theory.* Upper Saddle River, NJ: Prentice-Hall.

Bandura, A. (1982). Self-efficacy mechanism in human agency. *American Psychologist, 37,* 122–147.

Bandura, A. (1986). *Social foundations of thought and action: A social cognitive theory.* Upper Saddle River, NJ: Prentice-Hall.

Bandura, A. (1989). Human agency in social cognitive theory. *American Psychologist, 44,* 1175–1184.

Bandura, A. (1997). *Self-efficacy: The exercise of control.* New York: Freeman.

Bandura, A. (2000). Exercise of human agency through collective efficacy. *Current Directions in Psychological Science, 9,* 75–78.

Bandura, A. (2008). Toward an agentic theory of the self. In H. W. Marsh, R. G. Craven, & D. M. McInerney (Eds.), *Self-processes, learning, and enabling human potential* (pp. 15–49). Charlotte, NC: Information Age.

Bandura, A., Barbaranelli, C., Caprara, G. V., & Pastorelli, C. (2001). Self-efficacy beliefs as shapers of children's aspirations and career trajectories. *Child Development, 72,* 187–206.

Bandura, A., Ross, D., & Ross, S. A. (1961). Transmission of aggression through imitation of aggressive models. *Journal of Abnormal and Social Psychology, 63,* 575–582.

Bandura, A., Ross, D., & Ross, S. A. (1963). Imitation of film-mediated aggressive models. *Journal of Abnormal and Social Psychology, 66,* 3–11.

Bates, J. E., & Pettit, G. S. (2007). Temperament, parenting, and socialization. In J. E. Grusec & P. D. Hastings (Eds.), *Handbook of socialization: Theory and research* (pp. 153–177). New York: Guilford.

Bear, P., Torgerson, C., & Dubois-Gerchak, K. (2010). A positive procedure to increase compliance in the general education classroom for a student with serious emotional disorders. In G. S. Goodman (Ed.), *Educational psychology reader: The art and science of how people learn* (pp. 75–87). New York: Peter Lang.

Beirne-Smith, M., Patton, J. R., & Kim, S. H. (2006). *Mental retardation: An introduction to intellectual disabilities* (7th ed.). Upper Saddle River, NJ: Merrill/Prentice-Hall.

Belfiore, P. J., & Hornyak, R. S. (1998). Operant theory and application to self-monitoring in adolescents. In D. H. Schunk & B. J. Zimmerman (Eds.), *Self-regulated learning: From teaching to self-reflective practice* (pp. 184–202). New York: Guilford.

Berardi-Coletta, B., Buyer, L. S., Dominowski, R. L., & Rellinger, E. A. (1995). Metacognition and problem solving: A process-oriented approach. *Journal of Experimental Psychology: Learning, Memory, and Cognition, 21,* 205–223.

Berger. J.-L., & Karabenick, S. A.. (2010, April–May). *Changes and reciprocal causation of expectancy–value and learning strategy use in math over one term of high school.* Paper presented at the annual meeting of the American Educational Research Association, Denver.

Biemiller, A., Shany, M., Inglis, A., & Meichenbaum, D. (1998). Factors influencing children's acquisition and demonstration of self-regulation on academic tasks. In D. H. Schunk & B. J. Zimmerman (Eds.), *Self-regulated learning: From teaching to self-reflective practice* (pp. 203–224). New York: Guilford.

Blair, C. (2002). School readiness: Integrating cognition and emotion in a neurobiological conceptualization of children's functioning at school entry. *American Psychologist, 57,* 111–127.

Blair, C., & Razza, R. P. (2007). Relating effortful control, executive function, and false belief understanding to emerging math and literacy ability in kindergarten. *Child Development, 78,* 647–663.

Blanchard, F. A., Lilly, T., & Vaughn, L. A. (1991). Reducing the expression of racial prejudice. *Psychological Science, 2,* 101–105.

Bong, M., & Skaalvik, E. M. (2003). Academic self-concept and self-efficacy: How different are they really? *Educational Psychology Review, 15,* 1–40.

Boyer, E., Miltenberger, R. G., Batsche, C., & Fogel, V. (2009). Video modeling by experts with video feedback to enhance gymnastics skills. *Journal of Applied Behavior Analysis, 42,* 855–860.

Braaksma, M. A. H., Rijlaarsdam, G., & van den Bergh, H. (2002). Observational learning and the effects of model-observer similarity. *Journal of Educational Psychology, 94,* 405–415.

Braun, L. J. (1998). *The cat who saw stars.* New York: G. P. Putnam's Sons.

Bronson, M. B. (2000). *Self-regulation in early childhood: Nature and nurture.* New York: Guilford.

Bryan, J. H. (1975). Children's cooperation and helping behaviors. In E. M. Hetherington (Ed.), *Review of child development research* (Vol. 5, pp. 127–181). Chicago: University of Chicago Press.

Buckley, M., & Saarni, C. (2009). Emotion regulation: Implications for positive youth development. In R. Gilman, E. S. Huebner, & M. J. Furlong (Eds.), *Handbook of positive psychology in schools* (pp. 107–118). New York: Routledge.

Bushman, B. J., & Anderson, C. A. (2001). Media violence and the American public: Scientific facts versus media misinformation. *American Psychologist, 56,* 477–489.

Butler, D. L., & Winne, P. H. (1995). Feedback and self-regulated learning: A theoretical synthesis. *Review of Educational Research, 65,* 245–281.

Butler, R. (1990). The effects of mastery and competitive conditions on self-assessment at different ages. *Child Development, 61,* 201–210.

Butler, R. (1998a). Age trends in the use of social and temporal comparison for self-evaluation: Examination of a novel developmental hypothesis. *Child Development, 69,* 1054–1073.

Butler, R. (1998b). Determinants of help seeking: Relations between perceived reasons for classroom help-avoidance and help-seeking behaviors in an experimental context. *Journal of Educational Psychology, 90,* 630–644.

Butler, R. (2005). Competence assessment, competence, and motivation between early and middle childhood. In A. J. Elliot & C. S. Dweck (Eds.), *Handbook of competence and motivation* (pp. 202–221). New York: Guilford.

Carnagey, N. L., Anderson, C. A., & Bartholow, B. D. (2007). Media violence and social neuroscience: New questions and new opportunities. *Current Directions in Psychological Science, 16,* 178–182.

Carter, K., & Doyle, W. (2006). Classroom management in early childhood and elementary classrooms. In C. M. Evertson & C. S. Weinstein (Eds.), *Handbook of classroom management: Research, practice, and contemporary issues* (pp. 373–406). Mahwah, NJ: Erlbaum.

Carver, C. S., & Scheier, M. F. (1990). Origins and functions of positive and negative affect: A control-process view. *Psychological Review, 97,* 19–35.

Casella, R. (2001a). The cultural foundations of peer mediation: Beyond a behaviorist model of urban school conflict. In J. N. Burstyn, G. Bender, R. Casella, H. W. Gordon, D. P. Guerra, K. V. Luschen, R. Stevens, & K. M. Williams, *Preventing violence in schools: A challenge to American democracy* (pp. 159–179). Mahwah, NJ: Erlbaum.

Casey, W. M., & Burton, R. V. (1982). Training children to be consistently honest through verbal self-instructions. *Child Development, 53,* 911–919.

Castagno, A. E., & Brayboy, B. M. J. (2008). Culturally responsive schooling for Indigenous youth: A review of the literature. *Review of Educational Research, 78,* 941–993.

Chen, J., & Morris, D. (2008, March). *Sources of science self-efficacy beliefs among high school students in different tracking levels.* Paper presented at the annual meeting of the American Educational Research Association, New York.

Chen, P. P. (2003). Exploring the accuracy and predictability of the self-efficacy beliefs of seventh-grade mathematics students. *Learning and Individual Differences, 14,* 79–92.

Chen, X., & Wang, L. (2010). China. In M. H. Bornstein (Ed.), *Handbook of cultural developmental science* (pp. 429–444). New York: Psychology Press.

Coch, D., Dawson, G., & Fischer, K. W. (Eds.). (2007). *Human behavior, learning, and the developing brain: Atypical development.* New York: Guilford.

Cohen, R. L. (1989). Memory for action events: The power of enactment. *Educational Psychology Review, 1,* 57–80.

Cole, D. A., Martin, J. M., Peeke, L. A., Seroczynski, A. D., & Fier, J. (1999). Children's over- and underestimation of academic competence: A longitudinal study of gender differences, depression, and anxiety. *Child Development, 70,* 459–473.

Cole, P. M., Tamang, B. L., & Shrestha, S. (2006). Cultural variations in the socialization of young children's anger and shame. *Child Development, 77,* 1237–1251.

Cooney, C. (1997). *Wanted.* New York: Scholastic.

Cooper, J. O., Heron, T. E., & Heward, W. L. (2007). *Applied behavior analysis* (2nd ed.). Upper Saddle River, NJ: Pearson/Merrill/Prentice-Hall.

Corno, L., Cronbach, L. J., Kupermintz, H., Lohman, D. F., Mandinach, E. B., Porteu, A. W., et al. (2002). *Remaking the concept of aptitude: Extending the legacy of Richard E. Snow.* Mahwah, NJ: Erlbaum.

Corno, L., & Mandinach, E. B. (2004). What we have learned about student engagement in the past twenty years. In D. M. McInerney & S. Van Etten (Eds.), *Big theories revisited* (pp. 299–328). Greenwich, CT: Information Age.

Cosden, M., Morrison, G., Albanese, A. L., & Macias, S. (2001). When homework is not home work: After-school programs for homework assistance. *Educational Psychologist, 36,* 211–221.

Covington, M. V. (1992). *Making the grade: A self-worth perspective on motivation and school reform.* Cambridge, England: Cambridge University Press.

Cunningham, C. E., & Cunningham, L. J. (2006). Student-mediated conflict resolution programs. In R. A. Barkley, *Attention-deficit hyperactivity disorder: A handbook for diagnosis and treatment* (3rd ed., pp. 590–607). New York: Guilford.

Damon, W. (1988). *The moral child: Nurturing children's natural moral growth.* New York: Free Press.

Dapretto, M., Davies, M. S., Pfeifer, J. H., Scott, A. A., Sigman, M., Bookheimer, S. Y, et al. (2006). Understanding emotions in others: Mirror neuron dysfunction in children with autism spectrum disorders. *Nature Neuroscience, 9*(1), 28–30.

Deci, E. L., & Ryan, R. M. (1985). *Intrinsic motivation and self-determination in human behavior.* New York: Plenum.

Deci, E. L., & Ryan, R. M. (1992). The initiation and regulation of intrinsically motivated learning and achievement. In A. K. Boggiano & T. S. Pittman (Eds.), *Achievement and motivation: A social-developmental perspective* (pp. 9–36). Cambridge, England: Cambridge University Press.

Desoete, A., Roeyers, H., & De Clercq, A. (2003). Can offline metacognition enhance mathematical problem solving? *Journal of Educational Psychology, 95,* 188–200.

Deutsch, M. (1993). Educating for a peaceful world. *American Psychologist, 48,* 510–517.

Dijkstra, P., Kuyper, H., van der Werf, G., Buunk, A. P., & van der Zee, Y. G. (2008). Social comparison in the classroom: A review. *Review of Educational Research, 78,* 828–879.

Duckworth, A. L., & Seligman, M. E. P. (2005). Self-discipline outdoes IQ in predicting academic performance of adolescents. *Psychological Science, 16,* 939–944.

Dunning, D., Heath, C., & Suls, J. M. (2004). Flawed self-assessment: Implications for health, education, and the workplace. *Psychological Science in the Public Interest, 5,* 69–106.

DuPaul, G., & Hoff, K. (1998). Reducing disruptive behavior in general education classrooms: The use of self-management strategies. *School Psychology Review, 27,* 290–304.

Dweck, C. S. (2000). *Self-theories: Their role in motivation, personality, and development.* Philadelphia: Psychology Press.

Eccles, J. S., Wigfield, A., & Schiefele, U. (1998). Motivation to succeed. In W. Damon (Series Ed.) & N. Eisenberg (Vol. Ed.), *Handbook of child psychology: Vol. 3. Social, emotional, and personality development* (5th ed., pp. 1017–1095). New York: Wiley.

Eilam, B. (2001). Primary strategies for promoting homework performance. *American Educational Research Journal, 38,* 691–725.

Eisenberg, N., Vaughan, J., & Hofer, C. (2009). Temperament, self-regulation, and peer social competence. In K. H. Rubin, W. M. Bukowski, &

B. Laursen (Eds.), *Handbook of peer interactions, relationships, and groups* (pp. 473–489). New York: Guilford.

Elliott, R., & Vasta, R. (1970). The modeling of sharing: Effects associated with vicarious reinforcement, symbolization, age, and generalization. *Journal of Experimental Child Psychology, 10*, 8–15.

Elliott, S. N., & Busse, R. T. (1991). Social skills assessment and intervention with children and adolescents. *School Psychology International, 12*, 63–83.

Ellis, E. S., & Friend, P. (1991). Adolescents with learning disabilities. In B. Y. L. Wong (Ed.), *Learning about learning disabilities* (pp. 505–561). San Diego, CA: Academic Press.

Falco, L. D. (2008, March). *Improving middle school students' self-beliefs for learning mathematics: A Skill Builders intervention follow-up.* Paper presented at the annual meeting of the American Educational Research Association, New York.

Féry, Y.-A., & Morizot, P. (2000). Kinesthetic and visual image in modeling closed motor skills: The example of the tennis serve. *Perceptual and Motor Skills, 90*, 707–722.

Fitzsimmons, G. M., & Finkel, E. J. (2010). Interpersonal influences on self-regulation. *Current Directions in Psychological Science, 19*, 101–105.

Fletcher, J. M., Lyon, G. R., Fuchs, L. S., & Barnes, M. A. (2007). *Learning disabilities: From identification to intervention.* New York: Guilford.

Fletcher, K. L., & Cassady, J. C. (2010). Overcoming academic anxieties: Promoting effective coping and self-regulation strategies. In J. C. Cassady (Ed.), *Anxiety in schools: The causes, consequences, and solutions for academic anxieties* (pp. 177–200). New York: Peter Lang.

Ford, M. E. (1992). *Motivating humans: Goals, emotions, and personal agency beliefs.* Newbury Park, CA: Sage.

Försterling, F., & Morgenstern, M. (2002). Accuracy of self-assessment and task performance: Does it pay to know the truth? *Journal of Educational Psychology, 94*, 576–585.

Fries, S., Dietz, F., & Schmid, S. (2008). Motivational interference in learning: The impact of leisure alternatives on subsequent self-regulation. *Contemporary Educational Psychology, 33*, 119–133.

Gallese, V., Gernsbacher, M. A., Heyes, C., Hickok, G., & Iacoboni, M. (2011). Mirror neuron forum. *Perspectives on Psychological Science, 6*, 369–407.

Geiger, K. B., LeBlanc, L. A., Dillon, C. M., & Bates, S. L. (2010). An evaluation of preference for video and in vivo modeling. *Journal of Applied Behavior Analysis, 43*, 279–283.

George, T. R., & Feltz, D. L. (1995). Motivation in sport from a collective efficacy perspective. *International Journal of Sport Psychology, 26*(1), 98–116.

Gerst, M. S. (1971). Symbolic coding processes in observational learning. *Journal of Personality and Social Psychology, 19*, 7–17.

Goddard, R. D. (2001). Collective efficacy: A neglected construct in the study of schools and student achievement. *Journal of Educational Psychology, 93*, 467–476.

Goddard, R. D., Hoy, W. K., & Woolfolk Hoy, A. (2000). Collective teacher efficacy: Its meaning, measure, and impact on student achievement. *American Educational Research Journal, 37*, 479–507.

Goldstein, N. E., Arnold, D. H., Rosenberg, J. L., Stowe, R. M., & Ortiz, C. (2001). Contagion of aggression in day care classrooms as a function of peer and teacher responses. *Journal of Educational Psychology, 93*, 708–719.

Grace, D. M., David, B. J., & Ryan, M. K. (2008). Investigating preschoolers' categorical thinking about gender through imitation, attention, and the use of self-categories. *Child Development, 79*, 1928–1941.

Graham, S., & Golen, S. (1991). Motivational influences on cognition: Task involvement, ego involvement, and depth of information processing. *Journal of Educational Psychology, 83*, 187–194.

Graham, S., & Harris, K. R. (1996). Addressing problems in attention, memory, and executive functioning. In G. R. Lyon & N. A. Krasnegor (Eds.), *Attention, memory, and executive function* (pp. 349–365). Baltimore: Brookes.

Greene, J. A., & Azevedo, R. (2009). A macro-level analysis of SRL processes and their relations to the acquisition of a sophisticated mental model of a complex system. *Contemporary Educational Psychology, 34*, 18–29.

Guerra, N. G., Huesmann, L. R., & Spindler, A. (2003). Community violence exposure, social cognition, and aggression among urban elementary school children. *Child Development, 74*, 1561–1576.

Guskey, T. R. (1988). Teacher efficacy, self-concept, and attitudes toward the implementation of instructional innovation. *Teaching and Teacher Education, 4*, 63–69.

Hampson, S. E. (2008). Mechanisms by which childhood personality traits influence adult well-being. *Current Directions in Psychological Science, 17*, 264–268.

Harnishfeger, K. K. (1995). The development of cognitive inhibition: Theories, definitions, and research evidence. In F. N. Dempster & C. J. Brainerd (Eds.), *Interference and inhibition in cognition* (pp. 175–204). San Diego, CA: Academic Press.

Harris, K. R. (1982). Cognitive-behavior modification: Application with exceptional students. *Focus on Exceptional Children, 15*, 1–16.

Harris, K. R. (1986). Self-monitoring of attentional behavior versus self-monitoring of productivity: Effects of on-task behavior and academic response rate among learning disabled children. *Journal of Applied Behavior Analysis, 19*, 417–423.

Harris, K. R., Graham, S., Brindle, M., & Sandmel, K. (2009). Metacognition and children's writing. In D. J. Hacker, J. Dunlosky, & A. C. Graesser (Eds.), *Handbook of metacognition in education* (pp. 131–153). New York: Routledge.

Harris, P. L., & Want, S. (2005). On learning what not to do: The emergence of selective imitation in tool use by young children. In S. Hurley & N. Chater (Eds.), *Perspectives on imitation: From neuroscience to social science: Vol. 2. Imitation, human development, and culture* (pp. 149–162). Cambridge, MA: MIT Press.

Harter, S. (1999). *The construction of the self: A developmental perspective.* New York: Guilford.

Hatzigeorgiadis, A., Zourbanos, N., Galanis, E., & Theodorakis, Y. (2011). Self-talk and sports performance: A meta-analysis. *Perspectives on Psychological Science, 6*, 348–356.

Hawkins, F. P. L. (1997). *Journey with children: The autobiography of a teacher.* Niwot: University Press of Colorado.

Hayes, S. C., Rosenfarb, I., Wulfert, E., Munt, E. D., Korn, Z., & Zettle, R. D. (1985). Self-reinforcement effects: An artifact of social standard setting? *Journal of Applied Behavior Analysis, 18*, 201–214.

Hickey, D. J. (2011). Participation by design: Improving individual motivation by looking beyond it. In D. M. McInerney, R. A. Walker, & G. A. D. Liem (Eds.), *Sociocultural theories of learning and motivation: Looking back, looking forward* (pp. 137–161). Charlotte, NC: Information Age.

Hitchcock, C., Dowrick, P. W., & Prater, M. A. (2003). Video self-modeling interventions in school-based settings: A review. *Remedial and Special Education, 24*, 36–46.

Hofer, M. (2010). Adolescents' development of individual interests: A product of multiple goal regulation? *Educational Psychologist, 45*, 149–166.

Huston, A. C., Watkins, B. A., & Kunkel, D. (1989). Public policy and children's television. *American Psychologist, 44*, 424–433.

Iacoboni, M., & Woods, R. P. (1999). Cortical mechanisms of human imitation. *Science, 286*, 2526–2528.

Johnson, D. W., & Johnson, R. T. (1996). Conflict resolution and peer mediation programs in elementary and secondary schools: A review of the research. *Review of Educational Research, 66*, 459–506.

Johnson, D. W., & Johnson, R. T. (2006). Conflict resolution, peer mediation, and peacemaking. In C. M. Evertson & C. S. Weinstein (Eds.), *Handbook of classroom management: Research, practice, and contemporary issues* (pp. 803–832). Mahwah, NJ: Erlbaum.

Johnson, D. W., & Johnson, R. T. (2009a). An educational psychology success story: Social interdependence theory and cooperative learning. *Educational Researcher, 38*, 365–379.

Johnson, D. W., Johnson, R., Dudley, B., Ward, M., & Magnuson, D. (1995). The impact of peer mediation training on the management of school and home conflicts. *American Educational Research Journal, 32*, 829–844.

Jones, M. H., Estell, D. B., & Alexander, J. M. (2008). Friends, classmates, and self-regulated learning: Discussions with peers inside and outside the classroom. *Metacognition Learning, 3*, 1–15.

Jones, S. S. (2007). Imitation in infancy: The development of mimicry. *Psychological Science, 18*, 593–599.

Jordan, A. B. (2003). Children remember prosocial program lessons but how much are they learning? *Applied Developmental Psychology, 24,* 341–345.

Kehle, T. J., Clark, E., Jenson, W. R., & Wampold, B. (1986). Effectiveness of the self-modeling procedure with behaviorally disturbed elementary age children. *School Psychology Review, 15,* 289–295.

King, A. (1997). ASK to THINK—TEL WHY®©: A model of transactive peer tutoring for scaffolding higher level complex learning. *Educational Psychologist, 32,* 221–235.

Kitsantas, A., Zimmerman, B. J., & Cleary, T. (2000). The role of observation and emulation in the development of athletic self-regulation. *Journal of Educational Psychology, 92,* 811–817.

Klassen, R. (2002). Writing in early adolescence: A review of the role of self-efficacy beliefs. *Educational Psychology Review, 14,* 173–203.

Klassen, R. M., & Usher, E. L. (2010). Self-efficacy in educational settings: Recent research and emerging directions. In S. Karabenick & T. C. Urdan (Eds.), *Advances in motivation and achievement: Vol. 16A. The decade ahead: Theoretical perspectives on motivation and achievement* (pp. 1–33). Bingley, England: Emerald Group Publishing.

Kochanska, G., Gross, J. N., Lin, M.-H., & Nichols, K. E. (2002). Guilt in young children: Development, determinants, and relations with a broader system of standards. *Child Development, 73,* 461–482.

Krebs, D. L. (2008). Morality: An evolutionary account. *Perspectives on Psychological Science, 3,* 149–172.

Kuhl, J. (1985). Volitional mediators of cognition-behavior consistency: Self-regulatory processes and actions versus state orientation. In J. Kuhl & J. Beckmann (Eds.), *Action control: From cognition to behavior* (pp. 101–128). Berlin, Germany: Springer-Verlag.

Larson, R. W., & Brown, J. R. (2007). Emotional development in adolescence: What can be learned from a high school theater program? *Child Development, 78,* 1083–1099.

Leaper, C., & Friedman, C. K. (2007). The socialization of gender. In J. E. Grusec & P. D. Hastings (Eds.), *Handbook of socialization: Theory and research* (pp. 561–587). New York: Guilford.

Lee, J., & Shute, V. J. (2010). Personal and social-contextual factors in K–12 academic performance: An integrative perspective on student learning. *Educational Psychologist, 45,* 185–202.

Lenroot, R. K., Gogtay, N., Greenstein, D. K., Wells, E. M., Wallace, G. L., Clasen, L. S., et al. (2007). Sexual dimorphism of brain development trajectories during childhood and adolescence. *NeuroImage, 36,* 1065–1073.

Lewis, M. D., & Stieben, J. (2004). Emotion regulation in the brain: Conceptual issues and directions for developmental research. *Child Development, 75,* 371–376.

Liem, A. D., Lau, S., & Nie, Y. (2008). The role of self-efficacy, task value, and achievement goals in predicting learning strategies,

task disengagement, peer relationship, and achievement outcome. *Contemporary Educational Psychology, 33,* 486–512.

Liew, J., McTigue, E., Barrois, L., & Hughes, J. N. (2008, March). *I am, therefore I think: Effortful control, academic self-efficacy, and achievement in early grade school.* Paper presented at the annual meeting of the American Educational Research Association, New York.

Locke, E. A., & Latham, G. P. (1990). *A theory of goal setting and task performance.* Upper Saddle River, NJ: Prentice-Hall.

Lodewyk, K. R., & Winne, P. H. (2005). Relations among the structure of learning tasks, achievement, and changes in self-efficacy in secondary students. *Journal of Educational Psychology, 97,* 3–12.

Lowry, R., Sleet, D., Duncan, C., Powell, K., & Kolbe, L. (1995). Adolescents at risk for violence. *Educational Psychology Review, 7,* 7–39.

Mace, F. C., Belfiore, P. J., & Shea, M. C. (1989). Operant theory and research on self-regulation. In B. J. Zimmerman & D. H. Schunk (Eds.), *Self-regulated learning and academic achievement: Theory, research, and practice* (pp. 27–50). New York: Springer-Verlag.

Marchand, G., & Skinner, E. A. (2007). Motivational dynamics of children's academic help-seeking and concealment. *Journal of Educational Psychology, 99,* 65–82.

Martin, C. L., & Ruble, D. (2004). Children's search for gender cues: Cognitive perspectives on gender development. *Current Directions in Psychological Science, 13,* 67–70.

Mathews, J. (1988). *Escalante: The best teacher in America.* New York: Henry Holt.

Matthews, J. S., Ponitz, C. C., & Morrison, F. J. (2009). Early gender differences in self-regulation and academic achievement. *Journal of Educational Psychology, 101,* 689–704.

Mayer, R. E. (2011b). Instruction based on visualizations. In R. E. Mayer & P. A. Alexander (Eds.), *Handbook of research on learning and instruction* (pp. 427–445). New York: Routledge.

McCaslin, M., & Good, T. L. (1996). The informal curriculum. In D. C. Berliner & R. C. Calfee (Eds.), *Handbook of educational psychology* (pp. 622–670). New York: Macmillan.

McCaslin, M., & Hickey, D. T. (2001). Self-regulated learning and academic achievement: A Vygotskian view. In B. Zimmerman & D. Schunk (Eds.), *Self-regulated learning and academic achievement: Theory, research, and practice* (2nd ed., pp. 227–252). Mahwah, NJ: Erlbaum.

McDaniel, L. (1997). *For better, for worse, forever.* New York: Bantam.

McMillan, J. H. (2010). The practical implications of educational aims and contexts for formative assessment. In H. L. Andrade & G. J. Cizek (Eds.), *Handbook of formative assessment* (pp. 41–58). New York: Routledge.

Meichenbaum, D. (1977). *Cognitive-behavior modification: An integrative approach.* New York: Plenum..

Meichenbaum, D. (1985). Teaching thinking: A cognitive-behavioral perspective. In S. F.

Chipman, J. W. Segal, & R. Glaser (Eds.), *Thinking and learning skills: Vol. 2. Research and open questions* (pp. 407–426). Mahwah, NJ: Erlbaum.

Meichenbaum, D., & Goodman, J. (1971). Training impulsive children to talk to themselves: A means of developing self-control. *Journal of Abnormal Psychology, 77,* 115–126.

Meltzer, L. (Ed.). (2007). *Executive function in education: From theory to practice.* New York: Guilford.

Meltzer, L., Pollica, L. S., & Barzillai, M. (2007). Executive function in the classroom: Embedding strategy instruction into daily teaching practices. In L. Meltzer (Ed.), *Executive function in education: From theory to practice* (pp. 165–193). New York: Guilford.

Meltzoff, A. N. (2005). Imitation and other minds: The "like me" hypothesis. In S. Hurley & N. Chater (Eds.), *Perspectives on imitation: From neuroscience to social science* (pp. 55–77). Cambridge, MA: MIT Press.

Menéndez, R. (Director). (1988). *Stand and deliver* [Motion picture]. United States: Warner Studios.

Mercer, C. D., & Pullen, P. C. (2005). *Students with learning disabilities* (6th ed.). Upper Saddle River, NJ: Merrill/Prentice-Hall.

Middleton, M., & Abrams, E. (2004, April). *The effect of pre-service teachers' sense of efficacy on their self-reflective practice.* Paper presented at the Annual Meeting of the American Educational Research Association, San Diego, CA.

Miller, R. B., & Brickman, S. J. (2004). A model of future-oriented motivation and self-regulation. *Educational Psychology Review, 16,* 9–33.

Miller, S. D., Heafner, T., Massey, D., & Strahan, D. B. (2003, April). *Students' reactions to teachers' attempts to create the necessary conditions to promote the acquisition of self-regulation skills.* Paper presented at the annual meeting of the American Educational Research Association, Chicago.

Mineka, S., & Zinbarg, R. (2006). A contemporary learning theory perspective on the etiology of anxiety disorders: It's not what you thought it was. *American Psychologist, 61,* 10–26.

Mitchem, K. J., & Young, K. R. (2001). Adapting self-management programs for classwide use. *Remedial and Special Education, 22*(2), 75–88.

Mithaug, D. K., & Mithaug, D. E. (2003). Effects of teacher-directed versus student-directed instruction on self-management of young children with disabilities. *Journal of Applied Behavior Analysis, 36,* 133–136.

Moore, S., & Rosenthal, D. (2006). *Sexuality in adolescence: Current trends.* London: Routledge.

Morelli, G. A., & Rothbaum, F. (2007). Situating the child in context: Attachment relationships and self-regulation in different cultures. In S. Kitayama & D. Cohen (Eds.), *Handbook of cultural psychology* (pp. 500–527). New York: Guilford.

Moreno, R. (2006). Learning in high-tech and multimedia environments. *Current Directions in Psychological Science, 15,* 63–67.

Narciss, S. (2008). Feedback strategies for interactive learning tasks. In J. M. Spector,

M. D. Merrill, J. van Merriënboer, & M. P. Driscoll (Eds.), *Handbook of research on educational communications and technology* (3rd ed., pp. 125–143). New York: Erlbaum.

Nelson, J. R., Smith, D. J., Young, R. K., & Dodd, J. M. (1991). A review of self-management outcome research conducted with students who exhibit behavioral disorders. *Behavioral Disorders, 16,* 169–179.

Newman, R. S. (2008). Adaptive and nonadaptive help seeking with peer harassment: An integrative perspective of coping and self-regulation. *Educational Psychologist, 43,* 1–15.

Nielsen, M., & Tomaselli, K. (2010). Overimitation in Kalahari bushman children and the origins of human cultural cognition. *Psychological Science, 21,* 729–736.

Nikopoulos, C. K., & Keenan, M. (2004). Effects of video modeling on social initiations by children with autism. *Journal of Applied Behavior Analysis, 37,* 93–96.

Nolen, S. B. (1996). Why study? How reasons for learning influence strategy selection. *Educational Psychology Review, 8,* 335–355.

Nucci, L. P. (2001). *Education in the moral domain.* Cambridge, England: Cambridge University Press.

Obama, B. H. (2004). *Dreams from my father: A story of race and inheritance* (rev. ed.) New York: Three Rivers Press.

Pajares, F. (2009). Toward a positive psychology of academic motivation: The role of self-efficacy beliefs. In R. Gilman, E. S. Huebner, & M. J. Furlong (Eds.), *Handbook of positive psychology in schools* (pp. 149–160). New York: Routledge.

Pang, V. O. (1995). Asian Pacific American students: A diverse and complex population. In J. A. Banks & C. A. M. Banks (Eds.), *Handbook of research on multicultural education* (pp. 412–424). New York: Macmillan.

Paris, S. G., & Ayres, L. R. (1994). *Becoming reflective students and teachers with portfolios and authentic assessment.* Washington, DC: American Psychological Association.

Paris, S. G., & Paris, A. H. (2001). Classroom applications of research on self-regulated learning. *Educational Psychologist, 36,* 89–101.

Parker, W. D. (1997). An empirical typology of perfectionism in academically talented children. *American Educational Research Journal, 34,* 545–562.

Pea, R. D. (1993). Practices of distributed intelligence and designs for education. In G. Salomon (Ed.), *Distributed cognitions: Psychological and educational considerations* (pp. 47–87). Cambridge, England: Cambridge University Press.

Pekrun, R. (2006). The control-value theory of achievement emotions: Assumptions, corollaries, and implications for educational research and practice. *Educational Psychology Review, 18,* 315–341.

Perry, N. E. (1998). Young children's self-regulated learning and contexts that support it. *Journal of Educational Psychology, 90,* 715–729.

Perry, N. E., VandeKamp, K. O., Mercer, L. K., & Nordby, C. J. (2002). Investigating teacher-student interactions that foster self-regulated learning. *Educational Psychologist, 37,* 5–15.

Pietsch, J., Walker, R., & Chapman, E. (2003). The relationship among self-concept, self-efficacy, and performance in mathematics during secondary school. *Journal of Educational Psychology, 95,* 589–603.

Piirto, J. (1999). *Talented children and adults: Their development and education* (2nd ed.). Upper Saddle River, NJ: Merrill/Prentice-Hall.

Pintrich, P. R., & Schunk, D. H. (2002). *Motivation in education: Theory, research, and applications* (2nd ed.). Upper Saddle River, NJ: Merrill/Prentice-Hall.

Plante, I., & O'Keefe, P. A. (2010, April–May). *The relation among achievement goals and expectancy-value variables in predicting grades and career intentions.* Paper presented at the annual meeting of the American Educational Research Association, Denver.

Plavnick, J. B., Ferreri, S. J., & Maupin, A. N. (2010). The effects of self-monitoring on the procedural integrity of a behavioral intervention for young children with developmental disabilities. *Journal of Applied Behavior Analysis, 43,* 315–320.

Poche, C., McCubbrey, H., & Munn, T. (1982). The development of correct toothbrushing technique in preschool children. *Journal of Applied Behavior Analysis, 15,* 315–320.

Poche, C., Yoder, P., & Miltenberger, R. (1988). Teaching self-protection to children using television techniques. *Journal of Applied Behavior Analysis, 21,* 253–261.

Posner, M. I., & Rothbart, M. K. (2007). *Educating the human brain.* Washington, DC: American Psychological Association.

Powers, L. E., Sowers, J. A., & Stevens, T. (1995). An exploratory, randomized study of the impact of mentoring on the self-efficacy and community-based knowledge of adolescents with severe physical challenges. *Journal of Rehabilitation, 61*(1), 33–41.

Prater, M. A., Carter, N., Hitchcock, C., & Dowrick, P. (2011). Video self-monitoring to improve academic performance: A literature review. *Psychology in the Schools, 49*(1), 71–81.

Radke-Yarrow, M., Zahn-Waxler, C., & Chapman, M. (1983). Children's prosocial dispositions and behavior. In E. M. Hetherington (Ed.), *Handbook of child psychology: Vol. 4. Socialization, personality, and social development* (pp. 469–545). New York: Wiley.

Reid, R., Trout, A. L., & Schartz, M. (2005). Self-regulation interventions for children with attention deficit/hyperactivity disorder. *Exceptional Children, 71,* 361–377.

Richards, J. M. (2004). The cognitive consequences of concealing feelings. *Current Directions in Psychological Science, 13,* 131–134.

Roeser, R. W., Marachi, R., & Gehlbach, H. (2002). A goal theory perspective on teachers' professional identities and the contexts of teaching. In C. Midgley (Ed.), *Goals, goal structures, and patterns of adaptive learning* (pp. 205–241). Mahwah, NJ: Erlbaum.

Rosenthal, T. L., Alford, G. S., & Rasp, L. M. (1972). Concept attainment, generalization, and retention through observation and verbal coding. *Journal of Experimental Child Psychology, 13,* 183–194.

Rosenthal, T. L., & Bandura, A. (1978). Psychological modeling: Theory and practice. In S. L. Garfield & A. E. Begia (Eds.), *Handbook of psychotherapy and behavior change: An empirical analysis* (2nd ed., pp. 621–658). New York: Wiley.

Rosenthal, T. L., & Zimmerman, B. J. (1978). *Social learning and cognition.* San Diego, CA: Academic Press.

Rothbart, M. K. (2011). *Becoming who we are: Temperament and personality in development.* New York: Guilford.

Rothbart, M. K., Sheese, B. E., & Posner, M. I. (2007). Executive attention and effortful control: Linking temperament, brain networks, and genes. *Child Development Perspectives, 1,* 2–7.

Rushton, J. P. (1980). *Altruism, socialization, and society.* Upper Saddle River, NJ: Prentice-Hall.

Sands, D. J., & Wehmeyer, M. L. (Eds.). (1996). *Self-determination across the life span: Independence and choice for people with disabilities.* Baltimore: Brookes.

Sasso, G. M., & Rude, H. A. (1987). Unprogrammed effects of training high-status peers to interact with severely handicapped children. *Journal of Applied Behavior Analysis, 20,* 35–44.

Schneider, W. (2010). Metacognition and memory development in childhood and adolescence. In H. S. Waters & W. Schneider (Eds.), *Metacognition, strategy use, and instruction* (pp. 54–81). New York: Guilford.

Schraw, G., & Moshman, D. (1995). Metacognitive theories. *Educational Psychology Review, 7,* 351–371.

Schumaker, J. B., & Hazel, J. S. (1984). Social skill assessment and training for the learning disabled: Who's on first and what's on second? (Pt. 1). *Journal of Learning Disabilities, 17,* 422–431.

Schunk, D. H. (1983). Developing children's self-efficacy and skills: The roles of social comparative information and goal setting. *Contemporary Educational Psychology, 8,* 76–86.

Schunk, D. H. (1987). Peer models and children's behavioral change. *Review of Educational Research, 57,* 149–174.

Schunk, D. H. (1989a). Self-efficacy and achievement behaviors. *Educational Psychology Review, 1,* 173–208.

Schunk, D. H. (1989b). Self-efficacy and cognitive skill learning. In C. Ames & R. Ames (Eds.), *Research on motivation in education: Vol. 3. Goals and cognitions* (pp. 13–44). San Diego, CA: Academic Press.

Schunk, D. H. (1989c). Social cognitive theory and self-regulated learning. In B. J. Zimmerman & D. H. Schunk (Eds.), *Self-regulated learning and academic achievement: Theory, research, and practice* (pp. 83–110). New York: Springer-Verlag.

Schunk, D. H. (1998). Teaching elementary students to self-regulate practice of mathematical skills with modeling. In D. H. Schunk & B. J. Zimmerman (Eds.), *Self-regulated learning: From teaching to self-reflective practice* (pp. 137–159). New York: Guilford.

Schunk, D. H., & Hanson, A. R. (1985). Peer models: Influence on children's self-efficacy and achievement. *Journal of Educational Psychology, 77,* 313–322.

Schunk, D. H., Hanson, A. R., & Cox, P. D. (1987). Peer-model attributes and children's achievement behaviors. *Journal of Educational Psychology, 79,* 54–61.

Schunk, D. H., & Pajares, F. (2004). Self-efficacy in education revisited: Empirical and applied evidence. In D. M. McInerney & S. Van Etten (Eds.), *Big theories revisited* (pp. 115–138). Greenwich, CT: Information Age.

Schunk, D. H., & Pajares, F. (2005). Competence perceptions and academic functioning. In A. J. Elliot & C. S. Dweck (Eds.), *Handbook of competence and motivation* (pp. 85–104). New York: Guilford.

Schunk, D. H., & Swartz, C. W. (1993). Goals and progress feedback: Effects on self-efficacy and writing achievement. *Contemporary Educational Psychology, 18,* 337–354.

Schunk, D. H., & Zimmerman, B. J. (1997). Social origins of self-regulatory competence. *Educational Psychologist, 32,* 195–208.

Shih, S.-S., & Alexander, J. M. (2000). Interacting effects of goal setting and self- or other-referenced feedback on children's development of self-efficacy and cognitive skill within the Taiwanese classroom. *Journal of Educational Psychology, 92,* 536–543.

Shute, V. J. (2008). Focus on formative feedback. *Review of Educational Research, 78,* 153–189.

Silk, J. S., Steinberg, L., & Morris, A. S. (2003). Adolescents' emotion regulation in daily life: Links to depressive symptoms and problem behavior. *Child Development, 74,* 1869–1880.

Sinatra, G. M., & Mason, L. (2008). Beyond knowledge: Learner characteristics influencing conceptual change. In S. Vosniadou (Ed.), *International handbook on conceptual change* (pp. 560–582). New York: Routledge.

Skaalvik, E. M., & Skaalvik, S. (2008). Teacher self-efficacy: Conceptual analysis and relations with teacher burnout and perceived school context. In H. W. Marsh, R. G. Craven, & D. M. McInerney (Eds.), *Self-processes, learning, and enabling human potential* (pp. 223–247). Charlotte, NC: Information Age.

Slavin, R. E. (2011). Instruction based on cooperative learning. In R. E. Mayer & P. A. Alexander (Eds.), *Handbook of research on learning and instruction* (pp. 344–360). New York: Routledge.

Smith, D. J., Young, K. R., West, R. P., Morgan, R. P., & Rhode, G. (1988). Reducing the disruptive behavior of junior high school students: A classroom self-management procedure. *Behavioral Disorders, 13,* 231–239.

Spaulding, C. L. (1992). *Motivation in the classroom.* New York: McGraw-Hill.

Steinberg, L. (2009). Should the science of adolescent brain development inform public policy? *American Psychologist, 64,* 739–750.

Stevahn, L., Johnson, D. W., Johnson, R. T., Oberle, K., & Wahl, L. (2000). Effects of conflict resolution training integrated into a kindergarten curriculum. *Child Development, 71,* 772–784.

Stevenson, H. C., & Fantuzzo, J. W. (1986). The generality and social validity of a competency-based self-control training intervention for underachieving students. *Journal of Applied Behavior Analysis, 19,* 269–272.

Stipek, D. J. (1996). Motivation and instruction. In D. C. Berliner & R. C. Calfee (Eds.), *Handbook of educational psychology* (pp. 85–113). New York: Macmillan.

Stright, A. D., Neitzel, C., Sears, K. G., & Hoke-Sinex, L. (2001). Instruction begins in the home: Relations between parental instruction and children's self-regulation in the classroom. *Journal of Educational Psychology, 93,* 456–466.

Suina, J. H., & Smolkin, L. B. (1994). From natal culture to school culture to dominant society culture: Supporting transitions for Pueblo Indian students. In P. M. Greenfield & R. R. Cocking (Eds.), *Cross-cultural roots of minority child development* (pp. 115–130). Mahwah, NJ: Erlbaum.

Sullivan, J. R., & Conoley, J. C. (2004). Academic and instructional interventions with aggressive students. In J. C. Conoley & A. P. Goldstein (Eds.), *School violence intervention* (2nd ed., pp. 235–255). New York: Guilford.

Sweeny, K., Carroll, P. J., & Shepperd, J. A. (2006). Is optimism always best? Future outlooks and preparedness. *Current Directions in Psychological Science, 15,* 302–306.

Thomas, J. W. (1993b). Promoting independent learning in the middle grades: The role of instructional support practices. *Elementary School Journal, 93,* 575–591.

Trautwein, U., Lüdtke, O., Kastens, C., & Köller, O. (2006). Effort on homework in grades 5–9: Development, motivational antecedents, and the association with effort on classwork. *Child Development, 77,* 1094–1111.

Tschannen-Moran, M., Woolfolk Hoy, A., & Hoy, W. K. (1998). Teacher efficacy: Its meaning and measure. *Review of Educational Research, 68,* 202–248.

Turnbull, A. P., Turnbull, R., & Wehmeyer, M. L. (2010). *Exceptional lives: Special education in today's schools* (6th ed.). Upper Saddle River, NJ: Merrill.

Usher, E. L. (2009). Sources of middle school students' self-efficacy in mathematics: A qualitative investigation. *American Educational Research Journal, 46,* 275–314.

Usher, E. L., & Pajares, F. (2008). Sources of self-efficacy in school: Critical review of the literature and future directions. *Review of Educational Research, 78,* 751–796.

Usher, E. L., & Pajares, F. (2009). Sources of self-efficacy in mathematics: A validation study. *Contemporary Educational Psychology, 34,* 89–101.

Valentine, J. C., DuBois, D. L., & Cooper, H. (2004). The relation between self-beliefs and academic achievement: A meta-analytic review. *Educational Psychologist, 39,* 111–133.

Valiente, C., Lemery-Calfant, K., Swanson, J., & Reiser, M. (2008). Prediction of children's academic competence from their effortful control, relationships, and classroom participation. *Journal of Educational Psychology, 100,* 67–77.

van den Broek, P., Lorch, R. F., Jr., Linderholm, T., & Gustafson, M. (2001). The effects of readers' goals on inference generation and memory for texts. *Memory and Cognition, 29,* 1081–1087.

Velanova, K., Wheeler, M. E., & Luna, B. (2008). Maturational changes in anterior cingulate and frontoparietal recruitment support the development of error processing and inhibitory control. *Cerebral Cortex, 18,* 2505–2522.

Vintere, P., Hemmes, N. S., Brown, B. L., & Poulson, C. L. (2004). Gross-motor skill acquisition by preschool dance students under self-instruction procedures. *Journal of Applied Behavior Analysis, 37,* 305–322.

Volet, S., Vaura, M., & Salonen, P. (2009). Self- and social regulation in learning contexts: An integrative perspective. *Educational Psychologist, 44,* 215–226.

Vye, N. J., Schwartz, D. L., Bransford, J. D., Barron, B. J., Zech, L., & The Cognition and Technology Group at Vanderbilt. (1998). SMART environments that support monitoring, reflection, and revision. In D. J. Hacker, J. Dunlosky, & A. C. Graesser (Eds.), *Metacognition in educational theory and practice* (pp. 305–346). Mahwah, NJ: Erlbaum.

Vygotsky, L. S. (1986). *Thought and language* (rev. ed; A. Kozulin, Ed. and Trans.). Cambridge, MA: MIT Press. (Original work published 1934)

Walker, E., Shapiro, D., Esterberg, M., & Trotman, H. (2010). Neurodevelopment and schizophrenia: Broadening the focus. *Current Directions in Psychological Science, 19,* 204–208.

Wang, M.-T., & Holcombe, R. (2010). Adolescents' perceptions of school environment, engagement, and academic achievement in middle school. *American Educational Research Journal, 47,* 633–662.

Wang, J., & Lin, E. (2005). Comparative studies on U.S. and Chinese mathematics learning and the implications for standards-based mathematics teaching reform. *Educational Researcher, 34*(5), 3–13.

Ware, H., & Kitsantas, A. (2007). Teacher and collective efficacy beliefs as predictors of professional commitment. *Journal of Educational Research, 100,* 303–310.

Wartella, E., Caplovitz, A. G., & Lee, J. H. (2004). From Baby Einstein to Leapfrog, from Doom to The Sims, from instant messaging to Internet chat rooms: Public interest in the role of interactive media in children's lives. *Social Policy Report: Giving Child and Youth Development Knowledge Away, 18*(4), 3–19.

Webber, J., & Plotts, C. A. (2008). *Emotional and behavioral disorders: Theory and practice* (5th ed.). Boston: Allyn & Bacon.

Webber, J., Scheuermann, B., McCall, C., & Coleman, M. (1993). Research on self-monitoring as a behavior management technique in special education classrooms: A descriptive review. *Remedial and Special Education, 14*(2), 38–56.

Wehmeyer, M. L., Agran, M., Hughes, C., Martin, J., Mithaug, D. E., & Palmer, S. (2007). *Promoting self-determination in students with intellectual and developmental disabilities.* New York: Guilford.

Weissberg, R. P. (1985). Designing effective social problem-solving programs for the classroom. In B. H. Schneider, K. H. Rubin, & J. E. Ledingham (Eds.), *Children's peer relations: Issues in assessment and intervention* (pp. 225–242). New York: Springer-Verlag.

Wigfield, A., & Wagner, A. L. (2005). Competence, motivation, and identity development during adolescence. In A. J. Elliot & C. S. Dweck (Eds.), *Handbook of competence and motivation* (pp. 222–239). New York: Guilford.

Williams, K. M. (2001b). What derails peer mediation? In J. N. Burstyn, G. Bender, R. Casella, H. W. Gordon, D. P. Guerra, K. V. Luschen, R. Stevens, & K. M. Williams, *Preventing violence in schools: A challenge to American democracy* (pp. 199–208). Mahwah, NJ: Erlbaum.

Williams, T., & Williams, K. (2010). Self-efficacy and performance in mathematics: Reciprocal determinism in 33 nations. *Journal of Educational Psychology, 102,* 453–456.

Wilson, B. L., & Corbett, H. D. (2001). *Listening to urban kids: School reform and the teachers they want.* Albany: State University of New York Press.

Winne, P. H. (1995). Inherent details in self-regulated learning. *Educational Psychologist, 30,* 173–187.

Winne, P. H., & Hadwin, A. F. (1998). Studying as self-regulated learning. In D. J. Hacker, J. Dunlosky, & A. C. Graesser (Eds.), *Metacognition in educational theory and practice* (pp. 277–304). Mahwah, NJ: Erlbaum.

Winters, F. I., Greene, J. A., & Costich, C. M. (2008). Self-regulation of learning within computer-based learning environments: A critical analysis. *Educational Psychology Review, 20,* 429–444.

Wisner Fries, A. B., & Pollak, S. D. (2007). Emotion processing and the developing brain. In D. Coch, K. W. Fischer, & G. Dawson (Eds.), *Human behavior, learning, and the developing brain: Typical development* (pp. 329–361). New York: Guilford.

Wolters, C. A. (1998). Self-regulated learning and college students' regulation of motivation. *Journal of Educational Psychology, 90,* 224–235.

Wolters, C. A. (2003). Regulation of motivation: Evaluating an underemphasized aspect of self-regulated learning. *Educational Psychologist, 38,* 189–205.

Wolters, C. A., & Rosenthal, H. (2000). The relation between students' motivational beliefs and their use of motivational regulation strategies. *International Journal of Educational Research, 33,* 801–820.

Wong, B. Y. L., Hoskyn, M., Jai, D., Ellis, P., & Watson, K. (2008). The comparative efficacy of two approaches to teaching sixth graders opinion essay writing. *Contemporary Educational Psychology, 33,* 757–784.

Yell, M. L., Robinson, T. R., & Drasgow, E. (2001). Cognitive behavior modification. In T. J. Zirpoli & K. J. Melloy, *Behavior management: Applications for teachers* (3rd ed., pp. 200–246). Upper Saddle River, NJ: Merrill/Prentice-Hall.

Zeldin, A. L., & Pajares, F. (2000). Against the odds: Self-efficacy beliefs of women in mathematical,

scientific, and technological careers. *American Educational Research Journal, 37,* 215–246.

Ziegler, S. G. (1987). Effects of stimulus cueing on the acquisition of groundstrokes by beginning tennis players. *Journal of Applied Behavior Analysis, 20,* 405–411.

Zimmerman, B. J. (1998). Developing self-fulfilling cycles of academic regulation: An analysis of exemplary instructional models. In D. H. Schunk & B. J. Zimmerman (Eds.), *Self-regulated learning: From teaching to self-reflective practice* (pp. 1–19). New York: Guilford.

Zimmerman, B. J. (2004). Sociocultural influence and students' development of academic self-regulation: A social-cognitive perspective. In D. M. McInerney & S. Van Etten (Eds.), *Big theories revisited* (pp. 139–164). Greenwich, CT: Information Age.

Zimmerman, B. J., & Campillo, M. (2003). Motivating self-regulated problem solvers. In J. E. Davidson & R. J. Sternberg (Eds.), *The psychology of problem solving* (pp. 233–262). Cambridge, England: Cambridge University Press.

Zimmerman, B. J., & Kitsantas, A. (2005). The hidden dimension of personal competence: Self-regulated learning and practice. In A. J. Elliot & C. S. Dweck (Eds.), *Handbook of competence and motivation* (pp. 509–526). New York: Guilford.

Zimmerman, B. J., & Moylan, A. R. (2009). Self-regulation: Where metacognition and motivation intersect. In D. J. Hacker, J. Dunlosky, & A. C. Graesser (Eds.), *Handbook of metacognition in education* (pp. 299–315). New York: Routledge.

Zimmerman, B. J., & Risemberg, R. (1997). Self-regulatory dimensions of academic learning and motivation. In G. D. Phye (Ed.), *Handbook of academic learning: Construction of knowledge* (pp. 106–125). San Diego, CA: Academic Press.

Zusho, A., & Barnett, P. A. (2011). Personal and contextual determinants of ethnically diverse female high school students' patterns of academic help seeking and help avoidance in English and mathematics. *Contemporary Educational Psychology, 36,* 152–164.

## CHAPTER 11

Ablard, K. E., & Lipschultz, R. E. (1998). Self-regulated learning in high-achieving students: Relations to advanced reasoning, achievement goals, and gender. *Journal of Educational Psychology, 90,* 94–101.

Adam, J., Shirako, A., & Maddux, W. W. (2010). Cultural variance in the interpersonal effects of anger in negotiations. *Psychological Science, 21,* 882–889.

Adolphs, R., & Damasio, A. R. (2001). The interaction of affect and cognition: A neurobiological perspective. In J. P. Forgas (Ed.), *Handbook of affect and social cognition* (pp. 27–49). Mahwah, NJ: Erlbaum.

Ainley, M. (2006). Connecting with learning: Motivation, affect, and cognition in interest processes. *Educational Psychology Review, 18,* 391–405.

Ainley, M., & Ainley, J. (2011). Student engagement with science in early adolescence: The contribution of enjoyment to students' continuing interest in learning about science. *Contemporary Educational Psychology, 36,* 4–12.

Alexander, E. S. (2008). *How to hope: A model of the thoughts, feelings, and behaviors involved in transcending challenge and uncertainty.* Saarbrücken, Germany: VDM Verlag.

Alexander, J. M., Johnson, K. E., Leibham, M. E., & Kelley, K. (2008). The development of conceptual interests in young children. *Cognitive Development, 23,* 324–334.

Alexander, P. A., Kulikowich, J. M., & Schulze, S. K. (1994). How subject-matter knowledge affects recall and interest. *American Educational Research Journal, 31,* 313–337.

Alim, H. S. (2007). "The Whig party don't exist in my hood": Knowledge, reality, and education in the hip hop nation. In H. S. Alim & J. Baugh (Eds.), *Talkin Black talk: Language, education, and social change* (pp. 15–29). New York: Teachers College Press.

Amabile, T. M., & Hennessey, B. A. (1992). The motivation for creativity in children. In A. K. Boggiano & T. S. Pittman (Eds.), *Achievement and motivation: A social-developmental perspective* (pp. 54–74). Cambridge, England: Cambridge University Press.

Ames, C. (1992). Classrooms: Goals, structures, and student motivation. *Journal of Educational Psychology, 84,* 261–271.

Anderman, E. M., & Dawson, H. (2011). Learning with motivation. In R. E. Mayer & P. A. Alexander (Eds.), *Handbook of research on learning and instruction* (pp. 219–241). New York: Routledge.

Anderman, E. M., Griesinger, T., & Westerfield, G. (1998). Motivation and cheating during early adolescence. *Journal of Educational Psychology, 90,* 84–93.

Anderman, E. M., & Maehr, M. L. (1994). Motivation and schooling in the middle grades. *Review of Educational Research, 64,* 287–309.

Anderman, E. M., & Mueller, C. E. (2010). Middle school transitions and adolescent development. In J. Meece & J. Eccles (Eds.), *Handbook of research on schools, schooling, and human development* (pp. 198–215). Mahwah, NJ: Erlbaum.

Anderman, E. M., Noar, S., Zimmerman, R. S., & Donohew, L. (2004). The need for sensation as a prerequisite for motivation to engage in academic tasks. In M. L. Maehr & P. Pintrich (Eds.), *Advances in motivation and achievement: Motivating students, improving schools: The legacy of Carol Midgley* (Vol. 13, pp. 1–26). Greenwich, CT: JAI.

Anderman, L. H., & Anderman, E. M. (2009). Oriented towards mastery: Promoting positive motivational goals for students. In R. Gilman, E. S. Huebner, & M. J. Furlong (Eds.), *Handbook of positive psychology in schools* (pp. 161–173). New York: Routledge.

Anderman, L. H., Andrzejewski, C.E., & Allen, J. (2011). How do teachers support students' motivation and learning in their classrooms? *Teachers College Record, 113,* 969–1003.

Anderman, L. H., Patrick, H., Hruda, L. Z., & Linnenbrink, E. A. (2002). Observing classroom goal structures to clarify and expand goal theory. In C. Midgley (Ed.), *Goals, goal structures, and patterns of adaptive learning* (pp. 243–278). Mahwah, NJ: Erlbaum.

Anderson, L. W., & Pellicer, L. O. (1998). Toward an understanding of unusually successful programs for economically disadvantaged students. *Journal of Education for Students Placed at Risk, 3*, 237–263.

Andre, T., & Windschitl, M. (2003). Interest, epistemological belief, and intentional conceptual change. In G. M. Sinatra & P. R. Pintrich (Eds.), *Intentional conceptual change* (pp. 173–197). Mahwah, NJ: Erlbaum.

Archambault, I., Eccles, J. S., & Vida, M. N. (2010). Ability self-concepts and subjective value in literacy: Joint trajectories from grades 1 through 12. *Journal of Educational Psychology, 102*, 804–816.

Arnett, J. J. (1999). Adolescent storm and stress, reconsidered. *American Psychologist, 54*, 317–326.

Aronson, J., & Steele, C. M. (2005). Stereotypes and the fragility of academic competence, motivation, and self-concept. In A. J. Elliot & C. S. Dweck (Eds.), *Handbook of competence and motivation* (pp. 436–456). New York: Guilford.

Ashcraft, M. H. (2002). Math anxiety: Personal, educational, and cognitive consequences. *Current Directions in Psychological Science, 11*, 181–184.

Ashiabi, G. S., & O'Neal, K. K. (2008). A framework for understanding the association between food insecurity and children's developmental outcomes. *Child Development Perspectives, 2*, 71–77.

Assor, A., Vansteenkiste, M., & Kaplan, A. (2009). Identified versus introjected approach and introjected avoidance motivations in school and in sports: The limited benefits of self-worth strivings. *Journal of Educational Psychology, 101*, 482–497.

Babad, E. (1993). Teachers' differential behavior. *Educational Psychology Review, 5*, 347–376.

Bao, X., & Lam, S. (2008). Who makes the choice? Rethinking the role of autonomy and relatedness in Chinese children's motivation. *Child Development, 79*, 269–283.

Barab, S. A., Gresalfi, M., & Ingram-Goble, A. (2010). Transformational play: Using games to position person, content, and context. *Educational Researcher, 39*, 525–536.

Barron, B. (2006). Interest and self-sustained learning as catalysts of development: A learning ecologies perspective. *Human Development, 49*, 193–224.

Bartlett, M., Rudolph, K. D., Flynn, M., Abaied, J., & Koerber, C. (2007, March). *Need for approval as a moderator of children's responses to victimization.* Paper presented at the biennial meeting of the Society for Research in Child Development, Boston.

Battistich, V., Solomon, D., Kim, D., Watson, M., & Schaps, E. (1995). Schools as communities, poverty levels of student populations, and students' attitudes, motives, and performance: A multilevel analysis. *American Educational Research Journal, 32*, 627–658.

Becker, B. E., & Luthar, S. S. (2002). Social-emotional factors affecting achievement outcomes among disadvantaged students: Closing the achievement gap. *Educational Psychologist, 37*, 197–214.

Becker, M., McElvany, N., & Kortenbruck, M. (2010). Intrinsic and extrinsic reading motivation as predictors of reading literacy: A longitudinal study. *Journal of Educational Psychology, 102*, 773–785.

Beilock, S. L. (2008). Math performance in stressful situations. *Current Directions in Psychological Science, 17*, 339–343.

Beirne-Smith, M., Patton, J. R., & Kim, S. H. (2006). *Mental retardation: An introduction to intellectual disabilities* (7th ed.). Upper Saddle River, NJ: Merrill/Prentice-Hall.

Ben-Zeev, T., Carrasquillo, C. M., Ching, A. M. L., Kliengklom, T. J., McDonald, K. L., Newhall, D. C., et al. (2005). "Math is hard!" (Barbie™, 1994): Responses of threat vs. challenge-mediated arousal to stereotypes alleging intellectual inferiority. In A. M. Gallagher & J. C. Kaufman (Eds.), *Gender differences in mathematics: An integrative psychological approach* (pp. 189–206). Cambridge, England: Cambridge University Press.

Benes, F. M. (2007). Corticolimbic circuitry and psychopathology: Development of the corticolimbic system. In D. Coch, G. Dawson, & K. W. Fischer (Eds.), *Human behavior, learning, and the developing brain: Atypical development* (pp. 331–361). New York: Guilford.

Benner, A. D., & Graham, S. (2009). The transition to high school as a developmental process among multiethnic urban youth. *Child Development, 80*, 356–376.

Bergin, D. A., & Cooks, H. C. (2008). High school students of color talk about accusations of "acting White." In J. U. Ogbu (Ed.), *Minority status, oppositional culture, and schooling* (pp. 145–166). New York: Routledge.

Berlyne, D. E. (1960). *Conflict, arousal, and curiosity.* New York: McGraw-Hill.

Blackwell, L. S., Trzesniewski, K. H., & Dweck, C. S. (2007). Implicit theories of intelligence predict achievement across an adolescent transition: A longitudinal study and an intervention. *Child Development, 78*, 246–263.

Bleske-Rechek, A., Lubinski, D., & Benbow, C. P. (2004). Meeting the educational needs of special populations: Advanced Placement's role in developing exceptional human capital. *Psychological Science, 15*, 217–224.

Blumenfeld, P. C., Kempler, T. M., & Krajcik, J. S. (2006). Motivation and cognitive engagement in learning environments. In R. K. Sawyer (Ed.), *The Cambridge handbook of the learning sciences* (pp. 475–488). Cambridge, England: Cambridge University Press.

Boggiano, A. K., & Pittman, T. S. (Eds.). (1992). *Achievement and motivation: A social-developmental perspective.* Cambridge, England: Cambridge University Press.

Boman, P., Furlong, M. J., Shochet, I., Lilles, E., & Jones, C. (2009). Optimism and the school context. In R. Gilman, E. S. Huebner, & M. J. Furlong (Eds.), *Handbook of positive psychology in schools* (pp. 51–64). New York: Routledge.

Bong, M. (2009). Age-related differences in achievement goal differentiation. *Journal of Educational Psychology, 101*, 879–896.

Botelho, M. J., Cohen, S. L., Leoni, L., Chow, P., & Sastri, P. (2010). Respecting children's cultural and linguistic knowledge. In M. L. Dantas & P. C. Manyak (Eds.), *Home-school connections in a multicultural society: Learning from and with culturally and linguistically diverse families* (pp. 237–256). New York: Routledge.

Bower, G. H. (1994). Some relations between emotions and memory. In P. Ekman & R. J. Davidson (Eds.), *The nature of emotion: Fundamental questions* (pp. 303–305). New York: Oxford University Press.

Bower, G. H., & Forgas, J. P. (2001). Mood and social memory. In J. P. Forgas (Ed.), *Handbook of affect and social cognition* (pp. 95–120). Mahwah, NJ: Erlbaum.

Boyatzis, R. E. (1973). Affiliation motivation. In D. C. McClelland & R. S. Steele (Eds.), *Human motivation: A book of readings* (pp. 252–276). Morristown, NJ: General Learning Press.

Brody, G. H., Chen, Y.-F., Murry, V. M., Ge, X., Simons, R. L., Gibbons, F. X., et al. (2006). Perceived discrimination and the adjustment of African American youths: A five-year longitudinal analysis with contextual moderation effects. *Child Development, 77*, 1170–1189.

Brophy, J. E. (1986). *On motivating students* (Occasional Paper No. 101). East Lansing: Michigan State University, Institute for Research on Teaching.

Brophy, J. E. (2004). *Motivating students to learn* (2nd ed.). Mahwah, NJ: Erlbaum.

Brophy, J. E. (2006). Observational research on generic aspects of classroom teaching. In P. A. Alexander & P. H. Winne (Eds.), *Handbook of educational psychology* (2nd ed., pp. 755–780). Mahwah, NJ: Erlbaum.

Brophy, J. E. (2008). Developing students' appreciation for what is taught in school. *Educational Psychologist, 43*, 132–141.

Brophy, J., Alleman, J., & Knighton, B. (2009). *Inside the social studies classroom.* New York: Routledge.

Brown, B. B. (1993). School culture, social politics, and the academic motivation of U.S. students. In T. M. Tomlinson (Ed.), *Motivating students to learn: Overcoming barriers to high achievement* (pp. 63–98). Berkeley, CA: McCutchan.

Buehl, M. M., & Alexander, P. A. (2001). Beliefs about academic knowledge. *Educational Psychology Review, 13*, 385–418.

Burhans, K. K., & Dweck, C. S. (1995). Helplessness in early childhood: The role of contingent worth. *Child Development, 66*, 1719–1738.

Butler, R. (1994). Teacher communication and student interpretations: Effects of teacher responses to failing students on attributional inferences in two age groups. *British Journal of Educational Psychology, 64*, 277–294.

Cacioppo, J. T., Petty, R. E., Feinstein, J. A., & Jarvis, W. B. G. (1996). Dispositional differences in cognitive motivation: The life and times of individuals varying in need for cognition. *Psychological Bulletin, 119,* 197–253.

Cameron, J. (2001). Negative effects of reward on intrinsic motivation—A limited phenomenon: Comment on Deci, Koestner, and Ryan (2001). *Review of Educational Research, 71,* 29–42.

Cameron, J., & Pierce, W. D. (1994). Reinforcement, reward, and intrinsic motivation: A meta-analysis. *Review of Educational Research, 64,* 363–423.

Camras, L. A., Chen, Y., Bakeman, R., Norris, K., & Cain, T. R. (2006). Culture, ethnicity, and children's facial expressions: A study of European American, Mainland Chinese, Chinese American, and adopted Chinese girls. *Emotion, 6,* 103–114.

Carrasco, R. L. (1981). Expanded awareness of student performance: A case study in applied ethnographic monitoring in a bilingual classroom. In H. T. Trueba, G. P. Guthrie, & K. H. Au (Eds.), *Culture and the bilingual classroom: Studies in classroom ethnography* (pp. 153–177). Rowley, MA: Newbury House.

Carter, R., Williams, S., & Silverman, W. K. (2008). Cognitive and emotional facets of test anxiety in African American school children. *Cognition and Emotion, 22,* 539–551.

Carver, C. S., & Scheier, M. F. (1990). Origins and functions of positive and negative affect: A control-process view. *Psychological Review, 97,* 19–35.

Cassady, J. C. (2004). The influence of cognitive test anxiety across the learning-testing cycle. *Learning and Instruction, 14,* 569–592.

Cassady, J. C. (Ed.) (2010a). *Anxiety in schools: The causes, consequences, and solutions for academic anxieties.* New York: Peter Lang.

Cassidy, J., Ziv, Y., Mehta, T. G., & Feeney, B. C. (2003). Feedback seeking in children and adolescents: Associations with self-perceptions, attachment representations, and depression. *Child Development, 74,* 612–628.

Certo, J. L., Cauley, K. M., & Chafin, C. (2003). Students' perspectives on their high school experience. *Adolescence, 38,* 705–724.

Chabrán, M. (2003). Listening to talk from and about students on accountability. In M. Carnoy, R. Elmore, & L. S. Siskin (Eds.), *The new accountability: High schools and high-stakes testing* (pp. 129–145). New York: RoutledgeFalmer.

Chang, M.-L., & Davis, H. A. (2009). Understanding the role of teacher appraisals in shaping the dynamics of their relationships with students: Deconstructing teachers' judgments of disruptive behavior/students. In P. Schutz & M. Zembylas (Eds.), *Advances in teacher emotion research: The impact of teachers' lives* (pp. 95–125). New York: Springer.

Chen, J. A., & Pajares, F. (2010). Implicit theories of ability of grade 6 science students: Relation to epistemological beliefs and academic motivation and achievement in science. *Contemporary Educational Psychology, 35,* 75–87.

Chinn, C. A. (2006). Learning to argue. In A. M. O'Donnell, C. E. Hmelo-Silver, & G. Erkens (Eds.), *Collaborative learning, reasoning, and technology* (pp. 355–383). Mahwah, NJ: Erlbaum.

Chiu, C.-Y., & Hong, Y.-Y. (2005). Cultural competence: Dynamic processes. In A. J. Elliot & C. S. Dweck (Eds.), *Handbook of competence and motivation* (pp. 489–505). New York: Guilford.

Christenson, S. L., & Thurlow, M. L. (2004). School dropouts: Prevention, considerations, interventions, and challenges. *Current Directions in Psychological Science, 13,* 36–39.

Cizek, G. J. (2003). *Detecting and preventing classroom cheating: Promoting integrity in assessment.* Thousand Oaks, CA: Corwin.

Clani, K. D., Middleton, M. J., Summers, J. J., & Sheldon, K. M. (2010). Buffering against performance classroom goal structures: The importance of autonomy support and classroom community. *Contemporary Educational Psychology, 35,* 88–99.

Clark, B. (1997). *Growing up gifted* (5th ed.). Upper Saddle River, NJ: Merrill/Prentice-Hall.

Cleveland, M. J., Gibbons, F. X., Gerrard, M., Pomery, E. A., & Brody, G. H. (2005). The impact of parenting on risk cognitions and risk behavior: A study of mediation and moderation in a panel of African American adolescents. *Child Development, 76,* 900–916.

Clifford, M. M. (1990). Students need challenge, not easy success. *Educational Leadership, 48*(1), 22–26.

Clore, G. L., Gasper, K., & Garvin, E. (2001). Affect as information. In J. P. Forgas (Ed.), *Handbook of affect and social cognition* (pp. 121–144). Mahwah, NJ: Erlbaum.

Coddington, C. S., & Guthrie, J. T. (2008, March). *Intrinsic and avoidance motivation for school reading.* Paper presented at the annual meeting of the American Educational Research Association, New York.

Cohen, G. L., & Garcia, J. (2008). Identity, belonging, and achievement: A model, interventions, implications. *Current Directions in Psychological Science, 17,* 365–369.

Cohen, G. L., Garcia, J., Purdie-Vaughns, V., Apfel, N., & Brzustoski, P. (2009). Recursive processes in self-affirmation: Intervening the close the minority achievement gap. *Science, 324*(5925), 400–403.

Cole, P. M., Bruschi, C. J., & Tamang, B. L. (2002). Cultural differences in children's emotional reactions to difficult situations. *Child Development, 73,* 983–996.

Cole, P. M., Tamang, B. L., & Shrestha, S. (2006). Cultural variations in the socialization of young children's anger and shame. *Child Development, 77,* 1237–1251.

Cole, P. M., & Tan, P. Z. (2007). Emotion socialization from a cultural perspective. In J. E. Grusec & P. D. Hastings (Eds.), *Handbook of socialization: Theory and research* (pp. 516–542). New York: Guilford.

Collins, A., & Halverson, R. (2009). *Rethinking education in the age of technology: The digital revolution and schooling in America.* New York: Teachers College Press.

Combs, A. W., Richards, A. C., & Richards, F. (1976). *Perceptual psychology: A humanistic approach to the study of persons.* New York: Harper & Row.

Connell, J. P., & Wellborn, J. G. (1991). Competence, autonomy, and relatedness: A motivational analysis of self-system processes. In M. R. Gunnar & L. A. Sroufe (Eds.), *Self processes and development: The Minnesota Symposia on Child Psychology* (Vol. 23, pp. 43–77). Mahwah, NJ: Erlbaum.

Cook, P. J., & Ludwig, J. (2008). The burden of "acting White": Do Black adolescents disparage academic achievement? In J. U. Ogbu (Ed.), *Minority status, oppositional culture, and schooling* (pp. 275–297). New York: Routledge.

Corpus, J. H., McClintic-Gilbert, M. S., & Hayenga, A. O. (2009). Within-year changes in children's intrinsic and extrinsic motivational orientations: Contextual predictors and academic outcomes. *Contemporary Educational Psychology, 34,* 154–166.

Corpus, J. H., Tomlinson, T. D., & Stanton, P. R. (April, 2004). Does social-comparison praise undermine children's intrinsic motivation? Paper presented at the American Educational Research Association, San Diego, CA.

Costa, P. T., Jr., & McCrae, R. R. (1992). Trait psychology comes of age. In T. B. Sondereger (Ed.), *Nebraska Symposium on Motivation: Psychology and aging* (pp. 169–204). Lincoln: University of Nebraska Press.

Covington, M. V. (1987). Achievement motivation, self-attributions, and the exceptional learner. In J. D. Day & J. G. Borkowski (Eds.), *Intelligence and exceptionality.* Norwood, NJ: Ablex.

Covington, M. V. (1992). *Making the grade: A self-worth perspective on motivation and school reform.* Cambridge, England: Cambridge University Press.

Covington, M. V. (2000). Intrinsic versus extrinsic motivation in schools: A reconciliation. *Current Directions in Psychological Science, 9,* 22–25.

Covington, M. V., & Müeller, K. J. (2001). Intrinsic versus extrinsic motivation: An approach/avoidance reformulation. *Educational Psychology Review, 13,* 157–176.

Csikszentmihalyi, M. (1990). *Flow: The psychology of optimal experience.* New York: HarperPerennial.

Csikszentmihalyi, M. (1996). *Creativity: Flow and the psychology of discovery and invention.* New York: HarperCollins.

Csikszentmihalyi, M., Abuhamdeh, S., & Nakamura, J. (2005). Flow. In A. J. Elliot & C. S. Dweck (Eds.), *Handbook of competence and motivation* (pp. 598–608). New York: Guilford.

Csikszentmihalyi, M., & Nakamura, J. (1989). The dynamics of intrinsic motivation: A study of adolescents. In C. Ames & R. Ames (Eds.), *Research on motivation in education: Vol. 3. Goals and cognitions* (pp. 45–71). San Diego, CA: Academic Press.

Curtis, K. A. (1992). Altering beliefs about the importance of strategy: An attributional intervention. *Journal of Applied Social Psychology, 22,* 953–972.

Curtis, K. A., & Graham, S. (1991, April). *Altering beliefs about the importance of strategy: An attributional intervention.* Paper presented at the annual meeting of the American Educational Research Association, Chicago.

Dai, D. Y. (2010). *The nature and nurture of giftedness: A new framework for understanding gifted education.* New York: Teachers College Press.

d'Ailly, H. (2003). Children's autonomy and perceived control in learning: A model of motivation and achievement in Taiwan. *Journal of Educational Psychology, 95,* 84–96.

Damasio, A. R. (1994). *Descartes' error: Emotion, reason, and the human brain.* New York: Avon Books.

Danner, F. (2011, April). *School belonging and trajectories of depressive symptoms across adolescence and young adulthood.* Paper presented at the annual meeting of the American Educational Research Association, New Orleans, LA.

Daschmann, E. C., Nett, U. E., Wimmer, B. M., Goetz, T., & Stupnisky, R. H. (2010, April–May). *Students' and teachers' perspectives on the antecedents of boredom: An interview study.* Paper presented at the annual meeting of the American Educational Research Association, Denver.

Davies, P. G., & Spencer, S. J. (2005). The gender-gap artifact: Women's underperformance in quantitative domains through the lens of stereotype threat. In A. M. Gallagher & J. C. Kaufman (Eds.), *Gender differences in mathematics: An integrative psychological approach* (pp. 172–188). Cambridge, England: Cambridge University Press.

Davis, H. A. (2003). Conceptualizing the role and influence of student-teacher relationships on children's social and cognitive development. *Educational Psychologist, 38,* 207–234.

Davis, L. E., Ajzen, I., Saunders, J., & Williams, T. (2002). The decision of African American students to complete high school: An application of the theory of planned behavior. *Journal of Educational Psychology, 94,* 810–819.

Dawson, G., & Bernier, R. (2007). Development of social brain circuitry in autism. In D. Coch, G. Dawson, & K. W. Fischer (Eds.), *Human behavior, learning, and the developing brain: Atypical development* (pp. 28–55). New York: Guilford.

de Boer, H., Bosker, R. J., & van der Werf, M. P. C. (2010). Sustainability of teacher expectation bias effects on long-term student performance. *Journal of Educational Psychology, 102,* 168–179.

deCharms, R. (1972). Personal causation training in the schools. *Journal of Applied Social Psychology, 2,* 95–113.

Deci, E. L. (1992). The relation of interest to the motivation of behavior: A self-determination theory perspective. In K. A. Renninger, S. Hidi, & A. Krapp (Eds.), *The role of interest in learning and development* (pp. 43–70). Mahwah, NJ: Erlbaum.

Deci, E. L., Koestner, R., & Ryan, R. M. (2001). Extrinsic rewards and intrinsic motivation in education: Reconsidered once again. *Review of Educational Research, 71,* 1–27.

Deci, E. L., & Moller, A. C. (2005). The concept of competence: A starting place for understanding intrinsic motivation and self-determined extrinsic motivation. In A. J. Elliot & C. S. Dweck (Eds.), *Handbook of competence and motivation* (pp. 579–597). New York: Guilford.

Deci, E. L., & Ryan, R. M. (1985). *Intrinsic motivation and self-determination in human behavior.* New York: Plenum.

Deci, E. L., & Ryan, R. M. (1992). The initiation and regulation of intrinsically motivated learning and achievement. In A. K. Boggiano & T. S. Pittman (Eds.), *Achievement and motivation: A social-developmental perspective* (pp. 9–36). Cambridge, England: Cambridge University Press.

Deci, E. L., & Ryan, R. M. (1995). Human autonomy: The basis for true self-esteem. In M. H. Kernis (Ed.), *Efficacy, agency, and self-esteem* (pp. 31–49). New York: Plenum.

Deyhle, D., & LeCompte, M. (1999). Cultural differences in child development: Navajo adolescents in middle schools. In R. H. Sheets & E. R. Hollins (Eds.), *Racial and ethnic identity in school practices: Aspects of human development* (pp. 123–139). Mahwah, NJ: Erlbaum.

Diekman, A. B., Brown, E. R., Johnston, A. M., & Clark, E. K. (2010). Seeking congruity between goals and roles: A new look at why women opt out of science, technology, engineering, and mathematics careers. *Psychological Science, 21,* 1051–1057.

Dien, T. (1998). Language and literacy in Vietnamese American communities. In B. Pérez (Ed.), *Sociocultural contexts of language and literacy* (pp. 23–54). Mahwah, NJ: Erlbaum.

Dijkstra, P., Kuyper, H., van der Werf, G., Buunk, A. P., & van der Zee, Y. G. (2008). Social comparison in the classroom: A review. *Review of Educational Research, 78,* 828–879.

Dodge, K. A., Asher, S. R., & Parkhurst, J. T. (1989). Social life as a goal-coordination task. In C. Ames & R. Ames (Eds.), *Research on motivation in education: Vol. 3. Goals and cognitions* (pp. 107–138). San Diego: Academic Press.

Dotterer, A. M., McHale, S. M., & Crouter, A. C. (2009). The development and correlates of academic interests from childhood through adolescence. *Journal of Educational Psychology, 101,* 509–519.

Dowson, M., & McInerney, D. M. (2001). Psychological parameters of students' social and work avoidance goals: A qualitative investigation. *Journal of Educational Psychology, 93,* 35–42.

Doyle, W. (1986a). Classroom organization and management. In M. C. Wittrock (Ed.), *Handbook of research on teaching* (3rd ed., pp. 392–431). New York: Macmillan.

DuBois, D. L., Burk-Braxton, C., Swenson, L. P., Tevendale, H. D., & Hardesty, J. L. (2002). Race and gender influences on adjustment in early adolescence: Investigation of an integrative model. *Child Development, 73,* 1573–1592.

Dunlap, G., dePerczel, M., Clarke, S., Wilson, D., Wright, S., White, R., et al. (1994). Choice making to promote adaptive behavior for students with emotional and behavioral challenges. *Journal of Applied Behavior Analysis, 27,* 505–518.

Durik, A. M., & Harackiewicz, J. M. (2007). Different strokes for different folks: How individual interest moderates the effects of situational factors on task interest. *Journal of Educational Psychology, 99,* 597–610.

Durik, A., M., Vida, M., & Eccles, J. S. (2006). Task values and ability beliefs as predictors of high school literacy choices: A developmental analysis. *Journal of Educational Psychology, 98,* 382–393.

Dweck, C. S. (1986). Motivational processes affecting learning. *American Psychologist, 41,* 1040–1048.

Dweck, C. S. (2000). *Self-theories: Their role in motivation, personality, and development.* Philadelphia: Psychology Press.

Dweck, C. S. (2009). Foreword. In F. D. Horowitz, R. F. Subotnik, & D. J. Matthews (Eds.), *The development of giftedness and talent across the life span* (pp. xi-xiv). Washington, DC: American Psychological Association.

Dweck, C. S., & Elliott, E. S. (1983). Achievement motivation. In E. M. Hetherington (Ed.), *Handbook of child psychology: Vol. 4. Socialization, personality, and social development* (4th ed., pp. 643–691). New York: Wiley.

Dweck, C. S., & Leggett, E. L. (1988). A social-cognitive approach to motivation and personality. *Psychological Review, 95,* 256–273.

Dweck, C. S., Mangels, J. A., & Good, C. (2004). Motivational effects on attention, cognition, and performance. In D. Y. Dai & R. J. Sternberg (Eds.), *Motivation, emotion, and cognition: Integrative perspectives on intellectual functioning and development* (pp. 41–55). Mahwah, NJ: Erlbaum.

Dweck, C. S., & Molden, D. C. (2005). Self-theories: Their impact on competence motivation and acquisition. In A. J. Elliot & C. S. Dweck (Eds.), *Handbook of competence and motivation* (pp. 122–140). New York: Guilford.

Eccles, J. S. (2005). Subjective task value and the Eccles et al. model of achievement-related choices. In A. J. Elliot & C. S. Dweck (Eds.), *Handbook of competence and motivation* (pp. 105–121). New York: Guilford.

Eccles, J. S. (2007). Families, schools, and developing achievement-related motivations and engagement. In J. E. Grusec & P. D. Hastings (Eds.), *Handbook of socialization: Theory and research* (pp. 665–691). New York: Guilford.

Eccles, J. (2009). Who am I and what am I going to do with my life? Personal and collective identities as motivators of action. *Educational Psychologist, 44,* 78–89.

Eccles, J. S., & Midgley, C. (1989). Stage-environment fit: Developmentally appropriate classrooms for young adolescents. In C. Ames & R. Ames (Eds.), *Research on motivation in education: Vol. 3. Goals and cognition* (pp. 139–186). San Diego, CA: Academic Press.

Eccles, J. S., Wigfield, A., & Schiefele, U. (1998). Motivation to succeed. In W. Damon (Series Ed.) & N. Eisenberg (Vol. Ed.), *Handbook of child psychology: Vol. 3. Social, emotional, and personality development* (5th ed., pp. 1017–1095). New York: Wiley.

Eccles (Parsons), J. S., Adler, T. F., Futterman, R., Goff, S. B., Kaczala, C. M., Meece, J. L., et al. (1983). Expectancies, values, and academic behaviors. In J. T. Spence (Ed.), *Achievement and achievement motivation* (pp. 75–146). San Francisco: Freeman.

Efklides, A. (2011). Interactions of metacognition with motivation and affect in self-regulated learning: The MASRL model. *Educational Psychologist, 46*, 6–25.

Eid, M., & Diener, E. (2001). Norms for experiencing emotions in different cultures: Inter- and intranational differences. *Journal of Personality and Social Psychology, 81*, 869–885.

Eisenberg, N., Martin, C. L., & Fabes, R. A. (1996). Gender development and gender effects. In D. C. Berliner & R. C. Calfee (Eds.), *Handbook of educational psychology* (pp. 358–396). New York: Macmillan.

Elkind, D. (1981). *Children and adolescents: Interpretive essays on Jean Piaget* (3rd ed.). New York: Oxford University Press.

Elliot, A. J., & Dweck, C. S. (Eds.). (2005). *Handbook of competence and motivation.* New York: Guilford.

Elliot, A. J., Murayama, K., & Pekrun, R. (2011). A 3 × 2 achievement goal model. *Journal of Educational Psychology, 103*, 632–648.

Epstein, J. L. (1989). Family structures and student motivation. In R. E. Ames & C. Ames (Eds.), *Research on motivation in education: Vol. 3. Goals and cognitions* (pp. 259–295). New York: Academic Press.

Evans, G. W., Gonnella, C., Marcynyszyn, L. A., Gentile, L., & Salpekar, N. (2005). The role of chaos in poverty and children's socioemotional adjustment. *Psychological Science, 16*, 560–565.

Eysenck, M. W. (1992). *Anxiety: The cognitive perspective.* Hove, England: Erlbaum.

Fairweather, E., & Cramond, B. (2010). Infusing creative and critical thinking into the curriculum together. In R. A. Beghetto & J. C. Kaufman (Eds.), *Nurturing creativity in the classroom* (pp. 113–141). New York: Cambridge University Press.

Feather, N. T. (1982). *Expectations and actions: Expectancy-value models in psychology.* Mahwah, NJ: Erlbaum.

Ferrari, M., & Elik, N. (2003). Influences on intentional conceptual change. In G. M. Sinatra & P. R. Pintrich (Eds.), *Intentional conceptual change* (pp. 21–54). Mahwah, NJ: Erlbaum.

Fiske, A. P., & Fiske, S. T. (2007). Social relationships in our species and cultures. In S. Kitayama & D. Cohen (Eds.), *Handbook of cultural psychology* (pp. 283–306). New York: Guilford.

Fletcher, K. L., & Cassady, J. C. (2010). Overcoming academic anxieties: Promoting effective coping and self-regulation strategies. In J. C. Cassady (Ed.), *Anxiety in schools: The causes, consequences, and solutions for academic anxieties* (pp. 177–200). New York: Peter Lang.

Ford, M. E. (1992). *Motivating humans: Goals, emotions, and personal agency beliefs.* Newbury Park, CA: Sage.

Ford, M. E., & Smith, P. R. (2007). Thriving with social purpose: An integrative approach to the development of optimal human functioning. *Educational Psychologist, 42*, 153–171.

Försterling, F., & Morgenstern, M. (2002). Accuracy of self-assessment and task performance: Does it pay to know the truth? *Journal of Educational Psychology, 94*, 576–585.

Foster-Johnson, L., Ferro, J., & Dunlap, G. (1994). Preferred curriculum activities and reduced problem behaviors in students with intellectual disabilities. *Journal of Applied Behavior Analysis, 27*, 493–504.

Fowler, J. W., & Peterson, P. L. (1981). Increasing reading persistence and altering attributional style of learned helpless children. *Journal of Educational Psychology, 73*, 251–260.

Fredricks, J. A., Blumenfeld, P. C., & Paris, A. H. (2004). School engagement: Potential of the concept, state of the evidence. *Review of Educational Research, 74*, 59–109.

Fredrickson, B. (2009). *Positivity: Groundbreaking research reveals how to embrace the hidden strength of positive emotions, overcome negativity, and thrive.* New York: Crown.

Freeman, K. E., Gutman, L. M., & Midgley, C. (2002). Can achievement goal theory enhance our understanding of the motivation and performance of African American young adolescents? In C. Midgley (Ed.), *Goals, goal structures, and patterns of adaptive learning* (pp. 175–204). Mahwah, NJ: Erlbaum.

Frydenberg, E., & Lewis, R. (2000). Teaching coping to adolescents: When and to whom? *American Educational Research Journal, 37*, 727–745.

Fuligni, A. J., & Hardway, C. (2004). Preparing diverse adolescents for the transition to adulthood. *The Future of Children, 14*(2), 99–119.

Furrer, C., & Skinner, E. (2003). Sense of relatedness as a factor in children's academic engagement and performance. *Journal of Educational Psychology, 95*, 148–162.

Gabriele, A. J. (2007). The influence of achievement goals on the constructive activity of low achievers during collaborative problem solving. *British Journal of Educational Psychology, 77*, 1221–141.

Gabriele, A. J., & Boody, R. M. (2001, April). *The influence of achievement goals on the constructive activity of low achievers during collaborative problem solving.* Paper presented at the annual meeting of the American Educational Research Association, Seattle, WA.

Gallini, J. (2000, April). *An investigation of self-regulation developments in early adolescence: A comparison between non-at-risk and at-risk students.* Paper presented at the annual meeting of the American Educational Research Association, New Orleans, LA.

García, E. E. (1992). "Hispanic" children: Theoretical, empirical, and related policy issues. *Educational Psychology Review, 4*, 69–93.

Garner, R. (1998). Epilogue: Choosing to learn or not-learn in school. *Educational Psychology Review, 10*, 227–237.

Garner, R., Brown, R., Sanders, S., & Menke, D. J. (1992). "Seductive details" and learning from text. In K. A. Renninger, S. Hidi, & A. Krapp (Eds.), *The role of interest in learning and development* (pp. 239–254). Mahwah, NJ: Erlbaum.

Gaskill, P. J. (2001, April). *Differential effects of reinforcement feedback and attributional feedback on second-graders' self-efficacy.* Paper presented at the annual meeting of the American Educational Research Association, Seattle, WA.

Gay, G. (2010). *Culturally responsive teaching: Theory, research, and practice* (2nd ed.). New York: Teachers College Press.

Gentry, M., Gable, R. K., & Rizza, M. G. (2002). Students' perceptions of classroom activities: Are there grade-level and gender differences? *Journal of Educational Psychology, 94*, 539–544.

Goetz, T., Frenzel, A. C., Hall, N. C., & Pekrun, R. (2008). Antecedents of academic emotions: Testing the internal/external frame of reference model for academic enjoyment. *Contemporary Educational Psychology, 33*, 9–33.

Goldenberg, C. (1992). The limits of expectations: A case for case knowledge about teacher expectancy effects. *American Educational Research Journal, 29*, 517–544.

Goldstein, S., & Rider, R. (2006). Resilience and the disruptive disorders of childhood. In S. Goldstein & R. B. Brooks (Eds.), *Handbook of resilience in children* (pp. 203–222). New York: Springer.

Good, C., Aronson, J., & Inzlicht, M. (2003). Improving adolescents' standardized test performance: An intervention to reduce the effects of stereotype threat. *Journal of Applied Developmental Psychology, 24*, 645–662.

Good, T. L., & Brophy, J. E. (1994). *Looking in classrooms* (6th ed.). New York: HarperCollins.

Good, T. L., & Nichols, S. L. (2001). Expectancy effects in the classroom: A special focus on improving the reading performance of minority students in first-grade classrooms. *Educational Psychologist, 36*, 113–126.

Gottfried, A. E., Fleming, J. S., & Gottfried, A. W. (2001). Continuity of academic intrinsic motivation from childhood through late adolescence: A longitudinal study. *Journal of Educational Psychology, 93*, 3–13.

Graham, S. (1989). Motivation in Afro-Americans. In G. L. Berry & J. K. Asamen (Eds.), *Black students: Psychosocial issues and academic achievement* (pp. 40–68). Newbury Park, CA: Sage.

Graham, S. (1990). Communicating low ability in the classroom: Bad things good teachers sometimes do. In S. Graham & V. S. Folkes (Eds.), *Attribution theory: Applications to achievement, mental health, and interpersonal conflict* (pp. 17–36). Mahwah, NJ: Erlbaum.

Graham, S. (1991). A review of attribution theory in achievement contexts. *Educational Psychology Review, 3*, 5–39.

Graham, S., & Weiner, B. (1996). Theories and principles of motivation. In D. C. Berliner & R. C. Calfee (Eds.), *Handbook of educational psychology* (pp. 63–84). New York: Macmillan.

Greenspan, D. A., Solomon, B., & Gardner, H. (2004). The development of talent in different domains. In L. V. Shavinina & M. Ferrari (Eds.), *Beyond knowledge: Extracognitive aspects of developing high ability* (pp. 119–135). Mahwah, NJ: Erlbaum.

Hagtvet, K. A., & Johnsen, T. B. (Eds.). (1992). *Advances in test anxiety research* (Vol. 7). Amsterdam: Swets & Zeitlinger.

Hamre, B. K., & Pianta, R. C. (2005). Can instructional and emotional support in the first-grade classroom make a difference for children at risk of school failure? *Child Development, 76,* 949–967.

Hardré, P. L., Crowson, H. M., DeBacker, T. K., & White, D. (2007). Predicting the motivation of rural high school students. *Journal of Experimental Education, 75,* 247–269.

Hardré, P. L., & Reeve, J. (2003). A motivational model of rural students' intentions to persist in, versus drop out of, high school. *Journal of Educational Psychology, 95,* 347–356.

Hareli, S., & Weiner, B. (2002). Social emotions and personality inferences: A scaffold for a new direction in the study of achievement motivation. *Educational Psychologist, 37,* 183–193.

Harmon-Jones, E. (2001). The role of affect in cognitive-dissonance processes. In J. P. Forgas (Ed.), *Handbook of affect and social cognition* (pp. 237–255). Mahwah, NJ: Erlbaum.

Harter, S. (1990). Causes, correlates, and the functional role of global self-worth: A life-span perspective. In R. J. Sternberg & J. Kolligian, Jr. (Eds.), *Competence considered* (pp. 67–97). New Haven, CT: Yale University Press.

Harter, S. (1992). The relationship between perceived competence, affect, and motivational orientation within the classroom: Processes and patterns of change. In A. K. Boggiano & T. S. Pittman (Eds.), *Achievement and motivation: A social-developmental perspective* (pp. 77–114). Cambridge, England: Cambridge University Press.

Harter, S. (1999). *The construction of the self: A developmental perspective.* New York: Guilford

Hattie, J. (2008). Processes of integrating, developing, and processing self information. In H. W. Marsh, R. G. Craven, & D. M. McInerney (Eds.), *Self-processes, learning, and enabling human potential* (pp. 51–85). Charlotte, NC: Information Age.

Hattie, J. A. C. (2009). *Visible learning: A synthesis of over 800 meta-analyses relating to achievement.* London: Routledge.

Hattie, J., & Gan, M. (2011). Instruction based on feedback. In R. E. Mayer & P. A. Alexander (Eds.), *Handbook of research on learning and instruction* (pp. 249–271). New York: Routledge.

Hattie, J., & Timperley, H. (2007). The power of feedback. *Review of Educational Research, 77,* 81–112.

Hawley, C. A., (2005). Saint or sinner? Teacher perceptions of a child with traumatic brain injury. *Pediatric Rehabilitation, 8,* 117–129.

Hay, I., Ashman, A. F., van Kraayenoord, C. E., & Stewart, A. L. (1999). Identification of self-verification in the formation of children's academic self-concept. *Journal of Educational Psychology, 91,* 225–229.

Heine, S. J. (2007). Culture and motivation: What motivates people to act in the ways that they do?

In S. Kitayama & D. Cohen (Eds.), *Handbook of cultural psychology* (pp. 714–733). New York: Guilford.

Hemmings, A. B. (2004). *Coming of age in U.S. high schools: Economic, kinship, religious, and political crosscurrents.* Mahwah, NJ: Erlbaum.

Hennessey, B. A. (1995). Social, environmental, and developmental issues and creativity. *Educational Psychology Review, 7,* 163–183.

Heron, W. (1957). The pathology of boredom. *Scientific American, 196*(1), 52–56.

Hess, R. D., & Azuma, M. (1991). Cultural support for learning: Contrasts between Japan and the United States. *Educational Researcher, 29*(9), 2–8.

Heuer, F., & Reisberg, D. (1992). Emotion, arousal, and memory for detail. In S. Christianson (Ed.), *Handbook of emotion and memory* (pp. 151–180). Hillsdale, NJ: Erlbaum.

Heward, W. L. (2009). *Exceptional children: An introduction to special education* (9th ed.). Upper Saddle River, NJ: Merrill/Pearson Education.

Hickey, D. J. (2011). Participation by design: Improving individual motivation by looking beyond it. In D. M. McInerney, R. A. Walker, & G. A. D. Liem (Eds.), *Sociocultural theories of learning and motivation: Looking back, looking forward* (pp. 137–161). Charlotte, NC: Information Age.

Hidi, S., & Harackiewicz, J. M. (2000). Motivating the academically unmotivated: A critical issue for the 21st century. *Review of Educational Research, 70,* 151–179.

Hidi, S., & Renninger, K. A. (2006). The four-phase model of interest development. *Educational Psychologist, 41,* 111–127.

Hidi, S., Renninger, K. A., & Krapp, A. (2004). Interest, a motivational variable that combines affecting and cognitive functioning. In D. Y. Dai & R. J. Sternberg (Eds.), *Motivation, emotion, and cognition: Integrative perspectives on intellectual functioning and development* (pp. 89–115). Mahwah, NJ: Erlbaum.

Hidi, S., Weiss, J., Berndorff, D., & Nolan, J. (1998). The role of gender, instruction, and a cooperative learning technique in science education across formal and informal settings. In L. Hoffman, A. Krapp, K. Renninger, & J. Baumert (Eds.), *Interest and learning: Proceedings of the Seeon Conference on Interest and Gender* (pp. 215–227). Kiel, Germany: IPN.

Hill, K. T., & Sarason, S. B. (1966). The relation of test anxiety and defensiveness to test and school performance over the elementary school years: A further longitudinal study. *Monographs for the Society of Research in Child Development, 31*(2, Serial No. 104).

Hine, P., & Fraser, B. J. (2002, April). *Combining qualitative and quantitative methods in a study of Australian students' transition from elementary to high school.* Paper presented at the annual meeting of the American Educational Research Association, New Orleans, LA.

Hinkley, J. W., McInerney, D. M., & Marsh, H. W. (2001, April). *The multi-faceted structure of school achievement motivation: A case for social goals.* Paper presented at the annual

meeting of the American Educational Research Association, Seattle, WA.

Hinnant, J. B., O'Brien, M., & Ghazarian, S. R. (2009). The longitudinal relations of teacher expectations to achievement in the early school years. *Journal of Educational Psychology, 101,* 662–670.

Hofer, M. (2010). Adolescents' development of individual interests: A product of multiple goal regulation? *Educational Psychologist, 45,* 149–166.

Hom, A., & Battistich, V. (1995, April). *Students' sense of school community as a factor in reducing drug use and delinquency.* Paper presented at the annual meeting of the American Educational Research Association, San Francisco.

Hong, E., O'Neil, H. F., & Feldon, D. (2005). Gender effects on mathematics achievement: Mediating role of state and trait self-regulation. In A. M. Gallagher & J. C. Kaufman (Eds.), *Gender differences in mathematics: An integrative psychological approach* (pp. 264–293). Cambridge, England: Cambridge University Press.

Hong, Y., Chiu, C., & Dweck, C. S. (1995). Implicit theories of intelligence: Reconsidering the role of confidence in achievement motivation. In M. H. Kernis (Ed.), *Efficacy, agency, and self-esteem* (pp. 197–216). New York: Plenum.

Hsee, C. K., Yang, A. X., & Wang, L. (2010). Idleness aversion and the need for justifiable busyness. *Psychological Science, 21,* 926–930.

Huberty, T. J. (2008). Best practices in school-based interventions for anxiety and depression. In A. Thomas & J. Grimes (Eds.), *Best practices in school psychology–V* (pp. 1473–1486). Bethesda, MD: National Association of School Psychologists.

Hufton, N., Elliott, J., & Illushin, L. (2002). Achievement motivation across cultures: Some puzzles and their implications for future research. *New Directions for Child and Adolescent Development, 96,* 65–85.

Huguet, P., & Régner, I. (2007). Stereotype threat among schoolgirls in quasi-ordinary classroom circumstances. *Journal of Educational Psychology, 99,* 545–560.

Hulleman, C. S., Godes, O., Hendricks, B. L., & Harackiewicz, J. M. (2010). Enhancing interest and performance with a utility value intervention. *Journal of Educational Psychology, 102,* 880–895.

Hynd, C. (2003). Conceptual change in response to persuasive messages. In G. M. Sinatra & P. R. Pintrich (Eds.), *Intentional conceptual change* (pp. 291–315). Mahwah, NJ: Erlbaum.

Igoa, C. (1995). *The inner world of the immigrant child.* Mahwah, NJ: Erlbaum.

Ito, M., Baumer, S., Bittanti, M., Boyd, D., Cody, R., Herr-Stephenson, B., et al. (2009). *Hanging out, messing around, geeking out: Living and learning with new media.* Cambridge, MA: MIT Press.

Iyengar, S. S., & Lepper, M. R. (1999). Rethinking the value of choice: A cultural perspective on intrinsic motivation. *Journal of Personality and Social Psychology, 76,* 349–366.

Izard, C. (2007). Basic emotions, natural kinds, emotion schemas, and a new paradigm.

*Perspectives on Psychological Science, 2,* 260–280.

Jacobs, J. E., Davis-Kean, P., Bleeker, M., Eccles, J. S., & Malanchuk, O. (2005). "I can, but I don't want to": The impact of parents, interests, and activities on gender differences in math. In A. M. Gallagher & J. C. Kaufman (Eds.), *Gender differences in mathematics: An integrative psychological approach* (pp. 246–263). Cambridge, England: Cambridge University Press.

Jacobs, J. E., Lanza, S., Osgood, D. W., Eccles, J. S., & Wigfield, A. (2002). Changes in children's self-competence and values: Gender and domain differences across grades one through twelve. *Child Development, 73,* 509–527.

Jacobsen, B., Lowery, B., & DuCette, J. (1986). Attributions of learning disabled children. *Journal of Educational Psychology, 78,* 59–64.

Jagacinski, C. M., & Nicholls, J. G. (1984). Conceptions of ability and related affects in task involvement and ego involvement. *Journal of Educational Psychology, 76,* 909–919.

Jagacinski, C. M., & Nicholls, J. G. (1987). Competence and affect in task involvement and ego involvement: The impact of social comparison information. *Journal of Educational Psychology, 79,* 107–114.

Jain, S., & Dowson, M. (2009). Mathematics anxiety as a function of multidimensional self-regulation and self-efficacy. *Contemporary Educational Psychology, 34,* 240–249.

Jang, H., Reeve, J., & Deci, E. L. (2010). Engaging students in learning activities: It is not autonomy support or structure but autonomy support and structure. *Journal of Educational Psychology, 102,* 588–600.

Johnson, D. W., & Johnson, R. T. (2009a). An educational psychology success story: Social interdependence theory and cooperative learning. *Educational Researcher, 38,* 365–379.

Jussim, L., Eccles, J., & Madon, S. (1996). Social perception, social stereotypes, and teacher expectations: Accuracy and the quest for the powerful self-fulfilling prophecy. In M. P. Zanna (Ed.), *Advances in experimental social psychology* (Vol. 28, pp. 281–388). New York: Academic Press.

Juvonen, J. (2000). The social functions of attributional face-saving tactics among early adolescents. *Educational Psychology Review, 12,* 15–32.

Juvonen, J. (2006). Sense of belonging, social bonds, and school functioning. In P. A. Alexander & P. H. Winne (Eds.), *Handbook of educational psychology* (2nd ed., pp. 655–674). Mahwah, NJ: Erlbaum.

Kagan, J. (2010). Emotions and temperament. In M. H. Bornstein (Ed.), *Handbook of cultural developmental science* (pp. 175–194). New York: Psychology Press.

Kağıtçıbaşı, Ç. (2007). *Family, self, and human development across cultures: Theory and applications* (2nd ed.). Mahwah, NJ: Erlbaum.

Kaplan, A., & Midgley, C. (1999). The relationship between perceptions of the classroom goal structure and early adolescents' affect in school: The mediating role of coping strategies.

*Learning and Individual Differences, 11,* 187–212.

Kenrick, D. T., Griskevicius, V., Neuberg, S. L., & Schaller, M. (2010). Renovating the pyramid of needs: Contemporary extensions built upon ancient foundations. *Perspectives on Psychological Science, 5,* 292–314.

Kerns, L. L., & Lieberman, A. B. (1993). *Helping your depressed child.* Rocklin, CA: Prima.

Kesebir, S., Graham, J., & Oishi, S. (2010). A theory of human needs should be human-centered, not animal-centered: Commentary on Kenrick et al. (2010). *Perspectives on Psychological Science, 5,* 315–319.

Kiefer, S. M., & Ellerbrock, C. R. (2011, April). *Social goals: Relations with academic beliefs and school identification during early adolescence.* Paper presented at the annual meeting of the American Educational Research Association, New Orleans, LA.

Kim, H. S., Sherman, D. K., & Taylor, S. E. (2008). Culture and social support. *American Psychologist, 63,* 518–526.

King, N. J., & Ollendick, T. H. (1989). Children's anxiety and phobic disorders in school settings: Classification, assessment, and intervention issues. *Review of Educational Research, 59,* 431–470.

Knapp, M. S., Turnbull, B. J., & Shields, P. M. (1990). New directions for educating the children of poverty. *Educational Leadership, 48*(1), 4–9.

Knowlton, D. (1995). Managing children with oppositional behavior. *Beyond Behavior, 6*(3), 5–10.

Koestner, R., Ryan, R. M., Bernieri, F., & Holt, K. (1984). Setting limits in children's behavior: The differential effects of controlling versus informational styles on intrinsic motivation and creativity. *Journal of Personality, 52,* 233–248.

Kuhbandner, C., Spitzer, B., & Pekrun, R. (2011). Read-out of emotional information from iconic memory: The longevity of threatening stimuli. *Psychological Science, 22,* 695–700.

Kuhl, J., & Kraska, K. (1989). Self-regulation and metamotivation: Computational mechanisms, development, and assessment. In R. Kanfer, P. L. Ackerman, & R. Cudeck (Eds.), *Abilities, motivation, and methodology: The Minnesota Symposium on Learning and Individual Differences* (pp. 343–374). Mahwah, NJ: Erlbaum.

Kuhn, D., & Park, S.-H. (2005). Epistemological understanding and the development of intellectual values. *International Journal of Educational Research, 43,* 111–124.

Kuklinski, M. R., & Weinstein, R. S. (2001). Classroom and developmental differences in a path model of teacher expectancy effects. *Child Development, 72,* 1554–1578.

Kumar, R., Gheen, M. H., & Kaplan, A. (2002). Goal structures in the learning environment and students' disaffection from learning and schooling. In C. Midgley (Ed.), *Goals, goal structures, and patterns of adaptive learning* (pp. 143–173). Mahwah, NJ: Erlbaum.

Kunter, M., Frenzel, A., Nagy, G., Baumert, J., & Pekrun, R. (2011). Teacher enthusiasm:

Dimensionality and context specificity. *Contemporary Educational Psychology, 36,* 289–301.

Labouvie-Vief, G., & González, M. M. (2004). Dynamic integration: Affect optimization and differentiation in development. In D. Y. Dai & R. J. Sternberg (Eds.), *Motivation, emotion, and cognition: Integrative perspectives on intellectual functioning and development* (pp. 237–272). Mahwah, NJ: Erlbaum.

Ladd, G. W., & Dinella, L. M. (2009). Continuity and change in early school engagement: Predictive of children's achievement trajectories from first to eighth grade? *Journal of Educational Psychology, 101,* 190–206.

LaFontana, K. M., & Cillessen, A. H. N. (2010). Developmental changes in the priority of perceived status in childhood and adolescence. *Social Development, 19,* 130–147.

La Guardia, J. G., (2009). Developing who I am: A self-determination theory approach to the establishment of healthy identities. *Educational Psychologist, 44,* 90–104.

Lan, W. Y., Repman, J., Bradley, L., & Weller, H. (1994, April). *Immediate and lasting effects of criterion and payoff on academic risk taking.* Paper presented at the annual meeting of the American Educational Research Association, New Orleans, LA.

Landers, D. M. (2007). The arousal–performance relationship revisited. In D. Smith (Ed.), *Essential readings in sport and exercise psychology* (pp. 211–218). Champaign, IL: Human Kinetics.

Langer, E. J. (1997). *The power of mindful learning.* Reading, MA: Addison-Wesley.

Langer, J. A. (2000). Excellence in English in middle and high school: How teachers' professional lives support student achievement. *American Educational Research Journal, 37,* 397–439.

Lapan, R. T., Tucker, B., Kim, S.-K., & Kosciulek, J. F. (2003). Preparing rural adolescents for post-high school transitions. *Journal of Counseling and Development, 81,* 329–342.

Lapsley, D. K. (1993). Toward an integrated theory of adolescent ego development: The "new look" at adolescent egocentrism. *American Journal of Orthopsychiatry, 63,* 562–571.

Larson, R. W. (2000). Toward a psychology of positive youth development. *American Psychologist, 55,* 170–183.

Larson, R. W., & Brown, J. R. (2007). Emotional development in adolescence: What can be learned from a high school theater program? *Child Development, 78,* 1083–1099.

Larson, R. W., Moneta, G., Richards, M. H., & Wilson, S. (2002). Continuity, stability, and change in daily emotional experience across adolescence. *Child Development, 73,* 1151–1165.

Lau, S., & Nie, Y. (2008). Interplay between personal goals and classroom goal structures in predicting student outcomes: A multilevel analysis of person-context interactions. *Journal of Educational Psychology, 100,* 15–29.

Lawlor, M. S., & Schonert-Reichl, L. A. (2008, March). *The benefits of being good during early adolescence: Altruism, happiness, and the mediating role of relatedness.* Paper presented at the annual meeting of the American Educational Research Association, New York.

Lazarus, R. S. (1991). *Emotion and adaptation.* New York: Oxford University Press.

Leaper, C., & Friedman, C. K. (2007). The socialization of gender. In J. E. Grusec & P. D. Hastings (Eds.), *Handbook of socialization: Theory and research* (pp. 561–587). New York: Guilford.

Lee, J., & Shute, V. J. (2010). Personal and social-contextual factors in K–12 academic performance: An integrative perspective on student learning. *Educational Psychologist, 45,* 185–202.

Lee, J. Q., McInerney, D. M., Liem, G. A. D., & Ortiga, Y. P. (2010). The relationship between future goals and achievement goal orientations: An intrinsic–extrinsic motivation perspective. *Contemporary Educational Psychology, 35,* 264–279.

Lepper, M. R., Corpus, J. H., & Iyengar, S. S. (2005). Intrinsic and extrinsic motivational orientations in the classroom: Age differences and academic correlates. *Journal of Educational Psychology, 97,* 184–196.

Lepper, M. R., & Hodell, M. (1989). Intrinsic motivation in the classroom. In C. Ames & R. Ames (Eds.), *Research on motivation in education: Vol. 3. Goals and cognitions* (pp. 73–105). San Diego, CA: Academic Press.

Levy-Tossman, I., Kaplan, A., & Assor, A. (2007). Academic goal orientations, multiple goal profiles, and friendship intimacy among early adolescents. *Contemporary Educational Psychology, 32,* 231–252.

Lewis, M., & Sullivan, M. W. (2005). The development of self-conscious emotions. In A. J. Elliot & C. S. Dweck (Eds.), *Handbook of competence and motivation* (pp. 185–201). New York: Guilford.

Li, J. (2005). Mind or virtue: Western and Chinese beliefs about learning. *Current Directions in Psychological Science, 14,* 190–194.

Li, J. (2006). Self in learning: Chinese adolescents' goals and sense of agency. *Child Development, 77,* 482–501.

Li, J., & Fischer, K. W. (2004). Thought and affect in American and Chinese learners' beliefs about learning. In D. Y. Dai & R. J. Sternberg (Eds.), *Motivation, emotion, and cognition: Integrative perspectives on intellectual functioning and development* (pp. 385–418). Mahwah, NJ: Erlbaum.

Liem, A. D., Lau, S., & Nie, Y. (2008). The role of self-efficacy, task value, and achievement goals in predicting learning strategies, task disengagement, peer relationship, and achievement outcome. *Contemporary Educational Psychology, 33,* 486–512.

Lillard, A. S. (1997). Other folks' theories of mind and behavior. *Psychological Science, 8,* 268–274.

Linnenbrink, E. A. (2005). The dilemma of performance-approach goals: The use of multiple goal contexts to promote students' motivation and learning. *Journal of Educational Psychology, 97,* 197–213.

Linnenbrink, E. A., & Pintrich, P. R. (2002). Achievement goal theory and affect: An asymmetrical bidirectional model. *Educational Psychologist, 37,* 69–78.

Linnenbrink, E. A., & Pintrich, P. R. (2003). Achievement goals and intentional conceptual change. In G. M. Sinatra & P. R. Pintrich (Eds.), *Intentional conceptual change* (pp. 347–374). Mahwah, NJ: Erlbaum.

Linnenbrink, E. A., & Pintrich, P. R. (2004). Role of affect in cognitive processing in academic contexts. In D. Y. Dai & R. J. Sternberg (Eds.), *Motivation, emotion, and cognition: Integrative perspectives on intellectual functioning and development* (pp. 57–87). Mahwah, NJ: Erlbaum.

Lippa, R. A. (2002). *Gender, nature, and nurture.* Mahwah, NJ: Erlbaum.

Locke, E. A., & Latham, G. P. (2006). New directions in goal-setting theory. *Current Directions in Psychological Science, 15,* 265–268.

Lockhart, K. L., Chang, B., & Story, T. (2002). Young children's beliefs about the stability of traits: Protective optimism? *Child Development, 73,* 1408–1430.

Lopez, S. J., Rose, S., Robinson, C., Marques, S. C., & Pais-Ribeiro, J. (2009). Measuring and promoting hope in schoolchildren. In R. Gilman, E. S. Huebner, & M. J. Furlong (Eds.), *Handbook of positive psychology in schools* (pp. 37–50). New York: Routledge.

Luo, W., Paris, S. G., Hogan, D., & Luo, Z. (2011). Do performance goals promote learning? A pattern analysis of Singapore students' achievement goals. *Contemporary Educational Psychology, 36,* 165–176.

Mac Iver, D. J., Stipek, D. J., & Daniels, D. H. (1991). Explaining within-semester changes in student effort in junior high school and senior high school courses. *Journal of Educational Psychology, 83,* 201–211.

Maehr, M. L., & Anderman, E. M. (1993). Reinventing schools for early adolescents: Emphasizing task goals. *Elementary School Journal, 93,* 593–610.

Maehr, M. L., & McInerney, D. M. (2004). Motivation as personal investment. In D. M. McInerney & S. Van Etten (Eds.), *Big theories revisited* (pp. 61–90). Greenwich, CT: Information Age.

Mangels, J. (2004, May). *The influence of intelligence beliefs on attention and learning: A neurophysiological approach.* Invited address presented at the annual meeting of the American Psychological Society, Chicago.

Marachi, R., Friedel, J., & Midgley, C. (2001, April). "*I sometimes annoy my teacher during math*": Relations between student perceptions of the teacher and disruptive behavior in the classroom. Paper presented at the annual meeting of the American Educational Research Association, Seattle, WA.

Marcia, J. E. (1980). Identity in adolescence. In J. Adelson (Ed.), *Handbook of adolescent psychology* (pp. 159–187). New York: Wiley.

Marcus, G. (2008). *Kluge: The haphazard construction of the human mind.* Boston: Houghton Mifflin.

Marks, H. M. (2000). Student engagement in instructional activity: Patterns in the elementary, middle, and high school years. *American Educational Research Journal, 37,* 153–184.

Marsh, H. W., Martin, A. J., & Cheng, J. H. S. (2008). A multilevel perspective on gender in classroom motivation and climate: Potential benefits of male teachers for boys? *Journal of Educational Psychology, 100,* 78–95.

Martinez, R. S., & Huberty, T. J. (2010). Anxiety in students with learning difficulties and learning disabilities. In J. C. Cassady (Ed.), *Anxiety in schools: The causes, consequences, and solutions for academic anxieties* (pp. 137–152). New York: Peter Lang.

Maslow, A. H. (1943). A theory of human motivation. *Psychological Review, 50,* 514–539.

Maslow, A. H. (1973). Theory of human motivation. In R. J. Lowry (Ed.), *Dominance, self-esteem, self-actualization: Germinal papers of A. H. Maslow.* Monterey, CA: Brooks-Cole.

Maslow, A. H. (1987). *Motivation and personality* (3rd ed.). New York: Harper & Row.

Mason, L., Gava, M., & Boldrin, A. (2008). On warm conceptual change: The interplay of text, epistemological beliefs, and topic interest. *Journal of Educational Psychology, 100,* 291–309.

Masten, A. S. (2001). Ordinary magic: Resilience processes in development. *American Psychologist, 56,* 227–238.

Matthews, G., Zeidner, M., & Roberts, R. D. (2006). Models of personality and affect for education: A review and synthesis. In P. A. Alexander & P. H. Winne (Eds.), *Handbook of educational psychology* (2nd ed., pp. 163–186). Mahwah, NJ: Erlbaum.

McCall, R. B. (1994). Academic underachievers. *Current Directions in Psychological Science, 3,* 15–19.

McCaslin, M., & Good, T. L. (1996). The informal curriculum. In D. C. Berliner & R. C. Calfee (Eds.), *Handbook of educational psychology* (pp. 622–670). New York: Macmillan.

McClure, J., Meyer, L. H., Garisch, J., Fischer, R., Weir, K. F., & Walkey, F. H. (2011). Students' attributions for their best and worst marks: Do they relate to achievement? *Contemporary Educational Psychology, 36,* 71–81.

McDaniel, M. A., Waddill, P. J., Finstad, K., & Bourg, T. (2000). The effects of text-based interest on attention and recall. *Journal of Educational Psychology, 92,* 492–502.

McGregor, H. A., & Elliot, A. J. (2002). Achievement goals as predictors of achievement-relevant processes prior to task engagement. *Journal of Educational Psychology, 94,* 381–395.

McKown, C., & Weinstein, R. S. (2003). The development and consequences of stereotype consciousness in middle childhood. *Child Development, 74,* 498–515.

McLoyd, V. C. (1998). Socioeconomic disadvantage and child development. *American Psychologist, 53,* 185–204.

Meece, J. L. (1994). The role of motivation in self-regulated learning. In D. H. Schunk & B. J. Zimmerman (Eds.), *Self-regulation of learning and performance: Issues and educational applications* (pp. 25–44). Mahwah, NJ: Erlbaum.

Mellers, B. A., & McGraw, A. P. (2001). Anticipated emotions as guides to choice. *Current Directions in Psychological Science, 10,* 210–214.

Mendaglio, S. (2010). Anxiety in gifted students. In J. C. Cassady (Ed.), *Anxiety in schools: The causes, consequences, and solutions for academic anxieties* (pp. 153–173). New York: Peter Lang.

Mercer, C. D., & Pullen, P. C. (2005). *Students with learning disabilities* (6th ed.). Upper Saddle River, NJ: Merrill/Prentice-Hall.

Mesquita, B., & Leu, J. (2007). The cultural psychology of emotion. In S. Kitayama & D. Cohen (Eds.), *Handbook of cultural psychology* (pp. 734–759). New York: Guilford.

Meyer, D. K., & Turner, J. C. (2002). Discovering emotion in classroom motivation research. *Educational Psychologist, 37,* 107–114.

Meyer, D. K., & Turner, J. C. (2006). Re-conceptualizing emotion and motivation to learn in classroom contexts. *Educational Psychology Review, 18,* 377–390.

Mezulis, M. H., Abramson, L. Y., Hyde, J. S., & Hankin, B. L. (2004). Is there a universal positivity bias in attributions? A meta-analysic review of individual, developmental, and cultural differences in the self-serving attributional bias. *Psychological Bulletin, 130,* 711–747.

Middleton, M. J., & Midgley, C. (1997). Avoiding the demonstration of lack of ability: An under-explored aspect of goal theory. *Journal of Educational Psychology, 89,* 710–718.

Middleton, M. J., & Midgley, C. (2002). Beyond motivation: Middle school students' perceptions of press for understanding in math. *Contemporary Educational Psychology, 27,* 373–391.

Midgley, C. (1993). Motivation and middle level schools. In M. Maehr & P. R. Pintrich (Eds.), *Advances in motivation and achievement* (Vol. 8, pp. 217–274). Greenwich, CT: JAI.

Midgley, C. (Ed.). (2002). *Goals, goal structures, and patterns of adaptive learning.* Mahwah, NJ: Erlbaum.

Midgley, C., Kaplan, A., & Middleton, M. (2001). Performance-approach goals: Good for what, for whom, under what circumstances, and at what cost? *Journal of Educational Psychology, 93,* 77–86.

Midgley, C., Middleton, M. J., Gheen, M. H., & Kumar, R. (2002). Stage-environment fit revisited: A goal theory approach to examining school transitions. In C. Midgley (Ed.), *Goals, goal structures, and patterns of adaptive learning* (pp. 109–142). Mahwah, NJ: Erlbaum.

Miller, R. B., & Brickman, S. J. (2004). A model of future-oriented motivation and self-regulation. *Educational Psychology Review, 16,* 9–33.

Milner, H. R. (2006). Classroom management in urban classrooms. In C. M. Evertson & C. S. Weinstein (Eds.), *Handbook of classroom management: Research, practice, and contemporary issues* (pp. 491–522). Mahwah, NJ: Erlbaum.

Minsky, M. (2006). *The emotion machine: Commonsense thinking, artificial intelligence, and the future of the human mind.* New York: Simon & Schuster.

Miranda, A., Villaescusa, M. I., & Vidal-Abarca, E. (1997). Is attribution retraining necessary? Use of self-regulation procedures for enhancing the reading comprehension strategies of students with learning disabilities. *Journal of Learning Disabilities, 30,* 503–512.

Mitchell, M. (1993). Situational interest: Its multifaceted structure in the secondary school mathematics classroom. *Journal of Educational Psychology, 85,* 424–436.

Morales, J. R., & Guerra, N. G. (2006). Effects of multiple context and cumulative stress on urban children's adjustment in elementary school. *Child Development, 77,* 907–923.

Morelli, G. A., & Rothbaum, F. (2007). Situating the child in context: Attachment relationships and self-regulation in different cultures. In S. Kitayama & D. Cohen (Eds.), *Handbook of cultural psychology* (pp. 500–527). New York: Guilford.

Murayama, K., Elliot, A. J., & Yamagata, S. (2011). Separation of performance-approach and performance-avoidance achievement goals: A broader analysis. *Journal of Educational Psychology, 103,* 238–256.

Murdock, T. B. (1999). The social context of risk: Status and motivational predictors of alienation in middle school. *Journal of Educational Psychology, 91,* 62–75.

Murphy, P. K., & Alexander, P. A. (2000). A motivated exploration of motivation terminology. *Contemporary Educational Psychology, 25,* 3–53.

Nagengast, B., Marsh, H. W., Scalas, L. F., Xu, M. K., Hau, K.-T., & Trautwein, U. (2011). Who took the "x" out of expectancy–value theory? A psychological mystery, a substantive–methodological synergy, and a cross-national generalization. *Psychological Science, 22,* 1058–1066.

Nett, U. E., Goetz, T., & Hall, N. C. (2011). Coping with boredom in school: An experience sampling perspective. *Contemporary Educational Psychology, 36,* 49–59.

Newman, R. S., & Schwager, M. T. (1995). Students' help seeking during problem solving: Effects of grade, goal, and prior achievement. *American Educational Research Journal, 32,* 352–376.

Newmann, F. M., & Wehlage, G. G. (1993). Five standards of authentic instruction. *Educational Leadership, 50*(7), 8–12.

Nicholls, J. G. (1990). What is ability and why are we mindful of it? A developmental perspective. In R. J. Sternberg & J. Kolligian (Eds.), *Competence considered* (pp. 11–40). New Haven, CT: Yale University Press.

Nisbett, R. E. (2009). *Intelligence and how to get it.* New York: Norton.

Nolen, S. B. (1996). Why study? How reasons for learning influence strategy selection. *Educational Psychology Review, 8,* 335–355.

Nolen, S. B. (2007). Young children's motivation to read and write: Development in social contexts. *Cognition and Instruction, 25,* 219–270.

Nolen, S. B. (2011). Motivation, engagement, and identity: Opening a conversation. In D. M. McInerney, R. A. Walker, & G. A. D. Liem (Eds.), *Sociocultural theories of learning and motivation: Looking back, looking forward* (pp. 109–135). Charlotte, NC: Information Age.

Oakes, J., & Guiton, G. (1995). Matchmaking: The dynamics of high school tracking decisions. *American Educational Research Journal, 32,* 3–33.

Ogbu, J. U. (2003). *Black American students in an affluent suburb: A study of academic disengagement.* Mahwah, NJ: Erlbaum.

Ogbu, J. U. (2008b). Multiple sources of peer pressures among African American students. In J. U. Ogbu (Ed.), *Minority status, oppositional culture, and schooling* (pp. 89–111). New York: Routledge.

Osborne, J. W., & Simmons, C. M. (2002, April). *Girls, math, stereotype threat, and anxiety: Physiological evidence.* Paper presented at the annual meeting of the American Educational Research Association, New Orleans, LA.

Osborne, J. W., Tillman, D., & Holland, A. (2010). Stereotype threat and anxiety for disadvantaged minorities and women. In J. C. Cassady (Ed.), *Anxiety in schools: The causes, consequences, and solutions for academic anxieties* (pp. 119–136). New York: Peter Lang.

Osterman, K. F. (2000). Students' need for belonging in the school community. *Review of Educational Research, 70,* 323–367.

Otis, N., Grouzet, F. M. E., & Pelletier, L. G. (2005). Latent motivational change in an academic setting: A 3-year longitudinal study. *Journal of Educational Psychology, 97,* 170–183.

Oyserman, D. (2008). Possible selves: Identity-based motivation and school success. In H. W. Marsh, R. G. Craven, & D. M. McInerney (Eds.), *Self-processes, learning, and enabling human potential* (pp. 269–288). Charlotte, NC: Information Age.

Page-Voth, V., & Graham, S. (1999). Effects of goal setting and strategy use on the writing performance and self-efficacy of students with writing and learning problems. *Journal of Educational Psychology, 91,* 230–240.

Pajares, F. (2009). Toward a positive psychology of academic motivation: The role of self-efficacy beliefs. In R. Gilman, E. S. Huebner, & M. J. Furlong (Eds.), *Handbook of positive psychology in schools* (pp. 149–160). New York: Routledge.

Paley, V. G. (1984). *Boys and girls: Superheroes in the doll corner.* Chicago: University of Chicago Press.

Palmer, D. J., & Goetz, E. T. (1988). Selection and use of study strategies: The role of the studier's beliefs about self and strategies. In C. E. Weinstein, E. T. Goetz, & P. A. Alexander (Eds.), *Learning and study strategies: Issues in assessment, instruction, and evaluation* (pp. 41–61). San Diego: Academic Press.

Pang, V. O. (1995). Asian Pacific American students: A diverse and complex population. In J. A. Banks & C. A. M. Banks (Eds.), *Handbook of research on multicultural education* (pp. 412–424). New York: Macmillan.

Paris, S. G., & Cunningham, A. E. (1996). Children becoming students. In D. C. Berliner & R. C. Calfee (Eds.), *Handbook of educational psychology* (pp. 117–147). New York: Macmillan.

Paris, S. G., & Turner, J. C. (1994). Situated motivation. In P. R. Pintrich, D. R. Brown, & C. E. Weinstein (Eds.), *Student motivation, cognition, and learning: Essays in honor of Wilbert J. McKeachie* (pp. 213–238). Mahwah, NJ: Erlbaum.

Patall, E. A., Cooper, H., & Wynn, S. R. (2010). The effectiveness and relative importance of choice in the classroom. *Journal of Educational Psychology, 102,* 896–915.

Patrick, H. (1997). Social self-regulation: Exploring the relations between children's social relationships, academic self-regulation, and school performance. *Educational Psychologist, 32,* 209–220.

Patrick, H., Anderman, L. H., & Ryan, A. M. (2002). Social motivation and the classroom social environment. In C. Midgley (Ed.), *Goals, goal structures, and patterns of adaptive learning* (pp. 85–108). Mahwah, NJ: Erlbaum.

Patrick, H., Ryan, A. M., Anderman, L. H., Middleton, M. J., Linnenbrink, L., Hruda, L. Z., et al. (1997). *Observing Patterns of Adaptive Learning (OPAL): A scheme for classroom observations.* Ann Arbor, MI: The University of Michigan.

Patrick, H., Ryan, A. M., & Kaplan, A. M. (2007). Early adolescents' perceptions of the classroom social environment, motivational beliefs, and engagement. *Journal of Educational Psychology, 99,* 83–98.

Patton, J. R., Blackbourn, J. M., & Fad, K. S. (1996). *Exceptional individuals in focus* (6th ed.). Upper Saddle River, NJ: Merrill/Prentice-Hall.

Payne, R. K. (2005). *A framework for understanding poverty* (4th rev. ed.). Highlands, TX: aha! Process, Inc.

Pekrun, R. (2006). The control-value theory of achievement emotions: Assumptions, corollaries, and implications for educational research and practice. *Educational Psychology Review, 18,* 315–341.

Pekrun, R., Elliot, A. J., & Maier, M. A. (2009). Achievement goals and achievement emotions: Testing a model of their joint relations with academic performance. *Journal of Educational Psychology, 101,* 115–135.

Pekrun, R., Goetz, T., Daniels, L. M., Stupnisky, R. H., & Perry, R. P. (2010). Boredom in achievement settings: Exploring control–value antecedents and performance outcomes of a neglected emotion. *Journal of Educational Psychology, 102,* 531–549.

Pekrun, R., Goetz, T., Titz, W., & Perry, R. P. (2002). Academic emotions in students' self-regulated learning and achievement: A program of qualitative and quantitative research. *Educational Psychologist, 37,* 91–105.

Pellegrini, A. D., & Long, J. D. (2004). Part of the solution and part of the problem: The role of peers in bullying, dominance, and victimization during the transition from primary school through secondary school. In D. L. Espelage & S. M. Swearer (Eds.), *Bullying in American schools: A social-ecological perspective on prevention and intervention* (pp. 107–117). Mahwah, NJ: Erlbaum.

Perry, N. E., Turner, J. C., & Meyer, D. K. (2006). Classrooms as contexts for motivating learning. In P. A. Alexander & P. H. Winne (Eds.), *Handbook of educational psychology* (2nd ed., pp. 327–348). Mahwah, NJ: Erlbaum.

Perry, N. E., & Winne, P. H. (2004). Motivational messages from home and school: How do they influence young children's engagement in learning? In D. M. McInerney & S. Van Etten (Eds.), *Big theories revisited* (pp. 199–222). Greenwich, CT: Information Age.

Peterson, C. (1990). Explanatory style in the classroom and on the playing field. In S. Graham & V. S. Folkes (Eds.), *Attribution theory: Applications to achievement, mental health, and interpersonal conflict* (pp. 53–75). Mahwah, NJ: Erlbaum.

Peterson, C. (2006). *A primer in positive psychology.* New York: Oxford University Press.

Peterson, C., Maier, S., & Seligman, M. (1993). *Learned helplessness: A theory for the age of personal control.* New York: Oxford University Press.

Peterson, C., & Park, N. (2010). What happened to self-actualization? Commentary on Kenrick et al. (2010). *Perspectives on Psychological Science, 5,* 320–322.

Phalet, K., Andriessen, I., & Lens, W. (2004). How future goals enhance motivation and learning in multicultural classrooms. *Educational Psychology Review, 16,* 59–89.

Phelan, P., Yu, H. C., & Davidson, A. L. (1994). Navigating the psychosocial pressures of adolescence: The voices and experiences of high school youth. *American Educational Research Journal, 31,* 415–447.

Phelps, E. A., & Sharot, T. (2008). How (and why) emotion enhances the subjective sense of recollection. *Current Directions in Psychological Science, 17,* 147–152.

Pianta, R. C. (1999). *Enhancing relationships between children and teachers.* Washington, DC: American Psychological Association.

Pianta, R. C., & Hamre, B. K. (2009). Conceptualization, measurement, and improvement of classroom processes: Standardized observation can leverage capacity. *Educational Researcher, 38,* 109–119.

Piirto, J. (1999). *Talented children and adults: Their development and education* (2nd ed.). Upper Saddle River, NJ: Merrill/Prentice-Hall.

Pintrich, P. R. (2003). Motivation and classroom learning. In W. M. Reynolds, G. E. Miller (Vol. Eds.), & I. B. Weiner (Editor-in-Chief), *Handbook of psychology: Vol. 7. Educational psychology* (pp. 103–122). New York: Wiley.

Pintrich, P. R., & Schrauben, B. (1992). Students' motivational beliefs and their cognitive engagement in academic tasks. In D. Schunk & J. Meece (Eds.), *Students' perceptions in the classroom: Causes and consequences* (pp. 149–183). Mahwah, NJ: Erlbaum.

Plante, I., & O'Keefe, P. A. (2010, April–May). *The relation among achievement goals and expectancy-value variables in predicting grades and career intentions.* Paper presented at the annual meeting of the American Educational Research Association, Denver.

Pomerantz, E. M., Altermatt, E. R., & Saxon, J. L. (2002). Making the grade but feeling distressed: Gender differences in academic performance and internal distress. *Journal of Educational Psychology, 94,* 396–404.

Pomerantz, E. M., & Saxon, J. L. (2001). Conceptions of ability as stable and self-evaluative processes: A longitudinal examination. *Child Development, 72,* 152–173.

Pool, J., Dittrich, C., & Pool, K. (2011). Arts integration in teacher preparation: Teaching the teachers. *Journal for Learning through the Arts, 7*(1). Retrieved from http://escholarship.org/uc/item/65g5z7wp

Poortvliet, P. M., & Darnon, C. (2010). Toward a more social understanding of achievement goals: The interpersonal effects of mastery and performance goals. *Current Directions in Psychological Science, 19,* 324–328.

Posner, M. I., & Rothbart, M. K. (2007). *Educating the human brain.* Washington, DC: American Psychological Association.

Powell, S., & Nelson, B. (1997). Effects of choosing academic assignments on a student with attention deficit hyperactivity disorder. *Journal of Applied Behavior Analysis, 30,* 181–183.

Pressley, M., Borkowski, J. G., & Schneider, W. (1987). Cognitive strategies: Good strategy users coordinate metacognition and knowledge. In R. Vasta & G. Whitehurst (Eds.), *Annals of child development* (Vol. 5, pp. 80–129). New York: JAI.

Prout, H. T. (2009). Positive psychology and students with intellectual disabilities. In R. Gilman, E. S. Huebner, & M. J. Furlong (Eds.), *Handbook of positive psychology in schools* (pp. 371–381). New York: Routledge.

Pugh, K. J., & Bergin, D. A. (2006). Motivational influences on transfer. *Educational Psychologist, 41,* 147–160.

Qian, G., & Pan, J. (2002). A comparison of epistemological beliefs and learning from science text between American and Chinese high school students. In B. K. Hofer & P. R. Pintrich (Eds.), *Personal epistemology: The psychology of beliefs about knowledge and knowing* (pp. 365–385). Mahwah, NJ: Erlbaum.

Qin, L., Pomerantz, E. M., & Wang, Q. (2009). Are gains in decision-making autonomy during early adolescence beneficial for emotional functioning? The case of the United States and China. *Child Development, 80,* 1705–1721.

Radel, R., Sarrazin, P., Legrain, P., & Wild, T. C. (2010). Social contagion of motivation between teacher and student: Analyzing underlying processes. *Journal of Educational Psychology, 102,* 577–587.

Ratelle, C. F., Guay, F., Vallerand, R. J., Larose, S., & Senécal, C. (2007). Autonomous, controlled, and amotivated types of academic motivation: A person-oriented analysis. *Journal of Educational Psychology, 99,* 734–746.

Rawsthorne, L. J., & Elliot, A. J. (1999). Achievement goals and intrinsic motivation: A meta-analytic review. *Personality and Social Psychology Review, 3,* 326–344.

Ready, D. D., & Wright, D. L. (2011). Accuracy and inaccuracy in teachers' perceptions of young children's cognitive abilities: The role of child background and classroom context. *American Educational Research Journal, 48,* 335–360.

Reed, J. H., Schallert, D. L., Beth, A. D., & Woodruff, A. L. (2004). Motivated reader, engaged writer: The role of motivation in the literate acts of adolescents. In T. L. Jetton & J. A. Dole (Eds.), *Adolescent literacy research and practice* (pp. 251–282). New York: Guilford.

Reeve, J. (2006). Extrinsic rewards and inner motivation. In C. M. Evertson & C. S. Weinstein (Eds.), *Handbook of classroom management: Research, practice, and contemporary issues* (pp. 645–664.). Mahwah, NJ: Erlbaum.

Reeve, J. (2009). Why teachers adopt a controlling motivating style toward students and how they can become more autonomy supportive. *Educational Psychologist, 44,* 159–175.

Reeve, J., Bolt, E., & Cai, Y. (1999). Autonomy-supportive teachers: How they teach and motivate students. *Journal of Educational Psychology, 91,* 537–548.

Reeve, J., Deci, E. L., & Ryan, R. M. (2004). Self-determination theory: A dialectical framework for understanding sociocultural influences on student motivation. In D. M. McInerney & S. Van Etten (Eds.), *Big theories revisited* (pp. 31–60). Greenwich, CT: Information Age.

Régner, I., Escribe, C., & Dupeyrat, C. (2007). Evidence of social comparison in mastery goals in natural academic settings. *Journal of Educational Psychology, 99,* 575–583.

Renninger, K. A. (2009). Interest and identity development in instruction: An inductive model. *Educational Psychologist, 44,* 105–118.

Renninger, K. A., Hidi, S., & Krapp, A. (Eds.). (1992). *The role of interest in learning and development.* Mahwah, NJ: Erlbaum.

Reyna, C. (2000). Lazy, dumb, or industrious: When stereotypes convey attribution information in the classroom. *Educational Psychology Review, 12,* 85–110.

Reyna, C., & Weiner, B. (2001). Justice and utility in the classroom: An attributional analysis of the goals of teachers' punishment and intervention strategies. *Journal of Educational Psychology, 93,* 309–319.

Reyna, V. F., & Farley, F. (2006). Risk and rationality in adolescent decision making: Implications for theory, practice, and public policy. *Psychological Science in the Public Interest, 7*(1), 1–44.

Rhodewalt, F., & Vohs, K. D. (2005). Defensive strategies, motivation, and the self: A self-regulatory process view. In A. J. Elliot & C. S. Dweck (Eds.), *Handbook of competence and motivation* (pp. 548–565). New York: Guilford.

Riggs, J. M. (1992). Self-handicapping and achievement. In A. K. Boggiano & T. S. Pittman (Eds.), *Achievement and motivation: A social-developmental perspective* (pp. 244–267). Cambridge, England: Cambridge University Press.

Roberts, G. C., Treasure, D. C., & Kavussanu, M. (1997). Motivation in physical activity contexts: An achievement goal perspective. *Advances in Motivation and Achievement, 10,* 413–447.

Robertson, J. S. (2000). Is attribution training a worthwhile classroom intervention for K–12 students with learning difficulties? *Educational Psychology Review, 12,* 111–134.

Robinson, J. P., & Lubienski, S. T. (2011). The development of gender achievement gaps in mathematics and reading during elementary and middle school: Examining direct cognitive assessments and teacher ratings. *American Educational Research Journal, 48,* 268–302.

Roderick, M., & Camburn, E. (1999). Risk and recovery from course failure in the early years of high school. *American Educational Research Journal, 36,* 303–343.

Roeser, R. W., Marachi, R., & Gehlbach, H. (2002). A goal theory perspective on teachers' professional identities and the contexts of teaching. In C. Midgley (Ed.), *Goals, goal structures, and patterns of adaptive learning* (pp. 205–241). Mahwah, NJ: Erlbaum.

Rogoff, B. (2003). *The cultural nature of human development.* Oxford, England: Oxford University Press.

Roorda, D. L., Koomen, H. M. Y., Spilt, J. L., & Oort, F. J. (2011). The influence of affective teacher–student relationships on students' school engagement and achievement: A meta-analytic approach. *Review of Educational Research, 81,* 493–529.

Rose, A. J. (2002). Co-rumination in the friendship of girls and boys. *Child Development, 73,* 1830–1843.

Rose, S. C., & Thornburg, K. R. (1984). Mastery motivation and need for approval in young children: Effects of age, sex, and reinforcement condition. *Educational Research Quarterly, 9*(1), 34–42.

Rosenthal, R. (1994). Interpersonal expectancy effects: A 30-year perspective. *Current Directions in Psychological Science, 3,* 176–179.

Rosenthal, R. (2002). Covert communication in classrooms, clinics, courtrooms, and cubicles. *American Psychologist, 57,* 839–849.

Rosenthal, R., & Jacobson, L. (1968). *Pygmalion in the classroom: Teacher expectation and pupils' intellectual development.* New York: Holt, Rinehart & Winston.

Roth, W.-M. (2011). Object/motives and emotion: A cultural-historical activity theoretic approach to motivation in learning and work. In D. M. McInerney, R. A. Walker, & G. A. D. Liem (Eds.), *Sociocultural theories of learning and motivation: Looking back, looking forward* (pp. 43–63). Charlotte, NC: Information Age.

Rubie-Davies, C., Hattie, J., & Hamilton, R. (2006). Expecting the best for students: Teacher expectations and academic outcomes. *British Journal of Educational Psychology, 76,* 429–444.

Rudolph, K. D., Caldwell, M. S., & Conley, C. S. (2005). Need for approval and children's well-being. *Child Development, 76,* 309–323.

Rudolph, K. D., Lambert, S. F., Clark, A. G., & Kurlakowsky, K. D. (2001). Negotiating the transition to middle school: The role of self-regulatory processes. *Child Development, 72,* 929–946.

Rueda, R., & Moll, L. C. (1994). A sociocultural perspective on motivation. In H. F. O'Neil, Jr., & M. Drillings (Eds.), *Motivation: Theory and research* (pp. 117–137). Mahwah, NJ: Erlbaum.

Ryan, A. M., & Patrick, H. (2001). The classroom social environment and changes in adolescents' motivation and engagement during middle school. *American Educational Research Journal, 38,* 437–460.

Ryan, A. M., Pintrich, P. R., & Midgley, C. (2001). Avoiding seeking help in the classroom: Who and why? *Educational Psychology Review, 13,* 93–114.

Ryan, K. E., & Ryan, A. M. (2005). Psychological processes underlying stereotype threat and standardized math test performance. *Educational Psychologist, 40,* 53–63.

Ryan, K. E., Ryan, A. M., Arbuthnot, K., & Samuels, M. (2007). Students' motivation for standardized math exams: Insights from students. *Educational Researcher, 36*(1), 5–13.

Ryan, R. M., Connell, J. P., & Grolnick, W. S. (1992). When achievement is *not* intrinsically motivated: A theory of internalization and self-regulation in school. In A. K. Boggiano & T. S. Pittman (Eds.), *Achievement and motivation: A social-developmental perspective* (pp. 167–188). Cambridge, England: Cambridge University Press.

Ryan, R. M., & Deci, E. L. (2000). Self-determination theory and the facilitation of intrinsic motivation, social development, and well-being. *American Psychologist, 55,* 68–78.

Ryan, R. M., Mims, V., & Koestner, R. (1983). Relation of reward contingency and interpersonal context to intrinsic motivation: A review and test using cognitive evaluation theory. *Journal of Personality and Social Psychology, 45,* 736–750.

Sadker, M. P., & Sadker, D. (1994). *Failing at fairness: How our schools cheat girls.* New York: Touchstone.

Sapolsky, R. (2005). Stress and cognition. In M. Gazzaniga (Ed.), *The cognitive neurosciences* (3rd, ed, pp. 1031–1042). Cambridge, MA: MIT Press.

Sarason, I. G. (Ed.). (1980). *Test anxiety: Theory, research, and applications.* Mahwah, NJ: Erlbaum.

Savani, K., Markus, H. R., Naidu, N. V. R., Kumar, S., & Berlia, N. (2010). What counts as a choice? U.S. Americans are more likely than Indians to construe actions as choices. *Psychological Science, 21,* 391–398.

Schiefele, U. (1991). Interest, learning, and motivation. *Educational Psychologist, 26,* 299–323.

Schmidt, A. C., Hanley, G. P., & Layer, S. A. (2009). A further analysis of the value of choice: Controlling for illusory discriminative stimuli and evaluating the effects of less preferred items. *Journal of Applied Behavior Analysis, 42,* 711–716.

Schraw, G., Flowerday, T., & Lehman, S. (2001). Increasing situational interest in the classroom. *Educational Psychology Review, 13,* 211–224.

Schraw, G., & Lehman, S. (2001). Situational interest: A review of the literature and directions for future research. *Educational Psychology Review, 13,* 23–52.

Schultz, G. F., & Switzky, H. N. (1990). The development of intrinsic motivation in students with learning problems: Suggestions for more effective instructional practice. *Preventing School Failure, 34*(2), 14–20.

Schunk, D. H. (1990, April). *Socialization and the development of self-regulated learning: The role of attributions.* Paper presented at the annual meeting of the American Educational Research Association, Boston.

Schunk, D. H., & Pajares, F. (2004). Self-efficacy in education revisited: Empirical and applied evidence. In D. M. McInerney & S. Van Etten (Eds.), *Big theories revisited* (pp. 115–138). Greenwich, CT: Information Age.

Schunk, D. H., & Pajares, F. (2005). Competence perceptions and academic functioning. In A. J. Elliot & C. S. Dweck (Eds.), *Handbook of competence and motivation* (pp. 85–104). New York: Guilford.

Schutz, P. A. (1994). Goals as the transactive point between motivation and cognition. In P. R. Pintrich, D. R. Brown, & C. E. Weinstein (Eds.), *Student motivation, cognition, and learning: Essays in honor of Wilbert J. McKeachie* (pp. 113–133). Mahwah, NJ: Erlbaum.

Sedikides, C., & Gregg, A. P. (2008). Self-enhancement: Food for thought. *Perspectives on Psychological Science, 3,* 102–116.

Seiffge-Krenke, I., Aunola, K., & Nurmi, J.-E. (2009). Changes in stress perception and coping during adolescence: The role of situational and personal factors. *Child Development, 80,* 259–279.

Seligman, M. E. P. (1975). *Helplessness: On depression, development, and death.* San Francisco: Freeman.

Seligman, M. E. P. (1991). *Learned optimism.* New York: Knopf.

Senko, C., Hulleman, C. S., & Harackiewicz, J. M. (2011). Achievement goal theory at the crossroads: Old controversies, current challenges, and new directions. *Educational Psychologist, 46,* 26–47.

Shavinina, L. V., & Ferrari, M. (2004). Extracognitive facets of developing high ability: Introduction to some important issues. In L. V. Shavinina & M. Ferrari (Eds.), *Beyond knowledge: Extracognitive aspects of developing high ability* (pp. 3–13). Mahwah, NJ: Erlbaum.

Shepperd, J. A., & McNulty, J. K. (2002). The affective consequences of expected and unexpected outcomes. *Psychological Science, 13,* 85–88.

Shernoff, D. J., & Csikszentmihalyi, M. (2009). Flow in schools: Cultivating engaged learners and optimal learning environments. In R. Gilman, E. S. Huebner, & M. J. Furlong (Eds.), *Handbook of positive psychology in schools* (pp. 131–145). New York: Routledge.

Shernoff, D. J., Csikszentmihalyi, M., Schneider, B., & Shernoff, E. S. (2003). Student engagement in high school classrooms from the perspective of flow Theory. *School Psychology Quarterly, 18*(2), 158–176.

Shernoff, D. J., & Hoogstra, L. A. (2001). Continuing motivation beyond the high school classroom. In M. Michaelson & J. Nakamura (Eds.), *Supportive frameworks for youth engagement* (pp. 73–87). San Francisco: Jossey-Bass.

Shernoff, D. J., Knauth, S., & Makris, E. (2000). The quality of classroom experiences. In M. Csikszentmihalyi & B. Schneider, *Becoming adult: How teenagers prepare for the world of work* (pp. 141–164). New York: Basic Books.

Shernoff, D. J., Schneider, B., & Csikszentmihalyi, M. (2001, April). *An assessment of multiple influences on student engagement in high school classrooms.* Paper presented at the annual meeting of the American Educational Research Association, Seattle, WA.

Shim, S. S., & Ryan, A. M. (2006, April). *The nature and the consequences of changes in achievement goals during early adolescence.* Paper presented at the annual meeting of the American Educational Research Association, San Francisco, CA.

Shim, S. S., Ryan, A. M., & Anderson, C. J. (2008). Achievement goals and achievement during early adolescence: Examining time-varying predictor and outcome variables in growth-curve analysis. *Journal of Educational Psychology, 100,* 655–671.

Shute, V. J. (2008). Focus on formative feedback. *Review of Educational Research, 78,* 153–189.

Sideridis, G. D. (2005). Goal orientation, academic achievement, and depression: Evidence in favor of a revised goal theory framework. *Journal of Educational Psychology, 97,* 366–375.

Sinatra, G. M., & Mason, L. (2008). Beyond knowledge: Learner characteristics influencing conceptual change. In S. Vosniadou (Ed.), *International handbook on conceptual change* (pp. 560–582). New York: Routledge.

Sins, P. H. M., van Joolingen, W. R., Savelsbergh, E. R., & van Hout-Wolters, B. (2008). Motivation and performance within a collaborative computer-based modeling task: Relations between students' achievement goal orientation, self-efficacy, cognitive processing, and achievement. *Contemporary Educational Psychology, 33,* 58–77.

Sirin, S. R., & Ryce, P. (2010). Cultural incongruence between teachers and families: Implications for immigrant students. In E. L. Grigorenko & R. Takanishi (Eds.), *Immigration, diversity, and education* (pp. 151–169). New York: Routledge.

Skaalvik, E. (1997). Self-enhancing and self-defeating ego orientation: Relations with task avoidance orientation, achievement, self-perceptions, and anxiety. *Journal of Educational Psychology, 89,* 71–81.

Skaalvik, E. M., & Skaalvik, S. (2008). Teacher self-efficacy: Conceptual analysis and relations with teacher burnout and perceived school context. In H. W. Marsh, R. G. Craven, & D. M. McInerney (Eds.), *Self-processes, learning, and enabling human potential* (pp. 223–247). Charlotte, NC: Information Age.

Skinner, E., Furrer, C., Marchand, G., & Kindermann, T. (2008). Engagement and disaffection in the classroom: Part of a larger motivational dynamic? *Journal of Educational Psychology, 100,* 765–781.

Smith, J. L. (2004). Understanding the process of stereotype threat: A review of mediational

variables and new performance goal directions. *Educational Psychology Review, 16,* 177–206.

Snow, R. E., Corno, L., & Jackson, D., III (1996). Individual differences in affective and conative functions. In D. C. Berliner & R. C. Calfee (Eds.), *Handbook of educational psychology* (pp. 243–310). New York: Macmillan.

Spaulding, C. L. (1992). *Motivation in the classroom.* New York: McGraw-Hill.

Spear, L. P. (2000). Neurobehavioral changes in adolescence. *Current Directions in Psychological Science, 9,* 111–114.

Spera, C. (2005). A review of the relationship among parenting practices, parenting styles, and adolescent school achievement. *Educational Psychology Review, 17,* 125–146.

Stefanou, C. R., Perencevich, K. C., DiCintio, M., & Turner, J. C. (2004). Supporting autonomy in the classroom: Ways teachers encourage student decision making and ownership. *Educational Psychologist, 39,* 97–110.

Steinberg, L. (1996). *Beyond the classroom: Why school reform has failed and what parents need to do.* New York: Touchstone.

Steuer, G., & Dresel, M. (2011, April). *Dealing with errors in mathematics classrooms: The relevance of error climate and personal achievement motivation.* Paper presented at the annual meeting of the American Educational Research Association, New Orleans, LA.

Stevenson, H. W., Chen, C., & Uttal, D. H. (1990). Beliefs and achievement: A study of black, white, and Hispanic children. *Child Development, 61,* 508–523.

Stipek, D. J. (1984). Sex differences in children's attributions for success and failure on math and spelling tests. *Sex Roles, 11,* 969–981.

Stipek, D. J. (1993). *Motivation to learn: From theory to practice* (2nd ed.). Boston: Allyn & Bacon.

Stipek, D. J. (1996). Motivation and instruction. In D. C. Berliner & R. C. Calfee (Eds.), *Handbook of educational psychology* (pp. 85–113). New York: Macmillan.

Stodolsky, S. S., Salk, S., & Glaessner, B. (1991). Student views about learning math and social studies. *American Educational Research Journal, 28,* 89–116.

Stupnisky, R. H., Stewart, T. L., Daniels, L. M., & Perry, R. P. (2011). When do students ask why? Examining the precursors and outcomes of causal search among first-year college students. *Contemporary Educational Psychology, 36,* 201–211.

Suskind, R. (1998). *A hope in the unseen: An American odyssey from the inner city to the Ivy League.* New York: Broadway Books.

Swan, K., Mitrani, M., Guerrero, F., Cheung, M., & Schoener, J. (1990, April). *Perceived locus of control and computer-based instruction.* Paper presented at the annual meeting of the American Educational Research Association, Boston.

Tamir, M. (2009). What do people want to feel and why? Pleasure and utility in emotion regulation. *Current Directions in Psychological Science, 18,* 101–105.

Tamis-Lemonda, C. S., & McFadden, K. E. (2010). The United States of America. In

M. H. Bornstein (Ed.), *Handbook of cultural developmental science* (pp. 299–322). New York: Psychology Press.

Thomas, R. M. (2005). *High-stakes testing: Coping with collateral damage.* Mahwah, NJ: Erlbaum.

Thomas, S., & Oldfather, P. (1997). Intrinsic motivations, literacy, and assessment practices: "That's my grade. That's me." *Educational Psychologist, 32,* 107–123.

Thorkildsen, T. A., Golant, C. J., & Cambray-Engstrom, E. (2008). Essential solidarities for understanding Latino adolescents' moral and academic engagement. In C. Hudley & A. E. Gottfried (Eds.), *Academic motivation and the culture of school in childhood and adolescence* (pp. 73–98). New York: Oxford University Press.

Timm, P., & Borman, K. (1997). The soup pot don't stretch that far no more: Intergenerational patterns of school leaving in an urban Appalachian neighborhood. In M. Sellter & L. Weis (Eds.), *Beyond black and white: New faces and voices in U.S. schools.* Albany: State University of New York Press.

Tobias, S. (1994). Interest, prior knowledge, and learning. *Review of Educational Research, 64,* 37–54.

Tollefson, N. (2000). Classroom applications of cognitive theories of motivation. *Educational Psychology Review, 12,* 63–83.

Tomback, R. M., Williams, A. Y., & Wentzel, K. R. (2005, April). *Young adolescents' concerns about the transition to high school.* Poster presented at the annual meeting of the American Educational Research Association, Montreal.

Townsend, T. (2008, March). *Supporting students who struggle to learn: A community approach to development.* Paper presented at the annual meeting of the American Educational Research Association, New York.

Tryon, G. S. (1980). The measurement and treatment of anxiety. *Review of Educational Research, 50,* 343–372.

Tsai, J. L. (2007). Ideal affect: Cultural causes and behavioral consequences. *Perspectives on Psychological Science, 2,* 242–259.

Tsai, Y.-M., Kunter, M., Lüdtke, O., Trautwein, U., & Ryan, R. M. (2008). What makes lessons interesting? The role of situational and individual factors in three school subjects. *Journal of Educational Psychology, 100,* 460–472.

Tucker, V. G., & Anderman, L. H. (1999, April). *Cycles of learning: Demonstrating the interplay between motivation, self-regulation, and cognition.* Paper presented at the annual meeting of the American Educational Research Association, Montreal, Canada.

Tuominin-Soini, H., Salmela-Aro, K., & Niemivirta, M. (2011). Stability and change in achievement goal orientations: A person-centered approach. *Contemporary Educational Psychology, 36,* 82–100.

Turnbull, A. P., Turnbull, R., & Wehmeyer, M. L. (2010). *Exceptional lives: Special education in today's schools* (6th ed.). Upper Saddle River, NJ: Merrill.

Turner, J. C., Meyer, D. K., Cox, K. E., Logan, C., DiCintio, M., & Thomas, C. T. (1998). Creating contexts for involvement in mathematics. *Journal of Educational Psychology, 90,* 730–745.

Turner, J. C., & Patrick, H. (2008). How does motivation develop and why does it change? Reframing motivation research. *Educational Psychologist, 43,* 119–131.

Turner, J. C., Thorpe, P. K., & Meyer, D. K. (1998). Students' reports of motivation and negative affect: A theoretical and empirical analysis. *Journal of Educational Psychology, 90,* 758–771.

Turner, J. C., Warzon, K. B., & Christensen, A. (2011). Motivating mathematics learning: Changes in teachers' practices and beliefs during a nine-month collaboration. *American Educational Research Journal, 48,* 718–762.

Ulke-Kurcuoglu, B., & Kircaali-Iftar, G. (2010). A comparison of the effects of providing activity and material choice to children with autism spectrum disorders. *Journal of Applied Behavior Analysis, 43,* 717–721.

Urdan, T. (2004). Predictors of academic self-handicapping and achievement: Examining achievement goals, classroom goal structures, and culture. *Journal of Educational Psychology, 96,* 251–264.

Urdan, T. C., & Maehr, M. L. (1995). Beyond a two-goal theory of motivation and achievement: A case for social goals. *Review of Educational Research, 65,* 213–243.

Urdan, T. C., & Midgley, C. (2001). Academic self-handicapping: What we know, what more there is to learn. *Educational Psychology Review, 13,* 115–138.

Urdan, T. C., Midgley, C., & Anderman, E. M. (1998). The role of classroom goal structure in students' use of self-handicapping strategies. *American Educational Research Journal, 35,* 101–122.

Urdan, T. C., Ryan, A. M., Anderman, E. M., & Gheen, M. H. (2002). Goals, goal structures, and avoidance behaviors. In C. Midgley (Ed.), *Goals, goal structures, and patterns of adaptive learning* (pp. 55–83). Mahwah, NJ: Erlbaum.

Valente, N. (2001). *"Who cares about school?" A student responds to learning.* Unpublished paper, University of New Hampshire, Durham.

Valkenburg, P. M., & Peter, J. (2009). Social consequences of the Internet for adolescents: A decade of research. *Current Directions in Psychological Science, 18,* 1–5.

van den Bergh, L., Denessen, E., Hornstra, L., Voeten, M., & Holland, R. W. (2010). The implicit prejudiced attitudes of teachers: Relations to teacher expectations and the ethnic achievement gap. *American Educational Research Journal, 47,* 497–527.

van Laar, C. (2000). The paradox of low academic achievement but high self-esteem in African American students: An attributional account. *Educational Psychology Review, 12,* 33–61.

Vansteenkiste, M., Lens, W., & Deci, E. L. (2006). Intrinsic versus extrinsic goal contents in self-determination theory: Another look at the quality of academic motivation. *Educational Psychologist, 41,* 19–31.

Vermeer, H. J., Boekaerts, M., & Seegers, G. (2000). Motivational and gender differences: Sixth-grade students' mathematical problem-solving behavior. *Journal of Educational Psychology, 92,* 308–315.

Walls, T. A., & Little, T. D. (2005). Relations among personal agency, motivation, and school adjustment in early adolescence. *Journal of Educational Psychology, 97,* 23–31.

Walton, G. M., & Cohen, G. L. (2007). A question of belonging: Race, social fit, and achievement. *Journal of Personality and Social Psychology, 92,* 82–96.

Walton, G. M., & Spencer, S. J. (2009). Latent ability: Grades and test scores systematically underestimate intellectual ability of negatively stereotyped students. *Psychological Science, 20,* 1132–1139.

Wang, M.-T., & Holcombe, R. (2010). Adolescents' perceptions of school environment, engagement, and academic achievement in middle school. *American Educational Research Journal, 47,* 633–662.

Wehmeyer, M. L., Agran, M., Hughes, C., Martin, J., Mithaug, D. E., & Palmer, S. (2007). *Promoting self-determination in students with intellectual and developmental disabilities.* New York: Guilford.

Weiner, B. (1984). Principles for a theory of student motivation and their application within an attributional framework. In R. Ames & C. Ames (Eds.), *Research on motivation in education: Vol. 1. Student motivation* (pp. 15–38). San Diego, CA: Academic Press.

Weiner, B. (1986). *An attributional theory of motivation and emotion.* New York: Springer-Verlag.

Weiner, B. (2000). Intrapersonal and interpersonal theories of motivation from an attributional perspective. *Educational Psychology Review, 12,* 1–14.

Weiner, B. (2004). Attribution theory revisited: Transforming cultural plurality into theoretical unity. In D. M. McInerney & S. Van Etten (Eds.), *Big theories revisited* (pp. 13–29). Greenwich, CT: Information Age.

Weiner, B. (2005). Motivation from an attribution perspective and the social psychology of perceived competence. In A. J. Elliot & C. S. Dweck (Eds.), *Handbook of competence and motivation* (pp. 73–84). New York: Guilford.

Weinstein, C. E., Hagen, A. S., & Meyer, D. K. (1991, April). *Work smart . . . not hard: The effects of combining instruction in using strategies, goal using, and executive control on attributions and academic performance.* Paper presented at the annual meeting of the American Educational Research Association, Chicago.

Weinstein, R. S. (2002). *Reaching higher: The power of expectations in schooling.* Cambridge, MA: Harvard University Press.

Weinstein, R. S., Madison, S. M., & Kuklinski, M. R. (1995). Raising expectations in schooling: Obstacles and opportunities for change. *American Educational Research Journal, 32,* 121–159.

Weisgram, E. S., Bigler, R. S., & Liben, L. S. (2010). Gender, values, and occupational interests among children, adolescents, and adults. *Child Development, 81,* 778–796.

Wells, G. (2011). Motive and motivation in learning to teach. In D. M. McInerney, R. A. Walker, &

G. A. D. Liem (Eds.), *Sociocultural theories of learning and motivation: Looking back, looking forward* (pp. 87–107). Charlotte, NC: Information Age.

Wentzel, K. R. (1999). Social-motivational processes and interpersonal relationships: Implications for understanding motivation at school. *Journal of Educational Psychology, 91,* 76–97.

Wentzel, K. R., Filisetti, L., & Looney, L. (2007). Adolescent prosocial behavior: The role of self-processes and contextual cues. *Child Development, 78,* 895–910.

Wentzel, K. R., & Wigfield, A. (1998). Academic and social motivational influences on students' academic performance. *Educational Psychology Review, 10,* 155–175.

White, R. (1959). Motivation reconsidered: The concept of competence. *Psychological Review, 66,* 297–333.

Wigfield, A. (1994). Expectancy-value theory of achievement motivation: A developmental perspective. *Educational Psychology Review, 6,* 49–78.

Wigfield, A., Byrnes, J. P., & Eccles, J. S. (2006). Development during early and middle adolescence. In P. A. Alexander & P. H. Winne (Eds.), *Handbook of educational psychology* (2nd ed., pp. 87–113). Mahwah, NJ: Erlbaum.

Wigfield, A., & Eccles, J. (1992). The development of achievement task values: A theoretical analysis. *Developmental Review, 12,* 265–310.

Wigfield, A., & Eccles, J. (2000). Expectancy-value theory of achievement motivation. *Contemporary Educational Psychology, 25,* 68–81.

Wigfield, A., Eccles, J. S., Mac Iver, D., Reuman, D., & Midgley, C. (1991). Transitions at early adolescence: Changes in children's domain-specific self-perceptions and general self-esteem across the transition to junior high school. *Developmental Psychology, 27,* 552–565.

Wigfield, A., Tonks, S., & Eccles, J. S. (2004). Expectancy value theory in cross-cultural perspective. In D. M. McInerney & S. Van Etten (Eds.), *Big theories revisited* (pp. 165–198). Greenwich, CT: Information Age.

Wiles, J., & Bondi, J. (2001). *The new American middle school: Educating preadolescents in an era of change.* Upper Saddle River, NJ: Merrill/Prentice-Hall.

Williams, K. M. (2001a). "Frontin' it": Schooling, violence, and relationships in the 'hood. In J. N. Burstyn, G. Bender, R. Casella, H. W. Gordon, D. P. Guerra, K. V. Luschen, R. Stevens, & K. M. Williams, *Preventing violence in schools: A challenge to American democracy* (pp. 95–108). Mahwah, NJ: Erlbaum.

Wilson, B. L., & Corbett, H. D. (2001). *Listening to urban kids: School reform and the teachers they want.* Albany: State University of New York Press.

Wilson, T. D., & Gilbert, D. T. (2008). Explaining away: A model of affective adaptation. *Perspectives on Psychological Science, 3,* 370–386.

Winner, E. (1997). Exceptionally high intelligence and schooling. *American Psychologist, 52,* 1070–1081.

Winner, E. (2000a). Giftedness: Current theory and research. *Current Directions in Psychological Science, 9,* 153–156.

Winner, E. (2000b). The origins and ends of giftedness. *American Psychologist, 55,* 159–169.

Wlodkowski, R. J. (1978). *Motivation and teaching: A practical guide.* Washington, DC: National Education Association.

Wlodkowski, R. J., & Ginsberg, M. B. (1995). *Diversity and motivation: Culturally responsive teaching.* San Francisco: Jossey-Bass.

Wolters, C. A. (2003). Regulation of motivation: Evaluating an underemphasized aspect of self-regulated learning. *Educational Psychologist, 38,* 189–205.

Wolters, C. A. (2004). Advancing achievement goal theory: Using goal structures and goal orientations to predict students' motivation, cognition, and achievement. *Journal of Educational Psychology, 96,* 236–250.

Wong, B. Y. L. (Ed.). (1991). *Learning about learning disabilities.* San Diego, CA: Academic Press.

Yeager, D. S., & Walton, G. M. (2011). Social-psychological interventions in education: They're not magic. *Review of Educational Research, 81,* 267–301.

Yerkes, R. M., & Dodson, J. D. (1908). The relation of strength of stimulus to rapidity of habit-formation. *Journal of Comparative Neurology of Psychology, 18,* 459–482.

Youniss, J., & Yates, M. (1999). Youth service and moral-civic identity: A case for everyday morality. *Educational Psychology Review, 11,* 361–376.

Zahorik, J. A. (1994, April). *Making things interesting.* Paper presented at the annual meeting of the American Educational Research Association, New Orleans, LA.

Zajonc, R. B. (1980). Feeling and thinking: Preferences need no inferences. *American Psychologist, 35,* 151–175.

Zeelenberg, R., Wagenmakers, E.-J., & Rotteveel, M. (2006). The impact of emotion on perception: Bias or enhanced processing? *Psychological Science, 17,* 287–291.

Zeidner, M. (1998). *Test anxiety: The state of the art.* New York: Plenum.

Zeidner, M., & Matthews, G. (2005). Evaluation anxiety: Current theory and research. In A. J. Elliot & C. S. Dweck (Eds.), *Handbook of competence and motivation* (pp. 141–163). New York: Guilford.

Ziegert, D. I., Kistner, J. A., Castro, R., & Robertson, B. (2001). Longitudinal study of young children's responses to challenging achievement situations. *Child Development, 72,* 609–624.

Zimmerman, B. J. (1998). Developing self-fulfilling cycles of academic regulation: An analysis of exemplary instructional models. In D. H. Schunk & B. J. Zimmerman (Eds.), *Self-regulated learning: From teaching to self-reflective practice* (pp. 1–19). New York: Guilford.

Zimmerman, B. J. (2010). Self-efficacy: An essential motive to learn. In G. S. Goodman (Ed.), *Educational psychology reader: The art and science of how people learn* (pp. 223–230). New York: Peter Lang.

Zimmerman, B. J., Bandura, A., & Martinez-Pons, M. (1992). Self-motivation for academic attainment: The role of self-efficacy beliefs and

personal goal setting. *American Educational Research Journal, 29,* 663–676.

Zohar, A., & Aharon-Kraversky, S. (2005). Exploring the effects of cognitive conflict and direct teaching for students of different academic levels. *Journal of Research in Science Teaching, 42,* 829–855.

## CHAPTER 12

Afflerbach, P., & Cho, B.-Y. (2010). Determining and describing reading strategies: Internet and traditional forms of reading. In H. S. Waters & W. Schneider (Eds.), *Metacognition, strategy use, and instruction* (pp. 201–225). New York: Guilford.

Airasian, P. W. (1994). *Classroom assessment* (2nd ed.). New York: McGraw-Hill.

Alexander, P. A. (1997). Mapping the multidimensional nature of domain learning: The interplay of cognitive, motivational, and strategic forces. In P. R. Pintrich & M. L. Maehr (Eds.), *Advances in motivation and achievement* (Vol. 10, pp. 213–250). Greenwich, CT: JAI.

Alfassi, M. (2004). Reading to learn: Effects of combined strategy instruction on high school students. *Journal of Educational Research, 97,* 171–184.

Alfieri, L., Brooks, P. J., Aldrich, N. J., & Tenenbaum, H. R. (2011). Does discovery-based instruction enhance learning? *Journal of Educational Psychology, 103,* 1–18.

Alleman, J., & Brophy, J. (1998). Strategic learning opportunities during out-of-school hours. *Social Studies and the Young Learner, 10*(4), 10–13.

Alleman, J., Knighton, B., Botwinski, B., Brophy, J., Ley, R., & Middlestead, S. (2010). *Homework done right: Powerful learning in real-life situations.* Thousand Oaks, CA: Corwin.

Anderson, J. R., Reder, L. M., & Simon, H. A. (1996). Situated learning and education. *Educational Researcher, 25*(4), 5–11.

Anderson, L. W., Krathwohl, D. R., Airasian, P. W., Cruikshank, K. A., Mayer, R. E., Pintrich, P. R., et al. (Eds.). (2001). *A taxonomy for learning, teaching, and assessing: A revision of Bloom's taxonomy of educational objectives.* New York: Longman.

Anderson, R. C., Nguyen-Jahiel, K., McNurlen, B., Archodidou, A., Kim, S.-Y., Reznitskaya, A., et al. (2001). The snowball phenomenon: Spread of ways of talking and ways of thinking across groups of children. *Cognition and Instruction, 19,* 1–46.

Applebee, A. N., Langer, J. A., Nystrand, M., & Gamoran, A. (2003). Discussion-based approaches to developing understanding: Classroom instruction and student performance in middle and high school English. *American Educational Research Journal, 40,* 685–730.

Arlin, M. (1984). Time, equality, and mastery learning. *Review of Educational Research, 54,* 65–86.

Aronson, E., & Patnoe, S. (1997). *The jigsaw classroom: Building cooperation in the classroom* (2nd ed.). New York: Longman.

Aulls, M. W. (1998). Contributions of classroom discourse to what content students learn during curriculum enactment. *Journal of Educational Psychology, 90,* 56–69.

Ausubel, D. P., Novak, J. D., & Hanesian, H. (1978). *Educational psychology: A cognitive view* (2nd ed.). New York: Holt, Rinehart & Winston.

Azevedo, R., & Witherspoon, A. M. (2009). Self-regulated learning with hypermedia. In D. J. Hacker, J. Dunlosky, & A. C. Graesser (Eds.), *Handbook of metacognition in education* (pp. 319–339). New York: Routledge.

Barab, S. A., Gresalfi, M., & Ingram-Goble, A. (2010). Transformational play: Using games to position person, content, and context. *Educational Researcher, 39,* 525–536.

Battistich, V., Solomon, D., Kim, D., Watson, M., & Schaps, E. (1995). Schools as communities, poverty levels of student populations, and students' attitudes, motives, and performance: A multilevel analysis. *American Educational Research Journal, 32,* 627–658.

Beck, I. L., & McKeown, M. G. (1994). Outcomes of history instruction: Paste-up accounts. In M. Carretero & J. F. Voss (Eds.), *Cognitive and instructional processes in history and the social sciences* (pp. 237–256). Mahwah, NJ: Erlbaum.

Beck, I. L., & McKeown, M. G. (2001). Inviting students into the pursuit of meaning. *Educational Psychology Review, 13,* 225–241.

Belfiore, P. J., & Hornyak, R. S. (1998). Operant theory and application to self-monitoring in adolescents. In D. H. Schunk & B. J. Zimmerman (Eds.), *Self-regulated learning: From teaching to self-reflective practice* (pp. 184–202). New York: Guilford.

Bell, P., & Linn, M. C. (2002). Beliefs about science: How does science instruction contribute? In B. K. Hofer & P. R. Pintrich (Eds.), *Personal epistemology: The psychology of beliefs about knowledge and knowing* (pp. 321–346). Mahwah, NJ: Erlbaum.

Bellanca, J. A., & Stirling, T. (2011). *Classrooms without borders: Using Internet projects to teach communication and collaboration.* New York: Teachers College Press.

Bembenutty, H., & Karabenick, S. A. (2004). Inherent association between academic delay of gratification, future time perspective, and self-regulated learning. *Educational Psychology Review, 16,* 35–57.

Benware, C., & Deci, E. L. (1984). Quality of learning with an active versus passive motivational set. *American Educational Research Journal, 21,* 755–765.

Bereiter, C., & Scardamalia, M. (2006). Education for the Knowledge Age: Design-centered models of teaching and instruction. In P. A. Alexander & P. H. Winne (Eds.), *Handbook of educational psychology* (2nd ed., pp. 695–713). Mahwah, NJ: Erlbaum.

Biemiller, A., Shany, M., Inglis, A., & Meichenbaum, D. (1998). Factors influencing children's acquisition and demonstration of self-regulation on academic tasks. In D. H. Schunk & B. J. Zimmerman (Eds.), *Self-regulated learning: From teaching to self-reflective practice* (pp. 203–224). New York: Guilford.

Block, J. H. (1980). Promoting excellence through mastery learning. *Theory into Practice, 19,* 66–74.

Bloom, B. S. (1981). *All our children learning.* New York: McGraw-Hill.

Blumenfeld, P. C., Kempler, T. M., & Krajcik, J. S. (2006). Motivation and cognitive engagement in learning environments. In R. K. Sawyer (Ed.), *The Cambridge handbook of the learning sciences* (pp. 475–488). Cambridge, England: Cambridge University Press.

Blumenfeld, P. C., Marx, R. W., Soloway, E., & Krajcik, J. (1996). Learning with peers: From small group cooperation to collaborative communities. *Educational Researcher, 25*(8), 37–40.

Bransford, J., Stevens, R., Schwartz, D., Meltzoff, A., Pea, R., Reschelle, J., et al. (2006). Learning theories and education: Toward a decade of synergy. In P. A. Alexander & P. H. Winne (Eds.), *Handbook of educational psychology* (2nd ed., pp. 209–244). Mahwah, NJ: Erlbaum.

Bransford, J., D., Mosborg, S., Copland, M. A., Honig, M. A., Nelson, H. G., Gawel, D., et al. (2009). Adaptive people and adaptive systems: Issues of learning and design. In A. Hargreaves, A. Lieberman, M. Filan, & D. Hopkins (Eds.), *Second international handbook of educational change* (pp. 825–856). Dordrecht, Netherlands: Springer.

Brophy, J. E. (2006). Observational research on generic aspects of classroom teaching. In P. A. Alexander & P. H. Winne (Eds.), *Handbook of educational psychology* (2nd ed., pp. 755–780). Mahwah, NJ: Erlbaum.

Brophy, J. (2008). Developing students' appreciation for what is taught in school. *Educational Psychologist, 43,* 132–141.

Brophy, J., Alleman, J., & Knighton, B. (2009). *Inside the social studies classroom.* New York: Routledge.

Brown, A. L., & Palincsar, A. S. (1987). Reciprocal teaching of comprehension strategies: A natural history of one program for enhancing learning. In J. Borkowski & J. D. Day (Eds.), *Cognition in special education: Comparative approaches to retardation, learning disabilities, and giftedness* (pp. 81–132). Norwood, NJ: Ablex.

Brown, A. L., & Reeve, R. A. (1987). Bandwidths of competence: The role of supportive contexts in learning and development. In L. S. Liben (Ed.), *Development and learning: Conflict or congruence?* (pp. 173–223). Mahwah, NJ: Erlbaum.

Brown, M. C., McNeil, N. M., & Glenberg, A. M. (2009). Using concreteness in education: Real problems, potential solutions. *Child Development Perspectives, 3,* 160–164.

Bruner, J. S. (1966). *Toward a theory of instruction.* Cambridge, MA: Harvard University Press.

Bruning, R. H., Schraw, G. J., & Ronning, R. R. (1995). *Cognitive psychology and instruction* (2nd ed.). Upper Saddle River, NJ: Merrill/Prentice-Hall.

Bryan, T., Burstein, K., & Bryan, J. (2001). Students with learning disabilities: Homework problems and promising practices. *Educational Psychologist, 36,* 167–180.

Bulgren, J. A., Deshler, D. D., Schumaker, J. B., & Lenz, B. K. (2000). The use and effectiveness of analogical instruction in diverse secondary content classrooms. *Journal of Educational Psychology, 92,* 426–441.

Calderhead, J. (1996). Teachers: Beliefs and knowledge. In D. C. Berliner & R. C. Calfee (Eds.), *Handbook of educational psychology* (pp. 709–725). New York: Macmillan.

Calfee, R., Dunlap, K., & Wat, A. (1994). Authentic discussion of texts in middle grade schooling: An analytic-narrative approach. *Journal of Reading, 37,* 546–556.

Carney, R. N., & Levin, J. R. (2002). Pictorial illustrations *still* improve students' learning from text. *Educational Psychology Review, 14,* 5–26.

Carnine, D. (1989). Teaching complex content to learning disabled students: The role of technology. *Exceptional Children, 55,* 524–533.

Carr-Chellman, A. (2012, May). Why boys, why games? *Leading and Learning with Technology,* 12–26.

Castagno, A. E., & Brayboy, B. M. J. (2008). Culturally responsive schooling for Indigenous youth: A review of the literature. *Review of Educational Research, 78,* 941–993.

Certo, J. (2011). Social skills and leadership abilities among children in small group literature discussions. *Journal of Research in Childhood Education, 25*(1), 62–81.

Chiu, M. M. (2008). Effects of argumentation on group micro-creativity: Statistical discourse analyses of algebra students' collaborative problem solving. *Contemporary Educational Psychology, 33,* 382–402.

Clark, A.-M., Anderson, R. C., Kuo, L., Kim, I., Archodidou, A., & Nguyen-Jahiel, K. (2003). Collaborative reasoning: Expanding ways for children to talk and think in school. *Educational Psychology Review, 15,* 181–198.

Clark, R. E., Feldon, D. F., van Merriënboer, J. J. G., Yates, K. A., & Early, S. (2008). Cognitive task analysis. In J. M. Spector, M. D. Merrill, J. van Merriënboer, & M. P. Driscoll (Eds.), *Handbook of research on educational communications and technology* (3rd ed., pp. 577–593). New York: Erlbaum.

Clark, R. E., Yates, K., Early, S., & Moulton, (2009). An analysis of the failure of electronic media and discovery-based learning: Evidence for the performance benefits of guided training methods. In K. H. Silber & R. Foshay (Eds.), *Handbook of training and improving workplace performance: Vol. 1. Instructional design and training delivery* (pp. 263–297). New York: Wiley.

Cobb, P., Wood, T., Yackel, E., Nicholls, J., Wheatley, G., Trigatti, B., & Perlwitz, M. (1991). Assessment of a problem centered second-grade mathematics project. *Journal for Research in Mathematics Education, 22,* 3–29.

Cobb, P., & Yackel, E. (1996). Constructivist, emergent, and sociocultural perspectives in the context of developmental research. *Educational Psychologist, 31,* 175–190.

Cohen, E. G. (1994). Restructuring the classroom: Conditions for productive small groups. *Review of Educational Research, 64,* 1–35.

Cohen, E. G., Lockheed, M. E., & Lohman, M. R. (1976). The center for interracial cooperation: A field experiment. *Sociology of Education, 59,* 47–58.

Cohen, E. G., & Lotan, R. A. (1995). Producing equal-status interaction in the heterogeneous classroom. *American Educational Research Journal, 32,* 99–120.

Cole, N. S. (1990). Conceptions of educational achievement. *Educational Researcher, 19*(3), 2–7.

Collins, A., & Halverson, R. (2009). *Rethinking education in the age of technology: The digital revolution and schooling in America.* New York: Teachers College Press.

Connolly, F. W., & Eisenberg, T. E. (1990). The feedback classroom: Teaching's silent friend. *T.H.E. Journal, 17*(5), 75–77.

Connor, D. F. (2006). Stimulants. In R. A. Barkley, *Attention-deficit hyperactivity disorder: A handbook for diagnosis and treatment* (3rd ed., pp. 608–647). New York: Guilford.

Cooper, H. (1989). Synthesis of research on homework. *Educational Leadership, 47*(3), 85–91.

Cooper, H., Robinson, J. C., & Patall, E. A. (2006). Does homework improve academic achievement? A synthesis of research, 1987–2003. *Review of Educational Research, 76,* 1–62.

Cooper, H., & Valentine, J. C. (2001). Using research to answer practical questions about homework. *Educational Psychologist, 36,* 143–153.

Corkill, A. J. (1992). Advance organizers: Facilitators of recall. *Educational Psychology Review, 4,* 33–67.

Corno, L. (1996). Homework is a complicated thing. *Educational Researcher, 25*(8), 27–30.

Corno, L., & Snow, R. E. (1986). Adapting teaching to individual differences among learners. In M. C. Wittrock (Ed.), *Handbook of research on teaching* (3rd ed., pp. 605–629). New York: Macmillan.

Cosden, M., Morrison, G., Albanese, A. L., & Macias, S. (2001). When homework is not home work: After-school programs for homework assistance. *Educational Psychologist, 36,* 211–221.

Crook, C. (1995). On resourcing a concern for collaboration within peer interactions. *Cognition and Instruction, 13,* 541–547.

Cushing, L. S., & Kennedy, C. H. (1997). Academic effects of providing peer support in general education classrooms on students without disabilities. *Journal of Applied Behavior Analysis, 30,* 139–151.

Dansereau, D. F. (1988). Cooperative learning strategies. In C. E. Weinstein, E. T. Goetz, & P. A. Alexander (Eds.), *Learning and study strategies: Issues in assessment, instruction, and evaluation* (pp. 103–120). San Diego, CA: Academic Press.

Dansereau, D. F. (1995). Derived structural schemas and the transfer of knowledge. In A. McKeough, J. Lupart, & A. Marini (Eds.), *Teaching for transfer: Fostering generalization in learning* (pp. 93–122). Mahwah, NJ: Erlbaum.

de Jong, T. (2011). Instruction based on computer simulations. In R. E. Mayer & P. A. Alexander (Eds.), *Handbook of research on learning and instruction* (pp. 446–466). New York: Routledge.

de Jong, T., & van Joolingen, W. R. (1998). Scientific discovery learning with computer simulations of conceptual domains. *Review of Educational Research, 68,* 179–201.

Desberg, P., & Taylor, J. H. (1986). *Essentials of task analysis.* Lanham, MD: University Press of America.

Dettmers, S., Trautwein, U., Lüdtke, O., Goetz, T., Frenzel, A. C., & Pekrun, R. (2011). Students' emotions during homework in mathematics: Testing a theoretical model of antecedents and achievement outcomes. *Contemporary Educational Psychology, 36,* 25–35.

Dettmers, S., Trautwein, U., Lüktke, O., Kunter, M., & Baumert, J. (2010). Homework works if homework quality is high: Using multilevel modeling to predict the development of achievement in mathematics. *Journal of Educational Psychology, 102,* 467–482.

Deutsch, M. (1993). Educating for a peaceful world. *American Psychologist, 48,* 510–517.

Donnelly, C. M., & McDaniel, M. A. (1993). Use of analogy in learning scientific concepts. *Journal of Experimental Psychology: Learning, Memory, and Cognition, 19,* 975–987.

Doyle, W. (1983). Academic work. *Review of Educational Research, 53,* 159–199.

DuNann, D. G., & Weber, S. J. (1976). Short- and long-term effects of contingency managed instruction on low, medium, and high GPA students. *Journal of Applied Behavior Analysis, 9,* 375–376.

DuPaul, G. J., Ervin, R. A., Hook, C. L., & McGoey, K. E. (1998). Peer tutoring for children with attention deficit hyperactivity disorder: Effects on classroom behavior and academic performance. *Journal of Applied Behavior Analysis, 31,* 579–592.

Dymond, S. K., Renzaglia, A., & Chun, E. (2007). Elements of effective high school service learning programs that include students with and without disabilities. *Remedial and Special Education, 28*(4), 227–243.

Eccles, J. S. (2007). Families, schools, and developing achievement-related motivations and engagement. In J. E. Grusec & P. D. Hastings (Eds.), *Handbook of socialization: Theory and research* (pp. 665–691). New York: Guilford.

Edelson, D. C., & Reiser, B. J. (2006). Making authentic practices accessible to learners. In R. K. Sawyer (Ed.), *The Cambridge handbook of the learning sciences* (pp. 335–354). Cambridge, England: Cambridge University Press.

Edmonds, M. S., Vaughn, S., Wexler, J., Reutebuch, C., Cable, A., Tackett, K. K., et al. (2009). A synthesis of reading interventions and effects of reading comprehension outcomes for older struggling students. *Review of Educational Research, 79,* 262–300.

Eeds, M., & Wells, D. (1989). Grand conversations: An explanation of meaning construction in literature study groups. *Research in the Teaching of English, 23,* 4–29.

Egbert, J. (2009). *Supporting learning with technology: Essentials of classroom practice.* Upper Saddle River, NJ: Pearson/Merrill/Prentice-Hall.

Eilam, B. (2001). Primary strategies for promoting homework performance. *American Educational Research Journal, 38,* 691–725.

Esmonde, I. (2009). Ideas and identities: Supporting equity in cooperative mathematics learning. *Review of Educational Research, 79,* 1008–1043.

Fantuzzo, J. W., King, J., & Heller, L. R. (1992). Effects of reciprocal peer tutoring on mathematics and school adjustment: A

component analysis. *Journal of Educational Psychology, 84,* 331–339.

Fennema, E. (1987). Sex-related differences in education: Myths, realities, and interventions. In V. Richardson-Koehler (Ed.), *Educators' handbook: A research perspective* (pp. 329–347). White Plains, NY: Longman.

Ferguson, E. L., & Hegarty, M. (1995). Learning with real machines or diagrams: Application of knowledge to real-world problems. *Cognition and Instruction, 13,* 129–160.

Ferguson, R. (1998). Can schools narrow the Black-White test score gap? In C. Jencks & M. Phillips (Eds.), *The Black-White test score gap* (pp. 318–374). Washington, DC: Brookings Institute.

Fiedler, E. D., Lange, R. E., & Winebrenner, S. (1993). In search of reality: Unraveling the myths about tracking, ability grouping and the gifted. *Roeper Review, 16*(1), 4–7.

Finn, J. D., Pannozzo, G. M., & Achilles, C. M. (2003). The "why's" of class size: Student behavior in small classes. *Review of Educational Research, 73,* 321–368.

Fletcher, J. M., Lyon, G. R., Fuchs, L. S., & Barnes, M. A. (2007). *Learning disabilities: From identification to intervention.* New York: Guilford.

Fox, P. W., & LeCount, J. (1991, April). *When more is less: Faculty misestimation of student learning.* Paper presented at the annual meeting of the American Educational Research Association, Chicago.

Frederiksen, N. (1984a). Implications of cognitive theory for instruction in problem-solving. *Review of Educational Research, 54,* 363–407.

Fries, S., Dietz, F., & Schmid, S. (2008). Motivational interference in learning: The impact of leisure alternatives on subsequent self-regulation. *Contemporary Educational Psychology, 33,* 119–133.

Fuchs, D., Fuchs, L. S., Mathes, P. G., & Simmons, D. C. (1997). Peer-assisted learning strategies: Making classrooms more responsive to diversity. *American Educational Research Journal, 34,* 174–206.

Fuchs, L. S., Fuchs, D., Karns, K., Hamlett, C. L., Dutka, S., & Katzaroff, M. (1996). The relation between student ability and the quality and effectiveness of explanations. *American Educational Research Journal, 33,* 631–664.

Fueyo, V., & Bushell, D., Jr. (1998). Using number line procedures and peer tutoring to improve the mathematics computation of low-performing first graders. *Journal of Applied Behavior Analysis, 31,* 417–430.

Garbe, G., & Guy, D. (2006, Summer). No homework left behind. *Educational Leadership* (online issue). Retrieved February 23, 2009, from http://www.ascd.org/publications/educational_leadership/summer06/vol63/num09/toc.aspx

García, E. E. (1994). *Understanding and meeting the challenge of student cultural diversity.* Boston: Houghton Mifflin.

García, E. E. (1995). Educating Mexican American students: Past treatment and recent developments in theory, research, policy, and practice. In J. A. Banks & C. A. M. Banks (Eds.), *Handbook of research on multicultural education* (pp. 372–387). New York: Macmillan.

Gayford, C. (1992). Patterns of group behavior in open-ended problem solving in science classes of 15-year-old students in England. *International Journal of Science Education, 14,* 41–49.

Gehlbach, H., Brown, S. W., Ioannou, A., Boyer, M. A., Hudson, N., Niv-Solomon, A., et al. (2008). Increasing interest in social studies: Social perspective taking and self-efficacy in stimulating stimulations. *Contemporary Educational Psychology, 33,* 894–914.

Gillies, R. M. (2003). The behaviors, interactions, and perceptions of junior high school students during small-group learning. *Journal of Educational Psychology, 95,* 137–147.

Gillies, R. M., & Ashman, A. D. (1998). Behavior and interactions of children in cooperative groups in lower and middle elementary grades. *Journal of Educational Psychology, 90,* 746–757.

Ginsburg-Block, M. D., Rohrbeck, C. A., & Fantuzzo, J. W. (2006). A meta-analytic review of social, self-concept, and behavioral outcomes of peer-assisted learning. *Journal of Educational Psychology, 98,* 732–749.

Good, T. L., McCaslin, M. M., & Reys, B. J. (1992). Investigating work groups to promote problem solving in mathematics. In J. Brophy (Ed.), *Advances in research on teaching: Vol. 3. Planning and managing learning tasks and activities* (pp. 115–160). Greenwich, CT: JAI.

Graesser, A. C., D'Mello, S., & Cade, W. (2011). Instruction based on tutoring. In R. E. Mayer & P. A. Alexander (Eds.), *Handbook of research on learning and instruction* (pp. 408–426). New York: Routledge.

Graesser, A. C., McNamara, D. S., & VanLehn, K. (2005). Scaffolding deep comprehension strategies through Point&Query, AutoTutor, and iSTART. *Educational Psychologist, 40,* 225–234.

Graesser, A., & Person, N. K. (1994). Question asking during tutoring. *American Educational Research Journal, 31,* 104–137.

Greenwood, C. R., Carta, J. J., & Hall, R. V. (1988). The use of peer tutoring strategies in classroom management and educational instruction. *School Psychology Review, 17,* 258–275.

Griffin, M. M., & Griffin, B. W. (1994, April). *Some can get there from here: Situated learning, cognitive style, and map skills.* Paper presented at the annual meeting of the American Educational Research Association, New Orleans, LA.

Gronlund, N. E., & Brookhart, S. M. (2009). *Writing instructional objectives* (8th ed.). Upper Saddle River, NJ: Merrill/Pearson.

Guinee, K. (2003, April). *Comparison of second-graders' narrative stories written using paper-and-pencil and a multimedia computer-based writing tool.* Paper presented at the annual meeting of the American Educational Research Association, Chicago.

Guskey, T. R. (1985). *Implementing mastery learning.* Belmont, CA: Wadsworth.

Guskey, T. R. (2010). Formative assessment: The contributions of Benjamin S. Bloom. In H. L. Andrade & G. J. Cizek (Eds.), *Handbook of formative assessment* (pp. 106–124). New York: Routledge.

Gustafsson, J., & Undheim, J. O. (1996). Individual differences in cognitive functions. In D. C. Berliner & R. C. Calfee (Eds.), *Handbook of educational psychology* (pp. 186–242). New York: Macmillan.

Hacker, D. J., & Tenent, A. (2002). Implementing reciprocal teaching in the classroom: Overcoming obstacles and making modifications. *Journal of Educational Psychology, 94,* 699–718.

Hadjioannou, X. (2007). Bringing the background to the foreground: What do classroom environments that support authentic discussions look like? *American Educational Research Journal, 44,* 370–399.

Hansen, J., & Pearson, P. D. (1983). An instructional study: Improving the inferential comprehension of good and poor fourth-grade readers. *Journal of Educational Psychology, 75,* 821–829.

Hardy, I., Jonen, A., Möller, K., & Stern, E. (2006). Effects of instructional support within constructivist learning environments for elementary school students' understanding of "floating and sinking." *Journal of Educational Psychology, 98,* 307–326.

Hartley, J., & Trueman, M. (1982). The effects of summaries on the recall of information from prose: Five experimental studies. *Human Learning, 1,* 63–82.

Hatano, G., & Inagaki, K. (1991). Sharing cognition through collective comprehension activity. In L. B. Resnick, J. M. Levine, & S. D. Teasley (Eds.), *Perspectives on socially shared cognition* (pp. 331–348). Washington, DC: American Psychological Association.

Hatano, G., & Inagaki, K. (1993). Desituating cognition through the construction of conceptual knowledge. In P. Light & G. Butterworth (Eds.), *Context and cognition: Ways of learning and knowing* (pp. 115–133). Mahwah, NJ: Erlbaum.

Hatano, G., & Inagaki, K. (2003). When is conceptual change intended? A cognitive-sociocultural view. In G. M. Sinatra & P. R. Pintrich (Eds.), *Intentional conceptual change* (pp. 407–427). Mahwah, NJ: Erlbaum.

Hattie, J. A. C. (2009). *Visible learning: A synthesis of over 800 meta-analyses relating to achievement.* London: Routledge.

Hattie, J., & Gan, M. (2011). Instruction based on feedback. In R. E. Mayer & P. A. Alexander (Eds.), *Handbook of research on learning and instruction* (pp. 249–271). New York: Routledge.

Herrenkohl, L. R., & Guerra, M. R. (1998). Participant structures, scientific discourse, and student engagement in fourth grade. *Cognition and Instruction, 16,* 431–473.

Heward, W. L. (2009). *Exceptional children: An introduction to special education* (9th ed.). Upper Saddle River, NJ: Merrill/Pearson Education.

Hewitt, J., Brett, C., Scardamalia, M., Frecker, K., & Webb, J. (1995, April). *Schools for thought: Transforming classrooms into learning communities.* Paper presented at the annual meeting of the American Educational Research Association, San Francisco.

Hewitt, J., & Scardamalia, M. (1996, April). *Design principles for the support of distributed processes.* Paper presented at the annual meeting of the American Educational Research Association, New York.

Hewitt, J., & Scardamalia, M. (1998). Design principles for distributed knowledge building processes. *Educational Psychology Review, 10,* 75–96.

Hirsch, E. D., Jr. (1996). *The schools we need and why we don't have them.* New York: Doubleday.

Hmelo-Silver, C. E. (2006). Design principles for scaffolding technology-based inquiry. In A. M. O'Donnell, C. E. Hmelo-Silver, & G. Erkens (Eds.), *Collaborative learning, reasoning, and technology* (pp. 147–170). Mahwah, NJ: Erlbaum.

Hogan, D. M., & Tudge, J. R. H. (1999). Implications of Vygotsky's theory for peer learning. In A. M. O'Donnell & A. King (Eds.), *Cognitive perspectives on peer learning* (pp. 39–65). Mahwah, NJ: Erlbaum.

Hogan, K., Nastasi, B. K., & Pressley, M. (2000). Discourse patterns and collaborative scientific reasoning in peer and teacher-guided discussions. *Cognition and Instruction, 17,* 379–432.

Hoover-Dempsey, K. V., Battiato, A. C., Walker, J. M. T., Reed, R. P., DeJong, J. M., & Jones, K. P. (2001). Parental involvement in homework. *Educational Psychologist, 36,* 195–209.

Igoa, C. (1995). *The inner world of the immigrant child.* Mahwah, NJ: Erlbaum.

Inglis, A., & Biemiller, A. (1997, March). *Fostering self-direction in mathematics: A cross-age tutoring program that enhances math problem solving.* Paper presented at the annual meeting of the American Educational Research Association, Chicago.

Iran-Nejad, A., & Stewart, W. (2010). Understanding as an educational objective: From seeking and playing with taxonomies to discovering and reflecting on revelations. *Research in the Schools, 17,* 64–76.

Jadallah, M., Anderson, R. C., Nguyen-Jahiel, K., Miller, B. W., Kim, I.-H., Kuo, L.-J., et al. (2011). Influence of a teacher's scaffolding moves during child-led small-group discussions. *American Educational Research Journal, 48,* 194–230.

Johnson, D. W., & Johnson, R. T. (1991). *Learning together and alone: Cooperative, competitive, and individualistic learning* (3rd ed.). Upper Saddle River, NJ: Prentice-Hall.

Johnson, D. W., & Johnson, R. T. (2009a). An educational psychology success story: Social interdependence theory and cooperative learning. *Educational Researcher, 38,* 365–379.

Johnson, D. W., & Johnson, R. T. (2009b). Energizing learning: The instructional power of conflict. *Educational Researcher, 38,* 37–51.

Johnson-Glenberg, M. C. (2000). Training reading comprehension in adequate decoders/poor comprehenders: Verbal versus visual strategies. *Journal of Educational Psychology, 92,* 772–782.

Jonassen, D. H., Hannum, W. H., & Tessmer, M. (1989). *Handbook of task analysis procedures.* New York: Praeger.

Karpov, Y. V. (2003). Vygotsky's doctrine of scientific concepts: Its role for contemporary education. In A. Kozulin, B. Gindis, V. S. Ageyev, & S. M. Miller (Eds.), *Vygotsky's educational theory in cultural context* (pp. 65–82). Cambridge, England: Cambridge University Press.

Kim, H. S., & Kamil, M. L. (2004). Adolescents, computer technology, and literacy. In T. L. Jetton & J. A. Dole (Eds.), *Adolescent literacy research and practice* (pp. 351–368). New York: Guilford.

King, A. (1997). ASK to THINK—TEL WHY®©: A model of transactive peer tutoring for scaffolding higher level complex learning. *Educational Psychologist, 32,* 221–235.

King, A. (1998). Transactive peer tutoring: Distributing cognition and metacognition. *Educational Psychology Review, 10,* 57–74.

King, A. (1999). Discourse patterns for mediating peer learning. In A. M. O'Donnell & A. King (Eds.), *Cognitive perspectives on peer learning* (pp. 87–115). Mahwah, NJ: Erlbaum.

King, A., Staffieri, A., & Adelgais, A. (1998). Mutual peer tutoring: Effects of structuring tutorial interaction to scaffold peer learning. *Journal of Educational Psychology, 90,* 134–152.

Kintsch, W. (2009). Learning and constructivism. In S. Tobias & T. M. Duffy (Eds.), *Constructivist instruction: Success or failure?* (pp. 223–241). New York: Routledge.

Kirschner, F., Paas, F., & Kirschner, P. A. (2009). A cognitive load approach to collaborative learning: United brains for complex tasks. *Educational Psychology Review, 21,* 31–42.

Kirschner, P. A., Sweller, J., & Clark, R. E. (2006). Why minimal guidance during instruction does not work: An analysis of the failure of constructivist, discovery, problem-based, experiential, and inquiry-based teaching. *Educational Psychologist, 41,* 75–86.

Klahr, D. (2009). "To everything there is a season, and a time to every purpose under the heavens": what about direct instruction? In S. Tobias & T. M. Duffy (Eds.), *Constructivist instruction: Success or failure?* (pp. 291–310). New York: Routledge.

Koedinger, K., Aleven, V., Roll, I., & Baker, R. (2009). *In vivo* experiments on whether supporting metacognition in intelligent tutoring systems yields robust learning. In D. J. Hacker, J. Dunlosky, & A. C. Graesser (Eds.), *Handbook of metacognition in education* (pp. 383–412). New York: Routledge.

Koedinger, K. R., & Corbett, A. (2006). Cognitive tutors: Technology bringing learning sciences to the classroom. In R. K. Sawyer (Ed.), *The Cambridge handbook of the learning sciences* (pp. 61–77). Cambridge, England: Cambridge University Press.

Krajcik, J. S. (1991). Developing students' understanding of chemical concepts. In S. M. Glynn, R. H. Yeany, & B. K. Britton (Eds.), *The psychology of learning science* (pp. 117–147). Mahwah, NJ: Erlbaum.

Ku, Y.-M., Chan, W.-C., Wu, Y.-C., & Chen, Y.-H. (2008, March). *Improving children's comprehension of science text: Effects of adjunct questions and notetaking.* Paper presented at the annual meeting of the American Educational Research Association, New York.

Kuhn, D. (2007). Is direct instruction an answer to the right question? *Educational Psychologist, 42,* 109–113.

Kuhn, D., & Pease, M. (2008). What needs to develop in the development of inquiry skills? *Cognition and Instruction, 26,* 512–599.

Kuhn, D., & Pease, M. (2010). The dual components of developing strategy use: Production and inhibition. In H. S. Waters & W. Schneider (Eds.), *Metacognition, strategy use, and instruction* (pp. 135–159). New York: Guilford.

Kulik, C. C., Kulik, J. A., & Bangert-Drowns, R. L. (1990). Effectiveness of mastery learning programs: A meta-analysis. *Review of Educational Research, 60,* 265–299.

Lambert, M. C., Cartledge, G., Heward, W. L., & Lo, Y.-Y. (2006). Effects of response cards on disruptive behavior and academic responding during math lessons by fourth-grade urban students. *Journal of Positive Behavioral Interventions, 8,* 88–99.

Lamon, M., Chan, C., Scardamalia, M., Burtis, P. J., & Brett, C. (1993, April). *Beliefs about learning and constructive processes in reading: Effects of a computer supported intentional learning environment (CSILE).* Paper presented at the annual meeting of the American Educational Research Association, Atlanta, GA.

Lampert, M., Rittenhouse, P., & Crumbaugh, C. (1996). Agreeing to disagree: Developing sociable mathematical discourse. In D. R. Olson & N. Torrance (Eds.), *The handbook of education and human development: New models of learning, teaching, and schooling* (pp. 731–764). Cambridge, MA: Blackwell.

Leach, J. T., & Scott, P. H. (2008). Teaching for conceptual understanding: An approach drawing on individual and sociocultural perspectives. In S. Vosniadou (Ed.), *International handbook on conceptual change* (pp. 647–675). New York: Routledge.

Lee-Pearce, M. L., Plowman, T. S., & Touchstone, D. (1998). Starbase-Atlantis, a school without walls: A comparative study of an innovative science program for at-risk urban elementary students. *Journal of Education for Students Placed at Risk, 3,* 223–235.

Lepper, M. R., Aspinwall, L. G., Mumme, D. L., & Chabay, R. W. (1990). Self-perception and social perception processes in tutoring: Subtle social control strategies of expert tutors. In J. M. Olson & M. P. Zanna (Eds.), *Self-inference processes: The Ontario Symposium* (pp. 217–238). Mahwah, NJ: Erlbaum.

Leu, D. J., O'Byrne, W. I., Zawilinski, L., McVerry, J. G., & Everett-Cacopardo, H. (2009). Expanding the new literacies conversation. *Educational Researcher, 38,* 264–269.

Levin, J. R., & Mayer, R. E. (1993). Understanding illustrations in text. In B. K. Britton, A. Woodward, & M. Binkley (Eds.), *Learning from textbooks: Theory and practice* (pp. 95–113). Mahwah, NJ: Erlbaum.

Levstik, L. S. (2011). Learning history. In R. E. Mayer & P. A. Alexander (Eds.), *Handbook of research on learning and instruction* (pp. 208–126). New York: Routledge.

Levy, I., Kaplan, A., & Patrick, H. (2000, April). *Early adolescents' achievement goals, intergroup processes, and attitudes towards collaboration.* Paper presented at the annual meeting of the American Educational Research Association, New Orleans, LA.

Linn, M. C. (2008). Teaching for conceptual change: Distinguish or extinguish ideas. In S. Vosniadou (Ed.), *International handbook on conceptual change* (pp. 694–722). New York: Routledge.

Linn, M. C., & Eylon, B.-S. (2011). *Science learning and instruction: Taking advantage of technology to promote knowledge integration.* New York: Routledge.

Linn, M. C., Songer, N. B., & Eylon, B. (1996). Shifts and convergences in science learning and instruction. In D. C. Berliner & R. C. Calfee (Eds.), *Handbook of educational psychology* (pp. 438–490). New York: Macmillan.

Lorch, R. F., Jr., Lorch, E. P., Calderhead, W. J., Dunlap, E. E., Hodell, E. C., & Freer, B. D. (2010). Learning the control of variables strategy in higher and lower achieving classrooms: Contributions of explicit instruction and experimentation. *Journal of Educational Psychology, 102,* 90–101.

Lorch, R. F., Jr., Lorch, E. P., & Inman, W. E. (1993). Effects of signaling topic structure on text recall. *Journal of Educational Psychology, 85,* 281–290.

Lotan, R. A. (2006). Managing groupwork in heterogeneous classrooms. In C. M. Evertson & C. S. Weinstein (Eds.), *Handbook of classroom management: Research, practice, and contemporary issues* (pp. 525–539). Mahwah, NJ: Erlbaum.

Lou, Y., Abrami, P. C., Spence, J. C., Poulsen, C., Chambers, B., & d'Apollonia, S. (1996). Within-class grouping: A meta-analysis. *Review of Educational Research, 66,* 423–458.

Mac Iver, D. J., Reuman, D. A., & Main, S. R. (1995). Social structuring of the school: Studying what is, illuminating what could be. In J. T. Spence, J. M. Darley, & D. J. Foss (Eds.), *Annual review of psychology* (Vol. 46, pp. 375–400). Palo Alto, CA: Annual Review.

MacLean, D. J., Sasse, D. K., Keating, D. P., Stewart, B. E., & Miller, F. K. (1995, April). *All-girls' mathematics and science instruction in early adolescence: Longitudinal effects.* Paper presented at the annual meeting of the American Educational Research Association, San Francisco.

Marzano, R. J., & Kendall, J. S. (2007). *The new taxonomy of educational objectives* (2nd ed.). Thousand Oaks, CA: Corwin.

Mathes, P. G., Torgesen, J. K., & Allor, J. H. (2001). The effects of peer-assisted literacy strategies for first-grade readers with and without additional computer-assisted instruction. *American Educational Research Journal, 38,* 371–410.

Mayer, R. E. (1989). Models for understanding. *Review of Educational Research, 59,* 43–64.

Mayer, R. E. (2004). Should there be a three-strikes rule against pure discovery learning? *American Psychologist, 59,* 14–19.

Mayer, R. E. (2010a). Fostering scientific reasoning with multimedia instruction. In H. S. Waters & W. Schneider (Eds.), *Metacognition, strategy use, and instruction* (pp. 160–175). New York: Guilford.

Mayer, R. E. (2011a). *Applying the science of learning.* Boston: Allyn & Bacon.

Mayer, R. E., & Gallini, J. (1990). When is an illustration worth ten thousand words? *Journal of Educational Psychology, 82,* 715–726.

Mayer, R. E., Stull, A., DeLeeuw, K., Almeroth, K., Bimber, B., Chun, D., et al. (2009). Clickers in college classrooms: Fostering learning with questioning methods in large lecture classes. *Contemporary Educational Psychology, 34,* 51–57.

McAshan, H. H. (1979). *Competency-based education and behavioral objectives.* Englewood Cliffs, NJ: Educational Technology.

McDaniel, M. A., & Einstein, G. O. (1989). Material-appropriate processing: A contextualist approach to reading and studying strategies. *Educational Psychology Review, 1,* 113–145.

McDevitt, M., & Chaffee, S. H. (1998). Second chance political socialization: "Trickle-up" effects of children on parents. In T. J. Johnson, C. E. Hays, & S. P. Hays (Eds.), *Engaging the public: How government and the media can reinvigorate American democracy* (pp. 57–66). Lanhan, MD: Rowman & Littlefield.

McDevitt, T. M., & Ormrod, J. E. (2013). *Child development and education* (5th ed.). Upper Saddle River, NJ: Merrill/Pearson Education

McDonald, B. O., Robles-Piña, R., & Polnick, B. (2011, April). *A comparison of urban middle school mathematics teachers with high student gain scores and low student gain scores.* Paper presented at the annual meeting of the American Educational Research Association, New Orleans, LA.

McGee, K. D., Knight, S. L., & Boudah, D. J. (2001, April). *Using reciprocal teaching in secondary inclusive English classroom instruction.* Paper presented at the annual meeting of the American Educational Research Association, Seattle, WA.

McGee, L. M. (1992). An exploration of meaning construction in first graders' grand conversations. In C. K. Kinzer & D. J. Leu (Eds.), *Literacy research, theory, and practice: Views from many perspectives* (pp. 177–186). Chicago: National Reading Conference.

Meloth, M. S., & Deering, P. D. (1999). The role of the teacher in promoting cognitive processing during collaborative learning. In A. M. O'Donnell & A. King (Eds.), *Cognitive perspectives on peer learning* (pp. 235–255). Mahwah, NJ: Erlbaum.

Mercer, C. D., & Pullen, P. C. (2005). *Students with learning disabilities* (6th ed.). Upper Saddle River, NJ: Merrill/Prentice-Hall.

Mergendoller, J. R., Markham, T., Ravitz, J., & Larmer, J. (2006). Pervasive management of project based learning: Teachers as guides and facilitators. In C. M. Evertson & C. S. Weinstein (Eds.), *Handbook of classroom management: Research, practice, and contemporary issues* (pp. 583–615). Mahwah, NJ: Erlbaum.

Merrill, P. F., Hammons, K., Vincent, B. R., Reynolds, P. L., Christensen, L., & Tolman, M. N. (1996). *Computers in education* (3rd ed.). Boston: Allyn & Bacon.

Miller, M. D., Linn, R. L., & Gronlund, N. E. (2009). *Measurement and assessment in teaching* (10th ed.). Upper Saddle River, NJ: Merrill/Pearson.

Minstrell, J., & Stimpson, V. (1996). A classroom environment for learning: Guiding students' reconstruction of understanding and reasoning.

In L. Schauble & R. Glaser (Eds.), *Innovations in learning: New environments for education* (pp. 175–202). Mahwah, NJ: Erlbaum.

Moje, E. B., & Shepardson, D. P. (1998). Social interactions and children's changing understanding of electric circuits: Exploring unequal power relations in "peer"-learning groups. In B. Guzzetti & C. Hynd (Eds.), *Perspectives on conceptual change: Multiple ways to understand knowing and learning in a complex world* (pp. 225–234). Mahwah, NJ: Erlbaum.

Monte-Sano, C. (2008). Qualities of historical writing instruction: A comparative case study of two teachers' practices. *American Educational Research Journal, 45,* 1045–1079.

Moreno, R. (2006). Learning in high-tech and multimedia environments. *Current Directions in Psychological Science, 15,* 63–67.

Moreno, R., & Park, B. (2010). Cognitive Load Theory: Historical development and relation to other theories. In J. L. Plass, R. Moreno, & R. Brünken (Eds.), *Cognitive Load Theory* (pp. 9–28). Cambridge, England: Cambridge University Press.

Morgan, D. P., & Jenson, W. R. (1988). *Teaching behaviorally disordered students: Preferred practices.* Upper Saddle River, NJ: Merrill/Prentice-Hall.

Morra, S., Gobbo, C., Marini, Z., & Sheese, R. (2008). *Cognitive development: Neo-Piagetian perspectives.* New York: Erlbaum.

Munro, D. W., & Stephenson, J. (2009). The effects of response cards on student and teacher behavior during vocabulary instruction. *Journal of Applied Behavior Analysis, 42,* 795–800.

Murphy, P. K., Wilkinson, I. A. G., & Soter, A. O. (2011). Instruction based on discussion. In R. E. Mayer & P. A. Alexander (Eds.), *Handbook of research on learning and instruction* (pp. 382–407). New York: Routledge.

Murphy, P. K., Wilkinson, I. A. G., Soter, A. O., Hennessey, M. N., & Alexander, J. F. (2009). Examining the effects of classroom discussion on students' comprehension of text: A meta-analysis. *Journal of Educational Psychology, 101,* 740–764.

Narciss, S. (2008). Feedback strategies for interactive learning tasks. In J. M. Spector, M. D. Merrill, J. van Merriënboer, & M. P. Driscoll (Eds.), *Handbook of research on educational communications and technology* (3rd ed., pp. 125–143). New York: Erlbaum.

Newby, T. J., Ertmer, P. A., & Stepich, D. A. (1994, April). *Instructional analogies and the learning of concepts.* Paper presented at the annual meeting of the American Educational Research Association, New Orleans, LA.

Niederhauser, D. S. (2008). Educational hypertext. In J. M. Spector, M. D. Merrill, J. van Merriënboer, & M. P. Driscoll (Eds.), *Handbook of research on educational communications and technology* (3rd ed., pp. 199–210). New York: Erlbaum.

Nixon, A. S. (2005, April). *Moral reasoning in the digital age: How students, teachers, and parents judge appropriate computer uses.* Paper presented at the annual meeting of the American Educational Research Association, Montreal.

Nolen, S. B. (2011). Motivation, engagement, and identity: Opening a conversation. In D. M.

McInerney, R. A. Walker, & G. A. D. Liem (Eds.), *Sociocultural theories of learning and motivation: Looking back, looking forward* (pp. 109–135). Charlotte, NC: Information Age.

Nussbaum, E. M. (2008). Collaborative discourse, argumentation, and learning: Preface and literature review. *Contemporary Educational Psychology, 33,* 345–359.

O'Donnell, A. M. (1999). Structuring dyadic interaction through scripted cooperation. In A. M. O'Donnell & A. King (Eds.), *Cognitive perspectives on peer learning* (pp. 179–196). Mahwah, NJ: Erlbaum.

O'Donnell, A. M. (2006). The role of peers and group learning. In P. A. Alexander & P. H. Winne (Eds.), *Handbook of educational psychology* (2nd ed., pp. 781–802). Mahwah, NJ: Erlbaum.

O'Donnell, A. M., & O'Kelly, J. (1994). Learning from peers: Beyond the rhetoric of positive results. *Educational Psychology Review, 6,* 321–349.

Onosko, J. J. (1996). Exploring issues with students despite the barriers. *Social Education, 60*(1), 22–27.

Palincsar, A. S., & Brown, A. L. (1984). Reciprocal teaching of comprehension-fostering and comprehension-monitoring activities. *Cognition and Instruction, 1,* 117–175.

Palincsar, A. S., & Brown, A. L. (1989). Classroom dialogues to promote self-regulated comprehension. In J. Brophy (Ed.), *Advances in research on teaching* (Vol. 1, pp. 35–71). Greenwich, CT: JAI.

Palincsar, A. S., & Herrenkohl, L. R. (1999). Designing collaborative contexts: Lessons from three research programs. In A. M. O'Donnell & A. King (Eds.), *Cognitive perspectives on peer learning* (pp. 151–177). Mahwah, NJ: Erlbaum.

Palmer, E. L. (1965). Accelerating the child's cognitive attainments through the inducement of cognitive conflict: An interpretation of the Piagetian position. *Journal of Research in Science Teaching, 3,* 324.

Patall, E. A., Cooper, H., & Wynn, S. R. (2010). The effectiveness and relative importance of choice in the classroom. *Journal of Educational Psychology, 102,* 896–915.

Pea, R. D., & Maldonado, H. (2006). WILD for learning: Interacting through new computing devices anytime, anywhere. In R. K. Sawyer (Ed.), *The Cambridge handbook of the learning sciences* (pp. 427–441). Cambridge, England: Cambridge University Press.

Pellegrino, J. W., Chudowsky, N., & Glaser, R. (Eds.). (2001). *Knowing what students know: The science and design of educational assessment.* Washington DC: National Academy Press.

Pfeifer, J. H., Brown, C. S., & Juvonen, J. (2007). Teaching tolerance in schools: Lessons learned since Brown v. Board of Education about the development and reduction of children's prejudice. *Social Policy Report, 21*(2), 3–13, 16–17, 20–23. Ann Arbor, MI: Society for Research in Child Development.

Pianta, R. C., & Hamre, B. K. (2009). Conceptualization, measurement, and improvement of classroom processes: Standardized observation can leverage capacity. *Educational Researcher, 38,* 109–119.

Piirto, J. (1999). *Talented children and adults: Their development and education* (2nd ed.). Upper Saddle River, NJ: Merrill/Prentice-Hall.

Pittman, K., & Beth-Halachmy, S. (1997, March). *The role of prior knowledge in analogy use.* Paper presented at the annual meeting of the American Educational Research Association, Chicago.

Plass, J. L., Kalyuga, S., & Leutner, D. (2010). Individual differences and Cognitive Load Theory. In J. L. Plass, R. Moreno, & R. Brünken (Eds.), *Cognitive Load Theory* (pp. 65–87). Cambridge, England: Cambridge University Press.

Popham, W. J. (1995). *Classroom assessment: What teachers need to know.* Boston: Allyn & Bacon.

Portes, P. R. (1996). Ethnicity and culture in educational psychology. In D. C. Berliner & R. C. Calfee (Eds.), *Handbook of educational psychology* (pp. 331–357). New York: Macmillan.

Pugh, K. J., Schmidt, K., & Russell, C. (2010, May). *Fostering transformative experiences in science: A design-based study.* Paper presented at the annual meeting of the American Educational Research Association, Denver.

Quintana, C., Zhang, M., & Krajcik, J. (2005). A framework for supporting metacognitive aspects of online inquiry through software-based scaffolding. *Educational Psychologist, 40,* 235–244.

Redfield, D. L., & Rousseau, E. W. (1981). A meta-analysis of experimental research on teacher questioning behavior. *Review of Educational Research, 51,* 237–245.

Reeve, J. (2009). Why teachers adopt a controlling motivating style toward students and how they can become more autonomy supportive. *Educational Psychologist, 44,* 159–175.

Reinking, D., & Leu, D. J. (Chairs). (2008, March). *Understanding Internet reading comprehension and its development among adolescents at risk of dropping out of school.* Poster session presented at the annual meeting of the American Educational Research Association, New York.

Reynolds, R. E., & Shirey, L. L. (1988). The role of attention in studying and learning. In C. E. Weinstein, E. T. Goetz, & P. A. Alexander (Eds.), *Learning and study strategies: Issues in assessment, instruction, and evaluation* (pp. 77–100). San Diego, CA: Academic Press.

Rittle-Johnson, B. (2006). Promoting transfer: Effects of self-explanation and direct instruction. *Child Development, 77,* 1–15.

Robinson, A. (1991). Cooperation or exploitation? The argument against cooperative learning for talented students. *Journal for the Education of the Gifted, 14,* 9–27.

Robinson, D. R., Schofield, J. W., & Steers-Wentzell, K. L. (2005). Peer and cross-age tutoring in math: Outcomes and their design implications. *Educational Psychology Review, 17,* 327–362.

Roscoe, R. D., & Chi, M. T. H. (2007). Understanding tutor learning: Knowledge-building and knowledge-telling in peer tutors' explanations and questions. *Review of Educational Research, 77,* 534–574.

Rosenshine, B. (2009). The empirical support for direct instruction. In S. Tobias & T. M. Duffy (Eds.), *Constructivist instruction: Success or failure?* (pp. 201–220). New York: Routledge.

Rosenshine, B., & Meister, C. (1994). Reciprocal teaching: A review of the research. *Review of Educational Research, 64,* 479–530.

Rosenshine, B., & Stevens, R. (1986). Teaching functions. In M. C. Wittrock (Ed.), *Handbook of research on teaching* (3rd ed., pp. 376–391). New York: Macmillan.

Rowe, M. B. (1987). Wait-time: Slowing down may be a way of speeding up. *American Educator, 11,* 38–43, 47.

Ruef, M. B., Higgins, C., Glaeser, B., & Patnode, M. (1998). Positive behavioral support: Strategies for teachers. *Intervention in School and Clinic, 34*(1), 21–32.

Sadoski, M., & Paivio, A. (2001). *Imagery and text: A dual coding theory of reading and writing.* Mahwah, NJ: Erlbaum.

Sarama, J., & Clements, D. H. (2009). "Concrete" computer manipulatives in mathematics education. *Child Development Perspectives, 3,* 145–150.

Sawyer, R. K. (2006). Introduction: The new science of learning. In R. K. Sawyer (Ed.), *The Cambridge handbook of the learning sciences* (pp. 1–16). Cambridge, England: Cambridge University Press.

Scardamalia, M., & Bereiter, C. (2006). Knowledge building: Theory, pedagogy, and technology. In R. K. Sawyer (Ed.), *The Cambridge handbook of the learning sciences* (pp. 97–115). Cambridge, England: Cambridge University Press.

Scevak, J. J., Moore, P. J., & Kirby, J. R. (1993). Training students to use maps to increase text recall. *Contemporary Educational Psychology, 18,* 401–413.

Schiffman, G., Tobin, D., & Buchanan, B. (1984). Microcomputer instruction for the learning disabled. *Annual Review of Learning Disabilities, 2,* 134–136.

Schmidt, W. H. (2008, Spring). What's missing from math standards? *American Educator.* Retrieved March 3, 2008, from http://www.aft.org/pubs-reports/american_educator/issues/spring2008/schmidt.htm

Schofield, J. W. (2006). Internet use in schools: Promise and problems. In R. K. Sawyer (Ed.), *The Cambridge handbook of the learning sciences* (pp. 521–534). Cambridge, England: Cambridge University Press.

Schwartz, D. L., & Martin, T. (2004). Inventing to prepare for future learning: The hidden efficiency of encouraging original student production in statistics instruction. *Cognition and Instruction, 22,* 129–184.

Shuell, T. J. (1996). Teaching and learning in a classroom context. In D. C. Berliner & R. C. Calfee (Eds.), *Handbook of educational psychology* (pp. 726–764). New York: Macmillan.

Sinatra, G. M., & Mason, L. (2008). Beyond knowledge: Learner characteristics influencing conceptual change. In S. Vosniadou (Ed.), *International handbook on conceptual change* (pp. 560–582). New York: Routledge.

Sitko, B. M. (1998). Knowing how to write: Metacognition and writing instruction. In D. J. Hacker, J. Dunlosky, & A. C. Graesser (Eds.), *Metacognition in educational theory and practice* (pp. 93–115). Mahwah, NJ: Erlbaum.

Skinner, B. F. (1968). *The technology of teaching.* New York: Appleton-Century-Crofts.

Slater, W. H. (2004). Teaching English from a literacy perspective: The goal of high literacy for all students. In T. L. Jetton & J. A. Dole (Eds.), *Adolescent literacy research and practice* (pp. 40–58). New York: Guilford.

Slavin, R. E. (2011). Instruction based on cooperative learning. In R. E. Mayer & P. A. Alexander (Eds.), *Handbook of research on learning and instruction* (pp. 344–360). New York: Routledge.

Slavin, R. E., Hurley, E. A., & Chamberlain, A. (2003). Cooperative learning and achievement: Theory and research. In W. Reynolds & G. Miller (Eds.), *Handbook of psychology: Vol. 7. Educational psychology* (pp. 177–198). New York: Wiley.

Slavin, R. E., & Lake, C. (2008). Effective programs in elementary mathematics: A best-evidence synthesis. *Review of Educational Research, 78,* 427–515.

Small, M. Y., Lovett, S. B., & Scher, M. S. (1993). Pictures facilitate children's recall of unillustrated expository prose. *Journal of Educational Psychology, 85,* 520–528.

Smith, C. L. (2007). Bootstrapping processes in the development of students' commonsense matter theories: Using analogical mappings, thought experiments, and learning to measure to promote conceptual restructuring. *Cognition and Instruction, 25,* 337–398.

Snir, J., Smith, C. L., & Raz, G. (2003). Linking phenomena with competing underlying models: A software tool for introducing students to the particulate model of matter. *Science Education, 87,* 794–830.

Spicker, H. H. (1992). Identifying and enriching: Rural gifted children. *Educational Horizons, 70*(2), 60–65.

Spiro, R. J., & DeSchryver, M. (2009). Constructivism: When it's the wrong idea and when it's the only idea. In S. Tobias & T. M. Duffy (Eds.), *Constructivist instruction: Success or failure?* (pp. 106–123). New York: Routledge.

Spörer, N., & Brunstein, J. C. (2009). Fostering the reading comprehension of secondary school students through peer-assisted learning: Effects on strategy knowledge, strategy use, and task performance. *Contemporary Educational Psychology, 34,* 289–297.

Squire, K. (2011). *Video games and learning: Teaching and participatory culture in the digital age.* New York: Teachers College Press.

Stacey, K. (1992). Mathematical problem solving in groups: Are two heads better than one? *Journal of Mathematical Behavior, 11,* 261–275.

Staples, M. (2007). Supporting whole-class collaborative inquiry in a secondary mathematics classroom. *Cognition and Instruction, 25,* 161–217.

Stein, J. A., & Krishnan, K. (2007). Nonverbal learning disabilities and executive function: The challenges of effective assessment and teaching. In L. Meltzer (Ed.), *Executive function in education: From theory to practice* (pp. 106–132). New York: Guilford.

Sternberg, R. J., & Horvath, J. A. (1995). A prototype view of expert teaching. *Educational Researcher, 24*(6), 9–17.

Stevens, R. J., & Slavin, R. E. (1995). The cooperative elementary school: Effects of students' achievement, attitudes, and social relations. *American Educational Research Journal, 32,* 321–351.

Stokes, J. V., Luiselli, J. K., & Reed, D. D. (2010). A behavioral intervention for teaching tacking skills to high school football athletes. *Journal of Applied Behavior Analysis, 43,* 509–512.

Sullivan, J. R., & Conoley, J. C. (2004). Academic and instructional interventions with aggressive students. In J. C. Conoley & A. P. Goldstein (Eds.), *School violence intervention* (2nd ed., pp. 235–255). New York: Guilford.

Swan, K., Mitrani, M., Guerrero, F., Cheung, M., & Schoener, J. (1990, April). *Perceived locus of control and computer-based instruction.* Paper presented at the annual meeting of the American Educational Research Association, Boston.

Sweller, J. (2010). Cognitive Load Theory: Recent theoretical advances. In J. L. Plass, R. Moreno, & R. Brünken (Eds.), *Cognitive Load Theory* (pp. 29–47). Cambridge, England: Cambridge University Press.

Tamin, R. M., Bernard, R. M., Borokhovski, E., Abrami, P. C., & Schmid, R. F. (2011). What forty years of research says about the impact of technology on learning: A second-order meta-analysis and validation study. *Review of Educational Research, 81,* 4–28.

Tarver, S. G. (1992). Direct Instruction. In W. Stainback & S. Stainback (Eds.), *Controversial issues confronting special education* (pp. 143–165). Boston: Allyn & Bacon.

Tennyson, R. D., & Cocchiarella, M. J. (1986). An empirically based instructional design theory for teaching concepts. *Review of Educational Research, 56,* 40–71.

Tharp, R. G. (1989). Psychocultural variables and constants: Effects on teaching and learning in schools. *American Psychologist, 44,* 349–359.

Théberge, C. L. (1994, April). *Small-group vs. whole-class discussion: Gaining the floor in science lessons.* Paper presented at the annual meeting of the American Educational Research Association, New Orleans, LA.

Trautwein, U., & Lüdtke, O. (2007). Students' self-reported effort and time on homework in six school subjects: Between-student differences and within-student variation. *Journal of Educational Psychology, 99,* 432–444.

Trautwein, U., Lüdtke, O., Kastens, C., & Köller, O. (2006). Effort on homework in grades 5–9: Development, motivational antecedents, and the association with effort on classwork. *Child Development, 77,* 1094–1111.

Trautwein, U., Niggli, A., Schnyder, I., & Lüdtke, O. (2009). Between-teacher differences in homework assignments and the development of students' homework effort, homework emotions, and achievement. *Journal of Educational Psychology, 101,* 176–189.

Turnbull, A. P., Turnbull, R., & Wehmeyer, M. L. (2010). *Exceptional lives: Special education in today's schools* (6th ed.). Upper Saddle River, NJ: Merrill.

van Garderen, D. (2004). Reciprocal teaching as a comprehension strategy for understanding mathematical word problems. *Reading and Writing Quarterly, 20,* 225–229.

VanLehn, K. (2011). The relative effectiveness of human tutoring, intelligent tutoring systems, and other tutoring systems. *Educational Psychologist, 46,* 197–221.

van Merriënboer, J. J. G., Kirschner, P. A., & Kester, L. (2003). Taking the load off a learner's mind: Instructional design for complex learning. *Educational Psychologist, 38,* 5–13.

vanSledright, B., & Limón, M. (2006). Learning and teaching social studies: A review of cognitive research in history and geography. In P. A. Alexander & P. H. Winne (Eds.), *Handbook of educational psychology* (2nd ed., pp. 545–570). Mahwah, NJ: Erlbaum.

Verdi, M. P., & Kulhavy, R. W. (2002). Learning with maps and texts: An overview. *Educational Psychology Review, 14,* 27–46.

Wade, S. E. (1992). How interest affects learning from text. In K. A. Renninger, S. Hidi, & A. Krapp (Eds.), *The role of interest in learning and development* (pp. 255–277). Mahwah, NJ: Erlbaum.

Wade-Stein, D., & Kintsch, E. (2004). Summary Street: Interactive computer support for writing. *Cognition and Instruction, 22,* 333–362

Walker, J. M. T. (2001, April). *A cross-sectional study of student motivation, strategy knowledge and strategy use during homework: Implications for research on self-regulated learning.* Paper presented at the annual meeting of the American Educational Research Association, Seattle, WA.

Walshaw, M., & Anthony, G. (2008). The teacher's role in classroom discourse: A review of recent research into mathematics classrooms. *Review of Educational Research, 78,* 516–551.

Warschauer, M. (2011). *Learning in the cloud: How (and why) to transform schools with digital media.* New York: Teachers College Press.

Wasley, P. A., Hampel, R. L., & Clark, R. W. (1997). *Kids and school reform.* San Francisco: Jossey-Bass.

Watkins, C. L. (1997). *Project Follow Through: A case study of contingencies influencing instructional practices of the educational establishment.* Cambridge, MA: Cambridge Center for Behavioral Studies.

Webb, N. M. (1989). Peer interaction and learning in small groups. *International Journal of Educational Research, 13,* 21–39.

Webb, N. M., & Farivar, S. (1999). Developing productive group interaction in middle school mathematics. In A. M. O'Donnell & A. King (Eds.), *Cognitive perspectives on peer learning* (pp. 117–149). Mahwah, NJ: Erlbaum.

Webb, N. M., Franke, M. L., Ing, M., Chan, A., De, T., Freund, D., et al. (2008). The role of teacher instructional practices in student collaboration. *Contemporary Educational Psychology, 33,* 360–381.

Webb, N. M., & Mastergeorge, A. M. (2003). The development of students' helping behavior and learning in peer-directed small groups. *Cognition and Instruction, 21,* 361–428.

Webb, N. M., Nemer, K. M., Chizhik, A. W., & Sugrue, B. (1998). Equity issues in collaborative group assessment: Group composition and performance. *American Educational Research Journal, 35,* 607–651.

Webb, N. M., Nemer, K. M., & Zuniga, S. (2002). Short circuits or superconductors? Effects of group composition on high-achieving students' science assessment performance. *American Educational Research Journal, 39,* 943–989.

Webb, N. M., & Palincsar, A. S. (1996). Group processes in the classroom. In D. C. Berliner & R. C. Calfee (Eds.), *Handbook of educational psychology* (pp. 841–873). New York: Macmillan.

Weinert, F. E., & Helmke, A. (1995). Learning from wise Mother Nature or Big Brother Instructor: The wrong choice as seen from an educational perspective. *Educational Psychologist, 30,* 135–142.

Wentzel, K. R. (2009). Peers and academic functioning at school. In K. H. Rubin, W. M. Bukowski, & B. Laursen (Eds.), *Handbook of peer interactions, relationships, and groups* (pp. 531–547). New York: Guilford.

White, B. Y., & Frederiksen, J. R. (1998). Inquiry, modeling, and metacognition: Making science accessible to all students. *Cognition and Instruction, 16,* 3–118.

White, B. Y., & Frederiksen, J. R. (2005). A theoretical framework and approach for fostering metacognitive development. *Educational Psychologist, 40,* 211–223.

White, B., Frederiksen, J., & Collins, A. (2009). The interplay of scientific inquiry and metacognition: More than a marriage of convenience. In D. J. Hacker, J. Dunlosky, & A. C. Graesser (Eds.), *Handbook of metacognition in education* (pp. 175–205). New York: Routledge.

White, J. R., & McVeigh, J. (2010, April–May). Paper presented at the annual meeting of the American Educational Research Association, New Orleans, LA.

Wiggins, G., & McTighe, J. (2005). *Understanding by Design* (expanded 2nd ed.). Alexandria, VA: Association for Supervision and Curriculum Development.

Wilson, P. T., & Anderson, R. C. (1986). What they don't know will hurt them: The role of prior knowledge in comprehension. In J. Orasanu (Ed.), *Reading comprehension: From research to practice* (pp. 31–48). Mahwah, NJ: Erlbaum.

Windschitl, M. (2002). Framing constructivism in practice as the negotiation of dilemmas: An analysis of the conceptual, pedagogical, cultural, and political challenges facing teachers. *Review of Educational Research, 72,* 131–175.

Winn, W. (1991). Learning from maps and diagrams. *Educational Psychology Review, 3,* 211–247.

Winn, W. (2002). Current trends in educational technology research: The study of learning environments. *Educational Psychology Review, 14,* 331–351.

Winters, F. I., Greene, J. A., & Costich, C. M. (2008). Self-regulation of learning within computer-based learning environments: A critical analysis. *Educational Psychology Review, 20,* 429–444.

Wise, A. F., & O'Neill, K. (2009). Beyond more versus less: A reframing of the debate on instructional guidance. In S. Tobias & T. M. Duffy (Eds.), *Constructivist instruction: Success or failure?* (pp. 82–105). New York: Routledge.

Wittwer, J., & Renkl, A. (2008). Why instructional explanations often do not work: A framework for understanding the effectiveness of instructional explanations. *Educational Psychologist, 43,* 49–64.

Wixson, K. K. (1984). Level of importance of post-questions and children's learning from text. *American Educational Research Journal, 21,* 419–433.

Wood, J. W., & Rosbe, M. (1985). Adapting the classroom lecture for the mainstreamed student in the secondary schools. *Clearing House, 58,* 354–358.

Woolf, B. P. (2009). *Building intelligent interactive tutors: Student-centered strategies for revolutionizing e-learning.* Burlington, MA: Morgan Kaufmann/Elsevier.

Xu, J. (2008). Models of secondary school students' interest in homework: A multilevel analysis. *American Educational Research Journal, 45,* 1180–1205.

Zhang, J., Scardamalia, M., Reeve, R., & Messina, R. (2009). Designs for collective cognitive responsibility in knowledge-building communities. *Journal of the Learning Sciences, 18,* 7–44.

Zimmerman, B. J. (1998). Developing self-fulfilling cycles of academic regulation: An analysis of exemplary instructional models. In D. H. Schunk & B. J. Zimmerman (Eds.), *Self-regulated learning: From teaching to self-reflective practice* (pp. 1–19). New York: Guilford.

Zimmerman, B. J., & Didenedetto, M. K. (2008). Mastery learning and assessment: Implications for students and teachers in an era of high-stakes testing. *Psychology in the Schools, 45,* 206–216.

Zohar, A., & Aharon-Kraversky, S. (2005). Exploring the effects of cognitive conflict and direct teaching for students of different academic levels. *Journal of Research in Science Teaching, 42,* 829–855.

Zook, K. B. (1991). Effects of analogical processes on learning and misrepresentation. *Educational Psychology Review, 3,* 41–72.

Zook, K. B., & Di Vesta, F. J. (1991). Instructional analogies and conceptual misrepresentations. *Journal of Educational Psychology, 83,* 246–252.

## CHAPTER 13

Adger, C. T., Wolfram, W., & Christian, D. (2007). *Dialects in schools and communities* (2nd ed.). New York: Routledge.

Allday, R. A., Bush, M., Ticknor, N., & Walker, L. (2011). Using teacher greetings to increase speed to task engagement. *Journal of Applied Behavior Analysis, 44,* 393–396.

Allday, R. A., & Pakurar, K. (2007). Effects of teacher greetings on student on-task behavior. *Journal of Applied Behavior Analysis, 40,* 317–320.

Ames, C. (1984). Competitive, cooperative, and individualistic goal structures: A cognitive-motivational analysis. In R. Ames & C. Ames (Eds.), *Research on motivation in education: Vol. 1. Student motivation* (pp. 177–207). San Diego, CA: Academic Press.

Anderman, E. M. (2002). School effects on psychological outcomes during adolescence. *Journal of Educational Psychology, 94,* 795–809.

Anderman, L. H., Patrick, H., Hruda, L. Z., & Linnenbrink, E. A. (2002). Observing classroom goal structures to clarify and expand goal theory. In C. Midgley (Ed.), *Goals, goal structures, and patterns of adaptive learning* (pp. 243–278). Mahwah, NJ: Erlbaum.

Astor, R. A., Meyer, H. A., & Behre, W. J. (1999). Unowned places and times: Maps and interviews about violence in high schools. *American Educational Research Journal, 36,* 3–42.

Babad, E. (1995). The "teacher's pet phenomenon," students' perceptions of teachers' differential behavior, and students' morale. *Journal of Educational Psychology, 87,* 361–374.

Babad, E., Avni-Babad, D., & Rosenthal, R. (2003). Teachers' brief nonverbal behaviors in defined instructional situations can predict students' evaluations. *Journal of Educational Psychology, 95,* 553–562.

Baker, J. (1999). Teacher-student interaction in urban at-risk classrooms: Differential behavior, relationship quality, and student satisfaction with school. *Elementary School Journal, 100,* 57–70.

Bandura, A. (1986). *Social foundations of thought and action: A social cognitive theory.* Upper Saddle River, NJ: Prentice-Hall.

Barkley, R. A. (2006). *Attention-deficit hyperactivity disorder: A handbook for diagnosis and treatment* (3rd ed.). New York: Guilford.

Battistich, V., Solomon, D., Kim, D., Watson, M., & Schaps, E. (1995). Schools as communities, poverty levels of student populations, and students' attitudes, motives, and performance: A multilevel analysis. *American Educational Research Journal, 32,* 627–658.

Battistich, V., Solomon, D., Watson, M., & Schaps, E. (1997). Caring school communities. *Educational Psychologist, 32,* 137–151.

Becker, B. E., & Luthar, S. S. (2002). Social-emotional factors affecting achievement outcomes among disadvantaged students: Closing the achievement gap. *Educational Psychologist, 37,* 197–214.

Beirne-Smith, M., Patton, J. R., & Kim, S. H. (2006). *Mental retardation: An introduction to intellectual disabilities* (7th ed.). Upper Saddle River, NJ: Merrill/Prentice-Hall.

Bender, G. (2001). Resisting dominance? The study of a marginalized masculinity and its construction within high school walls. In J. N. Burstyn, G. Bender, R. Casella, H. W. Gordon, D. P. Guerra, K. V. Luschen, R. Stevens, & K. M. Williams, *Preventing violence in schools: A challenge to American democracy* (pp. 61–77). Mahwah, NJ: Erlbaum.

Blanton, H., & Burkley, M. (2008). Deviance regulation theory: Applications to adolescent social influence. In M. J. Prinstein & K. A. Dodge (Eds.), *Understanding peer influence in children and adolescents* (pp. 94–121). New York: Guilford.

Blugental, D. B., Lyon, J. E., Lin, E. K., McGrath, E. P., & Bimbela, A. (1999). Children "tune out" to the ambiguous communication style of powerless adults. *Child Development, 70,* 214–230.

Bornstein, M. H., & Cote, L. R. (2010). Immigration and acculturation. In M. H. Bornstein (Ed.), *Handbook of cultural developmental science* (pp. 531–552). New York: Psychology Press.

Borum, R., Cornell, D. G., Modzeleski, W., & Jimerson, S. R. (2010). What can be done about school shootings? A review of the evidence. *Educational Researcher, 39,* 27–37.

Brand, S., Felner, R., Shim, M., Seitsinger, A., & Duman, T. (2003). Middle school improvement and reform: Development and validation of a school-level assessment of climate, cultural pluralism, and school safety. *Journal of Educational Psychology, 95,* 570–588.

Brophy, J. E. (2006). Observational research on generic aspects of classroom teaching. In P. A. Alexander & P. H. Winne (Eds.), *Handbook of educational psychology* (2nd ed., pp. 755–780). Mahwah, NJ: Erlbaum.

Brophy, J. (2008). Developing students' appreciation for what is taught in school. *Educational Psychologist, 43,* 132–141.

Brown, R. P., Osterman, L. L., & Barnes, C. D. (2009). School violence and the culture of honor. *Psychological Science, 20,* 1400–1405.

Buchoff, T. (1990). Attention deficit disorder: Help for the classroom teacher. *Childhood Education, 67,* 86–90.

Burstyn, J. N., & Stevens, R. (2001). Involving the whole school in violence prevention. In J. N. Burstyn, G. Bender, R. Casella, H. W. Gordon, D. P. Guerra, K. V. Luschen, R. Stevens, & K. M. Williams, *Preventing violence in schools: A challenge to American democracy* (pp. 139–158). Mahwah, NJ: Erlbaum.

Campbell, D. E. (1996). *Choosing democracy: A practical guide to multicultural education.* Upper Saddle River, NJ: Merrill/Prentice-Hall.

Carbrera, N. J., Shannon, J. D., West, J., & Brooks-Gunn, J. (2006). Parental interactions with Latino infants: Variation by country of origin and English proficiency. *Child Development, 77,* 1190–1207.

Carini, P. F., & Himley, M., (with Christine, C., Espinosa, C., & Fournier, J.) (2010). *Jenny's story: Taking the long view of the child.* New York: Teachers College Press.

Carr, A. A. (1997, March). *The participation "race": Kentucky's site based decision teams.* Paper presented at the annual meeting of the American Educational Research Association, Chicago.

Carter, K., & Doyle, W. (2006). Classroom management in early childhood and elementary classrooms. In C. M. Evertson & C. S. Weinstein (Eds.), *Handbook of classroom management: Research, practice, and contemporary issues* (pp. 373–406). Mahwah, NJ: Erlbaum.

Casella, R. (2001b). What is violent about "school violence"? The nature of violence in a city high school. In J. N. Burstyn, G. Bender, R. Casella, H. W. Gordon, D. P. Guerra, K. V. Luschen, R. Stevens, & K. M. Williams, *Preventing violence in schools: A challenge to American democracy* (pp. 15–46). Mahwah, NJ: Erlbaum.

Cassady, J. C. (Ed.). (2010a). *Anxiety in schools: The causes, consequences, and solutions for academic anxieties.* New York: Peter Lang.

Castagno, A. E., & Brayboy, B. M. J. (2008). Culturally responsive schooling for Indigenous youth: A review of the literature. *Review of Educational Research, 78,* 941–993.

Cazden, C. B. (2001). *Classroom discourse: The language of teaching and learning* (2nd ed.). Portsmouth, NH: Heinemann.

Certo, J., Cauley, K. M., & Chafin, C. (2002, April). *Students' perspectives on their high school experience.* Paper presented at the annual meeting of the American Educational Research Association, New Orleans, LA.

Certo, J. L., Cauley, K. M., & Chafin, C. (2003). Students' perspectives on their high school experience. *Adolescence, 38,* 705–724.

Chang, M.-L., & Davis, H. A. (2009). Understanding the role of teacher appraisals in shaping the dynamics of their relationships with students: Deconstructing teachers' judgments of disruptive behavior/students. In P. Schutz & M. Zembylas (Eds.), *Advances in teacher emotion research: The impact of teachers' lives* (pp. 95–125). New York: Springer.

Chester, M. D., & Beaudin, B. Q. (1996). Efficacy beliefs of newly hired teachers in urban schools. *American Educational Research Journal, 33,* 233–257.

Christenson, S. L., & Sheridan, S. M. (2001). *Schools and families: Creating essential connections for learning.* New York: Guilford.

Cizek, G. J. (2003). *Detecting and preventing classroom cheating: Promoting integrity in assessment.* Thousand Oaks, CA: Corwin.

Clani, K. D., Middleton, M. J., Summers, J. J., & Sheldon, K. M. (2010). Buffering against performance classroom goal structures: The importance of autonomy support and classroom community. *Contemporary Educational Psychology, 35,* 88–99.

Clark, B. (1997). *Growing up gifted* (5th ed.). Upper Saddle River, NJ: Merrill/Prentice-Hall.

Cohen, G. L., & Garcia, J. (2008). Identity, belonging, and achievement: A model, interventions, implications. *Current Directions in Psychological Science, 17,* 365–369.

Coie, J. D., & Dodge, K. A. (1998). Aggression and antisocial behavior. In W. Damon (Series Ed.) & N. Eisenberg (Vol. Ed.), *Handbook of child psychology: Vol. 3. Social, emotional, and personality development* (5th ed., pp. 779–862). New York: Wiley.

Colvin, G., Ainge, D., & Nelson, R. (1997). How to defuse defiance, threats, challenges, confrontations. *Teaching Exceptional Children, 29*(6), 47–51.

Crone, D. A., Horner, R. H., & Hawken, L. S. (2004). *Responding to problem behavior in schools: The behavior education program.* New York: Guilford.

Dai, D. Y. (2010). *The nature and nurture of giftedness: A new framework for understanding gifted education.* New York: Teachers College Press.

Dantas, M. L., & Manyak, P. C. (Eds.). (2010). *Home–school connections in a multicultural society: Learning from and with culturally and linguistically diverse families.* New York: Routledge.

Davis, C., & Yang, A. (2005). *Parents and teachers working together.* Turners Falls, MA: Northeast Foundation for Children.

Davis, G. A., & Thomas, M. A. (1989). *Effective schools and effective teachers.* Boston: Allyn & Bacon.

Davis, H. A. (2003). Conceptualizing the role and influence of student-teacher relationships on children's social and cognitive development. *Educational Psychologist, 38,* 207–234.

Davis, H. A., Schutz, P. A., & Chambless, C. B. (2001, April). *Uncovering the impact of social relationships in the classroom: Viewing relationships with teachers from different lenses.* Paper presented at the annual meeting of the American Educational Research Association, Seattle, WA.

Deci, E. L. (1992). The relation of interest to the motivation of behavior: A self-determination theory perspective. In K. A. Renninger, S. Hidi, & A. Krapp (Eds.), *The role of interest in learning and development* (pp. 43–70). Mahwah, NJ: Erlbaum.

Dempster, F. N., & Corkill, A. J. (1999). Interference and inhibition in cognition and behavior: Unifying themes for educational psychology. *Educational Psychology Review, 11,* 1–88.

DeVoe, J. F., Peter, K., Noonan, M., Snyder, T. D., & Baum, K. (2005). *Indicators of school crime and safety: 2005* (NCES 2006–001/NCJ 210697). Washington, DC: U.S. Departments of Education and Justice. Retrieved February 6, 2007, from http://ojp.usdoj.gov/bjs/abstract/iscs05.htm

Deyhle, D., & LeCompte, M. (1999). Cultural differences in child development: Navajo adolescents in middle schools. In R. H. Sheets & E. R. Hollins (Eds.), *Racial and ethnic identity in school practices: Aspects of human development* (pp. 123–139). Mahwah, NJ: Erlbaum.

Diamond, S. C. (1991). What to do when you can't do anything: Working with disturbed adolescents. *Clearing House, 64,* 232–234.

Dien, T. (1998). Language and literacy in Vietnamese American communities. In B. Pérez (Ed.), *Sociocultural contexts of language and literacy* (pp. 23–54). Mahwah, NJ: Erlbaum.

Dishion, T. J., Piehler, T. F., & Myers, M. W. (2008). Dynamics and ecology of adolescent peer influence. In M. J. Prinstein & K. A. Dodge (Eds.), *Understanding peer influence in children and adolescents* (pp. 72–93). New York: Guilford.

Dodge, K. A., Lansford, J. E., Burks, V. S., Bates, J. E., Pettit, G. S., Fontaine, R., et al. (2003). Peer rejection and social information-processing factors in the development of aggressive behavior problems in children. *Child Development, 74,* 374–393.

Doyle, W. (1983). Academic work. *Review of Educational Research, 53,* 159–199.

Doyle, W. (1984). How order is achieved in classrooms: An interim report. *Journal of Curriculum Studies, 16,* 259–277.

Doyle, W. (1986a). Classroom organization and management. In M. C. Wittrock (Ed.), *Handbook of research on teaching* (3rd ed., pp. 392–431). New York: Macmillan.

Doyle, W. (1990). Classroom management techniques. In O. C. Moles (Ed.), *Student discipline strategies: Research and practice* (pp. 113–127). Albany: State University of New York Press.

Doyle, W. (2006). Ecological approaches to classroom management. In C. M. Evertson & C. S. Weinstein (Eds.), *Handbook of classroom management: Research, practice, and contemporary issues* (pp. 97–125). Mahwah, NJ: Erlbaum.

Dreikurs, R., & Cassel, P. (1972). *Discipline without tears* (2nd ed.). New York: Dutton.

Dwyer, K., & Osher, D. (2000). *Safeguarding our children: An action guide.* Washington, DC: U.S. Departments of Education and Justice, American Institutes for Research. Retrieved February 26, 2004, from http://www.ed.gov/pubs/edpubs.html

Dwyer, K., Osher, D., & Warger, C. (1998). *Early warning, timely response: A guide to safe schools.* Washington, DC: U.S. Department of Education. Retrieved February 26, 2004, from http://www.ed.gov/offices/OSERS/OSEP/earlywrn.html

Eaton, W. O., & Enns, L. R. (1986). Sex differences in human motor activity level. *Psychological Bulletin, 100,* 19–28.

Ellis, J., Fitzsimmons, S., & Small-McGinley, J. (2010). Encouraging the discouraged: Students' views for elementary classrooms. In G. S. Goodman (Ed.), *Educational psychology reader: The art and science of how people learn* (pp. 251–272). New York: Peter Lang.

Emmer, E. T., & Evertson, C. M. (1981). Synthesis of research on classroom management. *Educational Leadership, 38*(4), 342–347.

Emmer, E. T., & Evertson, C. M. (2009). *Classroom management for middle and high school teachers* (8th ed.). Upper Saddle River, NJ: Pearson.

Emmer, E. T., & Gerwels, M. C. (2006). Classroom management in middle and high school classrooms. In C. M. Evertson & C. S. Weinstein (Eds.), *Handbook of classroom management: Research, practice, and contemporary issues* (pp. 407–437). Mahwah, NJ: Erlbaum.

Emmer, E. T., & Stough, L. M. (2001). Classroom management: A critical part of educational psychology, with implications for teacher education. *Educational Psychologist, 36,* 103–112.

Epstein, J. L. (1996). Perspectives and previews on research and policy for school, family, and community partnerships. In A. Booth & J. F. Dunn (Eds.), *Family-school links: How do they affect educational outcomes?* (pp. 209–246). Mahwah, NJ: Erlbaum.

Espelage, D. L., Holt, M. K., & Henkel, R. R. (2003). Examination of peer-group contextual effects on aggression during early adolescence. *Child Development, 74,* 205–220.

Espinoza, G., & Juvonen, J. (2011). Perceptions of the school social context across the transition to middle school: Heightened sensitivity among Latino students? *Journal of Educational Psychology, 103,* 749–758.

Evertson, C. M., & Emmer, E. T. (1982). Effective management at the beginning of the year in junior high classes. *Journal of Educational Psychology, 74,* 485–498.

Evertson, C. M., & Emmer, E. T. (2009). *Classroom management for elementary teachers* (8th ed.). Upper Saddle River, NJ: Pearson.

Evertson, C. M., & Weinstein, C. S. (Eds.). (2006). *Handbook of classroom management: Research,* practice, and contemporary issues. Mahwah, NJ: Erlbaum.

Filax, G. (2007). Queer in/visibility: The case of Ellen, Michel, and Oscar. In S. Books (Ed.), *Invisible children in the society and its schools* (3rd ed., pp. 213–234). Mahwah, NJ: Erlbaum.

Finders, M., & Lewis, C. (1994). Why some parents don't come to school. *Educational Leadership, 51*(8), 50–54.

Fingerhut, L. A., & Christoffel, K. K. (2002). Firearm-related death and injury among children and adolescents. *The Future of Children, 12*(2), 25–37.

Finkelhor, D., & Ormrod, R. (2000, December). *Juvenile victims of property crimes.* Washington, DC: U.S. Department of Justice, Office of Justice Programs, Office of Juvenile Justice and Delinquency Prevention.

Flanagan, C. A., Cumsille, P., Gill, S., & Gallay, L. S. (2007). School and community climates and civic commitments: Patterns for ethnic minority and majority students. *Journal of Educational Psychology, 99,* 421–431.

Fletcher, K. L., & Cassady, J. C. (2010). Overcoming academic anxieties: Promoting effective coping and self-regulation strategies. In J. C. Cassady (Ed.), *Anxiety in schools: The causes, consequences, and solutions for academic anxieties* (pp. 177–200). New York: Peter Lang.

Forman, S. G., & Barakat, N. M. (2011). Cognitive-behavioral therapy in the schools: Bringing research to practice through effective implementation. *Psychology in the Schools, 48,* 283–296.

Fosnot, C. T. (1996). Constructivism: A psychological theory of learning. In C. T. Fosnot (Ed.), *Constructivism: Theory, perspectives, and practice* (pp. 833). New York: Teachers College Press.

Freiberg, H. J., & Lapointe, J. M. (2006). Research-based programs for preventing and solving discipline problems. In C. M. Evertson & C. S. Weinstein (Eds.), *Handbook of classroom management: Research, practice, and contemporary issues* (pp. 735–786). Mahwah, NJ: Erlbaum.

Fuller, M. L. (2001). Multicultural concerns and classroom management. In C. A. Grant & M. L. Gomez, *Campus and classroom: Making schooling multicultural* (2nd ed., pp. 109–134). Upper Saddle River, NJ: Merrill/Prentice-Hall.

Garbarino, J., Bradshaw, C. P., & Vorrasi, J. A. (2002). Mitigating the effects of gun violence on children and youth. *The Future of Children, 12*(2), 73–85.

García, E. E. (1995). Educating Mexican American students: Past treatment and recent developments in theory, research, policy, and practice. In J. A. Banks & C. A. M. Banks (Eds.), *Handbook of research on multicultural education* (pp. 372–387). New York: Macmillan.

Gettinger, M. (1988). Methods of proactive classroom management. *School Psychology Review, 17,* 227–242.

Gettinger, M., & Kohler, K. M. (2006). Process-outcome approaches to classroom management and effective teaching. In C. M. Evertson & C. S. Weinstein (Eds.), *Handbook of classroom management: Research, practice, and contemporary issues* (pp. 73–95). Mahwah, NJ: Erlbaum.

Glasser, W. (1969). *Schools without failure.* New York: Harper & Row.

Goddard, R. D., Hoy, W. K., & Woolfolk Hoy, A. (2000). Collective teacher efficacy: Its meaning, measure, and impact on student achievement. *American Educational Research Journal, 37,* 479–507.

Goldstein, L. S., & Lake, V. E. (2000). "Love, love, and more love for children": Exploring preservice teachers' understanding of caring. *Teaching and Teacher Education, 16,* 861–872.

Granger, D. A., Whalen, C. K., Henker, B., & Cantwell, C. (1996). ADHD boys' behavior during structured classroom social activities: Effects of social demands, teacher proximity, and methylphenidate. *Journal of Attention Disorders, 1*(1), 16–30.

Green, C. L., Walker, J. M. T., Hoover-Dempsey, K. V., & Sandler, H. M. (2007). Parents' motivation for involvement in children's education: An empirical test of a theoretical model of parental involvement. *Journal of Educational Psychology, 99,* 532–544.

Greenberg, M. T., Weissberg, R. P., O'Brien, M. U., Zins, J. E., Fredericks, L., Resnik, H., et al. (2003). Enhancing school-based prevention and youth development through coordinated social, emotional, and academic learning. *American Psychologist, 58,* 466–474.

Gregg, N. (2009). *Adolescents and adults with learning disabilities and ADHD: Assessment and accommodation.* New York: Guilford.

Hamovitch, B. (2007). Hoping for the best: "Inclusion" and stigmatization in a middle school. In S. Books (Ed.), *Invisible children in the society and its schools* (3rd ed., pp. 263–281). Mahwah, NJ: Erlbaum.

Hamre, B. K., & Pianta, R. C. (2005). Can instructional and emotional support in the first-grade classroom make a difference for children at risk of school failure? *Child Development, 76,* 949–967.

Hanley, G. P., Tiger, J. H., Ingvarsson, E. T., & Cammilleri, A. P. (2009). Influencing preschoolers' free-play activity preferences: An evaluation of satiation and embedded reinforcement. *Journal of Applied Behavior Analysis, 42,* 33–41.

Hattie, J., & Gan, M. (2011). Instruction based on feedback. In R. E. Mayer & P. A. Alexander (Eds.), *Handbook of research on learning and instruction* (pp. 249–271). New York: Routledge.

Henley, M. (2010). *Classroom management: A proactive approach* (2nd ed.). Columbus, OH: Merrill/Pearson.

Heward, W. L. (2009). *Exceptional children: An introduction to special education* (9th ed.). Upper Saddle River, NJ: Merrill/Pearson Education.

Hidalgo, N. M., Siu, S., Bright, J. A., Swap, S. M., & Epstein, J. L. (1995). Research on families, schools, and communities: A multicultural perspective. In J. A. Banks & C. A. M. Banks (Eds.), *Handbook of research on multicultural education* (pp. 498–524). New York: Macmillan.

Hiebert, E. H., & Raphael, T. E. (1996). Psychological perspectives on literacy and extensions to educational practice. In D. C. Berliner & R. C. Calfee (Eds.), *Handbook of educational psychology* (pp. 550–602). New York: Macmillan.

Hill, N. E., Castellino, D. R., Lansford, J. E., Nowlin, P., Dodge, K. A., Bates, J. E., & Pettit, G. S. (2004). Parent academic involvement as related to school behavior, achievement, and aspirations: Demographic variations across adolescence. *Child Development, 75,* 1491–1509.

Hill, N. E., & Craft, S. A. (2003). Parent-school involvement and school performance: Mediated pathways among socioeconomically comparable African American and Euro-American families. *Journal of Educational Psychology, 95,* 74–83.

Hill, N. E., & Taylor, L. C. (2004). Parental school involvement and children's academic achievement: Pragmatics and issues. *Current Directions in Psychological Science, 13,* 161–164.

Hogan, T., Rabinowitz, M., & Craven, J. A., III. (2003). Representation in teaching: Inferences from research of expert and novice teachers. *Educational Psychologist, 38,* 235–247.

Hom, A., & Battistich, V. (1995, April). *Students' sense of school community as a factor in reducing drug use and delinquency.* Paper presented at the annual meeting of the American Educational Research Association, San Francisco.

Hong, S., & Ho, H.-Z. (2005). Direct and indirect longitudinal effects of parental involvement on student achievement: Second-order latent growth modeling across ethnic groups. *Journal of Educational Psychology, 97,* 32–42.

Houts, R. M., Caspi, A., Pianta, R. C., Arseneault, L., & Moffitt, T. E. (2010). The challenging pupil in the classroom: The effect of the child on the teacher. *Psychological Science, 21,* 1802–1810.

Howell, J. C., & Lynch, J. P. (2000, August). Youth gangs in schools. *Juvenile Justice Bulletin* (OJJDP Publication NCJ-183015). Washington, DC: U.S. Department of Justice, Office of Juvenile Justice and Delinquency Prevention.

Hoy, W. K., Tarter, C. J., & Woolfolk Hoy, A. (2006). Academic optimism of schools: A force for student achievement. *American Educational Research Journal, 43,* 425–446.

Hughes, J. N., & Kwok, O. (2007). Influence of student-teacher and parent-teacher relationships on lower achieving readers' engagement and achievement in the primary grades. *Journal of Educational Psychology, 99,* 39–51.

Hughes, J. N., Luo, W., Kwok, O.-M., & Loyd, L. K. (2008). Teacher-student support, effortful engagement, and achievement: A 3-year longitudinal study. *Journal of Educational Psychology, 100,* 1–14.

Hyman, I., Kay, B., Tabori, A., Weber, M., Mahon, M., & Cohen, I. (2006). Bullying: Theory, research, and interventions. In C. M. Evertson & C. S. Weinstein (Eds.), *Handbook of classroom management: Research, practice, and contemporary issues* (pp. 855–884). Mahwah, NJ: Erlbaum.

Igoa, C. (1995). *The inner world of the immigrant child.* Mahwah, NJ: Erlbaum.

Ihlo, T., & Nantais, M. (2010). Evidence-based interventions within a multi-tier framework for positive behavioral supports. In T. A. Glover & S. Vaughn (Eds.), *The promise of response to intervention: Evaluating current science and practice* (pp. 239–266). New York: Guilford.

Jang, H., Reeve, J., & Deci, E. L. (2010). Engaging students in learning activities: It is not autonomy support or structure but autonomy support and structure. *Journal of Educational Psychology, 102,* 588–600.

Johnson, W., McGue, M., & Iacono, W. G. (2005). Disruptive behavior and school grades: Genetic and environmental relations in 11-year-olds. *Journal of Educational Psychology, 97,* 391–405.

Jones, V. (1996). Classroom management. In J. Sikula, T. J. Buttery, & E. Guyton (Eds.), *Handbook of research on teacher education* (2nd ed., pp. 503–521). New York: Macmillan.

Juvonen, J. (2006). Sense of belonging, social bonds, and school functioning. In P. A. Alexander & P. H. Winne (Eds.), *Handbook of educational psychology* (2nd ed., pp. 655–674). Mahwah, NJ: Erlbaum.

Kağitçibaşi, Ç. (2007). *Family, self, and human development across cultures: Theory and applications* (2nd ed.). Mahwah, NJ: Erlbaum.

Keller, H. R., & Tapasak, R. C. (2004). Classroom-based approaches. In J. C. Conoley & A. P. Goldstein (Eds.), *School violence intervention* (2nd ed., pp. 103–130). New York: Guilford.

Keogh, B. K. (2003). *Temperament in the classroom.* Baltimore: Brookes.

Kim, D., Solomon, D., & Roberts, W. (1995, April). *Classroom practices that enhance students' sense of community.* Paper presented at the annual meeting of the American Educational Research Association, San Francisco.

Kincheloe, J. L. (2009). No short cuts in urban education: Metropedagogy and diversity. In S. R. Steinberg (Ed.), *Diversity and multiculturalism: A reader* (pp. 379–409). New York: Peter Lang.

Kodluboy, D. W. (2004). Gang-oriented interventions. In J. C. Conoley & A. P. Goldstein (Eds.), *School violence intervention* (2nd ed., pp. 194–232). New York: Guilford.

Koegel, L. K., Koegel, R. L., & Dunlap, G. (Eds.). (1996). *Positive behavioral support: Including people with difficult behavior in the community.* Baltimore: Brookes.

Koestner, R., Ryan, R. M., Bernieri, F., & Holt, K. (1984). Setting limits in children's behavior: The differential effects of controlling versus informational styles on intrinsic motivation and creativity. *Journal of Personality, 52,* 233–248.

Kounin, J. S. (1970). *Discipline and group management in classrooms.* New York: Holt, Rinehart & Winston.

Kumar, R., Gheen, M. H., & Kaplan, A. (2002). Goal structures in the learning environment and students' disaffection from learning and schooling. In C. Midgley (Ed.), *Goals, goal structures, and patterns of adaptive learning* (pp. 143–173). Mahwah, NJ: Erlbaum.

Kupchik, A., & Bracy, N. L. (2009). The news media on school crime and violence: Constructing dangerousness and fueling fear. *Youth Violence and Juvenile Justice, 7,* 136–155.

Ladd, G. W., Herald-Brown, S. L., & Reiser, M. (2008). Does chronic classroom peer rejection predict the development of children's classroom participation during the grade school years? *Child Development, 79,* 1001–1015.

Ladson-Billings, G. (1994a). *The dreamkeepers: Successful teachers of African American children.* San Francisco: Jossey-Bass.

Lane, K., Falk, K., & Wehby, J. (2006). Classroom management in special education classrooms and resource rooms. In C. M. Evertson & C. S. Weinstein (Eds.), *Handbook of classroom management: Research, practice, and contemporary issues* (pp. 439–460). Mahwah, NJ: Erlbaum.

Lane, K. L., Kalberg, J. R., & Menzies, H. M. (2009). *Developing schoolwide programs to prevent and manage problem behaviors: A step-by-step approach.* New York: Guilford.

Lane, K. L., Menzies, H. M., Bruhn, A. L., & Crnobori, M. (2011). *Managing challenging behaviors in schools: Research-based strategies that work.* New York: Guilford.

Langer, J. A. (2000). Excellence in English in middle and high school: How teachers' professional lives support student achievement. *American Educational Research Journal, 37,* 397–439.

Learning First Alliance. (2001). *Every child learning: Safe and supportive schools.* Washington, DC: Association for Supervision and Curriculum Development.

Lee, J., & Shute, V. J. (2010). Personal and social-contextual factors in K–12 academic performance: An integrative perspective on student learning. *Educational Psychologist, 45,* 185–202.

Lee, J.-S., & Bowen, N. K. (2006). Parent involvement, cultural capital, and the achievement gap among elementary school children. *American Educational Research Journal, 43,* 193–218.

Lee, V. E., & Burkam, D. T. (2003). Dropping out of high school: The role of school organization and structure. *American Educational Research Journal, 40,* 353–393.

Levine, D. U., & Lezotte, L. W. (1995). Effective schools research. In J. A. Banks & C. A. M. Banks (Eds.), *Handbook of research on multicultural education* (pp. 525–547). New York: Macmillan.

Lewis, T. J., Newcomer, L. L., Trussell, R., & Richter, M. (2006). Schoolwide positive behavior support: Building systems to develop and maintain appropriate social behavior. In C. M. Evertson & C. S. Weinstein (Eds.), *Handbook of classroom management: Research, practice, and contemporary issues* (pp. 833–854). Mahwah, NJ: Erlbaum.

Lickona, T. (1991). Moral development in the elementary school classroom. In W. M. Kurtines & J. L. Gewirtz (Eds.), *Moral behavior and development: Vol. 3. Application* (pp. 143–161). Mahwah, NJ: Erlbaum.

Lipka, J. (1994). Schools failing minority teachers. *Educational Foundations, 8,* 57–80.

López, G. R. (2001). Redefining parental involvement: Lessons from high-performing migrant-impacted schools. *American Educational Research Journal, 38,* 253–288.

Mac Iver, D. J., Reuman, D. A., & Main, S. R. (1995). Social structuring of the school: Studying what is, illuminating what could be. In J. T. Spence, J. M. Darley, & D. J. Foss (Eds.), *Annual review of psychology* (Vol. 46, pp. 375–400). Palo Alto, CA: Annual Review, Inc.

Marachi, R., Friedel, J., & Midgley, C. (2001, April). "I sometimes annoy my teacher during math": Relations between student perceptions of the teacher and disruptive behavior in the classroom. Paper presented at the annual meeting of the American Educational Research Association, Seattle, WA.

Marzano, R. J., with Marzano, J. S., & Pickering, D. J. (2003). *Classroom management that works: Research-based strategies for every teacher.* Alexandria, VA: Association for Supervision and Curriculum Development.

Masten, A. S. (2001). Ordinary magic: Resilience processes in development. *American Psychologist, 56,* 227–238.

Mattingly, D. J., Prislin, R., McKenzie, T. L., Rodrigues, J. L., & Kayzar, B. (2002). Evaluating evaluations: The case of parent involvement programs. *Review of Educational Research, 72,* 549–576.

Mayer, M. J., & Furlong, M. J. (2010). How safe are our schools? *Educational Researcher, 39,* 16–26.

McCarty, T. L., & Watahomigie, L. J. (1998). Language and literacy in American Indian and Alaska Native communities. In B. Pérez (Ed.), *Sociocultural contexts of language and literacy* (pp. 69–98). Mahwah, NJ: Erlbaum.

McIntyre, E. (2010). Issues in funds of knowledge teaching and research: Key concepts from a study of Appalachian families and schooling. In M. L. Dantas & P. C. Manyak (Eds.), *Home–school connections in a multicultural society: Learning from and with culturally and linguistically diverse families* (pp. 201–217). New York: Routledge.

Meehan, B. T., Hughes, J. N., & Cavell, T. A. (2003). Teacher-student relationships as compensatory resources for aggressive children. *Child Development, 74,* 1145–1157.

Mehan, H. (1979). *Social organization in the classroom.* Cambridge, MA: Harvard University Press.

Mendaglio, S. (2010). Anxiety in gifted students. In J. C. Cassady (Ed.), *Anxiety in schools: The causes, consequences, and solutions for academic anxieties* (pp. 153–173). New York: Peter Lang.

Mercer, C. D., & Pullen, P. C. (2005). *Students with learning disabilities* (6th ed.). Upper Saddle River, NJ: Merrill/Prentice-Hall.

Miles, S. B., & Stipek, D. (2006). Contemporaneous and longitudinal associations between social behavior and literacy achievement in a sample of low-income elementary school children. *Child Development, 77,* 103–117.

Miller, A. (2006). Contexts and attributions for difficult behavior in English classrooms. In C. M. Evertson & C. S. Weinstein (Eds.), *Handbook of classroom management: Research, practice, and contemporary issues* (pp. 1093–1120). Mahwah, NJ: Erlbaum.

Miller, M. D., Linn, R. L., & Gronlund, N. E. (2009). *Measurement and assessment in teaching* (10th ed.). Upper Saddle River, NJ: Merrill/Pearson.

Milner, H. R. (2006). Classroom management in urban classrooms. In C. M. Evertson & C. S. Weinstein (Eds.), *Handbook of classroom management: Research, practice, and contemporary issues* (pp. 491–522). Mahwah, NJ: Erlbaum.

Minami, M., & Ovando, C. J. (1995). Language issues in multicultural contexts. In J. A. Banks & C. A. M. Banks (Eds.), *Handbook of research on multicultural education* (pp. 427–444). New York: Macmillan.

Moore, J. W., & Edwards, R. P. (2003). An analysis of aversive stimuli in classroom demand contexts. *Journal of Applied Behavior Analysis, 36*, 339–348.

Morgan, D. P., & Jenson, W. R. (1988). *Teaching behaviorally disordered students: Preferred practices.* Upper Saddle River, NJ: Merrill/Prentice-Hall.

Morrison, G. M., Furlong, M. J., D'Incau, B., & Morrison, R. L. (2004). The safe school: Integrating the school reform agenda to prevent disruption and violence at school. In J. C. Conoley & A. P. Goldstein (Eds.), *School violence intervention* (2nd ed., pp. 256–296). New York: Guilford.

Munn, P., Johnstone, M., & Chalmers, V. (1990, April). *How do teachers talk about maintaining effective discipline in their classrooms?* Paper presented at the annual meeting of the American Educational Research Association, Boston.

Murdock, T. B., Hale, N. M., & Weber, M. J. (2001). Predictors of cheating among early adolescents: Academic and social motivations. *Contemporary Educational Psychology, 26*, 96–115.

Narciss, S. (2008). Feedback strategies for interactive learning tasks. In J. M. Spector, M. D. Merrill, J. van Merriënboer, & M. P. Driscoll (Eds.), *Handbook of research on educational communications and technology* (3rd ed., pp. 125–143). New York: Erlbaum.

National Center for Education Statistics (2007, September). *Crime, violence, discipline, and safety in U.S. public schools: Findings from the School Survey on Crime and Safety, 2005–06.* Washington: U.S. Department of Education.

Newkirk, T. (2002). *Misreading masculinity: Boys, literacy, and popular culture.* Portsmouth, NH: Heinemann.

Nichols, J. D. (April, 2004). *Empowerment and relationships: A classroom model to enhance student motivation.* Paper presented at the American Educational Research Association, San Diego, CA.

Nucci, L. P. (2006). Classroom management for moral and social development. In C. M. Evertson & C. S. Weinstein (Eds.), *Handbook of classroom management: Research, practice, and contemporary issues* (pp. 711–731). Mahwah, NJ: Erlbaum.

Nucci, L. (2009). *Nice is not enough: Facilitating moral development.* Upper Saddle River, NJ: Merrill/Pearson.

O'Connor, E., & McCartney, K. (2007). Examining teacher-child relationships and achievement as part of an ecological model of development. *American Educational Research Journal, 44*, 340–369.

O'Connor, E. E., Dearing, E., & Collins, B. A. (2011). Teacher–child relationship and behavior problem trajectories in elementary school. *American Educational Research Journal, 48*, 120–162.

O'Donnell, D. A., Schwab-Stone, M. E., & Muyeed, A. Z. (2002). Multidimensional resilience in urban children exposed to community violence. *Child Development, 73*, 1265–1282.

Ogbu, J. U. (2003). *Black American students in an affluent suburb: A study of academic disengagement.* Mahwah, NJ: Erlbaum.

Osher, D., Bear, G. G., Sprague, J. R., & Doyle, W. (2010). How can we improve school discipline? *Educational Researcher, 39*, 48–58.

Osterman, K. F. (2000). Students' need for belonging in the school community. *Review of Educational Research, 70*, 323–367.

O'Toole, M. E. (2000). *The school shooter: A threat assessment perspective.* Quantico, VA: Federal Bureau of Investigation. Retrieved February 26, 2004, from http://www.fbi.gov/publications/school/school2.pdf

Patall, E. A., Cooper, H., & Robinson, J. C. (2008). Parent involvement in homework: A research synthesis. *Review of Educational Research, 78*, 1039–1101.

Patall, E. A., Cooper, H., & Wynn, S. R. (2010). The effectiveness and relative importance of choice in the classroom. *Journal of Educational Psychology, 102*, 896–915.

Patrick, H., Kaplan, A., & Ryan, A. M. (2011). Positive classroom motivational environments: Convergence between mastery goal structure and classroom social climate. *Journal of Educational Psychology, 103*, 367–382.

Patrick, H., & Pintrich, P. R. (2001). Conceptual change in teachers' intuitive conceptions of learning, motivation, and instruction: The role of motivational and epistemological beliefs. In B. Torff & R. J. Sternberg (Eds.), *Understanding and teaching the intuitive mind: Student and teacher learning* (pp. 117–143). Mahwah, NJ: Erlbaum.

Patrick, H., Ryan, A. M., & Kaplan, A. M. (2007). Early adolescents' perceptions of the classroom social environment, motivational beliefs, and engagement. *Journal of Educational Psychology, 99*, 83–98.

Patton, J. R., Blackbourn, J. M., & Fad, K. S. (1996). *Exceptional individuals in focus* (6th ed.). Upper Saddle River, NJ: Merrill/Prentice-Hall.

Payne, R. K. (2005). *A framework for understanding poverty* (4th rev. ed.). Highlands, TX: aha! Process, Inc.

Pekrun, R., Goetz, T., Daniels, L. M., Stupnisky, R. H., & Perry, R. P. (2010). Boredom in achievement settings: Exploring control–value antecedents and performance outcomes of a neglected emotion. *Journal of Educational Psychology, 102*, 531–549.

Pellegrini, A. D. (2002). Bullying, victimization, and sexual harassment during the transition to middle school. *Educational Psychologist, 37*, 151–163.

Pellegrini, A. D., & Horvat, M. (1995). A developmental contextualist critique of attention deficit hyperactivity disorder. *Educational Researcher, 24*(1), 13–19.

Peter, F., & Dalbert, C. (2010). Do my teachers treat me justly? Implications of students' justice experience for class climate experience. *Contemporary Educational Psychology, 35*, 297–305.

Pfiffner, L. J., Barkley, R. A., & DuPaul, G. J. (2006). Treatment of ADHD in school settings. In R. A. Barkley, *Attention-deficit hyperactivity disorder: A handbook for diagnosis and treatment* (3rd ed., pp. 547–589). New York: Guilford.

Pianta, R. C. (1999). *Enhancing relationships between children and teachers.* Washington, DC: American Psychological Association.

Pianta, R. C. (2006). Classroom management and relationships between children and teachers: Implications for research and practice. In C. M. Evertson & C. S. Weinstein (Eds.), *Handbook of classroom management: Research, practice, and contemporary issues* (pp. 685–709). Mahwah, NJ: Erlbaum.

Pianta, R. C., Belsky, J., Vandergrift, N., Houts, R., & Morrison, F. J. (2008). Classroom effects on children's achievement trajectories in elementary school. *American Educational Research Journal, 45*, 365–397.

Platts, J., & Williamson, Y. (2000). The use of cognitive-behavioural therapy for counseling in schools. In N. Barwick (Ed.), *Clinical counseling in schools* (pp. 96–107). New York: Routledge.

Polakow, V. (2007). In the shadows of the ownership society: Homeless children and their families. In S. Books (Ed.), *Invisible children in the society and its schools* (3rd ed., pp. 39–62). Mahwah, NJ: Erlbaum.

Polloway, E. A., & Patton, J. R. (1993). *Strategies for teaching learners with special needs* (5th ed.). Upper Saddle River, NJ: Merrill/Prentice-Hall.

Power, F. C., Higgins, A., & Kohlberg, L. (1989). *Lawrence Kohlberg's approach to moral education.* New York: Columbia University Press.

Reeve, J. (2009). Why teachers adopt a controlling motivating style toward students and how they can become more autonomy supportive. *Educational Psychologist, 44*, 159–175.

Reschly, A. L., & Christenson, S. L. (2009). Parents as essential partners for fostering students' learning outcomes. In R. Gilman, E. S. Huebner, & M. J. Furlong (Eds.), *Handbook of positive psychology in schools* (pp. 257–272). New York: Routledge.

Robers, S., Zhang, J., Truman, J., & Snyder, T. D. (2012). *Indicators of school crime and safety: 2011.* Washington, DC: National Center for Education Statistics and Bureau of Justice Statistics.

Robinson, D. R., Schofield, J. W., & Steers-Wentzell, K. L. (2005). Peer and cross-age tutoring in math: Outcomes and their design implications. *Educational Psychology Review, 17*, 327–362.

Robinson, S. L., & Griesemer, S. M. R. (2006). Helping individual students with problem behavior. In C. M. Evertson & C. S. Weinstein (Eds.), *Handbook of classroom management: Research, practice, and contemporary issues* (pp. 787–802). Mahwah, NJ: Erlbaum.

Rogers, C. R. (1983). *Freedom to learn for the 80's.* Upper Saddle River, NJ: Merrill/Prentice-Hall.

Roorda, D. L., Koomen, H. M. Y., Spilt, J. L., & Oort, F. J. (2011). The influence of affective teacher–student relationships on students' school engagement and achievement: A meta-analytic approach. *Review of Educational Research, 81*, 493–529.

Ross, S. W., & Horner, R. H. (2009). Bully prevention in positive behavior support. *Journal of Applied Behavior Analysis, 42*, 747–759.

Rothbart, M. K. (2011). *Becoming who we are: Temperament and personality in development.* New York: Guilford.

Rozalski, M. E., & Yell, M. L. (2004). Law and school safety. In J. C. Conoley & A. P. Goldstein (Eds.), *School violence intervention* (2nd ed., pp. 507–523). New York: Guilford.

Rudman, M. K. (1993). Multicultural children's literature: The search for universals. In M. K. Rudman (Ed.), *Children's literature: Resource for the classroom* (2nd ed., pp. 113–145). Norwood, MA: Christopher-Gordon.

Rumberger, R. W. (1995). Dropping out of middle school: A multilevel analysis of students and schools. *American Educational Research Journal, 32,* 583–625.

Ryan, A. M., & Patrick, H. (2001). The classroom social environment and changes in adolescents' motivation and engagement during middle school. *American Educational Research Journal, 38,* 437–460.

Sabers, D. S., Cushing, K. S., & Berliner, D. C. (1991). Differences among teachers in a task characterized by simultaneity, multidimensionality, and immediacy. *American Educational Research Journal, 28,* 63–88.

Salend, S. J., & Taylor, L. (1993). Working with families: A cross-cultural perspective. *Remedial and Special Education, 14*(5), 25–32, 39.

Sanchez, F., & Anderson, M. L. (1990). Gang mediation: A process that works. *Principal, 69*(4), 54–56.

Sanders, M. G. (1996). Action teams in action: Interviews and observations in three schools in the Baltimore School—Family—Community Partnership Program. *Journal of Education for Students Placed at Risk, 1,* 249–262.

Sapolsky, R. (2005). Stress and cognition. In M. Gazzaniga (Ed.), *The cognitive neurosciences* (3rd, ed, pp. 1031–1042). Cambridge, MA: MIT Press.

Sapon-Shevin, M., Dobbelaere, A., Corrigan, C., Goodman, K., & Mastin, M. (1998). Everyone here can play. *Educational Leadership, 56*(1), 42–45.

Scott, J., & Bushell, D. (1974). The length of teacher contacts and students' off-task behavior. *Journal of Applied Behavior Analysis, 7,* 39–44.

Scruggs, T. E., & Mastropieri, M. A. (1994). Successful mainstreaming in elementary science classes: A qualitative study of three reputational cases. *American Educational Research Journal, 31,* 785–811.

Serpell, R., Baker, L., & Sonnenschein, S. (2005). *Becoming literate in the city: The Baltimore Early Childhood Project.* Cambridge, England: Cambridge University Press.

Silberman, M. L., & Wheelan, S. A. (1980). *How to discipline without feeling guilty: Assertive relationships with children.* Champaign, IL: Research Press.

Silverberg, R. P. (2003, April). *Developing relational space: Teachers who came to understand themselves and their students as learners.* Paper presented at the annual meeting of the American Educational Research Association, Chicago.

Smith, A. K. (2009). *The art of possibility: Creating more successful learners.* Malibu, CA: Center

for Collaborative Action Research, Pepperdine University. Retrieved from http://cadres. pepperdine.edu/ccar/projects.school.html

Spaulding, C. L. (1992). *Motivation in the classroom.* New York: McGraw-Hill.

Spera, C. (2005). A review of the relationship among parenting practices, parenting styles, and adolescent school achievement. *Educational Psychology Review, 17,* 125–146.

Stack, C. B., & Burton, L. M. (1993). Kinscripts. *Journal of Comparative Family Studies, 24,* 157–170.

Stiggins, R. J., & Chappuis, J. (2012). *An introduction to student-involved assessment FOR learning* (6th ed.). Boston: Pearson Assessment Training Institute.

Stipek, D. J. (1996). Motivation and instruction. In D. C. Berliner & R. C. Calfee (Eds.), *Handbook of educational psychology* (pp. 85–113). New York: Macmillan.

Stipek, D., & Miles, S. (2008). Effects of aggression on achievement: Does conflict with the teacher make it worse? *Child Development, 79,* 1721–1735.

Stodolsky, S. S., Salk, S., & Glaessner, B. (1991). Student views about learning math and social studies. *American Educational Research Journal, 28,* 89–116.

Striepling-Goldstein, S. H. (2004). The low-aggression classroom: A teacher's view. In J. C. Conoley & A. P. Goldstein (Eds.), *School violence intervention* (2nd ed., pp. 23–53). New York: Guilford.

Strother, D. B. (Ed.). (1991). *Learning to fail: Case studies of students at risk.* Bloomington, IN: Phi Delta Kappa, Maynard R. Bemis Center for Evaluation, Development, and Research.

Sullivan-DeCarlo, C., DeFalco, K., & Roberts, V. (1998). Helping students avoid risky behavior. *Educational Leadership, 56*(1), 80–82.

Sutherland, K. S., & Morgan, P. L. (2003). Implications of transactional processes in classrooms for students with emotional/behavioral disorders. *Preventing School Failure, 48*(6), 32–45.

Sutton, R. E., & Wheatley, K. F. (2003). Teachers' emotions and teaching: A review of the literature and directions for future research. *Educational Psychology Review, 15,* 327–358.

Swanson, H. L., O'Connor, J. E., & Cooney, J. B. (1990). An information processing analysis of expert and novice teachers' problem solving. *American Educational Research Journal, 27,* 533–556.

Swearer, S. M., Espelage, D. L., Vaillancourt, T., & Hymel, S. (2010). What can be done about school bullying? Linking research to educational practice. *Educational Researcher, 39,* 38–47.

Syvertsen, A. K., Flanagan, C. A., & Stout, M. D. (2009). Code of silence: Students' perceptions of school climate and willingness to intervene in a peer's dangerous plan. *Journal of Educational Psychology, 101,* 219–232.

Tamis-Lemonda, C. S., & McFadden, K. E. (2010). The United States of America. In M. H. Bornstein (Ed.), *Handbook of cultural developmental science* (pp. 299–322). New York: Psychology Press.

Troop-Gordon, W., & Ladd, G. W. (2005). Trajectories of peer victimization and perceptions of the self and schoolmates:

Precursors to internalizing and externalizing problems. *Child Development, 76,* 1072–1091.

Turnbull, A. P., Pereira, L., & Blue-Banning, M. (2000). Teachers as friendship facilitators. *Teaching Exceptional Children, 32*(5), 66–70.

Turnbull, A. P., Turnbull, R., & Wehmeyer, M. L. (2010). *Exceptional lives: Special education in today's schools* (6th ed.). Upper Saddle River, NJ: Merrill.

Tutwiler, S. W. (2007). How schools fail African American boys. In S. Books (Ed.), *Invisible children in the society and its schools* (3rd ed., pp. 141–156). Mahwah, NJ: Erlbaum.

Tyler, K. M., Uqdah, A. L., Dillihunt, M. L., Beatty-Hazelbaker, R., Connor, T., Gadson, N., et al. (2008). Cultural discontinuity: Toward a quantitative investigation of a major hypothesis in education. *Educational Researcher, 37,* 280–297.

U.S. Secret Service National Threat Assessment Center, in collaboration with the U.S. Department of Education. (2000, October). *Safe school initiative: An interim report on the prevention of targeted violence in schools.* Washington, DC: Author.

Veenman, S. (1984). Perceived problems of beginning teachers. *Review of Educational Research, 54,* 143–178.

Vitaro, F., Brendgen, M., Larose, S., & Tremblay, R. E. (2005). Kindergarten disruptive behaviors, protective factors, and educational achievement by early adulthood. *Journal of Educational Psychology, 97,* 617–629.

Walker, H. M., Horner, R. H., Sugai, G., Bullis, M., Sprague, J. R., Bricker, D., et al. (1996). Integrated approaches to preventing antisocial behavior patterns among school-age children and youth. *Journal of Emotional and Behavioral Disorders, 4,* 194–209.

Walker, J. M. T., & Hoover-Dempsey, K. V. (2006). Why research on parental involvement is important to classroom management. In C. M. Evertson & C. S. Weinstein (Eds.), *Handbook of classroom management: Research, practice, and contemporary issues* (pp. 665–684). Mahwah, NJ: Erlbaum.

Wang, M.-T., & Holcombe, R. (2010). Adolescents' perceptions of school environment, engagement, and academic achievement in middle school. *American Educational Research Journal, 47,* 633–662.

Warren, J. S., Bohanon-Edmonson, H. M., Turnbull, A. P., Sailor, W., Wickham, D., Griggs, P., et al. (2006). School-wide positive behavior support: Addressing behavior problems that impeded student learning. *Educational Psychology Review, 18,* 187–198.

Watson, M. (2008). Developmental discipline and moral education. In L. Nucci & D. Narvaez (Eds.), *Handbook of moral and character education* (pp. 175–203). New York: Routledge.

Watson, M., & Battistich, V. (2006). Building and sustaining caring communities. In C. M. Evertson & C. S. Weinstein (Eds.), *Handbook of classroom management: Research, practice, and contemporary issues* (pp. 253–279). Mahwah, NJ: Erlbaum.

Watson, M. W., Andreas, J. B., Fischer, K. W., & Smith, K. (2005). Patterns of risk factors leading to victimization and aggression in children and adolescents. In K. A. Kendall-Tackett & S. M. Giacomoni (Eds.), *Child Victimization: Maltreatment, bullying and dating violence, prevention and intervention* (pp. 12.1–12.23). Kingston, NJ: Civic Research Institute.

Weinert, F. E., & Helmke, A. (1995). Learning from wise Mother Nature or Big Brother Instructor: The wrong choice as seen from an educational perspective. *Educational Psychologist, 30,* 135–142.

Wentzel, K. R., Battle, A., Russell, S. L., & Looney, L. B. (2010). Social supports from teachers and peers as predictors of academic and social motivation. *Contemporary Educational Psychology, 35,* 193–202.

Wentzel, K. R., Donlan, A. E., Morrison, D. A., Russell, S. L., & Baker, S. A. (2009, April). *Adolescent non-compliance: A social ecological perspective.* Paper presented at the annual meeting of the American Educational Research Association, San Diego, CA.

Williams, K. D. (2001). *Ostracism: The power of silence.* New York: Guilford.

Williams, K. M. (2001a). "Frontin' it": Schooling, violence, and relationships in the 'hood. In J. N. Burstyn, G. Bender, R. Casella, H. W. Gordon, D. P. Guerra, K. V. Luschen, R. Stevens, & K. M. Williams, *Preventing violence in schools: A challenge to American democracy* (pp. 95–108). Mahwah, NJ: Erlbaum.

Winner, E. (1997). Exceptionally high intelligence and schooling. *American Psychologist, 52,* 1070–1081.

Woolfolk, A. E., & Brooks, D. M. (1985). The influence of teachers' nonverbal behaviors on students' perceptions and performances. *Elementary School Journal, 85,* 513–528.

Woolfolk Hoy, A., Davis, H., & Pape, S. J. (2006). Teacher knowledge and beliefs. In P. A. Alexander & P. H. Winne (Eds.), *Handbook of educational psychology* (2nd ed., pp. 715–737). Mahwah, NJ: Erlbaum.

Woolfolk Hoy, A., & Weinstein, C. S. (2006). Student and teacher perspectives on classroom management. In C. M. Evertson & C. S. Weinstein (Eds.), *Handbook of classroom management: Research, practice, and contemporary issues* (pp. 181–219). Mahwah, NJ: Erlbaum.

Wynne, E. A. (1990). Improving pupil discipline and character. In O. C. Moles (Ed.), *Student discipline strategies: Research and practice* (pp. 167–190). Albany: State University of New York Press.

Zambo, D., & Brem, S. K. (2004). Emotion and cognition in students who struggle to read: New insights and ideas. *Reading Psychology, 25,* 1–16.

## CHAPTER 14

Airasian, P. W. (1994). *Classroom assessment* (2nd ed.). New York: McGraw-Hill.

Alleman, J., & Brophy, J. (1997). Elementary social studies: Instruments, activities, and standards. In G. D. Phye (Ed.), *Handbook of classroom assessment: Learning, achievement, and adjustment* (pp. 321–357). San Diego, CA: Academic Press.

Anderman, E. M., & Dawson, H. (2011). Learning with motivation. In R. E. Mayer & P. A. Alexander (Eds.), *Handbook of research on learning and instruction* (pp. 219–241). New York: Routledge.

Anderman, L. H., Freeman, T. M., & Mueller, C. E. (2007). The "social" side of social context: Interpersonal affiliative dimensions of students' experiences and academic dishonesty. In E. M. Anderman & T. B. Murdock (Eds.), *The psychology of academic cheating* (pp. 203–228). San Diego, CA: Elsevier.

Andrade, H. L. (2010). Students as the definitive source of formative assessment: Academic self-assessment and the self-regulation of learning. In H. L. Andrade & G. J. Cizek (Eds.), *Handbook of formative assessment* (pp. 90–105). New York: Routledge.

Andrade, H. L., & Cizek, G. J. (Eds.). (2010). *Handbook of formative assessment.* New York: Routledge.

Barkley, R. A. (2006). *Attention-deficit hyperactivity disorder: A handbook for diagnosis and treatment* (3rd ed.). New York: Guilford.

Baxter, G. P., Elder, A. D., & Glaser, R. (1996). Knowledge-based cognition and performance assessment in the science classroom. *Educational Psychologist, 31,* 133–140.

Beirne-Smith, M., Patton, J. R., & Kim, S. H. (2006). *Mental retardation: An introduction to intellectual disabilities* (7th ed.). Upper Saddle River, NJ: Merrill/Prentice-Hall.

Black, P., & Wiliam, D. (1998). Assessment and classroom learning. *Assessment in Education, 5*(1), 7–74.

Boschee, F., & Baron, M. A. (1993). *Outcome-based education: Developing programs through strategic planning.* Lancaster, PA: Technomic.

Brophy, J. E. (1986). *On motivating students* (Occasional Paper No. 101). East Lansing: Michigan State University, Institute for Research on Teaching.

Brophy, J. E. (2004). *Motivating students to learn* (2nd ed.). Mahwah, NJ: Erlbaum.

Brown, A. L., & Campione, J. C. (1996). Psychological theory and the design of innovative learning environments: On procedures, principles, and systems. In L. Schauble & R. Glaser (Eds.), *Innovations in learning: New environments for education* (pp. 289–325). Mahwah, NJ: Erlbaum.

Carbonneau, K. J., & Selig, J. P. (2011, April). *Teacher judgments of student mathematics achievement: The moderating role of student-teacher conflict.* Paper presented at the annual meeting of the American Educational Research Association, New Orleans, LA.

Carey, L. M. (1994). *Measuring and evaluating school learning* (2nd ed.). Boston: Allyn & Bacon.

Carter, R., Williams, S., & Silverman, W. K. (2008). Cognitive and emotional facets of test anxiety in African American school children. *Cognition and Emotion, 22,* 539–551.

Cassady, J. C. (2010b). Test anxiety: Contemporary theories and implications for learning. In J. C. Cassady (Ed.), *Anxiety in schools: The causes, consequences, and solutions for academic anxieties* (pp. 7–26). New York: Peter Lang.

Cassady, J. C., & Johnson, R. E. (2002). Cognitive test anxiety and academic performance. *Contemporary Educational Psychology, 27,* 270–295.

Castagno, A. E., & Brayboy, B. M. J. (2008). Culturally responsive schooling for Indigenous youth: A review of the literature. *Review of Educational Research, 78,* 941–993.

Chappuis, J. (2009). *Seven strategies of assessment for learning.* Boston: Pearson Assessment Training Institute.

Cheng, L. R. (1987). *Assessing Asian language performance.* Rockville, MD: Aspen.

Cizek, G. J. (2003). *Detecting and preventing classroom cheating: Promoting integrity in assessment.* Thousand Oaks, CA: Corwin.

Clifford, M. M. (1990). Students need challenge, not easy success. *Educational Leadership, 48*(1), 22–26.

Crehan, K. D. (2001). An investigation of the validity of scores on locally developed performance measures in a school assessment program. *Educational and Psychological Measurement, 61,* 841–848.

Crooks, T. J. (1988). The impact of classroom evaluation practices on students. *Review of Educational Research, 58,* 438–481.

Danner, F. (2008, March). *The effects of perceptions of classroom assessment practices and academic press on classroom mastery goals and high school students' self-reported cheating.* Paper presented at the annual meeting of the American Educational Research Association, New York.

Darley, J. M., & Gross, P. H. (1983). A hypothesis-confirming bias in labeling effects. *Journal of Personality and Social Psychology, 44,* 20–33.

Darling-Hammond, L., Ancess, J., & Falk, B. (1995). *Authentic assessment in action: Studies of schools and students at work.* New York: Teachers College Press.

Delandshere, G., & Petrosky, A. R. (1998). Assessment of complex performances: Limitations of key measurement assumptions. *Educational Researcher, 27*(2), 14–24.

Dempster, F. N. (1991). Synthesis of research on reviews and tests. *Educational Leadership, 48*(7), 71–76.

DiMartino, J., & Castaneda, A. (2007). Assessing applied skills. *Educational Leadership, 64,* 38–42.

diSessa, A. A. (2007). An interactional analysis of clinical interviewing. *Cognition and Instruction, 25,* 523–565.

D'Ydewalle, G., Swerts, A., & De Corte, E. (1983). Study time and test performance as a function of test expectations. *Contemporary Educational Psychology, 8*(1), 55–67.

Evans, E. D., & Craig, D. (1990). Teacher and student perceptions of academic cheating in middle and senior high schools. *Journal of Educational Research, 84*(1), 44–52.

Fall, R., Webb, N. M., & Chudowsky, N. (2000). Group discussion and large-scale language arts assessment: Effects on students' comprehension. *American Educational Research Journal, 37,* 911–941.

Feuerstein, R, Feuerstein, R. S., & Falik, L. H. (2010). *Beyond smarter: Mediated learning and the brain's capacity for change.* New York: Teachers College Press.

Foos, P. W., & Fisher, R. P. (1988). Using tests as learning opportunities. *Journal of Educational Psychology, 80,* 179–183.

Ford, D. Y., & Harris, J. J. (1992). The American achievement ideology and achievement differentials among preadolescent gifted and nongifted African American males and females. *The Journal of Negro Education, 61*(1), 45–64.

Frederiksen, J. R., & Collins, A. (1989). A systems approach to educational testing. *Educational Researcher, 18*(9), 27–32.

Frederiksen, N. (1984b). The real test bias: Influences of testing on teaching and learning. *American Psychologist, 39,* 193–202.

Fuchs, L. S., Compton, D. L., Fuchs, D., Hollenbeck, K. N., Craddock, C. F., & Hamlett, C. L. (2008). Dynamic assessment of algebraic learning in predicting third graders' development of mathematical problem solving. *Journal of Educational Psychology, 100,* 829–850.

Gaudry, E., & Bradshaw, G. D. (1971). The differential effect of anxiety on performance in progressive and terminal school examinations. In E. Gaudry & C. D. Spielberger (Eds.), *Anxiety and educational achievement.* Sydney, Australia: Wiley.

Geiger, M. A. (1997). An examination of the relationship between answer changing, testwiseness and examination performance. *Journal of Experimental Education, 66,* 49–60.

Glover, J. A. (1989). The "testing" phenomenon: Not gone but nearly forgotten. *Journal of Educational Psychology, 81,* 392–399.

Glover, T. A., & Vaughn, S. (Eds). (2010). *The promise of response to intervention: Evaluating current science and practice.* New York: Guilford.

Grant, C. A., & Gomez, M. L. (2001). *Campus and classroom: Making schooling multicultural* (2nd ed.). Upper Saddle River, NJ: Merrill/Prentice-Hall.

Gregg, N. (2009). *Adolescents and adults with learning disabilities and ADHD: Assessment and accommodation.* New York: Guilford.

Grolnick, W. S., & Ryan, R. M. (1987). Autonomy in children's learning: An experimental and individual difference investigation. *Journal of Personality and Social Psychology, 52,* 890–898.

Gronlund, N. E., & Waugh, C. K. (2009). *Assessment of student achievement* (9th ed.). Upper Saddle River, NJ: Merrill/Pearson.

Hagtvet, K. A., & Johnsen, T. B. (Eds.). (1992). *Advances in test anxiety research* (Vol. 7). Amsterdam: Swets & Zeitlinger.

Hamers, J. H. M., & Ruijssenaars, A. J. J. M. (1997). Assessing classroom learning potential. In G. D. Phye (Ed.), *Handbook of academic learning: Construction of knowledge* (pp. 550–571). San Diego, CA: Academic Press.

Hamp-Lyons, L. (1992). Holistic writing assessment for LEP students. In *Focus on evaluation and measurement* (Vol. 2, pp. 317–369). Washington, DC: U.S. Department of Education.

Hattie, J., & Gan, M. (2011). Instruction based on feedback. In R. E. Mayer & P. A. Alexander (Eds.), *Handbook of research on learning and instruction* (pp. 249–271). New York: Routledge.

Hay, P. J. (2008). (Mis)appropriations of criteria and standards-referenced assessment in a performance-based subject. *Assessment in Education: Principles, Policy, and Practice, 15,* 153–168.

Haywood, H. C., & Lidz, C. S. (2007). *Dynamic assessment in practice: Clinical and educational applications.* Cambridge, England: Cambridge University Press.

Hiebert, E. H., Valencia, S. W., & Afflerbach, P. P. (1994). Definitions and perspectives. In S. W. Valencia, E. H. Hiebert, & P. P. Afflerbach (Eds.), *Authentic reading assessment: Practices and possibilities* (pp. 6–25). Newark, DE: International Reading Association.

Hill, K. T. (1984). Debilitating motivation and testing: A major educational problem, possible solutions, and policy applications. In R. Ames & C. Ames (Eds.), *Research on motivation in education: Vol. 1. Student motivation* (pp. 245–274). San Diego, CA: Academic Press.

Hill, K. T., & Wigfield, A. (1984). Test anxiety: A major educational problem and what can be done about it. *Elementary School Journal, 85,* 105–126.

Hong, E., Sas, M., & Sas, J. C. (2006). Test-taking strategies of high and low mathematics achievers. *Journal of Educational Research, 99,* 144–155.

Hoover, J. J. (2009). *RTI assessment essentials for struggling learners.* Thousand Oaks, CA: Corwin.

Hughes, G. B. (2010). Formative assessment practices that maximize learning for students at risk. In H. L. Andrade & G. J. Cizek (Eds.), *Handbook of formative assessment* (pp. 212–232). New York: Routledge.

Johnson, R. L., Penny, J. A., & Gordon, B. (2009). *Assessing performance: Designing, scoring, and validating performance tasks.* New York: Guilford.

Khattri, N., & Sweet, D. (1996). Assessment reform: Promises and challenges. In M. B. Kane & R. Mitchell (Eds.), *Implementing performance assessment: Promises, problems, and challenges* (pp. 1–21). Mahwah, NJ: Erlbaum.

Klassen, S. (2006). Contextual assessment in science education: Background, issues, and policy. *Science Education, 90,* 820–851.

Lang, J. W. B., & Lang, J. (2010). Priming competence diminishes the link between cognitive test anxiety and test performance: Implications for the interpretation of test scores. *Psychological Science, 21,* 811–819.

Lenski, A., Husemann, N., Trautwein, U., & Lüdtke, O. (2010, April–May). *Academic cheating: A multidimensional point of view.* Paper presented at the annual meeting of the American Educational Research Association, Denver.

Lester, F. K., Jr., Lambdin, D. V., & Preston, R. V. (1997). A new vision of the nature and purposes of assessment in the mathematics classroom. In G. D. Phye (Ed.), *Handbook of classroom assessment: Learning, achievement, and adjustment* (pp. 287–319). San Diego, CA: Academic Press.

Li, J., & Fischer, K. W. (2004). Thought and affect in American and Chinese learners' beliefs about learning. In D. Y. Dai & R. J. Sternberg (Eds.), *Motivation, emotion, and cognition: Integrative perspectives on intellectual functioning and development* (pp. 385–418). Mahwah, NJ: Erlbaum.

Lidz, C. S., & Gindis, B. (2003). Dynamic assessment of the evolving cognitive functions in children. In A. Kozulin, B. Gindis, V. S. Ageyev, & S. M. Miller (Eds.), *Vygotsky's educational theory in cultural context* (pp. 99–116). Cambridge, England: Cambridge University Press.

Linn, R. L. (1994). Performance assessment: Policy promises and technical measurement standards. *Educational Researcher, 23*(9), 4–14.

Lovett, B. J. (2010). Extended time testing accommodations for students with disabilities: Answers to five fundamental questions. *Review of Educational Research, 80,* 611–638.

Lundeberg, M. A., & Fox, P. W. (1991). Do laboratory findings on test expectancy generalize to classroom outcomes? *Review of Educational Research, 61,* 94–106.

Mac Iver, D. J., Reuman, D. A., & Main, S. R. (1995). Social structuring of the school: Studying what is, illuminating what could be. In J. T. Spence, J. M. Darley, & D. J. Foss (Eds.), *Annual review of psychology* (Vol. 46, pp. 375–400). Palo Alto, CA: Annual Review.

Maehr, M. L., & Anderman, E. M. (1993). Reinventing schools for early adolescents: Emphasizing task goals. *Elementary School Journal, 93,* 593–610.

Magnusson, S. J., Boyle, R. A., & Templin, M. (1994, April). *Conceptual development: Re-examining knowledge construction in science.* Paper presented at the annual meeting of the American Educational Research Association, New Orleans, LA.

McDaniel, M. A., Agarwal, P. K., Huelser, B. J., McDermott, K. B., & Roediger, H. L., III (2011). Test-enhanced learning in a middle school science classroom: The effects of quiz frequency and placement. *Journal of Educational Psychology, 103,* 399–414.

McMillan, J. H. (2010). The practical implications of educational aims and contexts for formative assessment. In H. L. Andrade & G. J. Cizek (Eds.), *Handbook of formative assessment* (pp. 41–58). New York: Routledge.

Mellard, D. F., & Johnson, E. (2008). *RTI: A practitioner's guide to implementing response to intervention.* Thousand Oaks, CA: Corwin.

Mercer, C. D., & Pullen, P. C. (2005). *Students with learning disabilities* (6th ed.). Upper Saddle River, NJ: Merrill/Prentice-Hall.

Messick, S. (1994a). The interplay of evidence and consequences in the validation of performance assessments. *Educational Researcher, 23*(2), 13–23.

Meyer, L. H., Weir, K. F., McClure, J., & Walkey, F. (2008, March). *The relationship of motivation orientations to future achievement in secondary school.* Paper presented at the annual meeting of the American Educational Research Association, New York.

Miller, M. D., Linn, R. L., & Gronlund, N. E. (2009). *Measurement and assessment in teaching* (10th ed.). Upper Saddle River, NJ: Merrill/Pearson.

Millman, J., Bishop, C. H., & Ebel, R. (1965). An analysis of test-wiseness. *Educational and Psychological Measurement, 25,* 707–26.

Morgan, D. P., & Jenson, W. R. (1988). *Teaching behaviorally disordered students: Preferred practices.* Upper Saddle River, NJ: Merrill/ Prentice-Hall.

Murdock, T. B., Miller, A., & Kohlhardt, J. (2004). Effects of classroom context variables on high school students' judgments of the acceptability and likelihood of cheating. *Journal of Educational Psychology, 96,* 765–777.

Newmann, F. M. (1997). Authentic assessment in social studies: Standards and examples. In G. D. Phye (Ed.), *Handbook of classroom assessment: Learning, achievement, and adjustment* (pp. 360–380). San Diego, CA: Academic Press.

O'Connor, K. (2011). *A repair kit for grading: 15 fixes for broken grades* (2nd ed.). Boston: Pearson Assessment Training Institute.

Paris, S. G., & Ayres, L. R. (1994). *Becoming reflective students and teachers with portfolios and authentic assessment.* Washington, DC: American Psychological Association.

Paris, S. G., & Paris, A. H. (2001). Classroom applications of research on self-regulated learning. *Educational Psychologist, 36,* 89–101.

Paris, S. G., & Turner, J. C. (1994). Situated motivation. In P. R. Pintrich, D. R. Brown, & C. E. Weinstein (Eds.), *Student motivation, cognition, and learning: Essays in honor of Wilbert J. McKeachie* (pp. 213–238). Mahwah, NJ: Erlbaum.

Parkes, J. (2001). The role of transfer in the variability of performance assessment scores. *Educational Assessment, 7,* 143–164.

Petersen, G. A., Sudweeks, R. R., & Baird, J. H. (1990, April). *Test-wise responses of third-, fifth-, and sixth-grade students to clued and unclued multiple-choice science items.* Paper presented at the annual meeting of the American Educational Research Association, Boston.

Piirto, J. (1999). *Talented children and adults: Their development and education* (2nd ed.). Upper Saddle River, NJ: Merrill/Prentice-Hall.

Pintrich, P. R., & Schunk, D. H. (2002). *Motivation in education: Theory, research, and applications* (2nd ed.). Upper Saddle River, NJ: Merrill/ Prentice-Hall.

Popham, W. J. (1995). *Classroom assessment: What teachers need to know.* Boston: Allyn & Bacon.

Popham, W. J. (2006). *Assessment for educational leaders.* Boston: Pearson/Allyn and Bacon.

Putwain, D. W. (2007). Test anxiety in UK schoolchildren: Prevalence and demographic patterns. *British Journal of Educational Psychology, 77,* 579–593.

Quellmalz, E., & Hoskyn, J. (1997). Classroom assessment of reading strategies. In G. D. Phye (Ed.), *Handbook of classroom assessment: Learning, achievement, and adjustment* (pp. 103–130). San Diego, CA: Academic Press.

Ready, D. D., & Wright, D. L. (2011). Accuracy and inaccuracy in teachers' perceptions of young children's cognitive abilities: The role of child background and classroom context. *American Educational Research Journal, 48,* 335–360.

Reeve, J., Deci, E. L., & Ryan, R. M. (2004). Self-determination theory: A dialectical framework for understanding sociocultural influences on student motivation. In D. M. McInerney & S. Van Etten (Eds.), *Big theories revisited* (pp. 31–60). Greenwich, CT: Information Age.

Ritts, V., Patterson, M. L., & Tubbs, M. E. (1992). Expectations, impressions, and judgments of physically attractive students: A review. *Review of Educational Research, 62,* 413–426.

Robinson, J. P., & Lubienski, S. T. (2011). The development of gender achievement gaps in mathematics and reading during elementary and middle school: Examining direct cognitive assessments and teacher ratings. *American Educational Research Journal, 48,* 268–302.

Roediger, H. L., III, & Karpicke, J. D. (2006). The power of testing memory: Basic research and implications for educational practice. *Perspectives on Psychological Science, 1,* 181–210.

Rogoff, B. (2003). *The cultural nature of human development.* Oxford, England: Oxford University Press.

Rohrer, D., & Pashler, H. (2010). Recent research on human learning challenges conventional instructional strategies. *Educational Researcher, 39,* 406–412.

Russell, M. K. (2010). Technology-aided formative assessment of learning: New developments and applications. In H. L. Andrade & G. J. Cizek (Eds.), *Handbook of formative assessment* (pp. 125–138). New York: Routledge.

Sarason, I. G. (Ed.). (1980). *Test anxiety: Theory, research, and applications.* Mahwah, NJ: Erlbaum.

Sax, G. (2010). *Principles of educational and psychological measurement and evaluation* (4th ed.). Belmont, CA: Wadsworth.

Scarcella, R. (1990). *Teaching language-minority students in the multicultural classroom.* Upper Saddle River, NJ: Prentice Hall.

Scruggs, T. E., & Lifson, S. A. (1985). Current conceptions of test-wiseness: Myths and realities. *School Psychology Review, 14,* 339–350.

Shepard, L. (2000). The role of assessment in a learning culture. *Educational Researcher, 29*(7), 4–14.

Shepard, L., Hammerness, K., Darling-Hammond, L., & Rust, F. (with Snowden, J. B., Gordon, E., Gutierrez, C., & Pacheco, A.). (2005). Assessment. In L. Darling-Hammond & J. Bransford (Eds.), *Preparing teachers for a changing world: What teachers should learn and be able to do* (pp. 275–326). San Francisco: Jossey-Bass/Wiley.

Shriner, J. G., & Spicuzza, R. J. (1995). Procedural considerations in the assessment of students at risk for school failure. *Preventing School Failure, 39*(2), 33–38.

Sieber, J. E., Kameya, L. I., & Paulson, F. L. (1970). Effect of memory support on the problem-solving ability of test-anxious children. *Journal of Educational Psychology, 61,* 159–168.

Sireci, S. G., Scarpati, S. E., & Li, S. (2005). Test accommodations for students with disabilities: An analysis of the interaction hypothesis. *Review of Educational Research, 75,* 457–490.

Spaulding, C. L. (1992). *Motivation in the classroom.* New York: McGraw-Hill.

Spinelli, C. G. (2008). Addressing the issue of cultural and linguistic diversity and assessment: Informal evaluation measures for English language learners. *Reading and Writing Quarterly, 24,* 101–118.

Stein, J. A., & Krishnan, K. (2007). Nonverbal learning disabilities and executive function: The challenges of effective assessment and teaching. In L. Meltzer (Ed.), *Executive function in education: From theory to practice* (pp. 106–132). New York: Guilford.

Sternberg, R. J. (2005). Intelligence, competence, and expertise. In A. J. Elliot & C. S. Dweck (Eds.), *Handbook of competence and motivation* (pp. 15–30). New York: Guilford.

Stiggins, R. J., & Chappuis, J. (2012). *An introduction to student-involved assessment FOR learning* (6th ed.). Boston: Pearson Assessment Training Institute.

Stipek, D. J. (1993). *Motivation to learn: From theory to practice* (2nd ed.). Boston: Allyn & Bacon.

Stokes, J. V., Luiselli, J. K., Reed, D. D., & Fleming, R. K. (2010). Behavioral coaching to improve offensive line pass-blocking skills of high school football athletes. *Journal of Applied Behavior Analysis, 43,* 463–472.

Stupnisky, R. H., Stewart, T. L., Daniels, L. M., & Perry, R. P. (2011). When do students ask why? Examining the precursors and outcomes of causal search among first-year college students. *Contemporary Educational Psychology, 36,* 201–211.

Swanson, H. L., & Lussier, C. M. (2001). A selective synthesis of the experimental literature on dynamic assessment. *Review of Educational Research, 71,* 321–363.

Turnbull, A. P., Turnbull, R., & Wehmeyer, M. L. (2010). *Exceptional lives: Special education in today's schools* (6th ed.). Upper Saddle River, NJ: Merrill.

Turner, J. C., Meyer, D. K., Cox, K. E., Logan, C., DiCintio, M., & Thomas, C. T. (1998). Creating contexts for involvement in mathematics. *Journal of Educational Psychology, 90,* 730–745.

Tzuriel, D. (2000). Dynamic assessment of young children: Educational and intervention perspectives. *Educational Psychology Review, 12,* 385–435.

Usher, E. L. (2009). Sources of middle school students' self-efficacy in mathematics: A qualitative investigation. *American Educational Research Journal, 46,* 275–314.

Valdés, G., Bunch, G., Snow, C., & Lee, C. (with Matos, L.). (2005). Enhancing the development of students' language(s). In L. Darling-Hammond & J. Bransford (Eds.), *Preparing teachers for a changing world: What teachers should learn and be able to do* (pp. 126–168). San Francisco: Jossey-Bass/Wiley.

van den Bergh, L., Denessen, E., Hornstra, L., Voeten, M., & Holland, R. W. (2010). The implicit prejudiced attitudes of teachers: Relations to teacher expectations and the ethnic achievement gap. *American Educational Research Journal, 47,* 497–527.

van Kraayenoord, C. E., & Paris, S. G. (1997). Australian students' self-appraisal of their work samples and academic progress. *Elementary School Journal, 97,* 523–537.

Vye, N. J., Schwartz, D. L., Bransford, J. D., Barron, B. J., Zech, L., & The Cognition and Technology Group at Vanderbilt. (1998). SMART environments that support monitoring, reflection, and revision. In D. J. Hacker, J. Dunlosky, & A. C. Graesser (Eds.), *Metacognition in educational theory and practice* (pp. 305–346). Mahwah, NJ: Erlbaum.

Warren, G. (1979). Essay versus multiple-choice tests. *Journal of Research in Science Teaching, 16,* 563–567.

Warschauer, M. (2011). *Learning in the cloud: How (and why) to transform schools with digital media.* New York: Teachers College Press.

Wentzel, K. R. (2009). Peers and academic functioning at school. In K. H. Rubin, W. M. Bukowski, & B. Laursen (Eds.), *Handbook of peer interactions, relationships, and groups* (pp. 531–547). New York: Guilford.

Whitaker Sena, J. D., Lowe, P. A., & Lee, S. W. (2007). Significant predictors of test anxiety among students with and without learning disabilities. *Journal of Learning Disabilities, 40,* 360–376.

Wiggins, G. (1992). Creating tests worth taking. *Educational Leadership, 49*(8), 26–33.

Wiggins, G., & McTigue, J. (2007). *Schooling by design.* Alexandria, VA: Association of Supervision and Curriculum Development.

Wiley, D. E., & Haertel, E. H. (1996). Extended assessment tasks: Purposes, definitions, scoring, and accuracy. In M. B. Kane & R. Mitchell (Eds.), *Implementing performance assessment: Promises, problems, and challenges* (pp. 61–89). Mahwah, NJ: Erlbaum.

## CHAPTER 15

Adger, C. T., Wolfram, W., & Christian, D. (2007). *Dialects in schools and communities* (2nd ed.). New York: Routledge.

Airasian, P. W. (1994). *Classroom assessment* (2nd ed.). New York: McGraw-Hill.

American Educational Research Association, American Psychological Association, & National Council on Measurement in Education. (1999). *Standards for Educational and Psychological Testing* (2nd ed.). Washington, DC: American Educational Research Association.

Ames, C. (1984). Competitive, cooperative, and individualistic goal structures: A cognitive-motivational analysis. In R. Ames & C. Ames (Eds.), *Research on motivation in education: Vol. 1. Student motivation* (pp. 177–207). San Diego, CA: Academic Press.

Amrein, A. L., & Berliner, D. C. (2002, March 28). High-stakes testing, uncertainty, and student learning. *Education Policy Analysis Archives, 10*(18). Retrieved April 9, 2002, from http://epaa.asu.edu/epaa/v10n18/

Anderman, E. M., Anderman, L. H., Yough, M. S., & Gimbert, B. G. (2010). Value-added models of assessment: Implications for motivation and accountability. *Educational Psychologist, 45,* 123–137.

Anderman, E. M., Griesinger, T., & Westerfield, G. (1998). Motivation and cheating during early adolescence. *Journal of Educational Psychology, 90,* 84–93.

Aronson, J., & Steele, C. M. (2005). Stereotypes and the fragility of academic competence, motivation, and self-concept. In A. J. Elliot & C. S. Dweck (Eds.), *Handbook of competence and motivation* (pp. 436–456). New York: Guilford.

Arter, J. A., & Spandel, V. (1992). Using portfolios of student work in instruction and assessment. *Educational Measurement: Issues and Practice, 11*(1), 36–44.

Au, W. (2007). High-stakes testing and curricular control: A qualitative metasynthesis. *Educational Researcher, 36*(5), 258–267.

Baker, E. L. (2007). The end(s) of testing. *Educational Researcher, 36,* 309–317.

Balfanz, R., Legters, N., West, T. C., & Weber, L. M. (2007). Are NCLB's measures, incentives, and improvement strategies the right ones for the nation's low-performing high schools? *American Educational Research Journal, 44,* 559–593.

Ballou, D., Sanders, W., & Wright, P. (2004). Controlling for student background in value-added assessment of teachers. *Journal of Educational and Behavioral Statistics, 29,* 37–65.

Banta, T. W. (Ed.). (2003). *Portfolio assessment: Uses, cases, scoring, and impact.* San Francisco: Jossey-Bass.

Barkley, R. A. (2006). *Attention-deficit hyperactivity disorder: A handbook for diagnosis and treatment* (3rd ed.). New York: Guilford.

Beirne-Smith, M., Patton, J. R., & Kim, S. H. (2006). *Mental retardation: An introduction to intellectual disabilities* (7th ed.). Upper Saddle River, NJ: Merrill/Prentice Hall.

Bleeker, M. M., & Jacobs, J. E. (2004). Achievement in math and science: Do mothers' beliefs matter 12 years later? *Journal of Educational Psychology, 96,* 97–109.

Boykin, A. W. (1994). Harvesting talent and culture: African-American children and educational reform. In R. J. Rossi (Ed.), *Schools and students at risk: Context and framework for positive change* (pp. 116–138). New York: Teachers College Press.

Bracken, B. A., & Walker, K. C. (1997). The utility of intelligence tests for preschool children. In D. P. Flanagan, J. L. Genshaft, & P. L. Harrison (Eds.), *Contemporary intellectual assessment: Theories, tests, and issues* (pp. 484–502). New York: Guilford.

Brookhart, S. M. (2004). *Grading.* Upper Saddle River, NJ: Merrill/Prentice-Hall.

Brophy, J. E. (2004). *Motivating students to learn* (2nd ed.). Mahwah, NJ: Erlbaum.

Brown, A. B., & Clift, J. W. (2010). The unequal effect of adequate yearly progress: Evidence from school visits. *American Educational Research Journal, 47,* 774–798.

Brown, R. T., Reynolds, C. R., & Whitaker, J. S. (1999). Bias in mental testing since *Bias in Mental Testing. School Psychology Quarterly, 14,* 208–238.

Buck, G., Kostin, I., & Morgan, R. (2002). *Examining the relationship of content to gender-based performance differences in advanced placement exams* (Research Report No. 2002-12). New York: The College Board.

Carbonneau, K. J., & Selig, J. P. (2011, April). *Teacher judgments of student mathematics achievement: The moderating role of student-teacher conflict.* Paper presented at the annual meeting of the American Educational Research Association, New Orleans, LA.

Carhill, A., Suárez-Orozco, C., & Páez, M. (2008). Explaining English language proficiency among adolescent immigrant students. *American Educational Research Journal, 45,* 1045–1079.

Carter, R., Williams, S., & Silverman, W. K. (2008). Cognitive and emotional facets of test anxiety in African American school children. *Cognition and Emotion, 22,* 539–551.

Carver, S. M. (2006). Assessing for deep understanding. In R. K. Sawyer (Ed.), *The Cambridge handbook of the learning sciences* (pp. 205–221). Cambridge, England: Cambridge University Press.

Chabrán, M. (2003). Listening to talk from and about students on accountability. In M. Carnoy, R. Elmore, & L. S. Siskin (Eds.), *The new accountability: High schools and high-stakes testing* (pp. 129–145). New York: RoutledgeFalmer.

Cizek, G. J. (2003). *Detecting and preventing classroom cheating: Promoting integrity in assessment.* Thousand Oaks, CA: Corwin.

Cummins, J. (1981). Age on arrival and immigrant second language learning in Canada: A reassessment. *Applied Linguistics, 2,* 132–149.

Cummins, J. (2000). *Language, power, and pedagogy: Bilingual children in the crossfire.* Clevedon, England: Multlingual Matters.

Cummins, J. (2008). BICS and CALP: Empirical and theoretical status of the distinction. In B. Street & N. H. Hornberger (Eds.), *Encyclopedia of language and education* (2nd ed., Vol. 2, pp. 71–83). New York: Springer.

Dai, D. Y. (2010). *The nature and nurture of giftedness: A new framework for understanding gifted education.* New York: Teachers College Press.

Darling-Hammond, L., Ancess, J., & Falk, B. (1995). *Authentic assessment in action: Studies of schools and students at work.* New York: Teachers College Press.

Dempster, F. N., & Corkill, A. J. (1999). Interference and inhibition in cognition and behavior: Unifying themes for educational psychology. *Educational Psychology Review, 11,* 1–88.

DiMartino, J. (2007, April 25). Accountability, or mastery? *Education Week, 26*(34), 36, 44.

DiMartino, J., & Castaneda, A. (2007). Assessing applied skills. *Educational Leadership, 64,* 38–42.

Duckworth, A. L., & Seligman, M. E. P. (2005). Self-discipline outdoes IQ in predicting academic performance of adolescents. *Psychological Science, 16,* 939–944.

Duncan, G. J., Dowsett, C. J., Claessens, A., Magnuson, K., Huston, A. C., Klevanov, P., et al. (2007). School readiness and later achievement. *Developmental Psychology, 43,* 1428–1446.

Durost, W. N. (1961). How to tell parents about standardized test results. *Test Service Notebook* (No. 26). New York: Harcourt, Brace, & World.

Farran, D. C. (2001). Critical periods and early intervention. In D. B. Bailey, Jr., J. T. Bruer, F. J. Symons, & J. W. Lichtman (Eds.), *Critical thinking about critical periods* (pp. 233–266). Baltimore: Brookes.

Feuerstein, R, Feuerstein, R. S., & Falik, L. H. (2010). *Beyond smarter: Mediated learning and the brain's capacity for change.* New York: Teachers College Press.

Finnigan, K. S., & Gross, B. (2007). Do accountability policy sanctions influence teacher motivation? Lessons from Chicago's low-performing schools. *American Educational Research Journal, 44,* 594–629.

Ford, D. Y., & Harris, J. J. (1992). The American achievement ideology and achievement differentials among preadolescent gifted and nongifted African American males and females. *The Journal of Negro Education, 61*(1), 45–64.

Forte, E. (2010). Examining the assumptions underlying the NCLB federal accountability policy on school improvement. *Journal of Educational Psychology, 102,* 76–88.

Frisbie, D. A., & Waltman, K. K. (1992). Developing a personal grading plan. *Educational Measurement: Issues and Practice, 11*(3), 35–42. Reprinted in K. M. Cauley, F. Linder, & J. H. McMillan (Eds.), (1994), *Educational psychology 94/95.* Guilford, CT: Dushkin.

Garcia, E. E. (2005, April). *Any test in English is a test of English: Implications for high stakes testing.* Paper presented at the annual meeting of the American Educational Research Association, Montreal.

García, G. E., & Pearson, P. D. (1994). Assessment and diversity. In L. Darling-Hammond (Ed.), *Review of research in education* (Vol. 20, pp. 337–391). Washington, DC: American Educational Research Association.

Gilpin, L. (1968). *The enduring Navaho.* Austin: University of Texas Press.

Good, C., Aronson, J., & Inzlicht, M. (2003). Improving adolescents' standardized test performance: An intervention to reduce the effects of stereotype threat. *Journal of Applied Developmental Psychology, 24,* 645–662.

Gottfried, A. E., Fleming, J. S., & Gottfried, A. W. (1994). Role of parental motivational practices in children's academic intrinsic motivation and achievement. *Journal of Educational Psychology, 86,* 104–113.

Graham, S., & Golen, S. (1991). Motivational influences on cognition: Task involvement, ego involvement, and depth of information processing. *Journal of Educational Psychology, 83,* 187–194.

Gregg, N. (2009). *Adolescents and adults with learning disabilities and ADHD: Assessment and accommodation.* New York: Guilford.

Haertel, E., & Linn, R. (1996). Comparability. In G. Phillips (Ed.), *Technical issues in large-scale performance assessment* (pp. 59–78). Washington, DC: National Center for Education Statistics.

Halpern, D. F., Benbow, C. P., Geary, D. C., Gur, R. C., Hyde, J. S., & Gernsbacher, M. A. (2007). The science of sex differences in science and mathematics. *Psychological Science in the Public Interest, 8*(1), 1–51.

Haywood, H. C., & Lidz, C. S. (2007). *Dynamic assessment in practice: Clinical and educational applications.* Cambridge, England: Cambridge University Press.

Heath, S. B. (1989). Oral and literate traditions among black Americans living in poverty. *American Psychologist, 44,* 367–373.

Ho, A. D. (2008). The problem with "proficiency": Limitations of statistics and policy under No Child Left Behind. *Educational Researcher, 37,* 351–360.

Hoge, R. D., & Coladarci, T. (1989). Teacher-based judgments of academic achievement: A review of literature. *Review of Educational Research, 59,* 297–313.

Holme, J. J., Richards, M. P., Jimerson, J. B., & Cohen, R. W. (2010). Assessing the effects of high school exit examinations. *Review of Educational Research, 80,* 476–526.

Hursh, D. (2007). Assessing No Child Left Behind and the rise of neoliberal education policies. *American Educational Research Journal, 44,* 493–518.

Jacob, B. A. (2003). Accountability, incentives, and behavior: The impact of high-stakes testing in the Chicago Public Schools. *Education Next, 3*(1). Retrieved March 10, 2004, from http://www.educationnext.org/unabridged/20031/jacob.pdf

Johnson, R. L., Penny, J. A., & Gordon, B. (2009). *Assessing performance: Designing, scoring, and validating performance tasks.* New York: Guilford.

Johnson, R. S., Mims-Cox, J. S., & Doyle-Nichols, A. (2006). *Developing portfolios in education: A guide to reflection, inquiry, and assessment.* Thousand Oaks, CA: Sage.

Kieffer, M. J., Lesaux, N. K., Rivera, M., & Francis, D. J. (2009). Accommodations for English language learners taking large-scale assessments: A meta-analysis on effectiveness and validity. *Review of Educational Research, 79,* 1168–1201.

Koretz, D., Stecher, B., Klein, S., & McCaffrey, D. (1994). The Vermont portfolio assessment program: Findings and implications. *Educational Measurement: Issues and Practice, 13*(3), 5–16.

Kuhn, D. (2001a). How do people know? *Psychological Science, 12,* 1–8.

Kumar, R., Gheen, M. H., & Kaplan, A. (2002). Goal structures in the learning environment and students' disaffection from learning and schooling. In C. Midgley (Ed.), *Goals, goal structures, and patterns of adaptive learning* (pp. 143–173). Mahwah, NJ: Erlbaum.

La Guardia, J. G., (2009). Developing who I am: A self-determination theory approach to the establishment of healthy identities. *Educational Psychologist, 44,* 90–104.

La Paro, K. M., & Pianta, R. C. (2000). Predicting children's competence in the early school years: A meta-analytic review. *Review of Educational Research, 70,* 443–484.

Lester, F. K., Jr., Lambdin, D. V., & Preston, R. V. (1997). A new vision of the nature and purposes of assessment in the mathematics classroom. In G. D. Phye (Ed.), *Handbook of classroom assessment: Learning, achievement, and adjustment* (pp. 287–319). San Diego, CA: Academic Press.

Leu, D. J., O'Byrne, W. I., Zawilinski, L., McVerry, J. G., & Everett-Cacopardo, H. (2009). Expanding the new literacies conversation. *Educational Researcher, 38,* 264–269.

Lidz, C. S. (1991). Issues in the assessment of preschool children. In B. A. Bracken (Ed.), *The psychoeducational assessment of preschool children* (2nd ed., pp. 18–31). Boston: Allyn & Bacon.

Linn, R. L. (2000). Assessments and accountability. *Educational Researcher, 29*(2), 4–16.

Mastropieri, M. A., & Scruggs, T. E. (2007). *The inclusive classroom: Strategies for effective instruction* (3rd ed.). Upper Saddle River, NJ: Merrill/Prentice-Hall.

Mercer, C. D., & Pullen, P. C. (2005). *Students with learning disabilities* (6th ed.). Upper Saddle River, NJ: Merrill/Prentice-Hall.

Messick, S. (1983). Assessment of children. In W. Kessen (Ed.), *Handbook of child psychology* (Vol. 1, pp. 477–526). New York: Wiley.

Meyer, M. S. (2000). The ability-achievement discrepancy: Does it contribute to an understanding of learning disabilities? *Educational Psychology Review, 12,* 315–337.

Miller, M. D., Linn, R. L., & Gronlund, N. E. (2009). *Measurement and assessment in teaching* (10th ed.). Upper Saddle River, NJ: Merrill/Pearson.

Mintrop, H., & Sunderman, G. L. (2009). Predictable failure of federal sanctions-driven accountability for school improvement—And why we may retain it anyway. *Educational Researcher, 38,* 353–364.

National Commission on Excellence in Education. (1983). *A nation at risk: The imperative for educational reform.* Washington, DC: U.S. Government Printing Office.

Nichols, P. D., & Mittelholtz, D. J. (1997). Constructing the concept of aptitude: Implications for the assessment of analogical reasoning. In G. D. Phye (Ed.), *Handbook of academic learning: Construction of knowledge* (pp. 128–147). San Diego, CA: Academic Press.

Nitko, A. J., & Brookhart, S. M. (2011). *Educational assessment of students* (6th ed.). Boston: Pearson/Allyn & Bacon.

O'Connor, K. (2011). *A repair kit for grading: 15 fixes for broken grades* (2nd ed.). Boston: Pearson Assessment Training Institute.

Osborne, J. W., Tillman, D., & Holland, A. (2010). Stereotype threat and anxiety for disadvantaged minorities and women. In J. C. Cassady (Ed.), *Anxiety in schools: The causes, consequences, and solutions for academic anxieties* (pp. 119–136). New York: Peter Lang.

Padilla, A. M. (2006). Second language learning: Issues in research and teaching. In P. A. Alexander & P. H. Winne (Eds.), *Handbook of educational psychology* (2nd ed., pp. 571–591). Mahwah, NJ: Erlbaum.

Padilla-Walker, L. M. (2006). The impact of daily extra credit quizzes on exam performance. *Teaching of Psychology, 33,* 236–239.

Paris, S. G., Lawton, T. A., Turner, J. C., & Roth, J. L. (1991). A developmental perspective on standardized achievement testing. *Educational Researcher, 20*(5), 12–20, 40.

Parker, W. D. (1997). An empirical typology of perfectionism in academically talented children. *American Educational Research Journal, 34,* 545–562.

Paulson, F. L., Paulson, P. R., & Meyer, C. A. (1991). What makes a portfolio a portfolio? *Educational Leadership, 49*(5), 60–63.

Perkins, D. N., Tishman, S., Ritchhart, R., Donis, K., & Andrade, A. (2000). Intelligence in the wild: A dispositional view of intellectual traits. *Educational Psychology Review, 12,* 269–293.

Petersen, G. A., Sudweeks, R. R., & Baird, J. H. (1990, April). *Test-wise responses of third-, fifth-,* and sixth-grade students to clued and unclued multiple-choice science items. Paper presented at the annual meeting of the American Educational Research Association, Boston.

Phillips, B. N., Pitcher, G. D., Worsham, M. E., & Miller, S. C. (1980). Test anxiety and the school environment. In I. G. Sarason (Ed.), *Test anxiety: Theory, research, and applications.* Mahwah, NJ: Erlbaum.

Piirto, J. (1999). *Talented children and adults: Their development and education* (2nd ed.). Upper Saddle River, NJ: Merrill/Prentice-Hall.

Pitoniak, M. J., & Royer, J. M. (2001). Testing accommodations for examinees with disabilities: A review of psychometric, legal, and social policy issues. *Review of Educational Research, 71,* 53–104.

Popham, W. J. (1995). *Classroom assessment: What teachers need to know.* Boston: Allyn & Bacon.

Porter, A. C., & Polikoff, M. S. (2007). NCLB: State interpretations, early effects, and suggestions for reauthorization. *Social Policy Report, 21*(4) (Society for Research in Child Development).

Pulfrey, C., Buchs, C., & Butera, F. (2011). Why grades engender performance-avoidance goals: The mediating role of autonomous motivation. *Journal of Educational Psychology, 103,* 683–700.

Putwain, D. W. (2007). Test anxiety in UK schoolchildren: Prevalence and demographic patterns. *British Journal of Educational Psychology, 77,* 579–593.

Ricks, J. H. (1959). On telling parents about test results. *Test Service Bulletin* (No. 59). New York: Psychological Corporation.

Robinson, J. P. (2010). The effects of test translation on young English learners' mathematics performance. *Educational Researcher, 39,* 582–590.

Robinson, J. P., & Lubienski, S. T. (2011). The development of gender achievement gaps in mathematics and reading during elementary and middle school: Examining direct cognitive assessments and teacher ratings. *American Educational Research Journal, 48,* 268–302.

Rogoff, B. (2003). *The cultural nature of human development.* Oxford, England: Oxford University Press.

Ryan, R. M., & Brown, K. W. (2005). Legislating competence: High-stakes testing policies and their relations with psychological theories and research. In A. J. Elliot & C. S. Dweck (Eds.), *Handbook of competence and motivation* (pp. 354–372). New York: Guilford.

Sanders, C. E. (1997). Assessment during the preschool years. In G. D. Phye (Ed.), *Handbook of classroom assessment: Learning, achievement, and adjustment* (pp. 227–264). San Diego, CA: Academic Press.

Sarason, I. G. (Ed.). (1980). *Test anxiety: Theory, research, and applications.* Mahwah, NJ: Erlbaum.

Sattler, J. M. (2001). *Assessment of children: Cognitive applications* (4th ed.). San Diego, CA: Author.

Sax, G. (2010). *Principles of educational and psychological measurement and evaluation* (4th ed.). Belmont, CA: Wadsworth.

Scruggs, T. E., & Lifson, S. A. (1985). Current conceptions of test-wiseness: Myths and realities. *School Psychology Review, 14,* 339–350.

Shepard, L., Hammerness, K., Darling-Hammond, L., & Rust, F. (with Snowden, J. B., Gordon, E., Gutierrez, C., & Pacheco, A.). (2005). Assessment. In L. Darling-Hammond & J. Bransford (Eds.), *Preparing teachers for a changing world: What teachers should learn and be able to do* (pp. 275–326). San Francisco: Jossey-Bass/Wiley.

Shih, S.-S., & Alexander, J. M. (2000). Interacting effects of goal setting and self- or other-referenced feedback on children's development of self-efficacy and cognitive skill within the Taiwanese classroom. *Journal of Educational Psychology, 92,* 536–543.

Siskin, L. S. (2003a). Outside the core: Accountability in tested and untested subjects. In M. Carnoy, R. Elmore, & L. S. Siskin (Eds.), *The new accountability: High schools and high-stakes testing* (pp. 87–98). New York: RoutledgeFalmer.

Siskin, L. S. (2003b). When an irresistible force meets an immovable object: Core lessons about high schools and accountability. In M. Carnoy, R. Elmore, & L. S. Siskin (Eds.), *The new accountability: High schools and high-stakes testing* (pp. 175–194). New York: RoutledgeFalmer.

Smith, J. L. (2004). Understanding the process of stereotype threat: A review of mediational variables and new performance goal directions. *Educational Psychology Review, 16,* 177–206.

Solórzano, R. W. (2008). High stakes testing: Issues, implications, and remedies for English language learners. *Educational Researcher, 78,* 260–329.

Spandel, V. (1997). Reflections on portfolios. In G. D. Phye (Ed.), *Handbook of academic learning: Construction of knowledge* (pp. 573–591). San Diego, CA: Academic Press.

Stein, J. A., & Krishnan, K. (2007). Nonverbal learning disabilities and executive function: The challenges of effective assessment and teaching. In L. Meltzer (Ed.), *Executive function in education: From theory to practice* (pp. 106–132). New York: Guilford.

Sternberg, R. J. (2002). Raising the achievement of all students: Teaching for successful intelligence. *Educational Psychology Review, 14,* 383–393.

Stipek, D. J. (1996). Motivation and instruction. In D. C. Berliner & R. C. Calfee (Eds.), *Handbook of educational psychology* (pp. 85–113). New York: Macmillan.

Stipek, D. J. (2002). At what age should children enter kindergarten? A question for policy makers and parents. *Social Policy Report of the Society for Research in Child Development, 16*(2), 3–16.

Stringfield, S. C., & Yakimowski-Srebnick, M. E. (2005). Promise, progress, problems, and paradoxes of three phases of accountability: A longitudinal case study of the Baltimore City Public Schools. *American Educational Research Journal, 42,* 43–75.

Thomas, R. M. (2005). *High-stakes testing: Coping with collateral damage.* Mahwah, NJ: Erlbaum.

Thomas, S., & Oldfather, P. (1997). Intrinsic motivations, literacy, and assessment practices: "That's my grade. That's me." *Educational Psychologist, 32,* 107–123.

Turnbull, A. P., Turnbull, R., & Wehmeyer, M. L. (2010). *Exceptional lives: Special education in today's schools* (6th ed.). Upper Saddle River, NJ: Merrill.

Turner, J. C., Meyer, D. K., Cox, K. E., Logan, C., DiCintio, M., & Thomas, C. T. (1998). Creating contexts for involvement in mathematics. *Journal of Educational Psychology, 90,* 730–745.

Tyler, K. M., Uqdah, A. L., Dillihunt, M. L., Beatty-Hazelbaker, R., Connor, T., Gadson, N., et al. (2008). Cultural discontinuity: Toward a quantitative investigation of a major hypothesis in education. *Educational Researcher, 37,* 280–297.

Valla, J. M., & Ceci, S. J. (2011). Can sex differences in science be tied to the long reach of prenatal hormones? Brain organization theory, digit ratio (2D/4D), and sex differences in preferences and cognition. *Perspectives in Psychological Science, 6,* 134–146.

Valli, L., & Buese, D. (2007). The changing roles of teachers in an era of high-stakes accountability. *American Educational Research Journal, 44,* 519–558.

Venn, J. J. (2000). *Assessing students with special needs* (2nd ed.). Upper Saddle River, NJ: Merrill/Prentice-Hall.

Vucko, S., & Hadwin, A. (April, 2004). *Going beyond I like it in a portfolio context: Scaffolding the development of six grade-two students' reflections.* Paper presented at the American Educational Research Association, San Diego, CA.

Walton, G. M., & Spencer, S. J. (2009). Latent ability: Grades and test scores systematically underestimate intellectual ability of negatively stereotyped students. *Psychological Science, 20,* 1132–1139.

Wang, M.-T., & Holcombe, R. (2010). Adolescents' perceptions of school environment, engagement, and academic achievement in middle school. *American Educational Research Journal, 47,* 633–662.

Whitaker Sena, J. D., Lowe, P. A., & Lee, S. W. (2007). Significant predictors of test anxiety among students with and without learning disabilities. *Journal of Learning Disabilities, 40,* 360–376.

Wodtke, K. H., Harper, F., & Schommer, M. (1989). How standardized is school testing? An exploratory observational study of standardized group testing in kindergarten. *Educational Evaluation and Policy Analysis, 11,* 223–235.

Wright, W. E. (2006). A catch-22 for language learners. *Educational Leadership, 64*(3), 22–27.

Zwick, R., & Sklar, J. C. (2005). Predicting college grades and degree completion using high school grades and SAT scores: The role of student ethnicity and first language. *American Educational Research Journal, 42,* 439–464.

## APPENDIX A

Gottfried, A. E., Fleming, J. S., & Gottfried, A. W. (2001). Continuity of academic intrinsic motivation from childhood through late adolescence: A longitudinal study. *Journal of Educational Psychology, 93,* 3–13.

Janos, P. M., & Robinson, N. M. (1985). Psychosocial development in intellectually gifted children. In F. D. Horowitz & M. O'Brien (Eds.), *The gifted and talented: Developmental perspectives* (pp. 149–196). Washington, DC: American Psychological Association.

Marsh, H. W., Gerlach, E., Trautwein, U., Lüdtke, O., & Brettschneider, W.-D. (2007). Longitudinal study of preadolescent sport self-concept and performance reciprocal effects and causal ordering. *Child Development, 78*, 1640–1656.

McGrew, K. S., Flanagan, D. P., Zeith, T. Z., & Vanderwood, M. (1997). Beyond *g*: The impact of *Gf–Gc* specific cognitive abilities research on the future use and interpretation of intelligence tests in the schools. *School Psychology Review, 26*, 189–210.

# Name Index

# Subject Index

AAC (augmentative and alternative communication), 139, 149
ABA (applied behavior analysis), 290, 452, 456
Abstract ideas
    concrete examples of, 15, 255
    expository instruction and, 393
    formal operations stage and, 32, 35
    history and, 256, 257
    linguistic development and, 45
    mathematics and, 252, 255
    moral development and, 81, 83
    peer relationships and, 69
    Piaget on, 33
    science and, 255
    sense of self and, 60, 63
    students with general delays in cognitive and social functioning and, 145
    visual imagery and, 172
Academic achievement. *See also* Summarization of student achievement
    applied behavior analysis and, 290
    attributions and, 357
    behaviorism and, 293
    bilingual education and, 49, 51
    cooperative learning and, 409, 411, 417
    culture and, 93, 344
    delay of gratification and, 277
    dispositions and, 129
    doing-just-enough goals and, 352
    emotional and behavioral disorders and, 141
    gender differences and, 104
    group contingencies and, 283
    intellectual disabilities and, 144
    interests and, 346
    IQ scores and, 125
    learning strategies and, 204
    mastery orientation and, 360
    motivation and, 275, 335, 336, 343
    note taking and, 199
    peer mediation and, 323
    peer relationships and, 67, 68
    peer tutoring and, 412, 414, 417
    physical and health impairments and, 146
    popularity and, 70, 71
    reinforcement and, 274-275
    self-efficacy and, 310
    self-regulation and, 321
    sense of school community and, 441
    sense of self and, 65
    socioeconomic differences and, 109, 110
    students at risk and, 113, 115
    students in inclusive settings and, 132
    teacher expectations and, 361–364, 481
    teacher self-efficacy and, 313
    teacher-student relationships and, 426
    temperaments and, 56, 60
    transition to middle and secondary school and, 374
Accelerated Reader (www.renlearn.com/ar), 499
Acceleration approach, 150
Accommodation, 27, 28, 33, 44
Accountability
    definition of, 528
    high-stakes tests and, 527–531
    of teachers, 528, 529
Acculturation, 93
Achievement goals, 349–352, 354, 364

Achievement tests, 476, 507, 510, 511, 520–521, 522, B-1–B-2
Acquired immune deficiency syndrome (AIDS), 77, 146
Acting white, 65
Action research, 11–13
activation
    definition of, 165
    prior knowledge activation, 166, 176
Activity reinforcers, 273, 275
Actual achievement, 508
Actual developmental level, 38
Adaptive behavior, 119, 145
Adaptive testing, 523
Adequate yearly progress, 528
Adolescents
    achievement goals and, 350, 351
    affect and, 373
    aggression and, 454
    anxiety and, 372
    attention and, 162
    attention-deficit hyperactivity disorder and, 137, 138
    brain development and, 24, 25, 28, 158–159
    career goals and, 353
    classroom management and, 437–438
    cognitive development and, 26
    delay of gratification and, 275, 277
    elaboration and, 173
    epistemic beliefs and, 202
    expectancies and, 348
    formal operations stage and, 32, 33
    gender differences and, 107
    giftedness and, 149
    history and, 257, 259
    identity versus role confusion, 62
    learned helplessness and, 360
    linguistic development and, 46–47
    maps and, 258
    metacognition and, 197
    moral and prosocial behavior and, 79, 80, 83
    motivation and, 359
    peer relationships and, 67
    personal interests and, 346
    perspective taking and, 72
    reading and, 246
    reinforcers and, 276
    relatedness and, 342
    risk taking and, 63, 64
    romantic relationships and, 69–70
    self-handicapping and, 338
    self-regulated learning and, 321
    self-regulation and, 315, 316, 321, 324
    sense of self and, 63–65, 66
    standardized tests and, 524, 525
    storage processes, 174
    teacher expectations and, 362
    teacher praise and, 271
    transition to middle and secondary school, 10
    writing and, 248
Adults. *See also* Parents; Teachers
    attributions and, 358
    children's sense of self and, 61
    communities of practice and, 237
    co-regulated learning and, 321
    critical thinking and, 220
    Erikson's stages of psychosocial development and, 62
    eye contact and, 96
    formal operations stage and, 33
    guided participation and, 43

mediated learning experiences and, 229, 230–231
    self-actualization and, 345
    self-regulation and, 321
    sense of self and, 65
    stereotypes and, 108
    verbal assertiveness and, 95
    Vygotsky's cognitive development theory and, 36–37, 38, 39, 41–42, 44
Advance organizers, 393, 397
Affect. *See also* Emotions
    anxiety and, 370–372, 374–375
    classroom assessment and, 461
    definition of, 366
    developmental trends in, 373
    diversity and, 375–377
    learning and, 369, 370
    motivation and, 366, 368–369
African American English, 95
African Americans. *See also* Race and racism
    anxiety and, 376
    autonomy and, 343
    cognitive processes and, 189
    cooperation and, 438
    eye contact and, 96
    group achievement and, 97, 126
    history and, 256
    intelligence and, 126, 128
    learned helplessness and, 364
    linguistic development and, 48
    motivation and, 364
    peer relationships and, 76
    personal space, 96
    playing the dozens and, 93–94, 454
    students at risk and, 113
    talkativeness and, 95
    teasing and, 97
    verbal assertiveness and, 95–96
After-school detentions, 280
After-school programs, 325, 396
Age-equivalent scores, 506–507, 508, 511
Aggression. *See also* Violence
    competition and, 286
    gender differences and, 76, 105, 106, 438
    modeling and, 305–306
    peer relationships and, 67, 73–75
    physical aggression, 73, 75, 76, 78, 105
    prevalence of, 454
    psychological aggression, 73, 75, 78
    self-monitoring and, 318
    self-regulation and, 324
    three-level approach, 455–456
    time-out and, 278
Aggressive behavior, 57, 58, 73
Agreeableness, 59
AIMSweb (www.aimsweb.com), 499
Alcohol abuse, 110, 137, 140, 141
Alcohol use, 63, 64, 67, 125, 145, 338
Algorithms, 213–214, 251
Alternative-response items, 482
American Psychological Association, *Learner-Centered Psychological Principles,* 383n
American Sign Language (ASL), 77, 148, 534
Amusia, 135
Amygdala, 324, 369
Analogies, 213
Analytical intelligence, 122
Analytic scoring, 492
Analytic versus holistic processing, 128–129, 128n

*Animal Hospital: Pet Vet 3D,* 215
AnimalWatch, 216
Antecedent responses, 285–286
Antecedent stimuli, 285–286, 290–291
Anterior cingulate cortex, 324, 369
Antisocial students, 78, 110
Anxiety
    affect and, 370–372, 374–375
    classical conditioning and, 268, 269, 270, 292, 372
    classroom climate and, 429
    debilitating anxiety, 371, 372, 374
    definition of, 371
    developmental trends in, 372
    diversity and, 376
    facilitating anxiety, 371, 372, 374–375, 496
    high-stakes testing and, 530
    performance and, 5, 371
    positive behavior support and, 291
    sources of, 372
    test anxiety, 372, 376, 473, 495, 496, 533
Applied behavior analysis (ABA), 290, 452, 456
Apprenticeships, 43–44, 150, 242
Appropriation, 38
Arab Americans, 98
Argument analysis, 220
Arguments, 232
Arousal, 337–338, 344, 369, 433
Articulation, and apprenticeships, 44
Artifacts, 517
Asian Americans
    affect and, 375–376
    attributions and, 364
    authoritarian parenting and, 57, 445
    autonomy and, 343
    choices and, 343–344
    critical thinking and, 222
    cultural expectations and, 58
    cultural view of past events, 234
    family relationships and, 98
    group achievement and, 97, 126, 364
    history and, 260
    holistic thinking and, 129
    intelligence and, 126
    mastery goals and, 364
    motivation and, 364
    peer relationships and, 76
    personal space and, 96
    praise and, 293
    relatedness and, 344
    self-improvement and, 343
    self-regulation and, 323
    students at risk and, 113
    talkativeness and, 95
    teacher-directed instructional strategies and, 417
    verbal assertiveness and, 95–96
ASL (American Sign Language), 77, 148, 534
Asperger syndrome, 76, 142, 143, 149, 431
Assessment. *See also* Authentic assessment; Classroom assessment; Formative assessment; Informal assessment; Summarization of student achievement; Summative assessment
    administration of, 472, 473, 478
    anxiety and, 375
    bias in, 480, 481, 493, 531
    concept maps and, 171
    confidentiality of, 536–539
    definition of, 462